D0769613

Eastern Europe

Neal Bedford   Debra Herrmann   Simon Richmond
Yvonne Byron   Patrick Horton   Rachel Suddart
Steve Fallon   Cathryn Kemp   Mara Vorhees
Kate Galbraith   Steve Kokker   Kim Wildman
Paul Greenway   Alex Leviton   Nicola Williams
Paul Hellander   Craig MacKenzie   Neil Wilson
Jeanne Oliver

LONELY PLANET PUBLICATIONS
Melbourne • Oakland • London • Paris

Eastern Europe
7th edition – January 2003
First published – April 1989

Published by
Lonely Planet Publications Pty Ltd ABN 36 005 607 983
90 Maribyrnong St, Footscray, Victoria 3011, Australia

Lonely Planet Offices
Australia Locked Bag 1, Footscray, Victoria 3011
USA 150 Linden St, Oakland, CA 94607
UK 10a Spring Place, London NW5 3BH
France 1 rue du Dahomey, 75011 Paris

Photographs
Many of the images in this guide are available for licensing from
Lonely Planet Images.
w www.lonelyplanetimages.com

Front cover photograph
Something for the older gentlemen – a game of chess in the warm
waters of the Széchenyi Baths, Budapest, Hungary
(David Greedy, Lonely Planet Images)

ISBN 1 74059 289 1

Printed by The Bookmaker International Ltd
Printed in China

**Although the authors
and Lonely Planet try
to make the informa-
tion as accurate as
possible, we accept
no responsibility for
any loss, injury or
inconvenience sus-
tained by anyone
using this book.**

Contents – Text

HUNGARY 349

LATVIA 427

LITHUANIA 449

MACEDONIA 475

MOLDOVA 493

MOSCOW & ST PETERSBURG 517

POLAND 551

ROMANIA 643

SLOVAKIA 723

SLOVENIA 765

UKRAINE 797

Contents – Maps

The Authors

Neal Bedford

Neal updated the Danube Bend, Transdanubia, Lake Balaton and Great Plains sections of the Hungary chapter. Born in Papakura, New Zealand, Neal gave up an exciting career in accounting for the mundane life of a traveller. Travel led him through a number of countries and jobs, ranging from an au pair in Vienna to fruit picker in Israel. Deciding to give his life some direction, he landed the lucrative job of packing books in Lonely Planet's London office. One thing led to another and he managed to cross over into the mystic world of authoring. He now resides in Vienna.

Yvonne Byron

Yvonne updated the Getting There & Away chapter. After a quiet upbringing in rural Australia, Yvonne has travelled widely and lived in places as diverse as Dhaka, Oxford, Vancouver and Jakarta. After starting work as a defence analyst she has since been a pre-school teacher, university researcher and is now an editor with Lonely Planet. She has also co-authored or co-edited a number books on the relationship between people and forests. At Lonely Planet, Yvonne has been involved in the production of many guides, including 1st editions of the *Trans-Siberian Railway* and *Cyprus*. She now spends most weekends bushwalking in Victoria.

Steve Fallon

Steve updated the introductory, Budapest and Northern Hungary sections of the Hungary chapter. A native of Boston, he graduated from Georgetown University with a degree in languages and then taught at the University of Silesia near Katowice in Poland. After working for several years for an American daily newspaper and earning a master's degree in journalism, he travelled to Hong Kong, where he lived for over a dozen years, working for a variety of publications and running a travel bookshop. Steve lived in Budapest for 2½ years before moving to London in 1994. He has written or contributed to more than two dozen Lonely Planet titles, including the Lonely Planet Journeys title *Home with Alice: A Journey in Gaelic Ireland*.

Kate Galbraith

Kate updated the Bosnia-Hercegovina chapter. Kate fell in love with Bosnia in 1996, when she worked for a local news agency in Sarajevo. She has been astounded by the changes the city has undergone since then, from the development of inter-entity bus lines to the introduction of a Versace gallery in Sarajevo centre. Before settling back into Bosnia for Lonely Planet, she made a grand tour of Eastern Europe as a freelance writer. She suspects that she may forever be a wanderer.

Paul Greenway

Paul updated the Poland, Ukraine and Bulgaria chapters. Gratefully plucked from the blandness and security of the Australian Public Service, Paul has now worked on over 20 Lonely Planet titles, including *Jordan*, *Bulgaria* and *Botswana*, as well as various guides for India, Indonesia, Africa and the Middle East. During the rare times that he's not travelling – or writing, reading and dreaming about it – Paul relaxes to (and pretends he can play) heavy rock, eats and breathes Australian Rules Football, and will go to any lengths to avoid settling down.

Paul Hellander

Paul worked on the Albania and Macedonia chapters. He has never really stopped travelling since he first looked at a map in his native England. He graduated with a degree in Greek before heading for Australia where he trained interpreters and translators in Modern Greek before donning the hat of a travel writer. Paul has contributed to many LP titles including the following guides: *Greece, France, Cyprus, Israel & the Palestinian Territories, Singapore, Central America* and *South America*. His photos have also appeared in many LP guides. When not travelling, he lives in Adelaide, South Australia. He was last spotted heading once more to cover the prickly politics of Cyprus.

Debra Herrmann

Debra, who updated the Estonia chapter, started out from the Wimmera region of southeastern Australia, some distance south of the Baltic Sea. After subsisting as a junior in the design and advertising business, copywriting anything from seedy nightclubs to Swedish cars, she soon realised the value of a passport. Over 30 countries proved irresistible in the years that followed and, after a visa-friendly foray into publishing in London, led to the one employer who would regard this as a logical career path – Lonely Planet. Her other contributions to the Lonely Planet list include *Estonia, Lithuania and Latvia, Europe on a shoestring* and *Lonely Planet Unpacked Again.*

Patrick Horton

Patrick Horton explored Serbia, Montenegro and Kosovo for the Yugoslavia chapter and if that wasn't enough then went straight on to research an 'interesting' part of Russia for a different title. Patrick, writer and photographer, was born with restless feet. He travelled extensively in his native Britain before hitting the around-the-world trail in 1985. He prefers the more arcane areas of the world such as North Korea, Eritrea, East Timor or Tonga, or riding a motorcycle over the Himalaya. He now lives in Melbourne with his long-suffering partner Christine, another ardent traveller whom he met in Paris. Patrick has had photographs published in many Lonely Planet guides and has worked on the *Australia, Eastern Europe, Ireland* and *Delhi* guides.

Cathryn Kemp

Cathryn swapped tabloids for travel to update the Lithuania chapter. Cathryn started travelling in 1990 when she studied art at the Moscow Institute of Architecture. Several trips through Russia and Ukraine later, and a passion for travel was born. After a masters degree in fine art and photography in Barcelona and graduating from Winchester School of Art in 1995, with camera in hand, she backpacked across Asia, Europe, Australia, New Zealand and South America – interspersed with a budding career in journalism. For five years Cathryn has written for British national and regional newspapers with some freelance photography thrown in – but travel just keeps getting in the way.

Steve Kokker

Steve, who wrote the Belarus chapter of this book, was born in Montréal and studied psychology before becoming a film critic. Figuring it was best to live directly, not virtually, he moved to his ancestral home Tallinn, Estonia. He's been with Lonely Planet since 1998, writing about Russia, Estonia, Latvia and Lithuania, and has written guides to Russia's culture capital St Petersburg and Canada's French capital Québec.

Alex 'Pooky' Leviton

Alex updated the Slovenia chapter. Possibly Lonely Planet's shortest author ever at 4'9", Alex felt right at home in tiny Slovenia. She was raised in Los Angeles, but quickly escaped to the far reaches of Humboldt County. After college, she got a job at an alternative science/conspiracy theory magazine. This experience led her to leave the country, repeatedly. Alex has visited 46 countries on six continents. She worked on Slovenia while in her last semester at UC Berkeley's Graduate School of Journalism, and is currently a freelance writer and editor based in North Carolina and San Francisco.

Craig MacKenzie

Craig worked on the Introduction and Facts for the Visitor chapters. Born in Kinlochleven in the Scottish West Highlands, his parents told him he was on a two-week holiday back in 1963 when he arrived in Melbourne, Australia, as an unwitting migrant. He's still in Melbourne having spent over 15 years with the Fairfax media group as a sports journalist and subeditor with freelance stints on SBS radio and TV. Seeking a haven for industrial misfits he joined Lonely Planet as a book editor in June 1996. He's balding, fat, smokes long panatellas and drinks pints of Guinness.

Jeanne Oliver

Jeanne updated the Croatia chapter. Born in New Jersey, she spent her childhood mulling over the *New York Times* travel section and plotting her future voyages. After a BA in English and a stint at the *Village Voice* newspaper, Jeanne got a law degree. Her legal practice was interrupted by ever-more-frequent trips to far-flung destinations and eventually she set off on an around-the-world trip that landed her in Paris. A job in the tourist business led to freelance writing assignments for magazines and guidebooks. She joined Lonely Planet in 1996 and has written 1st editions of Lonely Planet's *Croatia, Normandy, Crete* and *Crete Condensed* as well as updating chapters in *Greece, Mediterranean Europe* and *France*.

Simon Richmond

Simon updated the St Petersburg and Around St Petersburg sections. After his first visit to St Petersburg in 1994, Simon knew this would not be his last encounter with this magical city and the fascinating country to which it belongs. The award-winning writer travelled from St Petersburg to Vladivostok for Lonely Planet's *Trans-Siberian Railway* guide in 2001, then returned in 2002 to research the new *Russia & Belarus* guide and contribute to this *Eastern Europe* guide. Co-author of other Lonely Planet titles including *İstanbul to Kathmandu, South Africa, Cape Town, Central Asia* and *Walking in Australia*, Simon also writes for several other guidebook publishers, magazines and newspapers.

Rachel Suddart

Rachel updated the Getting Around chapter. Originally from the Lake District (UK) and a graduate of Manchester University, she spent several years trying to work out how to combine her love for writing with her incurable wanderlust. In 2000 she had her first taste of authorship when she took part in a BBC documentary. After getting her foot stuck firmly in the door she took on a full-time role in Lonely Planet's London office, which is where you'll find her now (probably singing along to some dodgy rock music). She has contributed to several LP titles.

Mara Vorhees

Mara updated the Moscow and Around Moscow sections. Mara was born and raised in St Clair Shores, Michigan. Her fascination with world cultures and her penchant for good deeds led her into the field of international development and she set out to assist Russia in its economic transition. After two years in the field, mainly spent fighting with the tax police (and losing), she resorted to seeing and trying to save the world by other means. The pen-wielding traveller has since contributed to Lonely Planet's *Trans-Siberian Railway*, *Eastern Europe* and *Moscow* guides. When not traipsing around the former Soviet bloc, she resides in Somerville, Massachusetts, with her husband and her cat. She still dabbles in international development.

Kim Wildman

Kim, who updated the Romania and Moldova chapters, grew up in Toowoomba, Queensland, with parents who unwittingly instilled in her the desire to travel at a young age by extending the immediate family to include 11 exchange students. After graduating from Queensland College of Art, having studied photography, Kim packed her backpack and headed to the USA and Bermuda. But it was her next adventure to southern Africa that inspired her to combine her three loves: photography, writing and travel. Kim also has a BA in journalism and has co-authored Lonely Planet's *Europe on a shoestring*, *Romania & Moldova*, *South Africa, Lesotho & Swaziland*, *West Africa* and *Athens*.

Nicola Williams

Nicola worked on the Latvia chapter of this book – prompting a much-welcome return to a country she bussed the length and breadth of as features editor of the *Baltic Times* in 1995–96. After 12 more months exploring the Baltics as Vilnius-based editor-in-chief of the *In Your Pocket* city-guide series, she swapped Lithuanian *cepelinai* for Lyonnaise *andouillette*. Nicola has written several Lonely Planet titles including 1st editions of *Estonia, Latvia & Lithuania*, *Romania & Moldova*, *Provence & the Côte d'Azur*, *The Loire* and *Milan, Turin & Genoa*.

Neil Wilson

Neil updated the Slovakia and Czech Republic chapters. After working as a petroleum geologist in Australia and the North Sea and doing geological research at Oxford University, Neil gave up the rock business for the more precarious life of a freelance writer and photographer. Since 1988 he has travelled in five continents and written around 35 travel and walking guidebooks for various publishers. He has worked on Lonely Planet's *Georgia, Armenia & Azerbaijan*, *Czech & Slovak Republics*, *Slovenia*, *Scotland* and *Edinburgh* guides. Although he was born in Glasgow, in the west of Scotland, Neil defected to the east at the age of 18 and has lived in Edinburgh ever since.

AUTHOR ACKNOWLEDGMENTS

Neal Bedford Longest and loudest thanks go to Steve Fallon, for asking me to jump aboard the Hungary Express, for all his worldly advice and for the friendship and beer. Special thanks goes to Zsuzsa Gaspar for the brief Hungarian lessons, the critical praise of any Hungarian wines I smuggled home and for looking after the plant. A heartfelt thanks to all the Tourinform staff that helped me in so many ways, and thankfully spoke English and/or German. Also *köszönöm szépen* to the Hungarian folk I met along the way that made my trip all that more fun.

Yvonne Byron I'd like to thank Leonie Mugavin at Lonely Planet in Melbourne and Rachel Suddart, in the London office, for their assistance in navigating my way around the abundance of websites and other valuable sources providing information on how to actually get to Europe.

Steve Fallon Special thanks to Bea Szirti and to Erzsébet Tszai, who helped with the research of the Budapest and transport sections. Tourinform remains the most authoritative and knowledgable source of information on Hungary and things Hungarian; *köszönöm szépen* to Ágnes Padányi in Budapest and staff elsewhere in Magyarország. Dr Zsuzsa Medgyes of M&G Marketing in Budapest came forward with all those wonderful little details again. Many thanks. I am indebted to Michael Kovrig and to András Cseh for their hospitality in Budapest and Eger; Ildikó Nagy Moran was as welcoming and helpful as always. Once again, this chapter is dedicated to Michael Rothschild, with love and gratitude.

Kate Galbraith A special thanks to Dijana Radman in Sarajevo for insider tips; to Kendra Gregson for excellent restaurant suggestions and other pointers from her long experience; to the OHR crowd for a great day at Jahrina. In Banja Luka, huge thanks to John Crownover for showing me around the town; to Nevin Orange at Care Canada for putting me in touch with these wonderful folk; and to patient tourist offices around the country.

Paul Greenway In Poland, thanks to Piotr Kaminski; and to Marcin Ławrysz for showing me around Białowiecża and to his girlfriend Marta Kaminski for the grand tour of Warsaw. Also thanks to Tomasz Jędrzejewski for a drunken tour of Olsztyn.

In Ukraine, my gratitude goes to Lucy Tovchikh, Ksenia Tovchikh and Sara Stahl for being gracious hosts in Odesa. Also thanks to Yulia Tkachuk for showing me around Kyiv; and to Marta Pereyma and Paul Hacker from the US Embassy for their input. I appreciated the help offered by Ladislav Fornvald of Olymp Travel as well. Lastly, thanks to Scott Lewis of the *Kyiv Post* for keeping LP informed about what's going on in Ukraine.

And apologies if I have misspelt anyone's name.

Paul Hellander The Balkans can occasionally be a taxing yet fascinating place to travel and so I would like to thank the following people who made the trip just that bit easier: Mimi Apostolov (Ohrid); Dimitri Gligorov (Skopje); Alma & Josef Tedeschini (Durrës); Anton Bushati (Tirana). For sharing their homes with me as I put it all together my gratitude also goes out to my friends in Greece: Maria Haristou & Andonis Konstantinidis (Thessaloniki); Angeliki Kanelli (Athens); Giannis and Vasilis Kambouris (Ikaria); Helga & Dimitris Ioannidopoulos (Ikaria). Stella, Byron & Marcus – thanks again for being there when needed.

Debra Herrmann In Australia, special thanks to Sirje Jõgi for the introduction to Estonian language and culture, recipes and laughter and to Liz Filleul and Mark Griffiths for the kind invitation to a glimpse over the fence. In Estonia, thanks to Raivo Tõnissaar for generously sharing his Hiiumaa experience, to Marko Kaulder, Tõnu and crew for the adventures east and my newly acquired skills with *kala* and *õlu*. The inspired efforts of Ursula Toomri putting Tartu into perspective will long be remembered, as will the truly insightful Anne Kurepalu in Lahemaa. Finally, thanks to Steve Kokker, who travelled so well down these roads before me.

Patrick Horton I want to acknowledge the help given to me by Miroslav Maric in translating, transporting me around Serbia and Montenegro and providing much background information. I also want to thank Dren Shala for helping me in Kosovo. Thanks also to Leanne Smith of the Australian embassy in Belgrade for providing background information.

Cathryn Kemp Lithuania greeted me with open arms. In Vilnius, Rob and Laima – can I just say *ačiū*! Thanks to Livijus from the Old Town Hostel, my host family in Vilnius, American Paul and his army of friends. Many thanks to everyone at Vilnius TIC, Rimas from Rimas-Rent-A-Car, Sco and his gang from In Your Pocket, Dalia Bardauskienė (advisor to Vilnius mayor Artūras Zuokas) and Dr Shimon Alperovitch from the State Jewish Museum.

In Lithuania's heart, thanks to Barry who unravelled Panevėžys' charms and all in the Kaunas TIC. In the west, gratitude to Jurda at the Travellers Hostel, Dr Artūras Razinkovas from Klaipėda University, Antanas Kontautas from the Lithuanian Green Movement and the excellent Smiltynė and Nida TICs. And thanks to Nicola Williams who gave me brilliant contacts, excellent advice, and lent a sympathetic ear.

Steve Kokker In Brest, hats off to the incredible Zhanna Volkovicha at Belintourist. In Hrodna, heartfelt appreciation to Deacon Valera, a model for me of someone who truly strives for self improvement, and to Igor. In Minsk, thanks to Tatyana Shevstova and to Igor Popov, who was a big help before his bizarre disappearance. Final thanks to Etienne and Nick from London for being great companions and moonshine-drinking partners.

Alex Leviton This chapter would not have been possible without unending support from several incredibly wonderful and generous people, including my host Tanja Pajevic, my travelling partner and translator Freddy Wyss, and the helpful Ljubljana Tourist Board team of Tatjana Radovič and Petra Čuk. I'd also like to thank Tadeja Urbas, John Whaley, Jerry Wagner, Dave Barnes, Tim Steyskal, Sarah Isakson, Rok Krančnik, Brigita Mark, Miha Rott, Franci at the Ljubljana bus station, the tourist offices in Maribor, Ptuj and Bled, and Lonely Planet Slovenian pioneer Steve Fallon, for paving the way.

Craig MacKenzie I'm particularly grateful to Emma Sangster who provided invaluable assistance during a difficult period for her. Thanks also to Chris Adlam (Automobile Association), David Burnett, Yvonne Byron, Emma Cafferty (YHA England & Wales), Brigitte Ellemor, Paul Guy (HI Northern Ireland), Bibiana Jaramillo, Hilary Rogers and Joyce Turton (HI Canada).

Jeanne Oliver In Croatia, my thanks go first to Renata Janekovic and the National Tourist Board. The helpful staff of the local tourist associations deserve my eternal gratitude with a special nod to the indefatigable Stanka Kraljević in

Korčula and Goran Franinović in Pula. Jagoda Bracanović in Hvar, as well as Ratco Ojdanić and Aljoša Milat in Korčula, made my work a pleasure.

Simon Richmond Many thanks to following for their help, various insights and fun times: Peter Kozyrev, Steve Caron, Valudya Kovalev, Paul and Erica Marsh, Jan Krc, James Doty, Irina Volkova, Yegor Churakov, Nikolay Zag, Peter Morley, Chris Hamilton and Steve Kokker.

Rachel Suddart Thanks to the MTA staff (especially Adriana Cacciottolo in London), Philip Fenech (President of the GRTU's Hospitality and Leisure Division), Jacqui Roberts, Neil Wilson for his help and advice, Paul Gowen from the RAC for 'behind-the-wheel' knowledge, Mark Waters from the CTC for all things bicycle related, the UK IT team for all their patience and expertise, and Tom Hall for never getting sick of hearing 'Can I just run something past you...'. Thanks to Megan Hitchin for her tireless enthusiasm (and for saving me from being a billy-no-mates in the bars and restaurants), my Mum and Dad for their love and support and Paul for sending that all-important email. Thanks also to all the travellers that I met out on the road and those that took the time to write to our offices. Cheers to one and all.

Mara Vorhees On the ground in Moscow, I received valuable support from Viktor Orekhov and Natasha Lodyasova; Alexandra Lanskaya of Dom Patriarshy Tours was more than forthcoming with information and tips. Thanks also to my co-author Simon Richmond for his insights and oversight. I am ever indebted to friends and family at home, for keeping in touch while I'm on the road; to Theo Panayotou and Rob Faris at CID, for letting me go (again); and especially to my parents Roy and Ruth Vorhees, for never tiring of *russkie suveniri* (or at least for pretending). Most of all, to Gerald Easter – who may lose patience with Russia, but never seems to lose it with me – спасибо и целую.

Kim Wildman There were many people in Romania who generously donated their time and knowledge. Those to whom I am especially grateful include my two dearest friends Adriana Grigorut and Andrei Mahalinischi; Step by Step's Felicia Enache and Iulian Cozma; Colin Shaw; Radu Mititean; Elvis, Katarina, Ho Joon, Nathan and all the helpful staff at Elvis' Villa; YHR's Mátyás Ildikó; Florin Bărhălescu; OVR-Art-Tur's George Iurca, Ramona Ardelean and Nicolae Prisăcaru; and ANTREC's Petre Vasiliu. Also to all the travellers I met along the way thank you for becoming part of my Romanian odyssey – Theresa, Jordie and Travis – Maramureş would never have been the same without you.

Nicola Williams Many thanks to old friends who made me feel like I'd never left: Nomeda Navickaitė and Reine Ortiz, Renata Šutovaitė and sco, and Rimas in Vilnius; Ģirts Upenieks, Māris Petrēvics and Mārtiņš Zaprauskis (for ice hockey and beers at dawn) in Rīga. At home, the sweetest of thank-yous to Ingrida (Ligers) Rogal, my parents and Matthias Lüfkens. And kisses to Niko and Tomass for future Baltic explorations.

Neil Wilson *Mockrat děkuji* to the helpful staff at Prague Information Service, to Carol Downie for help with shops and restaurants, and to Richard Nebeský and Tomáš Harabíš for conversations over a cold *pivo* or six. Also, thanks to the editorial and cartographic staff at Lonely Planet.

This Book

Eastern Europe is part of Lonely Planet's Europe series, which includes *Western Europe*, *Mediterranean Europe*, *Central Europe*, *Scandinavian Europe* and *Europe on a shoestring*.

Many people have helped to create this 7th edition of *Eastern Europe*. Six new chapters have been included: Belarus, Estonia, Latvia, Lithuania, Moldova and Ukraine. Among the major contributors to past editions of *Eastern Europe* and to other guides that previously contained the new chapters were Peter Carney, Steve Fallon, Kate Galbraith, Mark Honan, Steve Kokker, Paul Hellander, Patrick Horton, Keti Japaridze, Steve Kokker, Jonathan Leff, Emma Miller, Richard Nebeský, Jeanne Oliver, David Rowson, Mara Vorhees, Kim Wildman, Nicola Williams and Neil Wilson.

FROM THE PUBLISHER

The coordinating editor of *Eastern Europe* was Yvonne Byron and the coordinating designer and cartographer was Sally Morgan. They were assisted by Susie Ashworth, Yvonne Bischofberger, Bridget Blair, Csanad Csutoros, Melanie Dankel, Tony Davidson, James Ellis, Susannah Farfor, Huw Fowles, Karen Fry, Kyla Gillzan, Jocelyn Harewood, Errol Hunt, Nancy Ianni, Birgit Jordan, Valentina Kremenchutskaya, Darren O'Connell, Leanne Peake, Adrian Persoglia, Cherry Prior, Nina Rousseau, Diana Saad, Anastasia Safioleas, Jacqui Saunders, Ann Seward, Sarah Sloane, Nick Stebbing, Julia Taylor, Ray Thomson, Gina Tsarouhas, Helen Yeates, Isabelle Young and Lonely Planet Images. The senior production staff were Gerilyn Attebery, Kerryn Burgess, David Burnett, Bruce Evans, Liz Filluel, Imogen Franks, Quentin Frayne, Mark Germanchis, Mark Griffiths, Kieran Grogan, James Hardy, Rachel Imeson, David Kemp, Emma Koch, Chris Lee Ack, Adriana Mammarella, Mary Neighbour, Daniel New, Robert Reid, Jane Thompson, Andrew Tudor and Celia Wood.

THANKS
Many thanks to the travellers who used the last edition and wrote to us with helpful hints, advice and interesting anecdotes. Your names appear in the back of this book.

Foreword

ABOUT LONELY PLANET GUIDEBOOKS

The story begins with a classic travel adventure: Tony and Maureen Wheeler's 1972 journey across Europe and Asia to Australia. There was no useful information about the overland trail then, so Tony and Maureen published the first Lonely Planet guidebook to meet a growing need.

From a kitchen table, Lonely Planet has grown to become the largest independent travel publisher in the world, with offices in Melbourne (Australia), Oakland (USA), London (UK) and Paris (France).

Today Lonely Planet guidebooks cover the globe. There is an ever-growing list of books and information in a variety of media. Some things haven't changed. The main aim is still to make it possible for adventurous travellers to get out there – to explore and better understand the world.

At Lonely Planet we believe travellers can make a positive contribution to the countries they visit – if they respect their host communities and spend their money wisely. Since 1986 a percentage of the income from each book has been donated to aid projects and human rights campaigns, and, more recently, to wildlife conservation.

> Although inclusion in a guidebook usually implies a recommendation we cannot list every good place. Exclusion does not necessarily imply criticism. In fact there are a number of reasons why we might exclude a place – sometimes it is simply inappropriate to encourage an influx of travellers.

UPDATES & READER FEEDBACK

Things change – prices go up, schedules change, good places go bad and bad places go bankrupt. Nothing stays the same. So, if you find things better or worse, recently opened or long-since closed, please tell us and help make the next edition even more accurate and useful.

Lonely Planet thoroughly updates each guidebook as often as possible – usually every two years, although for some destinations the gap can be longer. Between editions, up-to-date information is available in our free, quarterly *Planet Talk* newsletter and monthly email bulletin *Comet*. The *Scoop* section of our website covers news and current affairs relevant to travellers. Lastly, the *Thorn Tree* bulletin board and *Postcards* section carry unverified, but fascinating, reports from travellers.

Tell us about it! We genuinely value your feedback. A well-travelled team at Lonely Planet reads and acknowledges every email and letter we receive and ensures that every morsel of information finds its way to the relevant authors, editors and cartographers.

Everyone who writes to us will find their name listed in the next edition of the appropriate guidebook, and will receive the latest issue of *Comet* or *Planet Talk*. The very best contributions will be rewarded with a free guidebook.

We may edit, reproduce and incorporate your comments in Lonely Planet products such as guidebooks, websites and digital products, so let us know if you don't want your comments reproduced or your name acknowledged.

How to contact Lonely Planet:
Online: **e** talk2us@lonelyplanet.com.au, **w** www.lonelyplanet.com
Australia: Locked Bag 1, Footscray, Victoria 3011
UK: 10a Spring Place, London NW5 3BH
USA: 150 Linden St, Oakland, CA 94607

Introduction

No region in the world has undergone as much change in less than a generation as Eastern Europe. When the 1st edition of this book appeared in 1989, the region was by and large still locked behind the Iron Curtain – a destination primarily for the intrepid, curious or politically motivated. Less than one year later the communist regimes of Poland, Czechoslovakia, Hungary and Romania had collapsed, and by 1991 isolationist Albania, Bulgaria and Russia had democratically elected governments. Two years later Yugoslavia, Czechoslovakia and the Soviet Union had broken into some two dozen independent republics. A 'new world' had been created, with many of these countries making their own decisions for the first time in centuries – and, in some cases (eg, Macedonia and Slovenia), for the first time in history.

The very name of this region is troublesome. During the 19th century, Europe was viewed quite differently to how it is seen today. Until as late as 1945 there was the predominantly industrialised West at one end of the spectrum, an undeveloped and almost medieval Balkan region at the other, and in the middle sat the Mitteleuropa (meaning 'Middle Europe') of Prussian rule and the Habsburg Empire. The term 'Eastern Europe' gained common currency only with the Soviet domination of much of Central and Balkan Europe following WWII.

Our problem is coverage: about half the book deals with the Balkan region, which has never been considered part of Mitteleuropa, and there's also a chapter on Moscow and St Petersburg, which are much too far east. But from the traveller's point of view these countries have much in common, and basic things like accommodation, restaurants and public transport tend to work in similar ways throughout the region. Several countries also share the same bureaucratic hurdles and present occasional hassles.

You'll soon find, however, that the region's assets far outweigh its few drawbacks and for this 7th edition of *Eastern Europe* we have enhanced our coverage with the addition of Belarus, Estonia, Latvia, Lithuania, Moldova and the Ukraine.

From the Baltic to the Balkans and the Danube to the Don, a treasure trove of history and natural beauty awaits you. Eastern Europe has been the source of much of what we know as Western culture, while Moscow, St Petersburg, Warsaw, Budapest and Prague have been important cultural centres. And this volatile region has shaped world history. In the 20th century alone, both world wars began in Eastern Europe, and it was the primary 'battlefield' during the Cold War.

Apart from these legacies, the region also is home to vast forests, rugged mountains, pristine lakes, beautiful coastlines and mighty rivers just waiting to be discovered. An added incentive to visit the region is cost – prices almost everywhere are much lower than those in Western Europe.

The countries and cities covered in this book are fascinating for their diversity, and to gain some understanding of the region you should try to visit several. Spend time in the capitals, but also visit the provincial towns, which are usually much cheaper and less crowded. Also, the opportunity to meet local people is greater in the countryside. This is not a case of 'authentic' versus 'touristy'; a supermarket checkout in, say, Budapest is as much a part of the real Hungary of the 21st century as an old village shop on the Great Plain. But life in the provinces is more redolent of times past – simpler, slower and often more friendly.

Eastern Europe is a prominent notch in the belt of today's traveller. As this enticing region opens its arms to the world, there's never been a better opportunity for that trip of a lifetime. There's much in this region that beckons and this updated and expanded edition of *Eastern Europe* will be a travelling companion you can rely upon. All you have to do is go, so don't linger a second longer.

Facts for the Visitor

HIGHLIGHTS

There is so much to see in Eastern Europe that compiling a top 10 is next to impossible. Nevertheless, we've compiled this list. You may agree with some entries while some omissions may raise your hackles – it's OK, we've got broad shoulders:

1. Budapest
2. Prague
3. Rīga
4. Kraków's old town
5. St Petersburg and its white nights (late June)
6. Croatia's Dalmatian coast
7. Lake Ohrid in Macedonia
8. High Tatra Mountains of Poland and Slovakia
9. Latvia's Gauja River Valley
10. Škocjan Caves in Slovenia

Other possibilities include Brest Fortress, the painted churches of Bucovina in Romania, Lviv, the Rila Mountains in Bulgaria, Tallinn and the northern Lithuanian half of the Curonian Spit.

PLANNING
When to Go

Any time can be the best time to visit Eastern Europe, depending on what you want to see and do. Spring (from April to mid-June) is an excellent time to visit as the days are getting longer, the weather is good, the theatres and other cultural venues are open and in full swing, low-season rates still generally apply and local people are not yet jaded by waves of summertime visitors. The only drawback is that school outings often occur during this period; being crowded into a hostel, train carriage or museum with a bunch of raucous kids is no fun.

Summer (mid-June to early September) is the ideal time for hiking and camping, and is the peak season for budget travellers and just about everyone else. September can be an excellent month, with autumn colours on the trees, fruit and vegetables plentiful, shoulder-season tariffs in effect again and the tourist masses home and back at work. You can still swim comfortably in the Adriatic in September, but by mid-October most of the camping

grounds have closed down and the days are growing shorter.

From October to March it can be rather cold and dark throughout Eastern Europe with smoke belching from coal-burning furnaces and creating smog, though bear in mind that this is the peak theatre and concert season in the cities. And if you're keen on winter sports, resorts in the High Tatra Mountains of Poland and Slovakia, the Julian Alps in Slovenia and Otepää in Estonia generally begin operating in early December and move into full swing after New Year, closing down again when the snows begin to melt in March or even as late as April, depending on the altitude.

The Climate and When to Go sections in the individual country chapters explain what to expect and when, and the climate charts in country chapters will help you compare different destinations.

When summer and winter are mentioned throughout this book we generally mean high and low tourist seasons, ie, for summer read roughly May to September and for winter read October to April.

What Kind of Trip?

Travelling Companions If you decide to travel with others, bear in mind that travel can put any relationship to the test like few other experiences. Make sure to agree on itineraries and routines beforehand and try to remain flexible about everything – even in the heat of an August afternoon in Budapest. Travelling with someone else also has financial benefits as single rooms cost more per person than doubles in most countries.

If travel is a good way of testing established friendships, it's also a great way of making new ones. Camping grounds and hostels are good places to meet fellow travellers, so even if you're travelling alone, you need never be lonely.

The Getting Around chapter has information on organised tours.

Maps

Good maps are easy to come by once you're in Eastern Europe, but you might want to buy a few beforehand to plan and track your route. The maps in this book will help you get an idea of where you might want to go and will be a useful first reference when you arrive in a city. Proper road maps are essential if you're driving or cycling.

The Geocenter *Eastern Europe* map (1:2,000,000; UK£4.99) is very useful for getting an overview of the area but the one produced by Freytag & Berndt (same scale; UK£6.95) is better. Kümmerly + Frey and Hallwag also produce meticulously drawn maps of various parts of the region. Some of the best city maps are published by Falk; RV Verlag's EuroCity series is another good bet. For some European cities (eg, Budapest, Prague and St Petersburg) Lonely Planet now has detailed city maps. Tourist offices dispense free and useful (but usually fairly basic) maps.

What to Bring

It's relatively easy to find almost anything you need in Eastern Europe and, since you'll probably buy things as you go along, it's better to start with too little rather than too much.

A backpack is still the most popular method of carrying gear as it is convenient, especially for walking.

Travelpacks (combined backpack/shoulder bags) are very popular. The backpack straps zip away inside the pack when they are not needed, so you almost have the best of both worlds. Backpacks or travelpacks can be made reasonably theft-proof with small padlocks. Another alternative is a large, soft zip bag with a wide shoulder strap so it can be carried with relative ease. Forget suitcases unless you're travelling in style, but if you do take one, make sure it has wheels to allow you to drag it along behind you. Watch out on cobblestone streets, though.

The climate will have a bearing on what clothing you take. Remember that insulation works on the principle of trapped air, so several layers of thin clothing are warmer than a single thick one (and easier to dry). You'll also be much more flexible if the weather suddenly turns warm. Just be prepared for rain at any time of year. Bearing in mind that you can buy virtually anything on the spot, a minimum packing list could include:

- underwear, socks and swimming gear
- a pair of jeans and maybe a pair of shorts or skirt
- a few T-shirts and shirts
- a warm sweater
- a solid pair of walking shoes

- sandals or thongs for showers
- a coat or jacket
- a raincoat, waterproof jacket or umbrella
- a medical kit and sewing kit
- a padlock
- a Swiss Army knife
- soap and towel
- toothpaste, toothbrush and other toiletries

RESPONSIBLE TOURISM

In Eastern Europe's nature reserves and national parks, be sure to follow the local code of ethics and common decency and pack up your litter. Minimise the waste you must carry out by taking minimal packaging and taking no more food than you will need. Don't use detergents or toothpaste (even if they are biodegradable) in or near watercourses. Bear in mind that sensitive biospheres, both for flora and fauna, may be seriously damaged if you leave designated paths in protected areas. When camping in the wild (checking first to see that it's allowed), bury human waste in cat holes at least 15cm deep and at least 100m from any nearby watercourse.

Eastern Europe's cities get intolerably crowded in peak season. Traffic congestion on the roads is a major problem, and visitors will do themselves and residents a favour if they forgo driving and use public transport.

VISAS & DOCUMENTS
Passport

Your most important travel document is your passport, which should remain valid until well after you return home. If it's just about to expire, renew it before you go – having this done by your embassy in Prague or Warsaw can be inconvenient and time-consuming. Some countries insist your passport remain valid for a specified period (usually three months) beyond the expected date of your departure from that country.

Applying for or renewing a passport can take anything from an hour to several months, so don't leave it till the last minute. Bureaucratic wheels usually turn faster if you do everything in person rather than relying on the post, but check first what you need to take with you: photos of a certain size, birth certificate, population register extract, signed statements, exact payment in cash etc.

Australian citizens can apply at a post office or the passport office in their state capital; Britons can pick up application forms from major post offices, and the passport is issued

Eastern Europe World Heritage List

ALBANIA
Ancient ruins of Butrint
BELARUS
Belavezhskaja Pushcha
Mir Castle complex
BULGARIA
Boyana Church near Sofia
Ivanovo rock-hewn churches
  near Ruse
Kazanlâk Thracian tomb
Madara horseman relief
Nesebâr's old city
Pirin National Park
Rila Monastery
Srebarna Nature Reserve
Thracian Tomb of Svechtari
CROATIA
Dubrovnik's old city
Plitvice Lakes National Park
Poreč's Euphrasian Basilica
Šibenik's Cathedral of St James
Split's historic centre with
  Diocletian's Palace
Trogir's old town
CZECH REPUBLIC
Český Krumlov's historic centre
Holašovice historical village
Komeríz Castle and gardens
Kutná Hora medieval silver
  town & Church of St Barbara
Lednice-Valtice
Litomyšyl Castle
Prague's historic centre
Telč's old city
Pilgrimage Church of St John
  Nepomuk at Zelena Hora
Holy Trinity Column in
  Olomouc
Tugendhat Villa in Brno

ESTONIA
Tallinn's Old Town
HUNGARY
Budapest's Castle District and
  the banks of the Danube
Karst caves at Aggtelek
  (shared with Slovakia)
Hollókő (traditional village)
Hortobágy National Park
Pannonhalma Benedictine
  Abbey
Pécs' Early Christian Cemetery
Tokaj-Hegyalja wine-growing
  region
LATVIA
Rīga's historic centre
LITHUANIA
Vilnius' historic centre
Curonian Spit (shared with
  Russia)
MACEDONIA
Ohrid and its lake
**MOSCOW &
ST PETERSBURG**
Kremlin and Red Square in
  Moscow
St Petersburg's historic centre
Trinity Monastery of St Sergius
  in Sergiev Posad
Monuments of Vladimir and
  Suzdal
POLAND
Auschwitz concentration camp
Białowieża Forest
Churches of Peace in Jaworki
  and Świdnica
Mannerist architecture of
  Kalwaria Zebrzydowska
  pilgrimage site

Kraków's historic centre
Castle of the Teutonic Order in
  Malbork
Medieval town of Toruń
Warsaw's old city
Wieliczka salt mines near
  Kraków
Zamość's old city
ROMANIA
Biertan fortified church
Bucovina painted churches
Dacian fortresses in the
  Orastie Mountains
Danube Delta
Horezu Monastery
Maramureş' wooden churches
Sighişoara's historic centre
SLOVAKIA
Banská Štiavnica medieval
  mining centre
Bardejov Town Conservation
  Reserve
Slovakian Karst and Aggtelek
  Caves (shared with Hungary)
Spišský Hrad
Vlkolinec folk village near
  Ružomberok
SLOVENIA
Škocjan Caves
UKRAINE
St Sophia Cathedral and Caves
  Monastery in Kyiv
Historic centre of Lviv
YUGOSLAVIA
Durmitor National Park
Kotor and its gulf
Stari Ras and Sopoćani
  Monastery
Studenica Monastery

by the regional passport office; Canadians can apply at any regional passport office; New Zealanders can apply at any district office of the Department of Internal Affairs; US citizens must apply in person at a local US Passport Agency office or at some courthouses and post offices (but may usually renew by mail).

Once you start travelling, carry your passport at all times and guard it carefully (see Copies later in this section for advice about carrying copies of your passport and other important documents). Camping grounds and

hotels sometimes insist that you hand over your passport for the duration of your stay, which is very inconvenient, but a driving licence or Camping Card International usually solves the problem.

Citizens of European countries don't always need a valid passport to travel within the region. European Union (EU) and Swiss citizens, for example, can enter Slovenia on just a valid personal identity card for up to 30 days and nationals of Austria, Belgium, France, Italy, Liechtenstein, Luxembourg, Germany,

Slovenia, Spain and Switzerland need only produce a national ID card to enter Hungary. But if you want to exercise this kind of option, check with your travel agency or the embassies of the countries you plan to visit.

Note that Bulgaria, the Czech Republic, Estonia, Hungary, Latvia, Lithuania, Poland, Romania, Slovakia and Slovenia are among a group of countries negotiating to become EU members within the next few years, but the first wave of countries probably won't be admitted before 2004 at the earliest.

Visas

A visa is a stamp in your passport or a separate piece of paper permitting you to enter the country in question and stay for a specified period of time. Often you can get the visa at the border or at the airport on arrival, but not always, especially if you're travelling by train or bus and the procedure is likely to hold up others. Check first with the embassies or consulates of the countries you plan to visit; otherwise you could find yourself stranded at the border. With a valid passport and visa (if required) you'll be able to visit most Eastern European countries for up to three (and sometimes even six) months, provided you have some sort of onward or return ticket and/or 'sufficient means of support' (money).

In line with the Schengen Agreement, there are no longer passport controls at the borders between most EU countries, but procedures between EU and non-EU countries can still be fairly thorough (and between nations with less than sterling relations like Hungary and Slovakia even more so). For those who do require visas, it's important to remember that these will have a 'use-by' date, and you'll be refused entry after that period has elapsed.

Since February 2002, Russia has been running a trial scheme whereby tourists from Schengen countries, as well as from Britain, Switzerland and Japan, who wish to visit St Petersburg and Moscow for less than 72 hours, can receive their visas directly upon entry. Travellers must apply at one of 29 authorised tour operators in their home country 48 hours before departure. Check with the Russian embassy in your home country about details.

Visa requirements can change, so you should always check with the individual embassies or a reputable travel agency before travelling. See Visas & Documents under Facts for the Visitor in the individual country chapters, but always check these details before setting out; it is indeed perishable information.

Visas are *usually* issued immediately by consulates in Eastern Europe, although some could levy a 50% to 100% surcharge for 'express service'. Nationals requiring visas are strongly advised to get them at a consulate beforehand and not to rely on getting them at border crossings. They're often cheaper in your home country anyway.

Consulates are generally open weekday mornings (if there's both an embassy and a consulate, you want the consulate). Consulates in those countries not neighbouring the one you want to visit are far less crowded (for example, get your Polish visa in Bucharest, or your Slovakian visa in Zagreb). Take your own pen and be sure to have a good supply of passport photos that actually look like you (you may need from one to four every time you apply for a visa).

You can also apply for a visa from a consulate in your home country by registered mail, but this takes about two weeks unless you request express service at an additional fee. Write first for an application form and enclose a stamped, self-addressed envelope.

Visa fees must be paid in convertible cash. Most countries will issue double-entry visas upon request for double the normal fee. Visas may be used any time within three to six months from the date of issue.

Decide in advance if you want a tourist or transit visa. Transit visas, usually valid for just 48 or 72 hours, are often cheaper and issued faster, but it's usually not possible to extend a transit visa or change it to a tourist visa.

The visa form may instruct you to report to police within 48 hours of arrival. If you're staying at a hotel or other official accommodation (camping ground, hostel, private room arranged by a travel agency etc), this will be taken care of for you by the travel agency, hotel or camping ground. If you're staying with friends, relatives or in a private room arranged on the street or at the train station, you're supposed to register with the police yourself. During the communist days these regulations were strictly enforced, but things are pretty casual in most countries nowadays.

If you need a visa extension, ask the tourist office how to go about it. You'll probably have to report to the police in person. Office hours are short and the lines long, so don't leave it till the last minute.

Travel Insurance

A travel insurance policy to cover theft, loss and medical problems is a good idea. The policies written by STA Travel and other student travel organisations are usually good value. Some policies offer lower and higher medical expense options; the higher ones are chiefly for countries like the USA that have extremely expensive medical costs. There is a wide variety of policies available so check the fine print.

Although most medical treatment available in Belarus, Moldova, Romania and Ukraine is usually free to UK nationals, insurance is still recommended.

Some insurance policies will specifically exclude 'dangerous activities', which can include scuba diving, motorcycling and even trekking. Some even exclude entire countries (eg, Bosnia-Hercegovina or Yugoslavia). A locally acquired motorcycle licence is not valid under some policies.

You may prefer a policy that pays doctors or hospitals directly rather than you having to pay on the spot and claim later. If you have to claim later make sure you keep all documentation. Some policies ask you to call back (reverse charges) to a centre in your home country where an immediate assessment of your problem is made. Check that the policy covers ambulances and an emergency flight home.

Driving Licence & Permits

Many non-European driving licences are valid in Europe, but it's a good idea to bring along an International Driving Permit (IDP), which can make life much simpler, especially when hiring cars and motorcycles. Basically a multilingual translation of the vehicle class and the personal details noted on your local licence, an IDP is not valid unless accompanied by your original driving licence. An IDP is available for a small fee from your local automobile association. Make sure to bring along a passport photo and your valid licence.

Camping Card International

The Camping Card International (CCI) is a camping ground ID valid for a year that can be used instead of a passport when checking in and includes third-party insurance. As a result, many camping grounds will offer a small discount (usually 5% to 10%) if you have one. CCIs are issued by automobile associations, camping federations and, sometimes, on the spot at camping grounds. In the UK, the AA and RAC both issue them to members for UK£6.50. The CCI is also useful as it can sometimes serves as a guarantee so that you don't have to leave your passport at reception.

Hostel Cards

A hostelling card is useful – if not always mandatory – for staying at hostels. Most hostels in Eastern Europe don't require that you be a hostelling association member, but they sometimes charge less if you have a card. Some hostels will issue one on the spot or after a few days' stay, though this might cost a bit more than getting it in your home country. See Hostels under Accommodation later in this chapter for the addresses of hostelling associations in English-speaking countries.

Student, Youth & Teacher Cards

An International Student Identity Card (ISIC), a plastic ID-style card with your photograph, provides discounts on many forms of transport (including airlines and local transport), cheap or free admission to museums and sights, and inexpensive meals in some student cafeterias and restaurants. If you're under 26 but not a student, you are eligible to apply for an International Youth Travel Card (IYTC, formerly GO25), issued by the Federation of International Youth Travel Organisations, or the Euro<26 card (the latter card may not be recognised in Albania, Moldova, Romania and Yugoslavia). Both go under different names in different countries and give much the same discounts and benefits as an ISIC. An International Teacher Identity Card (ITIC) identifies the holder as an instructor and offers similar deals. All these cards are issued by student unions, hostelling organisations or youth-oriented travel agencies.

Seniors Cards

Many attractions offer reduced-price admission for people over 60 or 65 (sometimes as low as 55 for women). Make sure you bring proof of age. For a fee of around €20, European residents aged 60 and over can get a Railplus Card as an add-on to their national rail senior pass. It entitles the holder to train-fare reductions of around 25%.

International Health Certificate

You'll most likely need this yellow booklet only if you're entering Eastern Europe from those parts of Asia, South America and Africa where diseases like yellow fever can occur. See Immunisations under Health later in this chapter for more information on jabs.

Copies

The hassles created by losing your passport can be considerably reduced if you have a record of its number and issue date or, even better, photocopies of the relevant data pages. A photocopy of your birth certificate can also be useful.

Also note the serial numbers of your travellers cheques (cross them off as you cash them) and take photocopies of your credit cards, air ticket and other travel documents. Keep all this emergency material separate from your passport, cheques and cash, and leave extra copies with someone you can rely on at home. Add some emergency money (eg, US$50 to US$100 in cash) to this separate stash as well. If you do lose your passport, notify the police immediately to get a statement, and contact your nearest consulate.

There is another option for storing details of your vital travel documents before you leave – Lonely Planet's free online Travel Vault. This method can be safer than carrying photocopies of your important papers. It's the best option if you travel in a country with easy Internet access. Your own password-protected travel vault is accessible online at any time. Create your personal travel vault at **w** www.ekno.lonelyplanet.com.

EMBASSIES & CONSULATES

See the individual country chapters for the addresses of embassies and consulates.

It's important to realise what your embassy can and cannot do to help you if you get into trouble while abroad. Generally speaking, it won't be much help in emergencies if the trouble you're in is remotely your own fault. Remember that you are bound by the laws of the country you are visiting.

In genuine emergencies you might get some assistance, but only if other channels have been exhausted. For example, if you need to get home urgently, a free ticket home is exceedingly unlikely – the embassy would expect you to have insurance. If you have all your money and documents stolen, it might assist with getting a new passport, but a loan for onward travel is almost always out of the question.

MONEY

Money in Eastern Europe can be a bit tricky. Of the Eastern European currencies in circulation, only some (eg, Czech crowns, Estonian kroon, Hungarian forint, Latvian lati, Lithuanian litu and Slovenian tolar) are 100% fully convertible and easily exchanged abroad. Others are at various stages of convertibility; some can be exchanged relatively easily abroad (especially in neighbouring countries), others not at all. For the time being, the best policy is to spend whatever you have there and take out as little as possible. See Money in the individual country chapters for more details.

Exchanging Money

In the old days, Eastern Europe worked on a cash-only basis; cheques and credit cards were unheard of, banks kept true bankers' hours and the black market rates on the street (especially in Poland and Romania) were so attractive that even the most law-abiding traveller couldn't resist. That's all changed now with *bureaux de change* everywhere, banks keeping longer hours and currency-exchange machines and automated teller machines (ATMs) as ubiquitous as drunks on a weekend night in Warsaw.

Cash Nothing beats cash for convenience,or risk. If you lose it, it's gone forever and very few travel insurers will come to your rescue. Those that will usually limit the amount to about UK£200/US$300. For tips on carrying your money safely, see Theft under Dangers & Annoyances later in this chapter.

Despite all the changes in recent years, cash does remain more important in Eastern Europe than elsewhere on the Continent, and it's a good idea to carry some foreign currency with you (especially US dollars). Remember that banks will always accept paper money but very rarely coins in foreign currencies, so you should spend (or donate) your local coins before you cross a border. In some countries it's worth having plenty of small denomination banknotes as it's often difficult to make up change in hard currency. However, don't bring banknotes with any writing or rubber stamp marks on them, or that are damaged or badly worn, as these will often be rejected.

Travellers Cheques & Eurocheques

The main idea of carrying travellers cheques rather than cash is the protection they offer from theft, though they are losing their popularity as more travellers – including those on tight budgets – deposit their money in their bank at home and withdraw it through ATMs as they go along.

Banks usually charge from 1% to 2% commission to change travellers cheques (up to 5% in Bulgaria, Estonia, Latvia, Lithuania and Romania). Their opening hours are sometimes limited. In the individual chapters, we recommend the most efficient banks of each country.

The privately owned exchange offices in Albania, Bulgaria, Poland, Romania and Slovenia change cash at excellent rates without commission. Not only are their rates sometimes higher than those offered by the banks for travellers cheques but they stay open much longer hours, occasionally even 24 hours a day. However, do take care in Belarus, the Czech Republic, Estonia, Hungary, Latvia, Lithuania, Moldova, Slovakia and Ukraine, as some big exchange offices deduct exorbitant commissions unless you cash a small fortune with them. Before signing a travellers cheque or handing over any cash always check the commission and rate.

American Express and Thomas Cook representatives cash their own travellers cheques without commission, but both give rather poor rates of exchange. If you're changing more than US$20, you're usually better off going to a bank and paying the standard 1% to 2% commission to change there.

Guaranteed personal cheques are another way of carrying money or obtaining cash. Eurocheques, which are available if you have a European bank account, are guaranteed up to a certain limit. When you cash them (eg, at post offices), you will be asked to show your Eurocheque card bearing your signature and registration number, and perhaps a passport or ID card. Your Eurocheque card should be kept separately from the cheques. However, many hotels and merchants refuse to accept Eurocheques because of the relatively large commissions applied.

Carrying large amounts of cash on your person is always risky, so you will have to weigh up the advantages of the much greater convenience of cash against the greater security of cheques. If you decide to go with cash in hard currency you'll probably have to bring it with you from home as banks and American Express offices in Eastern Europe

charge anywhere from 7% commission upward to convert dollar travellers cheques into dollars cash, if they will do it at all.

ATMs & Credit Cards The hassle of trying to change travellers cheques at the weekend and rip-off *bureaux de change* are a thing of the past in most parts of Eastern Europe, with the arrival of ATMs that accept most credit and cash cards from the Balkans to the Baltic.

Credit cards are still not as commonly used as in Western Europe but they're gaining ground, especially American Express, Visa and MasterCard. You'll be able to use them at upmarket restaurants, shops, hotels, car-rental firms, travel agencies and most petrol stations.

With a credit card you can put big expenses like airline tickets on your account. Another major advantage is that they allow you to withdraw cash at selected banks or from ATMs that are linked internationally. However, if an ATM in Europe swallows a card that was issued outside Europe, it can be a major headache. Also, some credit cards aren't hooked up to ATM networks unless you specifically ask your bank to do this.

Cash cards, which you use at home to withdraw money directly from your bank account or savings account, can be used throughout Eastern Europe at those ATMs linked to international networks like Cirrus and Maestro.

If you use a credit – not a cash – card to get money from an ATM, you pay interest on the money from the moment you get it. You can get around that by leaving the card in credit when you depart or by having somebody at home pay money into the card account from time to time. On the plus side, you don't pay commission charges to exchange money and the exchange rate is usually at a better interbank rate than that offered for travellers cheques or cash exchanges. Bear in mind that if you use a credit card for purchases, exchange rates may have changed by the time your bill is processed, which can work out to your advantage or disadvantage.

Charge cards like American Express and Diners Club have offices in most countries, and they can generally replace a lost card within 24 hours. That's because they treat you as a customer of the company rather than of the bank that issued the card. In theory, the credit they offer is unlimited and they don't charge interest on outstanding accounts, but they do charge fees for to join and have an annual membership, and payment is due in full within a few weeks of the account statement date. Their major drawback is that they're not widely accepted off the beaten track of mainstream travel. Charge cards may also be hooked up to some ATM networks.

Credit and credit/debit cards like Visa and MasterCard are more widely accepted because they tend to charge merchants lower commissions. The major drawback of these cards is that they have a credit limit, based on your income, and this limit may not be high enough to cover all your major expenses like long-term car rental or long-distance airline tickets, especially if you're travelling for an extended period and using the card all the time. You can get around this by leaving your card account in credit when you leave home. Other drawbacks are that interest is charged on outstanding balances, either immediately or after a set period (always immediately on cash advances) and that the card can be very difficult to replace if lost abroad.

If you choose to rely on plastic, go for two different cards – a MasterCard or Visa, for instance, with an American Express or Diners Club backup. Better still is a combination of credit card and travellers cheques so you have something to fall back on if an ATM swallows your card or the banks in the area won't accept it (a not uncommon and always inexplicable occurrence).

A word of warning about credit cards: fraudulent shopkeepers have been known to make several charge-slip imprints with your credit card when you're not looking and then simply copy your signature from the authorised slip. There have also been reports of these unscrupulous people making quick and very high-tech duplicates of credit or debit card information with a machine. If your card leaves your possession for longer than you think necessary, consider cancelling it.

International Transfers While not very expensive, telegraphic transfers can be quite slow. Be sure to specify the name of the bank and the name and address of the branch where you'd like to pick it up.

Having money wired through American Express or MoneyGram used by Thomas Cook is faster and fairly straightforward; for the former you don't need to be a card-holder and it takes less than a day. You should know the sender's full name, the exact amount and

the reference number when you're picking up the cash. With a passport or other ID you'll be given the amount in US dollars or local currency. The sender pays the service fee (eg, US$20 for $100, US$40 for $500, US$60 for $1000 etc).

Black Market The conditions for a 'black market' exists whenever a government puts restrictions on free currency trading through regulations that prohibit banks and licensed foreign exchange dealers from changing the national currency into another. Now that most Eastern European currencies have reached (or are approaching) convertibility, the days when you could get five times the official rate for cash on the streets of Warsaw and Bucharest are well and truly over. Essentially there is no longer a black market in most countries of this region; anyone who approaches you offering such a deal (an uncommon occurrence these days) is your average, garden-variety thief.

Costs
This book provides a range of prices to suit every budget. See the Facts for the Visitor sections in the individual country chapters for specific information regarding travelling expenses.

Tipping & Bargaining
Throughout Eastern Europe you tip by rounding up restaurant bills and taxi fares to the next whole figure as you're paying. In some countries restaurants will already have added a service charge to your bill, so you needn't round it up much (if at all). A tip of 10% is quite sufficient if you feel you have been well attended. The waiters in any establishment catering mostly to foreign tourists will expect such a tip. If you're dissatisfied with the food or service at a restaurant, or feel you have been overcharged, you can convey the message by paying the exact amount without a gratuity included. If 'rounding up' means you're only giving honest waiters a couple of cents, add a few more coins to keep them happy. In general you don't leave a tip on the table in Eastern Europe (one exception is the Balkans), but you should tell your waiter how much you're prepared to give.

Some bargaining goes on in the markets, but the best you should hope for is a 20% reduction on the initial asking price.

Taxes & Refunds

A kind of sales tax called value-added tax (VAT) applies to most goods and services in many Eastern European countries; it can be as high as 25% in Hungary, 22% in the Czech Republic and 20% in Belarus, Moldova, Russia and Ukraine. In general, visitors can claim back the VAT on purchases that are being taken out of the country. The procedure for making the claim can be fairly straightforward (as in Slovenia) or rather complicated (as in Hungary), and there will be minimum-purchase amounts imposed. When making your purchase ask the shop attendant for a VAT refund voucher filled in with the correct amount and the date. This is usually refunded directly at international airports and border crossings, or validated and mailed back by the consumer for a refund.

CUSTOMS

While there's no problem with bringing in and taking out personal effects, be aware that antiques, books printed before 1945, crystal glass, gemstones, lottery tickets, philatelic materials, precious metals (gold, silver, platinum), securities and valuable works of art may still have to be declared in writing or even accompanied by a 'museum certificate' (available from the place of purchase) in many Eastern European countries. There may also be restrictions on the import/export of local currency, although the amounts these days are actually quite large (for example, the limit now is 350,000Ft in Hungary).

Throughout most of Eastern Europe, the usual allowances for tobacco (eg, 200 to 250 cigarettes, but a lung-busting 1000 cigarettes in Belarus), alcohol (2L of wine, 1L of spirits) and perfume (50g) apply to duty-free goods purchased at airports or on ferries. Customs checks are pretty cursory and you probably won't even have to open your bags, but don't be lulled into a false sense of security. When you least expect it…

POST & COMMUNICATIONS

Post

Details of post offices are given in the Information sections of each city or town in the individual country chapters. Postage costs vary from country to country as does postal efficiency – the Polish post office, while improving from the dark ages of a few years ago, is still not very reliable. Airmail from Belarus to Western Europe takes at least 10 days, is less efficient from Ukraine (two weeks or more) and carrier pigeons beat the Moldova post office (up to six weeks) wings down.

If you wish to receive snail mail while travelling you can have it sent care of poste restante (general delivery). Tell the sender to put the number 1 after the city name to insure that the letter goes to the main post office in that city. They should also underline your last name, as letters are often misfiled under first names. (The latter is particularly important when sending letters to Hungary where the family name *always* comes first.) The poste-restante offices seldom hold letters longer than a month and some charge a small fee for each letter picked up.

You can also have mail sent to you at American Express offices as long as you have an American Express card or are carrying its branded travellers cheques. When you buy American Express cheques, ask for a booklet listing all its office addresses worldwide. American Express will forward mail for a small fee, but what it won't do is accept parcels, registered letters, notices for registered letters, answer telephone inquiries about mail or hold mail longer than 30 days.

To send a parcel from Eastern Europe you usually have to take it unwrapped to a main post office. Parcels weighing over 2kg must often be taken to a special customs post office. Have the paper, string and tape ready. They'll usually ask to see your passport and note the number on the form. If you don't have a return address within the country put your name care of any large tourist hotel to satisfy them.

Telephone

Telephone service has improved throughout the region in a very short time. Telephone centres – where they exist – are generally in the same building as the main post office and may sometimes have Internet cafés. Here you can often make your call from one of the booths inside an enclosed area, paying the cashier as you leave. Public telephones are almost always found at post offices. Local telephone cards, available from post offices, telephone centres, newsstands or retail outlets, are popular everywhere in the region. In fact, in many countries they have become the norm.

There's a wide range of local and international phonecards. Lonely Planet's ekno global communication service provides low cost international calls, a range of messaging services, an online travel vault where you can store your important documents, free email and travel information, all in one easy service. Join online at **w** www.ekno.lonelyplanet.com, where you can also find the best local access numbers to connect to the 24-hour customer service centre to join or find out more. Once you have joined always check the ekno website for the latest access numbers for each country and updates on new features.

For local calls you're usually better off with a local phonecard.

To call abroad you simply dial the international access code for the country you are calling from (most commonly 00 in Eastern Europe, but 8/wait for tone/10 in Belarus, Moldova and Ukraine and 000 in Estonia), the country code for the country you are calling, the local area code (usually dropping the initial zero if there is one) and the number. If you are in Hungary (international access code 00) and want to make a call to the UK (country code 44), London (area code 020), local number ☎ 8123 4567, then you dial ☎ 00-44-20-8123 4567. To call from Bulgaria (international access code 00) to Australia (61), Sydney (02), number ☎ 1234 5678, you dial ☎ 00-61-2-1234 5678.

To make a domestic call to another city in the same country in Eastern Europe dial the area code with the initial zero and the number. Area codes for individual cities and regions are provided in the country chapters.

For country codes, see Appendix – Telephones at the end of the book.

Fax
You can send and receive faxes at main post offices throughout Eastern Europe.

Email & Internet Access
Major Internet service providers such as **AOL** (**w** www.aol.com), **CompuServe** (**w** www.compuserve.com) and **AT&T** (**w** www.att.com) have dial-in nodes throughout Europe; it's best to download a list of the dial-in numbers before you leave home. If you access your Internet email account at home through a small ISP or your office or school network, your best option is either to open an account with a global ISP, like those already mentioned, or to rely on Internet cafés and other public access points to collect your mail.

If you do intend to rely on Internet cafés, you'll need three pieces of information with

you to access your Internet mail account: your incoming (POP or IMAP) mail server name, your account name and your password. Your ISP or network supervisor will give you these. With this information, you should be able to access your Internet mail account from any Internet-connected machine across the world, provided it runs some kind of email software (remember that Netscape and Internet Explorer both have mail modules). Most ISPs also enable you to receive emails through its website, which only requires you to remember your account name and password. Become familiar with the process for doing this before you leave home.

You'll find Internet cafés throughout Eastern Europe – check out **w** www.netcafeguide.com for an up-to-date list. You may also be able to access the Web at telephone centres, post offices, hostels, hotels and universities.

DIGITAL RESOURCES
The Internet is a rich resource for travellers. You can research your trip, hunt down bargain air fares, book hotels, check on weather conditions or chat with locals and other travellers about the best places to visit (or avoid!).

Airline Information What airlines fly where, when and for how much.
w www.travelocity.com

Airline Tickets Name the price you're willing to pay for an airline seat and if an airline has an empty seat for which it would rather get something than nothing, US-based Priceline lets you know.
w www.priceline.com

Currency Conversions Exchange rates of hundreds of currencies worldwide.
w www.xe.net/ucc

Lonely Planet There's no better place to start your Web explorations than the Lonely Planet website. Here you'll find succinct summaries on travelling to most places on earth, postcards from other travellers and the Thorn Tree bulletin board, where you can ask questions before you go or dispense advice when you get back. You can also find travel news and updates to many of our most popular guidebooks, and the subWWWay section links you to the most useful travel resources elsewhere on the Web.
w www.lonelyplanet.com

Tourist Offices Lists tourist offices at home and around the world for most countries.
w www.towd.com

Train Information Train fares and schedules for the most popular routes in Europe, including information on rail and youth passes.
w www.raileurope.com

NEWSPAPERS & MAGAZINES

In larger city and towns you are able to buy the *International Herald Tribune* on the day of publication. Other English-language newspapers widely available are the colourful but superficial *USA Today*, the *Financial Times*, the European edition of the *Wall Street Journal* and the weekly *Guardian International*. News magazines like *Newsweek*, *Time* and the *Economist* are also readily available.

The *Central European Economic Review* is a monthly published by the *Wall Street Journal*. For more detailed coverage of Poland, the Czech Republic, Slovakia, Hungary and the Baltic countries, there's the *Central European Business Weekly*. It's sold at major newsstands in Eastern Europe.

For a local slant on international news and to learn lots more about the country you're visiting, pick up one of the English-language weeklies that have sprouted in Eastern Europe like mushrooms after rain: the *Prague Post*, *Slovenia Weekly*, *Budapest Sun*, *Slovak Spectator* and *Croatia Weekly*. In Russia there is the *St Petersburg Times* twice weekly, and the *Moscow Times* is a daily. See Newspapers & Magazines in the Facts for the Visitor sections of the individual country chapters for details on other local newspapers in English.

RADIO & TV

You can pick up a mixture of the BBC World Service and BBC for Europe on medium wave at 648kHz AM and on short wave at 1296kHz, 6195kHz, 9410kHz and 12095kHz (a good daytime frequency), depending on your location and the time of day. BBC Radio 4 broadcasts on 198kHz long wave.

You can usually find the Voice of America (VOA) on 1197kHz AM and at various times of the day on the other frequencies of 7170kHz, 9530kHz, 9760kHz, 11825kHz, 15205kHz and 15335kHz.

Cable and satellite TV have spread across Europe with more gusto than radio. Most larger hotels and pensions and even some hostels subscribe to satellite channels such as Sky News, CNN, Eurosport and MTV.

VIDEO SYSTEMS

If you want to record or buy videotapes to play back home, you won't get the picture if the image registration systems are different. Like Australia and most of the rest of Europe, Eastern Europe usually uses PAL (but sometimes the French SECAM system so check on your arrival), which is incompatible with the North American and Japanese NTSC system.

PHOTOGRAPHY & VIDEO

Eastern Europe and its people are extremely photogenic, but location and the weather will dictate what film to take or buy locally. In places such as northern Poland or the Czech Republic, where the sky can often be overcast, photographers should bring high-speed film such as 200 or 400 ASA. In sunny weather (or when the mountains are under a blanket of snow) slower film is the answer.

Film and camera equipment is available everywhere in Eastern Europe, but obviously shops in the larger places have a wider choice. Avoid buying film at tourist sites in Europe, such as the Castle District in Budapest or by Charles Bridge in Prague. It may have been stored badly or reached its sell-by date. It certainly will be more expensive than in shops.

In most Eastern European countries (as elsewhere) it's prohibited to take pictures of anything that might be considered of strategic importance – from bridges and tunnels to train stations and border crossings. Occasionally you will see a vintage sign showing a crossed-out camera indicating that there's something of interest in the vicinity. These days local officials are much less paranoid about photography than they were, but use common sense when it comes to this issue. And have the courtesy to ask permission before taking close-up photos of people.

Lonely Planet's *Travel Photography* by Richard I'Anson will help you capture the pictures you've always wanted.

Properly used, a video camera can give a fascinating record of your holiday. Unlike still photography, video 'flows' so, for example, you can shoot scenes of countryside rolling past the train window. Make sure you keep the batteries charged and have the necessary charger, plugs and transformer for the country you are visiting. In most countries, it is possible to obtain video cartridges easily in large towns and cities, but make sure you buy the correct format. It is usually worth buying at least a few cartridges duty-free at the start of your trip.

TIME

Many of the places covered in this book are on Central European Time (GMT/UTC plus one hour), the same time used from Spain to Poland. Belarus, Bulgaria, Estonia, Greece, Latvia, Lithuania, Moldova, Romania and Ukraine are all on Eastern European Time (GMT/UTC plus two hours), while Moscow and St Petersburg are on MSK (or Moscow) Time (GMT/UTC plus three hours).

Without taking daylight-saving times into account, if it's 6pm in Warsaw and Madrid, it will be 7pm in Bucharest and Sofia, 8pm in Moscow, 5pm in London, noon in New York, 9am in Los Angeles and 3am the next morning in Sydney.

Clocks are advanced for daylight-saving time in most countries on the last Sunday in March and set back one hour on the last Sunday in September.

ELECTRICITY

All the countries of Eastern Europe run on 220V, 50Hz AC. Check the voltage and cycle (usually 50Hz) used in your home country. Most appliances that are set up for 220V will handle 240V quite happily without modifications (and vice versa); the same goes for 110V and 125V combinations. It's preferable to adjust your appliance to the exact voltage if you can (some modern battery chargers and radios will do this automatically). Don't mix 110/125V with 220/240V without a transformer, which will be built in if the appliance can in fact be adjusted.

Several countries outside Europe (the USA and Canada, for instance) have 60Hz AC, which will affect the speed of electric motors even after the voltage has been adjusted, so CD and tape players (where motor speed is all-important) will be useless. But appliances such as electric razors, hair dryers, irons and radios will work fine.

Plugs in Eastern Europe and Russia are the standard round two-pin variety, sometimes called the 'europlug'. If your plugs are of a different design, you'll need an adapter.

WEIGHTS & MEASURES

The metric system is used throughout Eastern Europe; there's a conversion table at the back of this book.

HEALTH

Travel health depends on your predeparture preparations, your daily health care while travelling and how you handle any medical problem that does develop.

Predeparture planning

Immunisations Before you leave, find out from your doctor, a travel health centre or an organisation such as the US-based **Centers for Disease Control and Prevention** (**W** *www.cdc.gov*) what the current recommendations are for travel to your destination. Remember to leave enough time so that you can get any vaccinations you need – six weeks before travel is ideal. Discuss your requirements with your doctor, but generally it's a good idea to make sure your tetanus, diphtheria and polio vaccinations are up to date before travelling. Other vaccinations that may be recommended for your destination include typhoid, hepatitis A, hepatitis B, rabies and tick-borne encephalitis.

Although there is no risk of yellow fever in Europe, if you are arriving from a yellow-fever infected area (most of sub-Saharan Africa and parts of South America) you'll need proof of yellow fever vaccination before you will be allowed to enter some countries such as Albania.

All vaccinations should be recorded on an International Health Certificate (see that section under Visas & Documents earlier in this chapter).

Health Insurance Make sure that you have adequate health insurance. See Travel Insurance under Visas & Documents earlier in this chapter for details.

Travel Health Guides For advice on travel health for younger children consult Lonely Planet's *Travel with Children*.

There are also a number of excellent travel health sites on the Internet. The World Health Organization at **W** www.who.int and the US Centers for Disease Control and Prevention at **W** www.cdc.gov have good sites, while the Lonely Planet website at **W** www.lonelyplanet .com/weblinks/wlheal.htm has a number of excellent links.

Other Preparations Make sure you're healthy before you start travelling. If you are going on a long trip make sure your teeth are OK. If you wear glasses take a spare pair and your prescription.

If you require a particular medication take an adequate supply, as it may not be available locally. Take part of the packaging showing the generic name, rather than the brand, which

Travellers Thrombosis

Sitting inactive for long periods of time on any form of transport (bus, train or plane), especially if in cramped conditions, can give you swollen feet and ankles, and may increase the possibility of deep vein thrombosis (DVT).

DVT is when a clot forms in the deep veins of your legs. DVT may be symptomless or you may get an uncomfortable ache and swelling of your calf. What makes DVT a concern is that, in a minority of people, a small piece of the clot can break off and travel to the lungs to cause a pulmonary embolism, a very serious medical condition.

To help prevent DVT during long-haul travel, you should move around as much as possible and while you are sitting you should flex your calf muscles and wriggle your toes every half-hour. It's also a good idea to drink plenty of water or juices during the journey to prevent dehydration, and, for the same reason, avoid drinking caffeine-containing drinks or lots of alcohol. In addition, you may want to consider wearing support stockings if you have had leg swelling in the past or you are over 40.

If you are prone to blood clotting or are pregnant, you will need to discuss preventive measures with your doctor before you leave.

will make getting replacements easier. It's a good idea to have a legible prescription or letter from your doctor to show that you legally use the medication to avoid any problems.

Basic Rules

Food Salads and fruit should be safe throughout Eastern Europe though if you're avoiding tap water remember that leafy vegetables served in restaurants will have been washed with it. Take care with undercooked eggs or raw, which can cause intestinal illnesses. Ice cream is usually OK, but be wary if it has melted and been refrozen. Take great care with fish or shellfish (for instance, cooked mussels that haven't opened properly can be dangerous) and avoid undercooked meat.

If a place looks clean and well run and if the vendor also looks clean and healthy, then the food is probably safe. In general, places that are packed with travellers or local people will be fine. Be careful with food that has been cooked and left to go cold, as is often the case in old-style self-service restaurants in

Poland, the Czech Republic, Slovakia and Hungary. You could experience some gut problems in Poland where stuffed foods are common and tend to go off quickly in the warmer months; just avoid things like stuffed cabbage and meat *pierogi* (dumplings) in warm weather.

Mushroom-picking is a favourite pastime – some would say a religion – in some parts of Eastern Europe, but make sure you don't eat mushrooms that haven't been positively identified as safe. Some countries like Hungary and Slovenia set up free inspection tables at markets or at entrances to national parks to separate the good from the bad or even deadly. In a pinch, most pharmacists will be able to distinguish between the two.

Water In Eastern Europe it's best to stick to bottled or purified water, though always seek local advice (especially in polluted southwestern Poland and Romania). Never ever drink unboiled tap water in St Petersburg; it contains *Giardia lamblia*. Many Czechs prefer to drink reasonably priced bottled water, and water from the tap doesn't always look so good in Hungary. If you decide not to drink tap water, then you shouldn't use ice cubes either as even luxury hotels often make their ice from unboiled tap water.

Always be wary of natural water. The water in the flowing stream in the High Tatras may look crystal clear and very inviting, but before drinking it you need to be absolutely sure there are no settlements or cattle upstream. Run-off from fertilised fields is also a concern. If you are planning extended hikes where you have to rely on natural water, it may be useful to know about water purification.

The simplest way of purifying water is to boil it thoroughly. Technically this means bringing it to a rolling boil for 10 minutes, something that is rarely done. Remember that at high altitude water boils at a lower temperature, so germs are less likely to be killed. Boil it for longer in these environments.

Simple filtering will not remove all dangerous organisms, so if you cannot boil water it should be treated chemically. Chlorine tablets will kill many pathogens, but not some parasites like *Giardia lamblia* and amoebic cysts. Iodine is more effective in purifying water and is available in tablet form. Follow the directions carefully and remember that too much iodine can be harmful.

Medical Problems & Treatment

In emergencies you should try the casualty ward of any large general hospital. Finding the right hospital can sometimes take time, so in cases of real urgency you should have someone call an ambulance (see the Medical & Emergency Services sections of major cities in the country chapters). Hospital emergency (casualty) wards in Eastern Europe can cope with most medical problems, and the fees they ask are usually less than elsewhere in Europe. Most hospital doctors are eager to practise their English and will be very helpful, though in many cases the facilities are overcrowded.

Private medical practice is less common in Eastern Europe than it is in the West but with a private doctor you'll receive faster, more personalised attention than you would at a hospital. Embassies, tourist offices and receptionists in top-end hotels can often supply the name of an English-speaking doctor or dentist in the area.

If your problem isn't so serious try asking for advice at a pharmacy (chemist). Locally produced drugs and medicines are inexpensive – Hungary and Slovenia are leading producers of pharmaceuticals – and there's often someone there who understands a little English, German or, at the very least, sign language. Chemists also sell multivitamins, bottled medicinal water and even herbal teas and shampoos. Western brand names are expensive in Eastern Europe, so bring along any medicines you cannot do without, including something for headaches, common colds and stomach upsets. Prescriptions should be expressed in generic terminology.

Environmental Hazards

Altitude Sickness Lack of oxygen at high altitudes (over 3000m) affects most people to some extent. The effect may be mild or severe and occurs because less oxygen reaches the muscles and the brain, requiring the heart and lungs to compensate by working harder. Very few treks or ski runs in the High Tatras or the Julian Alps approach such heights, so it's unlikely to be a major concern.

Mild symptoms include headache, vomiting, dizziness, extreme faintness as well as difficulty in breathing and sleeping. Any mild altitude problems should abate after a day or so, but if symptoms persist or become worse the only treatment is to descend – even 500m can help – and seek medical advice.

Heat Exhaustion & Prickly Heat Salt deficiencyand dehydration can cause heat exhaustion. Take time to acclimatise to high temperatures, drink sufficient liquids and do not do anything too physically demanding.

Salt deficiency is characterised by fatigue, lethargy, headaches, giddiness and muscle cramps; salt tablets may help, but adding extra salt on your food is better.

Prickly heat is an itchy rash caused by excessive perspiration trapped under the skin. It usually strikes people who have just arrived in a hot climate. Try to keep cool, shower often, dry the skin and use a mild talcum or prickly heat powder, wear loose cotton clothing, or even resort to air-conditioning.

Sunburn You can get sunburnt surprisingly quickly, even through cloud and particularly at high altitude. Use a sunscreen, hat and barrier cream for your nose and lips. Calamine lotion or a sting-relief spray are good for mild sunburn. Protect your eyes with good-quality sunglasses, particularly if you will be near water, sand or snow.

Heatstroke This sometimes fatal condition can occur if the body's heat-regulating mechanism breaks down, and the body temperature rises to dangerous levels. Long, continuous periods of exposure to high temperatures and insufficient fluids can leave you vulnerable to heatstroke. You should avoid excessive alcohol or strenuous activity when you first arrive in a hot climate.

The symptoms are feeling unwell, not sweating very much or at all, and a high body temperature (39°C to 41°C). Where sweating has ceased, the skin becomes flushed and red. Severe, throbbing headaches and lack of co-ordination will also occur, and the sufferer may be confused or aggressive. If untreated, severe cases will eventually become delirious or convulse. Hospitalisation is essential, but in the meantime get victims out of the sun, remove their clothing, cover them with a wet sheet or towel and then fan them continually. Give fluids if they are conscious.

Hypothermia Too much cold is just as dangerous as too much heat, particularly if it leads to hypothermia. Cold combined with wind and moisture (ie, soaking rain) is particularly risky. If you are hiking at high altitudes or in a cool, wet environment, be prepared.

Hypothermia occurs when the body loses heat faster than it can produce it and the core temperature of the body drops. It is very easy to progress from very cold to dangerously cold through a combination of wind, wet clothing, fatigue and hunger, even when the air temperature is above freezing. It's best to dress in layers – silk, wool and some of the new artificial fibres are good insulating materials. A hat is important, as a lot of heat is lost through the head. A strong, waterproof outer layer is essential. Carry basic food supplies, including items that contain simple sugars to generate heat quickly and lots of fluids.

Symptoms of hypothermia are exhaustion, numb skin (particularly toes and fingers), shivering, slurred speech, irrational or violent behaviour, lethargy, stumbling, dizzy spells, muscle cramps and violent bursts of energy. Irrationality may take the form of sufferers claiming they are warm and trying to take off their clothes.

To treat a case of mild hypothermia, first get the person out of the wind and/or rain, remove their clothing if it's wet and replace it with dry, warm clothing. Give them hot, non-alcoholic liquids and some high-kilojoule (high-calorie), easily digestible food. Do not rub victims. Instead, allow them to slowly warm themselves. This should be enough for the early stages of hypothermia. Early recognition and treatment of mild hypothermia is the only way to prevent severe hypothermia, which is a critical condition.

Hay Fever Those who suffer from hay fever should be aware that the pollen count in certain parts of Eastern Europe – Romania is one place that springs to mind – is especially high during May and June.

Infectious Diseases
Diarrhoea Simple things like a change of water, food or climate can all cause a mild bout of diarrhoea, but a few rushed toilet trips with no other symptoms is not indicative of a major problem.

Dehydration is the main danger with any diarrhoea, particularly in the elderly or children as dehydration can occur quite quickly. Under all circumstances fluid replacement (at least equal to the volume being lost) is the most important thing to remember. Weak black tea with a little sugar, soda water, or soft drinks allowed to go flat and diluted 50%

with clean water are all good. With a severe case, a rehydrating solution is preferable to replace minerals and salts lost. Commercially available oral rehydration salts (ORS) are very useful; add them to boiled or bottled water. In an emergency you can make up a solution of six teaspoons of sugar and a half teaspoon of salt to a litre of boiled or bottled water. Keep drinking small amounts often. Stick to a bland diet as you recover.

Over-the-counter diarrhoea remedies such as loperamide or diphenoxylate (sold under many different brand names) can be used to bring relief from the symptoms, although they do not actually cure the problem. Only use these drugs if you do not have access to toilets, eg, if you *must* travel. Note that these drugs are not recommended for children under 12 years.

In certain situations antibiotics may be required: severe diarrhoea, diarrhoea with blood or mucus (dysentery), diarrhoea with fever, profuse watery diarrhoea, persistent diarrhoea not improving after 48 hours and severe diarrhoea. These suggest a more serious cause of diarrhoea and in these situations over-the-counter diarrhoea remedies should be avoided and you should consult a doctor.

Viral Gastroenteritis This is caused not by bacteria but, as the name suggests, by a virus. It is characterised by stomach cramps, diarrhoea and sometimes by vomiting and/or a slight fever. All you can do is rest and drink lots of fluids.

Fungal Infections These types of infections occur more commonly in hot weather and are usually found on the scalp, between the toes (athlete's foot) or fingers, in the groin and on the body (ringworm). You get ringworm (which is a fungal infection, not a worm) from infected animals or other people. Moisture encourages these infections.

To prevent fungal infections wear loose, comfortable clothes, avoid artificial fibres, wash frequently and dry carefully. If you do get an infection, wash the infected area at least daily with a disinfectant or medicated soap and water, and rinse and dry well. Apply an antifungal cream or powder like tolnaftate. Try to expose the infected area to air or sunlight as much as possible and wash all towels and underwear in hot water, change them often and let them dry in the sun.

Hepatitis This is a general term for inflammation of the liver. Symptoms include fever, chills, headache, feelings of weakness, fatigue and aches and pains, followed by loss of appetite, nausea, vomiting, abdominal pain, dark urine, light-coloured faeces, jaundiced (yellow) skin and yellowing of the whites of the eyes. People who have had hepatitis should avoid alcohol for some time after the illness, as the liver needs time to recover.

Hepatitis A is transmitted by contaminated food and drinking water. You should seek medical advice, but there is not very much you can do apart from resting, drinking lots of fluids, eating lightly and avoiding fatty foods. Hepatitis E is transmitted in the same way as hepatitis A; it can be particularly serious in pregnant women.

Hepatitis B is spread through contact with infected blood, blood products or body fluids, such as through sexual contact, unsterilised needles and blood transfusions, or contact with blood via small breaks in the skin. Other risk situations include having a shave, tattoo or body piercing with contaminated equipment. The symptoms of hepatitis B may be more severe than type A and the disease may lead to long-term problems such as chronic liver damage, liver cancer or a long-term carrier state. Hepatitis C and D are spread in the same way as hepatitis B and can also lead to long-term complications.

There are vaccines against hepatitis A and B, but there are currently no vaccines against the other types. Following the basic rules about food and water (hepatitis A and E) and avoiding risk situations (hepatitis B, C and D) are important preventative measures.

HIV & AIDS The 'human immunodeficiency virus' – HIV – may lead to AIDS, Acquired Immune Deficiency Syndrome, which is a fatal disease. Any exposure to blood, blood products or body fluids may put an individual at some risk. The disease is often transmitted through sexual contact or dirty needles – vaccinations, acupuncture, tattooing and body piercing can be as potentially dangerous as intravenous drug use. HIV/AIDS can also be spread through infected blood transfusions; blood used for transfusions in European hospitals is screened for HIV and should be safe.

An HIV test is required for all travellers planning to stay more than three months in Russia, HIV testing is required for foreigners requesting work permits or residency in Estonia, and an HIV test may be required for those staying more than one month in Bulgaria.

Sexually Transmitted Infections HIV/AIDS and hepatitis B can both be transmitted through sexual contact – see the relevant sections earlier for details. Other STIs include gonorrhoea, herpes and syphilis; sores, blisters or rashes around the genitals, discharges or pain when urinating are some common symptoms. In some STIs, such as wart virus or chlamydia, symptoms may be less marked or not observed at all, especially in women. Chlamydia infection can cause infertility in men and women before any symptoms have been noticed. Syphilis symptoms eventually disappear completely but the disease continues and can cause severe problems in later years. While abstinence from sexual contact is the only 100% sure prevention, using condoms is also effective. The treatment of both gonorrhoea and syphilis is with antibiotics.

STI clinics are widespread in Eastern Europe. Don't be shy about visiting if you think you may have contracted something; they are there to help and have seen it all before.

Cuts, Bites & Stings
Bedbugs & Lice Bedbugs live in various places, but particularly in dirty mattresses and bedding, evidenced by spots of blood on bedclothes or on the wall. Bedbugs leave itchy bites in neat rows. Calamine lotion or a sting relief spray may help.

All lice cause itching and discomfort. They make themselves at home in your hair (head lice), your clothing (body lice) or your pubic hair (crabs). You catch lice through direct contact with infected people or by sharing combs, clothing and the like. Powder or shampoo treatment will kill the lice and infected clothing should then be washed in very hot, soapy water and left in the sun to dry.

Insect Bites & Stings Mosquitoes will drive you almost insane during the late spring and summer months in Eastern Europe, so take some kind of insect repellent. If you are without a mosquito net, they will also cause sleepless nights in wet areas such as Lake Balaton in Hungary and the Great Masurian Lakes in Poland. Fortunately, mosquito-borne diseases like malaria are pretty much unknown in this part of the world, with the exception of the Danube Delta in Romania. Most people get used to mosquito bites after a few days as their bodies adjust, and the itching and swelling will become less severe. An antihistamine cream may help alleviate the symptoms. For some people, a daily dose of vitamin B seems to keep mosquitoes at bay.

Ticks You should always check all over your body if you have been doing any walking through a potentially tick-infested area as ticks can cause skin infections and other more serious diseases. If a tick is found attached, press down around the tick's head with tweezers, pinch the head and gently pull upwards. Avoid pulling the rear of the body as this may squeeze the tick's gut contents through the attached mouth parts into the skin, increasing the risk of infection and disease. Smearing chemicals on the tick will not make it let go and is not recommended.

Snakes In Eastern Europe, snakes tend to keep a very low profile but to minimise your chances of being bitten, try to wear boots, socks and long trousers when walking through undergrowth or rocky areas where snakes may be present. Tramp heavily and they'll usually slither away before you come near. Don't put your hands into holes and crevices, and be careful when collecting firewood.

Snake bites do not cause instantaneous death and antivenenes are usually available. Keep the victim calm and still, wrap the bitten limb tightly, as you would for a sprained ankle, and attach a splint to immobilise it. Then seek medical help, if possible with the dead snake for identification. Don't attempt to catch the snake if there is even a remote possibility of it biting again. Tourniquets and sucking out the poison are now completely discredited.

Women's Health

Antibiotic use, synthetic underwear, sweating and contraceptive pills can all lead to fungal vaginal infections when travelling in hot climates. Maintaining good personal hygiene, and loose-fitting clothes and cotton underwear will help to prevent these infections.

Fungal infections, characterised by a rash, itch and discharge, can be treated with a highly diluted vinegar or lemon-juice douche, or with yogurt. Antifungal pessaries or vaginal cream are the usual treatment.

Sexually transmitted infections are a major cause of vaginal problems. Symptoms include a smelly discharge, painful intercourse and sometimes a burning sensation when urinating. Male sexual partners must also be treated for the infection. Medical attention should be sought and remember in addition to these diseases HIV or hepatitis B may also be acquired during exposure. Besides abstinence, the best thing is to practise safe sex using condoms.

Less Common Diseases

Diphtheria There is an ongoing outbreak of diphtheria in the countries of the former Soviet Union. It mainly affects children and causes a cold-like illness, which is associated with a severe sore throat. A thick white membrane forms at the back of the throat, which can suffocate you, but what makes this a really nasty disease is that the diphtheria bug produces a very powerful poison that can cause paralysis and affect the heart. Vaccination against this serious disease is very effective.

Rabies The only Eastern European countries that are rabies-free are Albania and Macedonia. Many animals can be infected (such as dogs, cats, bats and monkeys) and it is their saliva that is infectious. Any bite, scratch or even lick from an animal should be cleaned immediately and thoroughly. Scrub with soap and running water, and then apply alcohol or iodine solution. Medical advice should be sought immediately as to the possibility of rabies in the region. A course of injections may then be required in order to prevent the onset of symptoms and death.

Lyme Disease This is a tick-transmitted infection, which may be acquired in parts of Eastern Europe. The illness usually begins with a spreading rash at the site of the tick bite and is accompanied by fever, headache, extreme fatigue, aching joints and muscles and mild neck stiffness. If untreated, these symptoms usually resolve over several weeks but over subsequent weeks or months disorders of the nervous system, heart and joints may develop. Treatment works best early in the illness. Medical help should be sought.

Tick-borne Encephalitis Ticks can carry encephalitis, a virus-borne cerebral inflammation. Tick-borne encephalitis can occur in most forest and rural areas of Eastern Europe, especially in Hungary and the Czech Republic. Symptoms include blotches around the bite, which is sometimes pale in the middle. Headache, stiffness and other flu-like symptoms, as well as extreme tiredness, appearing a week or two after the bite has been inflicted, can progress to more serious problems. Medical help must be sought.

Typhoid This dangerous gut infection is caused by contaminated water and food. Medical help must be sought. In its early stages sufferers may feel they as though they have a bad cold or flu on the way, as early symptoms are a headache, body aches and a fever, which rises a little each day until it is around 40°C (104°F) or more. The victim's pulse is often slow relative to the degree of fever present – unlike with a normal fever where the pulse rate increases. There may also be vomiting, abdominal pain, diarrhoea or constipation. In the second week the high fever and slow pulse continue and a few pink spots may appear on the body; trembling, delirium, weakness, weight loss and dehydration may occur. Complications such as pneumonia, perforated bowel or meningitis may also occur.

Tetanus This disease is caused by a germ that lives in soil and in the faeces of horses and other animals. It enters the body via breaks in the skin. The first symptom may be discomfort in swallowing, or stiffening of the jaw and neck; this is followed by painful convulsions of the jaw and whole body. The disease can be fatal. It can be prevented by vaccination.

WOMEN TRAVELLERS

Frustrating though it is, women travellers continue to face more challenging situations when travelling than men do. If you are a women traveller, especially a solo woman, you may find it helpful to understand the status of local women to better understand the responses you illicit from locals. Hopes of travelling inconspicuously, spending time alone and absorbing the surroundings are often thwarted by men who assume a lone woman desires company, or who seemingly find it impossible to avert their penetrating gaze. Bear in mind that most of this behaviour, which can come across as threatening, is more often than not harmless. Don't let it deter you! The more women that travel, alone or in pairs or groups, the less attention women

will attract and, in time, the more freedom women will feel to gallivant across the globe, *sans* beau in tow.

Despite feminism's grip on many European countries, women remain underrepresented in positions of power, in both governmental and corporate spheres. Despite the exciting progress to elevate the status of women in recent years, women's leadership at the upper levels of institutions still leaves a lot to be desired, and in many areas, you may notice the glut of women in low-paid, menial jobs. As is the case worldwide, women remain overrepresented among the illiterate and unemployed.

In Muslim countries, where conservative conceptions of the largely house-bound role of women still tend to prevail, women travelling alone or with other women will certainly be of interest or curiosity to both men and women. Unmarried men rarely have contact with women outside their family unit, which is why many men in, for example, Albania and Bosnia-Hercegovina, may afford travelling women so much attention. In such areas, women travelling with a male companion will often experience the opposite, and may need to pinch themselves as a reminder that yes, they actually exist.

GAY & LESBIAN TRAVELLERS

Eastern Europe lists contact addresses and gay and lesbian venues in the individual country chapters; look in the Facts for the Visitor and Entertainment sections.

The *Spartacus International Gay Guide* (Bruno Gmünder; US$39.95) is a good male-only international directory of gay entertainment venues in Europe and elsewhere. But use it in conjunction with listings in local gay papers, usually distributed for free at gay bars and clubs; as everywhere, gay venues in Eastern Europe change with the speed of summer lightning. *Women's Travel in Your Pocket* (Ferrari Publications; US$15.95) is one good international guide for lesbians.

DISABLED TRAVELLERS

If you have a physical disability, get in touch with your national support organisation (preferably the travel officer if there is one) and ask about the countries you plan to visit. They often have complete libraries devoted to travel, with useful things like access guides, and they can put you in touch with travel agencies who specialise in tours for the disabled. The British-based **Royal Association for Disability & Rehabilitation** *(RADAR;* ☎ *020-7250 3222, fax 7250 0212;* **W** *www .radar.org.uk; 12 City Forum, 250 City Rd, London EC1V 8AF)* is a very helpful association with a number of publications for the disabled on sale.

SENIOR TRAVELLERS

Senior citizens are entitled to many discounts in Eastern Europe on things like public transport, museum admission fees etc, provided they show proof of their age. In some cases they might need a special pass. The minimum qualifying age is generally 60 or 65 for men and slightly younger for women.

In your home country, a lower age may already entitle you to all sorts of interesting travel packages and discounts (on car hire, for instance) through organisations and travel agents that cater for senior travellers. Start hunting at your local senior citizens advice bureau. European residents over 60 are eligible for the Railplus Card.

TRAVEL WITH CHILDREN

Successful travel with young children requires planning and effort. Don't try to overdo things; even for adults, packing too much into the time available can cause problems. And make sure the activities include the kids as well – balance that morning at the Budapest Museum of Fine Arts with an afternoon at the nearby Grand Circus or a performance at the Puppet Theatre.

Include children in the trip planning; if they've helped to work out where you will be going, they will be much more interested when they get there. Lonely Planet's *Travel with Children* by Cathy Lanigan (with a foreword by Maureen Wheeler) is an excellent source of information.

In Eastern Europe most car-rental firms have children's safety seats for hire at a small cost, but it is essential that you book them in advance. The same goes for high chairs and cots (cribs); they're standard in many restaurants and hotels but numbers are limited. The choice of baby food, infant formulas, soy and cow's milk, disposable nappies (diapers) and the like can be as great in the supermarkets of many Eastern European countries as it is back home, but the opening hours may be quite different to what you are used to. Don't get caught out on the weekend.

DANGERS & ANNOYANCES

Eastern Europe is as safe – or unsafe – as any other part of the developed world. If you can handle yourself in the big cities of Western Europe, North America or Australia, you'll have little trouble dealing with the less pleasant sides of Eastern Europe. Look purposeful, keep alert and you'll be OK.

Whatever you do, don't leave friends and relatives worrying about how to get in touch with you in case of emergency. Work out a list of places where they can contact you or, best of all, phone home now and then or email.

Some local people will regale you with tales of how dangerous their city is and recount various cases of muggings, break-ins, kidnappings etc. Mostly they're comparing the present situation with that before 1989 when the crime rate was almost zero or, more usual, unreported in the press. Albania is one exception and crime is rife, especially in the north (muggings, carjackings, shootings). Bosnia and Kosovo have a unique form of danger – land mines. It's the only time Lonely Planet will ever advise you *not* to venture off the beaten track. Stray dogs in Bucharest are more of an annoyance than a danger, but steer clear of bitches with puppies.

Low-level corruption is disappearing fast as the back-scratching system so common during the communist regimes claims its rightful place in the dustbin of history, so do *not* pay bribes to persons in official positions, such as police, border guards, train conductors, ticket inspectors etc. If corrupt cops want to hold you up because some obscure stamp is missing from your documentation or on some other pretext, just let them and consider the experience an integral part of your trip.

Don't worry at all if they take you to the police station for questioning as you'll have a unique opportunity to observe the quality of justice in that country from the inside, and more senior officers will eventually let you go (assuming, of course, you haven't committed a real crime). If you do have to pay a fine or supplementary charge, insist on a proper receipt before turning over any money; this is now law in Hungary, for example, where traffic police were once notorious for demanding (and getting) gifts from motorists guilty of some alleged infraction. In all of this, try to maintain your cool as any threats from you will only make matters worse.

Theft

Theft is definitely a problem in Eastern Europe, and the threat comes both from local thieves and fellow travellers. The most important things to guard are your passport, other documents, tickets and money – in that order. It's always best to carry these next to your skin or in a sturdy leather pouch on your belt. Train-station lockers or luggage-storage counters are useful to store your luggage (but not valuables) while you get your bearings in a new town. Be very suspicious of people who offer to help you operate your locker. Carry your own padlock for hostel lockers.

You can lessen the risks further by being wary of snatch thieves. Cameras or shoulder bags are great for these people, who sometimes operate from motorcycles or scooters and slash the strap before you have a chance to react. A small daypack is better, but watch your rear. Be very careful at cafés and bars; loop the strap around your leg while seated.

Pickpockets are most active in dense crowds, especially in busy train stations and on public transport during peak hours. A common ploy in the Budapest and Prague metros has been for a group of well-dressed young people to surround you, chattering away while one of the group zips through your pockets or purse.

Be careful even in hotels; don't leave valuables lying around in your room. Also be wary of sudden friendships.

Parked cars containing luggage or other bags are prime targets for petty criminals in most cities, and cars with foreign number plates and/or rental agency stickers in particular. While driving in cities, beware of snatch thieves when you pull up at the lights – keep doors locked and windows rolled up high.

In case of theft or loss, always report the incident to the police and ask for a statement. Otherwise your travel-insurance company won't pay up.

Violence

Though it's unlikely that travellers will encounter any violence while in Eastern Europe, skinheads and neo-Nazis have singled out the resident Roma (Gypsies), blacks and Asians as scapegoats for their own problems, while foreigners have been attacked in Hungary and the Czech Republic. Avoid especially run-down areas in cities and *never* fight back. These people can be extremely dangerous.

Drugs

Always treat drugs with a great deal of caution. There are a lot of drugs available in the region, but that doesn't mean it's legal. The continual fighting in the former Yugoslavia in the 1990s forced the drug traders to seek alternative routes from Asia to Western Europe, sometimes crossing through Hungary, Slovakia, the Czech Republic and Poland. These countries, desperately seeking integration into the new Europe, do not look lightly upon drug abuse.

ACTIVITIES
Cycling

Along with hiking, cycling is the best way to really get close to the scenery and the people, keeping yourself fit in the process. It's also a good way to get around many cities and towns and to see remote corners of a country you wouldn't ordinarily get to.

The hills and mountains of Eastern Europe can be heavy going, but this is offset by the abundance of things to see. Physical fitness is *not* a major prerequisite for cycling on the plains of eastern Hungary (they're flatter than pancakes!) but the persistent wind might slow you down. Popular holiday cycling areas in Eastern Europe include the Danube Bend in Hungary, most of eastern Slovakia, the Karst region of Slovenia, and the Curonian Spit and Palanga in western Lithuania. The valleys of Maramureş in northern Romania are a great place for a cycling tour. If you are arriving from outside Eastern Europe, you can often bring your own bicycle along on the plane for a surprisingly reasonable fee. The Slovenian flag-carrier Adria, for instance, charges only UK£15 each way to transport a bicycle from London to Ljubljana. Alternatively, this book lists places where you can hire one.

See Bicycle in the Getting Around chapter for more information on bicycle touring, and the individual country chapters and destination sections for rental outfits as well as routes and tips on places to go.

Skiing

Eastern Europe's premier skiing areas are the High Tatra Mountains of Slovakia and Poland; the Carpathians near Braşov in Romania and Yablunytsia in Ukraine; Borovets in the Rila Mountains near Sofia; Pamporovo in the Rodopi Mountains in Bulgaria and Slovenia's Julian Alps. The skiing season generally lasts from early December to late March, though at higher altitudes it may extend an extra month either way. Snow conditions can vary greatly from one year to year and region to region, but January and February tend to be the best (and busiest) months. Snowboarding is especially popular in Slovakia, as is cross-country skiing in the Czech Republic and Ukraine.

Hiking

There's excellent hiking in Eastern Europe, with well-marked trails through forests, mountains and national parks. Public transport will often take you to the trailheads, and chalets or mountain huts in Poland, Bulgaria, Slovakia, Romania and Slovenia offer hikers dormitory accommodation and basic meals. In this book we include information about hiking in the High Tatra Mountains of Poland and Slovakia, the Malá Fatra of Slovakia, the Bucegi and Făgăraş Ranges in Romania's Carpathian Mountains, the Rila Mountains of Bulgaria, the Julian Alps of Slovenia and the spectacular Crimean mountain range of Ukraine, but there are many other hiking areas that are less well known, including the Bieszczady in Poland, Risnjak and Paklenica National Parks in Croatia and the Zemplén Hills in Hungary. The best months for hiking are from June to September, especially late in August and early September when the summer crowds will have disappeared.

Canoeing & Kayaking

Those with folding kayaks will want to launch them on the Krutynia River in Poland's Great Masurian Lakes district, on the Danube, Rába and Tisza Rivers in Hungary, the Soča River in Slovenia, the Vltava River in the Czech Republic and Latvia's Gauja, Salaca and Abava Rivers and its Latgale lakes region. Special kayaking and canoeing tours are offered in these countries, as well as in Croatia.

White-Water Rafting

This exciting activity is possible in summer on two of Eastern Europe's most scenic rivers: the Tara River in Montenegro and the Soča River in Slovenia. Rafting on the Dunajec River along the border of Poland and Slovakia is fun, but it's not a white-water experience.

Sailing

Eastern Europe's most famous yachting area is the passage between the long rugged islands off Croatia's Dalmatian coast. Yacht tours and rentals are available, though you certainly won't be doing this 'on a shoestring'. If your means are more limited, the Great Masurian Lakes of northeastern Poland are a better choice as small groups can rent sailing boats by the day for very reasonable rates. Hungary's Lake Balaton is also popular among sailing enthusiasts.

Horse Riding

Though horse riding is possible throughout Eastern Europe, the sport is best organised – and cheapest – in Hungary, whose people, they say, 'were created by God to sit on horseback'. The best centres are on the Great Plain though you'll also find riding schools in Transdanubia and northern Hungary. Horse riding is also very popular (and affordable) in the Baltic countries, Czech Republic, Poland and Slovenia.

Thermal Baths & Saunas

There are literally hundreds of thermal baths in Eastern Europe open to the public. The most affordable are in the Czech Republic, Hungary, Slovenia and along the Black Sea in Romania. Among the best are the thermal lake at Hévíz, the Turkish baths of Budapest and the spa town of Harkány in Hungary; the *fin-de-siécle* spas of Karlovy Vary (Karlsbad) and Mariánské Lázně (Marienbad) in the Czech Republic; and the spas at Dolenjske Toplice and Rogaška Slatina in Slovenia.

The Baltic countries are famous for the proliferation of saunas – both the traditional 'smoke' variety and the clean and smokeless modern sauna. A good example of the latter is in Hotel Olümpia in Tallinn while the traditionalist will find many opportunities to take in an old-style sauna in Lithuania.

COURSES

Apart from learning new physical skills by doing something like a ski course in Slovenia or horse riding in Hungary, you can enrich your mind with a variety of structured courses in Eastern Europe on anything from language to alternative medicine. Language courses are often available to foreigners through universities or private schools, and are justifiably popular since the best way to learn a language is in the country where it's spoken.

In general, the best sources of information are the cultural institutes maintained by many

European countries around the world; failing that, you could try national tourist offices or embassies. Student-exchange organisations, student travel agencies, and organisations such as Hostelling International (HI) can also put you on the right track.

WORK

With unemployment still a problem throughout the region, Eastern European countries aren't keen on handing out jobs to foreigners. The paperwork involved in arranging a work permit can be almost impossible, especially for temporary work.

That doesn't prevent enterprising travellers from topping up their funds occasionally, and they don't always have to do this illegally. If you do find a temporary job in Eastern Europe, though, the pay is likely to be abysmally low. Do it for the experience – not to earn your fortune – and you won't be disappointed. Teaching English is the easiest way to make some extra cash, but the market is saturated in places like Prague and Budapest. You'll probably be much more successful in less popular places like Sofia and Bucharest.

If you play an instrument or have other artistic talents, you could try working the streets. As every Peruvian pipe player (and his fifth cousin) *still* knows, busking is fairly common in major Eastern European cities like Prague, Budapest and Ljubljana. Some countries may require municipal permits for this sort of thing. Talk to other street artists before you start.

There are several references and websites that publicise specific positions across Eastern Europe. **Transitions Abroad** (w www.transabroad.com) publishes *Work Abroad: The Complete Guide to Finding a Job Overseas* and the *Alternative Travel Directory: The Complete Guide to Work, Study and Travel Overseas* as well as a colour magazine, *Transitions Abroad*. Its website lists paid positions and volunteer and service programmes. **Action Without Borders** (w www.idealist.org) and **GoAbroad.com** (w www.goabroad.com) list hundreds of jobs and volunteer opportunities.

Work Your Way Around the World by Susan Griffith gives good, practical advice on a wide range of issues. The publisher, **Vacation Work** (w www.vacationwork.co.uk), has many other useful titles, including *The Directory of Summer Jobs Abroad*, edited by

David Woodworth. *Working Holidays* by Ben Jupp, published by the Central Bureau for Educational Visits & Exchanges in the UK, is another good source, as is *Now Hiring! Jobs in Eastern Europe* (Perpetual Press) by Clarke Caufield.

Volunteer Work

Organising a volunteer work placement is a great way to gain a deeper insight into local culture. If you're staying with a family, or working alongside local colleagues, you'll probably learn much more about life here than you would if you were travelling through the country.

In some instances volunteers are paid a living allowance, sometimes they work for their keep and other programmes require the volunteer to pay.

There are several Internet sites that can help you search for volunteer work opportunities in Eastern Europe. As well as the websites mentioned earlier, try **WorkingAbroad** (w www.workingabroad.com) – it's a good resource for researching possibilities and applying for positions. The **Coordinating Committee for International Voluntary Service** (w www.unesco.org/ccivs) is an umbrella organisation with over 140 member organisations worldwide. It's useful if you want to find out about your country's national volunteer placement agency.

ACCOMMODATION

As in the rest of Europe, the cheapest places to find a place to rest your head in Eastern Europe are camping grounds, followed by hostels and student accommodation. Guesthouses, pensions, private rooms and cheap hotels are also good value. Self-catering flats in the city and cottages in the countryside are worth considering if you're in a group, especially if you plan to stay put for a while.

See the Facts for the Visitor sections in the individual country chapters for an overview of local accommodation options. During peak holiday periods, accommodation can be hard to find, and unless you're camping, it's advisable to book ahead where possible. Even camping grounds can fill up, particularly popular ones near large towns and cities.

Reservations

Hostels and cheap hotels in popular destinations, such as Prague, Budapest and Kraków, fill up quickly – especially the well-run ones in desirable or central neighbourhoods. It's a good idea to make reservations as many weeks ahead as possible – at least for the first night or two. An email or three-minute international phone call to book a bed or room is a lot more sensible use of time than wasting your first day in a city searching for a place to stay.

If you arrive in a country by air, there is often an accommodation-booking desk at the airport, although it rarely covers the lower strata of hotels. Tourist offices often have extensive accommodation lists, and the more helpful ones will go out of their way to find you something suitable. In most countries the fee for this service is very low, and if the accommodation market is tight, it can save you a lot of running around.

Camping

The cheapest way to go is camping, and there are numerous camping grounds throughout the region. Many are large sites intended mainly for motorists, though they're often easily accessible on public transport, and there's almost always space for backpackers with tents. Many camping grounds in Eastern Europe rent small on-site cabins, bungalows or caravans for double or triple the regular camping fee. In the most popular resorts all the bungalows will probably be full in July and August. Of the Baltic countries, Estonia has the most camping grounds and Latvia the least, while camping options are limited in Belarus and Moldova.

The standards of camping grounds in Eastern Europe vary from country to country. They're unreliable in Romania, crowded in Slovenia and Hungary (especially on Lake Balaton) and variable in Poland and Bulgaria. Coastal Croatia has nudist camping grounds galore (signposted 'FKK', the German acronym for 'naturist') and excellent places to stay because of their secluded locations – if you don't mind baring it all.

Camping grounds may be open from April to October, May to September, or perhaps only June to August, depending on the category of the facility, the location and demand. A few private camping grounds are open year-round. In Eastern Europe you are sometimes allowed to build a campfire (though ask first). Camping in the wild is usually illegal; ask local people the situation before you pitch your tent on a beach or in an open field.

Hostels

Hostels offer the cheapest (secure) roof over your head in Eastern Europe, and you do not have to be a youngster to take advantage of them. Most hostels are part of the national youth hostel association (YHA), which is affiliated with the Hostelling International (HI) umbrella organisation.

Hostels affiliated with HI can be found in most od the Eastern European countries. A hostel card is seldom required, though you sometimes get a small discount if you have one. If you don't have a valid HI membership card, you can buy one at some hostels.

To join the HI, you can ask at any hostel or contact your local or national hostelling office. There's a very useful website at w www .iyhf.org with links to most HI sites. The offices for English-speaking countries appear in the following text. Otherwise, check the individual country chapters for addresses.

Australia
Australian Youth Hostels Association (☎ 02-9261 1111, fax 9261 1969, e yha@yhansw.org.au) 422 Kent St, Sydney, NSW 2000

Canada
Hostelling International Canada (☎ 613-237 7884, fax 237 7868, e info@hihostels.ca) 205 Catherine St, Suite 400, Ottawa, Ont K2P 1C3

England & Wales
Youth Hostels Association (☎ 01629-592 600, fax 592 702, e customerservices@yha.org .uk) Trevelyan House, Dimple Rd, Matlock, Derbyshire DE4 3YH

Ireland
An Óige (Irish Youth Hostel Association; ☎ 01-830 4555, fax 830 5808, e mailbox@ anoige.ie) 61 Mountjoy St, Dublin 7

New Zealand
Youth Hostels Association of New Zealand (☎ 03-379 9970, fax 365 4476, e info@ yha.org.nz) PO Box 436, Level 3, 193 Cashel St, Christchurch

Northern Ireland
Hostelling International Northern Ireland (☎ 028-9031 5435, fax 9043 9699, e info@hini.org.uk) 22-32 Donegall Rd, Belfast BT12 5JN

Scotland
Scottish Youth Hostels Association (☎ 01786-891400, fax 891333, e info@syha.org.uk) 7 Glebe Crescent, Stirling FK8 2JA

South Africa
Hostelling International South Africa (☎ 021-424 2511, fax 424 4119, e info@hisa.org.za) PO Box 4402, St George's House, 73 St George's Mall, Cape Town 8001

USA
Hostelling International/American Youth Hostels
(☎ 202-783 6161, fax 783 6171,
e hiayhserv@hiayh.org) 733 15th St NW,
Suite 840, Washington DC 20005

At a hostel, you get a bed for the night, plus use of communal facilities, which often include a kitchen where you can prepare your own meals. You are sometimes required to have a sleeping sheet – simply using your sleeping bag is often not allowed. If you don't have your own sleeping sheet, you can sometimes hire one for a small fee.

Hostels vary widely in their character and quality. The hostels in Poland tend to be extremely basic but they're inexpensive and friendly. In the Czech Republic, and Slovakia many hostels are actually fairly luxurious 'junior' hotels with double rooms, often fully occupied by groups. Many Hungarian hostels outside Budapest are student dormitories open to travellers for six or seven weeks in summer only. In Budapest and Prague a number of privately run hostels now operate all year and are serious partying venues. The hostels in Bulgaria are in cities, resort and mountain areas.

There are many hostel guides with listings available, including the bible, HI's *Europe* (UK£8.50). Many hostels accept reservations by phone, fax or email, but not always during peak periods (though they might hold a bed for you for a couple of hours if you call from the train or bus station). You can also book hostels through national hostel offices.

University Accommodation

Some universities rent out space in student halls in July and August. This is quite popular in the Baltic countries, Croatia, the Czech Republic, Hungary, Macedonia, Poland, Slovakia and Slovenia. Accommodation will sometimes be in single rooms (but is more commonly in doubles or triples), and cooking facilities may be available. Inquire at the college or university, at the student information services or at local tourist offices.

Private Rooms

In most Eastern European countries, travel agencies arrange accommodation in private rooms in local homes. In Hungary you can get a private room almost anywhere, but in the other countries only the main tourist centres

have them. Some 1st-class rooms are like mini-apartments, with cooking facilities and private bathroom for the sole use of guests. Prices are low but there's often a 30% to 50% surcharge if you stay less than three nights. In Hungary, the Czech Republic and Croatia, higher taxation has made such rooms less attractive than they were previously, but they're still good value and cheaper than a hotel.

People will frequently approach you at train or bus stations in Eastern Europe offering a private room or a hostel bed. This can be good or bad – it's impossible to generalise. Just make sure it's not in some cardboard-quality housing project way out in a suburb somewhere and that you negotiate a clear price.

You don't have to go through an agency or an intermediary on the street for a private room. Any house, cottage or farmhouse with *Zimmer frei*, *sobe* or *szoba kiadó* displayed outside is advertising the availability of private rooms (these examples are in German, Slovene and Hungarian); just knock on the door and ask if any are available.

Pensions, Guesthouses & Farmhouses

Small private pensions are now very common in parts of Eastern Europe. Priced somewhere between hotels and private rooms, pensions typically have less than a dozen rooms and there's sometimes a small restaurant or bar on the premises. You'll get much more personal service at a pension than you would at a hotel at the cost of just a wee bit of privacy. If you arrive at night or on a weekend when the travel agencies assigning private rooms are closed, pensions can be a lifesaver. Call ahead to check prices and ask about reservations – German is almost always spoken, as is, increasingly, English.

'Village tourism', which means staying at a farmhouse, is highly developed in Estonia, Latvia, Lithuania and Slovenia and also popular in Hungary. In the Baltic countries and Slovenia, it's like staying in a private room or pension except that the participating farms are in picturesque rural areas and may offer such nearby activities as horse riding, kayaking, skiing and cycling. It's highly recommended.

Hotels

At the bottom of the bracket, cheap hotels may be no more expensive than private rooms or guesthouses in Eastern Europe, while at the other extreme they extend to five-star hotels with price tags to match. Categorisation varies from country to country and the hotels recommended in this book accommodate every budget. You'll often find cheap hotels clustered in the areas around bus and train stations, always good places to start hunting.

Single rooms can be hard to find in Eastern Europe, where you are generally charged by the room and not by the number of people in it; many local people still refuse to believe that anyone would actually take to the road alone. The cheapest rooms sometimes have a washbasin but shared bathroom, which means you'll have to go down the corridor to use the toilet and shower. Breakfast may be included in the price of a room or be extra – and mandatory.

FOOD

Sampling the local food is one of the most enjoyable aspects of travel. Eastern European cuisine, though often a heavy and stodgy one of goulash, sausages, dumplings, groats and schnitzel, comes into its own in soups, game, the use of forest products, like mushrooms and wild berries, and truly extravagant pastries. The Facts for the Visitor sections in the individual country chapters contain details of local dishes and specialities, and there are many suggestions on places to eat in the chapters themselves.

Restaurant types and prices vary enormously in Eastern Europe. The cheapest place for a decent meal is the self-service cafeteria – sometimes called *buffet* or some variation of the word (*büfé, bife* etc) – still found throughout much of Eastern Europe. Student *mensa* (university restaurants) are dirt cheap, but the food tends to be bland, and you may only be allowed in if you've got a local student ID. Kiosks often sell cheap snacks that can be as much a part of the national cuisine as more elaborate dishes.

It's worth trying the various folkloric restaurants where regional cuisine is usually on offer. It's called a *csárda* in Hungary, *gostišoe* or *gostilna* in Slovenia and *mehana* in Bulgaria.

Self-catering – buying your ingredients at a shop or market and preparing them yourself – is a cheap and wholesome way of eating. Even if you don't cook, a lunch on a park bench with a fresh stick of bread, some local

cheese and salami and a tomato or two, washed down with a bottle of local wine, can be particularly satisfying. It also makes a nice change from restaurant food.

If you have dietary restrictions – you're a vegetarian or you keep kosher, for example – tourist organisations may be able to advise you or provide lists of suitable restaurants. Some vegetarian and kosher restaurants are listed in the individual chapters in this book.

Vegetarianism remains in its infancy in Eastern Europe (a part of the world that has traditionally been *very* big on meat), though vegetarians won't starve. Many restaurants have one or two vegetarian dishes – deep-fried mushroom caps, pasta dishes with cheese, vegetable dumplings or Greek-style salads. Others might prepare special dishes on request as long as you approach them about this in advance.

DRINKS
Nonalcoholic Drinks

Most international soft drink brands are available in Eastern Europe, but coffee, mineral water and juice seem to be the most popular libations for teetotallers or just the thirsty at cafés, pubs and bars. Fruit juice is often canned or boxed fruit 'drink' with lots of sugar added, but it's of a high standard in the Balkans, especially Bulgaria.

Alcoholic Drinks

Eastern Europe boasts alcoholic beverages of a type and quality not usually found beyond its borders. Everyone knows about Polish *wódka* (vodka), Hungarian *bor* (wine) and Czech *pivo* (beer), but don't miss the opportunity of trying the many wonderful fruit and herbal brandies in Romania (where it is called *ţuică* or *palincă*, depending on the part of the country), Croatia and Slovenia (*žganje*) and Hungary (*pálinka*) and aniseed-flavoured *rakija* in the Balkans. Estonia boasts the ubiquitous Vana Tallinn, a syrupy and strong concoction whose mysteries are matched by Balzams from neighbouring Latvia – both recipes are closely guarded secrets.

In both Slovakia and Hungary wine bars/restaurants (*vinárna* or *borozó*) are common. Wines of Hungary, Moldova and Slovenia can be excellent, and quite good in Bulgaria and Croatia. Romanian and Slovakian wines generally range from plonk to acceptable.

Getting There & Away

Eastern Europe is becoming more accessible to the traveller. With severe competition between long-haul airlines and the advent of so many no-frills carriers in both Europe and the USA, there are plenty of cheap tickets available to a variety of gateway cities.

Some travellers still choose to arrive or depart overland – from or to the other parts of Europe, Africa, the Middle East and Asia via the Russian Federation (the Trans-Siberian, Trans-Mongolian and Trans-Manchurian express trains).

Only a handful of ships still carry passengers across the Atlantic; they don't sail often and are very expensive, even compared with full-fare air tickets. The days of ocean liners as a mode of transport are well and truly over. There are many ferry services operating in the Baltic Sea linking Scandinavia and Germany with countries like Poland, Lithuania, Latvia and Estonia. Other routes cross the Adriatic from Italy to Slovenia and Croatia.

You can find useful websites with information on travel planning and ticket prices under the Digital Resources section of the Facts for the Visitor chapter of this book.

AIR
Buying Tickets

With a bit of research – ringing around travel agencies, checking Internet sites, perusing the travel ads in newspapers – you can often get yourself a good travel deal. Start early as some of the cheapest tickets need to be bought well in advance and popular flights can sell out.

Generally, there is nothing to be gained by buying a ticket direct from the airline. Discounted tickets are released to selected travel agencies and specialist discount agencies, and these are usually the cheapest deals going. One exception to this rule is the expanding number of no-frills carriers, which mostly only sell direct to travellers. Unlike the full-service airlines, no-frills carriers often make one-way tickets available at around half the return fare, meaning that it is easy to put together an open-jaw ticket (flying to one place but leaving from another).

The other exception is booking over the Internet. Many airlines, full-service and no-frills, offer excellent fares to Net surfers. They may sell seats by auction or simply cut prices

Warning

The information in this chapter is particularly vulnerable to change: Prices for international travel are volatile, routes are introduced and cancelled, schedules change, special deals come and go, and rules and visa requirements are amended. Airlines and governments seem to take a perverse pleasure in making price structures and regulations as complicated as possible. You should check directly with the airline or a travel agent to make sure you understand how a fare (and ticket you may buy) works. In addition, the travel industry is highly competitive and there are many lurks and perks.

The upshot of this is that you should get opinions, quotes and advice from as many airlines and travel agents as possible before you part with your hard-earned cash. The details given in this chapter should be regarded as pointers and are not a substitute for your own careful, up-to-date research.

to reflect the reduced cost of electronic selling. Many travel agencies around the world have websites, which can make the Internet a quick and easy way to compare prices. There is also an increasing number of online agencies that operate only on the Internet. Online ticket sales work well if you want a simple one-way or return trip on specified dates. However, online superfast fare generators are no substitute for a travel agent who knows all about special deals, has strategies for avoiding layovers and can offer advice on everything from which airline has the best vegetarian food to the best travel insurance to bundle with your ticket.

You may find the cheapest flights are advertised by obscure agencies. Most such firms are honest and solvent, but there are some rogue fly-by-night outfits operating. Paying by credit card generally offers protection, as most card issuers provide refunds if you can prove you didn't get what you paid for. Similar protection can be obtained by buying a ticket from a bonded agency, such as one covered by the Air Travel Organisers' Licensing (ATOL) scheme in the UK. Agencies which accept only cash should hand over the tickets straight away and not tell you to 'come back tomorrow'. After you've made a booking or paid your deposit, call the airline and confirm that the booking was made. It's generally not advisable to send money (even cheques) through the post unless the agency is very well established – some travellers have reported being ripped off by fly-by-night mail-order ticket agencies.

If you purchase a ticket and later decide you want to make changes to your route or even to get a refund, you need to contact the original travel agency. Airlines issue refunds only to the purchaser of a ticket – usually the travel agency who bought the ticket on your behalf. Many travellers change their routes halfway through their trips, so think carefully before you buy a ticket that is not easily refunded. Don't bother buying half-used tickets from other travellers, no matter how low the price. You won't be able to board the flight unless the name on the ticket matches that on your passport.

You may decide to pay more than the rock-bottom fare by opting for the safety of one of the better-known travel agencies. Firms such as STA Travel, which has offices worldwide, are long-standing companies that generally offer good prices to most destinations.

Round-the-World (RTW) tickets are a useful option for long-haul travellers. Usually the tickets are valid for between 90 days and a year. Make sure you understand what restrictions may apply – there'll be a limit to how many stops (or kilometres/miles) you are permitted, and you won't be able to backtrack. Prices start at about UK£720, A$2250 or US$1450, depending on number of stops, the route and the season.

For short-term travel, cheaper fares are available by travelling mid-week, staying away at least one Saturday night or taking advantage of short-lived promotional fares.

Student & Youth Fares

Full-time students and people under 26 years (under 30 in some countries) have access to better deals than other travellers. The better deals may not be cheaper fares but can include more flexibility in changing flights and/or routes. You will have to show a document that proves your age or a valid International Student Identity Card (ISIC) or an International Youth Travel Card (IYTC) when buying your ticket, as well as when you board the plane. See W www.istc.org for more information.

Courier Flights

Another option is a courier flight, where an air-freight company uses your luggage allowance to send its parcels. The drawbacks are that your stay in Europe may be limited to one or two weeks, your luggage is usually restricted to hand luggage, and there is unlikely to be more than one courier ticket available for any given flight. Courier flights are occasionally advertised in newspapers, or check the telephone book for air-freight companies. You may even have to go to the air-freight company to get an answer – the companies aren't always keen to give out information over the phone.

You can find out more about courier flights from the **International Association of Air Travel Couriers** (in USA W www.courier.org, in UK W www.aircourier.co.uk). Joining the association costs US$45 or UK£32, but this does not guarantee a flight. *Travel Unlimited* (PO Box 1058, Allston, MA 02134, USA) is a US-based monthly travel newsletter that publishes many courier flight deals available from destinations worldwide.

Travellers with Special Needs

If they're warned early enough, airlines can often make special arrangements for travellers, such as wheelchair assistance at airports or vegetarian meals on the flight. Children under two years fly for 10% of the standard fare (or free on some airlines) as long as they don't occupy a seat. They don't get a baggage allowance. 'Skycots', baby food and nappies (diapers) should be provided by the airline if requested in advance. Children aged between two and 12 can usually occupy a seat for around two-thirds of the full fare, and do get a baggage allowance.

The disability-friendly website W www.everybody.co.uk has an airline directory that provides information on the facilities offered by various airlines.

The USA

The flight options available across the north Atlantic, the world's busiest long-haul air corridor, are bewildering. The *New York Times*, *LA Times*, *Chicago Tribune* and *San Francisco Chronicle* all have weekly travel sections in which you will find any number of budget travel agencies' advertisements. **Priceline** (W www.priceline.com) is a 'name-your-price' auction service on the Web.

STA Travel (☎ *800 781 4040;* W *www .statravel.com*) has offices in all major cities nationwide or check its website for your preliminary planning. You should be able to fly between New York and Europe (although not necessarily to an Eastern European city) for about US$450 in the low season (September to April) and US$750 during the high season; even lower promotional or restricted validity fares are sometimes on offer. The equivalent fares for flights departing from the west coast are US$150 to US$300 higher.

An interesting alternative to the boring New York to London flight is offered by **Icelandair** (☎ *800 223 5500;* W *www.icelandair.com*), which flies from northeastern USA to several European cities, including Frankfurt (about US$860 return). You can even include a three-night stopover in Iceland's capital, Reykjavík.

Stand-by, one-way fares can work out to be very reasonable. **Airhitch** (☎ *800 326 2009;* W *www.airhitch.org*) specialises in this sort of thing, with the cost of flying between Europe and the east coast/Midwest/west coast listed as US$165/199/233 each way, plus taxes and a processing fee.

Travelling as a courier, a New York to London return ticket can be had for as little as US$300 in the low season. You may also be able to fly one-way. See Courier Flights earlier in this chapter.

Canada

Travel CUTS (☎ *800 667 2887;* W *www .travelcuts.com*) has offices in all major Canadian cities. You might also scan the travel agencies' ads in the *Globe & Mail*, *Toronto Star* and *Vancouver Province*. From Toronto or Montreal, return flights to London are available from about C$950 in the low season; prices are C$150 or C$300 more from Vancouver. Airhitch (see the USA section) has stand-by fares to/from Toronto, Montreal and Vancouver.

The UK

If you're looking for a cheap way into or out of Eastern Europe, London is Europe's major centre for discounted fares. Throughout the year you should be able to fly to Berlin, Budapest, Munich, Prague, Vienna or Warsaw on British Airways for between UK£120 and about UK£200 return. To St Petersburg and Moscow count on from UK£200 to UK£350. British Airways flights to or from Rīga start

from around UK£180 and to or from Kyiv at about UK£235.

For destinations in or close to Eastern Europe, some of the best deals are offered by **British Midland** (W *www.britishmidland .com*) to Munich; **Buzz** (W *www.buzzaway .com*) to Berlin; **easyJet** (W *www.easyjet.co .uk*) to Athens; **Go** (W *www.go-fly.com*) to Prague and Munich; and **KLMuk** (W *www .klmuk.com*) to Budapest, Prague and Warsaw via Amsterdam.

You can often find air fares from London that either match or beat surface alternatives in terms of cost. Train journeys also involve several legs that need to be paid for separately. Long-distance trains no longer have the advantage of a central arrival point, as getting between airports and the city centres is rarely a problem in Eastern Europe thanks to the ever-improving tram and metropolitan train networks and good bus services.

If you are travelling alone, courier flights are a possibility. European Union (EU) integration and electronic communications means there's increasingly less call for couriers, but you might find something.

Plenty of budget travel agencies advertise in the travel sections of weekend newspapers and also in the entertainment listings magazine *Time Out* and the freebie *TNT Magazine*.

STA Travel (☎ *020-7361 6161;* W *www .statravel.co.uk; 86 Old Brompton Rd, London SW7*) has branches throughout the UK and sells tickets to all travellers but caters especially to young people and students.

Other recommended travel agencies are **Trailfinders** (☎ *020-7938 1234;* W *www .trailfinders.co.uk; 215 Kensington High St, London W8*), which has branch offices in Manchester, Glasgow and several other British cities; **Bridge the World** (☎ *020-7734 7447;* W *www.b-t-w.co.uk; 4 Regent Place, London W1*); and also **Flightbookers** (☎ *020-7757 2000;* W *www.ebookers.com; 34-42 Woburn Place, London WC1*).

Charter flights can be a cheaper alternative to scheduled flights, especially if you do not qualify for under-26 or student discounts. See your travel agency for possibilities.

Continental Europe

Although London is the travel discount capital of Europe, there are several other cities in the region where you'll find a wide range of good deals. STA Travel has offices throughout

Europe where cheap tickets can be purchased and STA-issued tickets can be altered (usually for a small fee). Check on the website for contact details. **Nouvelles Frontières** (w www .nouvelles-frontieres.com) also has branches throughout the world.

France has a network of student travel agencies that can supply discount tickets to travellers of all ages. **OTU Voyages** (☎ 0820 817 817; w www.otu.fr) and **Voyageurs du Monde** (☎ 01 42 86 16 00; w www.vdm .com) have branches throughout the country and offer some of the best services and deals.

CTS Viaggi (☎ 840 501 150; w www .cts.it) is a student and youth specialist in Italy; in Spain agencies include **Usit Unlimited** (☎ 902 25 25 75; w www.unlimited.es) and **Barcelo Viajes** (☎ 902 11 62 26; w www .barceloviajes.es).

Scheduled flights between Paris and Warsaw start at about €345 return and on the Barcelona to Warsaw route at around €300.

Australia

STA (☎ 131 776; w www.statravel.com.au) and **Flight Centre** (☎ 131 600; w www .flightcentre.com.au) are major dealers in the cheap air-fare game. **Student Uni Travel** (in Sydney ☎ 02-9232 7300, in Melbourne ☎ 03-0662 4666; w www.sut.com.au) specialises in the youth/backpacker market. Saturday's travel sections in the Sydney Morning Herald and Melbourne's Age have many ads offering cheap fares to Europe. With Australia's large and well-organised ethnic populations, it pays to check special deals in the ethnic press.

Thai Airways International, Malaysia Airlines, Qantas Airways and Singapore Airlines flights to Europe start from about A$1500 (low season) up to A$2500 return. All have frequent promotional fares. Flights from Perth are a couple of hundred dollars cheaper than from east-coast cities.

Another option for travellers to get to Britain between November and February is to hook up with a returning charter flight. These low-season, one-way fares do have restrictions, but may work out to be considerably cheaper. Ask your travel agency for details.

New Zealand

As in Australia, STA and Flight Centre are popular travel agencies in New Zealand. **Student Uni Travel** (☎ 09-379 4224; w www.sut .co.nz) has offices in Auckland, Christchurch and Hamilton. Also check the New Zealand Herald for ads. The cheapest fares to Europe are routed through Asia; a discounted return ticket to Europe from Auckland starts at around NZ$2100. A RTW ticket will you cost about NZ$2850.

Africa

Nairobi and Johannesburg are probably the best places in East and South Africa to buy tickets to Europe. One of the best agencies in Nairobi is **Flight Centre** (☎ 02-210 024; 2nd floor, Lakhamshi House, Biashara St). A return Nairobi to Zürich flight with Emirates Airlines starts as low as US$600, though with a limited period of validity. In Johannesburg **STA Travel** (☎ 011-447 5414; e rosebank@ statravel.co.za; Mutual Square, Rosebank) and also **Rennies Travel** (☎ 011-833 1441; w www.renniestravel.co.za; Unitas Bldg, 42 Marshall St) are recommended. Return flights to Berlin will cost from R7000.

Several West African countries, such as Gambia, Burkina Faso and especially Morocco offer cheap charter flights to France, from where you can travel to Central Europe.

Asia

Hong Kong, Singapore and Bangkok are the discount air-fare capitals of Asia, but ask the advice of other travellers before handing over any money for tickets in these cities. In Singapore **STA** (☎ 6737 7188; w www.statravel .com.sg; 35a Cuppage Rd, Cuppage Terrace) has competitive fares. In Hong Kong try **Phoenix Services** (☎ 2722 7378; room B, 6th floor, Milton mansion, 96 Nathan Rd, Tsimshatsui).

In India, cheap tickets can be bought from the bucket shops around Connaught Place in Delhi. Check with other travellers about the most trustworthy ones.

LAND

Before travelling to Eastern Europe by train, bus, car or motorcycle, check with the relevant consulates whether you'll need transit visas for countries you'll pass through. Generally, if you need a visa to visit a country, you'll need a transit visa to pass through it.

Bus

International bus travel tends to take second place to going by train. The bus has the edge in terms of cost, sometimes quite substantially, but is generally slower and less comfortable. Europe's largest network of international buses operates under the name of **Eurolines** (**w** www.eurolines.co.uk).

Eurolines offices or representatives in Eastern Europe include:

Czech Republic Sodeli CZ (☎ 02-24 23 93 18) Senovažne namesti 6, Prague
Estonia Mootor Reisi AS (☎ 641 0100) Suur Sojamae 4, Tallinn
Hungary Volánbusz (☎ 1-317 2562) Erzsebet ter, Budapest V
Latvia SIA Baltic Bus Lines (☎ 721 4080) Pragas iela 1, Rīga
Poland PKS (☎ 022-652 23 21) Dworzec Centralny (Central Bus Station), Warsaw
Russia Eurolines Russia (☎ 812-168 27 40) ulitsa Shkapina 10, St Petersburg

These companies may also be able to advise you on other bus companies and deals.

On Eurolines return trips, those under 26 and seniors over 60 pay around 10% less than the normal fare, and there are also off-peak and promotional discounts. The adult/youth return fares from London in the high season are UK£131/119 to Budapest, UK£95/86 to Prague, UK£97/91 to Warsaw, UK£228/188 to Tallinn and UK£188/152 to Vilnius. Return tickets are valid for six months.

Eurolines also offers passes, but they're neither as extensive nor as flexible as rail passes (see the Train section). The Eurolines pass covers 31 European cities but only Budapest, Kraków, Prague and Warsaw in Eastern Europe are included. Except for four popular Western European journeys, trips must be international (ie, you can't get on at Kraków and off in Warsaw). From 1 June to 15 September, the cost is UK£229 for 30 days (UK£186 for youths and seniors) or UK£267 for 60 days (UK£205). The passes are cheaper off-season. If you're planning a more extensive European trip, then this pass would be more cost-effective.

Busabout (☎ 020-7950 1661; **w** www.busabout.com; 258 Vauxhall Bridge Rd, London SW1) operates buses that complete set circuits around Europe, stopping at major cities. You get unlimited travel per sector, and can hop on and off at any scheduled stop, then resume with a later bus. While the circuits cover all countries in continental Western Europe, the only country included in Eastern Europe is the Czech Republic.

See the individual country chapters for more information about long-distance buses.

Other Bus Routes Coming from Western Europe, you can take a bus from Vienna to Brno in the Czech Republic or Bratislava in Slovakia. There are also buses travelling from Vienna to Sopron and Budapest in Hungary.

From Greece to Bulgaria a bus will cost less than the train. From Turkey, there are cheap buses from İstanbul to Bucharest.

Train

Taking the train is a more expensive but far more comfortable way to travel into Eastern Europe. Once you get to the region, train travel is a bargain (see the Getting Around chapter for more details).

International Tickets The regular international train tickets are usually valid for two months, and you may stop off as often as you wish. In Eastern Europe, international train tickets are often more easily purchased at a travel agency than at the train station.

Many express international trains between major cities – if not all – require seat reservations. On long hauls, sleepers are generally available in both 1st and 2nd class, and couchette compartments, sleeping four to six people, are available in 2nd class. Students without a national student ID card usually don't get discounts on domestic train tickets in Eastern Europe.

Rail Passes Shop around, as pass prices can vary between different outlets. Once you buy, make sure you take care of your pass, as it cannot be replaced or refunded if lost or stolen. Holders of European passes also get reductions on the *Eurostar*, the train that links England with France via the Channel Tunnel, and on ferries on certain routes (eg, Eurail pass-holders pay 50% of the adult pedestrian fare for crossings between Ireland and France on Irish Ferries).

Rail Europe in the UK (☎ 0870 584 8848; **w** www.raileurope.co.uk) and in the USA (☎ 877 257 2887; **w** www.raileurope.com) sell all sorts of rail passes, including many of the ones listed here.

Eurail These passes can be bought only by residents of non-European countries, and are supposed to be purchased before arriving in

Europe. If you've lived in Europe for more than six months, you are eligible for an Inter-Rail pass, which is a much better deal for Eastern Europe.

Of those countries in this book Eurail passes cover only Hungary. Still, if you will be travelling in both Western and Eastern Europe and want to use Hungary as your gateway, it might make sense. The passes offer reasonable value to people aged under 26. A Youthpass gives unlimited 2nd-class travel within a choice of five validity periods: 15/21 days' travel will cost UK£325/414 or one/two/three months are UK£525/740/925. The standard Eurail pass for those over 26 provides 1st-class travel and costs UK£470/605 for 15/21 days or UK£750/1065/1320 for one/two/three months. For two or more people travelling together a discount is available on the regular price.

Other Rail Passes Inter-Rail and Euro Domino passes are available to European residents of more than six months' standing (passport identification is required). These passess include several Eastern European and surrounding countries. The European East Pass and the Balkan Flexipass are both sold outside Europe and cover several Eastern European countries. For more details on these passes see the Getting Around chapter.

Continental Europe Railway tickets are expensive in Western Europe, so only buy a ticket as far as your first major stop within Eastern Europe and buy further tickets from there. There are dozens of trains daily between Germany and Poland; the most popular and quickest, and often the cheapest, is the Warsaw to Berlin line via Frankfurt and Poznań. See the individual country chapters for more details of routes and prices.

You can travel to a number of Eastern European countries using a German-Sparpreise ticket (see the International Guests page of the website **w** www.bahn.de). Travel from any German train station to Belarus, the Czech Republic, Croatia, Hungary, Latvia, Lithuania, Poland, Russia, Slovenia or Ukraine for between €134 and €300 2nd-class return (€30 extra if InterCity Express trains are used). The cost depends on distance from the border. You may travel any day, but your stay must include a Friday night or you need to travel on a Saturday or Sunday. There's 50% discount for a second adult. The ticket is valid for one month,

except to Belarus, Latvia, Lithuania, Russia and Ukraine, where it's valid for two months.

Other Train Routes For the Czech Republic or Slovakia, you can take a train from Linz in Austria to České Budějovice, or from Vienna to Bratislava. For Hungary there are trains from Vienna to Sopron and Budapest.

Railway lines from Austria and Italy converge on Ljubljana, from where you can reach Croatia and Yugoslavia by train or bus. The main line from Munich to Athens runs via Budapest and Belgrade.

There are a couple of trains per day between the town of Thessaloniki in Greece and Skopje. From Turkey, the main railway line from İstanbul northward passes through Sofia.

Asia & the Trans-Siberian Railway It *is* possible to get to Eastern Europe by rail from central and eastern Asia, though count on spending at least eight days doing it. You can choose from four different routes to Moscow. They are the Trans-Siberian (from Vladivostok), the Trans-Mongolian (from Beijing) and the Trans-Manchurian (from Beijing via Harbin), which all use the same tracks across Siberia but have different routes east of Lake Baikal. There's also the Trans-Kazakhstan, which runs between Moscow and Urumqi in northwestern China.

Prices vary enormously, depending on where you buy the ticket and what is included in the cost. Information is available from the **Russian National Tourist Office** (**w** www.interknowledge.com/Russia). The Lonely Planet *Trans-Siberian Railway* guide is a comprehensive guide to the route with details of costs, travel agencies who specialise in the trip and highlights. *The Big Red Train Ride* by Eric Newby is a good choice of reading material to take along for the ride.

There are countless travel options between Moscow and the rest of Europe. Most people will opt for the train, usually to/from Berlin, Helsinki, Munich, Budapest or Vienna.

Car & Motorcycle

Driving to and from Eastern Europe is pretty straightforward, and usually pleasurable, but there are specific rules you should know about once you've arrived (eg, keeping your headlights on throughout the day outside built-up areas in Hungary and Slovenia). For detailed information, turn to the introductory

Getting Around chapter or the Getting Around sections of the individual chapters.

SEA

There are Baltic ferries (mostly year-round) to Świnoujście, Gdynia and Gdansk in Poland from several Scandinavian cities and towns, including the Danish capital Copenhagen and, in Sweden, Karlskrona, Malmö and Öresund. You can sail directly from Finland to Estonia, from Germany and Sweden to Latvia, Lithuania and Estonia and also from Denmark to Lithuania. There is a wide range of companies operating on the Baltic routes, including **Silja Line** (w *www.silja.com*), **Scandlines** (w *www .scandlines.com*), **Tallink** (w *www.tallink.ee*) and **Krantas Shipping** (w *www.krantas.lt*).

There are also Adriatic ferries from the Greek island of Corfu and Italy to Albania, as well as several lines from Italy to Croatia and to Slovenia.

For details see Sea under Getting There & Away in the respective chapters.

RIVER

A hydrofoil service on the Danube between Budapest and Vienna via Bratislava operates daily between April and October. For details, see River under Getting There & Away in the Hungary chapter.

DEPARTURE TAX

Some countries in Eastern Europe charge you a fee for the privilege of leaving from their airports. Some also charge port fees when you're leaving by ship. Such fees are often included in the ticket price, but it always pays to check this when purchasing your ticket. If the fee is not included in the ticket price, you'll have to have it ready when you leave – usually in local currency. Details are given in the relevant country chapters.

Getting Around

AIR

Since 1997 air travel within the European Union (EU) has been deregulated. This 'open skies' policy allows greater flexibility in routing, wider competition and lower prices. However, such deregulation has had little impact on domestic air travel in the countries of Eastern Europe, none of which were EU members at the time of writing.

Domestic air travel remains a real luxury in Eastern Europe, especially when you consider how cheap local bus and train transport can be. Domestic flights operate within Bulgaria, Croatia, Poland, Slovakia, Romania, Russia and Yugoslavia. Fares are high, though the two-tier price system where foreign tourists pay more has largely been phased out (there's still a marginal difference in Russia).

Air-taxi services are taking off in a big way around the region, but these are even more expensive than scheduled flights. For domestic flights and prices see Getting Around in the individual chapters.

BUS

Buses are a viable alternative to the rail network in most Eastern European countries. Generally they tend to complement the rail system rather than duplicating it, though in some countries – notably Hungary, the Czech Republic and Slovakia – you'll almost always have a choice.

In general, buses are slightly more expensive and slower than trains; in Russia, Poland, Hungary, the Czech Republic and Slovakia they cost almost the same. Buses tend to be best for shorter hops such as getting around cities and reaching remote rural villages. They are often the only option in mountainous regions. The ticketing system varies in each country, but advance reservations are rarely necessary. It's always safest to buy your ticket in advance at the station, but on long-distance buses you usually just pay upon boarding.

Information on Eurolines is given in the Getting There & Away chapter. See also the individual country chapters for more details about long-distance buses.

TRAIN

You'll probably do most of your travelling within Eastern Europe by train. All countries have well-developed rail networks, and you will have a choice between local trains, that stop at every station, and express trains, including some EuroCity (EC) or InterCity (IC) trains. Local trains can cost less than express trains. Supplementary and reservation fees are *not* covered by the rail passes, and pass-holders must always carry their passport on the train for identification purposes.

In much of Eastern Europe domestic train travel is a bargain and tickets within the region are heavily discounted. In Hungary, for example, everyone gets a 20% to 50% discount on return fares to Bulgaria, the Czech Republic, Croatia, Estonia, Poland, Russia, Ukraine, Latvia, Lithuania and Belarus; it's a generous 60% to 75% to Slovakian destinations and 60% to 75% to certain locations in Romania. There's also a 40% concession on return fares from Budapest to six selected cities: Prague and Brno in the Czech Republic, and Warsaw, Kraków, Katowice and Gdynia in Poland.

Once you find a seat on a local train it's yours for the trip, and since passengers are constantly coming and going you eventually get a place even on a full train. First-class travel by local train costs about the same as 2nd class on an express and is quite comfortable, so long as you're in no hurry. First-class compartments usually have six padded seats, and 2nd-class ones have eight seats.

If you choose an express be sure to get an express ticket and ask if seat reservations are necessary. It's sometimes a hassle getting these tickets, so don't leave it too late. Express trains are often marked in red on posted timetables at stations, local trains in black. The symbol 'R' with a box around it means reservations are mandatory while an 'R' without a box may only mean reservations are possible. The boards listing departures are usually yellow, and those for arrivals are white.

Tickets for express trains are best purchased at the central train-ticket office one day before travelling. On overnight trains try to book a 2nd-class couchette or a 1st-class sleeper a few days in advance. Check that your ticket is in order before you board. If you have to arrange a reservation, buy a ticket or upgrade a local ticket to an express one once the trip has started, you'll pay a healthy supplement.

It's best to sit in the middle or front carriages of trains as many stations are poorly marked, often with only one sign on the main building. If there's any doubt, write the name of your destination on a piece of paper and show it to the other passengers so they can let you know when to get off.

If you plan to travel extensively by train, it might be worth getting hold of the *Thomas Cook European Timetable*, which gives a complete listing of train schedules and indicates where supplements apply or where reservations are necessary. It is updated monthly and is available from **Thomas Cook** (w *www.thomascook.com)* outlets in the UK, and from **Forsyth Travel Library** (☎ *800-367 7984;* w *www.forsyth.com)* in the USA. Check the websites. In Australia, look for it in one of the bigger bookstores, which can order in copies if they don't have any in stock. If you intend to stick to one or a handful of countries it might be worthwhile getting hold of the national timetable(s) published by the state railroad(s). A particularly useful online resource for timetables in Eastern Europe is the DeutcheBahn website at w www.bahn.de. Train fares and schedules in US and Canadian dollars on the most popular routes in Europe, including information on rail and youth passes, can be found on w www.raileurope .com. For fares in UK pounds go to w www .raileurope.co.uk.

Luggage

Almost every train station in Eastern Europe has a luggage room (left-luggage or cloakroom) where you can deposit your luggage as soon as you arrive. In Poland this can be expensive as you're charged 1% of the declared value of your luggage, but the fee in other countries is generally pretty cheap. You will usually pay the fee when you pick up your bag – handy if you're just arriving in a new country with no local currency on you. In main train stations the left-luggage office is usually open around the clock but this isn't always the case. Inquire before handing your bags over.

Some train stations also have quite complicated coin lockers. You have to compose a four-digit number on the keypad inside the door, insert a coin and close the locker. To open it again you arrange the same number on the outside and with luck the door will open. Don't forget the number or the location of your locker!

Overnight Trains

Overnight trains will usually offer a choice of couchette or sleeper – a good idea if you don't fancy sleeping in your seat with somebody else's elbow in your ear. Again, reservations are advisable as sleeping options are allocated on a first-come, first-served basis.

Couchette bunks are comfortable enough, if lacking a bit in privacy. There are four per compartment in 1st class and six in 2nd class. In addition to the price of the ticket, a bunk costs from around UK£10 for most of the international trains, irrespective of the length of the journey.

Sleepers are the most comfortable option, offering beds for one or two passengers in 1st class, and two or three passengers in 2nd class. Charges vary depending upon the journey, but they are significantly more expensive than couchettes.

Security

You should be quite safe travelling on most trains in Eastern Europe but it does pay to be security conscious. Keep an eye on your luggage at all times (especially when stopping at stations) and lock compartment doors at night. Take particular care on overnight IC trains in Russia.

Rail Passes

Not all countries in Eastern European are covered by rail passes, but they do include a number of destinations so are worthwhile if you are concentrating your travels around the region. They may also be useful for getting to or from neighbouring countries. Of the countries covered in this book, Eurail passes are valid only in Hungary; see the Getting There & Away chapter for more information.

Inter-Rail These passes are available to European residents of more than six months' standing (passport identification is required). Terms and conditions vary slightly from country to country, but when travelling in the country where you bought the pass, there is only a discount of around 50% on normal fares. The Inter-Rail pass is split into zones. Zone D is the Czech Republic, Slovakia, Poland, Hungary and Croatia; G includes Slovenia; and H is Bulgaria, Romania, Yugoslavia and Macedonia.

The normal Inter-Rail pass is for people under 26, though travellers over 26 can get the Inter-Rail 26+ version. The price for any single zone is UK£139 (UK£209 for those over 26) for 22 days. Multizone passes are valid for one month: two-zone passes costs UK£189 (UK£265), three zones UK£209 (UK£299) and the all-zone Global Pass is UK£249 (UK£355).

Euro Domino There is a Euro Domino pass for each of the countries covered by the Inter-Rail pass, and they are probably only worth considering if you're concentrating on a particular region. Adults (travelling 1st or 2nd class) and youths under 26 can opt for three to eight days' travel within one month. Some examples of adult/youth prices for eight days in 2nd class are UK£69/59 for Poland, UK£58/46 for the Czech Republic and UK£52/39 for Slovenia.

European East Pass This pass is sold in North America and Australia and is valid in Austria, Hungary, Poland, the Czech Republic and Slovakia. In the USA, **Rail Europe** (☎ 800 257 2887; W *www.raileurope.com*) charges US$220 for five days of 1st-class travel within one month; extra rail days (maximum five) cost US$25 each.

Balkan Flexipass This pass, also sold outside Europe, offers five/10/15 days unlimited travel within one month. It is valid in Bulgaria, Greece, Macedonia, Romania, Turkey and Yugoslavia and costs US$152/264/317 (US$90/156/190 for those under 26).

CAR & MOTORCYCLE

Travelling with your own vehicle allows increased flexibility and the option to get off the beaten track. Unfortunately, cars can be inconvenient in city centres when you have to negotiate strange one-way systems or find somewhere to park in a confusing concrete jungle.

Paperwork & Preparations

Proof of ownership of a private vehicle should always be carried (a Vehicle Registration Document for British-registered cars) when touring Europe. An EU driving licence is acceptable for driving throughout most of Eastern Europe as are North American and Australian ones. But to be on the safe side – or if you have any other type of licence – you should obtain an International Driving Permit

(IDP) from your motoring organisation (see Visas & Documents in the Facts for the Visitor chapter). You'll need a certified Russian translation for driving in Russia. Always check which type of licence is required in your chosen destination before departure.

Third-party motor insurance is compulsory throughout Europe. For non-EU countries make sure you check the requirements with your insurer. For further advice and more information contact the **Association of British Insurers** or check out its website (☎ 020-7600 3333; W *www.abi.org.uk*).

In general you should get your insurer to issue a Green Card (which may cost extra), an internationally recognised proof of insurance, and check that it lists all the countries you intend to visit. You'll need this in the event of an accident outside the country where the vehicle is insured. The European Accident Statement (known as the 'Constat Amiable' in France) is available from your insurance company and is copied so that each party at an accident can record the identical information for insurance purposes. The Association of British Insurers has more details. Never sign statements you cannot understand or read – insist on a translation and sign that only if it's acceptable. If the Green Card doesn't list one of the countries you're visiting and your insurer cannot (or will not) add it, you will have to take out separate third-party cover at the border of the country in question. This will probably be the case for Bulgaria and especially Russia. Note that the Green Card is also not accepted in the Baltic countries and you should allow extra time at borders to purchase insurance. Delays can sometimes last several hours.

Taking out a European breakdown assistance policy, such as the **AA** (in UK ☎ 0870 550 0600) Five Star Service or the **RAC** (in UK ☎ 0800 550 055; W *www.rac.co.uk*) Eurocover Motoring Assistance, is a good investment. Expect to pay about UK£50 for 14 days' cover with a 10% discount for members. Non-Europeans might find it cheaper to arrange for international coverage with their own national motoring organisation before leaving home. Ask your motoring organisation for details about free and reciprocal services offered by affiliated organisations around Europe.

Every vehicle travelling across an international border should display a sticker that shows country of registration. It's compulsory to carry a warning triangle almost everywhere in Europe, which must be displayed in the event of a breakdown. Recommended accessories are a first-aid kit (this is compulsory in Croatia, Slovenia and Yugoslavia), a spare bulb kit, and a fire extinguisher (compulsory in Bulgaria). Contact the RAC or the AA for more information.

Road Rules

Motoring organisations are able to supply their members with country-by-country information on motoring regulations, or they may produce motoring guidebooks for general sale. The RAC provides comprehensive destination-specific notes with a summary of national road rules and regulations. Contact it by telephone or check out its website.

According to statistics, driving in Eastern Europe is much more dangerous than in Western Europe. Driving at night can be especially hazardous in rural areas as the roads are often narrow and winding, and you may encounter horse-drawn vehicles, cyclists, pedestrians and domestic animals. In the event of an accident you're supposed to notify the police and file an insurance claim. If your car has significant body damage from a previous accident, point this out to customs upon arrival and have it noted somewhere, as damaged vehicles may only be allowed to leave the country with police permission.

The standard international road signs are used throughout Eastern Europe. You drive on the right-hand side of the road throughout the region and overtake on the left. Keep right except when overtaking, and use your indicators for any change of lane and when pulling away from the kerb. You're not allowed to overtake more than one car at a time, whether they are moving or stationary.

Speed limits are signposted, and are generally 110km/h or 120km/h on motorways (freeways), 100km/h on highways, 80km/h on secondary and tertiary roads and 50km/h or 60km/h in built-up areas. Motorcycles are usually limited to 90km/h on motorways, and vehicles with trailers to 80km/h. In towns you may only sound the horn to avoid an accident.

Everywhere in Eastern Europe, the use of seat belts is mandatory and motorcyclists (and their passengers) must wear a helmet. In most countries, children under 12 and intoxicated passengers are not permitted in the front seat. Driving after drinking *any* alcohol

is a serious offence – most Eastern European countries have a 0% blood-alcohol concentration (BAC) limit (0.02% in Poland).

Throughout Europe, when two roads of equal importance intersect, the vehicle coming from the right has right of way unless signs indicate otherwise. In many countries this also applies to cyclists, so take care. On roundabouts (traffic circles) vehicles already in the roundabout have the right of way. Public transport vehicles pulling out from a stop also have right of way. Stay out of lanes marked 'bus' except when you're making a right-hand turn. Pedestrians have the right of way at marked crossings and whenever you're making a turn. In Europe it's prohibited to turn right against a red light even after coming to a stop.

It's usually illegal to stop or park at the top of slopes, in front of pedestrian crossings, at bus or tram stops, on bridges or at level crossings. You must use a red reflector warning triangle when parking on a highway (in an emergency). If you don't use the triangle and another vehicle hits you from behind, you will be held responsible.

Beware of trams (streetcars) as these have priority at crossroads and when they are turning right (provided they signal the turn). Don't pass a tram that is stopping to let off passengers until everyone is out and the tram doors have closed again (unless, of course, there's a safety island). Never pass a tram on the left or stop within 1m of tram tracks. A police officer who sees you blocking a tram route by waiting to turn left will flag you over. Traffic police administer fines on the spot (always ask for a receipt).

Roads

Conditions and types of roads vary considerably across Eastern Europe, but it is possible to make some generalisations. The fastest routes are four- or six-lane dual carriageways, with two or three lanes either side – such as a motorway, *autópálya, avtocesta, autostradă* etc – though they are rare and of short length in the region. These roads are great in terms of speed and comfort but driving can be quite dull with little or no interesting scenery. Some of these roads also incur tolls. There's almost always an alternative (though much slower) route you can take if you don't want to pay a toll. Motorways and other primary routes are in good to fair condition depending on the country. Bulgaria, the Czech Republic and Slovakia levy a general tax on vehicles using their motorways.

Road surfaces on minor routes can be poor in some countries (eg, Romania, Bulgaria and Russia), and slow, and occasionally hazardous (beware of donkeys with no headlights). Watch out for speed traps and potholes off the main roads in the Baltics. As compensation for these irregularities you can expect much better scenery and plenty of interesting villages along the way.

Rental
The big international firms will give you reliable service and a good standard of vehicle. Prebooked rates are generally lower than walk-in rates at rental offices, but either way you'll pay around 20% to 40% more than in Western Europe.

You should be able to make advance reservations online. Check out the websites:

Avis w www.avis.com
Budget w www.budget.com
Europcar w www.europcar.com
Hertz w www.hertz.com

Brokers can cut hire costs. **Holiday Autos** *(in UK ☎ 0870 400 4477; w www.holidayautos .com • Kemwel Holiday Autos; in US ☎ 877 820 0668)* has low rates and representatives or offices in over 20 countries. See the website. In the UK, a competitor with even lower prices is **Autos Abroad** *(☎ 020-7287 6000; w www.autosabroad.co.uk)*.

If you're coming from North America, Australia or New Zealand, ask your airline if it has any special deals for rental cars in Europe, or check the ads in the weekend travel sections of major newspapers. You can often find very competitive deals.

Local companies not connected with any chain will usually offer lower prices than the multinationals, but when comparing rates beware of printed tariffs intended only for local residents, which may be lower than the prices foreigners are charged. If in doubt, ask. The chain companies sometimes offer the flexibility of allowing you to rent in one place and drop off the car at their locations in other cities at no additional charge.

If renting from abroad, you must tell the agency exactly which countries you plan to visit so it can make sure the insurance is in order. Many German agencies, for example, refuse to allow their cars to be taken to some parts of Eastern Europe because of high levels of car theft.

Purchase
Don't even consider buying a used car in Eastern Europe, where the paperwork is a nightmare. The after-sales care is nonexistent and the quality of vehicles is particularly poor.

Motorcycle Touring
If you are thinking of setting out on a tour of Europe by motorcycle contact the **British Motorcyclists Federation** *(☎ 0116-254 8818)* for some help and advice. An excellent source of information for those interested in more adventurous biking activities can be found at w www.horizonsunlimited.com.

Fuel
The problems associated with finding the right kind of petrol (or petrol of any kind without special coupons) are all but over in Eastern Europe. Fuel prices still vary considerably from country to country and may bear little relation to the general cost of living; relatively affluent Slovenia, for example, has very cheap fuel while the opposite is true in inexpensive Hungary. Savings can be made if you fill up in the right place. Russia is the cheapest place – then comes Romania, which has prices half those of neighbouring Hungary. Motoring organisations such as the RAC can give more details.

Unleaded petrol of 95 or 98 octane is now widely available throughout Eastern Europe, though maybe not at the odd station on back roads, or outside main cities in Russia. To be on the safe side in Russia, bring a 20L can in which to carry an extra supply, especially if your car is fitted with a catalytic converter, as this expensive component can be ruined by leaded fuel. Unleaded fuel is usually slightly cheaper than super (premium grade). Look for the pump with green markings and the word *Bleifrei*, German for 'unleaded'. Diesel is usually significantly cheaper in Eastern Europe.

Good-quality petrol is easy to find in the Baltics, but stations seem to be placed somewhat erratically. There can be several within a few miles of each other and then none for incredibly long stretches. Make sure you fill up your tank wherever possible – especially if you are travelling off the main highways.

TAXI

Taxis in Eastern Europe are much cheaper than in Western Europe. Although they are metered in most countries nowadays, scams and rip-offs (eg, in the Czech Republic and to some extent Hungary) can make taking a cab an unpleasant, expensive and even dangerous experience. See the individual country chapters for details. Taxis can be found idling near train stations or big hotels or you can hail one on the street. Don't underestimate the local knowledge that can be gleaned from most taxi drivers. They can often tell you about the liveliest places in town and know all about events happening during your stay.

BICYCLE

A tour of Western Europe by bike may seem like a daunting prospect but help is at hand. The **Cyclists' Touring Club** *(CTC; ☎ 0870 873 0060; w www.ctc.org.uk; Cotterell House, 69 Meadrow, Godalming, Surrey GU7 3HS)* is based in the UK and offers its members an information service on all matters associated with cycling (including maps, cycling conditions, itineraries and detailed routes). If it is not able to answer your questions the chances are it will know someone who can. The membership fee is UK£27 for adults, UK£10 for those aged under 25 and UK£16.50 for those over 65.

The key to a successful trip is to travel light. What you carry should be largely determined by your destination and type of trip. Even for the shortest and most basic trip it's worth carrying the tools necessary for repairing a puncture. Other things you might want to consider packing are spare brake and gear cables, spanners, Allen keys, spare spokes of the correct length and strong adhesive tape. Before you set off ensure that you are competent at carrying out basic repairs. There's no point in weighing yourself down with equipment that you haven't got a clue how to use. Always check over your bike thoroughly each morning and again at night when the day's touring is over. Take a good lock and always use it when you leave your bike unattended.

The wearing of helmets is not compulsory but is certainly advised.

A seasoned cyclist can average about 80km a day but this depends on the terrain and how much weight you are carrying. Don't overdo it – there's no point in burning yourself out during the initial stages.

One major drawback to cycling in Eastern Europe is the disgusting exhaust put out by Eastern European vehicles, especially buses and trucks. You'll often find yourself gasping in a cloud of blue or black smoke as these vehicles lumber along quiet country roads.

For more information on cycling, see Activities in the earlier Facts for the Visitor chapter and in the individual country chapters.

Rental

Except for in a few of the more-visited regions, it can be difficult to hire bikes in most of the countries of Eastern Europe. The best hunting grounds are often camping grounds and resort hotels in season. See the country chapters for more details.

Purchase

For major cycling tours, it's best to have a bike you're familiar with, so consider bringing your own (see the following section) rather than buying on arrival. If you can't be bothered with the hassle then there are places to buy in Eastern Europe (shops selling new and second-hand bicycles or you can check local papers for private vendors), but you'll need a specialist bicycle shop for a machine capable of withstanding touring. CTC can provide members with a leaflet on purchasing.

Transporting a Bicycle

If you want to bring your own bicycle to Europe, you should be able to take it on the plane. You can either take it apart and pack all the pieces in a bike bag or box, or simply wheel it to the check-in desk, where it should be treated as a piece of check-in luggage. You may have to remove the pedals and turn the handlebars sideways so that it takes up less space in the aircraft's hold; check all this with the airline well in advance, preferably before you pay for your ticket. If your bicycle and other luggage exceed your weight allowance, ask about alternatives or you may suddenly find yourself being charged a fortune for excess baggage.

Within Europe, bikes can usually be transported as luggage subject to a fairly small supplementary fee. If it's possible, book your tickets in advance.

HITCHING

Hitching is never entirely safe in *any* country, and we don't recommend it. Travellers who decide to hitch should understand that they are taking a small but potentially serious risk. People who do choose to hitch will be safer if they travel in pairs and let someone know where they plan to go.

Also, as long as public transport remains cheap in Eastern Europe, hitchhiking is more for the adventure than the transport. In Russia, Albania, Romania and sometimes Poland, drivers will expect riders to pay the equivalent of a bus fare. In Romania traffic is light, motorists are probably not going far, and almost everywhere you'll face small vehicles overloaded with passengers. If you want to give it a try, though, make yourself a small, clearly written cardboard destination sign, remembering to use the local name for the town or city ('Praha' not 'Prague'; 'Warszawa' not 'Warsaw'). Don't try to hitch from the city centres; city buses will usually take you to the edge of town. Hitchhiking on a motorway (freeway) is usually prohibited; you must stand near an entrance ramp. If you look like a Westerner your chances of getting a ride might improve.

Women will find hitchhiking safer than in Western Europe, but the standard precautions should be taken: never accept a ride with two men, don't let your pack be put in the boot (trunk), only sit next to a door you can open, ask drivers where they are going before you say where you're going etc. Don't hesitate to refuse a ride if you feel at all uncomfortable, and insist on being let out at the first sign of trouble. Best of all, try to find a travelling companion (although three people will have a very hard time getting a lift).

Travellers considering hitching as a way of getting around Eastern Europe may find the following websites useful. For general facts, destination-based information and rideshare options visit **w** www.bugeurope.com. The useful **w** www.hitchhikers.org connects hitchhikers and drivers worldwide.

BOAT

Croatia is the one country in Eastern Europe with significant (and affordable) sea routes. A boat trip along Croatia's heavily indented coast is one of the true scenic highlights of Eastern Europe.

Some of Eastern Europe's lakes and rivers are serviced by steamers and ferries; as you'd expect, schedules are more extensive in the summer months. In most cases, extended boat trips should be considered as relaxing and scenic excursions; as a means of transport, they can be grotesquely expensive. But getting out on the water for the day in countries like Hungary can be cheap and easy: local river ferries link Budapest with the picturesque towns of the Danube Bend to the north, and ferries serve all of the built-up areas on Lake Balaton. In southern Lithuania you can hop on the steamboat that runs along the Nemunas River. See the relevant country chapters for details.

PUBLIC TRANSPORT

Although ticket prices have increased substantially in recent years, public transport in Eastern Europe is still inexpensive and the low price is not at all indicative of the service, which is generally good. In most cities, buses and trams begin moving at 5am or earlier and continue until around 10.30pm or 11.30pm. There are metro (subway or underground) lines in Bucharest, Budapest, Prague, Warsaw, Moscow and St Petersburg.

For most forms of public transport you buy tickets in advance at a kiosk or from a machine. Information windows in bus and train stations sometimes have tickets for local transport. Once aboard you validate your own ticket by using a cancelling machine near the door. Watch how the locals do it but don't be surprised if you only see one or two in a carload punching their tickets; most commuters buy much cheaper weekly or monthly passes. Different tickets are sometimes required for buses, trolley buses, trams and the metro, but in most cases they're all the same. If all the kiosks selling tickets are closed, ask another passenger to sell you a ticket. It's also now possible to buy tickets from the driver or a conductor on some services.

Travelling 'black' (ticketless) is riskier than ever in Eastern Europe as public transport systems try to break even or turn a profit. With increased surveillance, there's a good chance you'll get caught, which can be both costly and embarrassing.

ORGANISED TOURS

A package tour is worth considering only if your time is very limited or you have a special interest such as skiing, canoeing, sailing, horse riding, cycling or spa treatments. Cruises on the Danube River are available but they're very expensive. Most tour prices are for double occupancy, which means singles have to share a double room with a stranger of the same sex or pay a supplement to have the room to themselves.

New Millennium Holidays *(☎ 0870 240 3217;* w *www.newmillennium-holidays.com; Icon House, 209 Yardley Rd, Birmingham B27 6LZ)* runs inexpensive bus or air tours all year from the UK to Central and Eastern Europe, including Russia. Packages vary from 10 to 17 days, some combining two or three countries, with half-board or B&B accommodation. Another British company highly experienced in booking travel to Eastern Europe is **Regent Holidays** *(☎ 0117-921 1711, fax 925 4866;* w *www.regent-holidays.co.uk; 15 John St, Bristol BS1 2HR)*. Check out the website.

For tours of the Baltic region, including weekend city breaks, activity holidays and cycling tours, **Lithuanian Holidays** *(☎ 0161-286 0830;* w *www.lithuanianholidays.com; 30 Cartwright Rd, Manchester M21 9EY)* is an option. It also arranges independent travel.

In Australia you can obtain a detailed brochure outlining dozens of upmarket tours (including to Russia) from the **Eastern Europe Travel Bureau** *(☎ 02-9262 1144;* e *eetb@ eetbtravel.com; Level 5, 75 King St, Sydney, NSW 2000)*.

Young revellers can party on Europe-wide bus tours. Contiki and Top Deck offer camping or hotel-based bus tours for the 18-to-35 age group. The duration of Contiki's tours that include Eastern Europe or Russia are 22 to 46 days. **Contiki** *(☎ 020-7290 6422;* w *www .contiki.com)* and **Top Deck** *(☎ 020-7370 4555;* w *www.topdecktravel.co.uk)* both have London offices, as well as offices or representatives in Europe, North America, Australasia and South Africa.

For people aged over 50, **Saga Holidays** *(in UK ☎ 0800 300 500; Saga Building, Middelburg Square, Folkestone, Kent CT20 1AZ, UK • in USA ☎ 617-262 2262; 222 Berkeley St, Boston, MA 02116, USA)* offers holidays ranging from cheap coach tours to luxury cruises (and has cheap travel insurance).

National tourist offices in most countries offer organised trips to points of interest. These may range from one-hour city tours to more extensive several-day circular excursions to regional areas of the country. They often work out more expensive than going it alone, but are sometimes worth it if you are pressed for time. A short city tour will give you a quick overview of the place and can be a good way to begin your visit.

Albania

Albania was a closed communist country until 1990, but caught world attention in November of that year as the last domino to tumble in Eastern Europe's sudden series of democratic revolutions. Long considered fair prey by imperialist powers, Albania chose a curious form of isolation, with everything centred on the Stalinist rule and personality cult of Enver Hoxha, Albania's iron-fisted dictator from 1944 to his death in 1985. Hoxha did save the country from annexation by Yugoslavia after WWII, but few Albanians have positive feelings about him.

Albanians call their country the Republika e Shqipërisë, or 'Land of the Eagle'. Albania is Europe's last unknown, with some enchanting classical ruins at Apollonia, Butrint and Durrës, the charming 'museum towns' of Gjirokastra and Berat, vibrant towns like Tirana, Shkodra, Korça and Durrës, colourful folklore and majestic landscapes of mountains, forests, lakes and sea.

Albania's first years of attempted democracy were troubled. The country spiralled into violence and anarchy following the collapse of fraudulent pyramid schemes in late 1996. Since that difficult beginning the economic situation has improved enormously and the country is open to travellers once more. Those who do decide to visit Albania should mingle curiosity with a healthy caution, but visiting this country, as it slowly opens up to the world, is a rare experience.

At a Glance

- **Tirana** – old bazaar town turned bustling metropolis
- **Ionian Coast** – towering mountains and dramatic ocean views
- **Gjirokastra** – picturesque fortress; the Drino Valley; tower houses
- **Butrint** – stunning well-preserved Roman ruins; an ancient Greek theatre; colourful mosaics

Capital	Tirana
Population	3.5 million
Official Language	Albanian (Tosk)
Currency	1 lekë (L) = 100 quintars
Time	GMT/UTC+0100
Country Phone Code	☎ 355

Facts about Albania

HISTORY

During the 2nd millennium BC, the Illyrians, who were ancestors of today's Albanians, occupied the western Balkans. The Greeks arrived in the 7th century BC to establish self-governing colonies at Epidamnos (now Durrës), Apollonia and Butrint. They traded peacefully with the Illyrians, who formed tribal states in the 4th century BC. The south became part of Greek Epirus.

In the second half of the 3rd century BC, an expanding Illyrian kingdom based at Shkodra came into conflict with Rome, which sent a fleet of 200 vessels against Queen Teuta (who ruled over the Illyrian Ardian kingdom) in 228 BC. A long war resulted in the extension of Roman control over the entire Balkan area by 167 BC.

Like the Greeks, the Illyrians preserved their own language and traditions despite centuries of Roman rule. Under the Romans, Illyria enjoyed peace and prosperity, though the large agricultural estates were worked by slave labour. The main trade route between Rome and Constantinople, the Via Egnatia, ran from Durrës to Thessaloniki.

When the Roman Empire was divided in AD 395, Illyria fell within the Eastern Roman

ALBANIA

YUGOSLAVIA

Podgorica

Mt Jezerce
(2694m)

Bajram
Curri

Djakovica

Kosova
(Kosovo)

Han i
Hotit

Fierza

Drin

River

Kruma

Prizren

Lake
Shkodra

Bar

Shkodra

Puka

Kukës

Morinë

To Ancona

Buna

River

Ulcinj

Mt Korab
(2751m)

Lezha

Rreshen

Peshkopi

ADRIATIC
SEA

Milot

Laç

Burrel

Maqellare

Drin

Debar

Kruja

Klos

River

Rinas

Durrës

TIRANA

To Bari

Kavaja

Librazhd

Struga

MACEDONIA

Rrogozhina

Qafa e
Thanës

Ohrid

Myzaqeja
Plain

Shkumbin River

Elbasan

Lake
Ohrid

Lushnja

Lake
Prespa

Seman

River

Gramsh

Pogradec

Apollonia

Fier

Kuçova

Devoll

Tushemisht

Patos

Osum

Berat

River

Maliq

Ballsh

Korça

Kapshtica

Vlora

Vjose

Poliçan

Çorovoda

River

Memaliaj

Erseka

IONIAN
SEA

Orikum

Tepelena

Kelçyra

Përmet

Leskoviku

Llogara
Pass

Dhërmi

Drino

Himara

River

Borsh

Gjirokastra

Delvina

GREECE

Saranda

Kakavija

0   25   50km
0   15   30mi

Corfu
(Kerkyra)

Butrint

Ioannina

Corfu

Konispoli

Empire, later known as Byzantium. Invasions by migrating peoples – Visigoths, Huns, Ostrogoths and Slavs – continued through the 5th and 6th centuries and only in the south did the ethnic Illyrians survive.

In 1344 Albania was annexed by Serbia, but after the defeat of Serbia by the Turks in 1389 the whole region was open to Ottoman attack. The Venetians occupied some coastal towns, and from 1443 to 1468 the national hero Skënderbeg (George Kastrioti) led Albanian resistance to the Turks from his castle at Kruja. Skënderbeg won all 25 battles he fought against the Turks, and even Sultan Mehmet-Fatih, conqueror of Constantinople, could not take Kruja.

From 1479 to 1912 Albania, the most backward corner of Europe, was under Ottoman rule. In the 15th and 16th centuries thousands of Albanians fled to southern Italy to escape Turkish rule and over half of those who remained converted to Islam.

In 1878 the Albanian League at Prizren, which is in present-day Kosova (Kosovo), began a struggle for autonomy that was put down by the Turkish army in 1881. Further Uprisings between 1910 and 1912 culminated in a proclamation of independence and the formation of a provisional government led by Ismail Qemali at Vlora in 1912. These achievements were severely compromised when Kosova, nearly half of Albania, was given to Serbia in 1913. With the outbreak of WWI, Albania was occupied by the armies of Greece, Serbia, France, Italy and Austria-Hungary in succession.

In 1920 the capital city was moved from Durrës to less-vulnerable Tirana. Thousands of Albanian volunteers converged on Vlora, forcing the occupying Italians to withdraw. Ahmet Zogu became the ruler of Albania and declared himself King Zogu I in 1928, but his close collaboration with Italy backfired in April 1939 when Mussolini ordered an invasion of Albania. Zogu fled to Britain and used gold looted from the Albanian treasury to rent a floor at London's Ritz Hotel.

On 8 November 1941 the Albanian Communist Party was founded with Enver Hoxha (pronounced Hodja) as first secretary, a position he held until his death in April 1985. The communists led the resistance against the Italians and, after 1943, against the Germans, ultimately tying down 15 combined German-Italian divisions.

The Rise of Communism

After the fighting had died down, the communists consolidated power. In January 1946 the People's Republic of Albania was proclaimed, with Enver Hoxha as president.

In September 1948 Albania broke off relations with Yugoslavia, which had hoped to incorporate the country into the Yugoslav Federation. Instead, Albania allied itself with Stalin's USSR and put into effect a series of Soviet-style economic plans.

Albania collaborated closely with the USSR until 1960, when a heavy-handed Khrushchev demanded that a submarine base be set up at Vlora. Albania broke off diplomatic relations with the USSR in 1961 and reoriented itself towards the People's Republic of China.

From 1966 to 1967 Albania experienced a Chinese-style cultural revolution. Administrative workers were suddenly transferred to remote areas and younger cadres were placed in leading positions. The collectivisation of agriculture was completed and organised religion banned.

Following the Soviet invasion of Czechoslovakia in 1968, Albania left the Warsaw Pact and embarked on a self-reliant defence policy. Some 750,000 igloo-shaped concrete bunkers and pillboxes with narrow gun slits, built by Hoxha, serve as a reminder of this policy.

With the death of Mao Zedong in 1976 and the changes that followed in China after 1978, Albania's unique relationship with China came to an end.

Post-Hoxha

Hoxha died in April 1985 and his long-time associate Ramiz Alia took over the leadership. Keenly aware of the economic decay caused by Albania's isolationist path, Alia began a liberalisation programme in 1986 and also broadened Albania's ties with foreign countries. Travellers arriving in Albania at this time no longer had their guidebooks confiscated and their beards and long hair clipped by border barbers, and short skirts were allowed.

In June 1990, inspired by the changes that were occurring elsewhere in Eastern Europe, some 4500 Albanians took refuge in Western embassies in Tirana. After a brief confrontation with the police and the Sigurimi (secret police) these people were allowed to board ships for Brindisi in Italy, where they were granted political asylum.

ALBANIA

After student demonstrations in December 1990, the government agreed to allow opposition parties. The Democratic Party, led by heart surgeon Sali Berisha, was formed. Further demonstrations won new concessions, including the promise of free elections and independent trade unions. The government announced a reform programme and party hardliners were purged.

In early March 1991, as the election date approached, some 20,000 Albanians fled to Brindisi by ship, creating a crisis for the Italian government, which had begun to view them as economic refugees. Most were eventually allowed to stay.

The March 1992 elections ended 47 years of communist rule. After the resignation of Ramiz Alia, parliament elected Sali Berisha president in April. In September 1992 former president Ramiz Alia was placed under house arrest after he wrote articles critical of the Democratic government. In August 1993 the leader of the Socialist Party, Fatos Nano, was also arrested on corruption charges.

A severe crisis developed in late 1996, when private pyramid investment schemes – widely thought to have been supported by the government – collapsed spectacularly. Around 70% of Albanians lost their savings – in total over US$1 billion – and nationwide disturbances and violence resulted. New elections were called, and the victorious Socialist Party under Fatos Nano – who had been freed from prison by the rampaging mob – was able to restore some degree of security and investor confidence.

Albania shuddered again during November 1998 when Azem Hajdari, a very popular Democratic Party deputy, was assassinated, but the riots following his death were eventually contained.

In spring 1999 Albania faced a crisis of a different sort. This time, it was the influx of 465,000 refugees from neighbouring Kosova during the NATO bombing and the Serbian ethnic-cleansing campaign in Kosova. While this put a tremendous strain on resources, the net effect has in fact been positive. Substantial amounts of international aid money have poured in, the service sector has grown and inflation has declined to single digits.

By 2002 the country found itself in a kind of miniboom with much money being poured into construction projects and infrastructure renewal.

GEOGRAPHY

More than three-quarters of this 28,748-sq-km country (a bit smaller than Belgium) consists of mountains and hills. There are three zones: a coastal plain, a mountainous region and an interior plain. The coastal plain extends approximately 200km from north to south and up to 50km inland. The 2000m-high forested mountain spine, which stretches for the entire length of Albania, culminates at Mt Jezerc (2694m) in the north, near the Yugoslav border. The country's highest peak is Mt Korab (2751m), which is located on the border with Macedonia to the east. Albania has been subject to some destructive earthquakes, such as the one that struck in 1979 leaving at least 100,000 people homeless.

The longest river in Albania is the Drin (285km), which drains Lake Ohrid. In the north the Drin flows into the Buna, Albania's only navigable river, which connects shallow Lake Shkodra to the sea. The Ionian littoral, especially the 'Riviera of Flowers' stretching from Vlora to Saranda, offers magnificent scenery. Forests cover 40% of the land, and the many olive trees, citrus plantations and vineyards give Albania a Mediterranean air.

CLIMATE

Albania has a warm Mediterranean climate. The summers are hot, clear and dry, and the winters, when 40% of the rain falls, are cool, cloudy and moist. In winter the high interior plateau can be very cold as continental air masses move in. Along the coast the climate is moderated by sea winds. Gjirokastra and Shkodra receive twice as much rain as Korça, with November, December and April being the wettest months. The sun shines longest from May to September and July is the warmest month, but even April and October are quite pleasant.

The average maximum temperature in Tirana is 23.5°C in summer and 9°C in winter.

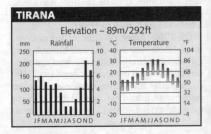

TIRANA

Elevation – 89m/292ft

ECOLOGY & ENVIRONMENT

Large parts of the country were subjected to ecological vandalism during the communist years, particularly near the Fier oilfields in central Albania where unregulated extraction caused massive surface damage from waste products. The huge petrochemical factory at Elbasan belched enormous amounts of toxic fumes over the valley for years.

Albanians are now turning their attention to cleaning up their act and foreign interests are taking an active role in monitoring industrial operations. However, issues such as improving roads still take precedence.

GOVERNMENT & POLITICS

Albania's political system is a presidential parliamentary democracy with Alfred Moisiu as president and head of state and Ilir Meta of the Socialist Party as prime minister. The main opposition, the Democratic Party, is chaired by Sali Berisha, the former president and rival to Socialist Party leader (and former prime minister) Fatos Nano.

ECONOMY

Albania is a country rich in natural resources such as crude oil, natural gas, coal, copper, iron, nickel and timber and is the world's third-largest producer of chrome, accounting for about 10% of the world's supply. The Central Mountains yield minerals such as copper (in the northeast around Kukës), chromium (farther south near the Drin River) and iron nickel (closer to Lake Ohrid). The government is now making preparations for Albania's mining industry to be privatised through sales to foreign interests.

There are textile industries at Berat, Korça and Tirana. Oil was discovered in Albania in 1917 and the country at one point supplied all its own petroleum requirements. Oil and gas from Fier also enabled the production of chemical fertilisers.

There are several huge hydroelectric dams on the Drin River in the north. Albania obtains 80% of its electricity from such dams and by 1970 electricity had reached every village in the country.

Following a period of neglect in the agricultural sector, Albanian farmers have begun the long task of rebuilding rural infrastructure, and agriculture currently accounts for 55% of the country's GDP, estimated in 2002 at US$10.5 billion.

Albania continues to be heavily dependent on remittances coming from the Albanian communities abroad, particularly in Greece and Italy. Albania is also angling for more international aid money, particularly in light of its generous intake of Kosovar Albanian refugees in 1998. Priority projects for aid money involve infrastructure improvement.

Despite many challenges, Albania's economy was projected to grow at 7% to 8% for the third straight year in 2002, making it one of the fastest-growing economies in Europe.

POPULATION & PEOPLE

Albanians are a hardy Mediterranean people, physically different from the more Nordic Slavs. Although the Slavs and Greeks look down on the Albanians, the Albanians themselves have a sense of racial superiority based on their descent from the ancient Illyrians, who inhabited the region before the Romans. The country's romanised name comes from the Albanoi, an ancient Illyrian tribe.

Approximately 95% of the country's population is Albanians. Over the years, the harsh economic conditions existing in Albania have unleashed waves of emigration: to Serbia in the 15th century, to Greece and Italy in the 16th century, to the USA in the 19th and 20th centuries and to Greece, Italy and Switzerland today. The Arbereshi, long-time Albanian residents of 50 scattered villages in southern Italy, fled west in the 16th century to escape the Turks. As many as two million ethnic Albanians live in Turkey today, emigrants from Serb-dominated Yugoslavia between 1912 and 1966. Since 1990 hundreds of thousands of Albanians have migrated to Western Europe (especially Greece and Italy) to escape the economic hardships at home. Minorities in Albania include the Greeks (3% of the population) and Vlachs, Macedonians and Roma (comprising a further 2% of the population).

The Shkumbin River forms a boundary between the Gheg cultural region of the north and the Tosk region in the south. The people in these regions still vary in dialect, musical culture and traditional dress.

ARTS
Music

Polyphony, the blending of several independent vocal or instrumental parts, is a southern Albanian tradition dating from ancient Illyrian times. Peasant choirs perform in a variety

ALBANIA

of styles, and the songs, usually with an epic-lyrical or historical theme, may be dramatic to the point of yodelling or slow and sober, with alternate male and female voices combining in harmonies. Instrumental polyphonic *kabas* are played by small Roma ensembles usually led by a clarinet. Improvisation gives way to dancing at colourful village weddings. One well-known group, which often tours outside Albania, is the Lela Family of Përmet.

An outstanding recording of traditional Albanian music is the CD *Albania, Vocal and Instrumental Polyphony* (LDX 274 897) in the series 'Le Chant du Monde' (Musée de l'Homme, Paris).

Literature
Prior to the adoption of a standardised orthography in 1909, very little literature was produced in Albania, though Albanians resident elsewhere in the Ottoman Empire and in Italy did write. Among these was the noted poet Naim Frashëri (1846–1900), who lived in İstanbul and wrote in Greek. Around the time of independence (1912), a group of romantic patriotic writers at Shkodra wrote epics and historical novels.

Perhaps the most interesting writer of the interwar period was Fan Noli (1880–1965). Educated as a priest in the USA, Fan Noli returned there to head the Albanian Orthodox Church in America after the Democratic government of Albania, in which he served as premier, was overthrown in 1924. Although many of his books are based on religion, the introductions he wrote to his own translations of Cervantes, Ibsen, Omar Khayyám and Shakespeare established him as Albania's foremost literary critic.

The poet Migjeni (1911–38) focused on social issues until his early death from tuberculosis. In his 1936 poem, *Vargjet e lira* (Free Verse), Migjeni seeks to dispel the magic of old myths and awaken the reader to present injustices.

Albania's best-known contemporary writer is Ismail Kadare, born in 1935, whose many novels have been translated into 20 languages. *Chronicle in Stone* (1971) relates wartime experiences in Kadare's birthplace, Gjirokastra, as seen through the eyes of a boy. *Broken April* (1990) deals with the blood vendettas of the northern highlands before the 1939 Italian invasion. Although Kadare lived in Tirana throughout the Hoxha years and even wrote a book, *The Great Winter* (1972), extolling Hoxha's defiance of Moscow, he sought political asylum in Paris in 1990. A more recent classic is *The Two-Arched Bridge* (1997), an ominous and beautiful 14th-century tale, told by a monk, of the troubled construction of a bridge during turbulent political times.

Cinema
A film worth seeing is *Lamerica*, a brilliant and stark look at Albanian post-communist culture. Despite its title, it is about Albanians seeking to escape to Bari, Italy, in the immediate postcommunist era. The title is a symbol for ordinary Albanians seeking a better and more materially fulfilling life in the West. Woven loosely around a plot about a couple of Italian scam artists, the essence of the film is the unquenchable dignity of the ordinary Albanian in the face of adversity.

SOCIETY & CONDUCT
Traditional dress is still common in rural areas, especially on Sunday and holidays. Men wear embroidered white shirts and knee trousers, the Ghegs with a white felt skullcap and the Tosks with a flat-topped white fez. Women's clothing is brighter than that of the men. Along with the standard white blouses with wide sleeves, women from Christian areas wear red vests, while Muslim women wear baggy pants tied at the ankles and coloured headscarves. Older Muslim women wear white scarves around the neck; white scarves may also be a sign of mourning.

The *Kanun* is an ancient social law, which outlines most aspects of social behaviour, including the treatment of guests. This has meant that Albanians can be hospitable in the extreme and will often offer travellers lodging and food free of charge. Travellers must be wary of exploiting this tradition and, while payment may well be acceptable in some cases, a small gift of a book or a memento from home will often suffice.

Be respectful when visiting the country's mosques – remove your shoes and try to avoid visits during prayer times.

RELIGION
From 1967 to 1990 Albania was the only officially atheist state in Europe. Public religious services were banned and many churches were converted into theatres or cinemas. In mid-1990 this situation ended and in December of

that year Nobel Prize-winner Mother Teresa of Calcutta, an ethnic Albanian from Macedonia, visited Albania and met with President Alia. Traditionally, Albania has been 70% Sunni Muslim, 20% Albanian Orthodox (mostly in the south) and 10% Roman Catholic (mostly in the north). It's the only country in Europe with an Islamic majority though the form of Islam is quite secular, similar to the situation in Turkey.

LANGUAGE

Albanian (Shqipja) is an Indo-European dialect of ancient Illyrian, with a number of Latin, Slavonic and (modern) Greek words. The two main dialects of Albanian have diverged over the past 1000 years. In 1909 a standardised form of the Gheg dialect of Elbasan was adopted as the official language, but since WWII a modified version of the Tosk dialect of southern Albania has been used.

Outside the country, Albanians resident in former Yugoslavia speak Gheg, those in Greece speak Tosk, whereas in Italy they speak another dialect called Arberesh. With practice you can sometimes differentiate between the dialects by listening closely for the nasalised vowels of Gheg. In 1972 the Congress of Orthography at Tirana established a unified written language based on the two dialects, which is now universally accepted.

You'll find that Italian is the most useful foreign language to know in Albania, and English is a strong second. Greek is also useful in the south.

Many Albanian place names have two forms because the definite article is a suffix. In this book we use the form most commonly used in English, but Tirana actually means *the* Tiranë. Albanians, like Bulgarians, shake their heads to say yes and usually nod to say no.

See the Language chapter at the back of the book for pronunciation guidelines and useful words and phrases.

Facts for the Visitor

HIGHLIGHTS

The beauty and mystique of Albania's mountains and coastal region makes the country a highlight in iteslef. The fortress town of Gjirokastra in the south is worth a visit, as are the stunning and well-preserved Roman ruins at Butrint, also in the far south.

PLANNING
Maps

The best map of the country is the 1:300,000 *Albania* map published by Euro Map. It also includes several city and town plans. The 1:450,000 *Albania World Travel Map* published by Bartholomew is also very detailed. Buy them before you arrive in Albania as they may be hard to find in the country.

TOURIST OFFICES

There are no tourist information offices in Albania, but hotel receptionists or travel agencies will sometimes help you with directions. You can buy city maps of Tirana in bookshops and larger kiosks in the capital, but in most of the other towns they're unobtainable. In addition, many streets lack signs and the buildings have no numbers marked on them! Some streets don't seem to have any name at all. However, you will find that most of the towns are small enough for you to get around without them.

VISAS & DOCUMENTS

No visa is required by citizens of EU countries or nationals of Australia, New Zealand and the USA. Travellers from other countries should check with an Albanian embassy for appropriate visa requirements. Citizens of most countries – even those entering visa-free – will be required to pay an 'entry tax' at the border. The entry tax for almost all visitors is US$10. Israeli citizens pay US$30.

Upon arrival you will fill in an arrival and departure card. Keep the departure card, which will be stamped, with your passport and present it when you leave.

EMBASSIES & CONSULATES
Albanian Embassies & Consulates

Listed below are some of the main addresses for Albanian embassies.

France (☎ 01-45 53 51 32) 13 rue de la Pompe, Paris 75016
Germany (☎ 0302-593 0550, fax 593 0599) Friedrichstrasse 231, D-10969 Berlin
Greece (☎ 21 0723 4412, fax 21 0723 1972) Karahristou 1, GR-114 21 Athens
UK (☎ 020-7730 5709, fax 7828 8869) 24 Buckingham Gate, 2nd Floor, London SW1 E6LB
USA (☎ 202-223 4942, fax 628 7342) 2100 S St NW, Washington DC 20008

Embassies & Consulates in Albania

The following embassies are in Tirana (area code ☎ 042):

Bulgaria (☎ 233 155, fax 232 272) Rruga Skënderbeg 12
Germany (☎ 232 048, fax 233 497) Rruga Skënderbeg 8
Greece (☎ 223 959, fax 234 443) Rruga Frederik Shiroka 3
Macedonia (☎ 233 036, fax 232 514) Rruga Lekë Dukagjini 2
Turkey (☎ 233 399, fax 232 719) Rruga E Kavajës 31
UK (☎ 234 973, fax 247 697) Rruga Skënderbeg 12
USA (☎ 247 285, fax 232 222) Rruga Elbasanit 103
Yugoslavia (☎ 232 089, fax 223 042) Rruga e Durrësit 192/196

MONEY
Currency

Albanian banknotes come in denominations of 100, 200, 500 and 1000 lekë. There are five, 10, 20 and 50 lekë coins. Notes that were issued after 1997 are smaller and contain a sophisticated watermark to prevent forgery. In 1964 the currency was revalued 10 times; prices on occasion may still be quoted at the old rate.

Everything in Albania can be paid for with lekë; however, bear in mind that most of the hotel and transport prices given in this chapter are quoted in US dollars or euros, both of which are readily accepted as alternative currencies for the lekë.

Exchange Rates

Conversion rates for major currencies at the time of publication are listed below:

country	unit		lekë
Australia	A$1	=	73.18 lekë
Canada	C$1	=	88.57 lekë
Euro Zone	€1	=	118 lekë
Japan	¥100	=	107.2 lekë
NZ	NZ$1	=	60 lekë
UK	UK£1	=	199.24 lekë
US	US$1	=	140 lekë

To find the most up-to-date exchange rates for the Albanian lekë, point your Web browser at **w** www.xe.com/ucc/full.shtml.

Exchanging Money

Some banks will change US-dollar travellers cheques into US dollars cash without any commission. Travellers cheques in small denominations may be used when paying bills at major hotels but cash is preferred everywhere. You'll find that credit cards are only accepted in the larger hotels and travel agencies, and a few places in Tirana and Durrës will offer credit-card advances (usually for MasterCard). At the time of research, one ATM had just opened in Tirana.

Every town has its free currency market, which usually operates on the street in front of the main post office or state bank. Look out for the men standing around with wads of money or pocket calculators in their hand. Such transactions are not dangerous and it all takes place quite openly, but be careful and make sure you count their money twice before tendering yours.

The advantages with changing money on the street are that you get a good rate and avoid the 1% commission some banks may charge. You also save time and don't have to worry about banking hours. Unlike the banks, private moneychangers never run out of currency notes.

In Albania, US dollars are the favourite foreign currency, though euros are also acceptable to all moneychangers. You will not be able to exchange Albanian currency outside of the country. Spend it or reconvert it before you leave.

Tipping

Albania is a moderately tip-conscious society. You should round up the bill in restaurants. However, with taxi drivers you will normally agree on a fare beforehand so an extra tip will not be considered necessary.

POST & COMMUNICATIONS
Post

There are few public mail boxes in Albania outside of main towns, but there is an increasing number of modern post offices springing up around the country where you can hand in your mail directly.

Letters to the USA and Canada cost 90 lekë and postcards 50 lekë. Letters to Australia, Africa and Asia cost 60 lekë and postcards 40 lekë. Within Europe letters cost 50 lekë to send and postcards 30 lekë, while to neighbouring countries the rates are 30 lekë and 20 lekë respectively. Within Albania the rates are 20 lekë and 15 lekë.

Telephone

Long-distance telephone calls made from main post offices are cheap, costing about 90 lekë a minute to Italy. Calls to the USA cost 230 lekë per minute. Phonecards are available from the post office in versions of 50 units (560 lekë), 100 units (980 lekë) and 200 units (1800 lekë). It's best not to buy the phonecards from the hawkers outside the post office.

Albania's country phone code is ☎ 355. Albania has two mobile/cellphone providers, and most areas of the country are now adequately covered. Roaming agreements with your home service provider may or may not exist. Owners of Greek mobile phones can roam in Albania. Local mobile numbers begin with 038 or 069.

To phone overseas from Albania, the international access code is ☎ 00. Dial ☎ 14 if you want domestic directory assistance and ☎ 12 for international directory assistance.

Fax

Faxing can be done from the main post office in Tirana, or from major hotels, though they will charge more.

Email & Internet Access

Places to access the Internet now abound in Tirana and most larger towns will have at least one place where you can access the Net. Rates are generally low – 300 lekë to 400 lekë an hour or part thereof. Some Internet centres also offer cheap international phone connections.

DIGITAL RESOURCES

Websites that you might find useful include **W** www.albanian.com and **W** www.albania.co .uk (a good info source on current events).

BOOKS

The Albanians – A Modern History (1999), by Miranda Vickers, is a comprehensive and very readable history of Albania from the time of Ottoman rule to the restoration of democracy after 1990.

Biografi (1993), by New Zealander Lloyd Jones, is a rather arresting story set in post-1990 Albania and is a mixture of both fact and fiction as the writer sets out to discover the alleged double of former communist dictator Enver Hoxha.

The Accursed Mountains: Journeys in Albania (1999), by Robert Carver, is a lively and colourful narrative about one journalist's entertaining, but occasionally credibility-stretching, journey through Albania in 1996.

The Best of Albanian Cooking (1999), by Klementina Hysa and R John Hysa, is one of scant few books on the subject of Albanian cuisine and contains a wide range of family recipes.

For a helpful list of Albanian words and phrases check out the *Mediterranean Europe phrasebook* from Lonely Planet, while *Colloquial Albanian* (1994), by Isa Zymberi, is a self-teach language course, accompanied by a cassette tape. It is part of the excellent Routledge teach-yourself language series.

An excellent source of rare and out-of-print books on Albania is **Harfield Books of London** (☎/fax 020-8871 0880; **W** www .harfieldbooks.com; *81 Replingham Rd, Southfields, London SW18 5LU).* Also try **Oxus Books** (☎/fax 020-8870 3854; *121 Astonville St, London SW18 5AQ),* which has a catalogue you can request.

NEWSPAPERS & MAGAZINES

A wide variety of newspapers are published in Tirana. The independent daily *Koha Jonë* is the paper with the widest readership.

The *Albanian Daily News* is a fairly dry, English-language publication that has useful information on happenings around Albania. It's generally available from major hotels for 300 lekë, or you can read it online at **W** www .AlbanianNews.com.

RADIO & TV

There are many TV channels available in Albania including the state TV service TVSH, the private station TVA and, among others, Eurosport, several Italian channels and even a couple of French ones.

The BBC World Service can be picked up in and around Tirana on 103.9FM, while the Voice of America's mainly music programme is on 107.4FM.

TIME

Albania is one hour ahead of GMT/UTC, the same as Yugoslavia, Macedonia and Italy, but one hour behind Greece. Albania goes on summer time at the end of March, when clocks are turned forward an hour. At the end of September, they're turned back an hour.

TOILETS

Public toilets should be used in dire circumstances only! There are only a handful in the whole of Tirana. Use hotel or restaurant toilets whenever you can. The ones in the main hotels in Tirana are very clean and modern. Plan your 'rest' stops carefully when travelling in the country.

HEALTH

Health services are available to tourists for a small fee at state-run hospitals, but service and standards are not crash hot. Make sure your travel or health insurance covers treatment in Albania includes evacuation. Use the private clinics where available; the ABS Health Foundation in Tirana is a good one (see Information in the Tirana section later in this chapter).

WOMEN TRAVELLERS

While women are not likely to encounter any predictable dangers, it is recommended that you travel in pairs or with male companions in order to avoid unwanted attention – particularly outside Tirana. Don't forget that Albania is a predominantly secular Muslim country. Dress should be conservative.

GAY & LESBIAN TRAVELLERS

Homosexuality became legal in Albania early in 1995, however attitudes are still highly conservative.

DISABLED TRAVELLERS

There are few special facilities for travellers in wheelchairs. However, there are toilets that cater for disabled people in the Tirana International and the Europapark Tirana hotels.

DANGERS & ANNOYANCES

The security level in the country is now generally stable. You are advised however to avoid independent travel in the far north of the country around Bajram Curri and along the road corridor from Shkodra to Kukës, as banditry may still occur. Be warned that there

---

Emergency Services

In the event of emergencies telephone ☎ 19 for the police, ☎ 17 for ambulance and ☎ 18 for the fire department. These numbers are valid nationwide.

---

may still be land mines near the northern border with Kosova around Bajram Curri.

Beware of pickpockets on crowded city buses and don't flash money around! Walking around larger towns is generally safe in the day, but at night beware of falling into deep potholes in the unlit streets, and occasional gangs of youths. Be aware of theft generally, but don't believe the horror stories you hear about Albania in Greece and elsewhere.

Take special care if accosted by Roma women and children begging; avoid eye contact and head to the nearest hotel.

As Albania was closed for so long, black travellers may encounter some curious stares. At worst, proprietors of small hotels may try to refuse service.

Corrupt police may attempt to extort money from you by claiming that something is wrong with your documentation, or they might try another pretext. Strongly resist paying them anything without an official receipt. If stopped, stay calm and smile. Allow the police to shoulder the onus of communication. They will probably give up if they can't make you understand. Always keep at least a copy of your passport with you.

You should also be aware of abysmal roads and chaotic driving conditions. Drive defensively and never at night.

Do not drink the tap water; plenty of bottled water is available.

BUSINESS HOURS

Most businesses open at 8.30am, and some close for a siesta from noon to 4pm, opening again from 4pm to 7pm. Banking hours are shorter (generally 8.30am to 2pm).

PUBLIC HOLIDAYS & SPECIAL EVENTS

Public holidays celebrated in Albania include New Year's Day (1 January), Easter Monday (March/April), Labour Day (1 May), Independence Day (28 November), Liberation Day (29 November) and Christmas Day (25 December).

Ramadan and Bajram, variable Muslim holidays, are also celebrated.

COURSES

The **University of Tirana** (fax 042-241 09) runs a summer-school programme in Albanian language and culture from mid-August to mid-September. The registration fee is US$100.

ACCOMMODATION

Accommodation has undergone a rapid transformation in Albania, with the opening of new, custom-built, private hotels to replace the dismal state hotels. Priced at about US$35 to US$50 and upwards per person per night (usually including breakfast), these are modern, well-appointed establishments.

Another positive development for visitors is the conversion of homes or villas into so-called private hotels. For budget travellers, these are without doubt the best way to go.

You can often find unofficial accommodation in private homes by asking around. However, for security reasons camping is not advisable.

FOOD

Lunch is the main meal of the day, although eating out in the evening is very common in Tirana. The quality of restaurants in the capital has improved greatly. In the country and other towns more places to eat are opening up, so you should have no problem getting a decent meal.

Albanian cuisine, like that of Serbia, has been strongly influenced by Turkey. Grilled meats like *shishqebap* (shish kebab), *romstek* (minced meat patties) and *qofte* (meat balls) are served across all the Balkan countries. Some local dishes include *çomlek* (meat and onion stew), *fërges* (a rich beef stew), *rosto me salcë kosi* (roast beef with sour cream) and *tavë kosi* (mutton with yogurt). Lake Shkodra carp and Lake Ohrid trout are the most common fish dishes. For dessert, try the *akullore* (ice cream), which is very popular everywhere.

DRINKS

Albanians take their coffee both as *kafe turke* (Turkish coffee) and *kafe ekspres* (espresso). If you ask for *kafe surogato* you will get what is the closest to filter coffee. Avoid unbottled drinks as they may contain tap water.

Albanian white wine is better than the vinegary red. However, the red *Shesi e Zi* from Librazhd or Berat is an excellent drop. Most of the beer consumed in Albania is imported from Macedonia or Greece, but look out for the locally produced and palatable Premium Tirana Pils. *Raki* (a clear brandy distilled from grapes) is taken as an aperitif – always ask for home-made if possible *(raki ë bërë në shtëpi)*. There's also *konjak* (cognac – the Skenderbey

cognac makes a good gift on your trip home), *uzo* (a colourless aniseed-flavoured liqueur like Greek ouzo) and various fruit liqueurs. *Fërnet* is a medicinal aperitif containing some herbal essences, made at Korça.

A good word to know is the favourite Albanian drinking toast – *gëzuar!*

ENTERTAINMENT

Check with the local theatre for performances. These are generally advertised on painted boards either in front of the theatre or on main streets, but performances are invariably only in Albanian.

There's usually a disco or two to complement the zillions of cafés in a given town; ask around for what's hot.

SPECTATOR SPORTS

Football (soccer) is played at local stadiums on weekend afternoons. As a foreigner, you may need someone to help you obtain tickets.

SHOPPING

Most hotels have tourist shops where you can buy Albanian handicrafts such as carpets, silk, ornaments (made from silver, copper and wood), embroidery, handmade shoes, shoulder bags, picture books, musical instruments, and CDs and cassettes of folk music.

Getting There & Away

AIR

Rinas airport is 26km northwest of Tirana. Taxis ply the route to Tirana.

Ada Air arrives in Rinas from Athens, Bari, Prishtina, Skopje and Ioannina; Adria Airways from Ljubljana; Albanian Airlines from Bologna, Frankfurt, İstanbul, Prishtina, Rome and Zürich; Austrian Airlines from Vienna; Hemus Air from Sofia; Lufthansa Airlines from Frankfurt and Munich; Malév-Hungarian Airlines from Budapest; Olympic Airways from Athens via Ioannina or Thessaloniki; Swiss Internationl Air lines from Zürich; and Turkish Airlines from İstanbul.

Some examples of return fares are US$308 from Rome flying with Albanian Airlines; US$220 from Athens with Olympic and Ada; US$322 from Budapest with Malév; US$155 from Prishtina with Ada Air (US$171 with

Albanian Airlines); and US$250 from İstanbul with Turkish Airlines.

Before investing in any of the above fares, compare them with the price of a cheap flight to Athens or Thessaloniki, from where Albania is easily accessible by local bus with a change of bus at the border. Another option is a charter flight to Corfu, from where you can take a ferry to Saranda in southern Albania.

See Getting There & Away in the Tirana section for the phone numbers of the main airlines.

LAND
Bus
Buses to Thessaloniki (€35, 10 hours) leave at 6am each morning from in front of **Albanian Interlines** (☎ 222 272; Bulevardi Zogu I). Buses to Athens (€50, 24 hours) also leave from here three times a week.

Buses to Prishtina, the capital of Kosova, leave daily from beside the Tirana International Hotel at 6pm (€30, 12 hours). If you're bound for Macedonia, you will need to take the daily bus to Tetovo (also from here) and from Tetovo you can take a frequent local bus to Skopje.

Buses for İstanbul and Sofia leave from **Albtransport** (☎ 223 026; Rruga Mine Peza, Tirana; open 8am-4pm Mon-Fri). The Sofia bus (€35, 15 hours) leaves at 10am on Wednesday. Two buses depart for İstanbul (€55, 24 hours) at 10am and 1pm on Monday, and go via Sofia.

Car & Motorcycle
Bringing a car or motorcycle to Albania is still a risky business as theft and the generally bad roads can be a problem. Additionally, your insurance Green Card may not cover Albania. But it is feasible to transit the country from, say, Yugoslavia to Macedonia or Greece in two days, if you are determined. You'll need to park the car in a secure park overnight in Tirana and continue the next day.

Roads are slowly being improved and there are quite decent sections between Tirana and Durrës and on the approaches to the main land borders. Drivers and riders will need to be extra careful of the poor driving techniques and be aware that traffic police regularly stop cars in an effort to extract fines for so-called infringements.

See also the Getting Around section later in this chapter for further information on local driving conditions.

The following highway border crossings are open to motorists, cyclists and pedestrians.

Yugoslavia The only border crossing is at Han i Hotit (between Shkodra and Podgorica), though a new crossing has been planned for some time at Muriqan/Sukobin, which would link Ulcinj, in Yugoslavia, and Shkodra much more conveniently.

Kosova/Kosovo The only really viable crossing for travellers is at Morinë/Vrbnica between Kukës and Prizren. However bear in mind that this whole area is not a good place to travel solo or independently as the corridor between Shkodra and the border can still be subject to random banditry and/or traveller harassment. Travellers on the through-buses should have no problems.

Macedonia The best two crossings are those on Lake Ohrid. The southern crossing is at Tushemisht (near Sveti Naum, 29km south of Ohrid), and the northern crossing is at Qafa e Thanës (between Struga and Pogradec). There is a third crossing at Maqellarë (between Debar and Peshkopi), but it is not recommended for travellers as Albanian-Macedonia tensions may flare up occasionally and delays or questioning of travellers may ensue.

Greece Border crossings are at Kapshtica/ Krystallopigi (between Korça and Florina) and Kakavija/Kakavia (between Ioannina and Gjirokastra). A new border crossing north of the Greek port of Igoumenitsa at Konispoli/ Sagiada is open, though facilities for vehicle crossings had not been completed at the time of research.

SEA
The Italian company of **Adriatica di Navigazione** operates ferry services to Durrës from Bari (US$60, 8½ hours) daily and from Ancona (US$85, 19 hours) four times a week. Cars cost US$90/100 respectively. Bicycles are carried free.

In Bari you are able to buy ferry tickets from **Agestea** (☎ 080-553 1555; e agestea .bari02@interbusiness.it; Via Liside 4); and in Ancona it's **Maritime Agency Srl** (☎ 071-204 915; e tickets.adn@maritime.it; Via XXIX Settembre 10). In Albania tickets are sold by any number of the travel agencies in Durrës or Tirana.

The car ferry C/F *Grecia* runs each Tuesday and Saturday at 1pm to Durrës from Trieste (and returns on Wednesday and Sunday at 7pm). The trip on deck costs US$40/50 in low/ high season. In Durrës contact **KAD Shipping** (☎ 052-25 154, fax 20 341) or any travel agency. In Trieste contact **Agemar** (☎ 39-40-363 222, fax 363 737; e *info@agemar.it)* or any travel agency selling ferry tickets.

The fastest ferry connection between Bari and Durrës is via the passenger catamarans operated by **Quality Lines** (€60, 3½ hours). These high-speed vessels leave Durrës daily at 10am and 4.30pm. The Durrës agent can be contacted on ☎ 052-24 571.

See the Saranda Getting There & Away section for information on travel between Corfu and the small southern Albanian port of Saranda.

ORGANISED TOURS

Package tours to Albania, which dwindled after the 1997 civil disturbances, currently are unavailable.

DEPARTURE TAX

Airport departure tax is US$10, payable in dollars or lekë. A US$4 tariff is imposed on people leaving Albania by ferry, and there's a US$1 daily tariff on vehicles, payable upon crossing the border out of the country.

Getting Around

BUS

Most Albanians travel around their country in private minibuses or larger buses. These run fairly frequently throughout the day between Tirana and Durrës (38km) and other towns north and south. Buses to Tirana depart from towns all around Albania at the crack of dawn. Pay the conductor on board; the fares are low (eg, Tirana-Durrës is 100 lekë). Tickets are rarely issued.

City buses operate in Tirana, Durrës and Shkodra (pay the conductor). Watch your possessions on crowded city buses.

TRAIN

Before 1948, Albania had no railways, but the communists built up a limited north-south rail network based at the port of Durrës. Today, however, nobody who can afford other types of transport takes the train, even though train fares are about a third cheaper than bus fares.

The reason will be obvious once you board – the decrepit carriages typically have broken windows and no toilets.

Daily passenger trains leave Tirana for Shkodra (3½ hours, 98km), Fier (4¼ hours), Ballsh (five hours), Vlora (5½ hours) and Pogradec (seven hours). Seven trains a day also make the 1½-hour trip between Tirana and Durrës.

CAR & MOTORCYCLE

Albania has only acquired an official road traffic code in recent years and most motorists have only learned to drive in the last five years. The road infrastructure is poor and the roads badly maintained, but the number of cars on the road is growing daily. There are plenty of petrol stations in the cities and increasing numbers in the country.

Hazards include: pedestrians who tend to use the roads as an extension of the footpaths; animals being herded along country roads; gaping potholes; a lack of road warnings and signs; and occasionally reckless drivers. Security is also an issue. Park your vehicle in a secure location, such as hotel grounds, or in a guarded parking lot. An immobiliser alarm is also a very good idea.

Banditry is still an occasional threat in the northern part of the country between Shkodra and Kukës, though the Tirana-Montenegro corridor is generally safe. Never drive at night in any part of Albania.

Unleaded fuel is generally widely available along all major highways, but fill up when you can. A litre of unleaded petrol costs 100 lekë, while diesel costs close to 70 lekë.

Avis (☎ 04-235 011, fax 235 042; e *gazi@ albaniaonline.net)*, based in the Europapark Tirana, is the only car-rental company in the country.

HITCHING

With buses so cheap, hitching will probably only be an emergency means of transport. You can afford to be selective about the rides you accept as everyone will take you if they possibly can.

You can get an indication of where a car might be going from the letters on the licence plate: Berat (BR), Durrës (DR), Elbasan (EL), Fier (FR), Gjirokastra (GJ), Korça (KO), Kruja (KR), Lezha (LE), Pogradec (PG), Saranda (SR), Shkodra (SH), Tirana (TR) and Vlora (VL).

Lonely Planet does not recommend hitching as a form of transport.

LOCAL TRANSPORT

Shared *furgon* (minibuses) run between cities when they are full or almost full. They usually cost about twice the bus fare, but for foreigners they're still cheap. Pay the driver or the driver's assistant once you leave the minibus.

Tirana

☎ 042 • pop 440,000

It wasn't too long ago that the capital city of Albania was just a dusty, languid town virtually unknown to the outside world. Few cars ran along its wide boulevards and there was no building more than four storeys tall. Today it is a bustling, busy metropolis, with more cars than its streets can cope with; restaurants and cafés have mushroomed like bunkers and tall buildings now creep skywards where once only the minaret of a mosque had been the city's most distinguishing feature. Tirana (Tiranë) today is a fascinating city in the way that it is emerging from anonymity to a new maturity.

Tirana lies close to midway between Rome and İstanbul. Mt Dajti (1612m) rises to the east. Founded by a Turkish *pasha* (military governor) in 1614, Tirana developed into a craft centre with a lively bazaar. In 1920 the city was made the capital of Albania and in the 1930s the bulky Italianate government buildings went up. In the communist era, larger-than-life 'palaces of the people' blossomed in and around Skënderbeg Square and along Bulevardi Dëshmorët e Kombit (Martyrs of the Nation Boulevard). You'll also see Italian parks and a Turkish mosque, but the market area on the eastern side of Tirana is also worth exploring. The city is compact and can be explored on foot.

Orientation

Orientation is easy in Tirana, as the whole city revolves around central Skënderbeg Square (Sheshi Skënderbeg). Running south from the square is Bulevardi Dëshmorët e Kombit, which leads to the three-arched university building. Running north Bulevardi Zogu I leads to the train station. Coming from the airport (26km) you will enter the city along Rruga Durrësit. Buses from the neighbouring countries will drop you off close to Skënderbeg Square. Most of the major services and hotels are within just a few minutes' walk of Skënderbeg Square.

Information

Tourist Offices Tirana does not have any official tourist office, but there are travel agencies (for details see Travel Agencies later in this Information section). One helpful publication is *Tirana In Your Pocket,* available at bookshops and some of the larger kiosks for 300 lekë.

Another useful reference is *Tirana 2003: The Practical Guide of Tirana.* This gives telephone numbers and addresses for everything from hospitals to banks to embassies, though many of the entries are only in Albanian. This is also available at the main hotels and bookshops for around 300 lekë.

Money While there are plenty of banks in Tirana, a free currency market operates directly in front of the main post office. At the time of research just one ATM at the Greek-owned **Alpha Bank** *(Bulevardi Zogu I)* was in operation.

If you would prefer to avoid the swarms of independent currency exchangers, the Hotel Europapark Tirana has a **currency exchange booth** *(open 10.30am-5pm Mon-Fri),* near the Swiss airline offices, which offers Master Card advances, cashes travellers cheques for 1% commission and exchanges cash. **American Bank of Albania** *(Rruga Ismail Qemali 27; open 9.30am-3.30pm Mon-Fri)* is also a reliable, secure place to cash your travellers cheques (2% commission). The American Express representative **World Travel** *(☎ 227 998; Mine Peza 2)* cashes travellers cheques for 2% commission.

The **Unioni Financiar Tiranë Exchange**, *(☎ 234 979; Rruga Dëshmorët e 4 Shkurtit),* just south of the main post office, offers Western Union wire transfer services.

Post & Communications The **main post office** *(☎ 228 262; Sheshi Çameria; open 8am-8pm Mon-Fri)* and telephone centre are adjacent on a street jutting west from Skënderbeg Square. Another telephone centre is on Bulevardi Zogu I, about 400m past Skënderbeg Square on the right-hand side. There are additional sub-branch post offices on Bulevardi Zogu I and on Rruga Mohamet Gjollesha.

International courier service **DHL** (☎ 232 816, fax 257 294; e DHLAlbania@tia-co .al.dhl.com; Rruga Dëshmorët e 4 Shkurtit 7/1 • ☎ 227 667, fax 233 934; Rruga Ded Gjo Luli 6) has two offices in Tirana.

Email & Internet Access There are several places to access the Internet in Tirana. The best is **Net 1** (☎ 257 433; Rruga Nikolla Tupe 1/b; open 9am-11pm), with banks of gleaming machines. Another good choice is **F@stech** (☎/fax 251 947; Rruga Brigada e VIII; open 8.30am-11pm) four blocks north. Two blocks south is **Interalb Internet** (☎ 251 747; Rruga Dëshmorët 4 Shkurtit. Pall. 25/1; open 8am-10pm). All charge around 300 lekë per hour or part thereof.

Travel Agencies A good place to arrange ferry tickets from Durrës (see under Sea in the Getting There & Away section earlier in this chapter), or to book private rooms, is **Albania Travel & Tours** (☎ 329 83, fax 339 81; Rruga Durrësit 102; open 8am-8pm Mon-Fri, 8am-2pm Sat & Sun).

Other travel agencies abound, but not all operators speak English.

Newspapers & Magazines Foreign newspapers and magazines, including the *Times,* the *International Herald Tribune* and the *Economist,* are sold at most major hotels and at some central street kiosks, though they tend to be a few days old.

The **International Bookshop** (open 9am-9pm daily), in the Palace of Culture on the right-hand side, is another option. It has a selection of Penguin literary classics, maps of Tirana and Albania, and an excellent selection of books about Albania.

The **Qëndra Stefan** (see Places to Eat) has an attached bookshop with a selection of foreign publications.

Medical & Emergency Services Most of Tirana's foreigners use **ABS Health Foundation** (☎ 234 105; 360 Rruga Qemali Stafa; open Mon-Fri); it's across the street from the 'New School', but watch carefully for the small sign. Staffed by doctors trained in the West, it offers a range of services including regular (US$60) and emergency (US$90) consultations. The fee goes down if you pay a 12-month registration of US$120. Patients are seen by appointment 8am to 4pm weekdays.

Things to See & Do

Most visits to Tirana begin at **Skënderbeg Square**, a great, open space in the heart of the city. Beside the 15-storey Tirana International Hotel, on the northern side of the square, is the **National Museum of History** (admission 300 lekë; open 8am-1pm Mon-Sat), the largest and finest museum in Albania. A huge, Stalinist-realism mosaic mural entitled *Albania* covers the facade of the museum building. Temporary exhibits are shown in the **gallery** (admission free) on the side of the building facing the Tirana International Hotel.

To the east is another massive building, the **Palace of Culture**, which has a theatre, shops and art galleries. Construction of the palace began as a gift from the Soviet people in 1960 and was completed in 1966, after the 1961 Soviet-Albanian split. The entrance to the **National Library** is on the south side of the building. Opposite this is the cupola and minaret of the **Et'hem Bey mosque** (1789–1823), one of the most distinctive buildings in the city. Inside the dome is beautifully painted. Built in 1830, Tirana's **clock tower** (☎ 243 292; open 9am-1pm & 4-6pm Mon, Wed & Sat) stands beside the mosque.

On the southern side of the square is the **Skënderbeg equestrian statue** (1968) looking straight up Bulevardi Zogu I north to the train station. Behind Skënderbeg's statue, the boulevard leads directly south to the three arches of **Tirana University** (1957). As you stroll down this tree-lined boulevard you'll see Tirana's **art gallery** (open Tues-Sun), a one-time stronghold of socialist realism, with a significant permanent collection that has been exhibited here since 1976.

Stalinist Tirana The wide and once vehicle-free Bulevardi Dëshmorët e Kombit was at one time the stomping ground of Albania's Stalinist *Nomenklatura* (political elite). It is along here and to the west of the boulevard that you can still see the sights of Tirana's not-too-distant Stalinist past.

Start your walk down Bulevardi Dëshmorët e Kombit, at the now brightly painted **government buildings**, housing various ministries. Just behind the last building on the left-hand side were the headquarters of the once much-feared **Sigurimi**, communist Albania's dreaded secret police.

Continue along Bulevardi Dëshmorët e Kombit to the bridge over the Lana River. On

ALBANIA

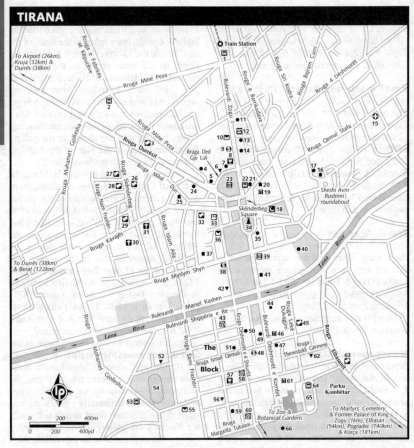

TIRANA

To Airport (26km),
Kruja (32km) &
Durrës (38km)

To Durrës (38km)
& Berat (122km)

The Block

To Zoo &
Botanical Gardens

To Martyrs' Cemetery
& Former Palace of King
Zogu (1km), Elbasan
(54km), Pogradec (140km)
& Korça (181km)

Sheshi Avni
Rustemi
roundabout

Skënderbeg
Square

Train Station

0   200   400m
0   200   400yd

the left just over the river you'll see the sloping, white-marble walls of the **former Enver
Hoxha Museum** (1988) – an expensive white
elephant later used as a disco and conference
centre. Just beyond and on the right, is the
dour, four-storey, former **Central Committee
building** (1955) of the Party of Labour, which
also houses various ministries.

Opposite the Central Committee building
is the **Prime Minister's Residence** now permanently guarded by strutting soldiers. On
the balcony on the 2nd floor Enver Hoxha
and cronies, such as Gog Nushi, Qemal Stafa
and Hysni Kapo, would stand and review
military parades.

Follow Rruga Ismail Qemali, the street on
the southern side of the Central Committee
building, and enter the once totally forbidden

Block – the former exclusive and strictly off-
limits residential district of the Communist-
party faithful. When the area was first opened
to the general public in 1991, great crowds of
Albanians flocked to see the style in which
their 'proletarian' leaders lived. The three-
storey pastel-coloured house on the corner of
Rruga Dëshmorët e 4 Shkurtit and Rruga Ismail Qemali is the **former residence of Enver
Hoxha**. The house is now guarded by a couple
of bored-looking soldiers and doesn't seem to
have any active function.

Other Sights   Beyond the university at the
end of Bulevardi Dëshmorët e Kombit is
Parku Kombëtar (National Park), with an
open-air theatre (Teatri Veror) and an artificial
lake. There's a superb view across the lake to

ALBANIA

TIRANA

PLACES TO STAY		12	Telephone Centre	39	Art Gallery
16	Qëndra Stefan	13	Albania Interlines	40	Parliament
20	Hotel Miniri	14	Olympic Airways	43	F@stech
21	Tirana International Hotel;	15	ABS Health Foundation	44	Former Enver Hoxha
	Turkish Airlines	17	Public Market		Museum
25	Hotel California	18	Et'hem Bey Mosque; Clock	45	Macedonian Embassy
37	Europa International		Tower	46	Prime Minister's
	Hotel	19	Palace of Culture;		Residence
41	Hotel Dajti		International Bookshop	47	Avis Car Rentals, Hotel
59	Hotel Endri	22	Bus Departure Point for		Europapark Tirana; Swiss;
			Prishtina		Austrian Airlines
PLACES TO EAT		23	National Museum of	48	American Bank of Albania
6	Piazza Restaurant		History; Alitalia	49	Former Central Committee
42	La Voglia	24	World Travel		Building
52	Ujevara	26	Bulgarian Embassy	50	DHL
56	Il Passatore	27	German Embassy	51	Former Residence of Enver
62	Villa Ambassador	28	UK Embassy		Hoxha
		29	Greek Embassy	53	Southern Bus Station
OTHER		30	Orthodox Church of	54	Selman Stërmasi (Dinamo)
1	Bus & Minibus Station to		Holy Evangelist		Stadium
	Durrës & North	31	Catholic Church of St	55	Post Office Sub Branch
2	Kruja Minibus Stop		Anthony	57	Murphy's
3	Yugoslavia Embassy	32	Turkish Embassy	58	Net 1
4	Albtransport	33	Kinema Millennium	60	Interalb Internet
5	Albania Travel & Tours	34	Skënderbeg Equestrian Statue	61	Palace of Congresses
7	DHL	35	Government Buildings;	63	US Embassy
8	London Bar		Former Sigurimi HQ	64	Minibuses to Elbasan,
9	Alpha Bank ATM	36	Main Post Office		Pogradec & Korça
10	Post Office Sub Branch	38	Unioni Financiar Tiranë	65	Qemal Stafa Stadium
11	Souvenir Stela		Exchange	66	Tirana University

the olive-coloured hills. Cross the dam retaining the lake to the rather moribund **Tirana Zoo**. Ask directions to the **botanical gardens**, just west of the zoo. If you're keen, you can hire a rowing boat and paddle on the lake.

About 1km southeast on Rruga Elbasanit is the **Martyrs' Cemetery** (Varrezat e Dëshmorëve), where some 900 partisans who died in WWII are buried. Large crowds once gathered here every 16 October, Enver Hoxha's birthday, since this is where he and other top Communist Party members were interred. (In May 1992 Hoxha's coffin was dug up and reburied in a common grave in a public cemetery on the other side of town.) The hill-top setting, with a great view over the city and mountains, is subdued, and a white figure of Mother Albania (1972) stands watch. Nearby, on the other side of the highway, is the **former palace of King Zogu**, now a government guesthouse.

Places to Stay
Private Rooms Staying in private, rented apartments or with local families is the best budget accommodation in Tirana, but they can be hard to find. Owners expect you to call

them and arrange a pick-up. Newer private hotels are pleasant but high priced.

Albania Travel & Tours (see Travel Agencies earlier in this section) has private rooms for around 2600 lekë per person. Other travel agencies may also find you a private room.

Tiny **Hotel Endri** (☎ 244 168, 229 334; *Pall 27, Sh. 3 Ap. 30, Rruga Vaso Pasha 27; rooms US$20*) is a decent deal. The 'hotel', essentially just two rooms next to manager Petrit Alikaj's apartment, is sparkling clean and new, with nice bathrooms and excellent showers. Handily, Petrit is also a taxi driver.

Qëndra Stefan (*Stephen Center; ☎/fax 253 924; e stephenc@icc.al.eu.org; Rruga Hoxha Tasim 1; singles/doubles including breakfast $30/50*) is a better option and much easier to find. Rooms are modern, bright and breezy and for nonsmokers and nondrinkers only. (See also Places to Eat later in this section.)

Hotels Just off Rruga Durrësit is the nifty **Hotel California** (*☎/fax 232 228; Rruga Mihal Duri 21; singles/doubles US$50/70 including breakfast*), which has clean rooms with minibar and TV.

ALBANIA

A quite pleasant private hotel is **Europa International Hotel** (☎/fax 227 403; Rruga Myslym Shyri 44/2; singles/doubles including breakfast US$60/70), with modern rooms and parking out front. It can be hard to find this place as it is actually off Rruga Myslym Shyri in a back street. Ask for directions.

For a taste of Stalinist decor step into the somewhat dour and ageing **Hotel Dajti** (☎ 251 031, fax 251 036; Bulevardi Dëshmorët e Kombit 6; singles US$50-60, doubles US$80). The Dajti was erected in the 1930s by the Italians and has changed very little since then.

Just off Skënderbeg Square is the small **Hotel Miniri** (☎ 230 930, fax 233 096; Rruga e Dibres 3; singles/doubles including breakfast US$60/96), with adequate but unexciting rooms with phone and TV. Its main advantage is its central location.

The **Tirana International Hotel** (☎ 234 185, fax 234 188; W www.hoteltirana.albnet .net; Skënderbeg Square; singles/doubles including breakfast US$140/190) has well-appointed rooms. The hotel accepts MasterCard, American Express and Diner's Club.

Places to Eat
There is no shortage of small restaurants, cafés and snack bars on and around Skënderbeg Square and Bulevardi Dëshmorët e Kombit.

Fancy breakfast, a cuppa or sandwich – perhaps a Chinese lunch, pizza, nachos or even fajitas? Call into **Qëndra Stefan** (☎ 253 924; Rruga Hoxha Tasim 1; open 8am-10pm; open Mon-Sat), a friendly, nonsmoking place run by Americans. Lunch specials are posted on a blackboard outside. It's near the fruit and vegetable market

Among Tirana's innumerable pizza places, the two-floor **La Voglia** (☎ 228 678; Rruga Dëshmorët e 4 Shkurtit; pizza 350-400 lekë; open 8am-11pm), close to the river, serves a very good pizza and has menus in English.

One of Tirana's more popular restaurants is **Il Passatore** (Antonella's; ☎ 233 420; Rruga Vaso Pasha 22/1; mains per person 1200 lekë; open noon-4pm & 7pm-11pm Mon-Sat). Convenient to Murphy's pub for the after-dinner wind-up, food and service here are excellent, with delicious specials of fish or pasta and a diverse salad bar.

Piazza Restaurant (☎ 230 706; Rruga Ded Gjo Luli; mains per person 1400 lekë; open noon-4pm & 7pm-11pm) is a tastefully designed and well-appointed establishment just north of Skënderbeg Square. The food and service are excellent and prices, for what you get, are reasonable.

The **Villa Ambassador** (☎ 038-202 4293; Rruga Themistokli Gërmenji; mains per person 1500 lekë; open noon-11.30pm), tucked away on a small street near the US embassy, is among Tirana's best for atmosphere. Try to sample a plateful of Albanian specialities like rice wrapped in grape leaves, burek (cheese or meat pie) and more.

A little out of the way is the **Ujevara** (☎ 243 702; Rruga Gjin Bue Shpata; open 12-11pm; pasta dishes 600-700 lekë). Italian pasta and fresh salads are the key ingredients at this pleasant eatery near the southern bus station.

Entertainment
For the low-down on events and exhibitions check out the leaflet ARTirana, which contains English, French, Italian and Albanian summaries of the cultural events currently showing in town.

Also check the posters outside the **Palace of Culture** (Skënderbeg Square; performances from 7pm, winter from 6pm) for ballet or opera. You can usually buy tickets half an hour before the show.

Tirana has an Irish pub: **Murphy's** (☎ 038-203 7854; Rruga Abdyl Frashëri; open 2pm until late) serves up Guinness on tap, Murphy's and a host of other brews, making it the before-and-after-dinner darling of the expat community.

London Bar (☎ 228 851; Bulevardi Zogu I 51), near the Tirana International Hotel, is also a popular hang-out with a restaurant.

Pop concerts and other musical events often take place in the **Qemal Stafa Stadium** next to the university. Look out for street banners bearing details of upcoming events. At the stadium there are also football matches held every Saturday and Sunday afternoon, except during July and August.

The biggest cinema in Tirana is the **Kinema Millennium** (☎ 248 647; Rruga e Kavajës; admission 200-400 lekë), near Skënderbeg Square, which shows recent box-office hits (earlier shows are cheaper).

Shopping
Tirana's **public market**, north of the Sheshi Avni Rustemi roundabout several blocks east of the clock tower, is largest on Thursday and Sunday. A few shops sell folkloric objects

such as carved wooden trays, small boxes, wall hangings and bone necklaces.

A good souvenir shop is **Souvenir Stela** (*Bulevardi Zogu I*), where the offerings include brass plates with the Albanian insignia and ashtrays that are very cleverly modelled on Hoxha's bunkers.

Getting There & Away

Air For information about routes and fares of flights to/from Rinas airport see the Getting There & Away section earlier in this chapter.

Many of the airline offices are on Rruga Durrësit, just off Skënderbeg Square. **Alitalia** (☎ 230 023; *Skënderbeg Square*) has an office behind the National Museum of History, and **Swiss International Air Lines** (☎/*fax 232 011*) and **Austrian Airlines** (☎/*fax 374 355*) are at Hotel Europapark Tirana. **Olympic Airways** (☎ 228 960; *Ve-Ve Business Centre, Bulevardi Zogu I*) is north of the Tirana International Hotel, and **Turkish Airlines** (☎ 234 185) is in the Tirana International Hotel.

Bus Buses and minibuses that run between Tirana and other towns are private. There are two main bus/minibus departure points: the Selman Stërmasi (Dinamo) Stadium for those buses heading to the south, and the lot in front of the train station for buses to Durrës and the north. Minibuses to Elbasan, Pogradec and Korça leave from the northern side of the Qemal Stafa Stadium, while minibuses to Kruja leave from a rather loosely defined area on Rruga Mine Peza.

The following table will give you an idea of distances and average costs of one-way bus trips from Tirana. Minibuses are usually 40% to 50% more expensive than buses, but buses do not cover all destinations.

destination	distance	duration	cost
Berat	122km	3½ hours	250 lekë
Durrës	38km	1 hour	100 lekë
Elbasan	54km	1½ hours	300 lekë
Fier	113km	3 hours	260 lekë
Gjirokastra	232km	7 hours	700 lekë
Korça	181km	4 hours	700 lekë
Kruja	32km	¾ hours	150 lekë
Kukës	208km	8 hours	1000 lekë
Pogradec	150km	3½ hours	600 lekë
Saranda	284km	8 hours	800 lekë
Shkodra	116km	2½ hours	300 lekë
Vlora	147km	4 hours	300 lekë

Note that both buses and minibuses normally leave when full. Departures tend to commence early (5am to 8am) and sometimes cease operation by mid-afternoon. Pay the driver or conductor on the bus.

Train The train station is at the northern end of Bulevardi Zogu I. Eight trains daily go to Durrës (55 lekë, one hour, 36km). Trains also depart for Elbasan (160 lekë, four hours, three daily), for Pogradec (245 lekë, seven hours, twice daily), for Shkodra (150 lekë, 3½ hours, twice daily) and for Vlora (210 lekë, 5½ hours, twice daily).

Getting Around

To/From the Airport A taxi to/from the airport should cost about €30 or US$20, depending on what currency you have in your pocket.

Car & Motorcycle Some of the major hotels offer guarded parking; others have parking available out the front. **Avis** (☎ 235 011, fax 235 024; e gazi@albaniaonline.net) in the Hotel Europapark Tirana is the only car-rental agency currently operating. Contact the office for rates.

Taxi Taxi stands dot the city and charge 400 lekë for a ride inside Tirana (600 lekë at night). Work out the price before getting in and reach an agreement with the driver *before* setting off. **Radio Taxi** (☎ 377 777), with 24-hour service, is particularly reliable. These local taxis are much cheaper than the Mercedes taxis parked at the large hotels.

The older, private taxis are usually found around the market or at bus and train stations, and the shiny, Mercedes, tourist taxis park outside the Hotel Europapark Tirana and Tirana International Hotel (which quote fares in US dollars but also take lekë).

Around Tirana

DURRËS
☎ 052 • pop 85,000

If the bustle, dust and confusion of Tirana are too much for you, consider basing yourself in Durrës. Once the grim, workaday main port of Albania, Durrës is now a relaxed, more laidback alternative to the capital, with some good places to eat and sleep. Moreover, Durrës still retains the time-honoured tradition of the *xhiro* – the evening street promenade, when the main drag is closed and all the town comes out to walk and talk, to see and to be seen.

Unlike Tirana, Durrës is an ancient city. In 627 BC the Greeks founded Epidamnos (Durrës), whose name the Romans changed to Dyrrachium. It was the largest port on the eastern Adriatic and the start of the Via Egnatia (an extension of the Via Appia to Constantinople). The famous Via Appia (Appian Way) to Rome began 150km southwest of Durrës at the town of Brindisi, Italy.

Durrës changed hands frequently before being taken by the Turks in 1501, under whom the port dwindled into insignificance. A slow revival began in the 17th century and from 1914 to 1920 Durrës was the capital of Albania. Landings here by Mussolini's troops on 7 April 1939 met fierce though brief resistance, and those who fell are regarded as the first martyrs in the War of National Liberation.

Today, Roman ruins and Byzantine fortifications embellish the town, which lies 38km west of Tirana. On a bay southeast of the city there are long, sandy beaches where a collection of tourist hotels and restaurants have sprung up like Hoxha's bunkers during the bad old days of communism.

Information
The **Savings Bank of Albania** *(open 8am-2pm Mon-Fri)*, across the bus parking lot from the train station, changes travellers cheques and offers MasterCard advances for a 1% commission.

The **post office** and **telephone centre** are located one block west of the train and bus stations. Several Internet cafés operate in the town. Among them are the **Interalb Internet** *(Rruga N Frashëri)*, the **Galaxy Internet Cafe** *(☎ 038-213 5637, Rruga Taulantia)* and **Patrik Internet** *(Rruga Aleksandër Goga)*. All charge around 240 lekë per hour.

Things to See
The **Archaeological Museum**, on the waterfront promenade near the port, is worth a visit. Look out for the Belle of Durrës mosaic, which gives a view of ancient Dyrrachium and is one of its more notable exhibits.

Beyond the museum are the 6th-century **Byzantine city walls**, built after the Visigoth invasion of AD 481 and supplemented by round Venetian towers in the 14th century.

The impressive but unrestored **Roman amphitheatre**, built between the 1st and 2nd centuries AD, is on the hillside just inside the walls of the city. Much of the amphitheatre has now been excavated and you are able to see a small, built-in, 10th-century Byzantine church decorated with wall mosaics. Farther up the hill you will come to the **citadel**, which is the highest point of what must have once been an impressive fortification used for protection of the city.

The former **palace of King Ahmet Zogu** is on the hill top west of the amphitheatre. However it is a military area and you cannot get into the palace grounds. The 20-minute walk up the hills and the views are worth it though. The next hill beyond the enclosure bears a **lighthouse** that would afford a splendid view of Albanian coastal defences, Durrës and the entire coast, if you could get past the fence surrounding it.

As you're exploring the centre of the city, stop to see the **Roman baths** directly behind Aleksandër Moisiu Theatre, on the central square. The large **Xhamia e Madhe Durrës** mosque on the square was erected with Egyptian aid in 1993, to replace one destroyed in the 1979 earthquake.

Places to Stay
Durrës has a handful of pleasant, mid-priced hotels in the centre and a string of new, resort-style hotels on the long, sandy beaches 8km south towards the settlement of Golem.

Albania Travel & Tours *(☎ 24 276, ☎/fax 254 50; Rruga Durrah; open 8am-8pm daily)*, near the port, may be able to help arrange a private room with advance notice.

The best budget choice is the **B&B Tedeschini** *(☎ 24 343, 038-224 6303;* e *ipmcrsp@ icc.al.eu.org; Dom Nikoll Kaçorri 5; B&B US$15)* in the gracious, 19th-century house of a personable Italian-Albanian couple. If you want lunch and dinner it's just US$10 more. The place is a bit hard to find; from the square fronting the mosque, walk towards the restaurant Il Castello. Take the first right, then a quick left, then a quick right. The house is 50m on the right down this street and has an unmarked red iron gate.

About 3km from Durrës and 400m back from the beach is the slightly more expensive **Green Villa** *(☎ 60 345;* e *bendushi_2001@ yahoo.com; singles/doubles from US$20/40)*. There are 16 rooms, all with private facilities.

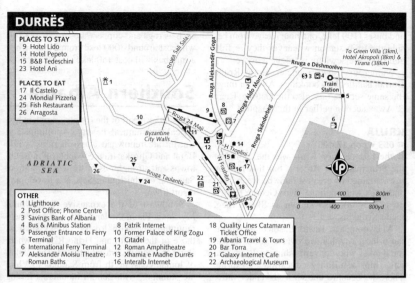

DURRËS

PLACES TO STAY
9 Hotel Lido
14 Hotel Pepeto
15 B&B Tedeschini
23 Hotel Ani

PLACES TO EAT
17 Il Castello
24 Mondial Pizzeria
25 Fish Restaurant
26 Arragosta

OTHER
1 Lighthouse
2 Post Office; Phone Centre
3 Savings Bank of Albania
4 Bus & Minibus Station
5 Passenger Entrance to Ferry
   Terminal
6 International Ferry Terminal
7 Aleksandër Moisiu Theatre;
   Roman Baths
8 Patrik Internet
10 Former Palace of King Zogu
11 Citadel
12 Roman Amphitheatre
13 Xhamia e Madhe Durrës
16 Interalb Internet
18 Quality Lines Catamaran
   Ticket Office
19 Albania Travel & Tours
20 Bar Torra
21 Galaxy Internet Cafe
22 Archaeological Museum

Another 5km south you will find the **Hotel Akropoli** (☎ 0579-22 142, 038-214 0070; *Golem; singles/doubles US$30/40*). This is a modern and pleasant resort-style hotel with an in-house restaurant. Ring beforehand for a complimentary chauffeur service.

The 13-room **Hotel Lido** (☎/fax 27 941; *Rruga Aleksandër Goga; singles/doubles US$35/46*), in the centre of town, has clean, pleasant rooms with TV, phone, fridge, heating and air-conditioning. The cheery **Hotel Pepeto** (☎ 24 190, ☎/fax 26 346; *singles/doubles US$40/60*), just east of the square fronting the mosque, is another good choice, with rates that include breakfast and laundry. The owner speaks English.

At the waterfront is the more upmarket **Hotel Ani** (☎ 24 288, fax 30 478; *Lagja 1, Rruga Taulantia; singles/doubles US$60/90*), where the comfy rooms all have air-con, TV, telephone and minibar.

Places to Eat
By far the best place to eat in town is the restaurant **Il Castello** (☎ 268 87; *Rruga H Troplini 3*), which has outstanding pastas (try the seafood pasta at 450 lekë) and a good selection of fish.

For a meal of fresh shrimp or fish on a patio overlooking the water, try the **Arragosta** (☎ 26 477, *Rruga Taulantia*), on the point about an 800m walk west of the town centre.

Mondial Pizzeria (☎ 27 946; *Rruga Taulantia*), which is on the waterfront on the way to Arragosta, is a busy little pizzeria serving good-sized pizzas and pasta dishes. Another option is the **Fish Restaurant** (*Rruga Taulantia*), which is universally recommended by the locals for its fresh fish. The Hotel Lido (see Places to Stay) also has its own restaurant for guests and outsiders alike.

Otherwise, if you happen to be along the beach strip south of Durrës, numerous restaurants offer seaside dining.

Entertainment
The niftiest place for a coffee or beer is **Bar Torra** in the tower beside the port entrance. You can sip your beverage of choice while inside or atop the tower. Alternatively, you could pay a visit to the **Aleksandër Moisiu Theatre** in the centre of Durrës. Its frequent theatrical productions are performed only in Albanian however.

Getting There & Away
Albania's 720km railway network centres on Durrës. There are eight trains a day to Tirana (55 lekë, one hour), two to Shkodra (150 lekë, 3½ hours) via Lezha, three to Pogradec (245 lekë, 6¾ hours) via Elbasan, and two to Vlora (210 lekë, five hours) via Fier. The train station is beside the Tirana highway, conveniently close to central Durrës.

Minibuses to Tirana (150 lekë, one hour) and buses (100 lekë, one hour) leave from beside the train station whenever they're full, and service elsewhere is frequent as well.

Numerous travel agencies along Rruga Durrah handle ferry bookings. All offer much the same service (see also the Getting There & Away section earlier in this chapter).

KRUJA
☎ 053 • pop 17,400

In the 12th century, Kruja was the capital of the Principality of Arberit, but this hill-top town attained its greatest fame between 1443 and 1468 when national hero George Kastrioti (1405–68), also known as Skënderbeg, made Kruja his seat.

At a young age, Kastrioti, son of an Albanian prince, was handed over as a hostage to the Turks, who converted him to Islam and gave him a military education at Edirne. There he became known as Iskënder (after Alexander the Great) and Sultan Murat II promoted him to the rank of *bey* (governor), thus the name Skënderbeg.

In 1443 the Turks suffered a defeat at the hands of the Hungarians at Niš, which gave the nationally minded Skënderbeg the opportunity he had been waiting for to abandon the Ottoman army and Islam and rally his fellow Albanians against the Turks. Among the 13 Turkish invasions he subsequently repulsed was that led by Murat II himself in 1450. Pope Calixtus III named Skënderbeg the 'captain general of the Holy See' and Venice formed an alliance with him. The Turks besieged Kruja four times. Though beaten back in 1450, 1466 and 1467, they took control of Kruja in 1478 (after Skënderbeg's death) and Albanian resistance was suppressed.

The main sight in Kruja is the impressive **castle** and its rather retro-modernistic **Skënderbeg Museum** *(admission 300 lekë; open 8am-1pm & 3pm-8pm daily)*. The displays are mainly replicas of paintings and armour depicting Skënderbeg's struggle against the Ottomans.

The **Ethnographic Museum** *(☎ 22 225; admission 300 lekë; open 8am-1pm & 3pm-8pm daily)* is also worth a look for its reconstruction of a 19th-century Albanian house as well as folk dress, pottery and copper goods.

Kruja is 6.5km off the main road to Tirana and is visited as much for its crucial historical importance and striking hill-side location as for its wide range of good-quality souvenirs, such as rugs and copperware. A cab to Kruja will cost around 3000 lekë from Tirana while a minibus will cost 150 lekë.

Southern Albania

The southern part of the country is rich in historical and natural beauty. Apollonia and Butrint are renowned classical ruins, while Berat and Gjirokastra are wonderful museum towns and strongholds of the Tosk tradition. Saranda, on the Ionian Sea, is a developing resort town.

Southeast of the expansive, agricultural Myzaqeja Plain, the land becomes extremely mountainous, with lovely valleys such as those of the Osum and Drino Rivers, where Berat and Gjirokastra are situated. The 124km of Ionian coast north from Saranda to Vlora are stunning, with 2000m mountains falling directly to the sea.

GJIROKASTRA
☎ 0762 • pop 24,500

Travellers from Greece may well find that this strikingly picturesque town, midway between Fier and Ioannina, is an ideal spot for the first night's stay in Albania. Gjirokastra (Gjirokastër) is reminiscent of an Albanian eagle perched on the mountainside with a mighty citadel for its head. The fortress surveys the Drino Valley above three- and four-storey tower houses clinging to the slopes. The town's Greek name of 'Argyrokastro' means 'silver castle'.

Gjirokastra was well established by the 13th century, but the arrival of the Turks during 1417 brought about a decline. By the 17th century Gjirokastra was thriving once again, with a flourishing bazaar where embroidery, felt, silk and the still-famous white cheese were traded. Ali Pasha Tepelena seized the town in the early 19th century and then he strengthened the citadel.

Gjirokastra was the birthplace of former dictator Enver Hoxha and for that reason special care was taken to retain its traditional architecture and both buildings and streets are made of the same white-and-black stone.

The old town, with its narrow, cobbled streets, sits high up on the hill side while the new town spills down to the main Kakavija-Tirana highway.

Things to See

Gjirokastra's **castle** *(500 lekë, open 8am-8pm daily)* is its main feature, although in fairness its main drawcard is the walk up and the views it affords. The grounds are rather overgrown and the desultory collection of WWII armaments in its interior colonnades are rather uninspiring. The bizarre sight of a long-downed and disintegrating US military jet on the ramparts adds a rather unreal air to the scene. The castle courtyards were used as a political prison during the Hoxha years. The tiny cells are particularly grim.

Places to Stay & Eat

The best place to stay is **Guest House Haxhi Kotoni** *(☎ 35 26; Lagja Palorto 8, Rruga Bashkim Kokona; singles/doubles 1500/2000 lekë)*. This neat but tiny B&B offers clean and comfy double rooms with bathroom, TV and heating in a traditional old house. Look for the B&B sign 220m northeast of the mosque in the old town.

Eating options in the old town are pretty thin on the ground. **Bar Fantazia** *(☎ 69 91)*, commanding the best view in the old town, is a café-bar and sometimes restaurant. Walk downhill to the new town to seek out a wider variety of choices. **First Pizza** is a Western-style fast-food place. It does excellent pizzas for around 280 lekë. Look for it on the north side of the long street leading from the old town to the main highway.

Getting There & Away

Buses to and from Gjirokastra depart from or stop on the main highway, 1½km from the old town. Taxis can take you into town for about 200 lekë. Buses to Tirana (1000 lekë, five hours) are fairly frequent while there are four a day to Saranda (200 lekë, one hour). You'll need to take a taxi to get to the Greek border at Kakavija (1500 lekë, 30 minutes).

SARANDA

☎ 0732 • pop 12,000

Saranda (Sarandë) is a small town on the Gulf of Saranda, between the mountains and the Ionian Sea, 61km southwest of Gjirokastra. An early Christian monastery dedicated to 40 saints (Santi Quaranta) gave Saranda its name. This southernmost harbour of Albania was once the ancient port of Onchesmos. It is now considered by most Albanians as their most 'exotic' holiday destination and in fact

it attracts a fair percentage of the domestic travel market. For foreigners Saranda's main attraction is that it is a useful entry point to and from Corfu in Greece. The sunny climate, a choice of good hotels and restaurants and the nearby ruins of Butrint also add to its traveller interest. The town's beaches are slowly being re-landscaped and the long promenade makes for some relaxed evening strolls.

Information

Change money at **Exchange Mario** *(☎ 23 61; Rruga Vangeli Gramoza)* or with the crowds of moneychangers that hang out near the central square. Receive money at the **Western Union** office in the modern **post office** *(☎ 23 45)* nearby. Cardphones abound while mobile-phone users can pick up Greek transmitters as well as Albanian ones. Check email at **Ecom Internet** *(☎ 39 95; Rruga Adem Shema)*, close to the centre.

Things to See

The ancient ruins of **Butrint** *(☎ 0732-46 00; 700 lekë; open 8am-7.30pm)*, 18km south of Saranda, are surprisingly extensive and interesting and are part of a 29-sq-km national park. The poet Virgil (70–19 BC) claimed that the Trojans founded Buthroton (Butrint), but no evidence of this has been found. Although the site had been inhabited long before, Greeks from Corfu settled on the hill in Butrint in the 6th century BC. Within a century Butrint had become a fortified trading city with an acropolis. The lower town began to develop in the 3rd century BC and many large stone buildings existed when the Romans took over in 167 BC. The site lies by a channel connecting salty Lake Butrint to the sea. A triangular **fortress**, erected by warlord Ali Pasha Tepelena in the early 19th century, watches over the ramshackle vehicular ferry that crosses the narrow channel.

Secluded in the forest below the acropolis is Butrint's 3rd-century BC **Greek theatre**, which was also in use during the Roman period. Close by are the small **public baths**, which have geometric mosaics. Deeper in the forest is a wall covered with crisp Greek inscriptions, and a 6th-century palaeo-Christian **baptistry** decorated with colourful mosaics of animals and birds. The mosaics are covered by protective sand. Beyond a 6th-century basilica stands a massive **Cyclopean wall** dating back to the 4th century BC. Over one gate is a splendid relief of a lion killing a bull, symbolic of a protective force vanquishing assailants.

In a crenellated brick building on top of the acropolis is a **museum** (if it is open) full of statuary from the site. There are good views from the terrace.

Butrint's prosperity continued throughout the Roman period and the Byzantines made it an ecclesiastical centre. Then the city declined; it was almost abandoned when Italian archaeologists arrived in 1927 and began carting off any relics of value to Italy until WWII interrupted their work. Some of these have been returned to Tirana's National Museum of History. A cab to Butrint will cost around 2000 lekë. There are no buses.

The **Blue Eye spring**, 15km east of Saranda, signposted *Syri i Kalter* to the left off the Gjirokastra road and before the ascent over the pass to the Drino Valley, is definitely worth seeing. Its iridescent blue water gushes from the depths of the earth and feeds into the Bistrica River. French divers have descended as far as 70m, but the spring's actual depth is still unknown.

Places to Stay & Eat

An excellent budget choice is **Hotel Lili** (*☎ 37 64; Lagja No. 3; singles/doubles 3000/5000 lekë*). All rooms have fridges, fans, TV and the use of a washing machine. There is a **restaurant** downstairs.

Excellent wood-oven pizzas are served up at **Pizzeri Evangjelos** (*☎ 54 29; ne Shetitore; pizzas 350-600 lekë*), at the southern end of the promenade, while farther south and right on the waterside is the small and friendly **Restaurant Emmanueli** (*ne Shetitore; meals 700-800 lekë*).

Getting There & Away

A daily ferry and hydrofoil service plies between Saranda and Corfu (€14 one way). Call **Finikas Lines** (*☎ 30-9-4485 3228*) in Corfu for schedules from Corfu. The hydrofoil normally leaves Saranda at 10am.

Buses to Tirana (1000 lekë, eight hours) and Gjirokastra (300 lekë, 1½ hours) leave from Saranda's bus station four times daily, while there are two to three services a week to Korça (1000 lekë, eight hours).

A taxi to the Greek border at Kakavija will cost 3500 lekë while a cab to the border near Konispoli will cost around 3000 lekë.

KORÇA
☎ 082 • pop 62,200

If you are heading to or from Greece via Florina or Kastoria then the small, breezy town of Korça may be the best stopover. Situated at the edge of a vast agricultural plain that stretches almost all the way to Lake Ohrid, this cultured, historical town is worth staying in for at least one day. Transport to and from the town is generally good and, while there's no specific drawcard, Korça's broad, tree-lined boulevards are a welcome respite from the often dreary, mud-stained streets of other rural Albanian towns.

Places to Stay & Eat

The best budget option is the signposted **Hotel Gold** (*☎ 46 894; Rruga Kiço Golniku 5; singles/doubles 1888/2830 lekë*). The clean rooms have TV and heating as well as private bathrooms. Follow the signs for 800m from the avenue leading from the bus stop to the main square.

In the centre of town you can't miss the modern **Hotel Grand** (*☎ 43 168, fax 42 677; Central Square; singles/doubles including breakfast 2950/4720 lekë*). Once a grim, Stalinist-era guesthouse, this renovated hotel is now quite pleasant and comfortable. The rooms all have bathroom and TV.

Both the above hotels have their own restaurants. **Restaurant Alfa** (*☎ 44 385; meals 700-800 lekë*) is just off the main square and is a pretty decent eating option. Fairly substantial Greek-style cuisine is on offer. Up a notch is the **Dolce Vita** (*☎ 42 480; pizzas 380 lekë*), 200m to the left of the large Orthodox church and just south of the main square. This is the poshest restaurant-pizzeria in town.

Getting There & Away

Buses and minibuses all congregate at the official – and thankfully mud-less – bus-parking area 200m, which is north of the main square. Arriving minibuses will normally drop their passengers off on the main square also. Minibuses to Tirana (700 lekë, four hours) depart when full.

For Greece there are three buses daily to Thessaloniki (€19, seven hours) and four a week to Athens (€30, 16 hours) at noon on Sunday, Monday, Thursday and Friday. Go to the **ticket office** in the street office behind the Grand Hotel to book your seat.

Note: you can take a minibus to the border for around 300 to 400 lekë, but a Greek taxi from the Albanian-Greek border to Florina or Kastoria alone will cost you a minimum of €30. There are only two to three inconveniently timed local buses daily linking the Greek border village of Krystallopigi with Florina, and none to Kastoria. The direct international bus from Korça is by far the best option.

FIER & APOLLONIA
☎ 0623 • pop 48,500

Fier is a large town by the Gjanica River at a junction of road and rail routes, 89km south of Durrës. Albania's oil industry is centred on Fier, with a fertiliser plant, an oil refinery and a thermal power plant fuelled by natural gas. Fier has a pleasant **riverside promenade,** the imposing 13th-century **Orthodox Monastery of St Mary**, with wonderful icons inside, and the rich **Museum of Apollonia**.

By far the most interesting sight in the vicinity is the ruins of ancient Apollonia (Pojan), 12km west of Fier, set on a hill top surrounded by impressive bunkers. Apollonia was founded by Corinthian Greeks in 588 BC and quickly grew into an important city-state, minting its own currency. Under the Romans the city became a great cultural centre with a famous school of philosophy.

Julius Caesar rewarded Apollonia with the title 'free city' for supporting him against Pompey the Great during a civil war in the 1st century BC, and sent his nephew Octavius, the future Emperor Augustus, to complete his studies there. After a series of military disasters, the population moved southward into present-day Vlora (the ancient Avlon), and by the 5th century only a small village with its own bishop remained at Apollonia.

Only a small part of ancient Apollonia has so far been excavated, but look out for the very picturesque 3rd-century BC **House of Mosaics**, one of the site's highlights.

Fier and Apollonia are best visited on day trips from Tirana or Durrës.

BERAT
☎ 062 • pop 47,700

Berat, Albania's second-most-important museum town, is sometimes called the 'city of a thousand windows' for the many openings in the white-plastered, red-roofed houses on terraces overlooking the Osum River. Along a ridge high above the gorge is a 14th-century **citadel** that shelters small Orthodox churches. On the slope below this, all the way down to the river, is **Mangalem**, the old Muslim quarter. A seven-arched stone bridge (1780) leads to **Gorica**, the Christian quarter.

In the 3rd century BC an Illyrian fortress called Antipatria was built here on the site of an earlier settlement. The Byzantines strengthened the hill-top fortifications in the 5th and 6th centuries, as did the Bulgarians 400 years later. The Serbs, who occupied the citadel in 1345, renamed it Beligrad, or 'White City', which has become today's Berat. In 1450 the Ottoman Turks took Berat. The town revived in the 18th and 19th centuries as a Turkish crafts centre specialising in woodcarving. For a brief time in 1944, Berat was the capital of liberated Albania.

While there is accommodation in the town, Berat is best visited on a day trip from Durrës or Tirana as the town does not really afford a convenient stopover for through travellers. You will need to retrace your steps as onwards travel is patchy and difficult at best.

Northern Albania

Visits to northern Albania still involve some element of risk due to continuing instability of security. The main road corridor from Tirana to the Yugoslav border is generally fine, but travellers are advised to avoid independent travel west of Shkodra, between that town and Kukës, and farther north around Bajram Curri.

Shkodra, the old Gheg capital near the lake of the same name, is a pleasant introduction to Albania for those who are arriving from Yugoslavia. South of here is Lezha and Skënderbeg's tomb.

SHKODRA
☎ 0224 • pop 91,300

Shkodra (also Shkodër and, in Italian, Scutari), the traditional centre of the Gheg cultural region, is one of the oldest cities in Europe. In 500 BC an Illyrian fortress already guarded the strategic crossing just west of the city where the Buna and Drin Rivers meet, and all traffic moving up the coast from Greece to Montenegro must pass. These rivers drain two of the Balkans' largest lakes: Shkodra, just northwest of the city, and Ohrid, far up the Drin River beyond massive hydroelectric dams. The route inland to Kosova also begins in Shkodra. North of Shkodra, line after line of cement bunkers point the way to the Han i Hotit border crossing into Yugoslavia (33km). Tirana is 116km south.

Queen Teuta's Illyrian kingdom was based here in the 3rd century BC. Despite wars with Rome in 228 and 219 BC, Shkodra was not taken by the Romans until 168 BC. Later the region passed to Byzantium before becoming the capital of the feudal realm of the Balshas in 1350. In 1396 the Venetians occupied Shkodra's Rozafa Fortress, which they held against Suleiman Pasha in 1473 but lost to Mehmet Pasha in 1479. The Turks lost 14,000 men in the first siege and 30,000 in the second.

As the Ottoman Empire declined in the late 18th century, Shkodra became the centre of a semi-independent pashalik, which led to a blossoming of commerce and crafts. In 1913 Montenegro attempted to annex Shkodra (it succeeded in taking Ulcinj), but this was not recognised by the international community and the town changed hands often during WWI. Badly damaged by the 1979 earthquake, Shkodra was subsequently repaired and now is Albania's fourth-largest town.

Quality private accommodation has been slow to emerge in Shkodra. Travellers are advised to head for Durrës or Tirana.

Rozafa Fortress

Two kilometres southwest of Shkodra, near the southern end of Lake Shkodra, is Rozafa Fortress, founded by the Illyrians in antiquity and rebuilt much later by the Venetians and Turks. From the highest point there's a marvellous view on all sides.

The fortress derived its name from a woman named Rozafa, who was allegedly walled into the ramparts as an offering to the gods so that the construction would stand. The story goes that Rozafa asked that two holes be left in the stonework so that she could continue to suckle her baby. Nursing women still come to the fortress to smear their breasts with milky water taken from a spring here.

Belarus Беларусь

Belarus has not exactly been a press darling in the West. The last dictatorship in Europe! A Soviet Union time-capsule!

True, the current government of Belarus is backwards and repressive in almost all ways, yet tourists will be undisturbed by its machinations. Instead, visitors can see what a safer, cleaner and more orderly Russia would look like. The capital, Minsk, rebuilt from scratch after WWII, is a shining testament to neoclassical Stalinist architecture but is straining to become cosmopolitan and Westernised – it's communism with a cappuccino.

Brest is a lively border town with a pleasant, timeless charm and Hrodna boasts a rich Catholic influence. The countryside – where you can see some of the planet's last remaining collective farms in action – is bereft of tourists, and historic towns such as Njasvizh and the reconstructed village at Dudutki make a relaxing day's excursion from the capital.

At a Glance

- **Brest** – cosmopolitan border town and amazing Soviet WWII memorial
- **Hrodna** – historic town boasting a stunning baroque cathedral
- **Minsk** – the best example of pure Soviet planning on a grand scale

Capital	Minsk
Population	9.95 million
Official Language	Belarusian
Currency	1 Belarusian rouble (BR)
Time	GMT/UTC+0200
Country Phone Code	☎ 375

Facts about Belarus

HISTORY

Evidence of human occupation in Belarus goes back to the early Stone Age. Eastern Slavs tribes were here by the 6th to 8th centuries AD. The area fell under the control of Kyivan Rus, but in the 14th century, Belarus was gradually taken over by Lithuania and became part of the Polish-Lithuanian Grand Duchy. It was to be 400 years before Belarus came under Russian control, a period in which Belarusians became linguistically and culturally differentiated from the Russians to their east and the Ukrainians to their south.

In this time, trade was controlled by Poles and Jews and most Belarusians remained peasants, poor and illiterate. After the Partitions of Poland (1772, 1793 and 1795–96), Belarus was absorbed into Russia and faced intense Russification policies. Due to their cultural stagnation, their absence from positions of influence and their historical domination by the Poles and Russians, any sense among speakers of Belarusian that they were a distinct nationality was slow to emerge.

During the 19th century Belarus was part of the Pale of Settlement, the area where Jews in the Russian Empire were required to settle,

and Jews formed the majority in many cities and towns before WWII.

In March 1918, under German occupation during WWI, a short-lived independent Belarusian Democratic Republic was declared, but the land was soon under the control of the Red Army. The 1921 Treaty of Rīga allotted roughly the western half of modern Belarus to Poland, which launched a programme of Polonisation that provoked armed resistance by Belarusians.

The area under Bolshevik control, the Belarusian Soviet Socialist Republic (BSSR), was a founding member of the USSR in 1922.

The Soviet regime in the 1920s encouraged Belarusian literature and culture but in the

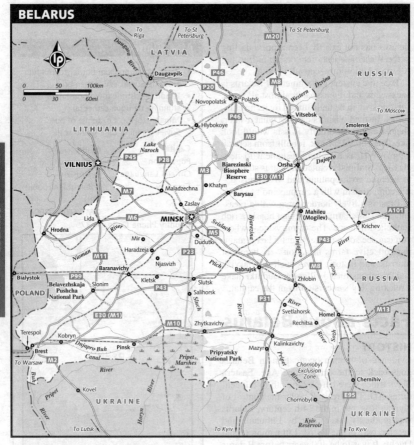

1930s under Stalin, nationalism and the Belarusian language were discouraged and their proponents ruthlessly persecuted. The 1930s also saw industrialisation, agricultural collectivisation, and purges in which hundreds of thousands were executed – most in the Kurapaty Forest, outside Minsk.

In September 1939, western Belarus was seized from Poland by the Red Army. When Nazi Germany invaded Russia in 1941, Belarus was on the front line and suffered greatly. German occupation was savage and partisan resistance widespread until the Red Army drove the Germans out in 1944, with massive destruction on both sides. Hundreds of villages were decimated, and barely a stone was left standing in Minsk. At least 25% of the Belarus population (over two million people)

died from 1939 to 1945. Many of them, Jews and others, died in 200-plus concentration camps; the third-largest Nazi concentration camp was set up at Maly Trostenets, where over 200,000 people were executed.

Western Belarus remained in Soviet hands at the end of the war, with Minsk developing into the industrial hub of the western USSR and Belarus becoming one of the Soviet Union's most prosperous republics.

The 1986 Chornobyl disaster left about a quarter of the country seriously contaminated, and its effects are still felt today, particularly in the southeastern regions of the country.

In response to the growth of nationalist feeling, on 27 July 1990 the republic issued a declaration of sovereignty within the USSR. On 25 August 1991 a declaration of full national independence was issued. With no history whatsoever as a politically or economically independent entity, the country of Belarus was one of the oddest products of the disintegration of the USSR.

Economic reform was slow, with the old communist guard opposing privatisation of state enterprises or state-run farms and advocating closer ties with Russia.

Since July 1994, Belarus has been governed by Alyaksandr Lukashenka, who is a former collective-farm director (a common derogatory nickname for him is *kolkhoznik*, from *kolkhoz*, collective farm). His presidential style has been autocratic and authoritarian and, in 1996, in a bid to increase his powers he held what the West still regards as an illegitimate referendum. This effectively stripped the authority of the parliament, now to be appointed by Lukashenka, and made the entire government subservient to him. It also extended his term for two years.

Since then, the opposition has been reduced to just a few (often opposed) groups, which hold rallies in the capital but have been unable to galvanise popular support into a unified whole. Numerous outspoken critics of the Lukashenka regime have been arrested, imprisoned or have simply disappeared.

Official elections were held in September 2001, despite international criticism and opposition calls of their illegality. Lukashenka again won a majority and is now scheduled to stay in power until (at least) 2006.

The country has become, politically, an isolated island in the centre of Europe.

GEOGRAPHY

Belarus has an area of 207,600 sq km, slightly smaller than the UK. It borders Russia in the north and east, Latvia and Lithuania in the northwest, Poland in the west and Ukraine in the south.

It's a low-lying, flat country, consisting of low ridges dividing broad, often marshy lowlands with many small lakes. The largest lake (79.6 sq km) is the Naroch, north of Minsk. In the south are the Pripet Marshes, Europe's largest marsh area. The country's major river is the Dnjapro.

CLIMATE

Belarus has a continental climate, which becomes marginally less temperate as you move from southwest to northeast. Average January temperatures are between -4 and -8°C, with frosts experienced for five to six months of the year. The warmest month is July, when temperatures can reach up to 30°C but the average temperature is 18°C. Rainfall is moderate at an average 670mm a year, with June to August the wettest months.

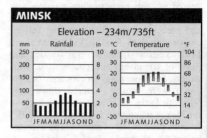

ECOLOGY & ENVIRONMENT

The 1986 disaster at Chornobyl has been the defining event for the Belarusian environment, if not for the republic as a whole. Some 70% of Chornobyl's released radioisotopes fell on Belarus (primarily but not exclusively in the Homel and Mahileu districts in the south and east). Some 1.8 million people still live in these areas.

The current government is downplaying the dangers inherent in living in these areas, encouraging resettlement and cutting benefits to those who suffered from the accident. The dangers of exposure to radiation for the casual tourist are negligible.

Most of the countryside is unspoiled, and old farmsteads have slowly been reclaimed by new forests. The marshland area known as Polesye in the south of the country are dubbed locally the 'lungs of Europe' as air currents passing over it are re-oxygenated and purified by the swamps.

GOVERNMENT & POLITICS

In theory, Belarus is a democracy with an executive president, chosen in direct popular elections. The president then chooses a prime minister, who is responsible for many of the day-to-day affairs of government. The country's parliament is the National Assembly, consisting of two chambers. However, in practice, the country is run by the sitting president, Alyaksandr Lukashenka.

Lukashenka has cracked down on media, halted or reversed economic reforms, stifled

BELARUS

political opposition and played chicken with the West – harshly condemning it while at the same time making moderate reforms to attract the funding he needs to keep the country running. He has effectively eliminated any real opposition and most voices of dissent.

Lukashenka's biggest efforts have been geared towards orchestrating a union with Russia. There are different models of union and partnership on offer, including full incorporation into Russia. Lukashenka and Boris Yeltsin signed several treaties and pacts of friendship and cooperation. Ultimately, grandiose plans for economic or legal union were mostly watered down, and Vladimir Putin is known to be lukewarm to the idea of union with Belarus. Still, the Belarusian press is full of reports of an eventual union, though the details of this are unclear.

The country is divided into six administrative regions centred on the cities of Minsk, Brest, Hrodna, Vitsebsk, Homel and Mahileu.

ECONOMY

Belarus has devolved continually under Lukashenka's spectacularly unsuccessful attempts at 'market socialism'. The figures actually show positive growth (the economy grew by 4.1% in 2001, and industrial output was up 5.4%) but this is largely due to the government pumping money into key industries. Byzantine regulations and corruption make small private business practically impossible.

Some of Belarus' major export items include potassium fertilisers, wood-fibre boards, chemicals, refrigerators, tractors and trucks.

Foreign investment was a meagre $16 million in the first quarter of 2002. Inflation for food goods at the close of 2001 was just under 50%; for nonfood products it was just under 30%.

Official unemployment in the country is very low: in 2001, 2.3%. While the average monthly wage in early 2002 was $95, a huge proportion of the populace earns much less than that.

POPULATION & PEOPLE

The Belarusian population is 81.2% Belarusian, 11.4% Russian, 4% Polish and 2.4% Ukrainian, with the remaining 1% consisting of other groups. This results in a rather homogeneous population, with many sharing characteristic physical attributes like fair hair and piercing blue eyes.

Prior to WWII, 10% of the national population was Jewish and in cities like Minsk, Hrodna, Brest and Vitsebsk, Jews made up between one-third and three-quarters of the population. They now make up less than 1% of the population.

As with other countries in the region, the death rate far exceeds the birth rate; in Belarus it is over 50% higher.

ARTS
Literature & Drama

The hero of early Belarusian literary achievement was Francyska Skaryny. Born in Polatsk but educated in Poland and Italy, the scientist, doctor, writer and humanist became the first person to translate the Bible into the Belarusian language. This, as well as other editions by Skaryny between 1517 and 1525, was one of the first books to be printed in all of Eastern Europe. In the late-16th century, the philosopher and humanist Simon Budny printed a number of works in Belarusian.

The 19th century saw the beginning of modern Belarusian literature with works by writers and poets such as Maxim Haradsky, Maxim Bohdanovish, Janka Kupala and most notably Jakub Kolas. Many of these writers had been active in the influential nationalist newspaper *Nasha Niva* (Our Cornfield). Kolas is considered to be the pioneer of classical Belarusian literature. Both he and Kupala are revered for having promoted the literary and poetic use of Belarusian.

Music

Belarusian folk music is well known and no visitor to the country should miss a performance. Modern folk music originated from ritualistic ceremonies – either based on peasant seasonal feasts or, more commonly, on the traditions of church music (hymns and psalms) which became highly developed in Belarus from the 16th century onwards. The band Pesnyary have been extremely popular since the 1960s for having put a modern twist on traditional Belarusian folk music.

SOCIETY & CONDUCT

Throughout history the Belarusian people have been the underclass in their own country, with little distinct culture or history of their own. As such, Belarusians are quiet, somewhat reserved people. Less demonstrative and approachable than Russians, they are just as friendly and generous, if not more so, once introductions are made. In further comparison to their Russian cousins, Belarusians tend to be harder workers, more aspiring in their personal goals and less likely to swear.

RELIGION

Belarus, like Ukraine, has always been a crossing point between Latin and Eastern Orthodox Christianity, with Polish Catholics to the west and Orthodox Russians to the east. Some 80% of the populace is Eastern Orthodox.

About 20% of the population (about two million people) is Roman Catholic, of whom 15% are ethnic Poles.

During the early 1990s the Uniate Church (an Orthodox sect that looks to Rome, not Moscow) was re-established and now it has a following of over 100,000 members. There's also a small Protestant minority, the remnant of a once large German population.

LANGUAGE

Belarusian belongs to the Eastern Slavonic branch of Indo-European, closely related to both Russian and Ukrainian. The centralised Soviet system subjected Belarus to a process of Russification.

Today, Russian dominates in nearly all aspects of social life and has been the second official language since 1995. There is little state support for keeping Belarusian alive and flourishing, and many citizens are quite apathetic, if slightly embarrassed about the subject. Only about 11% of school children are instructed in Belarusian.

While much of the signage is in Belarusian (street signs, inside train and bus stations, on museum displays), usage is indiscriminate.

See the Russian section in the Language chapter at the end of this book for some useful words and phrases.

Facts for the Visitor

HIGHLIGHTS

While Minsk is not a great tourist city, its cultural performances and festivals are usually outstanding and the events described at the Museum of the Great Patriotic War will stay with you a long time. Outside the capital, Hrodna has a pleasant old-town feel and a stunning cathedral. Brest's amazing fortress is a Soviet war monument whose scope defies

words, while the primeval forest of Belavezhskaja Pushcha National Park is home to the once near-extinct *zoobr*.

SUGGESTED ITINERARIES

Depending on time available and where you arrive you might visit the following:

Two Days
    Visit only Minsk, and a then take a quick trip to Dudutki
One Week
    Visit Minsk, Dudutki, Njasvizh as well as Brest and the Belavezhskaja Pushcha National Park
One Month
    In addition to the previous suggestions, and visiting other centres such as Vitsebsk and Hrodna, an extended stay in one of the country's national parks is recommended

PLANNING
What to Bring

While much organising can be accomplished face-to-face, planning your trip ahead of time can save frustration. Make sure all your official documents are in order.

It's not hard to find staple food, medicine and supplies in Belarus, but bring any special items you may require (specific medicine, high-speed film etc).

RESPONSIBLE TOURISM

Everyone comments on how clean the streets of Belarus' cities and towns are – keep up the tradition by disposing of your rubbish in appropriate places only. If you insist on talking politics, avoid brash statements that may seem obviously true to you, such as 'I can't believe that people here actually support that petty dictator of yours!'. Many people realise the state in which they live and may make some criticisms of their own but are nonetheless touchy when the same critiques are levelled by outsiders.

TOURIST OFFICES

There are no tourist information offices in the formal sense in Belarus, but there are some hotel service bureaus and excursion offices which may be helpful. Otherwise, travel agencies are your best bet.

VISAS & DOCUMENTS

The visa regulations change frequently, so check on Ⓦ www.belarusembassy.org, the Belarusian US embassy site, for details.

BELARUS

All foreigners visiting Belarus need to have a visa. Arranging one before you arrive in the country is absolutely essential. Visas are not issued at border points except at the Minsk-2 international airport – however, you will still need to show hotel reservations or your personal or business invitation.

There are three types of visas: tourist, issued if you have a tourist voucher or hotel reservation; visitor, if your invitation comes from an individual; and business, if your invitation is from a business. Tourist and visitor visas are issued for 30 days, while business visas are valid for 90 days and can be multi-entry.

Belarus requires foreigners to possess medical insurance from a pre-approved company covering their entire length of stay. Your local Belarusian embassy will tell you which local insurance companies are acceptable. Costs are reasonable ($15 for a 60-day stay). Insurance is also sold at border entry points, and is not required for holders of transit visas.

Once you enter the country you must be officially registered, a process hotels will do for a small fee. They'll give you small pieces of papers with stamps on them, which you keep to show to customs agents upon departure. In theory, you'll be fined if you do not prove that you've been registered. In practice, these are rarely asked for. If you've received a personal invitation, you'll need to seek out the nearest local passport office (OPVS; also known in Russian as OVIR) of the Ministry of the Interior. The main office (☎ 017-231 91 74; praspekt Francyska Skaryny 8) is in Minsk.

Transit Visas

All persons passing through Belarusian territory need a transit visa, which can be obtained at any Belarusian consulate upon presentation of travel tickets clearly showing the final destination as outside of Belarus. The possession of a valid Russian visa is no longer enough to serve as a transit visa. Transit visas are not available at the border.

Applying for a Visa

By far the simplest, but the most expensive, way to get a visa is to apply through a travel agency. Alternately, you can take a faxed confirmation from your hotel to the nearest Belarusian embassy and apply yourself.

Many Belarusian travel agencies (see Travel Agencies in the Minsk section) can send you an invitation. The Host Families Association (HOFA; see Homestays under accommodation) can do the same.

Visa costs vary. Typically, single-entry visas cost about $50 for five working days service and $90 for next-day service. Double entry visas usually cost double that. Transit visas typically cost from $20 to $35.

EMBASSIES & CONSULATES
Belarusian Embassies

Belarusian embassies abroad include:

France (☎ 01 44 14 69 79, fax 01 44 14 69 70) 38 blvd Suchet, 75016 Paris

Germany (☎ 030-5 36 35 929, fax 5 36 35 923, *Consular section:* ☎ 030-5 36 35 934, fax 5 36 35 924) Am Treptower Park 32, 12435 Berlin

Latvia (☎ 732 34 11, fax 732 28 91) Jezus baznicas iela 12, Rīga 1050

Lithuania (☎ 2-25 16 66, fax 25 16 62) Mimdaugo gatvė 13, Vilnius

Poland (☎ 022-617 23 91, fax 617 84 41) Ulica Atenska 67, 03-978 Warsaw

Russia (☎ 095-924 70 31, fax 928 66 33) Maroseyka ulitsa 17/6, 101000 Moscow

UK (☎ 020-7937 3288, fax 7361 0005) 6 Kensington Court, London W8 5DL

Ukraine (☎ 044-290 02 01, fax 290 34 13) vulitsya Sichnevogo povstannya 6, 252010 Kyiv

USA (☎ 202-986 1604, fax 986 1805) 1619 New Hampshire Ave NW, Washington, DC 20009

Embassies & Consulates in Belarus

The following addresses are all in Minsk; the telephone area code is ☎ 017.

France (☎ 210 28 68, fax 210 25 48) Ploshcha Svabody 11

Germany (☎ 284 87 14, fax 284 85 52) vulitsa Zakharava 26

Latvia (☎/fax 284 74 75) vulitsa Darashevicha 6

Lithuania (☎ 234 77 84, fax 234 72 00) vulitsa Varvasheni 17

Poland (☎ 213 41 14, fax 236 49 92) vulitsa Rumjantsava 6

Russia (☎ 250 36 66, fax 250 36 64) vulitsa Staravilenskaja 48

Ukraine (☎/fax 222 38 04) vulitsa Kirava 17

USA (☎ 210 12 83, fax 234 78 53) vulitsa Staravilenskaja 46

CUSTOMS

Upon arrival, you may be given a customs declaration form *(deklaratsia)* to fill out. You are allowed to bring in and out of the country currency up to $1500 without filling in a form.

If you are given a form to complete, keep it until your departure as you may be asked to show it before you leave. See the Belarus US embassy site at **w** www.belarus embassy.org for more detailed information.

MONEY

All prices are listed in Belarusian roubles (abbreviated to BR) in this book.

Currency

Belarusian roubles are better known as *zaichiki* or 'rabbits', named after the one rouble note first issued in 1992 that featured a leaping rabbit. There is no coinage in Belarus, but notes range from 1 to 20,000 roubles.

Exchange Rates

At the time of publication the exchange rates were:

country	unit		Belarusian rouble
Australia	A$1	=	BR999
Canada	C$1	=	BR1160
Euro Zone	€1	=	BR1819
Japan	¥100	=	BR1509
Lithuania	1 Lt	=	BR527
New Zealand	NZ$1	=	BR864
Russia	RR1	=	BR58
UK	UK£1	=	BR2891
USA	US$1	=	BR1842

Exchanging Money

In Minsk, there is a plethora of ATMs (along all major streets, inside metro stations, nightclubs etc) which accept all major credit cards and dispense roubles.

Costs

For travellers to Belarus, the major cost will be accommodation. In Minsk, dining in all but the cheapest café will also cost you more than you'd think – from $5 to $10 per average-sized meal. Almost everything else, including public transport, is inexpensive. Hanging out drinking beer is extremely cheap by most Western standards.

POST & COMMUNICATIONS
Post

The word for post office is *pashtamt*. Posting a 20g letter within Belarus costs $0.03 and to any other country $0.27. The best way to mail important, time-sensitive items is with the Express Mail Service (EMS), offered at most main post offices.

Telephone

There are two kinds of pay phones – the old-style, grey boxes that have been refitted so that they accept phonecards instead of kopecks, and the newer, blue pay phones that take another type of phonecard. Local calls can be made from both, but intercity and international calls, or calls to local mobile numbers with the ☎ 8 prefix, can only be made from the blue phones, which are few and far between. Both types of cards can be bought from post offices and some newspaper kiosks, and range in price from about BR3000 to BR10,000. Long-distance calls can also be made from the main post office or telephone offices like **Beltelekom** (☎ *017-236 71 24; vulitsa Enhelsa 14, Minsk; open 24hr)*.

To dial within Belarus, dial ☎ 8, wait for the new tone, then city code and the number. To dial abroad, dial ☎ 8, wait for the tone, then ☎ 10, country code, city code and the number. To phone Belarus from abroad, dial ☎ 375 followed by the city code and number.

BOOKS
Guidebooks

The English *Minsk What & Where* is a free annual magazine available at travel agencies and contains helpful general information on the city's museums and places to eat.

History & Politics

David Marples has written two excellent books that assess the enduring consequences of the Soviet regime, the Chornobyl disaster and Lukashenka's regime, which take into account Belarus' unique sociopolitical context: *Belarus: From Soviet Rule to Nuclear Catastrophe* (1996) and *Belarus: A Denationalized Nation* (1999).

Belarus: At a Crossroads in History by Jan Zaprudnik is one of the best reads about the conditions affecting the newly independent nation, though published in 1993. *Kurapaty: Articles, Comments and Photographs*, by the opposition leader Zjanon Paznjak, is a controversial 1994 expose of the Soviet slaughter of Belarusian citizens at Kurapaty, and its current cover-up. For the flipside of WWII atrocities, read Martin Dean's 1999 *Collaboration in the Holocaust: Crimes of the Local Police in Belorussia and Ukraine, 1941–44*.

BELARUS

NEWSPAPERS & MAGAZINES

State-run newspapers like *Sovetskaya Belorussya* dominate the market, usually featuring a photo of Lukashenka on the cover striking a commanding pose at least once a week. Popular among the independent press are the *Belorusskaya Gazetta* and *Vecherny Minsk* (Evening Minsk).

There are no English-language newspapers in Belarus.

TIME

Belarus is one hour behind Moscow time, ie, GMT/UTC plus two hours, and follows Daylight Savings Time.

LAUNDRY

There are no laundrettes in Belarus, though most hotels will wash your clothes for an extra fee.

TOILETS

There are many public toilets in the cities (BR100 to BR200), and they are predictably stinky. Bring your own toilet paper and stick to McDonald's.

HEALTH

Unboiled tap water is not recommended to drink, though for showering and brushing teeth it should pose no problems. Bottled mineral water is easily found across the country.

Chornobyl

Belarus suffered most severely from the 1986 Chornobyl disaster, with 70% of the fallout landing on its territory. About 20% of its forests and well over 250,000 hectares of agricultural land remain contaminated.

The risk to short-term visitors from the aftermath of the Chornobyl nuclear disaster is considered insignificant. The areas in Belarus to stay away from, at least for long-term exposure, are the southeastern regions.

WOMEN TRAVELLERS

Women travelling on their own are a rare sight in these parts, but those wishing to do so should encounter no particular problems or harassment. Travellers should be aware that traditional sex roles are quite firmly in place here, with both sexes straining to act in ways seen to be in accordance to their genders.

The **Discussion Women's Club** (☎ 017-263 77 36; e *beluwi@minsk.soram.com*) in

Minsk is an NGO that regularly hosts forums and meetings on women's issues in Belarus.

GAY & LESBIAN TRAVELLERS

Sex between consenting women is legal in Belarus from the age of 14; for men from 18. The state is not supportive of gay initiatives and organisations. However, there is a lively and popular gay bar in Minsk (see Entertainment in the Minsk section), and the **Belarus Lambda League** (☎ 017-221 92 05; e *uwb@user.unibel.by*) in Minsk can provide some assistance and advice.

DANGERS & ANNOYANCES

Crime levels in Belarus, partially thanks to the omnipresence of police on city centre streets, are relatively low, far below those of Western countries. As a foreigner you have a slightly higher chance of being targeted – don't flash your money around or put yourself in a vulnerable situation.

BUSINESS HOURS

Most shops close for lunch for an hour in the afternoon, any time between noon and 4pm. Most shops are open seven days a week, with slightly shorter hours on Saturday and Sunday.

PUBLIC HOLIDAYS & SPECIAL EVENTS

The main public holidays in Belarus are New Year's Day (1 January), Orthodox Christmas Day (7 January), International Women's Day (8 March), Constitution Day (15 March), Catholic Easter (March/April), Orthodox Easter (March/April), Radunitsa (ninth day after Orthodox Easter), International Labour Day (1 May), Victory Day 1945 (9 May), Day of the Coat of Arms and the State Flag of the Republic of Belarus (second Sunday in May), Independence Day (3 July), Dzyady or Memory Day (2 November), Anniversary of the October Revolution (7 November) and Catholic Christmas Day (25 December).

The night of 6 July is a celebration with pagan roots called Kupalye, when young girls gather flowers and throw them into a river as a method of fortune-telling, and everyone else sits by lake or riverside fires drinking beer.

In mid- to late July in Vitsebsk is the well-loved Slavyansky Bazar, a huge musical event which gathers singers and performers from many countries to sing in Slavic languages.

ACTIVITIES

Minsk's favourite watering hole and tanning area is Minskae Mora (Minsk Sea), a small lake 17km north of Minsk. This little getaway place has a free public beach, and has pedal boat and catamaran rental. Over a dozen buses make the 45-minute trip daily from Minsk's central bus station; by car, head north on P28 and watch for the signs after Ratomka village.

With over 10,000 small lakes and streams totalling more than 90,000km in length, fishing is obviously a national pastime. Belarus' flatness makes it a good, easy option for long-range cycling expeditions.

ACCOMMODATION
Camping

Farmers and villagers are generally generous about allowing campers to pitch a tent on their lot for an evening. Outside national parks you may camp in forests and the like, provided you don't make too much of a ruckus.

Hotels

While accommodation standards in Belarus tend to be lower than in the West, they are still generally acceptable and rooms almost always have private toilets. The prices for foreigners are, however, overpriced for what you get – in the cities, it's hard to find anything under BR40,000/55,000 for a single/double.

Homestays & Apartment Rentals

Host Families Association (HOFA; ☎/fax 812-275 1992; e alexei@hofak.hop.stu.neva .ru; w www.webcenter.ru/~hofa; 5-25 Tavricheskaya, St Petersburg, Russia) can set you up in a room with a local family.

Also, the **Harmony Agency** (☎ 029-282 60 08, 017-283 10 78; e harmony@europe.com; w www.russianlady.net/apartment1.html) has several excellent central apartments for rent ($15 to $30 a day).

FOOD & DRINKS

The Belarusians love their mushrooms, and mushroom-gathering is a traditional expedition in Belarus. It's pretty hard to avoid the fungus – they pop up in one way or another everywhere. *Hribnoy sup* is a mushroom and barley soup, and *kotleta pokrestyansky* is a pork cutlet smothered with a mushroom sauce. *Dranniki* are potato pancakes – a most traditional Belarusian dish. *Kolduni* are delicious, thick potato dumplings stuffed with meat. *Kletsky* are dumplings stuffed with either mushrooms, cheese or potatoes.

Try Belarusian *kvas*, a popular elixir made of malt, flour, sugar, mint and fruit. *Belovezhskaja* is a bitter herbal alcoholic drink. Most popular among alcoholic beverages are, of course, vodka and beer.

SHOPPING

Folk art is the main source of souvenirs, which include carved wooden trinkets, ceramics and woven textiles. Unique to Belarus are wooden boxes intricately ornamented with geometric patterns composed of multicoloured pieces of straw. These are easily found in city department stores and in some museum kiosks.

Getting There & Away

AIR

International flights entering and departing Belarus do so at the **Minsk-2 international airport** (☎ 017-279 10 32), about 40km east of Minsk. Some domestic flights as well as those to Kyiv, Kaliningrad and Moscow depart from the smaller **Minsk-1 airport** (☎ 017-22 54 18), only 6km from the city centre.

Belavia (☎ 017-210 41 00; w www .belavia.by; vulitsa Njamiha 14, Minsk), Belarus' national airline, has direct connections to a number of European destinations, including London ($390 return), St Petersburg, Stockholm, Warsaw, Prague, Vienna, Tel Aviv, Berlin, Frankfurt and Rome (all once to three times a week), and indirect connections with dozens of other international destinations. There are daily flights to Kyiv and Moscow ($165 return), and weekly flights to a number of other cities in Russia.

A number of other airlines service Minsk.

LAND
Border Crossings

Long queues are not uncommon. The most frequently used bus crossings are those on the four-hour trip between Vilnius and Minsk, and the seven-hour trip between Minsk and Bialystok in Poland.

Drivers should enter Belarus by one of the 10 main border crossings. International driving permits are recognised in Belarus. Roads in Belarus are predictably bad, but the main highways are decent. Fuel is available on the outskirts of most major cities but may be difficult to find elsewhere.

International trains cross into/out of Belarus at more than 10 crossing points and from five different countries.

Latvia, Lithuania & Estonia

The main road and rail crossing to the Baltic countries lies between Polatsk and Daugavpils (four to five hours).

There are two train lines that converge on Vilnius from Belarus. The busiest one is the Minsk-Vilnius line (four to five hours, several trains daily) which passes through Maladzechna. There are numerous daily buses that run between Vilnius and Minsk and between Vilnius and Lida.

From Tallinn, there is a weekly Eurolines bus, that passes through Pskov and Vitsebsk, as well as a twice weekly train travelling via Rīga and Vilnius.

Poland

The major train route to enter Belarus from Poland is the Brest crossing. Dozens of trains pull their loads adn passengers hrough each day, including the well used Warsaw-Minsk-Moscow route.

The other rail and road crossing is between Hrodna and Bialystok, the same crossing used by some of the St Petersburg-Vilnius-Warsaw trains.

Russia

The train and main road (M1) between Minsk and Moscow cross the border between Orsha (Belarus) and Smolensk (Russia), near the Russian town of Krasnoe. There are many regular services to Russian cities from all parts of Belarus.

Ukraine

There are only three main entry points to Ukraine from Belarus, the most heavily trafficked being the train and road link between Homel and Chernihov, Ukraine. The nightly Minsk-Kyiv train uses this route.

Getting Around

Travel within Belarus, although not always easy, is unrestricted. The country is linked by a system of train lines, bus routes and roads, and the cities themselves are navigable by trolleybus, tram, bus and, in Minsk, a metro. Local transport can often be crowded, grungy and slow.

AIR

There are several regional airports in Belarus, but as of 2002, only a Minsk-Homel flight was operating regularly, run by **Gomel Avia** (☎ 017-222 54 18). Contact the Minsk office of the Belarusian national air carrier, **Belavia** (☎ 017-229 28 38; vulitsa Njamiha 14), for the status of domestic flights in Belarus.

TRAIN

Trains between major cities are moderately frequent and cheap. A typical train ticket between Minsk and Brest (four to six hours) on a 2nd-class sleeper (kupe) costs around $6. Local electric trains are even cheaper, but much slower. Train stations are called zhelznadarazhniy or vokzal (station).

BUS

Buses are often the better option for travellers on most routes, because of their more convenient departure times, faster journey times and frequencies.

CAR & MOTORCYCLE

With spare parts rare, road conditions rugged and getting lost inevitable, driving or riding in Belarus is undeniably problematic, but is always an adventure and the best way to really see the country.

Road Rules

You will be instructed by signs to slow down when approaching GAI (road police) stations, and not doing so is a sure-fire way to get a substantial fine. You may see GAI signs in Russian (ГАЙ) or in Belarusian (ДАЙ).

Rental

Cars can be rented in Belarus with or without a driver – but it may be cheaper to bargain with a taxi driver if you just want to go to one destination and back for a day trip. The going city rate for taxis is BR450 per kilometre, and drivers will be happy to take you outside the city for a reasonable price. Prices for car rental average $15 an hour or $50 to $200 a day depending on the type of car and whether or not you have a driver.

HITCHING

Hitching is never entirely safe in any country in the world, and Lonely Planet doesn't recommend it. Nevertheless, it is a very common method of getting around in Belarus, especially for students. Avoid hitching at night or alone. Women should exercise caution.

LOCAL TRANSPORT

Local transport in Minsk is reasonably efficient, in Brest average, and in other cities infrequent. In any event it will be quite crowded.

Tickets (*kvitok* or *bilet*) cost BR120. You can buy them at most kiosks around bus stops. Plastic metro tokens (*zhetony*; BR150) are sold in Minsk's metro stations. Monthly passes are available. There are ticket inspectors but the fine for fare evasion is very small.

An Ä sign indicates a bus stop, T indicates a tram stop, Tp a trolleybus stop, and M a metro station.

Minsk Мінск

☎ 017 • pop 1.71 million

There's a palpable pride about Minsk, the pride of a survivor. It has come back from the dead several times in its almost millennium of existence (it's official birthday is 3 March 1067). It was frequently destroyed by fire throughout the centuries, sacked by Crimean Tatars in 1505, trampled to ruin by the French in 1812, and damaged by the Germans in 1918 and by the Poles in 1919–20. Its greatest suffering came in WWII, when half the city's people perished, including almost the entire population of 50,000 Jews. Virtually every building here has been erected since 1944, when Minsk's recapture by the Soviet army left barely a stone standing.

Moscow architects were given a blank slate after the war and they decided to make a model Soviet city out of Minsk's ruins. The excess of monumental classicism was supposed to give the impression of worker utopia. While the wide boulevards and grandiose proportions of the buildings in the city centre do initially impress, after a while they take on a cold, oppressive weightiness. Aside from a miniscule reconstructed Old Town, the city has no cosy corners or alleyways as an antidote to the concrete grandeur. However, there are several pleasant parks as well as a lovely promenade along the river Svislach.

Minsk is a safe (thanks partially to the fact that there are more police here per capita than in any other European city), ultra clean city, best enjoyed, as most youths do, hanging out in the parks and kicking back with a few beers.

Information

Tourist Offices There are no Western-style tourist information bureaus anywhere in Belarus, so travel agencies are your best source of information.

Post, Telephone & Fax Minsk's **central post office** (*glavpashtamt; praspekt Francyska Skaryny 10; open 8am-8pm Mon-Sat, 10am-5pm Sun*) is at the eastern end of Ploshcha Nezalezhnastsi. The **Express Mail Service** (☎ 227 85 12) is on the 2nd floor.

At the same address is also one of the city's numerous **telegraph offices** (*tsentralny telegraf; open 7am-11pm daily*), where you can make national and international calls. Another convenient one is **Beltelekom** (☎ 236 71 24; *vulitsa Enhelsa 14, open 24hr*).

Email & Internet Access There's round-the-clock access at **Beltelekom** (☎ 219-06 79; *vulitsa Enhelsa 14*), but you must call to reserve ahead. You have a better chance of getting online at **HP Invent** (☎ 226 42 43; *vulitsa Njamiha 8; open 9am-11pm daily*) inside the Na Nemige shopping centre.

Travel Agencies The helpful folks at **Belintourist** (☎ 226 98 85, fax 226 94 21; *w www.belarustourist.minsk.by; praspekt Masherava 19A; open 8am-8pm daily*) can arrange city or national tours of all kinds. A city tour costs around $45 per group; to Khatyn about $65. They also get about $10 knocked off the price of a room at Hotel Jubileynaja if they book it.

U Zheni (☎ 211 26 05; *w www.uzheni.com; vulitsa Kamsamolskaja 8/18*) deals mainly with Jewish tourists who come to Belarus to explore their family's roots. It offers 10 Jewish-themed tours (plus others) of the country. The staff are extremely resourceful and helpful, and can also get discounts at some Minsk hotels.

MINSK

PLACES TO STAY
7 Hotel Belarus
8 Hotel Planeta
10 Hotel Jubileynaya
38 Hotel Complex Oktjabrsky
59 Hotel Ekspress

PLACES TO EAT
3 Kamarowski Rynok
16 Stary Mlyn
20 Kitaiskoye Zhemchug
21 Karchma Stavravilenskaja
23 Tractkir Na Parkavoi
44 Express Kiritsa
50 Café Traktir Na Marxa

OTHER
1 Aquarium
2 Reactor
4 Belarusian State Philharmonia

5 US Embassy; Russian Embassy
6 Synagogue
9 Jewish Ghetto Monument
11 Belintourist Office
12 Sports Palace
13 National Academic Opera & Ballet Theatre
14 Former Residence of Lee Harvey Oswald
15 Ploshcha Peramohi & Victory Obelisk
17 Institute of Foreign Languages
18 German Embassy
19 Goethe Institute
22 Old Town (Traetskae Prodmestse)
24 SS Peter & Paul Church
25 Rakovsky Brovar

26 Na Nemige
27 Belavia
28 Tsentralny Universam
29 Air Grip
30 French Embassy
31 Holy Spirit Cathedral
32 Bernardine Church
33 Palats Respubliki
34 Museum of the Great Patriotic War
35 Trade Unions' Culture Palace; Zio Pepe
36 Tsentralny Skver
37 Presidential Administrative Building
39 Beltelekom
40 OVPS (OVIR)
41 GUM Department Store
42 Tsentralnaja Kniharnya Mahazin

43 KGB Building
45 Train Ticket Office
46 Belarusian State Art Museum
47 Dinamo Stadium
48 Ukraine Embassy
49 Belarus National Museum of History & Culture
51 Stary Mensk
52 Mastatsky Salon
53 Theatre Ticket Office
54 Central Post & Telegraph Office
55 U Zheni Travel Agency
56 Church of Sts Simon & Elena
57 Belarusian Government Building
58 Belarusian State University
60 Bus Station

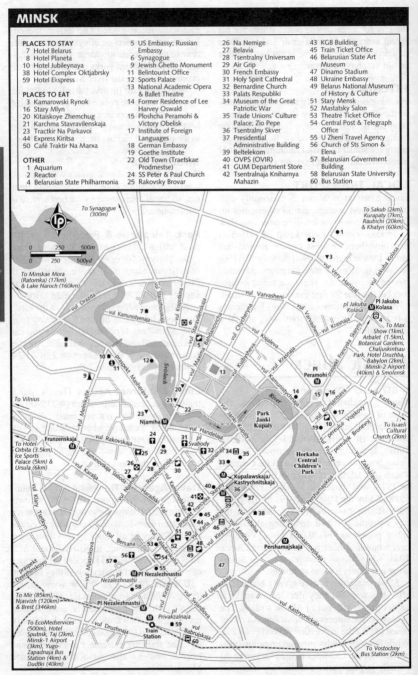

Bookshops A good selection of dictionaries, maps, postcards, souvenirs, English-language coffee-table books and posters of Lukashenka can be found at the **Tsentralnaja Kniharnya Mahazin** (☎ 227 49 18; praspekt Francyska Skaryny 19; open 10am-8pm Mon-Fri, 10am-6pm Sat).

Cultural Centres The following are good places to catch up on current events, swap stories with expats or just get your hands on a good book, newspaper or magazine.

Goethe Institute (☎ 236 34 33) vulitsa Frunze 5. Open 9am to 6pm Monday to Thursday and 8am to 4.30pm Friday.
Israeli Cultural Centre (☎ 230 18 74) vulitsa Uralskaja 3. Open 9am to 5pm Sunday to Friday. It has a small library of mostly Russian-language material.
Scientific Methodics Centre (☎ 236 79 53) Institute of Foreign Languages, vulitsa Zakharava 21. In place of the defunct British Council, this reading room is set to open by the end of 2002 and include some foreign-language books and journals.

Medical Services No reliable, Western-run clinics operate, but the **EcoMedservices** (☎ 220 45 81; vulitsa Tolstoho 4) is open around the clock and comes the closest.

Praspekt Francyska Skaryny

Minsk's main thoroughfare is hectic and huge: it's a six-lane monster extending over 11km from the train station to the outer city limits. The busiest section – and where the best architectural examples of Soviet monumentalism can be seen – is between Ploshcha Nezalezhnastsi and Ploshcha Peramohi.

The stubbornly austere and huge **Ploshcha Nezalezhnastsi** (Independence Square; or Ploshchad Nezavisimosti in Russian) is dominated by the Belarusian government building (behind the Lenin statue) on its northern side, and the equally proletarian Belarusian State University on the south side. When a current massive reconstruction project is completed, it promises to look more inviting.

Breaking the theme of Soviet classicism that dominates the square is the red-brick catholic **Church of Sts Simon & Elena** (1910), next to the Belarusian government building. Its tall, gabled bell tower and attractive detailing are reminiscent of many brick churches in the former Teutonic north of Poland.

Many of Minsk's main shops and cafés are northwest of the main square, including **GUM department store** (☎ 226 10 48; praspekt Francyska Skaryny 21). An entire block at No 17 is occupied by a yellow neoclassical building with an ominous, temple-like Corinthian portal – the **KGB headquarters**. On the other side of the street is a long narrow park with a **bust** of Felix Dzerzhynsky, the founder of the KGB's predecessor, the Cheka, and a native of Belarus.

Between vulitsa Enhelsa and vulitsa Janki Kupaly is a square that is still referred to by its Russian name, Oktyabrskaya ploshchad. Here you'll find the impressively severe **Palats Respubliki** (Palace of the Republic), a concert hall which opened in 2001 after some 15 years in construction.

Also on this square is the classical, multi-columned **Trade Unions' Culture Palace**, and next to this, the highly recommended **Museum of the Great Patriotic War** (☎ 277 56 11; praspekt Francyska Skaryny 25A; admission BR5000; open 10am-5pm Tues-Sun). The 28 well-designed rooms display the horrors of WWII. Particularly harrowing are the photographs of partisans being executed in recognisable central Minsk locations.

Across the street is **Tsentralny Skver** (Central Square), a small park on the site of a 19th-century marketplace. Behind this is the **Presidential Administrative Building**, where Lukashenka makes most of his wise decisions. It's also his residence and as such is well guarded.

As praspekt Francyska Skaryny crosses the Svislach River, it passes two of the city's main parks, **Park Janki Kupaly** on the southwest bank, and the larger **Park Horkaha** children's park, with attractions and fast-food kiosks. Just across the bridge, on the west bank of the river is the **apartment building** (vulitsa Kamunistychnaja 4) where Lee Harvey Oswald (the future alleged assassin of the US president John F Kennedy) lived for a few years in his early 20s.

Ploshcha Peramohi (Victory Square; Ploshchad Pobedy in Russian) is marked by a giant victory obelisk that rises up from the centre of the busy intersection. The eternal flame at its base is accessible by the underground passageway.

Further north is **Ploshcha Jakuba Kolasa**, another expansive square. Praspekt Francyska Skaryny continues northeast, becoming a bit

BELARUS

of a student ghetto around metro Akademija Navuk. Beyond the ho-hum **Botanical Gardens** *(Ploshcha Kalinina; admission BR500; open 10am-6pm daily early May-late Oct)* and the adjacent, sprawling, forest-like **Chaljuskintsau Park**, the praspekt's shops, cafés and commercial buildings become residential.

Old Town (Traetskae Prodmestse)

The congested overpass that now carries vulitsa Lenina over vulitsa Njamiha near the Njamiha metro station was the site of Minsk's main marketplace in the 12th century. In May 1999 the metro entrance was the site of a brutal stampede in which 53 people died. There is now a memorial at the site.

Ploshcha Svabody to the south-east became the new city centre in the 16th century. The baroque, twin-towered Orthodox **Holy Spirit Cathedral** off the northern end of the small square stands defiantly on a small hill overlooking its rather bleak surroundings. It was once part of a Polish Bernardine convent (founded in 1628) along with the former **Bernardine Church** next door, which now houses city archives.

Across the vulitsa Lenina overpass is the attractively restored 17th-century **SS Peter & Paul Church**, the city's oldest church (built in 1613, restored in 1871), awkwardly dwarfed by the surrounding morose concrete structures.

A miniscule area on the eastern bank of the Svislach River, bordered by vulitsa Maxima Bahdanovicha, has been rebuilt in 17th- and 18th-century styles to re-create the look and feel of much of Minsk during those eras. This Old Town is known as Traetskae Prodmestse (Trinity Suburb). There are a few cafés, bars, restaurants and craft/gift shops to tempt you for a lazy hour. Two blocks northeast is the bulky-looking, run-down **National Academic Opera & Ballet Theatre** set in a leafy park.

Other Museums

There is so much history and culture at the **Belarus National Museum of History & Culture** *(vulitsa Karla Marxa 12; admission BR5000; open 11am-7pm Thur-Tues)*, most visitors leave with their heads spinning. It takes you on a journey through the turbulent history of the nation.

More interesting is the **Belarusian State Art Museum** *(☎ 227 71 63; vulitsa Lenina 20; admission BR5000; open 11am-7pm Wed-Mon)*. Here you'll find the country's largest collection of Belarusian art as well as some minor European paintings and ceramics.

Places to Stay

With few exceptions, hotels in Minsk follow a predictable mould – unremarkable and overpriced.

Camping There are no longer any official camping sites near Minsk, though the authorities are not tough on those who pitch their tent unobtrusively in outlying wooded areas.

Hotels – Budget At the eastern end of the train station is **Hotel Ekspress** *(☎ 225 64 63; Privakzalnaja ploshcha 4; beds in 4-person room BR20,000, shared doubles per person BR26,000, luxury doubles BR118,000)*, a no-frills affair that may be your best bet, if you don't mind the absence of showers. All rooms have toilets.

If you can navigate yourself through the brazenly impolite service at the front desk and actually get some information about availability, the **Hotel Sputnik** *(☎ 229 36 19; vulitsa Brilevskaja 2; singles/doubles from BR40,000/57,000)* has some of the city's least expensive rooms.

Hotel Druzhba *(☎ 266 24 81; vulitsa Tolbukhina 3; singles/doubles/triples BR55,000/81,000/60,000)*, near the Park Chaljuskintsau metro station, has spartan rooms and a slightly seedy atmosphere, but its triple rooms are some of the best deals in the city.

Hotels – Mid-Range Rising above a concrete suburb near Metro Pushkinskaja is **Hotel Orbita** *(☎ 252 32 08, fax 257 14 20; praspekt Pushkina 39; singles/doubles from $35/50)*, which boasts friendly, attentive service and dull but decent rooms.

The snazzy, full-service lobby of the **Hotel Jubileynaya** *(☎ 226 90 24, fax 226 91 71; praspekt Masherava 19; singles/doubles from $47/58, renovated singles/doubles from $62/75)* may come as a welcome contrast to its dull, grey exterior but is sadly no indication of the rooms therein. Except for the luxury suites, they're all the same brand of mediocre.

About 200m away from the Jubileynaja is the **Hotel Planeta** *(☎ 226 78 55, fax 226 77 80; praspekt Masherava 31; singles/doubles from $70/80)*, with an equally pretty, marbled lobby and rooms that are more comfortable and modern.

Hotels – Top End The towering 23-storey Hotel Belarus (☎ 209 76 93, fax 239 12 33; e belarus@hotel.minsk.by; vulitsa Staraz-houskaja 15; singles $55-80, doubles $80-100, suites from $160) has several renovated floors, but aside from the best city views (ask for a room facing the centre), there is nothing noteworthy about this giant.

For years considered to be the tops in central Minsk, the **Hotel Complex Oktjabrsky** (☎ 222 32 89, fax 227 33 14; vulitsa Enhelsa 13; singles/doubles from $80/95, suites $135-190) has a rather humorous formality to it, perhaps due to its location right behind the President's Office. Rooms are starchly tasteful and comfortable.

Places to Eat

Your best bets for a good meal are the places listed under Belarusian cuisine.

Belarusian The city's best restaurant, hands-down, is **Stary Mlyn** (☎ 284 44 40; praspekt Francyska Skaryny 40; mains BR5000-8000; open noon-midnight daily), boasting four rarities in the Minsk restaurant world – a cosy atmosphere, creative and mouth-watering food, friendly service and reasonable prices. A great place to try some local food.

A good bet for traditional cuisine is the **Tractkir Na Parkavoi** (☎ 223 69 91; praspekt Masherava 11; mains BR6000-15,000; open noon-midnight daily), a pleasant early-20th-century country kitchen tucked behind a row of cement blocks.

Another excellent choice that serves decent Belarusian food like draniki is **Café Traktir Na Marxa** (☎ 226 03 61; vulitsa Karla Marxa 21; mains BR3000-7000), but it's the relaxed atmosphere in this cellar café-cum-bar that makes it a good hang-out.

Ethnic In the Trade Unions' Culture Palace is **Zio Pepe** (☎ 227 02 95; praspekt Francyska Skaryny 25; pizza BR3500-5500; open noon-4am daily) which has OK, thin-crust pizza and other Italian fare in an always-crowded, smoky basement.

Another winner is **Taj** (☎ 229 35 92; vulitsa Brilevskaja 2; mains BR6000-13,000; open noon-midnight daily), serving up delicious North Indian food in a subdued atmosphere – until the belly dancer comes on, that is. There's a good selection of vegetarian dishes (all under BR6000).

There are several Chinese eateries, including **Kitaiskoye Zhemchug** (☎ 234 94 41; vulitsa Staravilenskaja 10; mains from about BR12,000; open noon-11pm) which is seriously overplush but has authentic dishes.

Cafés Within the Old Town, try **Karchma Stavravilenskaja** (☎ 289 37 54; vulitsa Staravilenskaja 2; open 11am-midnight daily), along the riverfront, which has a breezy summer terrace and low-key interiors. The terrace at **Air Grip** (☎ 226 90 98; vulitsa Njamiha 3; open 10am-11pm daily) is ultra popular with poseurs and Italian tourists, who appreciate the excellent espresso and gelato.

Self Catering & Fast Food The immense **Kamarowski Rynok** (vulitsa Very Haruzaj 6) is a minicity of market mayhem with lots of fresh produce. The best-stocked grocery shop is the **Tsentralny Universam** (☎ 227 88 76; praspekt Francyska Skaryny 23; open 9am-11pm daily).

An interesting alternative to the standard nearby McDonald's is **Express Kiritsa** (☎ 226 17 08; praspekt Francyska Skaryny 18; meals under BR7000; open 11am-11pm daily), a two-floor cafeteria where all the food, happily swimming in grease, is visible.

Entertainment

Bars The best place for a Belarusian pint is **Rakovsky Brovar** (☎ 206 64 04; vulitsa Vitsebskaja 10; open noon-midnight daily). Because of the four beers brewed on site, this has become the city's most popular place for suds-lovers. The food is largely unsurprising.

You can get sauced in front of the KGB building at the tiny **Stary Mensk** (☎ 289 14 00; praspekt Francyska Skaryny 14; open 8.30am-11.30pm daily), which displays more photos of pre-WWII Minsk than you'll find at any museum.

Clubs Discos are widespread, but as prices are prohibitive for ordinary Belarusians, you are likely to face a predictable crowd – leather jackets, short skirts, wads of cash. **Reactor** (☎ 288 61 60; vulitsa Very Haruzaj 29; open 10pm-5am Tues-Sun), which often has live music, attracts a young crowd. One block north, **Aquarium** (☎ 231 20 53; vulitsa Kulman 14; open 10pm-5am daily) maintains a reputation for the city's best live shows and a fairly relaxed environment.

BELARUS

Probably the least pretentious and most fun-spirited club in town is the city's premier gay club, **Babylon** (☎ 8-029 677 04 45; vulitsa Tolbukhina 4; open 10pm-6am Tues-Sun), where people of all persuasions gather just to have a good time.

Classical Music, Opera & Ballet Minsk has quite a lively cultural life and its **Belarusian Ballet** is one of the best companies in the whole of Eastern Europe. Operas and ballets are regularly performed at the grand, ominous-looking **National Academic Opera & Ballet Theatre** (☎ 234 06 52; Ploshcha Parizhskoy Kamuni 1).

For classical music, the **Belarusian State Philharmonia** (☎ 284 44 27; praspekt Francyska Skaryny 50) also has a high reputation – it has folk ensembles as well as a symphony orchestra and performs everything from classical through to jazz. To buy advance tickets or to find out what's on, head to the **ticket office** (teatralnaja kasa; praspekt Francyska Skaryny 13). Same-day tickets are usually available only from the theatres.

The Belarusian Musical Autumn in the last 10 days of November is a festival of folk and classical music and dance.

Spectator Sports

Dinamo Minsk, Belarus' top soccer club (which often appears in European competitions), has a 55,000-capacity **stadium** (☎ 227 26 11; vulitsa Kirava 8). The **Ice Sports Palace** (☎ 252 50 22; vulitsa Prititskoho 27) and sometimes the **Sports Palace** (☎ 223 44 83; praspekt Masherava 4) host stellar ice-hockey matches.

Shopping

Souvenirs are often sold in hotel lobbies and department stores. **Mastatsky Salon** (☎ 227 83 63; praspekt Francyska Skaryny 12) has a good selection of porcelain and wooden souvenirs. Most days, a small outdoor tourist market operates in the small space between the Trade Unions' House of Culture and the Museum of the Great Patriotic War.

Getting There & Away

Air Most international flights use Minsk-2 airport, about 40km east of the city off the Moscow highway. A few shorter flights to neighbouring countries use Minsk-1 airport, at the end of vulitsa Chkalava, about 3km

south of Ploshcha Nezalezhnastsi (flights to Moscow and St Petersburg use both airports).

The Belarusian national airline, **Belavia**, has a downtown **office** (☎ 210 41 00; vulitsa Njamiha 14).

Train Minsk is located on the main Moscow-Warsaw-Berlin line, with at least 15 trains daily to Moscow (BR33,700, 12 hours), two to Warsaw (BR45,000, nine to 12 hours), and one daily to Berlin (BR105,000, 18 hours). Other trains go to St Petersburg, Kaliningrad, Kyiv, Vilnius, Prague, Tallinn and Rīga.

Domestic trains include about eight a day to Brest (BR14,000, 4½ to 10 hours). Three trains a day go to Hrodna (BR11,000, five to eight hours).

Ticket counters are on both sides of the main entrance hall of the **Minsk train station** (☎ 005 or 596 54 10). For the non-CIS international destinations like Prague and Warsaw, counter #13 sells tickets for the day of departure only (open 8pm to 8am every day); it's better to go to the **international ticket office** (☎ 225 30 67; vulitsa Voronyanskoho 6). To buy tickets for domestic and CIS destinations, you can also use the **ticket office** (☎ 225 61 24; praspekt Francyska Skaryny 18; open 9am-8pm Mon-Fri, 9am-7pm Sat-Sun). The tickets for slow electric trains to suburban destinations are sold in the smaller building just west (to the right) of the train station.

Bus Minsk has several bus stations. Most of those for international destinations depart from the central **long-distance bus station** (tsentralny avtovokzal; ☎ 004 or 227 37 25; vulitsa Babrujskaja 12), about 200m east of the train station. Other buses go to Bialystok, Kaunas, Vilnius, Rīga and Tallinn.

Vostochny (eastern) bus station (☎ 248 58 21) is about 3km southeast of the centre. Daily buses leaving Vostochny bus station include those to Warsaw (BR36,000, 11 hours). From the **Moskovsky bus station** (☎ 264 93 13), about 1km northeast of Chaljuskintsau Park, buses and minibuses leave twice daily to Vitsebsk (BR10,500, 6½ hours) and Polatsk (BR8000, five hours).

Intercars (☎ 226 90 22; w www.intercars .ru), inside the Hotel Jubileynaja, sells tickets for long-distance buses to Amsterdam ($105), Paris ($140), Rome ($200) and other European destinations. Intercars also offers a 10% student discount.

Getting Around

To/From the Airport The taxi drivers who lurk around Minsk-2 airport are vultures who all want about $40 for the 40-minute ride into the city (it should cost about $15 to $20). There are also hourly buses that cost BR2000 (but take 90 minutes) and bring you to the central bus station. There are also regular minibuses that make the trip in under an hour and cost only BR3500.

Bus & Trolleybus Busy buses and trolleybuses, operating 5.30am to 1am, serve all parts of the city. Trolleybus Nos 1, 2 and 18 ply praspekt Francyska Skaryny from Ploshcha Nezalezhnastsi to Ploshcha Peramohi.

AROUND MINSK
Dudutki Дудуткі

Near the sleepy, dusty village of Dudutki, which is 40km south of Minsk (15km east after a cut-off from the P23 highway) is an open-air **museum** (☎ 213-7 25 25, 017-269 09 60; admission BR9000, open 10am-8pm Tues-Sun May-Oct) where 19th-century Belarusian country life is re-created. Guided tours cost BR33,000 and an English-speaking guide costs $25 per group.

Traditional crafts such as carpentry, pottery, handicraft-making and bakery are on display in old-style wood and hay houses. You can wander around the grounds and spy on a working farm as it was a century ago. Nearby is a working windmill which you can climb. You can also go horse-ridding. Best of all, though, is the sumptuous traditional meal you can order, prepared on the premises. Homemade cheeses, bread, *draniki*, *kolduni*, and pork sausages all go down so well, especially with a shot of local *samagon* (moonshine). A full-course meal will cost only about BR10,000.

Getting There & Away Getting to Dudutki by public transport is iffy. There are about three buses daily which go to Ptich from Minsk's Yugo-Zapadnaja bus station, which let you off at the village of Dudutki, a 2km walk to the museum complex. Travel agencies will be happy to organise excursions for you. Hailing a cab from central Minsk there will cost about BR60,000 there and back.

Khatyn Хатынь

The hamlet of Khatyn, which is 60km north of Minsk, was burned to the ground with all its

inhabitants in a 1943 Nazi reprisal. The site is now a sobering memorial centred on a sculpture modelled on the only survivor, Yuzif Kaminsky. Also here are the Graveyard of Villages, commemorating 185 other Belarusian villages annihilated by the Fascists; the Trees of Life (actually concrete posts) commemorating a further 433 villages that were destroyed but rebuilt; and a Memory Wall listing the Nazi concentration camps in Belarus and some of their victims.

Khatyn is 5km east of the Minsk-Vitsebsk road (M3). The turn-off is about 15km north of Lohoysk, opposite the village of Kazyry. There's no reliable public transport out there, but a taxi will cost around BR60,000 for the return journey from Minsk. Organised trips are available through Minsk's Belintourist run during the summer and cost about $65 for small groups.

Mir Mip
☎ 01770

About 85km southwest of Minsk and 8km north off the Minsk-Brest road is the small town of Mir where, overlooking a pond, sits the 16th-century Mir Castle, once owned by the powerful Radziwill princes. Since 1994, it has been under Unesco protection. Built predominantly of stone and red brick, it's a walled complex with five towers surrounding a courtyard and keep. Today the castle is under restoration, but one tower is already open as an **archaeological museum** (admission BR250; open 10am-5pm Wed-Sun).

Due to the Unesco recognition, Lukashenka signed a decree in 2002 to turn Mir into Belarus' prettiest village, and consequently much reconstruction is underway. Most tourists, however, will find the area, including the castle, decidedly ho-hum, especially when compared to Njasvizh.

Getting There & Away From the central bus station in Minsk there are about 10 buses a day to the town of Navahrudak (Novogrudok in Russian), stopping in Mir (BR6000, two to 2½ hours) shortly after they turn off the main highway. (See directions for Njasvizh for an alternative way of getting to Mir.)

Njasvizh Нясвіж
☎ 01770

Njasvizh, 120km southwest of Minsk, is one of the oldest sites in the country, dating from the 13th century. It reached its zenith in the mid-16th century while owned by the mighty Radziwill magnates, who had the town redesigned and rebuilt with the most advanced system of fortification known at the time. Today it's a random mix of painted wooden cottages and bland housing, but with enough fine pieces of 16th-century architecture and a great park.

The impressive and sombre **Farny Polish Roman Catholic Church** was built between 1584 and 1593 in early baroque style and features a splendidly proportioned facade. Just beyond the church is the red-brick arcaded **Castle Gate Tower**. Built in the 16th century, the tower was part of a wall and gateway controlling the passage between the palace and the town. Here there's an **excursion bureau** where you pay to enter the **fortress grounds** (☎ 2 13 67; unguided admission BR450; open 8am-5pm daily). Farther on is a causeway leading to the **Radziwill Palace Fortress** (1583) designed by the Italian architect Bernardoni (who was also responsible for the Farny Church). In Soviet times it was turned into a sanatorium.

The splendid, lush parkland and nearby lake make for fitting surroundings. There's pedal and row-boat rental across another causeway, on the banks of Lake Dzikaya, a very nice picnic area.

Places to Stay & Eat Behind the town hall, **Hotel Njasvizh** (☎ 5 53 67; vulitsa Belaruskaja 9; singles/doubles BR40,000/66,000) is a friendly place with a shabby baroque quality and a sleepy restaurant. Rooms here are simple and decent.

You can probably find something decent at the **Kafe Njasvizh** (vulitsa Savetskaja 15; open 11am-7pm Tues-Sun).

Getting There & Away Buses that travel to Kletsk, about 16km south of Njasvizh, stop at Njasvizh (BR6700, 2½ to three hours) along the way, but only once or twice a day from Minsk.

Alternatively, take one of the six daily electric trains to Baranavichy and get off at the Haradzeja stop, about two hours (12 stops) from Minsk. At least 15 buses a day make the 30-minute trip from Haradzeja to Njasvizh. Every day there are also two buses running between Njasvizh and Mir, stopping in Haradzeja en route.

Elsewhere in Belarus

There remains much to entice the traveller off the beaten path. In cities such as Hrodna historic vestiges remain, and many of the small villages are still lost somewhere in the 18th century. The countryside is serene with great swathes of forest, clusters of lakes, streams and rivers, drawing many campers and hikers from the cities.

BREST БРЭСТ
☎ 0162 • pop 294,000

Brest, on the border with Poland, has always had a more cosmopolitan and Western feel than elsewhere in the country, Minsk included. It is on one of the busiest road and rail border points in Eastern Europe. Aside from its laidback pace, charming side streets and the friendliness of the locals, Brest will dazzle you with a true wonder of the Soviet era – Brest Fortress, an astounding war memorial.

First mentioned in 1019 and originally known as Bereste, Brest was sacked by the Tatars in 1241 and tossed between Slavic, Lithuanian and Polish control for several decades until it finally settled under the control of the Grand Duchy of Lithuania. In 1654, the Russians invaded.

The Treaty of Brest-Litovsk was negotiated here in March 1918. Brest was on the front line when Germany attacked the USSR on 22 June 1941. For its heroic defence, Brest was named one of the former Soviet Union's 11 'Hero Cities' of WWII.

Information

Brest Intourist (☎ 20 05 10; praspekt Masherava 15; open 9am-6pm Mon-Fri), inside Hotel Intourist, is super-friendly and can make organising tours much easier for you.

Nearby, **Beltelekom** (☎ 22 13 15; praspekt Masherava 21) has Internet access for BR1800 an hour; long-distance calls can be made from here as well.

Churches & Museums

The breathtakingly detailed, 200-year-old Orthodox **St Nikalaiv Church** (cnr vulitsa Savetskaja & vulitsa Mitskevicha) is one of many lovely churches in Brest. On Ploshcha Lenina, a **statue** of Lenin points east towards Moscow, but it appears more to be pointing

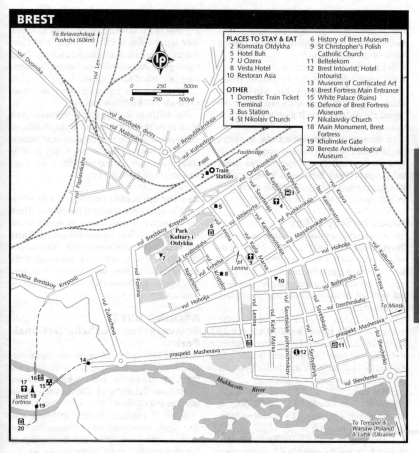

BREST

PLACES TO STAY & EAT		OTHER
2 Komnata Otdykha	6 History of Brest Museum	1 Domestic Train Ticket Terminal
5 Hotel Buh	9 St Christopher's Polish Catholic Church	3 Bus Station
7 U Ozera	11 Beltelekom	4 St Nikolaiv Church
8 Vesta Hotel	12 Brest Intourist; Hotel Intourist	13 Museum of Confiscated Art
10 Restoran Asia		14 Brest Fortress Main Entrance
		15 White Palace (Ruins)
		16 Defence of Brest Fortress Museum
		17 Nikalaivsky Church
		18 Main Monument, Brest Fortress
		19 Kholmskie Gate
		20 Bereste Archaeological Museum

BELARUS

across the street accusatorily to the 1856 **St Christopher's Polish Catholic Church**.

The Regional Museum has several branches throughout the city, the most interesting being the **History of Brest Museum** (☎ 23 17 65; *vulitsa Levatevskaha 3; admission BR160; open 10am-5pm Wed-Sun*), which has a small exhibit on the city in its different guises throughout history, and notably the great **Museum of Confiscated Art** (☎ 20 41 95; *vulitsa Lenina 39; admission BR160; open 10am-5pm Tues-Sun*), which displays valuable art pieces seized by Brest border guards as they were being smuggled out of the country.

Brest Fortress

If you are going to see only one Soviet WWII memorial in your life, make it **Brest Fortress**

(*Brestskaja krepost;* ☎ 20 41 09; *praspekt Masherava; admission free*). It's at the western end of praspekt Masherava, about a 20-minute walk from the centre; the hourly bus No 17 travels between here and Hotel Intourist.

Built between 1838 and 1842, by WWII the fortress was used mainly for housing soldiers. Nevertheless, two regiments bunking here at the time of the sudden German invasion in 1941 defended the aged fort for an astounding month.

Inside the complex, the enormous central monument comes into view – a stone soldier's head projecting from a massive rock, entitled 'Valour'. As you enter, to your right are the brick ruins of the **White Palace**, where the 1918 Treaty of Brest-Litovsk was signed. Farther to the right is the **Defence of Brest**

Fortress Museum (☎ 20 03 65; admission BR200; open 9.30am-6pm Tues-Sun). Its extensive and dramatic exhibits demonstrate the plight of the defenders.

Behind the Valour rock is the attractive, partly ruined shell of the Byzantine **Nikalaivsky Church**, the oldest church in the city, which dates from when the town centre occupied the fortress site. It now holds regular services.

To the south is **Kholmskie Gate**; its bricks are decorated with crenulated turrets and its outer face is riddled with hundreds of bullet and shrapnel holes. Beyond, is **Bereste archaeological museum** (☎ 20 55 54; admission BR160; open 9.30am-6pm Tues-Sun).

Places to Stay & Eat

For true and proud penny-pinchers, **Komnata Otdykha** (Rest Room; ☎ 27 39 67; beds in 8-person dorm BR3500) is a sort-of hostel on the 2nd floor of the train station's main building. Toilets are shared, there are no showers, and you can be assured colourful characters as roommates.

Perhaps the most pleasant hotel in the country is **Vesta Hotel** (☎ 23 71 69, fax 23 78 39; vulitsa Krupskoi 16; singles/doubles BR49,000/63,000). Rooms are quaint and comfortable (all have TV and fridge), and the surroundings are quiet and green.

Hotel Buh (☎ 23 64 17; vulitsa Lenina 2; singles/doubles from BR35,000/58,000) is set in a stately building. If your room faces the street, it'll be noisy.

A good bet for a meal is the **Restoran Asia** (☎ 26 63 25; vulitsa Hoholja 29; mains average BR6000; open noon-11pm Tues-Sun), which has a good selection of spicy Korean and Chinese dishes.

You can enjoy simple and cheap shashliks at **U Ozera** (☎ 23 57 63; Park Kultury I Otdykha; entrees BR3000-7500, mains BR7000-17,000; open 11am-1am daily), perched by a pond in the city's prettiest park. It also serves tasty, more elaborate fish and meat meals.

Getting There & Away

Train The impressive, classical Brest **train station** (☎ 005) is a busy place, as the city is an important border crossing on the Warsaw-Minsk-Moscow line. There are at least five trains a day to Warsaw (BR15,000, four to five hours) and Moscow (BR45,000, 12 to 15 hours), stopping at Minsk (BR14,000, five to

six hours) and Smolensk on the way. There are also much slower electric trains to Minsk four times a day (up to 10½ hours), and one express train called *Bereste* (4½ hours). Other trains go to Prague, Vienna, Berlin, St Petersburg, Kyiv and Kaliningrad.

Other domestic trains include a daily train to Hrodna (BR9200, 8¼ hours).

For all trains leaving Brest for Poland, you have to go through customs at the station, so get there early. Tickets for domestic electric trains are sold in the *passazhirsky pavilon* (passenger train terminal) behind the train station, away from the city.

Bus The **bus station** (☎ 004 or 23 81 42) is in the centre of town, next to the market. There are at least two daily buses or minibuses to Hrodna (BR10,500, four to 6½ hours). There are also about five buses daily to Warsaw (BR12,000, five hours) and at least once daily to Lviv (BR11,500, nine hours). Through-buses go on to Prague (BR100,000, 15 hours) once a week.

AROUND BREST
Belavezhskaja Pushcha National Park

About 1300 sq km of primeval forest survives in the Belavezhskaja Pushcha National Park (☎ 01631-56 370), which stretches north from the town of Kamjanjuky, about 60km north of Brest.

Some 55 mammal species including elk, deer, lynx, boar, wild horse, badger, ermine, wolf, marten, otter, mink and beaver live in the park but it is most celebrated for its 300 European bison, the continent's largest land mammal. These free-range *zoobr* were driven to extinction by 1919 and then bred back into existence from 52 animals that had survived in zoos. Now a total of about 2000 exist.

The reserve went from obscurity to the front page in late 1991, as the presidents of Belarus, Russia and Ukraine officially signed the death certificate of the USSR with a document creating the Commonwealth of Independent States (CIS) at the Viskuli dacha here.

You can take excursions, but these are best organised through Belarus Intourist (see Information in the Brest section earlier) for about $60 for a small group – particularly as this area is considered a border zone and visitors not in a pre-arranged group need special permission to be there.

HRODNA ГРОДНА

☎ 0152 • pop 290,000

Hrodna (Grodno in Russian), 282km west of Minsk, survived the war better than anywhere else in Belarus and has more historic buildings intact to prove it. As such, there are some picturesque corners. Settled since ancient times and first mentioned in 1128, it was absorbed by Lithuania in the late-14th century, and went to Russia in the late-18th century.

Overrun in WWI, the city was one of the first to be besieged by the invading Germans in 1941. It fell easily, suffering far less damage than it did when the Soviet forces came back through at the end of WWII. In the process, the once multiethnic population of Hrodna, including a large Jewish contingency, was wiped out.

Today it's an industrial and cultural centre and, with its proximity to both Lithuania (42km away) and Poland (24km), has a bit of a cosmopolitan atmosphere.

Information

The **main post office** (☎ 72 00 60; vulitsa Karla Marxa 29) also harbours a tiny and crowded **Internet club** (open 8am-8pm Mon-Fri, 10am-4pm Sat-Sun) with access for BR3200 an hour. The same building also has a currency exchange booth.

Churches & Museums

Near the train station, is the attractive 1904–5 **Pokrovsky Cathedral** (vulitsa Azhyeshka 23), a red-and-white candy house with blue-and-gold domes. Nearby, is the tiny **Museum**

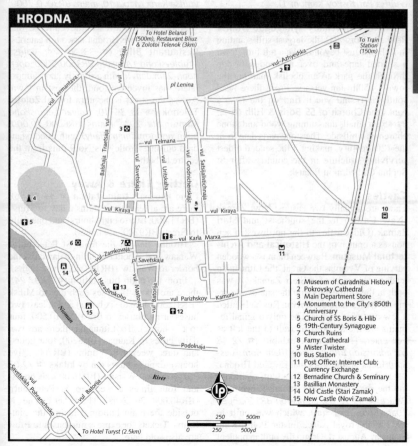

HRODNA

1 Museum of Garadnitsa History
2 Pokrovsky Cathedral
3 Main Department Store
4 Monument to the City's 850th Anniversary
5 Church of SS Boris & Hlib
6 19th-Century Synagogue
7 Church Ruins
8 Farny Cathedral
9 Mister Twister
10 Bus Station
11 Post Office; Internet Club; Currency Exchange
12 Bernadine Church & Seminary
13 Basilian Monastery
14 Old Castle (Stari Zamak)
15 New Castle (Novi Zamak)

BELARUS

of Garadnitsa History (☎ 72 16 69; vulitsa Azhyeshka 37; admission BR160; open 10am-6pm Tues-Sat), a good place to pick up handcrafted items and souvenirs.

At the northeastern corner of Ploshcha Savetskaja is the proud and pointy baroque Farny Cathedral (☎ 44 26 77), perhaps the most impressive church in Belarus. Built during Polish rule in the 18th century and still Catholic, it boasts a row of ornate altars leading to a huge main altarpiece constructed of multiple columns interspersed with sculpted saints. Another church once stood on the opposite side of the square. It was damaged in WWII and later razed by the Soviet regime; fragmented foundation ruins mark the spot.

Also worth a visit is the 16th-century Catholic Bernadine Church & Seminary (vulitsa Parizhskoy Kamuni 1).

Beyond the turn-off for the castle, is a dilapidated 19th-century synagogue (vulitsa Balshaja Troiskaja), the largest still standing in Belarus. Just beyond, take a left turn down a shaded lane and over a wooden bridge through the park to an obelisk marking the town's 850th anniversary. From there head south (left) and you'll find on the river's banks the Church of SS Boris & Hlib (☎ 72 31 45), a small, unassuming wood-and-stone church on a hillside. The stone parts date from the 12th century, making it the second oldest surviving structure in the country after St Sophia Cathedral in Polatsk.

Castles

There are actually two castles, Novi Zamak (New Castle) to the southeast and Stari Zamak (Old Castle) to the northwest. Each houses a branch of the Historical and Architectural Museum. Between them is a wooden carving of Vytautas the Great, the Lithuanian leader responsible for Stari Zamak. It was built in the 14th century on the site overlooking the river where the Kyivan Rus had settled a few centuries earlier. The only original remains are the sections of wall to the left as you enter. The extensive exhibits (☎ 72 18 51; admission BR570; open 10am-6pm Tues-Sun) focus on the wars that ravaged Hrodna.

On the opposite side of the bluff overlooking the river is the Novi Zamak (Governor's Palace; ☎ 44 72 69; admission BR160; open 10am-6pm Tues-Sun), which was built in 1737 as the royal palace for the Polish King Stanislav August II. Originally built in opulent rococo, it was completely gutted by fire and rebuilt in a subdued classical style.

Places to Stay

Of the limited choice, Hotel Belarus (☎ 44 16 74, fax 44 41 45; vulitsa Kalinovskoho 1; singles/doubles BR40,500/62,500) is the best. Staff are friendly and the rooms decent. Catch Bus No 15 from the train station.

More modern is the Hotel Turyst (☎ 26 99 48, fax 26 98 73; praspekt Janki Kupaly 63; singles/doubles from BR40,000/55,000), but it's in a dull, grey concrete suburban area 4km southeast of the centre.

Places to Eat

In the centre, virtually your only choice is the tacky bar-café Mister Twister (☎ 47 09 89; vulitsa Karla Marxa 10; mains BR3000-7000; open 11am-midnight daily).

About 4km northwest of the centre, beyond Hotel Belarus, are Hrodna's two top eateries. Restaurant Bliuz (☎ 33 29 74; vulitsa Vrublevskoho 1A; mains BR3500-9000; open noon-2am daily), with a slightly jazzy atmosphere, has inventive food, the best in town. Across the street is the ultra formal Zolotoi Telenok (☎ 33 36 10; bulvar Leninskoho Kamsamola 29A; mains BR6000-10,000; open noon-midnight daily) with good, standard cuisine. Trolleybus No 9 runs from the centre to both.

Getting There & Away

From Hrodna's train station (☎ 44 85 56), there are at least three trains a day to Minsk (BR11,000, five to eight hours) and one daily to Brest (BR9200, 8¼ hours).

Hrodna lies on the main St Petersburg-Warsaw line. About two trains a day cross the border to Warsaw (BR19,000, seven hours).

From the main bus station (☎ 72 37 24), there are about 14 buses each day to Minsk (BR10,300, five to six hours) and at least two buses or minibuses to Brest (BR10,500, four to 6½ hours). To Lithuania, there are two daily buses to Kaunas (BR8200, four hours) and three weekly to Vilnius (BR7000, five hours). Express buses run by Intaks (☎ 72 02 30) go daily to Warsaw (BR16,000, six hours) and four times a week to St Petersburg (BR40,000, 20 hours). The ticket counter is outside the main building, facing the platforms. Tickets for express minibuses to Brest are also sold here.

Bosnia-Hercegovina

Sandwiched between Croatia and Yugoslavia, the small mountainous country of Bosnia-Hercegovina has been a meeting point of east and west for nearly two millennia. Here the realm of Orthodox Byzantium mingled with Catholic Rome, and the 15th-century swell of Turkish power settled among the Slavs. One of the most fascinating cultures in Europe has resulted, with a heterogeneous population of Croats, Serbs and Slavic converts to Islam.

In the 20th century Bosnia-Hercegovina had more than its share of strife. WWI was sparked in Sarajevo when a Serbian nationalist assassinated an Austrian aristocrat, and much of the bitter partisan fighting of WWII took place in this region. Forty-five years of peace ensued, with Bosnia-Hercegovina the third-largest republic in Yugoslavia. This ended soon after Bosnia-Hercegovina declared independence in October 1991. Six months later Bosnian Serb ultranationalists, assisted by Yugoslavia's federal army, began a campaign of ethnic cleansing intended to bring Bosnia-Hercegovina into Belgrade's orbit.

When the three-way war ended in 1995, the country was physically devastated and ethnically divided. Of a prewar population of 4.5 million, over two million fled their former homes. Peace is currently enforced by 17,000 NATO troops, and a large international civilian presence is working hard to reintegrate and rebuild the country. Progress since peace has been substantial and, though much of its heritage has been destroyed, Bosnia-Hercegovina shows proud resilience through its scars.

At a Glance

- **Sarajevo** – colourful trams and lively cafés in a city recovering its vibrancy
- **Mostar** – old medieval buildings; charming cobbled streets; aqua-green Neretva River
- **Blagaj** – Dervish monastery where the river Buna gushes out of the mountainside

Capital	Sarajevo
Population	3.8 million (2000 estimate)
Official Language	Bosnian (Serbo-Croatian)
Currency	1 convertible mark (KM) = 100 convertible pfennigs
Time	GMT/UTC+0100
Country Phone Code	☎ 387

The Two Entities of Bosnia-Hercegovina p110

Facts about Bosnia-Hercegovina

HISTORY

The region's ancient inhabitants were Illyrians, who were followed by the Romans who settled around the mineral springs at Ilidža near Sarajevo. When the Roman Empire was divided in AD 395, the Drina River, today the border between Bosnia-Hercegovina and Yugoslavia, became the line that divided the Western Roman Empire from Byzantium.

The Slav groups arrived in the late 6th and early 7th centuries. In 960 the region became independent of Serbia, only to pass through the hands of other conquerors: Croatia, Byzantium, Duklja (modern-day Montenegro) and Hungary. The first Turkish raids came in 1383 and by 1463 Bosnia was a Turkish province with Sarajevo as its capital. Hercegovina is named after Herceg (Duke) Stjepan Vukčić, who ruled the southern part of the present republic from his mountain-top castle at Blagaj near Mostar until the Turkish conquest in 1482.

During 400 years of Turkish rule, Bosnia-Hercegovina was completely assimilated and became the boundary between the Islamic and Christian worlds. Wars against Venice and Austria were frequent. Many inhabitants converted to Islam, and the region still forms a Muslim enclave deep within Christian Europe.

As the influence of the Ottoman Empire declined in the 16th and 17th centuries, the Turks strengthened their hold on Bosnia-Hercegovina as an advance bulwark. During the mid-19th century, national revival movements led to a reawakening among the South Slavs, and in 1875–76 peasants rose against the Turkish occupiers in Bosnia-Hercegovina and Bulgaria. In 1878 Russia inflicted a crushing defeat on Turkey in a war over Bulgaria, and it was decided at the Congress of Berlin in the same year that Austria-Hungary would occupy Bosnia-Hercegovina. But the population wanted autonomy and had to be brought under Habsburg rule by force.

Resentment against foreign occupation intensified in 1908 when Austria annexed Bosnia-Hercegovina outright. The assassination of the Habsburg heir Archduke Franz Ferdinand by a Bosnian Serb in Sarajevo on 28 June 1914 led Austria to declare war on Serbia one month later. When Russia supported Serbia, and Germany backed Austria, the world was soon at war.

Following WWI, Bosnia-Hercegovina was taken into the Serb-dominated Kingdom of the Serbs, Croats and Slovenes (renamed as Yugoslavia in 1929). During 1941 the Axis powers annexed Bosnia-Hercegovina to the fascist Croatian state, but the area's mountains quickly became a wartime partisan stronghold. A conference in 1943 in Jajce laid the ground for postwar Yugoslavia. After the war Bosnia-Hercegovina was granted republic status within Yugoslavia, which was ruled until 1980 by Josip Broz Tito.

In the republic's first free elections in November 1990, the communists were defeated easily by nationalist Serb and Croat parties and by a predominantly Muslim party favouring a multiethnic Bosnia-Hercegovina.

The Croat and Muslim parties united their efforts against the Serb nationalists, and independence from Yugoslavia was declared on 15 October 1991. Serb parliamentarians withdrew and set up their own government at Pale, the 1984 Olympic village 20km east of Sarajevo. Bosnia-Hercegovina was recognised internationally and admitted to the UN, but talks between the parties broke down.

The War

War broke out in April 1992, shortly after Bosnian Serb snipers in the Sarajevo Holiday Inn killed a dozen unarmed civilians demonstrating for peace in Sarajevo.

The Serbs, inheritors of almost all the Yugoslav National Army's (JNA) arms, began seizing territory. Sarajevo came under siege by Serb irregulars on 5 April 1992 and shelling began soon after. Directed from nearby Pale, the brutal siege was to leave over 10,000 civilians dead and the city ravaged before ending in September 1995.

Serbian forces began a campaign of 'ethnic cleansing', expelling Muslims from northern and eastern Bosnia-Hercegovina to create a 300km corridor joining Serb ethnic areas in the west of Bosnia-Hercegovina with Serbia proper. Villages were terrorised and looted, and homes were destroyed to prevent anyone from returning. The Serbs also set up concentration camps for Muslims and Croats.

In 1992, the UN Security Council authorised the use of force to ensure the delivery of humanitarian aid, and by September 7500 UN troops were in Bosnia-Hercegovina. However, this UN Protection Force (Unprofor) was notoriously impotent. By mid-1993, with Serb 'ethnic cleansing' almost complete, the UN proposed setting up 'safe areas' for Muslims around five Bosnian cities, including Sarajevo. The Serbs, confident that the West would not intervene, continued their siege of Sarajevo.

Ethnic partition seemed increasingly possible, especially after a proposed peace plan that would have sliced Bosnia-Hercegovina into 10 ethnically based provinces. The Croats wanted their own share, and the Croatian Community of Herceg-Bosna was set up in July 1992. Eight months later, fighting erupted between the Muslims and Croats; the latter instigated a deadly minisiege of the Muslim quarter of Mostar, culminating in the destruction of Mostar's historic bridge in 1993.

Even as fighting between Muslims and Croats intensified, NATO finally began to take action against the Bosnian Serbs. A Serbian mortar attack on a Sarajevo market in February 1994 left 68 dead, and US fighters belatedly began enforcing the no-fly zone over Bosnia-Hercegovina by shooting down four Serb aircraft (the first actual combat in

BOSNIA-HERCEGOVINA

CROATIA
Glina
Plitvice
Bihać
Bosanski Novi
Prijedor
Banja Luka
Knin
CROATIA
Šibenik
Split
Brač
Hvar
Korčula
Mljet

Slavonski Brod
Derventa
Doboj
Jajce
Travnik
Zenica
Kupres
SARAJEVO
Ilidža
Pale
Jahorina (1913m)
Bjelašnica (2067m)
Konjić
Jablanica
Mostar
Međugorje
Blagaj
Počitelj
Ploče
Neum
Trebinje
Dubrovnik
ADRIATIC SEA
Herceg-Novi

Vinkovci
VOJVODINA
Županja
Orašje
Brčko
Bijeljina
Tuzla
SERBIA
Zvornik
Srebrenica
Žepa
Višegrad
Goražde
Foča
YUGOSLAVIA
MONTENEGRO
Nikšić
Podgorica

Sava River
Bosna
Vrbas
Una
Neretva River
Drina River

0 25 50km
0 15 30mi

BOSNIA-HERCEGOVINA

NATO's 45-year history). Two months later NATO aircraft made their first air strikes against Bosnian Serb ground positions after the Serbs advanced on a UN 'protected area'. When a British plane was shot down, the NATO raids ceased.

Meanwhile, at talks in Washington in March 1994, the USA pressured the Bosnian government to join the Bosnian Croats in a federation. Soon after, Croatia took the offensive against the Serbs, overrunning Croatian Serb positions and towns in western Slavonia, within Croatia, in 1995.

With Croatia now heavily involved, a pan-Balkan war seemed closer than ever. Again, Bosnian Serb tanks and artillery attacked Sarajevo, again UN peacekeepers requested NATO air strikes. When air strikes to protect

Bosnian 'safe areas' were finally authorised, the Serbs captured 300 Unprofor peacekeepers and chained them to potential targets to keep the planes away.

In July 1995 Bosnian Serbs attacked the safe area of Srebrenica, slaughtering an estimated 6000 Muslim men as they fled through the forest. This was the largest massacre in the war, and highlighted Unprofor's futility.

Nonetheless, the twilight of Bosnian Serb military dominance was at hand. European leaders loudly called for action. Croatia renewed its own internal offensive, expelling Serbs from the Krajina region.

With Bosnian Serbs battered by two weeks of NATO air strikes in September 1995, US president Bill Clinton's proposal for new peace talks was accepted.

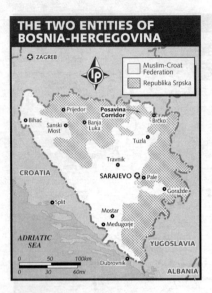

THE TWO ENTITIES OF BOSNIA-HERCEGOVINA

The Dayton Agreement

The peace conference in Dayton, Ohio, USA, began in November 1995 and the final agreement was signed in Paris in December.

The Dayton Agreement stipulated that the country would retain its prewar external boundaries, but would be composed of two parts or 'entities'. The Federation of Bosnia-Hercegovina (the Muslim and Croat portion) would administer 51% of the country, which included Sarajevo, and the Serb Republic of Bosnia-Hercegovina 49%. The latter is commonly referred to as Republika Srpska (RS).

The agreement emphasised the rights of refugees (1.2 million in other countries, and one million displaced within Bosnia-Hercegovina itself) to return to their prewar homes.

A NATO-led peace implementation force (IFOR) was installed as the military force behind the accords. IFOR's 60,000 international troops have been replaced by a 17,000-strong Stabilisation Force (SFOR), whose current mandate has no definite time limit.

After Dayton

Radovan Karadžić stepped down from the RS presidency in July 1996, after the international community threatened to impose sanctions unless he relinquished power. However, the first postwar national elections in Bosnia held in September 1996 essentially shored up the existing leadership.

Meanwhile Biljana Plavšić, then president of the RS, split from the hardline Karadžić during summer 1997. The RS itself seemed to be splintering along these lines, with the Pale-based eastern RS backing Karadžić, as Plavšić's domain in Banja Luka–based western RS became more open. Banja Luka emerged triumphant from the struggle and took over from Pale as the RS capital during January 1998.

Western hopes were given a further boost in January 1998 when a new, relatively liberal Bosnian Serb prime minister Milorad Dodik came to power. Dodik pushed several Dayton-compliant measures through the RS parliament, including common passports, a common licence plate and a new common currency called the convertible mark. Dodik lasted until November 2000; despite his efforts, reforms continue to stall.

Bosnia-Hercegovina today remains divided along ethnic lines, but tensions have ebbed, particularly between Muslims and Croats. More people are now crossing between the RS and the Federation. More Bosnians are returning home – 90,000 in 2001.

The Dayton Agreement also emphasised the powers of the Hague-based International Criminal Tribunal for the former Yugoslavia, which was established in 1993. At Dayton, NATO was authorised to arrest indicted war criminals. Action was initially slow but recently momentum has increased, especially with Slobodan Milošević, Yugoslavia's ex-leader, now in the dock. (He joins, among others, Biljana Plavšić, who gave herself up in January 2001.) The two most-wanted war criminals – Bosnian Serb leader Radovan Karadžić and his military henchman Ratko Mladić – remain at large.

GEOGRAPHY

Bosnia-Hercegovina is a mountainous country of 51,129 sq km on the western side of the Balkan Peninsula, almost cut off from the sea by Croatia. Most of the country's rivers flow north into the Sava; only the Neretva cuts south from Jablanica through the Dinaric Alps to Ploče on the Adriatic Sea. Bosnia-Hercegovina contains over 30 mountain peaks between 1700m and 2386m.

The larger region of Bosnia occupies the northern and central part of the republic, while Hercegovina occupies the south and southwest.

BOSNIA-HERCEGOVINA

CLIMATE

Bosnia-Hercegovina has a mix of Mediterranean and Central European climates; it gets hot in summer but quite chilly in winter, and snowfall can last until April.

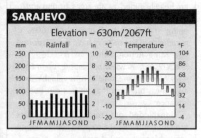

SARAJEVO

Elevation – 630m/2067ft

GOVERNMENT & POLITICS

The Dayton Agreement stipulated that the central government be headed by a rotating three-person presidency, with one elected by the Serb Republic and the others, a Muslim and a Croat, by the Federation. The House of Peoples is selected from the legislatures of the two entities and a House of Representatives that is directly elected by each entity. Two-thirds of each house are from the Federation, one-third from the Serb Republic, and a Council of Ministers implements government policies and decisions.

Despite ideals of a central government in Sarajevo, each division of the country maintains an essentially separate administration. The ethnically joint institutions called for by the Dayton Agreement rarely work smoothly, even those between Croats and Muslims. In a 2000 ruling, Bosnia's constitutional court spelled out the equality of each ethnic group in all entities, but putting that into practice has proved difficult.

In lieu of local cooperation, the West in essence rules Bosnia-Hercegovina, forcing the parties to come to decisions together. The Office of the High Representative (established by the Dayton Agreement) has made some headway. In the April 2000 local elections a multiethnic party made some gains, although voting on nationalist lines was still dominant. This trend continued in October 2002 national elections, but voter turnout was only 55%.

ECONOMY

Bosnia-Hercegovina was one of the poorest regions of Yugoslavia, its economy driven by mining, hydroelectricity and timber. War brought virtually all activity to a halt. While the situation is gradually improving, the unemployment rate still hovers around 40%.

The RS, which initially received less international assistance, is economically poorer than the Federation.

POPULATION & PEOPLE

Bosnia-Hercegovina's prewar population stood at around 4.5 million. In 1991 the largest cities were Sarajevo (525,980), Banja Luka (195,139), Zenica (145,577), Tuzla (131,861) and Mostar (126,067). The massive population shifts have changed the size of many cities, swelling the population of Banja Luka to 239,000 and initially shrinking Sarajevo and Mostar, though the former has been growing again and now nears its former size. Where available we have provided estimates of 2000 population figures.

The prewar population was incredibly mixed, but ethnic cleansing has concentrated Croats in Hercegovina (to the south), Muslims in Sarajevo and central Bosnia-Hercegovina, and Serbs in areas adjacent to Yugoslavia.

Serbs, Croats and Bosnian Muslims are all South Slavs of the same ethnic stock. Physically they are indistinguishable.

Terminology-wise, a Bosnian Serb denotes a Serb living in Bosnia, a Bosnian Croat means a Croat living in Bosnia, and Bosnian Muslims go by the term Bosniak.

ARTS

Bosnia's best-known writer is Ivo Andrić (1892–1975), winner of the 1961 Nobel Prize for Literature. His novels *The Travnik Chronicles* and *Bridge on the Drina*, both written during WWII, are fictional histories dealing with the intermingling of Islamic and Orthodox societies in the small Bosnian towns of Travnik and Višegrad.

SOCIETY & CONDUCT

Removing your shoes is usual in Muslim households; the host will provide slippers. When greeting acquaintances in Sarajevo or elsewhere in the Federation, it is customary to plant one kiss on each cheek. In the RS, three kisses (one-one-one) is the norm.

RELIGION

Of Bosnia-Hercegovina's current population of approximately 3.8 million, about 40% are Muslim, 31% Orthodox, 15% Roman Catholic

BOSNIA-HERCEGOVINA

and 14% are other religions. Most Serbs are Orthodox and most Croats are Catholic.

Across Bosnia-Hercegovina, churches and mosques are being built (or rebuilt) at lightning speed. This is more symptomatic of strong nationalism than religion, since most people are fairly secular.

LANGUAGE

Notwithstanding different dialects, the people of Bosnia-Hercegovina basically speak the same language. However, that language is referred to as 'Bosnian' in the Muslim parts of the Federation, 'Croatian' in Croat-controlled parts, and 'Serbian' in the RS. The Federation uses the Latin alphabet; the RS uses Cyrillic. See the Croatian & Serbian section of the Language chapter at the back of the book for pronunciation guidelines and useful words and phrases.

Facts for the Visitor

HIGHLIGHTS

Sarajevo, a major historic site, is recovering its vibrancy. Beautifully situated Mostar deserves a visit for its cobbled old town. Driving or taking the bus through Bosnia's ravaged but slowly recovering countryside is unforgettable.

SUGGESTED ITINERARIES

Depending on your time, you may want to take in the following:

Two days
Visit Sarajevo
One week
Visit Sarajevo and Mostar
Two weeks
Visit Sarajevo, Mostar, Travnik and Banja Luka

PLANNING
When to Go

The best time to visit is spring or summer. Don't worry about a seasonal crush of tourists just yet.

Maps

Freytag & Berndt produces a good 1:250,000 road map of Bosnia-Hercegovina. Some of the tourist offices and kiosks sell maps. The maps of the city centres may also be free from the tourist offices.

Warning: Land Mines

Over one million land mines are estimated to be in Bosnia-Hercegovina. They were mostly laid in conflict zones. All of Sarajevo's suburbs are heavily mined, as are areas around and/or in Travnik, Mostar and Bihać. The most frightening statistic is that only about 60% of minefields in the country have been reported. The **Mine Action Centre** (☎ *033-209 762, fax 209 763;* **W** *www.bhmac.org; open 8am-4pm Mon-Fri)* in Sarajevo runs valuable mine awareness briefings that visitors can book in advance.

Unexploded ordnance (UXOs, mortars, grenades and shells) also pose a huge danger around former conflict areas.

The golden rule for mines and UXOs is to stick to asphalt surfaces. Abandoned-looking areas are avoided for a reason. Do not drive off the shoulder of roads, do not poke around in abandoned villages or damaged houses, do not get curious about shiny metal objects on the grass, and regard every centimetre of ground as suspicious.

What to bring

Adaptor plugs are hard to come by, so bring one along if you want to use a computer.

TOURIST OFFICES

Bosnia's larger cities, including Sarajevo, Banja Luka, Mostar, Bihać and Međugorje, all have tourist offices – or travel agencies that serve just as well. The underemployed staff are generally delighted to see travellers and will dispense maps and advice.

VISAS & DOCUMENTS

No visas are required for citizens of the USA, Canada, Ireland, the UK and most other EU countries. Other nationals can obtain a one-month single-entry tourist visa at the cost of about UK£20 (ask your embassy for the exact amount in local currency). You will need to have a valid passport, a copy of a round-trip plane ticket and a bank statement. Apply to your nearest embassy for your visa. Allow at least two weeks for processing. Multiple-entry visas generally last three months and cost UK£36.

Visitors staying longer than three months will need to register with the local police once they arrive.

EMBASSIES & CONSULATES
Bosnian Embassies & Consulates
Bosnia-Hercegovina has embassies and/or consulates in the following countries; the website W www.mvp.gov.ba contains further listings.

Australia (☎ 02-6232 4646, fax 6232 5554) 6 Beale Crescent, Deakin ACT 2600

Canada (☎ 613-236 0028, fax 236 1139) 130 Albert St, Suite 805, Ottawa, Ontario K1P 5G4

Croatia *Consulate:* (☎ 01-48 19 420, fax 48 19 418) Pavla Hatza 3, PP27, 10001 Zagreb

France (☎ 01-42 67 34 22, fax 40 53 85 22) 174 Rue de Courcelles, 75017 Paris

Germany (☎ 030-814 712 33/4/5, fax 814 712 31) Ibsenstrasse 14, D-10439 Berlin
Consulate: (☎ 0228-35 00 60, fax 35 00 698) Friedrich-Wilhelm strasse 2, 53113 Bonn
Consulate: (☎ 089-982 80 64/5, fax 982 80 79) Montsalvat strasse 19, 80804 Munich

Slovenia *Consulate:* (☎ 01-432 23 70, 319 978) Likozarjeva 6, 1000 Ljubljana

UK (☎ 020-7255 3758, 7255 3760) 57 Lexham Gardens, London W8

USA (☎ 202-337 1500, fax 337 1502) 2109 E St NW, Washington DC 20037
Consulate: (☎ 212-593 1042, fax 751 9019) 866 UN Plaza, Suite 580, New York NY 10017

Embassies & Consulates in Bosnia-Hercegovina
The following embassies are in Sarajevo (area code ☎ 033), and the German consulate is in Banja Luka (area code ☎ 051):

Austria (☎ 279 400, fax 668 339) Džidžikovac 7

Bulgaria (☎ 668 191, fax 668 182, e possar@bih.net.ba) Trampina 12/2

Canada (☎ 447 900, fax 447 901) Logavina 7

Croatia (☎ 444 331, fax 472 434) Mehmeda Spahe 16

France (☎ 668 151, fax 668 103, e france-1@bih.net.ba) Mehmed-bega K. Lj 18

Germany (☎ 275 000, fax 652 978) Mejtaš Buka bb
Consulate: (☎ 277 949, fax 217 113) Kralja Karađorđevića 103, Banja Luka

Macedonia (☎/fax 206 004) Emerika Bluma 23

Slovenia (☎ 271 260, fax 271 270) Bentbaša 7

UK (☎ 444 429, fax 666 131, e britemb@bih.net.ba) Tina Ujevića 8

USA (☎ 445 700, fax 659 722, e opabih@pd.state.gov) Alipašina 43

Yugoslavia (☎ 260 090, fax 221 469) Obala Maka Dizdara 3A

MONEY
Currency
The convertible mark (KM), Bosnia's currency, is tied to the euro at a rate of 1KM to €0.51129. Most establishments (especially hotels) in the country accept euros as well as convertible marks and sometimes also list their prices in euros.

When buying convertible marks, it's best to ask for small bills as shops often are hard-pressed for change.

Exchange Rates
Conversion rates for major currencies at the time of publication were:

country	unit		convertible mark
Australia	A$1	=	1.18KM
Canada	C$1	=	1.34KM
Euro Zone	€1	=	1.96KM
Japan	¥100	=	1.65KM
NZ	NZ$1	=	1.01KM
UK	UK£1	=	3.04KM
USA	US$1	=	2.06KM

For up-to-date exchange rates go to W www.xe.net/ucc/full.shtml.

Travellers Cheques
Travellers cheques can be changed at banks in larger cities, though usually not in smaller cities (including Bihać or Travnik). Commission is generally 1.5%.

ATMs
ATMs have sprouted in Sarajevo; Banja Luka, Mostar and Međugorje each have one. MasterCard, Visa, Plus, Maestro and Cirrus are usually accepted. It is best to have a back-up option lest the machines malfunction.

Credit Cards
Major hotels, rental-car agencies and airlines accept major credit cards, as do a smattering of other establishments. MasterCard and Visa are most common. MasterCard advances are sometimes available from post offices.

Costs
Accommodation is the biggest factor in cost; budget travellers who stick to private accommodation might be able to squeeze by on 60KM to 70KM per day in Sarajevo, and 30KM to 40KM in other towns.

BOSNIA-HERCEGOVINA

Tipping & Bargaining

Tipping is customary at more the formal restaurants – round up the bill, or leave 1KM to 2KM extra. Taxi fares can be treated the same way.

Bargaining is sometimes possible in souvenir shops, such as those in Baščaršija (Sarajevo's Turkish bazaar area).

POST & COMMUNICATIONS
Post

Post and telephone offices are usually combined. Poste-restante service is available at all cities included in this book; letters should be addressed to: (Name), Poste Restante, (postcode), Bosnia-Hercegovina.

Postcodes are: Travnik 72270, Banja Luka 78101, Bihać 77000, Međugorje 88266, Mostar (Zapadni) 88000. A fee is usually charged at pick-up.

Telephone & Fax

To call Bosnia-Hercegovina from abroad, dial the international access code, ☎ 387 (the country code for Bosnia-Hercegovina), the area code (without the initial zero) and the number.

To make an international call from Bosnia-Hercegovina, it's cheapest to go to the post office. Dial the international access number (☎ 00), then the country code and number. A three-minute call to the USA costs 6.30KM.

Phonecards, useful for local or short international calls, can be purchased at post offices. Unfortunately, cards issued in the different parts of Bosnia-Hercegovina (ie, the RS, Hercegovina and the Muslim parts of the Federation) are not interchangeable.

Dial ☎ 900/901/902 for the international operator and ☎ 988 if you need local directory information.

Faxes can be sent from most post offices.

Email & Internet Access

Internet cafés abound in Sarajevo, and other large cities may have one or two Internet access spots.

DIGITAL RESOURCES

Bosnia-Hercegovina's natural and cultural wonders are talked up at W www.bhtourism .ba, administered by the Office of the High Representative, itself a good source of news (W www.ohr.int). The website W www.city.ba has istings and information on several Bosnian cities, including Sarajevo and Mostar.

BOOKS

Noel Malcolm's *Bosnia: A Short History* is a good country-specific complement to Rebecca West's mammoth classic *Black Lamb & Grey Falcon*, which exhaustively describes her 1930s trip through Yugoslavia. For a detailed account of the recent war, read *Yugoslavia: The Death of a Nation* by Laura Silber & Allan Little, or *The Fall of Yugoslavia* by Misha Glenny. Zoë Brân's *After Yugoslavia*, which is part of the Lonely Planet Journeys series, retraces the author's 1978 trip through the former Yugoslavia.

FILMS

Bosnia-Hercegovina captured an Oscar in 2002, when the film *No Man's Land*, made by Sarajevo-born Danis Tanović, won best foreign film. Shot in Slovenia and Italy, the film portrays the relationship between a Serb soldier and a Muslim soldier while Sarajevo was under siege. Another well-respected Bosnian film about the siege is *The Perfect Circle* (1997), whose protagonist is a poet.

NEWSPAPERS & MAGAZINES

All parts of Bosnia-Hercegovina have different papers. Sarajevo's independent daily *Oslobođenje* functioned throughout the war. *Dani*, the popular and outrageous biweekly magazine, keeps the government on its toes with colourful covers and entertaining political satire. English-language newspapers can be found in Sarajevo and Banja Luka.

RADIO & TV

Studio 99 is both a television and radio station; the latter carries some Radio Free Europe broadcasting. Radio Zid has some Voice of America news. Serb Radio Television (SRT) is broadcast out of Banja Luka.

PHOTOGRAPHY & VIDEO

Kodak and Fuji film is available in most cities; in Sarajevo, a 36-exposure colour film costs about 6KM a roll. It is common to take photographs of war damage, but use prudence and sensitivity.

TIME

Bosnia-Hercegovina is on Central European Time, which is GMT/UTC plus one hour. Daylight savings time in late March sets clocks forward one hour. In late October clocks are turned back one hour.

LAUNDRY
Laundrettes have yet to debut in Bosnia-Hercegovina, but pansions and hotels will usually do laundry if asked. The price varies by weight or quantity; expect about 10KM a load. Sarajevo has dry-cleaning facilities.

TOILETS
Public toilets are generally of the hole-in-the-ground, rather than the toilet-seat, variety. At train and bus stations they cost 0.50KM. Bring your own toilet paper.

HEALTH
Visiting a doctor will not be expensive, but make sure that your medical insurance plan includes evacuation from Bosnia-Hercegovina.

In the cities mentioned here, most locals and visitors drink the tap water.

WOMEN TRAVELLERS
Women travellers should feel no particular concern; indeed, people will go out of their way to help a woman alone.

GAY & LESBIAN TRAVELLERS
Homosexuality is not well-regarded in the Bosnian-Hercegovina society. However, there are rumours of a gay bar in the Sarajevo suburbs; ask a local in the know.

DISABLED TRAVELLERS
Those in wheelchairs will find few facilities; exceptions include Hotel Europa in Sarajevo and Hotel Ero in Mostar.

DANGERS & ANNOYANCES
Bosnia-Herzegovina's greatest danger is that some areas are heavily mined (see the 'Warning: Land Mines' boxed text earlier in this chapter). Nationalism runs strong in some parts of the country (notably the RS and Hercegovina), but this should not affect international travellers, who can expect a warm welcome almost everywhere.

PUBLIC HOLIDAYS
Bosnia-Hercegovina observes Independence Day (1 March), May Day (1 May) and the Day of the Republic (25 November). Bajram, a twice-yearly Muslim holiday, is observed in parts of the Federation (dates vary, so ask the tourist office). Catholic Christmas and Orthodox Christmas are observed by those individual religious groups.

Emergency Services

In the event of an emergency dial ☎ 92 for police, ☎ 93 for the fire department or ☎ 94 for emergency assistance

---

ACTIVITIES
Outdoor activities such as hiking and camping are severely compromised by the presence of mines. However, Jahorina and Bjelašnica, Bosnia-Hercegovina's ski resorts, are again open; stay on the groomed ski runs as there are mines in the vicinity of both resorts.

Rafting season runs from May to September. The Una River near Bihać is particularly popular for this.

Green Visions (☎/fax 033-207 169; Terezija bb; w www.greenvisions.ba) is a Sarajevo ecotoursim agency popular with expatriate workers. It runs outdoor trips (including rafting, skiing, hiking and camping) around the country. Ask about the company's mine policy and use your judgment about whether to sign up. It's impossible to be totally sure about mine safety. Trips cost from 65KM to 75KM, with student discounts available.

ACCOMMODATION
The reign of concrete Communist-era hotels is thankfully ending, as competition has arrived in the form of private hotels better suited to western tastes.

Larger towns also now have a smattering of *pansions* (pensions). These places are generally slightly humbler than the hotels, though more personable, and breakfast is usually included. Bathrooms are sometimes inside rooms and sometimes in the hallway. Confusingly, in Sarajevo some pansions now style themselves as 'hotels' or 'motels'; we therefore group pansions and small hotels together.

For both pansions and hotels, be sure to book in advance as they can fill with conference-goers. Most hotels and all but the cheapest pansions will have cable TV.

Private accommodation is easy to arrange in Sarajevo and is also possible in Mostar. Elsewhere, ask the local poeple at markets or shops. Staying in a home is not only cheaper, but also usually very pleasant. Likely as not, your hosts will ply you with coffee, pull out old pictures of Tito (depending on their politics), and regale you with many tales of Yugoslavia's past glory.

BOSNIA-HERCEGOVINA

Most accommodation attracts a tax of 2KM to 5KM, which is included in the prices listed in this chapter unless otherwise stated.

FOOD & DRINKS

Bosnia's Turkish heritage is savoured in grilled meats such as *bosanski lonac* (Bosnian stew of cabbage and meat). When confronted with the ubiquitous *burek* (a layered meat pie sold by weight), vegetarians can opt for *sirnica* (cheese pie) or *zeljanica* (spinach pie). *Ćevapčići*, another favourite, is lamb and beef rolls tucked into a half-loaf of spongy *somun* bread. For sugar-soaked desserts, try baklava or *tufahije*, an apple cake topped with walnuts and whipped cream. Many cities make good cheese (*sir*); feta-like Travnik cheese is especially well known.

Good wines from Hercegovina include Žilavka (white) and Blatina (red). These are best sampled in regional wineries; Međugorje has some fine offerings. A meal can always be washed down with a shot of *šljivovica* (plum brandy) or *loza* (grape brandy).

Getting There & Away

Travellers arriving by plane (and possibly those arriving by train) will be asked to fill out an arrival card consisting of two identical halves; hold onto one half to present when you are departing.

AIR

Bosnia-Hercegovina's main airport is in Sarajevo; smaller ones are in Mostar and Banja Luka. Airlines serving the country include Croatia Airlines, Swissair, Lufthansa, Austrian Airlines, Malev-Hungarian Airlines and Adria Airways, as well as Air Srpska (to Banja Luka) and Air Bosna (to Sarajevo from Istanbul, Gothenburg, Stockholm, Oslo and several destinations in Germany).

LAND

Buses are a reliable way to enter Bosnia-Hercegovina, and to see the countryside. Stowing luggage usually costs up to 2KM per item, depending on the route. Buses usually run on time, although they are slow due to winding roads and occasional stops for drivers and passengers to eat and smoke.

There are numerous bus routes to Bosnia-Hercegovina from Croatia (Zagreb, Split and Dubrovnik) and from Germany. The RS is well connected to Yugoslavia. Buses run every hour between Banja Luka and Belgrade, and seven more run daily from the Sarajevo suburb of Lukavica (in the RS) to Belgrade. Few bus stations, apart from Sarajevo and Mostar, have luggage storage.

One train daily travels from Sarajevo to Zagreb via Banja Luka, and another runs every day from Sarajevo to Ploče (five hours) via Mostar.

It is cheaper to buy a return ticket on buses and trains than a one-way fare (prices in this chapter are generally for one-way transport).

Getting Around

Trains are generally more comfortable than buses, although service is much more limited. About 10 trains per day chug out of Sarajevo, and trains from Banja Luka have a limited radius within the RS.

Bosnia-Hercegovina's bus network is quite comprehensive, particularly within each entity (the Federation and the RS) – though inter-entity travel is no longer a hassle.

Many car-rental places have sprung up, particularly in Sarajevo. Car rental is also available in Banja Luka, Mostar and Međugorje. Prices usually start at 100KM for one day with unlimited mileage; the rate may fall if you rent for longer.

Taxis are readily available and cheap, though outside Sarajevo and Banja Luka they may not have (or turn on) meters. If there is no meter, you may want to agree on the price before you set off.

As elsewhere in the Balkan countries, most people drive like maniacs, passing even on sharp curves.

Bosnia

SARAJEVO

☎ 033 • pop 500,000

Sarajevo, Bosnia-Hercegovina's capital, is tucked in the peaceful Miljacka River valley. Before the war, the city was an ethnic microcosm of Yugoslavia, where Muslims, Serbs, Croats, Turks, Jews and others had peacefully coexisted for hundreds of years.

From the mid-15th century until 1878, Turkish governors resided in Sarajevo. The city's name comes from *saraj*, Turkish for 'palace'. It is one of the most Oriental cities in Europe, retaining the essence of its rich history in its mosques, markets and the picturesque old Turkish bazaar called Baščaršija.

When the Turks finally withdrew, half a century of Austro-Hungarian domination began, culminating in the assassination of Archduke Franz Ferdinand and his wife Sophie by a Serbian nationalist in 1914. In 1984 Sarajevo again attracted world attention by hosting the 14th Winter Olympic Games.

Sarajevo's heritage of six centuries was pounded into rubble by Bosnian Serb artillery during the siege of 1992 to 1995, when Sarajevo's only access to the outside world was via a 1km tunnel under the airport. Over 10,500 Sarajevans died and 50,000 were wounded by Bosnian Serb sniper fire and shelling. The endless new graveyards near Koševo stadium are a silent record of the terrible years.

Despite the highly visible scars of war, Sarajevo is again bursting with energy. Colourful trams run down the road once called 'Sniper's Alley', innumerable cafés line the streets, and locals spend leisurely evenings strolling down the main pedestrian street, Ferhadija. A large international presence made up of government officials and humanitarian aid workers is also altering the face of the city. The energy poured into Bosnia-Hercegovina's recovery has rendered Sarajevo one of the fastest-changing cities in Europe.

Orientation

Surrounded by mountains, Sarajevo is near the geographic centre of Bosnia-Hercegovina. From the airport, 13km to the west, the main road runs through Novo Sarajevo, then past the turn-off to the bus and train stations and into the town centre. Baščaršija is at the eastern end of town.

Information

Tourist Offices The **Tourist Information Bureau** (☎ *220 724, 532 606, fax 532 281; Zelenih Beretki 22; open 9am-4pm Mon-Fri, 9am-1pm & 4pm-6pm Sat)* stocks books, maps and helpful brochures and can answer most questions about the city.

Money The **Central Profit Banka** (☎ *533 688; Zelenih Beretki 24; open 8am-7pm*

Mon-Fri, 8am-noon Sat), with branches around town, exchanges travellers cheques for 1% commission. Receiving wired money is also possible (1% commission), as are Diners Club, Visa and American Express cash advances. ATMs are sprinkled over the city centre, though some may have 100KM withdrawal limits.

Post & Communications Poste-restante mail is held at the **post office** near the bus and train stations, which also has phone booths. In town centre, the renovated **central post office** *(Obala Kulina Bana 8)* has post and telephone booths (the post part is closed Sunday).

Email & Internet Access 'Non-stop' Internet cafés are the latest rage. A handy one is at Ferhadija 12 *(open 24hr)*, and another at Pehlivanuša 2 *(open 24hr except Sunday morning)*. Both charge 3KM per hour.

Bookshops Near the eternal flame, **Šahinpašić** *(Mula Mustafe Bašeskije 1)* sells some English-language newspapers, magazines, cheap Penguin classics, maps and a sheaf of Lonely Planets. Don't miss the *Survival Map* (10KM), a cartoon-like depiction of wartime Sarajevo. **Buybook** *(Radićeva 4; open to 10pm Mon-Sat, to 6pm Sun)*, near the presidency, has a wider selection of books but no newspapers. Relax with an evening glass of wine in the in-house café.

Medical Services Try **Koševo Hospital** *(☎ 666 620; Bolnioka 25)* or the **City Hospital** *(☎ 664 724; Kranjčevića 12)*. Ask your embassy for a list of private doctors.

Things to See

Cobbled **Baščaršija** (the Turkish Quarter), where bronze artisans ply their trade, is the heart of Sarajevo. This is the only spot in the city where cafés serve real Turkish coffee in a *džežva* (brass pot), as opposed to espresso. **Morića Han**, now a café along Sarači, used to be a tavern and stable when Sarajevo was a crossroads between east and west. **Svrzo House** *(Glodžina 6; admission 2KM; open 10am-3pm Tues-Sat, Sun 10am-1pm)*, just above Baščaršija, shows the lifestyle of a well-to-do, 18th-century Muslim family.

The graceful Austro-Hungarian **National Library** is at the eastern end of Baščaršija along the river. The building was destroyed

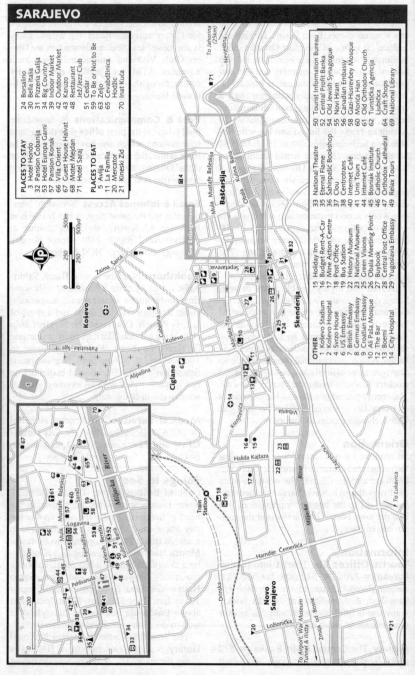

SARAJEVO

PLACES TO STAY
3 Hotel Hondo
32 Pansion Cobanija
53 Hotel Europa Garni
57 Pansion Konak
66 Villa Orient
67 Guest House Halvat
68 Motel Mejdan
71 Hotel Saraj

PLACES TO EAT
5 Avlija
11 La Familia
20 Mercator
21 Kineski Zid
24 Borsalino
30 Bella Italia
31 Pizzeria Galija
34 Big Country
39 Indoor Market
42 Outdoor Market
43 Karuzo
48 Restaurant
    Jež/Jezz Club
51 Cedar
59 To Be or Not to Be
63 Zeljo
65 Cevabdžinica
    Hodžic
70 Inat Kuca

OTHER
1 Koševo Stadium
2 Koševo Hospital
4 US Embassy
7 Svrzo House
8 British Embassy
9 German Embassy
10 Croatian Embassy
12 Ali Paša Mosque
13 The Bar
14 City Hospital
15 Holiday Inn
16 Budget Rent-A-Car
17 Mine Action Centre
18 Post Office
19 Bus Station
22 History Museum
23 National Museum
25 Green Visions
26 Obala Meeting Point
27 Buybook
28 Central Post Office
29 Yugoslavia Embassy
33 National Theatre
35 Eternal Flame
36 Šahinpašic Bookshop
37 Clou
38 Centrotrans
40 Internet Café
41 Unis Tours
44 Internet Café
45 Bosniak Institute
46 Catholic Church
47 Orthodox Cathedral
49 Relax Tours
50 Tourist Information Bureau
52 Central Profit Banka
54 Old Jewish Synagogue
55 Novi Hram
56 Canadian Embassy
58 Gazi-Husrevbey Mosque
60 Morica Han
61 Old Orthodox Church
62 Turisticka Agencija
    Ljubicica
64 Craft Shops
69 National Library

BOSNIA-HERCEGOVINA

by an incendiary shell on 25 August 1992, 100 years after construction began. It now has a postwar dome courtesy of Austria, but rebuilding still has far to go.

Austrian Archduke Franz Ferdinand and his wife Sophie paused at the National Library (then the town hall) on 28 June 1914, then rode west along the riverside in an open car to the second bridge (where Zelenih Beretki meets the river). It was here that they were shot. A plaque bearing the footprints of the assassin, Gavrilo Princip, was ripped out of the pavement during the recent war because Princip was a Bosnian Serb.

In the city centre, the **eternal flame** commemorates WWII. Places of worship for four different religions – Catholic, Orthodox, Muslim and Jewish – lie in close vicinity to each other, as Sarajevans proudly point out. These include the Catholic church on Ferhadija; the old **Orthodox Church** (Mula Mustafe Baškeskije), which predates the yellow and brown Orthodox cathedral (don't miss the **museum** inside the church, which showcases Russian, Greek and local icons, as well as tapestries and old manuscripts); the **Gazi-Husrevbey Mosque** (1531), built by masons from Dubrovnik; and the **Jewish synagogue** (Mula Mustafe Baškeskije). The Jewish Museum is closed, but the **Novi Hram Gallery** (Mula Mustafe Baškeskije 38) next door has dislays of historical documents relating to Bosnia-Hercegovina's Jews.

On the other side of the street, bibliophiles might enjoy a tour of the **Bosniak Institute** (☎ 279 800; e bosins@bih.net.ba; Mula Mustafe Baškeskije 21), which has a collection of old Bosnian and Turkish books; groups can request an English-language tour.

The three-year siege made Sarajevo itself a stunning sight. The road into the city from the airport (now Zmaja od Bosne) was dubbed 'Sniper's Alley' during the war because Serb snipers in the surrounding hills picked off civilians crossing the road. The bright yellow **Holiday Inn** was the wartime home to international journalists, as it was the city's only functioning wartime hotel. The side facing Sniper's Alley was heavily damaged, but the hotel has since been given a facelift. Across from the Holiday Inn is the **National Museum** (open 10am-2pm Tues-Fri; open Sun & longer hours Wed in summer), which has interesting ethnology and archaeology collections. A **History Museum** (open 9am-2pm Mon-Fri, 9am-1pm Sat & Sun) just up the road displays old photographs of Bosnia-Hercegovina and has rotating exhibits, some of which pertain to the recent war.

A **tree line** still rings the city, demarcating the former front line. Residents cut down trees and burned benches for heat during the siege. Watch the pavement for **Sarajevo roses**, which are skeletal hand-like indentations where a shell exploded. Some of these are symbolically filled in with red rubber. Most of the tunnel under the airport (Sarajevans' dangerous wartime exit) has collapsed, but a tiny **War Museum Tunnel** (☎ 628 591; Tuneli 1; admission 5KM), just beyond the airport, allows visitors to walk through an uncollapsed section.

Special Events
In late August, internationally produced films are shown at the annual **Sarajevo Film Festival** (☎ 524 127, fax 664 547). In February and March the Winter Festival features many theatrical and musical performances. Other festivals include Baščaršija Noči, when the old town erupts in song, dance and theatre.

Places to Stay
Sarajevo has plenty of accommodation, which has sprung up to house visiting international officials. However, hotel and pansion prices remain high, and reservations are wise. Private accommodation is a relative bargain at 40KM to 50KM per person, but the cheaper rooms will often be further from the centre.

Private Rooms For rooms in the centre, try **Unis Tours** (☎/fax 209 089; Ferhadija 16; singles/doubles 42/74KM), which accepts Visa and MasterCard.

Turistička Agencija Ljubičica (☎ 535 829, 066 131 813, ☎/fax 232 109; Mula Mustafe Baškeskije 65; rooms 32-62KM), in Baščaršija, has rooms both in the centre and farther out of town. Prices vary depending on location and room quality.

Relax Tours (☎/fax 263 330/331; Zelenih Beretki 22; rooms 50KM) can also help with accommodation bookings.

Pansions & Small Hotels The cheapest option is **Pansion Konak** (☎ 533 506; Mula Mustafe Baškeskije 48; singles/doubles 30/60KM), a quite basic but acceptable spot in the centre.

An excellent choice is **Guest House Halvat** (☎/fax 237 714; e halvat@bih.net.ba; Kasima Dobraoe 5; singles/doubles 89/119KM), with five cosy rooms and a cheery breakfast area. Children are welcome, and those up to 12 stay free.

The **Pansion Čobanija** (☎ 441 749, ☎/fax 203 937; Čobanija 29; singles/doubles 80/120KM), just past Pizzeria Galija on the southern side of the river, is a popular option. Request one of the nicer upstairs room (it's the same price), and enjoy the nearby sitting room. All have private bathrooms.

Motel Mejdan (☎ 232 421, fax 532 221; Mustaj Pašim Mejdan 11; singles/doubles 80/120KM), near the old library, is small but pleasant.

Hotel Hondo (☎ 666 564, ☎/fax 469 375; Zaima Šarca 23; singles/doubles 80/120KM) is a 20-minute walk uphill from the centre (head straight up Pehlivanuša behind the cathedral; it turns into Zaima Šarca). A good view, quiet neighbourhood and hearty breakfast are ample reward, though bathrooms are hallway rather than in-room.

Hotels At 150KM to 300KM a night, hotels are pleasant if not cost-effective.

Villa Orient (☎ 232 754, fax 441 044; Oprkanj 6; singles/doubles 150/200KM), in the midst of Baščaršija, has excellent, if compact, rooms (payment in cash only).

The white building visible on the hill behind the National Library is the **Hotel Saraj** (☎ 117 703/1, fax 172 691; e hotsaraj@bih.net.ba; Nevjestina 5; singles/doubles from 120/160KM). The rooms with a view of Sarajevo are more expensive, but all rooms are pleasant. MasterCard and Visa are accepted.

Hotel Europa Garni (☎ 232 855, fax 232 860; e europa-garni@smartnet.ba; Vladislava Skarića 3; singles/doubles 182/284KM), built behind its bombed-out predecessor, is perfect for deluxe stays. Perks include parking and disabled access. MasterCard, Maestro and Visa are accepted.

Places to Eat

Sarajevo's restaurants are the domain of internationals, as Bosnians socialise over coffee and eat at home. Most restaurant menus are in English, and main meals usually cost between 10KM and 15KM.

Karuzo, along Mehmeda Spahe, boasts Sarajevo's only sushi (10KM), and probably

its only meatless menu. Splurge on the exquisite seafood risotto (18KM).

To Be or Not to Be (Čizmedžiluk 5) in Baščaršija has generous, colourful salads in a candlelit setting. Vegetarians can opt for an omelette or spaghetti, while others can enjoy classic Bosnian steaks.

Avlija (Sumbul Avde 2) is a cosy den of wooden benches and hanging plants; its burgers and chicken wings (both around 5KM) draw raves.

Restaurant Jež (Zelenih Beretki 14; mains 20-25KM) does local classics generously and with flair. The name means 'hedgehog'.

Inat Kuća, opposite the National Library, offers fabulous, low-priced Bosnian specialities such as a whopping zeljanica (spinach pie; 5KM) in a lively old Turkish setting. Its story goes thus: when work began on the library, the authorities wanted to demolish the old house that stood in the way, but the owner insisted on having it moved piece by piece across the river and rebuilt. Hence the name, which translates as 'Spite House'.

Big Country (Branilaca Sarajeva) does a smashing weekend brunch; treats include real maple syrup and freshly squeezed juice from blood oranges.

Borsalino, in the Skenderija complex, has fabulous palačinke (3KM to 5KM) that make a meal in themselves.

Kineski Zid (Great Wall; Zvornička bb; mains from 11KM), in the suburb of Grbavica, offers elegant dining and dishes from duck to tofu; inquire about dumpling specials.

Cedar (Hadžiristićeva bb; mains 15-22KM) serves Lebanese classics, with the occasional live jazz show.

La Familia (Maršala Tita 12; mains 20-25KM), just across from the Bar, has an array of upmarket Italian options.

Bella Italia (Čobanija 1; pasta 10KM) has outdoor riverside seating in summer.

Pizzeria Galija (Čobanija 20) remains the local favourite for pizza.

For a quick meal, čevapi, burek and 'fast-food' joints are ubiquitous.

Ćevabdžinica Hodžić (Bravadžiluk 34), near the National Library, is a čevapi star. **Zeljo** (Bravadžiluk bb) is another very popular čevapi spot.

Self-Catering The huge Slovenian supermarket **Mercator** (Ložionička 16) stocks some Western-style supplies. Heading out of town on Zmaja od Bosne, take the first right after Hotel Bristol.

The **outdoor market** *(Mula Mustafe Bašeskije; open year-round)*, behind the cathedral, overflows with fruit and vegetables. Its indoor counterpart, with dairy products and meats, is across the street in the sandy-coloured building.

Entertainment

Jezz Club *(Zelenih Beretki 14)*, beside the Jež Restaurant, has live jazz performances on Thursday and Saturday.

Clou *(Mula Mustafe Bašekija 5; open from 6pm)* has occasional live jazz as well but is less roomy.

Boemi *(Valtera Periša 16)* is the current darling among Sarajevo's fickle disco-lovers.

The Bar *(Maršala Tita 7)*, near the intersection with Alipašina, is a popular hang-out for young Bosnians when they're not at other cafés in town.

The **National Theatre** *(Obala Kulina Bana 9)* often holds concerts, ballet and theatre; ask the tourist office for a monthly schedule.

Many cinemas show American films with subtitles; for extra comfort, try the **Obala Meeting Point** cinema in Skenderija. *Oslobođendje*, Sarajevo's daily paper, has daily cinema listings under the 'Kina' column.

Shopping

Metalworking craft shops line Kazandžiluk, at the end of Baščaršija. Turkish coffee sets and snazzy plates aside, the trendiest souvenirs are engraved shell cases (that is shell as in cartridge). Small ones sell for around 10KM. Bargaining is possible, and sometimes necessary, in these shops. Woollen Bosnian rugs are also popular.

Getting There & Away

Three buses a day run to Sarajevo from Zagreb (54KM, eight hours), four from Split (39KM, seven to eight hours) and three from Dubrovnik (8½ hours; four in summer). Three daily buses also go to and from Banja Luka. **Centrotrans** *(☎ 532 874; Niže Banje 1)*, at the intersection with Mula Mustafe Bašeskije, is helpful in providing bus times.

For buses to Belgrade (20KM, seven per day) and other parts of the RS, ask a taxi driver to take you to the station *(☎ 057-677 377)* in Lukavica, a suburb in the RS. The Sarajevo tourist office has a schedule for these buses.

Trains run once a day to Zagreb (44/71KM single/return, nine hours) via Banja Luka (22/35KM). One train daily travels to Ploče (18/28KM, five hours) with a stop at Mostar (12/19KM, 2½ hours).

Getting Around

To/From the Airport A taxi to the centre should cost about 15KM. Taxi drivers from the airport generally turn on their meters.

Public Transport An efficient tram network runs east-west between Baščaršija and Ilidža. Tram No 4 from Baščaršija peels off at the bus station; tram No 1 goes between the bus station and Ilidža. Buy tickets at kiosks near tram stations (1.20KM, 1.50KM if you buy them from the driver). Punch your ticket on board as there are inspectors about. Bus and trolleybus tickets work the same way.

Car Rental agencies at the airport include **Budget** *(☎ 427 670)*, **Hertz** *(☎ 235 050)*, **Avis** *(☎ 463 598)*, **Europcar** *(☎ 289 273)* and **Nektar** *(☎ 289 277)*. Prices are usually at least 100KM for one day, less for longer periods. These agencies and others also have offices downtown; the tourist office keeps a list.

Taxi All Sarajevo's ubiquitous taxis have meters that begin at 2KM and cost about 1KM per kilometre. Call **Radio Taxi** *(☎ 970)*.

AROUND SARAJEVO
Jahorina
☎ 057

Twenty-five kilometres southeast of Sarajevo, the nearly deserted slopes of Mt Jahorina, the site of the 1984 Winter Olympics, still offer some of the best skiing in Europe at bargain-basement prices. Due to the absence of large-scale development, the resort has a quaint, frozen-in-time feel. Ski rental is 10KM to 20KM; lift tickets are 10KM to 15KM. Lessons are similarly cheap. Do not stray from the groomed ski runs, as parts of Jahorina are mined.

For accommodation, the small cottages that dot the mountain roads are your best bet. Unfortunately, there is no organised rental process: it's a matter of knowing the right people. Try inquiring at **Pansion Sport** *(☎ 270 333, fax 270 444; rooms per person 22-37KM)*, a pleasant Swiss chalet–style guesthouse at the base of the ski runs. Rates are dependent on the season. Next door is immaculate **Hotel Kristal** (☎ 270 430, fax 270 431; singles/ doubles around 88/156KM), which accepts Visa and MasterCard.

Hotels and pansions tend to offer half- or full-board. There are also lunch spots by the ski lifts. Those with cars can search out the **trout restaurant** in nearby Pale (ask an international for directions). To relax after a long day on the slopes, stop in the atmospheric, bearskin-filled **Peggy's Bar**, which is 2km up the road behind Hotel Kristal.

Because Jahorina is in the RS, transport from Sarajevo is limited. One bus heads to Jahorina each morning from near the National Museum; the tourist office knows the times. **Green Visions** (☎ 033-207 169), a Sarajevo tour agency, sometimes organises ski trips.

TRAVNIK
☎ 030
Tucked into a narrow valley only 90km northwest of Sarajevo, Travnik served as the seat of Turkish viziers who ruled Bosnia-Hercegovina from 1699 to 1851. The town grew into a diplomatic crossroads, and earned fame more recently as the birthplace of Bosnia's best-known writer Ivo Andrić.

Although wartime fighting between Muslims and Croats went on in the surrounding hills, the town itself was mostly spared. With its lovely medieval castle and pristine natural springs, the town, in Muslim hands today, is well worth a day trip from Sarajevo or a stop on the way to Banja Luka.

Orientation & Information
Travnik's main street, Bosanska, runs east to west. The bus station is on the western end of town, within sight of the post office (which can issue MasterCard advances).

Things to See
The **medieval fort** at the top of the hill is believed to date from the 15th century. Head up Hendek in the east, turn right at the top of the steps and then right again; you'll see the walkway to the fort. It's open in the afternoons; if it's not, ask for the key in the anthropological-archaeological **museum** (worth a visit) on the right of Bosanska. This museum also has the key to the **Ivo Andrić Memorial Museum** (Zenjak bb), upstairs from Restaurant Divan, the birthplace of the famed Bosnian author of The Travnik Chronicles. On display you will

find Andrić's texts in many languages, photos of the 1961 Nobel Prize ceremonies, and a model 19th-century bedroom. Don't be fooled, though: the museum was reconstructed in 1974 and is not the original birth house.

Near the bottom of Hendek lies the famous **Many Coloured Mosque**, which allegedly contains hairs from the prophet Mohammed's beard. Just east of the mosque are the peaceful springs called **Plava Voda** (Blue Water), a favourite summer spot.

Places to Stay & Eat
Alfa DM (☎/fax 508 703, ☎ 061 133 800; Srednje Osoje br 2A; beds 20KM) is Bosnia's closest thing to a youth hostel, with clean beds, clean bathrooms, a tiny kitchen, a tub and (amazingly) a washing machine. Call ahead, as the office may be closed. To get there, cross the bridge behind the Many Coloured Mosque, take the middle fork, and look for the sign 'Prenocište').

The **Pansion Oniks** (☎ 618 546; singles/ doubles 35/70KM), behind the café of the same name near the Many Coloured Mosque, has rooms with bathrooms and is central.

Hotel Slon (☎/fax 811 008; Fatmić 11; singles/doubles 72/104KM) hosted Princess Diana shortly before her death but has aged in the meantime. Rooms have satellite TV.

Restaurant Divan (Mustafa Kundić), directly below the Ivo Andrić museum, has the best food in town. Coming from the bus station, turn left on Zenjak and go one block. Patio seating is available in summer.

To sample Travnički sir, the famed local cheese, head to the **market**.

Getting There & Away
Buses go almost hourly to Sarajevo and four per day go to Banja Luka.

BANJA LUKA
☎ 051 • pop 239,000
This important crossroads on the Vrbas in northwest Bosnia-Hercegovina is now known to the world as the capital of the RS. Banja Luka was never much of a tourist centre and in 1993 local Serbs made sure it never would be by blowing up all 16 of the city's mosques, adding to damage from WWII bombings and a 1969 earthquake. While not otherwise damaged in the recent war, the city is economically depressed and flooded with Serb refugees from the Bosnian Federation

and the Croatian Krajina. Still, Banja Luka is a good place to catch daily life in action, such as old men absorbed in an outdoor chess match or sipping Nektar, the local brew.

Orientation

Banja Luka is only 184km from Zagreb, 235km from Sarajevo and 316km from Belgrade. Many of Banja Luka's streets, which includes the main thoroughfare Kralja Petra I Karađorđevića (Kralja Petra), have been renamed since the war and locals still may have trouble remembering the new names.

Information

Tourist Office Turistički Savez (☎/fax 212 323, ☎ 218 022; Kralja Petra 75) sells maps of Banja Luka and staff speak some English.

Money An ATM on the pedestrian street in the centre takes Visa and Cirrus. The foreign banks can cash travellers cheques; try the **Zagrebačka Banka** (Nikole Pašića), which also handles Visa and MasterCard advances, or **Raiffeisen Bank** (Jevrejska bb), which does MasterCard advances.

Post & Communications The main post office (Kralja Petra 93) has numerous phone booths, sells phonecards and gives Master-Card advances.

There is an Internet café, which charges 3.20KM per hour, just around the corner from the tourist office.

For English-language newspapers, try the **Cambridge Center** (Zmaj Jovina 13) in Gymnasium high school (closed weekends).

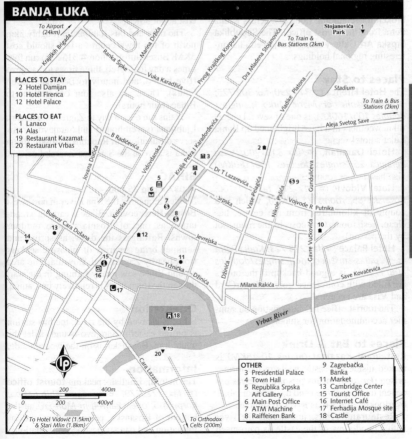

BANJA LUKA

To Airport (24km)

Stojanovića Park

To Train & Bus Stations (2km)

Stadium

To Train & Bus Stations (2km)

PLACES TO STAY
2 Hotel Damijan
10 Hotel Firenca
12 Hotel Palace

PLACES TO EAT
1 Lanaco
14 Alas
19 Restaurant Kazamat
20 Restaurant Vrbas

Vrbas River

0   200   400m
0   200   400yd

To Hotel Vidović (1.5km) & Stari Mlin (1.8km)

To Orthodox Celts (200m)

OTHER
3 Presidential Palace
4 Town Hall
5 Republika Srpska Art Gallery
6 Main Post Office
7 ATM Machine
8 Raiffeisen Bank
9 Zagrebačka Banka
11 Market
13 Cambridge Center
15 Tourist Office
16 Internet Café
17 Ferhadija Mosque site
18 Castle

BOSNIA-HERCEGOVINA

Things to See

The large 16th-century **castle** on the banks of the Vrbas River is an interesting place and hosts a summer drama and music festival in July. The benches of the overgrown amphitheatre were burned for fuel during the war.

War is the main theme of Banja Luka's sights. Atop Šehitluci Hill, 5km southeast of town, stands a huge white stone **WWII memorial**. This solitary and impressive slab affords a great view of the city.

In the city centre is the **presidential palace**, which has been the seat of government since January 1998. It faces the town hall. If you come across a bare patch of land in Banja Luka, most likely it is the site of one of the city's 16 destroyed mosques. The most famous of these was **Ferhadija** (1580), which was originally built with the ransom money for an Austrian count. Remarkably, ground has been broken for rebuilding (look just across Kralja Petra from the tourist office). The **Republika Srpska Art Gallery** along Kralja Petra has interesting regional holdings.

Places to Stay

The **Hotel Firenca** (☎ 311 290, fax 302 725; e firenca@blic.net; Marić Mirko 1; singles/doubles 105/160KM) is one of several cheerful newcomers that have brightened up Banja Luka's hotel scene.

Hotel Damijan, (☎/fax 313 200; Vase Pelagića 25; singles/doubles 130/180KM) also has dapper rooms.

Hotel Vidovič (☎ 217 217, fax 211 100; Kozarska 85; rooms 71-87KM), which is a couple of kilometres from the centre, has clean, fresh rooms (and costs by the room, not by the person).

Hotel Palace (☎/fax 218 723; Kralja Petra 1; e palas-sm@neco.net; singles/doubles 106/172KM) is a good backup if the others are filled with conference-goers. MasterCard and Visa are accepted.

The tourist office has information on summer accommodation for students.

Places to Eat & Drink

Restaurant Kazamat (mains 10-15KM) is tucked inside the castle walls in the former prison (kazamat means prison). It serves excellent traditional food and has outdoor tables overlooking the Vrbas River in summer.

Restaurant Vrbas, just across the river with a good view of the castle, is patronised by local politicians and known around town for its whopping portions.

Stari Mlin (Old Mill), west of town along the river and just beyond the Hotel Vidovič, occupies an even more secluded spot; opt for the meat roasted on the traditional sač.

Alas (Braće Mažar 47; dishes 9-28KM), off the transit road between Zagreb and Sarajevo, is the best place for fish.

Lanaco, in Stojanovića Park off Kralja Petra, is a popular pizza joint, with live bands at weekends.

Orthodox Celts (Stevana Bulajića 12), a lively Irish pub that sometimes features live bands, is good for a meal of Guinness.

Getting There & Away

The airport, some 25km north of Banja Luka, has flights to Vienna (Austrian Air) and Belgrade (Air Srpska). A taxi to the airport should cost about 30KM.

The train and bus stations lie roughly 3km north of the town centre; a taxi should cost 5KM. Buses (information ☎ 315 355) run four times a day to Zagreb, three times to Sarajevo (five hours), and hourly to Belgrade (seven hours). There are also four connections to Bihać (four hours).

Trains run once a day to Zagreb (4½ hours), Ljubljana (seven hours) and Sarajevo. Trains serve destinations in Republika Srpska; Banja Luka is also on the Sarajevo-Zagreb line.

BIHAĆ

☎ 037 • pop 75,000

Nestled alongside the Una River in northwest Bosnia-Hercegovina, Bihać is earning a reputation as one of Bosnia's more outdoor towns. Rafting is the draw, as spring and summer bring swarms of pleasure-seekers from nearby Zagreb and Slovenia. The area around Bihać saw heavy fighting in the war, though the town itself is relatively unscathed.

Orientation

Bihać is cleaved by the river; the bus station is on the eastern (Sarajevo-bound) side; the main drag, Bosanska, is on the western side.

Information

The helpful, English-speaking **tourist office** (☎/fax 322 079; e turizamb@bih.net.ba; Korpusa 5; open 8am-4pm Mon-Fri), at the bottom of Bosanska, provides maps and information and can suggest accommodation.

A few steps along Bosanska are the **post office**, with poste-restante facilities. It also does MasterCard, Maestro and Cirrus cash advances. The **telephone office** is at No 3. **Tasun** (*Branilaca bb*), a bar near the bus station, has four computers with Internet access.

Things to See & Do

The lofty, stone **captain's tower** (*admission 1KM*) on the western side of the river dates from the early 16th century. It was a prison from 1878 to 1959 but now holds a nifty multi-level **museum** featuring sarcophagi from the Bihać area and other early artefacts. If the museum is locked, call the number on the door and you can perhaps arrange to join a Bosnian-language tour.

Most visitors come for the Una's excellent, varied rapids; the rafting season usually runs from March to October. Groups can book with **Una Kiro Rafting** (*☎/fax 323 760;* **w** *www.una-kiro-rafting.com;* **M** *Ćazima Ćatića 1*). Prices range from 40KM to 80KM, depending on the type of trip. **Una Rafting** (*☎ 323 502;* **e** *raftbeli@bih.net.ba*) also does trips.

The **Una Regatta** festival during the last two weeks of July celebrates the river. For information on fishing, ask the tourist office.

Be very aware that the Bihać area was mined during the war.

Places to Stay & Eat

Uinski Biser (*☎ 333 732, 224 483; Djemala Bjedića 12; singles/doubles 53/73KM, with breakfast 55/83KM*), on the eastern side of the river, has four simple rooms in a gracious building.

Prednoćište Edo (*☎ 310 537; Hanovi br 6; singles/doubles/triples 30/40/60KM*), near the train station, is a good budget option, with plain but decent rooms; add 5KM per person for breakfast.

Hotel Ada (*☎ 311 570, fax 311 618; Husrefa Redžića 1; rooms from 72KM*), right on the river, has tidy rooms.

Ćordak Uni (*mains 7-13KM*), on Viteške Brigade on the western side of the river, has a selection of meats and fish.

River Unis (*Djemala Bjedića 6; mains 10-15KM*) offers a serene riverside setting in which to enjoy some well-garlicked squid and fine trout.

Express, nearby the telephone office on Bosanska, serves its ready-made hot meals cafeteria-style.

Getting There & Away

Buses run three times daily to Sarajevo (six hours) and five times daily to Zagreb (2½ hours). There are also buses to Banja Luka (four hours), Mostar and other towns.

Train service to Sarajevo and Zagreb is expected to begin by the end of 2002.

Hercegovina

MOSTAR
☎ 036 • pop 120,000

Mostar, the main city in Hercegovina, is a beautiful medieval town set in the valley of the aqua-green Neretva River. Its name is derived from the 16th-century Turkish bridge that used to arch over the river; *mostar* means keeper of the bridge. Sadly, the town was the scene of intense Muslim-Croat fighting during the recent war, which left many buildings destroyed or scarred. The bridge was destroyed by Croat shelling in November 1993. Once divided only by the Neretva River, Mostar is now segregated into Muslim and Croat sectors. Nonetheless, visitors are slowly drifting back to enjoy the old medieval buildings, cobbled streets and Turkish souvenir shops that give Mostar its charm.

Orientation

Mostar is a divided city. Though there are no physical barriers, Croats live on the western side of the Neretva River and Muslims on the east (though Muslims also control a small strip on the river's west bank). However, travellers can pass from one side to the other without any fuss. Maps are sold at kiosks and tourist agencies in the west for 6KM; a nicer map of the centre is available from the east-side tourist office near the bus station for 3KM.

Information

Tourist Offices The **Atlas Travel Agency** (*☎ 326 631,* **☎**/*fax 318 771*), in the same building as Hotel Ero, has useful suggestions. In the **tourist office** (*☎ 551 900*), on the eastern side beside the bus station, staff speak English and have information and maps of Mostar (3KM).

Money Adjacent to the Hotel Ero, **Hrvatska Banka**, changes travellers cheques for 1.5% commission and has a 24-hour ATM for Visa, MasterCard, Cirrus, Maestro and Plus.

BOSNIA-HERCEGOVINA

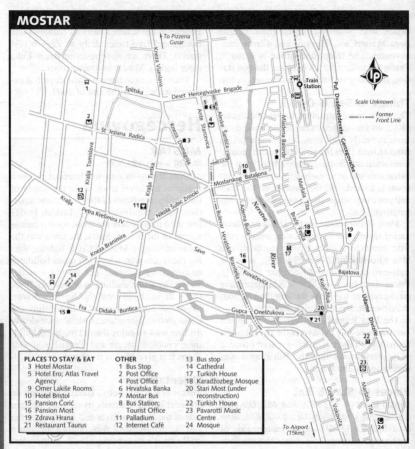

MOSTAR

PLACES TO STAY & EAT
3 Hotel Mostar
5 Hotel Ero; Atlas Travel
   Agency
9 Omer Lakiše Rooms
10 Hotel Bristol
15 Pansion Ćorić
16 Pansion Most
19 Zdrava Hrana
21 Restaurant Taurus

OTHER
1 Bus Stop
2 Post Office
4 Post Office
6 Hrvatska Banka
7 Mostar Bus
8 Bus Station;
   Tourist Office
11 Palladium
12 Internet Café

13 Bus stop
14 Cathedral
17 Turkish House
18 Karadžozbeg Mosque
20 Stari Most (under
   reconstruction)
22 Turkish House
23 Pavarotti Music
   Centre
24 Mosque

Post & Communications The large, modern **post office** on the western side, around the corner from Hotel Ero, has poste-restante mail; it's held for one month and pick-up is at window 12.

Email & Internet Access To log on there is an **Internet café** on Kralja Petra, just beyond the intersection with Kralja Tomislava. A small **post office** on Kralja Tomislava also has four Internet-linked computers. Hotels can often provide Internet access to guests.

Things to See
Stari Most (Old Bridge), now being slowly rebuilt, is still the heart of the old town. Sadly the small Crooked Bridge, which spanned a Neretva tributary nearby and was built a few years before Stari Most, was swept away in floods on the last day of 1999.

The cobbled old town, called **Kujundžiluk**, stretches down both sides of Stari Most and is filled with small shops selling Turkish-style souvenirs. Along the eastern side, the most famous mosque in Mostar is the **Karadžozbeg Mosque** (1557). The top of its minaret was blown off in the hostilities. Nearby, the 350-year-old **Turkish House** (Bišoevića) has colourful Turkish-style rugs and furniture. There is an even older **Turkish house** (Gaše Ilića 21), with a fascinating interior, behind the Pavarotti Music Centre.

The dramatic **front line**, which now essentially divides the town between Muslims and Croats, runs along the street behind Hotel Ero, then one street west to the main boulevard.

Places to Stay

Mostar's three hotels are expensive, but a few pleasant pansions offer relief. Many of their rooms have multiple beds. Reserve a week in advance, because groups occasionally fill the space. Most hotels have Internet access and accept major credit cards.

Private accommodation can be arranged through the east-side tourist office for 25KM per person.

Omer Lakiše, a retired professor who can speak a smattering of English, has eight beds in two rooms of in his **home** (☎ 551 627; Mladena Balorde 21A; beds 15KM including breakfast) and welcomes students.

Cheery **Pansion Most** (Adema Buća 100; ☎ 552 528, fax 552 660; singles/doubles 58/101KM) has eight rooms and is in a good central location.

Pansion Ćorić (☎ 331 077, fax 331 078; Fra Didaka Buntića; beds 50KM) is about 20 minutes' walk west of Stari Most. Rates include an excellent breakfast, and the friendly proprietors speak German but not English.

Zdrava Hrana (☎/fax 550 969, 551 444; Trg 1 maja 20; singles/doubles/triples/quads 30/40/60/80KM), a short walk uphill on the east side, is a good budget option. A handful of small apartments have very basic cooking equipment.

Across the river from the bus station, **Hotel Ero** (☎ 386 777, fax 386 700; e hotel.ero@ ero.ba; Ante Staroevića; singles/doubles 79/ 139KM) has polished rooms with porches and has disabled access.

The **Hotel Bristol** (☎ 500 100; e bristol@ cob.net.ba; Mostarskog Bataljona; singles/ doubles 63.50/97KM) is located on the river's west bank.

Hotel Mostar (☎ 322 679, fax 315 693; Kneza Domagoja bb; singles/doubles 52/ 84KM) is a plainer option.

Places to Eat

Čevapi spots are everywhere, and restaurants with divine views of the river cluster along the western riverbank near Stari Most; enjoy a *šopska salata* and a fresh trout there.

Restaurant Taurus overlooks where the Crooked Bridge used to stand and has tables on a covered porch. The food is hearty and traditional.

Pizzeria Gusar (Kneza Višeslava 8) is a trendy pizza joint, offering small, large and jumbo pizzas.

Entertainment

The **Pavarotti Music Centre** (☎ 550 7500, fax 552 081; Maršala Tita 179) has been the hub of Mostar's cultural activities since it opened in 1997. Music and dance courses for children are held in the large, modern building. The reception desk keeps a monthly schedule of free public concerts and events, and the centre's restaurant-café is always lively.

Palladium, off Kralja Tvrtka near the west-side roundabout, draws flocks of discoing youth. The Pavarotti Centre's receptionist is also bound to be up on the very latest hot spots to try.

Getting There & Away

Croatia Airlines has several flights weekly from Zagreb; the Mostar airport is about 15km south of the city centre.

Mostar lies on the route between Sarajevo and the coast. Eight buses per day run to Sarajevo, two to Split, one to Dubrovnik and one to Zagreb. Luggage storage is available in the bus station (2KM per item per day). Buses to Međugorje and other parts of Hercegovina depart from several bus stops on the western side. There's also a daily train (information ☎ 552 198) from Sarajevo to Ploče that stops in Mostar.

There are car-rental agencies in the airport; try **Europcar** (☎ 760 701).

AROUND MOSTAR

About 15km southeast of Mostar is the village of **Blagaj**, worth a day trip for its 16th-century *tekija* (Dervish monastery), beautifully sited at the point where the river Buna gushes out of the mountainside (2KM per visit). Afterwards, you can sit by the water and eat excellent trout at one of the restaurants.

Buses (20 minutes) run often from 'Mostar bus', which is beside Mostar's train station (on the opposite side to the bus station). From the stop in Blagaj the monastery is a 20-minute walk.

MEĐUGORJE
☎ 036

Međugorje is one of Europe's most remarkable sights. On 24 June 1981 six teenagers in this dirt-poor mountain village claimed they'd seen a miraculous apparition of the Virgin Mary, and Međugorje's instant economic boom began. Two decades later, Međugorje is awash with tour buses, souvenir stands, travel

BOSNIA-HERCEGOVINA

agencies, car-rental offices and pansions. The Catholic Church has not officially acknowledged the apparitions (the first in Europe since Lourdes, France, in 1858 and Fatima, Portugal, in 1917), but 'religious tourism' has developed as if this were a beach resort. Three of the original six still claim to see the vision daily, while the Virgin Mary only appears for the other three on special days.

After a wartime hiatus, the busloads of package pilgrims are returning with renewed fervour. Tourist facilities are fully intact, since the front line did not reach Međugorje – some locals attribute this to divine protection. The crowds are particularly heavy around Easter, the anniversary of the first apparition (24 June), the Assumption of the Virgin (15 August) and the Nativity of the Virgin (first Sunday after 8 September).

Orientation

Međugorje lies in the heart of Hercegovina, 125km and 129km from Split and Dubrovnik respectively and only 30 mountainous kilometres south from Mostar. Shops are clustered near the church. The streets have no names or numbers, but ask at tourist offices or hotels for the new topographical map that includes both Međugorje and Croatia.

Information

Tourist Offices Information centres thrive, but **Travel Agency Global** (☎ 651 489, fax 651 501; e OK@global-medjugorje.com), behind the central park, has Internet access. **Globtour** (☎/fax 651 393, 651 593), 50m from the post office towards the church, is also helpful. Both will arrange accommodation and find charter buses for groups from Split or Dubrovnik.

Money Almost any major currency will be accepted; menus are often priced in US dollars. It is often cheaper to pay in convertible marks, however. **Hrvatska Banka**, on the main street, has an ATM for Visa, MasterCard, Maestro, Cirrus and Plus. It charges 1.5% commission to change travellers cheques to convertible marks (more for other currencies).

Post & Communications The main post office (open 7am-9pm Mon-Sat, 10am-5pm Sun) by the bus stop has telephone booths and three computers with Internet access (4KM per hour).

Things to See & Do

Completed in 1969 before the apparitions began, **St James' Church** is a hub of activity. An information booth (☎ 651 988; w www .medjugorje.hr) beside the church has the daily schedule, plus multilingual printouts of the Virgin's monthly message.

Apparition Hill, where the Virgin was first seen on 24 June 1981, is near Podbrdo hamlet, southwest of town. A blue cross marks the place where the Virgin was supposedly seen with a cross in the background, conveying a message of peace. It's a place for silence and prayer. To reach Apparition Hill, take the road curving left (east) from the centre of town, and follow the signs to Podbrdo (3km away).

Mt Križevac (Cross Mountain) lies about 1.5km southwest of town. The 45-minute hike to the top leads to a white cross planted there in 1934 to commemorate the 1900th anniversary of Christ's death. Pilgrims stop to say the rosary at crosses along the trail. Wear sturdy shoes, as the path is extremely rocky. Candles are forbidden due to fire danger. After the hike, swing by **Pansion Stanko Vasilj**, 300m from the base of Mt Križevac, for a cool glass (1KM) of excellent home-made wine.

Wine-loving pilgrims might also wander over to **Cevrići**, a small residential area where superb *domaći vino* (home-made wine) is for sale (around 10KM per bottle). Arriving from Mostar, turn right on a small street about 40m after Pansion Ero. Just ask around; one house or another is sure to have some for sale.

Places to Stay

With 17,000 rooms, Međugorje probably has more accommodation than the rest of Bosnia-Hercegovina combined. Beds are fairly easy to find, except around major holidays. Pansions and hotels can fill unpredictably with large tour groups, so book in advance; if you're the only person in a pansion, service may not be quite as assiduous. Most pansion rooms look the same, though around the church is the most expensive. Friendly proprietors will usually offer the choice of B&B, half-board or full-board. Home-made meals are usually complemented with a bottle of *domaći vino*. Tourist offices can help arrange accommodation, but keep an eye on the price. Tour groups can find reduced rates.

The city's few hotels are blander and more expensive than the pansions, and the rooms are not much better.

Pansions Set about 100m back from the street, the large, whitewashed **Pansion Santa Maria** (☎ 651 523, fax 651 723; B&B/half-board/full-board per person 25/36/50KM), just past the turn by the post office, has pleasant rooms. Make sure you reserve early, as it is often filled with groups.

Pansion Martin (☎ 651 541, fax 651 505; e martin.ilic@st.tel.hr; half-board 65KM), very close to the church, is an excellent though pricier choice, with newly renovated rooms (some with balconies).

Pansion Međugorje (☎ 651 315, fax 651 452; B&B/half-board/full-board per person 20/30/40KM), is a homy, inexpensive gem on the road to Mt Križevac.

The **Pansion Pero Šego** (☎ 651-092); B&B/half-board/full-board per person 25/35/45KM) is another cheap choice for accommodation along this road.

Just 300m from Mt Križevac, **Pansion Stanko Vasilj** (☎ 651 042; B&B/ half-board/full-board per person 25/35/45KM) is a rambling house with a well-stocked wine cellar.

Hotels Most hotels offer group rates, and all include breakfast in the tariff.

Hotel Anna Maria (☎ 651 512, ☎/fax 651 023; singles/doubles 68/106KM) has rooms with satellite TV and phone.

The **Hotel Pax** (☎ 651 604, fax 650 874; singles/doubles 65/100KM), a comparatively ritzy choice that is closer to Apparition Hill, accepts most major cards; ask for a room with a balcony. Room rate is slightly less if you forego a TV.

Places to Eat
The half- or full-board options at the pansions include a very hearty, meat-and-bread meal. Restaurants can be expensive.

Colombo, near the church, is loved for its pizzas (11KM) and relatively low prices.

Galija, across the street, is good for a platter of steaming fish.

Getting There & Around
Most visitors come to Međugorje from Croatia. **Globtour** (☎/fax 651 393, 651 593) runs two buses daily from Split (3½ hours), one from Dubrovnik (three hours) and one from Zagreb (nine hours). Globtour also runs international bus services; ask for a schedule, and be sure to sign up well in advance. Four buses run daily between Međugorje and Mostar (40 minutes). There's no posted schedule, so ask at the post office. There are four buses daily from Sarajevo (three to four hours).

Taxis charge a flat fee of US$4 to anywhere in the town.

Bulgaria България

Bulgaria is a pleasant surprise. It boasts long, sandy beaches with plenty of top-class hotels, and the four major ski resorts usually offer plenty of snow. Sofia is a cosmopolitan city, with more than a dozen churches, as well as museums and art galleries to explore. The charming old towns of Plovdiv and Veliko Târnovo, and traditional villages such as Koprivshtitsa and Tryavna, just ooze an infectious historical ambience.

While some hotels, roads and buses may not be up to the standards expected in Western and northern Europe, Bulgaria is excellent value. And the country doesn't attract nearly as many Western tourists as it deserves, so visitors are assured of a cordial welcome. Importantly, Bulgaria is also cheap and safe.

Facts about Bulgaria

HISTORY

Archaeologists are now convinced that the earliest permanent settlers were the Neolithic people who lived in caves around 6000 BC. An amalgam of tribes, collectively known as the Thracians, started to settle around most of modern-day Bulgaria between about 6000 BC and the Bronze Age (about 2000 BC). From the 7th century BC, the Greeks made their way up the Black Sea coast, but avoided most of southern and central Bulgaria because of the unwelcoming Thracians.

By 345 BC, the Macedonians had conquered all of Bulgaria and subjugated the Thracians – but only for about 50 years. From 72 BC, the Romans successfully invaded and occupied major Greek ports in Bulgaria, but took over 100 years to control the Thracians. The demise of Roman power in Bulgaria was exacerbated by powerful, but ultimately short-lived, invasions by the Goths (AD 238–48), Vandals (378) and Huns (441–7).

Slavic tribes arrived in Bulgaria during the late 5th century. About 200 years later, the Bulgars, also known as the 'Proto-Bulgarians', migrated from Central Asia. This fierce Turkic tribe settled throughout the region and integrated with the Slavs and the few remaining Thracians.

At a Glance

- **Sofia** – surprisingly lively city with great museums
- **Vidin** – preserved stone fortresses overlooking the Danube
- **Tryavna** – delightful 19th-century village
- **Veliko Târnovo & Plovdiv** – fascinating old towns
- **Varna** – long Black Sea beaches; outstanding Archaeological Museum

Capital	Sofia
Population	7.97 million
Official Language	Bulgarian
Currency	1 leva (lv)
	= 100 stotinki
Time	GMT/UTC+0200
Country Phone Code	☎ 359

The Bulgar leader, Khan (Tsar) Asparukh, was responsible for establishing what became known as the First Bulgarian Empire (681–1018). In 865, Tsar Boris I (r. 852–89) tried to unify the fledgling Bulgar-Slav empire by converting it to Christianity. The empire reached its zenith under Tsar Simeon (r. 893–927), who created the largest and most powerful realm in Europe. Simeon's attempts to gain the Byzantine crown for himself, however, weakened the country. Veliki Preslav was eventually overrun by the Byzantines and the

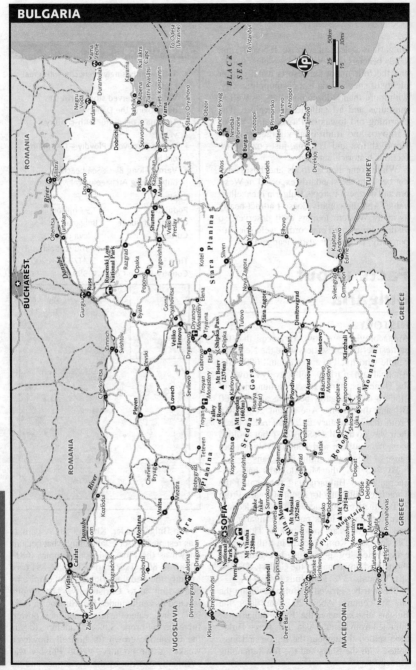

capital moved to Ohrid (in modern-day Macedonia) under Tsar Samuel (r. 997–1014).

In 1185, two aristocratic brothers, Asen and Petâr, spearheaded a general uprising against the Byzantines that resulted in the creation of the Second Bulgarian Empire (1185–1396). Asen's son, Tsar Ivan Asen II (r. 1218–1241), later became the most powerful ruler in southeastern Europe.

The Ottomans from Turkey started to invade the northern Balkan peninsula in 1362, and within 30 years had conquered all of Bulgaria. Turkish rule resulted in economic growth, but most churches and monasteries were destroyed or closed. Bulgarian national and cultural identity managed to survive, however, in isolated monasteries that were allowed to remain open or were never found, or controlled, by the Turks.

The so-called Bulgarian national revival period was prompted by a monk, known as Paisii Hilendarski, who wrote the first complete history of the Slav-Bulgarian people in 1762. He travelled across Bulgaria reading the history to illiterate people and igniting a long-forgotten national identity.

The most revered person in recent Bulgarian history is Vasil Levski. Born Vasil Ivanov Kunchev on 18 July 1837 in Karlovo, he was later given the *nom de guerre* Levski (from the Bulgarian word for 'lion') by his peers. He studied and worked as a monk, but moved to Belgrade in 1862 to join the anti-Turkish rebellion led by Georgi Rakovski. He later moved to Romania and then returned to Bulgaria. He travelled extensively to establish revolutionary cells. In early 1872, he was betrayed by a comrade and arrested by the Turks. In February 1873, Levski was hanged in Sofia.

The unsuccessful April Uprising against the Turks started prematurely at Koprivshtitsa in April 1876. The consequent carnage wreaked by the Turks outraged Western Europe, and led Russia to successfully defeat Turkey during the Russian-Turkish War (1877–78). Turkey ceded 60% of the Balkan peninsula to Bulgaria in the Treaty of San Stefano, but the powers of Western Europe later reversed these gains. These redefined borders have haunted the peninsula ever since: between 1878 and WWII each country in the Balkans, including Bulgaria, fought up to six wars over border issues.

The first Bulgarian National Assembly was convened at Veliko Târnovo on 16 April 1879, and on 26 June of that year Alexander Battenberg, a German prince, was elected head of state. On 6 September 1885, the principalities of Bulgaria and Eastern Rumelia were reunified after a bloodless coup. Complete independence from Ottoman control was declared on 22 September 1908, but only four years later the First Balkan War (1912) broke out as Bulgaria, Greece and Serbia declared war on Turkey. Squabbling among the victors led to the Second Balkan War (1913), from which Bulgaria emerged a loser.

At the beginning of WWII, Bulgaria declared its neutrality, but by 1941 German troops were stationed along the northern border with Romania. To avoid a war it could not win, the Bulgarian government joined the Axis. Bulgaria allowed the Nazis into the country, and officially declared war on the UK and France, but refused to declare war on Russia and to hand over thousands of Bulgarian Jews. A hastily formed coalition government sought peace with the Allies after WWII, but to no avail. Russia then invaded Bulgaria.

On 9 September 1944, the Fatherland Front, a resistance group coalition that included communists, assumed power. The Fatherland Front swept the November 1945 elections, but the communists within the Front achieved control of the new National Assembly and they proclaimed 'The People's Republic of Bulgaria' on 15 September 1946. Following the communist takeover, the royal family (including the king, Simeon Borisov Saxe-Coburgotski II) were forced to flee.

Simeon II became King of Bulgaria at the age of six following the death of his father, Tsar Boris III, in 1943. After leaving Bulgaria, Simeon II lived in Egypt for a while, before moving to Madrid where he became a successful businessman. Although he didn't return to his homeland again until 1996, he remained a popular figure. He is a distant relative of the Queen of England.

From the late 1940s, industrialisation and the collectivisation of agriculture were carried out, and Bulgaria became one of the most prosperous countries in the Soviet bloc. On 10 November 1989, an internal Communist Party coup led to the resignation of the ageing president, Todor Zhivkov. The Communist Party subsequently agreed to relinquish its monopoly on power and changed its name to the Bulgarian Socialist Party (BSP). The BSP defeated the Union of Democratic Forces (UDF) in the first parliamentary elections in 1990 – so Bulgaria had the dubious honour of being the first country from the former Soviet bloc to elect the communists back into power.

During the 1990s the UDF and BSP vied for power, while both unsuccessfully tried to keep some control of the economy. In June 2001, the National Movement Simeon II (NMSII) party, led by the former king of Bulgaria, Simeon II (who fled with his family in 1943), was voted prime minister in parliamentary elections. In a stunning reversal five months later, the popular president Petâr Stoyanov, was beaten by Georgi Parvanov, leader of the Coalition for Bulgaria and the BSP.

GEOGRAPHY

Bulgaria (110,912 sq km) lies at the crossroads of Europe and Asia in the heart of the Balkan peninsula. Bulgaria stretches 520km from the Serbian border to the Black Sea and 330km from Romania to Greece. About one-third of Bulgaria is mountainous – 5% of the terrain is over 1600m high.

The Stara Planina Mountains extend almost from the Yugoslav border to the Black Sea. Mt Musala (2925m) in the Rila Mountains is the highest peak between Transcaucasia and the Alps. The Rodopi Mountains stretch east along the Greek border from the Rila and Pirin Mountains, separating the Aegean from the Thracian Plain, and spilling over into Greece.

The 378km coast of the Black Sea is lined with some of Europe's finest beaches. The mighty Danube River mostly acts as a border with Romania.

CLIMATE

Generally, Bulgaria has a temperate climate with cold, damp winters and hot, dry summers. The Rodopi Mountains form a barrier to the moderating Mediterranean influence of the Aegean. Northern Bulgaria is open to the extremes of Central Europe, while the Black Sea

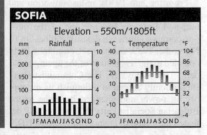

moderates temperatures in the east. Sofia's generally favourable climate is one of its main attributes, with average highs of 28°C in July and August and 3°C from December to February. Rainfall in Bulgaria is highest from April to June, while during winter the country is sometimes disrupted by heavy snowfalls.

ECOLOGY & ENVIRONMENT

Like most countries in Eastern Europe, the lure of fast cash and lax government controls have hindered any ecologically sustainable development: logging and animal poaching continues in protected areas; air and water pollution is rampant; Bulgarians often rely on nonrenewable fossil fuels, like coal, for heating, and on nuclear power for electricity; and farmers still illegally burn farmland.

Pollution in the Black Sea and the Danube River is appalling, though some resorts along the coast have received prestigious, international 'Blue Flag' awards for pollution-free beaches.

GOVERNMENT & POLITICS

Since 1990, Bulgaria has been a multiparty, democratic republic. Elections for the prime minister, who is also leader of the unicameral National Assembly, are usually held every four years; the president, as the head of state, is elected every five years. Traditionally, the cabinet consists of 16 ministers (currently three are women). Voting is not compulsory, but an admirable 67% of eligible voters participated in the 2001 parliamentary elections.

ECONOMY

Bulgaria's strategic location and highly skilled workforce are significant advantages, but those vested interests created by the old political system and inexperience from well-intentioned reformers continue to hinder any economic development. Tax reform and new banking laws have been enacted, but foreign investment is meagre and privatisation slow.

Since December 1999, Bulgaria has been frantically lobbying other European countries in an attempt to join the EU (and NATO). However, Bulgaria is 57th on the UN Development Programme's human development report, based on the wealth and life expectancy of its citizens and the government's commitment to education. Of the dozen or so European countries striving to join the EU and NATO, only Romania is rated lower.

POPULATION & PEOPLE

Nearly 70% of Bulgaria's population live in urban centres. Fertility rates are alarmingly low, which is one reason the population has actually *fallen* by about 503,000 since 1992. Bulgarians are Slavs and officially constitute 88.3% of the population. The largest minorities are Turks (8%); Macedonians (2.5%); Roma (2.6%), known as gypsies; Armenians (0.3%); and Russians (0.2%). About 250,000 Pomaks live in the Rodopi Mountains. They are Slavs who converted to Islam during the Ottoman occupation of the 15th century.

ARTS

Most of Bulgaria's earliest artists painted on walls of homes, churches and monasteries. The most famous was Zahari Zograf (1810–53), who painted magnificent murals in the monasteries at Rila, Troyan and Bachkovo. Many of his works were inspired by medieval Bulgarian art, but are more human than divine.

Bulgarian musical academies continue to churn out world-class opera stars, such as Nikolai Gyuzelev, Gena Dimitrova and Anna Tomova-Sintova. The most common traditional folk instruments are the *tambura*, a four-stringed long-necked lute akin to the Greek *bouzouki*; a goatskin bagpipe called a *gayda*; the *kaval*, a long, open flute; and the *tâppan*, a large, cylindrical, double-headed drum. But most of the modern Bulgarian sounds you're likely to hear are termed 'wedding music', a spirited pop-folk idiom also often called *chalga* (or 'truck driver music').

Probably the most obvious product of the Bulgarian national revival period (18th and 19th centuries) is its unique architecture. The ground floor of many homes normally consists of bare stone. The exterior of the upper floor(s) are often painted brown and white and feature rectangular windows with wooden shutters. Ceilings are usually intricately carved and/or painted with bright murals, and the interior also features small fireplaces and low doors.

SOCIETY & CONDUCT

Bulgarians shake their head in a curved, almost bouncy, motion to indicate 'yes', and, less often, nod to mean 'no'. To add to the confusion, some well-travelled Bulgarians may do the opposite to 'help' confused foreigners. If in doubt, ask *da ili ne* (yes or no)?

When visiting monasteries, mosques and churches, please dress conservatively and act appropriately. While shorts are mostly acceptable, revealing tops for females and tight shorts for both sexes are frowned upon, though you probably won't be refused entry. Topless sunbathing is permitted at most major beach resorts along the Black Sea, but before baring your top half, ladies, check that it's acceptable on that particular stretch of sand.

RELIGION

During the communist era Bulgaria was officially 'atheist' and only the elderly were left relatively unharassed to pursue their worship. These days, about 85% of the Bulgarian population claim to be Orthodox but not nearly as many as this regularly visit church. Officially, 13% of the population are Muslims and almost all of these are Sunni. Over the centuries, the Islam practised in Bulgaria has incorporated various local traditions and Christian beliefs and has become known as Balkan Islam.

LANGUAGE

Bulgarian is a South Slavonic language closely related to Macedonian. It became the official language in 1879, when the dialect spoken in the capital at the time, Veliko Târnovo, was chosen as the national language. Older Bulgarians may speak Russian and a few may get by in French or German, while others, especially those working in tourism and business, are more likely to speak English. Almost everything is written in Cyrillic, so it's essential to learn this strange alphabet. See the Language chapter at the end of this book for a list of useful Bulgarian words and phrases.

Facts for the Visitor

HIGHLIGHTS

The best museums are the Archaeological Museum in Varna, the Ethnographical Museum in Sofia and the Historical Museum in Smolyan. Of the 160 monasteries spread throughout the country, the big 'four' are the Rila Monastery, the Dryanovo Monastery, the Bachkovo Monastery and the Troyan Monastery. There are also numerous mosques and churches – none more spectacular than the Alexander Nevski Church in Sofia. The Romans left impressive reminders, such as the Roman Thermae in Varna and the Roman Amphitheatre in Plovdiv. Other must-see places are the traditional villages of Koprivshtitsa, Arbanasi and

Tryavna; Nesebâr and Sozopol along the Black Sea coast; and the fascinating old towns in Veliko Târnovo and Plovdiv.

SUGGESTED ITINERARIES

Your itinerary will obviously depend on your interests, where you arrive and/or depart, and the season, but you may wish to use this list as a guide:

One Week
  Sofia (two to three days), Plovdiv (two to three) and Veliko Târnovo (two)
Two Weeks
  Stay longer at the places listed above and visit Koprivshtitsa (one to two days), Tryavna (two) and Arbanasi (one)
One Month
  Most travellers choose a circular route between Sofia and the Black Sea coast, eg, Sofia (two to three days), Rila Monastery (one), Bansko (two), Plovdiv and around (four), Sliven (one to two), Burgas and around (two to three), Varna and around (four), Balchik (one), Dobrich (one), Shumen and around (two), Ruse and around (two), Veliko Târnovo (two to three), Tryavna (two) and Kazanlâk (two) and Koprivshtitsa (one to two).

PLANNING
When to Go

Spring (particularly April to mid-June) is an excellent time to visit. Summer (mid-June to early September) is ideal for hiking and festivals, but is the peak season for travellers from elsewhere in Europe. September can often be perfect; the autumn trees are glorious, fruit and vegetables are plentiful, shoulder-season tariffs are in effect, the tourist hordes have returned home, and you can still swim and sunbathe in the Black Sea.

The peak season along the Black Sea coast is mid-July to late August; at the ski resorts, it's Christmas/New Year and February to mid-March. If you avoid these places at these times, you may be astounded how few tourists there are in Bulgaria.

Maps

Baedeker Bulgaria (1:750,000) and Bartholomew's *Bulgaria* (1:750,000) are both printed in English and probably available in your home country. Proper road maps are absolutely *essential* if you're driving around the country – one of the best is *Bulgaria* (1:530,000), published in English by Datamap and available in Bulgaria. Detailed maps for most cities, towns and major attractions are available in Bulgaria, but mostly in Cyrillic.

What to Bring

The easy availability of consumer goods is Bulgaria's most enthusiastic expression of capitalism. If you bring a car or bicycle, it's worth carrying some spare parts, though these should be available. Bring a tent if you want to camp and a sleeping bag if you're staying at camping grounds and mountain huts. Except at hostels, basic hotels and mountain huts, towels are provided, but they're often threadbare and tiny so you may want to bring your own.

RESPONSIBLE TOURISM

The national **Bulgarian Association for Rural & Ecological Tourism** (☎/fax 02-971 3485; e baret@aster.net) has established several excellent hiking 'eco-trails' around the country. Information about these is also available from the regional tourist offices. Another progressive group based in Sofia and promoting ecotourism is the **Bulgarian Association for Alternative Tourism** (☎ 02-989 0538; e baat_bg@hotmail.com).

TOURIST OFFICES
Local Tourist Offices

The **National Information & Advertising Center** (☎ 02-987 9778, W www.bulgaria travel.org; ul Sveta Sofia, Sofia) is the closest thing to a tourist office in the capital. Several autonomous, regional tourist information centres (TICs) have also been established throughout Bulgaria, but most of these are associations of travel agencies rather than independent tourist offices.

Tourist Offices Abroad

Some offices worth contacting include:

Australia Consulate-General – see Embassies & Consulates
Canada (☎ 0613-789 5341, fax 789 3524) 325 Stewart St, Ottawa, Ontario K1N 6K5
France (☎ 01 45 51 05 32, fax 45 51 78 97) 1 Ave Rapp, 75007 Paris
Germany (☎ 069-295 284, fax 295 286) Eckenhemier Landstrasse 101, 60318 Frankfurt am Main
Netherlands (☎ 070-346 8872, fax 363 6704) Alexander Godelweg 22, 2517 JJ, The Hague
UK (☎ 020-7589 8402, fax 7589 4875) 186 Queen's Gate, London, SW7 5HL
US (☎/fax 0202-332 6609) 1621 22nd St NW, Washington DC 20008

VISAS & DOCUMENTS
Visas
Currently, citizens of the following countries can obtain a free, 30-day tourist visa at any Bulgarian border, international airport or sea port: all member countries of the EU, Australia, Canada, the Czech Republic, Hungary, Israel, Japan, New Zealand, Poland, Yugoslavia, Slovakia, Switzerland and the USA.

If you wish to stay longer than 30 days and don't want to leave Bulgaria to get another 30-day visa, or you come from a country not listed above, apply for a visa at one of the embassies or consulates listed later. Normally, the only option is a 90-day tourist visa that costs from US$30 to US$60 (depending on the country). Allow about one week for the visa to be processed.

Visa Extensions The 30-day tourist visa available on arrival *cannot* currently be extended within Bulgaria. If you want to stay longer, apply for a 90-day tourist visa, or just leave Bulgaria for Greece, Turkey or Romania and obtain another 30-day tourist visa on arrival. Extending a 90-day tourist visa costs the leva equivalent of about US$100. Apply at the **Passport Office** (*☎ 02-982 3316; bul Maria Luisa 48, Sofia)* or the **Foreign Citizens Bureau** (*☎ 032-234 835; ul Petko D Petkov 9, Plovdiv)*.

Registration
At all hotels, hostels, camping grounds and, often, private homes, staff will normally take details from your passport, fill out the registration form (in Cyrillic) and give you a copy. In theory, you must then show *all* of these forms to Immigration officials when you leave. However, this requirement is almost never enforced these days.

If you're staying with friends and relatives or, sometimes in a private home, you're supposed to personally register with the police within 48 hours. Ask a local where you're staying about the current requirements. If you're camping or staying in mountain huts, registration is clearly impossible – a fact that Immigration officials will grudgingly accept if they ask you about your registration forms.

Student, Youth & Teacher Cards
Holders of the International Student Identity Card (ISIC), International Youth Travel Card (IYTC) and International Teacher Identity

Card (ITIC) can obtain discounts of 10% to 20% at some museums, hotels, hostels, medical and dental clinics, and restaurants. There are selected travel agencies who also offer card-holders up to 50% off domestic flights and 10% off train and bus tickets.

A brochure listing (in Cyrillic) the places that offer these discounts is available from **Orbita** (*☎ 02-987 9128;* e *orbita@ttm.bg; bul Hristo Botev 48, Sofia)*. Orbita will also issue these cards to anyone with the correct documentation.

EMBASSIES & CONSULATES
Bulgarian Embassies & Consulates
Major Bulgarian diplomatic missions in other countries include:

Australia *Consulate-General:* (*☎/fax 02-9327 7581,* w www.users.bigpond.com/bulcgsyd) 4 Carlotta Rd, Double Bay, NSW 2028
Canada (*☎ 0613-789 3215,* e mailmn@storm .ca) 325 Stewart St, Ottawa, K1N 6K5 Consulate in Toronto
France (*☎ 01-45 51 85 90,* e bulgamb@ wanadoo.fr) 1 ave Rapp, 75007 Paris
Germany (*☎ 030-201 0922)* Mauerstrasse 11, 10117 Berlin Consulates in Bonn & Munich
Greece (*☎ 01-647 8106,* e embassbg@athserv .otenet.gr) 33a, Stratigou Kallari Str, Paleo Psychico 15452, Athens Consulate in Thessaloniki
Ireland (*☎ 01-660 3293)* 22 Burlington Rd, Dublin
Netherlands (*☎ 070-350 3051,* e bulnedem@ xs4all.nl) Duinrooseweg 9, 2597 KJ The Hague
Turkey (*☎ 0312-426 7455, fax 427 3178)* Atatürk Bulvari 124, Kavaklidere, Ankara Consulates in İstanbul & Edirne
UK (*☎ 020-7584 9400)* 186 Queen's Gate, London SW7 5HL
USA (*☎ 0202-387 0174,* w www.bulgaria -embassy.org) 1621 22nd St NW, Washington DC 20008 Consulate in New York

Embassies & Consulates in Bulgaria
All diplomatic missions detailed below are in Sofia (area code ☎ 02).

France (*☎ 965 1100,* w www.ambafrance-bg .org) ul Oborishte 27–29
Germany (*☎ 918 380)* ul Frederic Joliot-Curie 25
Greece *Consulate:* (*☎ 946 1562)* ul Oborishte 19 Consulate in Plovdiv

BULGARIA

Macedonia Consulate: (☎ 705 098) ul Frederic Joliot-Curie 17
Netherlands (☎ 962 5785) ul Galichitsa 38
Romania (☎ 973 3510) bul Sitnyakovo 4
Turkey (☎ 980 2270) bul Vasil Levski 80
  Consulates in Burgas & Plovdiv
UK (☎ 9339 2222) ul Moskovska 9
USA (☎ 963 2022) ul Kapitan Andreev 1
Yugoslavia (☎ 943 4590) ul Marin Drimov 17

CUSTOMS

Foreigners are allowed to take in and out 'gifts up to a reasonable amount', as well as souvenirs and articles for personal use.

MONEY

The local currency, leva (lv) – singular lev – comprises 100 stotinki. For major purchases, eg, organised tours, air fares, car rental, mid-range and top-end hotels, prices are almost always quoted by staff in US dollars (however, prices will probably be quoted in euros in the near future). In these cases only, we have listed prices throughout this chapter in US dollars though payment is possible in US dollars, leva or any major currency. While budget hotels and some private rooms also may quote their rates in US dollars, payment should be in leva.

Currency

Bulgarian banknotes come in denominations of one, two, five, 10, 20 and 50 leva, and coins come in one, two, five, 10, 20 and 50 stotinki. The prices for smaller items are always listed as a fraction of a lev, ie, '0.40 lv' rather than '40 stotinki'.

Since January 2002, the lev has been pegged to the euro.

Exchange Rates

Below are the official exchange rates for major currencies at the time of publication.

country	unit		leva
Australia	A$1	=	1.07 lv
Canada	C$1	=	1.25 lv
Euro Zone	€1	=	1.96 lv
Japan	¥100	=	1.67 lv
New Zealand	NZ$1	=	1.06 lv
Romania	10,000 lei	=	0.57 lv
Turkey	TL1,000,000	=	1.14 lv
UK	UK£1	=	3.05 lv
USA	US$1	=	1.93 lv
Yugoslavia	10DIN	=	0.32 lv

Exchanging Money

Cash The foreign currencies listed can be changed at the many foreign-exchange offices found at every city, town and major attraction. Most don't charge commission or fees, but some do despite claims to the contrary on notices outside. The best currencies to take are US dollars, UK pounds and euros. Foreign-exchange offices (and banks) will give you a receipt, but there's no need to keep it.

It's also easy to change cash at most larger banks. They may offer slightly higher rates than foreign-exchange offices, but many charge commission and queues are often long.

The lev is freely convertible, so there are no problems changing excess leva back into US dollars or other major foreign currencies.

Travellers Cheques Not all of the foreign-exchange offices and banks cash travellers cheques. Those that do sometimes only accept ones issued by American Express and Thomas Cook and will charge 3% to 5% commission. Some larger banks (eg, Bulbank in Sofia) will change US-dollar travellers cheques into US dollars cash for a fee (2% to 3%).

ATMs Automated teller machines (ATMs) that accept major credit cards (ie, Cirrus, Maestro, JCB, Visa, MasterCard and American Express) are increasingly common. The maximum withdrawal allowed per day by most ATMs is 200 lv.

Credit Cards American Express, Visa and MasterCard can be used at most upmarket of the hotels and restaurants, tourist-oriented souvenir shops, car-rental firms and travel agencies, and at some petrol stations, but rarely anywhere else. Some places, particularly the more expensive hotels, add a 5% surcharge to your bill for using a credit card.

Some larger banks (and occasional foreign-exchange offices) provide cash advances in leva over the counter using Visa or MasterCard. You will be charged about 4% commission and probably later hit with other fees by the credit-card company.

Black Market No black market exists in Bulgaria. You may still be approached to change money on the street, but this is unnecessary and illegal – and there's a high chance you'll be given counterfeit leva, short-changed or robbed.

Costs

If you stay in budget hotels or private rooms, eat at cheap Bulgarian restaurants and travel by public buses and 2nd-class trains, US$17/15 per person per day travelling as a single/couple should be enough. If you stay in the cheaper mid-range hotels, eat non-Bulgarian food at nice restaurants, charter occasional taxis, take 1st-class trains and buy souvenirs, allow from US$32/27 per person per day.

Dual Pricing One annoying aspect of travelling around Bulgaria is that foreigners are charged much more than Bulgarians for their accommodation and admission to tourist attractions. While these may eat into your daily budget, they are easily offset by the remarkably cheap food, drink and public transport.

Tipping & Bargaining

Waiters (and taxi drivers) normally round the bill (and fare) up to the nearest convenient figure and pocket the difference. In some restaurants a 10% service charge is already added. If not, and the service is good, add about 10%.

Haggling is not customary. An exception is at the Black Sea resorts where taxi drivers and landlords of private rooms habitually inflate prices for foreigners.

Taxes

The value-added tax (VAT) of 20% is included in all prices quoted in Bulgaria and all prices listed in this chapter.

POST & COMMUNICATIONS
Post

Sending a postcard to anywhere outside of Bulgaria costs 0.35 lv. The 'express service' is 0.45 lv to the UK and Europe and 0.60 lv to the rest of the world. Letters weighing up to 20g cost 0.68 lv to send out of Bulgaria; the 'express service' is 0.80 lv to the UK and Europe and 0.90 lv to anywhere else.

Telephone

To ring Bulgaria from abroad, dial the international access code from your home country, add ☎ 359 (the country code for Bulgaria), followed by the area code (minus the first zero) and then the number.

It's (normally) easy to telephone anywhere in the world from public telephone booths, telephone centres, private homes and hotels.

Every major settlement throughout the country has a Bulgarian Telecommunications Centre (BTC), normally inside or very near the main post office. From a BTC, a call costs 1.80 lv per minute to the UK and Europe, 2.25 lv per minute to North America and 3.05 lv per minute to Australia and New Zealand. No off-peak rates are available.

Most telephone booths are operated by Mobika and BulFon and use phonecards, while some Mobika booths also accept Visa and MasterCard for long-distance calls (and have instructions in English). Phonecards for both operators cost from 5 to 25 lv and are available at most kiosks and grocery shops. Mobika and BulFon booths can be used to make calls within Bulgaria, and direct long-distance calls to Europe and North America, but to anywhere else you have to use the international operator (☎ 0123).

Bulgarians have taken to mobile (cell) telephones like ducks to water and somehow manage to balance their cigarette and coffee while chatting away on a *handy* (as it's sometimes called). Mobile phone numbers have different codes (eg, ☎ 087 and ☎ 088) and are indicated by the abbreviations 'GSM' or 'mob' on signs and business cards etc. Each of the three operators, GloBul, Mobikom and MobilTel, cover most of the country, but contact your own mobile phone company about the usability of your phone in Bulgaria.

Fax

Faxes can be sent from most BTCs and post offices throughout Bulgaria. Incoming faxes can also be collected for a nominal fee.

Email & Internet Access

Even the smallest town in Bulgaria has at least one Internet centre. With about 150 Internet service providers throughout the country, competition is fierce and access is remarkably cheap: about 1 lv per 30 minutes.

DIGITAL RESOURCES

Useful websites (all in English) to access before you travel include:

- w **www.onlinebg.com** – news, shopping and great links
- w **www.dirbg.com** – excellent search facilities and links
- w **www.bulgarianspace.com/bmg** – best for anything cultural
- w **www.news.bg** – all sorts of useful information

BULGARIA

BOOKS

The Bulgarians from Pagan Times to the Ottoman Conquest by David Marshall Lang is well worth reading.

A Short History of Modern Bulgaria by RJ Crampton is incisive and detailed, if somewhat dry.

We the People by Timothy Garton Ash offers a clear and insightful interpretation of the collapse of communism throughout the region in 1989.

Bulgarian Cuisines by Dimitâr Mantov is the best recipe book (and souvenir), ideal for impressing friends with a traditional dish when you get home.

NEWSPAPERS & MAGAZINES

The English-language weekly the *Sofia Echo* (W www.sofiaecho.com) is published every Friday, and the perky *Sofia City Info Guide* (W www.sofiacityguide.com) comes out each month. Day-old copies of major British and German newspapers are available in central Sofia and at beach resorts along the Black Sea coast. *Time* and *Newsweek* are also sold at hotels and book stalls in central Sofia and at beach resorts along the coast.

RADIO & TV

Some radio stations worth listening to in Sofia include BG Radio (91.9FM), Radio Contact (106FM) and Jazz FM (104FM). Darrik Radio can be heard in Sofia (98.3FM), Varna (90.7FM), Plovdiv (94.6FM) and Veliko Târnovo (88.9FM). A number of international short-wave services are transmitted on the FM stations in Sofia: the Voice of America (103.9FM), BBC World Service (91FM), Deutsche Welle (95.7FM) and Radio France Internationale (103.6FM).

Bulgarian television is nothing to get excited about, which is why locals with enough money buy satellite dishes. Televisions in most hotel rooms can pick up a plethora of regional stations, so you can enjoy Israeli talent quests, Cypriot game shows and Russian soap operas, as well as CNN, BBC and MTV.

TIME

The whole of Bulgaria is on Eastern European Time, ie, GMT/UTC plus two hours – except the during daylight-saving period when the clocks are put forward by one hour between the last Sunday of March and the last Sunday in October.

LAUNDRY

Coin-operated laundrettes are virtually non-existent, but dry-cleaners can be found in most cities and major towns. Some budget and mid-range hotels also offer laundry services to guests.

TOILETS

Most toilets are the sit-down European variety. The standard of public toilets, especially at train and bus stations, is generally abominable. More acceptable, privately run toilets are available in central Sofia and at major tourist attractions for a small fee. All decent hotels provide toilet paper, but it's rarely offered anywhere else.

HEALTH

Every city and major town has an acceptable government-run hospital, while several high-quality and expensive private clinics are also located in Sofia. Citizens of Belgium, the Czech Republic, Hungary, Poland and the UK are able to receive emergency treatment at government-run hospitals for no charge (but medicines cost extra).

WOMEN TRAVELLERS

In general, travelling around Bulgaria poses no particular difficulties for women. Simply take the usual precautions. If you attract unwanted attention, *Omâzhena sâm* means 'I am married' and is a pretty firm message.

GAY & LESBIAN TRAVELLERS

Consensual homosexual sex is legal from the age of 14, but Bulgaria is generally far from gay-friendly. Same-sex couples should refrain from overt displays of affection and be discreet when booking into hotels. For details of gay clubs, contact the **Bulgarian Gay Organization Gemini** (☎ 02-987 6872; W *www .bgogemini.org; bul Vasil Levski 3, Sofia*).

DISABLED TRAVELLERS

Disabled travellers will have a rough time because few facilities exist for people with special needs. Uneven and broken pavements make wheelchair mobility problematic, and ramps and special toilets for those in wheelchairs are few and far between.

SENIOR TRAVELLERS

Bulgaria shouldn't cause too many obvious problems for able-bodied senior travellers. In all cities and major towns, and at most tourist attractions, there are commodious hotels, restaurants with staff who speak English, French or German, taxis, comfortable inter-city private buses and trains, and car-rental agencies. The resorts along the Black Sea coast are particularly well set up.

TRAVEL WITH CHILDREN

Most of the necessities for travelling with ankle-biters, such as nappies (diapers), baby food and fresh or powdered milk, are readily available. All cities and towns have parks with (dated) playground equipment, while children can also enjoy water slides, toy trains and paddle pools at the beach resorts.

USEFUL ORGANISATONS

You may wish to contact one of the following organisations in Sofia (area code ☎ 02):

Bulgarian Chamber of Commerce & Industry (☎ 981 1632) ul Parchevich 42
Bulgarian Red Cross (☎ 944 1443) ul Dondukov 61
UNICEF (☎ 544 730) bul Pencho Slaveikov 18b
UNHCR (☎ 980 2453) ul Denkoglu 19

DANGERS & ANNOYANCES

Some travellers see that Bulgaria is in the middle of the troublesome Balkans and feel slightly uneasy, but there's no need to worry; Bulgaria is as peaceful and trouble-free as Greece, Turkey and Romania.

Theft is not much of a problem, but parked cars are prime targets, especially those with foreign number plates and/or rental-agency stickers. The major traffic dangers are from cars hurtling through pedestrian crossings and from trams and trolleybuses shuttling stealthily along what appear to be pedestrian malls.

Bulgaria has harsh drug laws. It's a common route for drugs smuggled across the Black Sea from Russia and Armenia, and from Turkey to the south, so always treat the transport, trade and use of drugs with a *great* deal of caution.

LEGAL MATTERS

Foreigners are, of course, subject to the laws of the country, but no particular laws are unique to Bulgaria. The days of asking for bribes from foreigners are long gone, though residents do complain bitterly about corruption in some government departments.

Emergency Services

We certainly hope you don't need to contact any of these nationwide, toll-free 24-hour emergency numbers. Operators are unlikely to speak English.

For the fire brigade call ☎ 160; for Medical Rescue & Ambulance call ☎ 150. If you need the police call ☎ 166. You can contact the traffic police and notify them about road accidents on ☎ 165.

If you need roadside assistance outside Sofia call ☎ 146 or ☎ 048 146; for roadside assistance within Sofia call ☎ 1286.

BUSINESS HOURS

Government offices are normally open weekdays (ie, Monday to Friday) between 9am and 5pm, but often close for 45 to 60 minutes any time between noon and 2pm. Private businesses more or less keep the same hours, but staff rarely have time for a leisurely lunch break. Most shops open from about 9am to 7pm weekdays, and about 9am to 1pm on Saturday, but tend to open and close later during the summer.

Banks are open between 9am and 4pm weekdays, while foreign-exchange offices are generally open 9am to 6pm Monday to Saturday. BTCs and post offices are normally open 8am to 6pm daily, and Internet centres usually operate between about 10am and 9pm Monday to Saturday.

Many tourist attractions close for one or two days per week, usually between Sunday and Wednesday. Their opening times change regularly, so don't be surprised if a tourist attraction is closed even though it should be open (according to opening hours provided in this chapter or listed on their windows).

PUBLIC HOLIDAYS & SPECIAL EVENTS

Official public holidays are New Year's Day (1 January), Liberation Day (3 March; also known as National Day), Orthodox Easter Sunday & Monday (March/April; one week after Catholic/Protestant Easter), St George's Day (6 May), Cyrillic Alphabet Day (24 May; also known as Day of Bulgarian Culture), Unification (6 September; also known as National Day), Bulgarian Independence Day (22 September), National Revival Day (1 November) and Christmas (25 & 26 December).

BULGARIA

Special Events

Bulgaria hosts an inordinate number of festivals, the largest of which is the International Folk Festival held in Koprivshtitsa every five years (next in 2005). Other marvellous events are held annually in Sofia, Plovdiv, Bansko, Koprivshtitsa, Veliko Târnovo, Burgas, Sozopol and Varna – see those sections later for details. More information about these and other festivals can be obtained from **w** www.bulgariatravel.org and **w** www.bulgarian space.com/bmg and all the relevant regional tourist offices.

ACTIVITIES

Facilities at the ski resorts may not be world-class, but the snow is plentiful, the slopes are accessible and the prices are affordable (though foreigners are charged more than Bulgarians for accommodation, ski lifts and equipment rental). The ski season runs from about mid-December to mid-April at four major resorts: Bansko, Borovets, Vitosha National Park and Pamporovo. You can rent equipment and arrange ski instruction at any of the resorts, but it's less easy at Vitosha.

Bulgaria boasts about 37,000km of marked hiking trails. These trails are indicated on proper hiking maps in yellow, red, green or blue, which correspond to the colours on the signs along the trails. Most trails start and/or finish each day at one of the numerous mountain huts, so there's usually no need to bring a tent. *The Mountains of Bulgaria*, written by Julian Perry and available in Bulgaria, is the best book for long-distance trekking, but is of limited use for short hikes and the maps are inadequate. By far the best hiking/trekking maps available in Bulgaria are published by Kartografia (and available in Sofia).

Beaches along the Black Sea coast are long, wide, clean and developed, but the range of water sports is disappointing, however, though reasonably cheap.

COURSES

For learning Bulgarian, **Sts Cyril & Methodius University of Veliko Târnovo** (*☎/fax 062-628 023;* **w** *www.uni-vt.bg*) usually has a one-month 'International Seminar in Bulgarian Language and Culture' every August.

Each summer **Vedafolk** (*☎ 02-745 540*) presents an impressive range of residential seminars in traditional Bulgarian folk arts and languages in several villages.

WORK

Most foreigners working in Bulgaria are specialists with contracts arranged *before* they arrived. The websites mentioned in the Digital Resources section earlier, and the site run by the *Sofia Echo* (**w** www.sofiaecho.com), may list employment opportunities, but the frightening amount of paperwork required, and the fees for work permits (1000 lv!), are designed to dissuade foreigners from taking up temporary employment in Bulgaria.

ACCOMMODATION
Camping

Many of the few remaining camping grounds in Bulgaria are run down and closer to noisy main roads than anywhere peaceful or picturesque. Most close between November and April, and some along the Black Sea coast are only open June to early September. Pitching a tent outside a camping ground is technically prohibited, but normally accepted if you're discreet and you don't build wood fires.

Hostels

Most larger hostels and dormitories are only open in summer (June to August), and many only cater to Bulgarians on excursions and hiking trips. Therefore, getting information about the locations, opening times and costs of hostels is difficult unless you speak Bulgarian or know well-informed locals. No hostel in Bulgaria is part of any international organisation, such as the Youth Hostels Association (YHA) or Hostelling International (HI).

Mountain Huts

A dormitory bed in a mountain hut – called a *hizha* – is available to anyone. Most are only open in summer (May to October), but those situated at or near major ski slopes are often also open in winter. It's usually not necessary to book a bed in advance, but they can be reserved at the **Bulgarian Tourist Union** (*☎ 02-980 1285; bul Vasil Levski 75, Sofia*). (The office is inside a photo shop along the underpass at the junction of bul Vasil Levski and ul General Gurko.) It also sells hiking maps and a book (in Cyrillic) listing details about most mountain huts.

Private Rooms

Some families in a few cities, towns and villages offer rooms in private homes to visitors. These rooms are normally comfortable and clean, but bathroom facilities are often communal. The owners are almost always friendly, but rarely speak English. Rooms can be arranged through accommodation agencies in town/city centres or at bus/train stations. Alternatively, wait to be approached in the street or look out for relevant signs in shop windows or hanging outside homes.

Hotels

Hotels are rated from one to five stars, but one- and two-star places rarely advertise their rating. Most smaller and more remote hotels at the ski resorts are closed outside of the season (ie, closed mid-April to November), while almost nowhere along the Black Sea coast opens in winter (late October to early April). Reserving a room in any hotel in Bulgaria is not necessary, unless you're determined to stay at a particular hotel at peak times (eg, Nesebâr in August or Bansko at Christmas) or during a major festival. One reliable website for inquiring about mid-range and top-end accommodation is **w** www.hotelsbulgaria .com – there are often substantial discounts.

FOOD

It's important to note that all side dishes, such as chips, salads, rice and vegetables, must be ordered separately from the main dish, and will cost extra.

At cafeterias staff dollop out large helpings of simple, precooked meats, soups and salads. These places are ideal if you want to save money, taste some local food and also avoid deciphering a Bulgarian menu – simply point at what you want, pay the amount shown on the cash register and enjoy.

A *mehana* is a traditional tavern, often featuring authentic decor, waiters and waitresses dressed in folk costumes and live music.

As a starter, perhaps order *topcheta supa* (a creamy soup with meatballs), *tarator* (a cold dish with cucumbers, walnuts and yogurt), *bob* (bean soup) or a common *shopska* salad (chopped tomatoes, cucumbers and onions covered with grated cheese).

Popular Bulgarian main courses include such delights as *kebabche* (grilled spicy meat sausages); *kyufte*, which is basically the same thing but round and flat; *musaka*, which is shaped like the Greek equivalent but doesn't contain eggplants (aubergines); *kavarma* (meat and vegetables in a clay pot); and *plakiya* (rich fish stew).

Junk-food junkies won't suffer in Bulgaria; the big multinational chains can be found all over the country.

Vegetarians will not be disappointed with the number of meatless dishes available, but may be disaffected by the lack of imagination.

DRINKS

The average Bulgarian doesn't seem to be able to function properly without a serious fix of caffeine (and nicotine) each morning. Acceptable espresso coffee is available everywhere, and many places now serve cappuccinos. Tea is mostly the *bilkov* (herbal) and *plodov* (fruit) variety, while European-style *cheren chay* (black tea) is hard to find. Major international brands of soft drinks (sodas) and mineral water are widely available. The natural fruit juices are delicious.

Bulgaria is the world's fifth-largest exporter of wine. Palatable plonk includes Cabernet Sauvignon (from around Sliven and Melnik) and Sauvignon Blanc (from near Varna). Beers produced by the Zagorka, Astika and Kamenitsa breweries are available throughout Bulgaria, though provincial beers – such as *Pirinsko Pivo* (from Blagoevgrad) and *Shumensko Pivo* (Shumen) – are often better.

ENTERTAINMENT

There are numerous bars in the cities and towns in which to enjoy a drink, meet some locals and, maybe, hear bands play traditional Bulgarian folk music or passable versions of foreign pop. Most cities also have grand old theatres that feature (in Bulgarian) opera, drama and ballet. All cities and most larger towns have at least one cinema that shows recent foreign films in the original language (usually English). Tickets cost from 2 to 5 lv, depending on the film, session time and comfort of the cinema.

SPECTATOR SPORTS

The overwhelming sport is football (soccer). The season runs from late August to late May (with a break in January and February) and matches normally take place on Saturday and Sunday at 4pm and Wednesday at 7pm. Tickets cost from 4 to 9 lv.

SHOPPING

Exquisite mementoes include embroideries from Nesebâr, Varna and Sofia; paintings of the traditional village life or landscapes from

Nesebâr, Sofia, Varna and Plovdiv; wood-carvings from Tryavna; and carpets, rugs and bags from Koprivshtitsa. As the regional centre for the Valley of Roses, Kazanlâk is the best place to buy rose oils, perfumes, shampoos, liqueurs, tea bags and jams. For antiques, head to the old towns in Veliko Târnovo and Plovdiv.

Getting There & Away

AIR

Before buying a normal return air ticket to Bulgaria from Western or northern Europe, check the price of package tours to the resorts on the Black Sea coast (in summer) or the ski slopes (in winter). Airlines taking tourists to the beaches and mountains, via Sofia and/or Varna, include Britannia Airways (from Gatwick, Manchester and Birmingham), Hemus Air (from Leipzig), and Air Via and Condor Airlines (both from several German cities).

The national carrier, Balkan Airlines, flies between Sofia and most European cities. Other airlines that fly to Sofia all year include British Airways (from London), KLM (from Amsterdam), Lufthansa (from Frankfurt and Munich), Air France (from Paris) and Alitalia (from Rome and Milan).

There are no direct flights between Bulgaria and the USA or Canada, but Virgin Atlantic has a code-share agreement with Balkan Airlines. From Australia or New Zealand, get a connection through Europe or jump on an Aeroflot flight from Singapore.

LAND
Border Crossings

Below is a list of major road borders that accept foreigners and are open 24 hours.

Greece Between Kulata (Bulgaria) and Promahonas (Greece); and Svilengrad and Ormenion
Macedonia Between Gyueshevo and Deve Bair; Zlatarevo and Delčevo; and Stanke Lisichkovo and Novo Selo
Romania Between Vidin and Calafat; Ruse and Giurgiu; Kardam and Negru Vodă; and Durankulak and Vama Veche
Yugoslavia Between Kalotina and Dimitrovgrad; Vrâshka Chuka and Zajc; and Strezimirovtsi and Klisura
Turkey Between Malko Târnovo and Derekjoj; and Kapitan-Andreevo and Edirne

Bus

Greece & Macedonia From its office in Sofia, **MATPU** (☎ 02-953 2481; ul Damyan Gruev 23) operates a bus that leaves every day at 10.30am for Athens, via Thessaloniki (Greece), while **ATT** (bul Maria Luisa) also has daily buses from its office in Sofia to Athens and Thessaloniki. Other less comfortable but slightly cheaper buses to Athens leave from the bus terminals to the northwest and northeast of the Princess Hotel in Sofia.

City Local Transportation Co (☎ 032-624 274; pl Tsentralen) operates between one and three buses a day from Plovdiv to Thessaloniki, and runs another bus to Athens on Tuesday and Thursday. **Hemus Tours** (☎ 042-57 018; ul Tsar Simeon Veliki) in Stara Zagora also has regular buses to Athens.

MATPU and ATT offer several buses a day to Skopje (Macedonia) from Sofia, and **MATPU** (bul Sveti Dimitâr Solunski), opposite the bus terminal in Blagoevgrad, has daily buses to Bitola (Macedonia).

Romania Buses don't travel directly between Romania and Bulgaria because of long delays at the border near Ruse. Many buses, however, do travel between Bucharest (Romania) and İstanbul (Turkey), via Ruse and Veliko Târnovo. So, you could get off the bus after clearing Bulgarian customs, but you may have to pay the entire Bucharest-İstanbul fare. And you won't be able to get on an İstanbul-Bucharest bus within Bulgaria.

Yugoslavia ATT (see Greece & Macedonia earlier) offers buses from Sofia to Belgrade via Niš (Yugoslavia). Others to Belgrade and Niš leave from the bus terminals near the Princess Hotel in Sofia.

Turkey MATPU and ATT (see Greece & Macedonia earlier) have daily buses from Sofia to İstanbul, while others depart from the two terminals near the Princess Hotel in Sofia. Also to İstanbul, several private companies at the Yug Bus Terminal in Plovdiv offer daily buses; **Zlatni Piasaci Travel** (☎ 052-355 419), based at the main bus terminal in Varna, runs regular services; and **Enturtrans** (☎ 056-844 708; ul Bulair) in Burgas has daily buses.

Train

Tickets for international trains can be bought at any Rila Bureau (most open weekdays only) in the cities and major towns and/or at dedicated ticket offices (most open daily) at larger train stations with international connections. Tickets must be paid for in leva.

Greece & Macedonia The *Trans-Balkan Express* travels between Thessaloniki and Budapest (Hungary) daily, via Bucharest, Ruse, Gorna Oryahovitsa, Sofia and Sandanski. The Sofia-Thessaloniki service links the two cities daily during summer (15 June to 30 September) via Sandanski. There are also daily trains between Svilengrad and Athens.

No trains travel directly between Bulgaria and Macedonia, so the only way to Skopje by rail from Sofia is to get a connection in Niš.

Romania The *Bulgaria Express* runs between Sofia and Moscow, via Bucharest, Ruse and Pleven, every day. (Between Sofia and Bucharest, this train is called the *Grivitza*.) Also, every day in summer (15 June to 28 September), a train from Burgas and another from Varna connect with a train leaving Ruse for Bucharest, Budapest, Bratislava (Slovakia) and Prague (the Czech Republic).

Every day in summer (15 June to 28 September), the Sofia-Saratov service travels to Bucharest from Sofia, via Gorna Oryahovitsa and Ruse. Every day year-round, the *Bosfor* between İstanbul and Bucharest also passes through Bulgaria, via Stara Zagora, Veliko Târnovo and Ruse. And the *Trans-Balkan Express* (see Greece & Macedonia earlier) travels between Thessaloniki and Budapest, via Bulgaria and Bucharest.

Yugoslavia The daily *Balkan Express* between İstanbul and Belgrade goes via Plovdiv, Sofia and Niš and the Sofia-Beograd train goes every day between the two cities, via Niš.

Turkey To İstanbul, you can take the *Bosfor* or *Balkan Express* trains as mentioned in the previous Romania and Yugoslavia sections. There are also daily trains between Svilengrad and İstanbul.

CAR & MOTORCYCLE

Drivers of normal-sized cars (and motorbikes) are charged an entrance tax of US$10, except citizens from the Czech Republic, Denmark, France, Germany, Hungary, Italy, the Netherlands, Spain, Sweden, Switzerland and the UK. Drivers of private cars (and motorbikes)

from *all* countries must state on arrival which border they plan to exit, and pay a 'highway fee' of US$0.10 cents per km (minimum of US$5) when they depart Bulgaria. All drivers must also pay a 'disinfection fee' of US$3 when they enter the country. The above fees can be paid in US dollars, euros, leva and most other major European currencies.

Drivers of private and rented cars (and also motorbikes) must carry the registration papers in the vehicle. Your driving licence from home is valid in Bulgaria. Third-party 'liability insurance' is compulsory and can be purchased at any Bulgarian border. Better still, buy a Green (or Blue) Card before arrival – see the Getting Around chapter for details.

SEA & RIVER

Despite the long and inviting coastline, few of the international passenger boats ply the Black Sea to Bulgaria. Boats link Varna with İstanbul, Sochi (Russia), and Odesa, Sevastopol and Yalta (Ukraine) from May to September, but these are expensive luxury cruisers. Information is available from Etap Adress and Megatours, both on the ground floor of Cherno More Hotel, ul Slivnitsa 33, in Varna.

See the Vidin and Ruse sections later in this chapter for information about crossing the Danube River by boat to/from Romania.

ORGANISED TOURS

Most companies offering ski tours to Bulgaria are based in the UK, such as **Balkan Holidays** (☎ 020-7543 5555; **W** www.balkanholidays.co.uk) and **Crystal** (☎ 0870-160 6040; **W** www.crystalski.co.uk).

Most visitors to the Black Sea coast, however, are French or German. Two companies offering tours are **Slav Tours** (☎ 02 38 77 07 00; **W** www.slavtours.com; 6 rue de Jeanne d'Arc, 45000 Orleans) and **BG Tours** (☎ 030-706 2020; **W** www.bgtours.de; Maiendorfer Damm 147, 12107 Berlin).

Two British-based organisations that specialise in outdoor activities are **Balkan Eden** (☎ 01227-373 727; **e** balkan_eden@yahoo .com; 31a Canterbury Rd, Herne Bay, Kent UK CT6 6AU) and **Exodus** (☎ 020-8673 0859; **W** www.exodus.co.uk).

DEPARTURE TAX

The departure tax on all international flights is US$8. This tax is included in the price of all tickets bought in and outside of Bulgaria.

Getting Around

AIR

Hemus Air flies Monday to Saturday (15 March to 27 October) between Sofia and Varna (US$60/100 one way/return); it also lays on extra flights most days between 1 July and 15 September. All year, Balkan Airlines operates up to four flights a day between Sofia and Varna ($58/102). The quaintly named Dandy Airlines flies between Sofia and Varna (US$58/102) several times a day (14 July to 30 October) and between Sofia and Burgas (US$55/104) four times a week (15 April to 30 October). Tickets are available at the relevant airline offices, or from any travel agency, in Sofia, Varna and Burgas (see the destination sections for contact details).

The departure tax for domestic flights is US$2. This tax is included in the price of all tickets bought in and outside Bulgaria.

BUS & MINIBUS

Buses and minibuses link all cities and major towns and connect villages with the nearest transport hub. Buses run by the government are old, comparatively uncomfortable and slow, but newer, quicker and more commodious private buses and minibuses are more commonly available. And, surprisingly, they cost little more than the fare for a ramshackle public bus.

Tickets for public buses can rarely be booked in advance, but seats on private buses can be reserved one (or more) days in advance. Except for long-distance services at peak times, however, there's no need to book any bus more than a few hours ahead.

Whenever possible take a minibus, because they're quicker and more comfortable than public and private buses. Most minibuses leave from inside, or very close to, major public bus terminals. Tickets for minibuses cost about the same as for public buses, and are usually bought from the driver.

TRAIN

Trains are generally more comfortable than buses and minibuses and offer far nicer views. Except for the intercity express from Sofia to Varna and Burgas (and return), standards are not what you'd expect in Western and northern Europe, but trains are reasonably quick, often punctual and astoundingly cheap. Trains are classified as *ekspresen* (express), *bârz* (fast) or *pâtnicheski* (slow passenger). Use a fast or express train unless you absolutely thrive on train travel, or you want to visit a smaller village (and have no choice), or you're travelling on a really tight budget.

For frequent services, such as between Sofia and Plovdiv, there's rarely a problem if you just turn up at the station and buy a ticket for the next train. Advance tickets are sometimes advisable, however, to the Black Sea on the intercity express during a summer weekend. Advance tickets can be bought at specific counters inside larger train stations and at Rila Bureaus in cities and major towns.

Most Europe-wide rail passes can be used anywhere in Bulgaria – see the introductory Getting There & Away and Getting Around chapters for details. No special individual pass is available within Bulgaria, but the Bulgarian State Railways (BDZh) is part of the Euro Domino system. This pass is poor value, however, unless you plan to travel around Bulgaria by train for 10 hours every day.

First-class compartments seat six people, while eight are crammed into 2nd class. Sleepers and couchettes are available from Sofia to Burgas and Varna for an extra 8 to 15 lv per person, but should be booked in advance. Fares during the less-frequented 'regular' period (ie, Monday morning to Friday morning) are about 20% less, and fares for 1st class are around 25% higher than for 2nd class.

Here are two final tips. First, train stations are poorly marked, almost always signposted in Cyrillic, and no announcements are made on board in any language – so keep an eye out for your station. And second, only the intercity express between Sofia and the Black Sea coast reliably offers a buffet car, so bring your own food and drink.

CAR & MOTORCYCLE

The best way to travel around Bulgaria is to hire a car or bring your own car (or motorcycle), but driving is not as relaxing as it may be in Western and northern Europe. Road conditions are generally taxing, for example, and road signs (mostly in Cyrillic) are often frustratingly ambiguous or nonexistent.

Petrol is available in normal (91 octane), unleaded (95 octane) and super (98 octane). The normal petrol has an octane rating too low for Western cars, but unleaded (Euro 95) is easy to find. Diesel is also widely available.

Road Rules

The official speed limits are 50km/h in built-up areas, 90km/h on main roads and 120km/h on highways (50/80/100km/h for motorbikes/trucks/buses). Drivers and front-seat passengers must use seat belts, and motorcyclists must wear helmets. The blood-alcohol limit is 0.05%, and traffic police are *very* unforgiving about drink-driving. And please take care; every month about 100 people die on Bulgarian roads.

Rental

Cars can be rented in Albena, Burgas, Plovdiv, Ruse, Slânchev Bryag, Sofia, Sozopol, Sveti Konstantin, Varna, Veliko Târnovo and Zlatni Pyasâtsi, though sometimes it may be cheaper to return to Sofia and organise something from there. There's nowhere in Bulgaria to rent a motorbike.

Smaller Bulgarian rental agencies don't discriminate, so they charge foreigners the same rates as Bulgarians. These agencies are sometimes little more than a telephone in a garage in a remote suburb, however, so arrange everything through a travel agent (who may speak your language). For a basic Mazda 323, expect to pay from US$24 per day (for one to four days), US$20 per day (five to 10 days) or US$17 per day (11 to 20 days), including unlimited kilometres but not insurance (US$3 extra per day) or petrol.

Larger, more established Bulgarian car-rental companies offer more or less the same standard of vehicles and service as the major international agencies but are far cheaper (ie, about 50% more than the rates listed here for the smaller rental agencies). Two such reliable agencies in Sofia are **Drenikov** (*☎/fax 02-944 9532; w www.drenikov.com; ul Oborishte 55*) and **Rentaavto** (*☎ 02-929 5005; w www.rentauto-bg.com; ul Stamboliyski 219*). The rates offered by the major international companies, such as Avis and Hertz, are outrageous.

To rent a car, you normally need to have had a driving licence from your own country for at least one year, and be 21 years old or more. One-way rental within Bulgaria is possible with the more established companies for a negotiable fee. Most of the major international companies will allow some of their vehicles to be taken out of the country, but let them know beforehand so they can sort out the paperwork.

BICYCLE

Cycling is a viable way of getting around. The downside is that many roads are windy, steep, in poor condition and chock-a-block with traffic, and bikes aren't allowed on highways. On the other hand, traffic is light along routes between villages, and long-distance buses and trains will carry your bike for a small extra fee. Spare parts are available in cities and major towns, but it's probably better to bring your own.

HITCHING

Bearing in mind the general advice in the Getting Around chapter, hitching in rural Bulgaria may be preferable to being restricted by infrequent public transport. Hitching tends to be in fits and starts, however, because cars often only travel to the next village. Oh – and the pretty ladies standing along the major highways near Sofia waving down male drivers are *not* looking for, umm, a lift.

LOCAL TRANSPORT

All cities and major towns have buses, trolley-buses and trams, but they're generally decrepit and overcrowded. Tickets for these can be bought from kiosks (and sometimes from drivers), and don't forget to buy an extra ticket for each piece of large luggage. Newer minibuses operate in some cities, but most visitors will be confused by their ever-changing routes; tickets are available from the driver. Sofia boasts a modern metro (subway) system.

Taxis – which must be painted yellow and equipped with working meters – can be flagged down along most streets in every city and town. Taxis are generally cheap, but rates do vary enormously so it pays to shop around before jumping in. All taxis must clearly display their rates on their windows: the first line indicates the rate per kilometre between 6am and 10pm, while the last line shows the cost per minute for waiting. Taxis can be chartered for longer trips at negotiable rates of about 14 lv/h and 75 lv/day.

ORGANISED TOURS

Travel agencies and tourist offices that offer tours to foreigners can be found in Borovets, Burgas, Kazanlâk, Ruse, Sofia, Smolyan, Varna and Veliko Târnovo. Naturally, plenty of agencies at the Black Sea resorts of Albena, Slânchev Bryag and Zlatni Pyasâtsi offer (expensive) tours.

Enterprising Bulgarian travel agencies that offer a number of interesting tours around the country include:

Balkanfolk Tours (☎ 02-322 010, **W** www.balkan folk.com) ul Opalchenska 74, Sofia. This company specialises in folk tours.

Balkantourist (☎ 02-980 2324, **W** www.balkan tourist.bg) bul Vitosha 1, Sofia. This is an all-purpose travel agency.

Explorer Travel Company (☎/fax 02-430 852, **e** explorer@mail.bol.bg) Explorer specialises in bird-watching and photography trips.

Odysseia-In Travel Agency (☎ 02-989 0538, **W** www.newtravel.com) bul Stamboliyski 20, enter from ul Lavele. This is the best place for maps and advice, and to organise adventure-oriented trips.

Sofia София

☎ 02 • pop 1.18 million

Sofia, which sits on a 545m-high plateau in western Bulgaria at the foot of the imposing Mt Vitosha mountain range, is the highest capital in Europe. Almost all international flights start and finish in Sofia, and the capital is also the hub of much of Bulgaria's bus and rail transport, so most travellers end up here for a few days at least. There are enough museums, churches and art galleries to keep most visitors happy, and it's only an hour or so to excellent hiking and skiing spots – see the Vitosha National Park section later in this chapter. Sofia is also an ideal base for organised tours to the Rila Monastery.

History

The region around modern-day Sofia was first settled by the Thracian Serdi tribe, and later by the Macedonians and Romans. The Huns invaded in AD 441, but the city was soon retaken and rebuilt by the Byzantine rulers after Attila's death. The Slavs started to settle in the area during the 6th and 7th centuries. They renamed it Sredets, which means 'middle' (ie, of the Balkans).

The Bulgar king, Khan Krum, came through in 809 and made it a major town of the First Bulgarian Empire. Then, in 1018 the Byzantine rulers took the city and called it Triaditsa. In 1194, the Bulgars replaced the Byzantines and the city became a major trading centre for the Second Bulgarian Empire. It was at this time that the name of the city

was probably changed to Sofia after the Church of St Sofia (which still stands).

The Ottomans captured Sofia in 1382 and held it for nearly 500 years. During this time, it became the regional capital and regained some prominence as a market town because of its central location. Sofia officially became the capital of Bulgaria a year after the liberation of the city from the Turks in 1878.

Information

Tourist Offices The **National Information & Advertising Center** (☎ 987 9778; **W** www .bulgariatravel.org; ul Sveta Sofia; open 9am-5.30pm Mon-Fri) is across from Goody's restaurant. Although not a tourist office in the true sense of the word, staff are happy to help and they speak English.

Money You'll find **foreign-exchange offices** along bul Stamboliyski, bul Maria Luisa and bul Vitosha. Most are open from 8am to 8pm daily, though some along upper (northern) bul Maria Luisa are open 24 hours. The best bank for changing cash and travellers cheques, and obtaining cash advances over the counter with Visa and MasterCard, is **Bulbank** (cnr ul Lavele & ul Todor Alexandrov). Most banks around central Sofia have ATMs that accept all major credit cards.

Post & Telephone The **Central Post Office** (ul General Gurko 6; open 7.30am-8.30pm daily) has a poste-restante bureau. Inside the impressive **BTC** office (ul General Gurko; open 24hr), you will find plenty of telephone booths and an office for both sending and receiving faxes.

Email & Internet Access Internet access is pleasingly cheap and easy. Try the **BTC** office (ul General Gurko); the **Ultima Internet Center** (ul Lavele 16), just down from the entrance to the Odysseia-In Travel Agency; and the **Internet centres** inside, and along the underpass beneath, the NDK National Palace of Culture complex in Yuzhen Park.

Bookshops The **bookshop** inside the Fine Arts Gallery (ul Shipka 6) is the best place for guidebooks about the region. **Book World** (ul Graf Ignatiev 15) sells dictionaries, phrasebooks, local and international maps and foreign-language novels. Stalls crowded around pl Slaveikov along ul Graf Ignatiev

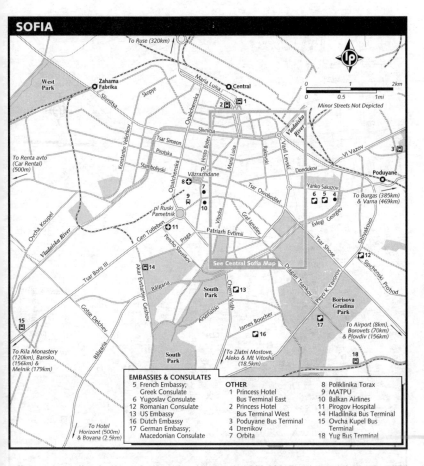

SOFIA

To Ruse (320km)

West Park

Zahama Fabrika

Central

Maria Luisa

Skopye

Silnitsa

2 ⬛ ⬛ 1

Vladaiska River

Tsar Simeon

Opalchenska

Silnitsa

Rakovski

Vl Vazov

3 ⬛

Pirotska

Hristo Botev

Maria Luisa

Vasil Levski

Dondukov

Poduyane

To Renta avto (Car Rental) (500km)

Konstantin Velichkov

Stamboliyski

Opalchenska

pl Vazrazhdane

Tsar Osvoboditel

Yanko Sakazov

6 5 4

To Burgas (385km) & Varna (469km)

8 ➕ 7

9

Vitosha

Graf Ignatiev

Evlogi Georgev

Chataldovo

10

pl Ruski Pametnik

Patriarh Evtimii

Tsar Shose

Gen Totleben

➕ 11

Pencho Slaveikov

Praga

Dragan Tsankov

Peyo K Yavorov

Sipchenski Prohod

⬛ 12

Ovcha Koupel

Vladaiska River

See Central Sofia Map

Tsar Boris III

Akat Evtatiev Geshov

Bålgaria

⬛ 14

Cherni Vrah

⬛ 13

Borisova Gradina Park

Gotse Delchev

South Park

Arsenalski

⬛ 17

To Airport (8km), Borovets (70km) & Plovdiv (156km)

15 ⬛

Bålgaria

South Park

James Boucher

⬛ 16

18 ⬛

To Rila Monastery (120km), Bansko (156km) & Melnik (179km)

To Zlatni Mostove, Aleko & Mt Vitosha (18.5km)

To Hotel Horizont (500km) & Boyana (2.5km)

0 1 2km
0 0.5 1mi
Minor Streets Not Depicted

EMBASSIES & CONSULATES
5 French Embassy;
 Greek Consulate
6 Yugoslav Consulate
12 Romanian Consulate
13 US Embassy
16 Dutch Embassy
17 German Embassy;
 Macedonian Consulate

OTHER
1 Princess Hotel
 Bus Terminal East
2 Princess Hotel
 Bus Terminal West
3 Poduyane Bus Terminal
4 Drenikov
7 Orbita

8 Poliklinika Torax
9 MATPU
10 Balkan Airlines
11 Pirogov Hospital
14 Hladilnika Bus Terminal
15 Ovcha Kupel Bus
 Terminal
18 Yug Bus Terminal

sell maps, as well as books and second-hand novels in English, French and German.

Emergencies The major public hospital for emergencies is **Pirogov Hospital** (☎ 51 531; bul Gen Totleben 21), while **Poliklinika Torax** (☎ 988 5259; bul Stamboliyski 57) is a competent, private clinic. For police matters (between 8am and 6pm), there are special contact numbers where operators speak English (☎ 988 5239) and French (☎ 982 3028).

Things to See
City Centre The best place to start a walking tour is **Aleksander Nevski Church** (pl Aleksander Nevski; admission free; open 7am-7pm daily). This massive building was created between 1892 and 1912 as a memorial to the 200,000 Russian soldiers who died fighting for Bulgaria's independence during the Russian-Turkish War (1877–78). Inside, the **Aleksander Nevski Crypt** (admission 8 lv; open 10.30am-noon & 2pm-6.30pm Wed-Mon) holds one of Bulgaria's best collections of religious icons. Over the road is the extensive **National Gallery for Foreign Art** (ul 19 Fevruari; admission 2 lv, free Sun; open 11am-6pm Wed-Mon).

Head down bul Vasil Levski and turn right for ul Tsar Osvoboditel, along which is the **National Assembly** (not open to the public) and the **Monument to the Liberators**. A bit further along ul Tsar Osvoboditel is the **St Nikolai Russian Church** (admission free; open 7am-7pm daily), built in 1912–13 by Russian emigres. Not far along the same

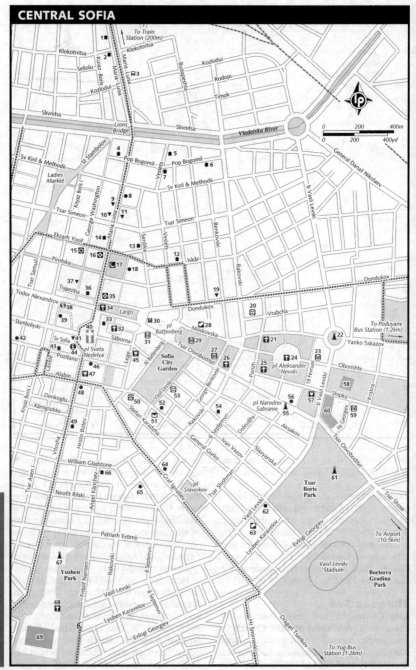

CENTRAL SOFIA

CENTRAL SOFIA

street is the **National Museum of Natural History** *(admission 3 lv; open 10am-6pm daily)*, which houses over one million specimens of animals, minerals and vegetables.

Soon you'll stumble across the **National Art Gallery** *(ul Tsar Osvoboditel; admission 2 lv, free Sun; open 10.30am-6.30pm Tues-Sun)*, which features a number of rooms of Bulgarian art. Sharing this former Royal Palace is the **Ethnographical Museum** *(admission 3 lv; open 10am-5.30pm Tues-Sun)*, which contains fascinating displays about Bulgarian arts and crafts from the last 300 years. Then head down ul Vasil Levski to admire the eye-catching neoclassical **Ivan Vazov National Theatre** *(ul Vasil Levski 5)*.

Cut through the **Sofia City Garden** and head west along trendy ul Sâborna to the magnificent **Sveta Nedelya Cathedral** *(pl Sveta Nedelya; admission free; open 7am-7pm daily)*. Built between 1856 and 1863, this cathedral features an exceptionally ornate interior. Further up bul Maria Luisa is the renovated **Central Hali Shopping Centre** and

the resplendent **Sofia Synagogue** *(ul Ekzarh Yosif 16)*, featuring a small **museum** *(admission free; open 10am-4pm Sun-Fri)*. Across the road from the Hali is the unmistakable **Banya Bashi Mosque** *(bul Maria Luisa; admission free; open dawn-dusk daily)*. The gorgeous 14th-century **Sveta Petka Samardjiiska Church** *(admission 6 lv; open 7am-6pm daily)* is accessible via an underpass.

Behind the monstrous Sheraton Hotel is the **Church of St George** *(admission free; open 8am-6pm daily)*. Originally built by the Romans as a rotunda in the 2nd or 3rd century BC, it was converted into a church during the Middle Ages. Perhaps continue east along the footpath to the modest **Archaeological Museum** *(ul Tsar Osvoboditel; admission 4 lv; open 10am-6pm Tues-Sun)*.

Across the road is the **President's Building** (not open to the public). Try to be outside the building on the hour (any day during daylight) for the serious (but rather humorous) **changing of the presidential guards**. Then head up ul Dondukov, turn right at ul Rakovski and

BULGARIA

left along ul Vrabcha to the **National Opera House**. Down ul Panzh is the 6th-century **Church of St Sofia** *(admission free; open 7am-7pm daily)*, the oldest Orthodox church in the capital. Nearby, is the **Tomb of the Unknown Soldier** *(admission free; open 24hr)*.

Boyana About 9km southwest of the city centre is the affluent little hillside village-cum-suburb of Boyana. Probably the most acclaimed (but, perhaps, the most overrated) museum in Bulgaria is the **National Museum of History** *(bul Okolovrusten Pat; admission 10 lv; open 10am-7pm daily Apr-Sept, 9.30am-5.30pm Oct-Mar)*. It houses fabulous Thracian gold treasures from 1000 to 100 BC, artefacts from several Roman ruins, and exhibits about Bulgarian history, religion and politics. The number of exhibits, however, is surprisingly small, and it's a hassle to get to.

The 13th-century **Boyana Church** *(ul Boyansko Ezero 3; admission 10 lv; open 9am-5pm Tues-Sun)* is listed as a World Heritage Site by Unesco. This is because the 90 murals are among the finest examples of Bulgarian medieval artwork (though some are in poor condition). To avoid the hefty admission fee admire the outside of the church from the pretty **gardens** for nothing and visit the adjacent **National Church Museum of Boyana** *(admission 3.50 lv; open 9am-5pm Tues-Sun)*, which houses copies of the murals and other religious icons.

For the National Museum of History, take bus No 63 from pl Ruski Pametnik, bus No 64 from the Hladilnika Bus Terminal or minibus No 21 from along bul Vitosha – the latter two services continue to Boyana Church. The church is a 45-minute walk uphill from the museum, so look for a taxi.

Special Events

St Sofia is the Mother of Hope, Love and Faith, so St Sofia's Day (17 September) is widely celebrated throughout the capital. The associated Sofia Fest (14 to 18 September) includes various cultural events, concerts and exhibitions. The Sofia International Folklore Festival takes places in and around the capital for five days during late August.

Places to Stay

Private Rooms The accommodation agency at the central train station can arrange rooms in local homes for about 35 lv per person. The accommodation agency at the airport is rarely staffed, but some readers have been impressed with the agency's service and the quality of rooms on offer from 30 lv per person.

Radost Tour Private Lodgings Office *(☎/fax 988 2631; e radostur@bol.bg; bul Vitosha 37)* offers a single/double rooms (35/58 lv) and apartments with TV in central Sofia. Look for the sign (in English) near the Reks Cinema.

Markella Accommodation Agency *(☎/fax 981 1833; ul Ekzarh Yosif 35)* is run by a helpful lady who can show you photographs of the available rooms that cost 25/35 lv for singles/doubles.

Hostels Above a Chinese restaurant, but not well signposted, **Sofia Hostel** *(☎/fax 989 8582; ul Pozitano 16; dorm beds with breakfast 25 lv)* offers basic accommodation around a communal kitchen and TV room.

Art Hostel *(☎ 987 0545; e art-hostel@art-hostel.com; ul Angel Kânchev 21a; dorm beds 22 lv)* is the sort of bohemian place where you're likely to meet some fascinating English-speaking locals, but never get any sleep before 3am.

Hotels For basic but comfortable rooms, try **Hotel Viki** *(☎ 983 9746; ul Veslets 56; beds with shared bathroom per person 12 lv)*. Each room has three beds, so a room to yourself will cost 36 lv.

Hotel Bolid *(☎ 983 3002; cnr ul Pop Bogomil & ul Veslets; singles/doubles with shared bathroom 25/45 lv)* is slowly undergoing renovations. Currently, the rooms (that have a TV and sink) are small, the ceilings are low and the floors squeak, but overall it's good value.

Hotel Horizont *(☎ 574 217; ul Gen Mihail Kutuzov 23; rooms with shared bathroom per person 25 lv)* is friendly, family-run and great value, but inconvenient. Contact the family about free transport from the bus or train station or airport, or take tram No 5 or 19 from along bul Vitosha.

Hotel Repos *(☎ 317 463; bul Klokotnitsa 1; singles/doubles 45/55 lv, with bathroom from 55/67 lv)* is convenient to the bus and train stations. The rooms are bright, quiet and nicely furnished, but most are on the upper floors (and there's no lift).

Hotel Enny *(☎ 983 3002; ul Pop Bogomil 46; singles/doubles with shared bathroom*

25/48 lv, doubles with TV and shower but no toilet 70 lv) is popular, friendly, central and quiet. It's a little overpriced and some rooms are small, but the courtyard is a convivial place to meet other travellers.

Hotel Maya *(☎ 989 4611; ul Trapezitsa 4; singles/doubles with bathroom 45/70 lv)* is a central and friendly guesthouse with cosy rooms (each containing a TV and fridge) either side of a rooftop courtyard. The downside is that the bathrooms are detached and minuscule, and single rates are not always available.

Hotel Iskâr *(☎ 986 6750; ul Iskâr 11)* and the associated **Hotel Pop Bogomil** *(☎ 983 7065; ul Pop Bogomil 5)* both offer doubles with a shared bathroom for US$28 as well as doubles with a private bathroom for US$33. The rooms are small and overpriced, but both places are well set up.

The **Hotel Slavyanska Beseda** *(☎ 988 0442, fax 875 6383; ul Slavyanska 3; singles/doubles with bathroom & breakfast US$37/53)* is a decent mid-range option. It's close to the city centre, but the rooms (which are air-conditioned and contain a fridge and TV) could do with some renovation.

Hotel Maria Luisa *(☎ 91 044; bul Maria Luisa 29; singles/doubles with bathroom & breakfast $80/90)* is in a central location and quiet, and wonderfully decorated with bathrooms fit for royalty.

Places to Eat
With several branches around the city **Trops Kâshta** is ideal for anyone who wants to try some local nosh without paying through the nose – just point, pay and enjoy. The most convenient branch *(bul Maria Luisa 26; salads 1 lv, mains 3 lv)* is next to the Modern Theatre cinema.

Folksy **Tsentral** *(ul George Washington; mains 3-4.50 lv)* is an outdoor mehana with a beer-garden setting. It offers Bulgarian dishes and a huge range of salads at reasonable prices. Staff can rustle up a menu in English.

San Valentino *(bul Maria Luisa; mains from 4 lv)* is a classy place that offers a decent range of Bulgarian and continental dishes (try the schnitzel). Prices are surprisingly reasonable, and the service is snappy. The menu is in English.

Birhale Gambrinus *(ul Dondukov 17; mains 8-9 lv)* is the sort of place where you can enjoy fine food and impeccable service without burning a hole in your pocket.

Happy Bar & Grill *(pl Sveta Nedelya; mains from 4 lv)* has spread its wings all over Bulgaria. It offers tasty Western meals, a terrific corner position and friendly staff. You can choose your meal from the handy 'photomenu'.

Goody's *(pl Sveta Nedelya; mains 3-4 lv)* is a central landmark. It offers more interesting meals, such as salads and scrumptious club sandwiches, than the usual junk-food place. It's large and clean, and provides plenty of outdoor seating.

Atlantik *(bul Maria Luisa 63; mains from 3 lv)* offers delicious cakes, tasty pizzas, cheap beer and its own brand of yummy ice-cream – all at very affordable prices.

To self-cater, try the **Oasis Supermarket** *(bul Maria Luisa)*, in the northern end of the TsUM shopping centre, the **Central Hali Shopping Centre** *(bul Maria Luisa 25)* and the chaotic **Ladies Market** *(ul St Stambolov)*.

Entertainment
The best source of information about what's going on (and where and when) is unquestionably the *Sofia Echo*.

The **National Opera House** *(ul Vrabcha; performances 9pm Tues & Sat Apr-Sept, 7pm daily Oct-Mar)* features the best that Bulgaria has to offer. The **NDK National Palace of Culture** *(Yuzhen Park)* maintains a regular programme of cultural events throughout the year, including summer (when most other theatres are closed).

The Library *(bul Vasil Levski)*, which is also called 'The Biblioteka', offers live music and a karaoke bar. It's in the basement of the National Library.

The smoky **La Cocaracha** *(ul Lege 19)* features a decent wine list and live music, while the **Svejk Pub** *(bul Vitosha 1)* offers an extensive range of beers, as well as meals every day and live music on weekends.

Two comfortable and convenient cinemas are in the **Euro-Bulgarian Cultural Centre** *(bul Stamboliyski 17)*, around the corner from the Happy Bar & Grill; and the **Modern Theatre** *(bul Maria Luisa 26)*, near the Trops Kâshta restaurant.

Shopping
The souvenir shop located on the ground floor of the **Ethnographical Museum** *(ul Tsar Osvoboditel)* sells folk art and Bulgarian music at reasonable prices. If you're in the

market for an original painting or sculpture by a Bulgarian artist, try the **Fine Arts Gallery** (ul Shipka 6). Charming landscape paintings are also sold at stalls in the park in front of the Holy Synod Church, on ul Panzh, and in the park between the Banya Bashi Mosque and Sofia Town Public Baths.

Stenata (ul Tsar Samuil 63) is the best place to buy hiking and mountain- and rock-climbing equipment, as well as mattresses, tents and sleeping bags, but it does not rent gear. The **Orion Ski Shop** (ul Pozitano), inside an arcade, sells (but does not rent) all sorts of ski gear.

Getting There & Away

For information about international flights, buses and trains to/from Sofia refer to the introductory Getting There & Away section earlier in the chapter. The three domestic airlines are **Balkan Airlines** (☎ 988 3595; ul Alabin • ☎ 659 517; NDK underpass); **Dandy Airlines** (☎ 943 3674; ul Shipka 42); and **Hemus Air** (☎ 981 8330; ul Rakovski 157). Offices for all major international airlines are listed in the *Sofia Echo*.

Air Refer to the Getting Around section earlier for details about domestic flights to/from Sofia. Offices for all major international airlines are listed in the *Sofia Echo*.

Bus The two major bus terminals in Sofia are either side of bul Maria Luisa and just north of Princess Hotel. In lieu of any official names for these terminals, we have dubbed them the **Princess Hotel Bus Terminal East** and the **Princess Hotel Bus Terminal West**. Both are fairly chaotic and disorganised – thankfully not an indication of bus terminals elsewhere in Bulgaria.

More buses leave from the western terminal, but if you can't find a bus at one terminal cross the road and look at the other. Because there are so many regular departures on public and private buses every day (especially in summer), it's usually easy enough to simply turn up at the western terminal and buy a ticket for a bus leaving within an hour or so.

From **Ovcha Kupel Bus Terminal** (bul Tsar Boris III), a few buses go south to Bansko, Blagoevgrad and Dupnitsa. This terminal is linked to the city centre by tram No 5 and bus No 60. Buses for Samokov leave from **Yug Bus Terminal** (bul Dragan Tsankov). From the

ramshackle **Poduyane Bus Terminal** (bul Vl Vazov), buses leave infrequently for small towns in central Bulgaria, such as Lovech and Troyan. **Hladilnika Bus Terminal** (bul Akar Evstartiev Geshov) handles buses to Boyana, and to Zlatni Mostove and Aleko in Vitosha National Park. It's near the southern terminus for tram Nos 2, 4, 9 and 12 from pl Sveta Nedelya. (From the final tram stop, cross the tiny park to the bus stop on the main road.)

Train Sofia's **Central Train Station** (bul Maria Luisa) can be as overwhelming as any station in a European capital, but it's a far cry from the old days (not that long ago) when travellers had to deal with destination signs in Cyrillic, platforms numbers in Roman numerals and tracks in Arabic numbers. Timetables for all domestic and international services are still in Cyrillic, but departures (for the next two hours) and arrivals (for the previous two hours) are listed in English on a large computer screen on the ground floor. The station can be reached from pl Sveta Nedelya on foot (30 minutes) or by tram Nos 1, 2 and 7.

Tickets for departure on the day of purchase to (and any place en route to) Vidin, Ruse and Varna are sold at counters on the ground floor. Same-day tickets to other destinations are sold downstairs. Advance tickets, seat reservations and sleepers for domestic services are available from another office downstairs. All the counters and offices are open 24 hours, and staff can usually understand a bit of English.

Tickets for international trains, and advance tickets for domestic services, are available from the **Rila Bureau** (☎ 932 3346) at the central train station and in the city centre (☎ 987 0777; ul General Gurko 5).

Getting Around

To/From the Airport The **Sofia Airport** is 12km southeast of the city centre. It can be reached by bus No 84 from opposite the Sofia University on bul Vasil Levski, or by minibus No 30 from along bul Maria Luisa and ul Tsar Osvoboditel. A taxi from the city centre should cost no more than 6 lv (with the meter).

Public Transport All forms of public transport operate daily from 5am to midnight. Most drivers on trams, buses and trolleybuses sell tickets (0.50 lv), but it's far easier and quicker to buy one ticket (or more) from any kiosk along a tram, bus or trolleybus route before boarding. Minibuses are quicker and more comfortable, but do cost a little more. Destinations and fares are indicated (in Cyrillic) on the front of the minibuses, and tickets are bought from the drivers. The suburban metro only has six stops and is of little use to visitors.

If you're going to use public transport often consider buying a pass – valid for all trams, buses and trolleybuses – for one day (2.50 lv), five days (10 lv) or one month (40 lv).

Taxi Taxis are an affordable and more comfortable alternative to public transport. The ones that wait around the airport, luxury hotels and pl Sveta Nedelya are often unscrupulous and will offer an unmetered fare.

VITOSHA NATIONAL PARK
НАЦИОНАЛЕН ПАРК ВИТОША
Only 22km south of Sofia is the Mt Vitosha mountain range, one of the most convenient skiing spots in Europe and part of the Vitosha National Park (227 sq km). Legions of hikers, berry pickers and sightseers flock to **Aleko** on summer weekends, from where there are dozens of clearly marked **hiking** trails. Bus No 66 regularly departs from the Hladilnika Bus Terminal in Sofia on Saturday and Sunday, and leaves four times a day on weekdays. It stops outside Hotel Moreni at Aleko.

A two-person **chairlift** to Aleko starts 5km up from **Dragalevtsi** village. One chairlift goes as far as Bai Krâstyo, from where another one carries on to Goli Vrâh. Both lifts operate all year, but most reliably run between 8.30am and 4.30pm from Friday to Sunday. From the start of the first chairlift, a trail (1km) leads to **Dragalevtsi Monastery**, built in about 1345. Bus Nos 64 and 93 from the Hladilnika terminal go to Dragalevtsi village, while bus No 93 continues to the first chairlift station.

Also, a **gondola** (six-person covered cabin) heads up the slopes from **Simeonovo** village. It operates 9am to 4.30pm Friday to Sunday from October to March and 8.30am to 6pm from May to September. Bus No 123 from the Hladilnika terminal goes directly to the gondola station.

Zlatni Mostove (Golden Bridges) is named after the extraordinary series of huge boulders dumped by glaciers many centuries ago. Bus No 261 from the Ovcha Kupel Bus Terminal in Sofia goes to Zlatni Mostove every 20 minutes on Saturday and Sunday, but less frequently on weekdays.

Southern Bulgaria

Southern Bulgaria is easily defined as the part of the country between the Sredna Gora Mountains and the borders with Greece and Turkey. In the southeast, between the Sredna Gora Mountains, Rodopi Mountains and Black Sea coast, is an area still known by its historical name of Thrace.

BOROVETS БОРОВЕЦ
☎ 07128
Borovets, 70km southeast of Sofia, is Bulgaria's oldest, most developed and also most compact **ski resort**. It's also an ideal starting point for **hikes** on the marked trails around the eastern Rila Mountains. The **travel agency** (☎ 306) inside the unmissable Hotel Samokov can arrange guides (which are not really necessary). Most hotels and eateries in Borovets close during the summer, but a few (including those mentioned below) open all year.

Pension Radenkov (☎ 737; camping per person 3 lv, rooms with shared bathroom per person 9 lv) is a rustic place that offers basic rooms with few amenities. It's a few metres up the *second* (minor) street which starts along the road from Samokov.

Siezhno Rano (☎ 087 442 459; doubles with bathroom 47 lv) is opposite Hotel Flora at the top of the (unnamed) main street. It offers bright and airy rooms each with a balcony, TV and fridge, and is remarkable value compared with other places nearby.

The cheapest **eateries** are at the turn-off to Borovets along the road from Samokov. Some of the more charming and less expensive places in Borovets are along the main street between the Borosports complex and Hotel Flora. Just up another (unnamed) street from the massive Hotel Rila, **Fantasy Restaurant** offers inexpensive and tasty food.

From the Yug Bus Terminal in Sofia, take a bus to Samokov, and then get a (regular) minibus to Borovets. A taxi between Samokov and Borovets costs a negotiable 6 lv.

RILA MONASTERY
РИЛСКИ МАНАСТИР
☎ 07054
Bulgaria's largest and most famous monastery is tucked away in a narrow, forested valley of the Rila Mountains, 120km south of Sofia. It's the holiest place in the country and

BULGARIA

probably *the* major attraction for Bulgarian pilgrims, as well as for the foreign tourists. It's best to avoid weekends in summer.

The monastery was built in 927, but was extensively restored in 1469. Under adverse conditions, the monastery helped to keep Bulgarian culture and religion alive during centuries of rule by the Turks. In 1833, a fire virtually engulfed all of the buildings, but it was rebuilt not long after. Rila Monastery has been included on the Unesco World Heritage list since 1983.

Many places to stay and eat are within 100m of the back (eastern) entrance called the **Samokov Gate**, while most cars and buses park near the front (western) entrance called the **Dupnitsa Gate**. A stall near the Dupnitsa Gate sells souvenirs and useful booklets in English about the monastery.

The monastery grounds are open 6am to 10pm daily, so bear this in mind if you're staying inside the monastery. Admission is free, but there is an entrance fee to the museum. No photos are allowed inside the Nativity Church, but are permitted elsewhere. And when visiting the monastery, please dress and behave appropriately.

Things to See

Four levels of colourful balconies, with some 300 monastic cells, as well as storerooms and a refectory, surround the large, irregular courtyard. The top balcony offers outstanding views of the surrounding Rila Mountains.

If you enter from the Samokov Gate, you'll soon see the 23m stone **Hrelyu Tower**, named after a significant benefactor. It is all that remains of the monastery that was built in 1335. The **kitchen**, built in 1816, is at courtyard level in the northern wing. The 22m chimney cuts through all storeys by means of 10 rows of arches crowned by a small dome.

Standing proudly in the middle of the courtyard is the magnificent **Nativity Church**, probably the largest monastery church in Bulgaria. The main building and its three great domes were built between 1834 and 1837, and now contain 1200 murals.

The two-storey **Ethnographic Museum** *(admission 6 lv; open 8.30am-4.30pm daily)* houses an impressive collection, including the **Rila Cross**, a double-sided cross, which Brother Raphael took over 12 years to create during the late 18th century.

Places to Stay & Eat

Zodiak Camping *(☎ 2291; camping per person 10 lv, singles/doubles in bungalows with shared bathroom 16/26 lv)* is not particularly private, and the bungalows are a bit shabby. However, the restaurant and riverside setting are superb. It's 1.6km past the Samokov Gate along the road to Kiril Meadow.

Rila Monastery *(☎ 2208; rooms from 25 lv)* has cheaper rooms in the older western wing with three or four beds. These rooms are sparsely furnished, but clean enough. The communal facilities for these rooms have toilets, but no showers. The newer rooms are far nicer and contain private bathrooms.

Hotel Tsarev Vrah *(☎/fax 2280; singles/doubles with bathroom 35/70 lv)* has been renovated but is still fairly unexciting. It's 150m beyond the Samokov Gate.

Rila Restaurant *(mains 5-8 lv)* is in a 120-year-old building close to Samokov Gate. It has a pleasant outdoor setting and extensive menu, but gets mixed reviews from readers. Nearby, the **bakery** is popular with hikers.

Getting There & Away

Currently, buses leave Rila village (22km west) for the monastery at 7.40am, 12.40pm and 3.50pm; they return to Rila village at 9am, 3pm and 5pm. From Dupnitsa, buses to Rila leave at 6.40am and 2.15pm, and return from the monastery at 9.40am and 5.15pm.

It's just about possible to make a (rushed) day trip from Sofia by public transport. Get on any bus that stops at Dupnitsa from the Princess Hotel Bus Terminal West or Ovcha Kupel Bus Terminal no later than 8am. In Dupnitsa, jump on the 10am (or 11am) bus to Rila village, and then catch the 12.40pm bus to the monastery. To return to Sofia, take the 5.15pm bus to Dupnitsa and one of the hourly buses (or trains) back to the capital. In summer, it's worth finding out from the Ovcha Kupel Bus Terminal (☎ 02-554 033) about direct buses between Sofia and the monastery.

Full-day tours (from US$30 per person) of Rila Monastery can be arranged through most travel agencies in Sofia.

BLAGOEVGRAD БЛАГОЕВГРАД
☎ 073 • pop 77,900

The university town of Blagoevgrad, 100km south of Sofia, boasts the sort of sophistication and cosmopolitan ambience that Sofia can only dream of.

The main square is pl Makedonia. An excellent resource for the whole region is the **Pirin Tourist Forum** (☎ 81 458; W www .pirin-tourism.bg). It's next to the laneway leading to the Kristo Hotel in the Varosha old quarter, 300m east across the bridge from pl Makedonia. There are plenty of **foreign-exchange offices** in the town centre, and the **First East International Bank** is along a laneway southwest of the main square.

Directly across the bridge from pl Makedonia is the worthwhile **History Museum** (bul Aleksandâr Stamboliyski; admission 3 lv; open 9am-noon & 3pm-6pm Mon-Fri). The serene **Church of the Annunciation of the Virgin** (ul Komitrov; admission free; open 6am-8pm daily), below the Kristo Hotel, is also worth a look. The vast **Forest Park** (admission free; open 24hr) is 700m up the road from the museum.

Alfatour Travel Agency (☎ 23 598, fax 62 841; ul Krali Marko 4) is the only accommodation agency and has private rooms for 25 lv per person. The office is 600m southwest on ul Todor Aleksandrov from pl Makedonia.

The **Hotel Alpha** (☎ 31 122; ul Kukush 7; doubles with bathroom from 32 lv) offers comfortable rooms with TVs and balconies. It's 500m southwest of the museum – you'll probably need to ask directions.

Every day, seven buses travel directly between Blagoevgrad and Sofia (6 lv, two hours), via Dupnitsa, but many more come through on their way between Kulata and Sandanski. From Blagoevgrad, there are also regular services to Plovdiv, Samokov, Bansko and Rila village. Every day, six trains travel from Sofia, via Dupnitsa; three of these continue to Sandanski and Kulata. The bus terminal and adjacent train station are 2.3km southwest of pl Makedonia.

BANSKO БАНСКО
☎ 07443 • pop 9740

Nestled at the base of the imposing Mt Vihren (2914m) in the Pirin Mountains, Bansko enjoys a climate of relatively short summers and long snowy winters. As a **ski resort** Bansko is not as developed as Borovets or Pamporovo, but is certainly a nicer place to stay.

The **tourist information centre** (☎ 5048) is inside a small room just to the northwest of pl Nikola Vaptsarov. (This main square is connected to pl Vûzhrazhdane by ul Pirin.) The office can assist with local hotel bookings and

provide information about regional **hiking** trails. Most **foreign-exchange offices** are around pl Nikola Vaptsarov; otherwise, try the **DSK Bank** (ul Tsar Simeon), along the mall southeast of the main square. An **Internet Agency** (cnr ul Pirin & ul Molerov) is 200m up from pl Vûzhrazhdane.

Things to See
The **House-Museum of Nikola Vaptsarov** (pl Nikola Vaptsarov; admission 3 lv; open 9am-noon & 2pm-5.45pm Mon-Sat) is dedicated to the respected antifascist poet and activist. The attached **Crafts & Textile Exhibition** displays (and sells) traditional arts, crafts and textiles from Bansko.

Velyanov's House (ul Velyan Ognev 5; admission 3 lv; open 9am-noon & 2pm-5pm Mon-Fri) is 100m southeast of pl Vûzhrazhdane. It features the sort of elaborately painted scenes and carved woodwork representative of the so-called Bansko school of art. The **House-Museum of Neofit Rilski** (ul Pirin 17; admission 3 lv; open 9am-noon & 2pm-5pm daily) is dedicated to Rilski, renowned as the father of Bulgarian secular education.

The **Sveta Troitsa Church** (pl Vûzhrazhdane; admission free; open 7am-7pm daily) features magnificent wooden floors and some period furniture surrounded by eerie, faded murals. The **Permanent Icon Exhibition** (ul Yane Sandanski; admission 3 lv; open 9am-noon & 2pm-5.30pm Mon-Fri), 50m from pl Vûzhrazhdane, contains a number of exquisite religious icons

Special Events
The Pirin Sings Folk Festival takes place near Bansko in August on every second (odd-numbered) year. The annual International Jazz Festival (7 to 15 August) attracts artists from all over Bulgaria.

Places to Stay & Eat
Unofficial **camping** is possible in the Pirin National Park, a few kilometres away at the end of ul Pirin.

KSV Ltd (☎ 3970; ul Tsar Simeon 68) can arrange rooms in local homes for about 25 lv per person.

Hotel Mir (☎ 2500; ul Neofit Rilski 28; singles/doubles with bathroom & breakfast 32/55 lv) is in a quiet spot 200m east of the House-Museum of Neofit Rilski. The rooms are bright and clean and have TVs.

Duata Smarcha (☎ 2632; ul Velyan Ognev 2; singles/doubles with bathroom & breakfast 25/45 lv) is set in a lovely garden only 50m southeast of pl Vûzhrazhdane. Traditional home-cooked meals are available (to guests and the public) at the **restaurant**.

Alpin Hotel (☎ 7443; ul Neofit Rilski 6; singles/doubles with bathroom 35/45 lv) offers clean and airy rooms. Staff are competent and it's good value.

Baryakova Mehana (ul Velyan Ognev 3; mains 5-6 lv), virtually on pl Vûzhrazhdane, offers quality food and a cheerful ambience. It's an ideal place to try some local cuisine and wine.

Bakanova Mehana (ul Pirin; mains 4-5 lv), overlooking pl Nikola Vaptsarov, offers a huge range of Bulgarian and Italian meals, though most locals go for the tasty pizzas.

Getting There & Away

From the **bus terminal** (ul Patriarh Evtimii), 350m north of pl Nikola Vaptsarov, six buses go every day to Sofia (5.50 lv, three hours), via Blagoevgrad. Also, four or five buses leave Bansko for Blagoevgrad only, and two more depart for Plovdiv.

Bansko is on the narrow-gauge railway between Septemvri and Dobrinishte. This train is painfully slow (five hours from Septemvri to Bansko), but popular with train buffs. The **train station** (bul Akad Yordan Ivanov) is 100m from the bus terminal.

MELNIK МЕЛНИК
☎ 07437 • pop 267

Tourists flock to Melnik to admire the unique architecture (the Bulgarian national revival period), to see the church ruins, to marvel at the strange 'sand pyramids' that surround the village and to sample regional food and wine.

But remember that Melnik is really only a village: there is no bank or foreign-exchange office (the nearest are in Sandanski) or Internet centre. Most places in Melnik are either side of the (mainly dry) creek that runs alongside the (unnamed) main street. About halfway along the northern side of the creek and street is the **post office**.

Things to See & Do

Bolyaskata Kâshta, 200m further east along from the post office, dates back to the 10th century, and it is one of the oldest homes in Bulgaria. Unfortunately, it is now completely ruined, and only some walls remain. In front of Bolyaskata Kâshta are the remains of the 19th-century **Sveti Antoni Church**.

Kordopulov House (admission 2 lv; open 8am-8pm daily) is one of the country's largest and most famous revival-period structures. It's another 150m east along the main street from Bolyaskata Kâshta.

The **City Museum** (admission 2 lv; open 9am-noon & 2pm-6pm Mon-Fri) features regional costumes, ceramics and jewellery. Look for the sign just before Hotel Despot Slav, 250m east of the post office.

Almost opposite the main entrance to Hotel Rodina (80m east of the post office), a path leads to the remains of the **Sveti Nikolai Church** and the **Slavova Krepost Fortress**. The trail then heads east (300m) along the ridge to the ruins of the **Sveta Zona Chapel**.

The **Mitko Manolev Winery** is an informal place to sample and buy the local wines. It's along the short hillside trail that runs up between the Bolyaskata Kâshta ruins and Kordopulov House.

Places to Stay & Eat

Many private **homes** in Melnik offer rooms for about 25 lv per person, but single travellers will often have to pay for a double room.

Lumparova Kâshta (☎ 0488-92 445; rooms with shared bathroom per person 12 lv) has cosy rooms and balconies with awesome views. The multilingual staff can offer wine-tasting and traditional food. It's 150m up a steep path behind Usunova Kâshta.

Usunova Kâshta (☎ 270; singles/doubles with bathroom & breakfast 22/44 lv) offers quiet and clean rooms. It's on the flat side of the creek (about 50m east of the post office), so no climbing is required to reach it.

Hotel Despot Slav (☎/fax 271; singles/doubles with bathroom & breakfast 33/44 lv) is a traditional place with large and well-furnished rooms.

The two largest restaurants are near each other opposite the creek from the post office. **Chinarite Restaurant** (mains 4-5 lv) is a bit cheerless, but the helpings are large. **Loznitsite Tavern** (mains 4-5 lv) has an inviting, vine-covered outdoor setting and an extensive menu.

Getting There & Away

Currently, one bus a day leaves Melnik for Sofia (7 lv, four hours) at 6am and returns to

Melnik from the Princess Hotel Bus Terminal West at about 10am. There are also regular buses between Melnik and Sandanski.

ROZHEN MONASTERY
РОЖЕНСКИ МАНАСТИР

This monastery *(admission free; open 7am-7pm daily)* was originally built in 1217, but most of what remains was reconstructed after 1732. The **Nativity of the Virgin Church**, originally built in 1600, contains some marvellous stained-glass windows, woodcarvings, murals and iconostases.

From Melnik to the monastery by road is 7.2km, including a steep 800m from Rozhen village. All buses from Sandanski to Melnik continue to Rozhen village. The popular **hiking** trail (6.5km) from Melnik to the monastery starts from near the track up to Boyaskata Kâshta and continues along the dry creek bed – look for the small white, orange and green signs.

PLOVDIV ПЛОВДИВ
☎ 032 • pop 376,500

Plovdiv is the second-largest road and railway hub and economic centre in Bulgaria. It's also the first/last stop for those travelling between Bulgaria and Greece or Turkey. Typically, the tourist authorities and travel agencies use cliches like 'you must see Plovdiv to see Bulgaria' – but, for once, these sort of phrases are not overstated. This modern, thriving city is based around a majestic old town crammed with 18th- and 19th-century homes, as well as dozens of museums, art galleries and churches. And to top it off, Plovdiv boasts the most remarkable Roman ruin in Bulgaria.

Information

Plenty of **foreign-exchange offices** can be found along the pedestrian mall (ul Knyaz Aleksandâr) and ul Ivan Vazov. Several offices along the mall also change travellers cheques and offer cash advances with major credit cards. There are a handful of banks near pl Dzhumaya, such as the **United Bulgarian Bank**, which has an ATM.

The **telephone centre** *(open 6am-11pm daily)* is inside the **main post office** *(pl Tsentralen)*. For 'cybermail', try **RNet Internet** *(ul Aleksandâr Ekzarh)* or **Net Burger**, which are both just down the steps from the overpass along ul Gladston.

Things to See

The best place to start a walking tour is pl Dzhumaya. The square is dominated by the **Dzhumaya Mosque** *(admission free; open dawn-dusk daily)*, one of 50 or so mosques built during the Turkish occupation.

Head east along ul Sâborna to the **Danov House** *(ul Mitropolit Paisii 2; admission 1.50 lv; open 9am-12.30pm & 2pm-4.30pm Mon-Sat)*, dedicated to a famous Bulgarian writer and publisher. Opposite is the massive 19th-century **Church of Sveta Bogoroditsa** *(admission free; open 8am-6pm daily)*, which contains a marvellous array of paintings and murals.

Further along ul Sâborna is the **State Gallery of Fine Arts** *(ul Sâborna 14a; admission 2.50 lv, free Tues; open 9am-12.30pm & 1pm-5.30pm)*, housed in a charmingly renovated home built in 1846.

A little further up is the **Zlatyo Boyadjiev House** *(ul Sâborna 18; admission 3 lv; open 9am-noon & 1pm-6pm daily Apr-Sept, closed Sat & Sun Oct-Mar)*, which contains massive works by this local artist.

Before the junction with ul Lavrenov look for the entrance to the charming **Church of St Konstantin & Elena** *(ul Sâborna 24; admission free; open 8am-6pm daily)*. It was constructed in AD 337, but mostly rebuilt in 1832. At the junction, turn left and check out the **Balabanov House** *(ul 4 Yanuari; admission 3 lv; open 9am-12.30pm & 2pm-5pm Mon-Fri)*. The **Hindlian House** *(ul A Gidikov 4; admission 3 lv; open 9am-noon & 1.30pm-4.30pm Mon-Fri)* features plenty of period furniture. Access is via an unnamed lane off the main street.

Head back up ul Dr Chomakov (the extension of ul Sâborna) to the dramatic **Ruins of Eumolpias** *(admission free; open 24hr)*. These remains of a Thracian settlement date from about 5000 BC. On the way down you will pass the excellent **Ethnographical Museum** *(ul Dr Chomakov 2; admission 3.50 lv; open 9am-5pm daily)*.

Turn left (southeast) along ul Lavrenov to the mildly interesting **Historical Museum** *(ul Lavrenov 1; admission 2.50 lv; open 8.45am-noon & 2pm-5pm Mon-Sat)* and the musty **Nedkovich House** *(admission 2.50 lv; open daily 9am-noon & 1pm-6pm Apr-Sept, closed Sat & Sun Oct-Mar)* next door.

Backtrack a little, stroll down ul Cyril Nektariev and then follow the 'Ancient Theatre'

BULGARIA

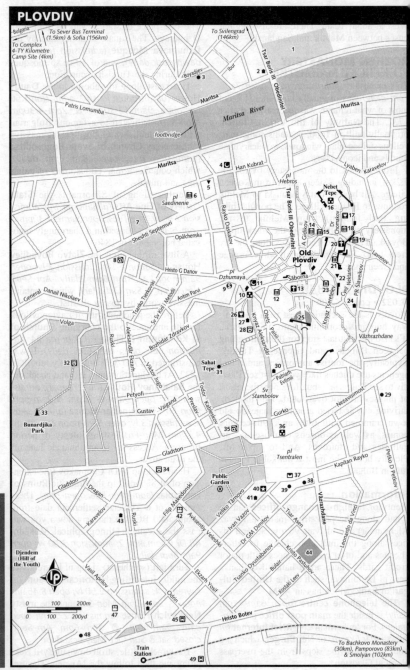

PLOVDIV

To Sever Bus Terminal
(1.5km) & Sofia (156km)

To Svilengrad
(146km)

To Complex
4-TY Kilometre
Camp Site (4km)

Bulgaria

Maritsa River

footbridge

Boyadjiev

Ibur

Tsar Boris III Obedinitei

Patris Lomumba

Maritsa

Maritsa

Maritsa

Maritsa

Han Kubrat

Lyaben Karavelov

pl
Hebros

Nebet
Tepe

Rayko Daskalov

pl
Saedinenie

Sheshti Septemvri

Opálchenska

A Gidikov

Tsar Boris III Obedinitei

Dr Chomakov

Old
Plovdiv

Nektariev

Lavrenov

PR Slaveikov

Hristo G Danov

pl
Dzhumaya

Sáborna

Knyaz Tsetelev

pl
Vázhrazhdane

General Danail Nikolaev

Tsanko Tserkovski

Sv Sv Kiril Metodi

Antim Parvi

Nezavisimost

Petko D Petkov

Volga

Ruski

Aleksandŭr Ekzarh

Bozhidar Zdravkov

Viktor Jugo

Otets
Paisii

Sahat
Tepe

Todor Kableshkov

Preslav

Patriah
Evtimii

Sv
Stambolov

Gurko

Kapitan Rayko

Bunardjika
Park

Petyofi

Gustav

Vajgand

Gladston

pl
Tsentralen

Vázrazhdane

Leonardo da Vinci

Djendem
(Hill of
the Youth)

Gladston

Dragan

Karavelov

Ruski

Filip Makedonski

Public
Garden

Veliko Tärnovo

Avksenty Veleshki

Ivan Vazov

Tsar Asen

Kristo Parttuhov

Vasil Aprilov

Ocin

Ekzarh Yosif

Tsanko Dyustabanov

Dr GM Dimitov

Bulair

Kotaki Leev

Hristo Botev

Train
Station

To Bachkovo Monastery
(30km), Pamporovo (83km)
& Smolyan (102km)

0   100   200m
0   100   200yd

BULGARIA

1
2
3
4
5
6
7
8
9
10
11
12
13
14
15
16
17
18
19
20
21
22
23
24
25
26
27
28
29
30
31
32
33
34
35
36
37
38
39
40
41
42
43
44
45
46
47
48
49

PLOVDIV

PLACES TO STAY & EAT
2 Hotel Maritsa
5 Totova Hrana
22 Pulden Restaurant
24 Tourist Hotel (Turisticheski Dom); Sportna Sretsha
27 Prima Vista Agency
30 Hotel Bulgaria
41 Esperantsa
43 Hotel Leipzig 91
46 Trakiya Hotel

OTHER
1 International Plovdiv Fairgrounds
3 Novotel; Avis
4 Imaret Mosque
6 Archaeological Museum
7 Market
8 RNet Internet
9 United Bulgarian Bank
10 Roman Stadium; I Claudius Cafe
11 Dzhumaya Mosque
12 Danov House
13 Church of Sveta Bogoroditsa; Restaurant Kambanata
14 Hindlian House
15 Balabanov House
16 Ruins of Eumolpias
17 Rahat Tepe Bar
18 Ethnographical Museum
19 Historical Museum; Nedkovich House
20 Church of St Konstantin & Elena
21 Zlatyo Boyadjiev House
23 State Gallery of Fine Arts
25 Roman Amphitheatre
26 Dive Club
28 Nikolai Masalitinov Dramatic Theatre
29 Foreign Citizens Bureau
31 Clock Tower
32 Open-Air Theatre
33 Monument to the Soviet Army
34 Plovdiv Opera House
35 Net Burger
36 Roman Forum
37 Main Post Office & Telephone Centre
38 Trimontium Princess Hotel; Tourist Service Rent-a-Car
39 City Local Transportation Co
40 Police
42 Cinemax
44 University
45 Yug Bus Terminal
47 Cinema Geo Milev
48 Rila Bureau
49 Rodopi Bus Terminal

signs to find the magnificent **Roman Amphitheatre** *(admission 2.50 lv; open 8am-6pm daily)*. It was built by the Romans in the early 2nd century AD, and partially restored to hold special events. On the way back to pl Dzhumaya have a look at the remarkable **Roman Stadium** *(ul Knyaz Aleksandâr)*, which can only be admired from the street level.

About 300m north of pl Dzhumaya is the disappointing **Archaeological Museum** *(pl Saedinenie; admission 2.50 lv; open 9am-12.30pm & 3pm-5.30pm Mon-Fri)*. It's worth noting, however, that the museum department does possess some 60,000 valuable archaeological items. Hopefully, these will be displayed here or elsewhere sometime in the future.

Special Events

Plovdiv hosts the Cultural Month Festival (late May to mid-July) and the International Folklore Festival (early August).

The week-long International Plovdiv Fair is held twice yearly in mid-May and late September in the massive fairgrounds north of the river.

Places to Stay

Complex 4-TY Kilometre *(☎ 951 360; camping per person 10 lv, bungalows with bathroom 32 lv)* is about 4km west of the river along the old Sofia Hwy. It provides some shade, privacy and tranquillity (if you can get away from the incessant traffic noise). Take bus No 4, 18 or 44 west along bul Bulgaria, or bus No 222 from the train station, for as far as it goes, and then walk 200m.

Prima Vista Agency *(☎ 272 778; ul Knyaz Aleksandâr 28)* arranges rooms for 20 to 25 lv. It has irregular opening hours, but staff are helpful. Look for the black 'accommodation agency' sign (in English) along the mall.

The **Esperantsa** *(☎ 260 653; ul Ivan Vazov 14)* accommodation agency can be a bit haphazard, but some readers have commented favourably about the quality of rooms on offer for 25 lv per person.

Tourist Hotel *(Turisticheski Dom; ☎ 633 211; ul PR Slaveikov 5; rooms with shared bathroom per person 25 lv)* is a remarkable old place. No-one minds the noisy nightclub at the back, the musty aroma and the saggy beds because it's so convenient and just *oozes* atmosphere.

Hotel Leipzig 91 *(☎ 632 250, fax 451 096; bul Ruski 70; singles/doubles with bathroom & breakfast 44/65 lv)* lacks charm, and the rooms need some renovation, but this is essentially a mid-range hotel at (almost) a budget price.

Trakiya Hotel *(☎ 624 101; ul Ivan Vazov 84; singles/doubles with bathroom & breakfast 43/85 lv)* is new and convenient. The rooms (which contain fans and TVs) are quiet despite the noisy location and popular bar downstairs.

The **Hotel Maritsa** (☎ 952 735, fax 952 770; bul Tsar Boris III Obedinitel 42; singles/ doubles with bathroom & breakfast US$50/ 73) has a garish decor that may not be to everyone's taste. However, the Maritsa offers comfortable rooms, each with a TV, fridge and air-conditioning, and is good value.

Hotel Bulgaria (☎ 633 599; e mng@ hotelbulgaria.net; ul Patriarh Evtimii 13; singles/doubles with bathroom & breakfast US$52/73) is very convenient. The modern rooms each feature a TV, fridge and air-con, but are a little charmless.

Places to Eat

Several **stalls** along the northern section of ul Rayko Daskalov sell tasty doner kebabs.

Totova Hrana (ul Han Kubrat; mains 2 lv) is an excellent choice for cheap, cafeteria-style food – just point at what you want and enjoy.

Pulden Restaurant (ul Knyaz Tseretelev 8; mains from 6 lv) has several unique dining rooms. Although predictably touristy and expensive, it's worth a visit.

Restaurant Kambanata (ul Sâborna; mains 7-8 lv) is a classy, yet rather bizarre, place virtually under the grounds of the Church of Sveta Bogoroditsa. The tables are set along small terraces so that diners can see the live music (on most nights).

I Claudius Cafe (ul Knyaz Aleksandâr; mains from 3.50 lv) overlooks and almost touches the Roman Stadium. Considering the extraordinary setting, the prices here really are quite reasonable.

Sportna Sretsha (ul PR Slaveikov 5; mains 4 lv) is ideal if you're staying at the Tourist Hotel (at the back) or traipsing around the Old Town.

Entertainment

One of the trendiest places to shake your booty is the **Dive Club**, at the end of a lane off pl Dzhumaya – look for the distinctive aquamarine murals on the front wall.

To enjoy a drink while admiring views of the Old Town, head to **Rahat Tepe Bar** (ul Dr Chomakov), which is almost at the top of Nebet Tepe hill.

From late May to early June, special events are often held at the **Roman Amphitheatre**, while the **Open-Air Theatre** (Bunardjika Park; Hill of the Liberators) hosts opera, music and drama throughout the summer. The **Nikolai Masalitinov Dramatic Theatre** (ul Knyaz Aleksandâr 38) is one of the most respected in the country.

Cinema Geo Milev (ul Vasil Aprilov) and **Cinemax** (ul Avksentiy Veleshki) show recent foreign films in comfortable surroundings.

Getting There & Away

Bus Every day from the **Yug Bus Terminal** (bul Hristo Botev), diagonally opposite the train station, there are two buses each to/from Bansko (3½ hours), Blagoevgrad (three hours), Burgas (four hours) and Varna (six hours); one to Ruse (six hours); six to Sliven (three hours); eight to Hisarya (one hour); and three to Veliko Târnovo (4½ hours). Buses also run hourly to Karlovo (one hour), Stara Zagora (1½ hours) and Sofia (7.50 lv, 2½ hours). Every day in summer, one or two buses also leave this terminal for most resorts along the Black Sea coast.

The **Rodopi Bus Terminal** is really only accessible on foot through the underpass by the train station. From this bus terminal, four buses a day go to Karlovo, and six to eight leave for Smolyan, via Bachkovo Monastery and Pamporovo.

From the **Sever Bus Terminal** in the northern suburbs (best accessible by taxi), one bus each day goes directly to Ruse, Troyan and Koprivshtitsa.

Train Each day from the **train station** (bul Hristo Botev), there are 19 trains to Sofia (1st/2nd class 7.50/5.80 lv, 2½ hours for the express train), five to Burgas, four to Svilengrad, six to Karlovo and Hisarya, and five to Veliko Târnovo. Advance tickets for domestic services are sold upstairs. For international tickets, go to the **Rila Bureau** (☎ 446 120), along a side street that runs parallel to bul Hristo Botev.

Getting Around

Plovdiv is pleasingly compact, so it's generally quickest to get around on foot. Happily, taxi drivers use their meters with little or no prompting.

Travelling around the region by car allows you to explore remote monasteries, caves and lakes. **Tourist Service Rent-a-Car** (☎ 623 496; Trimontium Princess Hotel, pl Tsentralen) and **Avis** (☎ 934 481; Novotel, ul Boyadjiev) are expensive, so ask one of the numerous travel agencies along ul Knyaz Aleksandâr about car rental.

BACHKOVO MONASTERY
БАЧКОВСКИ МАНАСТИР

Bulgaria's second-largest monastery *(admission free; open 6am-10pm daily)* is 30km south of Plovdiv. The courtyard is dominated by the 12th-century **Archangel Church** and the larger 17th-century **Church of the Assumption of Our Lady**, with 300-year-old iconostases and murals. On the northern side of the courtyard, the small **museum** *(admission 1 lv; open varying hours)* features weapons and icons. Through the gate beside the 17th-century **refectory** is the **St Nicholas Chapel**, built in 1836.

Take any of the regular buses to Smolyan from the Rodopi Bus Terminal in Plovdiv. Disembark at the obvious turn-off (about 1.2km south of Bachkovo village) and walk (500m) up the hill.

PAMPOROVO ПАМПОРОВО
☎ 3021

Set in the gorgeous eastern Rodopi Mountains, 83km south of Plovdiv, is Pamporovo, one of four major **ski resorts** in Bulgaria. The facilities are comparatively new and the slopes and lifts are well maintained, but the resort is expansive and expensive. Pamporovo is also worth visiting in summer, though many facilities (but not those listed below) are closed at this time. The centre of Pamporovo is the T-junction of the roads to Smolyan, Plovdiv and Devin. From this junction the resort spreads along several roads.

Hotel Perelik *(☎ 405; singles/doubles with bathroom & breakfast from 40/52 lv)* is a former government-run monolith. The more expensive rooms have been nicely renovated and feature spotless bathrooms.

Hotel Murgavets *(☎ 310; singles/doubles with bathroom & breakfast 35/70 lv)*, next to the Perelik, is large, new and is particularly good value.

Barbeque Lime Light *(mains from 5 lv)* at the T-junction is an easygoing place with comparatively reasonable prices.

Every hour, buses travelling between Smolyan and Chepelare pass through Pamporovo. The regular services between Smolyan and Plovdiv, and Smolyan and Sofia, also stop at Pamporovo. Every day, a couple of buses go directly to Pamporovo from Sofia (10 lv, four hours) and up to eight leave Plovdiv. The bus stop is at the 'Ski Lift No 1' chairlift at the T-junction.

SMOLYAN СМОЛЯН
☎ 0301 • pop 34,300

It's easy enough to stay in Smolyan and visit Pamporovo on day trips, though Smolyan has several worthwhile attractions and is an important transport hub for regional villages. The centre of this extremely spread-out town is Hotel Smolyan (see below). Nearby is the helpful **tourist office** *(☎ 25 040;* **w** *www .rodopi-bg.com)*. An **Internet centre** is in the same building.

Bulgaria's largest **planetarium** *(bul Bulgaria 20; admission 4 lv)* is about 200m west of Hotel Smolyan. It offers shows in English, French or German at 2pm from Monday to Saturday, but staff need one hour's notice and a minimum of 10 people (ie, a total payment of at least 40 lv).

The outstanding **Historical Museum** *(pl Bulgaria 3; admission 4 lv; open 9am-noon & 1pm-5pm Tues-Sun)* is a five-minute walk up the steps beside the Drama Theatre opposite Hotel Smolyan. Across from the museum is the extensive **Art Gallery** *(admission 2 lv; open 9am-noon & 1.30pm-5pm Tues-Sun)*.

The tourist office can provide details of the **private homes** that offer rooms for about 25 lv per person and the current rates for all the hotels in Smolyan.

Hotel Katerina *(☎ 28 805; ul N Filipov 16; singles/doubles with bathroom 27/37 lv)* is a two-star hotel with friendly staff and comfortable rooms. Take a taxi.

Hotel Smolyan *(☎ 2661; bul Bulgaria 3; singles/doubles with bathroom 35/45 lv)* hasn't been updated since the 1970s, but is not bad value. The **restaurants** are overpriced, however, so try the snack bar between the hotel and tourist office.

Most buses to/from Smolyan use the **Smolyan Bus Terminal** *(bul Bulgaria)* in the western suburbs. Each day, there are three or four buses to/from Sofia (11 lv, 3½ hours) and between six and eight to Plovdiv. About every hour something heads to Pamporovo.

Central Bulgaria

This part of the country was historically defined as the region between the Rodopi Mountains to the south and the Stara Planina Mountains further north. These days, however, central Bulgaria is determined more by transport routes, ie, the train lines and highways between Sofia and Varna, and between Sofia and Burgas. Centuries ago, these mountains were ideal locations for monasteries.

KOPRIVSHTITSA
КОПРИВЩИЦА
☎ 07184 • pop 2900

This picturesque village, 113km east of Sofia, has been carefully preserved as an open-air museum of the Bulgarian national revival period. It oozes charm and history and boasts nearly 400 buildings of 'architectural and historical' importance (according to Bulgaria's government). Koprivshtitsa is famous as the place where, on 20 April 1876, Todor Kableshkov (apparently) proclaimed the national uprising against the Turks.

The **tourist information centre** (☎/fax 2191; pl 20 April) is helpful. The only place to change money is the **DSK Bank**, behind the bus stop, and the only place to send emails is the **Heroes Internet Agency** (ul Hadzhi Nencho Palaveev).

Things to See

Six of the old, traditional homes have been turned into 'house-museums'. Admission to each costs 2.50 lv, so a combined ticket (6 lv) for all house-museums is better value. Tickets can be bought at the **souvenir shop** (ul Gereniloto), just up from the tourist office, or directly from one of the house-museums. Each is open 9.30am to 5.30pm daily from April to September, but most close for one or two days (often Sunday and/or Monday) October to March.

The most interesting and best-preserved are the three-sectioned **Karavelov House** (ul Hadzhi Nencho Palaveev 39), which includes a printing press; the **Oslekov House** (ul Gereniloto 4), probably the best example of Bulgarian national revival period architecture in the village; and the **Lyutov House** (ul Nikola Belovezhdov 2), reminiscent of the baroque homes found in Plovdiv. The other three are Debelyanov House, Kableshkov House and Benkovski House.

Special Events

The Folklore Days Festival (mid-August) and the Re-enactment of the April Uprising (1 to 2 May) are held every year. Check with the tourist office, or at the **Hadzhi Nencho Palaveev Cultural Centre** (☎ 2034; ul Hadzhi

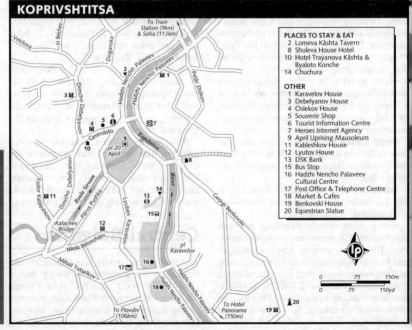

KOPRIVSHTITSA

To Train Station (9km) & Sofia (113km)

PLACES TO STAY & EAT
2 Lomeva Kâshta Tavern
8 Shuleva House Hotel
10 Hotel Trayanova Kâshta & Byaloto Konche
14 Chuchura

OTHER
1 Karavelov House
3 Debelyanov House
4 Oslekov House
5 Souvenir Shop
6 Tourist Information Centre
7 Heroes Internet Agency
9 April Uprising Mausoleum
11 Kableshkov House
12 Lyutov House
13 DSK Bank
15 Bus Stop
16 Hadzhi Nencho Palaveev Cultural Centre
17 Post Office & Telephone Centre
18 Market & Cafes
19 Benkovski House
20 Equestrian Statue

To Plovdiv (106km)

To Hotel Panorama (150m)

0   75   150m
0   75   150yd

BULGARIA

Nencho Palaveev 78), about these and other local festivals and cultural events.

Places to Stay & Eat

The tourist office can arrange rooms in **private houses** for 20 to 24 lv per person.

Shuleva House Hotel *(☎ 2122; ul Hadzhi Nencho Palaveev 37; singles/doubles with bathroom 20/25 lv)* is excellent value. The rooms are large, simple and clean, and readers have commented about the friendly staff.

Hotel Trayanova Kâshta & Byaloto Konche *(☎ 2250; ul Gereniloto 5; singles/doubles with shared bathroom from 25/45 lv)* offers huge, quiet rooms crammed with traditional furniture.

Hotel Panorama *(☎ 2035; ul Georgi Benkovski 40; singles/doubles with bathroom 35/50 lv)* is worth the walk (350m) from the bus stop. The rooms are comfortable and well furnished, and the French-speaking owners are amiable.

Lomeva Kâshta Tavern *(ul Hadzhi Nencho Palaveev 42; mains from 4 lv)* is a cosy place offering traditional cuisine at reasonable prices. The fireplace and low ceilings are reminiscent of a quaint English pub.

Chuchura *(ul Hadzhi Nencho Palaveev 66; mains 4-5 lv)* features an enticing streetside setting near the bus stop. The beer is alarmingly flat and warm, but the meals are tasty and cheap.

Getting There & Away

One bus leaves Koprivshtitsa for Sofia (4.50 lv, 2½ hours) at about 6.30am from Monday to Saturday and at 2pm on Sunday. It returns to Koprivshtitsa from the Princess Hotel Bus Terminal West in Sofia at 4pm (Monday to Saturday) and at 5pm (Sunday). Another bus departs from Koprivshtitsa for Plovdiv at 6.30am and returns from the Sever Bus Terminal in Plovdiv at 4.30pm. A bus schedule (in English), and a train timetable (in Bulgarian), are helpfully placed on the window of the **bus stop** *(ul Hadzhi Nencho Palaveev)*.

The **train station** is about 9km north of Koprivshtitsa at a place simply called 'Railway Station Koprivshtitsa'. To and from Sofia, five or six slow passenger trains stop at this station every day, but only one fast train from the capital stops on its way to Burgas, via Karlovo. If you're heading east from Koprivshtitsa, change trains at Karlovo for Plovdiv and at Tulovo for Veliko Târnovo.

TROYAN MONASTERY
ТРОЯНСКИ МАНАСТИР

Only 10km southeast of Troyan is Bulgaria's third-largest monastery *(admission free; open 6am-10pm daily)*. Although constructed in the 16th century, most of what remains was rebuilt in 1835. The colourful murals inside the **Church of the Holy Virgin** were painted in the 1840s by the renowned Zahari Zograf. The small **museum** *(admission 1 lv)* on the 3rd floor highlights the involvement of the monastery in the anti-Turkish rebellion during the 19th century.

Contact the reception office if you would like to stay in one of the basic **rooms** *(singles/doubles with shared bathroom 10/20 lv)*.

Every hour, a ramshackle bus from Troyan stops outside the monastery gates. A taxi from Troyan will cost about 5 lv.

KARLOVO КАРЛОВО
☎ 0335 • pop 27,700

Karlovo, about halfway between Sofia and Sliven, is not a bad place to break a journey. It's also easy to visit on a day trip from the larger, more interesting cities of Kazanlâk and Plovdiv. Karlovo is most famous as the birthplace of Vasil Levski (see History earlier).

From the train (or bus) station, walk about 700m up ul Vasil Levski to – yes, you guessed it – pl Vasil Levski. Here, the great man is immortalised with a bold **statue**. Turn right, and right again, to the **St Bogoroditsa Church** *(admission free; open 7am-7pm daily)*, which contains intricate wooden iconostases.

Opposite the church, the **History Museum** *(ul Vûzrozhdenska 4; admission 1 lv; open 9am-noon & 1pm-5pm Tues-Sun)* features a large array of ethnological displays. Further up ul Vasil Levski, a small park surrounds the decrepit, 15th-century **Kurshum Dzhamiya Mosque** (not open to the public). Continue up the mall to the town square (pl 20 Yuli) then head left past the **clock tower** to the inevitable **Vasil Levski Museum** *(ul Gen Kartzov 57; admission 1.50 lv; open 8.30am-1pm & 2pm-5.30pm Mon-Fri)*.

Hemus Hotel *(☎ 4597; ul Vasil Levski 87; singles/doubles with shared bathroom 15/30 lv)* is a small, family home with a handful of comfortable rooms.

Sherev Hotel *(☎ 3380; pl 20 Yuli; singles/doubles with bathroom & breakfast from US$17/27)* offers a fair range of rooms: the cheaper 'standard' rooms have nothing to get

BULGARIA

excited about, but the dearer 'luxury' rooms are spacious. Nearby you will find several quite appealing **cafés**.

Several buses a day travel between Karlovo and Stara Zagora, Kazanlâk, Sofia and Veliko Târnovo. About every hour, a bus travelling to/from Plovdiv (3 lv, one hour) stops in Karlovo, not far from the Vasil Levski Museum. From Sofia, two trains stop at Karlovo on the way to Burgas.

HISARYA ХИСАРЯ
☎ 0337 • pop 9180

Hisarya (Hisar), 17km southwest of Karlovo, is popular with Bulgarian tourists because of the **mineral waters**, which are used to cure all sorts of ailments. For foreigners, the main attractions are the ruins of the remarkable **Roman walls** (admission free; open 24hr). that protected the town and its springs. The walls are 300m down the main road from the bus terminal and adjacent train station.

Hotel Hisar (☎ 2727, fax 3634; singles/ doubles with bathroom 38/55 lv) is a massive place stuck in the 1950s, but the bathrooms are newish.

Hotel Augusta (☎ 3821; singles/doubles with bathroom US$33/38) is comfortable, but trapped in the 1970s (which at least makes it more modern than Hotel Hisar). Both are about 1km down ul General Gurko, which starts about 700m along the main road down from the bus and train stations.

To Hisarya, about eight buses a day travel from Plovdiv and Karlovo, and one or two depart from Sofia and Veliko Târnovo (via Kazanlâk).

KAZANLÂK КАЗАНЛЪК
☎ 0431 • pop 62,750

Kazanlâk is an important transport hub along the train line and highway between Sofia and Burgas. Although not a particularly appealing town, it does offer several worthwhile attractions. Kazanlâk is at the eastern end of the Valley of Roses and the centre for the production of rose oil.

The most reliable place to change money is **Magic Exchange** (ul Otets Paisii), not far from the main square (pl Sevtopolis). There's an **Internet centre** just west of this square.

Things to See

The **Thracian Tomb of Kazanlâk** is in the scruffy **Tyulbe Park** (admission free; open 24hr), 400m north of the main square. Built in the 4th century BC for a Thracian ruler, the tomb is now a Unesco World Heritage Site and not open to the public. To satisfy tourists, a full-scale replica is inside the unsatisfying **museum** (admission 2.50 lv; open 8am-6pm daily) nearby.

Just down the road from the park is the small but interesting **Kulata Ethnological Complex** (ul Knyaz Mirski; admission 2.50 lv; open 8am-noon & 1pm-6pm daily). The entrance is along the eastern section, opposite the impressive **stone church**.

The combined **Iskra Museum & Art Gallery** (ul Sv Sv Kiril i Metodii; admission 2.50 lv; open 9am-noon & 2pm-5.30pm daily May-Sept, Mon-Fri Oct-Apr) contains extensive archaeological displays and locally produced paintings. It's 100m north of the main square.

The tiny **Museum of the Roses** (admission free; open 9am-5pm daily May-Sept) explains the 300-year-old method of cultivating roses, picking the petals and processing the oil. The attached shop sells all sorts of 'rosy' items. It's about 3km north of the town centre – take a taxi or bus No 3 from the main square.

Places to Stay & Eat

Hadzhi Eminova Kâshta (☎ 42 095; ul Nikola Petkov 22; rooms 22 lv, apartment 45 lv) has a handful of spacious, traditionally furnished rooms. The (one) apartment is huge and worth booking ahead. The rooms and the apartment all have bathrooms. The charming **restaurant** is a little pricey. It's at the southern end of the Kulata Ethnological Complex.

Homy **Hotel Vesta** (☎ 20 350; ul Chavdar Vojvoda 3; singles/doubles with bathroom & breakfast US$33/43) is behind the House of Culture, 300m north of the main square. Some rooms are small, but the bathrooms are sparkling new. The **restaurant** is appealing.

Getting There & Away

From the **bus terminal** (ul Sofronii), 300m south of the main square, several buses a day go to Ruse, Plovdiv, Veliko Târnovo and Sofia (8 lv, 3½ hours). Most buses heading east to Burgas (via Sliven), and west to Sofia (via Karlovo), also pick up passengers in Kazanlâk. To Stara Zagora, catch one of the regular buses starting from Veliko Târnovo or a direct minibus from the specific stop near the bus terminal in Kazanlâk.

Every day, two trains stop at the **train station**, next to the bus terminal, on the way to both Burgas and Sofia.

ETÂR ЕТЪР

About 8km southeast of Gabrovo is the delightful **Etâr Ethnographic Village Museum** (W www.tourinfo.bg/etar; admission 7 lv; open 9am-6pm Mon-Fri, 9am-5.30pm Sat & Sun). This 'open-air museum' has nearly 50 shops and workshops designed in a style typical of the Bulgarian national revival period.

Hotel Perla (☎ 066-42 784; doubles with bathroom 40 lv) is one of the best deals in the region. The rooms are *huge* and each contains a bathroom that cannot be faulted. It's virtually opposite the Hotel Stannopriemintsa.

Hotel Stannopriemintsa, overlooking the northern (Gabrovo) end of the complex, has a **restaurant**. The decor is authentic (complete with deer antlers nailed to the wall), but the food is ordinary and overpriced.

Firstly, get to Gabrovo on any of the regular daily buses from Pleven, Stara Zagora or Plovdiv, or the hourly services from Tryavna, Veliko Târnovo or Kazanlâk. Then from along ul Aprilov in Gabrovo, bus Nos 1, 7 and 8 go directly to the complex. Alternatively, catch one of the hourly buses between Gabrovo and Kazanlâk, get off at the turn-off, and walk (2km). A taxi from Gabrovo costs about 5 lv one way.

STARA ZAGORA СТАРА ЗАГОРА
☎ 042 • pop 155,600

Bulgaria's sixth-largest city is a major transport hub, so many travellers find themselves passing through. It's a modern place with one of Bulgaria's nicest central parks, the **City Garden**, along the western end of the pedestrian mall (ul Tsar Simeon Veliki).

Plenty of **foreign-exchange offices** can be found along the mall; alternatively, try **Bulbank**, along the eastern end of ul Tsar Simeon Veliki. In the same building as the useful **Penguin Bookshop** (ul Tsar Simeon Veliki 110) is the trendy **Cafe Zagora** Internet centre.

Stara Zagora was rebuilt on the grid of an ancient Roman city, so some amazing discoveries have been unearthed – such as the massive **floor mosaic** (admission free; open 9am-noon & 2pm-5pm daily) displayed in the eastern entrance of the post office (ul Sv Knyaz Boris I), 100m north of the mall.

The **Neolithic Dwellings Museum** (admission 3.50 lv; open 9am-noon & 2pm-5pm Tues-Sat) houses the limited remains of two small, one-roomed, semidetached homes from the New Stone Age (about 6000 BC). Look for the grey-and-brown building surrounded by a wrought iron fence just down from ul Dr Todor Stoyanovich. It's about 800m west of the City Garden and hard to find, so take a taxi.

Hotel Zhelezhnik (☎ 22 158; ul Slavyanski; singles/doubles with bathroom 45/90 lv) probably hasn't been renovated since the 1950s, but it is the cheapest place in town. It's opposite the bus terminal.

Boasting the best location in town, **Hotel Ezeroto** (☎ 600 103; e stroitel@szeda.bg; ul Bratya Zhekovi 60; singles/doubles with bathroom & breakfast US$53/63) has wonderfully furnished rooms. The lakeside café and **restaurant** are also charming. It's one block north of the bus terminal.

From the **bus terminal** (ul Slavyanski), 250m south of the City Garden, buses leave every hour for Sofia (8 lv, four hours) and Plovdiv. There are also regular services each day to Sliven, Veliko Târnovo, Burgas and Ruse. For Kazanlâk, catch a bus towards Veliko Târnovo or get a direct minibus from the bus terminal. From outside its office 100m west of the City Garden, **Hemus Tours** (☎ 57 018; ul Tsar Simeon Veliki) also offers private buses to Sofia, Pleven and Plovdiv.

Every day, five trains travel in each direction between Sofia and Burgas and stop at the **train station**, about 200m south of the bus terminal.

TRYAVNA ТРЯВНА
☎ 0677 • pop 12,200

Tryavna, 40km southwest of Veliko Târnovo, is full of tree-lined and cobblestone streets, homes from the Bulgarian national revival period and quaint stone bridges. It's (currently) *far* less touristy than Arbanasi, costs nothing to wander around (unlike the Etâr complex) and prices are reasonable. The helpful **tourist office** (☎ 247; ul Angel Kânchev 22) is in the post office building.

Things to See

From the bus terminal, head east and turn right along ul Angel Kânchev. At No 128 is the impressive **St Georgi Church** (admission free; open 7.30am-12.30pm & 2.30pm-5.30pm daily). Further along at No 39 is the

Angel Kânchev House-Museum *(admission 2.50 lv; open 8am-noon & 1pm-5pm Tues-Sat)*, which contains exhibits relating to the Russian-Turkish War (1877–78).

Walk over the bridge, past the shady park and veer right to the picturesque **ploshtad Kapitan Dyado Nikola**. Facing this square is the **Staroto Shkolo** school, which will probably house the **Tryavna Museum School of Painting** in the future, and the **St Archangel Michael's Church** *(admission free; open 8am-4.30pm daily)*.

Continue over the stone **Arch Bridge** to the scenic thoroughfare, ul PR Slaveikov. At No 27a is the lovely **Daskalov House** *(admission 2.50 lv; open 8am-noon & 1pm-5pm daily)*, which contains the fascinating **Museum of Woodcarving & Icon Painting**. At No 50 is the **Slaveikov House-Museum** *(admission 2 lv; open 8am-noon & 1pm-6pm Wed-Sun)*, and at No 45, the **Summer Garden Kalinchev House** *(admission 1.50 lv; open 9am-1pm & 2pm-6pm Mon-Fri)* features a charming courtyard café.

Places to Stay & Eat
Several homes along ul Angel Kânchev from the bus terminal offer **private rooms**. The tourist office can also arrange private rooms from 20 lv per person.

The **Hotel Tigara** *(☎ 2469; ul D Gorov 7a; singles/doubles with bathroom 25/40 lv)* is about 200m from the (abandoned) Hotel Tryavna, which is at ul Angel Kânchev 46. The rooms are clean and comfortable, but ask for one of the newer ones at the back.

Hotel Family *(☎/fax 4691; ul Angel Kânchev 40; singles/doubles with bathroom & breakfast US$26/38)* is convenient and spotless, but expensive. The courtyard **restaurant** and bar are delightful.

Starata Loza *(ul PR Slaveikov 44; mains 4 lv)* is opposite the entrance to the Daskalov House. Although set up for the tourist crowd, prices are pleasingly reasonable.

Getting There & Away
Tryavna is linked by bus every hour to Gabrovo, but to nowhere else.

DRYANOVO MONASTERY
ДРЯНОВСКИ МАНАСТИР
About 5.5km south of Dryanovo is the captivating Dryanovo Monastery *(admission free; open 7am-10pm daily)*. Originally built in the

12th century, the monastery was destroyed by Turks and rebuilt by Bulgars several times during the subsequent 500 years.

The attached **Historical Museum** *(admission 2.50 lv; open 8.45am-12.30pm & 1pm-4.45pm Mon-Fri, 9.45am-3.45pm Sat & Sun)* features displays about the 1876 April Uprising and the 1877–78 war. From the bridge near the car park, a 400m path leads to the 1200m-long **Bacho Kiro** cave *(admission 2.50 lv; open 8am-6pm daily)*.

The **Komplex Bodopadi** *(☎ 0676-2314; doubles with bathroom 25 lv)* offers small but clean rooms, many of which feature huge balconies overlooking the monastery. About 100m from the car park is the delightful, riverside **Mehana Mecha Dupka** restaurant.

All buses travelling between Veliko Târnovo and Gabrovo will (if requested) stop at the turn-off (about 4km south of Dryanovo). From the turn-off, you then walk (1.5km) to the monastery.

VELIKO TÂRNOVO
ВЕЛИКО ТЪРНОВО
☎ 062 • pop 75,000
One of the most picturesque towns in Bulgaria is Veliko Târnovo. The Yantra River winds through a gorge, partially lined with traditional houses, and perched above the town is the ruined citadel on Tsarevets Hill – one of *the* highlights of Bulgaria. Veliko Târnovo is one place you should not miss – nowhere is the majesty of medieval Bulgaria more apparent.

Information
The **tourist information centre** *(☎ 22 148; ul Hristo Botev; open 8.30am-5pm Mon-Sat)* is very helpful. There's no problem changing cash because it seems that every third shop in the town centre is a **foreign-exchange office**. To change travellers cheques, obtain cash advances with a credit card or use an ATM, go to the **United Bulgarian Bank** *(ul Hristo Botev)*, near the Cinema Poltava complex. The **Internet Club Bezanata** *(ul Hristo Boltev)* is actually inside the Cinema Poltava complex.

Things to See
Museums The fine Bulgarian national revival period-style home **Sarafkina Kâshta** *(ul Gurko 88; admission 4.50 lv; open 8am-noon & 1pm-5pm Mon-Fri)* contains traditional arts and crafts.

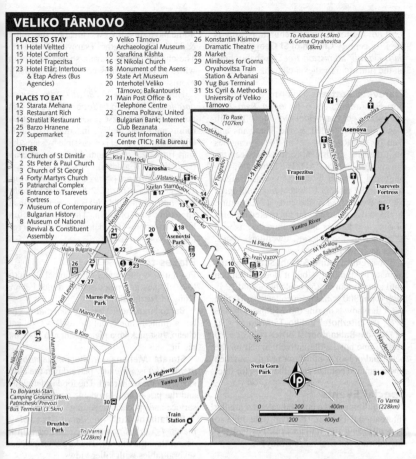

VELIKO TÂRNOVO

PLACES TO STAY
11 Hotel Veltted
15 Hotel Comfort
17 Hotel Trapezitsa
23 Hotel Etàr; Intertours & Etap Adress (Bus Agencies)

PLACES TO EAT
12 Starata Mehana
13 Restaurant Rich
14 Stratilat Restaurant
25 Barzo Hranene
27 Supermarket

OTHER
1 Church of St Dimitâr
2 Sts Peter & Paul Church
3 Church of St Georgi
4 Forty Martyrs Church
5 Patriarchal Complex
6 Entrance to Tsarevets Fortress
7 Museum of Contemporary Bulgarian History
8 Museum of National Revival & Constituent Assembly

9 Veliko Târnovo Archaeological Museum
10 Sarafkina Kâshta
18 Monument of the Asens
19 State Art Museum
20 Interhotel Veliko Târnovo; Balkantourist
21 Main Post Office & Telephone Centre
22 Cinema Poltava; United Bulgarian Bank; Internet Club Bezanata
24 Tourist Information Centre (TIC); Rila Bureau

26 Konstantin Kisimov Dramatic Theatre
28 Market
29 Minibuses for Gorna Oryahovitsa Train Station & Arbanasi
30 Yug Bus Terminal
31 Sts Cyril & Methodius University of Veliko Târnovo

The **Museum of National Revival & Constituent Assembly** (ul Ivan Vazov; admission 4.50 lv; open 8am-noon & 1pm-6pm Wed-Mon) contains books, costumes, icons and photos relating to the Old Town. Behind it, the uninspiring **Museum of Contemporary Bulgarian History** (admission 4 lv; open 8am-noon & 1pm-5pm Mon-Fri) features old photos, coins and war memorabilia.

The **Veliko Târnovo Archaeological Museum** (ul Ivan Vazov; admission 4.50 lv; open 8am-6.30pm Tues-Sat, 9am-5.30pm Sun) houses artefacts from Roman ruins, exhibits about medieval Bulgaria and some ancient gold from regional Neolithic settlements.

Dramatically situated in a tight bend of the Yantra River is the **State Art Museum** (admission 2.50 lv; open 10am-6pm Tues-Sun).

Nearby, the **Monument of the Asens** is an awe-inspiring commemoration of the establishment of the Second Bulgarian Empire.

Churches The churches mentioned below are open daily from about 9am to noon and 1pm to 6pm in summer (1 April to 30 September). To find out the opening hours at other times during the year, telephone the relevant authority (☎ 34 946).

The **Forty Martyrs Church** (ul Mitropolska; admission 2 lv) was originally built in 1230 to celebrate the victory of the Bulgars under Tsar Asen II against the Byzantines. A few blocks north, the 13th-century **Sts Peter & Paul Church** (ul Mitropolska; admission 4 lv) features three layers of remarkable murals. On the other side of the river is the renovated **Church**

BULGARIA

of St Dimitâr (ul Patriarh Evtimii; admission 4.50 lv), the town's oldest church. Nearby is the 17th-century **Church of St Georgi** (ul Patriarh Evtimii; admission free), probably built on the ruins of a medieval church.

Tsarevets Fortress Don't miss Tsarevets Fortress (admission 5 lv; open 8am-7pm daily Apr-Sept, 9am-5pm Oct-Mar). The hill was originally settled by the Thracians and then by the Romans, before the Byzantines built the first significant fortress between the 5th and 7th centuries AD. The fortress was rebuilt and fortified by the Slavs and Bulgars between the 8th and 10th centuries, and again by the Byzantines in the early 12th century. Archaeologists have so far uncovered remains of over 400 houses and 18 churches, as well as numerous monasteries, dwellings, shops, gates and towers.

The evening **Sound & Light Show** over the fortress is stunning – but it doesn't happen until a minimum of 25 people have paid 12 lv each (or at 300 lv has been collected). To find out if the show is on ring the organisers (☎ 636 828), the **Interhotel Veliko Târnovo** (☎ 630 571) or the **Balkantourist** office (☎ 633 975) in the same hotel. Alternatively, listen for the bells, and/or look for the laser beams, and then find a vantage point to enjoy the show for free!

Special Events
The highlights of the cultural calendar are the International Folklore Festival (late June to mid-July) and the Balkan Folk Festival (10 days during the first half of May).

Places to Stay
Bolyarski Stan Camping Ground (☎ 41 859; camping per person 10 lv, double bungalows 30 lv) is about 3.5km west of the town centre. It's OK, but the bungalows are not worth the money. Take bus No 5 or 110 from along ul Vasil Levski.

The tourist office (see earlier) can find **private rooms** in local homes for 15 to 25 lv per person. You may also be approached by locals with private rooms for about the same price.

Hotel Trapezitsa (☎ 22 061, fax 621 593; ul Stefan Stambolov 79; singles/doubles 15/30 lv, with bathroom 20/40 lv) is central, clean and outstanding value. Get a room at the back for the awesome views of the gorge.

Hotel Etâr (☎ 621 838, fax 621 890; ul Ivailo 2; singles/doubles with breakfast from 28/58 lv) offers clean but unexciting rooms. Some have superb views (ideal for the Sound & Light Show at the Tsarevets Fortress!). The cheaper rooms have a shared bathroom, while the dearer ones contain private bathrooms and TVs.

Hotel Veltted (☎ 29 788; ul Gurko; singles/ doubles with shared bathroom 20/30 lv) may not be the friendliest place in town, but the rooms are lovely and it's in a quiet part of the Old Town. The hotel is accessible by steps that start from near the Starata Mehana restaurant (see Places to Eat later).

Hotel Comfort (☎/fax 23 525; ul P Tipografov 5; dorm beds 22 lv, singles/doubles with bathroom 33/44 lv) is a new place in an appealing part of town. The rooms feature huge bathrooms and balconies with marvellous views.

Places to Eat
For a quick, cheap and filling meal it's hard to walk past any place selling doner kebabs along **ul Nezavisimost**.

Barzo Hranene (ul Vasil Levski; mains 3 lv) has a limited choice, but the food is tasty and cheap. Just pick up a plate, point at a dish and dig in.

Starata Mehana (ul Stefan Stambolov; mains 4 lv) is a friendly place down the cliffside from the main road. The food is delicious, and the prices are reasonable considering the service and spectacular setting.

Restaurant Rich (ul Stefan Stambolov; mains 4-5 lv) is newer, classier and a little dearer than the Starata. The larger terrace has several tables with killer views.

Stratilat Restaurant (ul Rakovski 11; snacks from 2.50 lv) offers 'Viennese apple pie' to die for and has toasted sandwiches that hang off the plate.

To self-cater, visit the **supermarket** (ul Vasil Levski).

Getting There & Away
Bus The Patnicheski Prevozi Bus Terminal (ul Nikola Gabrovski), about 4km west of the town centre, is accessible by bus Nos 10, 12, 14, 66, 70 and 110 on ul Vasil Levski. Veliko Târnovo is along the main highway between Sofia and Varna, so numerous public buses stop here on the way to Varna, Shumen and Sofia (9 lv, four hours). Also, buses regularly leave Veliko Târnovo for Karlovo, Kazanlâk, Stara Zagora, Plovdiv and Ruse.

From the **Yug Bus Terminal** (*ul Hristo Botev*), a 15-minute walk south of the town centre, private buses leave regularly for Sofia, Varna, Albena, Burgas, Plovdiv, Ruse and Stara Zagora. From outside its offices under Hotel Etâr (ul Ivailo 2), Etap Adress runs buses each day to Sofia, Dobrich, Varna, Albena and Balchik, and Intertours offers daily services to Burgas, Sofia and Kiten.

Train From the **train station**, about 1km south of central Veliko Târnovo, five slow trains plod along to Plovdiv daily, via Stara Zagora, and 10 crawl along to Gorna Oryahovitsa. This station is linked to the centre by bus Nos 10, 12, 14, 66, 70 and 110.

However, only 8.5km north of Veliko Târnovo, Gorna Oryahovitsa is one of the largest train stations in Bulgaria. Every day from this station, there are eleven trains (including four express and six fast) to Sofia, four to Varna and eleven to Ruse. To reach the station in Gorna Oryahovitsa from Veliko Târnovo, get a minibus from opposite the market along ul Vasil Levski, jump on bus No 10 from the town centre or hire a taxi.

Rila Bureau (☎ 22 042; ul Hristo Botev 13a), near the tourist office in Veliko Târnovo, sells tickets for domestic and international trains departing from Veliko Târnovo and Gorna Oryahovitsa.

ARBANASI АРБАНАСИ
☎ 062 • pop 1500

Arbanasi is only 5km northeast of Veliko Târnovo. This gorgeous village boasts nearly 90 churches, homes and monasteries that have been protected as 'cultural monuments' by the Bulgarian authorities.

Only three places are currently open to the public, but this may change if and when the renovations of other buildings are completed. One ticket (4.50 lv) allows you to visit all three; the ticket is available from the **kiosk** at the bus stop or directly from each of the three attractions. All are officially open 9am to noon and 1pm to 8pm every day from April to September. Check the opening times with the **Museums Department** (☎ 062-349 460) in Veliko Târnovo before visiting at other times.

The gorgeous, 17th-century **Konstantsalieva House** is 200m northwest of the bus stop. The upper floor contains several rooms of period furniture, while the ground floor has an impressive **souvenir shop**. The oldest

remaining church in the village is the 16th-century **Nativity Church**, 200m west of the bus stop. The interior is completely covered with lavishly coloured murals. Built in the 16th century on the ruins of a medieval church is **St Archangel Michael & Gabriel's Church**, 150m south of the bus stop. The dark interior is also covered with marvellous murals.

Places to Eat
Opposite the Nativity Church, **Konstantin & Elena Hotel** (☎ 600 217; doubles with bathroom US$37) is the best value in town.

Bolyarska Kâshta & Restaurant (☎ 20 484; singles/doubles with bathroom US$44/ 55), opposite the bus stop, is comfortable, but overpriced.

Pupyaka Restaurant (mains from 5 lv) is a classy place close to the bus stop. The setting is delightful, and it's an ideal place to try traditional Bulgarian cuisine.

Getting There & Away
From opposite the market on ul Vasil Levski in Veliko Târnovo, minibuses depart for Gorna Oryahovitsa train station and *may* detour through Arbanasi. If not, take this minibus anyway and disembark at the turn-off to Arbanasi along the road between Veliko Târnovo and Gorna Oryahovitsa. From the turn-off, walk about 700m to the village. A taxi from Veliko Târnovo costs about 2.50 lv one way.

SHUMEN ШУМЕН
☎ 054 • pop 107,650

Shumen (Shoumen) is about halfway between Ruse and Varna or Burgas. It doesn't boast the old towns, shady parks and long pedestrian malls of other places in the region, but the hilltop fortress is one of the highlights of central Bulgaria. Shumen is also an obvious base for day trips to Madara and Veliki Preslav (see the Around Shumen section later).

About 1km west along bul Slavyanski from the bus terminal and adjacent train station is the main square, pl Osvobozhdenie, where you'll find the **Internet Club & Café** in the Hotel Madara. To change money, try **Bulbank** (bul Slavyanski), half-way between the bus terminal and main square.

Things to See
The **Shumen Fortress** (admission 4 lv; open daily 8am-7pm May-Sept, 8.30am-5pm Oct-Apr) dates from the early Iron Age, and

has been fortified by the Thracians, Romans and Byzantines. It's about 5.5km uphill from the Tombul Mosque, so take a taxi.

From the entrance to the fortress, a reasonably flat 3km path leads to the **Creators of the Bulgarian State Monument**, which gets our award as the ugliest and most conspicuous monument in Bulgaria. It was built to commemorate the 1300th anniversary of the establishment of the First Bulgarian Empire. The best way up there is by taxi, while the best way down is along the obvious steps (about 2.5km) back to the city centre.

The **History Museum** (*bul Slavyanski 17; admission 2.50 lv; open 9am-5pm Mon-Fri*) contains a superb collection of artefacts and a scale model of the fortress. A pleasant **café** is in the ivy-covered courtyard.

The 18th-century **Tombul Mosque** (*ul Doiran; admission 2.50 lv; open 9am-6pm daily*) is 500m southwest of pl Osvobozhdenie. It's the most beautifully decorated mosque in Bulgaria.

Places to Stay & Eat

The **Orbita Hotel** (*☎ 52 398; Pripoden Park; doubles with bathroom 44 lv*) is excellent value. Rooms are clean and comfortable, but sparsely furnished. It's in a quiet, shady park about 2km (walk or take a taxi) from the city centre, along the road to the fortress.

Stariyat Grad Hotel & Café (*☎ 55 376; doubles with bathroom 35 lv*) is in a serene forest about 300m from the entrance to the fortress. The rooms are quiet and clean, and the owners are friendly.

A complex of quaint 19th-century buildings 200m west of pl Osvobozhdenie contains three traditional **mehanas** (*ul Tsar Osvoboditel*). Each offers indoor tables, a courtyard setting and almost identical service and prices (*mains 4 lv*).

Pizzeria Elit (*bul Slavyanski; pizzas from 2.50 lv*), 150m east of Bulbank, serves some of the tastiest pizzas in Eastern Europe. It's also an ideal place to enjoy a cheap drink at a streetside table.

Getting There & Away

Every day about three buses leave Shumen for Burgas, Ruse and Dobrich, and several head to Veliko Târnovo. Shumen is along the highway between Sofia (11 to 12 lv, six hours) and Varna, so numerous public and private buses come through in both directions. Many trains come through on their way to Varna and Sofia every day.

AROUND SHUMEN
Madara Мадара

This nondescript village, 16km east of Shumen, probably only exists because of the **Madara National Historical & Archaeological Reserve** (*admission 3 lv; open 8am-7pm daily*). This reserve surrounds the famous 'Madara horseman' bas-relief, which was carved into a cliff 23m above ground during the early 8th century to commemorate the creation of the First Bulgarian Empire. It is now protected as a World Heritage Site by Unesco.

The Horseman is 3km up a steep road from Madara village. Buses to Madara from Shumen are infrequent, so get a bus (five times a day) to Kaspichan and a minibus to Madara from there. A return taxi from Shumen costs from 15 lv, including waiting time. There are no taxis in Madara.

Veliki Preslav Велики Преслав

Veliki Preslav (sometimes known as 'Preslav'), 18km southwest of Shumen, is famous for the extensive ruins of this former Bulgar capital. The most distinguished building was the **Round Golden Church** (908), which has been partially restored in the last few years.

The **Archaeological Museum** (*☎ 0538-2630; admission 4 lv; open daily 9am-6pm May-Sept, 9am-5pm Oct-Apr*) has numerous artefacts from the old city; the prize exhibits are actually displayed in a walk-through safe. Guided tours (in English) by an archaeologist (10 lv per group) are worthwhile, but should be booked ahead. Otherwise, ask directions from the museum to the main sites or just head down the road (away from the modern town) towards the southern gate. It costs nothing to wander around, but bring your walking shoes because the ruins are spread over 2 or 3 sq km.

Eleven buses travel between Shumen and Veliki Preslav every day. From the bus terminal in Veliki Preslav, walk (2km) along ul Boris I, cross the road over to ul Ivanlo, turn right into ul Tsar Asen and look for the sign at the ruins of the northern gate. From there, the museum is another 300m down the road.

SLIVEN СЛИВЕН
☎ 044 • pop 109,600

Sliven is pleasantly located beneath several peaks over 1000m high. The city centre is the typically massive pl Hadzhi Dimitâr, from where ul Hadzhi Dimitâr heads southeast and the pedestrian mall (ul Tsar Osvoboditel) heads east. Several **foreign-exchange offices** can be found along the upper (northwestern) section of ul Hadzhi Dimitâr, while the **Internet Club** is just off the mall.

The delightful **Hadzhi Dimitâr Museum** *(ul Asenova 2; admission 2.50 lv; open 9am-noon & 2pm-5pm Mon-Fri)* is past the vibrant **market** and just across the bridge from the main square. The **History Museum** *(ul Tsar Osvoboditel 18; admission 2.50 lv; open 9am-noon & 2pm-5pm Mon-Fri)* is also worth a visit.

Most visitors head straight to the nearby hills, known as the **Blue Rocks**, which are accessible by chairlift. From the city centre, catch minibus No 13 from outside the train station or Hotel Sliven. You can also walk about 1km uphill (following the signs) from the end of the route for trolleybus Nos 18 and 20 from the city centre. Otherwise, take a taxi.

Hotel Sliven *(☎ 27 065, fax 25 112; pl Hadzhi Dimitâr; singles/doubles with bathroom & breakfast 45/70 lv)* offers the sort of standard and price you would expect at a former government-run hotel. The **dining room** (open to all) is typically charmless.

Chateau Alpina *(☎ 89 215, fax 73 016; singles/doubles with bathroom & breakfast 60/120 lv)* has luxurious rooms each with air-conditioning, as well as a balcony and TV. It's only 100m from the start of the chairlift, but far from the city centre.

Restaurant Maki *(ul Tsar Osvoboditel; mains from 5 lv)* has a useful 'photo-menu', so non-Bulgarian speakers can point at the meal they want.

From the **bus terminal** *(ul Hadzhi Dimitâr)*, 500m from the main square, buses regularly go to Veliko Târnovo, Plovdiv, Stara Zagora (also minibuses) and Karlovo. Most buses travelling between Burgas, Kazanlâk and Sofia (11 lv, five hours from Sliven) also pass through Sliven. Every day, two trains stop at Sliven on the way to both Sofia and Burgas.

Black Sea Coast

Foreigners have been visiting the Black Sea coast of Bulgaria since the 5th millennium BC. Initially, it was marauders from the Thracian, Roman and Greek empires lured by the attractive coastline and opportunities for trade; these days, it's masses of tourists from Germany, Poland, Russia and Britain attracted by the quality of sandy beaches, seemingly perpetual summer sunshine and the great variety of water sports.

Almost all hotels, restaurants, bars and cafés in the resorts close between mid-October and early April, while most of those in the cities and larger towns stay open all year.

BURGAS БУРГАС
☎ 056 • pop 210,000

Burgas is primarily a port, so it has fewer museums, beaches and parks than its rival to the north, Varna. While Burgas is a fairly relaxed place with good shopping and an abundance of restaurants and outdoor cafés, for most travellers the city is a convenient base for exploring the southern coast as far as Ahtopol and the northern coast up to Slânchev Bryag.

Information

Numerous **foreign-exchange offices** can be found along ul Aleksandrovska and ul Aleko Bogoridi. **Bulbank** *(ul Aleksandrovska)* has an ATM. The **ENet Internet Agency** *(ul Tsar Boris)* is cheap and reliable. **Helikon Bookshop** *(pl Troikata)* is one of the best places in Bulgaria for maps, while **Velkaimo Bookshop** *(ul Knyaz Al Battenberg)* offers an excellent variety of books.

Things to See & Do

The **Archaeological Museum** *(ul Aleko Bogoridi 21; admission 2.50 lv; open 9am-5pm daily, closed Sun Oct-Mar)* has a small collection of antiquities and bits and pieces from the Roman period. The highlight is probably the wooden tomb of a Thracian king.

The **Ethnographical Museum** *(ul Slavyanska 69; admission 2.50 lv; open 9am-5pm Mon-Sat Apr-Sept, closed Sat Oct-Mar)* features period furniture, regional costumes and exquisite jewellery. The small **Art Gallery** *(ul Mitropolit Simeon 24; admission 2.50 lv; open 9am-noon & 2pm-6pm Mon-Fri)* contains an eclectic collection of contemporary Bulgarian art and sculpture, as well as religious icons.

The **Maritime Park**, an extensive swathe of greenery running alongside the Black Sea coast, is particularly enjoyable and photogenic on a summer evening. The **beach**, however, is a disappointment.

BULGARIA

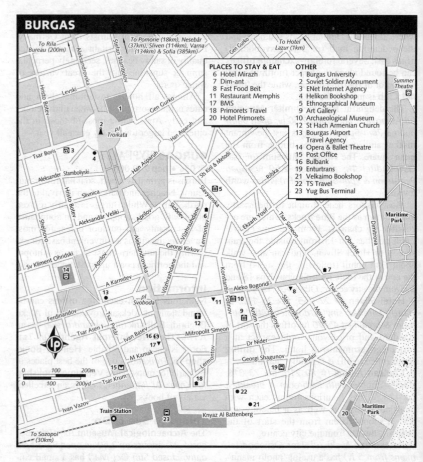

BURGAS

PLACES TO STAY & EAT
6 Hotel Mirazh
7 Dim-ant
8 Fast Food Beit
11 Restaurant Memphis
17 BMS
18 Primorets Travel
20 Hotel Primorets

OTHER
1 Burgas University
2 Soviet Soldier Monument
3 ENet Internet Agency
4 Helikon Bookshop
5 Ethnographical Museum
9 Art Gallery
10 Archaeological Museum
12 St Hach Armenian Church
13 Bourgas Airport
    Travel Agency
14 Opera & Ballet Theatre
15 Post Office
16 Bulbank
19 Enturtrans
21 Velkaimo Bookshop
22 TS Travel
23 Yug Bus Terminal

Special Events

Main events that occur throughout the year
include the International Folklore Festival
(late August), the Burgas Sea Song Festival
(July and August) and the Flora Flower Exhibition (April and September).

Places to Stay

There are two accommodation agencies in
Burgas that offer rooms in privates homes.

Primorets Travel (☎ 842 727; ul Bulair;
open 9.30am-5.30pm Mon-Fri) is in a bright
blue-green building opposite the Yug Bus
Terminal. Its rates are 12 lv per person.

Dim-ant (☎ 840 779, fax 843 748; ul Tsar
Simeon 15; open 8am-10pm daily) is inconvenient, but open weekends. It can organise
singles/doubles for 8/16 lv.

Hotel Mirazh (☎ 838 177; ul Lermontov
48; doubles with shared bathroom 45-50 lv)
is convenient and clean. Most rooms are large
and feature a balcony and seating, but those
facing the street are noisy during the day.

Hotel Lazur (☎ 838 196; ul Kalofer 1;
doubles with bathroom 50 lv) offers smallish
and unremarkable rooms. The area is quiet,
but a fair walk to any decent bar or restaurant.
It's about 2km northeast of the city centre:
catch bus No 12 or 15 from the bus or train
stations or, better, take a taxi.

Hotel Primorets (☎ 843 137, fax 842 934;
ul Knyaz Al Battenberg; singles/doubles with
bathroom & breakfast 90/125 lv) boasts a
pleasant and central location. Each room has
a balcony, and most of them have sparkling
new bathrooms.

Places to Eat

BMS (*ul Aleksandrovska; mains 3 lv*) is a cheap and cheerful cafeteria where you can tuck in to some traditional food without having to order in Bulgarian from a menu.

Fast Food Beit (*ul Aleko Bogoridi; mains from 2.50 lv*) offers a decent range of continental and oriental food at reasonable prices. It's ideal for vegetarians who don't want to resort to yet another salad.

Restaurant Memphis (*ul Aleko Bogoridi; mains from 3 lv*) provides huge servings of Bulgarian, Italian and other Western food. Prices are a little high, but a breakfast or lunch could fill you up for the rest of the day.

Getting There & Away

Air See the introductory Getting Around section earlier for information about flights from Burgas to Sofia. Tickets are available at the **Bourgas Airport Travel Agency** (☎ 842 631; cnr ul Hristo Botev & ul Ferdinandov).

Bus Most buses and minibuses arrive at/leave from the convenient **Yug Bus Terminal** (*ul Aleksandrovska*). To popular places along the Black Sea coast, such as Sozopol, Nesebâr and Slânchev Bryag, buses and minibuses leave every 30 to 40 minutes throughout the day. Buses also go to Primorsko every 30 minutes, to Kiten every 60 to 90 minutes, and four times a day to Ahtopol.

To Varna, buses depart every 30 to 40 minutes. Every day, there are also about 10 buses to Sofia (15 lv, eight hours), and regular services to Stara Zagora, Sliven and Plovdiv. **Enturtrans** (☎ 844 708; ul Bulair) operates daily buses to Sliven, Veliko Târnovo, Kazanlâk and Varna.

Train Every day from the **train station** (*ul Ivan Vazov*), seven trains head to Sofia – five via Plovdiv and two through Karlovo. Tickets for international services are available at **Rila Bureau** (☎ 820 523; ul Aleksandrovska 106), about 350m north of pl Troikata.

Getting Around

TS Travel (☎/fax 845 060; cnr ul Konstantin Fotinov & ul Bulair) can arrange car rental from US$42 per day including unlimited kilometres and insurance, but not including petrol. Any of the inordinate number of taxis in Burgas can be chartered to nearby beach resorts and villages.

SOZOPOL СОЗОПОЛ
☎ 05514 • pop 5000

Although the archaeological remains at Nesebâr are far more significant, Sozopol, 31km southeast of Burgas, is more relaxed and boasts two nice long, wide beaches. It's still as touristy as Nesebâr, but not quite as tacky, and prices for food and accommodation are far lower.

Many **foreign-exchange offices** can be found along the main streets in the Old Town and around the main square in the new town (Harmanite). The **United Bulgarian Bank** (*ul Apolonia 4*) cashes travellers cheques and has an ATM. The **Internet Club** (*ul Republikanska*) is small, but open every day.

Things to See & Do

The unimpressive **Archaeological Museum** (*ul Han Krum 2; admission 2 lv; open 9am-5pm daily Apr-Sept, Mon-Fri Oct-Mar*) has a limited array of artefacts from ancient settlements along the coast. The **Art Gallery of Sozopol** (*ul Kiril & Metodii 70; admission 1.50 lv; open 10am-7pm Mon-Sat*) is perched on a bluff with marvellous views of the sea. It features a collection of sea-motif paintings and sculptures.

Each of the numerous churches around Sozopol is open 6am to 10pm daily and the admission (where possible) is free. The 15th-century **Church of Sveta Bogoroditsa** (*ul Anaksimandâr 13*) contains exquisite wooden iconostases. The gates are mostly closed, however, so get the keys from the museum. The **Sveti Zossim Chapel** is a small working church in the shady gardens opposite the bus terminal. It was built in the 13th century to honour the patron saint of sailors. Also worth a quick look are the **Church of St George** (*ul Apolonia*) and the **St Nedelya Chapel** (*ul Anaksimandâr*).

The 6.6-sq-km **St John's (Ivan) Island** (*admission free; open 24hr*) is the largest along the Bulgarian coast. It is home to **ruins** of a 13th-century monastery and temple, a **lighthouse** that was built in 1884 and about 70 species of protected **birds**. The island can be visited by chartering a fishing boat (with boatman) or admired from the window of any restaurant along the northwestern side of the Old Town.

The southern **Harmanite Beach** and the more convenient **Town Beach** are clean and well frequented.

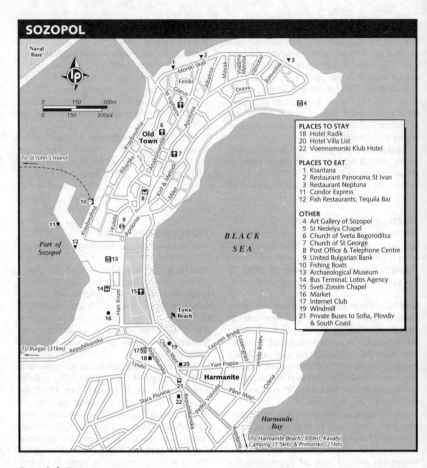

SOZOPOL

PLACES TO STAY
18 Hotel Radik
20 Hotel Villa List
22 Voennomorski Klub Hotel

PLACES TO EAT
1 Ksantana
2 Restaurant Panorama St Ivan
3 Restaurant Neptuna
11 Condor Express
12 Fish Restaurants; Tequila Bar

OTHER
4 Art Gallery of Sozopol
5 St Nedelya Chapel
6 Church of Sveta Bogoroditsa
7 Church of St George
8 Post Office & Telephone Centre
9 United Bulgarian Bank
10 Fishing Boats
13 Archaeological Museum
14 Bus Terminal; Lotos Agency
15 Sveti Zossim Chapel
16 Market
17 Internet Club
19 Windmill
21 Private Buses to Sofia, Plovdiv & South Coast

Special Events

The popular Apollonia Arts Festival (first half of September) features all sorts of jazz, pop and alternative music.

Places to Stay

The best-equipped camping ground in the area is **Kavatsi Camping** (☎ 2261; *camping per person 10 lv, bungalows with toilet 45 lv, double hotel rooms with bathroom 65 lv*). It's about 2km south of the main square in Harmanite, and along the coastal road on the way to Primorsko.

Lotos Agency (☎/fax 2429) is run by a helpful man who can show you photos of the rooms on offer in private homes for 15 to 45 lv per person. The agency is conveniently located at the bus terminal.

Hotel Radik (☎ 3706; *ul Republikanska 4; singles/doubles with bathroom from 30/55 lv*) is a bright place and is also immaculately clean. The rooms, which feature balconies, TVs and fridges, are tremendous value for the price you pay.

Voennomorski Klub Hotel (☎ 4362; *ul Republikanska 17; doubles with bathroom 54 lv*) is a large complex overlooking the main square in Harmanite. The rooms are quiet, comfortable and air-conditioned, but they are on the small side.

Hotel Villa List (☎/fax 2235; *ul Cherno More 5; singles/doubles with bathroom 40/60 lv*) is understandably popular with tour groups, and often full during the summer months of July and August. It's close to almost everything, and has excellent facilities.

Places to Eat

The cheapest **fish restaurants** are strung along the port – eg, **Tequila Bar** and the breezy **Condor Express** (on the top deck of a sailing boat).

Ksantana (ul Morski Skali; mains 7 lv) is a folksy establishment with a bird's-eye view of St John's Island.

Restaurant Panorama St Ivan (ul Morski Skali; mains from 5 lv) is a homy restaurant with reasonable prices and there's a small courtyard that provides glorious views and welcome breezes.

Restaurant Neptuna (ul Morski Skali; mains from 5.50 lv) is one of several similar places in the vicinity that offer tasty fish, superb views and cooling breezes.

Getting There & Away

From the **bus terminal** (ul Han Krum), buses and minibuses leave for Burgas about every 30 minutes between 6am and 9pm from April to September; about once an hour the rest of the year. Only one or two buses a day travel directly from Sozopol to Primorsko, Kiten and Ahtopol, and up to three each day head to Shumen, Stara Zagora and Sofia (17 lv, eight hours). From around the main square in Harmanite, comfortable private buses go to Sofia and Plovdiv and along the coast south of Sozopol. Note that almost all buses from Burgas, Sofia, Sliven, Plovdiv and Stara Zagora to anywhere along the southern coast stop in Sozopol.

SOUTH OF SOZOPOL

Places along the coast between Sozopol and the Turkish border offer none of the ambience and history of Sozopol or Nesebâr, but they attract far fewer tourists. Public transport is available from Burgas as far as Ahtopol, but less frequent the further south you go.

The beach at **Primorsko** is long, curved and sheltered, so it's ideal for swimming and boating. **See Desi Travel**, at the bus stop, offers rooms in private houses for 6 to 15 lv per person. **Hotel Koral** (☎ 05561-2230; ul Strandjha 17; singles/doubles with shared bathroom & breakfast 28/56 lv) is along a quiet street heading east from the main square.

About 5km further south is **Kiten**, pleasantly situated among pockets of forest. The northern **Atliman Beach** is one of the cleanest and prettiest along the coast, while the **Morski Beach** to the south is sheltered, ideal

for swimming and has plenty of beachside **cafés**. **Hotel Bohem** (☎ 088 512 481; ul Strandjha 14a; singles/doubles with bathroom 22/44 lv) is a cosy place just down from the bus stop.

Ahtopol, 30km further down the coast, has a long, curved and unspoiled beach. **Hotel Neptun** (☎ 05563-2164; singles/doubles with bathroom 12/24 lv) is on the corner of ul Sveti Nikola (which heads down from the bus stop) and ul Georgi Kondolov, and only metres from the sea.

NESEBÂR НЕСЕБЪР
☎ 0554 • pop 9500

Nesebâr sits on a small rocky island that is connected to the mainland by a causeway. Designated by Unesco as a World Heritage Site, Nesebâr is a glorious town with church ruins along cobblestoned streets and a couple of worthwhile museums. Unlike Sozopol, Nesebâr offers plenty of great hotels in the Old Town, though the beach here is nowhere near as good.

Every second or third shop seems to be a **foreign-exchange office**. The only bank, **Biochim Commercial Bank** (ul Mesembria), cashes travellers cheques and has an ATM. The **Internet Club** is inside Hotel the White House (see Places to Stay later).

Things to See & Do

Unless stated otherwise, every religious building mentioned below is open during daylight hours and admission is free.

The **Basilica** (ul Mitropolitska), which is now in ruins, was originally built in the early 6th century. It contained three naves and a spacious interior with high walls and wide windows. The well-preserved **Pantokrator Church** (ul Mesembria) was built in the mid-14th century. It's renowned for its bell tower and unusually conspicuous urban location.

Probably the most beautiful church in Nesebâr was the **St John Aliturgetos Church** (ul Mena). It was built in the mid-14th century, but mostly destroyed by an earthquake in 1913. The **Church of St John the Baptist** (ul Mitropolitska) was built during the 10th century and features some of the best-preserved murals in Bulgaria, dating from the 14th and 17th centuries. The **St Spa's Church** (ul Aheloi; admission 2 lv; open 10am-1pm & 2pm-5.30pm Mon-Fri, 10am-1.30pm Sat & Sun) features some more well-preserved murals.

BULGARIA

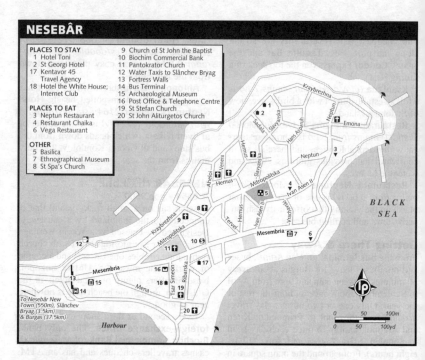

NESEBÂR

PLACES TO STAY
1 Hotel Toni
2 St Georgi Hotel
17 Kentavor 45
    Travel Agency
18 Hotel the White House;
    Internet Club

PLACES TO EAT
3 Neptun Restaurant
4 Restaurant Chaika
6 Vega Restaurant

OTHER
5 Basilica
7 Ethnographical Museum
8 St Spa's Church

9 Church of St John the Baptist
10 Biochim Commercial Bank
11 Pantokrator Church
12 Water Taxis to Slânchev Bryag
13 Fortress Walls
14 Bus Terminal
15 Archaeological Museum
16 Post Office & Telephone Centre
19 St Stefan Church
20 St John Aliturgetos Church

The **St Stefan Church** (ul Ribarska; admission 2 lv; open 9am-noon & 2pm-6pm daily) was built between the 10th and 12th centuries. It's almost completely covered inside with murals, and was one of the first churches in Bulgaria to be decorated with ceramics.

The **Archaeological Museum** (ul Mesembria 2; admission 2.50 lv; open 9am-1.30pm & 2pm-9pm Mon-Sat, also 9am-1pm & 2pm-7pm Sun Apr-Sept) houses artefacts detailing the naval history of previous civilisations. The **Ethnographical Museum** (ul Mesembria 32; admission 1.50 lv; open 10am-2pm & 3pm-6pm daily) features regional costumes and displays about weaving.

The **beaches** are small and rocky, and the water is often choked with seaweed. The beach at Slânchev Bryag, only 3km away, is far superior.

Places to Stay
Kentavor 45 Travel Agency (☎ 45 880) is along a laneway that starts northeast of ul Ribarska. It arranges rooms in a hotel/private home for 22/15 lv per person.

Hotel Toni (☎ 42 403; ul Kraybrezhna; doubles with bathroom from 33 lv) features the same sort of amenities, location and views as other hotels nearby costing far more.

Hotel the White House (☎ 333 103; ul Tsar Simeon 2; doubles with bathroom & breakfast 75 lv) is friendly, sparkling new and central. Each room features air-con and a TV and fridge.

St Georgi Hotel (☎/fax 44 045; ul Sadala 10; singles/doubles with bathroom & breakfast from 44/66 lv) is spotlessly clean and good value, though a bit charmless. The rooms are small but comfortable and have lovely bathrooms and balconies.

Places to Eat
Neptun Restaurant (ul Neptun 1; mains from 6 lv) is one of several excellent restaurants at the end of the main drag, mercifully distant from the noise and crowds.

Vega Restaurant (off ul Mesembria; mains 6 lv) is a waterside bar and restaurant almost on top of the sea. The private balconies are a delightful attraction.

Restaurant Chaika (ul Ivan Asen II; salads 3 lv, mains 6 lv) has a quiet, vine-covered courtyard. It's an ideal place to try fresh fish at reasonable prices.

Getting There & Away

From the obvious **bus terminal** at the end of the causeway, buses and minibuses go to Burgas every 30 to 40 minutes; to Varna about six times a day; and to Sofia (17 lv, seven hours) about 10 times every day. There are several ways to reach Slânchev Bryag: catch a taxi, take a bus (which leaves every 15 minutes), or jump into a water taxi (every 30 minutes) from a spot north of the fortress walls.

SLÂNCHEV BRYAG
СЛЬНЧЕВ БРЯГ

Slânchev Bryag (Sunny Beach) is a purpose-built resort based along a perfect stretch of beach only 3km from Nesebâr. There are about 120 hotels to chose from, but try to avoid any place too close to the main road. As an example, **Hotel Globus** (☎ 0554-22 018; doubles with bathroom & air-con from 50 lv) is a large three-star place only metres from the sea. It's comparatively excellent value and open all year.

Minibuses and buses travel between Burgas and Slânchev Bryag every 40 minutes and use the terminal just off the main road about 100m from Hotel Svejest in Slânchev Bryag. From this terminal, several buses also go to Sliven, Plovdiv, Stara Zagora, Sofia and Varna every day. See the Nesebâr section above for information about travelling between Nesebâr and Slânchev Bryag.

VARNA ВАРНА
☎ 052 • pop 350,000

Varna is an atmospheric city on a bay hemmed in by hills that offer scenic views. It boasts the largest and most impressive museum in Bulgaria, a marvellous seaside park, seemingly endless summer festivals, and the most extensive archaeological ruins in the country. Varna is also an ideal base for day trips to nearby beach resorts, as well as to Balchik and Dobrich.

Information

Bulbank (ul Slivnitsa) changes travellers cheques, gives cash advances on credit cards over the counter, and has an ATM. Oodles of **foreign-exchange offices** around the city centre offer competitive rates of exchange.

Send your mail from the **main post office** (bul Vladislav Varenchik). **Cyber X Internet Club** (ul Knyaz Boris I) is just around the corner from the McDonald's, while the **Skylark**

Internet Bar & Cafe (cnr ul Tsar Simeon & ul Asen Zlatarov) is also convenient.

Etap Adress and **Megatours** are both on the ground floor of the Cherno More Hotel complex at ul Slivnitsa 33. They are the best places to book organised tours, buy tickets for boats and private long-distance buses, and ask general questions in the absence of a proper tourist office. The **PS Bookshop** (ul Maria Luisa) offers an impressive array of books in English and German.

Things to See & Do

The **Roman Thermae** (ul Khan Krum; admission 2.50 lv; open 10am-5pm Tues-Sun Apr-Sept, Mon-Fri Oct-Mar) was built in the late 2nd century AD, and is now the largest ruins in Bulgaria. It can be admired for free from the grounds of the quaint **St Anastasios Orthodox Church** (ul Graf Ignatiev), but it's far better to pay the entrance fee and explore the ruins from within.

The mammoth **Cathedral of the Assumption of the Virgin** (pl Mitropolitska Simeon; admission 2.50 lv; open 6am-10pm daily) was built between 1880 and 1886. Although the location and size are impressive, the design and interior are fairly unremarkable.

Over 100,000 items are housed in the 39 rooms of the magnificent **Archaeological Museum** (ul Maria Luisa 41; admission 2.50 lv; open 10am-5pm Tues-Sun Apr-Sept, Tues-Sat Oct-Mar), one of the highlights of Bulgaria. All exhibits originate from the Varna area and are helpfully placed in chronological order.

The **Ethnographic Museum** (ul Panagyurishte 22; admission 2.50 lv; open 10am-5pm Tues-Sun Apr-Sept, Tues-Sat Oct-Mar) contains large, varied displays on wine-making, weaving and fishing, as well as exhibits of regional costumes and jewellery. The **National Naval Museum** (bul Primorski 2; admission 2.50 lv; open 10am-6pm Mon-Fri) explains the history of the Bulgarian Navy, and is the only one of its kind in the country.

Varna boasts the best suburban **beach** in Bulgaria. **Primorski Park**, stretching for 8km along the coast from Varna, is a marvellous place for an evening promenade.

Special Events

Varna hosts the renowned Varna Summer International Festival between May and October. It features outstanding events including

BULGARIA

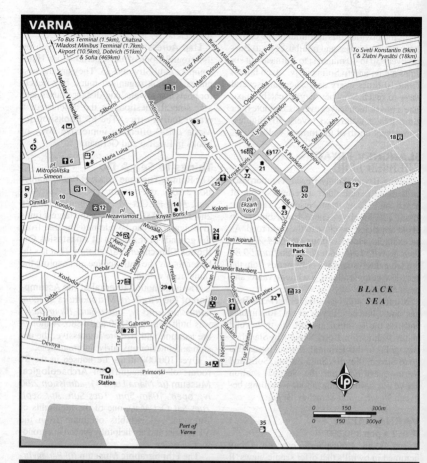

VARNA

PLACES TO STAY
8 Voennomorski Club
21 Cherno More Hotel; Etap
    Adress; Megatours;
    Vendor (Car Rental)
23 Hotel Santa Marina
28 Three Dolphins Hotel

PLACES TO EAT
13 Restaurant Chuchura
22 Trops Kâshta
25 Restaurant Arkitekta
32 Paraklisa

OTHER
1 Archaeological Museum
2 City Hall
3 PS Bookshop

4 Main Post Office &
   Telephone Centre
5 City Hospital
6 Cathedral of the
   Assumption of the
   Virgin
7 Mustang Cinema
9 Makedonia Dom
   (Minibuses to Albena)
10 Market
11 Clock Tower; Storya
    Bachvarov Dramatic
    Theatre
12 Varna Opera House;
    Night Club Danvi
14 Varna International
    Airport Travel Agency
15 St Nikolai Church

16 Cyber X Internet Club
17 Bulbank
18 Open-Air Theatre
19 Summer Theatre
20 Festival Hall
24 St Sarkis Armenian
    Apostolic Church
26 Skylark Internet Bar
    & Cafe
27 Ethnographic Museum
29 Rila Bureau
30 Roman Thermae
31 St Anastasios Orthodox
    Church
33 National Naval
    Museum
34 Roman Baths
35 Boat Passenger Terminal

BULGARIA

opera, the International Ballet Competition (held in even-numbered years) and choral, jazz and traditional music.

Places to Stay

Inside the train station, **Astra Tour** (☎ 605 861; e astratur@mail.vega.bg) and **Isak Accommodation Bureau** can arrange single/double rooms in local homes for 22/33 lv.

Voennomorski Club (☎ 238 312; ul Maria Luisa 1; doubles 24 lv, singles/doubles with bathroom 25/40 lv) is in the bright-blue building opposite the cathedral. It offers small, sparsely furnished but clean rooms in an unbeatable location.

Three Dolphins Hotel (☎ 600 911; ul Gabrovo 27; singles/doubles with bathroom & breakfast from 50/60 lv) is in a quiet area near the train station. This small, friendly guesthouse is great value.

Hotel Santa Marina (☎ 603 826, fax 603 825; ul Baba Rada 28; singles/doubles with bathroom & breakfast US$33/44) is cosy, convenient and good value. It's often full, especially on summer weekends. All rooms have air-con.

Cherno More Hotel (☎ 223 925, fax 236 311; ul Slivnitsa 33; singles/doubles with bathroom & breakfast from US$22/35) has so many rooms that it has probably never been full. The rooms are quiet, but small, and they offer magnificent views from the tiny balconies.

Places to Eat

Trops Kâshta (ul Knyaz Boris I; salads 1.50 lv, mains 2.50-4 lv) is the best place to enjoy a cheap, simple meal without needing to speak Bulgarian or plough through a menu in Cyrillic.

Paraklisa (☎ 223 495; bul Primorski 47; starters 4 lv, mains 7-10 lv) offers traditional Bulgarian cuisine and impeccable service. Reservations are a must; otherwise, dine here during off-peak hours.

Restaurant Arkitekta (ul Musala; mains from 3 lv) is based in a delightful house built during the Bulgarian national revival period. Although the helpings are not huge, it's worth visiting for the service and setting. The menu is in English.

Restaurant Chuchura (pl Nezavisimost; starters 2.50 lv, mains from 4 lv) is also based in a national revival period house and heartily recommended. Service is excellent (there's a

menu in English), and daily specials start from only 2 lv.

Entertainment

For some culture, find out what's happening at the **Varna Opera House** (pl Nezavisimost) or the **Storya Bachvarov Dramatic Theatre** (pl Mitropolitska Simeon), near the clock tower. The **Open-Air Theatre** and the temporary **Summer Theatre**, both in Primorski Park, host live music and drama. Otherwise, hit the **Night Club Danvi**, incongruously located under the Varna Opera House or catch a flick at the **Mustang Cinema** (bul Vladislav Varenchik).

Getting There & Away

Air See the introductory Getting Around section earlier for information on flights from Varna to Sofia. Tickets are available from the **Varna International Airport** travel agency (☎ 622 948; ul Knyaz Boris I 15).

Bus & Minibus The main **bus terminal** (bul Vladislav Varenchik) is 2km northwest of the city centre. From this terminal, buses to Sofia (16 lv, eight hours) leave every 45 minutes and travel via Shumen and Veliko Târnovo. Every day, there are also regular services to Burgas, Dobrich, Plovdiv, Sliven, Stara Zagora, Ruse and Durankulak (on the Romanian border). Most long-distance services are operated by private buses. Tickets for private buses can be bought at agencies in town (as well as at the bus terminal), but all services depart from the main bus terminal.

From the **Chatsna Mladost Minibus Terminal** (bul Vladislav Varenchik), minibuses frequently go to Dobrich, Balchik, Burgas, Nesebâr and Slânchev Bryag. This terminal is about 200m along a road that starts almost opposite the main bus terminal.

Train From the **train station** (bul Primorski), six trains a day go between Varna and Sofia – four via Gorna Oryahovitsa (for Veliko Târnovo) and Pleven, one through Plovdiv and another via Karlovo. Every day, there are also nine trains to Shumen and two each to Ruse and Dobrich. **Rila Bureau** (☎ 226 273; ul Preslav 13) sells tickets for international trains and advance tickets for domestic trains.

Getting Around

The bus terminal and train station are linked by bus Nos 1, 22 and 41. Bus No 409 connects

BULGARIA

the airport with Zlatni Pyasâtsi every 15 minutes between 6am and 11pm. This bus stops at the main bus terminal in Varna, near the main post office on bul Vladislav Varenchik and along ul Slivnitsa. It then stops along Primorski Park and near Sveti Konstantin.

Hertz (☎ 500 210) and **Avis** (☎ 500 832) have offices at the airport. **Vendor** (☎ 605 111; ul Slivnitsa 33), inside the Cherno More Hotel complex, is far cheaper for car rental.

AROUND VARNA

Along the coast north of Varna there are several upmarket beach resorts that cater almost exclusively to rich foreigners on package tours. Prices for hotels (and restaurants) are prohibitive for individual travellers, but the resorts are easy enough to visit on day trips from Varna or Balchik.

Sveti Konstantin
Свети Константин

Sveti Konstantin is only 9km from Varna. The hotels are attractively spaced out, but the beaches are not spectacular. One attraction is the tiny, 18th-century **Sv Konstantin & Sv Elena Monastery** (admission free; open dawn-dusk daily, except Sun morning).

Tourist Service Kapka 94 (☎ 052-361 003), near the post office, charges 20 lv per person for private rooms and 28 lv per person for a room in a two-star hotel. The **Estreya Hotel** (☎ 052-361 135, fax 361 316; singles/doubles with bathroom & breakfast 90/150 lv) is a modern place only metres from the monastery.

Bus No 409 from Varna stops outside Hotel Panorama at Sveti Konstantin. From this hotel, it's a short walk down to the hotels and beach.

Zlatni Pyasâtsi Златни Пясъци

Zlatni Pyasâtsi (Golden Sands), Bulgaria's second-largest resort, is situated 18km northeast of Varna.

The major attraction is the **Aladzha Monastery** (admission 2 lv; open 9am-6pm Tues-Sun Apr-Sept, 9am-4pm Tues-Sat Oct-Mar). Erosion has undoubtedly caused a lot of damage to this cave monastery, but it's still a remarkable place. If walking (one hour) from the resort, head up the road past the post office, cross the main road outside the Economic & Investment Bank, and follow the signs. The steep 3km road commences about

500m south from the start of the walking trail, along the Varna-Albena road.

The **accommodation office** (☎ 052-355 683), next to the Economic & Investment Bank, offers rooms in two-star hotels from 35 lv per person. **Hotel Rodina** (☎ 052-355 252, fax 355 587; singles/doubles with bathroom & breakfast 75/90 lv) is a modern, three-star place convenient to the beach.

Bus Nos 109, 209, 309 and 409 leave Varna every 15 minutes between 6am and 11pm for Zlatni Pyasâtsi. These buses stop along the Varna-Albena road at each of the resort's main entrances, from where it's a 10-minute walk to the beach and all major hotels.

Albena Албена

Albena's stunning **beach** is ideal for the abundance of **water sports** on offer; otherwise go **horse riding** or enjoy a spot of **tennis**. But beware: *everything*, including all activities, in Albena is horrendously overpriced.

Gorska Fey (☎ 0579-62 961; camping 8 lv, bungalows with bathroom 82 lv, A-frame bungalows 225 lv) is spread out along the forest just behind the bus terminal. The A-frame bungalows are large and luxurious.

The **accommodation office** (☎ 0579-62 920) at the bus terminal offers singles/doubles in hotels from 55/75 lv including breakfast. If you want a **private room**, look for the relevant signs outside homes along the Varna-Balchik road.

Minibuses to Albena leave every 30 minutes between 8am and 7.30pm from a spot known as Makedonia Dom (as indicated on the Varna map). From Albena, minibuses also leave regularly for Balchik and Dobrich, and three or four buses travel daily to Sofia.

BALCHIK БАЛЧИК
☎ 0579 • pop 13,760

Balchik is a picturesque old town huddled below white chalk bluffs. Although an easy day trip from Varna, Balchik is a cheap base from which to explore the nearby countryside and the beach resorts to the south. The downside is that Balchik has no natural beach.

The **Summer Palace Queen Marie & Botanical Gardens** (admission 5 lv; open 8am-6pm daily) was built between 1924 and 1926 by King Ferdinand of Romania because his wife, the UK-born Queen Marie, requested a place of solitude. (Balchik was then part of Romania.) The palace is deliberately designed in styles reminiscent of the Islamic faith and the Bulgarian national revival period. If coming by bus from the south coast, get off at the obvious bus stop opposite the palace, walk down the access road and enter at the main entrance. You can exit the palace at the beach (where there's another entrance) and stroll (3km) into town along the waterfront.

Three accommodation agencies located in the same building opposite the port area in Balchik can arrange rooms in local homes for approximately 13 lv per person: **Sea Foods Ltd** (☎ 72 531; e seafoods@hotmail.com), **Chaika** (☎ 73 775; e chaika@mail.bg) and **Zora Tours** (☎ 72 732; e zora_tour@abv.bg).

The **Balchik Hotel** (☎ 72 809, fax 72 862; singles/doubles with bathroom & breakfast from 17/20 lv) faces a small, quiet park near the main square. The rooms are large, clean and excellent value.

The waterfront between the port and palace is lined with modest **eateries** that serve fish fillets and kebabs with french fries.

Every day, minibuses regularly (more so in summer) link Balchik with Albena, Varna and Dobrich. From the **bus terminal**, a steep walk (1km) up ul Cherno More from the port, three or four buses a day also head to Sofia (20 lv, 10 hours).

Northern Bulgaria

Probably the most ignored region of the country is northern Bulgaria. Public transport is infrequent, so it's not easy to get around – but it is worth the effort. However, if you want to admire the Danube River in its glory from a riverside café, you may be disappointed. Few major towns are actually built along the Bulgarian side of the Danube because of perpetual flooding hundreds of years ago. The river is also polluted and unattractively shallow in summer.

BELOGRADCHIK БЕЛОГРАДЧИК
☎ 0936 • pop 6700

This gorgeous village is nestled in picturesque mountains in the remote northwestern corner. Half of Belogradchik is in the midst of dramatic reconstruction, though the rest of the village appears to have been permanently abandoned (including two major hotels).

The hilltop **Belogradchik Fortress** (admission 5.50 lv; open 8am-6pm daily) was orig-

inally constructed by the Romans during the 1st century BC, but most of what remains was rebuilt by the Turks between 1805 and 1837. The **History Museum** (pl 1850 Leto; admission 4 lv; open 8am-noon & 2pm-6pm Mon-Fri) contains numerous coins, jewellery and costumes, as well as 6000 artefacts from the fortress. **Belogradchiski Skali** are amazing rock formations that start only 100m down from the main square.

Hotel-Restaurant Madona (☎ 5546; ul Hristo Botev 26; singles/doubles with bathroom 33/44 lv) is small, friendly and quiet, but the rooms are *really* tiny. It's 600m up ul Vasil Levski from the main square, past the old Hotel Belogradchik Skali.

Hotel Rai (☎ 3735; singles/doubles most with shared bathroom 11/22 lv) is a comfortable place with a handful of small, cheap and clean attic-style rooms. It's one street from the bus terminal.

About 50m before the Madona, **Restaurant Eli** (ul Hristo Botev; mains 3-5 lv) is one of several cafés with a glorious hilltop position.

Every day, several buses travel between Sofia and Vidin, via Belogradchik.

VIDIN ВИДИН
☎ 094 • pop 69,400

Vidin is one of the few towns along the Danube River to offer worthwhile riverside views and ambience. Although it boasts several attractions and is a worthy alternative to Ruse for travelling to/from Romania, Vidin's remoteness is a disincentive.

From the main square (pl Bdintsi), ul Tsar Simeon Veliki heads northwest and ul Baba Vida hugs the river to the north. There are **foreign-exchange offices** along ul Tsar Simeon Veliki, and the **Bulgarian Post Bank** faces the main square. **Marc Internet** (ul Tsar Aleksandâr II) is 100m south of pl Bdintsi.

At the top end of ul Baba Vida, 1km north of the main square, is the magnificent **Baba Vida Museum-Fortress** (admission 1.50 lv; open daily 8.30am-5pm May-Sept, 10am-5pm Oct-April). The Bulgars constructed this fortress on the ruined walls of a Roman citadel, but most of what remains was rebuilt in the 17th century by the Turks.

The **Archaeological Museum** (admission 2 lv; ul Tsar Simeon Veliki 12; open 9am-noon & 2pm-6pm Tues-Sat) features Thracian and Roman artefacts and exhibits from the Bulgarian national revival period.

Places to Stay & Eat

Camping Nora (☎ 23 830; bungalows per person 20 lv) is beyond the abandoned fairgrounds 2.3km west of the main square, along ul Ekzarh Yosif I. This well-kept complex includes a swimming pool, bar and restaurant.

Voennomorski Klub Hotel (☎ 25 763; ul Baba Vida 15; rooms with shared bathroom per person 17 lv) offers basic accommodation on the top floor of a military club.

Hotel Dunav (☎/fax 24 448; ul Edelvais 3; singles/doubles with bathroom 22/44 lv) is quiet, clean and good value. It's 100m east of the southern tip of the main square.

Pizza Napoli (ul Tsar Aleksandâr II; mains from 3 lv) is a cosy place 100m south of pl Bdintsi. It offers some of the tastiest and best-value food in northern Bulgaria.

Getting There & Away

The **bus terminal** (ul Zhelezhnicharska) is two blocks southwest of pl Bdintsi. Buses to Sofia (11 lv, five hours) leave this terminal every 60 to 90 minutes, while many private buses to Sofia also leave from outside ticket counters in front of the train station. Four trains leave for Sofia every day from the **train station** (ul Saedinenie), between the main square and bus terminal.

To/from Romania From the port, 5km north of Vidin, ferries to Calafat in Romania leave about every hour (24 hours a day). Tickets cost US$13/2.50 per car/passenger (payable in US dollars, euros or leva). The port is accessible on bus No 1 from the train station in Vidin; the bus stop at the port is about 500m down the road from customs.

Far more convenient are the passenger boats (30 minutes) operated by **Eurokontact** (☎ 23 358). They leave every day from the riverboat terminal, 150m southeast of the main square in Vidin, at 8am, 10.30am and 6pm, and depart from Calafat at 9.30am, noon and 7.30pm. Tickets cost US$3.50 (payable in US dollars, euros or leva).

PLEVEN ПЛЕВЕН
☎ 064 • pop 138,500

Pleven is an unremarkable city with few redeeming features, but it's a reasonable place to break a journey. The town centre (pl Svoboda) is 1km south of the bus terminal and adjacent train station, along the pedestrian mall (ul Vasil Levski).

Most attractions commemorate the 1877–78 Russian-Turkish War. These include the **Museum of Liberation of Pleven 1877** (ul Vasil Levski 157; admission 2.50 lv; open 9am-noon & 1pm-6pm Tues-Sat); and the enormous **Historical Museum** (ul Stoyan Zaimov 3; admission 2.50 lv; open 9am-noon & 1pm-5pm Tues-Sat), about 400m south of the main square. The similar **Military-Historical Museum** (admission 2.50 lv; open 9am-5pm Tues-Sat) is on a hilltop in Skobelev Park, located about 1km southwest of the Historical Museum.

Miziya-95 (☎ 801 215; ul Ivan Vazov 5), next to Hotel Interrostov, organises double rooms in private homes for 17 to 25 lv.

Hotel Pleven (☎ 30 181; pl Republika; singles/doubles with bathroom 35/50 lv) is a dreary, two-star hotel just metres from the bus and train stations.

Hotel Interrostov (☎ 801 095; ul Osvobozhdenie 2; singles/doubles with bathroom 70/110 lv) faces pl Svoboda. The comfortable rooms each contain a fan, fridge and TV, but are small.

Mehana Bulgarski Koren (ul Naicho Tsanov 4; mains 5-7 lv) features one of the nicest courtyard settings in the country. It's tucked away along a side street just off ul Vasil Levski.

From the **bus terminal** (pl Republika), up to three public buses a day go to Burgas, Plovdiv, Ruse, Sliven, Sofia (8 lv, 2½ hours), Stara Zagora, Varna, Veliko Târnovo and Vidin. From the ticket offices in front of Hotel Pleven and the train station, private buses also go every hour to Sofia, but less frequently to Burgas, Ruse and Varna.

Pleven is has frequent train connections with Sofia, Varna and Gorna Oryahovitsa, from where there are four connections each day to Ruse.

RUSE ПУСЕ
☎ 082 • pop 182,500

Ruse (Rousse) is the fifth-largest city in Bulgaria and the major gateway for most people travelling to/from Romania. It's the nicest city along the Bulgarian side of the Danube River, and includes one of the most magnificent city squares (pl Svoboda) in the country. Disappointingly, however, the original town planners thought little of the Danube, so most of the riverside is dominated by ugly ports and disused train lines.

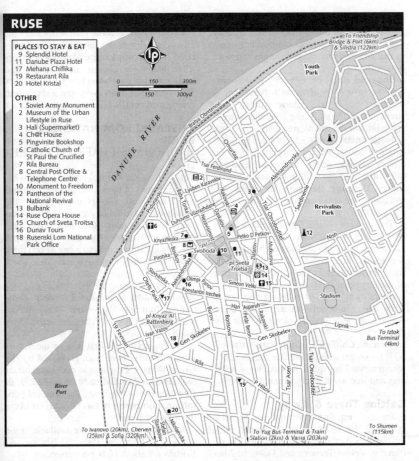

RUSE

PLACES TO STAY & EAT
9 Splendid Hotel
11 Danube Plaza Hotel
17 Mehana Chiflika
19 Restaurant Rila
20 Hotel Kristal

OTHER
1 Soviet Army Monument
2 Museum of the Urban
  Lifestyle in Ruse
3 Hali (Supermarket)
4 Ch@t House
5 Pingvinite Bookshop
6 Catholic Church of
  St Paul the Crucified
7 Rila Bureau
8 Central Post Office &
  Telephone Centre
10 Monument to Freedom
12 Pantheon of the
  National Revival
13 Bulbank
14 Ruse Opera House
15 Church of Sveta Troitsa
16 Dunav Tours
18 Rusenski Lom National
  Park Office

Information

Bulbank *(pl Sveta Troitsa)* cashes travellers cheques and has an ATM. Dozens of **foreign-exchange offices** can be found along ul Aleksandrovska and around pl Svoboda. One of the few Internet centres is **Ch@t House** *(ul Aleksandrovska)*.

Dunav Tours *(☎ 224 268; e dtbktu@dunavtours.bg; ul Olimpi Panov; open 9am-noon & 1pm-5pm Mon-Fri)* organises local tours. Just up from McDonald's, **Pingvinite Bookshop** *(ul Aleksandrovska)* offers one of the best ranges of maps in the country.

Things to See

The Russian-style **Church of Sveta Troitsa** *(pl Sveta Troitsa; admission free; open 7am-6pm daily)* is the oldest remaining building in

Ruse. It was built in 1632 and features several large and well-preserved murals, as well as 16th-century crosses and icons. The stained-glass windows are impressive. The bell tower in the grounds was added in the 19th century.

Currently, Ruse's only operating museum is the **Museum of the Urban Lifestyle in Ruse** *(ul Tsar Ferdinand 39; admission 3.50 lv; open 9am-noon & 2pm-5pm Mon-Fri)*. It contains sumptuous furniture from the early 20th century and displays of crockery, cutlery, porcelain and costumes.

The scruffy **Revivalists Park** is dominated by the gold-domed **Pantheon of the National Revival** *(admission free; open 9am-noon & 1pm-5pm Mon-Fri)*. It was built to commemorate the 100th anniversary of a battle against the Ottomans in 1878.

BULGARIA

Places to Stay & Eat

Dunav Tours (see Information) is a friendly and reliable travel-cum-accommodation agency that arranges single/double rooms in private homes from 35/50 lv.

Splendid Hotel (☎ 235 951; ul Aleksandrovska; singles/doubles with bathroom & breakfast 65/75 lv) is along a quiet, leafy street just off the mall. The Splendid is, well, splendid, but the rooms are small.

Hotel Kristal (☎ 824 333; ul Nikolaevska 1; singles/doubles with bathroom 50/70 lv, 'luxury' doubles 85 lv) has been extensively renovated and now offers sparkling new rooms. However, the downside is that the bathrooms are small and the hotel is along a noisy road.

The very convenient **Danube Plaza Hotel** (☎ 822 929; e plazahotel@mbox.digsys.bg; pl Svoboda; singles/doubles with bathroom & breakfast from US$32/42) offers (almost) four-star facilities for the same sort of rates offered by other three-star hotels.

Restaurant Rila (ul Borisova 49; mains from 3 lv) is a popular cafeteria-style place with cheap, tasty food. Just load up your tray and dig in.

Mehana Chiflika (ul Otets Paisii; mains 3 lv) is far bigger than the outside suggests. It's recommended for quick service, large helpings and live music every evening.

Getting There & Away

From the **Yug Bus Terminal** (ul Pristanishtna), 2.5km south of the city centre, public buses depart daily for Shumen, Varna, Plovdiv, Veliko Târnovo and Dobrich. Also from this terminal, private buses leave every hour for Sofia (12 lv, five hours). From the **Iztok Bus Terminal** (ul Ivan Vedur 10), 4.5km east of the city centre, buses go to regional villages.

The restored **train station** (ul Pristanishtna) is adjacent to the Yug Bus Terminal. Every day, two fast trains travel directly to Varna, via Shumen, while several others only go as far as the junction at Kaspichan. Eleven trains also depart from Ruse every day for Gorna Oryahovitsa, and a few continue on to Veliko Târnovo.

Tickets for international trains, and advance tickets for domestic services, are available at **Rila Bureau** (☎ 228 016) at the train station, and in the city centre (☎ 223 920; ul Knyazheska 33).

To/from Romania Ruse port is near the Friendship Bridge, about 7km northeast of the city centre. From this terminal, large ferries (US$27/6 per car/passenger) leave about every three hours for Giurgiu in Romania and smaller ferries leave when full (US$10/$1.50). Both operate 24 hours every day, and payment can be made in US dollars, euros or leva.

RUSENSKI LOM NATIONAL PARK
НАЦИОНАЛЕН ПАРК РУСЕНСКИ ЛОМ

This 32.6-sq-km national park is home to endemic species of birds and endangered mammals, but most visitors come to see the remarkable cave monasteries. The most famous is the **Ivanovo Rock Monastery** (admission 2.50 lv; open 8am-noon & 1pm-5pm Wed-Mon). It's signposted along a good road, and is 4km east of Ivanovo and 20km south of Ruse.

Also worth seeing are the remains of a 6th-century **citadel** (admission 3 lv; open 8am-noon & 1pm-5pm Wed-Mon). This is a short walk north of Cherven village, which is 15km south of Ivanovo.

All visitors should first pick up the *Naturpark Russenski Lom* map, published by the Green Danube Programme and available at the **National Park Office** (☎ 082-272 397; ul Gen Skobelev 7) in Ruse. The national park **information centre** (☎ 08116-2203) is in the town hall at Ivanovo.

Rooms in local homes are available in the villages of Cherven, Pisanets, Nisovo and Koshov for about 16 lv per person.

From the Iztok Bus Terminal in Ruse, three buses leave every weekday for Cherven, via Ivanovo and Koshov, while an extra bus departs at 11am on Saturday and Sunday. For Pisanets, take one of the frequent buses towards Razgrad from the Yug Bus Terminal in Ruse; for Nisovo, get a bus towards Opaka from the Iztok Bus Terminal.

DOBRICH ДОБРИЧ
☎ 058 • pop 113,800

Dobrich is a popular day trip from the resorts along the Black Sea coast and a cheaper, and more relaxed, base for exploring the region.

The **Stariyat Dobrich Ethnological Museum Complex** (ul Dr K Stoilov; admission free; open daily 8am-6pm May-Sept, 8am-5pm Oct-Apr) comprises 37 shops, cafés, bars, restaurants and souvenir stalls. It's north of the main square, pl Svoboda. You can wander in and watch artisans practise their trade.

Also worth visiting are both the **Art Gallery** *(ul Bulgaria 14; admission 1 lv; open 9am-12.30pm & 1.30pm-6pm Mon-Fri)*, 300m west of the main square, and the **Ethnological Museum** *(ul 25 Septemvri; admission 1 lv; open 9am-noon & 2pm-6pm Mon-Fri)*, 200m south of pl Svoboda.

The **Stara Dobrich Inn** *(☎ 43 611; singles/doubles with bathroom 45/70 lv)* is a charming guesthouse in the ethnological museum complex. On the town square, **Hotel Bulgaria** *(☎/fax 25 444;* e *ta@bulgaria.bergon.net; pl Svoboda; doubles with bathroom & breakfast US$45)* is central and comfortable. The **Bulgarsko Pivo Restaurant** *(ul 25 Septemvri; mains 3-5 lv)* has large serves of tasty food at reasonable prices.

From the **bus terminal** *(ul Gotse Delchev)*, 300m east of the main square, buses and minibuses leave every 30 to 60 minutes for Albena, Varna and Balchik. Every day, four or five buses also go to Ruse and a few head to Sofia (18 lv, eight hours). From the **train station**, 1km west of pl Svoboda, two slow trains a day plod along to Varna. It's also possible to get a same-day connection to Sofia, via Kaspichan, from Dobrich.

Croatia

Crystal-clear seas, lush islands, unspoilt fishing villages, beaches, vineyards, Roman ruins and medieval walled cities are some of the many treasures that make Croatia (Hrvatska) a traveller's paradise. When Yugoslavia split apart in 1991, no less than 80% of the country's tourist resorts ended up in Croatia, mostly along the Adriatic coast. There is almost 6000km of coastline that winds around innumerable bays and inlets, rising to steep mountainous backdrops or flattening out to shingle beaches. An abundance of natural harbours lures yachties, and naturists have a wide choice of secluded coves.

Croatia extends in an arc from the Danube River in the east to Istria in the west and south along the Adriatic coast to Dubrovnik. Roman Catholic since the 9th century, the Croatian interior fell under Austro-Hungarian influence while the Istrian and Dalmatian coast was marked by Venetian and Italian rule. Croatia only united with Orthodox Serbia in 1918 and split from Yugoslavia in a painful struggle that lasted from 1991 to 1995. The war disrupted the tourist industry, which had always been the main source of hard currency, but the country is beginning to pull out of the slump. Italian and Central European visitors fill the coastal resorts for most of July and August but at any other time of year the pace slows considerably.

Facts about Croatia

HISTORY

In 229 BC the Romans began their conquest of the indigenous Illyrians by establishing a colony at Solin (Salona), close to Split in Dalmatia. Emperor Augustus then extended the empire and created the provinces of Illyricum (Dalmatia and Bosnia) and Pannonia (Croatia). In AD 285, Emperor Diocletian decided to retire to his palace fortress in Split, today the greatest Roman ruin in Eastern Europe. When the empire was divided in 395, what is now known as Slovenia, Croatia and Bosnia-Hercegovina stayed with the Western Roman Empire, while present Serbia, Kosovo and Macedonia went to the Eastern Roman Empire, later known as the Byzantine Empire. Around 625, Slavic tribes migrated from present-day Poland. The Serbian tribe settled

in the region that is now southwestern Serbia and extended their influence south and west. The Croatian tribe moved into what is now Croatia and occupied two former Roman provinces: Dalmatian Croatia along the Adriatic and Pannonian Croatia to the north.

By the early part of the 9th century, both settlements had accepted Christianity but the northern Croats fell under Frankish domination while Dalmatian Croats came under the nominal control of the Byzantine Empire. The Dalmatian duke Tomislav united the two groups in 925 in a single kingdom that prospered for nearly 200 years.

Late in the 11th century, the throne fell vacant and a series of power struggles weakened central authority and split the kingdom. The northern Croats, unable to agree upon a ruler, united with Hungary in 1102 for protection against the Orthodox Byzantine Empire.

In 1242 a Tatar invasion devastated Hungary and Croatia. In the 14th century the Turks began pushing into the Balkans, defeating the Serbs in 1389 and the Hungarians in 1526. Northern Croatia turned to the Habsburgs of Austria for protection against the Turks in 1527 and remained part of their empire until 1918. To form a buffer against the Turks, in the 16th century the Austrians invited Serbs to settle the Vojna Krajina (military frontier) along the Bosnian border. The Serbs in the borderlands had an autonomous administration under Austrian control; these areas were reincorporated into Croatia in 1881.

The Adriatic coast fell under Venetian influence as early as the 12th century, although Hungary continued to struggle for control of the region. Some Dalmatian cities changed hands repeatedly until Venice imposed its rule on the Adriatic coast in the early 15th century and occupied it for nearly four centuries. Only the Republic of Ragusa (Dubrovnik) maintained its independence. The Adriatic coast was threatened but never conquered by the Turks and, after the naval Battle of Lepanto in 1571 when Spanish and Venetian forces wiped out the Turkish fleet, this threat receded.

After Venice was shattered by Napoleonic France in 1797, the French occupied southern Croatia, abolishing the Republic of Ragusa (Dubrovnik) in 1808. Napoleon's merger of Dalmatia, Istria and Slovenia into the 'Illyrian provinces' in 1809 stimulated the concept of South Slav (Yugoslav) unity. Following the defeat of Napoleon at Waterloo in 1815, Austria-Hungary moved in to pick up the pieces along the coast.

A revival of Croatian cultural and political life began in 1835. In 1848 a liberal democratic revolution, which was led by Josip Jelačić, was suppressed, but serfdom was abolished. An 1868 reform transferred northern Croatia from Austria to Hungary, united the territory with Hungarian Slavonia and granted a degree of internal autonomy. Dalmatia remained under Austria. In the decade before WWI, some 50,000 Croats emigrated to the USA.

With the defeat of the Austro-Hungarian empire in WWI, Croatia became part of the Kingdom of Serbs, Croats & Slovenes (called Yugoslavia after 1929), with a centralised government in Belgrade. This was strongly resisted by Croatian nationalists, who organised the Marseilles assassination of the royal dictator King Alexander I in 1934. Italy had been promised control of the Adriatic coast as an incentive to join the war against Austria-Hungary in 1915 and it held much of northern Dalmatia from 1918 to 1943.

After the German invasion of Yugoslavia in March 1941, a puppet government dominated by the fascist Ustaša movement was set up in Croatia and Bosnia-Hercegovina under Ante Pavelić (who fled to Argentina after WWII). At first the Ustaša tried to expel all Serbs from Croatia to Serbia. But when the Germans stopped this because of the problems it was causing, the Ustaša launched an extermination campaign that rivalled the Nazis in its brutality. Although the number of victims is controversial, estimates indicate that from 60,000 to 600,000 ethnic Serbs, Jews and Roma (gypsies) were murdered. The Ustaša programme called for 'one-third of Serbs killed, one-third expelled and one-third converted to Catholicism'.

Not all Croats supported these policies, however. Josip Broz, known as Maršal Tito, was himself of Croat-Slovene parentage and tens of thousands of Croats fought bravely with his partisans. Massacres of Croats conducted by Serbian Četniks in southern Croatia and Bosnia forced almost all antifascist Croats into the communist ranks, where they joined the numerous Serbs trying to defend themselves from the Ustaša. In all, about a million people died violently in a war that was fought mostly in Croatia and Bosnia-Hercegovina.

Recent History

After the war, Maršal Tito became the prime minister of the new Yugoslav Federation and divided it into five republics – Croatia, Serbia, Slovenia, Bosnia-Hercegovina and Macedonia. Even with a Stalin-style system of state planning, Croatia and Slovenia moved far ahead of the southern republics economically, leading to demands by reformers, intellectuals and students for greater autonomy. The 'Croatian Spring' of 1971 caused a backlash and purge of the reformers, who were jailed or expelled from the Communist Party.

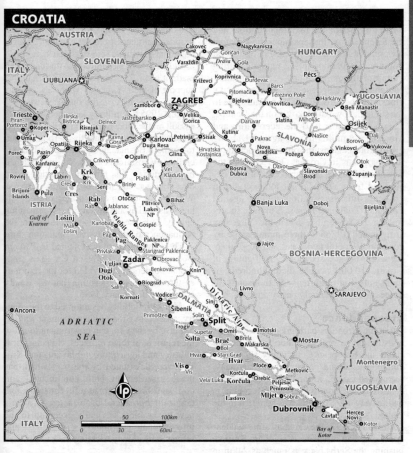

CROATIA

AUSTRIA

SLOVENIA

ITALY

LJUBLJANA

HUNGARY

YUGOSLAVIA

ZAGREB

SLAVONIA

BOSNIA-HERCEGOVINA

SARAJEVO

ADRIATIC
SEA

DALMATIA

Dinaric Alps

Split

Montenegro

YUGOSLAVIA

Dubrovnik

ITALY

0   50   100km
0   30   60mi

Tito's habit of borrowing from abroad to flood the country with cheap consumer goods produced an economic crisis after his death in 1980. The sinking economy provoked greater tension among Yugoslavia's ethnic groups, which came to a head when Serbian politician Slobodan Milošević whipped Serbs into a nationalistic frenzy over the aspirations of the Albanian majority in the province of Kosovo.

Fearing a renewal of Serbian hegemony, many Croats felt the time had come to end more than four decades of communist rule and attain complete autonomy into the bargain. In the free elections of April 1990 Franjo Tudjman's Croatian Democratic Union (Hrvatska Demokratska Zajednica) easily defeated the old Communist Party. On 22 December 1990 a new Croatian constitution was promulgated,

changing the status of Serbs in Croatia to a national minority.

The constitution's failure to guarantee minority rights, and mass dismissals of Serbs from the public service, led the 600,000-strong ethnic Serb community to demand autonomy. When Croatia declared independence on 25 June 1991, the Serbian enclave of Krajina proclaimed its independence from Croatia.

Heavy fighting broke out in Krajina (the area around Knin, north of Split), Baranja (the area north of the Drava River opposite Osijek) and Slavonia (the region west of the Danube). The 180,000-member, 2000-tank Yugoslav People's Army, dominated by Serbian communists, began to intervene on its own authority in support of Serbian irregulars under the pretext of halting ethnic violence.

In the three months following 25 June, a quarter of Croatia fell to Serbian militias and the federal army. In September the Croatian government ordered a blockade of 32 federal military installations in the republic, lifting morale and gaining much-needed military equipment. In response, the Yugoslav navy blockaded the Adriatic coast and laid siege to the strategic town of Vukovar on the Danube.

In early October 1991 the federal army and Montenegrin militia moved against Dubrovnik to protest against the ongoing blockade of their garrisons in Croatia. On 7 October the presidential palace in Zagreb was hit by rockets fired from Yugoslav air-force jets in an unsuccessful assassination attempt against President Tudjman. Heroic Vukovar finally fell on 19 November when the Yugoslav army ended a bloody three-month siege by concentrating 600 tanks and 30,000 soldiers there. During the six months of fighting in Croatia 10,000 people died, hundreds of thousands fled and tens of thousands of homes were deliberately destroyed.

Independence

After the Croatian parliament amended its constitution to protect minority and human rights the European Community (EC), succumbing to strong pressure from Germany, recognised Croatia in January 1992. This was followed three months later by US recognition and in May 1992 Croatia was admitted to the United Nations.

In January 1993 the Croatian army suddenly launched an offensive in southern Krajina, pushing the Serbs back as much as 24km in some areas and recapturing strategic points. The Krajina Serbs vowed never to accept rule from Zagreb and in June 1993 they voted overwhelmingly to join the Bosnian Serbs (and eventually Greater Serbia).

The self-proclaimed 'Republic of Serbian Krajina' held elections in December 1993, which no international body recognised as legitimate or fair. Continued 'ethnic cleansing' left only about 900 Croats in Krajina out of an original population of 44,000.

While the world's attention turned to the grim events unfolding in Bosnia-Hercegovina, the Croatian government quietly began procuring arms from abroad. On 1 May 1995, the Croatian army and police entered and occupied western Slavonia, east of Zagreb, and seized control of the region. As the Croatian military consolidated its hold in the west of Slavonia, some 15,000 Serbs fled the region despite assurances from the Croatian government that they were safe from retribution.

Belgrade's silence throughout this campaign made it clear that the Krajina Serbs had lost support of their Yugoslav sponsors, encouraging the Croats to forge on. At dawn on 4 August 1995 the military launched a massive assault on the rebel Serb capital of Knin. Outnumbered by two to one, the Serb army fled to northern Bosnia, along with about 150,000 civilians whose roots in the Krajina stretched back centuries. The military operation lasted days, but was followed by months of terror. Widespread looting and burning of Serb villages, as well as attacks on the few remaining elderly Serbs, seemed designed to ensure the permanence of this massive population shift.

The Dayton Agreement signed in Paris in December 1995 recognised Croatia's traditional borders and provided for the return of eastern Slavonia, a transition that was finally completed in January 1998.

Although stability has returned to the country, a key provision of the agreement was the promise by the Croatian government to allow the return of Serbian refugees. Housing, local industry and agriculture in Slavonia and Krajina were devastated by the war, which has made resettlement both complicated and costly. Although Serbian refugees face a real tangle of bureaucratic obstacles, Croatia's new government is finally acceding to the international community's demands and refugees are slowly trickling back.

GEOGRAPHY

Croatia is half the size of present-day Yugoslavia in area (56,538 sq km) and population. The republic swings around like a boomerang from the Pannonian plains of Slavonia between the Sava, Drava and Danube Rivers, across hilly central Croatia to the Istrian Peninsula, then south through Dalmatia along the rugged Adriatic coast.

The narrow Croatian coastal belt at the foot of the Dinaric Alps is only about 600km long as the crow flies, but it's so indented that the actual length is 1778km. If the 4012km of coastline around the offshore islands is added to the total, the length becomes 5790km. Most of the 'beaches' along this jagged coast consist of slabs of rock sprinkled with naturists. Don't come expecting to find sand, but

The Polish Catholic Church of Sts Simon & Elena, Minsk, Belarus, was built in 1910

A new day and future beckons for the people of battle-scarred Sarajevo, Bosnia Hercegovina

Berat, Albania's 'city of a thousand windows', overlooks the Osum River

The quiet village of Bansko in the Pirin Mountains is Bulgaria's newest ski resort

A hiker contemplates Bulgaria's Mt Vihren

Sociable summer in Sozopol, Bulgaria

Fishing boats line Sozopol port on the Black Sea

the waters are sparkling clean, even around large towns.

Croatia's offshore islands are every bit as beautiful as those off the coast of Greece. There are 1185 islands and islets along the tectonically submerged Adriatic coastline, 66 inhabited. The largest are Cres, Krk, Mali Lošinj, Pag and Rab in the north; Dugi Otok in the middle; and Brač, Hvar, Korčula, Mljet and Vis in the south. Most are barren and elongated from northwest to southeast, with high mountains that drop right into the sea.

CLIMATE

The climate varies from Mediterranean along the Adriatic coast to continental inland. The high coastal mountains help to shield the coast from cold northerly winds, making for an early spring and late autumn. In spring and early summer a sea breeze called the *maestral* keeps the temperature down along the coast. Winter winds include the cold *bura* from the north and the humid *široko* from the south.

The sunny coastal areas experience hot, dry summers and mild, rainy winters, while the interior regions are cold in winter and warm in summer. Because of a warm current flowing northward along the Adriatic coast, the sea temperatures never fall below 10°C in winter and can be as high as 26°C in August. You can swim in the sea from mid-June until late September. The resorts south of Split are the warmest.

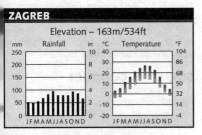

ECOLOGY & ENVIRONMENT

The lack of heavy industry in Croatia has left the country largely free of industrial pollution, but its forests are under threat from acid rain from neighbouring countries. The dry summers and brisk *maestral* winds pose substantial fire hazards along the coast. The sea along the Adriatic coast is among the world's cleanest but scavenging for coral has nearly eliminated coral reefs. Purchasing the coral

jewellery and decorative objects on sale in many resorts only exacerbates the problem.

NATIONAL PARKS

When the Yugoslav Federation collapsed, seven of its finest national parks ended up in Croatia. Brijuni near Pula is the most carefully cultivated park, with well-preserved Mediterranean holm oak forests. The mountainous Risnjak National Park near Delnice, east of Rijeka, is named after one of its inhabitants – the *ris*, or lynx.

Dense forests of beech trees and black pine in the Paklenica National Park near Zadar are home to a number of endemic insects, reptiles and birds, as well as the endangered griffon vulture. The abundant plant and animal life, including bears, wolves and deer, in the Plitvice Lakes National Park between Zagreb and Zadar has warranted its inclusion on Unesco's list of World Natural Heritage Sites. Both Plitvice Lakes and Krka National Parks (near Šibenik) feature a dramatic series of cascades and incredible turquoise lakes.

The 101 stark and rocky islands of the Kornati Archipelago and National Park make it the largest in the Mediterranean. The island of Mljet near Korčula also contains a forested national park.

GOVERNMENT & POLITICS

Croatia is a parliamentary democracy with a powerful presidency. Croatia's first president was Franjo Tudjman, who died in December 1999. Beleaguered by allegations of corruption and cronyism, his party, the Croatian Democratic Union or HDZ, was resoundingly defeated in parliamentary elections that took place in January 2000.

The election of Ivica Račan as the prime minister and Stipe Mesic as president was a rejection of the strongly nationalistic policies of the HDZ and has ushered in a rapprochement with the West. The new government has moved to end Croatia's international isolation by cooperating with the War Crimes Tribunal being conducted at The Hague, speeding the return of Serbian refugees and enacting legislation expanding minority rights. During May 2000, Croatia was admitted into NATO's Partnership for Peace and in October 2001 Prime Minister Račan signed a Stabilization and Association Agreement (SAA) with the EU bringing Croatia closer to its goal of membership in the EU.

ECONOMY

In addition to dealing with the residue of the banking crisis that occurred in the late 1990s, the current government is pushing ahead with a comprehensive privatisation of state assets. However, exports remain weak as the demand for Croatian products in Germany, Austria, Italy and Russia has slowed. Keeping inflation in check (2.6% in 2001) by limiting any wage increases in the public sector and maintaining a tight fiscal policy is now attracting international investment. There was a respectable 4.6% growth rate in the first quarter of 2002 but unemployment is high (22.3% in 2001) and the average wage is only about 3400KN (US$410) per month. Average Croatians have seen a steep decline in standard of living since the country's independence.

Tourism is expected to spearhead the new economy in Croatia. In the past, one-third of Croatia's national income came from tourism, but between 1991 and 1995 tourist numbers fell dramatically. Just as tourism was beginning to rebound, the 1999 war in Kosovo again labelled the region as a war zone and tourists stayed away in droves. Heavy investment in infrastructure and marketing is paying off; in 2002 tourism was expected to bring in US$4 billion, around 15% of the country's GDP.

POPULATION & PEOPLE

Before the war, Croatia had a population of nearly five million, of which 78% were Croats and 12% were Serbs. Today's population includes just 201,000 Serbs, slightly less than 5%. Most live in eastern Croatia (Slavonia). The next largest ethnic group is Bosnians, followed by Italians, Hungarians and Slovenes. Small communities of Czechs, Roma and Albanians complete the mosaic. The largest cities in Croatia are Zagreb (780,000), Split (188,700), Rijeka (144,000), Osijek (114,600) and Zadar (72,700).

ARTS

The Exhibition Pavilion in Zagreb is a good place to keep up with the latest developments in Croatian art.

Painting

Vlaho Bukovac (1855–1922) was the most notable Croatian painter in the late 19th century. Important early-20th-century painters include Miroslav Kraljević (1885–1913) and Josip Račić (1885–1908). Post-WWII artists experimented with abstract expressionism but this period is best remembered for the naive art that was typified by Ivan Generalić (1914–1992). Recent trends have included minimalism, conceptual art and pop art.

Sculpture

The work of sculptor Ivan Meštrović (1883–1962) is seen in town squares throughout Croatia. Besides creating public monuments, Meštrović designed imposing buildngs, such as the circular Croatian History Museum in Zagreb. Both his sculptures and architecture display the powerful classical restraint he learnt from Auguste Rodin. Meštrović's studio in Zagreb and his retirement home at Split have been made into galleries of his work (for details see Gradec in the Zagreb section and Museums & Galleries in the Split section later in this chapter).

Music & Dance

Croatian folk music has many influences. The kolo, a lively Slavic round dance where men and women alternate in the circle, is accompanied by Roma-style violinists or players of the tambura, a three- or five-string mandolin popular throughout the country. The measured guitar-playing and rhythmic accordions of Dalmatia have a gentle Italian air.

A recommended recording available locally on CD is Narodne Pjesme i Plesovi Sjeverne Hrvatske (Northern Croatian Folk Songs and Dances) by the Croatian folkloric ensemble Lado. The 22 tracks on this album represent nine regions, with everything from haunting Balkan voices reminiscent of Bulgaria to lively Mediterranean dance rhythms.

SOCIETY & CONDUCT

As the Yugoslav years and the bitter struggle for independence recede into the past, the country's real personality is beginning to emerge. The long coastline that spent centuries under Italian domination is infused with a Mediterranean insouciance while the interior has a Central European sense of orderliness and propriety. The contrasting attitudes create a society that operates efficiently even though there seem to be few rules and the prevailing spirit is 'nema problema' (no problem).

Croats take pride in keeping up appearances. Despite a fragile economy, money can usually be found in order to brighten up the town centre with a fresh coat of paint or to repair a historic building. Even as their bank accounts diminish, most people will cut out restaurants and movies to afford a shopping trip to Italy for some new clothes. The tidy streets and stylish clothes are rooted in the Croats' image of themselves as Western Europeans, not Yugoslavs, a word that makes Croats wince. Dressing neatly will go a long way towards gaining a traveller acceptance.

RELIGION

Croats are overwhelmingly Roman Catholic, while virtually all Serbs belong to the Eastern Orthodox Church. In addition to doctrinal differences, Orthodox Christians venerate icons, allow priests to marry and do not accept the authority of the Roman Catholic pope. Long suppressed under communism, Catholicism is undergoing a strong resurgence in Croatia and churches have good attendances on Sunday. Muslims make up 1.2% of the population and Protestants 0.4%, with a tiny Jewish population in Zagreb.

LANGUAGE

Croatian is a South Slavic language, as are Serbian, Slovene, Macedonian and Bulgarian. Prior to 1991 both Croatian and Serbian were considered dialects of a single language known as Serbo-Croatian.

As a result of history, tourism and the number of 'guest workers' who have returned from Germany, German is the most commonly spoken second language in Croatia. Most Istrians speak Italian and English is popular among young people.

The Lonely Planet *Mediterranean Europe phrasebook* includes a chapter on the Serbian and Croatian languages, with translations of key words and phrases from each appearing side by side, providing a clear comparison of the languages. For a basic rundown on words and phrases for the traveller, refer to the Language chapter at the end of this book.

Facts for the Visitor

HIGHLIGHTS
Museums & Galleries

Art museums and galleries are easier for a foreign visitor to enjoy than historical museums, which are usually captioned in Croatian only. In Zagreb, the Museum Mimara contains an outstanding collection of Spanish, Italian and Dutch paintings, as well as an archaeological collection, exhibits of ancient art from Asia and collections of glass, textiles, sculpture and furniture. The Strossmayer Gallery of Old Masters, also in Zagreb, is worthwhile for its exhibitions of Italian, Flemish, French and Croatian paintings.

The Meštrović Gallery in Split is worth a detour and in Zagreb the Meštrović Studio gives a fascinating insight into the life and work of this remarkable sculptor.

Beaches

Whether rocky, pebbly, gravelly or (rarely) sandy, Croatian beaches are often on the edge of a pine grove and slope into crystalline water that always seems to be the right temperature. The coastline is indented with wide bays and cosy coves where you just might be tempted to cast off your bathing suit along with the many naturists who flock to Croatian shores each summer.

Historic Towns

All along the Adriatic coast are white-stone towns with narrow, winding streets enclosed by defensive walls. Each has its own flavour: Hilly Rovinj looks over the sea; the peninsula of Korčula town burrows into it. While Zadar retains echoes of its original Roman street plan, Hvar and Trogir are traditional medieval towns. None can match the exquisite harmony of Dubrovnik, with its blend of elements of Renaissance and baroque architecture.

SUGGESTED ITINERARIES

Depending on how long you have in Croatia, you may like to visit the following places.

Two days
  Visit Dubrovnik
One week
  Visit Hvar or Korčula, Split and Dubrovnik
Two weeks
  Visit Zagreb, Istria and southern Dalmatia.

PLANNING
When to Go

May is a nice month to travel along the Adriatic coast, with good weather and few tourists. June is also good, but in the popular months of July and August all of Europe arrives and prices soar. September is perhaps the best month since it's not as hot as summer, though the sea remains warm, the crowds will have thinned out as children return to school, low-season accommodation rates apply and fruit, such as figs and grapes, will be abundant. In April and October it may be too cool for camping, but the weather should still be fine along the coast and private rooms will be plentiful and inexpensive.

Maps

Kúmmerley + Frey's map *Croatia & Slovenia* (1:500,000) is detailed and shows the country's latest borders. Most tourist offices in the country have local maps, but make sure the street names are up to date.

TOURIST OFFICES
Local Tourist Offices

The **Croatian National Tourist Board** (☎ 46 99 333, fax 45 57 827; W www.htz.hr; Iberov trg 10, Importanne Gallerija, 10000 Zagreb) is a good source of information. Regional tourist offices supervise tourist development and municipal tourist offices that have free brochures and information on local events. Some arrange private accommodation.

Tourist information is also dispensed by the commercial travel agencies, such as **Atlas** (W atlas-croatia.com), Croatia Express, Generalturist and Kompas, which also arranges private rooms and sightseeing excursions. The agencies often sell local guidebooks, which are excellent value if you'll be staying for a while. Ask for the schedule for coastal ferries.

Tourist Offices Abroad

Croatian tourist offices abroad include:

UK (☎ 020-8563 7979) Croatian National Tourist Office, 2 Lanchesters, 162-64 Fulham Palace Rd, London W6 9ER
USA (☎ 212-279 8672) Croatian National Tourist Office, Suite 4003, 350 Fifth Ave, New York, NY 10118

VISAS & DOCUMENTS

Visitors from Australia, Canada, New Zealand, the EU and the USA do not require a visa for stays of less than 90 days. For other nationalities, visas are issued free of charge at Croatian consulates. Croatian authorities require all foreigners to register with the local police when they first arrive in a new area of the country, but this is a routine matter that is normally handled by the hotel, hostel, camping ground or agency that organises your private accommodation.

EMBASSIES & CONSULATES
Croatian Embassies & Consulates

Diplomatic representation abroad includes:

Australia (☎ 02-6286 6988) 14 Jindalee Crescent, O'Malley, ACT 2601, Canberra
Canada (☎ 613-562 7820) 229 Chapel St, Ottawa, Ontario K1N 7Y6
Germany (☎ 030-219 15 514) Ahornstrasse 4, Berlin 10787
New Zealand (☎ 09-836 5581) 131 Lincoln Rd, Henderson, Box 83200, Edmonton, Auckland
South Africa (☎ 012-342 1206) 1160 Church St, 0083 Colbyn, Pretoria
UK (☎ 020-738 72 022) 21 Conway St, London W1P 5HL
USA (☎ 202-588 5899) 2343 Massachusetts Ave NW, Washington, DC 20008

Embassies & Consulates in Croatia

The following addresses are in Zagreb (area code ☎ 01), unless otherwise noted:

Albania (☎ 48 10 679) Jurišićeva 2a
Australia (☎ 48 36 600) Kršnjavoga 1
Bosnia-Hercegovina (☎ 46 83 761) Torbarova 9
Bulgaria (☎ 48 23 336) Novi Goljak 25
Canada (☎ 48 81 200) Prilaz Gjure Deželića 4
Czech Republic (☎ 61 77 246) Savska 41
Germany (☎ 61 58 105) avenija grada Vukovara 64
Hungary (☎ 48 34 990) Krležin Gvozd 11a
New Zealand (☎ 65 20 888) avenija Dubrovnik 15
Poland (☎ 48 34 579) Krležin Gvozd 3
Romania (☎ 24 30 137) Srebrnjak 150a
Slovakia (☎ 48 48 941) Prilaz Gjure Deželića 10
Slovenia (☎ 63 11 014) Savska 41
UK (☎ 45 55 310) Vlaška 121
  Consulate: (☎ 021-341 464) Obala hrvatskog narodnog preporoda 10, Split 21000
  Consulate: (☎ 020-412 916) Petilovrijenci 2, Dubrovnik 20000
USA (☎ 45 55 500) Andrije Hebranga 2
Yugoslavia (☎ 46 80 552) Mesićeva 19

CUSTOMS

Travellers can bring their personal effects into the country, along with 1L of liquor, 1L of wine, 500g of coffee, 200 cigarettes and 50mL of perfume.

MONEY
Currency

In May 1994 the Croatian dinar was replaced by the kuna. Visitors are allowed to import or export Croatian banknotes up to a value of around 2000KN but there's no reason to do either. Like other Continental Europeans, Croats indicate decimals with commas and thousands with points.

Exchange Rates

country	unit		kuna
Australia	A$1	=	4.25KN
Canada	C$1	=	4.94KN
Euro Zone	€1	=	7.65KN
Japan	¥100	=	6.53KN
NZ	NZ$1	=	3.65KN
UK	UK£1	=	12.25KN
USA	US$1	=	7.83KN

Exchanging Money

There are numerous places to change money, all offering similar rates; ask at any travel agency for the location of the nearest exchange. Banks and exchange offices keep long hours. Exchange offices may deduct a commission of 1% to change cash or travellers cheques but some banks do not. Kuna can be converted into hard currency only at a bank and if you submit a receipt of a previous transaction. Hungarian currency is difficult to change in Croatia.

Credit Cards American Express (AmEx), MasterCard, Visa and Diners Club cards are widely accepted in large hotels, stores and many restaurants but don't count on cards to pay for private accommodation or meals in small restaurants. ATMs accepting Master-Card, Maestro, Cirrus, Plus and Visa are available in most bus and train stations, airports, all major cities and most small towns. Many branches of Privredna Banka have ATMs that allow cash withdrawals on an AmEx card. Make sure you have a four-digit personal identification number (PIN).

Costs

Hotel prices, private accommodation and ferry fares are set in euros, though payment is in kuna calculated at the official daily rate. Accommodation is more expensive than it should be for a country trying to lure tourists, and real budget accommodation is in short supply. Transport, concert and theatre tickets, and meals are reasonably priced for Europe.

Accommodation costs vary widely depending on the season. If you travel in March you'll have no trouble finding a private room

for 90KN per person but prices climb to double that amount in July and August. Count on 25KN for a meal at a self-service restaurant and 35KN to 50KN for an average intercity bus fare. It's not that hard to survive on 250KN daily if you stay in hostels, private rooms or camping grounds. Unless you can survive on sandwiches, self-catering saves only a small amount of money since food is expensive in Croatia.

Tipping

If you're served fairly and well at a restaurant, you should round up the bill as you're paying, but a service charge is always included. (Don't leave money on the table.) Bar bills and taxi fares can also be rounded up. Tour guides on day excursions expect to be tipped.

Taxes & Refunds

A 22% Value Added Tax (VAT) is imposed upon most purchases and services and is included in the price. If your purchases exceed 500KN in one store you can claim a refund upon leaving the country. Ask the merchants for the paperwork but don't be surprised if they don't have it. You could try to bargain down the price if this happens.

POST & COMMUNICATIONS
Post

Mail sent to Poste Restante, 10000 Zagreb, Croatia, is held at the post office (open 24 hours) next to the Zagreb train station. A good coastal address to use is c/o Poste Restante, Main Post Office, 21000 Split, Croatia.

If you have an AmEx card, most Atlas travel agencies will hold your mail. Consult AmEx for a list of the cooperating agencies.

Telephone

To call Croatia from abroad, dial your international access code, ☎ 385 (the country phone code for Croatia), the area code (without the initial zero) and the local number. When calling from one region to another within Croatia, use the initial zero but do not use the area code if calling within the region.

To make a phone call from Croatia, go to the main post office – phone calls placed from hotel rooms are much more expensive. You'll need a phonecard to use public telephones.

Phonecards are sold according to units (*impulsa*) and you can buy cards of 25/50/100/200 units for 15/25/40/70KN. These can be purchased at any post office and most tobacco shops and newspaper kiosks. Many new phone boxes have a button on the upper left with a flag symbol. Press the button and you get instructions in English. Using a 100-unit phonecard, a three-minute call from Croatia will cost around 17KN to the UK and the USA, 25KN to Australia and 13KN to other European countries. The international access code is ☎ 00. For emergency and other useful service numbers see the boxed text 'Emergency Services' later.

Email & Internet Access
Internet cafés are becoming increasingly plentiful in Croatia; their locations are noted in each city entry. The going rate is about 30KN per hour and the connections are usually good. America Online (AOL) has access numbers in Zagreb, Split, Rijeka and Dubrovnik.

DIGITAL RESOURCES
All regions and many municipalities now have websites that range from collections of pretty pictures to detailed information on accommodation and activities. More hotels now have email addresses, which makes reservations easier. You can contact the Zagreb bus station at W www.akz.hr for information on schedules and fares. For train information check the Croatian Railways site on W www.hznet.hr and Croatian Telecom has an online phone directory in English at W imenik.hinet.hr. The useful website W www.visit-croatia.co.uk is a good stop for updated practical information.

BOOKS
For a comprehensive account of the personalities and events surrounding the collapse of the former Yugoslavia it would be hard to go past *Yugoslavia: Death of a Nation* by Laura Silber & Allan Little, based on the 1995 BBC television series of the same name. Richard Holbrooke's *To End a War* is a riveting look at the people and events surrounding the Dayton peace agreement. *Café Europa* is a series of essays by a Croatian journalist, Slavenka Drakulić, which provides an inside look at life in the country since independence. Rebecca West's 1937 travel classic, *Black Lamb & Grey Falcon*, contains a long section on Croatia as part of her trip through Yugoslavia. Robert Kaplan's *Balkan Ghosts* touches on Croatia's part in the tangled web of Balkan history. Marcus Tanner's *Croatia: A Nation*

Forged in War provides an excellent overview of Croatia's history.

For a more comprehensive guide to Croatia, pick up Lonely Planet's *Croatia*. There's also Zoë Brân's *After Yugoslavia*, part of the Lonely Planet Journeys series, which recounts the author's recent trip through the country.

NEWSPAPERS & MAGAZINES
The most respected daily in Croatia is *Vjesnik*, but the most daring is the satirical news weekly *Feral Tribune*. Its investigative articles and sly graphics keep Croatian politicians and businesspeople edgy. The English-language *Croatia Times* covers social, political and cultural developments and can be counted on for a rosy view of Croatian life. American, British and French newspapers and magazines can be hard to find outside large cities.

RADIO & TV
The three national television stations fill a lot of their air time with foreign programming, generally American and always in the original language. For local news, residents of Zadar, Split, Vinkovci and Osijek turn to their regional stations. Croatian Radio broadcasts news in English four times daily (8am, 10am, 2pm and 11pm) on FM frequencies 88.9, 91.3 and 99.3.

TIME
Croatia is on Central European Time (GMT/UTC plus one hour). Daylight saving comes into effect at the end of March, when clocks are turned forward an hour. At the end of September they're turned back an hour.

LAUNDRY
Self-service laundrettes are virtually unknown outside of Zagreb. Most camping grounds have laundry facilities, hotels will wash clothes for a (hefty) fee or you could make arrangements with the proprietor if you're staying in private accommodation.

TOILETS
Toilets in train or bus stations sometimes charge 2KN but it's usually not a problem to use the free toilets in a bar, café or restaurant.

HEALTH
Everyone must pay to see a doctor at a public hospital *(bolnica)* or medical centre *(dom zdravcja)* but charges are reasonable. Travel

insurance is important, especially if you have a serious accident and have to be hospitalised. Medical centres often have dentists on the staff, otherwise you can go to a private dental clinic *(zubna ordinacija)*.

WOMEN TRAVELLERS

Women face no special danger in Croatia although women on their own may be harassed and followed in the larger coastal cities. Some local bars and cafés seem like private men's clubs; a woman alone is likely to be greeted with sudden silence and cold stares. There are few rules about appropriate dress and topless sunbathing is considered acceptable.

GAY & LESBIAN TRAVELLERS

Homosexuality has been legal in Croatia since 1977 and is generally tolerated as long as it remains discreet. Public displays of affection between members of the same sex may meet with hostility, however, especially outside major cities. A small lesbian and gay community is developing in Zagreb but not to the extent of many Western European cities.

DISABLED TRAVELLERS

Because of the number of wounded war veterans, more attention is being paid to the needs of disabled travellers. Public toilets at bus stations, train stations, airports and large public venues are usually wheelchair accessible. Large hotels are wheelchair accessible but very little private accommodation is. Bus and train stations in Zagreb, Zadar, Rijeka, Split and Dubrovnik are wheelchair accessible but the local Jadrolinija ferries are not. For further information, get in touch with **Savez Organizacija Invalida Hrvatske** *(☎/fax 01-48 29 394; Savska cesta 3, 10000 Zagreb)*.

SENIOR TRAVELLERS

Although there are no transportation discounts available to seniors, most museums and attractions offer the same discounts to people over 60 as to students. Your passport usually suffices as proof of age.

DANGERS & ANNOYANCES

Land mines left over from the war in Croatia pose no threat to the average visitor but it's most important to be aware that the former confrontation line between Croat and federal forces is still undergoing de-mining operations. Eastern Slavonia was heavily mined and, out of

---

Emergency Services

In the event of an emergency call ☎ 92 for police, ☎ 93 for fire, ☎ 94 for emergency medical assistance and ☎ 901 for an operator-assisted call. Motorists can contact Hrvatski Autoclub (HAK; Croatian Auto Club) for help or advice – call ☎ 987 HAK *(vučna služba)* for road assistance.

These numbers can be dialled nationwide.

---

the main city of Osijek, de-mining is not yet complete. Main roads from Zagreb to the coast that pass through Karlovac and Knin are completely safe but it would be unwise to stray into fields or abandoned villages.

Personal security and theft are not problems in Croatia. The police and military are well disciplined and it's highly unlikely you'll have any problems with them in any of the places covered in this chapter.

See the boxed text 'Emergency Services' for emergency telephone numbers.

BUSINESS HOURS

Banking hours are 7.30am to 7pm on weekdays and 8am to noon on Saturday. Many shops are open 8am to 7pm on weekdays and until 2pm on Saturday. Along the coast, life is more relaxed; shops and offices frequently close around 1pm for an afternoon break. Croats are early risers and by 7am there will be lots of people on the street and many places will already be open.

PUBLIC HOLIDAYS & SPECIAL EVENTS

Public holidays are New Year's Day (1 January), Easter Monday (March/April), Labour Day (1 May), Bleiburg and Way of the Cross Victims Day (15 May), Statehood Day (30 May), Day of Antifascist Struggle (22 June), Homeland Thanksgiving Day (5 August), Feast of the Assumption (15 August), All Saints' Day (1 November) and Christmas and Feast of St Stephen (25 and 26 December). Statehood Day marks the anniversary of the declaration of independence in 1991, while Day of Antifascist Struggle commemorates the outbreak of resistance in 1941.

In July and August there are summer festivals in Dubrovnik, Opatija, Split and Zagreb. Mardi Gras celebrations marking the start of Lent have recently been revived in numerous towns with the attendant parades and festivities. The many traditional annual events held around Croatia are included under Special Events in the individual destination sections.

ACTIVITIES
Kayaking
There are countless possibilities for anyone with a folding sea kayak, especially in the Elafiti and Kornati Islands. Lopud is a good launching point to explore the Elafiti Islands and there's a daily ferry from Dubrovnik. Sali on Dugi Otok is close to the Kornati Islands and is connected by daily ferry to Zadar.

Hiking
Risnjak National Park at Crni Lug, 12km west of Delnice between Zagreb and Rijeka, is a good hiking area in summer. Because of the likelihood of heavy snowfalls, hiking is only advisable from late spring to early autumn. It's a 9km, 2½-hour climb from the entrance of the park at Bijela Vodica to Veliki Risnjak (1528m). The steep gorges and beech forests of Paklenica National Park, 40km northeast of Zadar, also offer excellent hiking.

Scuba Diving
The clear waters and varied underwater life of the Adriatic have led to a flourishing dive industry along the coast. Cave diving is the real speciality in Croatia; night diving and wreck diving are also offered and there are coral reefs in some places but in rather deep water.

You must get a permit for a boat dive but this is easy; go to the harbour captain in any port with your passport, certification card and 100KN. Permission is valid for a year in any dive spot in the country. If you dive with a dive centre it will take care of the paperwork.

Most of the coastal resorts mentioned in this chapter have dive shops. See the website for **Diving Croatia** (ⓦ *www.diving.hr*) for contact information.

ACCOMMODATION
Along the Croatian coast, accommodation is priced according to three seasons, which tend to vary from place to place. Generally October to May are the cheapest months, June and September are mid-priced, but count on paying top price for the peak season, which runs for a six-week period in July and August. Prices quoted in this chapter are for the peak period and do not include 'residence tax', which runs

from about 4KN to 7.50KN depending on the location and season. Deduct about 25% if you come in June, the beginning of July and September, about 35% for May and October and about 50% for all other times. Note that prices for rooms in Zagreb are pretty much constant all year and that many hotels on the coast close in winter. Some places offer half-board which is bed and two meals a day, usually breakfast and one other meal.

Camping
Nearly 100 camping grounds are scattered along the Croatian coast. Most operate only from mid-May to September, although a few are open in April and October. In May and late September, call ahead to make sure the camping ground is open before beginning the long trek out.

Many camping grounds, especially in Istria, are gigantic 'autocamps' with restaurants, shops and row upon row of caravans. Expect to pay up to 100KN for the site at some of the larger establishments but half that at most other camping grounds, in addition to 38KN to 48KN per person.

Nudist camping grounds (marked FKK) are among the best because their secluded locations ensure peace and quiet. However, bear in mind that freelance camping is officially prohibited.

Hostels
The **Croatian YHA** (☎ 01-48 47 472, fax 48 47 474; ⓦ *www.nncomp.com/hfhs/; Dežmanova 9, Zagreb*) operates youth hostels in Dubrovnik, Zadar, Zagreb and Pula. Non-members pay an additional 10KN per person daily for a stamp on a welcome card; six stamps entitles you to a membership. Prices in this chapter are for high season during July and August; prices fall the rest of the year. The Croatian YHA can also provide information about private youth hostels in Krk and Zagreb.

Private Rooms
Private rooms in local homes are the best accommodation in Croatia. Although you may be greeted by offers of *sobe* (rooms) as you step off your bus and boat, rooms are most often arranged by travel agencies. The most expensive rooms are three-star and have private facilities in a place resembling a small guesthouse. Some of the better ones are listed in this chapter. It's best to call in advance as

the owners often will meet you at the bus station or ferry dock. In a two-star room, the bathroom is shared with one other room; in a one-star room, the bathroom is shared with two other rooms or with the owner who is usually an elderly widow. Breakfast is usually not included but sometimes can be arranged for an additional 25KN. Be sure to clarify whether the price agreed upon is per person or per room. If you're travelling in a small group, it may be worthwhile to get a small apartment with cooking facilities, which are widely available along the coast.

It makes little sense to price-shop from agency to agency since prices are fixed by the local tourist association. Whether you deal with the owner directly or book through an agency, you'll pay a 30% surcharge for stays of less than four nights and sometimes 50% or even 100% more for a one-night stay, although you may be able to get them to waive the surcharge if you arrive in the low season. Prices for private rooms in this chapter are for a four-night stay.

Hotels

Hotels are ranked from one to five stars with the most in the two- and three-star range. Features, such as satellite TV, direct-dial phones, hi-tech bathrooms, minibars and air-con, are standard in four- and five-star hotels and one-star hotels have at least a telephone in the room. Many two- and three-star hotels offer satellite TV but you'll find better decor in the higher categories. Unfortunately the country is saddled with too many 1970s, concrete-block hotels, built to warehouse package tourists, but some entrepreneurs are starting up smaller, more personal establishments that can be good value. Prices for hotels in this chapter are for the pricey six-week period that begins in mid-July and lasts until the end of August. During this period, some hotels may demand a surcharge for stays of less than four nights but this surcharge is usually waived the rest of the year and prices drop steeply.

FOOD

A restaurant (restauracija) or pub may also be called a gostionica and a café is known as a kavana. Self-service cafeterias are quick, easy and inexpensive, though the quality of the food tends to vary quite a lot. Better restaurants aren't that much more expensive if you choose carefully. The cheapest dishes

are pasta and risotto, which can be a filling meal. Fish dishes are often charged by weight (from 220KN to 280KN a kilo), which makes it difficult to know how much a certain dish will cost but an average portion is about 250g. Some restaurants tack on a 10% cover charge, which is *supposed* to be mentioned on the menu.

Breakfast is included in the price of the hotels mentioned in this chapter and usually includes a juice drink, bread, cheese, yogurt, cereal and cold cuts, as well as coffee and tea. No restaurants serve breakfast. Throughout the former Yugoslavia the breakfast of the people is *burek* (a greasy layered pie made with meat) or *sira* (cheese), which is cut on a huge metal tray.

A load of fruit and vegetables from the local market can make a healthy, cheap picnic lunch. There are plenty of supermarkets in Croatia – cheese, bread, wine and milk are readily available and fairly cheap. The person behind the meat counter at supermarkets will make a big cheese or bologna sandwich for you upon request and you only pay the price of the ingredients.

Regional Dishes

The Adriatic coast excels in seafood, including scampi, *prstaci* (shellfish) and Dalmatian *brodet* (mixed fish stewed with rice), all cooked in olive oil and served with boiled vegetables or *tartufe* (mushrooms) in Istria. In the Croatian interior, watch for *manistra od bobića* (beans and fresh maize soup) or *štrukle* (cottage cheese rolls). A Zagreb speciality is *štrukli* (boiled cheesecake).

Italian pizza and pasta are good options in Istria and Dalmatia, costing about half of what you'd pay in Western Europe.

DRINKS

It's customary to have a small glass of brandy before a meal and to accompany the food with one of Croatia's fine wines. Ask for the local regional wine. Croatia is also famous for its *šljivovica* (plum brandies), *travarica* (herbal brandies), *vinjak* (cognacs) and liqueurs, such as maraschino, a cherry liqueur made in Zadar, or herbal *pelinkovac*. Italian-style espresso is popular in Croatia.

Zagreb's Ožujsko *pivo* (beer) is very good but Karlovačko beer from Karlovac is even better. You'll probably want to practise saying *živjeli!* (cheers!).

ENTERTAINMENT

Culture was heavily subsidised by the communists and admission to operas, operettas and concerts is still reasonable. The main theatres offering musical programmes are listed in this chapter, so note the location and drop by some time during the day to see what's on and to purchase tickets. In the interior cities, winter is the best time to enjoy the theatres and concert halls. The main season at the opera houses of Rijeka, Split and Zagreb runs from October to May. These close for holidays in summer and the cultural scene shifts to the many summer festivals. Ask at municipal tourist offices about cultural events in their area.

Discos operate in summer in the coastal resorts and all year in the interior cities, but the best way to mix with the local population is to enjoy a leisurely coffee or ice cream in a café. With the first hint of mild weather, Croatians head for an outdoor terrace to drink, smoke and watch the passing parade. In the summer season, many resort hotels sponsor free dances on their terraces.

SHOPPING

Tablecloths, pillowcases and blouses embroidered Croatian style in red geometric patterns make an easy souvenir to pack. Lavender and other fragrant herbs made into scented sachets or oils are found on most Dalmatian islands, especially Hvar, which is known for its lavender fields. Many of the jewellery stores are run by immigrants from Kosovo who have a centuries-old tradition in silver working. The workmanship on silver filigree earrings, bracelets and decorative objects is often of astonishingly high quality.

Getting There & Away

AIR

Croatia's main airline **Croatia Airlines** (☎ 01-48 19 633; **w** www.croatiaairlines.hr; Zrinjevac 17, Zagreb) has direct flights from Zagreb to Amsterdam, Berlin, Brussels, Frankfurt, İstanbul, London, Mostar, Munich, Paris, Prague, Sarajevo, Skopje, Tel Aviv, Vienna, Warsaw and Zürich. In summer there are also direct flights from London, Manchester and Rome to Dubrovnik and London and Manchester to Pula. There's a **Croatia Airlines**

minibus (*reservations* ☎ 051-330 207) that connects Zagreb airport with Rijeka daily (100KN). (Note that all batteries must be removed from checked luggage for all Croatia Airlines flights.)

LAND

Austria

Bus Eurolines Vienna runs a weekly bus from Vienna to Rijeka (€36, 8¼ hours), Split (€51, 15 hours) and Zadar (€43, 13 hours) and a twice daily bus (except Sunday) to Zagreb (€26, 4¾ hours).

Train The *Ljubljana* express travels daily from Vienna to Rijeka (€68.50, eight hours), via Ljubljana, and the EuroCity *Croatia* from Vienna to Zagreb (€62.30, 6½ hours); both services travel via Maribor, Slovenia.

Benelux

Budget Bus/Eurolines offers a weekly bus year-round from Amsterdam to Zagreb (€106, 26 hours) and another bus to Rijeka and Split with an extra weekly bus to both destinations during summer. Eurolines operates a twice-weekly service all year from Brussels to Zagreb, and another weekly bus to Rijeka and the Dalmatian coast.

Bosnia-Hercegovina

There are bus connections departing from Sarajevo (€21.50, six hours, daily) and Mostar (€10.50, three hours) for Dubrovnik; from Međugorje, Mostar and Sarajevo to Split (€16.50, seven hours), and also from Sarajevo to Zagreb (€26.50, eight hours) and Rijeka (€32).

Germany

Bus Deutsche Touring GmbH runs many buses German cities and Croatia, largely to service Croatian 'guest workers' in Germany. The prices and durations given below are for the entire journey from the German city where the bus originates to the final destination in Croatia.

There is a weekly bus leaving Frankfurt via Stuttgart, Ulm and Munich for Rijeka, Poreč, Rovinj and Pula (€85, 18½ hours); a daily bus from Bochum through Bonn, Düsseldorf, Frankfurt, Hamburg (twice weekly), Cologne, Stuttgart and Ulm to Rijeka, Zadar and Split (€115, 27½ hours); a twice-weekly bus from Berlin to Rijeka, Zadar and Split (€110, 24 hours); a weekly bus from Dortmund, Düsseldorf, Cologne, Bonn, Frankfurt, Stuttgart, Ulm and Munich to Dubrovnik (€125, 35 hours); a daily bus from Bochum that via Bonn, Hamburg (twice weekly) and Pforzheim to Zagreb (€105, 26 hours); and a direct bus from Berlin to Zagreb (€95, 17 hours, four times weekly). Information is available at bus stations in the cities mentioned. Baggage is €3 per piece.

Train There are three daily trains running from Munich to Zagreb (€75, nine hours) via Salzburg and Ljubljana and a daily train from Berlin to Zagreb (€162, 16 hours).

Hungary

The four daily trains from Zagreb to Budapest (€21, 6½ hours) stop in Nagykanizsa, the first main junction inside Hungary (€9). The price of the fare is the same for one way and return.

Italy

Bus Trieste is well connected with the Istrian coast. There are around six buses a day to Rijeka (€7.10, two to three hours), plus buses to Rovinj (€10.10, 3½ hours, three daily) Poreč (€8.05, 2¼ hours, three daily) and Pula (€13.75, 3¾ hours, four daily). There are fewer buses on Sunday. To Dalmatia there's a daily bus that leaves at 5.30pm and stops at Rijeka, Zadar (€23, 7½ hours), Split (€35.60, 10½ hours) and Dubrovnik (€53.20, 27 hours). There's also a bus from Venice leaving at 1.45pm Monday to Saturday that stops in Poreč (2½ hours), Rovinj (three hours) and Pula (€20, 3¼ hours). There's also a Friday night bus from Milan to Poreč, Rovinj and Pula (€49, 8½ hours).

For more information about bus travel, see **w** www.croazia travel.it.

Train Between Venice and Zagreb (€40, seven hours) there's an overnight direct train and a daily train via Trieste and Ljubljana.

Slovenia

Bus Slovenia is also well connected with the Istrian coast. There are two buses a day between Pula and Portorož (€11, 1½ hours) and Koper (€12, four hours), as well as one weekday bus between Rovinj and Koper (€10.75, three hours) and Poreč and Portorož (€5, 1½ hours), as well as a daily bus in summer from Rovinj to Ljubljana (128KN, 2½ hours).

Train There are seven trains daily between Ljubljana and Zagreb (3853 SIT, three hours) and seven between Ljubljana and Rijeka (2466 SIT, three hours).

Yugoslavia

Bus There's one bus each morning from Zagreb to Belgrade (€25, six hours). At Bajakovo on the border, a Yugoslav bus takes you on to Belgrade. The border between Montenegro and Croatia is open to visitors, allowing Americans, Australians, Canadians and Brits to enter visa-free. For further information regarding getting to/from Montenegro see the Dubrovnik Getting There & Away section of this chapter.

Train Five trains daily connect Zagreb with Belgrade (€16.50, six hours).

Car & Motorcycle

The main highway entry/exit points between Croatia and Hungary are Goričan (between Nagykanizsa and Varaždin), Gola (23km east of Koprivnica), Terezino Polje (opposite Barcs) and Donji Miholjac (7km south of Harkány). There are 29 crossing points to/from Slovenia, too many to list here. There are 23 border crossings into Bosnia-Hercegovina and 10 into Yugoslavia, including the main Zagreb to Belgrade highway. Major destinations in Bosnia-Hercegovina, like Sarajevo, Mostar and Međugorje, are accessible from Zagreb, Split and Dubrovnik.

SEA

Regular boats operated by several companies connect Croatia with Italy. All of the boat-company offices in Split are located inside the ferry terminal.

Jadrolinija (**☎** 51-211 444, fax 211 485, **w** www.jadrolinija.hr; Riva 16, Rijeka; in Ancona **☎** 071-20 71 465, in Bari **☎** 080-52 75 439), Croatia's national boat line, runs three to six car ferries a week between Ancona and Split (€36.50, 10 hours). From June to September these ferries stop twice a week at Stari Grad on Hvar and at Korčula. There's also a line from Ancona to Zadar (€34, seven hours) two or three times weekly and one line from Bari to Dubrovnik up to four times each week (€36.50, 6½ hours). Prices are for deck passage in the low season and does not include the embarkation fee of €3 in Italian ports. Prices increase by about 25% in July and August.

SEM (☎ 21-338 292, fax 338 291; Ⓦ www
.sem-marina.hr; Gat Sv Duje, Split; in Ancona ☎ 071-20 40 90) connects Ancona with
Split four times a week in winter and daily in
summer and Ancona with Stari Grad on Hvar
(8½ hours) in July and August.

SNAV (in Ancona ☎ 021-20 76 116, in
Naples ☎ 081-76 12 348, in Split ☎ 21-322
252; Ⓦ www.snavali.com) This company has
a fast car-ferry that links Ancona and Split in
only four hours (€62.50, daily) and a passenger boat that connects Split, Vela Luka on
Korčula and Stari Grad with the Italian cities
of Pescara, Vasto and Giulianova daily in
summer. One-way/return fares are €98.50/
150 in the low season and €114/181 in the
high season.

From May to mid-September **La Rivera** (in
Rome ☎ 06-509 16 061, in Naples ☎ 081-76
45 808; Ⓦ www.lariverabus.it), an Italian
company, offers a combination bus and boat
trip two or three times a week from Rome and
Naples to Korčula (both €117, 9¼ hours) and
Dubrovnik (€139, 12½ hours). In Croatia,
contact **Marko Polo Tours** (☎ 020-715 400,
fax 715 800; Ⓔ marko-polo-tours@du.tel.hr)
in Korčula and Jadroagent in Dubrovnik.

In addition to connecting Ancona and Split
two to four times a week for the same price
as Jadrolinija, **Adriatica Navigazione** (in
Venice ☎ 041-781 611, in Ancona 071-20
74 334; Ⓦ www.adriatica.it) runs the Marconi between Trieste and Rovinj (€15.49, 3½
hours) from May to September stopping at
the Brijuni Islands six times a week and stopping three times a week in July and August at
Poreč (from Trieste €13.94, 2¾ hours). Book
through **Aurora Viaggi** (☎ 040-631 300, Via
Milano 20, Trieste) and any Jadroagent office
in Croatia.

Until 2002 there was a regular ferry connecting Venice with Pula and Zadar. To see
if the service has re-commenced, check with
Agenzia Favret (☎ 041-25 73 511, via Appia
20) in Venice.

From mid-May to mid-September **Ustica
Lines** (in Venice ☎ 041-27 12 646, in Trieste
☎ 040-67 02 711; Ⓦ www.usticalines.it) runs
five passenger boats a week from Trieste to
Pula (€22, two hours) that stop twice a week
in Poreč (€20, one hour). There are also up to
six passenger boats a week mid-May to mid-
October between Venice and Rovinj (€40,
2½ hours) that stop three times a week in
Poreč (€40, one hour). In Croatia, Jadroagent

in Pula and **Istra Line** (☎ 52-451 067, Parti-
zansko 2) in Poreč sell tickets.

DEPARTURE TAX
Airport departure tax is US$11, which is in-
cluded in the cost of the ticket. There is no
port tax if you leave Croatia by boat but there
is an embarkation tax of €3 from Italian ports.

Getting Around

AIR
Croatia Airlines has daily flights between Zagreb and Dubrovnik (906KN, one hour), Pula
(483KN, 45 minutes), Split (627KN, 45 minutes) and Zadar (575KN, 40 minutes). Prices
are somewhat lower in the low season and
there are discounts for seniors and people aged
under 26.

BUS
Bus services in Croatia are excellent. Prices
can vary substantially between companies
and depend on the route taken, but the prices
in this book should give you an idea of costs
(and unless otherwise noted, all bus prices are
for one-way fares). Luggage stowed in the
baggage compartment under the bus costs
extra (6KN a piece, including insurance).

At large stations, bus tickets must be bought
at the office, not from drivers; try to book
ahead to be sure of a seat. Tickets for buses
that arrive from somewhere else are usually
purchased from the conductor. Since there are
several companies serving each route, buy
only a one-way ticket or you'll be locked into
one company's schedule for the return. On
Croatian bus schedules, vozi svaki dan means
'every day', and ne vozi nedjeljom ni prazni-
kom means 'not Sunday and public holidays'.

TRAIN
Train travel is about 15% cheaper than bus
travel and often more comfortable, though
slower. Local trains usually have only un-
reserved, 2nd-class seats but they're rarely
crowded. Reservations may be required on
express trains. 'Executive' trains have only
1st-class seats and are 40% more expensive
than local trains. Most train stations have left-
luggage offices charging about 10KN apiece
(passport required).

On timetables in Croatia the word for arrivals is dolazak and for departures odlazak or

polazak. Other terms you may find include *poslovni* (express train), *brzi* or *ubrazni* (fast train), *putnički* (local train), *rezerviranje mjesta obvezatno* (compulsory seat reservation), *presjedanje* (change of trains), *ne vozi nedjeljom i blagdanom* (no service Sunday and holidays) and *svakodnevno* (daily).

CAR & MOTORCYCLE

Motorists require vehicle registration papers and the green insurance card (see the introductory Getting Around chapter for details) to enter Croatia. Petrol is either leaded super, unleaded *(bezolovni)* or diesel. You have to pay tolls on the motorways around Zagreb, to use the Učka tunnel between Rijeka and Istria, the bridge to Krk Island, as well as the road from Rijeka to Delnice.

See the boxed text 'Emergency Services' earlier for emergency road assistance details.

Unless otherwise posted, the speed limits for cars and motorcycles are 50km/h in the built-up areas, 80km/h on main highways and 130km/h on motorways. On any of Croatia's winding two-lane highways, it's illegal to pass long military convoys or a line of cars caught behind a slow-moving truck. Drive defensively, as some local drivers lack discipline.

Rental

The large car-rental chains represented in Croatia are Avis, Budget, Europcar and Hertz. Throughout Croatia, Avis is allied with the Autotehna company, while Hertz is often represented by Kompas.

Independent local companies are often much cheaper than the international chains, but Avis, Budget, Europcar and Hertz have the big advantage of offering one-way rentals that allow you to drop the car off at any one of their many stations in Croatia free of charge.

Prices at local companies begin at around 260KN a day with unlimited kilometres. Shop around as deals vary widely and 'special' discounts and weekend rates are often available. Third-party public liability insurance is included by law, but make sure your quoted price includes full collision insurance, called collision damage waiver (CDW). Otherwise your responsibility for damage done to the vehicle is usually determined as a percentage of the car's value. Full CDW begins at 40KN a day extra (compulsory for those aged under 25), theft insurance is 15KN a day and personal accident insurance another 40KN a day.

Sometimes you can get a lower car-rental rate by booking the car from abroad. Tour companies in Western Europe often have fly-drive packages that include a flight to Croatia and a car (two-person minimum).

BOAT
Jadrolinija Ferries

Year-round Jadrolinija car ferries operate along the Bari–Rijeka–Dubrovnik coastal route, stopping at Zadar, Split, and the islands of Hvar, Korčula and Mljet, with less frequent services in winter. The most scenic section is Split to Dubrovnik, which all Jadrolinija ferries cover during the day.

Ferries are a lot more comfortable than buses, though considerably more expensive. From Rijeka to Dubrovnik the deck fare is 226KN, but it's at least 10% cheaper from October to May and there's a 20% reduction on the return portion of a return ticket. With a through ticket, deck passengers can stop at any port for up to a week, provided they notify the purser beforehand and have their ticket validated. This is much cheaper than buying individual sector tickets but is only good for one stopover. Cabins should be booked a week ahead, but deck space is usually available on all sailings.

Deck passage on Jadrolinija is just that: reclining seats *(poltrone)* are about 36KN extra and four-berth cabins (if available) begin at 355KN (Rijeka to Dubrovnik). Cabins can be arranged at the reservation counter aboard ship, but advance bookings are recommended if you want to be sure of a place. You must buy tickets in advance at an agency or Jadrolinija office since they are not sold on board.

Other Ferries

Local ferries connect the bigger offshore islands with each other and with the mainland. Some of the ferries operate only a couple of times a day and, once the vehicular capacity is reached, the remaining motorists must wait for the next available service. During summer the lines of waiting cars can be long, so it's important to arrive early.

Foot passengers and cyclists should have no problem getting on but you must buy your tickets at an agency before boarding since they are not sold on board. You should bear in mind that taking a bicycle on these services will incur an extra charge, which depends on the distance.

HITCHING

Hitching is never entirely safe in any country in the world, and we don't recommend it. Those travellers who decide to hitch should understand that they are taking a small but potentially serious risk. If you do choose to hitch you'll be safer travelling in pairs and let someone know where you are planning to go.

Hitching in Croatia is undependable. You will have better luck on the islands but in the interior cars are small and usually full. Tourists never stop. Unfortunately, the image many Croats have of this activity is based on violent movies like *The Hitcher*.

LOCAL TRANSPORT

Zagreb has a well-developed tram system as well as local buses but in the rest of the country you'll only find buses. In major cities, such as Rijeka, Split, Zadar and Dubrovnik buses run about every 20 minutes, and less often on Sunday. Small medieval towns along the coast are generally closed to traffic and have infrequent links to outlying suburbs.

Taxi

Taxis are available in all cities and towns but must be called or boarded at a taxi stand; note that it's usually not possible to hail them in the street. Prices are high (flag fall is 25KN) and are generally the same throughout the country.

ORGANISED TOURS

An interesting option for sailing enthusiasts is **Katarina Line** (☎ 051-272 110; w www .katarina-line.hr; Tita 75, Opatija), which offers week-long cruises from Opatija to Krk, Rab, Pag, Mali Lošinj and Cres or cruises from Split to Zadar that pass the Kornati Islands. Prices start at €250 a week per person and include half-board.

For specific tours in individual regions, see Organised Tours in the destination sections.

Zagreb

☎ 01 • pop 780,000

Zagreb is not a city that dazzles you with its charms at first glance – it requires time to appreciate its value. Spreading up from the Sava River, Zagreb sits on the southern slopes of Mt Medvednica and throbs with the energy you would expect from a capital city.

The nightlife is good, a wealth of outdoor cafés are packed from the first hint of mild weather and there's a decent assortment of museums and galleries to explore. Medieval Zagreb developed from the 11th to the 13th centuries in the twin villages of Kaptol and Gradec, which make up the city's hilly old town. Kaptol grew around St Stephen's Cathedral (now renamed the Cathedral of the Assumption of the Blessed Virgin Mary) and Gradec centred on St Mark's Church.

The lower town is all business with stately Austro-Hungarian buildings housing stores, restaurants and businesses. Parks, fountains and several imposing monuments lighten the sober architecture of the town centre before the scene deteriorates into glum apartment blocks in the suburbs. Since the town centre is the liveliest and most attractive part of the city, it's worthwhile to find central accommodation if at all possible.

Orientation

As you come out of the train station, you'll see a series of parks and pavilions directly in front of you and the twin neo-Gothic towers of the cathedral in the distance. Trg Jelačića, beyond the northern end of the parks, is the main city square. The bus station is 1km east of the train station. Tram Nos 2 and 6 run from the bus station to the nearby train station, with No 6 continuing to Trg Jelačića.

Information

Tourist Offices The Zagreb **main tourist office** (☎ 48 14 051, fax 48 14 056; e info@ zagreb-touristinfo.hr; Trg Jelačića 11; open 8.30am-8pm Mon-Fri, 9am-7pm Sat, 10am-2pm Sun) has city maps and the free leaflets, *Zagreb Info A-Z*, *Zagreb Events & Performances* and *City Walks*. There's a smaller **tourist office** (☎ 49 21 645; Zrinjskog 14) that has shorter opening hours. The tourist office also sells the Zagreb Card, which costs 60KN and includes 72 hours of free transport, a 50% discount on museums and sightseeing tours, and lists various discounts on car rentals, restaurants and parking.

The Croatian Auto Club (HAK) has an **information centre** (☎ 46 40 800; Derenčinova 20) in the city.

Plitvice Lakes National Park maintains an **information office** (☎ 46 13 586; Trg Tomislava 19). It also has information about other national parks around Croatia.

Jadrolinija (☎ 48 73 307; Zrinjevac 20) has information on coastal ferries.

Money There are ATMs at the bus and train stations and the airport as well as numerous locations around town. Exchange offices at the bus and train stations change money at the bank rate with 1.5% commission. Both the banks in the train station (open 7am to 9pm) and the bus station (open 6am to 8pm) accept travellers cheques.

The AmEx representative in Zagreb is **Atlas travel agency** (☎ 48 13 933; Zrinjevac 17).

Post & Communications Poste-restante mail is held (for one month) in the post office on the eastern side of the train station, which is open 24 hours Monday to Saturday and 1pm to midnight Sunday. Have your correspondence addressed to Poste Restante, 10000 Zagreb, Croatia.

This post office is also the best place for making long-distance telephone calls.

Email & Internet Access Zagreb's flashiest Internet café is **Art Net Club** (☎ 45 58 471; Preradovićeva 25; open 9am-11pm daily), which hosts frequent concerts and performances. There's also **Sublink** (☎ 48 11 329; Teslina 12; open 9am-10pm Mon-Sat, 3pm-10pm Sun), which charges 0.25KN a minute and offers a 10% discount to students. There are a number of smaller Internet cafés along Preradovićeva.

Travel Agencies **Dali Travel** (☎ 48 47 472, fax 48 47 474; e hfhs-cms@zg.hinet.hr; Dežmanova 9; open 9am-5pm Mon-Fri), the travel branch of the Croatian YHA, can provide information on HI hostels throughout Croatia and make advance bookings.

It also sells ISIC student cards (40KN) to those who have proof of attendance at an educational institution as well as Euro<26 cards for 30KN, which offer a variety of discounts in participating shops.

Bookshops The Algoritam bookshop in the Hotel Dubrovnik off Trg Jelačića has a wide selection of English-language books and magazines to choose from.

Laundry Predom (Draškovićeva 31; open 7am-7pm Mon-Fri) is one place to have your clothes cleaned. **Petecin** (Kaptol 11; open

---

Street Names

In Zagreb, you may notice a discrepancy between the names used in this book and the names you'll actually see on the street. In Croatian, a street name can be rendered either in the nominative or genitive case. The difference is apparent in the name's ending. Thus, Ulica Ljedevita Gaja (street of Ljudevita Gaja) becomes Gajeva ulica (Gaja's street). The latter version is the one most commonly seen on the street sign and used in everyday conversation. The same principle applies to a square (trg) which can be rendered as Trg Petra Preradovića or Preradovićev trg. Some of the more common names are: Trg svetog Marka (Markov trg), Trg Josipa Jurja Strossmayera (Strossmayerov trg), Ulica Andrije Hebranga (Hebrangova), Ulica Pavla Radića (Radićeva), Ulica Augusta Šenoe (Šenoina), Ulica Ivana Tkalčića (Tkalčićeva) and Ulica Nikole Tesle (Teslina). Be aware also that Trg Nikole Sća Zrinskog is almost always called Zrinjevac.

8am-8pm Mon-Fri) is another option and it is generally quicker than Predom. Expect to pay about 3KN for underwear, 4KN for a shirt and 10KN for a skirt.

Left Luggage There are **left-luggage offices** (open 24hr) in the train station, and a **left-luggage office** (open 5am-10pm Mon-Sat, 6am-10pm Sun) in the bus station. The price posted at the left-luggage office in the bus station is 1.20KN per hour, so be careful. At the train station you pay a fixed price of 10KN per day.

Medical & Emergency Services If you need to see a doctor, the closest health centre is **KBC Rebro** (☎ 23 88 888; Kišpatićeva 12; open 24hr year-round). It charges 200KN for an examination. The **police station** (☎ 45 63 311; Petrinjska 30) can assist foreigners with visa concerns.

Things to See
Kaptol Zagreb's colourful **Dolac vegetable market** (open daily) is just up the steps from Trg Jelačića and continues north along Opatovina. The twin neo-Gothic spires of the 1899 **Cathedral of the Assumption of the Blessed Virgin Mary** (formerly known as St Stephen's Cathedral) are nearby. Elements of

CROATIA

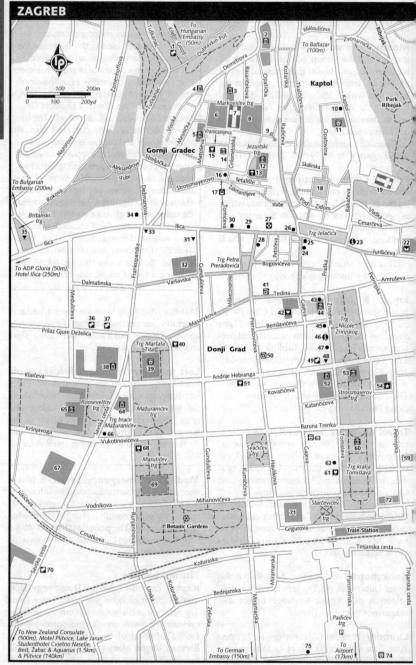

ZAGREB

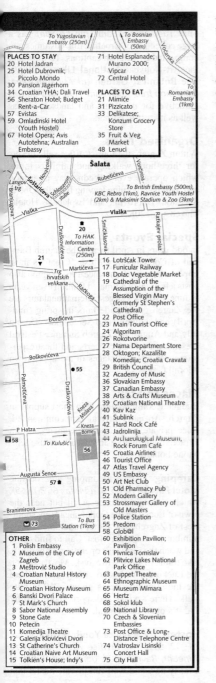

the medieval cathedral on this site, destroyed by an earthquake in 1880, can be seen inside, including 13th-century frescoes, Renaissance pews, marble altars and a baroque pulpit. The baroque **Archiepiscopal Palace** surrounds the cathedral, as do 16th-century fortifications constructed when Zagreb was threatened by the Turks.

Gradec From ul Radićeva 5, off Trg Jelačića, a pedestrian walkway called stube Ivana Zakmardija leads to the **Lotršćak Tower** *(open Mon-Sat)* and a funicular railway (1888), which connects the lower and upper towns (2KN one way). The tower has a sweeping 360-degree view of the city. To the right is the baroque **St Catherine's Church**, with Jezuitski trg beyond. The **Galerija Klovićevi Dvori** *(Jezuitski trg 4; open Tues-Sun)* is Zagreb's premier exhibition hall where superb art shows are staged. Further north and to the right is the 13th-century **Stone Gate**, with a painting of the Virgin, which escaped the devastating fire of 1731.

The colourful painted-tile roof of the Gothic **St Mark's Church** *(☎ 48 51 611; Markovićev trg; open 11am-4pm & 5.30pm-7pm daily)* marks the centre of Gradec. Inside are works by Ivan Meštrović, Croatia's most famous modern sculptor. On the eastern side of St Mark's is the **Sabor** (1908), Croatia's National Assembly.

West of the church is the 18th-century **Banski Dvori Palace**, the presidential palace with guards at the door in red ceremonial uniform. Between April and September there is a changing of the guard ceremony at noon on the weekend.

Not far from the palace is the former **Meštrović Studio** *(☎ 48 51 123; Mletačka 8; adult/concession 20/10KN; open 9am-2pm Tues-Fri, 10am-6pm Sat)*, now housing an excellent collection of some 100 sculptures, drawings, lithographs and furniture created by the artist. Other museums nearby include the **Croatian History Museum** *(☎ 48 51 900; Matoševa 9; temporary exhibitions adult/concession 10/5KN; open 10am-5pm Mon-Fri, 10am-1pm Sat & Sun)*; the **Croatian Naive Art Museum** *(☎ 48 51 911; Ćirilometodska 3; adult/concession 10/5KN; open 10am-6pm Tues-Fri & 10am-1pm Sat & Sun)*; and also the **Croatian Natural History Museum** *(☎ 48 51 700; Demetrova 1; adult/concession 15/7KN; open 10am-5pm*

Tues-Fri, 10am-1pm Sat & Sun). The best is the **Museum of the City of Zagreb** (☎ 48 51 364; Opatička 20; adult/concession 20/10KN; open 10am-6pm Tues-Fri, 10am-1pm Sat & Sun), with a scale model of old Gradec. Summaries in English and German are in each room of the museum, which is in the former Convent of St Claire (1650).

Lower Town Zagreb really is a city of museums. There are four in the parks between the train station and Trg Jelačića. The yellow **exhibition pavilion** (1897) across the park from the station presents changing contemporary art exhibitions. The second building north, also in the park, houses the **Strossmayer Gallery of Old Masters** (☎ 48 95 115; adult/student 20/15KN open 10am-1pm & 5pm-7pm Tues, 10am-1pm Wed-Sun), paintings by old masters. It's closed on Monday, but you can enter the interior courtyard to see the Baška Slab (1102) from the island of Krk, one of the oldest inscriptions in the Croatian language.

The fascinating **Archaeological Museum** (☎ 48 73 101; Trg Nikole Zrinjskog 19; adult/concession 20/10KN; open 10am-5pm Tues-Fri, 10am-1pm Sat & Sun) has a wide-ranging display of artefacts from prehistoric times through to the medieval period. Behind the museum is a garden of Roman sculpture that is turned into a pleasant open-air café in the summer.

West of the Centre The **Museum Mimara** (☎ 48 28 100; Rooseveltov trg 5; adult/concession 20/15KN; open 10am-5pm Tues, Wed, Fri & Sat, 10am-7pm Thur, 10am-2pm Sun) houses a diverse collection amassed by Ante Topić Mimara and donated to Croatia. Housed in a neo-Renaissance palace, the collection includes icons, glassware, sculpture, Oriental art and works by renowned painters, such as Rembrandt, Velasquez, Raphael and Degas. The **Modern Gallery** (☎ 49 22 368; Andrije Hebrangova 1; admission free; open 10am-6pm Tues-Sat & 10am-1pm Sun) has an excellent collection of paintings by Croatian masters created from 1850 to 1950 when Croatian art was at its zenith and also presents temporary exhibitions.

The neo-baroque **Croatian National Theatre** (Trg Maršala Tita 15), dates from 1895, and has Ivan Meštrović's sculpture *Fountain of Life* (1905) in front. The **Ethnographic Museum** (☎ 48 26 to 20; Trg Mažuranićev

14; adult/concession 15/10KN; open 10am-6pm Tues-Thur, 10am-1pm Fri-Sun) has a large collection of Croatian folk costumes, accompanied by English captions. To the south the Art-Nouveau **National Library** (1907). The **Botanical Garden** (ul Mihanovićeva; admission free; open 9am-7pm Tues-Sun) is attractive for its plants and landscaping, as well as its restful corners.

Organised Tours

Within Zagreb, the tourist office sells tickets for three-hour walking and minibus tours, which operate every Wednesday afternoon and Saturday morning leaving from the Opera, Sheraton, Dubrovnik and Esplanade Hotels. The cost is 120KN.

Special Events

In odd years in April there's the Zagreb Biennial of Contemporary Music, Croatia's most important music event since 1961. Zagreb also hosts a festival of animated films in even years in June. Croatia's largest international fairs are the Zagreb grand trade fairs in spring (mid-April) and autumn (mid-September). During July and August the Zagreb Summer Festival presents a cycle of concerts and theatre performances on open stages in the upper town (Gornji Gradec).

Places to Stay

Budget accommodation is in short supply in Zagreb. An early arrival is recommended, since private room-finding agencies are an attractive alternative and usually refuse telephone bookings.

Camping There's a camping area outside **Motel Plitvice** (☎ 65 30 444, fax 65 30 445), which is not in Plitvice at all but near the town of Lučko on the Obilazinica Hwy southwest of Zagreb. The motel sometimes runs a minibus from Savski Most. Call to find out if and when the service is operating. Otherwise, take tram No 7 or 14 to Savski Most and then the Lučko bus to Lučko village, from where the motel/camp site is about a 10-minute walk. There's a lake and sports centre nearby and it's open year-round.

Hostels The **Ravnice Youth Hostel** (☎/fax 23 32 325; e ravnice-youth-hostel@zg .hinet.hr; Ravnice 38d; dorm beds 99KN) is a fairly new and well-run private hostel that offers good value in its doubles, quads and one 10-bed dorm. Take either tram No 11 or 12 from Trg Jelačića.

Noisy **Omladinski Hotel** (*☎ 48 41 261, fax 48 41 269; Petrinjska 77; dorm beds 65KN, singles/doubles 149/197KN, with private bathroom 202/267KN; open year-round)* is actually a large youth hostel near the train station. Check-out is 9am.

Studenthotel Cvjetno Naselje (*☎ 45 93 587; singles/doubles 240/360KN, students 165/230KN)* is off Slavonska avenija in the southern part of the city. Breakfast is included. The rooms are good, each with private bathroom, although it's a long tram ride. To get there take tram No 4, 5, 14, 16 or 17 heading southwest on Savska cesta to 'Vjesnik'. Cvjetno Naselje is available to visitors only from mid-July to the end of September – for the rest of the year it's a student dormitory.

Private Rooms Convenient to the train station is **Evistas** (*☎ 48 39 554, fax 48 39 543;* e *evistas@zg.tel.hr; Šenoina 28; rooms with shared bathroom 254KN, studios 365KN; office open 9am-8pm Mon-Fri, 9.30am-5pm Sat)*. Prices are based on a two-night stay; there's a 10% surcharge for staying only one night. You could also try **ADP Gloria** (*☎ 48 23 567, fax 48 23 571;* e *gordana.gordic@ zg.tel.hr; Britanski trg 5; doubles with private bathroom 257KN, apartments from 365KN; open 9am-8pm Mon-Fri, 9am-2pm Sat)* It's wise to reserve in advance as accommodation in the town centre tends to fill rapidly.

Hotels For small hotels, you can't do better than the stylish **Hotel Ilica** (*☎ 37 77 522, fax 37 77 622;* e *info@hotel-ilica.hr; Ilica 102; singles/doubles 349/449KN, twins 549KN, apartments 749KN)*, two tram stops heading west from Trg Jelačića, which offers 12 quiet, pleasant rooms and two apartments – all with air-con, TV and telephone.

The 110-room **Central Hotel** (*☎ 48 41 122, fax 48 41 304;* e *hotel-central@zg .hinet.hr; Branimirova 3; singles/doubles 380/550KN)*, opposite the train station, is blandly modern. There are more expensive rooms available that have air-con.

The six-storey **Hotel Jadran** (*☎ 45 53 777, fax 46 12 151;* e *jadran@hup-zagreb.hr; Vlaška 50; singles/doubles 390/520KN)*, near the city centre, has rooms with TV, telephone and the price includes breakfast. For a little

more money, **Pansion Jägerhorn** (*☎ 48 33 877, fax 48 33 573; Ilica 14; singles/doubles 550/750KN, apartments 900KN)* offers comfortable, modern rooms with TV, telephone and air-con, and a three- or four-person, two-room apartment.

Hotel Dubrovnik (*☎ 48 73 555, fax 48 18 447;* e *hotel-dubrovnik@hotel-dubrovnik .tel.hr; Gajeva 1; singles/doubles from 585/ 890KN)* is a business-like hotel well-located in the centre of town.

For a memorable stay, try the five-star **Hotel Esplanade** (*☎ 45 66 666, fax 45 77 907;* e *esplanade@esplanade.hr; Mihano-vićeva 1; singles/doubles 954/1521KN)*, next to the train station. This six-storey, 215-room hotel, built in 1924, is a *belle époque* masterpiece where the stately rooms make very few concessions to the 21st century. A continental/ buffet breakfast will cost 90/135KN extra.

Places to Eat

Murano 2000 *(Hotel Esplanade; mains from 90KN)* offers the tastiest, most creative dishes in town. The vegetarian dishes that start at 60KN are truly wondrous and the restaurant specialises in *štrukli*, which could be a starter, main course or dessert.

Paviljon *(mains from 60KN)* is another elegant eatery with an Italian flavour – it's in the yellow exhibition pavilion across the park from the train station.

Piccolo Mondo *(Hotel Dubrovnik; mains from 35KN)* has an excellent location facing Trg Jelačića and the pastas and salads are surprisingly good. Pizza places are everywhere, but it would be hard to do better than the delicious, freshly made pizzas at **Pizzicato** *(Gundulićeva 4; pizzas from 18KN)* near the Academy of Music. The menu is translated into English.

For a change of pace, there's **Lenuci** *(Zrinjevac 16 19)*, which turns out decent fajitas for 59KN.

The best restaurant for a meaty Croatian speciality, prepared the Croatian way is **Baltazar** *(Nova Ves 4; mains from 60KN)*; to find it head north along Kaptol. **Mimiće** *(Jurišićeva 21)* has been a local favourite for decades, turning out plates of fried fish that cost from 11KN for 10 sardines and a hunk of bread.

Delikatese *(Ilica 39)* is a good place to pick up cheese, fruit, bread, yogurt and cold meat for a picnic. Next door is a **Konzum grocery**

store that sells whole roasted chickens, an assortment of prepared salads and Pag cheese. Farther along Ilica at Britanski trg, there's a **fruit and vegetable market** *(open to 3pm daily)* that sells farm-fresh produce. Don't hesitate to bargain.

Entertainment

Zagreb is a happening city. Its theatres and concert halls present a great variety of programmes throughout the year. Many (but not all) are listed in the monthly brochure *Zagreb Events & Performances*, which is available from the tourist office.

Cafés & Bars The liveliest scene in Zagreb is along bar-lined Bogovićeva, which turns into prime meet-and-greet territory each evening. Tkalčićeva, north of Trg Jelačića, attracts a slightly funkier crowd.

Pivnica Tomislav *(Trg Tomislava 18)*, facing the park in front of the train station, is a good local bar with inexpensive draught beer.

Rock Forum Café *(Gajeva 13; open summer)* occupies the rear sculpture garden of the Archaeological Museum, and across the street is **Hard Rock Café**, full of 1950s and '60s memorabilia. A couple of other cafés and music shops share this lively complex on the corner of Teslina and Gajeva Sts. Check out **BP Club** in the complex basement for jazz, blues and rock bands.

One of Zagreb's most pretentious cafés is Kazališna Kavana, known as **Kav Kaz** *(Trg Maršala Tita)*, opposite the Croatian National Theatre. **Old Pharmacy Pub** *(Andrije Hebranga 11a)* was once a pharmacy but now dispenses healthy doses of beer and spirits in a congenial environment. For a more offbeat experience, try **Tolkien's House** *(Vranicanijeva 8)*, which is decorated in the style of JRR Tolkien's books. **Indy's** *(Vranicanijeva 4)*, next door, presents a dazzling assortment of cocktails on an outdoor terrace.

Discos & Clubs Near the Hotel Sheraton, **Kulušić** *(Hrvojeva 6; open 8am-11pm Mon-Wed, 10pm-4am Thur-Sun)* is a casual, funky rock club that offers occasional live bands, fashion shows and record promos as well as standard disco fare.

A lot of the night action happens around Lake Jarun in the southwestern corner of the city. Take tram No 17 to the Jarun stop. Try **Best** *(☎ 36 91 601; Horvaćanski zavoj bb;*

open 10pm-4am Fri & Sat), **Žabac** *(Jarunska ulica bb)* or **Aquarius** *(☎ 36 40 231; open 10pm-4am Wed-Sun)* on Lake Jarun. In town, **Sokol klub** *(☎ 48 28 510; Trg Maršala Tita 6; admission free for before midnight; open 10pm-4am Wed-Sun)*, across the street from the Ethnographic Museum, is a more polished place to dance till dawn.

Gay & Lesbian Venues At present there are no exclusively gay and lesbian venues in Zagreb but **Glob@l** *(☎ 48 76 146; P Hatza 14; open noon-4am Mon-Fri, 4pm-4am Sat & Sun)* is a friendly, relaxed spot that welcomes gays and straights.

Theatre It's worth making the rounds of the theatres in person to check their programmes. Tickets are usually available for performances, even for the best shows. A small office marked 'Kazalište Komedija' (look out for the posters) also sells theatre tickets; it's in the Oktogon, a passage connecting Trg Petra Preradovićeva to Ilica 3.

The neobaroque **Croatian National Theatre** *(☎ 48 28 532; Trg Maršala Tita 15; box office open 10am-1pm & 5pm-7.30pm Mon-Fri, 10am-1pm Sat, ½hr before performances Sun)* was established in 1895. It stages opera and ballet performances. **Komedija Theatre** *(☎ 48 14 566; Kaptol 9)*, near the cathedral, stages operettas and musicals.

The **Vatroslav Lisinski Concert Hall** *(ticket office ☎ 61 21 166; Trg Stjepana Radica 4; open 9am-8pm Mon-Fri, 9am-2pm Sat)*, just south of the train station, is a prestigious venue where symphony concerts are held regularly.

Concerts also take place at the **Academy of Music** *(☎ 48 30 822; Gundulićeva 6a)* off Ilica. Another entertainment option is the **Puppet Theatre** *(ul Baruna Trenka 3; performances 5pm Sat, noon Sun)*.

Spectator Sports

Basketball is popular in Zagreb, and from October to April games take place in a variety of venues around town, usually on the weekend. The tourist office has the schedule.

Football (soccer) games are held every Sunday afternoon at the **Maksimir Stadium** *(Maksimirska 128; tram No 4, 7, 11 or 12 to Bukovačka)*, on the eastern side of Zagreb. If you arrive too early for the game, Zagreb's zoo is just across the street.

Shopping

Ilica is Zagreb's main shopping street. You can get in touch with true Croatian consumerism at the **Nama department store**, near the square Trg Jelačića.

Croatia is the birthplace of the necktie (cravat); **Kroata Cravata** *(Oktogon)* has locally made silk neckties at prices that run from 165KN to 360KN. **Rokotvorine** *(Trg Jelačića 7)* sells traditional Croatian handicrafts, such as red-and-white embroidered tablecloths, dolls and pottery.

Getting There & Away

Air For information about the flights to and from Zagreb, see the Getting There & Away and Getting Around sections at the start of this chapter.

Bus Zagreb's big, modern bus station has a large, enclosed waiting room and a number of shops, including grocery stores to stock up. You can buy most international tickets at window Nos 17 to 20.

Buses depart from Zagreb for most parts of Croatia, Slovenia and places beyond. Buy an advance ticket at the station if you're planning to travel far.

The following domestic buses depart from Zagreb:

destination	cost	duration	frequency
Dubrovnik	195KN	11 hours	7 daily
Korčula	209KN	12 hours	1 daily
Krk	126KN	5 hours	3 daily
Ljubljana	150KN	2½ hours	5 daily
Osijek	95KN	4 hours	6 daily
Plitvice	72KN	2½ hours	19 daily
Poreč	120–155KN	5 hours	6 daily
Pula	122–147KN	7 hours	13 daily
Rab	138KN	6 hours	2 daily
Rijeka	100KN	4 hours	21 daily
Rovinj	133–146KN	5–8 hours	8 daily
Split	120–132KN	7–9 hours	27 daily
Varaždin	50KN	1¾ hours	20 daily
Zadar	94–110KN	5 hours	20 daily

For international bus connections see the Getting There & Away section at the beginning of this chapter.

Train The following domestic trains depart from Zagreb:

destination	cost	duration	frequency
Osijek	88KN	4½ hours	4 daily
Pula	114KN	5½ hours	2 daily
Rijeka	77KN	5 hours	5 daily
Split	131KN	9 hours	3 or 4 daily
Varaždin	45KN	3 hours	13 daily
Zadar	131KN	11 hours	2 daily

Both daily trains to Zadar stop at Knin. Reservations are required on fast InterCity (IC) trains and there's a supplement that costs 5KN to 15KN for fast or express trains.

For international train connections see the Getting There & Away section at the beginning of this chapter.

Getting Around

Public transport is based on an efficient but overcrowded network of trams, though the city centre is compact enough to make them unnecessary. Tram Nos 3 and 8 don't run on weekends. Buy tickets at newspaper kiosks for 6KN or from the driver for 7KN. You can use your ticket for transfers within 90 minutes but only in one direction.

A *dnevna karta* (day ticket), valid on all public transport until 4am the next morning, is 16KN at most Vjesnik or Tisak news outlets. (See Tourist Offices under Information earlier for details on the Zagreb Card.)

To/From the Airport The Croatia Airlines bus to Zagreb airport, 17km southeast of the city, leaves from the bus station every half-hour or hour from about 5.30am to 7.30pm, depending on flights, and returns from the airport on about the same schedule (30KN). A taxi would cost about 250KN.

Car Of the major car-rental companies, you could try **Budget Rent-a-Car** (☎ 45 54 936) in the Hotel Sheraton, **Avis Autotehna** (☎ 48 36 006) at the Hotel Opera and **Hertz** (☎ 48 46 777; *Vukotinovićeva 1*). Bear in mind that local companies usually have lower rates. Try **Vipcar** (☎ 45 72 148; *Mihanovićeva 1*) at the Hotel Esplanade.

Taxi Zagreb's taxis ring up 7KN per kilometre after a flag fall of a whopping 25KN. On Sunday and at night from 10pm to 5am there's a 20% surcharge. Waiting time is 40KN an hour. The baggage surcharge is 5KN for every suitcase that the driver handles.

Istria

Istria (Istra to Croatians), which is the heart-shaped 3600-sq-km peninsula just south of Trieste, Italy, is graced with a 430km-long indented shoreline and an interior of green rolling hills, drowned valleys and fertile plains. The northern part of the peninsula belongs to Slovenia, while the Dinaric Range in the northeastern corner separates Istria from the continental mainland.

Istria has been a political basketball. Italy took Istria from Austria-Hungary in 1919, then had to give it to Yugoslavia in 1947. A large Italian community lives in Istria and Italian is widely spoken. Tito wanted Trieste (Trst) as part of Yugoslavia, too, but in 1954 the Anglo-American occupiers returned the city to Italy so that it wouldn't fall into the hands of the 'communists'. Today the Koper-Piran strip belongs to Slovenia while the rest is held by Croatia. Visit Piran quickly, then move south to Rovinj, a perfect base from which to explore Poreč and Pula.

If you'll be visiting a number of museums in Istria, it may pay to buy the Istra Card for 60KN, which allows free or discounted admission to most of the region's museums. It's available in most tourist offices and many travel agencies.

POREČ
☎ 052 • pop 17,460
Poreč (Parenzo in Italian), the Roman Parentium, sits on a low, narrow peninsula halfway down the western coast of Istria. The ancient Dekumanus with its polished stones is still the main street. Even after the fall of Rome, Poreč remained important as a centre of early Christianity, with a bishop and the famous Euphrasian Basilica, now a World Heritage Site. The town is the centre of a region packed with tourist resorts, but vestiges of earlier times and a quiet, small-town atmosphere (at least in the low season) make it well worth a stop. There are many places to swim in the clear water off the rocks north of the old town.

Orientation & Information
The bus station, with a **left-luggage office** (open 5am-9pm Mon-Sat, 7.30am-1pm & 2.30pm-9pm Sun), is directly opposite the small-boat harbour just outside the old town. Follow Obala Maršala Tita into the old town.

For visitor information, head to the **tourist office** (☎ 451 293, fax 451 665; **w** www .istra.com/porec; Zagrebačka 11; open 8am-10pm Mon-Sat Sept-June, 9am-1pm & 6pm-10pm Sun July & Aug). The **Atlas travel agency** (☎ 434 983; Eufrazijeva 63) represents AmEx. The **Sunny Way agency** (☎ 452 021; Alda Negrija 1) has information about boat connections to Italy.

The **telephone centre** (open 8am-3pm Mon-Fri, 8am-1pm Sat) is in the **main post office** (Trg Slobode 14). You can change money at any travel agency in town and there's an ATM at **Istarska Banka** (A Negrija 6). **Internet Center** (☎ 427 075; Grahalića 1) offers Internet access.

Things to See
The numerous historic sites in the old town include the ruins of two **Roman temples**, between Trg Marafor and the western end of the peninsula. Archaeology and history are featured in the **Regional Museum** (Dekumanus 9; adult/student 10/5KN; open 10am-1pm & 5pm-9pm daily July-Aug, 10am-1pm daily rest of year) in an old baroque palace. The captions are in German and Italian but there's an explanatory leaflet in English.

The main reason to visit Poreč, however, is to visit the 6th-century **Euphrasian Basilica** (☎ 431 635; admission free; open 7.30am-8pm daily, to 7pm Oct-Mar), which features some wonderfully preserved Byzantine gold mosaics. The sculpture and architecture of the basilica are remarkable survivors of that distant period. For a small fee you may visit the 4th-century mosaic floor of the adjacent Early Christian basilica or visit the baptistry and climb the bell tower.

From May to mid-October there are passenger boats (15KN return) every half-hour to **Sveti Nikola**, the small island opposite Poreč Harbour, departing from the wharf on Obala Maršala Tita.

Special Events
Annual events in Poreč include the day-long Folk Festival (June) and the Musical Summer (May to September). Ask about these at the tourist office.

Places to Stay
Accommodation in Poreč is tight in the summer but private-room prices are reasonable. Reserve in advance during July and August.

Camping There are two camping grounds at Zelena Laguna, 6km south of Poreč. Both **Autocamp Zelena Laguna** (☎ 410 541; camp sites 74KN plus per person 38KN) and **Autocamp Bijela Uvala** (☎ 410 5511; camp sites 74KN plus per person 38KN) are open from April to mid-October. Take the 'Zelena Laguna' resort tourist train (15KN) that runs half-hourly or hourly from the town centre between April and October.

Private Rooms In Poreč town centre **Di Tours** (☎ 432 100 or 452 018, fax 431 300; e di-tours@pu.tel.hr; Prvomajska 2) arranges private accommodation. Near the vegetable market at Partizanska there's also **Istra-Line** (☎ 451 067, fax 432 116) in a pink building. If you follow Nikole Tesle until it becomes Kalčića you'll come to Mate Vašića where you'll find **Fiore tours** (☎/fax 431 397; Mate Vašića 6), which also handles private accommodation. Expect to pay about 130/160KN for a single/double room with shared facilities in the high season plus a 30% surcharge for stays less than three nights.

Hotels Try the modern, five-storey **Hotel Poreč** (☎ 451 811, fax 451 730; e info@ hotelporec.com; singles/doubles 310/465KN) near the bus station, which has reasonably fresh rooms with TV. The front rooms are over a bar with a predictably noisy output during the summer. **Hotel Neptun** (☎ 400 800, fax 431 531; Obala Maršala Tita 15; singles/ doubles 375/675KN with half-board) overlooks the harbour and has more expensive rooms with harbour views. **Jadran** (☎ 431 236; Obala Maršala Tita; singles/doubles 325/600KN with half-board) has simpler rooms with no TV.

Places to Eat
The **Peškera Self-Service Restaurant** (open 10am-8pm year-round), just outside the northwestern corner of the old city wall, is good value and **Pizzeria Nono** (Zagrebačka 4; mains from 40KN) is a local favourite for its scrumptious pizzas.

There is a large **supermarket** and **department store** next to Hotel Poreč, near the bus station.

Getting There & Away
There are buses to Rovinj (22KN, one hour, seven daily), Zagreb (144KN, five hours, eight

daily) and Rijeka (53KN, 5½ hours, eight daily), and Pula (31KN, 1¼ hours, 12 daily). Between Poreč and Rovinj the bus runs along the Lim Channel, a drowned valley. To see it clearly, sit on the right-hand side if you're southbound, or the left if you're northbound.

The nearest train station is at Pazin, 30km east (five buses daily from Poreč).

For information about bus and boat connections to Italy and Slovenia see the Getting There & Away section at the start of this chapter. The cheapest price for car rental is at **Follis** (☎ 427 103; Istarskog razvoda 11).

ROVINJ
☎ 052 • pop 14,200
Relaxed Rovinj (Rovigno in Italian), with its high peninsula topped by the 60m tower of the massive Cathedral of St Euphemia, is perhaps the best place to visit in Istria. Wooded hills punctuated by low-rise luxury hotels surround the town, while the 13 green, offshore islands of the Rovinj archipelago make for pleasant, varied views. The cobbled, inclined streets in the old town are charmingly picturesque. Rovinj is still an active fishing port, so you see local people going about their day-to-day business, and you can swim from the rocks in the sparkling water below Hotel Rovinj.

Orientation & Information
The bus station is in the southeastern corner of the old town and there's an ATM next to the entrance, as well as Autotrans Travel Agency, which will change money. The Rovinj **tourist office** (☎ 811 566, fax 816 007; w www.tzgrovinj.hr; Obala Pina Budicina 12; open 8am-9pm Mon-Sat, 9am-1pm Sun) is just off Trg Maršala Tita. **Planet Tourist Agency** (☎ 840 494, Sv Križ 1) has a few computers to access the Internet and is in the centre of town. Otherwise, walk up Carducci about 500m to **Caffe-Bar Aurora** (☎ 830 333; Prolaz M Maretić 8). The AmEx representative is **Atlas travel agency** (☎ 813 463) next to Hotel Park at V Nazora BB.

Phone calls can be made from the post office that is across from the bus station. The bus station has a **left-luggage office** (open 6am-9pm daily) – ask at the ticket window.

Things to See
The **Cathedral of St Euphemia** (open 10am-6pm daily mid-June–mid-Sept, 10am-6pm Sun rest of year), which completely dominates

the town from its hill-top location and built in 1736, is the largest baroque building in Istria. It reflects the period during the 18th century when Rovinj was the most populous town in Istria, an important fishing centre and the bulwark of the Venetian fleet.

Inside the cathedral, don't miss the tomb of St Euphemia (martyred in AD 304) behind the right-hand altar. The saint's remains were brought from Constantinople in 800. On the anniversary of her martyrdom (16 September) devotees congregate here. A copper statue of her tops the cathedral's mighty tower.

Take a wander along the winding narrow backstreets below the cathedral, such as **ul Grisia**, where local artists sell their work. Each year in mid-August Rovinj's painters stage a big open-air art show in town.

The Rovinj **Regional Museum** (Trg Maršala Tita; adult/student 10/8KN; open 9.30am-12.30pm & 6pm-9.30pm Mon-Sat mid-June–mid-Sept, 10am-1pm Tues-Sat rest of year) contains an unexciting collection of paintings and a few Etruscan artefacts that have been found in Istria. Captions are only in Croatian and Italian.

Somewhat interesting is the **Rovinj Aquarium** (Obala Giordano Paliaga 5; admission 10KN; open 10am-6pm Mon-Sat mid-Apr–June & Sept–mid-Oct, 9am-9pm daily July & Aug), dating from 1891. It exhibits a collection of local marine life, from poisonous scorpion fish to colourful anemones.

When you've seen enough of the town, follow the waterfront south past the Park Hotel to **Punta Corrente Forest Park**, which was established in 1890 by Baron Hütterodt, an Austrian admiral who kept a villa on Crveni otok (Red Island). Here you can swim off the rocks, climb a cliff or just sit and admire the offshore islands.

Organised Tours

Delfin Agency (☎ 813 266), near the ferry dock for Crveni otok, runs half-day scenic cruises to the Lim Channel for 110KN per person, or you can go with one of the independent operators at the end of Alzo Rismondo that run half-day and full-day boat trips around the region. There's an hourly ferry to Crveni otok (20KN return) and a frequent ferry to nearby Katarina Island (15KN return) from the same landing. Get tickets on the boat or at the nearby kiosk. These boats operate only from May to mid-October.

Special Events

The city's annual events include the Rovinj-Pesaro Regatta (early May), 'Rovinj Summer' concert series (July and August) and Rovinj Fair (August).

Places to Stay

Camping The camping ground that is closest to Rovinj is **Porton Biondi** (☎ 813 557; per person/tent/car 30/16/16KN), less than a 1km from the town (on the Monsena bus route). Five kilometres southeast of Rovinj is **Polari Camping** (☎ 800 376; Villa Rubin bus; open May–mid-Oct).

Private Rooms The surcharge for a stay of less than three nights is 50% and guests who stay only one night are punished with a 100% surcharge, but you should be able to bargain the surcharge away outside of July and August. If not, it may be cheaper to stay in a hotel. **Natale-Lokva** (☎ 813 365, fax 830 239; e natale@pu.tel.hr; Via Carducci 4; singles/doubles with shared bathroom 185/315KN) is opposite the bus station.

You could also try **Futura Travel** (☎ 817 281; M Benussi 2) or **Marco Polo** (☎ 816 616, W www.marcopolo.hr; Trg Lokva 3), which have rooms at the same price. The prices are fixed by the local tourist association. Breakfast is an additional 30KN.

Hotels The **Hotel Rovinj** (☎ 811 288, fax 840 757; e hotel-rovinj@pu.hinet.hr; Svetoga Križa; singles/doubles from 352/487KN) has a splendid location overlooking the sea. Renovated rooms with air-con and/or sea view are more expensive. The cheapest hotel is the 192-room **Hotel Monte Mulin** (☎ 811 512, fax 815 882; singles/doubles with half-board 241/367KN), on the wooded hillside overlooking the bay just beyond Hotel Park. It's about a 15-minute walk heading south of the bus station. A new luxury hotel in a renovated Venetian building, **Hotel Villa Angelo D'Oro** (☎ 840 502, fax 840 112; e hotel.angelo@vip.hr; Via Svalba 38-42; singles/doubles 670/1160KN) offers plush, lavishly decorated rooms with air-con, satellite TV, minibar and a free sauna and Jacuzzi room.

Places to Eat

Most of the fish and spaghetti places along the harbour cater to the more upmarket crowd, while **Cantinon** (obala Alzo Rismondo 18) sells fresh grilled fish from 25KN to a local crowd. **Veli Jože** *(Svetoga Križa 1)* is somewhat more expensive, but is a good place to try Istrian dishes in an interior crammed with knick-knacks, or at tables outside.

Picnickers can buy supplies at the **supermarket** only about 25m downhill from the bus station or in one of the kiosks selling *burek* near the vegetable market.

Getting There & Away

There's a bus from Rovinj to Pula (22KN, 40 minutes to 1¼ hours) every hour or so. There are up to eight daily to Poreč (22KN to 39KN, one hour), eight daily to Rijeka (73KN, 3½ hours), nine daily to Zagreb (140KN, five to eight hours), one daily to Koper (69KN, 1½ hours) and Split (263KN, 11¼ hours), and one daily to Dubrovnik (373KN, 17½ hours) and Ljubljana (128KN, 2½ hours, July to August). Prices and durations vary between different companies and routes.

The closest train station is Kanfanar, 19km away on the Pula-Divača line.

Eurostar Travel *(☎ 813 144; Obala Pina Budicina 1)* is the agent for Adriatica Navigazione and has schedules and tickets for boats to Italy.

PULA

☎ 052 • pop 58,600

Pula (the ancient Polensium) is a large regional centre with some industry, a big naval base and a busy commercial harbour. An important base for the Romans, the city contains a wealth of Roman ruins topped by a remarkably well-preserved amphitheatre, which is now the centre of Pula's lively cultural scene. Nearby are some rocky wooded peninsulas overlooking the clear Adriatic waters, which explains the many resort hotels and camping grounds circling the city.

Orientation

The **bus station** *(ul Carrarina)* is in the centre of town. One block south is Giardini, the central hub, while the harbour is just north of the bus station. The train station is near the water about 1km north of town.

Information

Tourist Offices The helpful Pula **Tourist Information Centre** *(☎ 219 197, fax 211 955; W www.istra.com/pula; Forum 2; open 9am-8pm Mon-Sat, 10am-6pm Sun)* provides maps, brochures and schedules of upcoming events in Pula and around Istria.

Money You can exchange money in travel agencies and or the **post office** *(Istarska 5)* next to the bus station, where there is an ATM.

Post & Communications Long-distance telephone calls may be placed at the **main post office** *(Danteov trg 4; open to 8pm daily)*. You can check your emails at **Enigma** *(☎ 381 615; Kandlerova 19)*.

Travel Agencies The **Atlas travel agency** *(☎ 214 172, fax 214 090; ⓔ atl.pula@atlas .tel.hr; ul Starih Statuta 1)* organises tours to the Brijuni Islands (210KN), while **Jadroagent** *(☎ 210 431; ⓔ jadroagent-pula@pu .hinet.hr; Riva 14)* has schedules and tickets for boats connecting Istria with Italy and the islands.

Left Luggage The bus station has a **left-luggage office** *(open 4.30am-11.30pm daily with 2 half-hour breaks)*. The train station also has a **left-luggage service** *(open 9am-4pm Mon-Sat)*.

Things to See

Pula's most imposing sight is the 1st-century **Roman amphitheatre** *(Flavijevska ul; adult/concession 16/8KN; open 7.30am-9pm daily Jun-Sept, 8am-4.30pm rest of year)* overlooking the harbour and northeast of the old town. Built entirely from local limestone, the amphitheatre was designed to host gladiatorial contests and could accommodate up to 20,000 spectators. The 30m-high outer wall is almost intact and contains two rows of 72 arches. Around the end of July a Croatian film festival is held in the amphitheatre, and there are pop, jazz and classical events, often with major international stars, throughout summer.

The **Archaeological Museum** *(Ulica Cararina 3; adult/concession 12/6KN; open 9am-8pm Mon-Sat, 10am-3pm Sun June-Sept, 9am-3pm Mon-Fri rest of year)* is on the hill opposite the bus station.

Even if you don't get into the museum be sure to visit the large sculpture garden around it, and the **Roman theatre** behind the museum. The garden is entered through 2nd-century twin gates.

Along the street facing the bus station are **Roman walls** that mark the eastern boundary

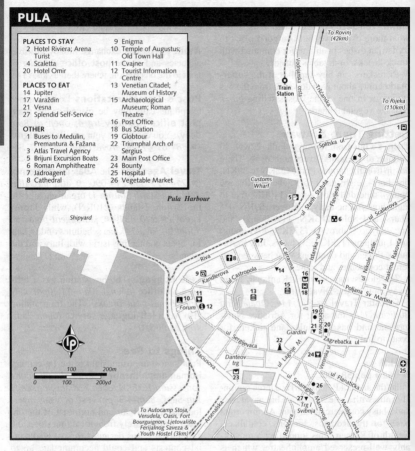

PULA

PLACES TO STAY
2 Hotel Riviera; Arena Turist
4 Scaletta
20 Hotel Omir

PLACES TO EAT
14 Jupiter
17 Varaždin
21 Vesna
27 Splendid Self-Service

OTHER
1 Buses to Medulin, Premantura & Fažana
3 Atlas Travel Agency
5 Brijuni Excursion Boats
6 Roman Amphitheatre
7 Jadroagent
8 Cathedral
9 Enigma
10 Temple of Augustus; Old Town Hall
11 Cvajner
12 Tourist Information Centre
13 Venetian Citadel; Museum of History
15 Archaeological Museum; Roman Theatre
16 Post Office
18 Bus Station
19 Globtour
22 Triumphal Arch of Sergius
23 Main Post Office
24 Bounty
25 Hospital
26 Vegetable Market

of old Pula. Follow these walls south and continue down Giardini to the **Triumphal Arch of Sergius** (27 BC). The street beyond the arch winds right around old Pula, changing names several times. Follow it to the ancient **Temple of Augustus** and the **old town hall** (1296).

The 17th-century **Venetian Citadel,** on a high hill in the centre of the old town, is worth the climb for the view if not for the meagre exhibits in the tiny **Museum of History** (Kaštel; admission 7KN; open 8am-7pm daily June-Sept, 9am-5pm Mon-Fri rest of year) inside.

Places to Stay

Camping The closest camping ground to the city centre is three kilometres southwest. **Autocamp Stoja** (☎ 387 144, fax 387 748; bus No 1 to Stoja terminus; per person/tent & car 50/100KN; open mid-Apr–mid-Oct) has lots of space along the shady promontory, with swimming possible off the rocks. There are more camping grounds at Medulin and Premantura, which are coastal resorts southeast of Pula (take the buses heading southeast from town).

Hostels In a great location overlooking a clean, pebble beach **Ljetovalište Ferijalnog Saveza Youth Hostel** (☎ 391 133, fax 391 106; e pula@hfhs.hr; tent sites 40KN, tent rental 10KN, B&B/half-board 90/155KN) is 3km south of central Pula. Take the No 2 or 7 Verudela bus to the 'Piramida' stop, walk back to the first street, then turn left and look for the sign. The rate for camping includes breakfast. The hostel is heated.

Private Rooms In the Hotel Riviera **Arena Turist** (☎ 529 400, fax 529 401, ⓦ www .arenaturist.hr; Splitska 1a), **Globtour** (☎ 211 255; Giardini 10) and Atlas travel agency have private rooms for 148/184KN per single/ double with private bathroom, plus a selection of apartments to rent.

Hotels Most accommodation is outside town in the sprawling resorts on the Verudela Peninsula. The cheapest hotel in town is **Hotel Omir** (☎ 210 614, fax 213 944; Dobricheva 6; singles/doubles 324/450KN), which has 14 small but adequate rooms. Prices stay the same year-round. For faded old-world elegance try **Hotel Riviera** (☎ 211 166, fax 211 166; Splitska ul 1; singles/doubles 465/ 705KN), overlooking the harbour. Neither the service nor the comfort justifies the price (which eases in the low season) in this one-star hotel, but the large front rooms have a view of the water and the wide shady hotel terrace is a relaxing place for a drink.

The most comfortable hotel in town is **Scaletta** (☎ 541 599, fax 541 025, ⓦ www .hotel-scaletta.com; Flavijeska 26; singles/ doubles 480/680KN), which offers beautifully decorated rooms with TV and telephone, including breakfast. The hotel restaurant is also excellent.

Places to Eat

Jupiter (Castropola 38) serves up the best pizza in town and the pasta is good too. **Varaždin** (Istarska 32; mains from 40KN) offers carefully prepared soups, pastas, risottos and salads, as well as an assortment of fish and meat dishes.

Splendid Self-Service (Trg I Svibnja 5; open 9.30am-8.45pm daily), opposite the vegetable market, is easy since you see what you're getting and you pay at the end of the line. The people at the cheese counter in **Vesna** (Giardini; open 6.30am-8pm Mon-Fri, 6.30am-1.30pm Sat) prepare healthy sandwiches while you wait.

Entertainment

Posters around Pula advertise live performances at the amphitheatre or the details of rave parties at two venues in Verudela: **Oasis** and **Fort Bourguignon**. The streets of Flanatička, Kandlerova and Sergijevaca, are lively people-watching spots and the Forum has several outdoor cafés that fill up in the early evening; the trendiest is café/gallery **Cvajner** with a stunning, art-filled interior.

Bounty (Veronska 8) is the place to go if Irish beer and cheer is your thing.

Getting There & Away

Bus The buses that travel to Rijeka (58KN, 2½ hours, 20 daily) are sometimes crowded, especially the eight that continue to Zagreb, so be sure to reserve a seat in advance. Going from Pula to Rijeka, be sure to sit on the right-hand side of the bus for a stunning view of the Gulf of Kvarner.

Other destinations for buses from Pula include: Rovinj (22KN, 40 minutes, 18 daily); Poreč (31KN, one hour, 12 daily); Zagreb (135KN, five hours, 11 daily); Zadar (161KN, seven hours, four daily), Split (248KN, 10 hours, four daily) and to Dubrovnik (354KN, 15 hours, one daily).

Train There are two daily trains to Ljubljana (110KN, four hours) and two to Zagreb (110KN, 6½ hours) but you must board a bus for part of the trip.

Boat Until 2002 there was a regular ferry connecting Pula and Venice. To see if the service has recommenced, check with Jadroagent on the harbour (see Travel Agencies earlier in this section).

Getting Around

The only city buses of use to visitors are bus No 1, which runs to the camping ground at Stoja, and bus Nos 2 and 7 to Verudela, which pass the youth hostel. Frequency varies from every 15 minutes to every 30 minutes, with service from 5am to 11.30pm daily. Tickets are sold at newsstands for 8KN and are good for two trips.

AROUND PULA
Brijuni Islands

The Brijuni (Brioni in Italian) island group consists of two main pine-covered islands and 12 islets off the coast of Istria and just northwest of Pula. Each year from 1949 until his death in 1980, Maršal Tito spent six months at his summer residences on Brijuni in a style any Western capitalist would have admired. In 1984 Brijuni was proclaimed a national park. Some 680 species of plants grow on the islands, including many exotic subtropical species, which were planted at Tito's request.

You may only visit Brijuni National Park with a group. Instead of booking an excursion with one of the travel agencies in Pula, Rovinj or Poreč, which costs 210KN, take a public bus from Pula to Fažana (8km), then sign up for a tour (170KN) at the **Brijuni Tourist Service** (☎ 525 883) office near the wharf. It's best to book in advance, especially in summer.

Also check along the Pula waterfront for excursion boats to Brijuni. The five-hour boat trips from Pula to Brijuni (60KN) may not actually visit the islands but only sail around them. Still, it makes a nice day out.

Gulf of Kvarner

The Gulf of Kvarner (Quarnero in Italian) stretches 100km south from Rijeka, between the Istrian Peninsula to the west and the Croatian littoral to the east. The elongated islands are the peaks of a submerged branch of the Dinaric Alps, the range that follows the coast south all the way to Albania. Rijeka is a busy commercial port and transport hub at the northern end of the gulf while Krk, Cres and Pag are among the largest islands in Croatia.

RIJEKA
☎ 051 • pop 144,000

Rijeka (Fiume in Italian), 126km south of Ljubljana, is such a transportation hub that it's almost impossible to avoid. The network of buses, trains and ferries that connect Istria and Dalmatia with Zagreb and points beyond all seem to pass through Rijeka. As Croatia's largest port, the city is full of boats, cargo, fumes, cranes and the bustling sense of purpose that characterises most port cities.

Although Rijeka is hardly one of the 'must see' destinations, the city does have a few saving graces, such as the pedestrian mall, Korzo, stately 19th-century buildings and a tree-lined promenade along the harbour.

Orientation
The **bus station** (Trg Žabica) is south of the Capuchin Church in the centre of town. The **train station** (ul Krešimirova) is a seven-minute walk west of the bus station.

The Jadrolinija ferry wharf (there's no left-luggage section) is just a few minutes east of the bus station. Korzo runs in an easterly direction through the city centre towards the fast-moving Rječina River.

Information
Tourist Offices The new and highly efficient **Turistička Zajednica** (☎ 335 882, fax 214 706, ⓦ www.multilink.hr/tz-rijeka; Korzo 33) distributes *Rijeka Tourist Route*, a walking-tour guide that is so well produced it makes you actually want to stay and look around. For boat information, there's **Jadroagent** (☎ 211 276, fax 335 172; Trg Ivana Koblera 2) and the head office of **Jadrolinija** (☎ 211 444; ⓦ www.jadrolinija.hr; Riva 16), the last word on its ever-changing schedule. **Hostelling International** (☎ 264 176; Korzo 22) sells HI cards and is a good source of information about Croatian hostels.

Money There's no ATM at the train station but the exchange offices adjacent to the train and bus stations keep long hours. There are a number of ATMs along Korzo and an exchange counter in the main post office.

Post & Communications The **telephone centre** (open 7am-9pm Mon-Fri, 7am-2pm Sat & Sun) is in the **main post office** (Korzo), opposite the old city tower. You can check your emails at **Ecomclub** (24a Ivana Zajca; open 7am-10.30pm daily) while enjoying a brew in a relaxed pub.

Left Luggage If the **left-luggage office** (open 5.30am-10.30pm daily) in the bus station is full, there's a **left-luggage office** (open 24hr) in the train station.

Laundry You'll find **Blitz** (Krešimirova 3a; open 7am-8pm Mon-Fri, 7am-1pm Sat) between the bus and train stations; it will do a small load of laundry for 60KN.

Things to See
Rijeka's main orientation point is the **City Tower** (Korzo), which was originally one of the main gates to the city and one of the few monuments to have survived the earthquake in 1750.

The **Modern Art Gallery** (Dolac 1; adult/concession 10/5KN; open 10am-1pm & 5pm-9pm Tues-Sun) is in the upstairs scientific library opposite Hotel Bonavia. The **Naval and Historical Museum** (Muzejski trg 1; adult/student 10KN/free; open 10am-1pm Tues-Sat) traces the development of sailing, with models and paintings of ships and portraits of the captains. The **Natural History**

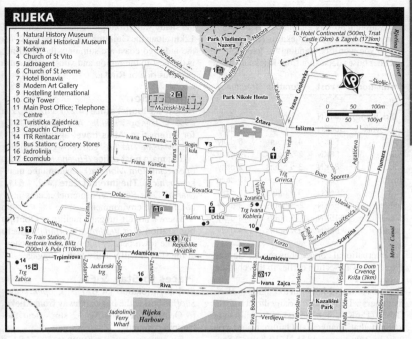

RIJEKA

1 Natural History Museum
2 Naval and Historical Museum
3 Korkyra
4 Church of St Vito
5 Jadroagent
6 Church of St Jerome
7 Hotel Bonavia
8 Modern Art Gallery
9 Hostelling International
10 City Tower
11 Main Post Office; Telephone Centre
12 Turistička Zajednica
13 Capuchin Church
14 ITR Rentacar
15 Bus Station; Grocery Stores
16 Jadrolinija
17 Ecomclub

Museum (*Lorenzov prolaz 1; adult/student 10/5KN; open 9am-7pm Mon-Fri, 9am-2pm Sat*) is devoted to regional geology and botany.

Worth a visit is the 13th-century **Trsat Castle** (*admission free; open daily*), which is on a high ridge overlooking Rijeka, and the canyon of the Rječina River. If you have some more time to kill, stroll into some of Rijeka's churches, such as **Church of St Vito** (*Trg Grivica 11*), **Church of St Jerome** (*Trg Riječke Rezolucije*) or the ornate **Capuchin Church** (*Trg Žabica*).

Places to Stay

The tourist office can direct you to the few options for private accommodation, most of which are a few kilometres out of town on the road to Opatija. It's just as easy to get to Opatija where there are more and better choices for hotels and private accommodation (for details on getting to/from Opatija see Getting There & Away in that section later).

The cheapest place to stay is **Dom Crvenog Križa** (*☎ 217 599, fax 335 380; Janka Polić Kamova 32; dorm beds 60KN*), a dorm run by the Red Cross, 3km east of town in Pećine. The only hotel in the centre is the four-star

Hotel Bonavia (*☎ 333 744, fax 335 969; Dolac 4; singles/doubles 967/1200KN*), which has all of the niceties that businesspeople on generous expense accounts find indispensable. **Hotel Continental** (*☎ 372 008; singles/doubles 315/390KN; Andrije Kašića Miočića*), northeast of the town centre, offers bland rooms in an unrenovated building.

Places to Eat

Restoran Index (*ul Krešimirova 18*), between the bus and train stations, has a good self-serve section. **Korkyra** (*Slogin kula 5; mains from 35KN*) is a local favourite for specialities, such as *brodetto* (fish stew), *bakalar* (codfish stew) and various pastas. There are several 24-hour **grocery stores** in and around the bus station.

Getting There & Away

Air The Croatia Airlines minibus (100KN) connects Zagreb with Rijeka. The bus goes to the central bus station in Rijeka and takes four hours.

Bus There are 13 buses daily between Rijeka and Krk (31KN, 1½ hours), via the huge Krk

Bridge. Buses to Krk are overcrowded and a reservation in no way guarantees a seat. Don't worry – the bus from Rijeka to Krk empties fast so you won't be standing for long.

Other buses departing from Rijeka include:

destination	cost	duration	frequency
Baška			
(Krk Island)	41KN	2 hours	1 daily
Dubrovnik	306KN	13 hours	2 daily
Poreč	53KN	4½ hours	5 daily
Pula	58KN	2½ hours	17 daily
Rab	87KN	3½ hours	2 daily
Rovinj	70KN	3½ hours	10 daily
Split	196KN	8½ hours	11 daily
Trieste	58KN	2-3 hours	3 daily
Zadar	115KN	5 hours	12 daily
Zagreb	98KN	3½ hours	24 daily

For international connections see the Getting There & Away section earlier in this chapter.

Train Four trains daily run to Zagreb (77KN, five hours). There's also a daily direct train to Osijek (156KN, eight hours) and a daily train to Split that changes at Ogulin where you wait for two hours (135KN, 10 hours). Several of the seven daily services to Ljubljana (80KN, three hours) require a change of trains at the Slovenian border and again at Bifka or Bistrica in Slovenia but there are also two direct trains. Reservations are compulsory on some *poslovni* (express) trains.

Car Close to the bus station **ITR Rent a Car** (☎ 337 544; Riva 20) has rental cars from about 300/1820KN per day/week with unlimited kilometres, including tax.

Boat Croatia's national boat line, Jadrolinija, has tickets for the large coastal ferries that run all year between Rijeka and Dubrovnik, as well as the weekly passenger boat that runs from Zadar to Rijeka (230KN, 5¼ hours) in the summer, but not the other way. The return trip from Rijeka does not stop in Zadar. For fares, see the Getting Around section at the beginning of this chapter.

OPATIJA
☎ 051 • pop 12,719

Opatija, just a few kilometres due west of Rijeka, was *the* fashionable seaside resort of the Austro-Hungarian empire until WWI. Many grand, old hotels remain from this time and the shady waterfront promenade stretches for 12km along the Gulf of Kvarner. The views of the indented coast are stunning, the nightlife is the best in the region and you're within an easy bus ride of Rijeka.

Information
Head to the **tourist office** (☎ 271 310, fax 271 699; **e** tzgr.op@ri.tel.hr; Maršala Tita 101) for information. **Atlas travel agency** (☎ 271 032; Maršala Tita 116) can also assist visitors.

The **main post office** (Eugena Kumičića 2; open 8am-7pm Mon-Sat) is behind the market (*tržnica*). **The Internet Cafe** (☎ 271 511; Maršala Tita 85) offers Internet access in a comfortable environment.

There's no left-luggage facility at **Opatija bus station** (Trg Vladimira Gortana), which is in the town centre, but Autotrans Agency at the station will usually watch luggage.

Places to Stay & Eat
Preluk Autokamp (☎ 621 913; open May-Sept) is beside the busy highway from Rijeka to Opatija. City bus No 32 stops near the camping ground.

For private rooms, try **Kompas** (☎ 271 912; Maršala Tita 110) or **GIT travel agency** (☎/fax 271 967; **e** gi-trade@ri.tel.hr; Maršala Tita 65). Both have rooms starting at 72/80KN per person for one-star accommodation inside/outside the town centre plus a 50% surcharge for single-room occupancy.

The hotel scene is competitive and offers good value for money especially outside of July and August. The two cheapest places to stay in town are **Hotel Paris** (☎ 271 911, fax 711 823; **e** lrh@lrh.tel.hr; Maršala Tita 198; singles/doubles from 262/405KN), and **Hotel Residenz** (☎ 271 399, fax 271 225; Maršala Tita 133; singles/doubles from 300/480KN). The **Hotel Kvarner** (☎ 271 233, fax 271 202; **e** hotel-kvarner@lrh.tel.hr; singles/doubles from 510/795KN) is a genteel 19th-century establishment with a swimming pool and easy access to the sea.

Maršala Tita is lined with a number of decent restaurants offering pizza, grilled meat and fish. There's the **supermarket/deli** (Maršala Tita 80) for self-caterers as well as the **Madonnina Pizzeria** (Pava Tomašića 3; mains from 35KN), not far from the Hotel Kvarner, which has a wide range of pizzas and pastas to choose from.

Entertainment

An **open air cinema** *(Park Angiolina)* screens films and presents occasional concerts nightly at 9.30pm from May to September. There's a boisterous bar scene centred around the harbour and the ever-popular **Caffé Harbour** or **Hemingways**.

Getting There & Away

Bus No 32 stops in front of the train station in Rijeka (11KN, ½ hour) and runs right along the Opatija Riviera, west of Rijeka, every 20 minutes until late in the evening. If you're looking for accommodation, it's easiest to get off at the first stop, opposite the GIT travel agency and walk downhill, passing hotels and other agencies on the way to the bus station.

KRK ISLAND

☎ 051 • pop 18,000

Croatia's largest island, the 409-sq-km Krk (Veglia in Italian), is very barren and rocky. In 1980 Krk was joined to the mainland by the enormous Krk Bridge, the largest concrete arch bridge in the world, with a span of some 390m. Since then, Krk has suffered from too-rapid development, from Rijeka airport and some industry at the northern end of Krk to big tourist hotels in the middle and far south. Still, the main town (also called Krk) is rather picturesque and the popular resort of Baška at the island's southern end has a 2km pebbly beach set below a high ridge.

Krk Town

Tiny Krk town has a compact medieval centre that opens onto a scenic port. From the 12th to 15th centuries, Krk town and the surrounding region remained semi-independent under the Frankopan Dukes of Krk, an indigenous Croatian dynasty, at a time when much of the Adriatic was controlled by Venice. This history explains the various medieval sights in Krk town, the ducal seat.

The bus from Baška and Rijeka stops by the harbour, a few minutes' walk from the old town of Krk. There's no left-luggage facility at Krk bus station. The **Turistička Zajednica** *(☎/fax 221 414; Velika Placa 1)* is in the city wall's Guard Tower. You can change money at any travel agency and there's an ATM accepting MasterCard and Cirrus in the shopping centre near the bus station.

The lovely 14th-century **Frankopan Castle** and 12th-century Romanesque **cathedral** are in the lower town near the harbour. In the upper part of Krk town are three old **monastic churches**. The narrow streets of Krk are worth exploring.

Places to Stay & Eat There is a range of accommodation in and around Krk, but many places only open during summertime. The closest camping ground is **Autocamp Ježevac** *(☎ 221 081; per person/tent/car 28/19/18KN)* on the coast, a 10-minute walk southwest of Krk town.

Private rooms can be organised through **Autotrans** *(☎ 221 172)* at the bus station. You can expect to pay from about 140/160KN for a single/double.

The new hostel **Veli Jože** *(☎/fax 220 212; Vitezića 32; dorm beds 132KN)* is located in a spruced-up older building and is open year-round. Rates go down considerably during the low season.

There are a number of restaurants around the harbour, but for something different, try **Konobo Nono** *(Krčkih iseljenika 8; mains around 50KN)* which offers *šurlice*, home-made noodles topped with goulash, as well as grilled fish and meat dishes.

Baška

At the southern end of Krk Island, Baška is popular for its 2km-long pebbly beach set below a dramatic, barren range of mountains. Although crowded in summer, the old town and harbour make a pleasant stroll and there's always that splendid beach. The bus from Krk stops at the top of a hill on the edge of the old town, between the beach and the harbour.

The main street of Baška is Zvonimirova, overlooking the harbour, and the beach begins at the western end of the harbour, continuing southwards past a big sprawling hotel complex. The town's **tourist office** *(☎ 856 817; e tz-baska@ri.tel.hr; Zvonimirova 114; open 8am-8pm daily mid-June–Sept, 8am-3pm Mon-Fri rest of year)* is just down the street from the bus stop.

Getting There & Away

About 14 buses a day travel between Rijeka and Krk town (31KN, 1½ hours), of which six continue on to Baška (up to one hour). One of the Rijeka buses is to/from Zagreb (four hours). To go from Krk to Zadar, take one of the many buses to Kraljevica and then change to a southbound bus.

Dalmatia

Dalmatia (Dalmacija) occupies the central 375km of Croatia's Adriatic coast, from the Gulf of Kvarner in the north to the Bay of Kotor in the south. With its Roman ruins, spectacular beaches, old fishing ports, medieval architecture and unspoilt offshore islands, Dalmatia offers an unbeatable combination of hedonism and historical discovery.

The dramatic coastal scenery is due to the rugged Dinaric Range, which forms a 1500m-long barrier that separates Dalmatia from Bosnia-Hercegovina. After the last Ice Age, part of the coastal mountains were flooded, creating the sort of long, high islands seen in the Gulf of Kvarner. The deep, protected passages between these islands are a paradise for sailors and cruisers.

Split is the largest city in the region and a hub for bus and boat connections along the Adriatic, as well as home to the late Roman Diocletian's Palace. Zadar has more Roman ruins and a wealth of churches. The architecture of Hvar and Korčula recalls the days when these places were outposts of the Venetian empire. None can rival majestic Dubrovnik, a cultural and aesthetic jewel. The ferry trip from Split to Dubrovnik is the Mediterranean at its best and one of the classic journeys of Eastern Europe.

ZADAR
☎ 023 • pop 72,700

Zadar (ancient Zara), the main city of northern Dalmatia, occupies a long peninsula separating the harbour on the east from the Zadarski Channel on the west. Its strategic position on the Adriatic coast made Zadar a target for the Romans, the Byzantine, Venetian, Austro-Hungarian empires and Italy. Although it was damaged by Allied bombing raids in 1943–44 and Yugoslav rockets in 1991, the resilient city has been rebuilt and restored, retaining much of its old flavour. The marble, traffic-free streets of the old town are replete with Roman ruins, medieval churches and several fascinating museums. Massive 16th-century fortifications still shield the city on the landward side, with high walls running along the harbour. The tree-lined promenade along Obala kralja Petra Krešimira IV is perfect for a lazy stroll or a picnic and there are several small beaches east of the old town. More beaches lie to the west at Borik as well as on the islands of Ugljan and Dugi Otok, within easy reach of the town. Don't forget to sample Zadar's famous maraschino cherry liqueur.

Orientation
The train and bus stations are adjacent and are a 15-minute walk southeast of the harbour and old town. From the stations, Zrinsko-Frankopanska ul leads northwest past the main post office to the harbour. Buses marked 'Poluotok' run from the bus station to the harbour. Narodni trg is the heart of Zadar.

Information
The main tourist office is **Turistička Zajednica** (☎ 212 222; e tzg-zadar@zd.tel.hr; Smiljanića 4; open 8am-8pm Mon-Sat, 8am-1pm Sun June-Sept, 8am-6pm Mon-Sat Oct-May).

The AmEx representative is **Atlas travel agency** (☎ 235 850; Branimirova Obala 12), across the footbridge over the harbour, and just northeast of Narodni trg. **Croatia Express** (☎ 250 502; Široka ul) is next to an ATM. **Croatia Airlines** (☎ 250 101; Poljana Natka Nodila 7) has flight information. You can exchange money at any travel agency, at the Jadrolinija office or in the main post office. There is also an exchange office and an ATM at the bus station.

Telephone calls can be made from the **post office** (Pojana Pape Aleksandra III). Computers and an Internet connection are available at **Cybercafe** (☎ 313 995; Špire Brusine 8; open 8am-10pm Mon-Sat).

There are **left-luggage** (open 24hr) facilities at the train station, a **left-luggage office** (open 7am-9pm Mon-Fri) at the bus station and yet another near the Jadrolinija dock (open 7am-8pm Mon-Fri, 7am-3pm Sat).

Things to See & Do
Most attractions are near **St Donatus Church** (Šimuna Kožičića Benje; admission 5KN; open 9.30am-2pm & 5pm-8pm daily Mar-Oct), a circular 9th-century Byzantine structure built over the Roman forum. Slabs for the ancient forum are visible in the church and there is a pillar from the Roman era on the northwestern side. In summer, ask about the musical evenings here (Renaissance and early baroque music). The outstanding **Museum of Church Art** (Poljana Opatice Čike bb; adult/student 20/10KN; open 10am-1pm daily, 6pm-8pm Mon-Sat), in the Benedictine

View over historic Dubrovnik to forested Lokrum Island, on the coast of Southern Dalmatia, Croatia

The imposing Museum Mimara in Zagreb, Croatia, houses outstanding European and Asian art

Dramatic cascades link 16 turquoise lakes in Croatia's Plitvice Lakes National Park

Prague Castle dominates the night sky above Malá Strana (the Small Quarter) and the Vltava River

The Old Town Square of Prague has been the heart of the city since the 10th century

Early-morning pedestrians mingle with the monuments on Prague's famous Charles Bridge

Prague's modern metro is designed to get you around at the speed of light (well, almost)

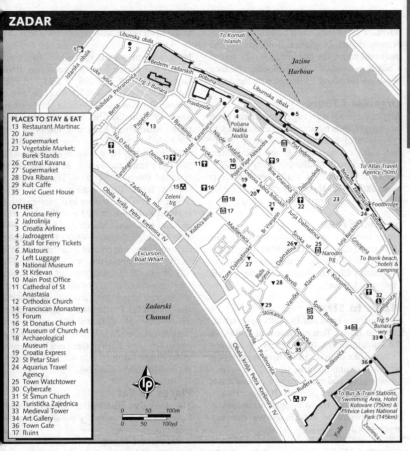

ZADAR

PLACES TO STAY & EAT
13 Restaurant Martinac
20 Jure
21 Supermarket
23 Vegetable Market;
   Burek Stands
26 Central Kavana
27 Supermarket
28 Dva Ribara
29 Kult Caffe
35 Jović Guest House

OTHER
1 Ancona Ferry
2 Jadrolinija
3 Croatia Airlines
4 Jadroagent
5 Stall for Ferry Tickets
6 Miatours
7 Left Luggage
8 National Museum
9 St Krševan
10 Main Post Office
11 Cathedral of St
   Anastasia
12 Orthodox Church
14 Franciscan Monastery
15 Forum
16 St Donatus Church
17 Museum of Church Art
18 Archaeological
   Museum
19 Croatia Express
22 St Petar Stari
24 Aquarius Travel
   Agency
25 Town Watchtower
30 Cybercafe
31 St Šimun Church
32 Turistička Zajednica
33 Medieval Tower
34 Art Gallery
36 Town Gate
37 Ruins

---

monastery opposite St Donatus, offers three floors of elaborate gold and silver reliquaries, religious paintings, icons and local lacework.

The 13th-century Romanesque **Cathedral of St Anastasia** *(Trg Svete Stoš; open only for Mass)* has some fine Venetian carvings in the 15th-century choir stalls. The **Franciscan Monastery** *(Zadarscog mira 1358; admission free; open 7.30am-noon & 4.30pm-6pm daily)* is the oldest Gothic church in Dalmatia (consecrated in 1280), with lovely interior Renaissance features and a large Romanesque cross in the treasury, behind the sacristy.

The most interesting museum is the **Archaeological Museum** *(Trg Opatice Čike 1; adult/student 10/5KN; open 9am-1pm & 6pm-8.30pm Mon-Fri, 9am-1pm Sat)*, across from St Donatus, with an extensive collection

of artefacts from the Neolithic period through the Roman occupation to the development of Croatian culture under the Byzantines. Some captions are in English and you are handed a leaflet in English when you buy your ticket.

Less interesting is the **National Museum** *(Poljana Pape Aleksandra III; admission 5KN; open 9am-2pm Mon-Fri)*, just inside the sea gate, featuring photos of Zadar from different periods, and old paintings and engravings of many coastal cities. The same admission ticket will get you into the **art gallery** *(Smiljanića; open 9am-noon & 5pm-8pm Mon-Fri, 9am-1pm Sat)*. Notable churches include **St Šimun Church** *(Trg Šime Budinica; open 8am-noon & 6pm-8pm daily June-Sept)*, with a 14th-century gold chest, and **St Petar Stari** with Roman-Byzantine frescoes.

There's a swimming area with diving boards, a small park and a café on the coastal promenade off Zvonimira. Bordered by pine trees and parks, the promenade takes you to a beach in front of Hotel Kolovare and then winds on for about a kilometre up the coast.

Organised Tours
Any of the many travel agencies around town can supply information on tourist cruises to the beautiful Kornati Islands, river-rafting and. half-day excursions to the Krka waterfalls. Check with **Miatours** (☎/fax 212 788; e miatrade@zd.tel.hr; Vrata Sveti Krševana) or **Aquarius Travel Agency** (☎/fax 212 919; e juresko@zd.tel.hr; Nova Vrata bb).

Special Events
Major annual events include the town fair (July and August), the Dalmatian Song Festival (July and August), the musical evenings in St Donatus Church (August) and the Choral Festival (October).

Places to Stay
Most visitors head out to the 'tourist settlement' at Borik, 3km northwest of Zadar, on the Puntamika bus (6KN, every 20 minutes from the bus station). Here there are hotels, a hostel, a camping ground and numerous 'sobe' signs; you can arrange a private room through an agency in town. If you arrive in the low season, try to arrange accommodation in advance, as some hotels and camping grounds will be closed.

Camping The huge autocamp **Zaton** (☎ 280 280; camp sites per person/tent & car 68/60KN; open May-Sept) is 16km northwest of Zadar on a sandy beach. There are 12 buses marked Zaton that leave daily from the bus station. Nearer to Zadar is **Autocamp Borik** (☎ 332 074; camp sites per person/tent/car 30/18/26KN), which is only steps away from Borik beach.

Hostels The Borik Youth Hostel (☎ 331 145, fax 331 190; Obala Kneza Trpimira 76; B&B/half-board 90/155KN) is near the beach at Borik.

Private Rooms Agencies that arrange private accommodation include Miatours and Aquarius Travel Agency (see under Organised Tours earlier in this section). Expect to pay about 140KN per person for accommodation in the town centre with private bathroom.

Hotels If you want to stay in the town, there is only one choice but it's a good one. **Jovic Guest House** (☎ 214 098, ☎ 098 330 958, Šime Ljubića 4a; rooms 150KN per person) is a new 12-room guesthouse in the heart of town with smallish but cool and attractive rooms with private bathroom. The price does not include breakfast but there are plenty of cafés around to have your morning meal. If you can't reach the owner, the rooms can be reserved through Aquarius Travel Agency (see Organised Tours, earlier).

Located right next door to the train station is **Hotel Kolovare** (☎ 203 200, fax 203 300, e hotel-kolovare-zadar@zd.tel.hr; Bože Peričića 14; singles/doubles 487/735KN), a more elaborate, but impersonal establishment. On Borik, **Hotel Mediteran** (☎ 337 500, fax 337 528; e info@hotelmediteran-zd.hr; M Gupca 19; singles/doubles 320/416KN) has comfortable rooms; dearer ones have air-con. You can also try **Hotel Puntamika** (singles/doubles 350/460KN), **Hotel Donat** or **Hotel Barbara** (singles/doubles 285/375KN), all in the Borik tourist complex. Each of these can be reserved at the **Hoteli Borik** (☎ 206 400, fax 332 065; e prodaja@hoteliborik.hr).

Places to Eat
The eatery **Dva Ribara** (Blaža Jurjeva 1; mains from 35KN) is justifiably popular with the local crowd.

Restaurant Martinac (Papavije 7; mains from 45KN) has a secluded backyard terrace behind the restaurant that provides a relaxed ambience to sample delicious risotto and fish.

Jure (Knezova Šubića Bribirskih 11; mains from 25KN) is a self-service restaurant.

There's a **supermarket** (cnr Široka & Sabora) that keeps long hours and you'll find a number of **burek stands** around the vegetable market.

Entertainment
Central Kavana (Široka ul) is a spacious café and hang-out with live music on the weekend. **Kult Caffe** (Stomarica) draws a young crowd; listen to rap music indoors or relax on the large shady terrace outside. In summer the many cafés along Varoška and Klaića place their tables on the street; it's great for people-watching.

Getting There & Away

Air Zadar's airport, 12km east of the city, receives charter flights and Croatia Airlines flights from Zagreb (575KN) daily. A Croatia Airlines bus meets all flights and costs 25KN. A taxi into town costs around 150KN.

Bus & Train Zadar is on the coastal route that goes from Rijeka down to Split and Dubrovnik. There are four daily trains to Zagreb (131KN, 11 hours) that change at Knin, but the bus to Zagreb is quicker and passes by Plitvice Lakes National Park (three hours).

Croatia Express (see Information earlier) sells bus tickets to many German cities. See the introductory Getting There & Away section earlier in this chapter for more information.

Boat The Jadrolinija coastal ferry from Rijeka to Dubrovnik calls at Zadar twice weekly (138/168KN low/high season, six hours). It arrives around midnight.

For information on the boat connections to Italy see the Getting There & Away section at the beginning of this chapter and contact **Jadroagent** (☎ 211 447; ul Natka Nodila), just inside the city walls. **Jadrolinija** (☎ 254 800; Liburnska obala 7), on the harbour, has tickets for all local ferries, or you can buy ferry tickets from the Jadrolinija stall on Liburnska obala.

AROUND ZADAR

Plitvice Lakes
☎ 053

Plitvice Lakes National Park (admission Oct-May/June-Sept 70/90KN, students 40/55KN) lies midway between Zagreb and Zadar. The 19.5 hectares of wooded hills enclose 16 turquoise lakes, which are connected by a series of waterfalls and cascades. The mineral-rich waters carve new paths through the rock, depositing tufa in continually changing formations. Wooden footbridges follow the lakes and streams over, under and across the rumbling water for an exhilaratingly damp 18km. Swimming is not allowed. Your park admission is valid for the entire stay and also includes the boats and buses you need to use to see the lakes. There is accommodation on the site, as well as private accommodation nearby. Check options with the Plitvice Lakes National Park information office in Zagreb (see Information in the Zagreb section earlier in this chapter).

Getting There & Away All buses from Zadar to Zagreb stop at Plitvice (three hours). It is possible to visit Plitvice for the day on the way to or from the coast but be aware that buses will not pick up passengers at Plitvice if they are full. Luggage can be left at the **tourist information centre** (☎ 751 015; open 7am-8pm daily) at the first entrance to the park.

SPLIT
☎ 021 • pop 188,700

Split (Spalato in Italian), the largest Croatian city on the Adriatic coast, is the heart of Dalmatia and lies on the southern side of a high peninsula sheltered from the open sea by many islands. Ferries to these islands are constantly coming and going. Within the ancient walls of Diocletian's Palace in the centre of town rises the majestic cathedral surrounded by a tangle of marble streets containing shops and businesses.

The entire western end of the peninsula is a vast, wooded mountain park, while industry, shipyards, limestone quarries and the ugly commercial-military port are mercifully far enough away on the northern side of the peninsula. High coastal mountains set against the blue Adriatic provide a striking frame to the scene.

Split achieved fame when Roman emperor Diocletian (AD 245–313), who was noted for his persecution of the early Christians, had his retirement palace built here from 295 to 305. After his death the great stone palace continued to be used as a retreat by Roman rulers. When the neighbouring colony of Salona was abandoned in the 7th century, many of the Romanised inhabitants fled to Split and barricaded themselves behind the high palace walls, where their descendants continue to live to this day.

Since 1945, Split has grown into a major industrial city ringed with apartment-block housing of stupefying ugliness, but the remarkable Diocletian's Palace (which is a now World Heritage Site) makes a visit to the city worthwhile. Split would make a great base for day trips to the surrounding islands, but finding some reasonable accommodation is a major problem.

Orientation

The bus, train and ferry terminals are adjacent on the eastern side of the harbour, a short walk from the old town. Obala hrvatskog narodnog

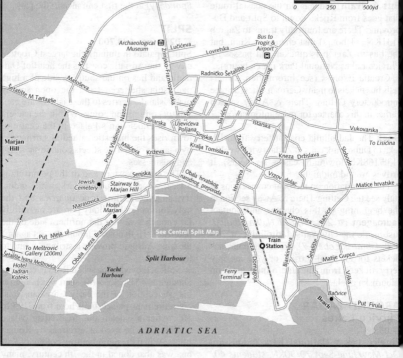

SPLIT

preporoda, the waterfront promenade, is your best central reference point in Split.

Information

Tourist Offices The **Turistička Zajednica** (☎/fax 342 606; ⓦ www.visitsplit.com; open 9am-8pm Mon-Fri, 9am-1pm Sat) on Peristyle has several brochures about Split but very little more. The **Turistička Biro** (☎/fax 342 142; Obala hrvatskog narodnog preporoda 12; ⓔ turist-biro-split@st.hinet.hr) arranges private accommodation and also sells guidebooks.

Money There are several ATMs around the bus and train station. The AmEx representative is **Atlas travel agency** (☎ 343 055; Nepotova 4). You can change money here or

at any travel agency. There's also an ATM next to the **Croatia Airlines office** (Obala hrvatskog narodnog preporoda 9).

Post & Communications Poste-restante mail can be collected from window No 7 at the **main post office** (Kralja Tomislava 9; open 7am-8pm Mon-Fri, 7am-3pm Sat). There's also a **telephone centre** (open 7am-9pm Mon-Sat) here. **Internet Games** (☎ 338 548; Obala Kneza Domagoja 3) caters to backpackers and offers an Internet connection.

Bookshop The **Algoritam** (Bajamontijeva 2) is a good English-language bookshop.

Left Luggage There's a **garderoba kiosk** (open 6am-10pm daily) at the bus station. The train station's **left-luggage office** (Domagoja 6; open 7am-9pm daily) is about 50m north of the station.

Things to See

The old town is a vast open-air museum and the new information signs at the important sights explain a great deal of Split's history. **Diocletian's Palace** (entrance: Obala hrvatskog narodnog preporoda 22), facing the harbour, is one of the most imposing Roman ruins in existence. It was built as a strong rectangular fortress, with walls measuring 215m from east to west and 181 m wide at the southernmost point and reinforced by square corner towers. The imperial residence, mausoleum and temples were south of the main street, connecting the east and west gates.

Enter through the central ground floor of the palace. On the left are the excavated **basement halls** (adult/concession 6/3KN; open 10am-6pm daily), which are empty but still impressive. Go through the passage to the **Peristyle**, a picturesque colonnaded square, with a neo-Romanesque cathedral tower rising above. The **vestibule**, an open dome above the ground-floor passageway at the southern end of the Peristyle, is overpowering. A lane off the Peristyle opposite the cathedral leads to the **Temple of Jupiter**, which is now a baptistry.

On the eastern side of the Peristyle is the **cathedral**, originally Diocletian's mausoleum. The only reminder of Diocletian in the cathedral is a sculpture of his head in a circular stone wreath below the dome directly above the baroque white-marble altar. The Romanesque wooden doors (1214) and stone pulpit are notable. Climb the tower for a small fee.

The west palace gate opens onto medieval Narodni trg, dominated by the 15th-century Venetian Gothic **old town hall**. Trg Braće Radića, between Narodni trg and the harbour, contains the surviving north tower of the 15th-century Venetian garrison castle, which once extended to the water's edge. The east palace gate leads into the market area.

In the Middle Ages the nobility and rich merchants built their residences within the old palace walls; the **Papalic Palace** (Papalićeva – also known as Žarkova – ul 5) is now the town museum. Go through the north palace gate to see the powerful **statue** (1929) by Ivan Meštrović of 10th-century Slavic religious leader Gregorius of Nin, who fought for the right to perform Mass in Croatian. Notice that

his big toe has been polished to a shine; it's said that touching it brings good luck.

Museums & Galleries Many of Split's museums have been closed for the last 10 years awaiting money for renovation.

The **town museum** (Papalićeva ul 5; adult/concession 10/5KN; open 9am-noon & 6pm-9pm Tues-Fri, 10am-noon Sat & Sun), east of Narodni trg, has a tidy collection of artefacts, paintings, furniture and clothes from Split; captions are in Croatian. The **Ethnographic Museum** (Narodni trg; adult/student 10/5KN; open 9am-noon & 6pm-9pm Tues-Fri, 9am-noon Sat-Mon) has a mildly interesting collection of photos of Old Split, traditional costumes and memorabilia of important citizens, but captions are in Croatian.

The **archaeological museum** (Zrinjsko-Frankopanska 25; adult/student 10/5KN; open 9am-noon & 5pm-8pm Tues-Fri, 9am-noon Sat & Sun), north of the town, is worth the walk for its exhibits devoted to burial sculpture and excavations at Salona.

The best art museum in Split is **Meštrović Gallery** (Šetalište Ivana Meštrovića 46; adult/student 15/10KN; open 10am-6pm Mon-Sat, 10am-2pm Sun). You'll see a comprehensive, well-arranged collection of works by Ivan Meštrović, Croatia's premier modern sculptor, who built the gallery as his home in 1931–39. Although Meštrović intended to retire here, he emigrated to the USA soon after WWII. Bus No 12 runs to the gallery from Trg Republike every 40 minutes.

From the Meštrović Gallery it's possible to hike straight up **Marjan Hill**. Go up ul Tonća Petrasova Marovića on the western side of the gallery and continue straight up the stairway to Put Meja ul. Turn left and walk west to Put Meja 76. The trail begins on the western side of this building. Marjan Hill offers trails through the forest, lookouts and old chapels.

Organised Tours

Atlas travel agency (see Information earlier) runs excursions to Krka waterfalls (225KN) and Zlatni Rat beach on the island of Brač (140KN), as well as other excursions.

Special Events

The Split Summer Festival (mid-July to mid-August) features open-air opera, ballet, drama and musical concerts. There's also the Feast of St Dujo (7 May), a flower show (May) and

CROATIA

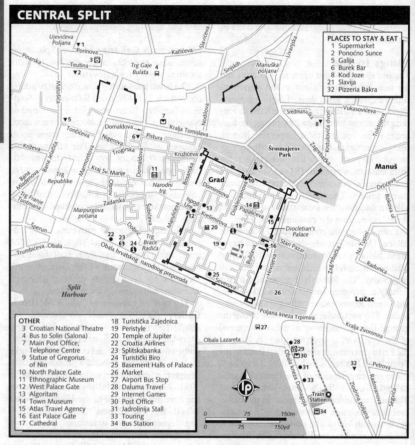

CENTRAL SPLIT

PLACES TO STAY & EAT
1 Supermarket
2 Ponoćno Sunce
5 Galija
6 Burek Bar
8 Kod Joze
21 Slavija
32 Pizzeria Bakra

OTHER
3 Croatian National Theatre
4 Bus to Solin (Salona)
7 Main Post Office; Telephone Centre
9 Statue of Gregorius of Nin
10 North Palace Gate
11 Ethnographic Museum
12 West Palace Gate
13 Algoritam
14 Town Museum
15 Atlas Travel Agency
16 East Palace Gate
17 Cathedral
18 Turistička Zajednica
19 Peristyle
20 Temple of Jupiter
22 Croatia Airlines
23 Splitskabanka
24 Turistički Biro
25 Basement Halls of Palace
26 Market
27 Airport Bus Stop
28 Daluma Travel
29 Internet Games
30 Post Office
31 Jadrolinija Stall
33 Touring
34 Bus Station

the Festival of Popular Music (end of June). The traditional February Carnival is from June to September and a variety of evening entertainment is presented in the old town.

Places to Stay

Budget travellers are out of luck in Split. There's only one one-star hotel in the town centre and the two-star hotels are a long bus or expensive taxi ride away. The closest camping ground is **Ribnjak** (☎ 864 430), 20km southeast of Split, near Omiš.

Turistička Biro (see Information) and **Daluma Travel** (☎/fax 338 439; e daluma-st@st.tel.hr; Obala Kneza Domagoja 1) have two-star singles/doubles for 145/265KN. **Slavija** (☎ 347 053, fax 591 558; Buvinova 3; singles/doubles 190/230KN, with private bathroom

230/280KN) has the cheapest rooms in town but they're still over-priced for the meagre amenities. Three-star **Hotel Marjan** (☎ 302 111, fax 302 930; Obala Kneza Branimira 8; singles/doubles 500/630KN) and the two-star **Hotel Jadran Koteks** (☎ 398 622, fax 398 586; e koteks-zvoncac@st.hinet.hr; Sustjepanski; singles/doubles 400/520KN), east of the town, offer rooms with TV and air-con but the Jadran Koteks has a swimming pool and is on the beach.

Places to Eat

The best pizza in town is at **Galija** (Tončićeva; pizzas from 26KN; open to 11pm daily), but **Pizzeria Bakra** (Radovanova 2; pizzas from 32KN), off ul Sv Petra Starog and just down from the vegetable market, is not bad either.

The vegetarian salad bar at **Ponoćno Sunce** *(Teutina 15)* is good value at 40KN. It also serves pasta and grilled meat. For some excellent Dalmatian specialities at a reasonable price, try **Kod Joze** *(Sredmanuška 4; mains from 40KN)*.

There's a spiffy **Burek Bar** *(Domaldova 13)*, near the main post office, and the vast **supermarket/delicatessen** *(Svačićeva 1)* has a wide selection of meat and cheese for sandwiches. The **vegetable market** has a wide array of fresh local produce.

Entertainment

In summer everyone starts the evening at one of the cafés along Obala hrvatskog narodnog preporoda and then heads towards the **Bačvice** complex on the beach. These former public baths offer restaurants, cafés, discos and venues for live rock and salsa. During winter, opera and ballet are presented at the **Croatian National Theatre** *(Trg Gaje Bulata; best seats about 60KN)*; tickets for the same night are usually available. Erected in 1891, the theatre was fully restored in 1979 in the original style; it's worth attending a performance for the architecture alone.

Getting There & Away

Air The country's national air carrier, **Croatia Airlines** *(☎ 362 997)*, operates flights between Zagreb and Split up to four times every day (627KN, one hour).

Bus Advance bus tickets with seat reservations are recommended. There are buses from the main bus station beside the harbour to:

destination	cost	duration	frequency
Dubrovnik	100KN	4½ hours	12 daily
Ljubljana	234KN	10 hours	1 daily
Međugorje	70KN	3 hours	4 daily
Mostar	74KN	4 hours	4 daily
Osijek	204KN	10½ hours	1 daily
Pula	250KN	10 hours	3 daily
Rijeka	104KN	8 hours	14 daily
Sarajevo	121KN	7 hours	11 daily
Zadar	78–88KN	3 hours	26 daily
Zagreb	130KN	8 hours	26 daily

Bus No 37 to Solin, Split airport and Trogir leaves from a local bus station on Domovinskog, 1km northeast of the city centre (see the Split map).

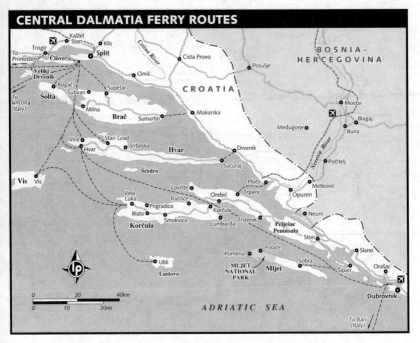

CENTRAL DALMATIA FERRY ROUTES

Touring (☎ 338 503; Obala Domagojeva 10), near the bus station, represents Deutsche Touring and sells tickets to German cities.

Train There are four trains daily that run between Split and Zagreb (90KN to 131KN, eight to nine hours depending on the service and the time of day), and Split and Šibenik (31KN, 90 minutes).

Boat In the large ferry terminal opposite the bus station, **Jadrolinija** (☎ 338 333) handles all car ferry services that depart from the docks around the ferry terminal. For passenger ferries, buy tickets at the Jadrolinija stall on Obala Kneza Domagoja near the train station and the departure point for passenger ferries. **Jadroagent** (☎ 338 335), in the ferry terminal, represents Adriatica Navigazione for its connections between Split and Ancona (see Sea in the Getting There & Away section at the beginning of this chapter). There's also an **SMC agency** (☎ 338 292) in the terminal for tickets between Ancona and Split, Hvar and Vis, as well as **SNAV** (☎ 322 252) for a four-hour connection to Ancona, and other connections to Pescara, Giulianova and Vasto. For details on connections to/from Italy see the Getting There & Away section at the beginning of this chapter

Getting Around

The bus to Split airport (30KN) leaves from Obala Lazareta 3, about 90 minutes before flight times or you can take bus No 37 from the bus station on Domovinskog (9.50KN for a two-zone ticket).

A one-zone ticket costs 7KN for one trip in Central Split if you buy it from the driver but 11KN for two trips and 55KN for 10 trips if you buy it from a kiosk. There's a kiosk that also distributes bus maps at the city bus stop.

SOLIN (SALONA)

The ruins of the ancient city of Solin (known as Salona by the Romans), among the vineyards at the foot of mountains 5km northeast of Split, are the most interesting archaeological site in Croatia. Today surrounded by noisy highways and industry, Salona was the capital of the Roman province of Dalmatia from the time Julius Caesar elevated it to the status of colony. Salona held out against the barbarians and was only evacuated in AD 614 when the

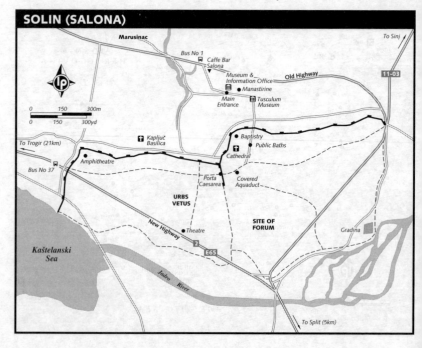

inhabitants fled to Split and neighbouring islands in the face of Avar and Slav attacks.

Things to See

A good place to begin your visit is at the main entrance near Caffe Bar Salona. There's a small **museum** (admission 10KN; open 8am-3pm Mon-Fri) at the entrance, which also provides a helpful map and some literature about the complex.

Manastirine, the fenced area behind the car park, was a burial place for early Christian martyrs before the legalisation of Christianity. Excavated remains of the cemetery and the 5th-century basilica are highlights, although .this area was outside the ancient city itself. Overlooking Manastirine is **Tusculum** with interesting sculptures embedded in the walls and in the garden.

The Manastirine-Tusculum complex is a part of an **archaeological reserve** (admission 10KN; open 7am-8pm daily). A path bordered by cypress trees runs south towards the northern **city wall** of Salona. Note the covered aqueduct along the inside base of the wall. The ruins in front of you as you stand on the wall were the Early Christian cult centre, which include the three-aisled, 5th-century **cathedral** and a small **baptistry** with inner columns. **Public baths** adjoin the cathedral on the east.

Southwest of the cathedral is the 1st-century east city gate, **Porta Caesarea**, later engulfed by the growth of Salona in all directions. Grooves in the stone road left by ancient chariots can still be seen at this gate.

Walk west along the city wall for about 500m to **Kapljuč Basilica** on the right, another martyrs' burial place. At the western end of Salona is the huge 2nd-century **amphitheatre**, destroyed in the 17th century by the Venetians to prevent it from being used as a refuge by Turkish raiders.

Getting There & Away

The ruins are easily accessible on Split city bus No 1 direct to Solin every half-hour from the city bus stop at Trg Gaje Bulata.

From the amphitheatre at Solin it's easy to continue to Trogir by catching a westbound bus No 37 from the nearby stop on the adjacent new highway. If, on the other hand, you want to return to Split, use the underpass to cross the highway and catch an eastbound bus No 37 (buy a four-zone ticket in Split if you plan to do this).

TROGIR
☎ 021 • pop 600

Trogir (formerly Trau), a lovely medieval town on the coast just 20km west of Split's city limits, is well worth a stop if you're coming south from Zadar. A day trip to Trogir from Split can easily be combined with a visit to the Roman ruins of Solin.

The old town of Trogir occupies a tiny island in the narrow channel lying between Čiovo Island and the mainland, and is just off the coastal highway. There are many sights on the 15-minute walk around this island.

Orientation & Information

The heart of the old town is a few minutes' walk from the bus station. After crossing the small bridge near the station, go through the north gate. Trogir's finest sights are around Narodni trg to the southeast.

A private tourist office, **Čipiko Tourist Office** (☎ 881 554; open 9am-12.30pm & 2.30pm-5pm Mon-Fri Sept-June, 9am-8pm Mon-Sat July & Aug) opposite the cathedral, sells a map of the area and arranges private accommodation. There's no left-luggage office in Trogir bus station, so you may end up toting your bags around town.

Things to See

The glory of the three-nave Venetian **Cathedral of St Lovro** (Trg Ivana Pavla II; open 8am-noon year-round & 4pm-7pm daily during summer) is the Romanesque portal of Adam and Eve (1240) by Master Radovan, the earliest example of the nude in Dalmatian sculpture. Enter the building via an obscure back door to see the perfect Renaissance Chapel of St Ivan and the choir stalls, pulpit, ciborium and treasury. You can even climb the cathedral tower, if it's open, for a great view. Also located on the square is the renovated **Church of St John the Baptist** with a magnificent carved portal and an interior showcasing a Pietá by Nicola Firentinac.

Getting There & Away

In Split, bus No 37 leaves from the local bus station. If you're making a day trip to Trogir also buy your return ticket back to Split, as the ticket window at Trogir bus station is often closed. Drivers will also sell tickets if you're stuck. The city bus No 37 runs between Trogir and Split every 20 minutes throughout the day, with a short stop at Split airport en route.

There's also a ferry once a week between Trogir and Split.

Southbound buses from Zadar (130km) will drop you off in Trogir. Getting buses north can be more difficult, as they often arrive full from Split.

HVAR ISLAND
☎ 021 • pop 12,600

Called the 'Croatian Madeira', Hvar is said to receive more sunshine than anywhere else in the country – 2724 hours each year. Yet the island is luxuriantly green, with brilliant patches of lavender, rosemary and heather. The fine weather is so reliable that hotels give a discount on cloudy days and a free stay if you ever see snow.

Hvar Town

Medieval Hvar lies between protective pine-covered slopes and the azure Adriatic, its Gothic palaces hidden among narrow backstreets below the 13th-century city walls. A long seaside promenade dotted with small, rocky beaches stretches from either end of Hvar's welcoming harbour. The traffic-free marble streets of Hvar have an air of Venice, and it was under Venetian rule that Hvar's citizens developed the fine stone-carving skills evident in a profusion of beautifully ornamented buildings.

Orientation & Information The town centre is Trg Sv Stjepana, 100m west of the bus station. Passenger ferries tie up on Riva, the eastern quay running south of Trg Sv Stjepana. Travel agencies, shops and banks are spread along the harbour and there is no lack of ATMs on the island.

The **tourist office** (☎/fax 742 977, 741 059; e tzg-hvar@st.tel.hr, w www.hvar.hr; open 8am-noon & 4pm-10pm daily, mornings only Oct-May) is located in the arsenal building on the corner of Trg Sv Stjepana. The travel agencies **Mengola Travel** (☎/fax 742 099; e mengola-hvar@st.tel.hr), on the western side of the harbour, and **Pelegrini** (☎/fax 742 250), on Riva, are generally more informative. There's a **left-luggage office** (open 7am-midnight daily) in the bathroom next to the bus station and Internet access at the hotel Slavija for 15KN an hour (for details see Places to Stay later in this section).

Atlas travel agency (☎ 741 670) is on the western side of the harbour. Public telephones are in the **post office** (open 7am-8pm Mon-Fri, 7am-3pm Sat) on Riva.

Things to See & Do The full flavour of medieval Hvar is best savoured on the backstreets of the old town. At each end of Hvar is a monastery with a prominent tower. The Domininican **Church of St Marko** at the head of the bay was largely destroyed by Turks in the 16th century but you can visit the local **archaeological museum** (admission 10KN; open 10am-noon daily) in the ruins. If it is closed you'll still get a good view of the ruins from the road just above, which leads up to a stone cross on a hill top offering a picture-postcard view of Hvar.

At the southeastern end of Hvar you'll find the 15th-century Renaissance **Franciscan monastery** (open 10am-noon & 5pm-7pm daily July & Aug, plus Christmas week & Holy Week), with a wonderful collection of Venetian paintings in the church and adjacent **museum** (admission 10KN; open 10am-noon & 5pm-7pm Mon-Sat), including The Last Supper by Matteo Ingoli.

Smack in the middle of Hvar is the imposing Gothic **arsenal**, its great arch visible from afar. The local commune's war galley was once kept here. Upstairs off the arsenal terrace is Hvar's prize, the first **municipal theatre** (admission 10KN; open 10am-noon & 5pm-7pm daily) in Europe (1612), rebuilt in the 19th century. Hours can vary and you enter through the adjoining **Gallery of Contemporary Croatian Art** (Arsenal; admission 10KN; open 10am-noon & 7pm-11pm July & Aug, plus Christmas week & Holy Week, 10am-noon low season).

On the hill high above Hvar town is a **Venetian fortress** (1551) and it's worth the climb for the sweeping panoramic views. The fort was built to defend Hvar from the Turks, who sacked the town in 1539 and 1571.

There is a small town beach next to the Franciscan Monastery but the best beach is in front of the Hotel Amphora, around the western corner of the cove. Most people take a launch to the offshore islands that include the naturist islands of Jerolim and Stipanska and lovely Palmižana; the cost is 20KN to 30KN.

In front of the Hotel Amphora, **Diving Centar Jurgovan** (☎ 742 490; w www.jurgovan.com) is a large operation that offers a certification course, dives (€34.15 with equipment) and all sorts of water sports (banana boating, snorkelling, water-skiing), as well as hotel packages. **Dinko Petrić** (☎ 741 792), in front of Hotel Bodul, is a smaller operator that offers day-long dive trips including lunch for about 220KN.

Places to Stay Accommodation in Hvar is extremely tight in July and August. A reservation is highly recommended.

The closest camping ground is **Mala Milna** (☎ 745 027), 2km southeast of town. For private accommodation, try Mengola Travel or Pelegrini. Expect to pay from 160/262KN per single/double with private bathroom in the town centre.

Jagoda & Ante Bracanović Guesthouse (☎ 741 416, 091 520 3796; e virgilye@ yahoo.com; Poviše Škole; singles/doubles 100/190KN) is a friendly place that offers six spacious rooms – each with a private bathroom, balcony and kitchen access – it's close to the town centre and is open all year.

About 1km southwest of the town centre is the two-star **Hotel Croatia** (☎ 742 707, fax 742 400; e croatia-hvar@st.tel.hr; singles/ doubles 290/510KN) that has 36 attractive and newly renovated rooms with telephones; the slightly more expensive rooms have balconies. The hotel is surrounded by a pine grove and has easy access to a small cove. Half-board is also available.

In town, there's the **Slavija** (☎ 741 820, fax 741 147; Riva; singles/doubles 444/664KN) right on the harbour and the century-old **Hotel Palace** (☎ 741 966, fax 742 420; singles/ doubles 544/878KN). One hotel or the other is open all year and the prices drop 50% during the low season. Reservations for both are handled by **Sunčani Hvar** (☎ 741 026, fax 742 014; w www.suncanihvar.hr), which also handles other hotels in town. The tourist office can also make hotel reservations.

Places to Eat Pizzerias along the harbour offer the most predictable but least expensive eating. **Bounty** (☎ 742 565; mains from 60KN), next to Mengola Travel Agency, is the cheapest of the options, but it's worthwhile to head up the stairs from the northern side of Trg Sv Stjepana to **Macondo** (☎ 741 851; mains from 50KN) or farther east to the **Paradise Garden** (☎ 741 310; mains from 60KN) up the stairs on the northern side of the cathedral, where dining is outdoors on an enclosed patio.

The **grocery store** (Trg Sv Stjepana) is a viable restaurant alternative and there's a morning **market** next to the bus station.

Getting There & Away The Jadrolinija ferries between Rijeka and Dubrovnik stop in Stari Grad before continuing to Korčula. The **Jadrolinija agency** (☎ 741 132) beside the landing sells tickets.

Car ferries from Split call at Stari Grad (32KN, one hour) three times daily (five daily in July and August) and there's an afternoon passenger boat from Split to Hvar town (23KN) that goes on to Vela Luka on Korčula Island (22KN, one hour). See the introductory Getting There & Away section of this chapter for information on international connections. Buses meet all ferries that dock at Stari Grad in July and August, but if you come in winter it's best to check first with one of the travel agencies to make sure the bus is running.

It's possible to visit Hvar on a (hectic) day trip from Split by catching the morning Jadrolinija ferry to Stari Grad, a bus to Hvar town, then the last ferry from Stari Grad directly back to Split.

KORČULA ISLAND
☎ 020 • pop 16,200

Korčula is the largest island in an archipelago of 48 islets. Rich in vineyards and olive trees, the island was named Korkyra Melaina (Black Korčula) by the original Greek settlers because of its dense woods and plant life. The southern coast is dotted with quiet coves and small beaches linked to the interior by winding, scenic roads.

Korčula Town

The town of Korčula (Curzola in Italian), at the northeastern tip of the island, hugs a small, hilly peninsula jutting into the Adriatic Sea. With its round, defensive towers and compact cluster of red-roofed houses, Korčula is a typical medieval Dalmatian town. Korčula Island was controlled by Venice from the 14th to the 18th centuries, as is evident from the Venetian coats of arms adorning the official buildings. The gated, walled old town is criss-crossed by narrow stone streets designed to protect its inhabitants from the winds swirling around the peninsula. If you didn't plan a stop in Korčula, one look at this unique town from the Jadrolinija ferry will make you regret it.

Orientation The big Jadrolinija car ferry drops you off either in the west harbour next to the Hotel Korčula or the east harbour next to Marko Polo Tours. The old town lies between the two harbours. The large hotels and main beach lie south of the east harbour and the residential neighbourhood Sveti Nikola (with a smaller beach) is southwest of the west harbour.

Information Korčula Turistička Agencija (☎ 711 067, fax 715 067; ⓦ www.korcula.net) is a good source of information on the west harbour as you enter the old town and the website gives a good range of accommodation options. **Atlas travel agency** (☎ 711 231) is the local AmEx representative and there's a **Jadrolinija office** (☎ 715 410) about 25m up from the west harbour.

The **post office** (with public telephones) is rather hidden next to the stairway up to the old town. There's Internet access at **Tino's Internet** (Ul Tri Sulara) or Tino's other outlet at the **ACI Marina**, both of which are open long hours.

There are ATMs in town at Splitska Banka and Dubrovačka Banka. You can change money there, at the post office or any of the travel agencies. There's no left-luggage office at the bus station.

Things to See Other than following the circuit of the former city walls or walking along the shore, sightseeing in Korčula centres on Cathedral Square. The Gothic **Cathedral of St Mark** features two paintings by Tintoretto (*Three Saints* on the altar and *Annunciation* to one side).

The **treasury** (☎ 711 049; Trg Sv Marka Statuta; admission 10KN; open 9am-7pm daily June-Aug) in the 14th-century Abbey Palace next to the cathedral is worth a look; even better is the **Town Museum** (☎ 711 420; Trg Sv Marka Statuta; admission 10KN) in the 15th-century Gabriellis Palace opposite. The exhibits of Greek pottery, Roman ceramics and home furnishings have English captions. It's said that Marco Polo was born in Korčula in 1254; you can climb the **tower** (admission 5KN) of what is believed to have been his house.

There's also an **Icon Museum** (Trg Svih Svetih; admission 8KN; open 10am-1pm Mon-Sat year-round) in the old town. It isn't much of a museum, but visitors are let into the

beautiful old **Church of All Saints**. Museums keep longer hours in the summer.

In the high summer season, water taxis at the east harbour collect passengers to visit various points on the island, as well as **Badija Island**, which features a 15th-century Franciscan monastery (now a dormitory), as well as Orebić and the nearby village of Lumbarda, which both have sandy beaches.

Organised Tours Both Atlas travel agency (for contact details see Information earlier) and **Marko Polo Tours** (☎ 715 400, fax 715 800; ⓔ marko-polo-tours@du.tel.hr) offer an Island Tour by boat (185KN), a tour to Mljet Island (170KN) or a half-day boat trip around the surrounding islands (100KN).

Places to Stay Korčula offers a range of accommodation, although prices are high in July and August. **Autocamp Kalac** (☎ 711 182, fax 711 146) is behind Hotel Bon Repos in a dense pine grove near the beach. Turistička Agencija and Marko Polo Tours arrange private rooms, charging 155/295KN per single/double with private bathroom and apartments starting at 335KN.

You may get a better deal from guesthouses, which are less likely to insist on a 30% surcharge for short stays. Try **Tarle** (☎ 711 712, fax 711 243; ⓔ croatia-osiguranje1@du.tel.hr; Stalište Frana Kršinića; doubles with/without kitchen 200/170KN, apartments 440KN) next to Hotel Marko Polo about 500m southeast of the bus station, which has a pretty enclosed garden and rooms with balconies. Air-con is planned.

Closer to the old town is the residential neighbourhood of Sveti Nikola, about 100m west of the bus station. Here you'll find the **Depolo** (☎/fax 711 621; ⓔ tereza.depolo@du.hinet.hr; doubles with/without sea view 200/160KN), which has spiffy rooms, some with air-con. Other guesthouses nearby for about the same price include **Peručić** (☎/fax 711 458; ⓔ tonci.perucic@du.hinet.hr) with great balconies and the homy **Ojdanić** (☎/fax 711 708; ⓔ roko-taxi@du.hinet.hr). Ratko Ojdanić also has a water taxi and much experience in fishing trips around the island.

The hotel scene is far from inspiring. The large **Hotel Park** (☎ 726 004, fax 711 746; ⓔ htp-korcula@du.tel.hr; singles/doubles 425/525KN) is the cheapest and can put you in touch with the four other large hotels.

Places to Eat Just around the corner from Marco Polo's house **Adio Mare** *(mains about 80KN)* is a reliable choice for fresh fish and has a charming maritime decor. **Marco Polo** *(mains from 35KN)* does a good job with its Italian-style dishes and is open year-round. **Gradski Podrum** *(mains from 65KN)* serves up local specialities, such as fish Korčula style – boiled with potatoes and topped with tomato sauce. There's a **supermarket** next to Marko Polo Tours.

Entertainment Between May and September there's **moreška sword dancing** *(tickets 50KN; 9pm Thur)* by the old town gate, more often during July and August. The clash of swords and the graceful movements of the dancers/fighters make an exciting show. Atlas, the Turistička Agencija or Marko Polo Tours sell tickets.

Getting There & Away Transport connections to Korčula are good. There's one bus every day to Dubrovnik and Zagreb (209KN, 12 hours) and one a week to Sarajevo (145KN, eight hours).

Boat There's a regular afternoon car ferry between Split and Vela Luka (35KN, three hours) on the island's western end that stops at Hvar most days. Six daily buses link Korčula town to Vela Luka (24KN, one hour) but services from Vela Luka are reduced on the weekend.

From Orebić, look for the passenger launch (10KN, 15 minutes, at least four times daily year-round), which will drop you off near Hotel Korčula right below the old town's towers. There's also a car ferry to Dominče (7KN, 15 minutes) which stops near the hotel Bon Repos where you can pick up the bus from Lumbarda or take a water taxi to town (6KN). For international connections see the Getting There & Away section at the beginning of this chapter.

OREBIĆ
Orebić, on the southern coast of the Pelješac Peninsula between Korčula and Ploče, offers better beaches than those found at Korčula, 2.5km across the water. The easy access by ferry from Korčula makes it the perfect place to go for the day. The best beach in Orebić is Trstenica cove, a 15-minute walk east along the shore from the port.

Getting There & Away
In Orebić the ferry terminal and the bus station are adjacent to each other. Korčula buses to Dubrovnik, Zagreb and Sarajevo stop at Orebić. See the Korčula section for additional bus and ferry information.

MLJET ISLAND
☎ 020 • pop 1111
Created in 1960, **Mljet National Park** occupies the western third of the green island of Mljet (Meleda in Italian), between Korčula and Dubrovnik. The park is centred around two saltwater lakes surrounded by pine-clad slopes. Most people visit the island on day trips from Korčula or Dubrovnik but it is possible to get here by the regular ferry from Dubrovnik, stay a few days and go hiking, cycling and boating.

Orientation
Tour boats and the Atlant passenger boats arrive at Pomena wharf at Mljet's western end, where a good map of the island is posted. Jadrolinija ferries arrive at Sobra on the eastern end and they are met by a local bus for the 1½-hour ride to Pomena. The admission price for the national park is 55/35KN per adult/concession during July and August, 38.50/24.50KN from September to June but there is no park admission price if you stay overnight on the island.

Things to See & Do
From Pomena it's a 15-minute walk to a jetty on **Veliko jezero**, the larger of the two lakes. Here you can board a boat (the price is included in the park admission fee) to a small lake islet and have lunch at a 12th-century **Benedictine monastery**, which is now a restaurant.

Those who don't want to spend the rest of the afternoon swimming and sunbathing on the monastery island can catch an early boat back to the main island and spend a couple of hours walking along the lakeshore before taking the late-afternoon excursion boat back to Korčula or Dubrovnik. There's a small landing opposite the monastery where the boat operator drops off passengers upon request. It's not possible to walk right around the larger lake because there's no bridge over the channel that connects the lakes to the sea.

Mljet is good for cycling; the Odisej hotel rents bicycles (70KN per half-day).

Organised Tours

See Organised Tours in the Korčula and Dubrovnik sections for agencies offering excursions to Mljet. The tour lasts from 8.30am to 6pm and includes the park entry fee. The boat trip from Korčula to Pomena takes at least two hours, less by hydrofoil. From Dubrovnik takes longer. Lunch isn't included in the tour price.

Places to Stay

There's no camping permitted inside the national park but **Marina** (☎ 745 071; open June-Sept) is a small camping ground in Ropa, about 1km from the park. The Polače **tourist office** (☎ 744 086; **e** np-mljet@np-mljet.hr) arranges private accommodation at 200KN per double room in peak season but it is essential to make arrangements before arrival. Don't count on 'sobe' signs and in high season you'll have trouble renting for less than four nights.

The only hotel option available on the island is the upmarket **Odisej** (☎ 744 022, fax 744 042; **e** odisej@plavalaguna.hr; 294KN per person) in Pomena. There's a 50% reduction on the rates in the low season.

Getting There & Away

It's possible to make a quick visit to Mljet by a regular morning ferry (32KN, two hours) from Dubrovnik in July and August. The rest of the year, the ferry leaves Dubrovnik in mid-afternoon Monday to Saturday or Sunday evening. The ferry docks in Sobra where it is met by a bus. The big Jadrolinija coastal ferries also stop at Mljet twice a week in summer and once a week during the rest of the year.

Atlant Shipping & Travel Agency (☎ 419 044; Radića 26) in Dubrovnik runs a fast boat, the *Nona Anna*, daily from June to September (30KN, one hour 40 minutes) to Pomena and Polače. It leaves from Gruž harbour, Dubrovnik, at 8am and returns at 7pm, allowing Mljet to be visited on a day trip. Tickets can be bought at the agency or on board the boat.

DUBROVNIK

☎ 020 • pop 43,770

Lord Byron called it 'the pearl of the Adriatic'; Agatha Christie spent her second honeymoon there; George Bernard Shaw said it was 'paradise on earth'. Behind the stone curtain of Dubrovnik's walls lay marble-paved squares, steps and streets ornamented with numerous

DUBROVNIK

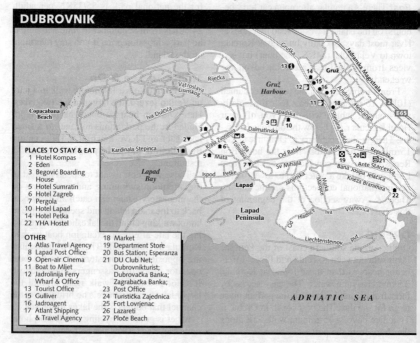

PLACES TO STAY & EAT
1 Hotel Kompas
2 Eden
3 Begović Boarding House
5 Hotel Sumratin
6 Hotel Zagreb
7 Pergola
10 Hotel Lapad
14 Hotel Petka
22 YHA Hostel

OTHER
4 Atlas Travel Agency
8 Lapad Post Office
9 Open-air Cinema
11 Boat to Mljet
12 Jadrolinija Ferry Wharf & Office
13 Tourist Office
15 Gulliver
16 Jadroagent
17 Atlant Shipping & Travel Agency
18 Market
19 Department Store
20 Bus Station; Esperanza
21 DU Club Net; Dubrovnikturist; Dubrovačka Banka; Zagrabačka Banka;
23 Post Office
24 Turistička Zajednica
25 Fort Lovrjenac
26 Lazareti
27 Ploče Beach

finely carved fountains and palaces. Churches, monasteries and museums recall an eventful history and a vibrant artistic tradition that is still flourishing. Beyond the walls stretch the crystal-blue waters of the southern Adriatic, sprinkled with tiny islands for the hedonistic.

Founded 1300 years ago by refugees from Epidaurus in Greece, medieval Dubrovnik (Ragusa until 1918) shook off Venetian control in the 14th century and became one of Venice's more important maritime rivals, trading with Egypt, Syria, Sicily, Spain, France and later Turkey. The double blow of an earthquake in 1667 and the opening of new trade routes to the east sent Ragusa into a slow decline, ending with Napoleon's conquest of the town in 1806.

The deliberate and militarily pointless shelling of Dubrovnik by the Yugoslav army in 1991 sent shockwaves through the international community but, when the smoke cleared in 1992, traumatised residents cleared the rubble and set about repairing the damage. With a substantial amount of international aid, the famous monuments were rebuilt and resculpted, the streets sealed and the clay roofs retiled. The reconstruction has been skilful but you will notice different shades of rose-tiled roofs as you walk around the city walls.

After a steep postwar decline, visitors are once again discovering Dubrovnik's magic. Tourism is the town's main (if not only) money-earner and its comeback has been striking, particularly in the warm summer months. Whatever the time of year the interlay of light and stone is enchanting. Don't miss it.

Orientation

The Jadrolinija ferry terminal and the bus station are a few hundred metres apart at Gruž, several kilometres northwest of the old town, which is closed to cars. The main street in the old town is Placa (also called Stradun). Most accommodation is on the leafy Lapad Peninsula, west of the bus station.

Information

Tourist Offices The main **Turistička Zajednica** (☎ 427 591, fax 426 253; e ured.pile@tzdubrovnik.hr; Starčevića 7; open 8am-8pm daily) is outside Pile Gate and there's another **tourist office** (☎ 417 983; Gruž) near the Jadrolinija dock. There's also a private **Tourist Information Centar** (☎ 323 350, fax 323 351; Placa 1) opposite the Franciscan monastery. Look for the booklet Dubrovnik Riviera Guide with useful information. **Jadrolinija** (☎ 418 000) sells ferry tickets.

Money You can change money at any travel agency or, if you arrive by a bus, at the post office in the department store near the bus station. There are ATMs southeast of the bus station at **Dubrovačka Banka** (Put Republike 9), for Visa and Plus, and at **Zagrabačka Banka** (Put Republike 5) for other cards. The same two banks also have ATMs on Gruž harbour near the Jadrolinija dock. There are also several ATMs on Placa.

Post & Communications The main post office (cnr Široka & Od Puća; open 8am-7pm Mon-Fri, 8am-2pm Sat) is in town and there's a branch at Ante Starčevića 2, a block from Pile Gate. There's another post office on the way to the Hotel Kompas, as well as one in Lapad. **DU Club Net** (☎ 356 894; Put Republike 7; open 8am-midnight daily) has Internet access and in town at the **Library** (cnr Od Puća & Miha Pracata; open 8am-8.30pm Mon-Fri, 8am-1pm Sat), which has cheaper access at 10/20KN per 30 minutes/one hour.

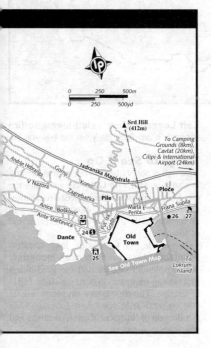

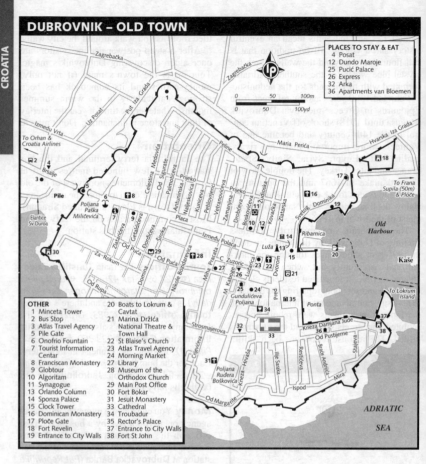

DUBROVNIK – OLD TOWN

PLACES TO STAY & EAT
4 Posat
12 Dundo Maroje
25 Pucić Palace
26 Express
32 Arka
36 Apartments van Bloemen

OTHER
1 Minceta Tower
2 Bus Stop
3 Atlas Travel Agency
4 Pile Gate
6 Onofrio Fountain
7 Tourist Information Centar
8 Franciscan Monastery
9 Globtour
10 Algoritam
11 Synagogue
13 Orlando Column
14 Sponza Palace
15 Clock Tower
16 Dominican Monastery
17 Ploče Gate
18 Fort Revelin
19 Entrance to City Walls
20 Boats to Lokrum & Cavtat
21 Marina Držlća National Theatre & Town Hall
22 St Blaise's Church
23 Atlas Travel Agency
24 Morning Market
27 Library
28 Museum of the Orthodox Church
29 Main Post Office
30 Fort Bokar
31 Jesuit Monastery
33 Cathedral
34 Troubadur
35 Rector's Palace
37 Entrance to City Walls
38 Fort St John

Travel Agencies The AmEx representative is **Atlas travel agency** (☎ 442 574; Sv Đurđa 1), outside Pile Gate next to the old town; it also holds mail. There are also other **Atlas offices** (☎ 418 001; Gruž harbour • ☎ 442 528; Lučarica 1). The travel agency closest to the bus station is **Dubrovnikturist** (☎ 356 959, fax 356 885; e dubrovnikturist@net.hr; Put Republike 7). **Globtour** (☎ 323 991; Placa) is in town and **Gulliver** is near Jadrolinija dock (☎ 313 300, fax 419 119; Radića 32).

Jadroagent (☎ 419 009, fax 419 029; Radića 32) handles tickets for most international boats from Croatia.

Bookshops You'll find a good selection of English-language books at **Algoritam** (Placa), including guidebooks.

Left Luggage There's a **left-luggage office** (open 5.30am-9pm daily) at the bus station.

Things to See & Do
You will probably begin your visit at the city bus stop outside **Pile Gate**. As you enter the city Dubrovnik's wonderful pedestrian promenade, Placa or Stradun, extends before you all the way to the clock tower at the other end of town.

Just inside Pile Gate is the huge **Onofrio Fountain** (1438) and **Franciscan monastery** with a splendid cloister and the third-oldest functioning pharmacy (operating since 1391) in Europe. The **monastery museum** (adult/concession 5/3KN; open 9am-4pm daily) has a collection of liturgical objects, paintings and pharmacy equipment.

In front of the clock tower at the eastern end of Placa, is the **Orlando Column** (1419) – a favourite meeting place. On opposite sides of Orlando are the 16th-century **Sponza Palace** (which was originally a Customs House then later a bank), which now houses the **State Archives** (☎ *321 032; admission free; open 8am-4pm Mon-Fri)*, and **St Blaise's Church**, a lovely Italian baroque building built in 1715 to replace an earlier church destroyed in the 1667 earthquake.

At the end of Pred Dvorom, the wide street beside St Blaise, is the baroque **Cathedral of the Assumption of the Virgin**. Between the two churches, the 1441 Gothic **Rector's Palace** *(adult/concession 15/10KN; open 9am-2pm Mon-Sat)* houses a museum with furnished rooms, baroque paintings and historical exhibits. The elected rector was not permitted to leave the building during his one-month term without permission of the senate. The narrow street opposite opens onto Gundulićeva Poljana, a bustling morning market. Up the stairs at the southern end of the square is the **Jesuit monastery** (1725).

As you proceed up Placa, make a detour to the **Museum of the Orthodox Church** *(adult/concession 10/5KN; open 9am-1pm Mon-Sat)* for a look at a fascination collection of 15th- to 19th-century icons.

By this time you'll be ready for a leisurely walk around the **city walls** *(adult/concession 15/5KN; open 9am-7pm daily)*, which has entrances just inside Pile Gate, across from the Dominican monastery and near Fort St John. Built between the 13th and 16th centuries and still intact, these powerful walls are the finest in the world and Dubrovnik's main claim to fame. They enclose the entire city in a protective veil over 2km long and up to 25m high, with two round towers, 14 square towers, two corner fortifications and a large fortress. The views over the town and sea are great – this walk could be the high point of your visit.

Whichever way you go, you'll notice the 14th-century **Dominican monastery** *(adult/concession 10/5KN; open 9am-6pm daily)* in the northeastern corner of the city, whose forbidding fortress-like exterior shelters a rich trove of paintings from Dubrovnik's finest 15th- and 16th-century artists.

Dubrovnik has many other sights, such as the unmarked **synagogue** *(ul Žudioska 5; admission free; open 10am-1pm Mon-Fri)*, near the clock tower, which is the second oldest

synagogue in Europe. The uppermost streets of the old town below the north and south walls are pleasant to wander along.

Beaches Ploče, the closest beach to the old city, is just beyond the 17th-century **Lazareti** (former quarantine station) outside Ploče Gate. There are also hotel beaches along the **Lapad Peninsula**, which you are able to use without a problem. The largest is outside the Hotel Kompas.

An even better option is to take the ferry that shuttles half-hourly in summer to lush **Lokrum Island** *(25KN return)*, a national park with a rocky nudist beach (marked FKK) and a botanical garden and the ruins of a medieval Benedictine monastery.

Organised Tours

Atlas offers full day tours to Mostar (240KN), Međugorje (220KN), the Elaphite Islands (210KN) and Mljet (320KN), among other destinations. Its tour to Montenegro (220KN) is a good alternative to taking the morning bus to Montenegro since the bus schedules make a day trip there impractical.

Special Events

The Dubrovnik Summer Festival from mid-July to mid-August is a major cultural event with over 100 performances at a number of different venues in the old city. The Feast of St Blaise (3 February) and carnival (February) are also celebrated.

Places to Stay

Camping The camping grounds that are closet to Dubrovnik are **Porto** (☎ *487 078; camp sites per person/tent/car 28/38/36KN)* and **Matkovica** (☎ *486 096; camp sites per person/tent/car 28/38/36KN)*, both 8km south of Dubrovnik near a quiet cove. Bus No 10 to Srebeno leaves you close to both.

Hostels The **YHA hostel** (☎ *423 241, fax 412 592; B&B/half-board 90/120KN)*, up Vinka Sagrestana from Bana Josipa Jelačića 17, is a party place. Full board can be arranged but the hostel is on one of the liveliest streets in Lapad, full of bars, cafés and pizzerias.

Private Rooms Agencies that organise private accommodation include Atlas, Globtour, Dubrovnikturist and Gulliver. Turistička Zajednica will put you in touch with proprietors but does not make reservations. In the high season, prices are about 93/76KN per person for rooms with private/shared shower with a 30% surcharge for single occupancy.

Hotels Staying in the old town is clearly desirable and there are a number of interesting options. The most personal and original accommodation to be found in Dubrovnik is **Apartments van Bloemen** (☎ 323 433, 91 33 24 106; e marc.van-bloemen@du.hinet.hr; Bandureva 1; apartments 680KN) with four beautifully decorated, air-conditioned apartments that sleep three. The **Pucić Palace** (☎/fax 324 111; e info@thepucicpalace .com; Od Puća 1; rooms from 1460KN) was about to open at the time of research and is clearly aiming to mine very deep pockets by offering the most deluxe digs in Croatia, which include the use of a private yacht.

Most hotels are in Lapad. Bus No 6 runs from the old town and the bus station to Lapad. From Jadrolinija wharf take bus No 7b. **Begović Boarding House** (☎ 435 191; Primorska 17; rooms per person 100KN, apartments per person 135KN), is a friendly place with three rooms with shared bathroom and three small apartments. There's a terrace out the back with a good view.

Hotel Sumratin (☎ 436 333, fax 436 006; singles/doubles 278/452KN), with a lift and parking, and **Hotel Zagreb** (☎ 436 146, fax 436 006; singles/doubles 307/510KN) are near each other in a tranquil part of Lapad, but Hotel Zagreb has a more traditional European flavour and its rooms also have TVs.

Renovated **Hotel Petka** (☎ 418 008, fax 418 058; Obala Stjepana Radića 38; singles/ doubles from 320/470KN), opposite the Jadrolinija ferry landing, has 104 nondescript rooms with air-con. **Hotel Lapad** (☎ 432 922, fax 424 782; e hotel-lapad@du.tel.hr; Lapadska Obala 37; singles/doubles 474/ 627KN) is a better bet with 200 rooms; the more expensive ones have air-con and satellite TV. The hotel is a solid, old limestone structure with simple but cheerful rooms and an outdoor swimming pool.

Places to Eat

The dining scene in the old town is not stupendous. Most places serve more or less the same thing at the same price.

The best dining in Lapad is at **Eden** (Kardinala Stepinca 54; mains 50-80KN). The leafy terrace upstairs is an agreeable spot to enjoy meat, pasta or fish dishes. **Pergola** (Tomislava 1; mains from 50KN) is another consistently satisfying place with an outdoor terrace and good seafood.

The spaghetti with shrimp and squid risotto at **Dundo Maroje** (Kovačka; mains from 45KN) are a cut above average. Vegetarians will like **Arka** (Uz Jezuite bb; mains from 40KN), which is Italian influenced but also has soybean-based dishes. **Express** (Kaboge 1; mains from 16KN) is a self-service restaurant that serves up freshly prepared food at unbeatable prices. **Posat** (Uz Posat 1; mains from 50KN) is the place to go for a romantic dinner on its outdoor terrace.

The cheapest way to fill up in Dubrovnik is to buy the makings of a picnic at a local supermarket, such as the one in the department store near the bus station.

Entertainment

Esperanza (☎ 357 144; Put Republike 30; open 10pm-4am daily), next to the bus station, is a popular disco and Jelačića, dubbed 'Bourbon' street, has a cluster of clubs on both sides of the youth hostel. The **open-air cinema** (Kumičića) in Lapad allows you to watch movies by starlight. **Troubadur** (☎ 412 154; Gundulićeva) is a local favourite for live music, which occasionally includes jazz.

Ask at the tourist office about concerts and folk dancing.

Getting There & Away

Air Daily flights to/from Zagreb are operated by Croatia Airlines. The fare is about 906KN one way in summer but less during the off-peak season.

There are also nonstop flights to Rome, and flights to Tel Aviv, London and Manchester from April to October.

Bus Buses from Dubrovnik include:

destination	cost	duration	frequency
Korčula	69KN	3 hours	1 daily
Mostar	77KN	3 hours	2 daily
Orebić	42KN	2½ hours	1 daily
Rijeka	295–309KN	12 hours	4 daily
Sarajevo	157KN	5 hours	1 daily
Split	72–111KN	4½ hours	14 daily
Zadar	131–185KN	8 hours	7 daily
Zagreb	165–199KN	11 hours	8 daily

There's a daily 11am bus to the Montenegrin border from where a Montenegrin bus takes you to Herceg-Novi (57KN, two hours) and on to Kotor (72KN, 2½ hours) and Bar (120KN, three hours). In the busy summer season and on the weekend, buses out of Dubrovnik can be crowded, so book a ticket well before the scheduled departure time.

Boat In addition to the Jadrolinija coastal ferry north to Hvar, Split, Zadar and Rijeka, there's a local ferry that leaves Dubrovnik for Sobra on Mljet Island (26KN to 32KN, 2½ hours, 2pm Monday to Saturday, 8.30pm Sunday) throughout the year. In summer there are two ferries a day. There are several ferries a day year-round to the outlying islands of Šipanska, Sugjuraj, Lopud and Koločep. Information on domestic ferries is available from **Jadrolinija** (☎ *418 000; Obala S Radića 40*). See also the Central Dalmatia Ferry Routes map in the Split Getting There & Away section earlier in this chapter.

For information on international connections see the Getting There & Away section at the beginning of this chapter.

Getting Around
Čilipi international airport is 24km southeast of Dubrovnik. The Croatia Airlines airport buses (25KN) leave from the main bus station 1½ hours before flight times. A taxi costs around 200KN.

Dubrovnik's buses run frequently and generally on time. The fare is 10KN if you buy from the driver but only 7KN if you buy a ticket at a kiosk.

AROUND DUBROVNIK
Cavtat is a small town that curves around an attractive harbour bordered by nice beaches. Although it does not have as many interesting sights as Dubrovnik, it does make a good alternative place to stay if Dubrovnik is fully booked out or the summer crowds become overwhelming. Don't miss the memorial chapel to the Račič family designed by Ivan Meštrović.

A day trip can be made from Dubrovnik to the resort town just to the southeast. Bus No 10 runs often to Cavtat from Dubrovnik's bus station and there are three daily boats during the summer (30KN).

Czech Republic

Deep in the heart of Europe lie the ancient lands of Bohemia and Moravia, which together make up the Czech Republic. It's one of Europe's most historic countries, full of fairytale castles, chateaux, manors and museums. The medieval cores of several dozen towns have been carefully preserved and there's so much to see that you could spend several months exploring.

The Czech Republic is doubly inviting for its cultured, generally friendly people and excellent facilities; the transportation network is both cheap and efficient. Although 90% of English-speaking visitors limit themselves to Prague, the clever few who escape the hordes and high prices in the capital soon experience just how helpful the Czech people can be. Almost everywhere outside Prague and Český Krumlov still feels off the beaten tourist track.

Facts about the Czech Republic

HISTORY

In antiquity the Bohemian Basin was inhabited by a Celtic tribe called the Boii, who gave their name to the land of Bohemia. Germanic tribes conquered the Celts in the 4th century AD, and between the 5th and 10th centuries the Western Slavs settled here. From 830 to 907, the Slavic tribes were united in the Great Moravian Empire. They adopted Christianity after the arrival in 863 of the Thessalonian missionaries Cyril and Methodius, who created the first Slavic (Cyrillic) alphabet.

In 995 the Czech lands were united under the native Přemysl dynasty as the principality of Bohemia. The Czech state became a kingdom in the 12th century and reached its peak under Přemysl Otakar II (1253–78). The rule of the Přemysls ended in 1306 and, in 1310, John of Luxembourg came to the Bohemian throne through marriage and annexed the kingdom to the German Empire. His son, Charles IV, became king of the Germans in 1346 and Holy Roman Emperor in 1355. Inclusion in this empire led to a blossoming of trade and culture. The capital, Prague, was made an archbishopric in 1344, and in 1348 Charles University was founded.

In 1415, the Protestant religious reformer Jan Hus, rector of Charles University, was burnt at the stake in Constance. His ideas inspired the religious and nationalist Hussite movement, which swept Bohemia betweeen 1419 and 1434.

After the defeat of the Hussites, the Jagiello dynasty ruled until 1526 when the Austrian Habsburg dynasty ascended the Bohemian throne. Thus Bohemia, strongly affected by the Protestant Reformation, was subject to the

CZECH REPUBLIC

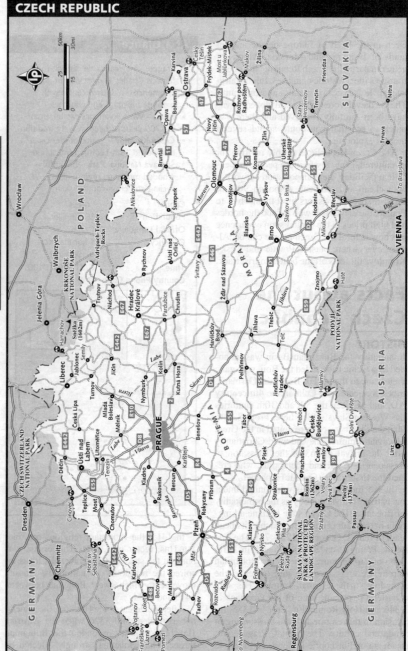

Catholic Counter-Reformation backed by the Habsburgs. The Thirty Years' War (1618–48), which devastated Central Europe, began in Prague, and the defeat of the uprising of the Czech Estates at the Battle of White Mountain in 1620 marked the start of a long period of forced re-Catholicisation, Germanisation and oppression of Czech language and culture.

The Czechs began to rediscover their linguistic and cultural roots at the start of the 19th century during the so-called National Revival. Despite defeat of the 1848 democratic revolution, the Industrial Revolution took firm hold here and a middle class emerged.

After WWI, during which Czech and Slovak nationalists strove for a common state, the Czechoslovak Republic was created on 28 October 1918. The first president was Tomáš Garrigue Masaryk. Three-quarters of the Austro-Hungarian empire's industrial power fell within Czechoslovakia, as did three million Germans, mostly in the border areas of Bohemia and Moravia (the *pohraniči*, known in German as the Sudetenland).

After annexing Austria in the Anschluss of March 1938, Hitler turned his attention to Czechoslovakia. Under the infamous Munich Pact of September 1938, Britain and France agreed not to oppose the annexation of the Sudetenland by Nazi Germany, and in March 1939 the Germans went onto occupy the rest of the country (calling it the Protectorate of Bohemia and Moravia). Slovakia became a fascist puppet state.

On 29 May 1942 the Nazi Reichs-Protector, Reinhard 'Hangman' Heydrich, was assassinated by Czechoslovak resistance fighters who had been parachuted in from London. In the reprisals, the Nazis razed the village of Lidice, 25km northwest of Prague, shot all the males and deported all the females and children to concentration camps. At the end of WWII, West Bohemia was liberated by US troops, and the rest of the country by the Soviet army.

Post-WWII

After the liberation of the regional capital of Košice (eastern Slovakia), a National Front was formed, which was covertly controlled by the Czechoslovak Communist Party and fully backed by the Soviets. This body laid out a blueprint for the takeover of the country. In the Constituent National Assembly elections of May 1946, the Communists won 36% of the vote and the Social Democrats 15.6%, and

together they formed a National Front majority. The Communist Party chairman Klement Gottwald became prime minister.

A power struggle developed between the communist and democratic forces. In early 1948, the Social Democrats withdrew from the coalition in protest against the antidemocratic activities of the communists. The result was the communist-staged and Soviet-backed 'February coup d'etat'. The new communist-led government set up the dictatorship of the proletariat and, in July, Gottwald also became the country's president.

The whole industrial sector was nationalised and the government's economic policies nearly bankrupted the country. The 1950s were years of harsh repression when thousands of noncommunists fled the country. Many people were imprisoned, and hundreds were executed or died in labour camps, often for little more than a belief in democracy or religion. A series of Stalinist purges was organised by the Communist Party, during which many people, including top members of the party itself, were executed.

In April 1968, the new first secretary of the Communist Party, Alexander Dubček, introduced liberalising reforms to create 'socialism with a human face' – referred to as the 'Prague Spring'. Censorship ended, political prisoners were released and decentralisation of the economy began. Dubček refused to bow to pressure from Moscow to withdraw the reforms, resulting in the occupation of Czechoslovakia by 200,000 Soviet and Warsaw Pact soldiers on the night of 20 August 1968, when Soviet tanks rumbled through the streets of Prague. The Czechs and Slovaks met the invaders with passive resistance.

Renewed dictatorship saw the expulsion of around 14,000 Communist Party functionaries and 500,000 party members lost their jobs. Many educated professionals were made street cleaners and manual labourers. Dissidents were routinely imprisoned.

In 1977 the trial of the rock group The Plastic People of the Universe inspired the formation of the human-rights group Charter 77. (The communists saw the musicians as a threat to the status quo, while others viewed the trial as part of a pervasive assault on human rights.) Made up of a small group of Prague intellectuals, including the playwright/philosopher Václav Havel, Charter 77 functioned as an underground opposition throughout the 1980s.

By 1989, Gorbachev's *perestroika* was sending shock waves through the region and the fall of the Berlin Wall on 9 November raised expectations of change in Czechoslovakia. On 17 November, an officially sanctioned student march in Prague in memory of students executed by the Nazis in 1939 was smashed by police. Daily demonstrations ensued, and protests widened, with a general strike on 27 November, culminating in the resignation of the Communist Party's Politburo. The 'Velvet Revolution' was over.

Civic Forum (Občanské Forum), an umbrella organisation of opponents of the regime formed in the wake of the 17 November violence, was led by Havel, Prague's best-known 'dissident' and ex-political prisoner. Havel took over as the country's interim president, by popular demand, and in the free elections of June 1990, Civic Forum and its counterpart in Slovakia, Society Against Violence, were successful. The Communist Party won 47 seats in the 300-seat federal parliament.

Velvet Divorce

With the strong central authority provided by the communists gone, old antagonisms between Slovakia and Prague re-emerged. The federal parliament tried to stabilise matters by approving a constitutional amendment in December 1990, which gave each of the Czech and Slovak Republics full federal status within the Czech and Slovak Federated Republic (ČSFR), as Czechoslovakia was now known. But these moves failed to satisfy Slovak nationalists. Meanwhile Civic Forum had split into two factions, the centrist Civic Movement, and the Civic Democratic Party (ODS). In Slovakia several separatist parties emerged.

The ODS instigated a purge of former communist officials and alleged secret-police informers in 1991, a process known as *lustrace*. However, the communists who had committed many crimes, including the torture and murder of many innocent people, have not been brought to trial.

The June 1992 elections sealed the fate of Czechoslovakia. Václav Klaus' ODS took 48 seats in the 150-seat federal parliament, while 24 seats went to the Movement for a Democratic Slovakia (HZDS), a left-leaning Slovak nationalist party led by Vladimír Mečiar.

The incompatibility of Klaus and Mečiar soon became apparent, with Klaus pushing for shock-therapy economic reform and Mečiar

for state intervention to save key industries in Slovakia. In August 1992, Klaus and Mečiar agreed that the Czechoslovak federation would cease to exist at midnight on 31 December 1992. The peaceful 'velvet divorce' was over.

In January 1993, the Czech parliament elected Václav Havel president for a five-year term, and re-elected him by a margin of one vote in 1998. Prime Minister Klaus staked his political future on the success of rapid economic reforms, but by 1996 the economy was slowing down. Among other major problems were corruption, an ineffective judiciary and a lack of openness in business, all contributing to hesitant foreign investment.

As the 21st century begins, the Czech Republic stands on the threshold of the EU, and in 2004 is expected to join, along with Poland, Hungary and Slovenia.

GEOGRAPHY

The Czech Republic is a landlocked country of 78,864 sq km squeezed between Germany, Austria, Slovakia and Poland. The Bohemian Massif forms the broad, rounded ranges of the Czech Republic with the Šumava Mountains along the Bavarian border, the Ore Mountains (Krušné hory) along the eastern German border and the Krakonos Mountains (Krkonoše) along the Polish border east of Liberec. The Czech Republic's highest peak, Sněžka (1602m), is in the Krkonoše. In between these ranges are rolling plains mixed with forests and farm land. The forests – mainly spruce, oak and beech – still cover one-third of the country. Dwarf pine is common near the tree line and above that (1400m) there is little but grasses, shrubs and lichens.

The Czech Republic has been called 'the roof of Europe' because no rivers or streams flow into the country. The three main rivers in the country – Morava, Vltava (Moldau) and Labe (Elbe) – all flow out into bordering Slovakia and Germany.

CLIMATE

The Czech climate is temperate, with cool and humid winters, warm summers and clearly defined spring and autumn seasons. Prague has average daily temperatures above 14°C from May to September, above 8°C in April and October, and below freezing point in December and January. In winter dense fog (or smog) can set in anywhere.

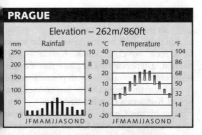

ECOLOGY & ENVIRONMENT

The forests of northern Bohemia and Moravia have been devastated by acid rain created by the burning of poor-quality brown coal at factories and thermal power stations. These industries spew sulphur dioxide, nitrogen dioxide and carbon monoxide into the atmosphere, creating one of Europe's most serious environmental disaster areas. The most affected region is the eastern Ore Mountains where the most trees are dead. In recent years sulphur dioxide levels in Prague have declined, while carbon monoxide pollution from cars and trucks has increased. There are two nuclear power-generating stations – the ageing Soviet reactor at Dukovany (between Znojmo and Brno), and the controversial Temelin reactor in South Bohemia, which came online in 2001 despite strong protest from Austria and environmental groups.

The most common types of wildlife in the mountains are wildcats, marmots, otters, marten and mink. Occasionally a bear makes an appearance in northeastern Moravia. In the woods and fields there are plenty of pheasants, partridges, deer, ducks and wild geese. Eagles, vultures, osprey, storks, bustards, grouse and lynx are rarer.

GOVERNMENT & POLITICS

The present constitution was passed by parliament in 1992. The country is a parliamentary democracy headed by President Havel who faces election by parliament every five years. Real power lies with the prime minister and the cabinet, and parliament can override the president's veto on most issues by a simple majority. There are two chambers in the parliament – the House of Representatives and the Senate – whose members are elected by Czech citizens every four and six years respectively.

The largest party is the left-of-centre Social Democrats (ČSSD) led by Vladimir Spidal, the current prime minister. Until 2002, the conservative opposition Civic Democratic Party (ODS) was led by Václav Klaus, prime minister from 1992 to 1997 and a pivotal character in economic reform; a poor performance in the June 2002 elections led to his decision not to stand in the 2003 presidential elections.

The Czech Communist Party of Bohemia & Moravia (KSČM) is one of the few communist parties left in the world that still adheres to Marxist-Stalinist doctrine; it has a solid core of mostly elderly followers.

The Social Democrats (ČSSD) remained the largest party at the June 2002 elections with an increased share of the vote (30.2% and 70 seats), led by its new leader and prime minister, Vladimir Spidl. Second was the right-wing Civic Democratic Party (ODS) with 24.5% and 58 seats. The Communist Party (KSČM) moved to third place (18.5% and 41 seats) and the Christian Democrat Coalition (Koalice; 14.3%, 31 seats) slipped to fourth. The turnout, however, was only 58%.

The traditional lands of the Czech Republic, Bohemia and Moravia, are divided into 14 administrative *kraje* (regions), consisting of Prague and nine regions in Bohemia, and four regions in Moravia. These are further subdivided into 76 *okresy* (districts).

ECONOMY

Bohemia and Moravia have specialised in light industry since the Industrial Revolution. Under communist rule, industry and agriculture were nationalised and heavy industry was introduced along Stalinist lines. Steel and machinery production are the main forms of heavy industry. Other important products include armaments, vehicles, cement, ceramics, plastics, cotton and beer.

Privatisation was carried out in three stages after the fall of communism. The first was the restitution of property to the original owners. Then, about 30,000 small retail outlets and service facilities were auctioned off. The third and most difficult stage of privatising 1500 medium- and large-sized companies is almost complete. Some companies were auctioned off and the majority were privatised by a voucher scheme – this, and other aspects of privatisation, have been dogged by corruption. In April 1993, the Prague stock market opened, and trading began in June of that year.

Agriculture is a small part of the Czech economy, employing about 2.9% of a workforce that is about one-third less productive than its EU counterparts. Most of the land has been returned to its previous owners or privatised, however many people formed their own cooperatives based on old government cooperatives. Major crops are sugar-beet, wheat, potatoes, corn, barley and hops, while cattle, pigs and chickens are the preferred livestock.

In 1998 the Czech economy, considered for years one of the best in the former Eastern Bloc, suffered a slump and has had budget deficits ever since. The unemployment rate stood at 9.5% in 2000, but had fallen to 8.8% by May 2002. Continuing problems include a drop in foreign investment, increasing public and government debt, and the lack of strong laws in the business sphere. The average monthly wage in May 2002 was approximately US$500 (16,219 Kč).

POPULATION & PEOPLE

The Czech Republic is fairly homogeneous; 95% of the people are Czech and 3% Slovak. A small Polish minority lives in the borderlands near Ostrava. After WWII three million Sudeten Germans were evicted from the country, and today only about 150,000 of this group remain.

The principal cities and their populations are: Prague (1,197,000), Brno (379,200), Ostrava (327,000), Plzeň (173,000) and Olomouc (106,000).

ARTS

Czech culture has a long and distinguished history. Charles University, the oldest in Central Europe, was founded in 1348, about the time that the Gothic architect Petr Parléř was directing the construction of St Vitus Cathedral, Karlův most (Charles Bridge) and other illustrious works.

In the early 17th century, the Thirty Years' War forced the educational reformer Jan Ámos Comenius (1592–1670) to flee Moravia. While in exile, Comenius (Komenský in Czech) produced a series of textbooks that were to be used throughout Europe for two centuries. *The Visible World in Pictures,* featuring woodcuts made at Nuremberg, was the forerunner of today's illustrated school book.

Literature

Another literary genius, Franz Kafka (1883–1924), wrote in German but was, nevertheless, a son of Prague. He was born and lived there most of his life, haunted by the city he both hated and needed. His novel *The Trial* (1925) gives an insight into his world.

After the 1968 Soviet invasion, the works of Czech novelist Milan Kundera were banned. *The Book of Laughter and Forgetting* combines eroticism with political satire, for which the communist government revoked Kundera's Czech citizenship.

One of the Czech Republic's foremost resident writers is Ivan Klíma, whose works were also banned from 1970 to 1989. Klíma's novels such as *Love and Garbage* (1986) tackle the human dimension behind the contradictions of contemporary Czech life.

Perhaps one of the best 20th-century Czech novelists is Bohumil Hrabal (1914–97; see Books in Facts for the Visitor), while by far the most brilliant plays are by the current president Václav Havel – among the most popular are *Audience* and *Largo Desolato.*

Music

During the 17th century, when Bohemia and Moravia came under Austrian domination and German was the official language, Czech culture survived in folk music. Moravian folk orchestras are built around the *cymbalum,* a copper-stringed dulcimer of Middle Eastern origin that stands on four legs and is played by striking the strings with two mallets.

Bohemia's pre-eminent baroque composer was Jan Dismas Zelenka (1679–1745) who spent some of his life in Dresden, where he was a composer to the Saxon court. The symbolism and subtle expression of Zelenka's last masses are unique expressions of his introverted, restrained character.

The works of the Czech Republic's foremost composers, Bedřich Smetana (1824–84) and Antonín Dvořák (1841–1904), express nostalgia, melancholy and joy. In his operas, Bedřich Smetana used popular songs displaying the innate peasant wisdom of the people to capture the nationalist sentiments of his time. His symphonic cycle *Má Vlast* (My Country) is a musical history of the country. Antonín Dvořák attracted world attention to Czech music through his use of native folk materials in works such as *Slavonic Dances* (1878).

Leoš Janáček (1854–1928) shared Dvořák's intense interest in folk music and created an original national style by combining the scales and melodies of folksongs with the inflections of the Czech language. One of his best known works is *Jenůfa* (1904).

Dance

Bohemia's greatest contribution to dance floors is the polka, a lively folk dance in which couples rapidly circle the floor in three-four time with three quick steps and a hop. Since its appearance in Paris in 1843, the polka has been popular worldwide. Smetana used it in his opera *The Bartered Bride* (1866). In some of Moravia's villages whirling couples dance the *vrtěná*, while the *hošije* and *verbuňk* are vigorous male solo dances.

SOCIETY & CONDUCT

The best way to see traditional Bohemian and Moravian folk customs, dress, song, dance, music and food is at any weekend folk festival held in villages around the country from spring to autumn (see Public Holidays & Special Events in the Facts for the Visitor section).

When it comes to attending classical music concerts, opera and traditional theatre, Czechs are quite conservative and dress formally. Foreign visitors are expected to dress the same. Contemporary dress is fine for other venues.

It is customary to say 'good day' (*dobrý den*) when entering a shop, café or quiet bar, and 'goodbye' (*na shledanou*) when leaving. If you are invited to a Czech home bring fresh flowers and when entering someone's home remember to remove your shoes, unless you're told not to bother. On public transport, young people readily give up their seats to the elderly, the sick, pregnant women or women carrying children.

RELIGION

Most Czechs are Catholic (40%), but church attendance is extremely low. Various Protestant sects makeup a small percentage of the population, while the Jewish community (1% of the population in 1918) today is only a few thousand. Religious tolerance is well established and the Catholic Church makes little attempt to involve itself in politics.

LANGUAGE

German is understood by many Czechs and is useful in most parts of the country, while in the capital you can get by with English. Under the communists everybody learned Russian at school but this has now been replaced by English.

Czech seems an outlandish language to native English-speakers, who must abandon linguistic habits to learn it. Its peculiarity is a lack of vowels, with many words containing nothing that we could identify as a vowel. One famous tongue twister goes *strč prst skrz krk* which means 'stick your finger through your neck' and is pronounced just as it's spelt!

An English-Czech phrasebook will prove invaluable, so consider Lonely Planet's *Czech phrasebook* or *Eastern Europe phrasebook*. Some useful Czech words that are frequently used in this chapter are: *most* (bridge), *nábřeží* (embankment), *nám* or *náměstí* (square), *nádraží* (station), *ostrov* (island), *třída* (avenue) and *ulice* (street). To open and close doors you will find the signs *sem* (pull) and *tam* (push). See the Language chapter at the back of the book for pronunciation guidelines and more useful words and phrases.

Facts for the Visitor

HIGHLIGHTS

The Czech Republic boasts many historic towns. The most authentic and picturesque include Prague, Litoměřice, Český Krumlov, Kutná Hora and Telč. There are magnificent castles at Karlštejn, Konopiště and Český Krumlov.

Some of the best museums are in Prague, where the Jewish Museum in the former Prague ghetto is easily the largest of its kind in Central Europe. Prague Castle is packed with art treasures, notably the collection of the National Gallery in the Šternberg Palace at the entrance of the castle. The Brewery Museum in Plzeň highlights one of the country's noblest contributions to humanity.

The Šumava National Park is a beautiful wooded mountain region great for hiking, cycling and cross-country skiing, while the Adršpach-Teplice Rocks have some of the country's most spectacular scenery.

SUGGESTED ITINERARIES

Depending on the length of your stay, you might want to see and do the following things in the Czech Republic:

Two days
Visit Prague
One week
Visit Prague, Český Krumlov, Litoměřice and Kutná Hora
Two weeks
Visit the places listed above, plus Adršpach-Teplice, Šumava and Telč

CZECH REPUBLIC

2002 Floods

In the summer of 2002 the Czech Republic, along with neighbouring Austria and Germany, suffered its worst floods in over a century. The country is facing an estimated clean-up bill of around €3 billion. Prague was severely affected with the famous Charles Bridge being threatened at one stage and the Jewish section of town badly damaged.

Visitors to Prague and the other affected regions may find some attractions limited by repair work into 2003. The former concentration camp at Terezín in North Bohemia also suffered severely, and may not be fully repaired until 2006. Check with tourist information offices for the latest situation.

PLANNING
When to Go
The weather is best in summer, but July and August as well as Christmas-New Year and Easter are very busy, so it's better to visit in May, June and September. Winter also has its charms. During the Prague Spring festival (in May), accommodation in Prague can be tight.

Maps
The Austrian publisher Freytag & Berndt publishes a good map of the Czech Republic. The best Czech road maps and city plans are the GeoClub series by SHOCart. Klub Cých Turistů produces excellent 1:50,000 hiking maps that cover the entire country.

TOURIST OFFICES
Local Tourist Offices
The municipal Prague Information Service (PIS) staff are very knowledgable about attractions, eateries and entertainment in the capital. There's also a network of municipal information centres (městské informační centrum/středisko) in all major tourist areas.

The travel agency Čedok, oriented towards the mid-range market, has offices around the country, which you can consult about exchanging money, accommodation, travel and sightseeing arrangements.

Within the Czech Republic there are several youth travel bureaus including CKM (Cestovní kancelář mládeže) in Prague. Former CKM offices in Plzeň, České Budějovice and Brno are now independently owned but still offer information on budget travel and ac-

commodation. GTS International is another agency that provides information on money-saving deals and also sells ISIC, ITIC, IYTC and Euro<26 cards.

Tourist Offices Abroad
The Czech Tourist Authority (ČCCR) offices abroad provide information about the whole of the Czech Republic, but do not book any hotels or transportation.

Canada (☎ 416-363 9928, fax 363 0239, ⓔ ctacanada@iprimus.ca) Czech Airlines Office, 401 Bay St, Suite 1510, Toronto, Ontario M5H 2Y4
France (☎ 01 53 73 00 32, fax 01 53 73 00 33, ⓔ bohmova@czech.cz) rue Bonaparte 19, 75006 Paris
Germany (☎/fax 030-204 4770, ⓔ tourinfo@czech-tourist.de) Karl Liebknecht Strasse 34, 10178 Berlin
UK (☎ 020-7291 9925, fax 7436 8300, ⓔ ctainfo@czechcentre.org.uk) 95 Great Portland St, London W1W 7NY
USA (☎ 212-288 0830, fax 288 0971, ⓔ travelczech@pop.net) 1109-1111 Madison Ave, New York, NY 10028

VISAS & DOCUMENTS
Everyone needs a passport valid until at least 90 days after your date of entry. Citizens of EU countries, Switzerland, the USA, Japan and New Zealand can stay for up to 90 days without a visa; for UK citizens the limit is 180 days. At the time of research, citizens of Australia, Canada and South Africa need a visa (even if you are only passing through by train or bus), which you should obtain in advance at a consulate in your own country. Visas are not available at border crossings or Prague's Ruzyně airport; you'll be refused entry if you need a visa and arrive without one.

Tourist visas valid for up to 90 days are readily available at Czech consulates for about US$24/88 for single/multiple entry. A five-day transit visa costs US$24/35 for single/double entry; it cannot be changed to a tourist visa upon arrival. You can use your visa at any time within six months of the date of issue.

Czech visa regulations change frequently, so check the latest situation on the Czech Ministry of Foreign Affairs website at ⓦ www.mzv.cz. If your country is *not* on the Visa Waiver list, then you *will* need a visa.

Arriving visitors are occasionally asked to show that they have the equivalent of at least 1100 Kč (US$30) for every day that they are intending to stay, or a credit card. You may also be asked to produce evidence of travel health insurance.

All foreign visitors must register with the Czech immigration police within three days of arrival; this is strictly enforced with a fine of 400 Kč. Hotels, hostels and camping grounds will automatically register you when you check in; otherwise – if you are staying with friends, for example – you will need to register yourself at a foreigners police office.

You can extend your stay in the country only once, for a fee of 1000 Kč, at foreigners police stations inside the Czech Republic.

EMBASSIES & CONSULATES
Czech Embassies & Consulates
The Czech Republic has diplomatic representation in the following countries:

Australia *Consulate:* (☎ 02-9371 0860) 169 Military Rd, Dover Heights, Sydney NSW 2030
Canada (☎ 613-562 3875) 251 Cooper St, Ottawa, Ontario K2P 0G2
France (☎ 01 40 65 13 01) 15 ave Charles Floquet, 75343 Paris Cedex 07
Germany (☎ 030-22 63 80) Wilhelmstrasse 44, 10117 Berlin
Ireland (☎ 031-668 1135) 57 Northumberland Rd, Ballsbridge, Dublin 4
Netherlands (☎ 070-346 9712) Paleisstraat 4, 2514 JA The Hague
New Zealand Contact the Czech consulate in Sydney
UK (☎ 020-7243 1115) 26 Kensington Palace Gardens, London W8 4QY
USA (☎ 202-274 9100) 3900 Spring of Freedom St NW, Washington, DC 20008

Embassies & Consulates in the Czech Republic
Most embassies and consulates are open at least 9am to noon Monday to Friday.

Australia (☎ 251 01 83 50) Klimentská 10, Prague 1 – this is an honorary consulate for emergency help only (eg, a stolen passport); otherwise contact the Australian embassy in Vienna
Austria (☎ 257 09 05 11) Viktora Huga 10, Prague 5
Canada (☎ 272 10 18 00) Mickiewiczova 6, Prague 6
France (☎ 251 17 17 11) Velkopřerovské nám 2, Prague 2
Germany (☎ 257 11 31 11) Vlašská 19, Prague 1
Ireland (☎ 257 53 00 61) Tržiště 13, Prague 1
Netherlands (☎ 224 31 21 90) Gotthardská 6/27, Prague 6

New Zealand (☎ 222 51 46 72) Dykova 19, Prague 10 – this is an honorary consulate that provides assistance (eg, a stolen passport) by appointment only; otherwise the nearest NZ embassy is in Berlin
Poland (☎ 224 22 87 22) Václavské nám 49, Prague 1
Slovakia (☎ 233 32 54 43) Pod Hradbami 1, Prague 6
UK (☎ 257 40 21 11) Thunovská 14, Prague 1
USA (☎ 257 53 06 63) Tržiště 15, Prague 1

CUSTOMS
Customs officers can be strict about antiques and will confiscate goods that are even slightly suspect. If you have any doubt about what you are taking out, talk to curatorial staff at the **National Museum** *(☎224 49 71 11; Václavské náměstí)* for coins, at the **National Gallery** *(☎ 224 30 11 11; Dukelských hrdinů 47)* for paintings and sculptures and at the **Museum of Decorative Arts** *(☎ 251 09 31 11; 17.listopadu 2)* for antiques. All these offices are in Prague.

There is no limit to the amount of Czech or foreign currency that can be taken in or out of the country, but amounts exceeding 350,000 Kč must be declared.

MONEY
Currency
The Czech crown or Koruna česká (Kč) is divided into 100 hellers or haléřů (h). Banknotes come in denominations of 20, 50, 100, 200, 500, 1000, 2000 and 5000 Kč; coins are of 10, 20 and 50 h and one, two, five, 10, 20 and 50 Kč. Keep a few 2 Kč, 10 Kč and 20 Kč coins handy for use in public toilets, telephones and tram-ticket machines.

Exchange Rates
Conversion rates for major currencies at the time of publication were:

country	unit		Czech crown
Australia	A$1	=	16.74 Kč
Canada	C$1	=	19.68 Kč
Euro Zone	€1	=	30.56 Kč
Japan	¥100	=	25.85 Kč
NZ	NZ$1	=	14.48 Kč
UK	UK£1	=	48.38 Kč
USA	US$1	=	30.94 Kč

For up-to-date exchange rates go to **W** www .xe.net/ucc/full.shtml.

Exchanging Money

There is no longer a black market in currency exchange; anyone who offers to change money in the street is a thief.

Remember when comparing exchange rates that you are interested in the 'buy' rate (they will be buying currency or travellers cheques from you).

Cash The main banks – Komerční banka, Česká spořitelna, ČSOB and Živnostenská banka – are the best places to change cash, charging 2% commission with a 50 Kč minimum (but always check, as commissions can vary from branch to branch). They will also provide a cash advance on Visa or MasterCard without commission. Most banks are open at least 8am to 4pm weekdays; in smaller towns they may close for lunch between noon and 1pm.

Hotels charge about 5% to 8% commission at poorer rates while Čedok travel agencies and post offices charge 2% at similar rates to the banks.

Many private-exchange offices, especially in Prague, charge exorbitant commissions (výlohy) of up to 10%. Some of these advertise higher rates and 0% commission but don't mention their sky-high 'handling fee', or charge no commission but have very poor exchange rates – if in doubt, ask first.

Travellers Cheques Banks charge 2% with a 50 Kč minimum for changing travellers cheques. American Express and Thomas Cook offices change their own-brand cheques without commission, but charge 2% or 3% for other brands, 3% or 4% for credit-card cash advances and 5% for changing cash.

ATMs There is a good network of ATMs, or *bankomaty,* throughout the country. Most accept Visa, Plus, Visa electron, MasterCard, Cirrus, Maestro, Euro and EC cards.

Credit Cards You'll find that credit cards are widely accepted in mid-range and top-end hotels and restaurants. You can use a card to get a cash advance in a bank or to withdraw money from ATMs. Your own bank may charge a fee of about US$3 and possibly a 1% commission for using an ATM, but this is still more favourable (if you take out large amounts) than the commissions and exchange rates charged on travellers cheques.

You can report any lost MasterCard/Euro cards on ☎ 261 35 46 50 and lost Visa cards on ☎ 224 12 53 53.

Costs

Food, transport and admission fees are fairly cheap, but accommodation in hotels is fairly expensive, at least in Prague. If you want to save money you'll have to spend a little more time looking for cheap pensions, hostels or camping grounds, and eat in pubs or stand-up cafeterias. You might be able to get away with US$15 a day in summer. Staying in private rooms or better pensions, eating at cheap restaurants and using public transport, you can count on US$25 to US$30. Get out of the capital and your costs will drop dramatically.

A disappointing side of the Czech concept of a 'free-market economy' is the official two-tier price system in which foreigners can pay up to double the local price for some hotel rooms, airline and bus tickets, and museum and concert tickets. In Prague most tickets are snapped up by scalpers and travel agencies who resell them to foreigners at several times the original price. Sometimes simply questioning the price difference results in an 'error correction'; if not, you either pay the higher price or go elsewhere. When you do get something for the local price (eg, beer or domestic train tickets), you'll find that it is inexpensive. Students usually get 50% off at museums, galleries, theatres, fairs, etc.

Tipping

Tipping in restaurants is optional but if there is no service charge and service is good you should certainly round up the bill to the next 10 Kč or 20 Kč (up to 10%). The same applies to tipping taxi drivers. If your driver is honest and turns on the meter then you should round up the fare at the end of your journey.

Taxes & Refunds

Value-added tax (VAT, or DPH in Czech) is 5% on food, hotel rooms and restaurant meals, but 22% on luxury items (including alcohol). This tax is included in the sticker price and not added at the cash register.

You can claim VAT refunds for purchases worth more than 1000 Kč made in shops displaying the 'Tax-Free Shopping' sticker. They will give you a VAT Refund Form, which you must present to customs for validation when you leave the country. You can then claim a refund from a collecting agency within three months of the purchase date.

POST & COMMUNICATIONS
Post

Main post offices are open 7am or 8am to 5pm or 7pm Monday to Friday, and until noon on Saturday.

Postcards and letters up to 20g cost 9 Kč to other European countries and 14 Kč to the USA and Canada. A 2kg parcel by airmail costs 348 Kč to other European countries and 691 Kč to North America.

In principle, anything can be posted internationally from any major post office. In practice, some postal employees still suffer from communist-era anxieties about 'regulations', and may send you off to the customs post office (usually open 8am to 3pm) to send anything over 2kg. Don't send parcels containing anything valuable by ordinary mail; for fast, secure delivery, use the more expensive Express Mail Service (EMS) or a courier service such as DHL.

General delivery mail can be addressed to Poste Restante, Pošta 1, in most major cities. For Prague, also include: Jindřišská 14, 11000 Praha 1, Czech Republic.

American Express card-holders can receive mail addressed c/o American Express, Václavské nám 56, 11000 Praha 1, Czech Republic; letters are held for 30 days, but parcels and registered mail are not accepted.

Telephone

Český Telecom has replaced its antiquated telephone network with a modern digital system. Beginning 22 September 2002 all Czech phone numbers will have nine-digits, without an initial zero and without a separate area code – you will have to dial all nine digits for any call, local or long distance. For example, all Prague numbers (former area code 02) will change from 02-xx xx xx xx to 2 xx xx xx xx, and you will have to the dial the '2' even if you are calling from within Prague. Czech mobile numbers will also drop the initial zero.

Local calls cost 4 Kč for two minutes at peak rate (7am to 7pm weekdays) using a coin-phone, 3.20 Kč with a cardphone; phonecards costing 175/320 Kč for 50/100 units are sold at newsstands and post offices.

You can make international telephone calls at main post offices or directly from cardphone booths. The international access code is ☎ 00. Three-minute direct-dial international calls at peak rate cost around 35 Kč to Germany; 42 Kč to the UK, France, Australia, the USA and Canada; and 63 Kč to New Zealand and Japan.

The Country Direct service is available in the Czech Republic (get a full list of countries and numbers from any telephone office or directory). Use the following numbers to make a charge-card or reverse-charge call to your home country:

Australia Direct	☎ 00420 06101
Canada Direct	☎ 00420 00151
Canada (AT&T)	☎ 00420 00152
France Direct	☎ 00420 03301
Deutschland Direct	☎ 00420 04949
Netherlands	☎ 00420 03101
UK Direct (BT)	☎ 00420 04401
USA (AT&T)	☎ 00420 00101
USA (MCI)	☎ 00420 00112
USA (Sprint)	☎ 00420 87187

See also 'Appendix – Telephones' at the back of this book.

Fax & Telegram

Telegrams can be sent from most post offices, while faxes can be sent from certain major post offices and hotel business centres. You can dictate telegrams on ☎ 0127.

Email & Internet Access

There are Internet cafés in most towns and cities; see the relevant sections for details. The usual charge is about 1 Kč to 2 Kč per minute.

DIGITAL RESOURCES

Websites at Ⓦ www.prague-info.cz, Ⓦ www.czechsite.com and Ⓦ www.ceskenoviny.cz/news are packed with useful information and lots of links. The Czech Press Agency (ČTK) has a website at Ⓦ www.ctknews.com and Ⓦ www.europeaninternet.com/czech also has Czech news and current affairs.

BOOKS

Lonely Planet's guides to *Czech & Slovak Republics* and *Prague* both have extensive information on travelling in the Czech Republic, while LP's *Czech phrasebook* is a good introduction to the language.

The Coasts of Bohemia by Derek Sayer is a very readable exploration of the ironies of Czech history from the 18th century to 1968.

CZECH REPUBLIC

The collection of essays entitled *Václav Havel, or Living in Truth* (1986), edited by Jan Vladislav, includes Havel's famous 1978 piece 'The power of the powerless'. Havel describes the conformity of those who simply accepted the 'post-totalitarian system' as 'living within the lie'. In contrast, the dissidents endured many difficulties but earned respect by 'living within the truth'. *The Reluctant President: A Political Life of Václav Havel*, by Michael Simmons, also portrays this captivating figure well.

In a classic Czech novel *The Good Soldier Švejk*, Jaroslav Hašek (1883–1923) satirises the pettiness of government and military service. A Prague dog-catcher is drafted into the Austrian army before WWI, and by carrying out stupid orders to the letter he succeeds in completely disrupting military life.

Probably the best Czech novelist of the 20th century is Bohumil Hrabal (1914–97). One of his finest works is *The Little Town Where Time Stood Still*, a novel set in a small town, which shows in a humorous way how the close-knit community interacts.

NEWSPAPERS & MAGAZINES

The *Prague Post* at **W** www.praguepost.cz is a good weekly newspaper founded by a group of US expats in October 1991. It has a 'Calendar' section with entertainment listings and practical visitor information. There are also several business papers, including the *Prague Business Journal* and the glossy *Prague Tribune*. Major European and US newspapers and magazines are on sale at newsstands in Prague and other tourist hot spots.

RADIO & TV

Between Czech programmes, the BBC World Service broadcasts news and other programmes in English hourly, throughout the day from 5am to midnight weekdays and from 8am on weekends. Tune into 101.1FM in Prague, 101.3FM in Brno and 98.6FM in Plzeň.

On TV, Euronews in English is on channel ČT 2 on some days at either noon or 1am. Cable and satellite TV has most of the English-language European stations.

TIME

The Czech Republic is on GMT/UTC plus one hour. On the last weekend in March the clocks go forward an hour. On the last weekend in October they're turned back an hour.

LAUNDRY

There are self-service laundrettes in Prague and Český Krumlov; anywhere else you will have to rely on laundries or dry cleaners *(prádelna or čistírna)* that can take up to a week to wash clothes. Some top-end hotels have an expensive overnight laundry service.

TOILETS

Public toilets usually charge 2 Kč to 5 Kč, but as there are only a few around you may have to resort to using the facilities in restaurants or pubs; in tourist areas some of these also charge 5 Kč. Toilets might be marked *záchody* or *WC*, while men's may be marked *páni* or *muži* and women's *dámy* or *ženy*.

The handful of public toilets in central Prague are mainly in metro stations.

HEALTH

Tap water is safe to drink, but many people prefer bottled water. The most popular brand is Dobra Voda ('Good Water') – blue bottle-caps for still, red for sparkling.

Thermal Baths

There are hundreds of curative mineral springs and dozens of health spas in the Czech Republic that use mineral waters, mud or peat. Most famous are the spas of West Bohemia – these include Karlovy Vary, Františkovy Lázně and Mariánské Lázně.

Unfortunately, the spas are reserved for the medical treatment of patients. Yet all have colonnades where you can join in the 'drinking cure', a social ritual that involves imbibing liberal quantities of warm spring water and then parading up and down to stimulate circulation. Admission is free but you need to bring your own cup or buy a special *lázeňský pohárek* (sap cup).

For medical treatment at a spa you must book in advance through a booking agency (see the Karlovy Vary section), a Čedok office, a Czech Tourist Authority office abroad or the **Czech Spas Association** (☎ 354 54 22 25, fax 354 54 23 56; **e** mip@mip.cz). The recommended stay is 21 days, although you can book for as few as three days. Daily prices begin at US$38 per person in the cheapest category during winter (October to April) and US$50 during summer. The price includes medical examination and care, spa curative treatment, room and board, and the spa tax. The clientele tends to be elderly.

WOMEN TRAVELLERS

Sexual violence has been on the rise in the Czech Republic but is still much lower than in the West. Nonetheless, solo female travellers should avoid deserted and unlit areas, especially at night. Women may experience cat calls and whistling.

GAY & LESBIAN TRAVELLERS

The bimonthly gay guide and contact magazine *Amigo* has a few pages in English, and a useful English-language website at w www .amigo.cz/indexe.htm. Gay Guide.Net Prague at w www.gayguide.net/Europe/Czech/Prague is another useful source of information.

Czechs are generally not accustomed to seeing homosexuals showing affection for each other in public, but their reaction will most likely be just a surprised look.

DISABLED TRAVELLERS

Facilities for disabled people are receiving some attention. Ramps for wheelchair users in Prague are becoming more common, especially at more expensive hotels, major street crossings, McDonald's and KFC entrances and toilets. Transport is a major problem as most buses and trams have no wheelchair access. In Prague, the Hlavní nádraží and Holešovice trains stations, and 23 metro stations, have lifts (that don't always work); bus Nos 1 and 3 are wheelchair accessible on weekdays only.

Elsewhere, only Plzeň's train station has a self-operating lift, while those at Brno, České Budějovice and Karlovy Vary have easy street and ramp access. For wheelchair assistance you need to inform the stationmaster 30 minutes before the train's departure.

The Stavovské Theatre (and several other theatres) in Prague has wheelchair access and is equipped for the hearing-impaired. Most pedestrian crossings with lights in city centres give off a steady ticking noise which speeds up when the light is green, signalling that it is OK to cross the street.

For more information, get in contact with the **Prague Wheelchair Users Organisation** (*Pražská organizace vozíčkářů;* ☎ 224 82 72 10; e pov@gts.cz; *Benediktská 6, Josefov*). It can organise a guide and transporta at about half the cost of a taxi, and has an online database of barrier-free places in Prague. Also visit w www.pov.cz; the site is currently in Czech only, but an English translation is planned.

Emergency Services

The telephone number for all emergency services is ☎ 112. For state police dial ☎ 158 and for local police ☎ 156.

For the fire brigade ring ☎ 150 and for the ambulance call ☎ 155.

Assistance for car breakdowns is available through ☎ 1230 and ☎ 1240.

All numbers are valid nationwide.

DANGERS & ANNOYANCES

Violent crime is low compared with the West, but theft and pickpocketing are a real problem in Prague's tourist zone (see that section for more details). Prague's international Ruzyně airport is also a haven for thieves. Another problem is the increasing number of robberies on international trains passing through the country. The victims are usually sleeping passengers, some of whom are gassed to sleep in their compartments and then relieved of their valuables. Groups of skinheads occasionally abuse and assault darker-skinned people.

Confusingly, buildings on some streets have two sets of numbers. The blue number is the actual street number while the red number is the old building-registration number. The streets themselves are sometimes poorly labelled.

BUSINESS HOURS

From Monday to Friday, shops open at around 8.30am (bakeries and some grocery stores at 7am) and close at 5pm or 6pm, though major department stores stay open until at least 8pm. Outside Prague, almost everything closes on Saturday afternoon and all day Sunday. Many department stores, some grocery stores and tourist-oriented shops (especially those in the centre of Prague) remain open on weekends until around 5pm. Most of the restaurants are open every day, but in the smaller towns it can be difficult to find a restaurant open on Sunday evening.

Most museums are closed on Monday and the day following a public holiday, but some are open seven days a week, especially in summer. Many gardens, castles and historic sites are closed from November to March and open on weekends only in April and October. In winter, before making a long trip out to an attraction in the countryside, be sure to check that it's open. At any sight where a guided tour is required the ticket office closes an hour or so before the official closing time, depending on the length of the tour.

PUBLIC HOLIDAYS & SPECIAL EVENTS

Public holidays are New Year's Day (1 January), Easter Monday (March/April), Labour Day (1 May), Liberation Day (8 May), Cyril and Methodius Day (5 July), Jan Hus Day (6 July), Czech Statehood Day (28 September), Republic Day (28 October), Struggle for Freedom and Democracy Day (17 November) and Christmas (24 to 26 December). On Christmas and New Year's Eves many restaurants and bars will either be rented out for private parties or closed.

Major festivals include the Prague Spring International Music Festival during the second half of May (most performances are sold out well in advance). Karlovy Vary holds an International Film Festival in July and the Dvořák Autumn Music Festival in September. Brno has an Easter Festival of Spiritual Music, as well as the International Moravian Music Festival in September.

Moravian folk-art traditions culminate in late June at the Strážnice Folk Festival. In mid-August the Chod Festival at Domažlice affords you a chance to enjoy the folk songs and dances of South and West Bohemia. Medieval festivals are held in Český Krumlov (June) and Tábor (September).

ACTIVITIES
Hiking

There are good hiking possibilities in the forests around Karlovy Vary and in the Moravian karst area, north of Brno. The Šumava hills in the southern part of Bohemia offers some of the best hiking in the country, while the Adršpach-Teplice Rocks in East Bohemia has the most spectacular scenery.

Cycling

The whole country is ideal for cycling and cycle-touring. For information on bicycle rentals and suggested trips, see Prague and Český Krumlov later in this chapter.

Canoeing

A number of rivers are good for canoeing, including the Otava. In summer, it is possible to transport canoes on trains. For canoeing possibilities, see the Český Krumlov section.

COURSES

The **Information-Advisory Centre of Charles University** (IPC; ☎ 224 49 18 96, 222 23 24 52, fax 222 23 22 52; e ipc@ruk.cuni.cz, Školská 13a, Prague 1), provides information about the university and its courses, and sells ISIC, IYTC and Euro<26 cards.

The **Institute of Linguistics & Professional Training** (Ústav jazykové a odborné přípravy, UJOP; ☎ 224 99 04 17/12, fax 224 99 04 40; e ujop@ruk.cuni.cz; Vratislavova 10, Prague 2), at the Charles University, runs four-week Czech-language courses for foreigners in July and August. The application deadline is mid-June. No prior knowledge of the Czech language is required, and the course fee is US$590, not including accommodation. You can also opt for individual lessons (45 minutes) at US$16 each. The university's website w www.cuni.cz/cuni/ujop/czech.htm has information.

WORK

Unless you speak Czech or have a job with an English-speaking company the most likely work is English teaching or assisting in one of the backpacker hostels in Prague or Český Krumlov. It's easier to find a teaching job in provincial towns and your living costs will be much lower. In Prague, look in the Czech advertising paper Annonce, the Prague Post, and around the expat cafés. Also try the **American Embassy Information Resource Center** (IRC; ☎ 224 23 10 85; Hybernská 7a, Nové Město) and the **British Council** (☎ 221 91 11 11; Národní 10, Nové Město).

To obtain work legally you need a working visa and residency permit, for which you must apply at a Czech embassy or consulate before entering the country. Your employer will need to obtain the permits. These visas can take some months to process.

The **Klub mladých cestovatelů** (KMC, Young Travellers Club; ☎/fax 222 22 03 47; w www.kmc.cz; Karolíny Světlé 30, Prague 1) organises international work camps from June to August renovating historic buildings, maintaining national parks and teaching children English etc. Contracts are for a minimum of three weeks with no pay, but room and board are provided. The registration fee, if you book ahead through a volunteer or Hostelling International organisation in your home country, is US$50 to US$100 (some are free). There's a list of upcoming camps on the KMC website.

ACCOMMODATION
Camping
At around 50 Kč to 100 Kč per person, pitching your own tent is definitely the cheapest form of accommodation. There are several hundred camping grounds in the Czech Republic, most of which are open from May to September only. The grounds are often accessible by public transport, but there's usually no hot water. Most have a small snack bar where beer is sold and many have small cabins for rent that are cheaper than a hotel room. Camping on public land is prohibited. Camping Gaz and Coleman gas canisters are widely available, as is Coleman fuel *(technický benzín)* and methylated spirits *(líh)*.

Hostels
The Hostelling International (HI) handbook lists an impressive network of associate hostels across the Czech Republic. In July and August many student dormitories become temporary hostels, while a number in Prague have been converted into all year, Western-style hostels. In central Prague, some normal schools also turn into temporary hostels during summer. Český Krumlov is the only place, apart from Prague, with a solid network of backpacker hostels.

Hostelling is controlled by **Klub mladých cestovatelů** *(KMC, Young Travellers Club;* ☎/fax 222 22 03 47; W *www.kmc.cz; Karolíny Světlé 30, Prague 1)*. It's usually best to book ahead. You can book hostels in Prague and Brno from anywhere in the world via the computerised international booking network (IBN) that is linked to the HI booking service. A HI membership card is not usually required to stay at hostels, although it will usually get you a reduced rate. An ISIC, ITIC, IYTC or Euro<26 card may also get you a discount. A dorm bed costs around 300 Kč to 400 Kč.

Another category of hostel not connected with HI is tourist hostels *(Turistické ubytovny)*, which provide very basic and cheap (200 Kč to 300 Kč) dormitory accommodation without the standards and controls associated with HI hostels. Ask about tourist hostels at information, CKM or GTS international offices and watch out for the letters 'TU' on accommodation lists published in languages other than English.

Private Rooms & Pensions
Private rooms (look for signs reading *'privát'* or *'Zimmer frei'*) are usually available in tourist towns, and many tourist information offices can book them for you; expect to pay from 250 Kč to 500 Kč per person outside Prague. Some have a three-night minimum-stay requirement.

In Prague, many private travel agencies offer private rooms, and the service is available daily and during evenings. This is the easiest way to find accommodation in Prague if you don't mind paying at least 500 Kč per person per night.

The are many small pensions (occasionally glorified private rooms), especially on the outskirts of Prague and in South Bohemia, and these offer a more personalised service at lower rates than the hotels.

Hotels
Hotels in Prague and Brno are expensive, whereas those in smaller towns are usually much cheaper. Czechs pay less than half as much as foreigners at some hotels.

Hotels are rated with stars, with four- and five-star hotels being luxury per single/double. Two-star hotels usually offer reasonable comfort for about 500/700 Kč for a single/double with shared bathroom, or 600/1000 Kč with private facilities (these prices are about 50% higher in Prague).

FOOD
The cheapest places to eat are self-service restaurants *(jídelna or samoobsluha)*. Sometimes they have tasty dishes like barbecued chicken or hot German sausage – handy for a quick lunch. Train stations in large cities often have cheap restaurants or buffets/bistros but the best-value meals are in busy beer halls. If the place is crowded with locals, is noisy and looks chaotic, chances are it will have great lunch specials at low prices. As a general rule, a restaurant calling itself *restaurace* is usually cheaper than a 'restaurant'. Also, with the exception of Prague, the food in most restaurants is the same no matter what the price. Your pork and dumplings will taste the same in a *hospoda* (pub) or *vinárna* (wine bar) for 60 Kč as in a four-star hotel for 180 Kč.

Lunches are generally bigger and cheaper than dinners in the less expensive places. Dinner is eaten early and latecomers may have little to choose from.

In Czech the word for menu is *jídelní lístek*. Menus are mostly in Czech, except in touristy areas where they are also in German and/or English. Anything that comes with *knedlíky* (dumplings) will be a hearty local meal. Some Prague restaurants are notorious for overcharging foreigners (see Places to Eat in the Prague section).

Most beer halls have a system of marking everything you eat or drink on a small piece of paper that is left on your table. Waiters in all Czech restaurants, including the expensive ones, whisk away empty plates from under your nose before you manage to swallow your last dumpling.

There are great little *cukrárna* (pastry shops) throughout the country. These offer cakes, pastries and puddings as good as anything you'll find in neighbouring Austria at a fraction of the price.

Local Specialities

Czech cuisine is strong on sauces and gravies and weak on fresh vegetables. *Pražská šunka* (smoked Prague ham) is often eaten as a starter with Znojmo gherkins, followed by a thick soup, such as *bramborová polévka* (potato soup) or *zeleninová polévka* (vegetable soup). *Drštková polévka* (tripe soup) is a treat not to be missed.

The Czechs love meat dishes with sauerkraut and/or *knedlíky*, dumplings made with *bramborové* (potato) or *houskové* (bread). Unfortunately, many of the bread dumplings are pre-made in factories and pale in comparison to home-made ones. In inexpensive pubs or restaurants bread dumplings taste fine, but the potato ones are usually tasteless and stodgy. However, in most expensive restaurants the potato dumplings are reasonably good.

Kapr (carp) from Bohemia's fish ponds is served fried or baked. Prague has a good range of vegetarian restaurants; elsewhere, *bezmasá* (vegie) dishes are limited to pizzas, *smažený sýr* (fried cheese) and *knedlíky s vejci* (scrambled eggs with dumplings). *Ovocné knedlíky* (Czech fruit dumplings), with whole fruit, are served as a dessert with cottage cheese or crushed poppy seeds and melted butter.

DRINKS

The Czech Republic is a beer drinker's paradise – where else could you get two or three 500mL glasses of top-quality Pilsner for under a dollar? One of the first words of Czech you'll learn is *pivo* (beer); alcohol-free beer (yuck!) is *nealkoholické pivo*. The Czechs serve their draught beer with a high head of foam.

Bohemian beer is probably the best in the world – the most famous brands are Budvar (the original Budweiser) and Plzeňský Prazdroj (Pilsner Urquell in German, the original Pilsner). The South Moravia and Mělník regions produce reasonable white wines *(bílé víno)*, but Czech red wines *(červené víno)* are not great.

Special treats include Becherovka (an exquisite bittersweet Czech liqueur), *zubrovka* (vodka with herb extracts) and *slivovice* (plum brandy). *Grog* is rum with hot water and sugar. *Limonáda* often refers to any soft drink, not just lemonade.

ENTERTAINMENT

Theatres and concert-hall admission prices are still well below those in Western Europe and most performances are first rate.

In Prague, most of the best theatre tickets are snapped up by scalpers and travel agencies who demand higher prices (these are still inexpensive), but in other towns such as Karlovy Vary, Plzeň, České Budějovice and Brno you can see top performances at minimal expense. Most theatres are closed in summer.

Outside Prague, the nightlife is rather limited, although after 9pm there's usually a band playing in the bar of the best hotel in town and on weekends a club will be pumping somewhere, so just ask. You often have to contend with overbearing door attendants and contemptuous waiters.

Cinema is always cheap and films are usually shown in the original language with local subtitles.

SPECTATOR SPORTS

European handball is the national sport but the most popular is *fotbal* (soccer). Outstanding soccer teams include SK Slavia Praha and AC Sparta Praha.

Ice hockey is followed with even more passion as the Czech national team is world class. Among the best ice hockey teams are HC Petra Vsetín (a South Moravian team) and HC Sparta Praha (a Prague city club).

Tennis is also popular, as is cross-country ski racing in winter.

SHOPPING

Good buys for the avid shopper include china, Bohemian crystal, costume jewellery, folk ceramics, lace, embroidery, wooden toys, shoes, colour-photography books, classical

CDs and souvenirs. Garnet, ruby and amber jewellery is a speciality in Bohemia.

Getting There & Away

AIR

The national air carrier, **Czech Airlines** (*ČSA;* ☎ *220 10 46 20; V celnici 5; metro Náměstí Republiky*), has direct flights to Prague from many European cities, including Sofia, Zagreb, Budapest, Rīga, Bucharest, Moscow, Bratislava, Ljubljana and Kyiv, and also from Beirut, Cairo, Dubai, İstanbul, Larnaca, Malta, Montreal, New York, Tel Aviv and Toronto. Return fares to Prague offered by ČSA include €342 from Paris, €252 from Frankfurt and UK£95 from London Stansted. Return fares from Prague include 1990 Kč to Bratislava, 9400 Kč to Budapest, 10,700 Kč to Sofia and 11,100 Kč to Kyiv.

The British airline **Go** (*in Prague* ☎ *296 33 33 33*) has direct flights to Prague from London Stansted, Bristol and East Midlands, with one-way fares from as little as UK£45. **KLM** (*in Prague* ☎ *233 09 09 33*) is also a good bet for low-cost flights to Prague via Amsterdam.

Flights from New York to Prague with Austrian Airlines or SAS start at around US$500.

LAND
Bus

Most of the international buses are operated by **Eurolines-Sodell CZ** (☎ *224 23 93 18;* W *www.eurolines.cz; Senovážné nám 6, Prague 1*) and **Bohemia Euroexpress International** (☎ *224 21 86 80;* W *www.bei.cz; Florenc Bus Station, Křižíkova 4-6, Prague 8*). Prague's main international bus station is Florenc (Autobusové nádraží Florenc), 600m northwest of the main train station, but some buses use stands at Holešovice train station or Želivského metro station – make sure you know where your bus departs from. It's easier to buy a bus ticket from a travel agency such as GTS (see the Prague section) than to struggle with the queues and grumpy salespeople at Florenc bus station.

The peak season for bus travel is from mid-June to the end of September, when there are daily Eurolines buses to Prague from London (UK£61/95 single/return, 23 hours), Paris (€68/122, 15 hours), Frankfurt (€44/69, 9½

hours), Vienna (€24/47, 4¾ hours) and Amsterdam (€73/130, 15 to 19 hours). Two buses a week link Kraków in Poland with Brno (80/130 zł, 6½ hours). Outside peak season daily services fall to two or three a week.

There are several buses daily to Bratislava from Prague (300 Kč one-way, 4¾ hours) and Brno (250 Kč, 1¾ hours), five a week from Prague to Budapest (1100 Kč, 7¼ hours) and three a week from Prague to Warsaw (550 Kč, 10½ hours) via Wrocław (350 Kč, five hours).

Kingscourt Express company (☎ *224 23 45 83;* W *www.kce.cz; Havelská 8, Prague 1*) runs four buses a week (six in summer) from Brno to London calling at Prague and Plzeň (1850/2900 Kč one way/return from all three Czech cities, 20 hours from Prague). **Capital Express** (☎ *020-7243 0488;* W *www.capital express.cz; 57 Princedale Rd, Holland Park, London W11 4NP*) has daily buses (twice daily in summer) from London to Plzeň, Prague (UK£40/60, 21 hours), Brno (UK£43/65, 24 hours), Olomouc and Ostrava.

Train

Train travel is the easiest and the most comfortable way to get from Western Europe to the Czech Republic, but it's expensive compared to the bus, and even budget airlines. Keep in mind that domestic Czech train fares are cheaper than what you might pay for the Czech section of a ticket to or from Western Europe. You can save a bit by buying a ticket that terminates at a border town, then continuing with a cheaper, Czech-bought ticket.

In the capital, international trains arrive at Prague's central station (Praha hlavní nádraží, or Praha hl. n.), Holešovice (Praha Hol.), Smíchov (Praha Smv.) or Masarykovo (Praha Mas.) stations. Make sure you know which station your train will arrive at or depart from.

Prague and Brno are on the main line used by daily express trains from Berlin and Dresden to Bratislava and Budapest, and from Hamburg and Berlin to Vienna. Trains from Frankfurt and Munich pass through Nuremberg, Cheb and Plzeň on the way to Prague. Local railcars shuttle between Cheb and Schirnding (15 minutes) in Germany several times a day. There are also daily express trains between Prague and Warsaw, Poland, via Wrocław or Katowice.

If you're planning to travel between Prague and Budapest check whether you need a Slovak transit visa (the train goes via Bratislava).

Sample one-way fares to Prague include €130 from Paris (15 hours); UK£95 from London (25 to 30 hours); €42 from Salzburg (eight hours); €122 from Amsterdam (12½ hours); €46 from Berlin (five hours); and €85 from Frankfurt (7½ hours).

One-way train fares from Prague include 400 Kč to Bratislava; 750 Kč to Vienna; 1150 Kč to Budapest; 750 Kč to Kraków; and 890 Kč to Warsaw.

You can buy tickets in advance from Czech Railways (ČD) ticket offices, ČD travel agencies or other travel agencies. International tickets are valid for two months with unlimited stopovers. Inter-Rail (Zone D) passes are valid in the Czech Republic, but Eurail passes are not. For travel within the Czech Republic only, the Czech Flexipass is available (from US$48 to US$78 for three to eight days' travel in a 15-day period).

Seat reservations are compulsory on all the international trains. First-class sleepers and 2nd-class couchettes are available on overnight services.

Car & Motorcycle

Motorists can enter the country at one of the many border crossings marked on most road maps (see the Czech Republic map for all major 24-hour crossings). Foreign driving licences are valid for up to 90 days; strictly speaking, licences that do not include a photo ID need an International Driving Permit as well, although this rule is rarely enforced.

A vehicle must be equipped with a first-aid kit, a red-and-white warning triangle and a nationality sticker on the rear; the use of seat belts is compulsory. Drinking and driving is strictly forbidden – the legal blood alcohol level is zero. Police can hit you with on-the-spot fines of up to 2000 Kč for speeding and other traffic offences (be sure to insist on a receipt).

You will need to buy a motorway tax coupon (nálepka), costing 100/200/800 Kč for 10 days/one month/one year for vehicles under 3.5 tonnes, in order to use Czech motorways; failure to display one risks a 5000 Kč fine. They are on sale at border crossings, petrol stations and post offices.

DEPARTURE TAX

The airport departure tax on international flights leaving the Czech Republic is included in the ticket price.

Getting Around

AIR

ČSA has flights between Brno and Prague but it is much cheaper, and almost as fast, to take the bus or the train.

BUS

Within the Czech Republic buses are often faster, cheaper and more convenient than the train, and by European standards both are cheap. Long-distance companies include the national carrier ČSAD, Čebus and Bohemia Euroexpress, and there are several buses a day from Prague to Brno (140 Kč, 2½ hours), Plzeň (60 Kč, 1½ hours), Karlovy Vary (100 Kč, 2¼ hours) and Český Krumlov (120 Kč, three hours). You sometimes have to pay a small additional charge for checked luggage.

A mass of complex footnotes often makes posted bus timetables difficult to read. Two crossed hammers means the bus only runs on weekdays; 'jede' means 'runs', 'nejede' means 'doesn't run', 'denně' means 'daily', 'so' and 'ne' mean 'Saturday' and 'Sunday'. As most buses leave in the morning, it's best to get an early start. Many buses don't operate on weekends, when trains are more reliable. Buses sometimes leave a few minutes early, so it's best to get to the station at least 15 minutes before the official departure time.

Bus ticketing at main stations such as Prague and Karlovy Vary is computerised, so you can often book a seat ahead and be sure of a comfortable trip. Way stations are rarely computerised and you must line up and pay the driver. Reservations can only be made at the bus' point of departure; at peak periods you may have to stand part of the way if you don't have a reservation.

TRAIN

Czech Railways (České dráhy, or ČD) provides efficient train services to almost every part of the country. However, some remote places are difficult or impossible to get to by train. One-way, 2nd-class fares cost around 64/120/224/424 Kč for 50/100/200/400km; 1st-class fares are 50% more expensive.

Some trains operate only on certain days, but the footnotes on the posted timetables are incomprehensible unless you speak Czech or have a timetable booklet (Jízdní řád) in English. The clerks at information counters very seldom speak English (even in the major stations), so to find out a departure time, try writing down your destination and the date you wish to travel, then point to your watch and pray. Alternatively, go to an Internet café and check train (and bus) timetables in English on W www.vlak.cz. All train ticket offices in the Czech Republic are computerised and will give you a print-out in English with information about your train.

Departures *(odjezdy)* notice boards in train stations are usually yellow, while the arrivals *(příjezdy)* boards are white. Both these and the posted timetables indicate the category and platform number *(č. nástupiště)* for each train. Categories include:

SC (SuperCity) – a few top-quality services with 1st-class coaches only; supplementary charge of 1000 Kč, reservations compulsory

EC (EuroCity) – fast, comfortable international trains, stopping at main stations only with 1st- and 2nd-class coaches; supplementary charge of 60 Kč, reservations recommended

IC (InterCity) – long-distance and international trains with 1st- and 2nd-class coaches; supplement of 40 Kč, reservations recommended

Ex (express) – as for IC, but no supplementary charge

R *(rychlík)* – the main domestic network of fast trains with 1st- and 2nd-class coaches and sleeper services; no supplement except for sleepers; express and *rychlík* trains are usually marked in red on timetables

Sp *(spěšný)* – slower and cheaper than *rychlík* trains; 2nd class only

Os *(osobní)* – slow trains using older rolling stock that stop in every one-horse town; 2nd class only

Only SC, IC, EC and express trains include a dining carriage *(restaurační vůz)*.

If there is a notice over the timetable or a footnote with the Slovakian *'Náhradní autobusová doprava'*, it means that a bus that is departing from outside the train station is replacing the train service.

A letter 'R' after the train name means that reservations are available; an 'R' inside a box or circle means that they are compulsory. Reservations are not available on *osobní* trains. In major cities, you usually have to make seat reservations *(místenka or rezervace míst)* for domestic travel at a separate counter, so make sure you're standing in the right queue. Reservations costs only 20 Kč, and are recommended whenever possible.

Domestic train tickets for distances of more than 50km are valid for 24 hours, but for distances under 50km only until 6am the next day. Note that domestic return *(zpáteční)* tickets (about 10% more expensive than singles) are only valid for 48 hours from the time of purchase. International train tickets are valid for two months with unlimited stopovers. If you have to purchase a ticket or pay a supplement on the train for any reason, you'll have to pay a fine if you do not tell the conductor *before* you're asked for your ticket.

Always check to see if your train is an SC, IC or EC and pay the surcharge in the station when buying your ticket. Staff at some ticket counters will happily sell you an invalid ticket and you'll have no recourse later.

In many stations, complete timetables for all services are posted on notice boards. Look at the map first and find the route number you want, then look for the table with the corresponding number. If you're going to be in the Czech Republic for any length of time, it's a good idea to purchase the national timetable from a train station information office.

One way to save on hotel bills while getting around is by using overnight trains. Sleepers *(lůžko* – more like a bed with sheets included) and couchettes *(lehátko* – narrower than a sleeper with only a blanket) are available on overnight trains. Book at least one day before departure at a train station ticket counter. On departure day, sleepers and couchettes can only be bought from the conductor, when available. Sleepers cost 518/222 Kč per person in a single/double compartment in 1st class and 148 Kč in 2nd class (double only), while couchettes are 134/89 Kč in a four/six-person compartment. All these charges are on top of the cost of the regular train ticket.

Annoyances

Some Czech train conductors try to intimidate foreigners by pretending there's something wrong with their ticket, usually in the hope that the confused tourists will give them some money to get rid of them. Always insure that you have the right ticket for your train and don't pay any 'fine', 'supplement' or 'reservation fee' unless you first get a written receipt *(doklad)*. When you arrive at your destination, take your ticket and the receipt to an information office and politely ask for an explanation.

Conductors have also been known to take passengers' tickets claiming they will return

CZECH REPUBLIC

them later. The only circumstance in which a conductor has the right to hold your ticket is when you board a train where you've reserved a couchette or sleeper, in which case the attendant will keep your ticket overnight so you don't have to be woken up for ticket controls. Don't forget to ask for your ticket back.

Several travellers have reported having problems with the lockers at the train and bus stations. Always remember to set the combination dial on the *inside* of the door *before* you close the locker; you then enter the same combination (write it down!) on the outside dial to open the locker.

CAR & MOTORCYCLE

Take care – there is a lot of dangerous driving on Czech roads. There are plenty of petrol stations, many open 24/7. Leaded petrol is available as *special* (91 octane) and *super* (96 octane), unleaded as *natural* (95 octane) or *natural plus* (98 octane); the Czech for diesel is *nafta* or just *diesel*. LPG gas *(autoplyn)* is available in every major town but at very few outlets. Natural 95 costs around 24.50 Kč a litre, diesel 22.30 Kč.

Road Rules

Speed limits are 30km/h or 50km/h in built-up areas, 90km/h on open roads and 130km/h on motorways; motorbikes are limited to 80km/h. At level crossings over railway lines the speed limit is 30km/h. Beware of speed traps, as the police are empowered to levy on-the-spot fines of up to 2000 Kč and foreigners are the preferred targets. You need a motorway tax coupon (see Car & Motorcycle in the Getting There & Away section of this chapter) to use the motorways; this is included with most rental cars.

Driving and parking in Prague are a nightmare so it's best to leave your vehicle somewhere safe and then use public transport. Unmetered parking in the historic centre of Prague is only allowed if you have a permit. Car theft by organised gangs is routine, with expensive Western cars disappearing across the country's borders within hours.

Rental

The major international car-rental chains including A-Rent-Car/Thrifty, Avis, Budget, Europcar and Hertz; all have outlets in the Czech Republic. A-Rent-Car is the cheapest, charging 1684/9666 Kč daily/weekly for a

Škoda Felicia including unlimited mileage, Collision Damage Waiver and tax. There's a 395 Kč surcharge to pick up your car from the airport; delivery to hotels in central Prague is free. Other major companies are up to 100% more expensive; Prague-based Dvorak Rent A Car has lower rates (from 1560/8400 Kč) but in Prague and Brno only. Most major companies allow one-way rentals in their other locations in the country at no extra cost.

Small local companies are much cheaper – from 680 Kč a day all inclusive – but are less likely to have English-speaking staff. See Getting Around in the Prague section.

BICYCLE

The Czech Republic offers some good opportunities for cycle touring. Cyclists should be careful, though, as minor roads are often very narrow and pot-holed, and in the towns cobblestones and tram tracks can be a dangerous combination, especially when it has been raining. Theft is a problem, especially in Prague and other large cities, so a good long chain and lock are essential.

It's fairly easy to transport your bike on Czech trains. First purchase your train ticket and then take it with your bicycle to the railway luggage office. There you fill out a card, which will be attached to your bike; on the card you should write your name, address, departure station and destination. You will be given a receipt that should include all the accessories that your bicycle has, such as lights and dynamo. You are not allowed to leave any luggage on the bicycle, and it is advisable to take with the pump and water bottles.

The cost of transporting a bicycle is 40 Kč to 60 Kč depending on the length of the journey. You can also transport bicycles on most buses if they are not too crowded and if the bus driver is willing.

HITCHING

The Czech Republic is no safer than other European countries when it comes to hitching; many hitchhikers are assaulted or raped, and each year a few are killed. Despite these dangers many Czechs, including young women, still choose to hitch.

LOCAL TRANSPORT

City buses and trams operate from around 4.30am to midnight daily. In Prague, buses and trains on some main routes operate every

40 minutes all night long. Tickets – sold at bus and train stations, newsstands and vending machines – must be validated using the time-stamping machines found on buses and trams and at the entrance to metro stations; failure to do so can result in a fine. Tickets are hard to find at night, on weekends and out in the residential areas, so carry a good supply. The yellow-ticket vending machines at Prague metro stations and some bus and tram stops sell tickets that can be used on all forms of public transport in Prague.

Taxi

Taxis have meters – just make sure the meter is switched on. Many Prague taxi drivers are highly experienced at overcharging tourists. See the Prague section for more details.

Prague

pop 1,197,000

Prague (Praha in Czech) has a magical feel about it, like a history lesson come to life. As you walk among the baroque palaces or across the Karlův most (Charles Bridge), with Smetana's Vltava flowing below and pointed towers all around, you'll feel as if history has stopped back in the 18th century. Goethe called Prague the prettiest gem in the stone crown of the world. The city is on the Unesco World Heritage list.

Prague enjoyed two architectural golden ages: a Gothic period under Holy Roman Emperor Charles IV, and a baroque period during the Habsburg Counter-Reformation. In the 18th century Czech culture was suppressed, so it's not surprising that Prague's two greatest baroque architects, Christopher and Kilian Dientzenhofer, were German.

Today Prague is the seat of government and the centre of much of the country's intellectual and cultural life. Unlike Warsaw, Budapest and Berlin, which were both major battlefields during WWII, Prague escaped almost unscathed, and after the war lack of modernisation prevented haphazard development. Since 1989, however, central Prague has been swamped by capitalism as the street vendors, cafés and restaurants take over pavements, streets and parks.

The way you feel about Prague's current tourist glut may depend on where you're coming from. If you're arriving from London,

Paris or Rome it may all seem quite normal, but if you've been elsewhere in Eastern Europe for a while, you'll be in for a bit of a shock. As you're being jostled by all the hawkers and hordes of tourists, you may begin to feel that Prague has become a tacky tourist trap, but try to overcome that feeling and enjoy this great European art centre for all it has to offer and all its beauty.

Remember, if you're in Prague on a Monday, many museums and galleries will be closed. However, the Jewish Quarter, the Mozart Museum, the National Museum, the Strahov Library, St Vitus Cathedral and many attractions in Prague Castle, the Old Town Hall and most sights in Vyšehrad citadel will still be open.

Orientation

Almost exactly midway between Berlin and Vienna, Prague nestles in a picturesque bend of the Vltava (Moldau) river, its seven hills topped by castles and churches. The Vltava swings through the centre of the city like a question mark, separating Malá Strana (Little Quarter) on the west bank from Staré Město (Old Town), the early Gothic city centre, on the east. North of Malá Strana is Hradčany, the medieval castle district, while Nové Město (New Town) is a late-Gothic extension of Staré Město to the east and south. Only in 1784 did these four royal towns unite within a single system of fortifications.

Prague Castle, visible from almost everywhere in the city, overlooks Malá Strana, while the twin Gothic spires of Týn Church dominates the wide, open space of Staroměstské nám, the old town square. The long broad avenue of Václavské nám (Wenceslas Square), Prague's Champs Elysées, stretches southeast from Staré Město towards the National Museum and the main train station. At its northwestern end is Na příkopě, a busy, pedestrian shopping street where most of the information offices are found.

Maps Our maps of Prague are for initial orientation only – for serious navigation you'll need a detailed street map. Lonely Planet's plastic-coasted *Prague City Map* is good value; other good maps include SHOCart's GeoClub *Praha – plán města* (1:15,000) and VKÚ's *Praha – mapa města* (1:10,000). PIS has a free *Welcome to the Czech Republic* pamphlet with a map of the city centre.

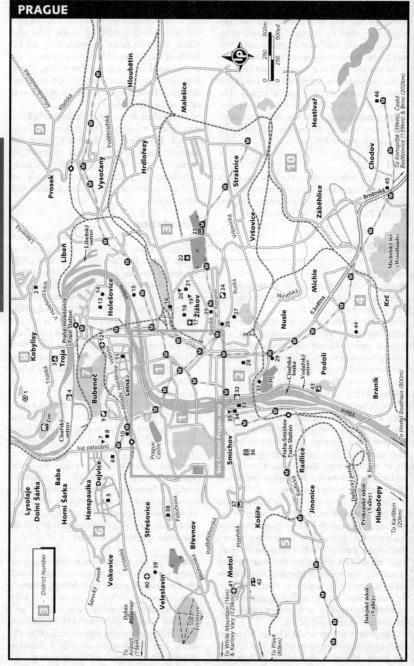

PRAGUE

CZECH REPUBLIC

0   250   500m
0   250   500yd

3 - District Number

Hloubětín

Malešice

Hostivař

Chodov

To Konopiště (39km), České
Budějovice (139km) & Brno (202km)

Podbradská

Strašnice

Brněnská

Vysočany

Hrdlořezy

Vršovice

Zábělice

Prosek

Strašnice

Michle

Michelský les
(Woodlands)

Libeň

Liberský
ostrov

Nuselská

Nusle

Krč

Kobylisy

Holešovice

Praha-Holešovice
Train Station

Ruská

Troja

Trojka

Letná

Podolí

Branik

Bubeneč

Prague Castle

See Central Prague map

Smíchov

Praha-Smíchov
Train Station

Radlice

To Hostel Boathaus (800m)

Lysolaje

Baba

Dolní Šárka

Horní Šárka

Dejvice

Hanspaulka

Střešovice

Břevnov

Košíře

Jinonice

Hlubočepy

Prokopské údolí
(Valley)

To Karlštejn
(20km)

Vokovice

Veleslavín

Motol

To White Mountain (1km)
& Karlovy Vary (129km)

To Plzeň
(80km)

Dalejské údolí
(Valley)

To Airport
(15km)

Šárecký potok

Dolní Šárka

Star
Enclosure

Jug patyzánů

PRAGUE

PLACES TO STAY		45	AV Pension Praha		22	Foreigners Police
2	Hotel Apollo	46	Hotel Business		23	Želivského Bus Station
3	Camp Dana Troja					(Eurolines) & Metro
5	Hotel Praha	**PLACES TO EAT**				Station
6	Welcome Hostel Dejvice	7	Pizzeria Grosseto		24	New Zealand Consulate
	& Accommodation	19	Mailsi		25	CKM Travel Centre
	Service	20	U radnice		26	Prague Laundromat
8	Hostel Orlík	35	Hospoda U Starého lva		29	Congress Centre
11	Hotel Belvedere				30	Vyšehrad Complex
13	Sir Toby's Hostel	**OTHER**			31	Institute of Linguistics &
16	Hostel Elf	1	Botanic Gardens			Professional Training
18	Clown & Bard Hostel	4	Zoo Boat Landing		32	PPS Riverboat Terminal
21	Hotel Golden City Garni	9	Dutch Embassy		36	Mozart Museum
27	Penzion Máchova	10	Laundry Kings		37	Customs Post Office
28	Hostel U Melounu	12	American Medical Center		39	West Car Praha Car Rental
33	Admirál Botel	14	Secco Car Rental		40	Canadian Medical Centre
34	Hotel Balkán	15	Bohemia Express Bus		41	Na Homolce Hospital
38	Hotel Markéta		Company Office		43	Swimming Pool
42	USK Caravan Camp	17	Palác Akropolis		44	ÚAMK

CZECH REPUBLIC

Information

Tourist Offices The municipal **Prague Information Service** (*Pražská informační služba, PIS;* ☎ 12444; ⓦ www.prague-info.cz; *open 9am-7pm Mon-Fri, 9am-5pm Sat & Sun Apr-Oct; 9am-6pm Mon-Fri, 9am-3pm Sat Nov-Mar*) has branches: at Na příkopě 20; in the Old Town Hall on Staroměstské nám (open to 6pm Saturday and Sunday in summer); at Malá Strana Bridge Tower (open 10am to 6pm daily from April to October only); and in the Praha-hlavní nádraží train station, next to the metro entrance.

The monthly *Culture in Prague* booklet in English is an invaluable guide to action in the city. All the PIS offices offer Ticketpro concert tickets and AVE accommodation services, while the Old Town Hall branch arranges guides and sells city tours (a three-hour tour is 500 Kč per person for two or more people).

For motoring matters, contact **Autoklub Bohemia Assistance** (*ABA;* ☎ 222 24 12 57; *Opletalova 29*), opposite the main train station, or **ÚAMK** (*☎ 261 10 43 33; Na Strži 6*).

Publications The English-language *Prague Post* (50 Kč, weekly) is a good source of information on what's happening in Prague; check out the website at ⓦ www.praguepost .cz. The irreverent *Prague Pill* (free, fortnightly) covers club culture and politics. *Think* (free, monthly) is a glossy magazine in Czech and English that covers art, music, fashion and subculture, along with good restaurant and bar reviews.

Money You can change American Express or Thomas Cook travellers cheques without commission at their respective city offices. **American Express** (*AmEx;* ☎ 222 80 02 37; *Václavské nám 56; open 9am-7pm daily*) changes non-AmEx travellers cheques for 2% commission. **Thomas Cook** (*☎ 221 10 53 71; Národní 28; open 9am-7pm Mon-Fri, 9am-6pm Sat, 10am-6pm Sun*) also changes Visa travellers cheques without commission. Both have poorer exchange rates than local banks.

Major banks are the best places for changing cash. Convenient branches include:

Česká spořitelna (Václavské nám 16) open 8am to 5pm Monday to Friday
ČSOB (Na příkopě 14) open 8am to 5pm Monday to Friday
Komerční banka (Václavské nám 42) open 8am to 5pm Monday to Friday
Živnostenská banka (Na příkopě 20) open 8am to 4.30pm Monday to Friday

Be on your guard against the exorbitant commission charged by private exchange offices in Prague such as Chequepoint and Change. Many charge from 4% to 12% commission (with a 95 Kč minimum), or advertise 0% commission but give a much poorer exchange rate and/or add on a hefty 'handling charge'.

Post & Communications To use the **main post office** (*Jindřišská 14; metro Můstek; open 7am-8pm daily*), take a ticket from one of the automated machines just outside the main hall (press button No 1 for stamps and parcels, No 4 for EMS). Wait until your number *(lístek číslo)* comes up on the electronic boards inside; these tell you which window to go to for service *(přepážka)*.

You can pick up poste-restante mail at window No 1 and buy phonecards at window No 28. Parcels weighing up to 2kg, as well as international and EMS parcels are sent from window Nos 7 to 10. (Note that these services close at 1pm on Saturday and all day Sunday.)

There's a telegraph and 24-hour telephone centre to the left of the right-hand post office entrance.

To reach the **customs post office** *(Pobočka Celního Úřadu; Plzeňská 139; open 7am-3pm Mon-Fri, to 6pm Wed)*, take the metro to Anděl, then go for three stops west on tram No 4, 7 or 9.

Email & Internet Access The centre of Prague is overflowing with Internet cafés. The cheapest places are **Bohemia Bagel** *(☎ 224 81 25 60; Masná 2, Staré Město • ☎ 257 31 06 94; Újezd 16, Malá Strana; both open 7am-midnight Mon-Fri, 8am-midnight Sat & Sun)* and **The Globe** (see Bookshops, later in this section), which both charge 1 Kč a minute with no minimum. The Globe also has network sockets where you can connect your own laptop (also 1 Kč a minute; cables provided, 50 Kč deposit).

Other convenient city-centre Internet cafés (with 10- or 15-minute minimum charges) include **Internet Cafe Prague** *(☎ 606 38 68 17; Liliová 18; open 9am-11pm Mon-Fri, 10am-11pm Sat & Sun)*, charging 120 Kč an hour; **Internet Nescafe Live** *(☎ 221 63 71 68; Rathova Pasaž, Na příkopě 23; open 9am-10pm Mon-Fri, 10am-8pm Sat & Sun)* where rates are 102 Kč an hour; and **Internet Kafe** *(☎ 220 10 81 47; Batalion Bar, 28.října 3; open 24hr)*, where it's just 80 Kč per hour.

Travel Agencies The **CKM Travel Centre** *(☎ 222 72 15 95; e ckmprg@login.cz; Mánesova 77, Vinohrady; metro Jiřího z Poděbrad; open 10am-6pm Mon-Thur, 10am-4pm Fri)* makes reservations for accommodation and books air and bus tickets, with discounts for those aged under 26 (it also sells youth cards). A similar agency for the younger traveller is **GTS International** *(☎ 222 21 12 04; e gts.smecky@gtsint.cz; Ve Smečkách 33; open 8am-6pm Mon-Fri, 11am-3pm Sat)*, which also sells train tickets and youth cards.

People aged under 26 can also purchase discounted train and bus tickets to Western Europe or book accommodation in Prague at **Wasteels** *(☎ 224 61 74 54; e wasteels@iol .cz; open 7.30am-8pm Mon-Fri, 8am-3pm Sat)* in Praha-hlavní nádraží train station.

Čedok *(☎ 224 19 71 21; Na příkopě 18; open 9am-6pm Mon-Fri, 10am-3pm Sat)* sells international air, train and bus tickets. **Bohemiatour** *(☎ 231 39 17; Zlatnická 7; open 8.30am-7pm Mon-Fri)* also sells international bus tickets to many European cities. **Eurolines-Sodeli CZ** *(☎ 24 23 93 18; Senovážné nám 6; open 8am-6pm Mon-Fri)* is the agency for Eurolines.

At the main train station, the **Czech Railways Travel Agency** *(CKČD; ☎ 224 21 79 48; Praha-hlavní nádraží, Wilsonova 80; open 8am-6pm daily)* sells air, train and bus tickets to points all over Western Europe, and also has cheap youth air fares.

Bookshops One of the city's best-stocked English-language bookshops is **Big Ben** *(Malá Štupartská 5; open 9am-6.30pm Mon-Fri, 10am-5pm Sat & Sun)*. Nearby **Anagram** *(Týn 4; open 10am-8pm Mon-Sat, 10am-6pm Sun)* is also good, and has a broad range of second-hand books as well.

Na můstku *(Na příkopě 3; open to 8am-7pm Mon-Fri, 9.30am-6pm Sat & Sun)* sells city maps, guides and souvenir books. **Kiwi** *(Jungmannova 23; open 9am-6.30pm Mon-Fri, 9am-2pm Sat)* has an excellent range of maps and Lonely Planet guidebooks. Famous expat hang-out **The Globe** *(Pštrossova 6; open 10am-midnight daily)* is a cosy English-language bookshop, bar and Internet café.

Laundry Most self-service laundrettes charge around 140 Kč to wash and dry a 6kg load of laundry. There's a convenient **Laundryland** *(Na příkopě 12; open 9am-8pm Mon-Fri, 9am-7pm Sat, 11am-7pm Sun)* on the 1st floor of Černá Růže shopping centre, above the Panská entrance.

Other self-service laundrettes in the city include: **Astera** *(Jindřišská 5)* off Vąlavské nám; **Laundryland** *(Londýnská 71)* and **Prague Laundromat** *(Korunní 14)* near nám Míru; and the **Laundry Kings** *(Dejvická 16)* in Dejvice.

Medical Services Emergency medical aid for foreigners is available at **Na Homolce Hospital** *(☎ 257 27 11 11, after hours ☎ 257*

The cruises run between 10.30am and 11pm daily in July and August and 10.30am to 8pm daily between March and June.

You can cruise the Vltava under your own steam in a rowing boat or pedalo rented from one of several places along the river.

Places to Stay

Prague is an extremely popular destination; if you're thinking of visiting during Christmas, Easter or May to September then bookings are strongly recommended, especially if you want to stay in or near the centre. Prices quoted are for 'high season', generally May, June, September and October; however, even these rates can increase by up to 15% on certain dates, notably during Christmas to New Year, Easter, and on weekends in May (during the Prague Spring festival). Some hotels (but not all) have slightly lower rates in July and August. November to March is low season, with the cheapest rates.

Accommodation Agencies There are dozens of agencies that will help you find a place to stay – some of which are better than others. Even if you turn up in peak period without a booking, these places should be able to find you a bed.

Look at the **TravelGuide website** (W *www .travelguide.cz*), which has a database of almost 400 hostels, pensions and hotels, and a straighforward online booking system.

The long-established **AVE** (☎ *224 22 32 26, reservations* ☎ *251 55 10 11, fax 224 22 34 63;* W *www.avetravel.cz*) has convenient booking offices at Praha-hlavní nádraží and Praha-Holešovice train stations, at Ruzyně airport and in PIS offices (see Tourist Offices, earlier in this section); the branch at Praha-hlavní nádraží is open 6am to 11pm daily. However, a few readers have reported problems using its reservation service.

Mary's Travel & Tourist Service (☎ *222 25 35 10,* ☎/*fax 222 25 22 15;* W *www .marys.cz; Italska 31, Prague 2*) offers a range of hostels, pensions, hotels and apartments, and has been recommended by travellers.

Stop City Accommodation (☎ *222 52 12 33,* ☎/*fax 222 52 12 52;* W *www.stopcity .com; Vinohradská 24, Prague 2; open 11am-8pm daily*), about six blocks away from the Praha-hlavní nádraží train station, has a large selection of private rooms and apartments available, with rates from €20 per person.

Welcome Accommodation Service (☎ *224 32 02 02, fax 224 32 34 89;* W *www.bed.cz; Zikova 13, Prague 6*) is in a student hostel in Dejvice – go in the main entrance, turn left, and it's the second door on the left; or just say 'Hostel?' to the lady at reception. It has rooms in student dormitories, hostels and hotels.

You can also rent a private room unofficially from householders who will approach you at the train and bus stations. They'll ask from about 300 Kč to 800 Kč per person, depending on the location. Check the location on a map before accepting – many places are way out in the suburbs.

Camping There are several camping grounds within reasonably easy reach of Prague's city centre. Most charge 75 Kč to 110 Kč for a small tent, plus a similar amount per person and also for a car.

The **USK Caravan Camp** (☎ *257 21 49 91; Plzeňská 279, Motol, Prague 5; tent sites 85 Kč plus per person 100 Kč; open year-round*), just west of Smíchov, is Prague's most convenient camping ground. Take tram No 7, 9 or 10 from the Andel metro to the Hotel Golf stop (10 minutes).

There are half-a-dozen camping grounds clustered together in Troja, in the north of the city, including **Camp Dana Troja** (☎/*fax 283 85 04 82;* e *campdana@volny.cz; Trojská 129, Troja, Prague 71; tent sites 75 Kč plus per person 115 Kč; open year-round*). Take tram No 5 from the Hlavní nádraží stop outside the main train station to the Trojská stop (20 minutes), then walk west along Trojská.

Hostels The central **Hostel Sokol** (☎ *257 00 73 97;* e *hostel@sokol-cos.cz; 3rd floor, Tyršův dům, Nostícova 2, Prague; dorm beds/doubles 270/1200 Kč*) in Malá Strana gets good reports from travellers. Take the metro to Malostranská and then tram No 12, 22 or 23 two stops south.

On the opposite side of the river to the Sokol in Staré Město is **Travellers Hostel Dlouhá** (*Roxy;* ☎ *224 82 66 62;* e *hostel@ travellers.cz; Dlouhá 33, Prague 1; dorm beds/singles/doubles 370/1120/1240 Kč*), with basic but clean accommodation and a 24-hour service that also includes lockers and Internet access. There are five other Travellers Hostels in central Prague, with cheaper dorm beds (220 Kč to 300 Kč) available from mid-June to August only.

Another good central place is **Hostel Týn** (☎ 222 73 45 90; e info@itastour.cz; *Týnská 19; dorm beds 370 Kč*), only a few minutes' walk from Staroměestské nám.

The popular **Clown & Bard Hostel** (☎ 222 71 64 53; e reservations@clownandbard .com; *Bořivojova 102, Prague 3; metro Jiřího z Poděbrad; dorm beds/doubles 250/900 Kč*) is in the heart of Žižkov's pub district. It's a party place, so don't come here seeking peace and quiet.

Also located in Žižkov, the friendly **Hostel Elf** (☎ 222 54 09 63; e info@hostelelf.com; *Husitská 11, Prague 3; dorm beds/doubles 260/840 Kč*) is recommended by readers.

The attractive **Hostel U Melounu** (☎/fax 224 91 83 22; e info@hostelumelounu.cz; *Ke Karlovu 7, Prague 2; dorm beds 380 Kč*) is in a historic building in a quiet back street, a ten-minute walk south of metro IP Pavlova.

Across the river in the Holešice area is the fairly new **Sir Toby's Hostel** (☎ 283 87 06 35; e info@sirtobys.com; *Dělnická 24, Prague 7; dorm beds/doubles 325/1150 Kč*), where the rooms include private shower and toilet, in a nicely refurbished apartment building.

Another popular place is the excellent **Hostel Boathaus** (☎ 402 10 76; *V náklích 1A, Prague 4; dorm beds 290 Kč*), with a peaceful riverside setting about 3km south of the city centre. To get there from Václavské nám take tram No 3 at Jindřišská in the direction of Modřany to the Černý kůň stop (20 minutes) and follow the hostel signs to the river.

Student Residences Many of the student residences *(koleje)* in Prague rent accommodation to tourists (students or not) year-round. As well as dormitory beds, they offer good-value single, double and triple rooms, often with four rooms sharing a small lounge, toilet, bathroom and cooking facilities.

The central **Hostel Jednota** (☎ 224 21 17 73, ☎/fax 224 81 82 00; *Opletalova 38, Prague 1; singles/doubles/triples/quads 550/ 680/1020/1240 Kč*) is only five minutes' walk from Praha-hlavní nádraží train station. You can arrange a bed through the **Alfa Tourist Service** (☎/fax 224 23 00 37; e info@ alfatourist.cz), which is based at the same address. It also offers accommodation at several other hostels and hotels in Prague.

There is plenty of accommodation at the student dormitory complex opposite the Strahov stadium west of the centre. Bus Nos 143,

149 and 217 run directly there from Dejvická metro station. As you get off the bus you'll see 11 huge blocks of flats. Although the capacity is enormous, the whole complex does occasionally get booked out by groups. The blocks of flats operate as separate hostels in July and August, while in the off season only five will be open at minimum capacity. Noisy nightclubs operate from 7pm to midnight downstairs in block Nos 7 and 11, and until 4am at No 1.

The main providers of year-round accommodation in the complex are **Hostel SPUS Strahov** (☎/fax 283 88 25 72; e reception@ spushostels.cz; *Chaloupeckého, Block 4, Prague 6; dorm beds/singles/quads 250/ 480/1160 Kč*), and the **Welcome Hostel Strahov** (☎ 224 32 02 02, fax 224 32 34 89; e welcome@bed.cz; *Vaníčkova, Block 3; dorm beds/singles/doubles 150/350/480 Kč*). Both of these hostels offer 10% discount to ISIC card-holders.

There's another concentration of student dorms in the suburb of Dejvice, only five minutes' walk from the Dejvická metro station, which includes **Hostel Orlík** (☎ 224 31 12 40; e praguehotel@atlas.cz; *Terronská 6, Prague 6; singles/doubles/triples 550/860/ 1250Kč; open July-Aug*), and **Welcome Hostel Dejvice** (☎ 224 32 02 02, fax 224 32 34 89; e welcome@bed.cz; *Zikova 13, Prague 6; singles/doubles 400/540 Kč*).

Pensions An interesting place to stay is **Unitas Pension** (☎ 224 21 10 20, fax 224 21 08 00; e unitas@cloisterinn.com; *Bartolomějská 9, Prague 1; metro Národní třída; singles/ doubles 1100/1400 Kč*) in Staré Město. This former convent has cramped rooms that were once used as prison cells (President Havel did time in one of them), with shared bathrooms and a generous breakfast included.

South of IP Pavlova metro station is **Pension Březina** (☎ 296 18 88 88, fax 224 26 67 77; e info@brezina.cz; *Legerova 41, Prague 2; economy singles/doubles 900/1100 Kč, luxury 1800/2000 Kč*). The economy rooms have shared bathrooms; luxury ones have private facilities, air-con and Ethernet sockets for your laptop (free use of Internet). Rooms facing the street can be pretty noisy.

Southeast of the centre and a five-minute walk east of Chodov metro station is the superb **AV Pension Praha** (☎ 272 95 17 26, fax 267 91 26 95; e votava@pension-praha.cz;

Malebná 75, Prague 4; singles/doubles with bath 1200/1630 Kč). It has just eight rooms.

The **Penzion Máchova** (☎ 222 51 01 07, fax 222 51 17 77; e machova@motylek.cz; Máchova 11, Prague 2; singles/doubles/triples 850/1400/1800 Kč) is in a quiet neighbourhood five minutes' walk south of metro Náměstí Míru.

Hotels – Budget There are no cheap hotels in central Prague; to get a double for under 2500 Kč you'll have to settle for the burbs.

The recently modernised **Hotel Golden City Garni** (☎ 222 71 10 08, fax 222 71 60 08; e hotel@goldencity.cz; Táboritská 3, Prague 3; singles/doubles/triples 1650/2450/2700 Kč), in the suburb of Žižkov, is three stops east of the main train station on tram No 5, 9 or 26, has friendly and helpful staff and is excellent value.

Hotel Balkán (☎ 257 32 21 50; e balkan@mbox.dkm.cz; třída Svornosti 28, Prague 4; singles/doubles/triples 2000/2400/2700 Kč), just south of the centre and two blocks from Anděl metro station, is a good deal. The hotel also has a decent restaurant.

Hotel Apollo (☎ 688 06 28, fax 688 45 70; Kubišova 23, Prague 8; singles/doubles/triples 1800/2300/2700 Kč) is a bland, modern place in a quiet housing estate north of the centre, 15 minutes from the centre on tram No 5, 14 or 17.

Modern **Hotel Markéta** (☎ 220 51 83 16, fax 220 51 32 83; e marketa@motylek.com; Na Petynce 45, Prague 6; singles/doubles/triples 1850/2500/3100 Kč) is in the suburb of Střešovice, about 10 minutes' walk west of Hradčany. From Hradčanská metro station take bus No 108 or 174 for three stops west to Kajetánka.

If a 20-minute metro ride doesn't deter you, consider the soulless but affordable **Hotel Business** (☎ 267 99 51 50, fax 267 99 51 33; e business3@motylek.com; Kupeckého 842, Prague 4; singles/doubles 980/1560 Kč, with bath 1140/1710 Kč). When you come out of Háje metro station, it's the tallest building you can see. It has very basic rooms sharing a toilet and shower between two, or renovated rooms with private bathrooms.

Hotels – Mid-Range There are several interesting hotels in Staré Město, including the appealing **Dům U krále Jiřího** (☎ 222 22 09 25, fax 222 22 17 07; e krak.jiri@telecom.cz;

Liliová 10, Prague 1; singles/doubles 1800/3100 Kč). The attic rooms with exposed wooden beams are especially attractive.

Not far from here is the small **Pension U medvídků** (☎ 24 21 19 16, fax 24 22 09 30; e pension@umedvidku.cz; Na Perštýně 7, Prague 1; singles/doubles 2300/3500 Kč), another historic building with appealing rooms.

Fancy retiring to a convent? About a block west is the **Cloister Inn** (☎ 224 21 10 20, fax 224 21 08 00; e cloister@cloister-inn.cz; Konviktská 14, Prague 1; singles/doubles/triples 3400/3800/4750 Kč), a comfortably refurbished convent with private parking and free Internet access.

The extravagant Art Nouveau facade of the **Grand Hotel Evropa** (☎ 224 22 81 17, fax 224 22 45 44; Václavské nám 25, Prague 1; metro Můstek; singles/doubles/triples 1600/2600/3100 Kč, with bathroom 3000/4000/5000 Kč) conceals a musty warren of run-down rooms that appear to have barely been touched since the 1950s. It still has a certain charm though, and considering its location is reasonable value.

The luxurious neo-Renaissance **Hotel Opera** (☎ 222 31 56 09, fax 222 32 14 77; e reception@hotel-opera.cz; Těš nov 13, Prague 1; metro Florenc; singles/doubles 3550/4200 Kč) is just 10 minutes' walk east of the Old Town.

Pleasant **Hotel Belvedere** (☎ 220 10 61 11, fax 233 37 23 68; e prague@belvedere-hotel.com; Milady Horákové 19, Prague 7; singles/doubles 2130/2850 Kč), north of the centre, has posh four-star rooms at reasonable rates. Take westbound tram No 1 or 25 two stops from Vltavská metro station.

Admirál Botel (☎ 257 32 13 02, fax 257 31 95 16; e info@admiral-botel.cz; Hořejš í nábřeží 57, Prague 5; metro Anděl; singles/doubles 2710/2840 Kč, triple/quad suites 4520/4910 Kč), about four blocks from Anděl metro station, offers an unusual alternative for a bed. It's a huge luxury riverboat permanently moored on the Vltava River with 82 double cabins and five suites.

Hotels – Top End The pretty little **Hotel Clementin** (☎ 222 22 17 98, fax 222 22 17 68; e hotel@clementin.cz; Seminářs ká 4, Prague 1; singles/doubles 4250/5250 Kč) – probably the narrowest hotel in Prague – has nine cosy rooms on a narrow street just off the tourist thoroughfare of Karlova.

On the other side of Staré Město is **Hotel Casa Marcello** (☎ 222 31 02 60, fax 222 31 33 23; **e** booking@casa-marcello.cz; Řásnovka 783, Prague 1; doubles 7500 Kč), a former aristocratic residence with stylishly furnished rooms and a pleasant courtyard where you can enjoy a drink or a snack. Prices can fall to almost half the advertised rack rate in July, August and winter.

South of here is the sumptuous Art Nouveau **Hotel Paříž** (☎ 222 19 51 95, fax 224 22 54 75; **e** booking@hotel-pariz.cz; U obecního domu 1, Prague 1; singles/doubles 9500/9800 Kč), a great place for a splurge. Facilities include a sauna and fitness room.

Hotel U tří pštrosů (☎ 257 53 24 10, fax 257 53 32 17; **e** info@utripstrosu.cz; Dražického nám 12, Prague 1; singles/doubles 5900/7900 Kč) is a grand old merchant's house at the foot of the Malá Strana tower on Charles Bridge, filled with interesting historical details. The rooms may be expensive, but it does have an unbeatable location and some splendid views.

Hotel Praha (☎ 224 34 11 11, fax 224 32 12 18; **e** reserv@htlpraha.cz; Sušická 20, Prague 6; singles/doubles 5900/6840 Kč) in Dejvice is a luxury complex with stunning views over the city that was built for the Communist Party apparatchiks in 1981. Tom Cruise stayed here during the filming of *Mission Impossible* in 1995.

Places to Eat

Tourism has had a heavy impact on the Prague restaurant scene. Cheaper restaurants have almost disappeared from the historical centre, while most of the restaurants in the Old Town, the castle district and along Václavské nám are now more expensive.

If you're on a tight budget it might be worth walking a few streets away from the tourist centres or taking the metro a few stops out of the centre and eating near there. Žižkov and Smíchov have plenty of inexpensive places.

Be aware that the serving staff in some Prague restaurants in the tourist centre shamelessly overcharge foreigners. Some restaurants in touristy areas have two menus, one in Czech and the other in German, English and French with higher prices. Insist on a menu with prices; if the waiter refuses to show you one listing specific prices, just get up and walk out. Don't be intimidated by the language barrier.

A good idea is to have a glance at the price of the beer on the menu, as this varies a lot and can cancel your savings on lower meal prices. If the drink prices aren't listed expect them to be sky high. At lunchtime the waiter may bring you the more expensive dinner menu.

Even if you do check the menu prices, the waiter may claim you were served a larger portion or may bring you a different, cheaper dish but still charge the higher price. Extras such as a side salad and bread and butter sometimes incur an added charge, so if you are served something you didn't order and don't want, send it back. Many of the tourist restaurants add about a 20 Kč cover charge (*couvert*) to the bill.

Hradčany & Malá Strana Five minutes' walk west of the castle is **Sate** (Pohořelec 3; mains 90-110 Kč; open 11am-10pm daily), which serves up some tasty Indonesian and Malaysian dishes.

There are many tourist places on and near Malostranské nám, including popular expat hang-out **Jo's Bar** (mains 100-150 Kč; open 11am-2am daily) at No 7, with Mexican food and burgers. Nearby is **Hostinec U kocoura** (cnr Nerudova & Zámecká; mains 70-100 Kč; open 11am-11pm daily) with inexpensive Bohemian beer snacks and pub grub.

Cosy and romantic **Vinárna U Maltézských rytířů** (Prokopská 10; mains 200-400 Kč; open 11am-11pm daily) offers top-notch food and professional service.

The elegant **Pálffy Palác** (Valdštejnská 14; mains 475-525 Kč; open 11am-midnight daily) is a Prague institution serving fish and meat dishes with mouth-watering sauces.

Informal **Bohemia Bagel** (Újezd 18, Malá Strana • Masná 2, Staré Město; mains 50-100 Kč; open 7am-midnight daily) is a great place to eat, and is one of the few places that offers early morning breakfast.

Staroměstské Nám & Around The **Staroměstská restaurace** (Staroměstské nám 19; mains 75-245 Kč; open 10am-11pm daily) has good Czech food and beer, and is easily the best of the restaurants on the square.

Behind Týn Church is an excellent French restaurant with pleasant service, **Le Saint-Jacques** (Jakubská 4; mains 400-800 Kč; open noon-3pm & 6pm-midnight Mon-Fri, 6pm-midnight Sat). **Pivnice Radegast** (Templová 2; mains 55-110 Kč; open 11am-12.30am *daily*), off Celetná, has good cheap Czech food; try the tasty *guláš* (goulash).

Five minutes' walk from the square is the **Orange Moon** (*Rámová 5; mains 150-220 Kč; open 11.30am-11.30pm daily*), with excellent Thai, Burmese and Indian dishes. Nearby is **U Benedikta** (*Benediktská 11; mains 60-180 Kč; open 11am-11pm daily*), another good Czech place.

There are a few good places around Betlémské nám. The popular, subterranean **Klub architektů** (*Betlémské nám 5; mains 100-220 Kč; open 11.30am-11pm daily*) serves tasty and inventive dishes, including vegetarian ones. Nearby is the top-notch **Vinárna v zátiší** (*Liliová 1; mains 500-900 Kč; open noon-3pm & 5.30pm-11pm daily*), offering Czech cuisine with a gourmet twist.

Václavské Nám & Around In a courtyard through a passage on Václavské nám 48 is the decent **Pizzeria Václavka** (*mains 65-120 Kč; open 11am-11pm daily*) with good inexpensive pizzas, pastas and salads.

Southwest of the square sample the Tex-Mex cuisine at **Buffalo Bill's Bar & Grille** (*Vodičkova 9; mains 180-280 Kč; open noon-midnight daily*), or try the excellent steaks and salads at **Titanic Steak House** (*Štěpánská 22; mains 90-190 Kč; open 11am-11pm Mon-Sat, 3pm-11pm Sun*).

A little bit farther away from the square is **Jihočeská restaurace u Šumavy** (*Štěpánská 3; mains 95-155 Kč; open 10am-11pm Mon-Fri, 11am-11pm Sat & Sun*), serving delicious, inexpensive South Bohemian dishes.

Národní Třída & Around The elegant **Café Louvre** (*Národní 22; breakfast 70-120 Kč; open 8am-11pm Mon-Fri, 9am-11pm Sat & Sun*) serves excellent breakfasts; it's also open for lunch and dinner but prices are higher. **Kmotra** (*V jirchářích 12; mains 100-180 Kč; open 11am-1am daily*) prepares mouth-watering pizzas in a wood-fired oven.

On the Staré Město side of the avenue is the inexpensive **Restaurace U Ampezonů** (*Konviktská 11; mains 70-100 Kč; open 11am-11pm daily*), whose solid Bohemian fare – such as roast chicken with potato dumplings – is good value.

U Fleků (*Křemencova 11*) is a German-style beer hall and garden where you can sit at long communal tables and drink the excellent dark ale brewed in-house. It's a Prague institution

but also a tourist trap; while the beer is good, the food is overpriced and forgettable.

Around Town A good Czech restaurant – with a sauna! – is **U radnice** (*Havlíčkovo nám 7, Žižkov, Prague 3; mains 50-85 Kč; open 11am-11pm Mon-Fri, 11am-10pm Sat & Sun*). Book ahead for the sauna. Nearby is **Mailsi** (*Lipanská 1; mains 150-300 Kč; open noon-11pm daily*), a great little Pakistani restaurant.

Pizzeria Grosseto (*Jugoslávsch patyzánů 8, Dejvice, Prague 6; mains 70-125 Kč; open 11.30am-11pm daily*) is a friendly place with excellent pizzas.

On the west bank of the river in Smíchov is **Hospoda U Starého lva** (*Lidická 13; mains 60-75 Kč; open 11am-11pm daily*), yet another reliable place for Czech pub grub.

Vegetarian In a passage south of Staroměstské nám, **Country Life** (*Melantrichova 15; mains 75-150 Kč; open 9am-8.30pm Mon-Fri*) has inexpensive salad sandwiches, pizzas, goulash and other vegetarian dishes. **Lotos** (*Platnéřská 13; mains 70-150 Kč; noon-10pm daily*), just north of the Klementinum, does gourmet vegie food with many dishes modelled on Bohemian cuisine.

Cafeteria-style **U Góvindy** (*Soukenická 27; open 11am-5.30pm Mon-Sat*) in the northern part of Nové Město is run by Hare Krishnas; a donation of at least 50 Kč gets you a hearty meal.

The best vegie food in Prague is served at **Radost Café** (*Belehradska 120; mains 110-230 Kč; open 11am-5am daily*), in the Club Radost FX (see Entertainment) where the menu ranges from Mexican to Italian to Thai.

Cafés Art Deco **Kavárna Slávia** (*Národní 1; open 8am-midnight Mon-Fri, 9am-midnight Sat & Sun*) is a classic but pricey Prague institution. A bit farther east on Národní is **Káva.Káva.Káva** (*open 7am-10pm daily*) in the Platýz courtyard at No 37, where you can indulge in huge cappuccinos along with carrot cake and other goodies. **Ebel Coffee House** (*Týn 2 • Řetězová 9; both open 9am-10pm daily*) offers superb coffee only a few minutes' walk from Staroměstské nám.

Prague also has several excellent oriental tearooms (*čajovny*) including **Dobra Čajovna** (*open 10am-11pm Mon-Sat, 2pm-11pm Sun*) in a passage at Václavské nám 14, and **Malý**

CZECH REPUBLIC

Buddha *(Úvoz 46; open 1pm-10.30pm Tues-Sun)* in Hradčany.

Self-Catering The Tesco, Kotva, Krone and Bílá Labuť department stores all have **supermarkets** in their basements. In the suburbs, the **Delvita** chain of supermarkets offers low prices and a wide selection of groceries.

Entertainment

Prague offers an amazing range of entertainment. While it has long been one of Europe's centres of classical music and jazz, it is now known for its rock and post-rock scenes as well. In such a vibrant city, it is quite possible that some places listed here will have changed by the time you arrive. For the most up-to-date information, refer to the *Prague Post, The Prague Pill, Culture in Prague* and the *Do města – Downtown* freesheet, and keep an eye on posters and bulletin boards.

For classical music, opera, ballet, theatre and some rock concerts – even the most 'sold-out' *(vyprodáno)* events – you can often find a ticket or two on sale at the box office 30 minutes or so before concert time. In addition, there are plenty of ticket agencies around Prague that will sell the same tickets at a high commission. Touts also sell tickets at the door, but avoid them unless you have no other option. Although some expensive tickets are set aside for foreigners, non-Czechs normally pay the same price as Czechs at the box office. Tickets can cost as little as 30 Kč for standing room only to over 900 Kč for the best seats in the house; the average price is about 500 Kč.

Cinema is good – films are usually screened in their original language with Czech subtitles – and tickets cost between 60 Kč and 130 Kč. The *Prague Post* lists what's on.

Ticket Agencies One of the largest ticket agencies is **Ticketpro** *(☎ 296 32 99 99, fax 296 32 88 88; ☒ www.ticketpro.cz; Salvátorská 10, Prague 1; open 9am-12.30pm & 1pm-5.15pm Mon-Fri)*, with branches in PIS offices (see Information earlier) and many other spots around Prague, including **Ticketcentrum** *(Rytířská 31; open 8.30am-8.30pm daily)*. Some music stores and other outlets also act as its agents – look for the Ticketpro sticker. The best place to buy your tickets for rock concerts is at Ticketpro's Melantrich outlet in the Rokoko passage at Václavské nám 38.

Other agencies include **Bohemia Ticket International** *(☎ 224 22 78 32, fax 221 61 21 26; ☒ www.ticketsbti.cz; Malé nám 13; open 9am-5pm Mon-Fri, 9am-2pm Sat • Na příkopě 16; open 10am-7pm Mon-Fri, 10am-5pm Sat, 10am-3pm Sun)*, American Express and Čedok (see Information, earlier).

Classical concert tickets are also available from the **FOK Box Office** *(☎ 222 00 23 36, fax 222 32 25 01; U obecního domu 2, Prague 1; open 10am-6pm Mon-Fri)*.

Most agencies charge similar prices for the following shows: the Laterna Magika (690 Kč), opera (230 Kč to 950 Kč), the National Theatre (600 Kč to 950 Kč) and the National Marionette Theatre (490 Kč).

Classical Music Prague's main concert venues include the Dvořák Hall in the neo-Renaissance **Rudolfinum** *(nám Jana Palacha; metro Staroměstská)*, and the Smetana Hall in the city's wonderful Art Nouveau **Obecní dům** *(nám Republiky 5)*. The latter always plays host to the opening concert of the Prague Spring festival.

Lots of organ concerts and recitals for tourists are performed in old churches and in historic buildings, but unfortunately many are of poor quality. You'll see stacks of fliers advertising these in every tourist office and travel agency around Prague. Seat prices begin at around 350 Kč, and the programmes change from week to week.

Jazz There are dozens of jazz clubs. The **Reduta Jazz Club** *(Národní 20; metro Národní Třída; cover charge 200 Kč; open 9pm-3am daily)* was founded in 1958 and is one of the oldest in Europe. You can hear live jazz every night at the unpretentious **AghaRTA jazz centrum** *(Krakovská 5; metro Muzeum; open 9pm-midnight daily)* and in the cosy basement at **U malého Glena** *(Karmelitská 23; metro Malostranská; music 9pm-2am daily)*.

Rock & Clubs Adjacent to the Reduta Jazz Club is the **Rock Café** *(Národní 20; open 10am-1am Mon-Fri, 8pm-3am Sat)*; wear black clothing if you can. **Batalion** *(28.října 3; open 24hr)* offers local rock, folk, jazz or blues bands downstairs, while DJs spin discs late at night or when there are no bands playing. **Lucerna Music Bar** *(Vodičkova 36; open 8pm-3am daily)*, inside the Lucerna passage, has live rock bands performing most nights.

Klub 007 Strahov (*Block 7, Chaloupeck-ého 7, Prague 6; open 8pm-1am daily*) has underground rock, punk, reggae bands or DJs playing nightly. Another place which has inexpensive beer and is popular with students is **Malostranská beseda** (*Malostranské nám 21; metro Malostranská; open 11am-1am daily*), where jazz, folk, country and rock can be heard nightly from 8.30pm.

Prague's prime club venue is **Radost FX** (**W** *www.radostfx.cz; Bělehradská 120, Prague 2; metro IP Pavlova*), with famous local and European guest DJs. The **Karlovy lázně** (*Novotného lávka, Prague 1*) complex, near the Smetana Museum, has a nightclub playing anything from 1960s hits to the latest techno on each of its three floors, while the basement hosts live bands.

Alternative Venues The **Roxy** (*Dlouhá 33, Prague 1; open 5pm-1am daily*) is a decrepit place with surprising longevity as an experimental venue – mostly avant-garde drama, dance and music.

One place with a difference is the **Palác Akropolis** (*Kubelíkova 27, Žižkov; metro Jiř-ího z Poděbrad*), where local bands perform. On some nights there are plays, films or other cultural shows.

Theatres Opera, ballet and classical drama (in Czech) are performed regularly at the neo-Renaissance **National Theatre** (*Národní 2; metro Národní Třída*). Next door is the modern **Laterna Magika** (*Národní 4*), established in 1983, which offers a widely imitated combination of theatre, dance and film.

Opera and ballet are also presented at the neo-Renaissance **State Opera** (*Wilsonova; metro Muzeum*). The neoclassical **Stavovské Theatre** (*Ovocný trh 1; metro Můstek*) also presents opera. Headphones providing simultaneous translation into English are available for some of its Czech plays.

For operettas and old-fashioned musicals in Czech go to the **Karlín Theatre of Music** (*Křižíkova 10; metro Florenc*), near Florenc bus station. Because it's a little out of the way and not as famous as some other venues, tickets are often available; it is highly recommended. The ticket office is open 10am to 1pm and 2pm to 6pm Monday to Saturday.

Several theatres around town stage 'black theatre' or 'magic theatre' performances combining mime, film, dance and music. **Black**

Theatre of Jiří Srnec (*Celetná 17, Nové Město; tickets from 370 Kč*) is one such place.

Plays by Václav Havel are often staged (in Czech) at **Na zábradlí Theatre** (*Anenské nám 5; metro Staroměstská*).

Puppet Theatres Children's theatre **Divadlo Minor** (*Vodičkova 6, Prague 1; metro Národní Třída*) has a fun mix of puppets and pantomime. Performances are at 9.30am, 3pm or 7pm Monday to Saturday and you can usually get a ticket at the door before the show.

What's Free

The National Museum is free on the first Monday of each month, and the City of Prague Museum is free on the first Thursday. All the galleries run by the City of Prague are free on the first Tuesday of the month.

Staroměstské nám and Karlův most are magical nocturnal attractions, and often have jazz bands busking for pennies. In the evening you can stroll along Na příkopě, where buskers play for the throng, or Václavské nám, where fast-food stands, cinemas and night bars stay open till late.

Shopping

You'll find many interesting shops along Karlova and Celetná, between Staroměstské nám and nám Republiky. One of the branches of **Česká lidová řemesla**, whose main shop is at Melantrichova 17, sells traditional Czech handicrafts. There are several good antique and bric-a-brac shops along Týnská and Týnská ulička, near Staroměstské nám.

For Bohemian crystal check the **Sklo** (*Václavské nám 28*) glass shop in the Alfa Cinema Arcade, or for the best-quality glass at premium prices there is **Moser** (*Na příkopě 17*). Ceramics with unusual Czech folk designs are worth checking out at **Tupesy** (*Havelská 21*). For all types of music **Bontonland** has the most choices – there is a major outlet at Václavské nám 1-3.

Getting There & Away

Air There are daily flights from Prague to Bratislava (from around 3000 Kč return) on **Czech Airlines** (*ČSA; ☎ 220 10 46 20; V celnici 5; metro Náměstí Republiky*).

Bus The **Florenc bus station** (*Florenc ÚAN; Křižíkova 4; metro Florenc*) is the departure point for buses that are travelling to Karlovy

CZECH REPUBLIC

CZECH REPUBLIC

Vary (110 Kč, 2½ hours), Brno (140 Kč, 2½ hours) and most other towns in the Czech Republic. Seven express buses a day go from Florenc to Bratislava (300 Kč). They take 4½ hours, compared to 5½ hours by train. Reservations are recommended on all these services.

The left-luggage room at Florenc station is upstairs above the information office (open 5am to 11pm daily).

Train Prague has four main train stations. International trains between Berlin and Budapest often stop at **Praha-Holešovice station** *(metro Nádraží Holešovice)* on the northern side of the city. Other important trains terminate at **Praha-hlavní nádraží** *(metro Hlavní Nádraží)* or **Praha-Masarykovo nádraží** *(metro Náměstí Republiky)*, both of which are close to the city centre. Some local trains to the southwest depart from **Praha-Smíchov station** *(metro Smíchovské Nádraží)*.

Praha-hlavní nádraží handles trains to České Budějovice (16 Kč, 2½ hours), Cheb via Plzeň (154 Kč, 3½ hours), Karlovy Vary (138 Kč, four hours), Košice (640 Kč, 10 hours), Kutná Hora (60 Kč, one hour), Plzeň (126 Kč, 1½ hours) and Tábor (80 Kč, 1½ hours). Trains to Brno (242 Kč, three hours) and Bratislava (400 Kč, 5½ hours) may leave from either Praha-hlavní nádraží, Praha-Holešovice or Masarykovo nádraží. Karlštejn (28 Kč, 35 minutes) trains depart from Hlavní nádraží and Smíchov.

This can be confusing, so study the timetables carefully to find out from which station you'll depart, then confirm the time and station at the information counter.

Praha-hlavní nádraží is Prague's largest train station with several exchange offices and accommodation services on levels 2 and 3, and a tourist information booth on level 2. The various snack stands on levels 2 and 3 are nothing special, but on level 4 is the pleasant Fantova kavárna, in a lovely Art Nouveau hall. Be extremely careful in and around the train station, as there are many thieves preying on unsuspecting foreigners.

The 24-hour left-luggage office (note its three half-hour breaks) is on level 1, so drop your bags off upon arrival and stroll into town to look for a room or a meal (you pay the fee – 15 Kč or 30 Kč per item per day depending on size – when you pick your bags up).

International tickets, domestic and international couchettes and seat reservations are sold on level 2 at the even-numbered windows from 10 to 24 to the right of the stairs leading to level 3. Domestic tickets are sold at the odd-numbered windows from 1 to 23 to the left of the stairs.

At Praha-Holešovice, windows marked ARES 1 and 2 are for booking international tickets and couchettes.

See the Getting There & Away and Getting Around sections earlier in this chapter introduction for more information.

Getting Around

To/From the Airport Prague's Ruzyně airport is 17km west of the city centre. City bus No 119 runs between the airport and Dejvická metro station (12 Kč, 20 minutes) daily from 5am to midnight. Buy tickets at the DPP desk in the airport (open 7am to 10pm daily), or from the vending machine at the bus stop (coins only).

Čedaz (☎ 220 11 42 96, 224 28 10 05; *open 5.30am-9.30pm daily*) has minibuses which depart every 30 minutes from nám Republiky, across from the Kotva department store (metro: Náměstí Republiky), and pick up passengers about 30 minutes later at Dejvická metro station on Evropská. Buy your ticket (90 Kč per person) from the driver. From the airport, they will take you to any address in central Prague (360 Kč for up to four people). To book a return trip to the airport, call at least two hours before your planned departure time.

Airport Cars taxi service, whose prices are regulated by the airport administration, charge 650 Kč (20% discount for return trip) into the centre of Prague (a regular taxi fare *from* central Prague should be about 450 Kč). Drivers accept Visa credit cards. If you take a regular taxi from the airport, there's a very good chance you will be ripped off, but going to the airport you should be safe taking a taxi with a reputable taxi company.

There's a 24-hour left-luggage office (40 Kč per day) in the terminal.

Public Transport All public transport is operated by **Dopravní podnik Praha** *(DP; ☎ 22 62 37 77; ₩ www.dp-praha.cz)*, which has information offices at Ruzyně airport and in five metro stations: Muzeum and Můstek (open 7am to 9pm daily), and Karlovo Náměstí, Nádraží Holešovice and Černý Most (open 7am to 6pm). Here you can get tickets, directions, a multilingual system map, a map of night services *(Noční provoz)* and a detailed and useful guide to the whole system.

Tickets are sold from machines at metro stations and major tram stops, at newsstands, Trafiky snack shops, PNS and other tobacco kiosks, hotels, all metro station ticket offices and DP information offices. The full-price ticket can also be bought from drivers on bus route Nos 300 to 399 only for 15 Kč; the exact fare is required.

A ticket *(jízdenka)* for one journey by tram, metro, bus or the Petřín funicular is 12 Kč, half-price for six- to 15-year-olds; large luggage and bicycles also need a 6 Kč ticket. Kids under six ride free. Validate (punch) your ticket by sticking it in the little yellow machine in the metro station lobby or on the bus or tram; this stamps the time and date on it. Once validated, tickets remain valid for 60 minutes from the time of stamping, if validated between 5am and 8pm on weekdays, and for 90 minutes at all other times. Within this time period, unlimited transfers are allowed on all types of public transport.

There's also a short-hop 8 Kč ticket, valid for 15 minutes on buses and trams, or for up to four metro stations or two zones. No transfers are allowed with these, and they're not valid on the Petřín funicular nor on night trams or buses. Being caught without a valid ticket entails a 400 Kč on-the-spot fine (50 Kč for not having a luggage ticket). Inspectors will often demand a higher fine from foreigners and pocket the difference, so insist on a receipt *(doklad)* before paying.

Travel tickets are available for periods of 24 hours (70 Kč) and three/seven/15 days (200/250/280 Kč). These tickets can be bought at the DP information desks, and at many other ticket offices in metro stations. You can also buy 24-hour tickets from vending machines. These must be validated on first use only.

On metro trains and newer trams and buses, an electronic display shows the route number and the name of the next stop and a recorded voice announces each station or stop. As the train, tram or bus pulls away, it says: *Příští stanice* (or *zastávka*) ... (The next station (or stop) is ...), perhaps noting that it's a *přestupní stanice* (transfer station). At metro stations, signs point you towards the *výstup* (exit) or to a *přestup* (transfer to another line).

Metro The metro operates from 5am to midnight daily. There are three lines: Line A runs from the northwestern side of the city at Dejvická to the east at Skalka; line B runs from the southwest at Zličín to the northeast at Černý Most; and line C runs from the north at Nádraží Holešovice to the southeast at Háje. Line A intersects line C at Muzeum, line B intersects line C at Florenc and line A intersects line B at Můstek.

After the metro closes at midnight, trams (Nos 51 to 58) and buses (Nos 501 to 512) still rumble across the city about every 40 minutes all night. If you're planning a late evening, find out if one of these services passes near where you're staying.

Car Local car-rental companies offer the best prices, although their staff may not speak fluent English; even so it's easy enough to book by email. Typical rates for a Škoda Felicia at the time of writing were 680 to 1150 Kč per day including unlimited kilometres, collision damage waiver and VAT; or 4600 Kč to 6300 Kč a week. Some companies ask for a deposit of 5000 Kč if they do not accept credit cards. Reputable local companies include:

Alimex ČR (☎ 800 150 170, e praha@ alimexcr.cz) Václavské nám, Prague 1
Secco Car (☎ 283 87 10 31, e info@ seccocar.cz) Přístavní 39, Prague 7
West Car Praha (☎ 235 36 53 07, e auto@ westcarpraha.cz) Veleslavínská 17, Prague 6

Mainstream international agencies charge at least twice the rates of local companies. All have airport pick-up points (where you may have to pay an extra 400 Kč surcharge), as well as central offices.

Bicycle Rental You can rents bicycles at **City Bike** *(☎ 776 180 284; Královská 5, Prague 1; metro Náměstí Míru; open 9am-7pm daily)* from 300 Kč a day. It also offers guided group rides.

Taxi The best way to avoid being ripped off by unscrupulous taxi drivers is to telephone for one using a reliable taxi company such as **AAA** *(☎ 221 11 11 11)* or **ProfiTaxi** *(☎ 261 31 41 51)*. If you feel you're being overcharged ask for a bill *(účet)*, which the driver is obliged to provide. Most taxi trips within the city centre should cost around 100 Kč to 150 Kč; a trip out to the suburbs should be no more than 250 Kč.

CZECH REPUBLIC

Central Bohemia

Although dominated by Prague, Central Bohemia has much to offer. Historic castles and chateaux rise out of the forests at Český Šternberk, Dobříš, Karlštejn, Kokořín, Konopiště, Křivoklát, Mělník and elsewhere, while Kutná Hora is a picturesque medieval town. Tourism is sharply focused on these sights. Transport around the region is good and all destinations can be visited as day trips from the capital.

KARLŠTEJN

An easy day trip from Prague is **Karlštejn Castle** (open 9am-noon & 12.30pm-6pm Tues-Sun July & Aug; 9am-noon & 12.30pm-5pm May, June & Sept; 9am-noon & 1pm-4pm Apr & Oct; 9am-noon & 1pm-3pm Nov-Mar), 33km to the southwest. Erected by Emperor Charles IV in the mid-14th century, this towering, fairy-tale castle crowns a ridge above the village, a 20-minute walk from the train station.

The highlight of Karlštejn Castle is the **Chapel of the Holy Rood** in the Great Tower, where the coronation jewels were kept until 1420. Some 128 painted panels by Master Theodoric and numerous precious stones covering the walls make this chapel a veritable gallery of 14th-century art.

The castle is closed on Monday, 24 December, 1 January and the day following public holidays. The 45-minute guided tours in English on Route I cost 200 Kč. Route II, which includes the chapel, runs from July to November only, and must be prebooked (☎ 274 00 81 54; e rezervace@spusc.cz) for a maximum of 10 people at 300 Kč per person plus a 20 Kč booking fee.

Trains leave for Karlštejn about once an hour from Praha-hlavní nádraží and Praha-Smíchov train stations (35 minutes).

KONOPIŠTĚ

Midway between Prague and Tábor, and 2km west of Benešov train station, is **Konopiště Chateau** (open 9am-12.30pm & 1pm-5pm daily May-Aug; 9am-12.30pm & 1pm-4pm daily Sept; 9am-12.30pm & 1pm-3pm Mon-Fri, 9am-12.30pm & 1pm-4pm Sat & Sun Apr & Oct; 9am-12.30pm & 1pm-3pm Sat & Sun Nov). The castle dates from the 14th century, but the Renaissance palace it shelters is from the 17th century.

Archduke Franz Ferdinand d'Este, heir to the Austro-Hungarian throne, had Konopiště renovated in 1894 and added a large English park and rose garden. His huge collection of hunting trophies and weapons, which are on display at the chateau, will disturb animal rights supporters.

There are three tours of the castle, each covering a different part. Tours I and II last 45 minutes each and in English cost 130 Kč; Tour III (one hour) is 260 Kč. Huge tour groups frequent the castle so get there early.

Twelve fast trains leave Prague's Praha-hlavní nádraží for Benešov (one hour, 49km) daily. Most trains going to and from Tábor (one hour, 54km) and České Budějovice (two hours, 120km) also stop here. There are occasional buses from Benešov train station to the castle, otherwise it's only a 10-minute walk to the west.

KUTNÁ HORA
pop 21,500
In the 14th century, Kutná Hora, 66km east of Prague, was the second-largest town in Bohemia after Prague. This was due to the rich veins of silver below the town itself, and the silver *groschen* minted here was the hard currency of Central Europe at the time. During the 16th century, Kutná Hora's boom ended, and mining ceased in 1726, so the medieval townscape is basically unaltered. In 1996 it was added to Unesco's World Heritage List.

Orientation & Information

The main train station, Kutná Hora hlavní nádraží, is 3km northeast of the centre. The bus station is more conveniently located just on the northeastern edge of the Old Town.

The easiest way to visit Kutná Hora on a day trip is to arrive on the morning express train from Prague's hlavní nádraží train station, then take a 10-minute walk from Kutná Hora hlavní nádraží train station to Sedlec to visit the ossuary (see the following Things to See section). From there it's another 15-minute walk or a five-minute bus ride to central Kutná Hora.

The municipal Kutná Hora **information centre** (☎ 327 51 23 78; e infocentrum@ kutnohorsko.cz; Palackého nám 377) sells local maps. Helpful staff can book accommodation and tours. There is also Internet access here for 1 Kč per minute (15 Kč minimum). **Komerční banka** (Tylova 9/390) has an ATM.

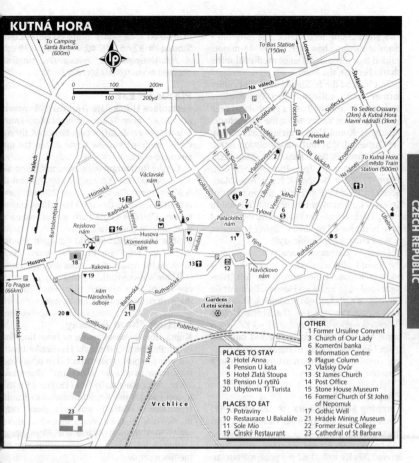

KUTNÁ HORA

OTHER
1 Former Ursuline Convent
3 Church of Our Lady
6 Komerční banka
8 Information Centre
9 Plague Column
12 Vlašský Dvůr
13 St James Church
14 Post Office
15 Stone House Museum
16 Former Church of St John
   of Nepomuk
17 Gothic Well
21 Hrádek Mining Museum
22 Former Jesuit College
23 Cathedral of St Barbara

PLACES TO STAY
2 Hotel Anna
4 Pension U kata
5 Hotel Zlatá Stoupa
18 Pension U rytířů
20 Ubytovna TJ Turista

PLACES TO EAT
7 Potraviny
10 Restaurace U Bakaláře
11 Sole Mio
19 Čínský Restaurant

Things to See

At Sedlec, 1km from Kutná Hora train station on the way into town (turn right when you come to a huge church on your left), is **Sedlec Ossuary** *(admission 30 Kč; open 8am-6pm daily Apr-Sept, 8am-noon & 1pm-5pm Oct, 9am-noon & 1pm-4pm Nov-Mar)*, decorated with the bones of some 40,000 people. In 1870, František Rint, a local woodcarver, arranged the bones in the form of a chandelier, bells, monstrances and even the Schwarzenberg coat-of-arms – a truly macabre sight.

Continue 2km southwest along Masarykova. As you enter the Old Town on Na náměti you'll see the Gothic **Church of Our Lady** on the left. Continue straight on and turn right on Tylova, which will take you to Palackého nám, the main square.

From the upper end of Palackého nám, Jakubská – a lane to the left – leads directly to **St James Church** (1330), just east of which is **Vlašský dvůr** *(Italian Court; admission 70 Kč; open 9am-6pm daily Apr-Sept, 10am-5pm Mar & Oct, 10am-4pm Nov-Feb)*, the former Royal Mint, now a museum. Master craftsmen from Florence began stamping silver coins here in 1300.

From the southern side of St James a narrow cobbled lane leads down and then up to the **Hrádek Mining Museum** *(admission with/without tour of mine 110/60 Kč; open 10am-6pm Tues-Sun July & Aug, 9am-6pm May, June & Sept, 9am-5pm Apr & Oct)*. This 15th-century palace contains an exhibit on the silver mining that made Kutná Hora wealthy. Note the huge wooden device used in the Middle Ages to lift up to 1000kg of rock from 200m-deep shafts. The museum's main attraction, however, is the 45-minute guided tour through 500m of **medieval mine shafts** beneath the town.

Just beyond the Hrádek is the 17th-century **former Jesuit college**, which has baroque sculptures in front of it and a good view of the Vrchlice River valley from the promenade. Nearby is Kutná Hora's greatest monument, the **Cathedral of St Barbara** (admission 30 Kč; open 9am-5.30pm Tues-Sun May-Sept, 10am-11.30am & 1pm-4pm Apr & Oct, 10am-11.30am & 2pm-3.30pm Nov-Mar), begun in 1388 by Petr Parléř, the architect of St Vitus Cathedral in Prague, and finished in 1547. The exquisite net vault above the central nave is supported by double flying buttresses in the French high-Gothic style.

From St Barbara retrace your steps past the Jesuit College and along Barborská till it ends at Komenského nám. Turn left, then right, and right again on Husova, then left on Lierova, which leads to Radnická. Downhill and across the street is the **Stone House** (Václavské nám 24; admission 40 Kč; open same hours as Hrádek), a fine old building from 1485 with a high triangular gable bearing figures of knights jousting. It's now a museum of local history.

Places to Stay

Camping Santa Barbara (☎ 327 51 20 51) is northwest of the town off Česká, and near the cemetery.

The private rooms in town cost from around 300 Kč to 500 Kč per person. **Pension U rytířů** (☎ 327 51 22 56; Rejskovo nám 123; rooms per person 250 Kč) is a friendly place to stay. Rooms vary in price but are mostly doubles with shared bathroom and toilet.

Ubytovna TJ Turista (☎ 327 51 49 61; nám Národního odboje 56; dorm beds with/without youth card 140/160 Kč; reception open 5pm-6pm) offers basic dormitory accommodation.

There are plenty of pensions and hotels to choose from. Rooms with shower and toilet at **Pension U kata** (☎ 327 51 50 96; Uhelná 569; singles/doubles 300/400 Kč) are pretty good value.

Hotel Anna (☎/fax 327 51 63 15; Vladislavova 372; singles/doubles/triples from 690/990/1465 Kč) offers comfortable, modern rooms with shower, TV and breakfast.

The most luxurious place that you can stay in town is the elegantly furnished **Hotel Zlatá Stoupa** (☎ 327 51 15 40, fax 327 51 38 08; e zlatastoupa@iol.cz; Tylova 426; singles/doubles from 1070/1800 Kč).

Places to Eat

Restaurace U Bakaláře (Husova 103; mains 85-110 Kč; open 10am-midnight Mon-Thur, 10am-6pm Fri & Sat) serves tasty and filling Czech grub, plus a few vegie dishes for the nonmeat-eater.

Čínský Restaurant (nám Národního odboje 48; mains 90-150 Kč; open 11am-2.30pm & 5.30pm-10pm Tues-Sat, 11am-2.30pm Sun) is a little heavy on the MSG but still manages a tasty Chicken Gung-Pao, which makes a change from dumplings.

Sole Mio (pizzas 80-100 Kč; open 11am-10pm Mon-Fri, 11am-11pm Sat, noon-10pm Sun), on the main square, does decent pizzas.

There's a convenient **potraviny** (grocery; open 6am-6pm Mon-Fri, 7am-noon Sat) on the eastern side of the main square.

Getting There & Away

Kutná Hora is on the main railway line between Prague and Brno via Havlíčkův Brod, but many express trains don't stop here (you may have to change at Kolín). There are seven direct trains daily from Prague's Praha-hlavní nádraží (62 Kč, 55 minutes) to Kutná Hora hlavní nádraží, which is about 3km northeast of the town centre. From here there are 15 local trains daily to Kutná Hora město station (8 Kč, seven minutes) on the edge of the town centre.

There are half-a-dozen buses to Prague (60 Kč, 1¼ hours) on weekdays but far fewer on weekends. If your timing doesn't coincide with a bus direct to Prague, take one to Kolín (12km), where there are better connections. At Kutná Hora bus station, buses to Prague leave from stand No 6, those to Kolín from stand Nos 2 and 10.

North Bohemia

Tourists tend to be shy of North Bohemia, perceived as little more than an arc of polluted factory towns, but away from the Chomutov-Most-Ústí nad Labem industrial region there are numerous unspoilt attractions, such as Litoměřice.

LITOMĚŘICE
pop 25,100

Litoměřice and was founded by German colonists in the 13th century, beneath the site of a 9th-century Slavic hill-top fortress. Five hundred years later, under Ferdinand III, the town's new status as a royal seat and bishopric brought it more prosperity. Today, the old town centre has many picturesque baroque buildings and churches, some of which were designed by the 18th-century architect Ottavio Broggio, who was born in the town.

Orientation & Information

The old centre is just across the road to the west of the adjacent train and bus stations, past the best-preserved parts of the 14th-century town walls. Walk down Dlouhá to the central square, Mírové nám.

The **information centre** (☎ 416 73 24 40; e info@mulitom.cz; Mírové nám 15; open 8am-6pm Mon-Sat, 9.30am-4pm Sun May-Sept; 8am-4pm Mon-Fri, 8am-11am Sat Oct-Apr) is in the distinctive House at the Chalice, the present town hall. The **Komerční banka** (Mírové nám 37) cashes travellers cheques and has an ATM. The **post and telephone office** is on Osvobození, two blocks north of Mírové nám.

Things to See

Dominating the broad and beautiful main square is the Gothic-turned-baroque **All Saints Church**. Across the street is the **Old Town Hall** with a small town museum, while the thin slice of pink baroque wedding cake at the uphill end of the square is the **House of Ottavio Broggio**. Compare it to the plain Gothic house at No 16, the oldest on the square, now the **Museum and Gallery of Litoměřice** (open 9am-noon & 1pm-6pm Tues-Sun Apr-Sept, to 5pm Oct-Mar) with a collection of religious art from St Stephen Cathedral. The green copper artichoke sprouting from the roof of the new town hall is actually a chalice, the traditional symbol of the Hussite church.

West of the square is another house where Broggio also left his touch, the excellent **North Bohemia Fine Arts Gallery** (Michalská 7; open 9am-noon & 1pm-6pm Tues-Sun) with its priceless panels from the Litoměřice Altarpiece.

Grassy, tree-lined, Domské nám on Cathedral Hill, southwest of the main square, is the town's historical centre. Pretty **St Wenceslas Church**, a true baroque gem, is just off the square at Domská. On top of Cathedral Hill is the town's oldest church, **St Stephen Cathedral**, dating from the 11th century.

Places to Stay

Autocamp Slavoj (☎ 416 73 44 81; open May-Sept), on Střelecký ostrov just south of the train and bus stations, has cheap bungalows as well as tent sites.

The best bargain in town is **Penzion U pavouka** (☎ 416 73 44 09; Pekařská 7; doubles 550 Kč), where the price includes breakfast. The new **Pension U svatého Václava** (☎ 416 73 75 00; Svatováclavská 12; singles/doubles 600/1000 Kč) is a bit more posh.

The top place in town, **Hotel Salva Guarda** (☎ 73 25 06, fax 73 27 98; Mírové nám 12; singles/doubles 920/1400 Kč), is in the historic House at the Black Eagle, where cosy rooms come with bathroom and TV.

Places to Eat

There's a **pekárna-potraviny** (bakery & grocery; open 7am-7pm Mon-Fri, 7am-noon Sat, 8am-noon Sun) at the top end of the square.

There is pleasant **café** (open 8am-10pm daily) in the arcade beneath the Old Town Hall. **Radniční sklípek** (Mírové nám 21; mains 85-125 Kč; open 10am-11pm daily) is a good cellar pub and restaurant serving cheap Czech grub.

Getting There & Away

There are no direct trains from Prague to Litoměřice, but there are hourly buses (61 Kč, one hour).

AROUND LITOMĚŘICE
Terezín

The huge 18th-century fortress town of Terezín is better known to history as Theriesenstadt – a notorious WWII concentration camp. It's only 3km south of Litoměřice and makes a deeply moving day trip.

Hourly buses from Litoměřice will drop you off at the main square, nám Československé armády, in the Main Fortress, where the **Museum of the Ghetto** (combined ticket to all museums 160 Kč; open 8am-6pm daily Apr-Sept, 8am-4.30pm Oct-Mar) documents daily life in the town in WWII. The Lesser Fortress is a 10-minute walk east across the Ohře River, where you can take a grimly fascinating self-guided tour through the prison barracks, isolation cells, workshops, morgues, execution grounds and former mass graves. During the floods of summer 2002, Terezín suffered severely, with buildings damaged and much original furniture destroyed. It is still partly open to visitors, but may not be fully repaired until 2006.

West Bohemia

Cheb and Plzeň are the western gateways to the Czech Republic. All trains from western Germany pass this way and the stately imperial spa of Karlovy Vary is nearby.

KARLOVY VARY
pop 53,900

Karlovy Vary (which means 'Charles' Hot Springs') is the largest and oldest of the Czech Republic's many spas. A local tradition says Emperor Charles IV discovered the springs by chance while hunting a stag. In 1358, he built a hunting lodge here and gave the town his name. From the 19th century, celebrities such as Beethoven, Bismarck, Brahms, Chopin, Franz Josef I, Goethe, Metternich, Paganini, Liszt, Peter the Great, Schiller, Tolstoy, Karl Marx and Yuri Gagarin came here to take the waters, and the busts of a few of them grace the promenades. Ludvík Moser began making glassware at Karlovy Vary in 1857 and today Bohemian crystal is prized around the world.

Karlovy Vary's 12 hot springs contain the various minerals used in the treatment of metabolic disorders and diseases of the digestive tract. The locally produced Becherovka herbal liqueur is known as the 13th spring.

Karlovy Vary still retains a 19th-century atmosphere despite being crowded with tourists. Elegant colonnades and boulevards complement the many peaceful walks in surrounding parkland. The picturesque river valley winds between wooded hills, yet the spa offers all the facilities of a medium-sized town.

Orientation

Karlovy Vary has two train stations. Express trains from Prague and Cheb use Karlovy Vary-horní nádraží, across the Ohře, just north of the city. Local trains stop at Karlovy Vary Dolní nádraží, which is beside the main ČSAD bus station. The Tržnice city bus station is in front of the market (*Městská tržnice*), three blocks east of Karlovy Vary Dolní nádraží.

TG Masaryka, the pedestrian mall in Karlovy Vary's city centre, runs east to the Teplá River. Upstream is the heart of the spa area.

If you decide to walk from town to Karlovy Vary-horní nádraží, you'll see a huge, pale pinkish-brown building directly in front of you as you cross the bridge leading to Sokolovska. Go around to the left behind this building and then straight ahead until you see a signposted way on the left which leads through a tunnel and straight up to the station

Both train stations have left-luggage rooms; the one at Karlovy Vary-horní nádraží is open 24 hours a day.

Maps One of the best city maps is SHOCart GeoClub's *Karlovy Vary* (1:12,000) available from Infocentrum and bookshops.

Information

The main information office is **Infocentrum** (☎ 353 22 40 97; **e** infocentrum@email.cz, *Lázeňská 1; open 8am-6pm Mon-Fri, 10am-4pm Sat & Sun*), which has brochures and maps, including the monthly *Promenáda* magazine full of all the latest information on Karlovy Vary. It can arrange spa treatment for visitors from 2500 Kč per person a day including room and board.

Money You'll find an exchange counter and an ATM at **Česká spořitelna** (*TG Masaryka 14*). **Incentives CZ** (☎ 353 22 60 27; *Vřídelní 51; open 10am-6pm Mon-Fri, 10am-4pm Sat*) is an American Express representative and has an exchange office.

Post & Communications The main post office (*TG Masaryka 1; open 7.30am-7pm Mon-Fri, 7am-1pm Sat, 7am-noon Sun*) includes a telephone centre; there's also a branch post office on Vřídelní. You can check email at the **Internet Café** (*open 10am-10pm daily*) in the Hotel Thermal for a minimum charge of 40 Kč or 80 Kč an hour.

Medical & Emergency Services There's a 24-hour **medical centre** (*lekárská pohotovost;* ☎ 353 22 46 79; *Krymská 2a*) near the Dolní nádraží train station; nearby **Aesculap** (*nám Dr M Horákové 8*) is a pharmacy. To get to the **Foreigners Police** (☎ 353 50 32 00; *Závodu míru 16; open 8am-5pm Mon & Wed*), take bus No 3 from Tržnice bus station and get off at the fifth stop.

KARLOVY VARY

PLACES TO STAY
6 W-Privat
   Accommodation
   Agency
10 Hotel Kavalerie
21 Pension Kosmos
25 Hotel Kolonáda
39 Hotel Embassy
42 Grandhotel Pupp

PLACES TO EAT
1 Městská tržnice
   (Market)
9 Parlament
12 Trumf Bakery
14 Bistro Pupík
17 VgR Vegetarian
   Restaurant
18 P & P Pizzeria
37 Café Elefant
45 Café

OTHER
2 ČSAD Long-Distance
   Bus Station
3 24-Hour Medical Centre
5 ČSAD Agency
7 Propaganda Music Club
8 Čedok Travel Agency
11 MHD Office (Public
   Transport Information)
13 Tržnice City Bus Station
15 Česká spořitelna
16 Kino Čas
19 Poštovní Bridge
20 Post & Telephone Office
22 Hotel Thermal; Internet
   Café
23 Open-Air Thermal Pool
24 Sadová Kolonáda
26 Church of SS Peter & Paul
27 Karl Marx Monument
28 Mlýnská Kolonáda &
   Bandstand
29 Infocentrum
30 Golden Key Museum
31 Incentives CZ
32 Branch Post Office
33 Zámecká Tower
34 House of the Three Moors
35 Vřídelní Kolonáda
36 Church of Mary
   Magdalene
38 Divadlo Vítězslava
   Nezvala
40 Karlovy Vary Museum
41 Lázně I (Spa No 1)
43 Diana Funicular Railway
44 Diana Tower

CZECH REPUBLIC

Things to See

As you follow the riverside promenade south, you'll pass the towering concrete **Hotel Thermal and Spa** (1976) and the neoclassical **Mlýnská Kolonáda** (1881), designed by Josef Zítek. The **Golden Key Museum** *(Lázeňská 3; admission 20 Kč; open 9am-noon & 1pm-5pm Wed-Sun)* is next, with paintings of the spa from the early 20th century. On a nearby hill is the old **Zámecká tower** (1608) on the site of Charles IV's 1358 hunting lodge; today it's a restaurant. Down the hill from the tower is the **House of the Three Moors** *(Dagmar House; Tržiště 25)*, where Goethe stayed during his many visits to Karlovy Vary.

Opposite this building is a bridge which leads to the pulsing heart of Karlovy Vary, the **Vřídelní Kolonáda**. A modern glass enclosure houses the Vřídlo or Sprudel (geyser), where spring water at 72.2°C spurts 12m into the air. Throngs of Czech tourists, little porcelain spa cups *(lázeňský pohárek)* in hand, pace up and down the neighbouring colonnade, taking the drinking cure (you're free to try it too, as long as you have your own cup).

Overlooking the Vřídelní Kolonáda is the baroque **Church of Mary Magdalene** (1736) designed by Kilian Dientzenhofer. Continue southwest along the river past the **Divadlo Vítězslava Nezvala** theatre (1886) to the **Karlovy Vary Museum** *(Nová Louka 23; admission 30 Kč; open 9am-noon & 1pm-5pm Wed-Sun)*, which has displays on local and natural history.

Beyond the park past the museum is the beautifully restored **Lázně I** (Spa No 1; 1895). Cross the bridge beside it and return north along the promenade on the far bank, past the **Grandhotel Pupp**, a former meeting place of the European aristocracy.

Just beyond the hotel you'll see Mariánská, a narrow alley on the left leading to the bottom station of the **Diana Funicular Railway** *(one way/return 25/40 Kč; open 9am-6pm daily)*, which climbs the 166m to the **Diana Tower** every 15 minutes. There are great views from the top, and pleasant walks back down through the forest. A café adjoins the Diana Tower.

Activities

Relax after your sightseeing with a swim in the large **open-air thermal pool** *(bazén; admission 30 Kč an hour; open 8am-8.30pm Mon-Sat, 9am-9.30pm Sun)* on the cliff top overlooking the Hotel Thermal.

The pool is closed every third Monday There's also a **sauna** *(10am-9.30pm daily)*, solarium and a fitness club.

Special Events

Cultural events include the Jazz Festival ir May, the Dvořák Singing Contest in June the International Film Festival (**w** www.kvif .com) in July, the Dvořák Autumn Festiva and Tourfilm (International Festival of Films about Tourism) in September.

Places to Stay

Camp Březový Háj (☎ 353 22 26 65, ☎ 602 120 477; **e** info@brezovy-haj.cz; Staromlýnská, Březová; tent sites 90 Kč; bungalow beds 150 Kč; open May-Sept) is in the Teplá valley 3km southwest of town. There are hourly buses (weekdays only) from the Tržnice bus station to Brežova (20 minutes)

On weekends Karlovy Vary fills up with German visitors and accommodation can be tight. **Čedok** (☎ 353 22 33 35; Dr Bechera 21, open 9am-6pm Mon-Fri, 9am-noon Sat, travel agency and **W-Privat Accommodation Agency** (☎/fax 353 22 77 68; nám Republiky 5; open 8.30am-5pm Mon-Fri, 9.30am-1pm Sat) can organise private rooms from 350 Kč per person.

A 15 Kč per person spa tax is added to regular hotel rates. The hostel-style **Penzión Hestia** (☎ 353 22 59 85, fax 353 22 04 82, Stará Kysibelská 45; beds 350 Kč) is a half-hour walk east of the centre, or you can take bus No 6 from Tržnice bus station. It has clean rooms, with shared facilities.

There are a number of reasonable pensions along Zahradní, such as **Pension Kosmos** (☎/fax 353 22 31 68; singles/doubles from 450/720 Kč) at No 39.

The two-star **Hotel Kavalerie** (☎ 353 22 96 13, fax 353 23 61 71; **e** kavalerie@volny .cz; TG Masaryka 43; singles/doubles 950/ 1350 Kč) is probably the best-value hotel in the town centre.

Hotel Embassy (☎ 353 22 11 61, fax 353 22 31 46; **e** embassy@mbox.vol.cz; Nová Louka 21; singles/doubles 2020/2980 Kč) is a good mid-range place with elegant 19th-century-style decor.

The attractive **Hotel Kolonáda** (☎ 353 34 55 55, fax 353 34 78 18; **e** reception@ kolonada.cz; IP Pavlova 8; singles/doubles 3355/5810 Kč), in the heart of the spa area, is even more luxurious.

Karlovy Vary's premier address is the opulent five-star **Grandhotel Pupp** (☎ 353 10 91 11, fax 353 22 40 32; e pupp@pupp.cz; *Mírové nám 2; singles/doubles US$180/220)*, an imposing 112-room hotel founded in 1701. Its annexe, the **Parkhotel Pupp**, has slightly less expensive rooms.

Places to Eat
P & P Pizzeria *(IP Pavlova 13; mains 75-90 Kč; open 10am-10pm Mon-Sat, 10am-8pm Sun)* is just across Poštovní Bridge. In a back court around the corner is the good **VgR Vegetarian Restaurant** *(IP Pavlova 23; open 11am-10pm daily)*.

Parlament *(cnr TG Masaryka & Zeyerova; mains 65-85 Kč; open 9am-10pm Mon-Sat)* is a good inexpensive place serving pork sauerkraut and dumplings and other Czech dishes.

The upmarket **Café Elefant** *(Stará Louka 30)* is perhaps Karlovy Vary's most popular and elegant café.

There's a good, cheap **bufet** inside the entrance to the market, which itself is a large supermarket. **Trumf** *(Zeyerova 17)* is a good cake shop and bakery. **Bistro Pupík** *(Horova 2)*, next to the Tržnice city bus station, has cheap beer on tap.

Entertainment
Karlovy Vary's main theatre is the **Divadlo Vítězslava Nezvala** *(Divadlo nám)*. From mid-May and mid-September concerts are held in Vřídelní Kolonáda Tuesday to Sunday.

Propaganda Music Club *(Jaltská 7)* has occasional live bands or DJs spinning rock/pop music nightly. Seeing a movie at the **Kino Čas** *(TG Masaryka 3)* is another option.

Getting There & Away
Bus There are direct trains to Prague, but it's faster and easier to take one of the five daily buses (110 Kč, 2½ hours). For Cheb, the bus (50 Kč, one hour) is also slightly faster than the train. The only way to get directly to Plzeň (1½ hours, 84km) and České Budějovice (four hours, 220km) is by bus. Seats on express buses should be reserved in advance at the **ČSAD agency** (☎ 353 22 36 62; *nám Republiky 7; open 6am-6pm Mon-Fri, 7am-noon Sat)* at the Dolní nádraží train station.

Train There are several direct trains daily from Karlovy Vary to Prague (168 Kč, 4½ hours). Hourly local trains connect Cheb (48 Kč, one hour) to Karlovy Vary. Heading west from Karlovy Vary to Nuremberg, Germany, and beyond, you'll have to change at Cheb.

Getting Around
You can buy local bus tickets (8 Kč) at the MHD office on Zeyerova and from automatic ticket machines. Bus No 11 runs hourly from Karlovy Vary-horní nádraží to the Tržnice city bus station at the market, then over the hills to Divadlo nám and the Vřídelní Kolonáda. Bus No 2 runs between Tržnice and Grandhotel Pupp (Lázně I) every half-hour or so from 6am to 11pm daily.

You can rent mountain bikes for 60/320 Kč per hour/day from Incentives CZ (see Money, earlier in this section).

AROUND KARLOVY VARY
Loket
If you have an afternoon free, take a ČSAD bus for Sokolov and get off 8km southwest of Karlovy Vary at Loket (20 Kč, 20 minutes). There's an impressive 13th-century **castle** *(English guided tours 100 Kč; open 9am-4.30pm daily Apr-Oct, 9am-3.30pm Nov-Mar)* on the hill in the town centre. A museum in the castle is dedicated to the china made in Loket since 1815. On the facade of Hotel Bílý Kůň, in Loket's picturesque town square, is a plaque commemorating Goethe's seven visits.

You can walk back to Karlovy Vary from Loket in three hours. Follow the scenic trail (blue waymarks) along the left bank of the Ohře to the **Svatošské Rocks**. Here, cross the river on a footbridge and follow the road to Doubí where you can catch Karlovy Vary city bus No 6 the rest of the way into town.

CHEB
pop 33,000
This medieval town (known as Eger in German) on the Ohře River, near the western tip of the Czech Republic, is an easy day trip on the train from Karlovy Vary. Only a few kilometres from the Bavarian border, Cheb retains a strong German flavour.

Orientation & Information
The train station and left-luggage office are at the southeastern end of třída Svobody.

The **Tourist Infocentrum** (☎ 354 42 27 05; e infocentrum.cheb@email.cz; *nám krále Jiřího z Poděbrad 33; open 9am-5pm Mon-Fri, 9am-noon Sat)* sells maps, guidebooks

CZECH REPUBLIC

and theatre and concert tickets, and can organise guides.

Česká spořitelna (cnr třída Svobody & Májová) has an exchange counter and an ATM. There's also a 24-hour ATM farther along třída Svobody towards nám krále Jiřího z Poděbrad.

The main post office is beside the train station. There's a telephone centre on nám krále Jiřího z Poděbrad at No 38.

The **24-hour pharmacy** (nám krále Jiřího z Poděbrad 6) has a red button to press in case of an emergency that happens outside normal business hours.

Things to See

Only a just few minutes' walk along třída Svobody from the ugly train-station area is the picturesque town square, nám krále Jiřího z Poděbrad, surrounded by burgher houses with red-tiled roofs. In the middle is the **Špalíček**, a cluster of 16th-century Gothic houses, which were once Jewish shops. Behind these is the **Cheb Museum** (admission 50 Kč; open 9am-12.30pm & 1pm-5pm Tues-Sun Mar-Dec), which has an excellent historical exhibition. The Thirty Years' War military commander Duke Albrecht Wallenstein was murdered in this building in 1634 and the museum devotes a room to him. Also on the square is the baroque, formerly new town hall (1728), now the **Museum of Fine Arts** (admission 20 Kč; open same hours as Cheb Museum) with changing art exhibits.

Behind Cheb Museum is **St Nicholas Church**, a massive Gothic structure with a sculpture-filled interior. Notice the portal (1270) and Romanesque features, such as the twin towers. West is **Cheb Castle** (admission 30 Kč; open 9am-6pm Tues-Sun June-Aug, 9am-5pm Tues-Sun May & Sept, 9am-4pm Tues-Sun Apr & Oct), erected in the 12th century by Friedrich I Barbarossa, leader of the Eastern Crusades. The Black Tower dates from 1222 but the exterior fortifications were built in the 17th century. In the castle is a 12th-century chapel, a rare sight in the Czech Republic.

Places to Stay

The nearest camping ground is **Autokempink Dřenice** (☎ 354 43 15 91; tent sites 190 Kč, plus per person 30 Kč; open May–mid-Sept) on Jesenice Lake, 5km east of Cheb. It also has bungalows for 170 Kč per person.

There are several pensions around town including the homely **Pension U kata** (☎ 354 42 34 65; Židovská 17; singles/doubles 350/700 Kč). The nearby **Hostel Židovská ulice** (☎ 354 42 34 01; Židovská 11; quads 1050 Kč) has basic accommodation in four-bed rooms; if available, a single costs 400 Kč.

The handful of hotels in Cheb includes just two in the city centre. The **Hotel Slávie** (☎/fax 354 43 32 16; třída Svobody 75) was undergoing renovation at the time of writing. **Hotel Hvězda** (☎ 354 42 25 49, fax 354 42 25 46; nám krále Jiřího z Poděbrad 4; singles/doubles 900/1500 Kč) on the main square is the most expensive place in town, although the rooms are still pretty basic.

Places to Eat

The Prior department store on třída Svobody has a basement **supermarket** in and there is a small open-air **market** on Obrněné brigády. There are a couple of tourist restaurants around nám krále Jiřího z Poděbrad; the best bet is **Kavárna Špalíček** (mains 90-150 Kč; open 9am-10pm daily) at No 499. The food is good, but the modern decor (and purple furniture) destroys any historical ambience.

Getting There & Away

Most trains arriving in the Czech Republic from Nuremberg and Leipzig stop here, and there are express trains to and from Stuttgart (six hours, 342km), Frankfurt am Main (five hours, 389km) and Dortmund (eight hours, 728km) daily. There are plenty of trains to Cheb from Prague (194 Kč, 3½ hours) via Plzeň (120 Kč, 1½ hours).

A railcar covers the 13km from Cheb to Schirnding, Germany (15 minutes, 13km), every two hours daily. To board an international train, enter through the door marked *zoll-douane* (customs) to one side of the main station entrance at least an hour before departure. If you miss the train to Schirnding you could take city bus No 5 to Pomezí (15 minutes), which is near the border 8km west of Cheb, and then cross into Germany on foot. The bus to Pomezí leaves from stand No 9 at the train station every hour or so.

PLZEŇ
pop 173,000

The city of Plzeň (Pilsen), midway between Prague and Nuremberg, is the capital of West Bohemia. At the confluence of four rivers, this town was once an active medieval trading centre. An ironworks was founded here in 1859, which Emil Škoda purchased 10 years later. The Škoda Engineering Works became a producer of high-quality armaments and was subject to heavy bombing at the end of WWII. The rebuilt Škoda Works now produces machinery and locomotives.

Beer has been brewed in Plzeň for 700 years and the town is famous as the original home of Pilsner. The only original Pilsner trademark is Pilsner Urquell (in German; Plzeňský Prazdroj in Czech). Connoisseurs of the brewer's art will not regret the pilgrimage.

Orientation

The main train station, Plzeň-hlavní nádraží, is on the eastern side of town. The central bus station is west of the centre on Husova, opposite the Škoda Works. Between these is the old town, which is centred on nám Republiky.

Tram No 2 goes from the train station to the centre of town and on to the bus station. The left-luggage office at the bus station is open 8am to 8pm Monday to Friday; the office at the train station is open 24 hours.

Information

The **city information centre** (☎ 377 03 27 50; e infocenter@mmp.plzen-city.cz; open 9am-6pm daily Apr-Sept, 10am-5pm Mon-Fri, 10am-3.30pm Sat & Sun Oct-Mar) is on the main square at nám Republiky 41.

Komerční banka (Zbrojnická 4) has an exchange desk, and there's a 24-hour ATM at the ČSOB on Americká.

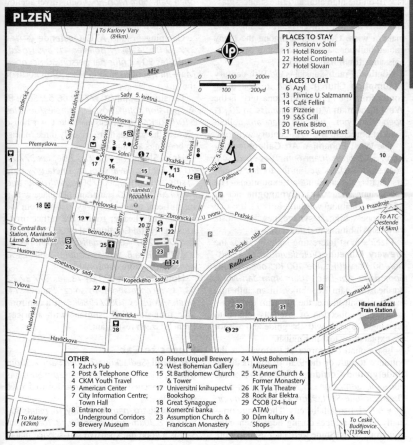

There's a telephone centre in the **main post office** *(Solní 20; open 7am-7pm Mon-Fri, 8am-1pm Sat, 8am-noon Sun),* and you can check email at the **American Center** *(☎ 377 23 77 22; Dominikánská 9; open 8am-6pm Mon-Fri)* for 30 Kč per half hour.

Universitní knihkupectví *(cnr Sedláčkova & Solní)* sells maps and a small collection of English books.

Things to See

Gothic **St Bartholomew Church** *(admission 20 Kč; open 10am-4pm Wed-Sat, noon-7pm Sun Apr-Dec)* in the middle of nám Republiky has the highest **tower** *(admission 20 Kč; open 10am-6pm daily)* in Bohemia at 102m; the view from the top is superb. Inside the soaring 13th-century structure are a Gothic Madonna (1390) on the high altar and fine stained-glass windows. On the back of the outer side of the church is an iron grille. Touch the angel and make a wish. Outstanding among the many gabled buildings around the square is the Renaissance **town hall** (1558).

South on Františkánská is the 14th-century **Assumption Church**. Behind it, around the corner from the Franciscan Monastery, is the **West Bohemian Museum** *(admission 20 Kč; open 9am-5pm Tues-Sun Mar-Jan)* collections of porcelain and 17th-century weapons.

The **West Bohemian Art Gallery** *(admission 20 Kč; open 10am-6pm Tues-Fri & Sun, noon-6pm Sat),* located in the former Butchers' Stalls, has changing art exhibitions. The neo-Renaissance **Great Synagogue** across Sady Pětatřicátníků was built in 1892. It is one of Europe's biggest synagogues, and hosts various exhibitions and concerts.

Plzeň's most interesting sight by far is the **Brewery Museum** *(Veleslavínova 6; admission 60 Kč, with guide 100 Kč; open 10am-6pm daily Apr-Dec, 10am-4pm Jan-Mar),* northeast of nám Republiky. In an authentic medieval malt house, the museum displays a fascinating collection of artefacts related to brewing. Dispense with the guide and ask for the explanatory text in English.

Just around the corner at Perlová 4 is the entrance to part of the 9km of the medieval **Underground Corridors** *(Plzeňské historické podzemí; admission 35 Kč; open 9am-5pm Tues-Sun June-Sept, 9am-5pm Wed-Sun Apr, May & Oct)* beneath the city. These were originally built as refuges during sieges, hence the numerous wells. Some were later used to store kegs of maturing beer. To enter you must wait for a group of at least five people to gather, then follow a tour (if there is no English-speaking guide ask for the text in English).

The very famous **Pilsner Urquell Brewery** *(☎ 377 06 11 11; tour 100 Kč; open 8am-4pm Mon-Fri, 8am-1pm Sat & Sun)* is only a 10-minute walk east along Pražská over the river. The twin-arched gate dated 1842–92, which appears on every genuine Pilsner label, is here. A one-hour tour of the brewing room and fermentation cellar is offered to individuals at 12.30pm on weekdays only. The rest of the day is reserved for organised groups.

Places to Stay

The **CKM** *(☎ 377 23 63 93, fax 377 23 69 09; e ckm-plzen@volny.cz; Dominikánská 1; open 9am-5pm Mon-Fri)* youth travel agency can book hostels in summer (from 200 Kč per person), pensions and hotels.

Camping ground **ATC Oestende** *(☎/fax 377 52 01 94; Malý Bolevec 41; bus No 20; tent sites 90 Kč plus per person 30 Kč; open May–mid-Sept)* is in Bílá Hora, 5km north of the city.

Pension v Solní *(☎ 377 23 66 52; Solní 8; e pension.solni@post.cz; singles/doubles 510/850 Kč)* is a pleasant little town house close to the square; there are only three rooms, so bookings are a must.

Hotel Slovan *(☎ 377 22 72 56, fax 377 22 70 12; e hotelslovan@iol.cz; Smetanovy sady 1; singles/doubles 500/750 Kč, with bath and TV 1420/2040 Kč)* is a grand old place with a magnificent central stairway, dating from the 1890s. The cheaper rooms are rather tired-looking. **Hotel Continental** *(☎ 377 23 52 92, fax 377 22 17 46; e mail@hotelcontinental .cz; Zbrojnická 8; singles/doubles 1490/2150 Kč)* is rather more comfortable.

Hotel Rosso *(☎ 722 64 73, fax 377 32 72 53; e recepce@hotel-rosso.cz; Pallova 12; singles/doubles 1080/1980Kč)* is a comfortable four-star establishment with a pricey French-Czech restaurant.

Places to Eat

S & S Grill *(Sedláčkova 7; open 9am-7.30pm Mon-Fri, 9am-3pm Sat, 10am-2pm Sun)* has great barbecued chicken for 45Kč to 55 Kč per 100g.

Fénix Bistro *(nám Republiky 18; mains 35-80 Kč; 8.30am-7pm Mon-Fri, 8.30am-3pm Sat)* is a good, inexpensive self-service place.

You can get decent, inexpensive pizzas at **Pizzerie** *(Solní 9; pizzas 52-62 Kč; open 10am-10pm Mon-Fri, 11am-11pm Sat, 11.30am-10pm Sun)*. Not far from the square is **Pivnice U Salzmannů** *(Pražská 8; mains 80-180 Kč; open 11am-11pm Mon-Sat, 11am-10pm Sun)*, a Plzeň institution known for its good-quality food and fine beer.

Café Fellini *(open 8am-midnight daily)* is the only place on the main square with decent coffee. **Azyl** *(Veleslavínova 17; open 8am-11pm Mon-Thur, 8am-1am Fri, 4pm-1am Sat, 4pm-10pm Sun)* is a cool café-bar and art gallery.

There is a **supermarket** *(open 7am-7pm Mon-Wed, 7am-8pm Thur & Fri, 8am-6pm Sat & Sun)* in Tesco, near the train station.

Entertainment
For entertainment, try **JK Tyla Theatre** or the ultramodern **Dům kultury** beside the river. There are also interesting tours of the backstage area, dressing rooms and below the stage of the Tyla Theatre, in Czech only, during July and August (20 Kč).

You can listen to local and foreign rock bands (till 11.30pm) or dance to pop tunes (till 5am) at **Rock Bar Elektra** *(Americká 24)*. **Zach's Pub** *(Palackého nám 2; open 11am-1am daily)* serves Guinness and English beers.

Getting There & Away
All international trains from Munich and Nuremberg to Prague stop at Plzeň. There are fast trains from here to České Budějovice (100 Kč, two hours) and Cheb (120 Kč, 1½ hours).

If you're heading for Karlovy Vary, take a bus (80 Kč, 1¾ hours). Buses also travel to Prague (60 Kč, 1½ hours) and České Budějovice (96 Kč, 2¾ hours).

South Bohemia

South Bohemia has many quaint little towns with a Bavarian or Austrian flavour mixed with local folk baroque buildings, enhanced by some 5000 carp ponds, many of them dating from the Middle Ages. In the Šumava hills, southwest of Prachatice, is the peak of Boubín (1362m) with its primeval forest of spruce, pine and beech trees. The Vltava River has its source among these hills.

After WWI, the southern part of South Bohemia was transferred to Czechoslovakia,
even though over half of its population was German; after WWII all German residents were expelled.

ČESKÉ BUDĚJOVICE
pop 98,900
České Budějovice (Budweis), the regional capital of South Bohemia, is a charming medieval city halfway between Plzeň and Vienna. Here the Vltava River meets the Malše and flows north to Prague. Founded in 1265, České Budějovice imported salt and wine from Austria and was a Catholic stronghold in the 15th century. Nearby silver mines made the town rich in the 16th century. After a fire in 1641 much of the town was rebuilt in the baroque style. In 1832, the first horse-drawn railway on the Continent arrived at České Budějovice from Linz. The city is famous as the original home of Budvar (Budweiser) beer.

The town is a good base for day trips to many local attractions, including picturesque little Bohemian towns such as Jindřichův Hradec, Písek, Prachatice, Tábor and Třeboň.

Orientation
It's a 10-minute walk west down Lannova třída, then Kanovnická, from the adjacent bus and train stations to nám Přemysla Otakara II, the main square. The left-luggage office at the bus station is open 7am to 7pm weekdays, to 2pm Saturday. The one at the train station is open 2.30am to 11pm daily.

Information
The helpful **city information centre** *(☎/fax 386 35 94 80; e infocb@c-budejovice.cz; nám Přemysla Otakara II 1; open 8.30am-8pm Mon-Fri, 9am-5pm Sat, 10am-4pm Sun June-Sept; 9am-5pm Mon-Fri, 9am-4pm Sun Oct-May)* sells maps and can arrange guides, theatre tickets and accommodation.

Also selling maps and tickets is the commercial **Tourist Information and Map Centre** *(☎/fax 386 35 25 89; e mapcentrum@ mbox.vol.cz; nám Přemysla Otakara II 28; open 7.45am-6pm Mon-Fri, 8.45am-4pm Sat, 1pm-4pm Sun)*. It can also arrange tour guides and book accommodation.

Motorists can go to **Jihočeský autoklub** *(☎ 635 65 66; Žižkova třída 13)* for help.

The **Raiffeisen Bank** *(open 8.30am-5pm Mon-Thur, 8.30am-4.30pm Fri)* on the main square changes travellers cheques and has an ATM.

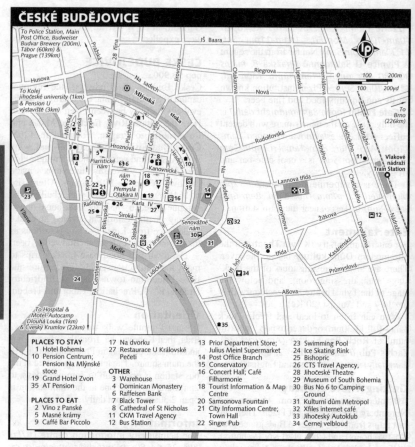

ČESKÉ BUDĚJOVICE

PLACES TO STAY
1 Hotel Bohemia
10 Pension Centrum;
   Pension Na Mlýnské
   stoce
19 Grand Hotel Zvon
35 AT Pension

PLACES TO EAT
2 Víno z Panské
5 Masné krámy
9 Caffé Bar Piccolo

17 Na dvorku
27 Restaurace U Královské
   Pečeti

OTHER
3 Warehouse
4 Dominican Monastery
6 Raffeisen Bank
7 Black Tower
8 Cathedral of St Nicholas
11 CKM Travel Agency
12 Bus Station

13 Prior Department Store;
   Julius Meinl Supermarket
14 Post Office Branch
15 Conservatory
16 Concert Hall; Café
   Filharmonie
18 Tourist Information & Map
   Centre
20 Samsonova Fountain
21 City Information Centre;
   Town Hall
22 Singer Pub

23 Swimming Pool
24 Ice Skating Rink
25 Bishopric
26 CTS Travel Agency,
28 Jihočeské Theatre
29 Museum of South Bohemia
30 Bus No 6 to Camping
   Ground
31 Kulturní dům Metropol
32 Xfiles internet café
33 Jihočeský Autoklub
34 Černej velbloud

The 24-hour **main post office** *(Pražská 69)* is north of the centre; there's a more convenient **branch post office** *(open 7am-7pm Mon-Fri, 8am-noon Sat)* on Senovážné nám. You can surf the Internet at **Xfiles internet café** *(Senovážné nám; open 10am-10pm Mon-Fri, 4pm-10pm Sat & Sun)* opposite the post office for 1 Kč a minute.

There's a **24-hour pharmacy** *(☎ 387 87 31 03)* at the **hospital** *(☎ 387 87 11 11; B Němcové 54)*.

The **police station** *(☎ 387 31 36 88; at Pražská 5)* is in the northern part of town.

Things to See

Nám Přemysla Otakara II, a vast, open square surrounded by 18th-century arcades, is one of the largest of its kind in Europe. At its centre is the **Samsonova Fountain** (1727), and on the western side stands the baroque **town hall** (1731). On the hour a tune is played from its tower. The allegorical figures of the cardinal virtues – Justice, Wisdom, Courage and Prudence – on the town hall balustrade, stand above four bronze dragon gargoyles. Looming above the opposite corner of the square is the 72m-tall **Black Tower** *(admission 15 Kč; open 10am-6pm daily July & Aug, 10am-6pm Tues-Sun Apr-June, Sept & Oct)*, dating from 1553, which has great views from the gallery. Beside it is the **Cathedral of St Nicholas**.

The streets around the square, especially Česká, are lined with old burgher houses. West near the river is the former **Dominican monastery** (1265) with another tall tower and a splendid pulpit. You enter the church from the Gothic cloister. Beside the church is a medieval warehouse where salt was stored before it was carried in barges down the Vltava to Prague. South along the riverside behind the warehouse are the remaining sections of the 16th-century walls. The **Museum of South Bohemia** (*admission 20 Kč; open 9am-12.30pm & 1pm-5pm Tues-Sun*) is just south of the old town.

The **Budweiser Budvar Brewery** (☎ 387 70 53 41; cnr Pražská & K Světlé; bus No 2; open 9am-5pm daily) is involved in a long-standing legal tussle with the US brewer Anheuser-Busch over the brand name 'Budweiser', which has been used by both breweries since the 19th century. However, there's no contest as to which beer is superior; one taste of Budvar and you'll be an instant convert. Tour groups need 10 or more people, except for the 2pm tour which is open to individual travellers. A one-hour tour in English costs 70/100 Kč on weekdays/weekends. If you miss the tour, the brewery's **beer hall** is open 10am to 10pm daily. The brewery is in an industrial area several kilometres north of the centre and lacks the picturesque appearance of the Urquell Brewery in Plzeň.

Places to Stay

Accommodation can be tight during the regular trade fairs held here throughout the year. Check with the tourist information centre before turning up without a booking.

Camping A 20-minute walk southwest of town (or take bus No 6 from opposite Kulturní dům Metropol to the fourth stop) is **Motel-Autocamp Dlouhá Louka** (☎ 387 21 06 01, fax 387 21 05 95; Stromovka 8; tent sites 50 Kč plus per person 50 Kč; open May-Sept). Bungalows with double rooms are available all year for 1080 Kč.

Hostels The **CKM** (☎ 386 35 12 70; Lannova třída 63; open 9am-5pm Mon-Thur, 9am-3.30pm Fri) youth travel agency and both tourist information offices can arrange dorm accommodation from 120 Kč per person. **Kolej jihočeské university** (☎ 387 77 42 01; Studentská 13-19; doubles 240 Kč), west of the centre, has beds available between July and September.

The closest thing to a travellers hostel is **Pension U výstaviště** (☎ 387 24 01 48; U výstaviště 17; beds 240 Kč). This place is 30 minutes from the city centre on bus No 1 from outside the bus station to the fifth stop (U parku); the pension is about 100m up the street (Čajkovského) on the right.

Private Rooms Both tourist information offices offer private rooms from around 300 Kč per person. Another good place with similarly priced rooms is **CTS Travel Agency** (☎ 386 35 39 68; nám Přemysla Otakara II 38; open 7.30am-7pm Mon-Thur).

Pensions The small private pensions around town are a better deal than the hotels, but the quality varies. **Pension Centrum** (☎ 386 35 20 30; Mlýnská stoka 6; doubles 850 Kč), just off Kanovnická, has been recommended by readers. Its neighbour **Pension Na Mlýnské stoce** (☎/fax 386 35 34 75; e penzion.garni@mybox.cz; Mlýnska stoka 7; singles 600-800 Kč, doubles 800-950 Kč) has also generated good feedback.

AT Pension (☎ 387 31 25 29; Dukelská 15; singles/doubles 650/980 Kč) has similar accommodation and is in a quiet street south of the centre.

Hotels The **Hotel Bohemia** (☎/fax 386 36 06 91; e hotel-bohemia@volny.cz; Hradební 20; singles/doubles 1290/1690 Kč) on a quiet side street has comfy rooms and a cellar wine bar with plenty of character.

The finest hotel in České Budějovice is the **Grand Hotel Zvon** (☎ 387 31 13 84, fax 387 31 13 85; e ghz@hotel-zvon.cz; nám Přemysla Otakara II 28; singles/doubles from 1780/2580 Kč).

Places to Eat

Try the local carp, which is on the menu of many restaurants.

Masné krámy (mains 40-60 Kč; open 10am-11pm daily) beer hall in the old meat market (1560), on the corner of Hroznová and 5.května, has been a local institution for centuries. Today it's a bit touristy but still worth a look. **Na dvorku** (Kněžská 11; mains 40-60 Kč; open 9.30am-10pm Mon-Fri, 10am-10pm Sat, 10am-3pm Sun) has a more genuine beer hall atmosphere.

Víno z Panské (Panská 14; restaurant open 5pm-1am Mon-Sat) is a good wine bar that serves vegetarian and chicken dishes. Its wine is served straight from the barrel.

In a higher price bracket is the **Restaurace U Královské Pečeti** *(Karla IV 8)* in the Hotel Malý Pivovar, serving excellent South Bohemian and Moravian food.

Café filharmonie *(cnr Kněžská & Karla IV; open 9am-10pm Mon-Sat)*, in the concert hall foyer, is the town's most elegant café; but the best coffee is at friendly little **Caffé Bar Piccolo** *(Mlýnská stoka 9; open 7.30am-7pm Mon-Thur, 7.30am-10pm Fri & Sat)*.

The Prior department store has a big **Julius Meinl supermarket** *(Lannova třída; open 8am-7pm Mon-Fri, 8am-1pm Sat)*.

Entertainment

Regular classical music concerts are staged by the Chamber Philharmonic Orchestra of South Bohemia at the **Concert Hall** *(Kněžská 6)* in the Church of St Anne, and also at the **Conservatory** *(Kanovnická 22)*.

The **Jihočeské Theatre**, by the river on Dr Stejskala, usually presents plays in Czech, but operas, operettas and concerts are also performed here.

Singer Pub *(Česká 55; open 11am-11pm daily)* is a lively Irish-type pub. Rock bands often play at **Černej velbloud** *(U tří lvů 4; open 6pm-1am Mon-Fri, 6pm-3am Sat)*.

Getting There & Away

There are fast trains from České Budějovice to Plzeň (100 Kč, two hours), Tábor (55 Kč, one hour) and Prague (126 Kč, 2½ hours). You can connect with trains between Prague and Vienna at České Velenice, 50km southeast of České Budějovice. For shorter trips you're probably better off travelling by bus. The bus to Brno (182 Kč, four hours) travels via Telč (86 Kč, two hours). Twice a week there's a bus to Linz, Austria (2¼ hours, 125km).

AROUND ČESKÉ BUDĚJOVICE
Hluboká nad Vltavou

One side trip not to miss is the neo-Gothic Tudor palace of Hluboká nad Vltavou *(open 9am-5pm daily July & Aug, 9am-5pm Tues-Sun June, 9am-4.30pm Tues-Sun Apr, May, Sept & Oct)*, 10km north, which is easily accessible by bus. The 13th-century castle was rebuilt by the Schwarzenberg family between 1841 and 1871 in the style of Windsor Castle. The palace's 144 rooms remained in use right up to WWII. To visit, you must join a guided tour, which costs 130/60 Kč with an English- or Czech-speaking guide.

The surrounding park is open throughout the year, as is the **Alšova jihočeská galerie** *(admission 30 Kč)*, an exceptional collection of Gothic paintings and sculptures housed in a former riding school. The **information centre** *(☎ 387 96 61 64; Masarykova 35)*, opposite the church, can help with accommodation.

ČESKÝ KRUMLOV
pop 14,600

Český Krumlov, a small medieval town 25km south of České Budějovice, is one of the most picturesque – and touristy – towns in Europe, its appearance almost unchanged since the 18th century. Built on a looping bend in the Vltava River, it has become a haven for Austrian tourists and backpackers. Its sprawling chateau occupies a ridge above the west bank of the river, while the old town centre sits on the tongue of land inside the loop on the east bank. To the southwest are the Šumava Hills, which separate Bohemia from both Austria and Bavaria.

Český Krumlov's Gothic border castle, rebuilt as a huge Renaissance chateau by 16th-century Italian architects, is second only to Prague Castle in size and splendour. The Renaissance lords of Rožmberk, whose seat this was, possessed the largest landed estate in Bohemia. In 1992 the town was added to Unesco's World Heritage List.

Orientation

Arriving by bus from České Budějovice, get off at the Český Krumlov Špičák bus stop, the first in town. The road on the bridge above this stop runs south to the Budějovická Gate, which leads directly into the old town.

The train station is 1.5km north of the old town centre. Bus Nos 1, 2 and 3 go from the station to the Špičák bus stop.

Information

The Český Krumlov **Infocentrum** *(☎ 380 70 46 22, fax 380 70 46 19; e infocentrum@ ckrf.ckrumlov.cz; nám Svornosti 2; open 9am-8pm daily July & Aug, 9am-7pm daily June & Sept, 9am-6pm daily Apr, May & Oct, 9am-5pm daily Nov-Mar; closed noon-1pm Sat, Sun & holidays)* is able to provide information about the town and region. It arranges accommodation, books tickets for concerts and the festivals, sells maps and guides, and organises tour guides. You can check email here for 10 Kč per 10 minutes.

ČESKÝ KRUMLOV

PLACES TO STAY
4 Hostel 99
6 Pension Ve Věži
23 Travellers' Hostel
25 Hotel Dvořák
33 Pension Myší Díra;
   Maleček Boat Rental
34 Hotel Růže
41 Krumlov House
42 U vodníka

PLACES TO EAT
14 Potraviny (Grocery)
24 Cikánská jizba

26 Dobrá Čajovna
27 Laibon
30 Restaurace Maštal
32 Krčma Barbakán
37 Hospoda Na louži

OTHER
1 24-Hour Pharmacy
   & Polyclinic
2 Špičák Bus Stop
3 Budějovická Gate
5 Post Office &
   Telephone Centre
7 Bus Station

8 Brewery
9 Minorite Monastery
10 Church of Božího
   Těla
11 Convent of the
   Poor Clares
12 Pension Lobo
   Laundrette
13 Café Internet
15 Red Gate
16 Bear Pit
17 Round Tower
18 First Courtyard
19 Chateau Ticket Office

20 Castle
21 Chateau Theatre
22 Former Riding School
28 Raiffeisen Bank
29 Infocentrum, Town
   Hall & Police
31 Regional Museum
35 Church of St Vitus
36 Plague Column
38 Vltava Travel
   Agency; Pension
   Vltava
39 U hada
40 M-club

CZECH REPUBLIC

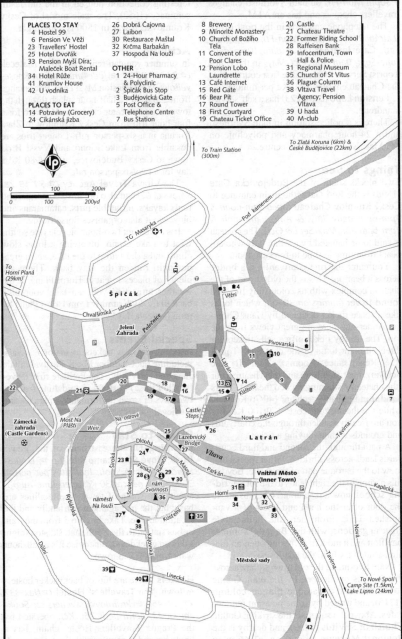

The **Raiffeisen Bank** (open 8.30am-4.30pm Mon-Fri) on nám Svornosti changes travellers cheques and has an ATM.

The telephone centre is in the **post office** (Latrán 81; 7am-6pm Mon-Fri, 7am-11am Sat). **Café Internet** (open 8am-10pm daily June-Sept, 9am-8pm Oct-May) in the Unios Tourist Service office in the first courtyard of the Chateau charges 1.50 Kč per minute.

Pension Lobo (Latrán 73) has a self-service laundrette.

There is a police station in nám Svornosti and a 24-hour pharmacy and polyclinic on TG Masaryka north of the centre.

Things to See

Two blocks south of the **Budějovická Gate** (1598) is the **Red Gate**, the main entrance to **Český Krumlov Chateau** (open 9am-noon & 1pm-6pm daily July & Aug, 9am-noon & 1pm-5pm Apr, May, Sept & Oct). The chateau is said to be haunted by a white lady who appears from time to time to forecast doom.

You enter the first courtyard via a bridge across a bear pit. This is the oldest part of the chateau complex with its colourfully frescoed **round tower** (admission 30 Kč), which looks like a space rocket designed by Hans Christian Andersen; there are great views from the top. The nearby ticket office sells tickets for three different tours of the chateau – Tour I (the Renaissance Rooms), Tour II (the Schwarzenberg Gallery) and the Theatre Tour (the chateau's stunning rococo theatre). Tours I and II in English/Czech are 140/70 Kč each, while the theatre tour costs 170/100 Kč. But you are free to wander through the courtyards and grounds without buying a ticket.

A path through the second and third courtyards leads across a bridge with a spectacular view to the baroque part of the castle. Beyond this a ramp to the right leads to the former **riding school**, now a restaurant. Cherubs above the door offer the head and boots of a vanquished Turk. From here the Italian-style chateau **gardens**, with the **'Bellarie' summer pavilion** and a modern revolving open-air theatre, stretch away to the southwest.

Nám Svornosti, the old town square across the river, is overlooked by the plain Gothic **town hall** and a baroque **plague column** (1716), and ringed by some pleasant outdoor cafés. Above the square is the striking Gothic **Church of St Vitus** (1439), and nearby is the **Regional Museum** (admission 20 Kč; open

10am-5pm Tues-Sun), with a surprisingly interesting collection housed in the old Jesuit seminary (1652). The scale model of Český Krumlov as it was in 1800 is a highlight.

Activities

In summer you can rent boats from **Maleček** (☎ 337 71 25 08; e lode@malecek.cz; Rooseveltova 28) at Pension Myší Díra. Prices range from 250 Kč for a half-hour splash through the town in a two-seater canoe, to 1650 Kč for a four-hour trip from Český Krumlov to Zlatá Koruna in a six-person raft. Longer trips are possible from Lake Lipno and Vyšší Brod down to Český Budějovice, at 380/980 Kč a day for a two/six-person raft.

The **Vltava Travel Agency** (☎ 71 19 78; Kájovská 62) can also organise boat trips, and rents kayaks, inflatable rafts, catamarans and bicycles; it also organises horse riding.

It's a pleasant two-hour bicycle ride southwest to Lake Lipno, involving a long, slow climb and a short drop to the lake, and a great downhill run on the way back. There are plenty of places to eat in Horní Planá. If the weather turns bad you can take your bike back to Český Krumlov from Horní Planá by train (seven a day).

Special Events

Infocentrum sells tickets to major festivals, including the Chamber Music Festival in late June and early July. The Pětilisté růže (Five-Petalled Rose) Festival in mid-June features two days of street performances, parades and medieval games.

Places to Stay

Camping On the east bank of the Vltava River, **Nové Spolí camp site** (no ☎; U Vlaštovičníku, Nové Spolí; tent sites per person 30 Kč, plus per car 30 Kč; open June-Aug) is about 2km south of town. The facilities are basic but the management is friendly and the location idyllic. Take bus No 3 from the train or bus station to the Spolí mat. šk. stop (eight a day on weekdays); otherwise it's a half-hour walk from the old town.

Hostels There are lots of backpacker hostels in town. The **Travellers' Hostel** (☎/fax 337 71 13 45; e krumlov@travellers.cz; Soukenická 43; dorm beds 250 Kč), operated by the Prague Travellers Hostel chain, has a lively bar and is popular with the party crowd.

Hostel 99 (☎ 377 71 28 12; e hostel99@ hotmail.com; Věžní 99; dorm beds 250 Kč, doubles 600 Kč) is another good place with a cool sun terrace to hang out on.

Right next to the river, U vodníka (☎ 377 71 19 35; e zukowski3@hotmail.com; Povodě 55; doubles 600 Kč) is a much more peaceful spot, down a cobbled lane off Rooseveltova. It has three double rooms, cooking facilities, a small English library and a nice garden. Nearby Krumlov House (Rooseveltova 68; dorm beds 250 Kč, doubles 800 Kč), at the top of the hill, is under the same management, with accommodation in dorms or in a suite with two double rooms. It has a potter's wheel, darkroom and a washing machine.

Private Rooms & Pensions The Infocentrum has private rooms from 400 Kč per person with breakfast. You may also be offered a private room by someone on the street. This is fine, but check the location before you agree to anything.

There are plenty of small pensions around the town, with new ones appearing all the time. In the same location as Vltava Travel Agency, the Pension Vltava (☎ 377 71 19 78; e ckvltava@ckvltava.cz; Kájovská 62; singles/ doubles 850/1200 Kč) is good.

In a great location overlooking the river, Pension Myší Díra (☎ 337 71 28 53, fax 337 71 19 00; e pension@ceskykrumlov-info.cz; Rooseveltova 28; singles/doubles 1390/ 1480) has bright, beautiful rooms with lots of pale wood. Rates fall by 40% in winter

For character, you can't beat Pension Ve Věži (☎/fax 337 71 17 42, ☎ 607 915 160; e info@reality-kolar.cz; Pivovarská 28; doubles/triples/quads 1200/1500/1800 Kč), set in a fairy-tale medieval round tower. There are only four rooms, so book well ahead.

Hotels Also overlooking the river, Hotel Dvořák (☎ 377 71 10 20, fax 377 71 10 24; e dvorak@ckmbox.vol.cz; Radniční 101; singles/doubles 2800/3500 Kč) is good for a splurge. The top place in town is the five-star Hotel Růže (☎ 377 77 21 00, fax 377 71 31 46; e info@hotelruze.cz; Horní 154; singles/ doubles 4000/4900 Kč), in a former Jesuit college building dating from 1588.

Places to Eat
Cikánská jizba (Dlouhá 31; mains 65-85 Kč; open 3pm-11pm Mon-Thur, 3pm-midnight Fri & Sat) is a very popular and inexpensive pub serving Czech food.

Restaurace Maštal (nám Svornosti 2; mains 80-150 Kč; open 10.30am-10pm daily) has a mixed menu that includes a few good vegetarian dishes.

Laibon (Parkán 105; mains 55-95 Kč; open noon-2pm & 6pm-10pm daily) is an excellent vegetarian restaurant with an attractive terrace beside the river.

You can enjoy good Czech food at the traditional Hospoda Na louži (Kájovaská 66; mains 60-100 Kč; open 9am-11pm daily) and the Gothic cellar tavern of Krčma Barbakán (Horní 26; mains 95-195 Kč; open 11am-midnight daily mid-Apr–Oct, 3pm-midnight Nov–mid-Apr). The latter has a superb terrace perched high above the river.

Dobrá Čajovna (open 1pm-10pm daily) tearoom opposite the bottom of the castle steps on Latrán has a wide range of teas.

There's a potraviny (grocery; open 7am-6pm Mon-Fri, 7am-noon Sat, 9am-3pm Sun) on Latrán, opposite the chateau entrance.

Entertainment
M-Club (cnr Rybářská & Plešivecké schody; 4pm-2am daily) offers pounding rock music and a pool table.

Just a few doors west, on the same side of Rybářská, is U hada (open 7pm-3am Mon-Thur, 7pm-4am Fri & Sat, 7pm-2am Sun), a hang-out for the rap/techno crowd.

Getting There & Away
The best way to get to Český Krumlov is by bus, with a fast service from České Budějovice (26 Kč, 45 minutes). Trains are slower (32 Kč, one hour) and the station is several kilometres north of town (although it's an easy downhill walk into town).

AROUND ČESKÝ KRUMLOV
Zlatá Koruna
Above the Vltava in the small village of Zlatá Koruna is one of the country's best-preserved Gothic Cistercian monasteries, founded in 1263 by Přemysl Otakar II. The monastery cathedral is clearly a Gothic building despite its baroque facelift.

The monastery complex also houses the Museum of South Bohemian Literature (admission 55 Kč; open 9am-noon & 1pm-4pm Tues-Sun Apr-Oct). Trains here from Český Krumlov are much more frequent than buses.

CZECH REPUBLIC

ŠUMAVA

The Šumava is a range of thickly wooded hills stretching for 125km along the border with Austria and Germany; the highest summit is Plechý (1378m), west of Horní Planá. The range is popular for hiking, cycling and cross-country skiing. You can hike the length of the national park, from Nová Pec, at the northern tip of Lake Lipno, up to Nýrsko, southwest of Klatovy.

Maps

The best hiking map is Klub Českých turistů's *Šumava* (1:50,000) and for cyclists there is SHOCart's *Šumava Trojmezí velká cykloturistická* (1:75,000) map.

National Park Walks

The **Povydří trail** along the Vydra (Otter) River is one of the most popular walks in the park. It is an easy 7km trail along a deep, forested river valley between Čeňkova Pila and Antýgl. The walk takes approximately two hours, with the Vydra itself running alongside between huge rounded boulders. There are about five buses a day running between Sušice and Modrava, stopping at Čeňkova Pila and Antýgl. Most of these places have plenty of accommodation.

Around the peak of **Boubín** (1362m), the 46-hectare *prales* (virgin forest) is the only part of the Šumava forest that is regarded as completely untouched. The trailhead is 2km northeast of the zastávka Zátoň train stop (not Zátoň town train station) at Kaplice, where there is a car park and a basic camping ground. From here it's an easy 2.5km to U pralesa Lake on a blue and green marked trail. To reach the top of Boubín peak, remain on the blue trail; it's a further 7.5km to the top. To return follow the trail southwest to complete the loop. The complete loop should take about five hours.

Getting There & Away

Šumava can be approached along three roads: road 169 via Sušice, road 4 via Strakonice and Vimperk, or road 141 via Prachatice and Volary. Regular buses and trains cover these routes. Up to eight trains a day run between the scenic route of Volary and Strakonice, stopping at Lenora, zastávka Zátoň and Horní Vltavice; the first two stops are several kilometres from their respective towns (Kubova Huť and Vimperk).

TÁBOR

pop 36,800

The Hussites – 'God's warriors' – founded Tábor in 1420 as a military bastion standing in defiance of Catholic Europe. The town was organised according to the precept that 'nothing is mine and nothing is yours, because the community is owned equally by everyone'. New arrivals threw all their worldly possessions into large casks at the marketplace and joined in communal work. This nonconformism helped to give the word 'Bohemian' its present-day connotations.

Planned as a bulwark against Catholics in České Budějovice and farther south, Tábor is a warren of narrow zigzag streets with protruding houses that were intended to disorient enemy attackers. Below ground, 14km of catacombs provided a refuge for the defenders. This friendly old town, 100km south of Prague, is well worth a brief stop.

Orientation & Information

From the train station walk west through the park past the bus station. Go west down třída 9.května, the main shopping street, till you reach a major intersection. Žižkovo nám, the old town square, is straight ahead on Palackého třída, 15 minutes' walk from the stations.

The municipal **Infocentrum** (☎ 381 48 62 30; e *infocentrum@mu.tabor.cz; Žižkovo nám 2; open 8.30am-7pm Mon-Fri, 9am-1pm Sat, 1pm-5pm Sun May-Sept, 9am-4pm Mon-Fri Oct-Apr*) is very helpful and informative. It sells maps and will organise your accommodation and guided tours.

Česká spořitelna (*třída 9.května 10*) changes travellers cheques and has an ATM.

The **post office**, icnluding the telephone centre, is in the pink building on the opposite side of Žižkovo nám from the museum. The **Internetový klub Euro** (*Farského 17; open 9am-8pm Mon-Thur, 9am-6pm Fri, 1pm-6pm Sat*) has Internet access at 60 Kč per hour.

Things to See

Unless otherwise stated, all museums are open from 8.30am to 5pm daily from April and October, and weekdays only during the rest of the year.

A statue of the Hussite commander Jan Žižka graces Žižkovo nám. Žižka's military successes were due to the novel use of peasant wagons (you can see one in the Hussite museum) against crusading Catholic knights.

Around the square are the homes of rich burghers, spanning the period from the late Gothic to the baroque. On the northern side is the Gothic **Church of the Transfiguration of Our Lord on Mt Tábor** (built between 1440 and 1512), with Renaissance gables and a baroque tower (1677).

The imposing early Renaissance town hall (1521) is now the **Museum of the Hussite Movement** (admission 40 Kč). Here also is the entrance to a 650m stretch of underground passages you can visit in groups of five (40 Kč per person). The passages, constructed in the 15th century as refuges during fire or times of war, were also used to store food and beer. The arch beside the Old Town Hall leads into Mariánská and then Klokotská, which runs southwest to the **Bechyně Gate** (admission 32 Kč; open May-Oct), now a small historical museum focusing on the lives of peasants.

Kotnov Castle, founded here in the 12th century, was destroyed by fire in 1532; in the 17th century the ruins were made into a **brewery** that's still operating today. The castle's remaining 15th-century **round tower** (open May-Oct) can be climbed from the Bechyně Gate museum for a sweeping view of Tábor, the Lužnice River and surrounding area.

Special Events

During the second weekend in September, Tábor holds a colourful Hussite Festival when locals dress in Hussite costumes.

Places to Stay

Around 1km north of town, near Lake Jordán, is **Autokemping Malý Jordán** (☎ 381 23 51 03; open mid-June–Sept), served by only a few buses a day.

The student hostel **Domov mládeže** (☎ 381 25 28 37; Martina Koláře 2118; dorm beds from 110 Kč) is 15 minutes' walk south of the train station.

The Infocentrum offers **private rooms** from 300 Kč per person.

There are two good pensions near the train and bus stations. **Pension Milena** (☎ 381 25 47 55, fax 381 25 11 33; e milena.sport@ volny.cz; Husovo nám 529; rooms per person from 200 Kč); and **Pension Dáša** (☎ 381 25 62 53; e pensiondasa@volny.cz; Bílkova 735; singles/doubles 700/990 Kč), a deluxe spot with a garden. The friendly **Pension Alfa** (☎ 381 25 61 65; Klokotská 107; 300 Kč

per person) is only a few minutes' walk from Žižkovo nám.

The classy **Hotel Kapitál** (☎ 381 25 60 96, fax 381 25 24 11; e hotel-kapital@volny.cz; třída 9.května 617; singles/doubles/triples 890/1190/1390 Kč) is on the main drag between the train station and the old town.

Places to Eat

Friendly little **Pizzeria Berka** (Kostnická 159; pizza 45-90 Kč; open 11am-10pm daily), to the left off Palackého třída, does tasty pizzas. The modern **Atrium Restaurace** (cnr třída 9.května & Kollárova; mains 60-100 Kč) offers traditional Bohemian cuisine.

Getting There & Away

Tábor is on the main railway line between Prague (80 Kč, 1½ hours) and Vienna. Trains from České Budějovice to Prague also pass through here. Buses to Prague cost much the same but are slightly faster (1¼ hours).

To get from Tábor to Telč by train you have to change at Horní Cerekev and Kostelec u Jihlavy. Although the connections are fairly good, the whole 107km trip by local train takes three or four hours. Otherwise take a bus to Jihlava (74km) and change there to reach Telč (29km).

Eastbound buses to Brno (140 Kč, three hours) leave four times a day.

East Bohemia

ADRŠPACH-TEPLICE ROCKS

The Czech Republic's most dramatic and rugged scenery is to be found at the Adršpach-Teplice Rocks (Adršpašsko-Teplické skály). They lie in the Broumov Hills (Broumovská vrchovina), in a knob of eastern Bohemia that juts into Poland. Deep layers of sandstone have been eroded and fissured by water and frost to form giant towers, pinnacles and walls – a scene fit for The Lord of the Rings.

You can hike well-marked paths that wind among the towers and pass through improbably narrow fissures, scramble up for the view of an outlaw's timber castle, or get join local guides for some serious rock-climbing. In summer the trails are busy, and you may have to book accommodation at least a week ahead, unless you're camping; in winter (snow stays as late as mid-April) you'll have this stunning landscape mostly to yourself.

There are actually two clusters of rock formations, hence the mouthful of a name – Adršpach Rock Town (Adršpašské skalní město) and Teplice Rock Town (Teplické skalní město). They now comprise of a single state nature reserve, lying about 15km east of the district capital of Trutnov.

At each 'rock town' you must pay a small admission charge of 25 Kč, and you can pick up an *Adršpašsko-Teplické skály a Ostaš* (1:25,000) trail map.

There are loop trails at both Adršpach (one hour) and Teplice (2½ hours), but the best route is the **Vlčí rokle** (Wolf Gorge), which links the two (four to five hours). You can return from Adršpach to Teplice (or vice versa) by walking along the road (one hour) or you can take the train (10 minutes).

Places to Stay

Autokemping Bučnice *(☎ 491 58 13 87; tent sites 30 Kč plus per person 50 Kč; open May-Sept)* is 300m northwest of the Teplice nad Metují-Skály train station.

In Teplice, the **Hotel Orlík** *(☎/fax 491 58 10 25; singles/doubles 400/800 Kč)* is a good-value choice.

Just east of the Orlík on the main road is the attractive **Pension Skály** *(☎ 491 58 11 74; rooms per person 550 Kč)* with comfortable en suite rooms.

At Adršpach, the **Hotel Lesní zátiší** *(☎/fax 491 58 60 18; 800/1400/1800 Kč)* sits right at the start of the rocks trail.

Getting There & Away

There are several direct buses a day from Prague to Trutnov (125 Kč, 3¼ hours).

Eight slow trains a day trundle back and forth between Trutnov and Adršpach (28 Kč, one hour), as well as Teplice and Metují-Skály (32 Kč, 70 minutes).

Moravia

The historic land of Moravia – Bohemia's eastern partner in the Czech Republic – is often overlooked by tourists. Yet Moravia has its own history and natural wonders, such as the karst area north of Brno, the Moravian capital, and the charming historic town of Telč. The north has some of the country's most fertile land. South Moravia is also famed for its excellent wines.

TELČ
pop 6000

Telč was founded in the 14th century by the feudal lords of Hradec as a fortified settlement with a castle separated from the town by a strong wall. The artificial ponds on either side of Telč provided security and a regular supply of fish. After a fire in 1530, Lord Zachariáš, then Governor of Moravia, ordered the town and castle rebuilt in the Renaissance style by Italian masons. Profits from gold and silver mines allowed Zachariáš to enjoy a regal lifestyle.

After the death of Zachariáš in 1589, the building activity stopped and the castle you see today remains largely as he left it. The main square of this most charming of Czech towns is unmarred by modern intrusions. Telč was added to Unesco's World Heritage List in 1992.

Orientation & Information

The bus and train stations are a few hundred metres apart on the eastern side of town. A 10-minute walk along Masarykova takes you to nám Zachariáš e z Hradce, the old town square. A left-luggage service is available at the train station 24 hours a day.

There's an **information office** *(☎ 567 24 31 45; e info@telc-etc.cz; open 8am-5pm Mon & Wed, 8am-2pm Tues, Thur & Fri)* in the town hall where you can book accommodation or check your email (1 Kč per minute, 10 Kč minimum).

The **Komerční banka** *(nám Zachariáš e z Hradce 40)* changes travellers cheques and has an ATM.

The **post office** is a block from the train station on Staňkova.

Things to See

Telč's wonderful old town square is surrounded by 16th-century Renaissance houses built on the ground-floor remains of their Gothic predecessors after the 1530 fire – the Gothic arches form a covered arcade running almost all the way around it. Although in different styles, the 49m Romanesque **tower** east of the square and the baroque **Marian column** (1717) in its centre do not detract from its character.

The greatest attraction in Telč for visitors is the Renaissance **Water Chateau** *(open 9am-noon & 1pm-5pm Tues-Sun May-Aug, 9am-noon & 1pm-4pm Apr, Sept & Oct)* at the

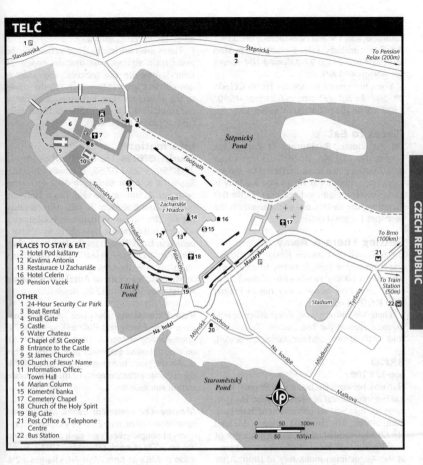

CZECH REPUBLIC

TELČ

PLACES TO STAY & EAT
2 Hotel Pod kaštany
12 Kavárna Antonia
13 Restaurace U Zachariáše
16 Hotel Celerin
20 Pension Vacek

OTHER
1 24-Hour Security Car Park
3 Boat Rental
4 Small Gate
5 Castle
6 Water Chateau
7 Chapel of St George
8 Entrance to the Castle
9 St James Church
10 Church of Jesus' Name
11 Information Office;
   Town Hall
14 Marian Column
15 Komerční banka
17 Cemetery Chapel
18 Church of the Holy Spirit
19 Big Gate
21 Post Office & Telephone
   Centre
22 Bus Station

square's northwestern end. To visit you need to join a guided tour, available in Czech (60 Kč) or English (120 Kč): Trasa (Tour) A takes you through the Renaissance chateau while Trasa B visits the aristocratic apartments. While you're waiting for your guide to arrive, you can visit the local **historical museum** (admission 20 Kč), which you can enter from the chateau courtyard. A scale model of Telč dated 1895 shows that the town hasn't changed since. The All Saints Chapel in the chateau houses the tombs of Zachariáš and his wife, Catherine of Valdštejn.

Opposite the chateau is the baroque **Church of Jesus' Name** (1655), in the former Jesuit college; **St James Church** (1372) beyond is Gothic. Through the gate beside St James Church is a large English-style park with some

restful walks and views of medieval towers; the duck ponds were once the town's defensive moat.

Places to Stay

The information office can book private rooms (from around 300 Kč per person) and pensions. There are several 'Zimmer frei' signs east along Štěpnická and on nám Zachariáš e z Hradce.

Friendly **Hotel Pod kaštany** (☎ 567 21 30 42, fax 567 22 30 65; Štěpnická 409; singles/doubles/triples without bath 400/660/780 Kč) is just outside the old town. It gives a 10% discount to ISIC card-holders.

If Pod kaštany has no room, try **Pension Relax** (☎ 721 31 26; Na posvátné 29; singles/doubles 450/900 Kč), which is further east along Štěpnická and where rooms come with bathroom and TV and rates include breakfast. Another similarly priced place is **Pension Vacek** (☎ *567 21 30 99; Mlýnská 104; rooms per person 400 Kč*).

For a little more luxury, try **Hotel Celerin** (☎ *567 24 34 77; singles/doubles 1050/1300 Kč*) on the main square at No 43.

Places to Eat
On the square, **Restaurace U Zachariáše** (*mains 80-110 Kč; open 10.30am-11pm daily*) is the place most preferred by the locals. The restaurant at **Hotel Pod kaštany** is good for Moravian food and beer. **Caffé Bar Piccolo** at the eastern end of the square is the best spot for good coffee.

Getting There & Away
Buses travelling between České Budějovice and Brno stop at Telč about two times a day – it's about a 100km, two-hour trip from Telč to either city. Five buses a day run to Prague (100 Kč, 2½ hours).

There's no information, ticket office or left-luggage area at the bus station. Tickets are sold by the drivers and timetables are posted.

BRNO
pop 379,200
Halfway between Budapest and Prague, Brno has been the capital of Moravia since 1641; its large fortress was an instrument of Habsburg domination. The botanist Gregor Mendel (1822–84) established the modern science of heredity through his studies of peas and bees at the Augustinian monastery in Brno. After the Brno-Vienna railway was completed in 1839, Brno developed into a major industrial centre for the country.

Brno has a rich cultural life and its compact centre (half is a pedestrian zone) has a variety of fascinating sights. The town has not been overwhelmed by tourism as Prague has. If you're a city slicker, you'll enjoy Brno.

Orientation
Brno's main train station is at the southern edge of the old town centre. Opposite the train station is the beginning of Masarykova, a main thoroughfare for trams and pedestrians into triangular nám Svobody, the city's main square. The main bus station is 800m south of the train station, beyond Tesco. To get there, go through the pedestrian tunnel

under the train tracks, then follow the crowd along the elevated walkway.

There are two left-luggage offices in the main train station, one upstairs (open 24 hours) opposite the lockers, and another downstairs (5am to 11pm daily) by the tunnel to the platforms. The left-luggage office at the bus station is open 5.15am to 10pm daily (to 6.15pm on weekends).

Information
Tourist Offices The **tourist office** (☎ *542 21 10 90, 542 21 07 58; e info@kicbrno.cz; Radnická 8; open 8am-6pm Mon-Fri, 9am-5pm Sat & Sun*) in the Old Town Hall can book accommodation. It sells the monthly *Kam v Brně* (also available in bookshops), which is full of information about what's happening in Brno. Watch for the free fortnightly *Do města – Downtown* leaflet that lists what's on in cinemas, theatres, galleries and clubs.

Motorists can turn to **Autoklub Bohemia Assistance** (*ABA; ☎ 1240; Bašty 8*).

Visa Extensions The place for visa extensions is the **Foreigners Police** (*Kounicova 24; open 8am-5pm Mon & Wed, 8am-1pm Fri*), on a northbound extension of Rašínova. This is also the place to report a lost visa. Look for the separate entrance north of the main police station entrance.

Money The **Komerční banka** (*open 8am-5pm Mon-Fri*) on nám Svobody changes travellers cheques, gives Visa cash advances and has an ATM. **Čedok** (*Nádražní 10/12; 9am-noon & 1.30pm-5pm Mon-Fri*) charges a 2% commission for exchange services.

Post & Communications There is a **post office** (*open 24hr daily*) at the western end of the train station. The telephone centre is at **Český telecom** (*Šilingrovo nám 3/4; open 7am-8pm Mon-Sat, 7am-1pm Sun*).

Surf the Web at **Internet Centrum** (*open 8am-midnight daily*) on Masarykova, or at **@ Internet café** (*Lidická tři 17; open 10am-10pm Mon-Fri, 2pm-10pm Sat & Sun*), just south of Hotel Slovan; both charge 1 Kč to 2 Kč a minute depending on total time used.

Travel Agencies The **České Dráhy Travel Agency**, next to the international ticket office in the train station, sells bus and train tickets to Western Europe.

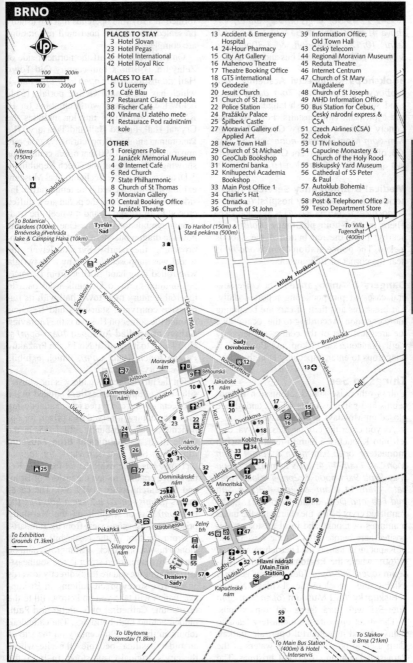

BRNO

PLACES TO STAY
3 Hotel Slovan
23 Hotel Pegas
26 Hotel International
42 Hotel Royal Ricc

PLACES TO EAT
5 U Lucerny
11 Café Blau
37 Restaurant Císaře Leopolda
38 Fischer Café
40 Vinárna U zlatého meče
41 Restaurace Pod radničním kole

OTHER
1 Foreigners Police
2 Janáček Memorial Museum
3 @ Internet Café
6 Red Church
7 State Philharmonic
8 Church of St Thomas
9 Moravian Gallery
10 Central Booking Office
12 Janáček Theatre

13 Accident & Emergency Hospital
14 24-Hour Pharmacy
15 City Art Gallery
16 Mahenovo Theatre
17 Theatre Booking Office
18 GTS international
19 Geodezie
20 Jesuit Church
21 Church of St James
22 Police Station
24 Pražákův Palace
25 Špilberk Castle
27 Moravian Gallery of Applied Art
28 New Town Hall
29 Church of St Michael
30 GeoClub Bookshop
31 Komerční banka
32 Knihupectví Academia Bookshop
33 Main Post Office 1
34 Charlie's Hat
35 Čtrnáčka
36 Church of St John

39 Information Office; Old Town Hall
43 Český telecom
44 Regional Moravian Museum
45 Reduta Theatre
46 Internet Centrum
47 Church of St Mary Magdalene
48 Church of St Joseph
49 MHD Information Office
50 Bus Station for Čebus, Český národní express & ČSA
51 Czech Airlines (ČSA)
52 Čedok
53 U Tří kohoutů
54 Capucine Monastery & Church of the Holy Rood
55 Biskupský Yard Museum
56 Cathedral of SS Peter & Paul
57 Autoklub Bohemia Assistance
58 Post & Telephone Office 2
59 Tesco Department Store

0   100   200m
0   100   200yd

To Alterna (150m)

To Botanical Gardens (100m); Brněvnska přehrada lake & Camping Hana (10km)

To Haribol (150m) & Stará pekárna (500m)

To Villa Tugendhat (400m)

Tyršův Sad

Sady Osvobození

Sokolská
Pekárenská
Smetanova
Antonínská
Slováková
Kounicova
Veveří
Marešova
Rašínova
Kozí
Milady Horákové
Lidická třída
Kolište
Bratislavská
Ponávka
Cejl

Moravské nám.
Joštova
Komenského nám.
Údolní
Roosveltova
Jakubské nám.
Běhounská
Jezuitská
Dvořákova
Solniční
Česká
Rašínova
Kozí
Dvořákova
Koblížná

Husova

To Exhibition Grounds (1.3km)

nám. Svobody
Postojská
Divadelní
Novobranská
Benešova

Pražská
Veselá
Dominikánské nám.
Jánská
Minoritská
Masarykova
Orlí
Josefská

Pellicova
Dominikánská
Starobrněnská
Pekařská
Šilingrovo nám.
Zelný trh

Denisovy Sady

Bašty
Nádražní
Kapucínské nám.

Hlavní nádraží (Main Train Station)

Kolište

To Ubytovna Pozemstav (1.8km)

To Main Bus Station (400m) & Hotel Interservis

To Slavkov u Brna (21km)

The youth travel agency **GTS International** (☎ 542 22 19 96; e gts.brno@gtsint.cz; Vachova 4) and **Čedok** (☎ 542 32 12 67; Nádražní 10/12; 9am-noon & 1.30pm-5pm Mon-Fri) sell international bus and tain tickets.

Bookshops Knihupectvi **Academia** (nám Svobody 13; open 9am-7pm daily) has a good selection of English-language fiction and a pleasant café upstairs. For maps and Lonely Planet guides, try **GeoClub** (open 9am-6pm Mon-Fri, 9am-noon Sat) in Pasaž KB, off the main square, or **Geodezie** (Vachova 8; open 9am-6pm Mon-Fri).

Medical & Emergency Services Brno's **accident and emergency hospital** (Urazova nemocnice; ☎ 545 53 81 11) is at Ponávka 6. There is a **24-hour pharmacy** (Koliště 47) nearby; press the red button if the door is locked. The **police station** (nám Svobody) is near the corner of Běhounská.

Dangers & Annoyances There are several cases of pickpocketing reported daily. Car break-ins and theft of cars are becoming more common. According to the local police the area just east of the centre, bordered by Cejl, Francouzská, Příkop and Ponávka, is dangerous to enter, especially at night.

Things to See

Unless otherwise stated, admission to museums and galleries costs 40 Kč, and all are closed on Mondays and Tuesdays.

As you enter the city on Masarykova, turn left into Kapučínské nám to reach **Capuchin monastery** (open 9am-noon & 2pm-4.30pm Mon-Sat, 11am-11.45am & 2pm-4.30pm Sun May-Sept; 9am-noon & 2pm-4.30pm Tues-Sat, 11am-11.45am & 2pm-4.30pm Sun mid-Feb–mid-Dec), dating from 1651. In the ventilated crypt below the church are the intact mummies of monks and local aristocrats deposited here before 1784. At the western end of Kapučínské nám is the Dietrichstein Palace (1760), where the **Regional Moravian Museum** (open 9am-5pm Tues-Sat) has geology exhibits and a mock medieval village. Nearby is **Biskupský Yard Museum** (open 9am-5pm Tues-Sat) with flora, fauna and coin exhibits.

The street opposite the monastery leads to Zelný trh and its colourful **open-air market**. Carp used to be sold from the waters of the Parnassus Fountain (1695) at Christmas. The

nearby **Reduta Theatre** is where Mozart performed in 1767 (the operettas that are usually presented here are on hold until restorations are completed).

On Radnická, just off the northern side of Zelný trh, is Brno's 13th-century **Old Town Hall** (admission 20 Kč; open 9am-5pm daily), which has a splendid Gothic portal (1511) below the tower (well worth climbing for 10 Kč). The town hall's interior includes the Crystal Hall, Fresco Hall and Treasury. The Panorama, another Brno curiosity, is a rare apparatus made in 1890 that offers continuous showings of images of the Czech Republic in 3-D, and is part of the Technological Museum exhibit that was moved here temporarily. Inside the passage behind the portal are a stuffed crocodile, or 'dragon', and a wheel, the traditional symbols of the city. One legend tells how the dragon once terrorised wayfarers approaching the nearby Svratka River; the wheel was supposedly made by a cartwright who rolled it by hand to Brno from Lednice.

Continue north to Dominikánské nám to the 16th-century **new town hall** with its impressive courtyard, stairways and frescoes. Around the corner on Husova is the **Moravian Gallery of Applied Art** (open 10am-6pm) at No 14 and, to its north at No 18, the **Pražákův Palace** (open 10am-6pm), which exhibits 20th-century Czech art.

On the hill above this gallery is the sinister silhouette of **Špilberk Castle**. Founded in the 13th century and converted to a citadel during the 17th century, it served as a prison for opponents of the Habsburgs until 1855. In the castle itself, the **Municipal Brno Museum** (open 9am-6pm Tues-Sun May-Sept, to 5pm Oct-Apr) has three exhibits: art from the Renaissance era until today; the history of Brno; and Brno architecture (1919–39). The **casemates** (admission 20 Kč; same hours as the museum) has an exhibit on the Habsburg prison. There's a good view from the ramparts.

From the foot of the castle hill go south along Husova one block to Šilingrovo nám on the left. An unmarked street in the southeastern corner of the square leads directly towards an old five-storey green building in Biskupská, which will take you up Petrov Hill to the neo-Gothic **Cathedral of SS Peter and Paul**, hidden behind high buildings. The cathedral, rebuilt in the late 19th century on the site of an older basilica, occupies the site where the city's original castle stood. In 1645, the

Swedish general Torstensson who was besieging Brno declared that he would leave if his troops hadn't captured the city by noon. At 11am the Swedes were about to scale the walls when the cathedral bell keeper suddenly rang noon. True to his word, the general broke off the attack; since that day the cathedral bells have always rung noon at 11am.

From Petrov Hill descend Petrská into Zelný trh and continue on Orlí to Minoritská and the **Church of St John** (rebuilt in 1733) which has fine altarpieces, an organ and painted ceilings. Nám Svobody – the city's broad main square – has a striking plague column (1680). North of the square is the parish church, **St James** (1473), with a soaring nave in the purest Gothic style. The **Church of St Thomas** and the former Augustinian monastery, which is now the **Moravian Gallery** (open 10am-6pm), are just north again on Moravské nám.

Also worth seeing is the **City Art Gallery** (Dům umění; Malinovského nám 2; admission 30 Kč; open 10am-6pm Tues-Sun), next to the Mahenovo Theatre east of the centre. Excellent art exhibitions are often staged here.

Other good museums are the **Janáček Memorial Museum** (Smetanova 14; open 8am-noon & 1pm-4pm Mon-Fri), which is a house-museum dedicated to the composer, and the **Mendelianum**, which records the work of Gregor Mendel (at the time of research the Mendelianum was closed and searching for new premises). The functionalist **Vila Tugendhat** (Černopolní 45; admission 80 Kč; open 10am-6pm), is a shrine for fans of modern architecture.

Language Courses

If you'd like to learn Czech, contact either **Lingua centrum** (☎ 543 23 44 34; Křenova 52), or **U tří kohoutů** (☎ 542 32 13 09; Masarykova 32). Rates begin at about 200 Kč per hour.

Special Events

The annual Brno Motorcycle Grand Prix is held at the end of August.

Places to Stay

Brno hosts international trade fairs all year round and accommodation is a problem during the main ones in February, March, April, August, September and October. Before you arrive, check carefully that your visit does not coincide with one of these three- or four-day fairs – as hotels fill, rates can almost double and all public facilities are very overcrowded.

Camping The attractive **Camping Hana** (☎/fax 549 42 03 31; e camping.hana@ quick.cz; Veverská bítýška; tent sites 40-60 Kč plus per person 80 Kč, car 60 Kč; open May-Sept) is at the northwestern end of Brněnska přehrada lake, about 10km northwest of the city centre. From the train station take tram No 4 eastbound to the third stop (Česká), then tram No 3 or 11 to the Přistavistě stop, then bus 103 to Veverská bítýška. In summer you can also take a boat along the lake from Přistavistě.

Hostels Both **Čedok** and **GTS International** (see Information, earlier) can arrange accommodation in student dormitories during July and August.

South of the centre, the HI-listed **Hotel Interservis** (☎ 545 23 42 32; Lomená; beds from 225 Kč) rents beds in double rooms. Take tram No 12 eastbound from the train station to the end of the line, go through the underpass and continue south on the main road, then turn left along Pompova. The hostel is the tall block of flats rising behind the houses on the right.

Ubytovna Pozemstav (☎ 543 21 47 63, fax 543 21 53 08; e hotel.brno@brn.czn.cz; Horní 19; singles/doubles 200/300 Kč) is a similar distance southwest of the centre. Take tram No 2 westbound from the train station to the Celní stop. Walk on about 100m, turn right on Celní and then take the second left on Horní; the hostel is near Hotel Brno at the end of the street.

Private Rooms From 550 Kč per person a night **Čedok** can arrange private rooms. Most are far from the centre but can easily be reached on public transport. **Infocentrum** also has private rooms from 350 Kč.

Hotels On a quiet street right in the centre of town is **Hotel Pegas** (☎ 542 21 01 04, fax 542 21 43 14; Jakubská 4; singles/doubles 1200/1700 Kč). Rooms are bright and clean and come with bath and breakfast.

Hotel Slovan (☎ 541 32 12 07, fax 541 21 11 37; e hotel@hotelslovan.cz; Lidická 23; singles/doubles 1200/1800 Kč) is a pleasant-enough business hotel just north of the centre.

CZECH REPUBLIC

One of the top hotels is the baroque **Hotel Royal Ricc** (☎ 542 21 92 62, fax 542 21 92 65; ℯ hotelroyalricc@brn.inecnet.cz; Staro-brněnská 10; singles/doubles 2500/2800 Kč), with smallish luxury historical rooms. Another is the Best Western **Hotel International** (☎ 42 12 28 11, fax 42 21 08 43; ℯ sales@ hotelinternational.cz; Husova 16; singles/ doubles 2490/2990 Kč) near the castle.

Places to Eat

The touristy **Pivnice Pegas** (Jakubská 4; mains 60-100 Kč; open 9am-midnight daily) is an attractive place with an extensive menu in English. The food is reasonable, and it brews its own beer on the premises.

An inexpensive and pleasant place to order a bottle of local wine with your meal is **Vinárna U zlatého meče** (Mečová 3; mains 60-110 Kč; open 11am-10pm Mon-Thur, 11am-2am Fri & Sat, 11am-4pm Sun). Nearby **Restaurace Pod radničním kole** (Mečová 5; mains 80-150 Kč; open 11am-midnight daily) is a red-brick cellar with good Moravian food and plenty of charming atmosphere.

Restaurant Císaře Leopolda (Orlí 3; mains 85-125 Kč; open 11am-11pm Mon-Thur, 11am-midnight Fri & Sat, noon-10pm Sun) serves hearty Italian dishes. The popular **U Lucerny** (Slovákova 2; mains 90-150 Kč; open 11am-midnight daily) is another excellent Italian restaurant with a garden out back in summer.

Haribol (Lužanecká 4; mains 50-90 Kč; open 11am-4pm Mon-Fri) is a vegetarian restaurant with some Indian dishes.

For good coffee, you can try the small and intimate **Café Blau** (Běhounská 18), or the stylish **Fischer Café** (cnr Masarykovo & Orlí).

There's a good **supermarket** in the basement of Tesco behind the train station on the way to the bus station.

Entertainment

Brno's theatres are excellent (although they close in midsummer). The tickets aren't cornered by scalpers and profiteers as they are in Prague, but you are expected to dress up a bit.

Opera, operettas and ballet are performed at the modern **Janáček Theatre** (Janáčkovo divadlo; Sady Osvobození), named after the composer Leoš Janáček, who spent much of his life in Brno.

The neobaroque **Mahenovo Theatre** (Mahenovo divadlo), a beautifully decorated old-style theatre in an 1882 building designed by the famous Viennese theatrical architects Fellner and Hellmer, presents classical drama in Czech and operettas.

The **Brno State Philharmonic** (Státní filharmonie Brno, SFB; Komenského nám 8), in Besední dům (the entrance is from Husova), has regular concerts. Tickets can be bought from **SFB** in Besední dům.

For tickets to the Janáček and Mahenovo theatres, go to the small **booking office** (předprodej; ☎ 542 32 12 85; Dvořákova 11; open 8am-5.30pm Mon-Fri, 9am-noon Sat) behind the Mahenovo Theatre.

The **Central Booking Office** (Centrální předprodej; Běhounská 17) sells tickets to classical, rock and folk concerts at a variety of venues.

Bars & Clubs Popular **Charlie's Hat** (Kobližná 12; open 11am-4am) is a cellar bar with many rooms and a small dance floor where DJs spin anything from heavy rock to dance music. Nearby restaurant and bar **Čtrnáčka** (Jánská 14; open 11am-11pm Mon-Sat) is hugely popular with students.

North of the city centre is **Stará pekárna** (Štefánikova 8; open 5pm-1am daily), with live bands playing a variety of styles, including jazz, funk and rock on most nights.

Alterna (Kounicova 48, block B; open 7pm-12.30am daily) is an alternative klub where you can enjoy some live rock, punk, jazz and other alternative entertainment. From Česká take trolleybus No 134 or 136 three stops north.

Getting There & Away

Bus The bus to Vienna–Mitte Bahnhof (350 Kč, 2½ hours) departs from platform No 20 at the main bus station twice a day. There are also buses to Prague (140 Kč, 2½ hours). For shorter trips such as Telč (86 Kč, two hours) buses are faster and more efficient than trains.

Train All trains running between Budapest and Berlin stop at Brno. If you're going to or from Vienna, change trains at Břeclav. To get to or from Košice, change trains at Přerov. There are also frequent direct trains between Brno and Bratislava (two hours, 141km) and Prague (242 Kč, 2¾ hours).

Three overnight trains with couchettes and sleepers travel between Brno and Košice. Reserve international tickets, couchettes or sleepers at windows to the right of the main entrance in the train station.

Getting Around

You can buy public transport tickets from shops, vending machines and the **MHD Information Office** *(Novobranská 18; open 6am-6pm Mon-Fri, 8am-3.30pm Sat & Sun).* Tickets valid for 10/40/60 minutes cost 7/12/15 Kč, 24-hour tickets are 48 Kč and seven-day tickets are 165 Kč.

AROUND BRNO
Slavkov u Brna

Slavkov u Brna, 21km east of Brno, is better known to history by its Austrian name – Austerlitz. On 2 December 1805, the famous 'Battle of the Three Emperors' took place in the open, rolling countryside between Brno and Slavkov u Brna, where Napoleon Bonaparte's French army defeated the combined forces of Emperor Franz I (Austria) and Tsar Alexander I (Russia). The battle was decided at **Pracký kopec**, a hill 12km west of Slavkov, marked by a monumental chapel (1912) and a small museum. After the battle Napoleon spent four days concluding an armistice at Slavkov's baroque **chateau** *(Slavkov Zámek; open 9am-6pm daily July & Aug; 9am-5pm May, June & Sept; 9am-4pm Apr, Oct & Nov; closed Mon Apr, May & Sept-Nov),* where you can visit the ornate rooms and gallery (route A), or the Napoleonic exhibit (route B). Tours in Czech/English cost 45 Kč/80 Kč.

Slavkov u Brna is easily accessible by bus or train from Brno, but Pracký kopec is difficult to reach by public transport. You can get a bus from Brno's bus station to Prace (nine a day – ask to get off at Náves stop), from where it is a 1.6km walk south to the top of the hill. On weekends it is better to catch one of the more frequent Brno–Slavkov trains (14km, 10 a day), getting off at Potovice and walking the 3.5km southeast through Prace.

Moravian Karst

The limestone plateau of the Moravský kras (Moravian Karst), 20km north of Brno, is riddled with caves and canyons carved by the Punkva River.

The **Ústřední informační služba** of Moravský kras *(☎ 516 41 35 75; Skalní Mlýn)* provides information and books accommodation and tickets for the caves.

The Caves A tour of the famous **Punkevní Cave** *(admission 80 Kč; open 8.20am-3.50pm daily Apr-Sept; 8.40am-2pm Mon-Fri, 8.20am-3.40pm Sat & Sun Oct; 8.40am-2pm daily Nov-Mar)* takes 75 minutes, and involves a 1km walk through caverns draped with stalactites and stalagmites to the bottom of the Macocha Abyss, where you board a small boat for a 400m ride along an underground river and out of the cave.

Kateřinská Cave *(admission 40 Kč)* has similar opening hours to Punkevní, except that it's closed from November to January. On weekends and in midsummer, all the tickets will usually have been sold two hours or more before the tours are due to commence, so be sure to arrive early. A shuttle 'train' covers the 2km road between the car park and the cave entrance (40 Kč), or you can walk there in 30 minutes.

From Punkevní it's a 15-minute hike, or an easy gondola ride (50 Kč return, 70 Kč for a combined ticket with the train), to the top of the 139m-deep Macocha Abyss. Other caves in the area include Balčárka and Sloupsko-Sošuvské (both have similar hours to Kateřinská – contact the information service). Traces of prehistoric humans have been found in the caves.

Places to Stay & Eat Near the Macocha Abyss is the hostel and restaurant **Chata Macocha** *(dorm beds 210 Kč);* book at Hotel Skalní Mlýn. The pricier **Hotel Skalní Mlýn** *(☎ 516 41 81 13, fax 516 41 81 14; e smk@smk.cz; singles/doubles from 990/1290 Kč)* is beside the car park in Skalní Mlýn.

Getting There & Away From Brno, take one of the frequent trains to Blansko (24 Kč, 30 minutes). From the nearby bus station, there are buses to Skalní Mlýn at 7.40am, 9.15am and 11.40am, returning at 3.25pm and 5.10pm (May to September); the rest of the year there is only the 7.40am bus there and the 3.25pm bus back. Check times at the Brno tourist office before setting off. You can also hike an 8km trail from Blansko to Skalní Mlýn (two hours).

Estonia

Estonia (Eesti) lies just 80km across the Gulf of Finland from Helsinki. Only fully independent since August 1991, Estonia's transition from a socialist republic of the Soviet Union to Western-style economy has been little short of miraculous. Even before independence, Estonia was known as the most 'Western' of the Soviet republics, partly because of its links with Finland.

Estonia is more Scandinavian in look and feel than its Baltic neighbours. However, its German past lingers and is particularly evident in Tallinn's medieval Old Town, now protected under the Unesco World Heritage List. Tallinn is the hub of Estonian life, but the university town of Tartu, the coastal resort of Pärnu and the islands of Saaremaa and Hiiumaa are also appealing destinations.

Facts about Estonia

HISTORY
Estonia's pagan clans encountered Scandinavians and Slavs between the 8th and 12th centuries but were little influenced from outside until German traders and missionaries, followed by knights, were unleashed by Pope Celestinus III's 1193 crusade against the 'northern heathens'. In 1202 the Bishop of Rīga established the Knights of the Sword to convert the region by conquest; southern Estonia was soon subjugated, the north fell to Denmark.

The Knights of the Sword were later subordinated to a second band of German crusaders, the Teutonic Order, which by 1290 ruled the eastern Baltic area as far north as southern Estonia, and most of the Estonian islands. Denmark sold northern Estonia to the knights in 1346, placing Estonians under servitude to a German nobility that lasted till the early 20th century. Hanseatic towns on the routes between Russia and the west prospered under the Germans, although many Estonians in rural areas were forced into serfdom.

By 1620 Estonia had fallen under Swedish control. The Swedes consolidated Estonian Protestantism and aimed to introduce universal education, however frequent wars were devastating. After the Great Northern War (1700–21), Estonia became part of the Russian empire. Repressive government from Moscow and economic control by German powers forged a national self-awareness among native Estonians. Serfs were freed in the 19th century and improved education and land-ownership rights promoted culture and welfare.

Independence
The Soviets abandoned the Baltic countries to Germany in WWI with the Treaty of Brest-Litovsk in March 1918. Estonian nationalists had originally declared independence on 24

ESTONIA

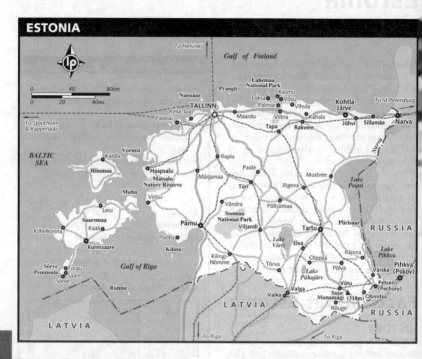

ESTONIA

February. The Bolsheviks failed to win back control, defeated by local opposition and outside military intervention from Britain and Scandinavia. This War of Independence led to the Tartu Peace Treaty on 2 February 1920, in which Russia renounced territorial claims to Estonia, supposedly forever.

Damaged by the war and hampered by trade disruptions with the USSR and a world slump, independent Estonia suffered economically even as it bloomed culturally. The anticommunist, antiparliamentary 'Vaps' movement won a constitutional referendum in 1933, but the prime minister, Konstantin Päts, outflanked it in a bloodless coup. He took over as a moderate, relatively benevolent dictator, who quietly safeguarded the USSR's interests.

Soviet Rule & WWII

The Molotov-Ribbentrop Pact of 23 August 1939 on Nazi-USSR nonaggression, secretly divided Eastern Europe into Soviet and German spheres of influence. Estonia fell into the Soviet sphere and by August 1940 was under occupation. Estonia was 'accepted' into the USSR after fabricated elections and, within a year, over 10,000 people in Estonia were killed or deported. When Hitler invaded the USSR in 1941, many saw the Germans as liberators, but during the German occupation about 5500 people died in concentration camps. Some 40,000 Estonians joined the German army to prevent the Red Army from reconquering Estonia, while nearly twice that number fled abroad.

Between 1945 and 1949, with Stalinism back on course, agriculture was collectivised and industry nationalised, and 60,000 more Estonians were killed or deported. An armed resistance, the *metsavennad* (forest brothers), fought Soviet rule until 1956.

New Independence

As early as 1980, Estonian students were demonstrating against 'Sovietisation', and widespread activism surged under *glasnost* (openness) in the late 1980s.

On 23 August 1989, on the 50th anniversary of the Molotov-Ribbentrop Pact, an estimated two million people formed a human chain across Estonia, Latvia and Lithuania and many called for secession from the USSR. In November of that year Moscow granted the three republics economic autonomy. Estonia's new

Supreme Council reinstated the pre-WWII constitution and, after observing events unfolding in nearby Lithuania, prepared Estonia for a cautious move towards independence.

Independence came suddenly, however, in the aftermath of the Moscow putsch against Gorbachev. Estonia's declaration of complete independence on 20 August 1991 was immediately recognised by the West and by the USSR on 6 September.

During October 1992, Estonia held its first democratic elections, which brought to the presidency Lennart Meri, a film maker and writer, who oversaw the removal of the last Russian troops in 1994. Simultaneously, elections were held for parliament (Riigikogu). Historian Mart Laar became prime minister, leading a government focused on launching radical reform policies, committed to European integration and NATO membership.

The decade since independence has seen frequent changes of government and no shortage of scandal. One of the stabilising influences in Estonian politics, Lennart Meri, ended his second term as president in 2001 (the constitution bars a third consecutive term). The elections that followed returned the last Soviet-era head of state Arnold Rüütel, in what was believed to be a reaction against the previous decade's drive towards the West. Rüütel maintains a commitment to EU accession and NATO, but is more cautious in his approach.

After a split in the ruling coalition Mart Laar resigned as prime minister early in 2002, believing that intraparliamentary conflicts threatened to undermine the country's progress to European integration and NATO membership. Siim Kallas, former head of the Bank of Estonia, was subsequently appointed Estonia's prime minister.

The EU and NATO remain the focus of Estonia's foreign policy. At the time of writing, it is anticipated Estonia will become a signatory to NATO before 2003 and accede to the EU by 2004.

GEOGRAPHY

With an area of 45,227 sq km, Estonia is only slightly bigger than Denmark. Mainly low-lying, with extensive bogs and marshes, Suur Munamägi (318m) in the southeast near Võru is the highest point. Nearly 50% of the land is forested and 22% is wetlands, with peat bogs in places 7m deep. The 3794km-long

coastline is heavily indented. Islands (1521) make up nearly 10% of Estonian territory and there are over 1400 lakes, the largest of which is Lake Peipsi (3555 sq km).

The Baltic Glint is Estonia's most prominent geological feature, 60-million-year-old limestone banks that extend 1200km from Sweden to Lake Ladoga in Russia, forming impressive cliffs along Estonia's northern coast.

CLIMATE

From May to September maximum temperatures are usually between 14°C and 22°C. July and August, the warmest months, are also the wettest with persistent showers. Snow is usually visible from December to late March.

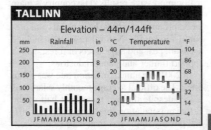

ECOLOGY & ENVIRONMENT

Since independence, the have been major 'clean-up' attempts to counter the effects of Soviet-era industrialisation, although the Baltic Sea remains extremely polluted. Toxic emissions in the industrialised northeast of Estonia have been reduced sharply and new environmental-impact legislation aims to minimise the effects of future development. Estonia's western islands boast some of the most unspoiled landscapes in Europe.

GOVERNMENT & POLITICS

Estonia is an independent republic with its own constitution. The head of state is the president, but his duties are mainly ceremonial. The 101-seat Riigikogu, or parliament, led by the prime minister, is elected every four years. The parliament comprises numerous parties and factions led by a coalition of the Centre and Reform Parties.

Successive governments over the decade since Estonia's independence have embraced free-market economics and European integration. This fast track towards the West has left critics feeling that Estonia is continuing its historical tradition of foreign dominance.

ESTONIA

Some feel alienated by progress, nostalgic for the Soviet days, while others have thrived in Estonia's new era of prosperity. The next presidential elections are due around 2006.

ECONOMY

During Soviet rule Estonia was transformed from an agrarian economy to an industrial one subservient to Moscow. Upon independence, the loss of the large Soviet market, subsidies and cheap fuel had a profound impact. The cost of living rose tenfold within the first year; spiralling inflation, shortages and unemployment followed. The introduction of the kroon in June 1992 was the start of a programme of stabilisation with dramatically impressive results. The country's main export products are machinery, timber and wood products, textiles, base metals and prepared foodstuffs. Natural resources include shale oil, peat and large tracts of forest, which support timber and paper industries.

In 2001, the annual inflation rate was about 5.8%. The official average monthly salary was €353, despite the fact that about half of the Estonian population live at or under the official poverty line – less than €100 a month.

POPULATION & PEOPLE

Estonia's population is 68% Estonian, 26% Russian, 2% Ukrainian, 1% Belarusian and 1% Finnish, with other groups making up the remainder. In 1934, over 90% of the population was native Estonian. Russian speakers are concentrated in Tallinn and in the industrial northeast, forming 40.5% and 96% of the respective populations.

It's believed the land that is now Estonia was settled immediately following the end of the last ice age, approximately 10,000 years ago. Recent theories suggest that ancestors of the Estonians and Finns arrived in small-scale migrations, moving northwards as opposed to westwards, and that there was intermingling between Finno-Ugric and other tribes. Estonians are closely related to the Finns, and more distantly to the Samis and Hungarians, but not to the Latvians and Lithuanians, who are of Indo-European heritage.

ARTS

Until the mid-19th century, Estonian culture existed only in the form of peasant, oral folk tales and chanted verses. Many were collected to form the national epic *Kalevipoeg* (The Son of Kalev), by Friedrich Reinhold Kreutzwald around 1861, inspired by Finland's *Kalevala*. The *Kalevipoeg* relates the adventures of the mythical hero, ends in his death, his land's conquest by foreigners and a promise to return to bring freedom. The epic played a major role in fostering the national awakening of the 19th century. Lydia Koidula (1843–86) is the revered poet and playwright of Estonia's national awakening.

AH Tammsaare, who wrote the monumental *Tõde ja õigus* (Truth and Justice) between 1926 and 1933, was the foremost writer of the first Independence. Artist Eduard Wiiralt produced fantastic and grotesque graphics between 1928 and 1935.

During Soviet times, Estonian poets and writers became figures of enormous spiritual significance. Novelist Jaan Kross *(The Czar's Madman)*, poet Jaan Kaplinski *(The Same Sea in Us All)* and playwright Paul-Eerik Rummo, whose *Four Kings' Day* was banned under the Soviets, gave inspiration and expression in greatly restrictive times.

In music, Veljo Tormis revives the ancient form of runic chanting to mesmerising effect. Composer Arvo Pärt has won international acclaim for his haunting sonic blend of tension and beauty, with outwardly simple but actually complex musical structures.

SOCIETY & CONDUCT

The Estonians are a rural people said to be happiest when their nearest neighbours are no closer than 1km away. Many urban-based Estonians retire to cottages outside of the city for as much of the summer as possible.

Attachment to the land is strong (almost every person's family name denotes a natural element) as is a reverence for nature. Estonians tend to take flowers whenever they go visiting or attend any kind of celebration.

RELIGION

Under Soviet rule religious practices were discouraged and there were limitations on study and work opportunities.

From 1987 to 1990 there was a surge of interest in religion as the state Lutheran Church allied itself to the independence cause, however that enthusiasm has now waned. Since independence the Russian Orthodox Church, largely comprised of Russians, has grown and the presence of various Western-backed, organised religions and sects has increased.

LANGUAGE

Like Finnish, Estonian is one of the Finno-Ugric languages. It's a difficult language to learn with 14 cases, a lack of gender, double infinitives, articles and future tense. Many Estonians speak at least some English. Only a small, yet growing, number of Russians in Estonia speak Estonian, but most Estonians also speak some Russian, although it is seen by some as the language of occupation.

See the Language Guide at the back of the book for pronunciation guidelines and useful words and phrases.

Facts for the Visitor

HIGHLIGHTS

Tallinn's Old Town with its winding cobbled streets and gingerbread-style facades is a definite high point of any trip to Estonia. Leaving the city – to Lahemaa National Park or to the western islands of Saaremaa and Hiiumaa – is the best way to experience something more essentially Estonian: solitude and nature.

SUGGESTED ITINERARIES

Depending on time available, you may like to take in the following:

Two days
Tallinn and on the second day visit Lahemaa National Park.

One week
Two days in Tallinn, down to Tartu spending the night in southeastern Estonia, a night or two on Saaremaa, and Pärnu.

PLANNING
When to Go

Between May and September is the best time of the year to travel to Estonia as there's better weather and longer days. You'll see the 'white nights' from mid-to-late June, when the skies darken for only a few hours each night.

Maps

Good, accurate town and regional maps are widely available. *Estonia, Latvia, Lithuania* (Bartholomew World Map Travel Series, Edinburgh) and *Baltische Staaten* (Ravenstein Verlag, Bad Soden am Taunas, Germany) are similar 1:850,000-scale maps, adequate for most travellers.

Local publishers EO have a large series of fold-out maps of every county and most larger towns in Estonia with detailed information on sites of interest. Bookshops stock these and other useful maps of Estonia and the region.

What to Bring

Even in summer evenings can be chilly and rain showers plentiful, so bring a warm pullover and a waterproof coat. Between September and May you will definitely need a warm jacket, during winter you will need thermal underwear and sturdy winter clothes to combat subzero temperatures.

Everything you will need is easily available in Estonia's urban centres including Western medications.

RESPONSIBLE TOURISM

Due both to the excessive pollution caused by Soviet-era industrialisation and a traditionally close link with nature, Estonians are quite sensitive to issues of environmental conservation. In protected areas, note the instructions given for tourists, keep to the prescribed trails and, wherever you go, don't leave your rubbish behind.

TOURIST OFFICES
Local Tourist Offices

Estonia has a well-coordinated tourism infrastructure. The **Estonian Tourist Board** (☎ 627 9770, fax 626 9777; **w** *www.visitestonia .com*) oversees the functioning of individual tourism information centres throughout the entire country.

VISAS & DOCUMENTS

Make sure your passport extends at least two months after the end of your travels as this may be a requirement for certain visas.

Visas

Estonia issues transit, single-entry, multiple-entry, tourist and business visas. Visa regulations are constantly changing so check with your local Estonian consulate or embassy or directly with the **Estonian Foreign Ministry** (☎ 631 7600, fax 631 7617; **w** *www.vm.ee*; *Islandi väljak 1, Tallinn*). For full details of Estonian visas and conditions, check the website. All requirements, with an up-to-date listing of which nationalities require a visa, are also given. Note that visas cannot be obtained at the border.

Embassies and consulates usually process visa applications in a few days at most, while

ESTONIA

immediate processing is a more expensive alternative. You will need to have your valid passport, a completed application form and one or two photos.

Estonia, Latvia and Lithuania established a 'common visa space' in 1992, meaning that for some nationalities a visa for one country is good for the other two. At time of printing, the common visa was available only to Canadian and South African passport holders.

Visa extensions are not readily available and applicants must prove valid grounds for an extension. Contact the Visa Extension Department of the **Citizenship & Immigration Board** *(☎ 612 6963; Endla tänav 13, Tallinn)*.

EMBASSIES & CONSULATES
Estonian Embassies & Consulates
Estonia maintains diplomatic representation in the following countries:

Australia (☎ 02-9810 7468, fax 9818 1779, e eestikon@ozemail.com.au) 86 Louisa Rd, Birchgrove, NSW 2041
Canada (☎ 416-461 0764, fax 461 0353, e estconsu@ca.inter.net) 202-958 Broadview Ave, Toronto, Ontario M4K 2R6
Finland (☎ 9-622 0260, fax 622 02610, e embassy.helsinki@mfa.ee) Itäinen Puistotie 10, 00140 Helsinki
Germany (☎ 30-25 460 600, fax 25 460 101, e embassy.berlin@mfa.ee) Hildebrand-strasse 5 10785 Berlin
  Consulate: (☎ 40 450 40 26, fax 40 450 40 515) Badestrasse 38, 20143 Hamburg
Latvia (☎ 781 20 20, fax 781 20 29, e embassy.riga@mfa.ee) Skolas iela 13, Rīga
Lithuania (☎ 5-278 0200, fax 278 0201; e embassy.vilnius@mfa.ee) Mickeviciaus gatvė 4a, Vilnius
Russia (☎ 095-290 5013, 737 3640, fax 737 3646, e embassy.moskva@mfa.ee) Maly Kislovsky 5, 103009 Moscow
  Consulate: (☎ 812-102 0920, fax 102 0927, e consulate.peterburg@mfa.ee) Bolsaja Monetnaja 14, St Petersburg
Sweden (☎ 08-5451 2280, fax 5451 2299, e embassy@estemb.se) Tyrgatan 3, Stockholm
UK (☎ 020-7589 3428, fax 7589 3430, e embassy.london@mfa.ee) 16 Hyde Park Gate, London SW7 5DG
USA (☎ 202-588 0101, fax 588 0108)
  To mid-2003: 1730 M St, Suite 503, NW, Washington, DC 20036
  From mid-2003: 2131 Massachusetts Ave, NW, Washington DC 20008
  Consulate: (☎ 212-883 0636, fax 883 0648) 660 3rd Ave, 26th floor, New York, NY

Foreign Embassies & Consulates in Estonia
Following is a list of some foreign embassies and consulates with offices in Tallinn. For information on other countries and their representatives, or for visa-related information, contact the **Estonian Foreign Ministry** *(☎ 631 7600, fax 631 7617; w www.vm.ee; Islandi väljak 1, Tallinn)*.

Australia (☎ 650 9308, fax 667 1333, e mati@standard.ee) Kopli tänav 25
Canada (☎ 627 3311, fax 627 3312, e canembt@unint.ee) Toom-Kooli tänav 13
Finland (☎ 610 3200) Kohtu tänav 4
  Consulate: (☎ 610 3300, fax 610 3281; e info@datanet.ee) Pikk jalg 14
Germany (☎ 627 5300, fax 627 5304, e deutchland@online.ee) Toom-Kuninga tänav 11
Latvia (☎ 646 1310, fax 631 1366, e embassy.estonia@mfa.gov.lv) Tõnismägi tänav 10
Lithuania (☎ 631 4030, 641 2014 for visas, fax 641 2013; e amber@anet.ee) Uus tänav 15
Russia (☎ 646 4175, 646 4178, e vensaat@online.ee) Pikk tänav 19
  Consulate in Narva: (☎ 035-60 652, fax 60 654) Rüütli tänav 8
Sweden (☎ 640 5600, fax 640 5695, e swedemb@estpak.ee) Pikk tänav 28
UK (☎ 667 4700, fax 667 4755, e information@britishembassy.ee) Wismari tänav 6
USA (☎ 668 8100; fax 668 8134, e tallinn@usemb.ee) Kentmanni tänav 20

CUSTOMS
In general, travellers over 21 years of age are allowed to bring in and take out duty free 1L of hard alcohol over 22% by volume, or 1L of alcohol of up to 22% plus 2L of wine. 200 cigarettes are the maximum permitted. Phone the **Customs Department** *(☎ 696 7435; w www.customs.ee)* in Tallinn for up-to-date regulations or check the website.

There are restrictions on taking antiques and works of art, which are subject to duty, out of the county. Permits can be obtained from the **Division of the Export of Cultural Objects** *(☎ 644 6578; Sakala tänav 14, Tallinn)*.

MONEY
Currency
The kroon (EEK; pronounced 'krohn') is pegged to the euro and comes in two, five, 10, 25, 50, 100 and 500EEK denomination notes. One kroon is divided into 100 sents, and there are coins of five, 10, 20 and 50 sents, as well as one and five kroon coins.

Exchange Rates

The Estonian kroon is pegged to the euro. At the time of publication the following exchange rates prevailed:

country	unit		kroon
Australia	A$1	=	9.22EEK
Canada	C$1	=	10.70EEK
Denmark	1Dkr	=	2.10EEK
Euro Zone	€1	=	15.64EEK
Iceland	Ikr1	=	5.40EEK
Latvia	1Ls	=	26.98EEK
Lithuania	1Lt	=	4.53EEK
Norway	1Nkr	=	2.11EEK
Sweden	1SKr	=	1.72EEK
UK	UK£1	=	24.51EEK
USA	US$1	=	16.58EEK

Exchanging money

The best currencies to bring into Estonia are US dollars or euros, although almost all Western currencies are readily exchangeable.

Private exchange bureaus offer the most favourable rates. All major credit cards are widely accepted, although Visa is most common. Most banks accept travellers cheques but commissions can be unpleasantly high.

Costs

Accommodation and food costs constantly rise, particularly in Tallinn, but bus and train services within Estonia are quite inexpensive by Western standards. Students, pensioners, groups and those travelling with children should ask about concessions, available for most transport services and sights.

The *käibemaks* consumption tax, levied on most goods and services ranges from 5% to 18% and makes its presence felt. Prices for imported goods are comparable to those in Scandinavia. Bargains still exist but now take a little longer to find.

Tipping

Tipping has become the norm in the last few years, but generally no more than 5% to 10% is expected.

POST & COMMUNICATIONS
Post

Mail service in and out of Estonia is quite reasonable; letters or postcards should take about four days to Western Europe or a week to North America. Air-mail rates for letters that weigh up to 20g are between 6.5EEK and 8EEK. There is a poste-restante bureau at the **central post office** (*Narva maantee 1, Tallinn*) where mail is kept for one month.

Telephone

To call other cities in Estonia, simply dial ☎ 0, followed by the area code and telephone number. Tallinn now has no area code and all Tallinn numbers have seven digits.

Estonia's country code when calling from abroad is ☎ 372, followed by the local city code and subscriber number. For example, to call Tartu, dial ☎ 3727 followed by the subscriber number. For Tallinn, simply dial ☎ 372 plus the seven-digit number.

Public telephones accept chip cards available at post offices, hotels and most kiosks (50EEK or 100EEK). For placing calls outside Estonia, an international telephone card, available at many kiosks, is far better value.

Fax & Telegraph

Post offices throughout Estonia generally include the sending of faxes and telegrams among their many services.

Email & Internet Access

Most cities and towns in Estonia and even some rural dots on the map have at least one place to log on. See Tallinn, Tartu and Pärnu sections for Internet access points.

DIGITAL RESOURCES

Anything truly Estonian has a presence on the Web, for background information or travel planning, go to Ⓦ www.ee/www/welcome .html and Ⓦ www.visitestonia.com. Useful websites for tourist services include Ⓦ www .turismiweb.ee and Ⓦ www.inyourpocket .com. The English Estonian dictionary available at Ⓦ www.ibs.ee/dict may also come in handy.

BOOKS

For anyone interested in a comprehensive account of the region *The Baltic Revolution* by Anatol Lieven is essential reading. Another excellent historical analysis is provided by John Hiden & Patrick Salmon's *The Baltic Nations and Europe*. Estonian photographer Ann Tenno has produced a series of fascinating books, that include *Tallinna Album* and *Pictures of Estonia*, which evoke the delicate spirit of the land.

ESTONIA

With more than 80 useful maps and 400 pages of invaluable information, Lonely Planet's *Estonia, Latvia & Lithuania* will make a helpful travelling companion.

NEWSPAPERS & MAGAZINES

The Rīga-based weekly *Baltic Times* (**w** www .baltictimes.com) is an authoritative English-language digest of Baltic news and information. The bimonthly *City Paper* contains some good informative features and listings.

RADIO & TV

Along the north coast of Estonia it's possible to pick up Finnish TV channels which broadcast many English-language programmes. See the local press for schedules. Most hotels have satellite TV offering an onslaught of European and English language programmes.

Estonian Radio broadcasts 15 minutes of local news in English at 6pm on weekdays on 103.5 FM, or on its website at **w** www.er.ee. Alternatively, your favourite online media service will keep you informed.

PHOTOGRAPHY & VIDEO

Good-quality print film is freely available in towns and cities at photo shops and kiosks. There are many quick print-processing outlets. Camcorder videocassettes are expensive and the selection is not wide – do bring extras.

TIME

In 2002, Estonia introduced daylight-saving time. Standard time is GMT/UTC plus two hours, with GMT/UTC plus three hours from the last Sunday in March to the last Sunday of October.

LAUNDRY

While the better hotels offer laundry services, you will find laundrettes *(pesumajad)* in most towns and cities. In Tallinn there are two options close to the city centre (see the Tallinn section for details).

TOILETS

Public toilets throughout Estonia are well signposted and usually clean but some horrors await at regional bus and train stations. Expect to pay 2EEK to 3EEK in exchange for a few sheets of rough toilet paper (bringing your own isn't a bad idea).

The letter *M* marks a men's toilet and *N* indicates a women's toilet. Some toilets sport a triangle for women and an inverted triangl for men.

HEALTH

It's wise to carry a small, basic medical kit i your destination lies beyond the beaten track In the major towns and cities however, yo will find all you need. No immunisations ar required but bear in mind tuberculosis is fa more prevalent in Estonia than in Wester Europe. Emergency care is not free in Estoni so it is a good idea to have medical insuranc (see Travel Insurance under Visas & Docu ments in the introductory Facts for the Visito chapter).

Tap water in Estonia is clean and drinkable

WOMEN TRAVELLERS

Western women are unlikely to experienc aggravation from men in Estonia, but trad itional gender role expectations are somewha entrenched. Notions of feminism and equa opportunity resonate much more quietly her and acts of chivalry are not uncommon.

GAY & LESBIAN TRAVELLERS

While open displays of same-sex affectio are discouraged in Estonia, the overall atti tude is more of curiosity than antagonism; th media have run several gay-positive article since the early 1990s. For more informatio about the gay scene in the country, contac the **Estonian Gay League** (*PO Box 142 Tallinn 10502;* **e** *gayliit@hotmail.com*).

The **Estonian Union for Lesbian and Bi sexual Women** (**☎** *055 11 132*) can also b contacted through the Estonian Gay League

DISABLED TRAVELLERS

For information on all services available i Estonia, contact the **Tallinn Association fo the Disabled** (**☎** *644 2804; Tatari tänav 14)* The **Invaühing** (**☎** *7-366 762*) in Tartu and it **information centre** (**☎** *7-401 226*) can als provide information. Specially equipped taxi and minibuses can be ordered in advance i Tallinn through **Linnataxo** (**☎** *644 2442*).

Emergency Services

In case of emergencies call **☎** 110 for police and **☎** 112 for fire, ambulance and urgent medical advice. These numbers are national.

Call **☎** 1188 for 24-hour car assistance.

ESTONIA

DANGERS & ANNOYANCES

Theft from hotel rooms is a danger in the Baltics, more significantly in cheap hotels. Keep valuables with you or in a hotel safe.

Most of the surly, rude, obstructive goblins employed in service industries during the Soviet era have miraculously changed character now that pleasing the customer has become worthwhile, but you are still likely to encounter apathetic service from time to time; just grit your teeth and quietly persist.

Drunks on the streets, around stations and in hotels can be a nuisance. Steer clear and don't get involved.

PUBLIC HOLIDAYS & SPECIAL EVENTS

The biggest occasion of the year is the night of 23 June, Jaanipäev (St John's Eve), a celebration of the pagan Midsummer's Night, best experienced out in the country where huge bonfires are lit for all-night parties. June 23 is also the Victory Day holiday (anniversary of Battle of Võnnu, 1919). The official Jaanipäev holiday is 24 June. Good Friday, Christmas, Boxing Day and New Year's Day are celebrated as elsewhere in the West and 1 May is the traditional May Day holiday.

Independence is celebrated twice, on 24 February Independence Day, the anniversary of the 1918 declaration, and on 21 August New Independence Day, celebrating the 1991 declaration of independence from the USSR.

Estonia also has a busy calendar of festivals encompassing all aspects of contemporary and folk culture. The Baltika International Folk Festival (which alternates between Estonia, Latvia and Lithuania, usually in mid-July) is a week of music, dance and displays focusing on Baltic and other folk traditions, next due in Estonia in 2004. The All-Estonian Song Festival convenes every four years and culminates in a 30,000-strong traditional choir.

Smaller annual festivals include: the Tallinn Old Town Days, Pärnu's international music and theatre festival FiESTa and Tartu's popular Jazz Festival, which all take place in June.

ACTIVITIES

Cycling

The bicycle shop **Jalgrattakeskus** (☎ 623 7799; Tartu maantee 73, Tallinn) rents bicycles by the hour with better deals for long-term rentals. Bicycle tours througout Estonia can be arranged through **Alutaguse Matkaklubi** (☎ 051-41 692, fax 23 70 568), which is based in Kohtla-Järve.

Sailing

Existing harbour facilities are constantly being upgraded in ports throughout Estonia. For information on western Estonian ports and conditions visit ⓦ www.tt.ee/renza/sadamad. Yachts can be hired from **Kalevi Jahtklubi** (☎ 623 9158; Pirita tee 17) for trips around Tallinn Bay and also to neighbouring islands, with spectacular views of Tallinn from the sea.

Skiing

Skiing (predominantly cross-country) is extremely popular. The main skiing centre is Otepää in southeastern Estonia where there are several centres that hire equipment. Contact the Otepää **Tourist Information Centre** (☎ 76-55 364; ⓔ otepaa@visitestonia.com) for more information.

Sauna

The sauna is an Estonian institution and comes close to being a religious experience. The most common type of sauna here is the dry, Finnish style. Most hotels have saunas; the most luxurious can be experienced on the 26th floor of cetnral Tallinn's **Hotel Olümpia** (☎ 631 5585; Liivalaia tänav), along with some fantastic views. **Kalma Saun** (☎ 627 1811; Vana-Kalamaja 9A; open 10am-11pm daily) is the best of Tallinn's public saunas.

ACCOMMODATION

Tallinn Tourist Information Centre (☎ 645 7777, fax 645 7778; ⓔ turismiinfo@tallinlv .ee; Raekoja plats 10) keeps lists of camping grounds, hotels, motels and guesthouses all throughout Estonia.

It's worth trying to book ahead wherever you plan to stay as vacancies, particularly during summer, can be scarce. Agencies in other countries as well as in Tallinn can make bookings, although top-end categories are their speciality.

Camping

There are a few camping grounds (kämpingud) that allow you to pitch a tent, but most consist mainly of permanent wooden cabins. Showers and toilets are usually communal. Camping grounds are generally open from mid-May to early September.

ESTONIA

Hostels

The **Estonian Youth Hostels Association** (☎ 646 1457; W www.baltichostels.net) will take online bookings for hostels throughout Estonia. Accommodation is mainly in small, two- to four-bed rooms.

Hotels

Estonia's budget hotels are generally bare and dowdy, but usually have tolerably clean rooms, with private or shared bathrooms. The mid-range and top-end hotels often exceed Western standards and expectations. During summer, rooms can be booked out well in advance in major centres and resort towns, so be sure to check ahead in these areas.

Private Homes & Apartments

There are a number of organisations that will organise rooms in a private home – an excellent way to experience local life – or your own apartment with a shared bathroom. **Rasastra** (☎/fax 661 6921; W www.bedbreakfast.ee; Mere puiestee 4, Tallinn), near Rotermanni Shopping Centre, is a good place to start.

Farmstays

The best information about farmstays can be obtained from regional tourist information centres throughout Estonia. Farms offer more than a choice of rooms; in many cases meals, sauna and a wide range of activities are also available.

FOOD

The Estonian diet relies heavily on *sealiha* (pork), red meat, chicken, sausage and potatoes. Fish appears most often as a smoked or salted starter. *Forell* (smoked trout) is one good speciality. *Sült*, jellied meat, will likely be served as well. At Christmas time, *verivorst* (sausages) are made from fresh blood and wrapped in pig intestine (joy to the world indeed!). Those really in need of a transfusion will find blood sausages, blood bread and blood dumplings, all available in most traditional Estonian restaurants and shops year-round.

Unless you're a vegetarian, or on a modified diet, no significant challenges lie ahead. The mayonnaise or sour cream that used to engulf most meals now increasingly appears as a polite condiment. Delicious and inexpensive freshly baked cakes, breads and pastries are available everywhere.

Restaurants are plentiful and pubs will often serve meals. A *puffet* (buffet) will provide a cheaper cafeteria-style meal. Menu are commonly available in English or are readily translated.

DRINKS

Õlu (beer) is the favourite alcoholic drink in Estonia and the local product is very much in evidence. Best brands are Saku and A Le Coq which come in a range of brews. *Viin* (vodka) and *konjak* (brandy) are also popular drinks Vana Tallinn, the very sweet and very strong (40% alcohol) liqueur of unknown extraction is an integral part of any Estonian gift pack Saare Dzinn (gin made from Saaremaa-grown juniper berries) is also well worth trying for a of sample local beverages.

Eesti Kali is the favourite (Estonian) brand of Baltic cola.

ENTERTAINMENT

The university city of Tartu and the resorts of Pärnu and Otepää, are giving the capital some serious competition as party centres in Estonia. At the end of the day Tallinn prevails with its legions of clubs, pubs, bars theatres and casinos. Regular free events take place in the Old Town square over the warmer months.

Classical music, opera and ballet feature strongly in most major centres; festivals of music, dance and theatre are an integral part of the entertainment and arts calendar throughout the country. See the individual city sections for more details.

SPECTATOR SPORTS

To witness a truly unique Estonian sport, be on the lookout for **kiiking** events, where the gentle pleasure of riding a swing becomes something of an extreme sport based on the number of rotations a competitor can achieve Visit W www.kiiking.ee for the kiiking story

SHOPPING

In Tallinn and most major centres all survival needs are met and some fine souvenirs and gift ideas abound. Traditional items to take home as a memento are hand-knitted garments, lace, leather-bound books, ceramics, amber, silverware and objects carved out of limestone.

Markets provide a good local shopping experience and some genuine bargains.

27 25 27; 5th floor, Foreign Pavilion, Roentgenova 2), with some of the best facilities in the country. Staff speak English, German, French and Spanish, but there are no English speakers on the after-hours telephone number. Take bus No 167 from Anděl metro station and get off at the sixth stop.

District clinics have after-hours emergency services (from 7pm to 7am, and 24 hours on weekends and holidays). The **Polyclinic at Národní** (☎ 222 07 51 20; Národní 9; metro Národní Třída) has staff who speak English, French and German. Expect to pay around 800 Kč to 1200 Kč for an initial consultation.

There are several private centres that have English and German-speaking staff providing emergency medical and dental care. An initial consultation will cost US$50 to US$200; you can pay by cash or credit card. Reputable establishments include the **American Medical Center** (24hr ☎ 220 80 77 56; Janovského 48, Prague 7; metro Vltavská) and the **Canadian Medical Centre** (☎ 235 36 01 33, after hours ☎ 60321 23 20; Veleslavínská 1; tram No 20 or 26 west from metro Dejvická).

There are several 24-hour pharmacies (lékárna) in the city centre, including the **Praha lékárna** (☎ 224 94 69 82; Palackého 5) and **Lékárna U sv Ludmily** (☎ 222 51 33 96; Belgická 37; metro Náměstí Míru). For emergency service after hours, ring the bell (usually a red button with a sign saying 'zvonek léka' or 'první pomoc').

Police Official police reports for stolen belongings (needed for insurance claims) can only be obtained at the main police station in the district in which the theft occurred. This process can take a couple of hours and the officer on duty will probably have to call an interpreter. In central Prague the **police station** (☎ 261 45 17 60; Jungmannovo nám 9) can arrange for an interpreter. Unless you can speak Czech, forget about telephoning any other police station as English is rarely spoken.

Dangers & Annoyances The crime rate is low by Western standards but theft is rife. Pickpockets regularly work the crowds at the astronomical clock on the Old Town Hall, at Prague Castle, Karlův most (Charles Bridge), the entrance to the Old Jewish Cemetery, Václavské nám, Na příkopě and on the central metro and tram lines, especially tourists getting on or off crowded tram Nos 9 and 22.

We've also had reports of bogus police who approach tourists and ask to see their money, claiming that they are looking for counterfeit notes. They then run off with substantial amounts of cash. If in doubt, ask the 'policeman' to go with you to the nearest police station; a genuine cop will happily do so.

Being ripped off by taxi drivers is another hazard. Most taxi drivers are honest, but a large minority who operate from tourist areas greatly overcharge their customers (even Czechs). Try not to take a taxi from Václavské nám, Národní and other tourist areas. It is better to phone for a taxi (see Getting Around later in this section) or walk a couple of streets into the suburbs before hailing one.

Be aware that the park outside the main train station is a hang-out for drunks and questionable characters and should be avoided late at night.

Hradčany

Prague's finest churches and museums are in Hradčany, the wonderful castle district stretching along a hill top west of the river. During weekends and summer, Prague Castle is packed with sightseers. Early morning is a good time to visit, and evening is even better (although all the museums will be closed). Unless otherwise indicated, museums and galleries are closed on Monday; concession prices are for children under 16 and students.

The easiest way to get to this area is by metro to Malostranská, then tram No 22 up the hill to the back of Hradčany as far as the fourth stop, Památník Písemnictví. From here Pohořelec and Loretánská slope down to the castle gate.

A passage at Pohořelec 8 leads up to the **Strahov Library** (adult/concession 50/30 Kč; open 9am-noon & 1pm-5pm daily), the largest monastic library in the country, built in 1679. The Philosophy Hall features beautifully carved shelves and a gorgeous frescoed ceiling. Look out for the books on tree-growing bound in the bark of the trees they describe. The lane east of the monastery leads to a terrace with a good view over the city.

Nearby on Loretánské nám is the splendid baroque **Černín Palace** (1687), now the Ministry of Foreign Affairs. The exuberantly baroque **Loreta** (adult/concession 80/60 Kč; open 9.15am-12.15pm & 1pm-4.30pm daily), opposite the palace, is a convent with a fabulous treasure of diamonds, pearls and gold, and a

1631 replica of the Santa Casa in the Italian town of Loreto, itself said to be the replica of the Virgin Mary's house in Nazareth, carried to Italy by angels in the 13th century. The convent gets very crowded with tourists.

Loretánská soon opens onto Hradčanské nám, with the main gate to Prague Castle at its eastern end. On the square at No 2 is the imposing Renaissance **Schwarzenberg Palace** (1563) with its sgraffito decoration. Just across the square at No 15 is the 18th-century Šternberg Palace, the main branch of the **National Gallery** *(adult/concession 60/30 Kč; open 10am-6pm)*. This houses the country's main collection of 14th- to 18th-century European paintings, including Cranachs and Goyas.

Prague Castle

Founded in the 9th century, Prague Castle *(☎ 224 37 33 68; adult/concession 220/110 Kč; buildings open 9am-5pm daily Apr-Oct, 9am-4pm Nov-March; grounds open 5am-midnight daily Apr-Oct, 6am-11pm Nov-Mar)* was rebuilt and extended many times. Always the centre of political power, it's still the official residence of the president. The full-price ticket (valid for one day) allows entry to St Vitus Cathedral, the Old Royal Palace, Basilica of St George, Powder Gate (Mihulka), Golden Lane and Dalibor Tower. Guided tours in English cost 400 Kč for up to five people. Cheaper tickets are available for

more limited sightseeing. Note that cameras and videos cannot be used inside the buildings without official permission.

Matthias Gate leads from the first courtyard under an arch dated 1614 to the second courtyard and the **Chapel of the Holy Cross** (with the castle ticket and information office). On the north side of this courtyard is the **Prague Castle Gallery** *(adult/concession 100/50 Kč; open 10am-6pm daily)*, with a good collection of European baroque paintings.

The third courtyard is dominated by **St Vitus Cathedral**, a glorious French Gothic structure begun in 1344 by order of Emperor Charles IV and finally completed in 1929. Its stained-glass windows, frescoes and tombstones (including that of its founder inside the crypt) merit careful attention. The 14th-century chapel on the cathedral's southern side with the black imperial eagle on the door contains the **tomb of St Wenceslas**, the Czech's patron saint and the 'Good King Wenceslas' of the Christmas carol. Wenceslas' zeal in spreading Christianity and his submission to the German King Henry I led to his murder by his brother, Boleslav I. Alarmed by reports of miracles at Wenceslas' grave, Boleslav had the remains re-interred in St Vitus Cathedral in 932, and the saint's tomb soon became a great pilgrimage site. The small door beside the chapel windows leads to a chamber where the Bohemian crown jewels are kept (not open to

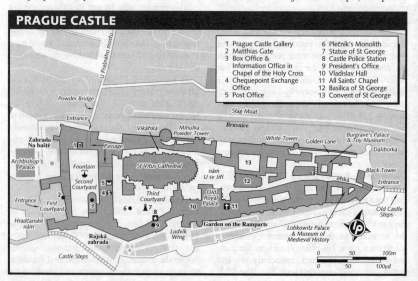

PRAGUE CASTLE

1 Prague Castle Gallery
2 Matthias Gate
3 Box Office & Information Office in Chapel of the Holy Cross
4 Chequepoint Exchange Office
5 Post Office
6 Plečník's Monolith
7 Statue of St George
8 Castle Police Station
9 President's Office
10 Vladislav Hall
11 All Saints' Chapel
12 Basilica of St George
13 Convent of St George

U Prašného mostu

Powder Bridge

Entrance

Stag Moat

Brusnice

Zahrada Na baště

Vikářská

Mihulka Powder Tower

White Tower

Golden Lane

Burgrave's Palace & Toy Museum

Daliborka

Archbishop's Palace

Fountain

Passage

St Vitus Cathedral

nám U sv Jiří

13

12

Jiřská

Black Tower

Entrance

Second Courtyard

Entrance

First Courtyard

Third Courtyard

Old Royal Palace

10

11

Old Castle Steps

Hradčanské nám

Rajská zahrada

Ludvík Wing

Garden on the Ramparts

Lobkowicz Palace & Museum of Medieval History

Castle Steps

0   50   100m
0   50   100yd

CZECH REPUBLIC

the public). You can climb the 287 steps of the cathedral's **Great Tower** *(open 9am-4.15pm daily Apr-Oct)*.

On the southern side of the cathedral is the entrance to the **Old Royal Palace** with the huge and elegantly vaulted Vladislav Hall, built between 1486 and 1502. A ramp up to one side allowed mounted horsemen to ride into the hall for indoor jousts. On 23 May 1618 two Catholic councillors were thrown from the window of an adjacent chamber by irate Protestant nobles, the so-called 'Defenestration of Prague' that touched off the Thirty Years' War.

As you leave the palace, the **Basilica of St George** (1142), Prague's finest Romanesque church, is right in front of you. Next to the church, in the **Convent of St George** *(adult/ concession 50/20 Kč; open 10am-6pm)*, you'll find the National Gallery's collection of Czech art from the 16th to 18th centuries.

Beyond the basilica, follow the crowd into **Golden Lane**, a 16th-century tradesmen's quarter of tiny houses built into the castle walls. Franz Kafka, who was born in Prague in 1883, lived and wrote in the tiny house at No 22 from 1916 to 1917.

On the right, just before the gate leading out of the castle, is **Lobkowitz Palace** *(adult/ concession 40/20 Kč; open 9am-5pm)*, which houses a museum of Czech history with replicas of the crown jewels. From the eastern end of the castle, the Old Castle Steps lead back down towards Malostranská metro station. Alternatively, you can turn sharp right and then wander back through the lovely **Castle Gardens** *(admission free; open 10am-6pm daily Apr-Oct)*.

Malá Strana

Malá Strana (The Small Quarter), sheltered beneath the protective walls of Prague Castle, was built in the 17th and 18th centuries by victorious Catholic clerics and nobles on the foundations of the Renaissance palaces of their Protestant predecessors.

From Malostranská metro station, follow Valdštejnská around to Valdštejnské nám, past many impressive buildings, notably the **Wallenstein Palace** (1630), now home to the Senate of the Czech Republic, which fills the entire eastern side of the square.

Albrecht Wallenstein, a famous figure in the Thirty Years' War, started out on the Protestant side then went over to the Catholics

and built this palace with the expropriated wealth of his former colleagues. In 1634 the Habsburg Emperor Ferdinand II learned that Wallenstein was about to switch sides again and had him assassinated at Cheb. The **palace gardens** *(admission free; open 10am-6pm daily Mar-Sept)* are through a gate at Letenská 10, a block to the east.

Continue south on Tomášská and round the corner to Letenská to reach **St Thomas Church**, a splendid baroque edifice built in 1731. Beyond nearby Malostranské nám is the formerly Jesuit **St Nicholas Church** *(admission 45 Kč; open 9am-6pm daily Apr-Oct, 9am-4pm daily Nov-Mar)*, built in 1755, one of the greatest baroque buildings in Prague, its dome visible from afar.

Once you have had a wander around the square, follow the tram tracks south along Karmelitská. At No 9 is the **Church of Our Lady Victorious** (1613), with the venerated wax figure of the Holy Infant of Prague (1628). Originally erected by Lutherans, the church was taken over by the Carmelite Order following the Catholic victory at the Battle of White Mountain (1620).

Backtrack a little and take narrow Prokopská east towards the river. You'll soon reach a beautiful square surrounded by fine baroque palaces. Bear left on Lázeňská towards the massive stone towers of the **Church of Our Lady Below the Chain**. To the left of the church, Lázeňská leads to Mostecká.

Turn right to reach **Charles Bridge** (Karlův most). This enchanting structure, which was built in 1357 and graced by 30 statues dating from the 18th century, was the only bridge in Prague until 1841. Take a leisurely stroll across it, but first climb the **Malá Strana bridge tower** *(admission 30 Kč; open 9am-6pm Tues-Sun, 11am-5pm Mon)* on the Malá Strana side for a great bird's-eye view of the city. In the middle of the bridge is a bronze statue (1683) of St John Nepomuk, a priest who was thrown to his death from the bridge in 1393 for refusing to reveal the queen's confessions to King Wenceslas IV. The bridge's atmosphere is best appreciated at dawn, before the crowds arrive.

Staré Město

On the Staré Město side of Charles Bridge is the 17th-century **Klementinum**, once a Jesuit college but now the State Library, the largest historic building in the city after the Prague

CZECH REPUBLIC

CZECH REPUBLIC

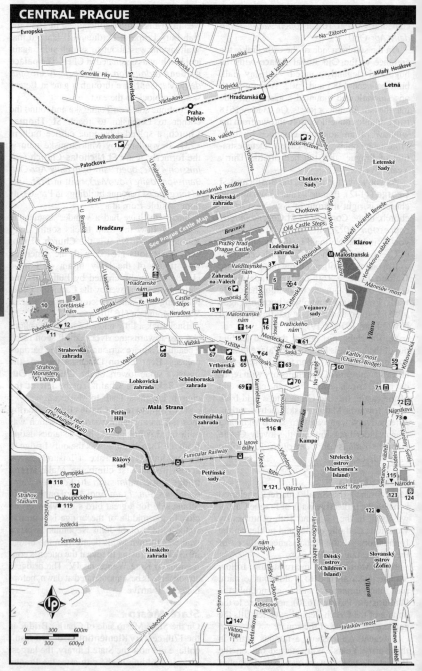

CENTRAL PRAGUE

Evropská

Generála Píky

Dejvická

Svatovítská

Václavová

Podhradbami

1

Patočkova

Jaselská

Pod kaštany

Dejvická

Na valech

Milady Horákové

Letná

Hradčanská M

Praha-
Dejvice

Mickiewiczova 2

Chotkovy
Sady

Letenské
Sady

U Prašného mostu

Jeleni

Mariánské hradby

Královská
zahrada

Chotkova

Brusnice

Chotkova

nábřeží Edvarda Beneše

Old Castle Steps

Klárov

Hradčany

U Brusnice

See Prague Castle Map

Pražký hrad
(Prague Castle)

Ledeburská
zahrada

Valdštejnská

Malostranská M

Klárova

Kosárkovo nábřeží

Nový Svět

Keplerova

Černínská

U kasáren

Valdštejnské-
nám

3

Mánesův most

Zahrada
na Valech

5 4

Vltava

7

Hradčanské
nám

8

Loretánské
nám

Ke Hradu

Castle
Steps

Thunovská

Snemovní

Tomášská

Letenská

17

Vojanovy
sady

10

9

Loretánská

Úvoz

Nerudova

13

Malostranské
nám

14

16

Dražického
nám

61

Karlův most
(Charles Bridge)

59

Pohořelec

12

11

Vlašská

15

Tržiště

Mostecká

Josefská

Saská

62

Křižovnická

Strahovská
zahrada

Vlašská

68

67
66

65

64

Prokopská

Lázeňská

63

60

71

Vrtbovská
zahrada

Karmelitská

70

Na Kampě

Čertovka

72

Náprstkova

73

Lobkovická
zahrada

Schönbornská
zahrada

69

Nosticova

Strahov
Monastery
& Library

Hladová zeď
(The Hunger Wall)

Malá Strana

Seminářská
zahrada

Hellichova

116

Kampa

Petřín
Hill

117

Růžový
sad

Funicular Railway

U lanové
dráhy

Újezd

Vlašská

Střelecký
ostrov
(Marksmen's
Island)

Smetanovo nábřeží

Dívadelní

115

Národní

123

124

Olympijská

118
120

Chaloupeckého

119

Strahov
Stadium

Vaníčkova

Jezdecká

Šermířská

Kinského
zahrada

Petřínské
sady

Říční

121

Vítězná

most 'Legii'

Zborovská

Janáčkovo nábřeží

Dětský
ostrov
(Children's
Island)

122

Slovanský
ostrov
(Žofín)

Vltava

nám
Kinských

Eliščky

Peškové

Drtinova

Holečkova

147

Viktora-
Huga

Štefánikova

Arbesovo
nám

Jiráskův most

Rašínovo nábřeží

0   300   600m
0   300   600yd

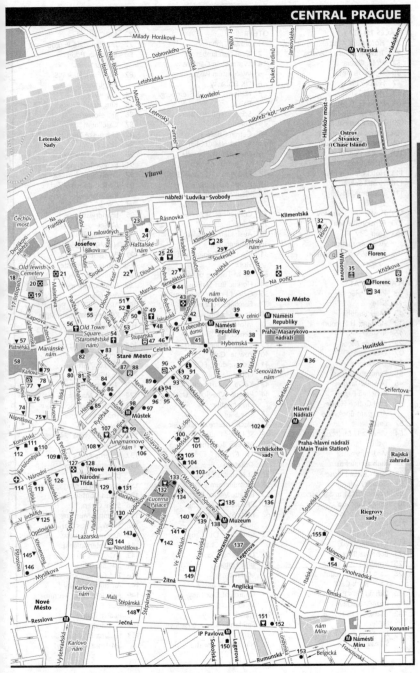

CZECH REPUBLIC

Castle. Just south of Charles bridge is the **Smetana Museum** (adult/concession 50/20 Kč; open 10am-noon & 12.30pm-5pm Wed-Mon), in a former waterworks building beside the river. The view from the terrace in front of the museum is one of the best in Prague.

Beside the Klementinum, narrow and crowded Karlova leads east towards Staroměstské nám, Prague's old town square and still the heart of the city. Below the clock tower of the **Old Town Hall** (admission 30 Kč) is a Gothic astronomical clock (1410) that entertains the crowds with its parade of Apostles and bell-ringing skeleton every hour on the hour. Climb up the **tower** (admission 30 Kč; open 9am-6pm Tues-Sun, 11am-5pm Mon) for an outstanding view.

At the centre of Staroměstské nám is the **Jan Hus Monument**, erected in 1915 on the 500th anniversary of the religious reformer's death by fire at the stake. On one side of the square is the baroque wedding cake structure of **St Nicholas Church**, designed by Kilian Dientzenhofer in the 1730s. More striking are the twin Gothic steeples of **Týn Church** (1365); the tomb of the 16th-century Danish astronomer Tycho Brahe is in front of the main altar.

Leaving the square near the astronomical clock, head southeast along Železná to the **Carolinum**, the oldest remaining part of the Charles University, and the neoclassical **Stavovské Theatre** (1783), where the premiere of Mozart's *Don Giovanni* took place on 29 October 1787 with the maestro himself conducting. Return to the square and then follow Celetná east to the Gothic Powder Gate and Prague's unrivalled Art Nouveau masterpiece, the **Obecní Dům** (Municipal House; 1912).

Tucked away in the northern part of Staré Město's narrow streets is one of Prague's oldest Gothic structures, the magnificent **Convent of St Agnes** (adult/concession 100/50 Kč; open 10am-6pm) housing the National Gallery's collection of Czech and Central European medieval art.

Josefov

Josefov – the area north and northwest of Staroměstské nám, bordered by Kaprova, Dlouhá and Kozí streets – was once the city's Jewish Quarter. It retains a fascinating variety of monuments, all now part of the **Prague Jewish Museum** (adult/concession 500/340 Kč; open 9am-5.30pm Sun-Fri) complex.

Men must cover their heads to enter the synagogues; bring a cap of your own or buy a paper cap at the entrance.

The collections of the Prague Jewish Museum have a remarkable origin. In 1942 the Nazis brought the objects here from 153 Jewish communities in Bohemia and Moravia for a planned 'museum of an extinct race' to be opened once their extermination programme was completed. The combined ticket allows entry to all the sights; alternatively, the 200/140 Kč adult/concession ticket gets you into the Staronová Synagogue only, and the 300/200 Kč ticket gives access to all the others.

The early Gothic **Staronová Synagogue** (1270) is one of the oldest in Europe; opposite is the pink Jewish town hall with its picturesque 16th-century clock tower. The **Klaus Synagogue** (1694), west along crowded U starého hřbitova, houses an exhibition on Jewish customs and traditions. The walls of the **Pinkas Synagogue**, a block south on Široká, bear the names of 77,297 Czech Jews – including Franz Kafka's three sisters – and the names of the camps where they perished. The synagogue is likely to be closed until winter 2003 as a result of the 2002 floods.

The **Old Jewish Cemetery** (entered from the Pinkas Synagogue), with its 12,000 tombstones, is the most evocative corner of the Josefov area. The oldest grave is dated 1439. By 1787 when the cemetery stopped being used, it had become so crowded that burials were carried out one on top of the other, up to 12 layers deep!

Nové Město

If Staroměstské nám and Charles Bridge are the heart of tourist Prague, the fashionable boulevard of **Václavské nám** (Wenceslas Square) is the city's focus for local residents, its majestic Art Nouveau facades rising above a bustle of shoppers, trams and taxis. At its upper end stands an **equestrian statue** of the 10th-century king Václav I, or St Wenceslas, patron saint of Bohemia. In the 20th century, this broad avenue was often the scene of public protests – on 16 January 1969, a Czech student named Jan Palach publicly burned himself to death in protest against the Soviet invasion, and in 1989 demonstrators again gathered at this spot. Just below the statue is a simple memorial with photos and flowers dedicated to those who resisted the communists.

Looming over the southeastern end of Václavské nám is the **National Museum** *(adult/concession 80/40 Kč; open 10am-6pm May-Oct, 9am-5pm Nov-Apr)*, with some ho-hum collections covering prehistory, mineralogy and stuffed animals. The captions on the exhibits are in Czech only and the grand interior of this neo-Renaissance museum building (1890) is more interesting than the displays.

Vyšehrad

Take the metro to Vyšehrad station where the concrete **Congress Centre** (1981) rises above a deep ravine crossed by the Nuselský Bridge. Pass to the north of the centre and along Na Bučance to the gates of the 17th-century **Vyšehrad Citadel**, built on a crag above the Vltava, and once the seat of the 11th-century Přemysl princes of Bohemia. You pass the Romanesque **Rotunda of St Martin** before reaching the twin towers of **SS Peter and Paul Church**, founded in the 11th century but rebuilt in neo-Gothic style between 1885 and 1903. **Slavín Cemetery**, beside the church, contains the graves of many distinguished Czechs, including the composers Smetana and Dvořák. The view of the Vltava Valley from the citadel battlements along the southern side of the Vyšehrad ridge is superb.

Other Museums

The **Mozart Museum** *(Mozartova 169; adult/concession 90/50 Kč; open 9.30am-6pm daily Apr-Oct, 9.30am-5pm Nov-Mar)* in Vila Bertrámka, is where Mozart finished composing *Don Giovanni* in 1787. To get there take metro Anděl, then head west on Plzeňská three blocks and left on Mozartova. Czech film maker Miloš Forman's Oscar-winning movie *Amadeus,* about the life of Mozart, was shot mostly in Prague.

The **City of Prague Museum** *(Na Poříčí 52; adult/concession 30/15 Kč; open 9am-6pm Tues-Sun)*, in a grand, neo-Renaissance building near Florenc metro station, contains maps and photos of the city's monuments, plus interesting artefacts to put them in perspective, such as the original Mánes calendar wheel from the Old Town Hall clock tower. The museum's crowning glory is a huge scale model of Prague made in 1834. Don't miss it!

Petřín Hill

On a hot summer afternoon you can escape the tourist throngs via the **funicular railway** from Újezd up to the rose gardens of **Petřínské sady**. You can climb the iron **Petřín Tower** *(adult/concession 40/30 Kč; open 10am-7pm daily Apr-Oct)*, built in 1891 in imitation of the Eiffel Tower, for one of the best views of Prague. A stairway behind the tower leads down into a series of picturesque lanes and back to Malostranské nám.

Organised Tours

Pragotur *(☎ 224 48 25 62; Old Town Hall, Staroměstské nám)* in the PIS office arranges personal guides fluent in all major European languages. **City Walks** *(☎ 608 200 912, 222 24 45 31;* w *www.praguewalking tours.com)* offers guided walks for 300 Kč to 450 Kč per person and **Prague Walks** *(☎ 261 21 46 03;* w *www.praguewalks.com)* charges 300 Kč per person. The walks last from 75 minutes to four hours with themes ranging from 'Mysterious Prague' to Prague pubs to the Velvet Revolution. Most walks begin at the astronomical clock in the Old Town Hall square.

Pragotur and various private companies operating from kiosks along Na příkopě offer three-hour city bus tours for 560 Kč per person. These are fine if your time is very short, but the castle and other major sights get so crowded that you can't enjoy the tour or even hear your guide.

Boat Trips From May to early September **Prague Passenger Shipping** *(PPS; ☎ 224 93 00 17; Rašínovo nábr; metro Karlovo Náměstí)* runs all-day cruises upriver to Slapy (250 Kč return, 9½ hours), departing at 9am Friday to Sunday. The riverboat terminal is on the right bank of the Vltava between Jiráskův most and Palackého most.

Shorter trips downriver to the zoo (Troja landing; 60 Kč return, 1¼ hours each way) depart three or four times daily between May and August, and Saturday and Sunday only in April, September and October. Allow 15 minutes to walk from the zoo to the landing. From the Kampa landing next to Charles Bridge there are 50-minute cruises (200 Kč) hourly from 11am to 8pm between March and December.

Prague Venice *(☎ 603 819 947; Křížovnické nám 3 • Čertovka, Kampa Island, Malá Strana)* operates 30-minute cruises (270 Kč per person including drink) in small boats under the hidden arches of Charles Bridge, and along the Čertovka mill stream in Kampa.

Getting There & Away

Numerous daily flights and ferries link Helsinki with Tallinn. Scheduled flights connect Estonia with many destinations; consider also options such as a ferry from Sweden or the Baltic corridor overland through Lithuania and Latvia. Estonia also has direct connections with Warsaw, Moscow, St Petersburg and Minsk.

Trains and buses are definitely the way to go if you are travelling within the region. Check the Getting There & Away sections of particular towns for more details.

AIR

The national carrier **Estonian Air** (☎ 640 1101 at the airport, fax 601 6092; w www .estonian-air.ee) links Tallinn with many destinations throughout Europe, also via code share arrangement with SAS and airBaltic. Flights service Stockholm and Copenhagen three to four times daily; London and Moscow six times weekly; Vilnius five times weekly; Frankfurt four times weekly; and Kyiv three times a weekly. Check the website for details.

Stockholm and Copenhagen are also served by Finnair with increasing frequency and at least six flights every day connect Helsinki with Tallinn.

Western airlines also offer worldwide connections via their hubs. Lauda Air flies direct from Vienna to Tallinn daily.

LAND
Bus

Buses link Estonia with most parts of Europe. Concession prices for children, students and pensioners are available on most international tickets.

Europe Buses are the cheapest but the least comfortable way of reaching the Baltic area. **Eurolines** (☎ 601 7000, 601 0909; w www .eurolines.ee; Lastekodu tänav 46, Tallinn) runs direct buses daily to Tallinn from Stuttgart, Frankfurt, Berlin and a number of other destinations in Germany, with connecting services to cities throughout Western Europe. Direct services connect Tallinn with Rīga (200EEK to 250EEK, six hours, eight daily) and Vilnius (300EEK, 10½ hours, two daily).

Some German-bound buses stop at Rīga and either Vilnius or Kaunas.

Russia Buses leave Tallinn for St Petersburg several times daily (200EEK, eight hours). There is also one bus daily from Tallinn to Kaliningrad (300EEK, 15 hours).

Train

The twice-weekly Tallinn to Minsk train passes through Rīga and Vilnius. The *Baltic Express* between Warsaw and Tallinn no longer operates.

St Petersburg and Tallinn are serviced by an overnight train on alternate evenings (228/ 390EEK 3rd/2nd class, 1st class not available, nine hours). An overnight train every evening runs between Moscow and Tallinn (724/ 1459EEK 2nd/1st class, around 14 hours).

Car & Motorcycle

See the introductory Getting Around chapter for general comments on driving and riding in Europe. From Finland it's easier to put your vehicle on a Helsinki to Tallinn ferry than to drive via St Petersburg with possible border delays and visa requirements.

SEA
Finland

About 25 ferries and hydrofoils cross between Helsinki and Tallinn every day. Ferries make the crossing in 2½ to 3½ hours, hydrofoils in less than 1½ hours. All companies provide some concessions, charge higher prices for any weekend travel and also have business-class tickets. You can expect to pay around the price of an adult ticket extra to take a car on many services.

Tallink (☎ 640 9808; w www.tallink.ee) runs several ferries and hydrofoils daily. Ferry tickets start from 235EEK; hydrofoils from 345EEK. **Lindaline** (☎ 641 2412; w www .lindaline.fi) makes six hydrofoil crossings each way daily. A one-way trip costs from 310EEK. **Eckerö Line** (☎ 631 8606; w www .eckeroline.fi) operates a daily vehicle catamaran making the crossing in 3½ hours, with one-way tickets starting at 190EEK. **Nordic Jet Line** (☎ 613 7000; w www.njl.fi) has several vehicle catamarans, making the trip in around 1½ hours, several times a day; one-way/return tickets cost between 280EEK and 580EEK. **Silja Line** (☎ 611 6661; w www .silja.com) ferries make the crossing between

Tallinn and Helsinki in 1½ hours with worthwhile day-trip packages available to Helsinki. Prices start from 370EEK.

Sweden
Tallink runs two former Estline ferries each day to Sweden; *Regina Baltica* from Tallinn to Stockholm (from 650EEK, 15 hours) and *Baltic Kristina* from Paldiski, 52km west of Tallinn, to Kappelskär near Stockholm (from 450EEK, 12 hours). There are small student reductions. Tickets should be booked well in advance through the **Tallink** city office (☎ 64 9808; *Pärnu Maantee*) or **Frihamnen** *(Free Harbour;* ☎ 08-667 0001) in Stockholm.

DEPARTURE TAX
There are no departure taxes to be paid and no other formalities to be completed before leaving Estonia.

Getting Around

AIR
The only domestic flights opertaing within Estonia connect the mainland to the islands of Hiiumaa, Saaremaa, Kihnu and Ruhnu. Contact **Air Livonia** *(in Tallinn* ☎ *605 8888, in Pärnu 45-75 007;* **w** *www.airlivonia.ee)* or **Avies** (☎ *605 8022).* Charter flights are also widely available. Air Livonia, Avies or the nearest airport can advise on your options.

BUS
Long-distance buses serve all major Estonian towns. Buses are generally cheaper, more frequent and definitely faster than trains, and cover many destinations not serviced by trains. For a listing of current bus schedules throughout Estonia visit **w** www.bussireisid.ee. Some terms you will find on the site are: *sõidu algus* (journey begins); *sõidu lõpp* (journey ends); *kestvus* (duration); *hind* (cost); and *sõidupäevad* (service days).

Most stations post listings at platforms (for the services that depart from that platform) and display timetables inside the station. English is spoken at the information desks of most larger bus stations.

TRAIN
Throughout Estonia train services have been dramatically reduced with privatisation in recent years. Trains are slower and rarer than buses, the most frequent trains service the suburbs of Tallinn.

CAR & MOTORCYCLE
Travelling by car is by far the best way to see Estonia. Western-quality petrol is widely available and repair outlets are increasingly common. Parking tickets can be bought from kiosks or parking attendants in larger centres.

An International Driving Permit (IDP) is necessary to drive in Estonia, as is carrying your vehicle's registration papers and having compulsory accident insurance, which can be bought at border crossings. Your biggest concern is likely to be security as theft both from and of vehicles is common, bring as many car security devices as you can muster.

Headlights need to be kept on at all times in Estonia.

BICYCLE
Estonia is predominantly flat, with good roads and light traffic, and distances between urban centres are relatively small – all factors which make cycling an ideal way of getting around. As few locals cycle within main cities, be wary of inconsiderate motorists. For organised bike trips through Estonia, see the Activities section earlier in this chapter.

HITCHING
Hitching is a common way of getting around but is never entirely safe or recommended. For more information, see the Getting Around chapter at the beginning of the book.

LOCAL TRANSPORT
Estonia's cities have good networks of buses, trolleybuses and trams usually running from 6am to midnight. In Estonia tickets *(piletid)* are sold from street kiosks displaying them in the window or can be purchased from the driver. Validate your ticket using the hole punch inside the vehicle.

Taxi
Taxis cost a minimum of 7EEK per kilometre in Estonia and are by far the most efficient in the Baltic region. In Tallinn call **Klubi Takso** (☎ *638 0638)* or **Raadiotakso** (☎ *601 1111).*

ORGANISED TOURS
Local tourist information centres (see individual sections for details) are the best place to find information on organised tours. It's also a

good idea to contact your destination directly, especially if your visit extends to a national park. Information on activities is readily available from all regional visitor and information centres throughout Estonia.

Contact the following organisations for more information on tours:

Biosphere Reserve of the West Estonian Archipelago (BKA; ☎ 46-22 101, **W** www.bka.ee/hiiumaa) Vabriku väljak 1. Based in Kärdla, on the island of Hiiumaa, BKA can assist with advice on exploring Hiiumaa or connect you with BKA branches covering Saaremaa and other places along Estonia's west coast.

Estonian Ecotourism Association (☎ 44-66 405, 050 61 896, **e** estecas@ecotourism.ee) This association organises rewarding cultural and nature tours based on low-impact tourism to protected areas around Estonia.

Lahemaa National Park See the section on the park later in this chapter for details.

Matsalu Nature Reserve (☎ 47-78 114, **e** matsalu@matsalu.ee) This reserve in Penijõe is one of Europe's prime bird migration and breeding grounds; staff can arrange bird-watching tours.

Tallinn

☎ no code • pop 398,434

Tallinn fronts a bay on the Gulf of Finland and is defined by Toompea (**tom**-pe-ah), the hill over which it has tumbled since the Middle Ages. The aura of the 14th and 15th centuries survives intact in central Tallinn's jumble of medieval walls and turrets, spires and winding cobbled streets; the area has been judiciously restored and is protected under Unesco's World Heritage programme.

History

In 1219, the Danes set up a castle and installed a bishop on Toompea. German traders arrived and Tallinn joined the Hanseatic League in 1285, becoming a vital link between east and west. By the mid-14th century, after the Danes had sold northern Estonia to the German knights, Tallinn was a major Hanseatic town. The merchants and artisans in the lower town built a fortified wall to separate themselves from the bishop and knights on Toompea.

Prosperity faded in the 16th century as Swedes, Russians, Poles and Lithuanians all fought over the Baltic region. Sweden held Tallinn between 1561 and 1710, then Russia, under Peter the Great, took control after the devastating Great Northern War. The city grew in the 19th century and by WWI had a population of 150,000. In 1944 Soviet bombing brought massive destruction. After WWII, industry developed and Tallinn expanded quickly, with much of its population growth due to immigration from outside Estonia. Just over half of Tallinn's population today is Estonian.

Orientation

Tallinn spreads south from Tallinn Bay, which lies between two promontories jutting north into the Gulf of Finland. The medieval town, just south of the bay, is made up of two parts: Toompea (the upper town) and the lower town. Toompea was traditionally the centre of Tallinn and the medieval seat of power. The lower town spreads around the eastern foot of Toompea, still surrounded by much of its 2.5km defensive wall. Its centre is Raekoja plats (Town Hall square).

Around the Old Town is a belt of green parks which follows the line of the city's original moat defences. Along this green belt are a number of places useful for getting your bearings: Vabaduse väljak, the new modern centre; the train station (Balti jaam), northwest of the Old Town, and the tall slab of the Viru Hotel, just outside the eastern edge of the Old Town.

Information

Tourist Offices The **Tallinn Tourist Information Centre** (☎ 645 7777, fax 645 7778; **e** turismiinfo@tallinnlv.ee; Raekoja plats 10; open 9am-6pm Mon-Fri, 10am-4pm Sat & Sun, closed Sun Nov-Mar) is right in the Old Town's centre and offers a range of services. Here you can purchase the Tallinn Card, which gives free admission to all museums in the city, the zoo and free rides on public transport. A sightseeing tour is included with cards valid for a minimum of 24 hours.

Infotelefon (☎ 626 1111) provides practical information in English 24 hours a day, as can **1182** (☎ 1182; **W** www.1182.ee), which is a second information service that can also facilitate Web-based searches.

During summer a countrywide Welcome to Estonia Visitor Centre sets up in Tallinn to provide specialist tourist information to visitors. Check with the main tourist information centre at Raekoka plats because the location may change.

ESTONIA

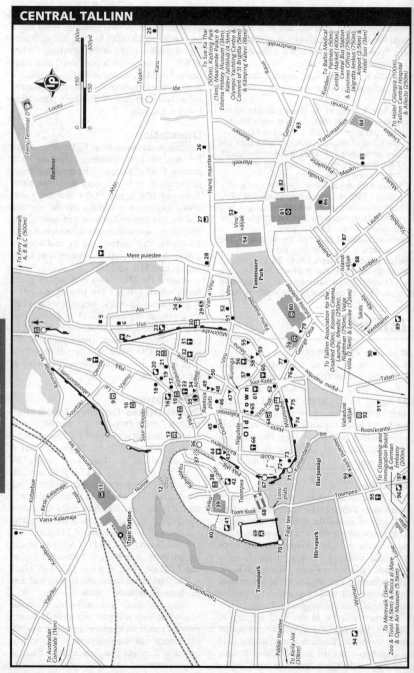

CENTRAL TALLINN

CENTRAL TALLINN

PLACES TO STAY
5	Hostel
6	Old House
21	Parc Consul Schlössle
25	Dorell
26	Hotel Central
28	Rasastra
45	Hotel Eeslitall & Restaurant
54	Viru Hotel
57	Vana Tom
86	SAS Radisson; SAS Office
90	Helke; Division of the Export of Cultural Objects

PLACES TO EAT
24	Kaubahall
34	Balthasar & Raeapteek
43	Vanaema Juures
47	Olde Hansa
48	Troika
49	Café Anglais
50	Elevant
53	Nehatu
55	Crêperie Sans Nom
58	Must Lammas
59	Buongiorno
72	Mõõkala
74	Pizza Americana
75	Gloria Wine Cellar
79	Armaada Sandwicherie
83	Poliina
87	Eesti Maja
91	Peetri Pizza
93	Võiroos

OTHER
1	Kalma Saun
2	Maritime Museum; Fat Margaret Bastion; Great Coast Gate
3	Estonia Ferry Disaster Memorial
4	Levi'st Väljas
7	Levi'st Väljas
8	Oleviste Church
9	Linnateater
10	Applied Art Museum
11	Local Bus Station
12	Patkuli Trepp (Steps)
13	Puppet Theatre
14	State History Museum
15	Draakon Gallery; Maiasmokk Café
16	Russian Embassy
17	St Canutus' Guild Hall
18	Baltic Tours
19	Brotherhood of Blackheads; St Olaus' Guild
20	Swedish Embassy
22	City Museum
23	Lithuanian Embassy
27	Central Post Office
29	Tavid
30	Kinomaja
31	Dominican Monastery
32	Kloostri Ait
33	Holy Spirit Church
35	Tourist Information Centre
36	Pikk Jalg Gate Tower
37	Lookout Point
38	National Art Museum
39	Toomkirik
40	Lookout Point
41	Canadian Embassy
42	Finnish Embassy
44	Von Krahli Baar & Theatre
46	Town Hall; Tristan ja Isolde
51	Viru Gate
52	Apollo
56	X-Baar
60	Nimega Baar
61	Nimeta Baar
62	Estravel
63	Sõprus; Hollywood
64	Arvutisaal
65	Kupar
66	Niguliste Church
67	Neitsitorn
68	Alexander Nevsky Cathedral
69	Toompea Castle; Riigikogu
70	Pikk Hermann
71	Kiek-in-de-Kök
73	Mr Kolk Bookshop
76	Rahva Raamat
77	Estonian Holidays; Tallink
78	Estonian Drama Theatre
80	Estonia Theatre; Concert Hall
81	Kaubamaja; @5
82	Euro Publications
84	Stockmann
85	Sauberland
88	Estonian Foreign Ministry
89	US Embassy
92	Russian Drama Theatre
94	UK Embassy
95	Kaarli Kirik Church
96	Latvian Embassy
97	Tõnismäe 24-Hour Pharmacy

ESTONIA

Money Currency exchanges are available at all transport terminals, the post office and inside all banks and major hotels. One of many private exchange bureaus with competitive rates is **Tavid** (☎ 627 9900; Aia tänav 5; open 9am-7pm Mon-Fri, 10am-5pm Sat & Sun).

Most central ATMs also accept major cards. **Estravel** (see Travel Agencies later) is the official agency for American Express.

Post & Communications The **central post office** (☎ 625 7300; Narva maantee 1; open 7.30am-8pm Mon-Fri, 8am-6pm Sat) is on the northern side of Viru väljak. Express mail, faxes and telegrams can be sent from here, and there's a postal shop on site.

Email & Internet Access On the 5th floor of the Kaubamaja shopping centre, **@5** (open 9am-9pm Mon-Fri, 10am-8pm Sat, 10am-6pm Sun) is a lively central place to connect

with the Net for 40EEK an hour. **Internet salon** (open 7.30am-8pm Mon-Fri, 8am-6pm Sat) on the 2nd floor of the main post office charges 1EEK per minute. **Arvutisaal** (2nd floor, Vana-Posti tänav 2; open 10am-8pm daily) is ideal for lengthy sessions at 30EEK an hour; every 3rd hour is free.

Travel Agencies City tours, guided trips to provincial Estonia and accommodation in other towns are all part of most of the many travel agencies' stock in trade. Leading agencies to try include:

Baltic Tours (☎ 630 0400, fax 630 0411, e baltic.tours@bt.ee) Pikk tänav 31. This is one of the longest-established firms with offices in other cities.
Estonian Holidays (☎ 631 4106, fax 631 4109, e holidays@holidays.ee) Pärnu maantee 12
Estravel (☎ 626 6285, fax 626 6202, w www .estravel.ee) Suur-Karja tänav 15

Bookshops The best selection of English-language books is at **Allecto** (☎ 660 6493; Juhkentali tänav 32) – and you can order books as well. Art books are the speciality at **Euro Publications** (☎ 661 2210; Tartu maantee 1). Travel books abound at **Apollo** (☎ 654 8485; Viru tänav 23). The largest choice of Estonian-language books is at **Rahva Raamat** (☎ 644 3682; Pärnu maantee 10) and **Kupar** (☎ 644 8309; Harju tänav 1). For used or antique books and photos, a visit to the friendly **Mr Kolk** (☎ 641 8005; Rüütli tänav 28/30) will fulfil any 'old bookstore' fantasy you may have harboured.

Laundry Two laundrettes close to the city centre provide self-service or full-service washes; one (Pärnu maantee 48) is opposite the Kosmos cinema, while **Sauberland** (Maakri tänav 23), near Stockmann, also offers a dry-cleaning service.

Left Luggage There's a left-luggage room (pakihoid) at the main ferry terminal and another at the bus station, but currently no facilities are available at the train station.

Medical & Emergency Services Just south of Liivalaia tänav and some 300m west of the Hotel Olümpia, **Tallinn Central Hospital** (☎ 620 7015 24hr; Ravi tänav 18) has a full range of services, a polyclinic and a 24-hour emergency room.

Western in price, service and attitude are Tallinn's privately run medical centres, like **Meedic** (☎ 646 3390; Pärnu maantee 48A), and **Baltic Medical Partners** (☎ 601 0550; Tartu maantee 32), an excellent dental clinic.

All pharmacies sell Western medicines. **Tõnismäe Apteek** (☎ 644 2282; Tõnismägi 5; open until 8pm daily) runs a night service (just ring the bell).

Raekoja Plats & Around

Wide Raekoja plats (Town Hall square) has been the centre of Tallinn life since markets began here probably in the 11th century (the last was held in 1896). It's dominated by the only surviving Gothic **town hall** (1371–1404) in northern Europe.

The **Raeapteek** (Town Council Pharmacy), on the northern side of Raekoja plats, is another ancient Tallinn institution; there's been a pharmacy or apothecary's shop here since at least 1422, though the present facade is 17th century. An arch beside it leads into short, narrow Saia käik (White Bread Passage), at the far end of which is the lovely, 14th-century Gothic **Holy Spirit Church** (Pühavaimu Kirik), used by Lutherans. Its clock is the oldest in Tallinn, with carvings from 1684 and a tower bell cast in 1433.

A medieval merchant's home, on the corner of Pühavaimu tänav, houses Tallinn's most interesting museum. The **City Museum** (Linnamuuseum; ☎ 644 6553; Vene tänav 17; adult/student 25/10EEK; open 10.30am-5.30pm Wed-Mon Apr-Oct, 11am-4.30pm Nov-Mar) traces Tallinn's development from its beginnings through to 1940 with some informative displays and curious artefacts.

Also on Vene tänav (Estonian for 'Russian', named for the many Russian merchants who lived in the street), at No 16, is an 1844 Catholic church, set back from the street. A door in the courtyard leads into the **Dominican Monastery** (☎ 644 4606; e kloostri@hot.ee; Vene tänav 16; adult/student 25/15EEK; open 9.30am-6pm daily mid-May–mid-Sept, other times by arrangement), founded in 1246 as a base for Scandinavian monks. Today the monastery complex houses Estonia's largest collection of **stone carvings**.

The majestic **Niguliste Church** (☎ 631 4330; admission 35EEK; open 10am-5pm Wed-Sun), a minute's walk south of Raekoja plats, has an early Gothic north doorway, but is a mostly 15th-century construction. It's now used to stage concerts and serves as a **museum** of medieval church art.

At the foot of the slope below the Niguliste is the carefully exposed wreckage of the buildings that stood here before the Soviet bombing of Tallinn on the night of 9 March 1944. A sign details the damage caused that night.

Toompea

A regal approach to Toompea is through the red-roofed 1380 **Pikk jalg gate tower** at the western end of Pikk tänav in the lower town, and along Pikk jalg (Long Leg). Nineteenth-century Russian Orthodox **Alexander Nevsky Cathedral** dominates Lossi plats at the top of Pikk jalg, built as a part of Alexander III's policy of Russification, and sited strategically across from **Toompea Castle**, Estonia's traditional seat of power. The parliament meets in the pink Baroque-style **Riigikogu** opposite the cathedral, an 18th-century addition to the castle. Nothing remains of the original 1219

Danish castle. Still standing are three of the four corner towers of its successor, the Knights of the Sword's Castle. Finest of these towers is the 14th-century **Pikk Hermann** (Tall Hermann) at the southwestern corner. Sixteenth-century shell scars from are visible on its walls.

The Lutheran **Toomkirik** (Dome Church) is Estonia's oldest church; at the northern end of Toom-Kooli, on the site of a 1219 Danish church, it dates from the 14th century. Inside are finely carved tombs and coats of arms. Across the street from Toomkirik, an 18th-century noble's house, is now the **National Art Museum** (Kunstimuuseum; ☎ 644 9340; Kiriku plats 1; adult/student 30/20EEK; open 11am-6pm Wed-Sun).

A path leads down from Lossi plats through an opening in the wall to the Danish King's Courtyard where, in summer, artists set up their easels. One of the towers, the **Neitsitorn** (Virgin's Tower), has been become a popular café, with good views.

Nearby **Kiek-in-de-Kök** (adult/student 10/7EEK; open 10.30am-6pm Wed-Sun mid-May–Sept, 11am-5pm Oct–mid-May), a tall tower built in about 1475, is a museum that holds several floors of maps and models of old Tallinn, weapons and a photographic gallery. Its name is Low German for 'Peep into the Kitchen' – from the upper floors of the tower, medieval voyeurs could see into the kitchens of the Old Town.

Lower Town

Pikk tänav, running north from Raekoja plats to the **Great Coast Gate** – the medieval exit to Tallinn's port – is lined with 15th-century houses of medieval merchants and gentry. Also here are the buildings of several old Tallinn guilds. No 17 is the 1440 building of the Great Guild, to which the most important merchants belonged. Today it is the **State History Museum** (Ajaloomuuseum; ☎ 641 1412; adult/student 10/5EEK; open 10am-6pm Thur-Tues) featuring Estonian history up to the mid-19th century, with labelling in English. No 18, is the 1911 **Draakon gallery** with its fantastically sculpted facade.

Pikk tänav 20, **St Canutus' Guild Hall** with statues of Martin Luther and St Canutus, dates only from the 1860s, but the site had previously housed St Canutus' Guild for several centuries. Its members were mainly German master artisans.

The **Brotherhood of Blackheads** and **St Olaus' Guild** are in adjoining buildings at Pikk tänav 24 and 26. The Blackheads were unmarried, mainly foreign merchants whose patron saint, Mauritius, appears with his head between two lions on the building's facade (dating from 1597).

At the northern end of Pikk tänav stands a chief Tallin landmark, the **Oleviste Church**. The church is dedicated to the 11th-century king Olav II of Norway, but linked in local lore with another Olav (Olaf), the church's legendary architect, who fell to his death from the 120m tower. It's said that a toad and snake then crawled out of his mouth. The incident is recalled in one of the carvings on the east wall of the 16th-century **Chapel of Our Lady**, which adjoins the church. Most of the church was rebuilt after a fire during the 1820s. Just south of the church on Lai tänav 46/48, is the former KGB headquarters; the basement windows were bricked up to conceal the sounds of interrogations from those on the street above.

The Great Coast Gate is joined to **Paks Margareeta** (Fat Margaret), the rotund 16th-century bastion which protected this entrance to the Old Town. Inside the bastion is the **Maritime Museum** (Meremuuseum; ☎ 641 1408; adult/student 25/10EEK; open 10am-6pm Wed-Sun, closed July). There are great views from the platform on the roof.

In the grounds stands a white cross erected in 1995 in memory of victims of the Estonia ferry disaster. In September 1994, 852 people died when the popular ferry sank en route from Stockholm to Tallinn.

While Pikk was the street of traders, **Lai tänav**, running roughly parallel, was the street of artisans, whose traditions are recalled in the **Applied Art Museum** (Tarbekunstimuuseum; open 11am-6pm Wed-Sun). It's housed in a 17th-century granary at No 17, with excellent ceramics, glass, rugs, metal and leatherwork.

Suur-Kloostri leads to the longest-standing stretch of the **Lower Town Wall**, with nine towers along Laboratooriumi to the northern end of Lai.

Kadriorg

To reach the pleasant, wooded **Kadriorg Park** 2km east of the Old Town along Narva maantee, take tram No 1 or 3 to the last stop, or bus No 1 from Pärnu maantee. The park and the 1718–36 Kadriorg Palace were designed for Peter the Great. In one of the palace buildings

ESTONIA

is the **Estonian Foreign Art Museum** (☎ 606 6400; Weizenbergi tänav 37; adult/student 35/20EEK; open 11pm-5pm Tues-Sun). A walk through the streets around Kadriorg, with their charming but dilapidated wooden architecture, is definitely recommended.

Maarjamäe & Pirita

One kilometre north of Kadriorg, Maarjamäe Palace (Maarjamäe Loss; Pirita tee 56) contains the part of the **Estonia History Museum** (☎ 601 4535; Pirita tee 56; admission 25/10EEK; open 11am-6pm Wed-Sun) covering the mid-19th century onwards.

Pirita Yacht Club, some 1.5km beyond Maarjamäe Palace and the **Olympic Yachting Centre** were venues for the 1980 Olympic sailing events. International regattas are still held here. In summer you can rent rowing boats and pedalos beside the bridge over the river. North of the bridge are a beach backed by pine woods and the 15th-century Swedish **Convent of St Brigitta** (adult/student 25/10EEK; open 10am-6pm daily) ruined by war in 1577. The long stretch of clean beaches on the other side of Pirita tee are popular in the summer. Particularly recommended is a late-evening walk along Pirita tee to watch the summer sun set across the bay. Bus Nos 1, 8 and 34 run between the city centre and Pirita.

Zoo & Rocca al Mare

The **Tallinn Zoo** (☎ 694 3300; Paldiski maantee 145; adult/child 35/20EEK; open 9am-5pm daily) boasts the world's largest collection of wild goats and 334 different species of animals, birds, reptiles and fish. Opposite the zoo is **Tivoli** a small amusement park for the kids.

A kilometre beyond the zoo, Rannamõisa tee turns right towards Rocca al Mare and its **Open Air Museum** (☎ 654 9100; Vabaõhumuuseumi tee 12; adult/child 25/9EEK; buildings open 10am-6pm daily May-Oct, grounds open year-round). Most of Estonia's oldest wooden structures, mainly farmhouses, and a chapel (1699) and windmill, are preserved here. On Sunday mornings there are folk song and dance shows. There's also a restaurant serving traditional Estonian meals.

Places to Stay

Camping Eight kilometres from the city is **Kämping Kalevi** (☎/fax 623 9191; Kloostrimetsa tee 56a; tent & parking/caravans 200/275EEK, 2-/4-bed cabins 320/400EEK; open mid-May– mid-Sept), with a good range of budget accommodation. Meals are available in the pub nearby and there's also a handy shop for self-caterers. Take bus No 34 or 38 from Viru Väljak in the centre and get off at the Motorklubi stop.

Leevike (☎ 493 294; Pärnu maantee 600; 2-person/3-person/4-person cabins 200/350/500EEK), 12km south of the centre, has decent cabins with full facilities on site. Camping with tents is possible but call ahead to confirm.

Hostels The Estonian Youth Hostels Association (☎ 646 1457; w www.baltichostels .net) has a few good choices in the city. It can also book hostel stays for you in neighbouring countries.

The **Merevaik** (☎ 655 3767; 5th floor, Sõpruse puiestee 182; dorm beds HI member/nonmember 108/120EEK), around 5km from the centre of Tallinn, offers basic lodgings with a common room and self-catering kitchens. Take trolleybus No 2 or 3 from the stop diagonally opposite the Hotel Palace and get off at the Linnu tee stop.

Vana Tom (☎ 631 3252; Väike-Karja tänav 1; dorm beds HI member/nonmember 210/225EEK, rooms from 590EEK) has an unbeatable location – 30 seconds' walk from Raekoja plats. Some rooms may provide a second-hand experience of the strip club upstairs.

Hostel (☎ 641 1281; Uus tänav 26; dorm beds/singles/doubles 220/500/650EEK) has a great Old Town location and friendly reception, although the bathrooms are small and the presence of passing traffic may be felt.

Hotels – Budget A favourite in the Old Town, **Hotel Eeslitall** (☎ 631 3755; Dunkri tänav 4; singles/doubles 450/585EEK) is a minute's walk from Raekoja plats. Below it is the popular Eeslitall restaurant, giving guests the chance to pop downstairs to the courtyard for breakfast in the sun.

Helke (☎ 644 5802; fax 644 5792; Sakala 14; singles/doubles 400/490EEK) is a friendly place on the southern fringe of the Old Town. The rooms are comfortable and breakfast is also included.

The **Old House** (☎ 641 1464; e info@ oldhouse.ee; Uus tänav 22; singles/doubles 450/650EEK) is a very well-positioned and professional B&B offering warm and friendly hospitality in clean surroundings. Apartment rental is also available.

Hotels – Mid-Range Another good central choice is **Dorell** (☎ 626 1200, fax 662 3578; *Karu tänav 39; singles/doubles 650/750EEK*), with clean renovated rooms, sauna access and a bar serving inexpensive meals.

Valge Villa (☎/fax 654 2302; *Kännu tänav 26/2; singles/doubles 780/980EEK*) is a super-friendly, family-run place, a 3km ride from the centre on trolleybus No 2, 3 or 4 to the Teadre stop. Each of its comfy rooms have Internet connections. Weekend or long-stay specials are offered and bookings via the website attract a 10% discount.

The **Hotel Susi** (☎ 630 3200; e susi@susi .ee; *Peterburi tee 48; singles/doubles 600/800EEK, with bathroom 800/1000EEK*), 4km from the centre, is one of the wackiest, liveliest places in town, has colourful fully equipped rooms in a place that should appeal to the eccentric in everyone. Its Green Spider nightclub reveals a lighter side of Tallinn.

The single and double rooms in Hostel (see the Hostels section earlier) are also good mid-range options.

Hotels – Top End There's no shortage of choice in this category, just have your credit cards ready. Inquire about special offers or reduced prices if travelling in numbers.

The **Parc Consul Schlössle** (☎ 699 7700; e schlossle@consul-hotels.com; *Pühavaimu tänav 13-15; singles/doubles from 3560/4150EEK, children 0-12 years free*) is in the Old Town's centre, with sparkling rooms in a complex of buildings that have witnessed 600 years of Tallinn life. All needs are catered for under its five stars.

SAS Radisson (☎ 669 0000; e info .tallinn@radissonsas.com; *Rävala puiestee 3; singles/doubles/suites 2321/2632/5592EEK*), the most expensive construction project ever mounted in Estonia, is meticulous in presentation and attention to detail. Free morning saunas rate among the indulgences offered.

Hotel Central (☎ 633 9800, fax 633 9900; e central.sales@revalhotels.com; *Narva maantee 7; singles/doubles 1100/1300EEK*), the cheapest of the expensive city-centre hotels, has friendly service without pretence, and is a short walk from the Old Town.

The old **Hotel Olümpia** (☎ 631 5333, fax 631 5325; e olympia.sales@revalhotels.com;

Liivalaia tänav 33; singles/doubles from 1950/2300EEK) is well known for its glass-windowed sauna and its buffet breakfasts.

Viru Hotel (☎ 630 1311; e reservation@ viru.ee; *Viru väljak; singles/doubles from 1560/1875EEK*) remains ever popular, due largely to its prominent location, impeccable service and cultured ugliness.

Places to Eat
Restaurants Some fine dining options exist in the capital, with satisfying rewards for courageous palates and treats for those more timid. Generally, restaurants in the Old Town are better value for lunch than dinner.

Eesti Maja (☎ 645 5252; *Lauteri tänav 1; buffet 75EEK, meals 120EEK; open 11am-11pm daily*) offers genuine Estonian cuisine. The weekday buffet allows for a sampling of some exotic carnivoria without demanding a full-plate commitment.

Vanaema Juures (*Grandma's Place;* ☎ 626 9080; *Rataskaevu tänav 12; meals 140EEK; open noon-10pm Mon-Fri, noon-6pm Sun*) was one of Tallinn's most stylish restaurants in the 1930s and still ranks today as offering authentic Estonian fare.

Balthasar (☎ 627 6400; *Raekoja plats 11; meals 150EEK; open noon-midnight daily*) is a haven for garlic lovers where succulent main meals are lavished with the healthy stuff.

Must Lammas (☎ 644 2031; *Sauna tänav 2; meals 170EEK; open noon-11pm Mon-Sat, noon-6pm Sun*) has the feeling of casual sophistication, with a wholesome Caucasian menu that goes well with Georgian wine.

Elevant (☎ 631 3132; *Vene tänav 5; meals 170EEK; open noon-11pm daily*) is one of the city's truly sophisticated restaurants, with its winding staircase, East-meets-Scandinavia pastel walls and rarefied taste in music. The subdued elegance carries over to the food.

Buongiorno (☎ 640 6858; *Müürivahe tänav 17; meals 110EEK; open 10am-11pm daily*) is an unprepossessing little cellar space. The meals are simple, reasonably priced and quite delicious. Try its bruschettas, paninis or pasta specials.

Maiasmokk (*Sweet-Tooth Café & Restaurant;* ☎ 646 4070; *Pikk tänav 16; meals 190EEK; open noon-midnight daily*) held a place of honour as Tallinn's most elite café during Estonia's pre-WWII period of independence. The upstairs restaurant has popular old-world dishes.

ESTONIA

Sue Ka Thai (☎ 641 9347; Vilmsi tänav 6; 120EEK; open noon-11pm Mon-Sat, noon-10pm Sun) is a rarity in Tallinn – inexpensive and pleasantly spicy Thai and generally Asian-inspired meals, best enjoyed after a stroll through surrounding Kadriorg. Deliveries can be made.

Troika (☎ 627 6245; Raekoja plats 11; meals 140EEK; open noon-midnight daily) leads in ambience, with evocative otherworldly decor and authentic Russian meals. An interesting and extensive array of vodkas grace the tavern bar.

Olde Hansa (☎ 627 9020; Vanaturg tänav 1; meals from 190EEK; open 11am-midnight daily) is one of the most popular of the jovial medieval-theme restaurants, with sumptuous meals with some surprise menu items.

Mõõkala (☎ 631 3583; Rüütli tänav 16/18; meals from 220EEK; open noon-midnight daily) serves an exquisite array of ordinary and exotic fish in a cosy cellar setting once the domain of Tallinn's executioner.

Cafés & Light Meals Overlooking Town Hall square, **Café Anglais** (2nd floor, Raekoja plats 14; open 11am-11pm daily) is a relaxed meeting place for some of Tallinn's eccentric types. The coffees and pastries are heavenly as are the generous servings of cake.

Crêperie Sans Nom (Müürivahe 23A) serves fine savoury and dessert crepes in tastefully understated surroundings.

Poliina (Gonsiori tänav 10) has ready-made salads, tasty meat and vegetable dishes and some excellent French pastries.

Tristan ja Isolde (Town Hall building, Raekoja plats) is an essential stop for lovers of fine coffee in intimate medieval surroundings.

Gloria Wine Cellar (Müürivahe tänav 2) has a cosy ambience, with just a few tables among the wine barrels.

Võiroos (Kaarli puiestee 4; open 24hr) is a Tallinn institution for those with late-night munchies, a shack serving decent food to an interesting and diverse crowd.

Fast Food & Pizza The **Armaada Sandwicherie** (Georg Otsa tänav; open 24hr), a window in the wall beside the Estonian Drama Theatre, serves original hot baguettes, often precariously loaded with sour cream. Burgers abound at the Finnish chain **Hesburgers** and Estonian alternatives can be found at **Nehatu** (open 24hr) in the middle of Viru väljak.

Peetri Pizza (☎ 641 8203 delivery) has a number of outlets doling out thin-crusted and pan pizzas, including one at Pärnu maantee 22 (takeaway only). **Pizza Americana** (☎ 644 8837 delivery; Müürivahe tänav 2) also gets the job done.

Self-caterers will find a good selection of groceries inside **Stockmann** (Liivalaia tänav 53), Kaubamaja (off Vabaduse Väljak) and **Kaubahall** (Aia tänav 7) in the Old Town, open daily from 9am to 9pm.

Entertainment

Bars & Discos Retaining its popularity with expats and visitors, **Nimeta Baar** (Bar with No Name; Suur-Karja tänav 4/6) has a central location and offers flavoursome meals, a good choice of music, sports telecasts and, of course, beers.

Nimega Baar (Bar with a Name; Suur-Karja tänav 13), Nimeta's sister pub, is also a very popular choice and is a good alternative to the Nimeta bar.

Kloostri Ait (Vene tänav 14) is another veteran on the scene and a focal meeting place for an alternative crowd.

Von Krahli Baar (Rataskaevu tänav 10-12), one of the city's best hang-outs inside an experimental theatre is highly worth a visit. It often has live bands and is a good place to meet interesting locals.

Levi'st Väljas (Olevimägi tänav 12), which roughly translates as 'out of range', is a cellar space in the Old Town but off the tourist path and refreshingly raw.

The hot club event in Tallinn is the once-a-month event **Vibe** (W www.vibe.ee), where Tallinners revel under the influence of some imported DJs. Check on the website for the dates and locations.

Otherwise, the mainstream clubs are the most popular and usually open from 10pm to late, Wednesday to Saturday.

Hollywood (Vana-Posti tänav 8), in the Sõprus cinema, attracts the largest crowds of youth and beauty.

Spirit (Mere puiestee 6A; W www.spirit.ee) is a sophisticated Scandinavian-inspired bar with a rave arena upstairs hosting a fluid list of guest DJs.

Nightman (Vineeri tänav 4) is Tallinn's main gay and lesbian club but is also a hang-out for a straight and alternative crowd.

X-Baar (Sauna tänav 1) is a more exclusively gay venue.

Cinema The worst of US blockbusters and comedies are shown here, but all in original English, with subtitles. The main cinemas are the **Sõprus** (Vana-Posti tänav 8), in a beautiful Stalin-era building, and the **Kosmos** (Pärnu maantee 45). Foreign, cult and alternative films are shown at the **Kinomaja** (☎ 646 4510; Uus tänav 3).

Opera, Ballet & Theatre Tallinn has several companies staging performances from September until the end of May, sometimes with simultaneous translation into English.

The **Estonia Theatre** (box office ☎ 626 0215; Estonia puiestee 4) is Tallinn's main theatre, and the theatre building also houses the Estonian National Opera and Ballet.

Other theatres include the **Estonian Drama Theatre** (☎ 680 5555; Pärnu maantee 5); the **Russian Drama Theatre** (☎ 644 3716; Vabaduse väljak 5); the **Puppet Theatre** (Nukuteater; ☎ 667 9555; Lai tänav 1); the **Von Krahli Theatre** (☎ 626 9090; Rataskaevu tänav 10-12), which is known for its fringe productions; and the most beloved theatre in town, **Linnateater** (City Theatre; ☎ 665 0800; Lai tänav 23), which always puts on something memorable.

Getting There & Away

Air For information on flights in and out of Tallinn check out the Getting There & Away section earlier in this chapter. **Tallinn airport** (☎ 605 8888; W www.tallinn-airport.ee) is 3km southeast of the city centre on Tartu maantee. Schedules are on its website.

Airline offices in Tallinn include:

Estonian Air (☎ 640 1101, W www.estonian-air .ee) Airport
Finnair (☎ 605 8353) Airport
SAS (☎ 666 3030) Rävala puiestee 2, beside the SAS Radisson.

Bus Buses to places within about 40km of Tallinn depart from the **local bus station** beside the train station. You can get information and timetables around the clock from **Harju Linnid** (☎ 644 1801). For detailed bus information and to buy advance tickets for all other destinations, contact the central bus station **Autobussijaam** (☎ 680 0900; Lastekodu tänav 46). Tram No 2 south from Mere puiestee or tram No 4 east from Tammsaare Park will take you there.

For information on buses to places outside Estonia see the Getting There & Away section earlier in this chapter. Domestic services include:

Haapsalu 52EEK, 1½ hours, 100 km, 20 buses daily
Kärdla 130EEK, 4½ hours, 160 km, three buses daily
Kuressaare 160EEK, 220 km, 4½ hours, nine buses daily
Narva 75EEK, four hours, 210 km, 15 buses daily
Pärnu 60EEK, two hours, 130 km, more than 20 buses daily
Tartu 80EEK, three hours, 190 km, around 50 buses daily
Võru 85EEK, 4½ hours, 250 km, 12 buses daily

Train Tallinn's **Baltic station** (Balti jaam; Toom puiestee 35) is on the northwestern edge of the Old Town – a short walk from Raekoja plats, or a ride of three stops on tram No 1 or 2 north from the Viru Hotel.

For information about trains to places outside Estonia see the Getting There & Away section earlier in this chapter. Services within Estonia include two trains daily to Tartu (70EEK, three to four hours); two daily to Pärnu (40EEK, three hours); and each day to Narva (70EEK, four hours).

Car & Motorcycle There are 24-hour petrol stations at strategic spots within the city and along major roads leading to and from Tallinn. The Pärnu maantee Neste has a car-repair service.

Car rental in Tallinn is spectacularly overpriced. You can rent cars in Tartu, Pärnu or Võru for half the price you would pay in Tallinn (contact the tourist information centres in each city). If you can read Estonian, check out the *Kuldne Börs* classified-ad newspaper for individuals renting their cars privately.

Some of the major agencies to check out for car rental are:

Avis (☎ 605 8222, fax 638 8221) Airport
Hertz (☎ 605 8923, fax 605 8953) Airport
Tulika Rent (☎ 612 0012, fax 612 0041) Tulika tänav 33 – bookings through Palace, Olümpia and Central Hotels.

Boat See the Getting There & Away section earlier in this chapter for information about the many services available between Tallinn and Helsinki or Stockholm. Tallinn's **sea-passenger terminal** is at the end of Sadama, about 1km northeast of the Old Town. Tram Nos 1 and 2 and bus Nos 3, 4 and 8 go to the Linnahall stop (by the Statoil petrol station), five minutes' walk from terminals A, B and C. Terminal D is at the end of Lootsi tänav, better accessed from Ahtri tänav. A taxi between the centre and any of the terminals will cost about 40EEK.

Getting Around

To/From the Airport Tallinn airport is on Tartu maantee, 3km from the centre. Bus No 2 runs every 30 minutes from the eastern side of the Kaubamaja department store. A taxi to/from the centre should cost about 80EEK.

Public Transport The train station and many hotels are an easy walk from the city centre. Buses, trams and minibuses will take you everywhere else. See also Local Transport in the Getting Around section earlier in this chapter.

AROUND TALLINN

There are several pleasant options for day trips to places easily accessible from Tallinn. The tourist information centre can provide details on day trips and cruises to the nearby islands of Aegna, Naissaar and Prangli.

Keila-Joa

About 30km west of Tallinn, the small village of Keila-Joa boasts 'Estonia's Niagara Falls' (at 6.1m the second highest waterfall in the country). There's a manor house (1883) on the banks of the falls and the large park and forest that surround it are perfect for a day's picnicking or hiking.

The road from Tallinn runs right along cliff tops to a very popular lookout called Türisalu, some 2km after the Naage bus stop. Bus Nos 108, 110, 136 and 172 from Tallinn's train station run to Keila-Joa. Call **Harju Linnid** (☎ 644 1801) for timetables.

Northeastern Estonia

While the area to the near east of Tallinn is an attractive unspoilt national park, closer to Narva an industrial landscape emerges. Despite some heavily polluted areas, the region has some fine lookouts, historic sites and a number of picturesque towns (like Sillamäe, a living museum of Stalin-era architecture). The population of Eastern Estonia is predominantly Russian-speaking.

LAHEMAA NATIONAL PARK
☎ 32

Lahemaa National Park encompasses a rocky stretch of the north coast, with 220 sq km of marine areas, plus 480 sq km of hinterland with 14 lakes, eight rivers and many waterfalls, 70km east of Tallinn. The landscape is 24% cultivated, 68% forest or heath and 8% bog. Roads crisscross the park from the Tallinn to Narva highway and some places within the park are accessible by bus.

Information

Lahemaa National Park Visitors Centre (*Lahemaa Rahvuspark Külatuskeskus;* ☎ 95 555, *fax 95 556;* ⓔ *info@lahemaa.ee; open 9am-7pm daily May-Aug, 9am-5pm daily Sept, 9am-5pm Mon-Fri Oct-Apr*) is in a converted wagon-house and stable in Palmse, 8km north of Viitna in the southeast of the park. Entry to the park is free. It's worth contacting the visitors centre before heading out as it can help you make the most of your trip. For an outstanding and highly recommended guide to the park, contact **Anne Kurepalu** (ⓔ *anne@ phpalmse.ee*) at Park Hotel Palmse.

Things to See

There is an unlimited amount of sightseeing, hiking, biking and boating to be done here; remote islands can also be explored. The park has several well-signposted nature trails and cycling paths winding through it. The small coastal towns of **Võsu**, **Käsmu** and **Loksa** are popular seaside spots in summer. There are also **prehistoric stone barrows** (tombs) at Kahala, Palmse and Vihula, and a **boulder field** on the Käsmu Peninsula.

Lahemaa also features some historic **manor houses**: Kolga, Vihula, Palmse and Sagadi. Two are open to the public. **Palmse Manor** (*open 10am-7pm daily summer*), near the visitors centre, was once a wholly self-contained Baltic-German estate and **Sagadi** (*open 10am-7pm daily summer*) was another opulent residence that now houses the **Forest Museum** (☎ 58 8888; entry to the museum & manor adult/student 30/10EEK; open 11am-6pm Tues-Sun 15 May-30 Sept, by arrangement 1 Oct-May 14).

Places to Stay

The visitors centre arranges accommodation to suit every budget. It can also advise on the best places for camping.

Ojaäärse hostel (☎ 34 108; e sagadi .hotell@rmk.ee; dorm beds 150EEK; open year-round) is a converted 1855 farmhouse in a picturesque setting, which is 1.5km southeast of Palmse.

Redefining the notion of a hostel, **Sagadi Manor** (☎ 58 8888; e sagadihotell@rmk.ee; dorm beds from 200EEK, singles/doubles 700/900EEK) has a range of accommodation in a luxurious setting.

Viitna Holiday Centre (☎ 93 651; dorm beds/singles/doubles/cabins 60/110/150/ 300EEK) is in a tranquil wooded area beside a clean lake.

Merekalda Boarding House (☎/fax 38 451; e info@merekalda.ee; Neeme tee 2, Käsmu; singles/doubles/cabins 290/590/ 890EEK) has elegant rooms and cabins overlooking the sea.

Park Hotel Palmse (☎/fax 34 167; singles/ doubles with breakfast 690/890EEK) offers pristine and pine-fresh rooms inside Palmse Manor distillery, but book well ahead.

Getting There & Away

There are 19 buses daily from Tallinn to Rakvere, which stop at Viitna (30EEK, one hour). For an update on bus services between Tallinn, Käsmu and Võsu, contact the visitors centre.

NARVA & AROUND
☎ 35

Estonia's easternmost town is separated only by the thin Narva River from Ivangorod in Russia and is almost entirely populated by Russians. Narva (population 68,117) was a Hanseatic League trading point by 1171. Later it became embroiled in Russia's border disputes with the German knights and Sweden. Ivan III of Muscovy founded Ivangorod in 1492 and the large castle still stands. Narva was almost completely destroyed in WWII.

While there are some lovely areas outside Narva, today the region is blighted by phosphorite and oil-shale industries (although emissions have been cut back greatly in more recent years).

The city itself is pleasant and friendly. There is a **tourist information centre** (☎ 60 184, fax 60 186; e narva@visitestonia.com; Puškini 13) in the city centre.

The **bus** and **train stations** are located together at Vaksali tänav 2, and opposite the Russian Orthodox Voskresensky Cathedral. Walk north up Puškini tänav to the castle (500m) and the centre.

Things to See

Restored after being damaged in WWII, **Narva Castle**, guarding the road bridge (Friendship Bridge) over the river, dates from Danish rule in the 13th century. The castle houses the **Town Museum** (☎ 99 247; adult/ student 50/10EEK; open 10am-6pm Wed-Sun). The baroque **town hall** (1668–71), on Raekoja väljak north of the bridge, has also been restored. On the square in front of the train station is a monument to the Estonians deported to Siberia in 1941, who were loaded into cattle wagons here.

About 12km north of Narva is the pretty but dilapidated holiday resort of **Narva-Jõesuu**, popular since the 19th century for its long white sandy beaches. There are many unique, impressive early-20th-century wooden houses and villas throughout the town.

Places to Stay & Eat

The **Hostel Lell** (☎ 73 461; e lell77@hot.ee; Partisani tänav 4; singles/doubles/deluxe doubles with bathroom 150/300/500EEK) has neat, basic rooms and a restaurant serving reasonable Russian cuisine.

Hotel Vanalinn (☎ 22 486; Koidula tänav 6; singles/doubles 490/750EEK), just north of the castle, is in a renovated 17th-century building. Generous child discounts are available.

There are a few restaurants and cafés in the centre serving decent meals and snacks.

German Pub (Puškini tänav 10; meals 70EEK) is a good choice for a light meal or sundae treat in comfortable pub surroundings.

Gulliver Pub (Lavretsov tänav 7; meals 60EEK) gives a warm welcome with delicious meals and friendly service.

Rossan Baar (Puškini 12) is a popular bar with locals and gives a fair insight into life across the border.

Getting There & Away

Narva is 210km east of Tallinn on the road and train line to St Petersburg, 140km away. From Tallinn there are about 15 buses and one train daily. There are also 10 daily buses to Tartu and many to nearby cities. Buses and microbuses go to Narva-Jõesuu throughout the day.

ESTONIA

Southeastern Estonia

The focus of southeastern Estonia is the historic university town of Tartu, the country's second city. Beyond Tartu is an attractive region of gentle hills, beautiful lakes and the traditional lands of the Setu people.

TARTU

☎ 7 • pop 101,140

Tartu lies 190km southeast of Tallinn on the Emajõgi River and lays claim to being the spiritual capital of Estonia. The Estonian nationalist revival during the 19th century had its origins here and Tartu was the location for the first Estonian Song Festival in 1869. This is also a classic university town and students inject a vitality into the serene surroundings.

Around the 6th century, there was an Estonian stronghold on Toomemägi Hill. In 1030, Yaroslav the Wise of Kyiv is said to have founded a settlement here called Yuriev. By the early 13th century the ruling Knights of the Sword had placed a bishop, castle and cathedral on Toomemägi Hill. The town that grew up between the hill and the river became a member of the Hanseatic League. In the 16th and 17th centuries Tartu sustained repeated attacks and underwent periods of rule by Russia, Sweden and Poland-Lithuania. Classical architecture rose from the city's rebuilding after most of the town burnt down in 1775.

The university, founded in 1632 during Swedish rule to train Protestant clergy and government officials, became one of the foremost 19th-century seats of learning. During the Soviet occupation, Westerners were not allowed to stay overnight in Tartu because of the 'security risk' to a military airfield nearby.

Orientation & Information

Toomemägi Hill and the area of older buildings between it and the Emajõgi River are the focus of Tartu. At the heart of this area are Raekoja plats (Town Hall square) and Ülikooli tänav, the main shopping area, which runs across the square's western end.

The **tourist information centre** (☎/fax 432 141; e tartu@visitestonia.com; Raekoja plats 14; open 10am-6pm Mon-Fri, 10am-3pm Sat) has an good range of local maps, books and brochures and sells the entertainment and accommodation listings booklet *Tartu Today*.

All **Hansapanks** accept travellers cheques (the central one is in the Kaubahall Shopping Centre next to the main post office). **Estravel** (☎ 440 300, fax 440 301; e tartu@estravel .ee; Vallikraavi tänav 2) is the official agency for American Express.

The **central post office** (Vanemuise tänav 7; open 8am-7pm Mon-Sat) is just off Ülikooli tänav. Tartu's coolest Internet café is **Café Virtuaal** (Pikk tänav 40; open 11am-midnight daily), which charges 30EEK/hour.

Travel agencies that can organise tours or arrange bookings include Estravel and **Hermann Travel** (☎ 301 444; e tartu@hermann .ee; Lossi tänav 3), which specialises in nature tours. The helpful **South Estonian Travel** (Lõuna Eesti Reisburoo; ☎ 474 553; e lets .travel@kiirtee.ee), on the 2nd floor of the bus station, sells bus tickets for European destinations and can arrange tours in southern Estonia.

Mattiesen (☎ 309 721; Vallikraavi tänav 4) stocks an extensive range of books.

Things to See & Do

Tartu, as the major repository of Estonia's cultural heritage, has an abundance of museums and cultural institutions.

At the centre of town on Raekoja plats is the beautifully proportioned **Town Hall** (1782–89), topped by a tower and weather vane. The buildings at Nos 6, 8, 12 and 16 are also neoclassical but No 2, one of the first to be built after the 1775 fire, is late baroque. Formerly the home of Colonel Barclay de Tolly (1761–1818), No 18 is a wonderfully crooked building now housing **Kivisilla Art Gallery** (☎ 441 080; Raekoja plats 18; adult/student 10/5EEK; open 11am-6pm Wed-Sun).

The main **university** building (☎ 375 100; Ülikooli tänav 18), with six Corinthian columns, was built between 1803 and 1809. It houses the **Art Museum of Tartu University** (☎ 375 384; adult/child 7/4EEK; open 11am-5pm Mon-Fri) and the **Students' Lock-Up** museum (adult/child 5/2EEK; open 11am-5pm Mon-Fri) where you can see the place 19th-century students were held as punishment for their misdeeds.

Further north, the 1330 Gothic brick **Jaani Kirik** (St John's Church) is undergoing extensive restoration after Soviet bombing in 1944. It has rare **terracotta sculptures** surrounding the main portal. The **Botanical Gardens** (Lai tänav 40; greenhouse adult/student 18/5EEK;

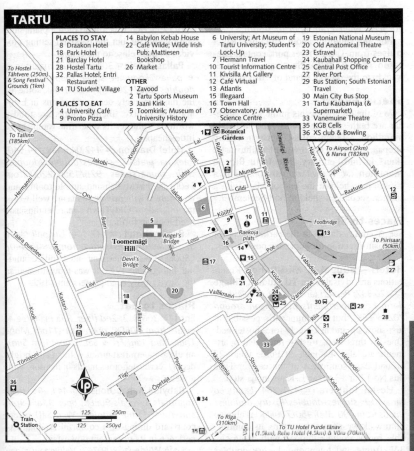

TARTU

PLACES TO STAY
8 Draakon Hotel
18 Park Hotel
21 Barclay Hotel
28 Hostel Tartu
32 Pallas Hotel; Entri Restaurant
34 TU Student Village

PLACES TO EAT
4 University Café
9 Pronto Pizza

14 Babylon Kebab House
22 Café Wilde; Wilde Irish Pub; Mattiesen Bookshop
26 Market

OTHER
1 Zavood
2 Tartu Sports Museum
3 Jaani Kirik
5 Toomkirik; Museum of University History

6 University; Art Museum of Tartu University; Student's Lock-Up
7 Hermann Travel
10 Tourist Information Centre
11 Kivisilla Art Gallery
12 Café Virtuaal
13 Atlantis
15 Illegaard
16 Town Hall
17 Observatory; AHHAA Science Centre

19 Estonian National Museum
20 Old Anatomical Theatre
23 Estravel
24 Kaubahall Shopping Centre
25 Central Post Office
27 River Port
29 Bus Station; South Estonian Travel
30 Main City Bus Stop
31 Tartu Kaubamaja (& Supermarket)
33 Vanemuine Theatre
35 KGB Cells
36 XS club & Bowling

To Hostel Tähtvere (250m) & Song Festival Grounds (1km)

To Tallinn (185km)

Botanical Gardens

To Airport (2km) & Narva (182km)

Footbridge

To Piirisaar (50km)

Toomemägi Hill

Angel's Bridge

Devil's Bridge

Raekoja plats

To Riga (310km)

To TU Hotel Purde tänav (1.5km), Rehe Hotel (4.5km) & Võru (70km)

Train Station

0   125   250m
0   125   250yd

ESTONIA

open 9am-5pm daily, grounds open 9am-9pm), established in 1803, is home to 6500 different species of plants.

Rising to the west of Raekoja plats is Toomemägi Hill, landscaped in the manner of a 19th-century English park. The thirteenth-century Gothic **Toomkirik** (cathedral) at the top was rebuilt in the 15th century, despoiled during the Reformation in 1525, and partly rebuilt in 1804–07 to accommodate the university library, which today is the **Museum of University History** (☎ 375 677; adult/student 20/5EEK; open 11am-5pm Wed-Sun).

Also on Toomemägi Hill are the **Angel's Bridge** (Inglisild; 1838), with a good view of the city, the 1913 **Devil's Bridge** (Kuradisild) and the **observatory**. Science-based exhibitions are regularly held in the Observatory's

AHHAA Science Centre (☎ 375 798; w www .ahhaa.ee); contact the observatory for details. On the southwestern side of Toomemägi is the **Old Anatomical Theatre** currently not accessible to the public.

Among the country's finest museums is the **Estonian National Museum** (☎ 421 311; w www.erm.ee; Kuperjanovi tänav 9; adult/student 12/5EEK; open 11am-6pm Wed-Sun), which traces the history, traditions and life of the Estonian people.

To the west of Toomemägi Hill is the country's most interesting museum. **Tartu Sports Museum** (☎ 300 750; Rüütli tänav 15; adult/student 10/5EEK; open 11am-6pm Mon-Fri) showcases Estonian Olympic excellence. The former KGB headquarters on Riia maantee now houses the sombre **KGB Cells** museum

(☎ 461 717; Riia maantee 15b; adult/student 20/5EEK; open 11am-6pm Tues-Sun).

For information about Emajõgi River **cruises** from Tartu's river port, contact **Laevatöö** *(☎ 340 025)*. Services run twice-weekly to the remote island of Piirissaar.

Special Events

Two of the biggest events in the local calendar are both sporting events. The **Tartu ski marathon**, a 60km cross-country trek from Otepää, involves hundreds of enthusiastic skiers in mid-February. The **Tartu Bicycle Marathon** (W *www.tartumaraton.ee)* is a 136km race held at the end of May, with a shorter, second one held in mid-September.

Places to Stay

See Accommodation in the earlier Facts for the Visitor section for homestay possibilities.

Hotels – Budget & Mid-Range Reservations are advisable for **TU Student Village** *(☎ 420 337; Pepleri tänav 14;* e *telts@ut.ee; dorm beds/apartments per person around 70/150EEK)*, but in summer it's possible to just show up and ask nicely for a hostel bed. One- to three-bed, freshly renovated apartments are also available at Purde tänav 27 around 2km southwest of the centre. Take bus No 12 or 13 to the E-Kaubamaja stop.

Hostel Tähtvere *(☎ 421 364; Laulupeo tänav 19; singles/doubles/luxury doubles/ quads from 200/350/450/700EEK)* is about a 1km walk west from the centre. Its comfortable rooms come equipped with bathroom, TV, fridge and telephone, luxury doubles have a fireplace. Many activities are offered at its adjoining sports complex.

Hostel Tartu *(☎ 432 091; Soola tänav 3; singles/doubles 375/640EEK, with shower 660/990EEK)* does have the location and reasonable rooms but beware, this charm-free old Soviet is undergoing large-scale and lengthy renovations.

Rehe Hotel *(☎ 412 234, fax 412 355; Võru tänav 235; singles/doubles/deluxe doubles 400/600/1200EEK)* offers comfortable rooms and security parking with signage inspired by Hollywood no one could miss 5km from the centre on the road to Võru.

Hotels – Top End Nestled into the side of Toompea, you'll find the **Park Hotel** *(☎ 433 663, fax 434 382; Vallikraavi tänav 23; basic singles/singles/doubles/suites from 460/800/ 980/1250EEK)*. It is a little on the plain side, and overpriced, but the parkland setting provides a haven close to the centre.

Pallas Hotel *(☎ 301 200; Riia maantee 4;* e *pallas@kodu.net; singles/doubles/deluxe doubles 880/1200/1600EEK)* has some of the most uniquely decorated rooms in Estonia. The deluxe 'theme' suites are totally worth the splurge. Its other fine rooms are a little cheaper.

Hotel Draakon *(☎ 442 045, fax 434 540; Raekoja plats 2; singles/doubles/doubles with sauna/suites 975/1550/2200/from 2600EEK)* has stylish and simple rooms, and the doubles with private sauna are well worth the upgrade – Old Town square enthusiasts need look no further.

Barclay Hotel *(☎ 447 100; Ülikooli tänav 8; singles/doubles/suites from 990/1440/ 1800EEK)* is in a charming and dignified building dating from 1912. It was requisitioned as the Soviet army headquarters until 1992.

Places to Eat

Entri *(☎ 306 812; 2nd floor, Riia maantee 4; meals from 70EEK; open 7am-11pm Mon-Thur, 7am-1am Fri & Sat, 8am-11pm Sun)*, an ultramodern restaurant with an airy bright decor, serves delicious meals in its room with a view.

Babylon Kebab house *(☎ 441 295; Raekoja plats 3; meals 90EEK; open 11am-9pm Sun-Tues, 11am-midnight Wed-Sat)* offers courtyard dining or a colourful Arabian experience in its restaurant downstairs.

Café Wilde *(☎ 309 762; Vallikraavi tänav 4; open 9am-9pm Sun-Thur, 9am-10pm Fri & Sat)* is Tartu's finest café, serving creamy cappuccinos, home-made cakes and baguettes in sublime surroundings. Its namesake is Peter Ernst Wilde, who opened a publishing house here in the 18th century, but it is Oscar Wilde who is celebrated at the popular **Wilde Irish Pub** serving decent meals upstairs.

Café Virtuaal (see Information earlier) also has some excellent meals.

University Café *(Ülikooli tänav 20)* is an old-world café with beautiful wooden floors that's a must for a light lunch or afternoon tea. It's in the original part of the university (dating from 1632).

Pronto Pizza *(☎ 442 085; Küütri tänav 3)* serves interesting pizza and has a decent salad bar.

The **central market**, about 150m north-west of the bus station, is a vast indoor space offering a wide variety of fresh produce.

Entertainment

Illegaard (☎ 434 424; Ülikooli tänav 5; open 5pm-2am daily) is a new-wave inspired jazz vault attracting an artsy crowd; check posters around town for live sessions.

Zavood (☎ 441 321; Lai tänav 30; open 4pm-2am daily) is another popular spot for late-night carousing, offering the best chance to see a student band.

Atlantis (Narva maantee 2; open 10pm-3am Sun-Thur; 10pm-4am Fri & Sat) is a popular nightclub overlooking the Emajõgi River.

XS (Vaksali tänav 21) attracts a very mixed, fun crowd. You even can go ten-pin bowling here until it's time to hit the club.

For theatre selections, check what's on at the **Vanemuine Theatre** (☎ 442 272; Vanemuise tänav 6). The first Estonian-language theatre troupe performed here when the theatre was founded in 1870.

Getting There & Away

Some 50 buses a day run to/from Tallinn, taking 2½ to 3½ hours depending on the service, and costing around 80EEK. There are also two trains daily.

While no scheduled flights service the **Tartu airport** (☎ 309 210), charter flights are regularly available; contact the airport for details.

OTEPÄÄ & AROUND
☎ 76

The small hill-top town of Otepää (population 2197), 44km south of Tartu, is the centre of a pretty area much loved by the Estonians for its hills and lakes, and often referred to jokingly as the 'Estonian alps'. It is an excellent place to enjoy the Estonian countryside. In winter, Otepää also becomes a popular **skiing** centre.

Orientation & Information

The centre of town is the triangular main 'square', Lipuväljak, with the bus station just off its eastern corner. On the square there is a **tourist information centre** (☎ 55 364, fax 61 246; e otepaa@visitestonia.com; open 9am-6pm Mon-Fri, 9am-3pm Sat & Sun) and the post office, bank and main food shop are beside the bus station. Staff at the **Otepää Travel Agency** (☎ 54 060; e otepaarb@hot .ee) are efficient and friendly.

Things to See & Do

Otepää's pretty little 17th-century **church** is on a hill top about 100m northeast of the bus station. It was in this church in 1884 that the Estonian Students' Society consecrated its new blue, black and white flag, which later became the flag of independent Estonia. The former vicar's residence now houses two museums: **Flag Museum** (Eesti Lipu Muuseum; ☎ 55 075) and **Ski Museum** (Suusamuuseum; ☎ 63 670; e suusamuuseum@hot.ee). Both can be visited by appointment.

The best views are along the shores of the 3.5km-long **Pühajärv** (Holy Lake) in the southwest of town. The lake was blessed by the Dalai Lama and a monument on the eastern shore commemorates his visit in 1992.

Otepää is home to many rare species of birds including the black stork, osprey and the white-backed woodpecker.

Places to Stay & Eat

In the heart of town, **Edgari** (☎ 54 275; Lipuväljak 3; singles/doubles 200/300EEK) offers clean, freshly renovated rooms, a dining area and kitchenette, with a TV in the communal lounge.

One of the region's finest hotels, **Karupesa** (☎ 61 500; e karupesa@scandichotels.ee; Tehvandi tänav 1a; singles/doubles/triples/suites with breakfast 700/800/1000/1400-2200EEK) has luxurious rooms and an à la carte restaurant.

Better known for its Irish Pub, the **Setanta Guesthouse** (☎ 68 200; e setanta@estpak .ee; doubles from 650EEK) has views from its terrace over Lake Pühajärv that are worth writing home about.

Just outside Otepää, the **Tehvandi Sports Centre** (☎/fax 69 500; e tehvandi@ tehvandi.ee; off Tehvandi tänav; singles/doubles/triples 380/490/690EEK) has neat and functional rooms with an exhaustive range of activities for both guests and visitors.

About 25km from Otepää is **Sangaste Loss** (☎ 79 300; e sloss@hot.ee; singles/doubles 200/400EEK), a lovely, fairy-tale brick castle modelled on England's Windsor Castle. It's in parkland close by a river where you can hire boats and bicycles. There is also a **museum** (adult/student 10/5EEK; open 9am-6pm daily) inside the castle. There are three to five buses daily between Otepää and Sangaste, and one daily to/from Tartu. The castle is also open to visitors not staying.

ESTONIA

Many hotels have a café or restaurant and a quick stroll through the town centre will acquaint you with popular local haunts **Oti Pubi** (☎ 69 840; Lipuväljak 26; meals 70EEK) and **Hermanni Pubi** (☎ 79 241; Lipuväljak 10; meals 60EEK; open 11am-11pm daily).

Getting There & Away
Buses are Otepää's only public transport. There are 11 daily buses to/from Tartu (¾–1½ hours), three to/from Tallinn (3½ hours) and one bus daily to/from Võru.

VÕRU
☎ 78 • pop 14,800
Võru, 64km south of Tartu, is a good base for visiting some interesting points in Estonia's far southeast, such as Suur Munamägi (the highest point in the Baltics), the picturesque village of Rõuge, or the area of Setumaa along the Russian border, one of Estonia's culturally most interesting places.

Võru lies on the eastern shore of Lake Tamula. The central square, on Jüri, is dominated by the Lutheran church. The bus station is half a kilometre east along Tartu tänav.

Võru has a **tourist information centre** (☎/fax 21 881; w www.visitestonia.com/werro; Tartu maantee 31; open 10am-6pm Mon-Fri, 10am-2pm Sat & Sun May-Sept; 9am-5pm Mon-Fri Oct-Feb) to help visitors. Try the **South Estonian Tourism Agency** (☎ 28 580; e tourism@wk.ee; Jüri tänav 22a) for all kinds of tours, including excursions to the nearby Haanja Nature Reserve, Setumaa and day trips to Setu lands in Russia.

Friedrich Reinhold Kreutzwald, honoured for his verse epic *Kalevipoeg*, lived in Võru. His home, an 18th-century wooden building, houses the **Kreutzwald Memorial Museum** (Kreutzwaldi tänav 31; adult/student 10/5EEK; open 10am-5pm Wed-Sun). **Võrumaa Museum** (Katariina tänav 11; adult/student 8/3EEK; open 11am-4pm Wed-Sun), displaying local history, is also worth a visit.

Places to Stay & Eat
Hermes Guesthouse (☎ 21 326; Jüri tänav 32A; singles/doubles/suites with shared bathroom 410/520/700-900EEK) has reasonable rooms despite a characterless exterior.

Hotel Tamula (☎ 30 430; e hotell@tamula.ee; singles/doubles & twins 500/800EEK) is a pristine new complex on the 'beach' with a tennis court; it welcomes pets.

Bevega (☎ 25 960; Mäe tänav 11; meals 100EEK; open 11am-1am Mon-Wed, 11am-6am Thur-Sat) is a fine semiformal restaurant with a wide menu selection complemented by a well-stocked bar.

Hundijalg (☎ 24 073; Jüri tänav 18B; meals 75EEK) is a local favourite for lunches. Its open grill behind the bar makes a very tasty meal.

Getting There & Away
There are about 28 buses to/from Tartu daily (1½ hours), 12 to/from Tallinn (4½ hours) and about four to Rõuge and Haanja. Schedules are posted around the bus station or call (☎ 21 018) for details of other services.

SETUMAA
Lying in the far southeastern part of Estonia is the (politically unrecognised) area of Setumaa. Unlike the rest of Estonia, this part of the country never came under the control of the Teutonic and German tribes, but fell under Novgorod's and later Pskov's subjugation. The Setu people, originally Finno-Ugric, then became Orthodox, not Lutheran. The whole of Setumaa was contained within independent Estonia between 1920 and 1940, but the greater part of it is now in Russia. Today, the Setu culture is tragically in decline. There are approximately 4000 Setu in Estonia (about another 3000 in Russia), half the population of the early 20th century. Museums of Setu culture are in **Obinitsa** and **Värska**. The **tourist information centre** (☎ 78-54 190) in Obinitsa is a good source of information and can advise on a number of local places to stay.

Southwestern Estonia & The Islands

PÄRNU
☎ 44 • pop 45,040
Pärnu (**pair**-nu), 127km south of Tallinn on the road to Rīga, is Estonia's leading seaside resort and a magnet for party-loving Estonians and mud-cure-seeking Finns. With wide leafy streets and white sandy beaches Pärnu has much to offer.

In the 13th century the Knights of the Sword built a fort at Pärnu. It became a Hanseatic port in the 14th century and flourished in the 17th century under Swedish rule. From 1838 the town grew as a resort, with mud baths, the beach and relatively good weather. During the 1930s Pärnu was favoured by Finns and Swedes. In the Soviet era all the guesthouses, hotels and villas were converted to sanatoriums providing treatments for visitors throughout the Soviet Union. Many now have now been revived as hotels.

Orientation & Information

Pärnu lies either side of the estuary of the Pärnu River, which empties into Pärnu Bay. The **tourist information centre** (☎ 73 000; ⓦ www.parnu.ee; Rüütli tänav 16) is on the main commercial street in the heart of the Old Town, about 100m southwest of the bus station. Running southward the streets get wider and greener before ending at Ranna puiestee and the beach.

Ühispank (Rüütli tänav 40a), in the building behind the bus station, cashes travellers cheques and gives cash advances on credit cards; it also has an ATM.

The **central post office** (Akadeemia 7; open 8am-6pm Mon-Fri, 9am-3pm Sat & Sun) is near Vallikäär Park. **Rüütli Internetipunkt** (Rüütli tänav 25; open 11am-9pm Mon to Fri, 10am-6pm Sat & Sun) provides access to Internauts for 20EEK an hour.

Things to See & Do

Punane Torn (Red Tower; Hommiku tänav; adult/student 10/5EEK; open 10am-6pm Mon-Fri, 10am-3pm Sat) is a survivor from

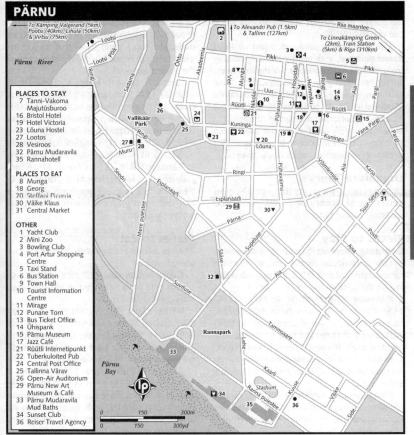

PÄRNU

PLACES TO STAY
7 Tanni-Vakoma Majutüsburoo
16 Bristol Hotel
19 Hotel Victoria
23 Lõuna Hostel
27 Lootos
28 Vesiroos
32 Pärnu Mudaravila
35 Rannahotell

PLACES TO EAT
8 Munga
18 Georg
20 Steffani Pizzeria
30 Väike Klaus
31 Central Market

OTHER
1 Yacht Club
2 Mini Zoo
3 Bowling Club
4 Port Artur Shopping Centre
5 Taxi Stand
6 Bus Station
9 Town Hall
10 Tourist Information Centre
11 Mirage
12 Punane Torn
13 Bus Ticket Office
14 Ühispank
15 Pärnu Museum
17 Jazz Café
21 Rüütli Internetipunkt
22 Tuberkuloited Pub
24 Central Post Office
25 Tallinna Värav
26 Open-Air Auditorium
29 Pärnu New Art Museum & Café
33 Pärnu Mudaravila Mud Baths
34 Sunset Club
36 Reiser Travel Agency

To Kämping Valgerand (5km), Pootsi (40km), Lihula (50km) & Virtsu (75km)

To Alexandri Pub (1.5km) & Tallinn (127km)

To Linnakämping Green (2km), Train Station (5km) & Riga (310km)

Pärnu River

Vallikäär Park

Pärnu Bay

Rannapark

ESTONIA

the days of the Knights of the Sword and now houses a small museum.

Parts of the 17th-century Swedish moat and ramparts remain in Vallikäär Park, including the tunnel-like **Tallinna Värav** (Tallinn Gate) at the western end of Kuninga. Local history features at **Pärnu Museum** (☎ 33 231; Rüütli tänav 53; adult/student 30/15EEK; open 10am-6pm Wed-Sun). An eclectic collection of cute, colourful reptiles and passive pythons reside at Pärnu's **Mini Zoo** (☎ 055 16 033; Akadeemia tee 1; adult/child 25/10EEK; open 10am-6pm Mon-Fri, 10am-4pm Sat & Sun).

The **Pärnu New Art Museum** (☎ 30 772; e aip@chaplin.ee; Esplanaadi tänav 10; adult/student 15/10EEK; open 9am-9pm daily), southwest of the centre, is among the cultural bright spots in all of Estonia, with its café, arts bookshop and some quite intriguing exhibitions. With some of the higher-profile temporary exhibitions the admission price can rise to 50EEK.

The wide, white-sand beach just south of Ranna puiestee, with nearby buildings dating from the first independence, are Pärnu's finest attractions. The grand neoclassical building at Ranna puiestee 1 is **Pärnu Mudaravila Mud Baths** (☎ 25 525, fax 25 521; Ranna puiestee 1), offering a range of 'cures'. It is possible to walk west along the coast from here to the 2km stone breakwater that stretches out into the mouth of the river.

Organised Tours

Nature-related tours are the speciality of **Reiser Travel Agency** (☎ 71 480; e reiser@reiser.ee; Kuuse tänav 1).

Places to Stay

Camping There are several camping options to choose from around the city, all of which have cabins and possibly tent space, depending on the conditions.

Kämping Valgerand (☎ 44 004, fax 40 135; 2-person/4-person tents 50/100EEK, caravans/2-bed & 4-bed cabins 300/400EEK) is 7km west of Pärnu in a lovely wooded strip beside the sea. It's best accessed using private transport; the buses en route to Lihula stop on the main road at Valgerand and from there it's a 3km walk.

Linnakämping Green (☎ 38 776; Suure-Jõe 50b; cabins per person 95EEK), 3km from Pärnu at the rowing centre on the river, also offers boat and bike rentals.

Hostels & Homestays To organise rooms in local homes, contact **Tanni-Vakoma Majutüsburoo** (☎ 31 070; e tanni@online.ee; Hommiku tänav 5).

The **Lõuna Hostel** (☎ 30 943, fax 30 944; e hostellouna@hot.ee; Lõuna tänav 2; dorm beds 200-250EEK, doubles 400EEK) is a fresh, new hostel in a grand old building that overlooks a park. It offers the quality budget accommodation Pärnu so desperately needed. The gleaming new bathrooms will impress.

Hotels – Mid-Range & Top End Accommodation at **Pärnu Mudaravila** (☎/fax 25 523; e info@mudaravila.ee; Sääse tänav 7; singles/doubles 380/500EEK, accommodation with treatments from 460EEK) redefines the notion of bed, bath and breakfast.

The **Lootos** (☎/fax 31 030; Muru tänav 1; singles/doubles 600/800EEK) and, across the street, the **Vesiroos** (☎ 30 940; Esplanaadi tänav 42A; doubles/triples 900/1100EEK) are under the same management. Both are hygienically clean and guests at either can use the swimming pool.

Centrally located, **Hotel Victoria** (☎ 43 412, fax 43 415; e victoria@hot.ee; Kuninga tänav 25; singles/doubles from 690/990EEK) is a highly dignified establishment in the town centre. **Bristol Hotel** (☎ 31 450, fax 43 415; Rüütli tänav 45; singles/doubles 860/1150EEK) likewise has exquisite rooms.

Rannahotell (☎ 38 950, fax 38 318; Ranna puiestee 5; singles/doubles from 1130/1430EEK) is a stunning functionalist mansion reposing quietly on the seafront. Expect all sorts of comforts.

Places to Eat

The beachfront is lined with café-kiosks that serve fast food.

Georg (Rüütli tänav 43; meals 50EEK) is a stylish café in the city centre offering good soups, salads and meals.

Väike Klaus (Supeluse tänav 3; meals 80EEK; open 11am-midnight Mon-Fri, 11am-2am Sat & Sun), a hearty, German-inspired pub, is a great place for a meaty lunch to offset those healthy mud treatments.

Alexandri Pub (Vana Rääma tänav 8; meals under 70EEK; open noon-11pm daily) may look like a biker bar but it's a friendly place very popular with locals. Go north across the bridge and turn right on the first street past the traffic lights.

ESTONIA

Munga *(Munga tänav 9; meals 50EEK; open 10am-midnight daily)*, a small café and restaurant with a warm old-world ambience, is in an old home on a charming side street.

Pärnu New Art Museum café *(Esplanaadi tänav 10; open 11am-5pm daily)* serves delicious food daily with an arts ambience.

Steffani Pizzeria *(Nikolai tänav 24)* does Pärnu's best fast pizza and pasta.

For self-catering, there is a **central market** *(cnr Karja tänav & Suur-Sepa tänav)*.

Entertainment

On the seafront in a grandiose building dating from 1939, **Sunset Club** *(Ranna puiestee 3; open 10pm-4am Thur-Sat)*, brings in the numbers as a club or venue for touring musicians.

Tuberkuloited Pub *(Kuninga tänav 11; open 11am-midnight Mon-Fri, 11am-2am Sat)* may sound like a sick potato but is a fine place for catching local live music, its namesake is one of Estonia's favourite bands.

Jazz, sand and mud form quite a trio at **Jazz Café** *(☎ 27 546; Ringi tänav 11; open 10am-midnight daily)*. Spontaneous live performances here may surprise.

Mirage *(Rüütli tänav 40; open 10pm-3am Fri, 10pm-3am Sat)* retains its popularity despite the dazzling Vegas foyer lights and a few shady types in its casino.

A healthier time can probably be had at the **Bowling Club** *(☎ 71 222; Aida tänav 5)*.

Getting There & Away

More than 20 buses daily connect Pärnu with Tallinn (60EEK, two hours). Details about a multitude of other destinations are available at the Pärnu bus station **ticket office** *(open 5am-8.30pm)* on Ringi tänav, across from the bus station.

KIHNU & RUHNU ISLANDS

☎ 44 • pop 497 & pop 66

Six-kilometre-long Kihnu Island in the Gulf of Rīga 40km southwest of Pärnu, is almost a living museum of Estonian culture. Many of the islands' women still wear traditional colourful striped skirts and the community adheres to Orthodox traditions.

Ruhnu Island, smaller than Kihnu, is 100km southwest of Pärnu. For several centuries the island supported a mainly Swedish population of around 300, who abandoned the island on 6 August 1944 to escape the advancing Red Army. Traces of the community,

including a **wooden church** from 1644, poignantly remain.

Reiser Travel Agency (see Organised Tours in the Pärnu section) arranges trips to the islands of Ruhnu and Kihnu. **Kihnurand Travel Agency** *(☎/fax 69 924)* on Kihnu organises full-day excursions to the islands.

There are regular ferries from the Munalaiu port *(☎ 96 312)* in the village of Pootsi, 40km southwest of Pärnu. The journey takes about an hour and a half.

HIIUMAA

☎ 46 • pop 10,385

Hiiumaa, Estonia's second biggest island is a quiet, sparsely populated haven with some delightful stretches of coast rich in birdlife. The commercial centre of the island is Kärdla, where you'll find the useful **tourist information centre** *(☎ 22 233; w www.hiiumaa .ee; Keskväljak 1; open 9am-6pm Mon-Fri, 10am-4pm Sat & Sun mid-Apr–mid-Sept; 9am-5pm Mon-Fri mid-Sept–mid-Apr)* and most of the island's services, including a bank, post office and supermarket.

Things to See & Do

The Hiiumaa headquarters of the **Biosphere Reserve of the West Estonian Archipelago** *(☎ 22 101; w www.bka.ee/hiiumaa; Vabriku väljak 1)* and the tourist information centre can advise on the bird-watching opportunities around the Takhuna Peninsula, Käina Bay and Hiiumaa Islets reserve.

Off the mainland west coast, the **Matsalu Nature Reserve** *(☎ 47-78 114; e matsalu@ matsalu.ee)* is a prime migration stopover and an essential destination for birding enthusiasts.

Other attractions on Hiiumaa are its lighthouses; **Kõpu Peninsula** was the site of an ancient 16th-century lighthouse (although the present one dates from 1845). The picturesque **Sääre Tirp** on the southern coast of Kassari will also reward a visit.

At **Suuremõisa**, 6km inland from Heltermaa port, you can see the late-baroque **Suuremõisa manor and park** *(adult/student 8/4EEK; open 10am-4pm June-Sept)*.

Places to Stay & Eat

The Kärdla tourist information centre can advise on a range of accommodation options throughout Hiiumaa.

Eesti Posti Puhkekeskus *(☎ 91 871; Posti tänav 13; beds from 100EEK)* has well-kept rooms in a homely building that until recently was the local post office.

Hotel Liilia (*☎ 36 146, fax 36 546;* e *liilia hotell@hot.ee; Hiiu maantee 22; singles/ doubles 490/690EEK*) in Käina offers rooms with bathroom and satellite TV. Its restaurant boasts an Estonian and international menu.

Priiankur (*Sadama tänav 4; meals 70EEK; open 11.30am-10pm Mon-Fri, noon-10pm Sat & Sun*) has an ample dining area separate from its bar and hearty meals to match.

Getting There & Away
Ferries make the 1½-hour trip between Rohu-küla and Heltermaa seven times daily (six times on Saturday). Two to three daily buses from Tallinn travel with the ferry directly to Kärdla or Käina, taking about 4½ hours.

SAAREMAA
☎ 45 • pop 35,746
Soviet-era industry and immigration barely touched Saaremaa, Estonia's biggest island, which retains the appearance of agricultural pre-WWII Estonia. Although Saaremaa has long been a popular local holiday retreat, during Soviet times it was closed to foreigners. Even mainland Estonians needed a permit to visit because of an early-warning radar system and rocket base on the island.

Orientation & Information
To reach Saaremaa you must first cross Muhu, the small island where the ferry from the mainland docks and which is connected to Saaremaa by a 2.5km causeway. Kuressaare, the capital of Saaremaa, on the south coast is a natural base for visitors.

Kuressaare's **tourist information office** (*☎/fax 33 120;* w *www.visitestonia.com/ saaremaa; Tallinna tänav 2; open 9am-7pm Mon-Fri, 9am-5pm Sat, 9am-3pm Sun May-Sept; 9am-5pm Mon-Fri Oct-Apr*) can assist with anything you may require to get oriented on the island.

You can change money at the bus station or at any of the several banks in the Town Hall square. The **post office** (*Torni maantee 1*) is north of the town square.

Things to See & Do
The yellow **town hall** in the main Old Town square dates from 1654. Opposite stands the baroque **Weighing House** built in 1663. To the left is a converted, 18th-century firehouse,

which now houses the Kuressaare tourist information centre.

The island's most distinctive landmark is the restored **Bishop's Castle** (1338–80) at the southern end of the town – an impressive, regal structure. It now houses the **Saaremaa Regional Museum** (*adult/child 30/15EEK; open 10am-7pm Wed-Sun*).

At Angla, 40km from Kuressaare on the Leisi road, is a most photogenic group of five **windmills** by the roadside. Two kilometres away, along the road opposite the windmills, is **Karja church**, the island's most striking 13th- to 14th-century German Gothic church. At Kaali, 18km from Kuressaare on the road to the harbour, is a 100m-wide, water-filled **crater** formed by a meteorite 2700 years ago. In ancient Scandinavian mythology, the site was known as 'the sun's grave'.

Saaremaa's magic can really be felt along the **Sõrve Peninsula**, jutting out south and west of Kuressaare. This sparsely populated strip of land saw some of the heaviest fighting in WWII. By the lighthouse at the southern tip, you can walk around the ruins of an old Soviet army base. Other bases and antitank defence lines still stand. A bike or car trip along the coastline provides some of the most spectacular sights on the island. Several daily buses from Kuressaare bus station head down the coast to the village of Sõrve.

Organised Tours
Arensburg travel agency (*☎ 33 360;* e *abr@ tt.ee; Tallinna maantee 25*) is extremely knowledgable about the island and specialises in boat trips to remote islands such as Abruka.

Places to Stay
The tourist information centre can organise beds in private apartments in Kuressaare and throughout the region. There are also numerous farmstays available in the area.

Behind a quiet, sandy beach about 10km on the road west of Kuressaare, **Kämping Mändjala** (*☎ 44 193;* e *mandjala@saaremma.ee; camping/cabin beds 40/180EEK*) is a pleasant camping ground also with cabins. Buses from Kuressaare to Torgu or Sääre (three a day) go to the Mändjala bus stop, about 500m beyond the site.

The **Saaremaa School Hostel** (*☎ 54 388;* e *marika@syg.edu.ee; Hariduse tänav 13; floor/singles/doubles per person 50/145/ 290EEK*) understands backpackers, offering a place to crash on a gym floor if a bed is not necessary and good news if Internet access is something you need.

The family-run **Pärna Guesthouse** (☎/fax 57 521; e perhoht@hot.ee; Pärna tänav 3; singles/doubles 400/550EEK) is on a quiet street just a few minutes' walk from the centre. The guesthouse has a kitchen available for guests' use.

Places To Eat
Cafe Hansa (Tallinna maantee 9; meals 70EEK) is one of Kuressaare's finest, with its old-world Bohemian ambience and memorable home-made pastries.

You can lose track of time over a memorable meal at **Raekelder** (town hall basement, Raekoja plats; meals from 120EEK; open noon-midnight daily).

Veski (☎ 33 776; Pärna tänav 19; meals from 120EEK; open noon-midnight Sun-Thur, noon-2am Fri & Sat) has a variable menu with some wholesome choices but mostly satisfies intrigue about a windmill-dining experience.

The **central market** in Kuressaare, offers a fine array of fresh produce (and Estonian handicrafts) and is just north of the town hall square.

Getting There & Around
A vehicle ferry runs throughout the day from Virtsu on the mainland to Muhu Island, which is joined by a causeway to Saaremaa. At least nine direct buses daily travel each way via the ferry between Tallinn and Kuressaare (160EEK, 4½ hours). There are also three daily buses to/from Tartu, and two a day to/from Pärnu.

Hungary

Hungary is just the place to kick off an Eastern or Central European trip. Just a short hop from Vienna, the land of Franz Liszt and Béla Bartók, Gypsy music, the romantic Danube River and piquant paprika continues to entice and enchant visitors. The allure of Budapest, once an imperial city, is apparent on arrival, but other cities such as Pécs, the sunny heart of the south, and Eger, the wine capital of the north, have much to offer travellers, as does the beautiful countryside.

In Hungary you'll find much of the glamour and excitement of Western Europe – at half the cost.

Facts about Hungary

HISTORY
Early Settlements & the Middle Ages
The Celts occupied the Carpathian Basin in the 3rd century BC but were conquered by the Romans just before the Christian era. Until the early 5th century AD, all of today's Hungary west of the Danube (Transdanubia) was in the Roman province of Pannonia. The Roman legion stationed at Aquincum, in what is now Óbuda, guarded the northeastern frontier of the empire. The Romans brought writing, planted the first vineyards in Hungary and built baths near the region's thermal waters.

The Romans were forced to abandon Pannonia in 451 by the Huns, whose short-lived empire had been established by Attila. The Huns were followed by the Goths, Longobards and the Avars, a powerful Turkic people who were subdued by Charlemagne in 796.

Exactly a century later, seven Magyar tribes swept in from the area between the Dnieper and lower Danube Rivers above the Black Sea and occupied the Danube Basin. The Magyars terrorised much of Europe with raids reaching as far as Spain, northern Germany and southern Italy until they were stopped at the Battle of Augsburg in 955 and subsequently converted to Christianity. Hungary's first king and its patron saint, Stephen (István), was crowned on Christmas Day in 1000, which marked the foundation of the Hungarian state. After the

Mongols sacked Hungary in 1241–42, killing an estimated one-third of its population of two million, many cities were fortified.

Medieval Hungary was a powerful state that included Transylvania (now in Romania), Slovakia and Croatia. The so-called Golden Bull, a kind of Magna Carta limiting some of the king's powers in favour of the nobility, was signed at Székesfehérvár in 1222, and universities were founded in Pécs in 1367 and in Óbuda in 1389.

HUNGARY

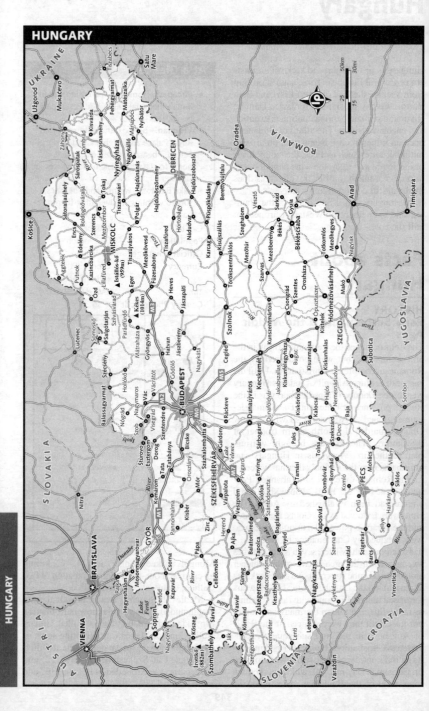

HUNGARY

In 1456 at Nándorfehérvár (today's Belgrade), Hungarians under János Hunyadi (r. 1445–56) stopped the Ottoman Turkish advance through Hungary to Vienna; under Hunyadi's son, Matthias Corvinus (1458–90), Hungary experienced a brief flowering of Renaissance culture. Then in 1514 what had started as a crusade by peasants turned into a revolt against landowners. The peasants were eventually suppressed, with tens of thousands massacred and their leader, György Dózsa, burned alive on a red-hot iron throne.

Turkish Occupation & Habsburg Rule

Hungary was seriously weakened by the revolt, and the Turks defeated the Hungarian army at Mohács in 1526. Buda Castle was seized in 1541 and Hungary divided in three. The central part, including Buda, was in Turkish hands while Transdanubia and present-day Slovakia were under the Austrian House of Habsburg, aided by Hungarian nobility based in Pozsony (Bratislava). The principality of Transylvania, east of the Tisza, prospered as a vassal state of the Ottoman Empire.

After the Turks were expelled from Buda in 1686, Habsburg domination of Hungary began. From 1703 to 1711 Ferenc Rákóczi II, prince of Transylvania, led an unsuccessful war of independence but united Hungarians against the Austrians for the first time.

Hungary never fully recovered from these disasters and from the 18th century had to be rebuilt from the ground up. Under the 'enlightened absolutism' of the Habsburg monarchs Maria Theresa (r. 1740–80) and her son Joseph II (r. 1780–90), the country made great steps forward economically and culturally.

The revolution of 1848, led by the lawyer Lajos Kossuth and poet Sándor Petőfi, demanded freedom for serfs and independence. Although it was put down a year later, the uprising shook the oligarchy. In 1865 Austria was defeated by Prussia and the next year a compromise was struck, creating the Dual Monarchy of Austria (the empire) and Hungary (the kingdom). This 'Age of Dualism' continued until 1918 and spurred economic, cultural and intellectual rebirth in Hungary.

Trianon & WWII

After WWI and the collapse of the Habsburg Empire in November 1918, Hungary was proclaimed a republic. However, the 1920 Trianon Treaty stripped the country of more than two-thirds of its territory.

In August 1919, a brutal communist government led by Béla Kun was overthrown after five months in power. In March of the next year, Admiral Miklós Horthy established a repressive rightist regime that attacked Jews and communists, imprisoning and executing many and forcing still more to flee the country.

Horthy immediately embarked on a 'white terror' – every bit as brutal as the red one of Béla Kun – that attacked communists and Jews for their roles in supporting the Republic of Councils. As the regime was consolidated over the next decade, it showed itself to be extremely rightist and conservative, advocating the status quo and 'traditional values' – family, state, religion. Though the country had the remnants of a parliamentary system, Horthy was all-powerful, and very few reforms were enacted. On the contrary, the lot of the working class and the peasantry worsened.

In 1941 Hungary's ambition to recover its lost territories drew the nation into war on the side of Nazi Germany. When Horthy tried to negotiate a separate peace with the Allies in 1944, the Germans occupied Hungary and brought the fascist Arrow Cross Party to power. The Arrow Cross then began deporting hundreds of thousands of Jews to Auschwitz.

In December 1944 a provisional government was established at Debrecen, and by early April 1945 all of Hungary had been liberated by the Soviet army.

The Communist Era

In 1947 the communists assumed complete control of the government and began nationalising industry and dividing up large estates among the peasantry.

On 23 October 1956 student demonstrators demanding the withdrawal of Soviet troops were fired upon. The next day Imre Nagy, the reformist minister of agriculture, was named prime minister. On 28 October Nagy's government offered amnesty to all those involved in the violence and promised to abolish the ÁVH (known as ÁVO until 1949), the hated secret police. But the fighting intensified, with some Hungarian military units joining rebels. Soviet troops, who had become involved in the conflict, began a slow withdrawal.

On 31 October hundreds of political prisoners were released, and widespread reprisals began against ÁVH agents. On 1 November

HUNGARY

Nagy announced that Hungary would leave the Warsaw Pact and assume neutral status. At this, the Soviet forces began to redeploy and on 4 November tanks moved into Budapest, crushing the uprising. When the fighting ended on 11 November, some 25,000 people were dead. Then the reprisals began: an estimated 20,000 people were arrested; 2000 were executed, including Nagy; and another 250,000 fled to Austria.

After the revolt, the Hungarian Socialist Workers' Party was reorganised, and János Kádár, proclaiming a new social unity, named party president and premier. After 1968 Hungary abandoned strict central economic control in favour of a limited market system.

In June 1987 Károly Grósz took over as premier and in May 1988, after Kádár's forced retirement, became party secretary general. Under Grósz and other reformers, Hungary began moving towards full democracy.

The Republic of Hungary

At their party congress in February 1989 the communists agreed to give up their monopoly on power, the Republic of Hungary was proclaimed in October, and democratic elections were scheduled for March 1990. Though they had changed their name and now advocated a free-market economy, the communists could not shake the stigma of four decades of autocratic rule, and the elections were won by the centrist Hungarian Democratic Forum (MDF), which advocated a gradual transition towards capitalism. Hungary had changed political systems with scarcely a murmur, and the last Soviet troops left the country in June 1991.

In coalition with two smaller parties, the MDF oversaw the painful transition to a full market economy, which resulted in declining living standards for most people. In 1991 most state subsidies were removed, leading to a severe recession. Beggars and homeless people appeared on the streets, and free education and health-care programmes were cut.

Disillusionment with this ugly side of capitalism brought the Hungarian Socialist Party (MSZP) to power in the 1994 elections. This in no way implied a return to the past, and party leader Gyula Horn was quick to point out that it was the socialists who had initiated the reform process in the first place.

In the elections of 1998, the once left-wing Alliance of Young Democrats (Fidesz) moved significantly to the right and then added the extension 'MPP' (Hungarian Civic Party) to its name in order to attract the support of the burgeoning middle class. It won government by forming a coalition with the MDF and the agrarian conservative Independent Smallholders Party (FKgP). Fidesz-MPP's youthful leader, Viktor Orbán, became prime minister.

Despite the astonishing economic growth and other gains made by the coalition government, the electorate grew increasingly hostile to Fidesz-MPP's – and Orbán's – strongly nationalistic rhetoric and arrogance. In April 2002 the largest turnout of voters in Hungarian history unseated the government and returned the MSZP, allied with the Alliance of Free Democrats (SZDSZ), to power under Prime Minister Péter Medgyessy, a free-market advocate who had served as the finance minister in the Horn government.

Hungary became a fully fledged member of NATO in 1999 and hopes to join the European Union (EU) by 2004.

GEOGRAPHY

Hungary occupies the Carpathian Basin in the very centre of Eastern Europe. It covers just over 93,000 sq km and shares borders with Austria, Slovakia, Ukraine, Romania, Yugoslavia, Croatia and Slovenia.

The longest rivers are the Tisza (597km in Hungary) and the Danube (417km), which divide the country into three parts. The country has well over 1000 lakes (of which the largest is Lake Balaton at 596 sq km) and is riddled with thermal springs.

The Danube separates the Great Plain (Nagyalföld, or *puszta*) in the east and Transdanubia (Dunántúl) in the west. Hungary's 'mountains' to the north are merely hills, with the highest peak being Kékes (1014m) in the Mátra Range.

CLIMATE

Hungary has a temperate Continental climate with Mediterranean and Atlantic influences. Winters are cold, cloudy and damp or windy, and summers are warm – sometimes very hot. March, April and November are the wettest months. The number of hours of sunshine averages 2209 a year – among the highest in Europe. From late April to the end of September, you can expect the sun to shine for about 10 hours a day. August is the hottest month (average temperature 23.9°C) and January the coldest (-0.7°C).

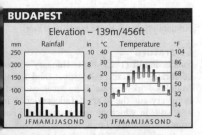

ECOLOGY & ENVIRONMENT

Pollution is a large and costly problem. Low-grade coal that fuels some industry and heats some homes creates sulphur dioxide and acid rain. Nitrogen oxides emitted by cars on the highways and in city centres cause severe air pollution. The over-use of nitrate fertilisers in agriculture has caused the ground water beneath the plains to become contaminated with phosphates and has even threatened Lake Balaton. But there has been marked improvement in air and water quality in recent years as Hungary attempts to conform to EU environmental standards. Between 1990 and 1997, for example, sulphur dioxide emissions fell by one-third while levels of nitrogen oxide decreased by one-fifth over the same period.

The most serious environmental disaster in recent years occurred in January 2000, when cyanide from a gold mine in Baia Mare in Romania emptied into the Tisza River, poisoning the water and killing fish and other animals and plant life for hundreds of kilometres downstream. Environmentalists now say the heavy-metal contamination will affect the food chain for years and the regeneration of the flora and fauna of the Tisza could take decades. The Szentendre-based Regional Environmental Center for Central and Eastern Europe is developing a common ecosystem strategy for the five nations sharing the Tisza.

FLORA & FAUNA

Hungary is home to over 2000 flowering plant species, many of which are not normally found at this latitude. There are a lot of common European animals (deer, wild hare, boar, otter) as well as some rarer species (wild cat, lake bat, Pannonian lizard), but three-quarters of the country's 450 vertebrates are birds, especially waterfowl.

There are 10 national parks in Hungary, including three on the Great Plain and two in the hilly north.

GOVERNMENT & POLITICS

Hungary's 1989 constitution provides for a parliamentary system of government. The unicameral assembly consists of 386 members chosen for four years in a complex, two-round system that balances direct ('first past the post') and proportional representation. The head of state, the president, is elected by the house for five years. The prime minister is head of government.

The main political parties are: the rightist Fidesz-MPP (Alliance of Young Democrats-Hungarian Civic Party); the conservative MDF (Hungarian Democratic Forum); the agrarian conservative FKgP (Independent Smallholders Party); the socialist MSZP (Hungarian Socialist Party); the liberal SZDSZ (Alliance of Free Democrats); and the xenophobic and ultra-nationalist MIÉP (Hungarian Justice and Life Party).

ECONOMY

With the strongest economy in Eastern and Central Europe, Hungary's painful restructuring appears to be over. The spiralling inflation and unemployment levels of the early to mid-1990s have finally settled, with figures now approaching those in the West. As long as economic targets are met and administrative reform continued, Hungary should be one of the first countries admitted to the EU when it expands its membership, possibly by 2004.

Behind the economic surge are European, Asian and North American companies that have invested more than US$20 billion over the past decade, mainly because wages and operational costs are relatively low. Hungary's workforce is also considered flexible, skilled and highly educated.

Still, it's not all rosy. Wages growth lags behind inflation and the country's poorer areas – the northeast and southeast, in particular, are yet to feel the boom that has buoyed Budapest and the western counties.

POPULATION & PEOPLE

Neither a Slavic nor a Germanic people, the Ugric Hungarians were the last major ethnic group to arrive in Europe during the period of the Great Migrations. Some 10.2 million Hungarians live within the national borders, and another five million Hungarians and their descendants are abroad. The estimated 1.65 million Hungarians in Transylvania (now Romania) constitute the largest ethnic minority

HUNGARY

in Europe, and there are another 600,000 in Slovakia, 350,000 in Yugoslavia, 180,000 in Ukraine and 35,000 in Austria. Hungarian immigrants to the USA, Canada, Australia and Israel add up to more than half a million.

Ethnic Magyars make up some 97.7% of the population. Minorities include Germans (0.3%), Slovaks (0.1%), Croatians (0.1%) and Romanians (0.1%). The number of Roma is officially put at 1.4% of the population (or 132,600 people) though some sources place it as high as 3%.

ARTS

While the Renaissance flourished briefly in the late 15th century, rump Hungary was isolated from the mainstream of European culture during Turkish rule. Then came domination by the Habsburgs, Nazi Germany and the Soviet Unión. It's not surprising that the works of Hungarian writers and artists have tended to reflect the struggle against oppression.

Music

Franz (or Ferenc) Liszt (1811–86) described himself as 'part Gypsy', and some of his works, notably *Hungarian Rhapsodies*, echo Romani music. Ferenc Erkel (1810–93) is the father of Hungarian opera, and two of his works – the stirringly nationalist *Bánk Bán* and *László Hunyadi* – are standards at the Hungarian State Opera House in Budapest.

Béla Bartók (1881–1945) and Zoltán Kodály (1882–1967) made the first systematic study of Hungarian folk music, travelling and recording throughout the linguistic region in 1906. Both integrated some of their findings into their compositions.

Hungarian folk musicians play violins, zithers, hurdy-gurdies, bagpipes and lutes on a five-tone diatonic scale. There are lots of different performers – watch out especially for Muzsikás and the incomparable Marta Sebestyén. Anyone playing the haunting music of the Csángó, pockets of Hungarians living in eastern Transylvania and Moldavia, is a good bet.

Gypsy music, as it is known and played in Hungarian restaurants from Budapest to Boston, is urban schmaltz and based on recruiting tunes played during the Rákóczi independence war. At least two fiddles, a bass and a cymbalom (a curious stringed instrument played with sticks) are *de rigueur*. Real Romani music usually doesn't employ instruments but

is sung a cappella. One of the best modern Romani groups is Kalyi Jag (Black Fire).

Literature

Sándor Petőfi (1823–49) is Hungary's most celebrated and accessible poet, and a line from his work *National Song* became the rallying cry for the War of Independence in 1848–49, in which he fought and died. His comrade-in-arms, János Arany (1817–82), wrote epic poetry *(Toldi Trilogy)* and ballads. Another friend, the prolific novelist and playwright Mór Jókai (1825–1904), gave expression to heroism and honesty in such wonderful works as *The Man with the Golden Touch* and *Black Diamonds*.

Hungary's finest 20th-century lyric poet, Endre Ady (1877–1919), attacked narrow materialism, provoking a storm of indignation from right-wing nationalists. The work of the poet Attila József (1905–37) expresses the alienation felt by individuals in the modern age. The novels of Zsigmond Móricz (1879–1942) examine the harsh reality of peasant life in Hungary.

Three important contemporary writers are György Konrád (1933–), Péter Nádas (1942–) and Péter Esterházy (1950–), whose works now appear in English translation.

Painting

Favourite painters from the 19th century include realist Mihály Munkácsy (1844–1900), the so-called painter of the *puszta*; Tivadar Kosztka Csontváry (1853–1919), who has been compared with Van Gogh, and József Rippl-Rónai (1861–1927), the key exponent of Secessionist art in Hungary. Győző Vásárhelyi (1908–97), who changed his name to Victor Vasarely when he emigrated to Paris in 1930, is considered the 'Father of Op Art'.

SOCIETY & CONDUCT

In general Hungarians are not uninhibited like the extroverted Romanians or the sentimental Slavs. They are a reserved, somewhat formal people. Forget about the impassioned, devil-may-care Gypsy-fiddling stereotype – it does not exist. The overall mood is one of *honfibú*, literally 'patriotic sorrow' but really a penchant for the blues, with a sufficient amount of hope to keep most people going. Family is very important in Hungarian society. If you're invited to someone's home, bring a bunch of flowers and/or a bottle of good local wine.

RELIGION
Of those Hungarians declaring religious affiliation, about 68% are Roman Catholic, 21% Reformed (Calvinist) Protestant and nearly 6% Evangelical (Lutheran) Protestant. There are also small Greek Catholic and Orthodox congregations. Hungary's Jews number about 100,000, down from a prewar population of nearly 10 times that size.

LANGUAGE
Hungarians speak Magyar, a member of the Ugric group of the Uralic family of languages that is related very, very distantly to Finnish, Estonian and about a dozen other very minor languages in Russia and western Siberia. Hungarian is not an Indo-European language, so you'll recognise very few words.

Many older Hungarians, particularly in the western part of the country, can understand German and more and more young people, particularly in Budapest, speak some English. Any travel-related business will have at least one staff member who can speak English.

Some useful words to learn are: *utca* or *utcája* (street), *út* or *útja* (road), *tér* or *tere* (square), *körút* (boulevard), *sétány* (promenade) and *híd* (bridge).

Hungarians always put surnames before given names. To avoid confusion, all Hungarian names in this chapter are written in the Western manner – Christian name first – including the names of museums and theatres if they are translated into English. For example, Budapest's Arany János színház is Hungarian, but it's the János Arany Theatre in English. Addresses are always written in Hungarian: Kossuth Lajos utca, Arany János tér etc.

See the Language chapter at the back of the book for pronunciation guidelines and more useful words and phrases in Hungarian. Lonely Planet's *Eastern Europe phrasebook* contains a chapter on the language.

Facts for the Visitor

HIGHLIGHTS
Historic Towns
Many historic towns, including Eger, Győr and Veszprém, were rebuilt in the baroque style during the 18th century. Sopron and Kőszeg are among the few towns in Hungary with a strong medieval flavour. The greatest monuments of the Turkish period are in Pécs.

Budapest has wonderful examples of all architectural styles but especially Secessionist (Art Nouveau).

Castles & Palaces
Hungary's most famous castles are those that resisted the Turkish onslaught in Eger, Kőszeg and Siklós. Though in ruins, the citadel at Visegrád evokes the power of medieval Hungary. Esterházy Palace at Fertőd and the Festetics Palace at Keszthely are among the finest in the land.

Museums & Galleries
The following museums and galleries are among the best: the Christian Museum (Gothic paintings) in Esztergom, the Imre Patkó Collection in Győr (Asian and African art), the Storno House Collection (Romanesque and Gothic furnishings) in Sopron, the Zsolnay Porcelain Museum (Art Nouveau porcelain) and the Vasarely Museum in Pécs (op art), the Ferenc Móra Museum in Szeged (Avar finds and a mock yurt), and the Museum of Applied Arts (Art Nouveau furnishings) and Museum of Fine Arts (foreign art) in Budapest.

SUGGESTED ITINERARIES
Depending on the length of your stay, you could see and do the following:

Two days
   Visit Budapest
One week
   Visit Budapest, the Danube Bend and one or two of the following places: Sopron, Pécs, Eger, Kecskemét or Szeged
Two weeks
   Visit Budapest, Győr, Sopron, the northern shore of Lake Balaton, Pécs, Szeged and Eger

PLANNING
When to Go
Every season has its attractions. Though it can be pretty wet in April and even May, spring is excellent as the weather is usually mild and the crowds of tourists have not yet arrived. Summer is warm, sunny and unusually long, but the resorts are crowded. If you avoid Lake Balaton, you'll do OK. Budapest comes to a grinding halt in August. Autumn is beautiful, particularly in the hills around Budapest and in the north. In Transdanubia and on the Great Plain this is harvest and vintage time. Avoid winter; apart from being cold and often bleak, winter sees museums

HUNGARY

and other tourist sights closed or their hours sharply curtailed.

Maps

In this small country you could easily get by with the *Road Map Hungary*, available free from branches of the Hungarian National Tourist Office (HNTO) abroad and from Tourinform offices in Hungary.

The Hungarian map-making company **Cartographia** (**W** *www.cartographia.hu*) publishes a useful 1:450,000 scale sheet map (800Ft) and its *Magyarország autóatlasza* (Road Atlas of Hungary) is indispensable if you plan to do a lot of travelling in the countryside by car. It comes in two sizes and scales – 1:360,000 (1600Ft) and 1:250,000 (2000Ft). The smaller scale atlas has thumbnail plans of virtually every community in the land, while the larger one has 23 city maps.

Discount Cards

Those planning extensive travel in Hungary might consider the **Hungary Card** (**☎** *1-266 3741;* **W** *www.hungarycard.hu*), which gives 50% discounts on all return train fares, some bus and boat travel, and some museums and attractions; up to 25% off selected accommodation; and 20% off the price of the Budapest Card (see Information in the Budapest section). The card, available at Tourinform and Volánbusz offices, larger train stations, some newsagents and petrol stations throughout Hungary, costs 6888Ft and is valid for a year.

What to Bring

A swimsuit for use in the mixed-sex thermal spas and pools is a good idea as are sandals or thongs (flip flops). If you plan to stay in hostels, pack a towel and a plastic soap container. Bedclothes are usually provided, though you might want to bring your own sheet bag and padlock for storage cupboards.

TOURIST OFFICES
Local Tourist Offices

The Hungarian National Tourist Office (HNTO) has a chain of 120 Tourinform information bureaus across the country, and these are the best places to ask general any questions and pick up brochures. The main **Tourinform office** (**☎** *1-438 8080*, fax *318 9059;* **W** *www.hungarytourism.hu; V Vigadó utca 6*) in Budapest is open 24 hours a day, seven days a week.

If your query is about private accommodation, flights or international train travel, you may have to ask a commercial travel agency; most towns have at least a couple. The oldest, Ibusz, is arguably the best for private accommodation. Others include Cooptourist and Vista. The Express travel agency, with branches in many cities, issues student, youth, teacher and hostel cards (1600Ft) and sells discounted Billet International de Jeunesse (BIJ) train tickets and cheap airfares. Some local Express offices can tell you about university accommodation as well.

Tourist Offices Abroad

The HNTO has offices in some 19 countries, including the following:

Austria (**☎** 01-585 20 1213, fax 585 20 1214, **e** htvienna@hungarytourism.hu) Opernring 5/2, A-1010 Vienna
Czech Republic (**☎** 02-2109 0135, fax 2109 0139, **e** htpragaue@hungarytourism.hu) Rumunská 22, 22537 Prague 2
France (**☎** 01 53 70 67 17, fax 01 47 04 83 57, **e** htparis@hungarytourism.hu) 140 ave Victor Hugo, 75116 Paris
Germany (**☎** 030-243 146 0, fax 243 146 13, **e** htberlin@hungarytourism.hu) Karl Liebknecht Strasse 34, D-10178 Berlin
Netherlands (**☎** 070-320 9092, fax 327 2833, **e** htdenhaga@hungarytourism.hu) Laan van Nieuw Oost Indie 271, 2593 BS The Hague
UK (**☎**/fax 020-7823 1032, fax 7823 1459, **e** htlondon@hungarytourism.hu) 46 Eaton Place, London SW1X 8AL
USA (**☎** 212-355 0240, fax 207 4103, **e** htnewyork@hungarytourism.hu) 33rd floor, 150 East 58th St, New York, NY 10155-3398

In countries without an HNTO office, contact Malév Hungarian Airlines, which has offices or associated agencies in some 40 countries worldwide.

VISAS & DOCUMENTS

Everyone needs a valid passport or, for citizens of certain European countries, a national identification card, to enter Hungary. Citizens of virtually all European countries, the USA, Canada, Israel, Japan and New Zealand do not require visas to visit Hungary for stays of up to 90 days. UK citizens do not need a visa for a stay of up to six months. Nationals of Australia and now South Africa (among others) require visas. Check current visa requirements at a consulate, any HNTO or Malév office or on the website of the **Foreign Ministry** (W *www.kum.hu*) as these can change without notice.

Visas are issued at Hungarian consulates or missions, most international highway border crossings, Ferihegy airport and the International Ferry Pier in Budapest. Visas are never issued on trains and rarely on buses. Be sure to retain the separate entry and exit forms issued with the visa stamped in your passport.

Single-entry tourist visas are issued at Hungarian missions in the applicant's country of residence upon receipt of the equivalent of US$40 and three photos (US$65 at a mission outside the country of residence or at the border). A double-entry tourist visa costs US$75/100, and you must have five photos. A multiple-entry visa is US$180/200. Express service (10 minutes as opposed to overnight) costs US$15 extra. Single- and double-entry visas are valid for six months prior to use. Multiple entries are good for a year.

Be sure to get a tourist rather than a transit visa; the latter – available for single (US$38/50), double (US$65/90) and also multiple (US$150/180) entries – is only good for a stay of 48 hours each time, you must enter and leave through different border crossings and already hold a visa (if required) for the next country you visit.

Tourist visas can only be extended (3000Ft) in emergencies (eg, medical reasons) and must be done at the central police station (*rendőrkapitányság*) of any city or town 15 days before the original one expires. It's no longer an option to go to a neighbouring country like Austria or Slovakia and then re-enter; as of January 2002, tourist visas now allow visitors to stay for 90 days within a six-month period only.

EMBASSIES & CONSULATES
Hungarian Embassies & Consulates
Hungarian embassies around the world include the following:

Australia (☎ 02-6282 2555) 17 Beale Crescent, Deakin, ACT 2600
Consulate: (☎ 02-9328 7859) Suite 405, Edgecliff Centre, 203-233 New South Head Rd, Edgecliff, NSW 2027
Austria (☎ 01-537 80 300) 1 Bankgasse 4–6, 1010 Vienna
Canada (☎ 613-230 9614) 299 Waverley St, Ottawa, Ontario K2P 0V9

Consulate: (☎ 416-923 8981) Suite 1115, 121 Bloor St East, Toronto, Ontario M4W 3M5
Croatia (☎ 01-489 0900) Krlezin gvozd 11/a, 10000 Zagreb
Germany (☎ 030-203 100) Unter den Linden 76, 10117 Berlin
Consulate: (☎ 089-911 032) Vollmannstrasse 2, 81927 Munich
Ireland (☎ 01-661 2902) 2 Fitzwilliam Place, Dublin 2
Romania (☎ 01-311 0062) Strada Jean-Louis Calderon 63–65, Bucharest 70202
Slovakia (☎ 02-544 30541) ul Sedlárska 3, 81425 Bratislava
Slovenia (☎ 01-512 1882) Konrada Babnika ulica 5, 1210 Ljubljana-Sentvid
South Africa (☎ 012-430 3030) 959 Arcadia St, Hatfield, 0083 Pretoria
UK (☎ 020-7235 5218) 35 Eaton Place, London SW1X 8BY
Consulate: (☎ 020-7235 2664) 35/b Eaton Place, London SW1X 8BY
Ukraine (☎ 044-212 4134) ul Rejtarszkaja 33, Kyiv 01034
USA (☎ 202-362 6730) 3910 Shoemaker St NW, Washington, DC 20008
Consulate: (☎ 212-752 0661) 223 East 52nd St, New York, NY 10022
Consulate: (☎ 310-473 9344) Suite 410, 11766 Wilshire Blvd, Los Angeles, CA 90025
Yugoslavia (☎ 011-444 0472) ul Ivana Milutinovica 74, Belgrade 11000

Embassies & Consulates in Hungary
Countries with representation in Budapest (phone code ☎ 1) include the following (hours indicate when consular or chancellery services are available):

Australia (☎ 457 9777) XII Királyhágó tér 8–9 (open 9am-noon Mon-Fri)
Austria (☎ 352 9613) VI Benczúr utca 16 (open 9am-11am Mon-Fri)
Canada (☎ 392 3360) XII Budakeszi út 32 (open 8.30am-11am & 2pm-3.30pm Mon-Thur)
Croatia (☎ 354 1315) VI Munkácsy Mihály utca 15 (open 1pm-3pm Mon, Tues, Thur & Fri)
Germany (☎ 488 3500) I Úri utca 64-66 (open 9am-noon Mon-Fri)
Ireland (☎ 302 9600) V Szabadság tér 7–9 (open 9.30am-12.30pm & 2.30pm-4.30pm Mon-Fri)
Romania (☎ 352 0271) XIV Thököly út 72 (open 8.30am-noon Mon-Fri)
Slovakia (☎ 460 9010) XIV Stefánia út 22–24 (open 8am-noon Mon-Fri)
Slovenia (☎ 438 5600) II Cseppkő utca 68 (open 9am-noon Mon-Fri)
South Africa (☎ 392 0999) II Gárdonyi Géza út 17 (open 9am-12.30pm Mon-Fri)

HUNGARY

UK (☎ 266 2888) V Harmincad utca 6 (open
9.30am-12.30pm & 2.30pm-4.30pm Mon-Fri)
Ukraine (☎ 355 2443) XII Nógrádi utca 8 (open
9am-noon Mon-Wed & Fri by appointment
only)
USA (☎ 475 4400) V Szabadság tér 12 (open
8.15am-5pm Mon-Fri)
Yugoslavia (☎ 322 9838) VI Dózsa György út
92/b (open 9am-1pm Mon-Fri)

CUSTOMS

You can bring the usual personal effects, 200
cigarettes, 1L of wine or champagne and 1L
of spirits. You are not supposed to export
valuable antiques without a special permit;
this should be available from the place of
purchase. You must declare the import/export
of any amount of cash exceeding the sum of
1,000,000Ft.

MONEY
Currency

The unit of currency is the Hungarian forint
(Ft). Coins come in denominations of one,
two, five, 10, 20, 50 and 100Ft, and notes are
denominated 200, 500, 1000, 2000, 5000,
10,000 and 20,000Ft.

Exchange Rates

Exchange rates at the time of going to press
were:

country	unit		forint
Australia	A$1	=	139Ft
Canada	C$1	=	163Ft
Euro Zone	€1	=	245Ft
Japan	¥100	=	206Ft
New Zealand	NZ$1	=	120Ft
UK	UK£1	=	378Ft
USA	US$1	=	247Ft

Exchanging Money

You'll find automated teller machines
(ATMs) accepting most credit and cash cards
throughout the country; all banks mentioned
in this chapter have them unless indicated
otherwise. It's always prudent to carry a little
foreign cash, preferably euros or US dollars,
and perhaps some travellers cheques (eg,
American Express, Visa or Thomas Cook).

Banks and bureaux de change generally
don't take a commission, but exchange rates
vary tremendously; private agencies are always the most expensive. The national savings
bank, Országos Takarékpénztár (OTP), has
branches everywhere and offers some of the
best rates; Ibusz is also a good bet. Many
banks, including K&H and Postabank (at post
offices nationwide), give cash advances on
most credit cards.

The use of credit cards is gaining ground,
especially Visa, MasterCard and American
Express. You'll be able to use them at upmarket restaurants, shops, hotels, car-rental firms,
travel agencies and petrol stations but not museums, supermarkets or train and bus stations.

Money can be wired to Hungary through
American Express – you don't need to be an
Amex card-holder but the sender does. The
procedure takes less than 30 minutes. You
should know the sender's full name, the exact
amount and the reference number when
you're picking up the cash. You'll be given
the amount in US dollars travellers cheques
or forint. The sender pays the service fee
(about US$50 for US$1000 sent).

Security

Overall, Hungary is a very safe country but
pickpocketing can be a problem, especially in
Budapest (see the Dangers & Annoyances section). Always put your wallet in your front
pocket, hold your purse close to your body and
keep your backpack or baggage in sight. And
watch out for tricks. The usual method on the
street is for someone to distract you by running
into you and then apologising profusely – as
an accomplice takes off with the goods. We
have received amny reports of unscrupulous
waiters and shop assistants making high-tech
duplicates of credit- or debit-card information
with a machine. If your card leaves your possession for a considerable length of time, think
about having it cancelled.

Costs

Prices may have risen over the past few years,
but Hungary remains a bargain destination for
Western travellers. If you stay in private
rooms, eat at medium-priced restaurants and
travel on public transport, you should get by
on US$30 a day without scrimping. Those
staying at hostels, dormitories or camping
grounds and eating at food stalls or self-
catering will cut costs substantially.

Because of the changing value of the
forint, many hotels quote their rates in euros,
as does the national rail company. In such
cases, we have followed suit.

HUNGARY

Tipping

Hungarians routinely give tips of about 10% to waiters, hairdressers, taxi drivers and even doctors, dentists and petrol station attendants manning the pumps. In restaurants, do this on payment of the bill; leaving money on the table is considered rude in Hungary. If you were less than impressed with the service, don't feel obliged to leave a gratuity. Some upmarket places add a 10% service charge to the bill, which makes tipping unnecessary.

Taxes & Refunds

ÁFA, a value-added tax of 11% to 25%, covers the purchase of all new goods. It's usually included in the quoted price but not always, so it pays to check. Visitors can claim refunds for total purchases of more than 50,000Ft on one receipt as long as they take the goods out of the country within 90 days. The ÁFA receipts (available from the shops where you made the purchases) should be stamped by customs at the border, and the claim has to be made within 183 days of exporting the goods.

Budapest-based **Global Refund Hungary** (☎/fax 1-468 2965, fax 468 2966; **W** www .globalrefund.com; XIV Zászlós utca 54) can help you with refunds for a fee.

POST & COMMUNICATIONS
Post

Letters/postcards sent within Hungary and to neighbouring countries cost 38/30Ft. Airmail letters within Europe cost 150/240Ft for up to 20/50g and 160/260Ft for the rest of the world. Postcards cost 100Ft and 110Ft respectively.

Mail addressed to poste restante in any town or city will go to the main post office (főposta), which is listed under Information in the destination sections. When collecting poste-restante mail, look for the sign 'postán maradó küldemények'. Don't forget identification and write your full name on a piece of paper; otherwise the clerk might look under your first name.

If you hold an American Express credit card or are carrying their travellers cheques, you can have your mail sent to **American Express** (Deák Ferenc utca 10, 1052 Budapest), where it will be held for one month.

Telephone

You can make domestic and international calls from public telephones. They work with both coins and phonecards, though the latter are now more common. Phonecards (800Ft or 1800Ft) are available from post offices, newsagents, hotels and petrol stations. Telephone boxes with a black and white arrow and red target on the door and the word 'Visszahívható' display a telephone number, so you can be phoned back.

All localities in Hungary have a two-digit area code, except for Budapest, which has '1'. Local codes appear under the destination headings in this chapter.

To make a local call, pick up the receiver and listen for the continuous dial tone, then dial the phone number. For an intercity call within Hungary, dial ☎ 06 and wait for the second, more musical, tone. Then dial the area code and phone number. You must always dial ☎ 06 when ringing a mobile telephone, whose area codes are ☎ 06-20 (Pannon), ☎ 06-30 and ☎ 06-60 (Westel), and ☎ 06-70 (Vodafone).

The procedure for making an international call is the same except that you dial ☎ 00, followed by the country code, the area code and then the number. International phone charges from a phone box are: 131Ft per minute to neighbouring countries and 136Ft to Europe, North America, Australia and New Zealand.

Useful phone numbers include domestic (☎ 198) and international operator/directory inquiries (☎ 199).

Fax

You can send faxes from most main post offices and Internet cafés for 150/500Ft per page within/outside Hungary.

Email & Internet Access

Internet cafés have sprouted in Budapest (see that section) like mushrooms after rain and all the capital's year-round hostels offer access. Public Internet connections in the provinces are harder to find, though most major towns now have a Matáv Pont outlet, which usually has at least a couple of terminals available (300/500Ft for 30/60 minutes).

DIGITAL RESOURCES

Tourinform's informative website **W** www .hungarytourism.hu should be your initial portal of call. For information on hotels, try **W** www.hotelshungary.com, **W** www.hotels info.hu or **W** www.szallasinfo.hu. Check out **W** www.youthhostels.hu for hostel accommodation and also **W** www.camping.hu for camping grounds in Hungary.

HUNGARY

The website [w] www.budapestinfo.hu is the best overall site for information about Budapest, and Budapest Week Online, at [w] www .budapestweek.com, has events, music and movie listings. Budapest Sun Online, found at [w] www.budapestsun.com, is similar but with a focus on local news, interviews and features. For national news, visit the website at [w] www.insidehungary.com.

BOOKS
An excellent overall guidebook is Lonely Planet's *Hungary*, while the *Budapest* guide takes an in-depth look at the capital.

An Illustrated History of Hungary by István Lázár is an easy introduction to the nation's past, but more serious students will pick up a copy of Miklós Molnár's *A Concise History of Hungary*.

Budapest: A Cultural Guide by Michael Jacobs is a history-cum-walking guide that sometimes borders on the academic. Imre Móra's *Budapest Then & Now*, now in its second edition, is a collection of essays that has some esoteric bits of information relating to the capital.

NEWSPAPERS & MAGAZINES
Budapest has two English-language weeklies: the fluffy *Budapest Sun* (298Ft), with a useful 'Style' arts and entertainment supplement, and the *Budapest Business Journal* (550Ft). *The Hungarian Spectator* (100Ft), an unsuccessful mix of the two, appears twice a month.

A number of Western English-language newspapers, including the *International Herald Tribune*, are available on the day of publication in Budapest and in certain other large western Hungary cities. Many more, mainly British, French and German, are sold a day late. International news magazines are also widely available.

RADIO & TV
With the sale of the state-owned TV2, Magyar Televízió (MTV) controls only one TV channel (M1). There are also the public channels M2 and Duna TV and a host of cable and satellite ones (such as RTL Klub and Magyar ATV) broadcasting everything from game and talk shows to Pokemon, all in – or dubbed into – Hungarian. Most larger hotels and pensions have satellite TV, mainly German, but sometimes Sky News, CNN, Eurosport and BBC News.

Hungarian Radio has three stations, named after Lajos Kossuth (jazz, news; 98.6AM), Sándor Petőfi (1960s to 80s music, news; 94.8FM) and Béla Bartók (classical music, news; 105.3FM). Est.fm (98.6FM) is a popular alternative music station while Radio © (88.8FM) is super for Romani music as well as jazz, Latino and North African sounds. Budapest Rádió is on 88.1 FM and 91.9FM.

PHOTOGRAPHY & VIDEO
Major brands of film are readily available and one-hour processing places are common in Budapest and larger cities and towns.

Film prices vary but basically 24 exposures of 100 ASA Kodacolor II, Agfa or Fujifilm costs 1000Ft, and 36 exposures is 1290Ft. Ektachrome 100 costs 1790Ft for 36 exposures. Developing print film is 1099Ft a roll; for the prints themselves, you choose the size and pay accordingly (eg, 10cm x 15cm prints cost 89Ft each). Slide film costs 1100Ft to process. Videotape such as TDK EHG 30/45 minutes costs 990/1310Ft.

TIME
Time is GMT plus one hour. Clocks are advanced at 2am on the last Sunday in March and set back at the same time on the last Sunday in October. In Hungarian, 'half eight' means 7.30 and not 8.30.

LAUNDRY
Most hostels and camping grounds have some sort of laundry facilities; expect to pay about 1000Ft per good-sized load. Commercial laundries often take days to do your wash and are never cheap. Self-service laundries are virtually nonexistent.

TOILETS
Public toilets, which always levy a user's fee (usually 50Ft), are invariably staffed by an old *néné* (auntie), who continuously mops the floor, hands out sheets of Grade AAA sandpaper and has seen it all before.

Public toilets *(WC* or *toalett)* are signposted *női* or *nők* for women and *férfi* or *férfiak* for men.

WOMEN TRAVELLERS
Hungarian men can be very sexist in their thinking, but women do not suffer any particular form of harassment (though domestic violence and rape get little media coverage).

For assistance and/or information ring the **Women's Line** (*Nővonal;* ☎ 06-80 505 101) or **Women for Women against Violence** (*NANE;* ☎ 1-267 4900), which operates from 6pm to 10pm daily.

GAY & LESBIAN TRAVELLERS

For up-to-date information on venues, events, parties etc, pick up the pamphlet *Na végre!* (At Last!) at gay venues in Budapest or contact the group directly ([e] navegre@hotmail.com). The websites [w] www.pride.hu, [w] www.gay guide.net/europe/hungary/budapest, [w] english .gay.hu and [w] masprogram.freeweb.hu are good sources of information.

For one-to-one contact, ring either the **Gay Switchboard** (☎ 06-30 932 3334, 1-351 2015; *open 4pm-8pm Mon-Fri*) or **Háttér Gay & Lesbian Association** (☎ 1-329 3380; *open 6pm-11pm daily*).

DISABLED TRAVELLERS

Most of Hungary has a long way to go before it becomes accessible to the disabled. Wheelchair ramps, toilets fitted for the disabled and inward opening doors are virtually nonexistent, though audible traffic signals for the blind are becoming increasingly commonplace and the higher-denominated forint notes have markings in Braille.

For more information, contact the **Hungarian Disabled Association** (*MEOSZ;* ☎ 1-388 5529, 388 2387; [e] meosz@matavnet.hu; *San Marco utca 76, Budapest 1035; open 8am-4pm Mon-Fri*).

DANGERS & ANNOYANCES

Hungary is not a violent or dangerous society, but crime has increased fourfold from a communist-era base of virtually nil over the past 15 years. Racially motivated attacks against Roma, Africans and Arabs are not unknown, but violence is very seldom directed against travellers in the country.

As a traveller you are most vulnerable to pickpockets and taxi louts (see Getting Around in the Budapest section) and possibly car thieves.

BUSINESS HOURS

With some rare exceptions, the opening hours (*nyitvatartás*) of any concern to the ordinary traveller are posted on the front door of establishements; *nyitva* means 'open' and *zárva* is 'closed'.

Emergency Services

In the event of an emergency anywhere in Hungary, phone the central emergency number on ☎ 112 (English spoken).

For police call ☎ 107, for fire ☎ 105 and for ambulance ☎ 104. The English-language crime hotline is ☎ 1-438 8000.

Car assistance (24 hours) is available by calling ☎ 188.

Grocery stores and supermarkets open from about 7am to 6pm or 7pm on weekdays, and department stores 10am to 6pm. Most shops stay open until 8pm on Thursday; on Saturday they usually close at 1pm. Main post offices are open 8am to 6pm weekdays, and to noon or 1pm Saturday. Banking hours vary but are usually 8am to about 4pm Monday to Thursday and to 1pm on Friday. With few exceptions, museums are open 10am to 6pm Tuesday to Sunday from April to October and to 4pm on the same days the rest of the year.

Most places have a 'nonstop' convenience store, which opens late (but not always 24 hours), and many of the hyper-supermarkets open on Sunday.

PUBLIC HOLIDAYS & SPECIAL EVENTS

Hungary's 10 public holidays are: New Year's Day (1 January), 1848 Revolution Day (15 March), Easter Monday (March/April), International Labour Day (1 May), Whit Monday (May/June), St Stephen's Day (20 August), 1956 Remembrance Day (23 October), All Saints' Day (1 November) and Christmas and Boxing Days (25 and 26 December).

The best annual events include: the Budapest Spring Festival (March); the Balaton Festival based in Keszthely (May); the Hungarian Dance Festival in Győr (late June); Sopron Festival Weeks (late June to mid-July); Győr Summer Cultural Festival (late June to late July); Hortobágy International Equestrian Days (July); Szeged Open-Air Festival (July); Kőszeg Castle Theatre Festival (mid- to late July); Pepsi Sziget Music Festival on Obudai hajógyár-sziget (Óbuda Shipbuilding Island) in Budapest (late July to early August); Hungaroring Formula-1 races at Mogyoród, 24km northeast of Budapest (mid-August); and the Budapest Autumn Festival (mid-October to early November).

HUNGARY

ACTIVITIES

Thermal Baths

More than 100 thermal baths are open to the public. The thermal lake at Hévíz is Hungary's most impressive. Public thermal pools at Budapest, Eger, Győr and Harkány are also covered in this chapter.

Water Sports

The main places for water sports in Hungary are Lake Balaton (Keszthely, Balatonszabadi, Balatonvilágos and Balatonaliga) and Lake Velence. Qualified sailors can rent yachts on Balaton; motorboats are banned.

Many canoe and kayak trips are available. Following the Danube from Rajka in the northwest to Mohács in the southwest (386km) or the Tisza River from Tiszabecs on the border with Ukraine southward to Szeged (570km) are popular runs, but there are less congested waterways and shorter trips, such as the Rába River from Szentgotthárd north to Győr (205km).

The HNTO publishes a brochure titled *Water Tourism: 3500km of Waterways*, which introduces what's available on Hungary's rivers, streams and canals, and offers practical information.

Cycling

Hungary now counts 2500km of dedicated bicycle lanes around the country, with more on the way. In addition there are thousands of kilometres of roads with light traffic and dikes suitable for cycling. The HNTO produces the useful *Cycling in Hungary* brochure, with 12 recommended routes with maps, as well as a 60-page insert crammed with all sorts of practical information.

Cartographia produces a series of 1:100,000 regional Tourist Maps (*Turistatérkép*; 650Ft), with cycling routes marked and explanatory notes in English. Another possibility is the 1:250,000-scale *Cycling around Hungary* (*Kerékpártúrák Magyarországon*; 2600Ft), with 100 tours outlined and places of interest and service centres listed in English.

For information and advice in Budapest, contact the helpful **Hungarian Bicycle Touring Association** (*MKTSZ*; ☎ 1-311 2467; e *mktsz@dpg.hu; VI Bajcsy-Zsilinszky út 31*). Also in the capital, the enthusiastic **Friends of Nature Bicycle Touring Association** (*TTE*; ☎ 1-316 5867; II Bem rakpart 51*) can help organise bike tours and supply guides.

Hiking

You can enjoy good hiking in the forests around Visegrád, Esztergom, Badacsony, Kőszeg and Budapest. North of Eger are the Bükk Hills and south of Kecskemét the Bugac Puszta, both with marked trails. Cartographia publishes three dozen hiking maps (average scales 1:40,000 and 1:50,000; 650/1600Ft folded/spiral-bound) to the hills, forests, rivers and lakes of Hungary. Most are available from its outlet in Budapest (see Orientation in the Budapest section).

The HNTO produces the free *The Beauty of Nature: 11,000 kms of Marked Rambling Paths*, with ideas for treks and walks around the country and an insert with practical information and tips.

Horse Riding

The Magyars say they were 'created by God to sit on horseback' and that still holds true today. But it's risky to show up at a riding centre without a booking, particularly in the high season. Book through a local tourist office or the **Hungarian Equestrian Tourism Association** (*MLTSZ*, ☎ 1-456 0444, fax 456 0445; w *www.equi.hu; IX Ráday utca 8*) in Budapest. Also in the capital, **Pegazus Tours** (☎ 1-317 1644, fax 266 2827; e *orycsilla@ pegazus.hu; V Ferenciek tere 5*) organises riding tours.

The HNTO produces a useful 64-page brochure called *Riding in Hungary* with both general and very detailed information.

LANGUAGE COURSES

Language schools teaching Hungarian to foreigners are in abundance, but they do vary tremendously in quality, approach and their success rates.

Hungarian Language School (☎ 1-351 1191, fax 351 1193; w *www.hls.hu; VI Rippl-Rónai utca 4*) is a good choice for those wanting to learn the basics.

Debrecen Summer University (*Debreceni Nyári Egyetem;* ☎/fax 52-489 117; w *www .nyariegyetem.hu; Egyetem tér 1, PO Box 35, Debrecen 4010*), in eastern Hungary, is the granddaddy of all the Hungarian language schools. It organises intensive two- and four-week courses during July and August and 80-hour, two-week advanced courses during winter. There is now a **Budapest branch** (☎/fax 1-320 5751; *Jászai Mari tér 6*) that puts on regular and intensive courses.

WORK

Travellers on tourist visas in Hungary are forbidden from taking any form of employment, but some end up teaching or even working for foreign firms without permits.

Check the English-language telephone book or ads for English schools in the *Budapest Sun*; there are also job listings but pay is generally low. You can do much better teaching privately (2000Ft to 4000Ft per hour).

Obtaining a work permit *(munkavállalási engedély)* involves a Byzantine paper chase. You'll need a letter of support from your prospective employer, copies of your birth certificate, academic record officially translated into Hungarian and results of a recent medical examination (including a test for HIV exposure). The employer then submits these to the local labour centre *(munkaügyi központ)*, and you *must* return to your country of residence and apply for the work permit (US$40) at the Hungarian embassy or consulate there.

ACCOMMODATION

Many cities and towns levy a local tourist tax of around 250Ft per person per night, though sometimes only after the first 48 hours. People under 18 years of age or staying at camping grounds may be exempt. Breakfast is usually included in the price of a hotel or hostel.

Camping

Hungary has more than 400 camping grounds. Small, private camping grounds are usually preferable to the large, noisy, 'official' sites. Prices vary widely and around Lake Balaton they can be exorbitant in summer.

Most camping grounds open from April or May to September or October and also rent small bungalows. In midsummer the bungalows may all be booked, so it check with the local Tourinform office before making the trip. A Camping Card International will sometimes get you a 10% discount. Camping 'wild' is prohibited in Hungary. Tourinform's *Camping Hungary* map/brochure lists every camping ground in the land.

Farmhouses

'Village tourism', which means staying at a farmhouse, can be cheap but most of the places are truly remote. Contact Tourinform or the **National Association of Village Tourism** *(FAOS; ☎/fax 1-268 0592; VII Király utca 93)* in Budapest for information.

Hostels & Student Dormitories

Despite all the places that are listed by the Budapest-based **Hungarian Youth Hostel Association** *(MISZSZ; ☎ 1-413 2065, fax 321 4851; ⓦ www.youthhostels.hu; VII Baross tér 15, 3rd floor)*, a hostel card isn't particularly useful as most of the associated hostels are remote, although it occasionally gets 10% off the quoted price.

There's no age limit at hostels and they stay open all day. Generally the only year-round hostels are in Budapest.

From 1 July to about 20 August, the cheapest rooms are in vacant student residences (dorm beds and sometimes private rooms too).

Private Rooms

Private rooms are usually assigned by travel agencies, which give you a voucher bearing the address and sometimes even the key to the house or flat. In Budapest, individuals at train stations approach anyone looking vaguely like a traveller and offer private rooms. Unless you find out the exact location, you're probably better off getting a room from an agency.

There's usually a 30% supplement on the first night if you stay less than four nights, and single rooms are hard to come by.

You'll probably share the house or flat with a Hungarian family. The toilet is usually communal but otherwise you can close your door and enjoy as much privacy as you please. Some places offer kitchen facilities. In Budapest and elsewhere, the distinction between the more expensive private rooms and pensions is becoming blurred.

In resort areas look for houses with signs reading *'szoba kiadó'* or the German *'Zimmer frei'* that advertise private rooms.

Pensions

Quaint, often family-run, pensions *(panziók)* are abundant across Hungary, and most towns have at least one. In Budapest they are mostly in the Buda Hills. Pensions are really just little hotels. They are usually new and clean and often have a restaurant attached.

Hotels

Hotels, called *szállók* or *szállodák*, run the gamut from luxurious five-star palaces to the run-down old communist-era hovels that still survive in some towns.

A cheap hotel will be more expensive than a private room, but it may be the answer if

HUNGARY

you're only staying one night or if you arrive too late to get a private room through an agency. Two-star hotels usually have rooms with a private bathroom; it's down the hall in a one-star place. Three- and four-star hotels, many of which are brand-new or are newly renovated old villas, can be excellent value compared with other European countries.

FOOD

Inexpensive by Western European standards and served in huge portions, traditional Hungarian food is heavy and rich. Meat, sour cream and fat abound and, except in season, *saláta* generally means a plate of pickled beets, cabbage and/or peppers. But things are improving for the health-conscious traveller, with vegetarian, 'New Hungarian' and ethnic cuisines more available (at least in Budapest).

The most famous traditional meal is *gulyás* (or *gulyásleves*), a thick beef soup cooked with onions and potatoes and usually eaten as a main course. *Pörkölt* (stew) is closer to what we call 'goulash' abroad. Pork, turkey and chicken are the most common meats and can be breaded and fried or baked.

Many dishes are seasoned with paprika, which appears on restaurant tables as a condiment beside the salt and pepper shakers. It's quite a mild spice and is used predominantly with sour cream or in *rántás*, a heavy roux of pork lard and flour added to cooked vegetables. Things stuffed *(töltött)* with meat and rice, such as cabbage or peppers, are cooked in rántás, tomato sauce or sour cream.

Another Hungarian favourite is *halászlé* (fisherman's soup), a rich mix of several kinds of poached freshwater fish, tomatoes, green peppers and paprika. Noodle dishes with cheese, such as *sztrapacska*, go well with fish.

Some dishes for vegetarians to request are *rántott sajt* (fried cheese), *gombafejek rántva* (fried mushroom caps), *gomba leves* (mushroom soup), *gyümölcs leves* (fruit soup), *sajtos kenyer* (sliced bread with soft cheese) and *túrós csusza* (Hungarian pasta with cheese). *Bableves* (bean soup) usually contains meat. *Palacsinta* (pancakes) may be savoury and made with *sajt* (cheese) or *gomba* (mushrooms) or sweet and prepared with *dió* (nuts) or *mák* (poppy seeds). *Lángos*, a deep-fried dough with various toppings, is a cheap meatless snack sold on streets throughout the land.

An *étterem* is a restaurant with a large selection. A *vendéglő* is smaller and is supposed to serve inexpensive regional dishes. An *étkezde* is even smaller, often with counter seating, while the over-used term *csárda*, originally a rustic country inn with Gypsy music, can now mean anything.

DRINKS

Wine has been produced in Hungary for thousands of years and you'll find it available by the glass or bottle everywhere. For dry whites, look for Badacsonyi Kéknyelű or Szürkebarát, Mőcsényi or Boglári Chardonnay or Debrői Hárslevelű. Olasz Rizling and Egri Leányka tend to be sweet , though nowhere near Tokaji Aszú dessert wines. Dependable reds include Villányi Merlot, Pinot Noir and Cabernet Sauvignon, Szekszárdi Kékfrankos and Nagyrédei Cabernet Franc. Celebrated Egri Bikavér (Eger Bull's Blood) is a full-bodied red high in acid and tannin. Hangover in a bottle.

A popular spirit is *pálinka*, a strong brandy distilled from a variety of fruits, but most commonly plums or apricots. Hungarian liqueurs are usually unbearably sweet and taste artificial, though the Zwack brand is reliable. Zwack also produces Unicum, a bitter aperitif that has been around since 1790.

Hungarian beers sold nationally include Dreher and Kőbanyai; others are distributed only near where they are brewed (eg, Kanizsai in Nagykanizsa and Szalon in Pécs). Bottled Austrian, German and Czech beers are readily available.

A *borozó* is a place (usually a dive) serving wine, a *pince* is a beer or wine cellar, while a *söröző* is a pub that offers *csapolt sör* (draught beer).

ENTERTAINMENT

Hungary is a paradise for culture vultures. In Budapest there are several musical events every night and excellent opera tickets cost between 600Ft and 7000Ft. Besides traditional opera, operetta and classical concerts, there are rock and jazz concerts, folk dancing, pantomime, puppet shows, movies in English, discos, floor shows and circuses to keep you entertained.

Excellent cultural performances can also be seen in provincial towns like Eger, Győr, Kecskemét, Pécs, Veszprém, Szombathely adn Szeged all of which have fine theatres. Information about events is readily available at Tourinform offices, in the monthly *Programme in Ungarn/in Hungary* and the *Pesti*

Est listings magazines available at the Tourinform offices and entertainment venues everywhere. The free *Pesti Est* listings magazine for Budapest publishes editions to almost 18 other cities and regions – from *Békés Est* to *Zalai Est*. You can pick them up for free in the tourist offices and at entertainment venues throughout the country. Some useful words to remember are *színház* (theatre), *pénztár* (box office), *jegy* (ticket) and *elkelt* (sold out).

In mid-June many theatres close for the summer holidays, reopening in late September or October. Summer opera, operetta and concert programmes specially designed for tourists are more expensive than the normal productions the rest of the year.

Be aware that many foreign films are dubbed into Hungarian, so try asking the ticket seller if the film retains the original soundtrack and has Hungarian subtitles *(feliratos)* or is dubbed *(szinkronizált* or *magyarul beszélő)*.

SHOPPING

Books and folk-music tapes and CDs are affordable, and there is an excellent selection. Traditional products include folk-art embroidery and ceramics, wall hangings, painted wooden toys and boxes, dolls, all forms of basketry and porcelain (especially Herend, Zsolnay or the cheaper Kalocsa). Feather or goose-down pillows and duvets (comforters) are of exceptionally high quality.

Foodstuffs that are expensive or difficult to buy elsewhere – goose liver (both fresh and potted), caviar and some prepared meats like Pick salami – make nice gifts (if you are allowed to take them home), as do the many varieties of paprika. Some of Hungary's 'boutique' wines – especially those that have imaginative labels – make good, inexpensive gifts. A bottle of dessert Tokay always goes down well.

Getting There & Away

AIR

Budapest's **Ferihegy airport** (☎ *1-296 9696)*, 24km southeast of the city centre, has two modern terminals side by side. Terminal 2A is reserved for the national carrier, **Malév Hungarian Airlines** (Ⓦ *www.malev.hu)*, and its code-share partners. Terminal 2B handles all other foreign airlines. For flight information at Terminal 2A, ring ☎ 1-296 7000 for departures or ☎ 1-296 8000 for arrivals. For Terminal 2B, ring ☎ 1-296 5882 (departures) or ☎ 1-296 5052 (arrivals).

Malév flies nonstop to Ferihegy from North America, the Middle East and many cities in Continental Europe and the British Isles. It has links to Asia and Australia via its European gateways. The airline has ticketing desks at Terminal 2A (☎ 1-296 7211) and at Terminal 2B (☎ 1-296 5767).

Malév doesn't offer student discounts on flights originating in Hungary, but youth fares are available to people aged under 26 (in summer only). These might not always be cheaper than a discounted ticket, however. Some sample return air fares to other cities in Eastern Europe include: Moscow (75,000Ft), Warsaw (63,000Ft) and Prague (63,000Ft).

LAND

Hungary has excellent land transport connections with its seven neighbours. Most of the departures are from Budapest, though other cities and towns closer to the various borders can also be used as springboards.

Bus

Most international buses are run by **Eurolines** (☎ *1-219 8080, 219 8000)* or its Hungarian associate, **Volánbusz** (☎ *1-485 2162, 485 2100;* ☎ *www.volanbusz.hu)*. The Eurolines passes include Budapest. For more information on these bus passes see the introductory Getting There & Away chapter.

Some Eurolines services between Budapest and Western Europe, with high-season (mid-June to mid-September) one-way fares quoted, include the following:

Amsterdam: 25,900Ft; 19 hours (1435km) via Frankfurt (21,900Ft) and Düsseldorf (23,500Ft), continuing on to Rotterdam (25,900Ft); four days a week year-round, six or seven weekly from early June to late September

Berlin: 19,900Ft; 15 hours (915km) via Prague (8900Ft), then continuing on to Hamburg (22,900Ft); three days a week year-round, five weekly from early June to late October

London: 33,900Ft; 26 hours (1755km) via Vienna (6390Ft) and Brussels (22,900Ft); four days a week year-round, five to seven weekly from early June to late October

Paris: 27,900Ft; 22 hours (1525km) via Strasbourg (25,900Ft) and Reims (27,900Ft); two to three days a week from April to late October

HUNGARY

Rome: 23,500Ft; 15 hours (1330km) via Bologna (16,900Ft) and Florence (18,900Ft), continuing on to Naples (25,500Ft) four days a week year-round, five to six weekly from early April to late October to Rome; two days a week year-round to Naples

Vienna: 6390Ft; 3½ hours (254km) via Győr (4400Ft); three buses daily (four on Saturday)

To Romania, there are regularly scheduled buses on Saturday year-round to Arad (4000Ft, seven hours, 282km) and Timişoara (Hungarian: Temesvár; 4900Ft, eight hours).

Other useful international buses include those to: Bratislava (Pozsony; 3100Ft, four hours, 213km, daily year-round) in Slovakia; Prague (8900Ft, eight hours, 535km, three days a week year-round, five weekly from early June to late September) in the Czech Republic; Belgrade (4100Ft, nine hours, 422km, daily year-round) via Subotica (Szabatka; 3300Ft, four hours, 227km) in Yugoslavia; Pula (9900Ft, 14½ hours, 775km, Friday from late June to early September) via Rijeka (7900Ft, 10 hours, 546km) in Croatia; and Kraków (6900Ft, 10 hours, Saturday year-round) via Zakopane (5600Ft, 8½ hours, 387km) in Poland.

Train

Magyar Államvasutak (ⓦ *www.mav.hu*), which translates as Hungarian State Railways and is known as MÁV, links up with the European rail network in all directions, running trains as far as London (via Cologne and Brussels), Paris (via Frankfurt), Stockholm (via Hamburg and Copenhagen), Moscow, Rome and Istanbul (via Belgrade).

In Budapest, most international trains arrive at and depart from **Keleti station** *(Eastern; ☎ 1-313 6835; VIII Kerepesi út 2-4)*; trains to some places in Romania and Germany leave from **Nyugati station** *(Western; ☎ 1-349 0115; VI Nyugati tér)*, while **Déli station** *(Southern; ☎ 1-355 8657; I Krisztina körút 37/a)* handles trains to/from Zagreb and Rijeka in Croatia. But these are not hard-and-fast rules, so *always* check from which station the train leaves when you buy a ticket. For 24-hour information on the international train services call ☎ 1-461 5500 in Budapest. For the domestic schedules, ring ☎ 1-461 5400.

Tickets & Discounts To avoid confusion, specify your train by the name listed under the following destinations or on the posted schedule when seeking information or buying a ticket. You can buy tickets at the three international train stations in Budapest, but it's easier at MÁV's central ticket office in Budapest (see Getting There & Away in that section).

There are big discounts on return fares only between Hungary and former communist countries: 30% to Bulgaria, the Czech Republic and Poland; 40% to Yugoslavia and the Baltic countries; 50% to Belarus, Russia and Ukraine; up to 65% to Slovakia and Slovenia; and up to 75% to Romania.

For tickets to Western Europe you'll pay the same as everywhere else unless you're aged under 26 and qualify for the 30% to 50% BIJ discount. Ask at MÁV, Express or the Wasteels office (☎ 1-210 2802) in Keleti Station in Budapest

The following are minimum return, 2nd-class fares from Budapest: Amsterdam €212; Berlin €126 (via Prague) and €198 (via Vienna); London €352; Munich €91; Rome (via Ljubljana) €172; and Vienna €41. Three daily EuroCity (EC) trains to Vienna and points beyond charge a supplement of 1000Ft to 1500Ft. The 1st-class seats are usually 50% more expensive than 2nd class. Costs for sleepers depend on the destination, and how many beds are in the carriage.

International seat reservation costs vary according to the destination (eg, €6.60 to Prague, €10.60 to Warsaw). Fines are levied on passengers without tickets or seat reservations on trains where they are mandatory. Tickets are valid for 60 days from the date of purchase, and stopovers are permitted.

MÁV sells Inter-Rail passes from one to eight zones to European nationals (or residents of at least six months). The price for any one zone is €226/158/113 for adult/youth 12 to 26/child four to 12. Hungary is in Zone D along with the Czech Republic, Slovakia, Poland and Croatia. Multizone passes are better value and are valid for one month: two zones cost €296/211/148 and three zones €336/239/168. All eight zones (a 'Global' pass) cost €398/281/199. Eurail passes are valid but not sold in Hungary.

Western Europe Seven trains a day link Vienna and Budapest (three hours, 273km) via Hegyeshalom and Győr. Most depart from Vienna's Westbahnhof, including the *Arrabona*, the EuroCity *Bartók Béla* and the EuroNight *Kálmán Imre* from Munich (7½ hours, 742km)

via Salzburg (six hours, 589km); the EC *Liszt Ferenc* from Cologne (11 hours, 1247km) via Frankfurt (10 hours, 1026km); the *Dacia Express* to Bucharest (15½ hours, 874km); and the InterCity *Avala* to Belgrade (10 hours, 647km). The early morning EC *Lehár* departs from Vienna's Südbahnhof. None requires a seat reservation, though they're highly recommended in summer.

Up to nine trains leave Vienna's Südbahnhof every day for Sopron (75 minutes, 76km) via Ebenfurt; as many as 10 a day also serve Sopron from Wiener Neustadt (easily accessible from Vienna). Some five milk trains daily make the four-hour, 136km trip from Graz to Szombathely.

The EC *Hungária* travels from Berlin (Zoo and Ostbahnhof stations) to Budapest (12½ hours, 1002km) via Dresden, Prague and Bratislava. The express *Spree-Donau Kurier* arrives from Berlin via Nuremberg.

Czech Republic, Slovakia & Poland In addition to being served by the EC *Hungária*, Prague (seven hours, 611km) can be reached from Budapest on the EC *Comenius*, the IC *Csárdás*, the *Slovan* and the *Pannónia Express*, which then carries on to Bucharest. The *Amicus* runs directly to/from Bratislava (three hours, 215km) every day.

Each day the EC *Polonia* and the *Báthory* head for Warsaw from Budapest (12 hours, 802km) passing through Katowice and either Bratislava or Štúrovo. The *Cracovia* runs to Kraków (10½ hours, 598km) via Košice. From Miskolc in northern Hungary, you can pick up the *Karpaty* to Warsaw via Kraków and Košice.

Another train, the *Rákóczi*, links Budapest with Košice and Bratislava. The *Bem* connects Budapest with Szczecin (17 hours, 1019km) in northwestern Poland via Wrocław and Poznań.

Three local trains a day cover the 90km from Miskolc to Košice (two hours). The 2km journey from Sátoraljaújhely to Slovenské Nové Mesto (two a day) is only a four-minute ride by train.

Romania To Bucharest there are six trains: the EC *Traianus*, the *Dacia Express*, the *Ovidius*, the EN *Ister*, the *Muntenia* and the *Pannonia*. All go via Arad (5½ hours, 253km) and some require seat reservations. The *Karpaty* goes to Bucharest from Miskolc.

There are two daily connections to Cluj-Napoca (eight hours, 402km) via Oradea: the *Ady Endre* and the *Corona*. The *Partium* only goes as far as Oradea. All three trains require a seat reservation.

Two local trains a day link Budapest with Baia Mare (8¾ hours, 285km) in northern Romania via Satu Mare and Debrecen.

Bulgaria & Yugoslavia The *Transbalkan* links Budapest with Sofia (25 hours, 1366km) via Bucharest, before continuing on to Thessaloniki in Greece. Trains between Budapest and Belgrade (seven hours, 374km) via Subotica include the *Beograd*, the *Ivo Andri* and the IC *Avala*.

You must reserve your seats on some of these trains.

Two local trains a day make the 1¾-hour, 45km journey between Szeged and Subotica.

Croatia, Bosnia-Hercegovina & Slovenia You get to Zagreb (seven hours, 386km) on two trains that go via Siófok on Lake Balaton's southern shore: the *Maestral*, which ends in Split; and the *Venezia Express*, which carries on to Ljubljana (10 hours, 504km) and Venice. Two other trains to Ljubljana are the IC *Citadella* and the IC *Dráva*, which continues on to Venice. The IC *Kvarner* links Budapest with Rijeka (nine hours, 591km) via Siófok on Lake Balaton and Zagreb. The no-name train linking Budapest and Sarajevo (616km) via Pécs takes 14 hours.

Ukraine & Russia To Moscow (42 hours, 2106km) there's only the *Tisza Express*, which travels via Kyiv and Lviv in Ukraine.

Car & Motorcycle

Of the 50-odd international border crossings Hungary maintains with its neighbours, some 20 (mostly in the north and northeast) are restricted to local citizens on both sides of the border, though some allow EU citizens to cross as well.

For the latest list of border crossings check out **w** www.hungarytourism.hu, the website of Tourinform.

Walking & Cycling

Many border guards frown on walking across borders, particularly in Romania, Yugoslavia and Ukraine; in those places, try hitching a ride instead. Cyclists may have a problem crossing at Hungarian border stations connected to main roads since bicycles are banned on motorways and national highways with single-digit route numbers.

If you're heading north, there are three crossings to and from Slovakia where you should not have any problems. Bridges link Esztergom with Štúrovo and Komárom with Komárno. At Sátoraljaújhely, northeast of Miskolc, there's a highway border crossing over the Ronyva River which links the centre of town with Slovenské Nové Mesto.

RIVER
A Danube hydrofoil service between Budapest and Vienna (5½ hours, 282km), with the possibility of disembarking at Bratislava (on request), runs daily between April and early November, with an extra sailing in August. Adult one-way/return fares for Vienna are €65/89 and for Bratislava €59/83. Students with ISIC cards pay €51/75, and children under six go free. A bicycle is €16 each way.

In Budapest, ferries arrive and depart from the International Ferry Pier (Nemzetközi hajóállomás) on V Belgrád rakpart, between Erzsébet and Szabadság Bridges on the Pest side. In Vienna, the boat docks at the Reichsbrücke pier near Mexikoplatz.

For detailed information and tickets, contact **Mahart PassNave** (☎ 1-484 4013; ⓦ www .maharttours.com) at the Belgrád rakpart in Budapest and **Mahart PassNave Wien** (☎ 01-72 92 161, 72 92 162; Handelskai 265/3/ 517) in Vienna.

DEPARTURE TAX
An air passenger duty of between 8000Ft and 10,000Ft is levied on all airline tickets issued in Hungary. The one exception is JFK airport in New York, which attracts a tax of 20,000Ft. The tax is usually included in the quoted fare.

Getting Around

AIR
There are no scheduled flights within Hungary. Domestic air taxis is a possibility but the cost is prohibitive – eg, 150,000Ft from Budapest to Szeged and back (you must pay the return) for up to three people – and the trips can take almost as long as an express train when you add the time required to get to/from the airports.

BUS
Volán buses are a good alternative to trains, and fares are only slightly more than comparable 2nd-class train fares. Bus fares average 994/1992/2974Ft per 100/200/300km.

In southern Transdanubia or parts of the Great Plain, buses are essential unless you are prepared to make several time-consuming changes on the train. For short trips in the Danube Bend or Lake Balaton areas, buses are also recommended. Tickets are usually available from the driver, but ask at the station to be sure. There are sometimes queues for intercity buses so it's probably wise to arrive early.

Timetables are posted at stations and stops. Some footnotes you could come across include *naponta* (daily), *hétköznap* (weekdays), *munkanapokon* (on work days), *munkaszüneti napok kivételével naponta* (daily except holidays), *szabadnap kivételével naponta* (daily except Saturday), *szabad és munkaszüneti napokon* (on Saturday and holidays), *munkaszüneti napokon* (on holidays), *iskolai napokon* (on school days) and *szabadnap* (on Saturday). Check carefully before buying.

A few large bus stations have left-luggage rooms, but they generally close by 6pm.

TRAIN
MÁV operates reliable, comfortable and not overcrowded train services on its 8000km of track, much of which converges in Budapest. For details on buying tickets, see that section under Budapest – Getting There & Away.

Second-class train fares are 302/732/1482/ 2390Ft for 50/100/200/400km. First class is 50% more. If you buy your ticket on the train rather than in the station, there's a 500Ft surcharge (1500Ft on InterCity trains). Seat reservations may be compulsory (indicated on the timetable by an 'R' in a box), mandatory on trains departing from Budapest (an 'R' in a circle) or simply available (just a plain 'R').

There are several types of train. The InterCity Express (ICE) and InterCityRapid (ICR) trains levy a supplement of 250Ft to 400Ft, which includes a seat. IC trains stop at main centres only and are the fastest and most comfortable trains. *Gyorsvonat* (fast trains) and *sebesvonat* (swift trains), indicated on the timetable by boldface type, a thicker route line and/or an 'S', often require a seat reservation (110Ft). *Személyvonat* (passenger trains) are the real milk runs and stop at every city, town, village and hamlet along the way.

If you plan to do a lot of travelling by train, get yourself a copy of MÁV's official timetable *(Menetrend)* to help with planning. It is available at most large stations and at the MÁV ticket office in Budapest for 650/1350Ft in small or large format.

In all stations a yellow board indicates departures *(indul)* and a white board arrivals *(érkezik)*. Express and fast trains are indicated in red, local trains in black. In some stations, large black-and-white schedules are plastered all over the walls. To locate the table you need, first find the posted railway map of the country, which indexes the route numbers at the top of the schedules.

All train stations have left-luggage offices (150Ft to 200Ft per item per day), some of which stay open 24 hours a day.

The following are distances and approximate times to provincial cities from Budapest (usually via express trains).

destination	duration	distance
Transdanubia		
Győr	1¾ hours	131km
Sopron	3 hours	216km
Szombathely	3½ hours	236km
Pécs	3 hours	228km
Danube Bend		
Esztergom	1½ hours	53km
Szentendre	40 minutes	20km
(HÉV commuter line)		
Vác	1½ hours	49km
Lake Balaton Area		
Siófok	1½ hours	115km
Balatonfüred	2 hours	132km
Veszprém	1¾ hours	112km
Székesfehérvár	50 minutes	67km
Great Plain		
Szolnok	1¼ hours	100km
Kecskemét	1½ hours	106km
Debrecen	3 hours	221km
Békéscsaba	2½ hours	196km
Szeged	2½ hours	191km
Northern Hungary		
Nyíregyháza	4 hours	270km
Eger	2 hours	143km
Miskolc	2¼ hours	183km
Sátoraljaújhely	3½ hours	267km

CAR & MOTORCYCLE

Motorways, preceded by an 'M', link Budapest with Lake Balaton and Vienna via Győr. They also run part of the way to Miskolc and Szeged and along the eastern bank of the Danube Bend. National highways are numbered by a single digit and fan out mostly from Budapest. Secondary and tertiary roads have two or three digits.

You must obtain a motorway pass to access the M1 and M3 (1500Ft for nine days). Passes are available at petrol stations, post offices and some motorway entrances and border crossings. The M5 is a toll road (400Ft to 1820Ft).

Petrol *(benzin)* of 91 and unleaded *(ólommentes)* 95 and 98 octane is available all over the country and costs 219/222/231Ft per litre respectively. Most stations also have diesel fuel *(gázolaj)* costing 203Ft. Payment by credit card is now possible.

Third-party insurance is compulsory. If your car is registered in the EU, it's assumed you have it. Other motorists must show a Green Card or will have to buy insurance at the border.

The so-called 'Yellow Angels' of the Hungarian Automobile Club do basic breakdown repairs for free if you belong to an affiliated organisation such as AAA in the USA or AA in the UK. You can telephone 24 hours a day on ☎ 188 nationwide.

Many cities and towns require that you 'pay and display' when parking. The cost averages about 100Ft an hour in the countryside, and up to 180Ft on central Budapest streets.

Road Rules

You must drive on the right. The use of seat belts in the front (and in the back, if fitted) is compulsory in Hungary, but this is often ignored. Motorcyclists must wear helmets.

Speed limits are strictly enforced: 50km/h in built-up areas, 80km/h on secondary and tertiary roads, 100km/h on highways and 120km/h on motorways. Exceeding the limit can earn you a fine of between 5000Ft and 30,000Ft.

All vehicles must have their headlights switched on throughout the day outside built-up areas. Motorcyclists must illuminate them at all times. Using a mobile phone while driving is prohibited in Hungary.

There is virtually a 100% ban on alcohol when you are driving, and this rule is *very* strictly enforced. Do not think you will get

HUNGARY

away with even one glass of wine at lunch; if caught with any – 0.001%! – alcohol in the blood, you will be fined up to 30,000Ft. If the level is high, you will be arrested and your licence almost certainly taken away.

Rental

In general, you must be at least 21 years old and have had your licence for at least a year to rent a car. Drivers under 25 sometimes have to pay a surcharge. All the big international firms have offices in Budapest, and there are scores of local companies throughout the country, but don't expect too many bargains. For more details, see Getting There & Away in the Budapest section.

HITCHING

Hitching is never entirely safe in any country in the world, and we don't recommend it. Travellers who decide to hitch are taking a small but potentially serious risk. Hitchhiking is, however, legal in Hungary except on the motorways. A service in Budapest matches drivers and passengers – see the Budapest Getting There & Away section for details.

BOAT

In summer there are regular passenger ferries on Lake Balaton and on the Danube from Budapest to Szentendre, Visegrád and Esztergom. Details of the schedules are given in the relevant destination sections.

LOCAL TRANSPORT

Public transport is efficient and cheap, with city bus and, in many towns, trolleybus services. Four cities, including Budapest and Szeged, also have trams, and there's an extensive metro (underground or subway) and a suburban commuter railway in Budapest. You must purchase tickets for all these at newsstands or ticket windows beforehand and validate them once aboard. Inspectors are everywhere.

Taxi

Taxis are plentiful and, if you are charged the correct fare, very reasonably priced. Flag fall varies, but a fair rate is 150Ft to 200Ft, with the charge per kilometre about the same, depending on whether you book by telephone (cheaper) or hail a cab on the street. The best places to find taxis are in ranks at bus and train stations, near markets and around main

squares. But you can flag down cruising taxis anywhere at any time. At night, vacant taxis have an illuminated sign on the roof.

In Budapest, and in touristy places outside the capital, it is not uncommon for taxi drivers to try to rip foreigners off. See Getting Around in the Budapest section for tips on how to avoid this.

Budapest

☎ 1 • pop 1.8 million

There's no other city in Hungary like Budapest. Home to almost a fifth of the national population, the *főváros* (capital) is also the country's administrative, business and cultural centre. For better or for worse, virtually everything in Hungary starts, finishes or is taking place in Budapest.

But it is the beauty of the city that makes it stand apart. More romantic than Warsaw and more cosmopolitan than Prague, Budapest straddles a gentle curve in the Danube, with the Buda Hills to the west and the start of the Great Plain to the east. Architecturally, it is a gem. Add to this parks brimming with attractions, museums filled with treasures, boats sailing upriver to the scenic Danube Bend and the Turkish-era thermal baths and you have one of Europe's most delightful cities to visit.

Strictly speaking, the story of Budapest begins only in 1873 when hilly, residential Buda and historic Óbuda (the oldest part of Buda) on the west bank of the Danube merged with flat, industrial Pest on the eastern side to form what was at first called Pest-Buda. But a lot of water had flowed under the Danube bridges by that time. The Romans built the settlement of Aquincum here, the Turks arrived uninvited and stayed for 150 years, the Austrians did the same and hung around for even longer. Today it is the increasingly sophisticated capital of a proud and independent republic that makes its own decisions and policies.

People come to Budapest for all sorts of reasons. Russians and Asians come here to make money or to get a taste of the West; Westerners revel in the affordable nightlife, theatres, museums, restaurants, cafés and bathhouses. Whatever your motives, there's no doubt that the 'Queen of the Danube' will be among the highlights of your travels around Eastern Europe.

ORIENTATION

Budapest is a well laid-out city and it is almost difficult to get lost. The Danube (Duna), the city's traditional artery, is spanned by nine bridges that link hilly, historic Buda with bustling, commercial and very flat Pest.

Two ring roads – the big one (Nagykörút) and the semicircular Kiskörút (little ring road) – link three of the bridges across the Danube and essentially define central Pest. Important boulevards such as Rákóczi út and leafy Andrássy út fan out from these, creating large squares and circles. The most central square in Pest is Deák tér. Buda is dominated by Castle and Gellért Hills; the main square is Moszkva tér.

Budapest is divided into 23 kerület (districts). The Roman numeral appearing before each street address signifies the district.

Maps

Lonely Planet's Budapest City Map covers the more popular parts of town in detail.

The best folding maps to the city are Cartographia's 1:20,000 (550Ft) and 1:28,000 (450Ft) Budapest ones. If you plan to see the city thoroughly, the Budapest Atlas, also from Cartographia, is indispensable. It comes in two scales: the pocket-size 1:25,000 (1900Ft) and the larger format 1:20,000 (2900Ft).

Many bookshops, including Libri Könyvpalota (see Bookshops later), stock a wide variety of maps, or go directly to Cartographia (☎ 312 6001; VI Bajcsy-Zsilinszky út 37; open 9am-5pm Mon-Wed, 9am-6.30pm Thur, 9am-3.30pm Fri).

INFORMATION
Tourist Offices

The best source of information about Budapest is Tourinform (☎ 438 8080, fax 356 1964; W www.hungarytourism.hu; V Vigadó utca 6; open 24hr). It has a nearby branch (Sütő utca 2; open 8am-8pm daily) and a 24-hour information hotline (☎ 06-80 66 0044).

See Travel Agencies later for details on other outfits that can book accommodation and transport and change money.

Discount Cards

The Budapest Card (☎ 266 0479; W www .budapestinfo.hu) offers free admission to most museums and galleries in town and unlimited travel on all forms of public transport. It also gives discounts on organised tours, at

thermal baths and at selected shops and restaurants. A 48-/72-hour card costs 3700/ 4500Ft. The card is sold at Tourinform offices and travel agencies, hotels and train, bus and main metro stations.

Also worth considering is the Hungary Card (see Discount Cards under Planning in the Facts for the Visitor section).

Money

OTP bank (V Nádor utca 6; open 7.45am-5pm Mon, 7.45am-4pm Tues-Fri) has among the best exchange rates for cash and travellers cheques, but be sure to get there at least an hour before closing time to ensure the bureau de change counter is still open. K&H (V Váci utca 40; open 8am-5pm Mon, 8am-4pm Tues-Thur, 8am-3pm Fri) often offers good rates too.

There are ATMs all around the city, including in the train and bus stations, and quite a few foreign-currency exchange machines too, including ones at V Károly körút 20 and V Váci utca 40. In touristed areas private exchange offices such as Interchange are abundant, but they always give very poor rates.

American Express (☎ 235 4330; V Deák Ferenc utca 10; open 9am-5.30pm Mon-Fri, 9am-2pm Sat) changes its own travellers cheques without commission, but its rates are poor. Its commission on converting US dollar travellers cheques into cash dollars is 7%.

Tribus (see Private Rooms under Places to Stay later) is handy if you arrive late at night and need to change money.

Post & Communications

The main post office (V Petőfi Sándor utca 13-15 or V Városház utca 18; open 8am-8pm Mon-Fri, 8am-2pm Sat) is just a few minutes' walk from Deák tér and the Tourinform branch office. This is where you can pick up poste-restante mail.

The best place to make international phone calls is from a phone box with a phonecard. The phone boxes just inside the front door of the post office are relatively quiet.

Email & Internet Access

Internet cafés abound in Budapest.

Ami Internet Coffee (☎ 267 1644; W www .amicoffee.hu; V Váci utca 40; open 9am-2am daily) is very central and has 50 terminals. The costs are 200/400/700Ft for 15/30/60 minutes; five/10 hours cost 3250/6400Ft.

HUNGARY

BUDAPEST

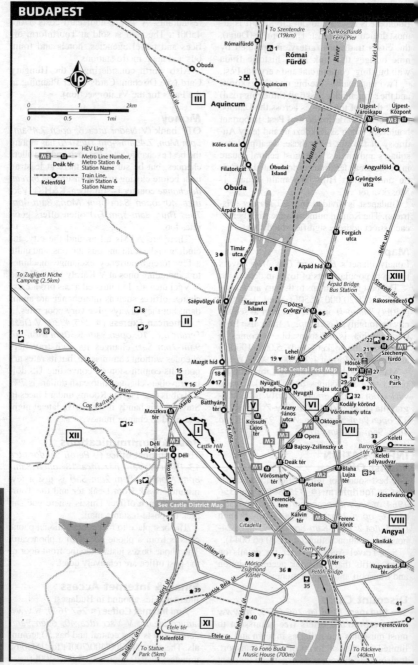

To Szentendre (19km)

Rómaifürdő

Pünkösdfürdő
Ferry Pier

Római
Fürdő

Óbuda

Aquincum

III Aquincum

Újpest-
Városkapu

Újpest-
Központ

Újpest

Köles utca

Filatorigát

Óbudai
Island

Óbuda

Angyalföld

Gyöngyösi
utca

Árpád híd

Forgách
utca

Tímár
utca

Árpád híd

Árpád Bridge
Bus Station

Rákosrendező

XIII

Szépvölgyi út

Margaret
Island

Dózsa
György út

Szilágyi Erzsébet fasor

To Zugligeti Niche
Camping (2.5km)

II

Lehel
utca

Széchenyi
fürdő

Lehel
tér

Hősök
tere

City
Park

Margit híd

Margit körút

Nyugati
pályaudvar

Nyugati

Bajza utca

Cog Railway

Moszkva
tér

Batthyány
tér

Arany
János
utca

Kodály körönd

Vörösmarty utca

VI

Déli
pályaudvar

Déli

I

Castle Hill

Kossuth
Lajos
tér

Oktogon

VII

Keleti

Opera

Bajcsy-Zsilinszky út

Keleti
pályaudvar

XII

Deák tér

Vörösmarty
tér

Blaha
Lujza
tér

Astoria

Józsefváros

Ferenciek
tere

Kálvin
tér

Citadella

Ferenc
körút

VIII

Móricz
Zsigmond
Körtér

Ferry Pier

Boráros
tér

Petőfi Bridge

Nagyvárad
tér

Angyal

Klinikák

Budafoki út

Bartók Béla út

Fehérvári út

XI

Etele tér

Kelenföld

Etele út

Ferencváros

To Statue
Park (5km)

To Fonó Buda
Music House (700m)

To Ráckeve
(40km)

See Central Pest Map

See Castle District Map

HUNGARY

Legend

HÉV Line

M3 M Metro Line Number,
Metro Station &
Station Name
Deák tér

Kelenföld Train Line,
Train Station &
Station Name

0   1   2km
0   0.5   1mi

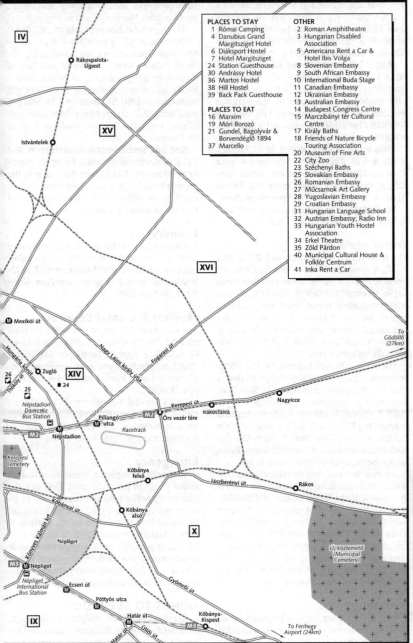

BUDAPEST

PLACES TO STAY
1 Római Camping
4 Danubius Grand Margitsziget Hotel
6 Diáksport Hostel
7 Hotel Margitsziget
24 Station Guesthouse
30 Andrássy Hotel
36 Martos Hostel
38 Hill Hostel
39 Back Pack Guesthouse

PLACES TO EAT
16 Marxim
19 Móri Borozó
21 Gundel, Bagolyvár & Borvendéglő 1894
37 Marcello

OTHER
2 Roman Amphitheatre
3 Hungarian Disabled Association
5 Americana Rent a Car & Hotel Ibis Volga
8 Slovenian Embassy
9 South African Embassy
10 International Buda Stage
11 Canadian Embassy
12 Ukrainian Embassy
13 Australian Embassy
14 Budapest Congress Centre
15 Marczibányi tér Cultural Centre
17 Király Baths
18 Friends of Nature Bicycle Touring Association
20 Museum of Fine Arts
22 City Zoo
23 Széchenyi Baths
25 Slovakian Embassy
26 Romanian Embassy
27 Műcsarnok Art Gallery
28 Yugoslavian Embassy
29 Croatian Embassy
31 Hungarian Language School
32 Austrian Embassy; Radio Inn
33 Hungarian Youth Hostel Association
34 Erkel Theatre
35 Zöld Párdon
40 Municipal Cultural House & Folklór Centrum
41 Inka Rent a Car

IV

Rákospalota-Újpest

XV

Istvántelek

XVI

Mexikói út

Hungária körút

Zugló

Thököly út

XIV

★ 24

Nagy Lajos király útja

Fogarasi út

To Gödöllő (27km)

Népstadion Domestic Bus Station

Népstadion

Pillangó utca

Kerepesi út

Rákoskava

Nagyicce

Órs vezér tére

Racetrack

Kerepesi Cemetery

Köbánya felső

Jászberényi út

Rákos

Köbányai út

Köbánya alsó

X

Könyves Kálmán krt

Népliget

Népliget

Népliget International Bus Station

Ecseri út

Gyömrői út

Új köztemető (Municipal Cemetery)

IX

Pöttyös utca

Határ út

Köbánya-Kispest

Határ út

Üllői út

To Ferihegy Airport (24km)

HUNGARY

Budapest Net (☎ 328 0292, fax 328 0294; e info@budapestnet.hu; V Kecskeméti utca 5; open 10am-10pm daily) attracts students from ELTE university nearby. With over 50 terminals, it charges 150/350/700Ft for 10/30/60 minutes and 2400/4600Ft for five/10 hours.

Matáv Telepont Internet Kávézó (☎ 485 6612; V Petőfi Sándor utca 17-19; open 9am-8pm Mon-Fri, 10pm-3pm Sat) is a smallish café (eight terminals) run by the national telecommunications company. The rates are 300/500Ft for 30/60 minutes. A 10-hour pass is 4000Ft.

Vista Internet Café (☎ 429 9950, fax 429 9951; e icafe@vista.hu; VI Paulay Ede utca 7; open 10am-10pm Mon-Fri, 10am-8pm Sat), at the Vista Visitor Center (see Travel Agencies), charges 11/660Ft per minute/hour.

Most of the year-round hostels (see Places to Stay later) offer Internet access.

Travel Agencies

The main office of **Ibusz** (☎ 485 2723, 485 2767; w www.ibusz.hu; V Ferenciek tere 10; open 8.15am-5.30pm Mon-Fri, 9am-1pm Sat in summer; 8.15am-4.30pm Mon-Fri in winter) supplies travel brochures, changes money, books all types of accommodation and accepts credit-card payments. Its nearby branch (☎ 322 7214; VII Dob utca 1) is good for booking train tickets.

The main office of **Express** (☎ 317 8600; w www.extress-travel.hu; V Semmelweiss utca 1-3; open 8am-6pm Mon-Fri, 9am-1pm Sat) books accommodation in Budapest, especially hostels and colleges; while the **Express branch** (☎ 311 6418; V Zoltán utca 10; open 8.30am-4.30pm Mon-Thur, 8.30am-4pm Fri) books international and domestic trains, Eurolines buses and sells cheap airline tickets.

An excellent one-stop shop for all your outbound needs (air tickets, package tours etc) is the massive **Vista Travel Center** (☎ 429 9760; w www.vista.hu; VI Andrássy út 1; open 9am-6.30pm Mon-Fri, 9am-2.30pm Sat). The **Vista Visitor Center** (☎ 429 9950; VI Paulay Ede utca 7; open 9am-8pm Mon-Fri, 10am-6pm Sat) handles tourist information, room bookings and organised tours. There's a popular café and Internet centre here too.

Bookshops

Top of the pops for English-language bookshops in Budapest is the recently expanded **Bestsellers** (☎ 312 1295; V Október 6 utca 11; open 9am-6.30pm Mon-Fri, 10am-5pm Sat, 10am-4pm Sun), with novels, magazines, travel guides, Hungarica and newspapers.

The huge **Libri Könyvpalota** (☎ 267 4844; VII Rákóczi út 12; open 10am-7.30pm Mon-Fri, 10am-3pm Sat), on two floors, really is a 'book palace' with a wonderful selection of English-language novels, art books, guidebooks and maps on the 1st floor. Try the more central **Libri Studium** (☎ 318 5680; V Váci utca 22; open 10am-7pm Mon-Fri, 10am-3pm Sat & Sun) for books in English on Hungarian subjects.

Red Bus Second-hand Bookstore (☎ 337 7453; V Semmelweiss utca 14; open 10am-6pm Mon-Fri, 10am-3pm Sat), below the popular hostel of that name (see Places to Stay later), is the only shop in town selling used English-language books.

Laundry

If your hostel or hotel does not have laundry facilities, about the only self-service laundrette in the city is **Irisz Szalon** (☎ 317 2092; V Városház utca 3-5; open 7am-7pm Mon-Fri, 7am-1pm Sat).

Medical & Dental Services

The **American Clinics** (☎ 224 9090; I Hattyú utca 14, 5th floor; open 8.30am-7pm Mon-Thur, 8.30am-6pm Fri, 8am-noon Sat, 10am-2pm Sun) can help you in an emergency but it's not cheap: a basic consultation will cost you 28,600Ft.

S.O.S Dental Service (☎ 267 9602; VI Király utca 14; open 24hr) charges 2000Ft for a consultation, 5000Ft to 6000Ft for extractions and from 6000Ft for fillings.

Emergency

If you need to report a crime or a lost or stolen passport or credit card, first call the emergency police help number at ☎ 107 or go to the police station of the district you're in. In central Pest that would be the **District V Police Station** (☎ 302 5935; V Szalay utca 11-13). If possible, ask a Hungarian speaker to accompany you. In the high season, police officers pair up with university students, who act as translators, and patrol the busiest areas.

THINGS TO SEE & DO

If you plan to visit lots of sights in a few days, consider buying the Budapest Card (see Discount Cards under Information earlier).

When your head begins to spin from all the museums, take a walk (or bus No 26 from Nyugati train station) over to **Margaret Island**, which is in the Danube between Buda and Pest, or to the **City Park** at the top of Andrássy út and accessible on the little yellow metro line (M1). Both of these 'green lungs' offer any number of sights and recreational facilities – from bicycle rentals, the ruins of two medieval monasteries and Olympic-size swimming pools on the island to the sprawling Széchenyi Baths (see the Thermal Baths section later), the **City Zoo** (☎ 363 3797; XIV Állatkerti körút; adult/child/student/family 900/650/750/2800Ft; open 9am-4pm daily Nov-Feb, 9am-5pm March & Oct, 9am-6pm Apr-Sept) and still more museums in the park.

Buda

Most of what remains of medieval Budapest is on **Castle Hill** (Várhegy) perched above the Danube and now on Unesco's list of World Heritage Sites. The easiest way to get there from Pest is to stroll across Chain Bridge and board the **funicular railway** (uphill/downhill ticket adult 450/250Ft, child 2-10 350/250Ft; open 7.30am-10pm daily) from Clark Ádám tér up to Szent György tér near the Royal Palace. The funicular does not run on the first and third Monday of the month.

Another option is to take the metro to Moszkva tér, cross the footbridge above the square and walk up Várfok utca to **Vienna Gate**. A minibus with a logo of a castle and labelled 'Várbusz' or 'Dísz tér' follows the same route from the start of Várfok utca.

At the Vienna Gate, turn west (right) onto Petermann bíró utca and walk past the **National Archives**, with its majolica-tiled roof, to Kapisztrán tér. The **Magdalen Tower** is all that's left of a Gothic church destroyed here during WWII. The white neoclassical building facing the square is the **Military History Museum** (☎ 356 9522; I Tóth Árpád sétány 40; adult/child 250/80Ft; open 10am-6pm Tues-Sun April-Sept, 10am-4pm Oct-Mar).

Walk southeast along Tóth Árpád sétány, the ramparts promenade, and to the east you'll glimpse the neo-Gothic tower of **Matthias Church** (☎ 489 0717; Szentháromság tér; adult/child 300/150Ft; open 9am-5pm Mon-Fri, 9am-1pm Sat, 1pm-5pm Sun). The church, rebuilt in 1896, has a colourful tiled roof and lovely murals inside. Franz Liszt's *Hungarian Coronation Mass* was played here for the first time at the coronation of Franz Joseph and Elizabeth in 1867.

Just south of the church is an equestrian **statue of St Stephen**, Hungary's first king. Behind it is **Fishermen's Bastion** (adult/child 250/120Ft; open 8.30am-11pm daily), a neo-Gothic structure built in 1905 with stunning views of Pest and the Parliament building.

From the **Holy Trinity statue** in the centre of Szentháromság tér, Tárnok utca runs southeast to Dísz tér and the **Royal Palace**. The palace enjoyed its greatest splendour under King Matthias in the second half of the 15th century and has been destroyed and rebuilt half a dozen times since then.

Today it contains several important museums, including the **National Gallery** (☎ 375 7533; Wings B, C & D, Szent György tér 6; adult/child 600/300Ft; open 10am-6pm Tues-Sun Mar-Nov, 10am-4pm Dec-Feb), with a huge collection of Hungarian works of art from the Gothic period to the present, and the **Budapest History Museum** (☎ 375 7533; Wing E, Szent György tér 2; adult/child, student & senior/family 600/300/1000Ft; open 10am-6pm Wed-Mon Mar–mid-May, mid-Sept–Oct, 10am-6pm daily mid-May–mid-Sept, 10am-4pm daily Nov-Feb), which traces the city's 2000-year history.

To the south is Gellért Hill and the **Citadella** (admission 300Ft; open 8am-10pm daily) built by the Habsburgs after the 1848–49 revolution to 'defend' the city from further insurrection but never used as a fortress. To get there from Pest, cross Erzsébet Bridge and take the stairs leading up behind the waterfall and **statue of St Gellért** or go over Independence (Szabadság) Bridge and follow the path through the park opposite the entrance to the Gellért Baths. Bus No 27 runs almost to the top of the hill from Móricz Zsigmond körtér, southwest of the Gellért Hotel (and accessible using tram Nos 18, 19, 47 and 49).

The **Independence Monument**, the lovely lady with the palm leaf proclaiming freedom throughout the city at the eastern end of the Citadella, was erected as a tribute to the Soviet soldiers who died liberating Hungary in 1945, but both the victims' names in Cyrillic letters on the plinth and the memorial statues of Soviet soldiers were removed a decade ago. The most memorable views of Budapest and the Danube are from Gellért Hill; try to get up here at night.

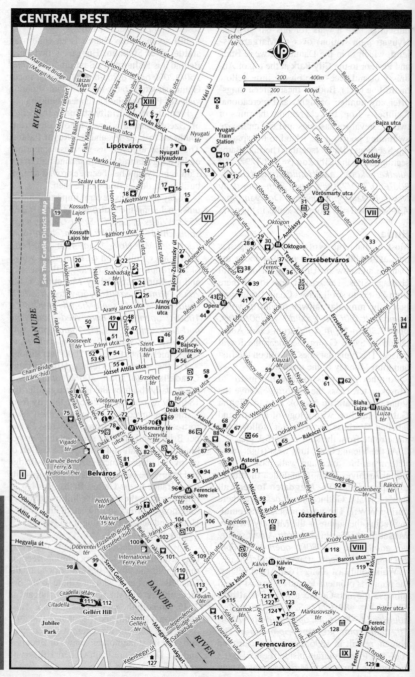

CENTRAL PEST

CENTRAL PEST

PLACES TO STAY
12 Best Hostel
13 Yellow Submarine Youth Hostel
15 Bánki Hostel
28 Hotel Medosz
64 Hostel Marco Polo
68 Carmen Mini Hotel
74 Inter-Continental Hotel
80 Budapest Marriott Hotel
81 Tribus Nonstop Hotel Service
87 Red Bus Hostel & Second-Hand Bookstore
95 Leo Panzió
111 Citadella Hotel & Hostel
117 Hotel Ibis Centrum
118 Museum Castle Guest House
127 Gellért Hotel & Baths
129 Hotels Corvin & Sissi

PLACES TO EAT
2 Rothschild Supermarket
3 Művész Bohém
6 Okay Italia
7 Wabisabi
9 Okay Italia Branch
14 Kaiser's Supermarket
17 Semiramis
29 Teaház a Vörös Oroszlánhoz
36 Café Vian
37 Fortuca
40 Felafel Faloda
41 Két Szerecsen
42 Művész
48 Kisharang
50 Gandhi
54 Coquan's Branch
60 Hannah
63 Match Supermarket
72 Gerbeaud
93 Múzeum
106 Centrál Kávéház
113 Rembetiko Piraeus
116 Marie Kristensen Sandwich Branch Bar
119 Stex Alfred
121 Teaház a Vörös Oroszlánhoz
122 Soul Café
123 Pink Cadillac
124 Coquan's
125 Shiraz Gyros Takeaway
126 Shiraz

BARS & CLUBS
5 Trocadero
10 Bank Music Club
16 Beckett's Irish Pub
30 Cactus Juice
34 Angyal
62 Old Man's Music Pub
75 Columbus Irish Pub
88 Café Eklektika
101 Capella Café
110 Limo Café
114 Közgáz Pince Klub

OTHER
1 Debrecen Summer University Branch
4 Gaiety Theatre
8 West End City Centre Shopping Mall
11 Post Office
18 District V Police Station
19 Parliament
20 Express Branch (Transport Tickets)
21 Hungarian Television Building
22 Soviet Army Memorial
23 US Embassy
24 National Bank Building
25 Irish Embassy
26 Hungarian Bicycle Touring Association
27 Cartographia Map Shop
31 House of Terror
32 Bábszínház (Budapest Puppet Theatre)
33 National Association of Village Tourism
35 Liszt Academy of Music
38 Budapest Operetta Theatre
39 MÁV Ticket Office
43 Hungarian State Opera House
44 Ticket Express
45 Budatours
46 St Stephen's Basilica
47 Bestsellers Bookshop
49 To-Ma Travel Agency
51 Central European University
52 Duna Palota
53 OTP Bank
55 La Boutique des Vins
56 Vista Travel Center
57 Vista Internet Café & Visitor Centre
58 S.O.S. Dental Service
59 Concerto Music Shop
61 BKV Office
65 Libri Könyvpalota Bookshop
66 Great Synagogue & Jewish Museum
67 Ibusz Branch
69 Lutheran Church
70 Tourinform Branch
71 American Express
73 UK Embassy
76 Tourinform (24 Hours)
77 Malév Ticket Office
78 Vigadó Jegyiroda (Ticket Office)
79 Pesti Vigadó (Concert Hall)
82 Rózsavölgyi Music Shop
83 Libri Studium Bookshop
84 Matáv Telepont Internet Kávézó
85 Main Post Office
86 Merlin Theatre
89 K&H Bank & Foreign Currency Exchange Machine
90 Express Main Office
91 East-West Business Centre
92 Kenguru (Car Pooling)
94 Irisz Szalon Laundrette
96 Ibusz Main Office
97 Inner Town Parish Church
98 St Gellért Statue
99 Rudas Baths
100 Mahart PassNave Ticket Office
102 Aranytíz Youth Centre & Kalamajka Táncház
103 Ami Internet Coffee
104 K&H Bank & Foreign Currency Exchange Machine
105 Pegazus Tours
107 National Museum
108 Budapest Net
109 Folkart Centrum
112 Independence Monument
115 Nagycsarnok (Great Market)
120 Hungarian Equestrian Tourism Association
128 Museum of Applied Arts

Many monuments to the Soviet liberators and socialist heroes that once filled Budapest's streets and squares are on display in the **Statue Park** (☎ 227 7446; XXII Szabadkai út; adult/child 300/200Ft; open 10am-dusk daily Mar-Nov, 10am-dusk Sat & Sun Dec-Feb) in south-west Buda. To reach this socialist Disneyland, take tram No 19 or 49 (or a red-numbered bus

No 7 from Ferenciek tere in Pest) to the terminus at XI Etele tér. From there catch a yellow Volán bus from stand No 2 or 3 to Diósd-Érd. From June to August a direct bus (1250Ft, including admission to the park) leaves from in front of Hotel Le Meridien at V Erzsébet tér 9–10 at 9am, 10am and 11am and again at 3pm, 4pm and 5pm.

THE CASTLE DISTRICT

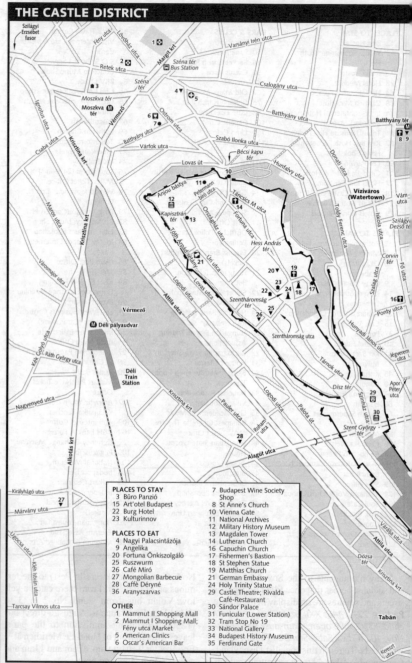

PLACES TO STAY
3 Büro Panzió
15 Art'otel Budapest
22 Burg Hotel
23 Kulturinnov

PLACES TO EAT
4 Nagyi Palacsintázója
9 Angelika
20 Fortuna Önkiszolgáló
25 Ruszwurm
26 Café Miró
27 Mongolian Barbecue
28 Caffé Déryné
36 Aranyszarvas

OTHER
1 Mammut II Shopping Mall
2 Mammut I Shopping Mall;
  Fény utca Market
5 American Clinics
6 Oscar's American Bar

7 Budapest Wine Society
  Shop
8 St Anne's Church
10 Vienna Gate
11 National Archives
12 Military History Museum
13 Magdalen Tower
14 Lutheran Church
16 Capuchin Church
17 Fishermen's Bastion
18 St Stephen Statue
19 Matthias Church
21 German Embassy
24 Holy Trinity Statue
29 Castle Theatre; Rivalda
   Café-Restaurant
30 Sándor Palace
31 Funicular (Lower Station)
32 Tram Stop No 19
33 National Gallery
34 Budapest History Museum
35 Ferdinand Gate

HUNGARY

Pest

The most attractive boulevard in Budapest is leafy Andrássy út, which stretches northeast from Bajcsy-Zsilinszky út to Heroes' Square (Hősök tere) and City Park and is home to many important sights, including the neo-Renaissance **Hungarian State Opera House** (☎ 332 8197; VI Andrássy út 22), completed in 1884. Daily tours in English at 3pm and 4pm (1500/900Ft adult/student) are 'second-best' to attending a performance here. Many of the other great buildings along this section of Andrássy út date from Budapest's Golden Age, including **Drechsler House** (VI Andrássy út 25), now being turned into a hotel, and the sublime Art Nouveau **New Theatre** (VI Paulay Ede utca 35) around the corner.

A bit farther afield, Budapest's newest museum is the **House of Terror** (☎ 374 2600; Andrássy út 60; adult/child 1000/500Ft; open 10am-6pm Tues-Sun). Once the headquarters of the dreaded ÁVH secret police, it focuses on the crimes and atrocities committed by Hungary's fascist and Stalinist regimes.

The neo-Renaissance dome of **St Stephen's Basilica** (☎ 311 0839; V Szent István tér; treasury adult/child 200/150Ft; open 9am-7pm Mon-Sat, 1pm-4pm Sun) (1905) looms some 96m over Bajcsy-Zsilinszky út. The mummified right hand – the so-called Holy Right or Holy Dexter – of St Stephen is kept in the chapel at the rear of the church; take the passage on the left of the main altar. To reach the **dome** (adult/child 500/400Ft; open 10am-5pm Apr-May & Sept-Oct, 10am-6pm June-Aug) take the lift near the entrance and then scale 150-odd steps to the top.

To the northwest of the basilica, through stately Szabadság tér, is the neo-Gothic **Parliament** (☎ 441 4904; V Kossuth Lajos tér 1-3; adult/student 1700/800Ft), built in 1902 and housing the Crown of St Stephen, the nation's most important national icon. English language tours are held at 10am, noon and 2pm daily.

Several other museums in Pest are worth your time and consideration. The **National Museum** (☎ 338 2122; VIII Múzeum körút 14-16; adult/student 600/300Ft; open 10am-6pm Tues-Sun mid-Mar–mid-Oct, 10am-5pm mid-Oct–mid-Mar) contains the nation's most important collection of historical relics (including King Stephen's crimson silk coronation robe) in a large neoclassical building purpose-built in 1847.

The **Museum of Applied Arts** (☎ 456 5100; IX Üllői út 33-37; adult/child 500/ 250Ft; open 10am-6pm Tues-Sun Apr-Oct, 10am-4pm Nov-Mar) has a wonderful array of Hungarian furniture dating from the 18th and 19th centuries, Art Nouveau and Secessionist artefacts and bric-a-brac. The building itself, built in 1896, is covered in colourful Zsolnay ceramic tiles and has a central hall of white marble modelled on the Alhambra in southern Spain.

Facing monument-filled **Heroes' Square**, which was constructed in 1896 to mark the millennium of the Magyar conquest of the Carpathian Basin, the **Museum of Fine Arts** (☎ 363 2675, 469 7100; adult/student & child 6-12 700/350Ft; open 10am-5.30pm Tues-Sun) houses Hungary's richest collection of foreign art. The collection of Old Masters is the most complete, and there are more works by El Greco here than anywhere outside Spain.

The twin-towered, Romantic-style **Great Synagogue** (☎ 324 1335; VII Dohány utca 2), dating from 1859, is the largest functioning synagogue in Europe. It contains the **Jewish Museum** (☎ 342 8949; adult/student 600/ 200Ft; open 10am-5pm Mon-Thur, 10am-3pm Fri, 10am-2pm Sun mid-April–Oct; 10am-3pm Mon-Thur, 10am-2pm Fri, 10am-2pm Sun Nov–mid-April), with a particularly harrowing exhibit on the Holocaust.

Thermal Baths

Budapest is a major spa centre with many thermal baths open to the public. The Danube follows the geological fault separating the Buda Hills from the Great Plain and over 40 million litres of warm mineral water gush forth daily from more than 120 thermal springs.

Some bathhouses require you to wear a bathing suit while others do not; take one just in case. Most of the public baths hire out bathing suits and towels (500Ft) if you don't have your own; bathing caps are provided for use in the swimming pools. Note that some of the baths become gay venues on male-only days – especially the Király and on Sunday the Gellért.

The city's most famous thermal spa is the **Gellért Baths** (☎ 466 6166; XI Kelenhegyi út; thermal baths admission 1600Ft, swimming pool & baths admission 2000-2400Ft; thermal baths open 6am-7pm Mon-Fri, 6am-5pm Sat & Sun May-Sept; 6am-7pm Mon-Fri, 6am-2pm Sat & Sun Oct-Apr; swimming pool open 6am-7pm daily May-Sept; 6am-7pm Mon-Fri, 6am-5pm Sat & Sun Oct-Apr). Soaking in this Art Nouveau palace has been likened to taking a bath in a cathedral. The pools here maintain a constant temperature of 44°C and a large outdoor pool is open from April to September.

Close to the Buda side of Erzsébet Bridge is a thermal bath where you'll meet more locals than tourists. The **Rudas Baths** (☎ 356 1322; I Döbrentei tér 9; admission 1000Ft; thermal baths open to men only 9am-7pm Mon-Fri, 6am-noon Sat & Sun; swimming pool open to all 6am-6pm Mon-Fri, 6am-1pm Sat & Sun), close to the river, were built by the Turks in 1566 and retain a strong Turkish atmosphere.

The **Király Baths** (☎ 202 3688, 201 4392; II Fő utca 84; admission 800Ft; open to men 9am-8pm Mon, Wed & Fri; to women 6.30am-6pm Tues & Thur, 6.30am-12.30pm Sat) are genuine Turkish baths built in 1570 and have a wonderful sky-lit central dome.

The **Széchenyi Baths** (☎ 363 3210; XIV Állatkerti út 11; admission deposit before/after 3pm 1500/900Ft; open 6am-7pm daily May-Sept; 6am-7pm Mon-Fri, 6am-5pm Sat & Sun Oct-Apr), with nine indoor and outdoor pools, are just outside the Széchenyi fürdő metro station in City Park. The entry fee is actually a kind of deposit; you get back 900/ 600/300Ft if you leave within two/three/ four hours before 3pm and 600/300Ft if you exit within two/three hours after 3pm.

ORGANISED TOURS

Budatours (☎ 353 0558; W www.budatours .hu; VI Andrássy út 2) runs seven bus tours a day in both open and covered coaches in July and August (between two and three the rest of the year). It's a two-hour nonstop tour with taped commentary in 16 different languages and costs 4800/2400Ft for an adult/child from six to 12.

Queenybus (☎ 247 7159) departs twice daily (11am and 2.20pm) from St Stephen's Basilica, V Bajcsy-Zsilinszky út, for two-hour city tours (5000/4000/2500Ft per adult/ student/child six to 16).

From April to September **Mahart Pass-Nave** (☎ 484 4013; V Belgrád rakpart) has 1½-hour cruises on the Danube at noon and 7pm daily for 1200/600Ft per adult/child. In April the noon cruise is on Saturday and holidays only, and from mid-June to August the evening programme begins at 7.45pm and includes music and dance (1500/750Ft). More expensive cruises also operate on the river, including **Legenda** (☎/fax 317 2203; **w** *www .legenda.hu*), which runs day (3400/1600Ft per adult/child) and night (4000Ft) tours with taped commentary in up to 30 languages.

Highly recommended for tours is **Absolute Walking Tours** (☎ 06-30 211 8861; **w** *www .budapestours.com*), a 3½-hour guided promenade through City Park, central Pest and Castle Hill. Tours (3500/3000Ft adult/student & under 26) depart at 9.30am and 1.30pm daily from the steps of the yellow Lutheran church on Deák tér and at 10am and 2pm from the steps of the Műcsarnok art gallery in the Heroes' Square from mid-May to September. During the rest of the year they leave from the Deák tér church at 10.30am and the Műcsarnok at 11am, with tours curtailed over Christmas and in January.

PLACES TO STAY
Camping
Római Camping (☎ 388 7167, fax 250 0426; III Szentendrei út 189; per person/tent site/caravan 990/1990/3300Ft, 2-bed cabins 3600-6000Ft; camping open year-round, cabins mid-Apr–mid-Oct) is a large site in a leafy park north of the city. To get there take the HÉV suburban railway from Batthyány tér metro station to the Rómaifürdő station, which is just about opposite the camping ground. Use of the adjacent swimming pool is included in the rates.

Zugligeti Niche Camping (☎ 200 8346, XII Zugligeti út 101; tent site for 2 people 2900-3000Ft, caravan 3950-4400Ft, bungalow for 2 people 4000Ft; open year-round) is in the Buda Hills at the bottom station of the chair lift (take bus No 158 from Moszkva tér to the terminus).

Hostels
There are two types of hostel in Budapest: year-round private hostels, many in old apartments in or near central Pest; and student dormitories open to travellers during summer holidays (July to late August). Year-round hostels generally have laundry facilities (about 1000Ft per load), a fully equipped kitchen, storage lockers, TV lounge, no curfew and computers for accessing the Internet.

Dormitory accommodation in both year-round and summer hostels ranges from 1700Ft to 3300Ft; expect to pay from 2800Ft to 4700Ft for doubles (book these in advance). High season usually means April to October. Prices almost always include breakfast.

Express is the best travel agency to contact for hostel information (see Travel Agencies under Information earlier).

Year-Round Hostels – Buda The **Back Pack Guesthouse** (☎ 385 8946; **w** *www .backpackbudapest.hu*; XI Takács Menyhért utca 33; dorm beds 1800-2300Ft, doubles 2800Ft) is a colourful place with 50 beds and a friendly, much-travelled manager. There are dormitories with between five and 11 beds and one small double, a lovely garden and very laid-back clientele. It's in south Buda and not central, but transport is reliable. Get here on the black-numbered bus No 7 or 7A from Keleti train station, tram No 49 from the little ring road in central Pest, or tram No 19 from Batthyány tér in Buda.

Citadella Hotel (☎ 466 5794; **w** *www .citadella.hu*; XI Citadella sétány; dorm beds 2200Ft), in the fortress atop Gellért Hill, has a room with 14 beds as well as hotel rooms (see Hotels – Budget later). Solo travellers may prefer somewhere more central, as it's a bit isolated. To get here catch bus No 27 from XI Móricz Zsigmond körtér in Buda.

Student accommodation is available all year at the large **Martos Hostel** (☎ 209 4883, fax 463 3650; **e** *reception@hotel.martos.bme .hu*; XI Sztoczek utca 5-7; singles 3500Ft, doubles/triples/quads per person 2200Ft). It's reasonably well situated, near the Danube and a few minutes' walk from Petőfi Bridge (tram No 4 or 6). There are also doubles with shower and toilet (8000Ft) and small apartments with four beds (14,000Ft).

Year-Round Hostels – Pest The Travellers' Youth Hostels-Mellow Mood group, which runs a number of summer hostels (see that section following) for individuals and groups, also has two year-round hostels. More central (and expensive) is **Hostel Marco Polo** (☎ 413 2555; **w** *www.marcopolohostel.com*; VII Nyár utca 6; bed in 12-bed dorm low/high season €17/19, singles €46/51; doubles/triples/quads per person low season €31/26/22, high season €34/29/24). Almost like a mid-range hotel, it has telephones in the rooms, a lovely courtyard and bar and restaurant (set meals 1000Ft).

The same group operates **Diáksport Hostel** (☎ 340 8585, 413 2062; W www.backpackers .hu; XIII Dózsa György út 152; bed in 6-bed dorm 3300Ft, singles & doubles with bath per person 4600Ft, doubles/triples & quads with shared bath per person from 3600/3500Ft) is a bit far from the action (M3 metro stop: Dózsa György út), but compensates by having its own 24-hour bar. This is definitely a party place so go elsewhere if you've come to Budapest for a good rest. Student, youth and hostel card-holders get a 10% discount.

Another place a tad off the beaten track but with a great atmosphere is **Station Guesthouse** (☎ 221 8864; e station@matavnet.hu; XIV Mexikói út 36/b; bed in 14-/8-bed dorms 1700/2400Ft, doubles & triples/quads per person 3200/2700Ft). It's another party place with a 24-hour bar, pool table and occasional live entertainment. HI card-holders get 200Ft off the quoted prices and rates drop by 100Ft a night from the second to sixth night of stay. Get here on the M1 metro (stop: Mexikói út) or red-numbered bus No 7 from Keleti train station.

For a central, well-managed place, look no further than the **Red Bus Hostel** (☎/fax 266 0136; e redbusbudapest@hotmail.com; V Semmelweiss utca 14, 1st floor; dorm beds 2700Ft, singles 6000/7000Ft winter/summer, doubles 7000Ft), with large airy rooms cobbled from two flats, a modern kitchen and exceptionally friendly management.

Another very central place, close to the restaurants and bars of Ráday utca, is the **Museum Castle Guest House** (☎ 318 9508, 266 8879; e museumgh@freemail.C3.hu; VIII Mikszáth Kálmán tér 4, 1st floor; dorm beds 2800Ft), a poky but creatively decorated and friendly place, with six to nine dorm beds in three rooms.

Two similar places close to Nyugati station almost face one another on the intersection of Teréz körút and Podmaniczky utca. **Yellow Submarine Youth Hostel** (☎/fax 331 9896; W www.yellowsubmarinehostel.com; VI Teréz körút 56, 3rd floor; dorm beds 2500Ft, doubles/quads per person 3750/2800Ft) has lots of facilities. However, it overlooks one of Pest's busiest boulevards and there's no lift. The **Best Hostel** (☎ 332 4934; e bestyh@ mail.datanet.hu; VI Podmaniczky utca 27, 1st floor; dorm beds 2800Ft, doubles/quads per person 4000/3400Ft) is a bit dearer but rooms are bigger, airier and quieter.

Summer Hostels Affiliated with Hostelling International (HI), **Travellers' Youth Hostels-Mellow Mood** (☎ 413 2062, 215 0660; W www.backpackers.hu) runs many summer hostels in student accommodation. Its booths at Keleti train station (☎ 343 0748; open 7.30am-11pm daily during summer, 7.30am-9pm rest of year) make bookings and may arrange to transport you there. All the hostels are open 24 hours a day, and there's no curfew. An HI card is not required, but having one usually gets you a 10% discount.

The group's summer hostels include **Bánki Hostel** (VI Podmaniczky utca 8; bed in 8-bed dorms 3300Ft, quads/doubles per person from 3500/3800Ft), near Nyugati train station in Pest; and **Hill Hostel** (XI Ménesi út 5; doubles with shower 4700Ft per person) below leafy Gellért Hill in Buda.

Private Rooms

Private rooms in Budapest generally cost from 3600Ft to 5000Ft for a single, 5000Ft to 7000Ft for a double and 8000Ft to 14,000Ft for a small apartment, with a 30% supplement if you stay less than four nights. To get a room in the centre of town, you may have to try several offices. There are lots of rooms, and even in July and August you'll be able to find something. You'll probably need an indexed city map to find the flat housing your room.

Among the best places to try for private rooms are Ibusz and Vista (see Travel Agencies under Information earlier). Another good place is **To-Ma** (☎ 353 0819; W www.toma tour.hu; V Október 6 utca 22; open 9am-noon & 1pm-8pm Mon-Fri, 9am-5pm Sat & Sun). After hours try **Tribus Nonstop Hotel Service** (☎ 318 3925, 318 4848; W www .tribus.hu; V Apáczai Csere János utca 1; open 24hr) near the Budapest Marriott Hotel. It books all types of accommodation and cashes travellers cheques around the clock.

Hotels – Budget

In Buda, **Büro Panzió** (☎ 212 2929, fax 212 2928; e buro-panzio@axelero.hu; II Dékán utca 3; singles/doubles with shower 9000/ 13,500Ft), a pension just a block off the northern side of Moszkva tér, looks basic from the outside but its 10 rooms are comfortable and have TVs and telephones.

The 12-room **Citadella Hotel** (☎ 466 5794; W www.citadella.hu; XI Citadella sétány; doubles with/without bath from €55/50) has big, clean, dark-wood rooms, although we've heard complaints about the noisy dance club below.

In Pest, the most central cheap place is the **Hotel Medosz** (☎ 374 3000, fax 332 4316; VI Jókai tér 9; singles/doubles/triples 10,000/13,000/15,500Ft), right near Oktogon metro station and the restaurants and bars of Liszt Ferenc tér. The 70 rooms are well worn but have private bath and satellite TV; the best ones are in the main block, not in the labyrinthine wings.

Not very far from the square Deák tér, the **Carmen Mini Hotel** (☎ 352 0798, fax 318 3865; e carmen@axelero.hu; Károly körút 5/b, 2nd floor; singles/doubles €50/60) has nine large and spotless rooms all of which are protected from the noise of the little ring road by double-glazing.

Excellent value for its location and immaculate 14 rooms is **Leo Panzió** (☎ 266 9041, fax 266 9042; e panzioleo@mail .datanet.hu; V Kossuth Lajos utca 2/a, 2nd floor; singles €45-66, doubles €69-82).

Up close to leafy Andrássy út, the **Radio Inn** (☎ 342 8347, fax 322 8284; e radioinn@elender.hu; VI Benczúr utca 19; singles €43-48, doubles €48-65) is a real find, with 33 large suites with bathroom, kitchen and bed (or beds).

Hotel Margitsziget (☎ 329 2949, fax 340 4846; e hotelmargitsziget@axelero.hu; XIII Margitsziget; singles €43-45, doubles €43-54), in the middle of Margaret Island, is good value and almost feels like a budget resort, with free use of tennis courts, swimming pool and sauna.

Hotels – Mid-Range

For location and price in Buda, you can't beat the **Kulturinnov** (☎ 355 0122, fax 375 1886; e mka3@axelero.hu; I Szentháromság tér 6; singles/doubles/triples €65/80/110), a 16-room hotel in the former Finance Ministry in the Castle District. Chandeliers and a sprawling marble staircase greet you on entry, though the rooms are not so nice.

The nearby **Burg Hotel** (☎ 212 0269, fax 212 3970; e hotel.burg@mail.datanet.hu; I Szentháromság tér 7-8; singles €73-97, doubles €85-10⁹) is a new, 26-room hotel with all mod cons, opposite Matthias Church.

In Pest, two small three-star hotels sit side by side on a street close to the Ferenc körút metro station and the Danube. **Hotel Corvin** (☎ 218 6566, fax 218 6562; e corvin@mail .datanet.hu; IX Angyal utca 31; singles/doubles/triples €80/100/120) has 40 very comfortable rooms with all the mod cons, while the 44-room **Hotel Sissi** (☎ 215 0082; w www .hotelsissi.hu; IX Angyal utca 33; singles €67-90, doubles €78-100) next door has nicer and cheaper rooms.

The appropriately named **Hotel Ibis Centrum** (☎ 215 8585; w www.ibishotel.com; IX Ráday utca 6; singles €78-98, doubles €85-106) faces central Kálvin tér. The rooms are light and airy and there's a pleasant garden.

Hotels – Top End

Choose any of the following for their location, special amenities and ambience: the old-world 234-room **Gellért Hotel** (☎ 385 2200; w www.danubiusgroup.com; XI Szent Gellért tér 1; singles €115-150, doubles €190-235); the almost-London **Art'otel Budapest** (☎ 487 9487; w www.parkplazaww.com; I Bem rakpart 16-19; singles & doubles from €198), a new trendy place with 165 rooms; the totally revamped Art Deco **Andrássy Hotel** (☎ 462 2100; w www.andrassyhotel.com; VI Andrássy út 111 or Munkácsy Mihály utca 5-7; singles €100-145, doubles €175-250), with 70 stunning rooms; or the 164-room **Danubius Grand Hotel Margitsziget** (☎ 452 6264; w www.danubiusgroup.com; XIII Margitsziget; singles €136-176, doubles €168-208), built in 1873 on Margaret Island along the Danube and connected to the thermal spa.

PLACES TO EAT
Buda

Restaurants If you are going to splash out in the touristy, expensive Castle District, choose **Rivalda** (☎ 489 0236; I Színház utca; mains 2900-5200Ft; open 11.30am-11.30pm daily), an international café-restaurant next to the Castle Theatre, with a thespian theme and garden courtyard. **Café Miró** (☎ 375 5458; I Úri utca 30; light meals 1200Ft; open 9am-midnight daily) is a bright, modern place, good for a light meal.

Aranyszarvas (☎ 375 6451; I Szarvas tér 1; mains 1500-2500Ft; open noon-11pm daily) is set in an old 18th-century inn at the foot of Castle Hill and serves game dishes. The outside terrace is lovely in summer.

Near Moszkva tér, **Marxim** (☎ 316 0231; II Kisrókus utca 23; pizzas 490-950Ft; open noon-10pm Mon-Sat) is a veritable temple of

HUNGARY

communist memorabilia and campy Stalinist decor. For more serious (but affordable) Italian fare head for **Marcello** (☎ 466 6231; XI Bartók Béla út 40; pizzas & pasta 720-850Ft; open 11am-midnight Mon-Thur, 11am-1pm Fri & Sat), popular with students from the nearby university and nonsmoking.

South of Déli train station, the **Mongolian Barbecue** (☎ 353 6363; XII Márvány utca 19/a; buffet before/after 5pm 1990/3690Ft) is another one of those all-you-can-eat pseudo-Asian places that includes as much beer and wine as you can sink too.

Cafés The perfect place for coffee and cakes in the Castle District is the very crowded **Ruszwurm** (☎ 375 5284; I Szentháromság utca 7; open 10am-7pm daily). Two other charming cafés are **Angelika** (☎ 212 3784; I Batthyány tér 7; open 9am-midnight daily) and the untouristed **Caffè Déryné** (☎ 212 3864; I Krisztina tér 3; open 8am-10pm Mon-Fri, 8am-9pm Sat, 9am-9pm Sun).

Fast Food For a cheap and quick weekday lunch while in the Castle District try **Fortuna Önkiszolgáló** (☎ 375 2401; I Hess András utca 4; open 11.30am-2.30pm Mon-Fri), a self-service place above the Fortuna. **Nagyi Palacsintázója** (Granny's Palacsinta Place; ☎ 201 8605, 212 4866; I Hattyú utca 16; menus 568-888Ft; open 24hr) serves Hungarian pancakes – both savoury (148Ft to 248Ft) and sweet (78Ft to 248Ft) – throughout the day.

Self-Catering Budapest counts some 20 markets though the lion's share of them are in Pest. The **Fény utca market** (II Fény utca) is conveniently located next to the huge Mammut shopping mall.

Pest

Restaurants For good, old-fashioned Hungarian home cooking try **Móri Borozó** (☎ 349 8390; XIII Pozsonyi út 37; mains 500-750Ft; open 10am-8pm Mon-Thur, 10am-3pm Fri), a little wine bar-restaurant just a short walk north of Szent István körút.

If you want a bit more style (antique furniture, photos of Magyar actors on the walls and piano music), head for the **Művész Bohém** (☎ 339 8008; XIII Vígszínház utca 5; mains 750-1700Ft; open 11am-11pm daily), directly behind the Gaiety Theatre.

Stex Alfred (☎ 318 5716; VIII József körút 55-57; mains 710-1980Ft; open 8am-6am daily) is a big, noisy place. The extensive menu includes soups, sandwiches, pasta, fish and meat dishes and it transforms into a lively bar late at night. Best of all there's breakfast (320Ft to 860Ft).

Two pedestrian areas in Pest popular with Budapest's young-bloods are Ráday utca and Liszt Ferenc tér. On or near the former, try the upbeat **Pink Cadillac** (☎ 216 1412; IX Ráday utca 22; pizzas 650-1055Ft; open 11am-12.30am Sun-Thur, 11am-1am Fri & Sat) for pizza; or **Shiraz** (☎ 218 0881; IX Mátyás utca 22; mains 1350-1950Ft; open noon-midnight daily), a Persian restaurant with a **gyros take-away** (☎ 217 4547; IX Ráday utca 21; gyros 460-550Ft) round the corner.

Soul Café (☎ 217 6989; IX Ráday utca 11-13; mains 1200-2300Ft; open noon-1am daily) is a good choice for inventive Continental food and decor.

Of the many places on Liszt Ferenc tér, **Café Vian** (☎ 268 1164; VI Liszt Ferenc tér 9; open 9am-midnight daily), with an eight-page drinks menu, is a good choice. **Fortuca** (☎ 413 1612; VI Liszt Ferenc tér 10; pizzas & pasta 990-1290Ft; open 11am-1am daily) is the recommended new kid on the block. Nearby, but more subdued, is **Két Szerecsen** (☎ 343 1984; VI Nagymező utca 14; mains 800-2000Ft; open 8am-1am Sun-Thur, 11am-1am Fri & Sat), which also serves breakfast (from 600Ft).

Okay Italia (☎ 349 2991; XIII Szent István körút 20; pizzas & pasta 1090-1640Ft; mains 1390-2480Ft) is a perennially popular Italian-run place with a nearby **branch** (☎ 332 6960; V Nyugati tér 6). For excellent Greek food go to the **Rembetiko Piraeus** (☎ 266 0292; V Fővám tér 2-3; mains 990-2990Ft; open noon-midnight) overlooking a leafy square and the Great Market Hall.

Budapest has some decent vegetarian restaurants. **Gandhi** (☎ 269 1625; V Vigyázó Ferenc utca 4; set menu small/large 980/1680Ft; open noon-10pm Mon-Sat), in a cellar near Chain Bridge, serves a daily Sun and Moon plate set menu as well as wholesome salads, soups and desserts. **Wabisabi** (☎ 412 0427; XIII Visegrádi utca 2; mains 1080-1480Ft; open 9am-11pm Mon-Sat) offers wonderful Asian-inspired vegan dishes.

For a kosher meal, head for **Hannah** (☎ 342 1072; VII Dob utca 35; lunch 2500Ft; open

1.30am-3pm Sun-Fri), in a courtyard near the Great Synagogue.

If you want to dine in style, the **Múzeum** (☎ 338 4221; *VIII Múzeum körút 12; mains 1700-4100Ft; open noon-midnight Mon-Sat)* is still going strong after more than a century at the same location near the National Museum.

Gundel (☎ 468 4040; *XIV Állatkerti út 2; mains 3500-8800Ft; open noon-4pm & 5.30pm-midnight)* is Budapest's fanciest eatery, but these days the cognoscenti eschew it for its little sister and brother next door: **Bagolyvár** (☎ 343 0217; *mains 1180-2380Ft; open noon-11pm)*, with excellent reworked classics; and **Borvendéglő 1894** (☎ 468 4044; *mains 1600-2100Ft; open noon-11pm Tues-Sat)*, a new wine cellar and restaurant.

Cafés & Teahouses Try **Gerbeaud** (☎ 429 9000; *V Vörösmarty tér 7; open 9am-9pm daily)*, which has been the city's most fashionable café for the city's elite since 1870. **Művész** (☎ 352 1337; *VI Andrássy út 29; open 9am-11pm daily)*, almost opposite the State Opera House, is a more interesting place to people-watch and has cheaper (though with inferior) cakes.

Centrál Kávéház (☎ 266 4572; *V Károlyi Mihály utca 9; mains 1990-3590Ft; open 8am-1am Mon-Sat, 8am-midnight Sun)* is another reopened grande dame jostling to reclaim her title as *the* place to sit and look intellectual. It serves meals as well as fine coffee and cakes.

Budapest has a growing number of hip modern cafés and teahouses whose patrons take their hot beverages very seriously indeed. For the former, try **Coquan's** (☎ 215 2444; *IX Ráday utca 15; open 7.30am-7pm Mon-Fri, 9am-5pm Sat)*, with a long list of brews, cakes, bagels and a second branch (☎ 266 9936; *V Nádor utca 5; open 9am-7pm Mon-Fri, 9am-5pm Sat)*. One of the best teahouses in the city (usually nonsmoking) is **Teaház a Vörös Oroszlánhoz** (Teahouse at the Red Lion; ☎ 269 0579; *VI Jókai tér 8; open 11am-11pm Mon-Sat, 3pm-11pm Sun)*, with an Asian vibe and a **branch** (☎ 215 2101; *IX Ráday utca 9)* that keeps the same hours.

Fast Food American fast-food joints proliferate in Budapest but a much better choice are the wonderful little *étkezde* serving simple dishes that change every day. A central one is

Kisharang (☎ 269 3861; *V Október 6 utca 17; mains 500-820Ft; open 11am-8pm Mon-Fri, 11.30am-4.30pm Sat & Sun)*.

An inexpensive place to nosh Israeli-style is **Falafel Faloda** (☎ 267 9567; *VI Paulay Ede utca 53; large/small sandwiches 450/270Ft, salads 420-1050Ft; open 10am-8pm Mon-Fri, 10am-6pm Sat)*, where you pay a fixed price to stuff a piece of pita bread or fill a plastic container from the great assortment of salad options. Cheaper Middle Eastern food can be found at **Semiramis** (☎ 311 7627; *V Alkotmány utca 20; open noon-9pm Mon-Sat)*.

If you're craving for a Western-style sandwich, **Marie Kristensen Sandwich Bar** (☎ 218 1673; *IX Ráday utca 7; sandwiches 220-550Ft; open 8am-9pm Mon-Fri, 11am-8pm Sat)* has a large selection and does salads (from 490Ft) too.

Self-Catering Budapest's biggest market, the **Nagycsarnok** (*Great Market; IX Fővám tér)*, has become a bit of a tourist trap. Still, plenty of locals head here for fruit and vegetables, deli items, fish and meat. There are good food stalls on the upper level.

Large supermarkets are everywhere in Pest, including **Match** (*VIII Rákóczi út; open 6am-9pm Mon-Fri, 7am-8pm Sat, 7am-4pm Sun)* facing Blaha Lujza tér; and **Kaiser's** (*VI Nyugati tér 1-2; open 7am-8pm Mon-Sat, 7am-3pm Sun)* opposite Nyugati train station. **Rothschild** (*XIII Szent István körút 4; open 6am-8pm Mon-Fri, 7am-4pm Sat, 9am-5pm Sun)* is another chain, with a good supply of kosher products.

ENTERTAINMENT
Ticket Agencies
Tickets for concerts, dance performances and theatre are available from **Vigadó Jegyiroda** (☎ 327 4322; *V Vörösmarty tér 1; open 9am-7pm Mon-Fri, 10am-5pm Sat)*. **Ticket Express** (information ☎ 312-0000, bookings ☎ 06-30 303 0999; **W** www.tex.hu) has half a dozen outlets, including a District VI branch (*VI Andrássy út 18; open 9.30am-6.30pm Mon-Fri, 9am-1pm Sat)*.

Classical Music
Koncert Kalendárium lists all concerts in town each month. Major venues include the **Liszt Academy of Music** (☎ 342 0179; *VI Liszt Ferenc tér 8)* in Pest and the **Budapest Congress Centre** (☎ 372 57000; *XII Jagelló út 1-3)* in

Buda. The **Pesti Vigadó** (☎ 318 9167; V Vigadó tér 2) usually has light classical music and touristy musical revues. Concerts are also held regularly in the city's churches, including **Matthias Church** on Castle Hill.

Opera

You should pay at least one visit to the **State Opera House** (☎ 332 7914; W www.opera .hu; VI Andrássy út 22) to see a performance and the incredible interior decor. Budapest's second opera house is the modern (and ugly) **Erkel Theatre** (☎ 333 0540; III Köztársaság tér 30). The **Budapest Operetta Theatre** (☎ 269 0118; VI Nagymező utca 17) puts on operettas – always a riot, particularly campy ones like the *Queen of the Csárdás* composed by Imre Kálmán.

Folk & Traditional Performance

Authentic folk-music workshops (*táncház*, literally 'dance house') are held at various locations throughout the week but less frequently in summer. Venues in Buda include the **Fonó Buda Music House** (☎ 206 6296; W www.fono.hu; XI Sztregova utca 3), the **Folklór Centrum** (☎ 203 3868; XI Fehérvári út 47) in the Municipal Cultural House and the **Marczibányi tér Cultural Centre** (☎ 212 2820; W www.marczi.hu; II Marczibányi utca 5/a). In Pest there is the wonderful **Kalamajka Táncház** (☎ 317 5928; V Molnár utca 9) at the Aranytíz Youth Centre.

Hungária Koncert (☎ 317 1377) organises folk and Gypsy concerts featuring the Hungarian State Folk Ensemble and two other groups at the **Duna Palota** (V Zrínyi utca 5) and the **Bábszínház** (Budapest Puppet Theatre; VI Andrássy út 69) throughout the year. Tickets cost 5600Ft (5100Ft for students).

Theatre

In Pest, **Merlin Theatre** (☎ 317 9338; W www .szinhaz.hu/merlin; V Gerlóczy utca 4) regularly stages comedies and dramas in English. A more recent arrival, the **International Buda Stage** (☎ 391 2525; II Tárogató út 2-4; tickets 300-800Ft) in Buda has English-language theatre, films and music programmes.

Pubs & Clubs

Budapest has a number of 'Irish' pubs, including **Becketts** (☎ 311 1035; V Bajcsy-Zsilinszky út 72; open 10am-1am Sun-Thur, 10am-3am Fri & Sat) and **Columbus** (☎ 266

9013; open noon-1am daily), which sits on a boat moored in the Danube opposite the Inter-Continental hotel.

In Pest, **Cactus Juice** (☎ 302 2116; V Jókai tér 5; open 11am-2am Mon-Thur, 11am-4am Fri & Sat, 4pm-2am Sun) is in 'American rustic' drag and a good place to sip and sup with no distractions. There's dancing at weekends.

Old Man's Music Pub (☎ 322 7645; VI Akácfa utca 13; open 3pm-4am daily) pulls in the best live blues and jazz acts in town; shows are from 9pm to 11pm.

In Buda, **Oscar's American Bar** (☎ 212 8017; I Ostrom utca 14; open 5pm-2am Sun-Thur, 5pm-4am Fri & Sat), with some film memorabilia on the wood-panelled walls and leather directors' chairs on the floor, is a cocktail oasis up from the desert of Moszkva tér

A wonderful spot to chill out along the banks of the Danube is **Zöld Párdon** (W www .zp.hu), an outdoor dancing and drinking venue on the Buda side of Petőfi Bridge. The 'world's longest summer festival' runs from 9am to 6am daily from May to September. Concerts begin at 8pm and then DJs take over until dawn.

Bank Music Club (☎ 414 5025; VI Teréz körút 55; open 9pm-5am Thur-Sat), in the south wing of Nyugati train station next to McDonald's, has a floor with international hits and another with Hungarian pop music and concerts. The **Közgáz Pince Klub** (☎ 218 6855; IX Fővám tér 8; open 9pm-5am Mon-Sat) has fewer frills and charges cheap covers but there's plenty of room to dance.

Trocadero (☎ 311 4691; VI Szent István körút 15; open 9pm-2am Tues-Thur, 9pm-5am Fri & Sat) attracts one of the most diverse crowds in Budapest with its great canned Latin, salsa and concert nights. Best parties are at weekends.

Gay & Lesbian Venues Budapest's flagship gay club is **Angyal** (☎ 351 6490; VII Szövetség utca 33; open 10pm-5am Fri-Sun), which welcomes girlz on Friday and Sunday. **Capella Café** (☎ 318 6231; V Belgrád rakpart 23; open 10pm-5am Wed-Sat) and its new extension, **Limo Café** (☎ 266 5455; V Belgrád rakpart 9; open noon-5am Sun-Thur, noon-6am Fri & Sat), are twin clubs frequented by gays, lesbians and fellow travellers.

The only real lesbian venue is **Café Eklektika** (☎ 266 3054; V Semmelweiss utca 21;

open noon-midnight Mon-Fri, 5pm-midnight Sat & Sun), though it attracts a mixed crowd.

SHOPPING

Upstairs at the **Nagycsarnok** *(IX Fővám tér)* here are dozens of stalls selling Hungarian folk costumes, dolls, painted eggs, embroidered tablecloths and so on. If you prefer your prices clearly labelled, head for the **Folkart Centrum** *(☎ 318 4697; V Váci utca 58; open 10am-7pm daily).*

There's an excellent selection of Hungarian wines at the **Budapest Wine Society Shop** *(☎ 212 2569; I Batthyány utca 59; open 10am-8pm Mon-Fri, 10am-6pm Sat)* in Buda and **La Boutique des Vins** *(☎ 317 5919; V József Attila utca 12; open 10am-6pm Mon-Fri, 10am-3pm Sat)* in Pest.

Many record shops sell CDs and tapes of traditional folk music, including **Rózsavölgyi** *(☎ 318 3500; V Szervita tér 5; open 9.30am-7pm Mon-Fri, 10am-5pm Sat).* For locally produced classical CDs, tapes and vinyl, try **Concerto** *(☎ 268 9631; VII Dob utca 33; open noon-7pm Mon-Fri, noon-4pm Sun).*

GETTING THERE & AWAY

Air

In Budapest, the main ticket office for **Malév Hungarian Airlines** *(☎ 235 3534, 235 3417; w www.malev.hu; V Dorottya utca 2; open 8.30am-5.30pm Mon-Wed & Fri, 8.30am-6pm Thur)* is near Vörösmarty tér. Other major carriers and their locations include:

Aeroflot (☎ 318 5892) V Váci utca 4
Air France (☎ 318 0441) V Kristóf tér 6
British Airways (☎ 411 555) VIII Rákóczi út 1–3 (East-West Business Centre)
KLM Royal Dutch Airlines (☎ 373 7737) VIII Rákóczi út 1–3 (East-West Business Centre)
Lufthansa (☎ 266 4511) V Váci utca 19–21
SAS (☎ 266 2633) V Bajcsy-Zsilinszky út 12
Swiss International Air Lines/Brussels Airlines (☎ 328 5000) V Kristóf tér 7–8

For details of international flights to/from Budapest, see the general Getting There & Away section earlier in this chapter. For information on getting to/from Ferihegy airport, see the Getting Around section later.

Bus

For details of international bus services see the general Getting There & Away section earlier in this chapter.

All international buses and some – but not all – buses to/from southern and western Hungary now arrive at and depart from the new **Népliget bus station** *(☎ 264 3939; IX Üllői út 131; metro Népliget)* in Pest. The **ticket office** *(open 6am-6pm Mon-Fri, 6am-4pm Sat & Sun)* is upstairs. **Eurolines** *(☎ 219 8080, 219 8000)* is represented here, as is its Hungarian associate, **Volánbusz** *(☎ 1-485 2162, 485 2100; w www.volanbusz.hu).* There's a **left-luggage office** *(open 6am-9pm daily)* downstairs, which charges 150Ft per piece per day.

Népstadion bus station *(☎ 252 4498; XIV Hungária körút 48-52; metro Népstadion)* in Pest now serves most buses to domestic destinations. Things were in a state of flux at the time of research while the adjacent Budapest Sportcsarnok, destroyed by fire in 1999, was being rebuilt, but you should find the **ticket office** *(open 6am-6pm Mon-Fri, 6am-noon Sat & Sun)* as well as the **left-luggage office** *(open 6am-6pm daily)* here.

Most buses to the Danube Bend and parts of northern Hungary (eg, Balassagyarmat, Szécsény) arrive at and leave from the **Árpád Bridge bus station** *(☎ 329 1450, off XIII Róbert Károly körút; metro Árpád híd; ticket office open 7am-4pm Mon-Fri)* in Pest. The small **Széna tér bus station** *(☎ 201 3688, I Széna tér 1/a; metro Moszkva tér)* in Buda handles some traffic to and from the Pilis Hills and towns northwest of the capital, with some departures to Esztergom.

Train

For details of international trains, see the introductory Getting There & Away section earlier in this chapter. For general information on intercity train travel within Hungary, see the introductory Getting Around section.

The three main train stations are each on a metro line. **Keleti station** *(Eastern; ☎ 333 6342, 313 6835; VIII Kerepesi út 2-4; metro Keleti pályaudvar)* handles most (but not all) international trains, plus domestic trains to/from the north and northeast. For some Romanian and German destinations as well as domestic ones to/from the Great Plain and the Danube Bend, head for **Nyugati station** *(Western; ☎ 349 0115; VI Nyugati tér; metro Nyugati pályaudvar).* For trains bound for Transdanubia and Lake Balaton, go to **Déli station** *(Southern; ☎ 375 6293, 355 8657; I Krisztina körút 37/a; metro Déli pályaudvar).* Some trains to/from western and southern

Transdanubia also pass through Budapest's 'fourth' station – Kelenföld in Buda – but most of these services start or end at Déli or Keleti stations. Always check which station the train leaves from when you buy a ticket.

Buying Tickets Go to the **MÁV ticket office** (☎ 461 5500, 461 5400; w www.mav.hu; VI Andrássy út 35; open 9am-6pm Mon-Fri Apr-Sept, 9am-5pm Oct-Mar) for international train tickets and to make advance seat reservations for domestic express trains. The prices are the same as you would pay at the station and it accepts credit cards.

MÁV, Express (see Travel Agencies under Information earlier) and **Wasteels** (☎ 210 2802; open 8am-7pm Mon-Fri, 8am-1pm Sat) in Keleti station sell BIJ train tickets to those under 26, giving a 25% to 50% discount on fares to Western Europe. You must show your passport as proof of age.

You must have an ISIC card to get the student fare on international tickets. There are no student fares on domestic train travel.

Car & Motorcycle

Car rental costs have risen in recent years and are now usually charged in euros. One of the cheapest companies for renting cars is **Inka Rent a Car** (☎ 456 4666, fax 456 4699; e mail@inkarent.hu; IX Könyves Kálmán körút; open 8am-7pm Mon-Sat, 8am-2pm Sat). Although it is more expensive than Inka, **Americana Rent a Car** (☎ 350 2542, fax 320 8287; e americana@mail.matav.hu; XIII Dózsa György út 65) in the Ibis Volga hotel is reliable and has American cars with automatic transmissions.

The 25% ÁFA (value-added tax) on car rentals doesn't apply to nonresidents paying with foreign currency or credit card.

Hitching

Kenguru (☎ 266 5837, 483 0105; w www .kenguru.hu; VIII Kőfaragó utca 15; open 8am-6pm Mon-Fri, 10am-2pm Sat & Sun) matches up drivers and riders for a fee – mostly to points abroad. Approximate one-way fares include: Amsterdam 13,800Ft, London 15,200Ft, Munich 7300Ft, Paris 14,400Ft, Prague 5400Ft and Vienna 2800Ft.

Boat

Hydrofoils linking Budapest with Vienna via Bratislava run daily between April and early November; see River in the introductory Getting There & Away section of this chapter.

Mahart ferries link Budapest with the towns of the Danube Bend – see Getting There & Away under Szentendre in The Danube Bend section later in this chapter fo fares and schedules. In Budapest, boats leave from below Vigadó tér on the Pest side. The first stop is at Batthyány tér in Buda.

GETTING AROUND
To/From the Airport

The **Airport Minibus Service** (☎ 296 8555 fax 296 8993) ferries passengers in eight-sea vans from the airport directly to their hotel hostel or residence. The fare is 1800/3300F one way/return, and tickets are available at a clearly marked desk in the arrival halls. You need to book your journey to the airport 24 hours in advance.

The cheapest but most time-consuming method to get into town is to take the airpor bus (look for the stop marked 'BKV Plusz Reptér Busz' on the pavement between terminals 2A and 2B), which terminates a Kőbánya-Kispest metro station. From there take the blue metro line (M3) into the centre The total cost should be 190Ft.

If you want to take a taxi to the airport telephone **Tele 5** (☎ 355 5555). There is a fla fare of 2800Ft to or from the airport from Pes (3200Ft or from Buda).

Public Transport

All public transport in Budapest is run by **BKV** (Budapest Public Transport Company; ☎ 342 2335, 06-80 406 688; w www.bkv.hu).

The three underground metro lines meet a Deák tér: the little yellow line (M1) from Vörösmarty tér to Mexikói út; the red line (M2) from Déli train station to Örs vezér tere; and the blue line (M3) from Újpest-Központ to Kőbánya-Kispest. A possible source of confusion on the yellow line is that one stop is called Vörösmarty tér and another is Vörös-marty utca. The HÉV above-ground suburban railway, which runs north from Batthyány tér, is almost like a fourth metro line.

There's also an extensive network of buses, trams and trolleybuses. On certain bus lines the same numbered bus may have a black or a red number. The red-numbered bus is the express, which makes limited stops. A useful transit map detailing all services is available at most metro ticket booths.

The metro operates from 4.30am until 11.30pm. There are also some 17 night buses (marked with an É after the designated number) running every half-hour or so along the main routes.

Travelling 'black' (without a valid ticket) is risky; with better surveillance (especially in the metro), there's a good chance you'll get caught. The on-the-spot fine is 1600Ft, which rises to 4000Ft if you pay later at the BKV office (☎ 461 6800; VII Akácfa utca 22; open 6am-8pm Mon-Fri, 8am-2pm Sat).

Fares & Travel Passes To travel on the metro, trams, trolleybuses, buses and the HÉV (as far as the city limits), which is the Békásmegyer stop to the north) you must have a valid ticket, which you can buy at kiosks, newsstands or metro entrances. The basic fare for all forms of transport is 106Ft (1000/1910Ft for a block of 10/20 tickets), allowing you to travel as far as you like on the same metro, bus, trolleybus or tram line without changing. A ticket allowing unlimited stations with one change in 90 minutes costs 190Ft.

On the metro exclusively, the 106Ft base fare drops to 75Ft if you are just going three stops within 30 minutes. For 120Ft you can travel five stops and transfer at Deák tér to another metro line within one hour. Unlimited stations travelled with one change within 60 minutes costs 175Ft. You must always travel in one continuous direction on a metro ticket; return trips are not allowed. Tickets have to be validated in machines at metro entrances and on other forms of transport – inspectors will also fine you for not validating your ticket.

Life is much simpler if you buy a pass. Passes are valid on all trams, buses, trolleybuses, HÉV (within the city limits) and metro lines, and you don't have to worry about validating your ticket each time you get on.

A one-day pass is poor value at 850Ft, but the three-day pass (touristajegy, or tourist ticket) for 1700Ft and the seven-day pass (hetijegy, or one week) for 2100Ft are worthwhile for most people. You'll need a photo for the fortnightly (2650Ft) or monthly (4050Ft) passes.

Taxi
Overcharging (due to rigged meters or long detours) is quite common in Budapest. Never get into a taxi that does not have a yellow licence plate (as required by law), the logo of a reputable taxi firm on the side doors and a table of fares posted prominently.

Taxi firms apply different tariffs, but prices cannot exceed the legally enforced ceiling rates. Between 6am and 10pm the maximum flag fall allowed is 200Ft, the per-kilometre fee is 200Ft, and the waiting fee 50Ft a minute. From 10pm to 6am, the maximum charges are 280/280/70Ft. Hungarians rarely flag down taxis in the street – they almost always ring for them, and fares are actually cheaper if you book. Make sure you know the number of the landline phone you're calling from as that's how they establish your address (though you can call from a mobile too). Dispatchers usually speak English.

Following are the telephone numbers of several reliable taxi firms in order of preference: **City** (☎ 211 1111), **Fő** (☎ 222 2222), **Tele 5** (☎ 355 5555), **Rádió** (☎ 377 7777) and **Buda** (☎ 233 3333).

Boat
Between May and mid-September **BKV passenger ferries** (☎ 369 1359; ⓦ www.ship-bp .hu) depart from Boráros tér beside Petőfi Bridge and head to Pünkösdfürdő north of Aquincum, with many stops along the way. Tickets (500/400Ft adult/child from end to end or 400/200Ft from intermediate stops) are usually sold on board. The ferry stop closest to the Castle District is Batthyány tér, and Petőfi tér is not far from Vörösmarty tér, a convenient place to pick up the boat on the Pest side.

The Danube Bend

Between Vienna and Budapest, the Danube breaks through the Pilis and Börzsöny Hills in a sharp bend. Here medieval kings once ruled Hungary from majestic palaces overlooking the river at Esztergom and Visegrád. East of Visegrád, the river divides, with Szentendre and Vác on different branches and long, skinny Szentendre Island in the middle. Today the historic monuments, easy access, good facilities and forest trails combine to put this scenic area at the top of any visitor's list.

SZENTENDRE
☎ 26 • pop 21,400
Szentendre (St Andrew in English) is a pretty little town 19km north of Budapest on an arm of the Danube. With its charming old centre,

HUNGARY

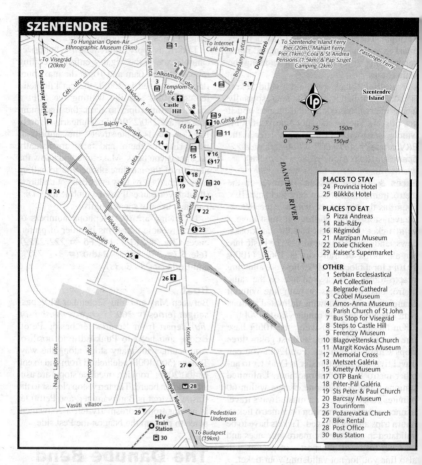

SZENTENDRE

To Hungarian Open-Air Ethnographic Museum (3km)
To Internet Café (50m)
To Szentendre Island Ferry Pier (20m), Mahart Ferry Pier (1km), Cola & St Andrea Pensions (1.5km) & Pap Sziget Camping (2km)
Passenger Ferry
To Visegrád (20km)
Dunakanyar körút
Pátriárka utca
Bogdányi utca
Duna korzó
Céh utca
Alkotmány utca
Rákóczi F utca
Templom tér
Castle Hill
Bajcsy - Zsilinszky
Fő tér
Görög utca
Szentendre Island
DANUBE RIVER
Kanonok utca
Duna korzó
Bükkös part
Paprikabíró utca
Kucsera Ferenc utca
Dumtsa Jenő utca
Bükkös Stream
Nagy Lajos utca
Ortonty utca
Kossuth Lajos utca
Dunakanyar körút
Vasúti villasor
Pedestrian Underpass
HÉV Train Station
To Budapest (19km)
Bus Station

0   75   150m
0   75   150yd

PLACES TO STAY
24 Provincia Hotel
25 Bükkös Hotel

PLACES TO EAT
5 Pizza Andreas
14 Rab-Ráby
16 Régimódi
21 Marzipan Museum
22 Dixie Chicken
29 Kaiser's Supermarket

OTHER
1 Serbian Ecclesiastical Art Collection
2 Belgrade Cathedral
3 Czóbel Museum
4 Ámos-Anna Museum
6 Parish Church of St John
7 Bus Stop for Visegrád
8 Steps to Castle Hill
9 Ferenczy Museum
10 Blagoveštenska Church
11 Margit Kovács Museum
12 Memorial Cross
13 Metszet Galéria
15 Kmetty Museum
17 OTP Bank
18 Péter-Pál Galéria
19 Sts Peter & Paul Church
20 Barcsay Museum
23 Tourinform
26 Požarevačka Church
27 Bike Rental
28 Post Office
30 Bus Station

Serbian Orthodox churches, art and craft galleries and easy accessibility from the capital, the place swells with tourists during the summer. Just try to avoid it at weekends.

Orientation & Information

From the HÉV and bus stations, it's a short walk under the subway and up Kossuth Lajos utca to Fő tér, the centre of the old town. The Duna korzó – the river embankment – is a block east of this square. There are no left-luggage offices at the HÉV or bus stations.

Tourinform (☎ 317 965; e szentendre@tourinform.hu; Dumtsa Jenő utca 22; open 9.30am-4.30pm Mon-Fri year-round, 10am-2pm Sat & Sun in summer) has brochures and information. The **OTP bank** (Dumtsa Jenő utca 6) is just off Fő tér, and the main **post**

office (Kossuth Lajos utca 23-25) is across from the bus and train stations.

There's an **Internet café** (Bogdányi utca 40), north of Fő tér, with Web access for 500Ft an hour.

Things to See

Begin your sightseeing at Fő tér, the town's central focus. Many of the buildings around this colourful square date from the 18th century, as does the **memorial cross** (1763) in the centre and the 1752 Greek Orthodox **Blagoveštenska Church** (☎ 310 554; admission 100Ft; open daily mid-Mar–Oct) on the northeastern corner.

The **Ferenczy Museum** (☎ 310 790; Fő tér 6; adult/child 300/150Ft; open 10am-6pm Wed-Sun Apr-Sept) displays artwork of the influential Ferenczy clan; paintings from Károly Ferenczy and sculptures, weaving and paintings from his three children.

Just east of Fő tér is the **Margit Kovács Museum** (☎ 310 244; Vastagh György utca 1; adult/child 450/220Ft; open 10am-6pm daily Feb-Oct). Kovács (1902–77) was a ceramicist who combined Hungarian folk, religious and modern themes to create Gothic-like figures. Narrow stepped lanes lead up from between Fő tér 8 & 9 to Castle Hill and the **Parish Church of St John** (rebuilt in 1710), from where you get great views of the town. Just north, the tall red tower of the Serbian **Belgrade Cathedral** (Pátriárka utca), from 1764, casts its shadow over the next-door **Serbian Ecclesiastical Art Collection** (☎ 312 399; adult/child 200/100Ft; open 10am-6pm Tues-Sun May-Oct, 10am-4pm Tues-Sun Mar & Apr, 10am-4pm Fri-Sun Jan & Feb).

The large **Hungarian Open-Air Ethnographic Museum** (☎ 502 500; adult/child 600/300Ft; open 9am-5pm Tues-Sun Apr-Oct, 9am-7pm July & Aug), which includes reassembled houses and buildings from around the country, is quite a way northwest on Sztaravodai út. Guided tours in English, French and German are available for 7000Ft. There's often a seasonal festival or everyday village activities going on; Tourinform stocks brochures with details. Up to 15 buses daily leave for the museum from stand No 7 at the bus station (about a 15-minute trip).

Szentendre has a plethora of museums and galleries not mentioned here; check with Tourinform for more details.

Activities

Szentendre Island has oodles of kilometres of uncrowded cycling – **rental bicycles** are available in the courtyard behind Kossuth Lajos utca 17-19 from 400Ft for one hour to 2500Ft for the day. **Canoes** and **motor boats** can be rented from **Dunabogdány** (☎/fax 390 086) for 1700Ft and 6000Ft per day respectively; boats are delivered, for which there's a minimal charge.

Places to Stay & Eat

You can easily see Szentendre on a day trip from Budapest, but if you want to stay the options range from inexpensive camping to pricey hotels.

About 2km north of Szentendre on Pap Island is **Pap Sziget Camping** (☎ 310 697; bus No 1, 2 or 3; camp sites per tent/adult/child 1900/900/500Ft, hostel singles/doubles 2600/3800Ft, bungalows & 4-person motel rooms 6000Ft; open May–mid-Oct). Generally the accommodation options of this leafy camping ground has shared bathrooms.

For rooms in **private houses** head west of the town centre around the Dunakanyar körút ring road, and look for 'Zimmer frei' signs.

If pensions are more your style there are a couple of places not far north. Take your pick between **Cola** (☎ 310 410, fax 500 539; Dunakanyar körút 50; singles/doubles €23/32), with comfy rooms (some with terrace), but is on a busy road; and **St Andrea** (☎ 311 989, fax 500 804; Egres utca 22; singles/doubles €20/25), which has simpler rooms but is on a quiet street.

More a pension than a hotel, **Bükkös Hotel** (☎ 312 021, fax 310 782; Bükkös part 16; singles/doubles €40/45) is central and has good rooms.

The three-star **Provincia Hotel** (☎ 301 082, fax 301 085; Paprikabíró utca 21-23; singles/doubles €50/61) has modern rooms and a sauna, swimming pool and garage.

In a tourist hub like Szentendre, you're not going to starve. **Régimódi** (☎ 311 105; Dumtsa Jenő utca 2), just down from the Margit Kovács Museum, has a filling Hungarian set menu for 1500Ft. Another old stand-by is **Rab-Ráby** (☎ 310 819; Péter-Pál utca 1; mains 1000-2000Ft).

For a simple affair with outdoor seating try **Pizza Andreas** (☎ 310 530; Duna korzó 5; pizzas from 700Ft).

Dixie Chicken (☎ 311 008; Dumtsa Jenő utca 16; burgers from 240Ft) is your standard fast-food joint, but it does have a salad bar. A large **Kaiser's supermarket** is next to the HÉV station if you want to give Szentendre's touristy restaurants a miss and have a riverside picnic.

The unusual **Marzipan Museum** (☎ 310 931; Dumtsa Jenő utca 12; admission to museum 250Ft) is a good place to stop for cake and ice cream.

Getting There & Away

Bus & Train Take the HÉV from Budapest's Batthyány tér metro station to the end of the line (40 minutes). You'll never wait longer than 20 minutes, and the last train leaves Szentendre for Budapest at 11.10pm. Some HÉV trains run only as far as Békásmegyer, where you cross the platform to catch the Szentendre train.

Buses from Budapest's Árpád híd bus station, which is on the blue metro line, also run to Szentendre frequently. Some buses continue on to Visegrád (eight buses daily) and Esztergom (17 a day).

Boat From late May to early September, one daily Mahart ferry plies the Danube to/from Budapest's Vigadó tér (830/1660Ft one way/return), departing from Budapest at 9am and Szentendre at 11.45am and 5.55pm. From mid-June to early September two extra ferries leave Budapest at 10.30am (express hydrofoil; 1300Ft one way; Tuesday to Sunday only) and 2pm and one from Szentendre at 5.45pm (express hydrofoil; Tuesday to Sunday only). From April to late May and September until seasonal shutdown, one boat daily leaves Budapest at 9am and Szentendre at 5.15pm. There is one departure from Szentendre (10.40am) to Visegrád during the low season and two in the high season (10.40am and 3.30pm). The 3.30pm departure continues on to Esztergom. The riverboat terminal is 1km north of town at the end of Czóbel Béla sétány.

VISEGRÁD
☎ 26 • pop 1540

Visegrád is superbly situated on the Danube's abrupt loop between the Pilis and Börzsöny Hills. After the 13th-century Mongol invasions, Hungarian kings built a mighty citadel on the hill top and a lower castle near the river. In the 14th century a royal palace was built on the flood plain at the foot of the hills and in 1323 King Charles Robert of Anjou, whose claim to the local throne was being fiercely contested in Buda, moved the royal household here. For nearly two centuries Hungarian royalty alternated between Visegrád and Buda.

The destruction of Visegrád came with the Turks and later the Habsburgs who destroyed the citadel to prevent Hungarian independence fighters from using it. All trace of the palace was lost until 1934 when archaeologists, by following descriptions in literary sources, uncovered the ruins that you can visit today.

The small town has two distinct areas; one to the north around Mahart ferry pier and another, the main town, about 1km to the south. There's a bank in the main centre at Rév utca, but it isn't always open and doesn't have an ATM.

Things to See & Do
The partly reconstructed **Royal Palace** (☎ 398 026; Fő utca 29; adult/child 400/200Ft; open 9am-4.30pm Tues-Sun), 400m south of the Mahart pier, doesn't come anywhere near its former glory, but is still worth a look. Highlights include the working Hercules Fountain in the Gothic courtyard and a small museum devoted to the history of the palace and its reconstruction.

The palace's original Gothic fountain is in the museum at **Solomon's Tower** (☎ 398 233; adult/child 400/200Ft; open 9am-4.30pm Tues-Sun May-Sept), a few hundred metres north of the palace ruins. This was part of a lower castle controlling river traffic.

Visegrád Citadel (adult/child 500/250Ft; open 9.30am-6pm daily mid-Mar–mid-Oct, weekends only rest of year) is high on a hill directly above Solomon's Tower. While the citadel (1259) itself is not particularly spectacular, the view of the Danube Bend from the walls is well worth the climb. There's a small museum on torture and some quasi-medieval activities. From the town centre a trail leads to the citadel from behind the Catholic church on Fő tér; this is less steep than the arduous climb from Solomon's Tower. **Citibus** (☎ 311 996), a local bus service, runs up to the citadel from the Mahart ferry pier three times daily (more often in July and August).

Places to Stay & Eat
On Mogyoróhegy (Hazelnut Hill), just about 2km northeast of the citadel, **Jurta Camping** (☎ 398 217; camp sites per tent/adult/child 420/550/350Ft; open May-Sept) is nicely situated but far from the centre, and buses only run there between June and August.

Visegrád Tours (☎ 398 160; Rév utca 15), near the bank, can organise private rooms starting at 4000/5900Ft for singles/doubles. Many houses along Fő utca and Széchenyi utca in the main centre have signs advertising 'Zimmer frei'.

Haus Honti (☎ 398 120, fax 397 274; Fő utca 66; singles/doubles 7000/8000Ft) is a friendly pension with homely rooms. Backing onto the pension, and accessible from the main road to Esztergom, is the pension's newer and more expensive cousin, **Hotel Honti** (singles/doubles 9000/10,000Ft), with its modern, spacious rooms.

If you go in for men in tights and silly hats, the medieval-style **Reneszánsz** (☎ 398 081;

Fő utca 11; mains 900-1500Ft), opposite the Mahart pier, can be a lot of fun. A better and cheaper deal is **Grill Udvar** *(Rév utca 6; pizzas & mains from 500Ft)*, opposite the bank. **Gulás Csárda** *(☎ 398 329)*, in town at the start of Mátyás király utca, serves reliable Hungarian standards for around 1000Ft.

Getting There & Away

Bus & Train Buses are very frequent (up to 16 daily) to and from Budapest's Árpád híd station, the Szentendre HÉV station and Esztergom. No railway line reaches Visegrád, but you can take one of many trains bound for Szob from Budapest's Nyugati station. Get off at Nagymaros-Visegrád, and hop on the ferry across to Visegrád.

Boat Between mid-June and early September, three daily Mahart ferries (7.30am, 9am and 2pm) leave Budapest for Visegrád (870/1740Ft one way/return, 3½ hours). Two of these ferries continue on to Esztergom at 10.55am and 5pm. Ferries to Budapest depart from Visegrád at 10.30am, 4.30pm and 5.30pm; only the first two stop in Szentendre on the way. On weekends from July to mid-August there is a high-speed hydrofoil from Budapest to Visegrád (1790/2990Ft, one hour), departing from Budapest at 9.30am and Visegrád at 3.55pm.

Hourly ferries cross the Danube to Nagymaros (170/170/700Ft per person/bicycle/car). The ferry operates all year except when the Danube freezes over or fog descends.

ESZTERGOM

☎ 33 • pop 29,300

Esztergom, at the western entrance to the Danube Bend, is one of Hungary's most historically important cities and has been the seat of Roman Catholicism here for more than a millennium. Second-century Roman emperor-to-be Marcus Aurelius wrote his *Meditations* while he camped here. Stephen I, founder of the Hungarian state, was born and crowned at Esztergom, and it was the royal seat from the late 10th to the mid-13th centuries. Originally the clerics lived by the river bank while royalty lived in the hill-top palace. When the king departed for Buda after the Mongol invasion, the archbishop moved up and occupied the palace, maintaining Esztergom's prominence. In 1543 the Turks ravaged the town and much of it was rebuilt in the 18th and 19th centuries.

Orientation & Information

The train station is on the southern edge of town, about a 10-minute walk south of the bus station. From the train station, walk north on Baross Gábor út, then along Ady Endre utca to Simor János utca. The ticket clerk at the train station holds luggage (open 24 hours).

Gran Tours *(☎/fax 502 000; Széchenyi tér 25; open 8am-6pm Mon-Fri, 9am-noon Sat June-Aug, 8am-4pm Mon-Fri Sept-May)* is best in town for information. You could also try **Cathedralis Tours** *(☎ 415 260; cnr Bajcsy-Zsilinszky utca & Batthyány Lajos utca; open 8am-5pm Mon-Fri, 9am-noon Sat)*.

The **OTP bank** *(Rákóczi tér)* does foreign exchange transactions. The **post office** *(Arany János utca 2)* is just off Széchenyi tér.

Things to See & Do

You can't miss **Esztergom Basilica** *(☎ 411 895; admission free; open 7am-6pm daily)*, built on a hill high above the Danube – it's the largest church in Hungary. The colossal building was rebuilt in the neoclassical style in the 19th century, but the white and red marble **Bakócz Chapel** (1510) on the south side was moved here from an earlier church. Underneath the cathedral is a large **crypt** *(admission 50Ft; open 9am-5pm daily)*; among those buried in the crypt is the controversial Cardinal Mindszenty who, among other things, was imprisoned by the communists for refusing to allow Hungary's Catholic schools to be secularised. The **treasury** *(adult/child 250/150Ft; open 9am-4.30pm daily mid-Mar–Oct, 11am-3.30pm Nov–mid-Mar)* contains priceless and beautiful medieval objects, including the 13th-century Hungarian coronation cross. It's worth making the twisting climb up to the **cupola** *(admission 100Ft)* for outstanding views over the city – this is not for the faint-hearted, particularly when it's windy.

At the southern end of the hill is the **Castle Museum** *(☎ 415 986; adult/child 400/200Ft; open 9am-4.30pm Tues-Sun Apr-Oct, 10am-4pm Nov-Mar)*, with partially reconstructed remnants of the medieval royal palace (1215) and archaeological finds from the region.

Southwest of the cathedral along the banks of the Little Danube is the pretty Víziváros (Watertown) district, home to the **Watertown Parish Church** (1738), with its fairy-tale air. Esztergom's **Christian Museum** *(☎ 413 880; Berényi Zsigmond utca 2; adult/child 250/150Ft; open 10am-6pm Tues-Sun)* is in the

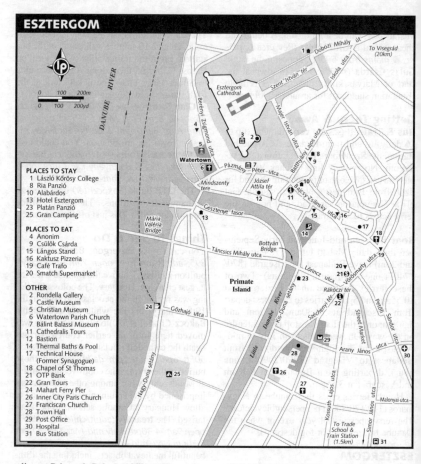

ESZTERGOM

PLACES TO STAY
1 László Kőrösy College
8 Ria Panzió
10 Alabárdos
13 Hotel Esztergom
23 Platán Panzió
25 Gran Camping

PLACES TO EAT
4 Anonim
9 Csülök Csárda
15 Lángos Stand
16 Kaktusz Pizzeria
19 Café Trafo
20 Smatch Supermarket

OTHER
2 Rondella Gallery
3 Castle Museum
5 Christian Museum
6 Watertown Parish Church
7 Bálint Balassi Museum
11 Cathedralis Tours
12 Bastion
14 Thermal Baths & Pool
17 Technical House
   (Former Synagogue)
18 Chapel of St Thomas
21 OTP Bank
22 Gran Tours
24 Mahart Ferry Pier
26 Inner City Paris Church
27 Franciscan Church
28 Town Hall
29 Post Office
30 Hospital
31 Bus Station

adjacent Primate's Palace (1882). It houses the best collection of medieval religious art in the country. Nearby is the **Bálint Balassi Museum** (☎ 412 185; Pázmány Péter utca 13; adult/child 100/50Ft; open 9am-5pm Tues-Sun), with objects of local interest.

Cross the bridge south of Watertown Parish Church and about 100m farther south is the recently completed **Mária Valéria Bridge**. Destroyed during WWII, it once again connects Esztergom with the Slovakian city of Štúrovo.

The Moorish Romantic-style **Technical House** (Imaház utca 4), dating from 1888, once served as a synagogue for Esztergom's Jewish community, the oldest in Hungary.

Esztergom has some outdoor **thermal baths** (☎ 312 249; Bajcsy-Zsilinszky utca 14;

adult/child 350/150Ft; open 9am-6pm daily May-Sept). You can use the **indoor pool** (open 6am-6pm Mon & Sat, 6am-7pm Tues-Fri, 9am-4pm Sun) the rest of the year.

Places to Stay

Gran Camping (☎ 411 953; fax 402 513; Nagy-Duna sétány 3; camp sites per tent/adult/child/car 950/950/500/1000Ft, dorm beds 1700Ft, bungalows 9000-13,000Ft, doubles 6500Ft; open May-Sept), down a quiet lane by the Danube, is small and central. Bungalows sleep four to six.

Contact Gran Tours (see Information earlier) for **private rooms** (from 2000Ft) or **apartments** (about 6000Ft). From July to late August dormitory rooms become available at the **trade school** (☎ 411 746; Budai Nagy

HUNGARY

Antal utca 38; dorm beds 1200Ft) near the train station; and at the **László Kőrösy College** *(☎ 400 005; Szent István tér 16; dorm beds 2700Ft)*, opposite the cathedral.

The large, plain **Platán Panzió** *(☎ 411 355; Kis-Duna sétány 11; rooms from 4200Ft)* has doubles with a shared bathroom. It's central and relatively cheap.

Comfortable **Alabárdos** *(☎/fax 312 640; Bajcsy-Zsilinszky utca 49; singles/doubles 6000/9000Ft)* is close to the basilica. The nearby but flashier **Ria Panzió** *(☎ 313 115; fax 401 429, Batthyány Lajos utca 11; singles/doubles 8500/10,500Ft)* has private parking and good-sized rooms.

Hotel Esztergom *(☎ 412 555, fax 412 853; Nagy-Duna sétány; singles/doubles €42/56)* looks like it might be a 1970s hotel in decline, but it's actually quite good. There's a rather fancy restaurant, roof terrace and sports centre.

Places to Eat

The cheapest place in town to grab a bite to eat is the small **lángos stand** at the entrance to the baths.

For something less casual try **Csülök Csárda** *(☎ 312 420; Batthyány Lajos utca 9; mains from 850Ft)*, popular with both visitors and locals and serving good home cooking and huge main courses.

Anonim *(☎ 411 880; Berényi Zsigmond utca 4; mains 1000-2400Ft; open until 10pm daily)*, in a historical townhouse, serves small but excellent dishes. For pizza, pasta and salads, head to the small **Kaktusz Pizzeria** *(Bajcsy-Zsilinszky utca 25-27; pizzas from 450Ft; open until 10pm daily)*.

Modern **Cafe Trafó** *(Vörösmarty utca 15; coffee from 100Ft)* is a little island oasis (literally) – *the* place to take a breather, sit back and relax. There's a **Smatch supermarket** on Bajcsy-Zsilinszky utca.

Getting There & Away

Bus & Train Buses to/from Budapest's Árpád híd bus station run about every half-hour from around 4am to 6.30pm. Buses from Budapest to Esztergom may travel via Dorog (75 minutes) or Visegrád and Szentendre (two hours). Buses to Visegrád and Szentendre depart almost hourly from 6am to 8.40pm and to Sopron and Győr once daily.

Trains to Esztergom depart from Budapest's Nyugati train station (1½ hours) up to 13 times a day. To get to western Transdanubia

from Esztergom, take one of the three daily trains to Komárom (1½ hours) where you can pick up connecting trains to Győr, Sopron and Lake Balaton.

Boat Mahart riverboats travel to/from Budapest (910/1820Ft one way/return, five hours) once a day from late May to mid-June, and twice a day beween mid-June and late September. From April to late May and late September to seasonal shutdown, they only run on Saturday and bank holidays, leaving Budapest at 8am and Esztergom at 3pm. A speedy hydrofoil makes the run from Budapest to Esztergom (1990/3390Ft, 1½ hours) weekends only between early July and mid-August, departing from Budapest at 9.30am and from Esztergom at 3.30pm.

Western Transdanubia

Beyond the Bakony Hills, northwest of Lake Balaton, lies western Transdanubia, a region that's bounded by the Danube and the Alps. Conquered by the Romans but never fully occupied by the Turks, this enchanting corner of Hungary contains picturesque small towns and cities with a decidedly Central European air. The old quarters of Sopron and Győr are brimming with what were once the residences of prosperous burghers and clerics, Kőszeg offers an intact medieval castle, Fertőd a magnificent baroque palace and Pannonhalma a functioning Benedictine monastery.

GYŐR

☎ 96 • pop 129,500

Győr (pronounced **jyeur**) is Hungary's third-largest industrial centre, but you'd never know it standing in its charming old centre. This historic city, midway between Budapest and Vienna at the point where the Mosoni-Danube, Rábca and Rába Rivers meet, was the site of a Roman town named Arrabona. In the 11th century, Stephen I established a bishopric here and in the 16th century a fortress was erected to hold back the Turks.

Orientation & Information

The large neobaroque City Hall (1898) rises up across from the train station. The **left-luggage office** *(open 5am-11pm daily)* at the

HUNGARY

GYŐR

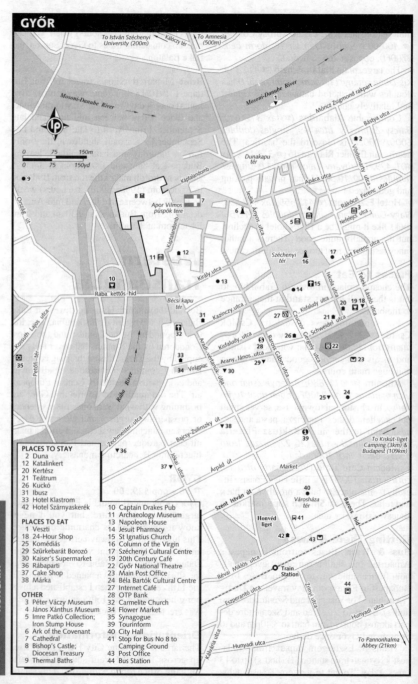

To István Széchenyi University (200m)
Kalóczy tér
To Amnesia (500m)

Mosoni-Danube River

Mosoni-Danube River

Mórcz Zsigmond rakpart

Bástya utca

Vörösmarty utca

Apáca utca

Rákóczi Ferenc utca

Nefelejcs utca

Dunakapu tér

Káptalandomb

Apor Vilmos püspök tere

Kálptalandomb

Jedlik Ányos utca

Liszt Ferenc utca

Teleki László utca

Iskola utca

Széchenyi tér

Király utca

Bécsi kapu tér

Kazinczy utca

Czuczor Gergely utca

Kisfaludy utca

Kisfaludy utca

Schweidel utca

Baross Gábor utca

Arany János utca

Virágpiac

Zechmeister utca

Bajcsy-Zsilinszky út

Jókai utca

Árpád út

Market

Váróscsháza tér

Szent István út

Honvéd liget

Révai Miklós utca

Eszperantó utca

Kálvária utca

Hunyadi utca

Barcs hid

Train Station

Zrínyi utca

Hunyadi utca

To Kiskút-liget Camping (3km) & Budapest (109km)

To Pannonhalma Abbey (21km)

Mosoni-Danube River

Rába River

Kossuth Lajos utca

Petőfi-tér

Ország út

Aradi vértanúk útja

PLACES TO STAY
2 Duna
12 Katalinkert
20 Kertész
21 Teátrum
26 Kuckó
31 Ibusz
33 Hotel Klastrom
42 Hotel Szárnyaskerék

PLACES TO EAT
1 Veszti
18 24-Hour Shop
25 Komédiás
29 Szürkebarát Borozó
30 Kaiser's Supermarket
36 Rábaparti
38 Márka

OTHER
3 Péter Váczy Museum
4 János Xánthus Museum
5 Imre Patkó Collection; Iron Stump House
6 Ark of the Covenant
7 Cathedral
8 Bishop's Castle; Diocesan Treasury
9 Thermal Baths
10 Captain Drakes Pub
11 Archaeology Museum
13 Napoleon House
14 Jesuit Pharmacy
15 St Ignatius Church
16 Column of the Virgin
17 Széchenyi Cultural Centre
19 20th Century Café
22 Győr National Theatre
23 Main Post Office
24 Béla Bartók Cultural Centre
27 Internet Café
28 OTP Bank
32 Carmelite Church
34 Flower Market
35 Synagogue
39 Tourinform
40 City Hall
41 Stop for Bus No 8 to Camping Ground
43 Post Office
44 Bus Station

HUNGARY

station is next to the exit from one of the two tunnels under the tracks (the one directly opposite the start of Aradi vértanúk útja). This same tunnel leads directly through to the main bus station, just south of the train station.

Baross Gábor utca, which leads to the old town and the rivers, lies diagonally across from City Hall. Much of central Győr is pedestrianised, making parking difficult but walking the city a real pleasure.

There's a **Tourinform** (☎ 311 771; e gyor@ tourinform.hu; *Árpád út 32; open 8am-8pm Mon-Fri, 9am-6pm Sat & Sun June–mid-Sept; 8am-6pm Mon-Fri, 9am-2pm Sat Apr & May; 9am-4pm Mon-Fri, 9am-2pm Sat mid-Sept– Mar)* office on the corner of Árpád út and Baross Gábor utca.

OTP bank *(Baross Gábor 16)* has a branch on the main pedestrian street. There are several ATMs around the town centre.

There's a post office next to the train station and the **main post office** *(Bajcsy-Zsilinszky út 46)* is to the northeast of this. A small **Internet café** *(Czuczor Gergely utca 6)* is bizarrely located above a clothes shop and charges 200Ft per hour.

Things to See

The enchanting **Carmelite church** (1725) and many fine baroque palaces line Bécsí kapu tér. On the northwestern side of the square are the fortifications built in the 16th century to stop the Turks. A short distance east is **Napoleon House** *(Király utca 4)*, where Bonaparte spent his only night in Hungary in 1809.

Head north along one of the narrow, pedestrianised lanes that lead up to Chapter Hill (Káptalandomb), the oldest part of Győr. The solid baroque **Cathedral** *(open 10am-noon & 2pm-5pm daily)* on the hill was originally Romanesque, but most of what you see inside dates from the 17th and 18th centuries. Don't miss the Gothic **Hédervárý Chapel** on the southern side of the cathedral, which contains a glittering 15th-century bust of King (and St) Ladislas. West of the cathedral is the fortified **Bishop's Castle** in a mixture of styles, which now houses the **Diocesan Treasury** *(☎ 312 153; adult/child 300/100Ft; open 10am-4pm Tues-Sun)*.

The streets behind the cathedral are full of old palaces, and at the bottom of the hill on Jedlik Ányos utca is the **Ark of the Covenant**, an outstanding baroque statue dating from 1731. From here you can head north to a

bridge overlooking the junction of the city's three rivers.

One of the nicest things about Győr is its atmospheric old streets. Stroll down Bástya utca, Apáca utca, Rákóczi Ferenc utca, Liszt Ferenc utca and Király utca, where you'll see many fine buildings. The late-Renaissance palace was once a charity hospital, and now houses the **Péter Váczy Museum** *(☎ 318 141; Rákóczi Ferenc utca 6; admission free; open 10am-6pm Tues-Sun Mar-Oct, 10am-5pm Nov-Feb)*. Enter around the back at Nefelejcs utca 3.

Széchenyi tér is the heart of Győr and features the **Column of the Virgin** (1686) in the middle. **St Ignatius Church** (1641) is the finest in the city with a superb pulpit, pews and ceiling frescoes. The **Jesuit Pharmacy** *(☎ 320 954; Széchenyi tér 9; admission free; open 7.30am-4pm Mon-Fri)* is a fully operational baroque institution.

Cross the square to the **János Xantus Museum** *(☎ 310 588; Széchenyi tér 5; adult/child 400/200Ft; open 10am-6pm Tues-Sun)*, which is in a palace built in 1743. Beside it is the **Iron Stump House** *(Széchenyi tér 4)*, which still sports the beam onto which itinerant artisans would drive a nail to mark their visit. The building now houses the **Imre Patkó Collection** *(☎ 310 588; adult/child 300/150Ft; open 10am-6pm Tues-Sun)* of paintings and Asian and African art, one of Hungary's finest small museums.

Pannonhalma Abbey If you have a half-day to spare, it's worth visiting Pannonhalma Abbey *(☎ 570 191; open 8.30am-6pm daily June-Sept, 8.30am or 9.30am-4.30pm or 5pm Tues-Sun Oct-May)*, a Unesco World Heritage listed site on top of a 282m hill some 21km south of Győr. Highlights include the Gothic cloister (1486), the Romanesque basilica (1225) and the 11th-century crypt.

Because it's a working monastery, the abbey must be visited with a guide. Tours in Hungarian with foreign-language text cost 1000/300Ft per adult/child, while tours in foreign languages are 2000/1000Ft. From late March to mid-November tours are available at 11am and 1pm in English, Italian, German, French and Russian. In the low season, tours in foreign languages are available only by request. The entry fee includes the tour.

Pannonhalma is best reached from Győr by bus (almost every hour) as the train station is

2km southwest of the abbey. To be safe, allow one hour to travel the 18km by bus.

Activities

Győr's **thermal baths** (☎ 522 646; Ország út 4; adult/child 500/400Ft; open 9am-6pm daily May-Sept), west of the Rába River, was undergoing a major face-lift at the time of research, but should be ready by the end of 2003. There is also a **covered pool** (open 6am-8pm Mon-Fri year-round).

Places to Stay

Camping Some 3km northeast of town is the **Kiskút-liget Camping** (☎ 318 986; camp sites including tent & one person 1470Ft, 4-person bungalows 4300Ft; motel doubles 3800Ft; bungalows open mid-Apr–mid-Oct, motel open year-round) in suburban Győr. Take bus No 8 from beside City Hall.

Private Rooms & Hostels Private rooms are available from the friendly **Ibusz** (☎ 311 700; Kazinczy utca 3) office from 2000Ft per person. Dormitory accommodation is available year-round at the huge **István Széchenyi University** (☎ 503 447; Héderváry út 3; dorm beds around 1000Ft) north of the town centre. Check with Tourinform for other possibilities.

Pensions Győr is full of small private pensions and, while not the cheapest places to stay, they are usually very central and in some of the city's most atmospheric old buildings.

Kuckó (☎ 316 260, fax 312 195; Arany János utca 33; singles/doubles 5900/7490Ft) has nine rooms with private bath in a lovely old townhouse. The new kid on the block is **Katalinkert** (☎/fax 542 088; Sarkantyú köz 3; singles/doubles 5800/7500Ft), with six nice modern rooms tucked away above a pleasant courtyard restaurant.

Kertész (☎/fax 517 461; Iskola utca 11; singles/doubles 6000/8000Ft) is bigger with nine rooms, all with bath. Other fine choices, and under the same management, are **Teátrum** (☎ 310 640, fax 328 827; Schweidel utca 7; singles/doubles/triples 6200/7900/9500Ft), on a pedestrianised mall; and the pretty **Duna** (☎/fax 329 084; Vörösmarty utca 5; singles/doubles/triples 6200/7900/9500Ft).

Hotels Convenient to the train and bus stations is **Hotel Szárnyaskerék** (☎ 314 629; Révai Miklós utca 5; doubles with/without bath 6900/4650Ft), a large, institutional-like place. Only four rooms have en suite baths.

If your budget is bigger, you shouldn't go past **Hotel Klastrom** (☎ 516 910, fax 327 030; e klastrom@arrabonet.gyor.hu; Zechmeister utca 1; singles/doubles/triples €49/66/76), wonderfully positioned by the river just off Bécsí kapu tér. It has rooms in a beautifully restored 250-year-old Carmelite convent, and a sauna and solarium for guests.

Places to Eat

Komédiás (☎ 527 217; Czuczor Gergely utca 30; mains around 1000Ft) is a cellar restaurant worth a try, as is atmospheric **Veszti** (☎ 337 700; Móricz Zsigmond rakpart 3; pizzas from 390Ft, mains from 760Ft; open 11am-1pm daily). Situated on an old paddle-steamer on the Mosoni-Duna River, it has a huge range of pizzas and Tex-Mex/Americana mains.

For a cheap and filling meal, try **Rábaparti** (Zechmeister utca 15; mains from 700Ft), an unpretentious (though rather gloomy) restaurant. For a self-service meal, head for **Márka** (☎ 320 800; Bajcsy-Zsilinszky út 30; salads & mains around 430Ft; buffet open 11am-5pm Mon-Sat).

A decent wine cellar is **Szürkebarát Borozó** (☎ 311 548; Arany János utca 20; mains from 600Ft). A stairway in the courtyard leads down into this vaulted restaurant. There's an excellent ice-cream stand in the same courtyard. For cakes, don't go past the tiny **cake shop** at Jókai utca 6. It's so popular people line up along the footpath.

A massive **Kaiser's supermarket** (cnr Arany János utca & Aradi vértanúk útja) and department store takes up much of the block on this corner.

There's a **24-hour shop** on the corner of Teleki László utca and Schweidel utca and another at the train station.

Entertainment

The celebrated Győr Ballet and the city's opera company and philharmonic orchestra all perform at the modern **Győr National Theatre** (☎ 314 800; Czuczor Gergely utca 7), a technically advanced though rather unattractive structure covered in op art tiles by Victor Vasarely.

In summer there's a month-long festival of music, theatre and dance from late June to late July. In March, Győr hosts many events in conjunction with Budapest's Spring Festival.

Captain Drakes Pub *(Radó sétány)* on the little island in the Rába River is a great spot for a drink on balmy summer evenings. **Amnesia** *(Héderváry utca 16)* is a club/bar north of the city centre that attracts a student crowd, while the **20th Century Café** *(Schweidel utca 25)* is central and caters to a more mature audience.

Getting There & Away

Bus Buses travel to Balatonfüred (four daily), Budapest (every hour), Esztergom (one per day), Hévíz (two daily), Keszthely (five daily), Pannonhalma (hourly), Pécs (two daily) and Vienna (one to three daily). To get to Fertőd, you must take the Sopron bus to Kapuvár (up to 12 a day) and change there.

Train Győr is well connected by express train to Budapest's Déli, Kelenföld and Keleti train stations (1½ hours) and to Sopron (1½ hours). Other trains go to Szombathely (1¾ hours) via Celldömölk. To go to Lake Balaton take one of the six trains daily heading south to Veszprém (2½ hours) via Pannonhalma.

For Vienna's Westbahnhof you may have to change trains at Hegyeshalom since some express trains don't pick up passengers at Győr. Another route to Austria requires a change at Sopron and passes through Wiener Neustadt before arriving at Vienna's Südbahnhof.

SOPRON

☎ 99 • pop 55,000

Sopron (Ödenburg in German) sits right on the Austrian border, only 69km south of Vienna. In 1921 the town's residents voted in a referendum to remain part of Hungary, while the rest of Bürgenland (the region to which Sopron used to belong) went to Austria.

Sopron has been an important centre since the time of the Romans, who called it Scarbantia. The Mongols and Turks never got this far, so numerous medieval structures remain intact. In the small, horseshoe-shaped old town, still partially enclosed by medieval walls built on Roman foundations, almost every building is historically important.

Orientation & Information

From the main train station, walk north on Mátyás király utca, which becomes Várkerület after a few blocks. Várkerület and Ógabona tér form a loop right around the old town, following the line of the former city walls. Előkapu (Front Gate) and Hátsókapu (Back Gate) are

the two main entrances to the old town and Fő tér, the town's central square.

The bus station is northwest of the old town on Lackner Kristóf utca. There is a **left-luggage office** *(open 3am-11pm daily)* in the main train station. There's no left-luggage area at the bus station.

Tourinform *(☎/fax 338 892;* e *sopron@ tourinform.hu; Előkapu 11; open 9am-5pm daily June-Aug, 9am-4pm daily Sept-May)* is right near the Fire Tower.

There is an **OTP bank** *(Várkerület 96/a)* outside the old town. For Internet access head to **Internet Sopron** *(Új utca 3; open 11am-8pm Mon-Fri, 10am-5pm Sat)*, which charges 400Ft for an hour's surfing.

Things to See

The 60m-high **Fire Tower** *(☎ 311 327; Fő tér; adult/child 300/150Ft; open 10am-6pm Tues-Sun Apr-Oct)*, above the old town's northern gate, is a true architectural hybrid. The 2m-thick square base, built on a Roman gate, dates from the 12th century, the middle cylindrical and arcaded balcony was built in the 16th century and the baroque spire was added in 1680. You can climb up to the top for a marvellous view of the city. **Fidelity Gate** at the bottom of the tower pictures Hungary receiving the *civitas fidelissima* (most loyal citizenry) of Sopron. It was erected in 1922 after that crucial plebiscite.

In the centre of Fő tér is the magnificent **Holy Trinity Column** (1701) and beyond this the 13th-century **Goat Church**, whose name comes from the heraldic animal of its chief benefactor. Below the church is the **Chapter Hall** *(☎ 338 843; Templom utca 1; admission free; open 10am-noon & 2pm-5pm Tues-Sun May-Sept)*, part of a 14th-century Franciscan monastery with frescoes and stone carvings.

Of the several excellent museums on Fő tér, two stand out (both are open 10am to 6pm Tuesday to Sunday April to September, and 10am to 2pm October to March). **Fabricius House** *(☎ 311 327; adult/child 300/150Ft)* at No 6 is a comprehensive historical museum with rooms on the upper floors that are devoted to domestic life in the 17th and 18th centuries and has impressive Roman sculpture in the Gothic cellar. **Storno House** *(☎ 311 327; adult/child 500/250Ft)* at No 8 is a famous Renaissance palace (1560) that is now a museum and gallery of Romanesque and Gothic decorative art.

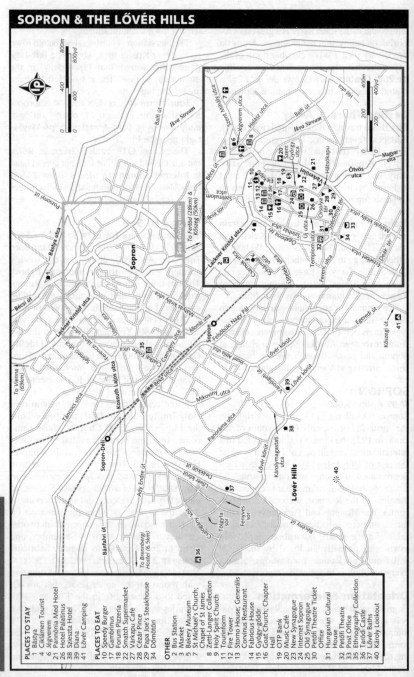

SOPRON & THE LŐVÉR HILLS

PLACES TO STAY
1 Bástya
4 Ciklámen Tourist
6 Jégverem
21 Pannónia Med Hotel
26 Hotel Palatinus
38 Szieszta Hotel
39 Diana
41 Lővér Camping

PLACES TO EAT
10 Speedy Burger
17 Gambrinus
18 Forum Pizzeria
22 Smatch Supermarket
27 Várkapu Café
28 Cézár Pince
29 Papa Joe's Steakhouse
34 Dömötöri

OTHER
2 Bus Station
3 Market
5 Bakery Museum
7 St Michael's Church;
   Chapel of St James
8 Zettl-Langer Collection
9 Holy Spirit Church
11 Tourinform
12 Fire Tower
13 Storno House; Generális
   Corvinus Restaurant
14 Fabricius House
15 Gyógy-gödör
16 Goat Church; Chapter
   Hall
19 OTP Bank
20 Music Café
23 New Synagogue
24 Internet Sopron
25 Old Synagogue
30 Petőfi Theatre Ticket
   Office
31 Hungarian Cultural
   House
32 Petőfi Theatre
35 Post Office
36 Ethnography Collection
37 Járdó Castle
38 Lővér Baths
40 Károly Lookout

A unique museum of Jewish life is housed in the 14th-century Old Synagogue (Új utca 22; adult/child 200/100Ft; open 9am-5pm Wed-Mon Mar-Sept), and it is in better condition than many others scattered throughout the country.

In the Ikva district north of the old town are several more interesting museums, including the excellent Zettl-Langer Collection (☎ 335 123; Balfi út 11; admission 200Ft; open 10am-noon Tues-Sun) of ceramics, paintings and furniture; and the hunger-inducing Bakery Museum (☎ 311 327; Bécsí út 5; adult/child 200/100Ft; open 10am-2pm Tues-Sun May-Aug).

To visit the hills surrounding Sopron, take bus No 1 or 2 to the Szieszta Hotel and hike up through the forest to the Károly Lookout (394m) for the view. To the northwest is the slightly bizarre Taródi Castle (Csalogány köz 8), a 'self-built private castle' owned by the obsessed Taródi family.

Places to Stay

On Pócsi-domb about 2.5km south of the city centre is Lővér Camping (☎/fax 311 715; Kőszegi út; bus No 12 from bus & train stations; camping per adult/child 600/300Ft; bungalow doubles 2688Ft; open mid-Apr–mid-Oct) in a quiet rural spot. The bungalows and camp sites are shaded.

The Brennbergi Hostel (☎/fax 313 116; Brennbergi út; bus No 3; dorm beds 1200Ft, bungalows per person 2000Ft; open mid-Apr–mid-Oct) is pretty far west of the city centre, but a bed is cheap and there are also bungalows here.

Ciklámen Tourist (☎ 312 040; Ógabona tér 8) travel agency has private rooms for about 3000/4000Ft a single/double, though singles are scarce in summer.

Sopron has plenty of pensions and hotels to choose from. A good bet is Jégverem (☎/fax 510 113; e haspart@axelero.hu; Jégverem utca 1; singles/doubles 4000/8000Ft) with five large rooms in an 18th-century ice warehouse and cellar, in the Ikva district.

Bástya (☎ 325 325, fax 334 061; Patak utca 40; singles/doubles 6000/8000Ft) has 16 modern rooms and is a 10-minute walk north of the old town. Another wise choice but out near the Lővér Hills is Diana (☎ 329 013; Lővér körút 64; singles/doubles 5400/8000Ft). Its eight rooms are large and comfortable, and there's a restaurant.

Hotel Palatinus (☎ 523 816; Új utca 23; singles/doubles €40/52) couldn't be more central, but it's not a particularly attractive place. Sopron's grand old dame is the 100-year-old Pannónia Med Hotel (☎ 312 180, fax 340 766; Várkerület 75; singles/doubles from 16,800/18,900Ft). It's a nice place with all the trimmings, but is a tad overpriced.

Places to Eat

Generális-Corvinus (☎ 314 841; Fő tér 7-8; mains 1000-1900Ft), with its café tables on the square, is a great place for a meal in the warm months. Opposite is Gambrinus (☎ 339 966; Fő tér 3; mains 800-1500Ft; open to midnight daily), with solid Hungarian and Austrian fare. Fórum Pizzéria (☎ 340 231; Szent György utca 3; dishes under 1000Ft) is a good bet for decent pizza, pasta and salads.

The burgers at Speedy Burger (Várkerület 36; burgers 260-380Ft) are big, filling and served before you know it. A great place for an inexpensive lunch or light meal is Cézár Pince (☎ 311 337; Hátsókapu 2; dishes 330-690Ft; open to 11pm daily), in a medieval cellar off Orsolya tér. Around the corner is Papa Joe's Steakhouse (☎ 340 933; Várkerület 108; mains 900-1500Ft), with grills, steaks, soups and salads and an inviting courtyard.

Stop in at Várkapu Café (Várkerület 108/a; cakes from 50Ft) for cake and coffee on the corner of Hátsókapu. For ice cream, line up at the old-world ice creamery and cake shop Dömötöri (Széchenyi tér 13; ice cream 60Ft per scoop), by far the most popular in town.

For self-catering heading for the Smatch supermarket (Várkerület 100).

Entertainment

The Hungarian Cultural House (Széchenyi tér), undergoing renovation at the time of research, is usually the place for music and other cultural events. The beautiful Petőfi Theatre (☎ 511 700; Petőfi tér 1), with its National Romantic-style decor, is in constant use. Its ticket office (☎ 511 730; open 9am-5pm Mon-Fri, 9am-noon Sat) is at Széchenyi tér 17.

For less highbrow entertainment, head to the Music Café (Várkerület 49), which often has live jazz in the evenings. If you're feeling a bit more raucous you can head to the 'saloon bar' at Papa Joe's Steakhouse (see Places to Eat). But before leaving town be sure to sample Sopron's wines in the deep, deep cellar of Gyógy-gődőr (Fő tér 4).

HUNGARY

Getting There & Away

Bus Bus connections are good. There are hourly buses (sometimes more) to Fertőd and Győr, and less frequent buses to Balatonfüred (two daily), Budapest (four), Esztergom (two), Hévíz and Keszthely (three), Kőszeg (eight), Pécs (one) and Szombathely (nine). There is an 8am bus to Vienna daily, plus an extra 9.25am departure on Monday and Thursday, and 8.55am and 9.25am on Friday. Two buses a week make the trip to Munich and Stuttgart (8.05pm Thursday and 9.05pm Sunday).

Train Express trains en route to Vienna's Südbahnhof pass through Sopron up to nine times daily; five local services a day depart for Wiener Neustadt (where you can transfer for Vienna). Eight express trains a day depart for Keleti in Budapest, travelling via Győr and Komárom, and seven to nine trains to Szombathely.

FERTŐD
☎ 99 • pop 2700

Don't miss the 126-room **Esterházy Palace** (☎ 537 640; adult/child 1000/600Ft; open 10am-6pm Tues-Sun mid-Mar–Oct, 10am-4pm Fri-Sun Nov–mid-Mar) at Fertőd, 27km east of Sopron and easily accessible by bus. Built in 1766, this magnificent Versailles-style baroque palace, easily the finest in Hungary, must be visited with a guide, and information sheets in various languages are available. From May to October piano and string quartets perform in the concert hall regularly, and the Haydn Festival takes place here in early September (Joseph Haydn was court musician to the Esterházy family from 1761 to 1790). Programmes are available from the palace or from **Tourinform** (☎ 370 544; e fertod@tourinform.hu; Madách Sé-tány 1), opposite the palace inside the old Grenadier House.

Places to Stay & Eat

Dori Hotel & Camping (☎/fax 370 838; Po-mogyi út 1; camp sites per tent €2-2.60, per person €1.20-1.70; bungalow singles €17-21, doubles €30-34; hotel singles €15-19, doubles €27-30) has a good range of accommodation possibilities 100m north of the palace. Price depends on the season.

You can spend the night in the palace at the **Kastély Hotel** (☎ 537 640; doubles/triples/quads 4200/5800/6600Ft), but don't expect palace standards. The rooms are clean, simple and booked well in advance.

Two decent restaurants occupying the palace's Grenadier house are **Gránátos** and **Kastélykert** (mains around 1000-1500Ft at both). For ice cream head to **Elit** (Fő utca 1; ice cream from 80Ft), west of the palace in town.

KŐSZEG
☎ 94 • pop 11,900

Kőszeg (Güns in German) is a small town at the foot of the Kőszeg Hills just 3km from the Austrian border. Mt Írottkő (882m), southwest of town and straddling the border, is the highest point in Transdanubia. At Kőszeg's centre is the old town, a well-preserved medieval precinct with a main square that's hardly changed since the 18th century. The Várkör rings the centre along the old castle walls.

In 1532 Kőszeg's castle garrison held off a Turkish army of 100,000, and this delay gave the Habsburgs time to mount a successful defence of Vienna, ensuring Kőszeg's place in Hungarian history.

Orientation & Information

The train station is a 15-minute walk to the southeast of the old town on Alsó körút; buses stop just a block from Várkör on Liszt Ferenc utca. The train station doesn't have a left-luggage office, but the staff will probably agree to hold your bags for the usual fee.

There's a helpful **Tourinform** office (☎ 563 120; e koszeg@tourinform.hu; Jurisics tér 7; open 8am-6pm Mon-Fri, 10am-6pm Sat & Sun mid-June–mid-Sept; 8am-4pm Mon-Fri mid-Sept–mid-June) on the main square. The **OTP bank** (Kossuth Lajos utca 8) has a foreign currency exchange machine.

Things to See

Heroes' Gate, leading into Jurisics tér, was erected in 1932 to mark the 400th anniversary of the Turkish onslaught. In the General's House next to the gate is the **Városi Museum** (☎ 360 240; Jurisics tér 4-6; adult/child 100/50Ft; open 10am-5pm Tues-Sun), containing exhibits on folk art, trades and crafts, and the natural history of the area.

Buildings of note on the town's main square include the striking **Town Hall** at No 8, the **Church of St Henry** (1615) and behind it the **Church of St James** (1403), a splendid Gothic structure with three 15th-century frescoes. There's a baroque **pharmacy** (☎ 360 337;

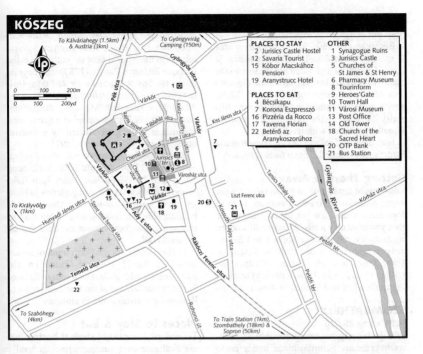

KŐSZEG

| 0 | 100 | 200m |
| 0 | 100 | 200yd |

PLACES TO STAY
2 Jurisics Castle Hostel
12 Savaria Tourist
15 Kóbor Macskához Pension
19 Aranystrucc Hotel

PLACES TO EAT
4 Bécsikapu
7 Korona Eszpresszó
16 Pizzéria da Rocco
17 Taverna Florian
22 Betérő az Aranykoszorúhoz

OTHER
1 Synagogue Ruins
3 Jurisics Castle
5 Churches of St James & St Henry
6 Pharmacy Museum
8 Tourinform
9 Heroes'Gate
10 Town Hall
11 Városi Museum
13 Post Office
14 Old Tower
18 Church of the Sacred Heart
20 OTP Bank
21 Bus Station

Jurisics tér 11; admission free; open 10am-5pm Tues-Sun), which is now a museum. The square also contains a statue of the Virgin Mary (1739) and the town fountain (1766).

The other main highlight of Kőszeg is the Gothic and baroque **Jurisics Castle** (☎ 360 240; Rajnis utca 9; adult/child 100/60Ft; open 10am-5pm Tues-Sun), dating from 1263 and now a historical museum.

A pleasant way to spend a few hours is walking in the hills west of the town. Of particular interest in this area is the baroque chapel on 393m **Kálváriahegy** (Calvary Hill), the vineyards of **Királyvölgy** (King's Valley) and 458m **Szabóhegy** (Tailor's Hill). A copy of Cartographia's A Kőszegi-hegység és környéke (The Kőszeg Hills & Surrounds) 1:40,000 map (No 13; 650Ft) will prove useful when exploring the area.

Places to Stay
Gyöngyvirág Camping (☎ 360 454, fax 364 574; Bajcsy-Zsilinszky utca 6; camp sites per adult/child/tent/car 500/300/300/300Ft; pension rooms from 3500Ft; open year-round), by the little Gyöngyös River, has a basic camping ground and clean, modern rooms.

Jurisics Castle Hostel (☎ 360 113; Rajnis József utca 9; doubles 3000Ft), in a small building near the entrance to the castle, is well worn, but the location makes it attractive.

Savaria Tourist (☎ 563 048; Várkör 69) can arrange private rooms from about 4000Ft a double and pensions from 4000Ft to 8000Ft. Plus every second restaurant seems to have some pension rooms upstairs.

Kóbor Macskához (☎/fax 362 273; Várkör 100; singles/doubles 5000/6300Ft) has nine charming rooms with bath. It is above a sometimes noisy restaurant-cum-pub. **Aranystrucc Hotel** (☎ 360 323, fax 563 330; Várkör 124; singles/doubles 4700/7700Ft), in an 18th-century building overlooking Fő tér, has large rooms with bath and TV, which can also be rather noisy.

Places to Eat
Pizzéria da Rocco (☎ 362 379; Várkör 55; pizzas 400-1500Ft; open 10am-midnight daily), with its huge garden inside the old castle walls, is a great place for pizza or just a drink. For fine dining, head next door to **Taverna Flórián** (☎ 563 072; Várkör 59; pasta around 700Ft; mains around 1500Ft),

HUNGARY

which serves quality Mediterranean food in beautiful cellar-like surroundings.

Bécsikapu *(☎ 360 297; Rajnis József utca 5; mains around 800Ft)*, almost opposite St James Church, is a pleasant place close to the castle. **Betérő az Aranykoszorúhoz** *(Temető utca 59; open daily; mains around 800Ft)* proves quite a mouthful not only in name (literally 'Visitor at the Sign of the Golden Wreath'), but also with its dishes.

For coffee and cakes you can't beat **Korona Eszpresszó** *(Várkör 18; open 8am-6pm daily)*.

Getting There & Away

Kőszeg is at the end of an 18km railway spur from Szombathely, to which there are 14 to 15 departures a day. To get to/from anywhere else, you must take a bus. At least half a dozen buses a day run to/from Sopron and Szombathely, and there is one daily to Keszthely. Three buses a week (7.05am Wednesday, 8.10am Friday and 4.45am Saturday) head for Oberpullendorf and Vienna in Austria.

SZOMBATHELY
☎ 94 • pop 85,600

Szombathely (pronounced roughly as **sombot-hay**) means 'Saturday place' and refers to the important weekend markets held here in the Middle Ages. It's a pretty, relaxed city and, though it's not packed with sights, you might find yourself passing through as it is a transport crossroad.

Orientation & Information

Szombathely is made up of narrow streets and squares with the town centre at leafy Fő tér, one of the largest squares in Hungary. The train station is five blocks east of Mártírok tere at the end of Széll Kálmán út. The bus station is north of the cathedral at Petőfi Sándor utca.

There's a **Tourinform** office *(☎ 514 451; e szombathely@tourinform.hu; Király utca 11; open 9am-6pm Mon-Fri, 9am-5pm Sat & Sun June–mid-Sept; 9am-5pm Mon-Fri mid-Sept–May)*, north of Fő tér, which may have moved to the **City Hall** *(Kossuth Lajos utca)* by the time you read this.

OTP bank has branches at Király utca 10 and on Fő tér.

Things to See

The rebuilt **Szombathely Cathedral** (1797) is on Templom tér. Behind the cathedral is the

Garden of Ruins *(☎ 313 369; Templom tér; adult/child 300/150Ft; open 9am-5pm Tues-Sun Mar-Nov)*, with Roman Savaria relics. On the other side of the cathedral is the baroque **Bishop's Palace** (1783), and beyond this is the **Smidt Museum** *(☎ 311 038; Hollán Ernő utca 2; adult/child 300/150Ft; open 10am-5pm Tues-Sun Mar-Dec, 10am-5pm Tues-Fri Jan & Feb)*, containing a fascinating assortment of things collected by a squirrel physician before his death in 1975.

Szombathely Gallery *(☎ 508 800; Rákóczi Ferenc utca 12; adult/child 300/150Ft; open 10am-5pm Tues & Fri-Sun, 10am-7pm Thur)* is one of the best modern art galleries in Hungary. The lovely twin-towered Moorish-style building (1881) across the street at No 3, a former synagogue, now houses the **Béla Bartók Concert Hall**.

In **Ják**, a small village 12km south of Szombathely, is the 1214 **Abbey Church** *(☎ 356 217; adult/child 200/100Ft; open 8am or 9am-5pm daily)*, one of the finest examples of Romanesque architecture in Hungary.

Places to Stay & Eat

Tourinform has a list of **student hostels** that are available over summer; beds generally cost between 800Ft and 1400Ft. **Savaria Tourist** *(☎ 511 435; Mártírok tere 1)* and **Ibusz** *(☎ 314 141; Fő tér 44)* may have private rooms available (doubles from 3000Ft).

Liget Hotel *(☎ 509 323; Szent István park 15; singles/doubles from 5000/6000Ft)*, west of the centre and accessible on bus No 27 from the train station, is a quiet hotel that's more like a motel.

The faded Art Nouveau splendour of the **Hotel Savaria** *(☎ 311 440; Mártírok tere 4; singles/doubles without bath, 4900/6900Ft, singles with bath 7900-12,900Ft doubles with bath 10,900-15,900Ft)*, well positioned in the very centre of town, is reasonable value.

Surprisingly for a town of this size, there isn't a big selection of eateries. For a cheap meal head to **Mensa** *(Mártírok tere 5/b; light meals from 300Ft)* near Hotel Savaria, or for something more substantial and upmarket try **Paradicsom** *(☎ 342 012; Belső Uránia Udvar; mains 600-1500Ft)*, an above-average Italian restaurant off Mártírok tere.

Getting There & Away

Bus Up to 16 buses leave every day for Ják (they drop you at the bottom of the hill, a short walk from the church) and there are half-hourly departures to Kőszeg. Other destinations include: Budapest (three departures daily), Győr (six), Keszthely via Hévíz (two), Pécs (three) and Sopron (four). One bus a week departs for Graz in Austria (7am Friday) and three to Vienna (6.40am Wednesday, 7am Friday and 3.55am Saturday).

Train Express trains to Déli and Kelenföld stations in Budapest go via Veszprém and Székesfehérvár. Up to four express trains run to Győr via Celldömölk daily, and up to three to Pécs. Frequent local trains run to Kőszeg and Sopron.

Szombathely is only 13km from the Austrian border, and there are direct trains that travel to/from Graz.

Lake Balaton

Lake Balaton, which is 77km long, is the largest freshwater lake in Europe, outside Scandinavia. The southeastern shore is quite shallow and in summer the warm, sandy beaches are a favourite holiday spot. Better scenery, more historic sites and deeper water are found on the northwestern side. Balaton's very popularity is its main drawback, with the southeastern shore particularly crowded during July and August.

The lake is also a favourite centre for yachting enthusiasts. Other common activities are horse riding, cycling and hiking – *A Balaton* 1:40,000 map (No 41; 550Ft) is handy for this. The thermal baths of Hévíz are also nearby. Many towns and villages on the lake, particularly along its northern shore, are important wine-making centres.

Getting Around
From April to mid-October, Mahart ferries run between Siófok, Balatonfüred and Tihany, as well as Fonyód and the Badacsony area. During the main summer season (between mid-May and early September), ferries ply the entire length of the lake from Balatonkenese to Keszthely and make frequent stops on both shores.

There are also car ferries across the lake between Tihanyi-rév and Szántódi-rév from March to mid-November. It costs 280/230/460/920Ft per person/bicycle/motorcycle/car.

BALATONFÜRED
☎ 87 • pop 13,200
Balatonfüred, a spa town with the easy-going grace that highly commercialised Siófok on the opposite shore totally lacks, has attracted heart patients for centuries because of its curative thermal waters. It has been the most fashionable bathing resort on the lake since the late 18th century, when a medicinal bathing centre

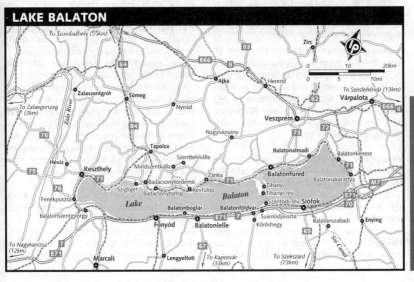

was established here. Unfortunately the mineral baths are now reserved for patients. During the early 19th century it became an important meeting place for many of Hungary's intellectuals, and some parts of town still bear an aristocratic air.

Orientation & Information

The adjacent bus and train stations are on Dobó István utca, 1km northwest of the spa centre and lake. From the stations it's an easy walk to the lakefront, first northeast along Dobó István utca, then southeast along Jókai Mór utca.

Tourinform (e balatonfured@tourinform .hu) has two offices in Balatonfüred. One is inconveniently located 1km northwest of the centre (☎ 580 480; Petőfi Sándor utca 68; open 9am-2pm or 4pm Mon-Fri) and another annoyingly situated about 1.5km to the southwest (☎ 580 480; Széchenyi utca 47; open 9am-5pm Mon-Fri, 9am-1pm Sat May-Sept; 9am-3pm Mon-Fri Oct-Apr).

The **OTP bank** (Petőfi Sándor utca 8) and **post office** (Zsigmond utca 14) are northwest of the ferry pier.

Things to See

The heart of the old spa town is **Gyógy tér**. In the centre of this leafy square, **Kossuth Spring** (1853) dispenses slightly sulphuric water that you can drink.

The **park** along the nearby lakeshore is worth a promenade. Near the wharf you'll encounter a bust of the Bengali poet Rabindranath Tagore before a lime tree that he planted in 1926 to mark his recovery from illness after treatment in Balatonfüred.

Diagonally opposite the **Round Church** (1846), on the corner of Jókai Mór utca and Honvéd utca, is **Mór Jókai Museum** (☎ 343 426; adult/child 200/100Ft; open 10am-6pm Tues-Sun May-Oct), in the acclaimed novelist's former summer house.

Veszprém The picturesque buildings and surrounding area of Veszprém (pop 63,900), 16km north of Balatonfüred, make it a worthwhile day trip from the lake area. You'll be able to get information about attractions at **Tourinform** (☎ 88-404 548; e veszprem@ tourinform.hu; Vár utca 4) in the old town. The best way to get here is by bus, as the bus station in Veszprém is central and the train station is 3km from town.

Activities

Balatonfüred has three **public beaches** (adult/ child 260/160Ft); the best is Kisfaludy Strand along Aranyhíd sétány northeast of the pier. There are other beaches attached to various places to stay.

In July the Anna Ball is held at the Sanatorium, near Gyógy tér, and it's a prime event on the Hungarian social calendar. Tickets cost from 25,000Ft. Concerts and other events accompany the ball; keep your eyes peeled if you're here in July.

Places to Stay

Camping Massive **Füred Camping** (☎ 580 241; Széchenyi utca 24; camp sites 2900-4900Ft, adult 600-1300Ft, child 500-1050Ft, 3-4 person bungalows or motel rooms 5460-22,490Ft; open Apr–mid-Oct) is about 2km southwest of the train station. It has every type of accommodation you need, but is ridiculously expensive during the summer months.

Hostels & Private Rooms The **Lajos Lóczy Gymnasium** (☎ 343 428; Bartók Béla utca 4; dorm beds 1500Ft), near the stations, and the far-flung **Ferenc Széchenyi College** (☎ 343 844; dorm beds 1500Ft), on Hősök tere, 3km to the northeast of the resort, usually have accommodation in summer.

Balatontourist (☎ 580 031; Petőfi Sándor utca 2), near the OTP Bank, has private rooms for €25-30 per double.

Pensions & Hotels Prices for accomodation fluctuate throughout the year and usually peak between early July and late August.

The friendly **Ring Pension** (☎ 342 884; Petőfi Sándor utca 6a; singles/doubles from 7200/8000Ft) is so-named because the owner was a champion boxer. Neat, clean rooms with shared bathrooms vary in price, depending on the size of the room and its amenities. Closer to the lake is another excellent choice, **Zöld Tető** (☎ 341 701; Huray utca 4; singles/ doubles €35.50/45.50). It's more expensive, but the rooms are a cut above and there's a lovely garden.

One of the nicest places in town, and also reasonably priced, is the central **Hotel Blaha Lujza** (☎ 581 210; Blaha Lujza utca 4; singles 7300-8200Ft, doubles 9300-12,300Ft). This hotel was once the holiday home of the much-loved 19th-century Hungarian actress-singer Lujza Blaha.

With less soul, but right on the water, is the high-rise **Hotel Uni** (☎ 581 360; Széchenyi utca 10; singles 4520-9880Ft, doubles 5610-11,850Ft). Every room in the nearby **Tagore Hotel** (☎ 342 603; Deák Ferenc utca 56; singles €22-35, doubles €29-50) has a balcony, and it's also close to the lake.

Places to Eat
The eastern end of Tagore sétány is a strip of pleasant bars and terraced restaurants, including **Bella** (☎ 481 815; pizzas 600-800Ft), with good pizza and pasta. For cheap eats, head west along the lake and Zákonyi Ferenc utca where you'll come across a plethora of **food stalls**.

Balaton (☎ 481 319; Kisfaludy utca 5; mains 1000-2000Ft), just north of the pier, isn't the cheapest place in town but the selection is wide and so is the shaded terrace.

Halászkert (☎ 343 039; Zákonyi Ferenc utca 3; mains 800-1000Ft), west of Vitorlás tér and the pier, still serves one of the best 'drunkard's fish soups' (korhely halászlé) in Hungary.

Escape the crowds down by the lake and head to popular **Cafe Bergman** (☎ 341 087; Zsigmond utca 3) near the post office for cake and ice cream.

Getting There & Away
Buses to and from Tihany and Veszprém leave continually throughout the day, and there are also departures for Hévíz (six daily), Győr (seven), Esztergom (one), Sopron (two) and Kecskemét (one).

Balatonfüred is 2½ hours by express train from Déli and Kelenföld stations in Budapest and three hours by local train. The line goes to Tapolca via Badacsony. There are a number of towns on the train line with 'Balaton' or 'Füred' somewhere in the name, so double-check which station you're getting off at.

Mahart ferries travel on the lake from Balatonfüred to Badacsony (900ft), Siófok (760Ft) and Tihany (480Ft).

SIÓFOK
☎ 84 • pop 22,200
Siófok is the largest and busiest settlement on Balaton's southeastern shore. It's a useful transit point, but there's no reason to stay. A strip of pricey high-rise hotels, a half-dozen large camping grounds, holiday cottages, tacky discos and a sleazy nightlife attract big crowds. In midsummer, bedlam reigns; in winter Siófok is all but dead.

Siófok can be convenient, however, if you're just passing through, as the train and bus stations are adjacent in the centre of town on Váradi Adolf tér, just off Fő utca (the main drag), and the Mahart ferry pier is an easy 10-minute walk to the northwest. The **Tourinform** (☎ 315 355; ⓔ siofok@tourinform.hu; Szabadság tér) office is in the base of the landmark water tower in the town centre.

TIHANY
☎ 87 • pop 1300
Tihany village sits on a peninsula of the same name, which juts 5km into Lake Balaton, almost linking its northern and southern shores. The whole peninsula is a nature reserve, and many people consider it the most beautiful place on the lake. After visiting the quaint town and famous Abbey Church, you can easily shake the tourist hordes by hiking to the Inner Lake (Belsőtó) or the reedy (and almost dried up) Outer Lake (Külsőtó). Both have abundant birdlife.

Orientation & Information
Tihany village sits on a ridge on the eastern side of the peninsula's high plateau. The Inner Harbour (Belső kikötő), where ferries to/from Balatonfüred and Siófok dock, is below the village. Car ferries to/from Szántódi-rév and passenger ferries to/from Balatonföldvár dock at Tihanyi-rév, the port at the southern end of the peninsula.

For information, there is a **Tourinform** (☎ 448 804; ⓔ tihany@tourinform.hu; Kossuth Lajos utca 20; open 9am-8pm Mon-Fri, 9am-6pm Sat & Sun June-Aug; 9am-5pm Mon-Fri, 9am-3pm Sat May & Sept; 9am-3pm Mon-Fri Oct-Apr) office in the centre. The **post office** (Kossuth Lajos utca 37) has an ATM and will exchange money.

Things to See & Do
Tihany's twin-towered **Abbey Church** (☎ 448 405; adult/child 260/130Ft; open 9am-6pm daily May-Sept, 10am-5pm Apr & Oct, 10am-3pm Nov-Mar), dating from 1754, is outstanding for its carved baroque altars, pulpit and organ. The 11th-century **crypt** below the front of the church contains the tomb of the abbey's founder, King Andrew I. The abbey's Deed of Foundation, now in the archives of the Benedictine Abbey at Pannonhalma near Győr, is the earliest document in existence containing Hungarian words.

HUNGARY

The monastery beside the church contains the **Abbey Museum**, with exhibits relating to Lake Balaton and a library of manuscripts. Archaeological finds are in the cellar. The view of Lake Balaton from behind the abbey is superb. The admission fee includes entry to the museum and crypt.

Pisky sétány, a promenade running along the ridge north from the church to Echo Hill, passes a cluster of folk houses, which have now been turned into a small **open-air museum** (☎ 714 960; adult/child 200/100Ft; open 10am-6pm Tues-Sun May-Sept).

From Echo Hill you can descend Garay utca to the inner harbour or continue up to a couple of **hiking trails**. The red-marked trail crosses the peninsula between the two lakes to **Csúcs Hill** (two hours), which offers fine views over the surrounding countryside.

Following the green trail northeast of the church for an hour will bring you to a **Russian Well** (Oroszkút) and the ruins of the **Old Castle** (Óvár), where the Russian Orthodox monks, brought to Tihany by Andrew I, hollowed out cells in the soft basalt walls. Study the map near the front of the Abbey Church before heading off.

Places to Stay & Eat
Tihany Tourist (☎ 448 481; Kossuth Lajos utca 11) has **private rooms** from 4000Ft per double in the low season and 5000Ft in the high season. Many houses along Kossuth Lajos utca and on the little streets north of the Abbey Church have 'Zimmer frei' signs.

The swish, 16-room **Erika** (☎ 448 010; Batthyány utca 6; doubles €60) has rooms with bath and all the mod cons. It also has a small swimming pool.

Club Tihany (☎ 538 500; Rév utca 3; bungalows from €50, singles/doubles from €45/56) is a 13-hectare resort near the car ferry. Bungalows accommodate two to four people, and prices skyrocket during the summer months of July and August.

Rege Café (☎ 448 280; Kossuth Lajos utca 22; mains 1000-2000Ft), in the former monastery stables next to the Abbey Church, is modern and expensive but offers a panoramic view from its terrace. Also good are **Kecskeköröm Csárda** (Kossuth Lajos utca 13; mains around 1200Ft), a few hundred metres northwest of Rege Café on the main road, and **Kakas Csárda** (☎ 448 541; Batthyány utca 1; mains around 1500Ft).

Getting There & Away
Buses cover the 11km from Balatonfüred's train station to and from Tihany about 20 times every day.

Passenger ferries to/from Siófok and Balatonfüred stop in Tihany from late April to late October. Catch them at the pier below the abbey or at Tihanyi-rév. From early March to late November the car ferry crosses the narrow stretch of water between Tihanyi-rév and Szántódi-rév.

BADACSONY
☎ 87 • pop 2600

Four different towns actually make up the Badacsony region, but when Hungarians say Badacsony, they usually mean the little resort at the Badacsony train station, near the ferry pier southwest of Badacsonytomaj. Lying between Balatonfüred and Keszthely, this picturesque region of basalt peaks can claim some of the best hikes in Hungary. Vineyards hug the sides of Badacsony's extinct volcanic cone, and the gentle climate and rich soil make this an ideal wine-making area.

Orientation & Information
Route No 71, the main road along Balaton's northern shore, runs through Badacsony as Balatoni út; this is where the bus lets you off. The ferry pier is on the south side of this road; almost everything else is north. Above the village, several pensions and houses with private rooms ring the base of the hill on Római út. Szegedi Róza utca branches off to the north from Római út through the vineyards to Kisfaludy House and the base of the hill.

Tourinform (☎ 431 046; e badacsony tomaj@tourinform.hu; Park utca 6; open 9am-6pm Mon-Fri, 9am-1pm Sat & Sun June-Aug; 8am-4pm Mon-Fri Sept-May), northwest of the bus stops and pier, is the first port of call for information. From October to April or as late as mid-May almost the whole town shuts up shop.

You can change money at the nearby **post office** (Park utca 3). The ticket clerk at the train station will mind your bags for a fee.

Things to See & Do
The **József Egry Museum** (Egry sétány 12) in town is normally devoted to the Balaton region's leading painter (1883–1951), but it was in meltdown mode at the time of research, and no one is sure when it will reopen.

The slopes and vineyards above the town are sprinkled with little press houses and 'folk-baroque' mansions. One of these is the **Róza Szegedi House** (1790), which belonged to the actress wife of the poet Sándor Kisfaludy of Sümeg. It contains a literature museum.

If you'd like a running start on your hiking, catch one of the topless jeeps marked 'Badacsony hegyi járat'. They depart from diagonally opposite Tourinform from 9am to dusk from May to September whenever at least six paying passengers climb aboard (600/1000Ft one way/return). The jeep will drop you at Kisfaludy House, where a map of the trails is posted by the parking lot. **Kisfaludy Tower**, 1km or so above, offers splendid views.

The tiny **beach** *(adult/child 300/150Ft)* is reedy; you would do better to head a few kilometres east to Badacsonytomaj or Badacsonyörs for a swim.

Places to Stay & Eat

The closest camping ground is **Badacsony Camping** *(☎ 531 041; camp sites per tent 655-990Ft, per adult 655-930Ft, per child 520-700Ft; open May-early Sept)*, at the water's edge, about 1km west of the ferry pier. Price depends on the season.

There are plenty of travel agencies organising **private rooms**, including **Miditourist** *(☎ 431 028; Egry sétány 3)* and **Balatontourist** *(☎ 531 021; Park utca 4)*, both near Tourinform; doubles are around €18 to €25. There are several small **pensions** in town and among the vineyards on Római út.

The best place for a meal or drink is the terrace of **Kisfaludy House** *(☎ 431 016; Szegedi Róza utca 87; mains 1000-2500Ft)*, on the hill overlooking the vineyards and the lake. **Halászkert** *(☎ 431 054; Park utca 5; mains around 1500Ft)* is crowded and touristy, but the fish dishes are excellent.

There are **food stalls** with picnic tables dispensing sausage and fish soup between the train station and Park utca.

Getting There & Away

Three buses a day head for Balatonfüred. Other destinations include: Budapest (once daily), Hévíz (one), Keszthely (one) and Veszprém (one).

Badacsony is on the rail line linking all the towns on Lake Balaton's northern shore with Déli and Kelenföld stations in Budapest and Tapolca. To get to Keszthely you must change

at Tapolca, but there's often an immediate connection.

Ferries to Fonyód are fairly frequent and reasonably regular to Keszthely between late April and late October; in Fonyód you can get a connection to southern Transdanubia by taking a train direct to Kaposvár. Other ferry destinations include Tihany and Balatonfüred.

KESZTHELY
☎ 83 • pop 23,000

Keszthely (pronounced **kest**-hay) is a fairly large old town, which boasts the incredible Festetics Palace, some good facilities and boat services on the lake from June to early September. It's the only town on Lake Balaton that has a life of its own; since it isn't entirely dependent on tourism, it's 'open' all year.

Orientation & Information

The bus and train stations, side by side at the end of Mártírok útja, are fairly close to the ferry pier. There is a **left-luggage office** *(open 24hr)* at the train station. From the stations follow Mártírok útja up the hill, then turn right onto Kossuth Lajos utca into town.

Tourinform *(☎/fax 314 144; e keszthely@ tourinform.hu; Kossuth Lajos utca 28; open 9am-8pm Mon-Fri, 9am-6pm Sat mid-June– mid-Sept; 9am-5pm Mon-Fri, 9am-1pm Sat mid-Sept–mid-June)* is an excellent source of information on the whole Balaton area.

There's a huge **OTP bank** facing the park south of the Catholic church and close by is the **main post office** *(Kossuth Lajos utca 48)*.

Things to See

Keszthely's most impressive sight is the **Festetics Palace** *(☎ 312 190; Kastély utca 1; adult/student 1500/750Ft; open 9am-6pm daily July-Aug, 9am-5pm Tues-Sun Sept-May)*, the one-time residence of the wealthy Festetics family, which was built in 1745 and extended 150 years later. The palace boasts 100 rooms, but only the **Helikon Palace Museum** and the renowned **Helikon Library**, in the baroque south wing, are open to visitors. One-hour guided tours of the palace will set you back 5000Ft.

In 1797 Count György Festetics, an uncle of the reformer István Széchenyi, founded Europe's first agricultural institute, the Georgikon, here in Keszthely. Part of the original school is now the **Georgikon Farm Museum** *(☎ 311 563; Bercsényi Miklós utca*

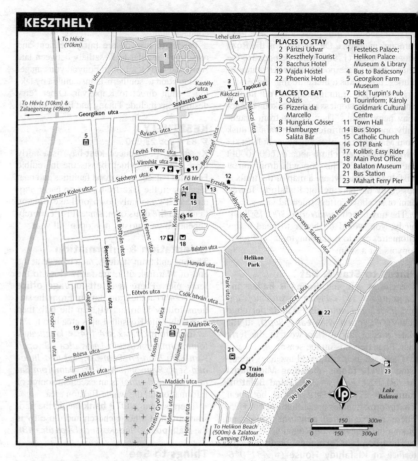

KESZTHELY

PLACES TO STAY	OTHER
2 Párizsi Udvar	1 Festetics Palace;
9 Keszthely Tourist	Helikon Palace
12 Bacchus Hotel	Museum & Library
19 Vajda Hostel	4 Bus to Badacsony
22 Phoenix Hotel	5 Georgikon Farm
	Museum
PLACES TO EAT	7 Dick Turpin's Pub
3 Oázis	10 Tourinform; Károly
6 Pizzeria da	Goldmark Cultural
Marcello	Centre
8 Hungária Gösser	11 Town Hall
13 Hamburger	14 Bus Stops
Saláta Bár	15 Catholic Church
	16 OTP Bank
	17 Kolibri; Easy Rider
	18 Main Post Office
	20 Balaton Museum
	21 Bus Station
	23 Mahart Ferry Pier

67; adult/child 300/150Ft; open 10am-5pm Mon-Sat, 10am-6pm Sun May-Oct).

The **Balaton Museum** (☎ 312 351; Múzeum utca 2; adult/child 200/150Ft; open 10am-6pm Tues-Sat May-Oct, 10am-5pm Nov-Apr) has exhibits on the history of navigation on the lake and photographs of summer frolickers at the lake early in the 20th century.

Places to Stay

Zalatour Camping (☎/fax 312 782; Ernszt Géza sétány; camp sites per tent 650-790Ft, per adult 650-790Ft, per child 270-300Ft; bungalows 3000-4200Ft, apartments 7900-9300Ft), about 1km south of town, is a big place with large bungalows for four people and smaller but better equipped apartments. There are also tennis courts, and the site has

access to Helikon Beach. Prices depend on the season.

Vajda Hostel (☎ 311 361; Gagarin utca 4; dorm beds 1000-1200Ft; open mid-June–late Aug) is what János Vajda College becomes over the summer break.

Private rooms are available from **Keszthely Tourist** (☎ 312 031; Kossuth utca 25; doubles around 4000Ft). If the agencies are closed, a good place to look for a room is Móra Ferenc utca, to the east of the town centre near the lake. Look out for the usual 'szoba kiadó' or 'Zimmer frei' signs.

In the off season it's worth checking for specials at the upmarket hotels along the lakefront. **Phoenix Hotel** (☎ 312 631; Balatonpart 5; singles €20-24, doubles €25-40) is a two-star place with low off-season rates.

HUNGARY

Párizsi Udvar (☎/fax 311 202; Kastély utca 5; rooms from 6900Ft) pension is a good choice near the Festetics Palace. Its 14 rooms were originally part of the palace complex.

Bacchus Hotel (☎/fax 314 097; ⓦ www .bacchushotel.hu; Erzsébet királyné utca 18; singles €28-41, doubles €36-54) has 26 lovely rooms and houses a wine museum where you can have tastings. Prices for rooms vary depending on the season.

Places to Eat
Burgers, salads and outdoor seating are available at the **Hamburger Saláta Bár** (Erzsébet királyné utca; burgers from 300Ft). **Pizzeria da Marcello** (☎ 313 563; Városház utca 4; pizzas from 650Ft), in a cellar with rustic furniture, has made-to-order pizzas and salads.

Oázis (☎ 311 023; Rákóczi tér 3; open 11am-4pm Mon-Fri; mains 650-950Ft), incredibly for this carnivorous country, serves only vegetarian dishes. A real oasis.

Hungária Gösser (☎ 312 265; Kossuth Lajos utca 35; mains from 800Ft) is a pub-restaurant in a lovely historical building with stained-glass windows. It has German and Hungarian dishes and a salad bar.

Entertainment
On Sunday at 8.30pm between July and mid-August, there's Hungarian folk dancing in the courtyard of the **Károly Goldmark Cultural Centre** (☎ 314 286; Kossuth Lajos utca 28).

There are several interesting places for a drink along Kossuth Lajos utca. **Easy Rider** at No 79 attracts the local young bloods, while **Kolibri** cocktail bar at No 81 is for an older crowd. **Dick Turpin's Pub** (Városház utca 2) plays the best music and is more central.

Getting There & Away
There are about 10 daily buses to Hévíz and Veszprém, one to Szombathely and two to Siófok. Other towns served by buses include Badacsony (three daily), Budapest (six), Győr (two), Pécs (three) and Sopron (three).

Some of these buses – including those to Hévíz – can be boarded at the bus stops in front of the Catholic church on Fő tér. For buses to the lake's northern shore you can catch the bus along Tapolcai út.

Keszthely is on a branch rail line linking Tapolca and Balatonszentgyörgy, from where up to 17 daily trains continue along the southern shore to Siófok and Budapest. To reach Szombathely or towns along Lake Balaton's northern shore by train, change at Tapolca.

Mahart ferries link Keszthely with most places on the lake from late May to early September.

HÉVÍZ
☎ 83 • pop 4400
Hévíz, 7km northwest of Keszthely, is the site of Europe's largest thermal lake, Gyógytó. The people of this town have made use of the warm mineral water for centuries, first as a tannery in the Middle Ages and later for curative purposes (it was developed as a private resort in 1795).

The bus station is on Somogyi Béla utca, opposite the northern entrance to the thermal lake. For information head to the travel agency **Hévíz Tourist** (☎ 341 348; Rákóczi utca 2; open 8.30am-5.30pm Mon-Fri, 9am-1pm Sat). The town has an **OTP bank** (Erzsébet királynő utca 7) in the centre of town, and a **post office** (Kossuth Lajos utca 4) northwest of the lake.

Thermal Lake
The Gyógytó (admission 3 hours/whole day 600/1200Ft; open 8.30am-5.30pm daily in summer, 9am-4.30pm in winter) is an astonishing sight: a milky blue-green surface of about five hectares, covered for most of the year in water lilies. The spring is a crater some 40m deep that disgorges up to 80 million litres of warm water a day, renewing the lake every two days or so. The surface temperature here averages 33°C and never drops below 26°C, allowing bathing throughout the year. The water and the mud on the bottom are slightly radioactive and are said to alleviate various medical conditions. A covered bridge leads to the pavilion, from where catwalks and piers fan out. Hold onto your ticket for the lake as you will have to show it to get out. There is an **indoor spa** (adult/child 490/270Ft; open 7am-4pm daily year-round) not far from the lake to the northwest.

Places to Stay & Eat
During the summer period, accommodation may prove a problem and it is generally more expensive.

Castrum Camping (☎ 343 198; Tó-part; camp site per tent 580-860Ft, per adult 720-1150Ft, per child 430-720Ft; pension singles 5800-10,100Ft, doubles 7200-11,500Ft) is close to the lake's southern end and is the most central of Hévíz's several camping grounds.

Hévíz Tourist can find you a **private room** for around €20 to €25 a double. You'll see *'Zimmer frei'* and *'szoba kiadó'* signs on Kossuth Lajos utca and Zrínyi utca, to the west of the lake.

One kilometre northwest of the lake is **Pannon Hotel** *(☎ 340 482; Széchenyi utca 23; singles €29, doubles €40-54)*, with colourful rooms and a pleasant garden. Across the road is another good option, **Hotel Napfény** *(☎ 340 642; Széchenyi utca 21; singles 4200-5600Ft, doubles 7100-9900Ft)*. The high-rise **Hotel Panoráma** *(☎ 341 074; Petőfi Sándor utca 9; singles €29-39, doubles €38-46)* is closer to the lake but less personal.

The best places for a quick bite are the **food stalls** selling *lángos* (dough snack), sausages and other fast-food treats at the bottom of Rákóczi utca.

For a proper meal, try **Liget** *(Dr Moll Károly tér; pizzas and mains around 1000-1200Ft)* in the centre of town; or **Piroska** *(☎ 343 942; Kossuth Lajos utca 10; mains 700-1400Ft)*, a quiet spot west of the lake with a shady terrace. For cake and ice cream the **Astoria** *(Rákóczi utca 13; ice cream 80Ft)* is popular, with a terrace for watching the passing parade.

Getting There & Away

Hévíz doesn't have a train station, but a bus goes to Keszthely almost every half-hour from stand No 3 in the bus station. There are frequent departures to towns such as Badacsony (eight daily), Balatonfüred (seven) and Veszprém (eight). Other destinations include Budapest (five), Győr (three), Pécs (two), Sopron (two) and Szombathely (three).

Southern Transdanubia

Southern Transdanubia is bordered by the Danube River to the east, the Dráva River, Croatia and Slovenia to the south and west, and Lake Balaton to the north. It's generally flatter than Western Transdanubia, with the Mecsek and Villány Hills rising in isolation from the plain.

Near Mohács on the Danube in 1526, the Hungarian army under young King Lajos II was routed by a vastly superior Ottoman force. The gracious city of Pécs still bears the imprint of Turkish rule.

PÉCS
☎ 72 • pop 166,500

Pécs (pronounced **paich**) was an important historical city early – for 400 years the settlement was the capital of the Roman province of Lower Pannonia. Christianity flourished here in the 4th century and by the 9th century the town was known as Quinque Ecclesiae for its five churches (it's still called Fünfkirchen in German). In 1009 Stephen I made Pécs a bishopric. The first Hungarian university was founded here in the mid-14th century.

City walls were erected after the Mongol invasion of 1241, but 1543 marked the start of almost a century and a half of Turkish domination. The Turks left their greatest monuments at Pécs and these, together with imposing churches and a lovely synagogue, over a dozen museums, possibilities for hiking through the Mecsek Hills and a lively student atmosphere, make Pécs the perfect place to spend a couple of days.

Orientation

The bus and train stations are three blocks apart on the southern side of the centre of town. Find your way north to Széchenyi tér, the centre of the old town where a dozen streets meet.

The **left-luggage office** at the main train station is in a separate building, to the west of the station. It's open 4am to midnight, while the one at the bus station is open 6am to 6pm.

Information

For information about attractions **Tourinform** *(☎ 213 315; e baranya-m@tourinform.hu; Széchenyi tér 9; open 9am-7pm Mon-Fri, 9am-6pm Sat & Sun mid-June–mid-Sept; 8am-4pm Mon-Fri, 9am-2pm Sat mid-Sept–mid-June)* has copious amounts on Pécs and Baranya County. Unless otherwise indicated, museums and other sites are open 10am to 6pm Tuesday to Saturday and 10am to 4pm Sunday from April to October and 10am to 4pm the rest of the year. They generally cost 200Ft to 400Ft for adults and 100Ft to 200Ft for children.

There are plenty of ATMs scattered around town. The main **OTP bank** *(Rákóczi út)* has a currency-exchange machine and there's a branch on Király utca. The **M&M Exchange**

(Király utca 16; open 8.30am-5pm Mon-Fri, 8.30am-1pm Sat) offers decent rates.

The **main post office** *(Jókai Mór utca 10)* is in a beautiful Art Nouveau building (1904). **Mac Café**, inside the Dante Café (see Entertainment later), charges 500Ft for Internet connection.

Things to See
Széchenyi tér is the bustling heart of Pécs, dominated to the north by the former Gazi Kassim Pasha Mosque, the largest Turkish building in Hungary. Today it's the Inner Town Parish Church and more commonly known as the **Mosque Church** *(☎ 321 976; open 10am-4pm Mon-Sat, 11.30am-4pm Sun mid-Apr–mid-Oct; 10am-noon Mon-Sat, 11.30am-2pm Sun mid-Oct–mid-Apr)*. Islamic elements inside, such as the mihrab (prayer niche) on the southeastern side, are easy to spot. Behind the Mosque Church is the **Archaeology Museum** *(☎ 312 719; Széchenyi tér 12; open 10am-4pm Tues-Sun Apr-Oct, 10am-2pm Nov-Mar)*. Southwest of Széchenyi tér is another important Turkish building, the 16th-century **Hassan Jakovali Mosque** *(Rákóczi út 2)*. It comes complete with minaret and a small museum of Ottoman history.

From the Hassan Mosque head northeast to Szent István tér where you'll find an excavated 4th-century **Christian tomb** *(☎ 312 7190)*, with striking frescoes of Adam and Eve, and Daniel in the lion's den. The **Roman mausoleum** *(Apáca utca 14)* a little farther south, and the **Jug mausoleum** *(Dom tér)* to the north, are other fine examples of underground tombs – all three have been declared World Heritage Sites by Unesco.

A stone's throw east of the Christian tomb is the **Csontváry Museum** *(☎ 310 544; Janus Pannonius utca 11)*, displaying the work of the incomparable painter Tivadar Kosztka Csontváry (1853–1919).

Dóm tér is dominated by the huge four-towered **Basilica of St Peter**. The oldest part of is the 11th-century crypt, but the whole complex was rebuilt in a neo-Romanesque style in 1881. The **Bishop's Palace** (1770) is in front of the cathedral, and west is a 15th-century **barbican**, the only stone bastion to survive from the old city walls.

Káptalan utca, which climbs northeast from here, is lined with museums. Behind the **Endre Nemes Museum** *(☎ 310 172; open 10am-2pm Tues-Sun)* at No 5 is the Erzsébet Schaár Utca or 'Street', a complete artistic environment in which the sculptor has set her whole life in stone. The **Vasarely Museum** *(☎ 324 822)* at No 3 houses the op art of Victor Vasarely, who was born here in 1908. The cellar labyrinth of the Vasarely Museum hosts the **Mecsek Mine Museum**. Across the street at No 2 is the **Zsolnay Porcelain Museum**, which has examples of famous porcelain from the factory's early days in the mid-19th century to the present.

Attractions in the eastern part of the city include the neo-rococo **National Theatre** and **Church of St Stephen** (1741), both on Király utca. If you turn right from Király utca into Felsőmalom utca, you'll find an excellent **City History Museum** *(☎ 310 165; open 10am-4pm Tues-Sat)* at No 9.

Pécs' beautifully preserved 1869 **synagogue** *(☎ 315 881; Kossuth tér; adult/child 150/50Ft; open 9am-5pm Sun-Thur, 9am-4pm Fri May-Oct)* is south of Széchenyi tér.

Mecsek Hills Bus No 35 from in front of the train station (or from Aradi vértanúk útja) climbs hourly to the 194m **TV Tower** *(adult/child 280/180Ft; open 9am-9pm Sun-Thur, 9am-11pm Fri & Sat June-Aug, 9am-7pm rest of year)* on Misina Peak (534m) in the Mecsek Hills.

Well-marked hiking trails fan out from the TV Tower – the 1:40,000 *A Mecsek* topographical map (No 15; 650Ft) shows them all. Armed with this map, you could also take a bus from the bus station to **Orfű** (with an attractive lake) or **Abaliget** (with a 450m-long cave) and hike back over the hills. Much of this area has been logged, but doesn't attract many visitors, so it is quite peaceful.

Places to Stay
Camping Up in the Mecsek Hills, **Mandulás Camping** *(☎ 315 981; Ángyán János utca 2; bus No 34; tent sites 600Ft, motel doubles 3500Ft, bungalows per person 1600Ft, hotel doubles with bath 6000Ft; open mid-Apr–mid-Oct)* has a good selection of accommodation options.

Hostels & Private Rooms During July and August, central **Mátyás Kollégium** *(☎ 315 846; Széchenyi tér 11; dorm beds around 1200Ft)* and **János Kollégium** *(☎ 251 234; Szánto Kovács János utca 1/c; dorm beds around 1000Ft)*, both west of the town centre,

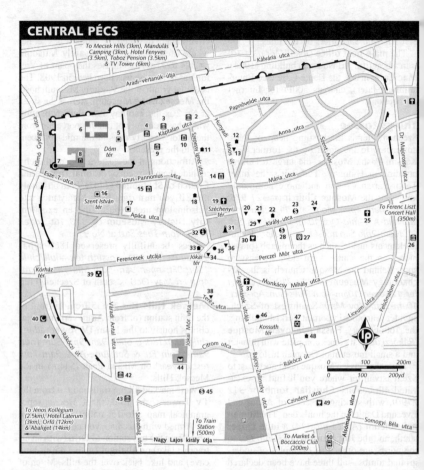

CENTRAL PÉCS

accommodate travellers in dormitory rooms with two to five beds. Ask Tourinform about other college dorms.

Ibusz (☎ 212 157; Apáca utca 1) arranges **private rooms** from 2000Ft per person and apartments for a little bit more.

Pensions & Hotels The **Centrum** (☎/fax 311 707; Szepessy Ignác utca 4; singles/ doubles 4500/5600Ft) has seven rooms that aren't particularly modern, but it's a friendly place and very central.

Another central place to try is **Főnix Hotel** (☎ 311 682, fax 324 113; Hunyadi János út 2; singles/doubles 4790/7290Ft), with 15 accommodating rooms. South of the synagogue is the friendly **Diana** (☎ 328 594, fax 333 373; Tímár 4a; dorm beds 2000Ft,

singles/doubles 5600/8600Ft), with eight excellent hotel-style rooms and dorm rooms that sleep up to four.

The big 1960s-style **Hotel Laterum** (☎ 252 108, fax 252 131; bus No 4; Hajnóczy utca 37-39; dorm beds 2000-2500Ft, doubles 5500-8000Ft) is on the far western side of town. Dorm-bed rates depend on the season and doubles on the amenities.

The landmark **Hotel Palatinus** (☎ 514 260, fax 514 738; Király utca 5; singles/doubles from €51/58) is an opulent old place, but it's overpriced considering the rooms aren't nearly as grand as the impressive foyer.

Up in the Mecsek Hills, the lovely **Toboz Pension** (☎ 510 555, fax 510 556; Fenyves sor 5; singles/doubles 7600/10,200Ft) has a retreat feel to it and good rooms. The nearby

CENTRAL PÉCS

PLACES TO STAY		OTHER			
11	Centrum	1	St Augustine Church	26	City History Museum
12	Fönix Hotel	2	Zsolnay Porcelain Museum	27	National Theatre
18	Mátyás	3	Modern Hungarian Art	28	M&M Exchange
	Kollégium		Gallery I	30	Murphy's Pub
22	Hotel Palatinus	4	Ferenc Martyn Museum	31	Trinity Column
33	Ibusz	5	Jug Mausoleum	32	Tourinform
48	Diana	6	Basilica of St Peter	35	Artists' House; Corvina
		7	Barbican		Art Bookshop
PLACES TO EAT		8	Bishop's Palace	37	Church of the Good
13	Cellárium	9	Endre Nemes Museum		Samaritan
20	Mecsek Cukrászda	10	Vasarely Museum &	39	Pasha Memi Bath Ruins
21	Dóm Vendéglö		Mecsek Mine Museum	40	Hassan Jakovali Mosque
24	Oazis	14	Archaeology Museum	42	Ethnology Museum
29	Dóm Snack	15	Csontváry Museum;	43	Modern Hungarian Art
34	Az Elefánthoz;		Dante Café; Mac Café		Gallery II
	Morik Caffè	16	Christian Tomb	44	Main Post Office
36	Virág	17	Roman Mausoleum	45	Main OTP Bank
38	Tex-Mex Café	19	Mosque Church	46	Town Hall
41	Nonstop Grocery	23	OTP Bank	47	Synagogue
	Store	25	Church of St Stephen	49	Soul 6
				50	Bus Station

Hotel Fenyves (☎/fax 315 996; Szölö utca 64; singles/doubles from 6800/9800Ft) has fading rooms, compensated by great views of the city and terraces. Take bus No 34 or 35 from the train station for both places.

Places to Eat
Király utca is lined with eateries. **Dóm Snack** (Király utca 3; dishes around 700Ft) has pizza and pasta. Down the alleyway next door, **Dóm Vendéglö** (☎ 210 088; mains 800-1600Ft) is the place to splurge on fine food and ornate surrounds. Further east at No 17 is **Oázis** (kebabs & dishes 500-800Ft), a small takeaway spot (it also has pavement seating) serving Middle Eastern dishes at the right price.

Housed in an attractive cellar is **Tex-Mex Café** (☎ 215 427; Teréz utca 10; mains 900-1500Ft), with tasty enchiladas and fajitas, and tequila to wash it down.

Az Elefánthoz (☎ 215 026; Jókai tér 6; mains around 1000Ft) is a bustling Italian restaurant with excellent pizza, pasta and meal-sized salads. Occupying the same building and sharing a terrace is the **Morik Caffè** (☎ 215 026), a great place to people-watch. Behind the Fönix Hotel, the underground **Cellárium** (☎ 314 453; Hunyadi János út 2; mains 800-1200Ft) is a reliable choice.

For coffee and cake, try **Mecsek Cukrászda** (☎ 315 444; Széchenyi tér 16) near to the Mosque Church or **Virág** (☎ 313 793; Irgalmasok utcája) not far south.

There are several **nonstop grocery stores**, including one at Rákóczi út 8.

Entertainment
The biweekly freebie Pécsi Est will tell you what's on in Pécs and surrounding towns. Pécs has well-established opera and ballet companies. If tickets to the **National Theatre** (☎ 310 539; Király utca) are sold out, try for a cancellation an hour before the performance.

The **Artists' House** (☎ 315 388; Széchenyi tér 7-8) advertises its many programmes outside. This is the place to ask about classical music concerts. Another venue is the **Ferenc Liszt Concert Hall** (☎ 311 557; Király utca 83), east of the centre.

There are pubs and bars along Király utca, many with outside tables in summer. **Murphy's Pub** (Király utca 2) is a poor attempt at an Irish pub, but it attracts the crowds. **Dante Café** (Janus Pannonius 11), occupying the ground floor of the Csontváry Museum, is a good place to meet local students, and has a huge garden and occasional live music. Clubs worth checking include **Boccaccio** (Bajcsy-Zsilinszky utca 45), a large place with three dance floors; and **Soul 6** (Czindery utca 6), a small but popular venue.

Getting There & Away
There are hourly buses in summer to Abaliget and Orfü in the Mecsek Hills, but only seven to 10 a day during winter. Other destinations

include Hévíz (two daily), Keszthely (three), Kecskemét (two), Siklós (12 or more), Siófok (four), Sopron (one) and Szeged (seven). Buses run three to four times every day from Barcs on the border to Zagreb in Croatia. There are also three buses dailyy (at 11.50am, 4.30pm and 4.45pm) from Pécs to Osijek, which is in Croatia.

Up to 13 trains a day connect Pécs with Budapest. You can reach Nagykanizsa and other points northwest via a rather circuitous but scenic line along the Dráva River. From Nagykanizsa, up to eight trains a day continue on to Szombathely. One early morning express (at 5.35am) follows this route from Pécs all the way to Szombathely. Two daily trains run from Pécs (10.50am and 1pm) to Osijek.

HARKÁNY
☎ 72 • pop 3500

The hot springs at Harkány, 26km south of Pécs, have medicinal waters with the richest sulphuric content in Hungary. There are large outdoor thermal pools open in summer and indoor baths open year-round.

For information on the town and the area go to **Tourinform** (☎ 479 624; e harkany@ tourinform.hu; Kossuth Lagos utca 2/a; open 9am-6pm Mon-Fri, 10am-6pm Sat & Sun mid-June– mid-Sept; 9am-4pm Mon-Fri mid-Sept–mid-June). **K&H Bank** has an exchange office at the entrance to the spa.

There's not much to see in town, but **Sik-lós**, 6km east of Harkány, is surrounded by the wine-producing Villány Hills. On a hill top stands a well-preserved 15th-century castle, now the **Castle Museum** (adult/child 450/250Ft; open 9am-4pm or 6pm Tues-Sun), with a Gothic chapel and a dungeon.

Places to Stay & Eat
Thermál Camping (☎ 480 117; Bajcsy-Zsilinszky utca 6; camp sites per tent/person 700/700Ft, 4-person bungalows 8000Ft, motel rooms 3500Ft, hotel rooms 5000Ft; open mid-Mar–mid-Oct) occupies a leafy space just north of the baths.

Tourinform has a comprehensive list of **private rooms** (from 3000Ft), but doesn't make bookings. If the office is shut, Bartók Béla utca has a proliferation of 'Zimmer frei' signs.

There's a bunch of hotels along Bajcsy-Zsilinszky utca opposite the baths entrance. The **Baranya Hotel** (☎/fax 480 160; singles/ doubles €18/36) is typical.

You're not going to starve in this town of sausage stands and wine counters, but if you want to sit down, go to **Robinson** (Kossuth Lajos utca 7; mains 1000-1500Ft). For something cheaper, try **Éden** (Kossuth Lajos utca 7; pizzas 750-1000Ft) just across the road.

Getting There & Away
All buses between Pécs and Siklós stop in Harkány. Harkány is a transit point for people travelling between Croatia and Yugoslavia. Three buses a day link Harkány with Croatia: two go to Osijek (at 12.30pm and 5.30pm) and one to Našice (10am weekdays).

The Great Plain

The Great Plain (Nagyalföld) of southeastern Hungary is a wide expanse of level *puszta* (prairie) drained by the Tisza River. For many centuries it has appeared in poems, songs, paintings and stories. Parts of the plain have been turned into farmland, but other regions are little more than grassy, saline deserts.

Visitors to the region are introduced to the lore of the Hungarian horse, cow and shepherds and their unique animals: Nonius horses, long-horned grey cattle and *racka* sheep. Two national parks protect the unique environment: Kiskunság in the Bugac Puszta and Hortobágy in the Hortobágy Puszta, which was listed as a World Heritage Site by Unesco in 1999.

KECSKEMÉT
☎ 76 • pop 108,500

Lying exactly halfway between Budapest and Szeged and near the geographical centre of Hungary, Kecskemét is a clean, leafy city famous for its apricots, potent *barack pálinka* (apricot brandy), fine architecture and level puszta. A vast quantity of average-quality wine is also produced here.

Orientation & Information
Kecskemét is a city of squares running into one another. The main bus and train stations are opposite each other in József Katona Park. A 10-minute walk southwest along Nagykőrösi utca will bring you to the first of the squares, Szabadság tér. The train station has a **left-luggage office** (open 7am-7pm).

Tourinform (☎ 481 065; e kecskemet@ tourinform.hu; Kossuth tér 1; open 8am-8pm Mon-Fri, 9am-1pm Sat & Sun July-Aug;

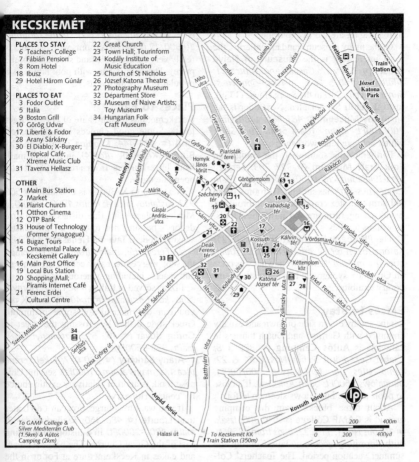

KECSKEMÉT

PLACES TO STAY
6 Teachers' College
7 Fábián Pension
8 Rom Hotel
18 Ibusz
29 Hotel Három Gúnár

PLACES TO EAT
3 Fodor Outlet
5 Italia
9 Boston Grill
10 Görög Udvar
17 Liberté & Fodor
28 Arany Sárkány
30 El Diablo; X-Burger;
   Tropical Café;
   Xtreme Music Club
31 Taverna Hellasz

22 Great Church
23 Town Hall; Tourinform
24 Kodály Institute of
   Music Education
25 Church of St Nicholas
26 József Katona Theatre
27 Photography Museum
32 Department Store
33 Museum of Naive Artists;
   Toy Museum
34 Hungarian Folk
   Craft Museum

OTHER
1 Main Bus Station
2 Market
4 Piarist Church
8 Otthon Cinema
12 OTP Bank
13 House of Technology
   (Former Synagogue)
14 Bugac Tours
15 Ornamental Palace &
   Kecskemét Gallery
16 Main Post Office
19 Local Bus Station
20 Shopping Mall;
   Piramis Internet Café
21 Ferenc Erdei
   Cultural Centre

8am-5pm Mon-Fri, 9am-1pm Sat May, June & Sept; 8am-5pm Mon-Fri Oct-Apr) is on the northeastern corner of the Town Hall.

The **OTP bank** (Szabadság tér 1/a), on the corner of Arany János utca, does foreign exchanges. There are plenty of ATMs around town. The **main post office** (Kálvin tér 10) is to the southeast. **Piramis Internet Café** (Csányi utca 1-3; open 10am-8pm Mon-Fri, noon-8pm Sat & Sun) is upstairs in the small shopping mall at the western end of Szabadság tér. Surfing costs 480Ft per hour.

Things to See
Kossuth tér is surrounded by historic buildings. Dominating the square is the massive Art Nouveau **Town Hall** (1897), which is flanked by the **Great Church** (1806) and the

earlier **Church of St Nicholas**, dating (in parts) from the 13th century. Nearby is the magnificent 1896 **József Katona Theatre** (Katona József tér) with a baroque statue of the Trinity (1742) in front of it.

Facing Szabadság tér, the Art Nouveau **Ornamental Palace** (1902) is covered in multicoloured majolica tiles. It houses the **Kecskemét Gallery** (☎ 480 776; Rákóczi út 1; adult/child 260/130Ft; open 10am-5pm Tues-Sat, 1.30pm-5pm Sun), but more impressive than the art is the building's aptly named **Decorative Hall**, with its amazing stucco peacock, bizarre windows and tiles.

A few doors up, the imposing Moorish-style **House of Technology** (☎ 487 611; Rákóczi út 2; open 10am-6pm Mon-Fri) was once a synagogue and now holds exhibitions. The little

HUNGARY

streets (some paved with brick) northwest of Szabadság tér are worth exploring.

Of the many museums and art galleries, the most interesting is the **Museum of Naive Artists** (☎ 324 767; *Gáspár András utca 11; adult/child 150/50Ft; open 10am-5pm Tues-Sun mid-Mar–Oct)* in the Stork House (1730), just off Petőfi Sándor utca. Next door is the small **Toy Museum** (☎ 481 469; *adult/child 200/100Ft; open 10am-5pm Tues-Sun)*, which holds regular workshops.

Farther to the southwest, the **Hungarian Folk Craft Museum** (☎ 327 203; *Serfőző utca 19a; adult/child 200/100Ft; open 10am -5pm Tues-Sat)* has around 10 rooms of an old farm complex crammed with embroidery, woodcarving, furniture and agricultural tools, as well as textiles.

The **Photography Museum** (☎ 483 221; *Katona József tér 12; adult/child 150/100Ft; open 10am-5pm Wed-Sun)* in what was once an Orthodox synagogue has interesting temporary exhibits.

Places to Stay

On the southwestern side of town and usually crammed with German and Dutch tourists in caravans is **Autós Camping** (☎ 329 398; *Csabai Géza körút 5; bus Nos 1, 11 & 22; camp sites per tent/person 500/600Ft, bungalows 5500Ft; open Apr-Oct)*. It's close to pools and the bungalows sleep up to four.

About three blocks from the camping ground is **GAMF College** (☎ 510 300; *Izsáki út 10; bus Nos 1, 11 & 22; beds from 1250Ft)*, with dormitory accommodation during the summer vacation period. The **Teachers' College** (☎ 486 977; *Piaristák tere 4; beds 1600Ft)* is more central. Both colleges are open mid-June to August, but you can sometimes get a bed at other times. Tourinform has a list of other colleges.

Ibusz (☎ 486 955; *Kossuth tér 3)* has private rooms from 1500Ft to 2500Ft per person.

Fábián Pension (☎ 477 677; *fax 477 175; Kápolna utca 14; singles/doubles 5500/ 7500Ft)* is a fab place – all 10 rooms are modern, clean and have a bath and the friendly staff speak a multitude of languages.

Rom Hotel (☎ 483 174; *Széchenyi tér 14; rooms 5000Ft, apartment 10,000Ft)* is above a solarium in a small shopping plaza, across from the local bus station. The apartment, which sleeps four and has a small kitchen, is great value.

The charming **Hotel Három Gúnár** (☎ 483 611; *Batthyány utca 1-7; singles/doubles 10,900/12,000Ft)* has rooms with bath and is really very comfortable (and should be for the price). The hotel's bar, with pool tables, is a popular place with guests.

Places to Eat

Kecskemét has its fair share of cheap burger joints. Some good choices include **Boston Grill** (☎ 484 444; *Kápolna utca 2)* and **X-Burger** (*Kisfaludy utca 4)*, in a small mall. Both have burgers from around 250Ft and open late daily.

Next door to X-Burger is **El Diablo** (☎ 500 922; *Kisfaludy utca 4; mains 1000-2000Ft)*, a Mexican place with fine dishes and bizarre decor – be sure not to step on the plastic snakes. Modern **Taverna Hellasz** (☎ 417 213; *Deák Ferenc tér; mains from 750Ft)*, behind the shopping centre, has excellent Greek meals and snacks, including generous gyros.

Pizzas served at **Italia** (☎ 484 627; *Hornyik János körút 4; pizzas from 400Ft)* are OK but you can opt instead for some mammoth Greek-style dishes by crossing the street to **Görög Udvar** (☎ 492 513; *Széchenyi tér 9; mains 950-1500Ft)*.

Arany Sárkány (☎ 320 037; *Erkel Ferenc utca 1/a; mains around 1000Ft)*, serving Chinese food, is another relatively exotic choice for central Hungary.

If you want to splurge, you can't do better than **Liberté** (☎ 480 350; *Szabadság tér 2; mains 1000-2000Ft)* in a historical building east of the Great Church. The best ice cream and cakes in Kecskemét are at **Fodor** in the same building as Liberté. Fodor has another outlet at Nagykőrösi utca 15.

Entertainment

The **Ferenc Erdei Cultural Centre** (☎ 484 594; *Deák Ferenc tér 1)* sponsors some events and is a good source of information. The 19th-century **József Katona Theatre** (☎ 483 283; *Katona József tér)* stages dramatic works as well as operettas and concerts by the Kecskemét Symphony Orchestra.

A chilled-out place for a drink in the evenings is the **Tropical Café** (*Kisfaludy utca 4)*; once you're ready to go clubbing, head next door to the **Xtreme Music Club** or the to the student-friendly **Silver Mediterrán Club** (*Izsáki út 2)* near GAMF College (see Places to Stay).

Getting There & Away

There are buses almost hourly to Budapest, every couple of hours to Szeged and at least two a day to Pécs and Eger.

Kecskemét is on the rail line that links Budapest's Nyugati station with Szeged. To get to Debrecen and other cities and towns east, you must change at Cegléd.

KISKUNSÁG NATIONAL PARK

Totalling 76,000 hectares, Kiskunság consists of half a dozen 'islands' of land. Much of the park's alkaline ponds, dunes and grassy 'deserts' are off limits to casual visitors, but you can get a close look at this environmentally fragile area – and see the famous horse herds go through their paces – at **Bugac**, 30km southwest of Kecskemét.

Bugac Tours (☎ 482 500; Szabadság tér 5; open 8am-4.30pm Mon-Fri) in Kecskemét is the place to go for bus timetables, tour prices and general information. It also has an office at the park entrance.

The main attraction at the park is the **horse show** (adult/child 1100/550Ft, with horse-drawn carriage tour 2200/1100Ft; 3.15pm daily June-Aug, 1.15pm daily May & Sept). The horse herders crack their whips, race one another bareback and ride 'five-in-hand', a breathtaking performance in which one *csikós* (cowboy) gallops five horses at full speed while standing on the backs of the rear two. The show takes place 3km from the park entrance; you can either walk or catch a ride with the horse-drawn carriage.

Bugaci Karikás Csárda (☎ 482 500; mains from 1000Ft), with its folk-music ensemble and goulash, is a lot more fun than it might appear. It has horse riding (2000Ft per hour), a **camping ground** (camp sites per person 500Ft) and also rustic **cottages** (per double 8000Ft) nearby.

The best way to get there on your own is by bus from Kecskemét. The 11am bus from the main terminal gets you to the park entrance around noon. After the show, the first bus back to Kecskemét passes by the park entrance at 4pm on weekdays, and 6.35pm on weekends (a change at Jakabszállás is required). More convenient on weekends is the narrow-gauge train; it leaves from Bugac felső station, 15 minutes' walk south of the park entrance, at 6.20pm and will get you to Kecskemét KK train station (south of the town centre) around 7.45pm.

SZEGED

☎ 62 • pop 175,500

Szeged (Segedin in German), the most important city on the southern Great Plain, straddles the Tisza River just before it enters Yugoslavia. The Maros River from Romania enters the Tisza just east of the centre.

But all this water has been known to prove hazardous. Disaster struck in 1879 when the Tisza swelled its banks and almost washed the city off the map. Szeged was redesigned with concentric boulevards and radial avenues. Flooding can still be a problem; in April 2000 the river burst its banks again, causing most damage in New Szeged.

Szeged is more architecturally homogeneous than many other cities, with few modern buildings intruding on the stately city centre. It's large and lively with lots of students, and produces paprika and Pick, which is Hungary's finest salami.

Orientation & Information

The main **train station** (Indóház tér) is south of the city centre; tram No 1 will take you to the centre of town. The **bus station** (Mars tér) is to the west of the centre and is within easy walking distance via pedestrian Mikszáth Kálmán utca. There is a **left-luggage office** (open 4am-11pm) at the train station.

Tucked away in a quiet courtyard is **Tourinform** (☎ 488 690; e szeged@tourinform .hu; Dugonics tér 2; open 10am-6pm Mon-Fri May-Sept, 9am-4pm Oct-Apr). It also has a pavilion (open 9am-9pm daily May-Sept) on the square.

The **K&H Bank** (Klauzál tér 2) has a foreign currency exchange machine. Next door is an **OTP Bank** (Klauzál tér 4).

There is a **main post office** (Széchenyi tér 1) in the centre of town. **Cyber Café** (Dugonics tér 11; open until midnight daily) is a dark basement bar where Internet use costs 480Ft per hour.

Things to See & Do

Begin your tour of Szeged in Dom tér, dominated by the twin-towered **Votive Church**, an ugly brown brick structure that was pledged after the flood of 1879 but not completed until 1930. The Romanesque **St Demetrius Tower** nearby is all that remains of a church dating from the 13th century, which was demolished to make room for the present one. Running along three sides of the square is the **National**

HUNGARY

SZEGED

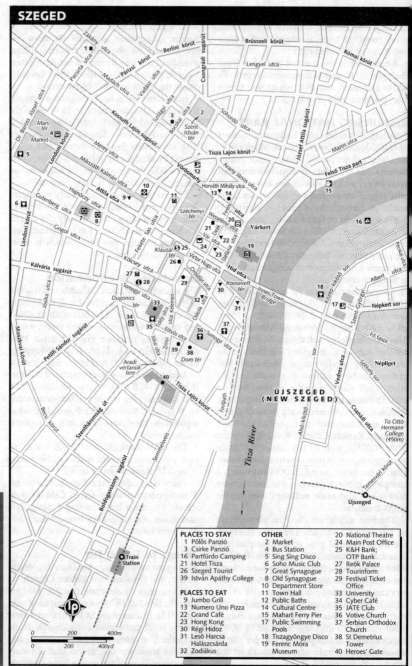

ÚJSZEGED
(NEW SZEGED)

Tisza River

To Ottó
Hermann
College
(450m)

Újszeged

PLACES TO STAY
1 Pölös Panzió
3 Csirke Panzió
16 Partfürdő Camping
21 Hotel Tisza
26 Szeged Tourist
39 István Apáthy College

PLACES TO EAT
9 Jumbo Grill
13 Numero Uno Pizza
22 Grand Café
23 Hong Kong
30 Régi Hídoz
31 Leső Harcsa
Halászcsárda
32 Zodiákus

OTHER
2 Market
4 Bus Station
5 Sing Sing Disco
6 Soho Music Club
7 Great Synagogue
8 Old Synagogue
10 Department Store
11 Town Hall
14 Cultural Centre
15 Mahart Ferry Pier
17 Public Swimming
Pools
18 Tiszagyöngye Disco
19 Ferenc Móra
Museum

20 National Theatre
24 Main Post Office
25 K&H Bank;
OTP Bank
27 Reök Palace
28 Tourinform
29 Festival Ticket
Office
33 University
34 Cyber Café
35 JATE Club
36 Votive Church
37 Serbian Orthodox
Church
38 St Demetrius
Tower
40 Heroes' Gate

Pantheon – statues and reliefs of 80 Hungarian notables. The **Szeged Open-Air Festival** is held here from mid-July to late August.

Inside the **Serbian Orthodox Church** *(adult/child 100/80Ft)*, dating from 1778 and behind the Votive Church, have a look at the fantastic iconostasis – a central gold 'tree' with 60 icons hanging off its 'branches'. Get the key at Somogyi utca 3 (flat I/5) towards the river.

Head north to the **Ferenc Móra Museum** *(☎ 549 040; Várkert; adult/child 300/150Ft; open 10am-3pm Tues, 10am-5pm Wed-Sun)*, in a huge neoclassical building (1896). Downstairs is a good collection of Hungarian paintings and an exhibit on the Avar people, who occupied the Carpathian Basin from the 5th to 8th centuries. The upper floor is dedicated to folk art.

There are many fine buildings around Széchenyi tér in the centre of town, including the **Town Hall**. Don't miss the **Reök Palace** *(Kölcsey utca)*, a mind-blowing Art Nouveau structure from 1907.

The 1903 **Great Synagogue** *(☎ 423 849; Gutenberg utca 13; adult/child 200/100Ft; open 10am-noon & 1pm-5pm Sun-Fri Apr-Sept, 9am-2pm Oct-Mar)* is the most beautiful Jewish house of worship in Hungary and is still in use. Free organ concerts here are common on summer evenings.

Places to Stay
The most central camping ground is **Part-fürdő Camping** *(☎ 430 843; Közép-kikötő sor; camp sites per tent/adult/child 600/600/430Ft; bungalows from 6000Ft)* on the eastern banks of the Tisza and near the public swimming pools and thermal baths.

Plenty of student accommodation is open to travellers in July and August, including the central **István Apáthy College** *(☎ 545 896; Eötvös utca 4; dorm beds 1250Ft, rooms per person from 2500Ft)* near the Votive Church. **Ottó Hermann College** *(☎ 544 309; Temesvári körút 52; bus No 2; dorm beds from 700Ft, doubles 2000Ft)* is a cheaper option but is east of the town centre in New Szeged.

Contact **Szeged Tourist** *(☎ 420 428; Klauzál tér)* for **private rooms** from 2000Ft to 3000Ft per person.

If you arrive by bus you'll be within walking distance of **Pölös Panzió** *(☎/fax 498 208; Pacsirta utca 17a; singles/doubles 4500/5500Ft)*, which has well-worn yet comfortable rooms. The rooms at **Csirke Panzió** *(☎ 426 188; Bocskai utca 3b; singles/doubles 5000/6000Ft)* are quite large but are often taken, so call ahead.

The grand old three-star **Hotel Tisza** *(☎/fax 478 278; Wesselényi utca 1; singles 5880-11,900Ft, doubles 8760-14,900Ft)*, just off Széchenyi tér, is a glorious place to stay and its large bright rooms are still reasonable value (price depends on bathroom facilities).

Places to Eat
Jumbo Grill *(Mikszáth Kálmán utca 4; dishes from 270Ft)*, with salads and excellent grilled chicken, is a good spot for a cheap meal.

The **Leső Harcsa Halászcsárda** *(Eager Catfish Fishermen's Inn; ☎ 555 980; Roosevelt tér 14; mains around 1500Ft)* is a little on the expensive side but is a Szeged institution and serves up *halászlé* (fisherman's soup) by the cauldron.

Nearby **Régi Hídhoz** *(At the Sign of the Old Bridge; ☎ 420 910; Oskola utca 4; mains 800-1200Ft)* serves standard Hungarian fare and has a pleasant garden.

A popular Chinese restaurant is **Hong Kong** *(Deák Ferenc utca 24; mains 700-1000Ft)*. Head here at lunchtime, when there's a great set menu (990Ft). **Numero Uno Pizza** *(☎ 424 745; Széchenyi tér 5; pizzas from 275Ft)* has good pizzas and its garden is a fine place for a drink.

Zodiákus *(☎ 420 914; Oskola utca 13; mains 1000-2000Ft)* is a cut above, with an excellent international menu and zodiac symbols everywhere you look.

For coffee, cake and a bit of peace and quiet, head to **Grand Café** *(☎ 420 578; Deák Ferenc utca 18, 2nd floor)*.

Entertainment
The best sources of information in culturally active Szeged are the **Cultural Centre** *(☎ 479 566; Vörösmarty utca 3)* and the free bi-weekly *Szegedi Est*. The **National Theatre** *(☎ 479 279; Deák Ferenc utca 12-14)* has always been the centre of cultural life in the city and usually stages opera and ballet.

There's a vast array of bars, clubs and other nightspots in this student town, especially around Dugonics tér. The cover charge for these clubs ranges from free entry to 500Ft. The clubs generally open until 4am almost daily. **JATE Club** *(Toldy utca 1)* is the best place to meet students on their own turf.

HUNGARY

Sing Sing Disco *(cnr Mars tér & Dr Baross József utca; open Wed-Sat)* has lots of rave parties, while **Soho Music Club** *(Londoni körút 3)* is best for drum & bass. The huge **Tiszagyöngye Disco** *(Közép-kikötő sor)* in New Szeged is another popular hangout.

Getting There & Away
Bus Bus services are good, with departures to Budapest (seven daily), Eger (two), Győr (two), Kecskemét (10) and Pécs (seven).

If you're heading for Romania, buses run to Arad at 6.30am daily, with extra departures at 8.45am on Friday, 10.10am on Saturday and 8.10am on Sunday. There are buses to Timişoara on Tuesday and Friday at 6.30am and Saturday at 10.10am. Buses run to the Yugoslavian destinations of Novi Sad once daily and Subotica three times daily. A 9.30am bus on Friday departs for Vienna.

Train Szeged is on the main train line to Nyugati station in Budapest. Another line connects the city with Hódmezővásárhely and Békéscsaba, where you can change trains for Gyula or Romania. Southbound local trains leave Szeged for Subotica twice daily (6.35am and 4.20pm).

Northern Hungary

Northern Hungary is the most mountainous part of the country. The southern foothills of the Carpathian Mountains stretch east along the Slovakian border in a chain of wooded hills (maximum height 1000m) from the Danube Bend almost as far as Ukraine. Historic Eger offers an ideal base for sightseers and wine-tasters; Szilvásvárad, the Hungarian home of the snow-white Lipizzaner horses, is just to the north. To the northeast is Tokaj, celebrated for its legendary sweet wines.

EGER
☎ 36 • pop 61,500
Eger (Erlau in German) is a lovely baroque city full of historic buildings. It was here in 1552 that Hungarian defenders temporarily stopped the Turkish advance into Western Europe and helped preserve Hungary's identity. The Turks returned in 1596 and managed to capture Eger Castle but were evicted in 1687. Eger played a central role in Ferenc Rákóczi II's attempt to overthrow the Habsburgs early

in the 18th century, and it was then that a large part of the castle was razed by the Austrians.

Credit goes to the bishops of Eger for erecting most of the town you see today. Eger has some of Hungary's finest architecture, especially examples of Copf (Zopf in Hungarian), a transitional style between late baroque and neoclassicism found only in Central Europe.

Today Eger is famous for its potent Bull's Blood (Egri Bikavér) red wine. Dozens of wine cellars are to be found in Szépasszonyvölgy (Valley of the Beautiful Women), just a 20-minute walk southwest of the centre.

Orientation & Information
The **main train station** *(Vasút utca)* is a 15-minute walk south of town, just east of Deák Ferenc utca. The **Egervár train station** *(Vécseyvölgy utca)*, which serves Szilvásvárad and other points north, is a five-minute walk north of the castle along Bástya utca. The **bus station** *(Pyrker János tér)* is west of Széchenyi István utca, Eger's main drag.

The friendly staff at **Tourinform** *(☎ 517 715, fax 518 815; e eger@tourinform.hu; Bajcsy-Zsilinszky utca 9; open 9am-7pm Mon-Fri, 10am-6pm Sat & Sun June-Aug; 9am-5pm Mon-Fri, 9am-1pm Sat Sept-May)* can supply lots of information and recommend agencies for finding private rooms.

Due west is a branch of **OTP bank** *(Széchenyi István utca 2; open 7.45am-5pm Mon, Tues, Thur & Fri, 7.45am-6pm Wed)*. The main **post office** *(Széchenyi István utca 20-22; open 8am-8pm Mon-Fri, 8am-1pm Sat)* is 350m to the north. **Egri Est Café** (see Entertainment later) doubles as an Internet café *(300/500Ft for 30/60 minutes)*.

Things to See & Do
The first thing you see as you come into town from the bus or train station is the neoclassical **Eger Cathedral** *(Pyrker János tér 1)*, built in 1836. Directly opposite is the Copf-style **Lyceum** *(☎ 520 400; Eszterházy tér 1; open 9.30am-3pm Tues-Sun Apr-Sept, 9.30am-1.30pm Sat & Sun Oct-Mar)*, dating from 1765, with a 20,000-volume frescoed **library** *(adult/student 300/150)* on the 1st floor and an 18th-century **observatory** and **Astronomy Museum** *(adult/student 300/150Ft)* on the 6th floor. Climb three more floors up to the observation deck for a great view of the city and to try out the **camera obscura**, the 'eye of Eger', designed in 1776 to entertain the locals.

EGER

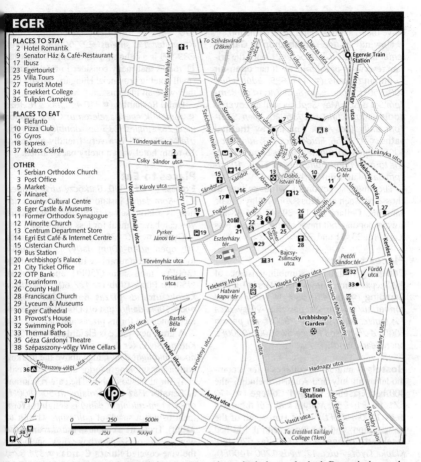

PLACES TO STAY
2 Hotel Romantik
9 Senator Ház & Café-Restaurant
17 Ibusz
23 Egertourist
25 Villa Tours
27 Tourist Motel
34 Érsekkert College
36 Tulipán Camping

PLACES TO EAT
4 Elefanto
10 Pizza Club
16 Gyros
18 Express
37 Kulacs Csárda

OTHER
1 Serbian Orthodox Church
3 Post Office
5 Market
6 Minaret
7 County Cultural Centre
8 Eger Castle & Museums
11 Former Orthodox Synagogue
12 Minorite Church
13 Centrum Department Store
14 Egri Est Café & Internet Centre
15 Cistercian Church
19 Bus Station
20 Archbishop's Palace
21 City Ticket Office
22 OTP Bank
24 Tourinform
26 County Hall
28 Franciscan Church
29 Lyceum & Museums
30 Eger Cathedral
31 Provost's House
32 Swimming Pools
33 Thermal Baths
35 Géza Gárdonyi Theatre
38 Szépasszony-völgy Wine Cellars

Kossuth Lajos utca to the south has some superb buildings, including the rococo **Provost's House** at No 4, the baroque **County Hall** at No 9 (check out the frilly wrought-iron gates in the passageway) and the former **Orthodox synagogue** (1893) at No 17.

At the northern end of Kossuth Lajos utca, across Dózsa György tér, a cobblestone lane leads to **Eger Castle** (☎ 312 744; *Vár 1; adult/ student combined ticket 500/250Ft; grounds only 200/100Ft; open 8am-8pm Tues-Sun Apr-Aug, 8am-7pm Sept, 8am-6pm Oct & Mar, 8am-5pm Nov-Feb)*, erected in the 13th century after the Mongol invasion. Inside are the foundations of St John's Cathedral, which was destroyed by the Turks. Models and drawings in the **István Dobó Museum**, housed in the former Bishop's Palace (1470), show how

the cathedral once looked. Beneath the castle are underground **casemates** hewn from solid rock, which you may tour with a Hungarian-speaking guide (included in the admission price; English-language guide 400Ft extra). Other exhibits include the **Waxworks** *(adult/ student 250/150Ft)* and **Minting Exhibit** *(adult/student 100/50Ft)*. You can still tour the castle grounds for 200/100Ft on Monday, when all the other exhibits are closed.

The **Minorite church** *(Dobó István tér)*, built in 1771, is one of the most glorious baroque buildings in the world. In the square in front are statues of national hero István Dobó and his comrades-in-arms routing the Turks in 1552. Due north in the old town is the 40m **Minaret** *(Knézich Károly utca; admission 100Ft; open 9am-6pm daily Apr-Oct)*, topped

HUNGARY

with a cross. Only non-claustrophobes will brave the 97 narrow spiral steps to the top.

Unwind in the **Archbishop's Garden** (enter from Petőfi Sándor tér 2), once the private reserve of papal princes. It has **open-air swimming pools** (☎ 411 699; adult/child 500/350Ft; open 6am-8pm Mon-Fri, 8am-7pm Sat & Sun May-Sept) as well as **covered pools** (adult/child 500/350Ft; open 9am-7pm daily Oct-Apr). The nearby **thermal baths** (☎ 413 356; Fürdő utca 1-3; admission 500Ft; open to women noon-6pm Wed & Fri; to men noon-6pm Tues & Thur, 10am-2pm Sat) date from Turkish times.

The huge selection of **wine cellars** to chosse between at Szépasszony-völgy can be daunting. Cellars 16, 17, 29, 42 and 48 are always popular, but there's better wine at Nos 5, 13, 18, 23, 31 and 32.

Places to Stay

Camping Within easy stumbling distance of the Szépasszony-völgy wine cellars is **Tulipán Camping** (☎/fax 410 580; ⓦ www.home/zonnet.hu/tulipan; Szépasszony-völgy utca 71; tent/caravan sites 600/800Ft, per person 600Ft, 4-/5-person bungalows 5000/9000Ft; open year-round).

Hostels A number of colleges offer accommodation in July and August, including the 400-bed **Erzsébet Szilágyi College** (☎ 410 571, fax 310 259; Mátyás király út 62; dorm beds 1100-1500Ft), about 1km south of the train station; and the more central 132-bed **Érsekkert College** (☎ 413 661, fax 520 440; Klapka György utca 12; beds 1200-1400Ft).

Private Rooms Agencies that can organise private rooms for between 2100Ft and 2500Ft a night per person include: **Egertourist** (☎ 510 270, fax 411 225; Bajcsy-Zsilinszky utca 9; open 9am-5pm Mon-Fri, 9am-1pm Sat Jun-Sept); **Ibusz** (☎ 311 451, fax 312 652; Széchenyi István utca 9; open 8am-4pm Mon-Fri, 9am-1pm Sat June-Sept); and **Villa Tours** (☎ 410 215, fax 518 038; Jókai utca 1; open 8am-4pm Mon-Fri).

Hotels The **Tourist Motel** (☎ 411 101, fax 429 014; Mekcsey István utca 2; singles/doubles/triples with shared bathroom 3000/5000/6000Ft) is a frayed though spotlessly clean place south of the castle with 34 rooms. Breakfast costs 500Ft extra.

In Eger's main square, **Senator Ház** (☎/fax 320 466; ⓔ hotelsen@axelero.hu; Dobó István tér 11; singles €27.50-48, doubles €39-57) is a delightful 18th-century inn with 11 rooms that many consider to be the finest small hotel in provincial Hungary. Would that they were all like this...

Hotel Romantik (☎ 310 456, fax 516 362; ⓔ romantik-eger@axelero.hu; Csíky Sándor utca 26; singles €35-55, doubles €40-65, triples €50-75) is a very friendly and cosy 16-room hotel with a pretty back garden.

Places to Eat

Express (☎ 517 920; Barkóczy utca 4; open 7am-8pm daily), just northeast of the bus station, is a large self-service restaurant where you can have a meal for less than 400Ft.

Gyros (☎ 310 135; Széchenyi István utca 10; open noon-10pm daily) is a friendly local café-restaurant with Greek salads (360Ft), moussaka (750Ft) and souvlaki (750Ft). **Pizza Club** (☎ 427 606; Dr Hibay Károly utca 8; pizzas 650-1200Ft; open noon-10pm daily), just off Dobó István tér, is recommended for its pizzas and pasta.

A great new place is **Elefanto** (☎ 411 031; Katona István tér 2; mains 950-1800Ft; open noon-midnight daily), high above the market, with a nonsmoking interior and covered balcony for al fresco dining. The café-restaurant at **Senator Ház** hotel (mains 1050-1800Ft; open 11am-midnight daily) is delightful for a meal or just a snack of palacsinta (130Ft to 350Ft). There are a couple of csárdas amid the wine cellars of Szépasszony-völgy, including the vine-covered **Kulacs Csárda** (☎ 311 375; Szépasszony-völgy utca; mains 900-1500Ft; open noon-11pm Tues-Sun).

Entertainment

The Tourinform office, the **County Cultural Centre** (☎ 510 020; Knézich Károly utca 8) opposite the minaret, or the city's **ticket office** (☎ 518 347; Széchenyi István utca 5; open 9am-4pm Mon-Fri) can tell you what concerts and plays are on. Venues are the **Géza Gárdonyi Theatre** (☎ 310 026; Hatvani kapu tér 4), the Lyceum and Eger Cathedral (see Things to See & Do). From mid-May to mid-October there are half-hour organ concerts at 11.30am daily from Monday to Saturday and at 12.45pm on Sunday in the cathedral.

Of the many cafés and bars in the centre, among the best is **Egri Est Café** (☎ 411 105;

Széchenyi István utca 16; open 11am-midnight Sun-Thur, 11am-4am Fri & Sat), with parties at the weekend.

Getting There & Away

Buses leave Eger for Szilvásvárad about every half-hour, for Budapest and Miskolc about once an hour, for Szeged twice a day, for Kecskemét three times a day and for Debrecen five times a day.

Eger is on a minor train line linking Putnok and Füzesabony; for Budapest, Miskolc or Debrecen you usually have to change at Füzesabony. There are up to five direct trains a day to and from Budapest's Keleti station (2½ hours) that do not require a change.

SZILVÁSVÁRAD

☎ 36 ● pop 1950

The Bükk Hills, most of which falls within the 43,000-hectare Bükk National Park, lie to the north of Eger. A good place to begin a visit is the village of Szilvásvárad, 28km from Eger. It's an ideal base for hiking and the centre of horse breeding in Hungary, with some 250 prize Lipizzaners in local stables.

Orientation & Information

Arriving in Szilvásvárad, get off the train at Szilvásvárad-Szalajkavölgy, the first of the town's two stations, and follow Egri út northeast for about 10 minutes to town. The bus from Eger will drop you off in the centre.

There's no tourist office, but Tourinform in Eger can provide information and sells Cartographia's three 1:40,000 maps of the Bükk region (1250Ft each): *A Bükk-fennsík* (Bükk Plateau; No 33); *A Bükk – északi rész* (Bükk – northern section; No 29); and *A Bükk – déli rész* (Bükk – southern section; No 30).

Along the main drag, you'll find an **OTP bank** *(Egri út 30a; open 8am-4pm Mon-Fri)* and the **post office** *(Egri út 12; open 8am-4pm Mon-Fri)*.

Things to See & Do

Some people come to Szilvásvárad just to ride the open-air **narrow-gauge railway** *(☎ 355 197; adult/child one way 160/80Ft, steam train 320/240Ft)* into the Szalajka Valley. It departs seven times a day from May to September (10 times at the weekend), with three daily departures in April and October. The station is approximately 300m south of Egri út at Szalajka-völgy 6.

The little train chugs along for about 5km to **Szalajka-Fátyolvízesés**. Stay on the train for the return trip or you can walk back along well-trodden, shady paths, taking in the sights along the way, including the trout-filled streams. On the way, the **Forestry Museum** *(☎ 355 112; open 8.30am-4.30pm Tues-Sun mid-Apr–Sept, 8.30am-3pm Tues-Sun Oct, 9am-2pm daily Nov–mid-Apr)* deals with everything that the forest contains or surrenders: timber, game, plant life etc.

From Szalajka-Fátyolvízesés, you can walk for 15 minutes to the **Istállóskő Cave**, where Palaeolithic pottery shards have been discovered, or climb 958m **Mt Istállóskő**, the highest peak in the Bükk.

In Szilvásvárad, both the covered and the open **racecourses** *(adult/child 150/100Ft)* put on Lipizzaner parades and coach races on weekends throughout the summer, but times are not fixed.

For horse riding (1800-2500Ft per hour) or coach rides (from 4300Ft), head for the **Lipizzaner Stud Farm** *(☎ 355 155; Fenyves utca; open 8am-4pm daily)* to the northwest. You'll learn more about these intelligent creatures at the **Horse Museum** *(☎ 355 135; Park utca 8; adult/child 80/50Ft; open 9am-noon & 1pm-4pm daily)* in an 18th-century working stable.

Mountain Bike Rentals *(☎ 06-30 335 2695; Szalajka-völgy)* rents out bicycles from a stand opposite the narrow-gauge train station. The rates are 700/900/1100/1300/1500Ft for 1/2/3/4/5 hours, or 1800Ft per day.

Places to Stay & Eat

Hegyi Camping *(☎/fax 355 207;* w *www .hegyicamping.com; Egri út 36/a; tent site per person 550-750Ft, caravan 2000Ft, 2-/3-/4-bed houses 3900/4900/5600Ft; open mid-Apr–mid-Oct)* is on the way to the centre from Szilvásvárad-Szalajkavölgy train station.

Hotel Lipicai *(☎ 355 100, fax 355 200; Egri út 12-14; singles/doubles 5100/6100Ft)* is a basic-looking place that's a little bit on the dark and dingy side, although the rooms are reasonable.

The **Hotel Szilvás** *(☎ 355 159, fax 355 324;* e *reserve@hotelszilvas.hunguest.hu; Park utca 6; singles 4600-6300Ft, doubles 6900-9200Ft)* is a 40-room hotel just beyond the Horse Museum in the former Palavicini mansion. Prices depend on the season and if your room has a bath, shower and/or toilet.

HUNGARY

Szalajka-völgy is lined with food stalls and restaurants, including the pretty **Lovas** (☎ *355 555; mains 860-2620Ft; open noon-10pm daily*). Many of them serve trout (45Ft to 50Ft/100g), the speciality of the area.

Getting There & Away
Buses to/from Eger are frequent and faster than the train. Up to eight trains a day link Szilvásvárad with Egervár station.

TOKAJ
☎ 47 • pop 4650
Although it's just a picturesque little town at the bottom of the Zemplén Hills, Tokaj has been synonymous with fine wine since the 17th century. Tokaj is, in fact, just one of 28 towns and villages of the Tokaj-Hegyalja, a 6600-hectare vine-growing region that produces wine along the southern and eastern edges of the Zemplén Hills. In 2002 it was the eighth site in Hungary to be added to the Unesco World Heritage List.

King Louis XIV famously called Tokaj 'the wine of kings and the king of wines'; to modern tastes it's often overly sweet and oxidised. The dessert wines are especially sugary and rated based on the number of *puttony* (butts) of sweet Aszú added. Tokaj also produces less-sweet wines: Szamorodni (like dry sherry), Furmint and Háslevelú, the driest of all.

Information
Tourinform (☎ *552 070, fax 352 259;* e *tokaj@tourinform.hu; Serház utca 1; open 9am-4pm Mon-Fri*) is just off Rákóczi út. It sits between the **OTP bank** (*Rákóczi út 35; open 8am-4pm Mon-Fri*) and the **post office** (*Rákóczi út 24; open 8am-5pm Mon-Fri, 8am-noon Sat*).

Things to See & Do
The **Tokaj Museum** (☎ *352 636; Bethlen Gábor utca 13; adult/child 300/200Ft; open 9am-4pm Tues-Sun May-Nov*) leaves nothing unsaid about the history of Tokaj, the region and its wines. Just up the road in an 18th-century Greek Orthodox church, the **Tokaj Gallery** (☎ *352 003; Bethlen Gábor utca 17; admission free; open 10am-4pm daily May-Oct*) exhibits works by local artists. The Eclectic **Great Synagogue** (*Serház utca 55*) is a short distance to the east.

Private cellars (*pincék*) offering **wine tastings** are scattered throughout town, including

those at Rákóczi út 2 and 6, Óvári utca 40 and Bem József utca 2 and 16. For the ultimate in tasting venues head for the 600-year-old **Rákóczi Cellar** (☎ *352 408; Kossuth tér 15; open 10am-7pm or 8pm daily Apr-Oct*), where bottles of wine mature in long corridors (one measures 28m by 10m). Tastings of six Tokaj wines cost 1800Ft or, if you prefer only Aszú, 2750Ft.

The correct order of sampling Tokaj wines is: Furmint, dry Szamorodni, sweet Szamorodni and then the Aszú wines – from three to six puttony.

Places to Stay
Pelsőczi-Tiszavirág Camping (☎ *352 626, fax 352 017; Horgász út 11; tent/caravan sites 450/900Ft, per person 40Ft, 2-/3-bed bungalows 4000/6000Ft*) is along the river just north of Tisza Bridge opposite town.

North of the Tourinform office, **Lux** (☎/fax *352 145; Serház utca 14; doubles 4550Ft*) is a friendly six-room pension.

Tokaj Hotel (☎ *352 344, fax 352 759; Rákóczi út 5; singles 4600-5700Ft, doubles 5000-6200Ft*), at the confluence of the Bodrog and Tisza Rivers, has 42 no-frills rooms. Come armed with insect repellent.

Places to Eat
Makk Marci (☎ *352 336; Liget köz 1; pizzas 430-900Ft; open 8am-10pm daily*) is a cheap and friendly pizzeria. **Róna** (☎ *352 116; Bethlen Gábor utca 19; starters 290-450Ft, mains 700-1650Ft; open 11am-10pm daily*) specialises in fish dishes.

Tokaj can now boast one of provincial Hungary's finest restaurants. **Degenfeld** (☎ *553 050; Kossuth tér 1; mains 950-2200Ft; open 11.30am-10pm daily*), in a lovely 19th-century townhouse on the main square, has inventive New Hungarian cuisine, an excellent wine list and lovely decor.

Getting There & Away
Up to nine buses a day go to Szerencs, the chocolate capital of Hungary, with two to Nyíregyháza and one to Debrecen.

Up to 14 trains a day connect Tokaj with Miskolc and Nyíregyháza; change at the latter for Debrecen. To travel north to Sárospatak and Sátoraljaújhely, take the Miskolc-bound train and change at Mezőzomb. Only two direct trains a day travel to and from Budapest's Keleti station.

Latvia

Latvia (Latvija), the man in the middle for far too long, is making heads turn at last – not least in the world of pop music where 160 million people watched Latvia scoop the 2002 Eurovision Song Contest, making it Eurovision host for 2003. With roots in a past that has seen Lutheran Germans and Swedes, Catholic Poles and Orthodox Russians dominate, this small Baltic nation is charting a course set firmly towards Europe – European Union (EU) membership is slated for 2004.

Wedged between Estonia and Lithuania, Latvia stands out for its vibrant capital Rīga, the Baltics' largest and most cosmopolitan city with more preserved Art Nouveau buildings than any other city in the world. Within easy striking distance lie sandy white beaches, the stunningly beautiful Gauja National Park and a rash of palaces and castles evocative of the former Soviet republic's chequered and often painful past.

Facts about Latvia

HISTORY
The idea of Latvia being a discrete political entity inhabited by speakers of Latvian did not become current until the late 19th century. For centuries, the country was divided into the regions of Courland (west of Rīga) and Livonia (eastern Latvia and southern Estonia), governed by various rulers.

Peoples who arrived from the south to the southeastern Baltic around 2000 BC introduced settled agriculture to Latvia and they eventually grouped into what are called the 'Baltic' tribes. The Knights of the Sword, also known as the Livonian Order, were founded in Rīga in AD 1202 and subjugated Latvia. Having been defeated by the Latvian and Lithuanian tribes at Saule in 1236, these knights were reorganised in 1237 as a branch of a second band of German crusaders, the Teutonic Order. By 1290 they controlled the seaboard from modern Poland to Estonia, plus inland Latvia. The existing inhabitants became serfs to a German nobility.

Latvia fell under Polish control in 1561 following an appeal by the Livonian Order to Poland-Lithuania for protection against Ivan the Terrible. In the 1620s Sweden took control

At a Glance

- **Rīga** – picturesque 17th-century old town with wonderful architecture on the Daugava River
- **Sigulda** – pretty Gauja Valley village with medieval castles and legendary caves
- **Kurzeme Region** – beautiful coastal tip with historic towns and white sandy beaches

Capital	Rīga
Population	2.36 million
Official Language	Latvian
Currency	1 lats (Ls) = 100 santīmi
Time	GMT/UTC+0200
Country Phone Code	☎ 371

of most of Latvia until the Great Northern War (1700–21), after which Latvia became part of the Russian empire. An awakening of Latvian national consciousness marked the 19th century. Serfs were freed and Latvian interests were promoted.

After WWI, fighting between the Latvian nationalists (who had declared their independence in November 1918), Bolsheviks who were trying to incorporate Latvia into Soviet Russia, and lingering German occupation forces continued until 1921, when Moscow signed a peace treaty with the independent Latvian parliamentary republic. From 1934 the

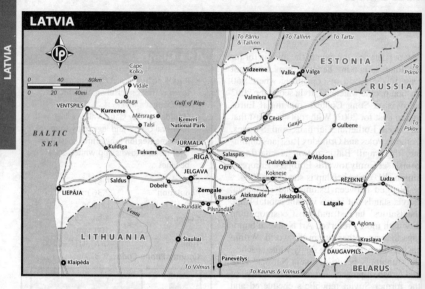

authoritarian leader Kārlis Ulmanis headed a non-parliamentary government of unity.

The period from 1939 to 1941 witnessed the Molotov-Ribbentrop Pact, occupation by Soviet troops, a Communist 'election' victory, incorporation into the USSR, nationalisation, mass killings and about 35,000 deportations. Latvia was occupied partly or wholly by Nazi Germany from 1941 to 1945, and its Jewish population was nearly wiped out. Conquest by the Red Army was followed by farm collectivisation. An estimated 175,000 Latvians were killed or deported.

The first major public protest of the *glasnost* (openness) era was on 14 June 1987 when 5000 people rallied at Rīga's Freedom Monument to commemorate the 1941 Siberia deportations. On 23 August 1989 about two million Latvians, Lithuanians and Estonians formed a 650km human chain from Vilnius, through Rīga, to Tallinn, to mark the 50th anniversary of the Molotov-Ribbentrop Pact.

A reformist, pro-independence Latvian Popular Front was formed. After its supporters won a big majority in the March 1990 elections to Latvia's Supreme Soviet (now the parliament), the pre-WWII constitution was reinstated. Hardliners regained the ascendancy in Moscow in winter 1990–91 and on 20 January 1991 Soviet troops, trying to destabilise the Baltics, stormed the Interior Ministry building in Rīga, killing four people.

The August 1991 coup attempt in Moscow turned the tables and Latvia declared full independence on 21 August. It was recognised first by the West then, on 6 September, by the USSR. Latvia's first democratic elections were held in June 1993.

Initially it was only citizens of the pre-1940 Latvian Republic and their descendants who became citizens of the modern Latvia, which left 35% of the population noncitizens without the right to vote. The first amendments in 1994 introduced Latvian language and history tests to vet wannabe citizens. Applications were restricted to noncitizens of stipulated ages, and it was not until 1998 that all noncitizens – irrespective of age – could apply. The same law also granted automatic citizenship to all children born in Latvia after 1991. By April 2002 Latvia had naturalised 50,386 people – but 55% of Russians remained noncitizens.

Merriment spilled across the capital's streets in 2001 as Rīga celebrated its 800th birthday. The rash of commercial development enveloping the historic centre prompted a warning from Unesco that the city could lose its World Heritage status – bestowed upon Latvia's capital in 1997.

Latvia started accession talks with the EU in December 1999 and hopes to become a fully fledged member by 2004. Its entry into NATO was expected at the end of 2002.

GEOGRAPHY

Green and rolling, Latvia embraces 64,600 sq km. Its four regions are Kurzeme (west), Zemgale (south), Vidzeme (east) – with an upland of mixed farmland and forest that includes Gaiziņkalns (312m), the country's highest point – and Latgale (southeast), with over 40% of Latvia's several thousand lakes.

The Daugava River flows from Belarus to the sea at Rīga. The 452km Gauja, flowing from the northeast, is Latvia's longest river.

CLIMATE

Latvia has a damp climate, with over 600mm of precipitation a year. July is the warmest month, with temperatures reaching 28°C, but also the wettest. Late June is noted for its thunderstorms. Winter starts in November and lasts until late March, with temperatures rarely above 4°C.

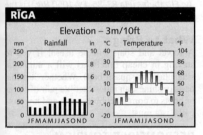

RĪGA
Elevation – 3m/10ft

ECOLOGY & ENVIRONMENT

Woodland, half of it pine, covers 46% of Latvia. Northern Kurzeme and Vidzeme are the most forested areas. About one million hectares of land are protected as nature and national parks and reserves.

Latvia's post-Soviet fight with pollution continues – as new dangers crop up. The drive towards commercialism, which is manifested in increased forestry and property development, is posing more of a threat to relatively untouched areas like the Slītere National Park in western Latvia than communism ever did.

Coastal regions tend to be polluted but beaches in Majori, Bulduri (both in Jūrmala), Ventspils and Liepāja are clean enough to warrant a European blue flag. Seek local advice before swimming in lakes and rivers.

State expenditure on environmental protection has more than doubled in the past five years – rising from 13.7 million Ls in 1996 to 29.6 million Ls in 2000 (86% of which was spent on water protection).

GOVERNMENT & POLITICS

The Latvian political scene is a mosaic of 40-odd parties jostling for power. The 100-seat parliament, the Saeima (w www.saeima.lv), was elected in June 1993 by proportional representation. The president is elected every four years by parliament. In 1995 Latvia's first post-Soviet president, Guntis Ulmanis, was elected for a second term. In 1999 Vaira Vike-Freiberga became president – the first woman to head a former Soviet republic. In power since April 2000, the current government is a four-party coalition, led by former Rīga mayor Andris Berzins of the Latvian Way (LC), and including the People's Party, Latvia's Way and For Fatherland & Freedom. Parliamentary elections took place in late 2002.

ECONOMY

The economy is on track for Latvia to become an EU member state in 2004 – a step that will yield massive financial benefits for the former Soviet republic. Accession negotiations have yet to be completed, but the Latvian Foreign Ministry reckons on paying between €118 to €128 million into the EU pot each year – and taking €261 to €447 million a year out.

Foreign investment totalled €1015 per capita in the third quarter of 2001. Estonia, Norway, Sweden, the USA and Germany remain Latvia's largest foreign investors. Latvia has been a member of the Word Trade Organization (WTO) since 1999. Germany, Russia, Sweden, the UK and Finland are key trading partners. Agricultural output has fallen by 20% since 1995.

In April 2002 the gross monthly average wage was 162 Ls and the average monthly pension was 58 Ls. Unemployment was 8.1% and annual inflation clocked in at 3.3%.

POPULATION & PEOPLE

Latvia's population is only 57.7% ethnic Latvian. In all the major cities, Latvians are in a minority; in Rīga they comprise 41.2% and Russians 43.7%. Russians account for 29.6% of the national population. Since 1987 the natural growth rate of Latvia's population has plunged – the death rate is almost double the (falling) birth rate among ethnic Latvians. Latvians (along with Lithuanians) are the only surviving members of the Baltic ethnic family, an Indo-European but non-Slavic group whose third branch – the old Prussians – was exterminated by the Teutonic Knights.

ARTS

The earliest remnants of Latvian culture are the 1.4 million *dainas* (folk songs), which were identified and collected by Krišjānis Barons (1835–1923). The cornerstone of the new culture was the epic *Lāčplēsis* (The Bear Slayer), formed from traditional folk tales by Andrējs Pumpurs in 1888. The beginings of the nationalist movement in 1988 were accompanied by a rock opera *Lāčplēsis*. A play about the same theme, *Uguns un nakts* (Fire and Night), was written by the most celebrated figure in Latvian literature, Jānis Rainis (1865–1929). His criticism of social and political oppression forced him to live much of his life in exile in Siberia and Switzerland.

SOCIETY & CONDUCT

The Latvian national character can be best described as stoic, enigmatic and unsmiling, but don't mistake a reserved attitude for indifference or hostility. Latvians like flowers, so if you go to a special event, it's nice to bring a bouquet – but make sure it's an odd number of flowers; even-numbered offerings, including 12 red roses, are for mournful occasions! Traditional gender roles are still more intact than in the West.

RELIGION

Lutheranism is the predominant faith, but there's a significant Roman Catholic community too. Among the Russian community, Russian Orthodoxy holds sway. There are 46 other registered denominations in Latvia.

LANGUAGE

Latvian is one of two languages of the Baltic branch of the Indo-European language family, making its language something of an endangered species. English is widely spoken in Rīga and other large cities – and not at all in the countryside.

See the Language chapter at the back of the book for help.

Facts for the Visitor

HIGHLIGHTS

Apart from the obvious destination of Rīga, the other highly recommended spot is the Gauja Valley – take a canoe trip down the Gauja River or – for those pressed for time – hike or bungee jump from Sigulda's cable car.

SUGGESTED ITINERARIES

Depending on time available and where you arrive you might visit the following:

Two days
  Rīga with a day trip to Sigulda
One week
  Rīga, Jūrmala, Sigulda, Cēsis and Kurzeme

PLANNING
When to Go

Summer and spring are the best times to visit. Winter brings little daylight and heaps of snow. The big thaw usually begins in wet and slushy March, which is best to avoid.

Maps

Latvia is well covered by many available large-scale Baltic country maps. Within Latvia, **Jāņa sēta** (☎ 709 22 77; W www.kartes .lv; Elizabetes iela 83-85, LV-1050 Rīga) is the place for maps.

What to Bring

A towel and soap will be useful if you're staying in cheap hotels, as will a universal sink plug (or squash ball). Whether it rains, hails or shines, an indestructible pair of shoes or boots to combat cobblestones and icy footpaths is a must.

RESPONSIBLE TOURISM

In Livonia don't venture off the beaten path without permission, as the land is a preservation area dedicated to Latvia's ancient peoples. In national parks only pitch your tent in designated camp sites and take your rubbish with you.

Rīga's Old Town is on the Unesco World Heritage list; pay it the due respect it deserves.

TOURIST OFFICES
Local Tourist Offices

The **Latvian Tourism Development Agency** (☎ 72 29 945, fax 75 08 468; W www.latvia tourism.lv; Pils laukums 4, LV-1050 Rīga) has a tourist office in most towns and cities (see the individual Information sections throughout this chapter) where staff generally speak English.

Tourist Offices Abroad

Latvian tourist offices in **Finland** (☎ 09-278 47 74; e latviatravel@kolumbus.fi; Mariankatu 8B, SE-00170 Helsinki) and **Germany**

(☎ 0251-21 50 742; e *info@baltic-info.de; Salzmannstrasse 152, D-48159 Münster)* can assist Latvia-bound travellers.

VISAS & DOCUMENTS

Citizens of most EU and Schengen countries don't need a visa to enter Latvia; before leaving on your travels, check on the latest visa developments with the Latvian **Ministry of Foreign Affairs** (w *www.mfa.gov.lv/en).*

In mid-2002, nationalities that could travel visa-free included citizens of Andorra, Austria, Belgium, Croatia, Cyprus, the Czech Republic, Denmark, Estonia, Finland, France, Germany, Greece, Hungary, Iceland, Ireland, Italy, Israel, Japan, Liechtenstein, Lithuania, Luxembourg, Malta, Monaco, Netherlands, Norway, Poland, Portugal, Slovakia, Slovenia, Spain, Sweden, Switzerland, UK, the USA and Vatican City. Note that Australian and New Zealander passport holders still need a visa to enter Latvia.

Ten-day visas are sold for 12 Ls on-the-spot at Rīga's international airport. To extend a visa once in Latvia, contact the visa office in the **Department of Immigration & Citizenship** *(☎ 721 96 39;* w *www.pmlp.gov.lv; Raiņa bulvāris 5, LV-1181 Rīga).*

EMBASSIES & CONSULATES
Latvian Embassies & Consulates Abroad

Latvian representation abroad includes:

Australia (☎ 02-9744 5981) 32 Parnell St, Strathfield 2135, Sydney
Belarus (☎ 0172-84 93 93) 6a Doroshevica Str, BY-220013 Minsk
Canada (☎ 613-238 6014) 208 Albert St, Suite 300, Ottawa, K1P 5G8 Ontario
Estonia (☎ 646 13 13) Tõnismägi 10, EE10119 Tallinn
Finland (☎ 09-476 472 44) Armfeltintie 10, SF-00150 Helsinki
France (☎ 01 53 64 58 10) 6 Villa Said, F-75116 Paris
Germany (☎ 030-826 00 211) Reinerzstrasse 40-41, D-14193 Berlin
Lithuania (☎ 5-213 1260) Čiurlionio 76, LT-2600 Vilnius
Russia (☎ 095-925 27 03) ul Chapligina 3, RUS-103062 Moscow
Sweden (☎ 08-700 63 00) Odengatan 5, Box 19167, S-10432 Stockholm
UK (☎ 020-731 20 040) 45 Nottingham Place, London W1U 5LR
USA (☎ 202-726 82 13) 4325 17th St NW, Washington, DC 20011

Embassies & Consulates in Latvia

The following diplomatic offices are in Rīga:

Australia (☎ 722 23 83) Raiņa bulvāris 3
Belarus (☎ 732 34 11) Jēzusbaznīcas iela 12
Canada (☎ 722 63 15) Doma laukums 4
Estonia (☎ 781 20 20) Skolas iela 13
Finland (☎ 733 20 05) Kalpaka bulvāris 1
France (☎ 703 66 00) Raiņa bulvāris 9
Germany (☎ 722 90 96) Raiņa bulvāris 13
Lithuania (☎ 732 15 19) Rūpniecības iela 24
Netherlands (☎ 732 61 47) Torņa iela 4
Poland (☎ 732 16 17) Elizabetes iela 2a
Russia (☎ 733 21 51) Antonijas iela 2
Sweden (☎ 733 87 70) Andreja Pumpura iela 8
UK (☎ 777 47 00) Alunāna iela 5
USA (☎ 703 62 00) Raiņa bulvāris 7

CUSTOMS

People over 18 can bring in and take out 1L of alcohol and 200 cigarettes, 20 cigars or 200g of tobacco without paying duty tax. You can import and export duty-free any amount of hard currency. Customs rules are posted on the Latvian Tourism Development Agency's website at w www.latviatourism.lv.

MONEY

The lats (plural: lati, designated Ls) is the country's only legal tender and comes in one and two lati coins, and five, 10, 20, 50, 100 and 500 lats notes. One lats is divided into 100 santīmi and there are one, two, five, 10, 20 and 50 santīmi coins.

After Latvia joins the EU in 2004, it will retain its national currency, at least for the initial period. If it is able to meet the strict economic criteria set down by the EU, it could theoretically adopt the euro after 2006.

National bank **Latvijas Bankas** *(Latvian Bank;* w *www.bank.lv)* posts daily exchange rates on its website. Exchange rates at the time of publication were as follows:

country	unit	lati
Australia	A$1	0.35 Ls
Belarus	1000 BR	0.34 Ls
Canada	C$1	0.40 Ls
Estonia	10 EEK	0.37 Ls
Euro Zone	€1	0.57 Ls
Lithuania	1 Lt	0.16 Ls
Poland	1 zł	0.15 Ls
Russia	10R	0.20 Ls
UK	UK£1	0.91 Ls
USA	US$1	0.62 Ls

Exchanging Money

Western and Eastern European currencies are perfectly acceptable and can be exchanged easily. Make sure it is in pristine condition. Tattered notes will be refused.

Automated teller machines (ATMs) accepting Visa and/or MasterCard/Eurocard are widespread. Credit cards are accepted in many hotels, restaurants and shops

Costs

Accommodation in Rīga will be your biggest cost. Eating out in the capital is approaching Western norms. Overland travel remains pleasantly affordable.

POST & COMMUNICATIONS
Post

To send a postcard or letter under 20g within Latvia costs 0.15 Ls, and to Europe and the USA it costs 0.30 Ls. A letter weighing 20g to 100g costs 0.50 Ls to send within Latvia or Europe, and 0.80 Ls to the USA. Mail to North America takes about 10 days, to Europe about a week. Stamps are sold at the *pasts* (post office).

The poste-restante desk at the train station **post office** (☎ *701 88 04; Stacijas laukums 1*) keeps mail for one month. Address letters to Poste Restante, Rīga 50, LV-1050, Latvia.

Telephone

There are public phones countrywide that accept chip cards worth 2, 3 or 5 Ls, sold at kiosks, shops and post offices.

Latvian telephone numbers have seven digits and require no city or area code. Mobile telephones have seven digits, require no area code and start with the digit 9. To make a local or national call, simply dial the seven-digit number. To make an international call, dial the international access code (00), the country and city codes, followed by the subscriber's number. To call a Latvian telephone number from abroad, dial the country code for Latvia (371) and the subscriber's seven-digit number.

Telephone rates are on the website of **Lattelekom** (ⓦ *www.lattelekom.lv*). **ZL Hotline** (ⓦ *www.7770777.lv*) is an online telephone directory with an English-language version.

Email & Internet Access

Internet cafés – many open 24 hours – are abundant in Rīga, large towns and seaside resorts. Access costs about 0.50 Ls per hour.

DIGITAL RESOURCES

Start your virtual trip to Latvia at ⓦ www .latviatourism.lv, which oozes oodles of cultural, historical and practical information.

The detailed music reviews on ⓦ www .Latvians.online.com stand out. Another inspirational site for tuning in to the happening music scene is ⓦ www.music.lv. The ⓦ www .sportsnews.lv website will take sports fans through the highs and lows of Latvian football, basketball and ice hockey.

Cheeky hotel, restaurant, bar and nightclub listings make the ⓦ www.inyourpocket.com site worth a click.

BOOKS

If you are going to follow a Baltic or Scandinavian route Lonely Planet's *Estonia, Latvia & Lithuania* and *Scandinavian Europe* are recommended.

The Holocaust in Latvia 1941–1944: The Missing Centre, by Andrew Ezergailis, presents a balanced account of this provocative subject. For a history of the revolution, Anatol Lieven's *The Baltic Revolution* is a classic.

Robert G Darst's *Smokestack Diplomacy* tackles the dirty issue of environmental protection in Latvia and four other former Soviet republics.

Vieda Skultan's *The Testimony of Lives: Narrative and Memory in Post-Soviet Latvia* (1998) examines themes of belonging and independence in modern Latvian literature.

Latvian National Kitchen, written by Ņina Masiļūne, tells you at exactly what time of year you should boil up your pig's trotters to make *pirāgi* (Latvian meat pasties).

FILMS

Latvia has a strong film-making tradition. Sergei Eisenstein was born in Rīga, as was the documentary maker Jūris Podnieks, who died young in 1992 but not before producing some outstanding, haunting documentaries of life in the late Soviet era, including *Is it Easy to be Young?*, *Hello Do You Hear Us?* and *Homeland*. The most recent film by film director Jānis Streičs, *The Mystery of the Old Parish Church* (2000), stars the lead singer of Latvian boy band Brainstorm.

NEWSPAPERS & MAGAZINES

The English-language weekly newspaper, the *Baltic Times*, published every Thursday, reports on Latvia and its Baltic neighbours. The online version is at **W** www.baltictimes.com. City guide *Rīga In Your Pocket*, sold for 1.20 Ls at news kiosks, is credited with opinionated eating, drinking and entertainment reviews.

Western newspapers and magazines of the day are sold in Rīga at **Narvesen** *(Brīvibas iela 78 • K Barona iela 11).*

RADIO & TV

The BBC World Service can be picked up on 100.5FM. The Latvian State Radio station, Latvijas radio I (with Internet relay at **W** www .radio.org.lv), transmits short-wave broadcasts at 5935kHz in English. The most popular commercial channels in Latvia are Mix FM on 102.7FM, Radio SWH at 105.2FM and Super FM on 104.3FM.

There are two state TV channels and several private channels to choose from. In Rīga, TV5 broadcasts programmes relating to the capital and its inhabitants – watch it at **W** www.tv5.lv or you can even record your own two-minute broadcast at the **TV5 self-recording street booth** *(Smilšu iela 1-3).*

TIME

Latvia adheres to Eastern European Time (GMT/UTC plus two hours), with daylight saving in force from the last Sunday in March to the last Sunday in October.

LAUNDRY

Top hotels tout laundry services – at a price – and there are laundrettes in major cities.

TOILETS

Most public toilets are vile, stinking black holes. The letter 'V' marks a men's toilet in Latvian and 'S' is for women. Many sport triangles: a skirt-wearing triangle (point up) for women and a broad-shouldered one (point down) for men.

WOMEN TRAVELLERS

Women are not likely to receive aggravation from men in Latvia, although unaccompanied women should avoid a few of the sleazier bars. Those who are scantily dressed risk being treated as prostitutes.

GAY & LESBIAN TRAVELLERS

Rīga is fairly gay-friendly, but open displays of same-sex affection remain rare. **Latvian Gay & Lesbian** *(☎ 959 22 29; **W** www.gay baltics.com; Pastkasteiela 380)* offers advice.

Emergency Services

The nationwide emergency phone number for police is ☎ 02 and for ambulance is ☎ 03.

LATVIA

DISABLED TRAVELLERS

With its cobbled streets, rickety pavements and old buildings, Rīga is not user-friendly for disabled travellers.

TRAVEL WITH CHILDREN

Many larger hotels have family rooms or will put an extra bed in the room for you. Kidding around in the capitals kicks off with Rīga circus and Lido atpūtas centrs – great for little and big kids alike.

DANGERS & ANNOYANCES

Pickpockets and car thieves are rife in the Latvian capital, and you're sure to hear about the 'mafia' when in town. But don't be alarmed. Latvia is generally a fairly safe place and the mafia doesn't bother with dull tourists. Snail-slow service in restaurants, the odd street drunk and bureaucratic border guards can be very annoying.

LEGAL MATTERS

It is illegal to buy alcohol anywhere except restaurants, cafés, bars and clubs between the hours of 10pm and 8am.

PUBLIC HOLIDAYS & SPECIAL EVENTS

Latvia's national holidays are New Year's Day (1 January), Good Friday (March/April), Labour Day (1 May), Mother's Day (second Sunday in May), Ligo (Midsummer Festival; 23 June), Jāni (St John's Day; 24 June), Day of Proclamation of the 18 November Latvian Republic, 1918 (18 November), Christmas Eve and Day (24 and 25 December), Boxing Day (26 December) and New Year's Eve (31 December)

Key events in the country include the Baltika International Folk Festival, which Latvia hosts every three years, and the All-Latvian Song and Dance Festival, held every five years. Both should fall in 2003.

Smaller annual festivals include Gadatirgus, a folklore fair held the first weekend of June at Rīga's Open-air Ethnography Museum; and Rīga Summer – a festival of symphonic and chamber music – in July. Sigulda hosts an

Opera Music Festival and a Festival of Ancient Music fills Bauska Castle with music every July. The international film festival, Arsenāls, takes place in the capital in mid-September. Cultural events are listed online at w www.km.gov.lv.

ACTIVITIES

Berry-picking and bird-watching, skiing and sweating it off in a steaming sauna are fun ways to discover Latvia's wild side.

Cycling is popular in this flat land – a track runs from Rīga to Jūrmala.

The Gauja, Salaca and Abava Rivers offer uninterrupted water routes of several days' duration. Organised trips are 3km to 85km long and cost 10 to 39 Ls per boat, including equipment and transport to the tour's starting point. Makars in Sigulda and Valmiera's Sporta Bāze Baiļi and Hostelis Eži all run trips (see Eastern Latvia later in this chapter).

The Gauja Valley is Latvia's winter sports centre. Hire equipment once you arrive.

COURSES

Learn Latvian at Rīga's **Public Service Language Centre** (☎ 721 22 51, fax 721 37 80; w www.vmc.lv; Smilšu iela 1-3).

ACCOMMODATION
Camping

Latvian *kempings* (camping grounds) usually have wooden cottages as well as space for tents. **Lauku Ceļotājs** (see B&Bs following) can direct you to places in rural Latvia where you can pitch a tent.

Hostels

The hostel scene is undeveloped. **Hostelling Latvia** (☎ 921 85 60, fax 722 40 30; w www .hostellinglatvia.com; Ciekurkalna iela 1-7, LV-1026 Rīga) is the only association.

B&Bs

In Rīga several agencies organise B&Bs with or without a local host.

Lauku Ceļotājs (☎ 761 76 00, fax 783 00 41; w www.traveller.lv; Ku-u iela 11, Rīga) arranges B&B accommodation for 5 to 16 Ls a night in farmhouses, manor houses, palaces and guesthouses in rural Latvia.

Hotels

Rīga has a vast choice of hotels – most nearer the top-end price bracket. Elsewhere, decent modern hotels tout reasonable rates, alongside a handful of cheap grey concrete Soviet dinosaurs with drab beige rooms.

Homestays & Rental Accommodation

Overseas, **American-International Homestays** (☎ 303-258 3234; w www.aihtravel .com/homestays; PO Box 1754, Nederland, CO 80466, USA) and **Gateway Travel** (☎ 02-9745 3333; w www.russian-gateway.com .au; 48 The Boulevarde, Strathfield, NSW 2135, Australia) organise homestays in Latvia.

Rīga-based **Patricia** (☎ 728 48 68, 923 82 67, fax 728 66 50; w www.rigalatvia.net; Elizabetes iela 22) arranges rooms/apartments from 12.50/23 Ls per person.

FOOD

The Latvian diet leans towards fatty dairy products, grains and fish, though meat is common. *Šprotes* (sprats) crop up as a starter in many places. You may also find *siļe* (herring), *līdaka* (pike) and *lasis* (salmon). *Cepts,* fish or meat, is fried; *kūpināts* means that it's smoked. *Zupa* (soups) and *desa* (sausage) are popular. During summer and autumn good use is made of the many available types of berry. Throughout Latvia you will find a mouth-watering choice of freshly baked cakes, breads and pastries for as little as 0.20 Ls a piece.

DRINKS

The best *alus* (beer) is produced by Aldaris. A 330mL bottle of Aldaris Zelta costs 0.40 Ls. A Latvian speciality for the brave-hearted is Rīga Black Balsam, a thick, dark, vaguely noxious liquid with supposedly medicinal properties. Revolting on its own, it's better when mixed 50/50 with vodka, coffee or, best of all, with white grape juice.

ENTERTAINMENT

Rīga has a well-developed night life: theatres and cinemas are abundant, and its symphony orchestra and opera are highly regarded. Elsewhere, evening entertainment rarely extends beyond a handful of bars and cafés.

SPECTATOR SPORTS

Latvia's sporting forte is ice hockey and it will host the IIHF World Ice Hockey Championships in 2006. But both basketball and football also draw crowds.

SHOPPING

Amber ranks among Latvia's top souvenirs, so much so that **Nordwear** (**w** *www.nordwear .com; Kaļķu iela 2, Rīga*), which sells hand-knitted Nordic sweaters with Latvian national symbols, proclaims itself amber-free.

Getting There & Away

AIR

Rīga is served by several international airlines, including the national carrier **airBaltic** (**w** *www.airbaltic.com*), which operates in partnership with SAS. AirBaltic sells tickets on the Internet (only for journeys originating in Rīga) and at SAS offices worldwide.

Cities linked by daily scheduled flights with the Latvian capital include Copenhagen, Helsinki, Stockholm, Vienna, Tallinn, Vilnius, Moscow, Warsaw and London Gatwick. There are also weekly flights to/from Berlin, Frankfurt, Kyiv and Vienna.

LAND

For any travel through Russia, Belarus or Kaliningrad, look into the visa situation well ahead of departure.

Bus

Eurolines (**☎** *721 40 80;* **w** *www.eurolines .lv; Prāgas iela 1*), inside Rīga bus station, operates several daily buses to Tallinn, Vilnius, St Petersburg, Kaliningrad and Berlin; an overnight bus to Warsaw; several a week to various German cities; and one bus each week to Prague.

Buses to Stuttgart and Bremen in Germany, and to Amsterdam, Brussels, Paris, Minsk, Kyiv and Moscow are all handled by **Ecolines** (**☎** *721 45 12;* **w** *www.ecolines.lv*) in the bus station in Rīga. **TAK Reisid** (**☎** *7212 402*) operates a twice-weekly bus to Kiel, via Berlin and Hamburg.

In mid-2002 a one-way fare from Rīga to Amsterdam/Brussels/St Petersburg costs 60/63/11 Ls. One-way fares to Tallinn (7 to 8.50 Ls, six hours, five daily) and Vilnius (6 Ls, six hours, four daily) are available.

Train

Latvia is not included in the Inter-Rail, Eurail, ScanRail or other European pass networks, or

the Wasteels/BIJ (Billets Internationales de Jeunesse) ticket network.

The easiest way to reach Latvia's neighbouring Baltic capitals is by bus, although there is a snail-slow overnight train to/from Vilnius (6/8/11 Ls for a seat/couchette/bunk in four-bed compartment, 7½ hours) via Kaunas. The *Baltija* travels overnight between Rīga and St Petersburg (10/20/31/50 Ls for a seat/couchette/bunk in four-bed compartment/1st class, 12 hours), and the *Latvijas Ekspresis* and *Jūrmala* travels to and from Moscow (11/23/36/61 Ls general seating/couchette/compartment/1st class, 16½ hours).

Other rail services serving Rīga include a twice-weekly train to/from Lviv and Odesa via Gomel.

Car & Motorcycle

Latvia demands compulsory accident insurance for drivers. The Green Card – a routine extension of domestic motor insurance to cover most European countries – is not valid in Latvia. Insurance policies with limited compensation rates can be bought at Latvian borders.

SEA

Rīga's **ferry terminal** (**☎** *732 98 82;* **w** *www .rop.lv; Eksporta iela 1*) is about 1.5km downstream of Akmens Bridge. Tickets for the twice-weekly ferry to/from Kiel are available at **Hanza Maritime Agency** (**☎** *732 35 69;* **w** *www.hanza.lv; Eksporta iela 3a*), based at the terminal. There is also a twice-weekly ferry to/from Lübeck.

Between mid-April and mid-September **Rīgas Jūras Līnija** (**☎** *720 54 60;* **w** *www .rigasealine.lv; Eksporta iela 3a*) sails every second day to/from Nynashamn, 60km south of Stockholm.

ORGANISED TOURS

Leading tour specialists include:

Australia
Gateway Travel (**☎** 02-9745 3333, fax 02-9745 3237, **w** www.russian-gateway.com.au) PO Box 451, Strathfield, NSW 2135 – Baltics, ex-USSR and Trans-Siberian specialist offering tours of Eastern Europe
UK
Regent Holidays (**☎** 0117-921 1711, fax 0117-925 4866, **w** www.regent-holidays.co.uk) 15 John St, Bristol BS1 2HR – leading British Baltic specialist

The USA & Canada
Baltic Design Tours (☎ 888-226 36 28, 416-221 9212, fax 416-2216989, w www.baltic-design-tours.on.ca) 5650 Yonge St, Toronto, Ontario M2M 4G3 – city, country and regional tours and Baltic Sea cruises
Vytis Tours (☎ 718-423 6161, 800-778 9847; fax 718-423 3979, w www.vytistours.com) 40–24 235th St, Douglaston, New York NY 11363

Getting Around

AIR
There are no domestic flights within Latvia.

BUS
The country is well-served by buses, although services to off-the-beaten track villages are infrequent. Bus stations in towns and cities have information windows with staff who speak some English. Very occasionally, they charge (per question) for their services.

Updated timetables are online at w www.autoosta.lv. Domestic bus fares average 1.50 Ls per 100km.

TRAIN
An excellent network of suburban trains provide the best transport option for many places within about 50km of Rīga. The regular long-distance rail services link major cities and towns. Suburban or *elektrovilcienci* ('electric' trains) are slower and stop more frequently than *dīzeļvilcienci* (long-distance trains), of which there are three types – 'fast' (international routes only), passenger and diesel.

Latvian Railways (w www.ldz.lv) posts an updated timetable on the Internet. Train tickets for a bum-numbing seat in the cheapest 'general seating' cost around 1.20 Ls per 100km. For longer journeys a bunk in couchette class costs about 3 Ls per 100km.

CAR & MOTORCYCLE
Driving in the countryside is a world apart from Rīga's manic motorists – zig-zag along gravel roads, admire the movie-style dust trail in your mirror and wonder where on earth that solitary passer-by is walking to.

Main roads linking the cities and towns are generally good, distances are not great and traffic is light. Petrol stations open 24 hours abound. You must have your headlights switched on when driving on highways, even during the day. It is illegal to use a mobile telephone while operating a vehicle.

BICYCLE
Latvia is flat and easy to pedal. Seek advice from the **Latvian Bicycle Tourism Information Centre** (VIC; ☎ 750 70 41, fax 750 70 42; w www.velokurjers.lv; Jēkabpils iela 19a, LV-1003 Rīga).

LOCAL TRANSPORT
A mix of trams, buses and trolleybuses (buses run by electricity from overhead wires) provide thorough public transport around towns and cities. Most run from about 5.30am to 12.30am. Tickets cost 0.20 Ls and must be punched in a machine on board the tram, bus or trolleybus.

Taxis cost around 0.30 Ls per kilometre. Higher night-time tariffs apply between 10pm and 6am.

ORGANISED TOURS
In-country tour operators include:

Country Holidays (Lauku ceļotājs; ☎ 761 76 00, ☎/fax 783 00 41, e lauku@celotajs.lv) Ku-u iela 11, LV-1048 Rīga – bird-watching, berry-picking, walking and other nature expeditions
Latvia Tours (☎ 708 50 01, w www.latviatours.lv) Kaļķu iela 8 – daily day trips May to September from Rīga to Sigulda (13 Ls) and Rundāle (18 Ls); and weekly trips to Latgale and Kurzeme (21 Ls)

Rīga

pop 753,000
Rīga is the big boy of the Baltics – a major metropolis with a big-city atmosphere. In the 1930s it was the West's major post for listening in to 'the Russian bear' to the east, and the city became a thrumming mix of diplomats, traders and intrigue – earning it the accolade 'the Paris of the east'. Rīga's postcard-pretty historic old quarter is a Unesco World Heritage site, and its collection of stunning Art Nouveau architecture is Europe's finest.

A fascinating mix of Latvian, Russian and German influences, Rīga has changed dramatically since independence. More office blocks and swanky hotels are sprouting than mushrooms after the rain (occasionally to the peril of the city's historical integrity), the restaurant scene is thriving and nightlife is glitzy. The success of the city's 800th birthday party in 2001 was sealed by Maria N who won the Eurovision Song Contest for Latvia in 2002.

Fewer than half of Rīgan residents are ethnic Latvians (41.2% in 2001), with Russians accounting for nearly 44% of the population. Despite Latvians being a minority in their own capital, ethnic harmony presides.

History

Rīga was founded in 1158 as a river-mouth storehouse for Bremen merchants. In 1201, Bishop Albert of Buxhoevden founded the first German fort in the Baltics. He also founded the Knights of the Sword, who made Rīga their base for subjugating Livonia. Rīga became an important fortified port and joined the Hanseatic League in 1282.

After the Knights' decline in the 16th century, Rīga fell under Polish, Swedish and then (in 1710) Russian control, though it's still dominated by the old German nobility. It grew into an important trading city and by WWI it was Russia's third most important industrial city and the world's greatest timber port.

Rīga was seriously damaged in WWI (also in WWII). The Germans departed in 1939. After WWII, the city was turned into a Soviet industrial centre, becoming the main source of the USSR's railway engines and carriages, and a big supplier of radios, telephone exchanges and computers.

Orientation

Rīga straddles the Daugava River. On the eastern bank you'll find Old Rīga (Vecrīga), the city's historic heart with a skyline dominated by three steeples: St Peter's, Dome Cathedral and St Jacob's. East of the old city is a ring of parks and boulevards.

The train and bus stations are five minutes' walk apart on the southeastern edge of Old Rīga. The ferry terminal is about 500m north of Old Rīga.

Information

Tourist Offices The **tourist office** (☎ 703 79 00, fax 703 79 10; **w** www.rigatourism .com; Rātslaukums 6; open 10am-7pm daily), inside the House of Blackheads, sells the Rīga Card that for one/two/three days costs 8/12/16 Ls and gets you into many museums for free.

Money There are exchange offices at Rīga airport and throughout the centre. **Bastejkubs**

(Basteja bulvāris 12; open 24hr) is on the old-town fringe. ATMs accepting MasterCard, Visa, Cirrus and Plus abound in central Rīga.

Banks change travellers cheques and Eurocheques for 3% commission. Latvia Tours (see Travel Agencies), the agent for American Express, cannot cash travellers cheques, but issues them and replaces lost American Express cheques and cards.

Post & Communications The **central post office** (Brīvības bulvāris 19) is not far from Milda. There's another **post office** (Stacijas laukums 1) next to the train station.

Internet access at **Arēna** (☎ 731 45 14; Ģertrūdes iela 46; open 24hr) and **Dual Net Café** (☎ 781 44 40; Peldu iela 17; open 24hr) costs 0.50 Ls an hour. **Poligons** (☎ 724 22 12; Dzirnavu iela 55; open 24hr) charges 0.40 Ls an hour.

Travel Agencies Latvia Tours (☎ 708 50 01; **e** hq@latviatours.lv; Kaļķu iela 8) is among Latvia's largest agencies and offers a bounty of services.

Others agencies are **World Travel Service** (☎ 733 22 33; K Valdemāra iela 33) and **Via Rīga** (☎ 728 59 01; K Barona iela 7-9). ISIC cards are handled by **Student & Youth Travel Bureau** (SJCB; ☎ 728 48 18; **w** www.sjcb.lv; Lāčplēsa iela 29).

Bookshops For Lonely Planet guides, maps and other travel titles **Jāņa sēta** (Elizabetes iela 83-85) is a good source.

Jāņa Rozes (Elizabetes iela 85a) stocks a good selection of English-language novels, classical literature and also Latvian-language learning cassettes. Its branch shop (K Barona iela 5) sells reference books in English on Rīga and Latvia.

Globuss (Vaļņu iela 26) sells the Penguin classics and has a reading café upstairs.

Laundry For your clothes, the laundrette **City Clean** (K Barona iela 52; open 8am-8pm Mon-Fri, 10am-5pm Sat) dry-cleans too.

Left Luggage At the train station the **left-luggage room** (open 4.30am-midnight daily) in the basement charges 0.50/1 Ls per day for a small/large bag.

The **left-luggage room** (open 6am-11pm daily) at the bus station charges 0.20 Ls per hour for a bag up to 10kg.

LATVIA

CENTRAL RĪGA

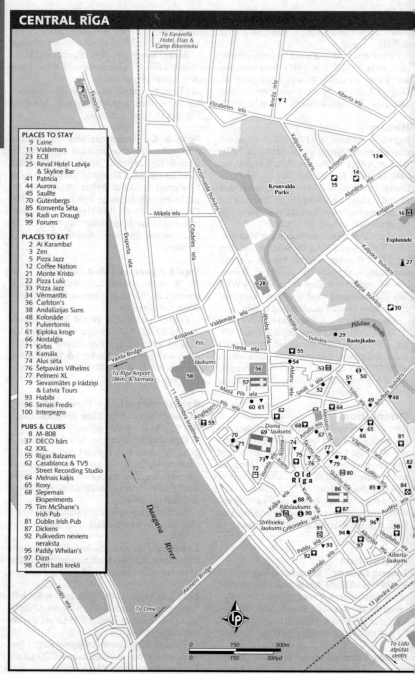

To Karavella
Hotel, Elias &
Camp Bikernieku

Elizabetes iela

▼2

Briẽža iela

Alberta iela

Kalpaka bulvāris

Antonijas iela

13●

Kronvalda bulvāris

Eksporta iela

Citadeles iela

Mikela iela

14
15

Alunāna iela

Kronvalda
Parks

16

Krišjāna

Esplanāde

Kalpaka bulvāris

27

Raina bulvāris

Eksporta iela

28

30

Valdemāra iela

Jēkaba iela

Bastēja

Pilsētas kanāls

bulvāris

29

Bastejkalns

Krišjāna

Valdemāra iela

Pils

Torna iela

55

Vanšu Bridge

laukums

54

53

51
50

To Rīga Airport
(8km) & Jūrmala

58

Mazā Pils iela

56
57

Aldaru

Smilš u iela

52

Valnu iela

49

48

Brīvības bulvāris

11 novembra krastmala

Pils iela

60 61

62

63

64

65
66

81

82

Anglikāņu

59

Doma
laukums

Rozena

68
67

Amatu iela

Meistaru iela

77

78

79

Vāgnera iela

70

69

74

75
76

Skūnu iela

Kalēju iela

80

85

71

Jauniela

73

72

Kramu

Old
Rīga

Skārņu iela

86

84

Rātslaukums

88

87

89

90

Kaļķu iela

Rātslaukums

Audēju iela

95

96

98

Strēlnieku
laukums

Grēcinieku iela

91

94

97

Peldu iela

92

93

Vecpilsētas iela

Alksnāja iela

Alberta
laukums

Mārstaļu iela

13 janvāra iela

Daugava River

Kuğu iela

To Oma

Akmens Bridge

To Lido
atpūtas
centrs

0   150   300m
0   150   300yd

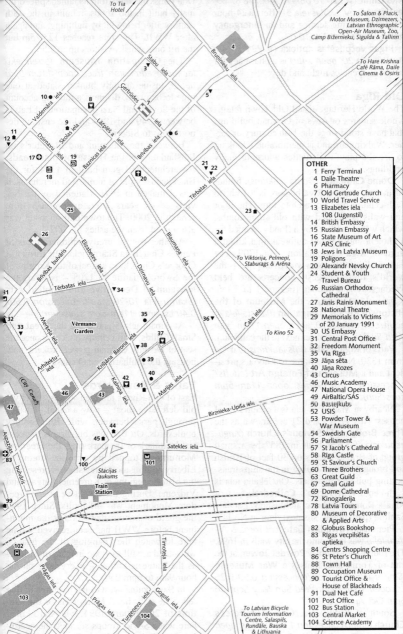

CENTRAL RĪGA

To Tia
Hotel

To Šalom & Placis,
Motor Museum, Dzimezers,
Latvian Ethnographic
Open-Air Museum, Zoo,
Camp Bižernieku, Sigulda & Tallinn

To Hare Krishna
Café Rāma, Daile
Cinema & Osiris

Slūbu iela

Brunmieku iela

Gertrūdes iela

Valdemāra iela

Lāčplēša iela

Skolas iela

Dzirnavu iela

Baznīcas iela

Brīvības iela

Tērbatas iela

Blaumana iela

Dzirnavu iela

To Viktorija, Pelmeņi,
Staburags & Arēna

Brīvības bulvāris

Elizabetes iela

Tērbatas iela

Merķeļa iela

Vērmanes
Garden

Arhitektu iela

(City Canal)

Kr̄išjāņa Barona iela

Čaka iela

To Kino 52

Aspazijas
bulvāris

Marijas iela

Birznieka-Upīša iela

Satekles iela

Stacijas
laukums

Train
Station

Timoteja iela

Prāgas iela

Prāgas iela

Turgeņeva iela

Gogoļa iela

To Latvian Bicycle
Tourism Information
Centre, Salaspils,
Rundāle, Bauska
& Lithuania

OTHER
1 Ferry Terminal
4 Daile Theatre
6 Pharmacy
7 Old Gertrude Church
10 World Travel Service
13 Elizabetes iela
   108 (Jugenstil)
14 British Embassy
15 Russian Embassy
16 State Museum of Art
17 ARS Clinic
18 Jews in Latvia Museum
19 Poligons
20 Alexandr Nevsky Church
24 Student & Youth
   Travel Bureau
26 Russian Orthodox
   Cathedral
27 Janis Rainis Monument
28 National Theatre
29 Memorials to Victims
   of 20 January 1991
30 US Embassy
31 Central Post Office
32 Freedom Monument
35 Via Rīga
39 Jāņa sēta
40 Jāņa Rozes
43 Circus
46 Music Academy
47 National Opera House
49 AirBaltic/SAS
50 Bastejkubs
52 USIS
53 Powder Tower &
   War Museum
54 Swedish Gate
56 Parliament
57 St Jacob's Cathedral
58 Rīga Castle
59 St Saviour's Church
60 Three Brothers
63 Great Guild
67 Small Guild
69 Dome Cathedral
72 Kinogalerija
78 Latvia Tours
80 Museum of Decorative
   & Applied Arts
82 Globuss Bookshop
83 Rīgas vecpilsētas
   aptieka
84 Centrs Shopping Centre
86 St Peter's Church
88 Town Hall
89 Occupation Museum
90 Tourist Office &
   House of Blackheads
91 Dual Net Café
101 Post Office
102 Bus Station
103 Central Market
104 Science Academy

Medical & Emergency Services The **ARS Clinic** (☎ 720 10 06/7/8, fax 728 87 69; e ars@delfi.lv; Skolas iela 5) offers a 24-hour English-speaking service and an **emergency home service** (☎ 720 10 03).

Rīgas vecpilsētas aptieka (☎ 721 33 40; Audēju iela 20; open 24hr) is a pharmacy for your emergencies night and day.

Old Rīga

The World Heritage-listed Old Town retains whole squares or rows of German buildings that have stood since the 17th century or earlier. Walking around is memorable – look up to see the playful statuettes adorning many buildings.

Dome Cathedral (Doma laukums), founded in 1211 for the Rīga bishop, is a 13th- to 18th-century blend of architecture. The floor and walls are dotted with old stone tombs, which were inundated by a flood – blamed for a cholera and typhoid outbreak that killed a third of Rīga's population – in 1709. The cathedral's 1880s organ with 6768 pipes is the world's fourth largest; concerts are held Wednesday and Sunday (tickets: 1 to 3 Ls). Rīga's oldest museum, the **Museum of the History of Rīga & Navigation** (Palasta iela 4; adult/concession 1/0.50 Ls; open 11am-5pm Wed-Sun), is in a cloister next to the cathedral.

Parts of **Rīga Castle** (Pils laukums 3) dates from 1330. Now it is home to Latvia's president and a **Museum of Foreign Art** (adults/concession 1.20/0.70 Ls; open 11am-5pm Tues-Sun).

Nearby at Mazā Pils iela is a quaint row of houses: Nos 17, 19 and 21 are known as the **Three Brothers**. **St Saviour's Church** (Anglikāņu iela 2a) was built in 1857 by a small group of British traders on 30 feet of British soil brought over as ballast in the ships transporting building materials. On Jēkaba iela is 13th-century **St Jacob's Cathedral**, seat of Rīga's Roman Catholic archbishop. Latvia's **Saeima** (parliament) sits next door at No 11.

Picturesque **Swedish Gate** (cnr Torņa & Aldaru iela) was built onto the city walls in 1698. The round 14th-century **Powder Tower**, at the end of Torņa iela, houses a **War Museum** (Smilšu iela 20; adult/concession 0.50/0.25 Ls; open 10am-6pm Wed-Sun May-Sept, to 5pm Oct-Apr).

South of Kaļķu iela, Gothic **St Peter's Church** (adult/concession 1.60/0.50 Ls; open 10am-6pm Tues-Sun May-Sept, to 5pm Oct-April) dominates the southern half of Old Rīga. Don't miss the view from its famed spire, originally built in the 1660s, rebuilt in the 18th century after being hit by lightning, and again after WWII. The spire reaches 123.25m but the lift only whisks visitors up to 72m.

The **Occupation Museum** (Strēlnieku laukums; admission free; open 11am-5pm daily), inside an ugly bunker slated at one time to be razed, displays a moving account of the Soviet and Nazi occupations of Latvia between 1940 and 1944 and the ensuing deportations to Siberia.

Between the museum and St Peter's on Rātslaukums is the **House of Blackheads**. An architectural gem built in 1344 for the Blackheads' guild of unmarried merchants, it was damaged in 1941, flattened by the Soviets seven years later, and rebuilt from scratch in 2000. The town hall opposite was also raised from the ashes in 2002.

Another row of pretty buildings faces St Peter's Church on Skārņu iela. The former St George's Church – a chapel of the Knights of the Sword dating to 1208 – is today the **Museum of Decorative and Applied Arts** (Skārņu iela 10-20; adult/concession 0.50/0.40 Ls; open 11am-5pm Tues-Sun).

At Amatu iela 5 and 6 are the **Great and Small Guilds**, 14th-century buildings once the seat of wealthy German power brokers, now housing the Philharmonic Orchestra.

Parks & Boulevards

East of Old Rīga's jumbled streets, the city's old defensive moat – now a canal – snakes through parks between wide 19th-century boulevards. On Brīvības bulvāris is the central landmark of the park ring, the **Freedom Monument**, topped by a bronze statue of Liberty holding aloft three stars, representing the historic regions of Kurzeme, Latgale and Vidzeme. During the Soviet years the Freedom Monument was off limits. Since 1992 the guard of honour that stood at the monument before WWII has been revived. Come here to watch the changing of the guards, who stand as still as stone in front of Milda – as the statue is known – every hour on the hour 9am to 6pm daily.

In Bastejkalns, west of the monument, five red stone slabs lie as **Memorials to the Victims of 20 January 1991**, who were killed here when Soviet troops stormed the nearby Interior Ministry.

The old 19th-century **Russian Orthodox cathedral** is on Brīvības bulvāris.

The **State Museum of Art** (K Valdemāra iela 10a; adult/concession 1.20 Ls; open 11am-5pm Wed-Mon) houses Russian and Latvian work.

New Rīga

The commercial soul of the city lies beyond the ring of Elizabetes iela in a grid of broad streets lined by six-storey buildings. The boulevards here are lined with impressive and flamboyant 19th- and early-20th-century buildings in Rīga's characteristic *Jugendstil* (Art Nouveau) style. One of the best examples, designed by Mikhail Eisenstein, father of the renowned film maker Sergei, is at Elizabetes iela 10b. Around the corner, on nearby Alberta iela, Eisenstein's work on No 2a is only one of the highlights of this fantastic street.

The **Jews in Latvia Museum** (Skolas iela 6; admission by donation; open 10am-5pm Mon-Fri) has a captivating exhibition, not only of the extermination of the Jews in Latvia during wartime, but also of their historical cultural presence in the country. Ask to see the 10-minute introductory video that contains some chilling footage shot by an amateur German soldier. This museum is currently closed for renovation and at the time of research there was no clear date for its reopening.

Suburbs

Rīga's **Motor Museum** (Eizenšteina iela 6; adult/concession 1/0.50 Ls; open 10am-3pm Mon, 10am-6pm Tues-Sun), 8km east of the Old City, is worth the trip to see cars that belonged to Stalin and Brezhnev. Bus No 21 from the Russian Orthodox cathedral goes to the Pansionāts stop on Šmerļa iela, 500m from the museum.

The **Latvian Ethnographic Open-Air Museum** (Brīvības gatve 440; adult/concession 1/0.50 Ls; open 11am-5pm daily mid-May–mid-Oct, closed last day of each month), on the city's eastern edge, houses over 90 buildings from rural Latvia. Take bus No 1 from the corner of Merķeļa iela and Tērbatas iela to the Brīvdabas muzejs stop.

Places to Stay

Hostels If you stay at **Placis** (☎ 755 18 24, fax 754 13 44; e placis@delfi.lv; Laimdotas iela 2a; singles/doubles/triples with shared bathroom 5/7/15 Ls, doubles with shower &

toilet 20 Ls) there's a 10% discount with a Hostelling International (HI) card. Hop on Trolleybus No 4 from the Circus stop at Merķela iela and go to the Teika stop.

B&Bs With its entrance opposite Ģertrūdes iela 39, **ECB** (☎ 729 85 55, 912 56 57, fax 729 85 25; e ecb@ecb.apollo.lv; Kr Barona iela 37-18; singles/doubles/triples 27/32/38 Ls) is a British-run B&B agency with spacious rooms in central Rīga. Rates include an evening meal as well as breakfast.

Patricia (☎ 728 48 68, 923 82 67, fax 728 66 50; w www.rigalatvia.net; Elizabetes iela 22; rooms without breakfast 12.50 Ls per person, self-catering apartments from 23 Ls per person) arranges rooms in private flats all over Latvia.

Hotels – Budget Budget hotels are like gold dust in Rīga.

The good **Viktorija** (☎ 701 41 11; w www.hotel-viktorija.lv; A Čaka iela 55; singles/doubles 12/17 Ls, with bathroom & breakfast 30/40 Ls) takes out the prize for Rīga's best-value budget accommodation. Shared showers are new, clean and pleasant to use.

The flip side is **Aurora** (☎ 722 44 79; Marijas iela 5; singles/doubles/triples with shared bathroom 8/9/12 Ls), a miserable joint by the train station with poky noisy rooms that won't make you smile.

Around the corner, paint wore away many moons ago at the run-down **Saulīte** (☎ 722 45 46; Merķeļa iela 12; singles/doubles with shared bathroom from 7/16 Ls).

Mežaparks (☎ 755 79 88; Sakses iela 19, Mežaparks; doubles with shared bathroom 7 Ls, luxury doubles 17-30 Ls) comes complete with outstanding lake views. Take trolleybus No 2 from K Barona iela to the last stop.

Another out-of-town option is **Elias** (☎ 751 81 17; Hamburgas iela 14; doubles 16 Ls), close to Lake Ķīsezers. Take tram No 11 from K Barona iela.

Hotels – Mid-Range & Top End Prices include breakfast. The rooms with bathrooms at the Viktorija (see Hotels – Budget) offer excellent value mid-range accommodation.

The **Radi un Draugi** (☎ 722 03 72, fax 724 22 39; w www.draugi.lv; Mārstaļu iela 1; singles/doubles from 33/42 Ls), owned by British-Latvians, is clean, popular and often fully booked.

On a par is **Laine** (☎ 728 88 16, 728 98 23, fax 728 76 58; ⓦ www.laine.lv; Skolas iela 11; singles/doubles/triples 15/25/30 Ls, singles/doubles with private bathroom 35/40 Ls, luxury singles/doubles 40/45 Ls), tucked in a courtyard off the main street. Outside it appears run down, but inside jolly green-and-yellow candy-striped corridors lead to comfortable rooms.

Old Town **Forums** (☎ 781 46 80, fax 781 46 82; ⓦ www.hotelforums.lv; Vaļņu iela 45; doubles from 33 Ls) has rooms warranting no complaints inside a terracotta townhouse.

Along K Valdemāra iela is the hotel **Valdemārs** (☎ 733 44 62, 733 21 32, fax 733 30 01; ⓦ www.valdemars.lv; K Valdemāra iela 23; singles/doubles without breakfast 25/35 Ls) with age-old furnishings and creaky corridors; and **Tia** (☎ 733 39 18, fax 783 03 90; ⓦ www.tia.lv; Valdemāra iela 63; singles/doubles/triples from 32/40/64 Ls), which touts simple but soulful rooms.

One notch up, give **Konventa Sēta** (☎ 708 75 01/2/3, fax 708 75 06; Kalēju iela 9/11; singles/doubles 46/55 Ls) a whirl. The unique hotel is in the restored courtyards of a 15th-century convent, with 10 medieval buildings each named after their original uses.

Gutenbergs (☎ 781 40 90, fax 750 33 26; ⓦ www.gutenbergs.lv; Doma Laukums 1; doubles from 55 Ls) is an irresistibly slurge-worthy choice. Its stunning rooftop restaurant overlooking St Peter's Church wins the prize for rooms with the best view.

Reval Hotel Latvija (☎ 777 22 22, fax 777 22 21; ⓦ www.revalhotels.com; Elizabetes iela 55; doubles from 65 Ls), the city's former Intourist hotel, is a sparkling 27-storey tower of wealth and luxury today. City views from the bar on the 27th floor are better than those atop St Peter's.

If you don't mind being on the other side of the river, the **Oma** (☎ 761 33 88, fax 761 32 33; ⓔ oma@com.latnet.lv; Ernestīnes iela 33; singles/doubles from 33/43 Ls) is a pleasing hotel in a quiet neighbourhood where rooms have fresh wood furniture.

At the port is the modern **Karavella** (☎ 732 31 30, fax 783 01 87; ⓦ www.karavella.lv; Katrīnas dambis iela 27; singles/doubles from 24/33 Ls), run by the Latvian Shipping Company. Tram Nos 5 and 9 north on Aspazijas and Kronvalda bulvāris, go to the Eksporta stop, on the corner of Pētersalas iela and Katrīnas dambis, 500m south of Karavella.

Places to Eat

Dining out in Rīga offers a tongue-tickling range of choices.

Restaurants For cheap and tasty Latvian food, lick your lips in Lido, a chain of buffet-style restaurants where a titillating array of all kinds of foods, salads and desserts, many prepared in front of you, will keep you purring. **Alus sēta** (☎ 722 24 31; Tirgoņu iela 6; meals 3 Ls; open 10am-1am daily), overlooking Doma laukums, is Lido's only Old Town outlet. **Vērmanītis** (☎ 728 62 89; Elizabetes iela 65; meals 2-3 Ls; open 8am-1am daily) and **Staburags** (A Čaka iela 57; meals 3 Ls; open noon-1am daily) are central.

Out of town, Lido runs the fabulous **Lido atpūtas centrs** (☎ 728 21 87; Krasta iela 76; meals 2-3 Ls; open 10am-11pm daily), loved by Latvian families who flood the vast eating and entertainment complex at weekends. Spend the day here discovering Latvia. Take bus No 107 from in front of the train station to the Lido stop.

Back in Old Rīga, **Ķiploka krogs** (☎ 721 14 51; Jēkaba iela 3; meals 3 Ls; open noon-midnight daily) cooks up garlic in all shapes, sizes and guises. Equally eccentric **Nostal-ija** (☎ 722 23 38; Kaļķu iela 22; open 10am-2am daily) is a retro Soviet restaurant.

Exuding spiritualism is the chilled **Kamāla** (☎ 721 13 32; ⓔ kamala@delfi.lv; Jauniela 14; meals 5 Ls; open 8.30am-midnight daily), named after the wife of Vishnu and the daughter of the milk ocean. It's vegetarian.

European-style safe bets are easy to find. **Osiris** (☎ 724 30 02; K Barona iela 31; meals 5-7 Ls; open 8am-midnight Mon-Fri, 10am-midnight Sat & Sun) is great for breakfast or a romantic glass of wine. **Čarlston's** (☎ 777 05 72; ⓦ www.charlstons.lv; Blaumaņa iela 38-40; meals 6-8 Ls; open 8am-midnight daily) has a cappuccino bar and Tex-Mex grill; **Andalūzijas Suns** (Andalusian Dog; ☎ 728 84 18; Elizabetes iela 83/85; meals 4-8 Ls; open 11am-1am daily) is a trendy bistro in Berga bazārs mall; and **Ai Karamba!** (☎ 733 46 72; Brieža iela 2; open 8am-midnight Mon-Sat, 9am or 10am-midnight Sun) is an American diner with breakfast, knock-back nightcaps and everything in between.

Cafés Hare Krishna café **Rāma** (K Barona iela 56; open 9am-midnight, Sun 11am-7pm) dishes up a healthy, gut-busting vegetarian meal for 1.50 Ls. Wash it down with home-made ginger tea for 0.15 Ls. **Ķirbis** (*The Pumpkin; Doma laukums 1; open 9am-11pm Mon-Fri, 10am-11pm Sat & Sun*) is the other vegetarian fave.

Favoured for its range of coffee beans and cake is **Monte Kristo** (*Ģertrūdes iela 27; open 9am-9pm Mon-Sat, noon-9pm Sun*). The tea equivalent is laid-back **Zen** (*Stabu iela 6; open noon-midnight daily*) where you can loll on floor cushions and watch – for a thirsty 20 minutes – your tea being prepared.

The **Habibi** (*Peldu iela 24; open noon-midnight daily*) is run by an English- and Russian-speaking Egyptian and is another spot to take it easy. Habibi serves Arabian dishes out front and belly dancers shake their stuff out back to a water-pipe-smoking clientele. Fruit-flavoured tobacco costs 5 Ls a pipe.

Modern coffee bar **Coffee Nation** (*Valdemāra iela 21; open 8am-10pm daily*) is great for sinking into an armchair with a good book and a cappuccino. Its freshly squeezed beetroot juice is marketed to customers as inducing a good mood, and no, there's nothing in it besides beetroot.

Old favourites include **Kolonāde** (*Brīvības bulvāris 26*), with a terrace garden overlooking the opera house, and **Senais Fredis** (*Audēju iela 5*) in the Old Town.

Pulvertornis (*Vaļņu iela 3; open 8am-8pm Mon-Fri, 9am-6pm Sat & Sun*) is a dirt-cheap café where soups/salads/meat dishes cost upwards of 0.17/0.19/0.75 Ls. Rīga's Jewish community hangs out at **Šalom** (*Brīvības iela 158; open noon-11pm daily*); kosher food must be ordered in advance.

Fast Food Latvia's answer to fast food can be found stuffed inside *pelmeņi* (meat dumplings fried, boiled or swimming in soup), *pīrāgi* (meat pasties baked in the oven) and *pankuki* (pancakes). This is may be why big international fast-food chains are refreshingly few and far between in the Latvian capital.

Pelmeņi (*A Čaka iela 38a*) and **Pelmeņi XL** (*Kaļķu iela 7*) are two calorie-heavy places where you can eat to your heart's content for 0.55 Ls a dumpling. The mother-in-law bakes the best *pīrāgi* at **Sievasmātes p īrādziņi** (*Kaļķu iela 10*), quite literally called Mother-in-Law's *pīrāgi*. The cute little pasties come stuffed with meat, mushrooms, fruit or cheese.

Pancakes with sweet and savoury toppings and fillings are the reason behind lunchtime queues that linger outside **Šetpavārs Vilhelms** (*Šķūņu iela 6*), another cafeteria-style place in Old Rīga.

Pizza-wise, bag a table in advance at the packed-out **Pizza Jazz** (*Raiņa iela 15 • Brīvibas bulvāris 76*); or opt for a giant pizza slice at **Pizza Lulū** (*Ģertrūdes iela 27 • K Valdemāra iela 143-145;* w *www.lulu.lv; open 24hr*) any time of the day or night.

Self Catering Rīga's bustling **central market** (*open 7am-4pm daily*) is located in five great zeppelin hangars on Prāgas iela behind the bus station. The **Interpegro** grocery store opposite the train station opens 24 hours.

Entertainment

The *Baltic Times* and *Rīga In Your Pocket* list upcoming events.

Bars & Clubs Pubs generally open 11am to midnight Sunday to Thursday, and until 2am Friday and Saturday. Most clubs throb until 5am at weekends.

Anglophiles kick off the night at British pub **Dickens** (*Grēcinieku iela 9/1*), where a pint of Guinness/Kilkenny costs 1.70/1.60 Ls. After that, there's a trio of Irish pubs – **Paddy Whelan's** (*Grēcinieku iela 4*), **Dublin** (*Vāgnera iela 16*) and **Tim McShane's** (*Tirgoņu iela 10*) – to drink away a Friday night.

Party animals often end up at **Pulkvedim neviens neraksta** (*Noone Writes to the Colonel; Peldu iela 26-28*), an off-beat dance bar. Watch the sun rise at **Melnais kaķis** (*Meistaru iela 10-12; open 9pm-7am daily*) where punters play pool, eat or bask in the early-morning sun with a pint in hand.

Ordering anything other than black balzams (see Food & Drink earlier) at **Rīgas Balzams** (*Torņa iela 4*) is sacrilege. **DECO bārs** (*Dzirnavu iela 84*) has a slick industrial decor, chic pavement terrace and ultra-hip dance floor come the early hours.

Music clubs in the capital include: **M-808** (w *m.808.lv; Lāčplēša iela 5*), where techno and house beats; house-music hideout **Dizzi** (*Mārstaļu iela 10*); and also **Četri balti krekli** (w *www.krekli.lv; Vecpilsētas iela 12*), where the best of Latvian bands play.

The more mainstream nightclubs in Rīga include **Roxy** (*Kaļķu iela 24*) and the flash brash **Casablanca** (w *www.casablanca.lv; Smilšu iela 1-3*), which is next door to TV5's recording studio.

The only gay club, generically replete with Tom of Finland drawings and a darkroom, is **XXL** (☎ 728 22 76; Kalniņa iela 4).

Opera, Ballet & Classical Music The performances at Rīga's **National Opera House** (☎ 707 377 77; w www.opera.lv; Aspazijas bulvāris 3) start at 7pm. The venue is home to the highly rated Rīga Ballet, where Mikhail Baryshnikov made his name. The concert hall of the renowned Latvia National Symphonic Orchestra is the **Great Guild** (Lielā -ilde; Amatu iela 6). Tickets for the twice-weekly organ concerts at Dome Cathedral are sold from the cathedral **ticket office** (☎ 721 32 13; tickets 1-3 Ls), opposite the west door.

Cinema The Daile (☎ 728 38 54; K Barona iela 31) and **Kino 52** (☎ 728 87 78; Lāčplēsa iela 52-54) cinemas show films in English with Latvian or Russian subtitles. ISIC card-holders get 10% discount.

Circus Rīga's permanent circus (Cirks; ☎ 721 32 79, e circusriga@Apollo.lv; Merķeļa iela 4; tickets 1-3 Ls; shows twice daily Fri-Sun Oct-April) is close to the train station.

Getting There & Away
Air International flights to/from **Rīga airport** (Lidosta Rīga; ☎ 720 70 09; w www.riga -airport.com), 8km west of the city centre, are covered in the Getting There & Away section earlier in this chapter. **AirBaltic** (☎ 720 77 77; w www.airbaltic.com; Kaļķu iela 15) has an office at the airport too.

Bus Both national and international buses use Rīga's **bus station** (w www.autoosta.lv; Prāgas iela 1). Timetables are in the station and on its website. **Information office** (☎ 900 00 09; open 6am-11pm daily) staff speak English. Domestic bus services include:

Bauska 1.20 Ls, 1½ hours, 65km, more than 30 daily
Cēsis 1.30 Ls, two hours, 90km, 26 daily
Daugavpils 3 Ls, four hours, 230km, up to seven daily
Jelgava 0.55-0.78 Ls, one hour, 40km, one or two daily
Kolka 2.35-2.98 Ls, 5¾ hours, 160km, three daily
Kuldīga 2.20 Ls, three to four hours, 150km, six to 10 daily
Liepāja 2.98 Ls, four to six hours, 220km, about 20 buses daily

Sigulda 0.90 Ls, one hour, 50km, 12 daily
Talsi 1.65 Ls, 2½ hours, 115km, about 12 daily
Valmiera 1.30 Ls, 2½ hours, 120km, about 12 daily
Ventspils 2.70 Ls, 2½ to four hours, 200km, about 12 daily

Train Rīga's **train station** (centrālā stacija; ☎ 583 30 95; Stacijas laukums) enjoyed a US$5.5 million facelift in 2002–03. Find the timetable on the Latvian Railways' website at w www.ldz.lv.

Tickets are sold in the main departures hall: window Nos 1 to 6 sell tickets for international trains; window Nos 7 to 9 sell tickets for mainline services; and window Nos 10 to 13 sell tickets for slower suburban trains, including Sigulda, Cēsis, Valmiera, Jelgava and Jūrmala. Mainline services include:

Daugavpils 2.42 to 3 Ls, 3½ to 4¼ hours, 218km, four daily
Liepāja 2.45 Ls, five to 5¾ hours, 220km, two daily
Valga (via Sigulda, Cēsis & Valmiera) 2 Ls, three to 3½ hours, 168km, one daily
Ventspils 2.17 Ls, 4¼ hours, 200km, two daily

Car & Motorcycle Motorists must pay 5 Ls/hour to enter the Old Town. All the major car-rental firms have offices at the Rīga airport and in town.

Getting Around
To/From the Airport Bus No 22 runs about every 20 minutes between Rīga airport (see earlier) and the stop on 13 Janvāra iela opposite the bus station in central Rīga. Tickets (0.20 Ls) are sold by the bus driver. A taxi to the centre should cost no more than 8 Ls.

Public Transport All the routes of buses, trolleybuses and trams are clearly marked on Jāņa sēta's Rīga City Map. Tickets (0.20 Ls) are sold at news kiosks and by drivers. City transport runs 5.30am to 12.30am daily.

Bicycle Hire two wheels from **Antīvās atpūtas** (☎ 955 41 55; Pāvu iela 2) for 2/1.50 Ls for first/subsequent hours.

AROUND RĪGA
Jūrmala
pop 56,000
Jūrmala (Seashore) is a string of resorts that stretch 30km west along the coast. Its sandy beaches, backed by dunes and pine woods,

have seduced the holiday-makers since the 19th century.

Of its 14 townships, the 4km-stretch between Bulduri and Dubulti is the hub. Jomas iela, the pedestrian street in **Majori** (tourist office ☎ 776 46 76, fax 776 46 72; e jurmala info@mail.bkc.lv; Jomas iela 42) is key Sunday strolling territory. Ķemeri, 6km inland, is the starting point for bog walks in the **Ķemeri National Park** (visitors centre ☎/fax 776 53 87; Meža māja; e nacionalparks@kemeri .apollo.lv; open May–mid-Oct).

During Soviet times the Rīga-Jūrmala highway, Latvia's only six-laner, was dubbed '10 minutes in America' – locally made films set in the USA were always filmed on it.

Things to See To stroll along the beach, play volleyball and suntan, or walk over the dunes and through pine forests is reason enough to visit Jūrmala. The highest **dunes** are at Lielupe. In Vaivari the **Nemo Water Park** (☎ 773 63 92; e nemo@apollo.lv; Atbalss iela 1) has slides, a sauna, large pool and bicycles to rent (5 Ls per hour).

The country cottage where the poet Jānis Rainis died in 1929 is in Majori and is now a **museum** (Plieksāna iela 5-7; open 11am-6pm Wed-Sun).

Places to Stay & Eat At the water park, **Kempings Nemo** (☎ 773 63 92; e nemo@ apollo.lv; Atbalss iela 1, cottage beds 12.50 Ls, tent sites 1 Ls per person) has little cottages and tent sites

In Majori, **Dārta** (☎ 766 23 91; e darta@ latnet.lv; Jūras iela 59; singles/doubles/triples with shared bathroom & breakfast 12/18/26 Ls, doubles with bathroom 25-45 Ls) and **Elina** (☎/fax 776 16 65; Lienes iela 43; doubles 15 Ls Sept-May, 25 Ls June-Aug) offer good-value accommodation in typical wooden houses.

Jomas iela in Majori has dozens of eating and drinking options. Stop at **Salmu krogs** (Jomas iela 70-72) for a beer and ķiploku grauzdiņi (Latvian black-bread garlic sticks). **Jūras Zaķis** (Sea Rabbit; Vienibas prospekts 1), 30m from Bulduri beach, is a good place for local fish.

Getting There & Away Two to five trains an hour travel from Rīga to Jūrmala along the Ķemeri to Tukums line starting at 5.45am until 11.10pm. All stop at Dubulti (0.52 Ls, 35 minutes), but not all at Majori (0.51 Ls, 40 minutes) and other stations.

Salaspils

Between 1941 and 1944 an estimated 45,000 Jews from Rīga and approximately 55,000 other people, including Jews from other Nazi-occupied countries and prisoners of war, were murdered in the concentration camp that was set up at Salaspils, 15km southeast of Rīga, on the Daugava River. Giant, gaunt sculptures stand on the site as a memorial, and there's a small museum inside the huge concrete bunker. The inscription reads 'Behind this gate the earth groans'. In the shadow of the memorial lies a 6m-long block of polished stone with a metronome inside, ticking a haunting heartbeat that never stops.

From Rīga take a suburban train (10 daily) on the Ogre-Krustpils line to Dārziņi (not Salaspils) station. A path leads from the station to the piemineklis (memorial), which is a 15-minute walk.

Rundāle Palace

The 18th-century **Rundāle Palace** (Rundāles pils; ☎ 39 62 197; w www.rpm.apollo.lv; adult/concession 1.50/1 Ls; open 10am-6pm daily May-Oct, to 5pm Nov-Apr), in Pilsrundāle, 77km south of Rīga, is definitely the architectural highlight of provincial Latvia. It was designed and was built for Baron Ernst Johann von Bühren (1690–1772), Duke of Courland, by Bartolomeo Rastrelli, the baroque genius from Italy who created many of St Petersburg's finest buildings. Some 40 of the palace's 138 rooms are open to visitors, as are the gardens.

Rundāle can be easily combined in a day trip with Bauska (population 10,600), a country town just 12km east, on the main Rīga to Vilnius road. The imposing **Bauska Castle** (1443–56) was constructed for the Livonian Knights, blown up in 1706 during the Great Northern War, and rebuilt in the 1970s. Merriment fills the castle grounds during July's Festival of Ancient Music.

Unless you have your own transport, the best way to reach Rundāle is from Bauska – its **bus station** (☎ 39 22 477; Slimnīcas iela 11) is served by hourly buses between 5.30am and 5.30pm both to and from Rīga (1.20 Ls, 1¼ hours). Once you reach Bauska take a bus west to Rundālespils (not Rundāle, which is 2.5km farther west).

Eastern Latvia

Two of the country's three historic regions lie east of Rīga. In the northeast, Vidzeme, which is Latvia's most scenically varied region, is dominated by the beautiful Gauja Valley. Dubbed the 'Switzerland of Latvia', the valley is partly protected by a national park and bespeckled with castles. The small towns of Sigulda, Cēsis and Valmiera all make excellent bases for delving into its scenic depths. Sigulda is the gateway to the Gauja National Park, although older Cēsis, 30km northeast, is the only town actually in the park. **Valmiera** (population 28,730), 30km north of Sigulda lures outdoor enthusiasts with its ski resort and canoeing centre, both managed by **Sporta Bāze Baiļi** (☎ 42 21 861; w www.baili.lv) on the town's eastern fringe. In town, Latvia's best-run hostel **Hostelis Eži** (☎ 42 81 764, 42 07 263; e ezi@ezi.lv, w www.ezi.lv; Valdemāra iela 1; dorm beds 5 Ls) in a red-brick water tower dating from the early 1900s, rents bicycles and canoes.

Scenic Vidzeme is also home to a long sandy stretch of largely unspoilt coast along the Gulf of Rīga; Latvia's highest terrain known as the Vidzeme Upland; and to one of Europe's oddest border towns, Valka, split between Latvia and Estonia.

In the southeast of the country is industrial Latgale, which was Latvia's main bastion of Roman Catholicism under the Polish control from 1561 to 1772. **Daugavpils** (population 114,000) is Latvia's second-largest city as a result of extensive industrial development since WWII and is predominantly Russian – only 16.1% of its population is Latvian.

Latgale's far southeastern corner is blessed with the Latgale Upland, a scenic lake district. Some of the best scenery is around **Lake Rāzna**, Latvia's largest lake at 55 sq km. On Ascension Day (15 August) thousands of people flock to Aglona Basilica, Latvia's leading Roman Catholic shrine built on the shores of Lake Egles in 1699.

SIGULDA
pop 10,855

Known locally as the 'Switzerland of Latvia', Sigulda is 53km east of Rīga. Inhabited by Finno-Ugric Liv tribes as early as 2000 BC, the pretty town stands on the southern edge of a picturesque, steep-sided, wooded section of the Gauja Valley and is spanned by a string of medieval castles and legendary caves.

A minor health resort and winter sports centre, Sigulda sports an Olympic bobsled run and is the primary gateway to the beautiful Gauja National Park that stretches northeast as far as Valmiera.

Orientation & Information

Gauja National Park **visitors centre** (☎ 79 71 345, fax 79 71 344; w www.gnp.lv; Baznīcas iela 3; open 9.30am-5pm Mon, 9.30am-6pm Tues-Sun) is able to arrange accommodation, guided tours and a wealth of exciting outdoor activities.

The Sigulda **tourist office** (☎/fax 79 71 335; w www.sigulda.lv; Pils iela 6; open 10am-7pm daily May-Oct, to 5pm Nov-Apr) also stocks reams of information.

Sigulda Castle

Built between 1207 and 1226, there remains little of Sigulda Castle, the Knights' stronghold – but its ruins (Siguldas pilsdrups) are perhaps all the more evocative for this. On the way to the ruins from town you pass the 1225 **Sigulda Church**, rebuilt in the 18th century, and the 19th-century New Sigulda Castle, the former residence of Prince Kropotkin. To the west of Raiņa iela is a **cable car**, which runs every 15 or 30 minutes between 7.30am and 6.30pm across to Krimulda Castle (0.5 Ls one way). Those with a stomach of steel can bungee jump 43m from the cable car from 6.30pm on Saturday and Sunday, May to September. Baptism jumps cost 13 Ls.

Turaida Museum Reserve

The centrepiece of Sigulda's **Turaida Museum Reserve** (Turaidas muzejrezervats; ☎/fax 79 71 402; w www.turaida-muzejs.lv; admission 1 Ls Mon & Tues, 1.20 Ls Wed-Fri, 1.50 Ls Sat & Sun May-Oct, 1 Ls daily Nov-Apr; open 9.30am-8pm daily May-Oct, 10am-5pm Nov-April) is **Turaida Castle** (Turaidas pils; ☎ 79 71 402; open 10am-6pm daily May-Oct, to 5pm Nov-Apr), a red-brick archbishops' castle founded in 1214 on the site of a Liv stronghold. The museum inside its 15th-century granary offers an interesting account of the Livonian state from 1319 to 1561. Exhibitions can also be viewed in the Donjon. The castle is in Turaida's **Dainu Hill Song Garden**, studded with 23 sculptures dedicated to characters in Latvian folklore.

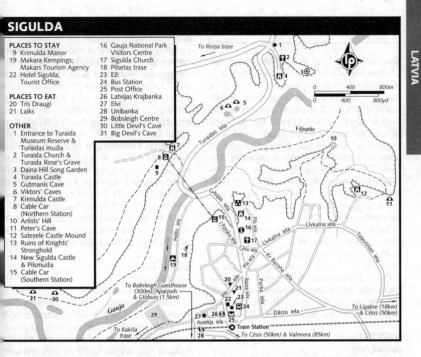

SIGULDA

PLACES TO STAY	16 Gauja National Park
9 Krimulda Manor	Visitors Centre
19 Makara Kempings;	17 Sigulda Church
Makars Tourism Agency	18 Pilsetas trase
22 Hotel Sigulda;	23 Eži
Tourist Office	24 Bus Station
	25 Post Office
PLACES TO EAT	26 Latvijas Krajbanka
20 Tris Draugi	27 Elvi
21 Laiks	28 Unibanka
	29 Bobsleigh Centre
OTHER	30 Little Devil's Cave
1 Entrance to Turaida	31 Big Devil's Cave
Museum Reserve &	
Turaidas muiža	
2 Turaida Church &	
Turaida Rose's Grave	
3 Daina Hill Song Garden	
4 Turaida Castle	
5 Gutmanis Cave	
6 Viktors' Caves	
7 Krimulda Castle	
8 Cable Car	
(Northern Station)	
10 Artists' Hill	
11 Peter's Cave	
12 Satezele Castle Mound	
13 Ruins of Knights'	
Stronghold	
14 New Sigulda Castle	
& Pilsmuiža	
15 Cable Car	
(Southern Station)	

Between the tower and road, near the small wooden-spired **Turaida Church**, two lime trees shade the grave of the 'Turaida Rose' – a legendary beauty who met her untimely death in Gūtmaņa Ala.

Activities

Cheap thrill-seekers can fly down Sigulda's fun 16-bend **bobsled track** (☎ 79 73 813; Šveices iela 13; open 11am-6pm Sat & Sun) at 80km/h.

Makars (at Makara Kempings – see Places to Stay) organises **canoeing** and **rafting trips** along the Gauja River. In winter it rents equipment for **cross-country** and **downhill skiing**.

Eži (☎ 94 28 846; Pils iela 4a; open 10am-8pm daily May-Oct), in a kiosk behind the tourist office, rents bicycles and roller blades for 5 Ls a day.

Places to Stay & Eat

Makara Kempings (☎ 92 44 948, ☎ 79 73 724; w www.makars.lv; Peldu iela 1; person/tent/car/caravan 1/1/1/2 Ls; open 15 May-15 Sept) is a riverside camping ground in the national park. For hostel accommodation, head for the **Krimulda Manor** (☎ 79 72 232;

e krimulda@ls.lv; camping per tent 1 Ls; bed in furnished summer house 5 Ls; beds in 2-, 4- or 6-bed dorms 5-7 Ls), which functions partly as a children's hospital. Breakfast will cost 1 Ls extra.

The prices reflect luxury at the impressive **Hotel Sigulda** (☎ 79 72 263, fax 72 45 165; w www.hotelsigulda.lv; Pils iela 6; singles/doubles 24/30 Ls), a snazzy place with a modern pink, glass facade.

Canteen-style **Trīs Draugi** (Pils iela 9) is the place to fill up on the cheap. **Laiks** (Pils iela 8) opposite cooks up some light dishes in a pub-style setting.

Pilsmuiža (☎ 79 71 395; Pils iela 16; meals 3.50 Ls; open noon-2am daily), overlooking the ruins of the castle, is a feast for the eyes. Ask the waiter for the key to the castle tower (1937) for the ultimate view.

Getting There & Away

Ten trains a day on the Rīga-Sigulda-Cēsis-Valmiera line stop at **Sigulda train station**; a Rīga-Sigulda fare costs 0.86 Ls and the journey takes 1¼ hours.

Six to eight buses daily trundle between Sigulda and Rīga (0.90 Ls, two hours).

Western Latvia

Kurzeme (Courland in English), the entire western region of Latvia, is one of Latvia's least densely settled regions, and the northern part – crowned by stunning Cape Kolka where the Baltic Sea majestically meets the Gulf of Rīga – is still heavily forested. The largely untouched Baltic coast, lined with white-sand beaches and fishing villages, is home to Latvia's tiny ethnic minority, the Livs. The Slītere National Park, with its **information centre** (*☎ 32 49 211, 32 81 066;* **w** *www.slitere.gov.lv*) inside a lighthouse, protects spectacular sand dunes and forests on the northern tip.

Inland, pretty **Talsi**, 75km south, is wedged between two lakes in a shallow valley. **Kuldīga**, 75km southwest again, is a small town on the Venta River with a clutch of 16th- to 18th-century buildings, a charming Old Town and Europe's widest waterfall. It was the first capital of the Duchy of Courland, albeit briefly, from 1561 to 1573.

VENTSPILS
pop 44,000

Latvia's wealthiest industrial town (not to mention the USSR's primary oil and chemical export port) it might be, but filthy-rich Ventspils, 60km north of Kuldīga on the Baltic coast, is looking pretty smart these days. More than 10% of Russian oil and oil products still passes through the ice-free port but the town itself has had a massive facelift.

The Ventspils **tourist office** (*☎/fax 36 22 263;* **w** *www.tourism.ventspils.lv; Tirgus iela 7; open 8am-7pm Mon-Fri, 8am-5pm Sat, 10am-5pm Sun May-Oct, 9am-5pm Mon-Fri, 10am-3pm Sat Nov-April*) can book accommodation for you.

Ventspils' Old Town is small but pretty; its 13th-century **Livonian Order Castle** *(Jana*

iela 17) houses the country's most cutting edge, interactive display of its history; the beach is clean and the seaside **water amusement park** is wild. The **city stadium** hosted the national Eurovision Song Contest final in 2002. Latvia, as winners of the international Eurovision Song Contest in 2002 are designated hosts for 2003. Ventspils city stadium could host the real thing in 2003 should Rīga fail to find a venue.

Piejūras Kempings (*☎ 36 27 925;* **w** *www.camping.ventspils.lv; Vasarnicu iela 56; tent site per person 1.50 Ls, 4-person cottage 10-20 Ls*) must be Latvia's best camping ground. **Bugins** *(Lielā iela 1/3)*, with its funky log-cabin interior, is the place to eat and drink.

Ventspils' sparkling **bus station** (*☎ 36 22 789; Kuldīga iela 5*) is served by hourly buses to/from Rīga (2.70 Ls, 2½ to four hours).

LIEPĀJA
pop 89,400

Liepāja, 11km south on the Baltic coast, is Latvia's second port and third-largest city. Though lacking in sightseeing attractions, it has a pleasant beach front, a glut of fun places to drink and dine at, and a naval port built by Russian Tsar Alexander III in 1890 and used as a Soviet military base until the early 1990s.

The Liepāja **tourist office** (*☎/fax 34 80 808;* **w** *www.liepaja.lv; Lielā iela 11; open 9am-6pm Mon-Fri, 9am-5pm Sat*) can assist with accommodation.

In August the city hosts Latvia's largest annual rock festival, **Liepājas Dzintars** (Amber of Liepāja).

Liepāja's **bus** and **train stations** (*☎ 34 72 633, 34 27 552; Rīgas iela*) are served by hourly buses to/from Rīga (2.65 Ls, 3½ to 4½ hours); and six buses daily to/from Kuldīga (1.10 to 1.55 Ls, 2¼ hours), Talsi (2.10 to 2.45 Ls, 4½ hours) and Ventspils (1.95 to 2.45 Ls, 3 to 3¾ hours). The website at **w** *www.liepaja-online.lv/lap* has timetables.

Lithuania

Enigmatic and eccentric, Lithuania (Lietuva) is one of Europe's best-kept secrets. Tenacious little Lithuania stunned the world when it played David and Goliath with the might of the Soviet Union – and won its independence just over a decade ago. But this Baltic sister once had an empire stretching from the Baltic to the Black Sea.

Raw pagan roots fuse with fervent Catholicism, the Polish inheritance that sets Lithuania apart from Latvia and Estonia, as it looks once again to Europe.

Vilnius charms with its opulent baroque Old Town, and there are other fascinating cities such as Kaunas, briefly the capital in the early 20th century, and the seaport Klaipėda, formerly the German town Memel. The natural treasures of the Curonian Spit (Neringa) and Nemunas Delta glitter alongside the strange Hill of Crosses near Šiauliai.

Facts about Lithuania

HISTORY

Lithuania's troubled history is one of rags to riches – and back again. From early settlement in 9000 BC, Lithuania became a powerful state in the 14th to 16th centuries. It then disappeared off the maps of Europe as it became a subservient cousin of Poland, then was under the iron rule of Russia from the 18th century. Lithuania waited until just over a decade ago before achieving long-awaited independence.

Gediminas, leader of united Lithuania from 1316 to 1341, pushed Lithuania's borders south and east. In 1386 marriage forged an alliance with Poland against the German knights, which lasted 400 years. In 1410 the Teutonic Order was decisively defeated at the battle of Grünwald in Poland. The alliance controlled a huge swathe of land from the Baltic to the Black Sea by the 16th century, with Lithuania as the junior partner.

The Reformation sent a wave of Protestant zeal across Lithuania and Poland, which had petered out by the 1570s.

In the 18th century, the Polish-Lithuanian state was so weakened by division that it was carved up by Russia, Austria and Prussia

At a Glance

- **Vilnius** – skyline of church spires; atmospheric cobbled streets
- **Šiauliai** – eccentric character; memorable Hill of Crosses
- **Curonian Spit** – a magnificent world of wind-swept sand dunes and pine trees

Capital	Vilnius
Population	3.7 million
Official Language	Lithuanian
Currency	1 litas (Lt) = 100 centu
Time	GMT/UTC+0200
Country Phone Code	☎ 370

(successor to the Teutonic Order) in the Partitions of Poland (1772, 1793 and 1795–96).

Vilnius was a bastion of Polish culture in the 19th century and focus of uprisings against Russia. Lithuanian nationalists declared independence on 16 February 1918 with Kaunas as the capital, since Polish troops had annexed Vilnius from the Red Army in 1919.

In 1940, following the Molotov-Ribbentrop Pact, Lithuania was forced into the USSR. Within a year 40,000 Lithuanians were killed or deported. Up to 300,000 more people, mostly Jews, died in concentration camps and ghettos during the 1941–44 Nazi occupation.

The USSR ruled again between 1945 and 1952. An estimated 200,000 people were

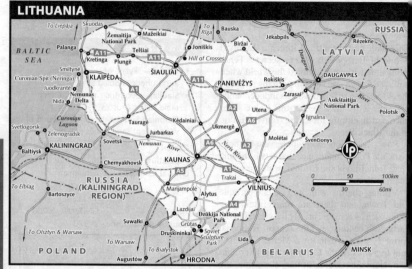

LITHUANIA

murdered or deported to Siberia. Armed partisans resisted Soviet rule from the forests but tens of thousands of 'forest brothers' were massacred by 1953.

In the late 1980s Lithuania lead the Baltic push for independence. The popular front, Sajūdis, won 30 seats in the March 1989 elections for the USSR Congress of People's Deputies. Lithuania was the first Soviet state to legalise noncommunist parties. In February 1990 Sajūdis was elected to form a majority in Lithuania's new Supreme Soviet (now the parliament), which on 11 March declared Lithuania independent.

Moscow marched troops into Vilnius and cut off Lithuania's fuel supplies until president Vytautas Landsbergis agreed to a 100-day moratorium in exchange for independence talks. In January 1991, Soviet troops stormed key buildings in Vilnius. Fourteen people were killed at the TV tower and Lithuanians barricaded their parliament (Seimas). In the wake of heavy condemnation from the West, the Soviets recognised Lithuanian independence on 6 September, bringing about the first of the Baltic republics.

Since the last Soviet troops left the country on 31 August 1993, Lithuania has struggled with the highs and lows of political and economic independence. Domestic and foreign policy has been focused on EU and NATO membership. Lithuania's currency,

the litas, replaced the Russian rouble, Lithuania joined the NATO Partnership for Peace programme and in 1995 Lithuanian became the official language and an association agreement was signed with the EU.

Lithuania is expected to join NATO in November 2002 and the EU by 2004. Debate still rages with the EU on closing controversial nuclear power station Ignalina and stopping farming subsidies but laws have been fine-tuned to meet Europe's requirements. The litas was pegged to the euro in February 2002 and there was growing optimism for the future with foreign investment and EU aid.

GEOGRAPHY

Lithuania can be described in two words: flat and fertile. The largest of the Baltics is 65,300 sq km, dotted with lush forests, 4000 lakes and a 100km-wide lowland centre. Retreating glaciers left higher areas in the northwest (the Žemaičių Upland), across the southeast (the Baltic highlands) and in the east (stretches of the Lithuanian-Belarusian uplands including the country's highest hill, 294m Juozapinė). Forest covers a third of the country.

Half of Lithuania's short Baltic Coast lies along the mesmerising Curonian Spit (Kuršių Nerija) 4km-wide sand bar stretching 98km with 60m-high sand dunes. Behind the spit is the wide (up to 35km) Curonian Lagoon fed by the Nemunas River.

CLIMATE

Snow, showers and sunshine dominate Lithuania's climate. Between mid-November and mid-March temperatures barely rise above freezing. Its beautiful, fleeting summers from June to August bring temperatures of around 20°C – and rain. In the inland east of the country, winter lasts about six weeks longer than on the coastal west.

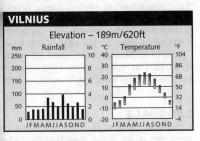

ECOLOGY & ENVIRONMENT

That warm glow of happiness you feel in Lithuania may be Ignalina nuclear power plant, 120km north of Vilnius. It's a Soviet-era reactor similar to Chornobyl in Ukraine, the site of the world's worst nuclear disaster in 1986. Lithuania, the most nuclear power–dependent country in the world, gets 80% of its electricity from the plant near the Belarus border. Experts rank it among the world's most dangerous nuclear installations. Despite the EU spending €236 million in the last decade to improve safety, including €10 million to shut the first of the two reactors by 2004, it now wants the plant shut completely by 2009 at a cost of €3.2 billion – which Lithuania says it can't pay.

A terrifying arsenal of decomposing chemical weapons could wreak damage to the coast of Lithuania – and poison the entire Baltic Sea. About 40,000 bombs and mines lie on the seabed 70 nautical miles off Klaipėda where Soviet forces sank German ships.

The Būtingė oil terminal, off the northwestern coast near Latvia, continues to enrage both environmentalists, with a 60-ton oil spill in November 2001, and economists, with its huge losses. The state owns 60% of the terminal and it cost €266 million to build.

GOVERNMENT & POLITICS

Lithuanians know irony. They are credited with causing the collapse of the Soviet Union, but at their first democratic elections in 1992

they promptly voted in the ex-communist Lithuanian Democratic Labour Party (LDDP)! Presidential elections followed in 1993; former Communist Party first secretary Algirdas Brazauskas won with 60% of the votes.

In January 1998 Valdas Adamkus, who had lived most of his life in the USA having fled the Soviets with his parents at the end of the war, won presidential elections by a slim majority. There were hopes he would inject some American oomph into the failing economy.

In May 1999 Adamkus appointed Rolandas Paksas, Vilnius mayor and champion stunt pilot, as his prime minister. He resigned five months later over the controversial sale of a state oil company to a US firm.

In October 2000 elections, the Conservative faction lost to the Social Democratic Coalition, which won 31% of the vote and holds 52 seats in the Seimas, headed by former president, Algirdas Brazauskas. Paksas, chairman of the Lithuanian Liberal Union, became Prime Minister again. Presidential elections were due in December 2002. At the time of research Lithuanians seemed happy with the country's relative stability and the SDC was looking the favourite to be re-elected.

ECONOMY

Post-independence was a painful time for Lithuania as the Baltic economic underdog. Inflation ran at 1000% and thousands of jobs were lost from inefficient heavy industry. In 1993, Lithuania was the first post-Soviet Baltic state to open a stock exchange.

However, Lithuania has become the Baltic top dog, its economy is one of the world's fastest growing. The collapse of Russia's economy, its biggest trading partner, in 1998 sparked depression but forced diversification into new EU electronic, manufacturing and chemical markets. The average monthly income is €284, but this supply of cheap, skilled labour attracted foreign investment; €3216 million from abroad in 2001.

GDP growth was 5.9% in 2001 with predictions of 4.4% for 2002, 4.9% for 2003 and 5.3% for 2004. Inflation was 2.1% in late 2001 but the country remains dogged by high unemployment, estimated 11% in 2002 (but as much as 30% in rural areas). In February, 2002, the litas was pegged to the euro at 3.4528 to 1, ending a seven-year peg to the US dollar, to make exports more competitive and show determination to join Europe.

LITHUANIA

POPULATION & PEOPLE

Lithuania's population in 2002 was 3.7 million. Lithuanians form 81% of the population. The main minority groups are Russians (8%), Poles (7%) and Jews (0.1%).

The Lithuanian Diaspora is the biggest of the Baltics, with over 800,000 Lithuanians in the USA alone (mainly in Chicago) and other communities living in Canada, South America and Australia.

A public education centre for Roma was set up in 2000 in Vilnius as part of a government-funded project to integrate this group into Lithuanian society.

ARTS

Lithuanian fiction began with the late 18th-century poem *Metai* (The Seasons) by Kristijonas Donelaitis. Antanas Baranauskas' 1860 poem *Anykščiai Pine Forest* uses the forest as a symbol of Lithuania. Literature suffered persecution from the Tsarist authorities, who banned use of the Latin alphabet. Nineteenth-century nationalists drew their inspiration from Polish writer Adam Mickiewicz who began his great poem *Pan Tadeusz* with 'Lithuania, my fatherland…'(he regarded himself part Lithuanian).

National revival poet Maironis heralded the start of modern Lithuanian poetry with the romantic *Pavasario balsai* (Voices of Spring). The Lithuanian Diaspora has also produced major cultural figures, including the poet Tomas Venclova and the novelist Antanas Škėma, whose *A White Shroud* has been compared to the work of James Joyce.

Lithuani's national artist will always be Mikalojus Konstantinas Čiurlionis (1875-1911), a depressive painter who also composed symphonic poems and piano pieces.

Contemporary Lithuania is the jazz giant of the Baltics with its highlight, the Kaunas Jazz Festival. Europas Parkas Sculpture Park at the geographical centre of Europe, 19km from Vilnius, and the Užupis district in the capital are part of a thriving art scene.

SOCIETY & CONDUCT

Lithuanians are emotional people with a tendency towards mysticism. They are fiercely proud of their national identity, as a backlash from brutal attempts to eradicate it and memories of their long-lost empire.

Lithuanian pride in being the (disputed) geographical centre of Europe shows in their willingness to speak English, German and even Russian.

Make sure only to give odd numbers of flowers as a gift, keep eye contact when making a toast and never, ever shake hands across a doorway if you want to stay friends with your exuberant hosts.

RELIGION

The Lithuanians are predominantly Roman Catholic. While church leaders played an important role in the drive for independence, Lithuanians were the last pagans in Europe. Grand Duke Mindaugas accepted Christianity in 1251 in order to be crowned king, but the new religion wasn't widespread for over a century.

LANGUAGE

Lithuanian is one of the only two surviving languages of the Baltic branch of the Indo-European language family (the other one is Latvian). Most Lithuanians – both young and old – speak Russian and outside Vilnius it's used more than English. See the Language Guide at the back of this book for useful words and phrases.

Facts for the Visitor

HIGHLIGHTS

Wander the cobbled streets of charming Vilnius Old Town flanked by colourful baroque creations. Wonder at the natural magic of the Curonian Spit's towering sand dunes and whispering pine trees. Discover the strength of Lithuanian spirit at the strange Hill of Crosses near Šiauliai and see Lenin strike a pose at the unique Soviet Sculpture Park in the south.

SUGGESTED ITINERARIES

Now your toothbrush is packed, here are some ideas for a magical trip:

Two days
  Vilnius with a trip to Trakai
One week
  Two days in Vilnius including a trip to Trakai or the Soviet Sculpture Park; Klaipėda; and the Curonian Spit
Two weeks
  Several days exploring Vilnius; Klaipėda; then discover the dunes and forests of the Curonian Spit; back to Vilnius via Kaunas and the Hill of Crosses near Šiauliai

PLANNING

Unless you're happy donning thermals, the best time to catch those fragile Baltic sun rays is between May and September.

Maps

The *Lietuva Road Map* (1:500,000), published by Rīga-based map publishers Jāņa sēta includes small inset city maps of Šiauliai, Panevėžys, Vilnius, Kaunas and Klaipėda; and is sold in TIC offices and kiosks for 8 Lt. Jāņa sēta also does individual city plans *(miesto planas)* at a scale of 1:25,000 with a 1:10,000 inset of the centre costing 6 to 8 Lt.

RESPONSIBLE TOURISM

Lithuania's coastal and inland wildernesses are delicate (especially the Curonian Spit) so leave nothing, take nothing and respect it.

TOURIST OFFICES

Tourist information sources abroad include Lithuanian embassies and specialist travel agencies. In Lithuania the tourist information centres (TICs) are dotted around the country. They are coordinated by the **Lithuanian Tourist Board** (☎ 5-262 2610; **w** www .tourism.lt; *Vilniaus gatvė 4/35, Vilnius*).

VISAS & DOCUMENTS

Double check before you leave home as more countries sign visa-free agreements with Lithuania. The **Foreign Ministry** (**w** www .urm.lt) has up-to-date details.

A valid passport is the only entry requirement for citizens of many countries, including Lithuania's Baltic sisters, Nordic countries, Europe, Australia, Canada, Iceland, Ireland, Israel, Japan, New Zealand, the UK and USA. Lithuania no longer issues visas at its border points. Visas are generally for stays of up to 90 days within a period of either six or 12 months.

If you plan on travelling on to, or through, Poland check whether your bus or train passes through Belarus as you will need a Belarusian transit visa.

Extend your Lithuanian visa at the **immigration department** *(imigracijos tarnyba;* ☎ 5-271 7749; *Verkių gatvė 3, Vilnius)*.

EMBASSIES & CONSULATES
Lithuanian Embassies & Consulates

Lithuania has representatives in the following countries:

Australia (☎ 02-9498 2571) 40B Fiddens Wharf Rd, Killara, NSW 2071
Canada (☎ 613-567 5458, **e** litemb@storm.ca) 130 Albert St, Suite 204, Ottawa, Ontario K1P 5G4
Estonia (☎ 2-631 4030, **e** amber@anet.ee) Uus tn 15, Tallinn
Finland (☎ 09-608 210, **e** embassylt@kolumbus .fi) Rauhankatu 13a, Helsinki 20180
France (☎ 01 48 01 00 33, **e** amb.lituanie@ magic.fr) 14 blvd Montmartre, 75009 Paris
Germany (☎ 030-890 6810) Charitestrasse 9, 10711 Berlin
Latvia (☎ 2-732 1519, **e** lithemb@ltemb.vip.lv) Rūpniecibas iela 22, 1010 Rīga
Poland (☎ 022-625 3368, **e** konslt@waw.pdi .net) aleje Jana Chrystiana Szucha 5, Warsaw
Russia (☎ 095-785 8605/25, **e** amb.ru@urm.lt) Borisoglebsky per 10, Moscow 121069 *Consulate:* (☎ 0112-551 444) ul Proletarskaya 133, Kaliningrad
Sweden (☎ 08-667 5455, **e** litemb@telia.com) Strandvagen 53, 11523 Stockholm
UK (☎ 020-7486 6402, **e** lralon@globalnet.co .uk) 84 Gloucester Place, London W1H 3HN
USA (☎ 202-234 5860, **e** amb.us@urm.lt) 2622 16th St NW, Washington, DC 20009

Embassies & Consulates in Lithuania

The following embassies and consulates are in Vilnius. The area code for Vilnius is 5.

Australia (☎ 266 0730, **e** aust.con.vilnius@post .omnitel.net) Vilniaus gatvė 23
Belarus (☎ 266 2200, **e** bpl@post.5ci.lt) Mindaugo gatvė 13
Canada (☎ 249 6853, **e** vilnius@canada.lt) Gedimino prospektas 64
Estonia (☎ 278 0200, **e** sekretar@estemb.lt) A Mickevičiaus gatvė 4a
Finland (☎ 212 1621, **e** sanomat.vil@formin.fi) Klaipėdos gatvė
Germany (☎ 265 0272, **e** germ.emb@takas.lt) Sierakausko gatvė 24
Latvia (☎ 213 1260, **e** lietuva@latvia.balt.net) MK Čiurlionio gatvė 76
Poland (☎ 270 9001, **e** ambpol@tdd.lt) Smėlio gatvė 20a
Russia (☎ 272 1763, **e** rusemb@rusemb.lt) Latvių gatvė 53/54
Sweden (☎ 268 5010, **e** ambassaden.vilnius@ foreign.ministry.se) Didžioji gatvė 16
UK (☎ 212 2070/1, **e** be-vilnius@britain.lt) Antakalnio gatvė 2
USA (☎ 266 5500, **e** mail@usembassy) Akmenų gatvė 6

CUSTOMS

Customs regulations are subject to change. In Vilnius, check with the **customs department**

LITHUANIA

(☎ 5-212 6415; W www.cust.lt; Jakšto gatvė 1/25) about the regulations.

Lithuania has limits on amber exports, but a few souvenirs are fine if their value doesn't exceed €266. You'll need a Culture Ministry permit, and pay 20% duty, to export artworks over 50 years old. Modern works of art also need special permission. Contact the **Committee of Cultural Heritage** *(☎ 5-272 4005; Snipiškių gatvė 3, Vilnius)* for information.

MONEY
Currency
Lithuania's currency, the litas (plural: litų; Lt), is pegged to the euro at a rate of 3.4528 Lt to €1.

The litas comes in 10, 20, 50, 100, 200 and 500 Lt notes and one, two and five litų coins. One litas is 100 (almost worthless) centų (ct).

Exchanging Money
Most currencies can be exchanged but US dollars, euros or British pounds are best. At the time of printing exchange rates were:

country	unit		litų
Australia	A$1	=	1.90 Lt
Canada	C$1	=	2.32 Lt
Euro Zone	€1	=	3.45 Lt
Japan	¥1	=	2.80 Lt
Sweden	1 Skr	=	0.46 Lt
UK	£1	=	5.52 Lt
USA	$1	=	3.8 Lt

Costs
Travelling in Lithuania is relatively cheap. Budget travellers staying at camp sites/hostels can spend €20/30 a day with food and transport. Mid-range accommodation and a few Baltic blowouts will push it up to €50. Use student cards for discounts on museums and travel fares. As a general guide to real costs, a Big Mac meal costs 9.80 Lt, a bottle of local beer 4 to 8 Lt, a hostel 32 Lt and 100km by bus/train 11.50/9.80 Lt.

POST & COMMUNICATIONS
Post
Lithuania's post is quick and cheap. Letters/postcards cost 1.70/1 Lt internationally and 1/0.80 Lt internally. Mail to America takes 10 days, to Europe about a week. EMS is the cheapest express mail service, available at Vilnius' central post office.

Telephone & Fax
The Lithuanian telephone network was digitalised in 2002 and all the area access codes were changed. If you are in doubt about a code check on the website W www.telecom .lt. To call other cities in Lithuania, dial ☎ 8 wait for the tone, then dial the area code and telephone number.

To make an international call dial ☎ 00 before the country code. To call Lithuania from abroad, dial ☎ 370 then the area code, follow with the city code and telephone number.

All blue public phones are card-only, sold in denominations of 50/75/100/200 units costing 9/13/16/30 Lt. Lithuanians do seem to have their mobile phones surgically attached to their ears though.

Faxes can be sent from main post offices or from good hotels. International telegrams (incoming or outbound) arrive the same or next day and can be sent from most post offices.

Email & Internet Access
Internet cafés have grown like mushrooms (as they say in Lithuania) across Vilnius (2 to 8 Lt per hour). Outside the capital, prices and speed are higher and lower respectively.

DIGITAL RESOURCES
Check the cheeky online version of *In Your Pocket* guides to Vilnius and Klaipėda/Kaunas at W www.inyourpocket.com. Try W www .baltictimes.com for news and views and, of course, check out W www.lonelyplanet.com.

BOOKS
See Facts for the Visitor in the Estonia chapter for titles that cover the Baltics generally.

Of Gods & Holidays: The Baltic Heritage (1999), edited by Jonas Trinkūnas, concentrates on Lithuania's pagan roots. The readable *Lithuania – Independent Again: The Autobiography of Vytautas Landsbergis* (1998) is a chronicle of the life of one of the country's most colourful political figures.

Forest of the Gods by dramatist Balys Sruoga, is a moving recollection of the author's time in a Nazi concentration camp.

Don't forget your trusty Lonely Planet guide to *Estonia, Latvia and Lithuania*.

NEWSPAPERS & MAGAZINES
The *Baltic Times* is sold at news kiosks for 4 Lt (free from tourist offices). Read excellent features in *Lithuania in the World*, Lithuanian

Airlines' in-flight magazine that's available in bookshops for 9 Lt. Foreign newspapers are generally available from good hotels. The British *Financial Times* can be purchased for 15 Lt. Day-late tabloids can be read at the **British Council** (*Vilniaus gatvė 39/6, Vilnius*).

RADIO & TV
Baltic TV screens CNN news in English at midnight and World Net at 1pm. Newcomers LNK TV and TV3 are popular for American films and soap operas.

M1 (106.8FM), the first independent radio station to broadcast in Soviet times, has launched a sister station M1 Plus (106.2FM) dedicated to music.

Radiocentras (101.5FM) is one of the country's upbeat favourites.

Radio Vilnius (102.6FM) has local news in English at 10pm and Voice of America at 10.30pm. The BBC World Service (95.5FM) is available 24 hours a day, as is Radio France Internationale (98.3FM).

TIME
Lithuania is on Eastern European time (GMT/UTC plus two hours).

HEALTH
It may be wise to drink bottled rather than tap water, especially after diesel fuel was spilled into the Voke River, which feeds into the Vilnius water supply, in 2000 and the degree of contamination is uncertain. Avoid swimming in the Curonian (Kuršių) Lagoon

WOMEN TRAVELLERS
Lithuanians are generally polite people and hassle is rare.

GAY & LESBIAN TRAVELLERS
The scene is still low-key. For general information and guides go to **w** www.gay.lt or call the **Gay Information Line** (☎ 5-233 3031).

The country's first gay club only opened in 2000 in Vilnius, **Men's Factory** (☎ 5-231 0687; *Žygimantų 1*).

DISABLED TRAVELLERS
Lithuania is not the most friendly country for disabled travellers; the cobbled streets of Vilnius Old Town make it difficult for wheelchair users and the visually impaired. Public transport is not easily accessible, although a few hotels and bars do cater for the disabled.

DANGERS & ANNOYANCES
There have been disturbing reports of anti-Semitic attacks, both verbal and physical, in Lithuania. Gay people and those from ethnic backgrounds are also targets.

PUBLIC HOLIDAYS & SPECIAL EVENTS
National holidays include New Year's Day (1 January), Independence Day (16 February, anniversary of 1918 independence declaration), the Restoration of Lithuania's 11 March Independence, Good Friday and Easter Monday (April), Labour Day (1 May), State Holiday (6 July, commemoration of Grand Duke Mindaugas' coronation), All Saints' Day (1 November), Christmas Day (25 December) and Boxing Day (26 December).

The Lithuanian Song Festival, which ends with a gala parade from Katedros aikštė to Vingis parkas, will take place from 1 to 7 July 2003. The Baltika International Folk Festival will be next held in Vilnius in July 2005. Other annual festivals include Kaunas International Jazz Festival in April; the week-long Life Theatre Festival in Vilnius in late May; Vilnius Summer Music Festival throughout July; Vilnius City Masks Festival celebrating the autumnal equinox at the end of September; and Vilnius International Jazz Festival in October.

In Vilnius, the **Lithuanian Folk Culture Centre** (☎ 5-261 2594; **w** www.lfcc.lt; *Barboros Radvilaitės gatvė 8*) has information on cultural events.

ACTIVITIES
As ancient oak trees were still being worshipped a mere six centuries ago, the pagan roots of Lithuanians are revealed by their love of nature. Travellers can hike in the wilderness, sweat in traditional saunas and enjoy the frozen experiences of ice-fishing or skiing.

Bird-Watching
The **Lithuanian Ornithological Society** (☎ 5-213 0498; **e** birdlife@post.5ci.lt; *Naugarduko gatvė 47/3*) is based in Vilnius.

Krantas Travel (**w** www.krantas.lt), with offices in several cities, organises tours of the western Nemunas Delta wetlands, which are rich in birdlife.

Cycling

There are new cycling tracks around Vilnius with bike hire from the **TIC** *(Vilniaus gatvė 22)* for 1 Lt per day. Most towns/cities have bike hire either from Litinterp, the TICs or private hotels/guest houses.

Mushrooming

Mushrooming is a relic of Lithuania's traditional way of life. There are deadly poisonous varieties so only eat what you know is safe.

ACCOMMODATION

Camping

Lithuanian camping grounds *(Kempingas)* are basic, cheap (5 to 20 Lt to pitch a tent, 15 to 30 Lt for a wooden cabin) and run down. There are moves by the Lithuanian Tourist Board to spruce up facilities. The national parks have basic camp sites and there are private ones dotted around Palanga and Trakai.

Hostels

The **Lithuanian Hostels Association** *(☎ 5-215 4627, fax 212 0149; e filaretai@post .omnitel.net; Filaretų gatvė 17, Vilnius)* is based at the largest hostel it runs. The association runs a second hostel in Vilnius Old Town, and has an affiliated hostel in Klaipėda. A bed in a shared room costs 32 Lt a night.

Private Homes

Litinterp offers B&Bs and self-catering facilities in Vilnius, Klaipėda, Kaunas and Palanga. In Vilnius prices start at 80 Lt per person, while outside the capital city the rates range from 70 Lt.

Tourist centres can book countryside home-stays from 100 Lt a double.

FOOD & DRINKS

Long, miserable winters are to blame for the hearty, waist-widening Baltic diet based on potatoes, meat and dairy products. Lithuanian food is epitomised in the Zeppelin *cepelinai*, an airship-shaped parcel of thick potato dough, filled with cheese, meat or mushrooms.

Artery-furring staples are *bulvinai blynai*, pancakes of grated potato stuffed with dairy products, including *varškė* (curd) and *rūgusis pienas* (sour milk), though meat and other vegies are standard. Another good stand-by is

koldūninė, small ravioli-like dumplings that are stuffed with cheese, mushrooms or meat.

Beer is *alus* in Lithuanian and the best local brands are Utenos and Kalnapilis. No drink would be complete without a bar snack, *kepta duona*, which reaches new fattening heights with deep-fried bread drowning in garlic.

Lithuanians drink *midus* (mead), such as Žalgiris and Suktinis, which are as much as 60% proof, and *gira*, made from fermented grains or fruit and brown rye bread. *Vynas* is wine, *arbata* tea, *kava* coffee and *mineralinis vanduo* mineral water.

ENTERTAINMENT

Vilnius has a new €10 million **Akropolis** shopping complex with ice-skating rink and multiscreen **cinema** *(☎ 5-248 4848; Ozo 25)*.

The more adventurous could try Europe's highest **bungee jump** from Vilnius' TV Tower *(☎ 6-284 171 67)* for 250 Lt.

In Kaunas the plush new cinema **Planeta** has surround sound and shows top English-language films.

SPECTATOR SPORTS

Basketball is religion. The worshipped national team won bronze medals in the last three Olympics. The team came within seconds of pulling off the basketball coup of the century by almost defeating the American Dream Team at Sydney 2000. Žalgiris Kaunas tops the domestic league.

SHOPPING

Amber – pine resin fossilised 50 million years ago – is one of Lithuania's treasures.

Vilnius' main markets are Gariūnai, off the Kaunas road, and Kalvarijų, north of the city centre, where you can join the scrum of *babushkas* jostling for bargains.

Getting There & Away

There are growing numbers of direct flights to/from Vilnius around Europe, including London and Moscow. Lithuania has cheap bus and rail links with Warsaw, which in turn has flights, trains and cheap buses to/from many western European cities. You can also easily reach Lithuania overland through Latvia or by sea from Germany and Sweden.

AIR

Routes

Lithuanian Airlines (*Lietuvos Avialinijos, LAL;* ⓦ *www.lal.lt*) flights to/from Vilnius include: daily to Amsterdam, two daily (except Saturday) to Berlin, daily (except Saturday) to Copenhagen, four daily to Frankfurt, daily to Helsinki, three weekly to Kyiv, daily to London Gatwick, four weekly to Moscow, three weekly to Paris; daily to Prague, two or three daily (except Saturday) to Stockholm, two to five daily (weekdays only) to Tallinn and daily to Warsaw.

The Latvian state airline, airBaltic, flies from Vilnius to Rīga three times weekly. Estonian Air flies to Tallinn on weekdays.

Fares

Hunt out cheaper fares through discount air travel agencies (see the Getting There & Away chapter). In 2002, LAL's Vilnius to Prague flight cost 1390 Lt one way, Vilnius to Rīga 936/1061 Lt one way/return, Vilnius to Tallinn 870/560 Lt and Vilnius to London 1400 Lt return.

LAND

Bus

Three buses run daily between Vilnius and Rīga (40 Lt) and two daily between Vilnius and Tallinn (90 Lt).

Eurolines (☎ *5-215 1377, fax 215 1376;* ⓦ *www.eurolines.lt*) is based inside Vilnius bus station. It sells tickets for destinations in mainland Europe, Scandinavia, Moscow and the UK, as well as for other bus companies.

Train

There is no rail link between Vilnius and Tallinn. There's one train daily between Vilnius and Rīga (46 Lt, eight hours, 300km), the Warsaw-bound train on even days to Šeštokai (three hours, 198km), and one to three trains daily from Vilnius to Moscow (14 hours, 944km). The excellent website ⓦ www.litrail .lt has details in English. There are two to five daily trains from Vilnius to Kaliningrad (seven hours), one to three daily to St Petersburg (15 to 17 hours) and several weekly to Lviv.

Car & Motorcycle

See the Getting Around chapter at the start of this book for information about driving in Europe generally. The wait for motorists on the Lithuanian-Polish borders at Kalvarija and Lazdijai can be from two minutes to two days. The Lithuanian-Belarusian border crossings are notoriously slow.

SEA

Lisco and Scandlines ferries sail from Klaipėda to/from Kiel (Germany) daily (31 to 33 hours). Lisco has services to/from Mukran (Germany) daily except Monday (19 hours) and to/from Karlshamn (Sweden) three times weekly (17 hours). For tickets and schedules contact **Krantas Travel** (see the following section).

ORGANISED TOURS

Krantas Travel (☎ *46-395 111;* ⓔ *travel@ krantas.lt; Lietuvininkų aikštė 5, Klaipėda*) organises specialist bird-watching, cycling and hiking tours in national parks including the Nemunas Delta and Curonian Spit. Tourist information centres have details of tours.

DEPARTURE TAXES

There are no departure taxes payable for travellers leaving Lithuania.

Getting Around

AIR

Between May 25 and September 14 there are four domestic LAL flights between Vilnius and Palanga every Saturday. **Air Lithuania** (☎ *5-212 1322;* ⓦ *www.airlithuania.lt*) also does a once-weekly Palanga-Vilnius-Palanga run for 115/195 Lt one way/return.

BUS

Lithuania boasts a cheap, efficient and plentiful supply of long-distance buses linking it internally and to its Baltic sisters.

TRAIN

Cheaper, slower and rarer than buses, trains are the dinosaurs of Lithuanian transport. For anorak-wearing trainspotters only!

Vilnius

☎ 5 • pop 600,000

Bizarre, beautiful and bewitching; the capital city of Vilnius seduces visitors with its Unesco World Heritage baroque Old Town, skyline of church spires and underlying oddness. Where else but this devilishly attractive city 250km

LITHUANIA

inland could be the world's only statue of psychedelic musician Frank Zappa? Or a self-proclaimed independent republic of artists? Where else will you find the spirit of resistance that existed during Soviet occupation?

Crumbling archways frame the life of the narrow, cobbled streets. Change is under way but new infrastructure won't disguise the curious charm of soulful Vilnius, in Lithuania's southeastern corner.

History

According to legend, Vilnius was founded in the 1320s by Duke Gediminas after a dream. But it was probably already a political and trade centre. The Teutonic Knights attacked the city, which sat on the slopes of Gediminas Hill, at least six times between 1365 and 1402 but their defeat in 1410 at Grünwald prompted an era of prosperity.

Following Tatar attacks, a 2.4km stone wall was built between 1503 and 1522 around the new part of the town south of Gediminas Hill. Sixteenth-century Vilnius was one of the biggest cities in Eastern Europe, a population of 30,000. It blossomed with buildings in late-Gothic and Renaissance styles as Lithuanian monarchs Žygimantas I and II occupied the Polish-Lithuanian throne.

In the 17th and early 18th centuries Vilnius suffered war, famine and plague, and shrank in population and importance. The 19th century saw industry develop as it became a refuge for dispossessed Polish-Lithuanian gentry. It was devastated in WWI during the German occupation and by the subsequent Bolshevik/Polish/Lithuanian fighting.

When the fighting ended, Vilnius found itself in Poland, where it remained till 1939. By then its population was one-third Jewish and it developed into one of the world's major centres of Jewish culture and scholarship, earning it the nickname 'Jerusalem of Lithuania'. WWII saw another three-year German occupation when Vilnius' Jews were slaughtered in its ghetto or at Paneriai death camp.

In 2000 flamboyant Artūras Zuokas, from the Liberal Union Party, was elected Vilnius mayor. His radical plans raised the city's status internationally. Wacky world champion acrobatic pilot Jurgis Kairys flew under the city's 10 bridges spanning the Neris in 2001.

In 2002, the European bank agreed on a €10 million loan for new train links, an Old Town bypass and new highways that will link Vilnius to Kyiv and Minsk. The same year saw work begin on the controversial reconstruction of the Jewish ghetto.

Orientation

The heart of Vilnius is Katedros aikštė, the cathedral square, with Gediminas Hill rising behind it. Southwards are the streets of the Old Town; to the west Gedimino prospektas is the axis of the newer part of the city. The train and bus stations are 1.5km south of Katedros aikštė.

Maps Jāņa sēta's 2001/02 *Vilnius City Plan* (1:25,000), which includes a city centre map (1:10,000), costs about 8 Lt in bookshops and tourist centres.

Information

Tourist Offices The Vilnius **Tourist Information Centre** (☎ 262 9660, fax 262 8169; w www.vilnius.lt; Vilniaus gatvė 22; open 9am-6pm Mon-Thur, 9am-5pm Fri) has a touch-operated infokiosk with information in English and German. There's a **smaller branch** (☎ 262 6470; Pilies gatvė 42; open 10am-6pm Mon-Fri, 10am-4pm Sat & Sun), which will move to the Old Town Hall. Both offer accommodation bookings, excursions to Trakai, and car and bike rental.

Kelvita Tourist Information (☎/fax 231 0229; Geležinkelio gatvė 16; open 8am-6pm Mon-Fri) is in the international hall of the train station and sells visas for Belarus, Russia and Ukraine.

Bright yellow buses do city tours (10 Lt) from the Town Hall square; call ☎ 273 8625 for information.

Vilnius' **International Police Commission** (☎ 272 6159, 271 6221) has staff who speak English, French and German do deal with foreigners who are victims of crime. Ring ☎ 02 in an emergency.

The city now has tourist signs in English and Lithuanian around the Old Town.

Money You will find a **24-hour currency exchange** (Parex Bankas; ☎ 213 5454; Geležinkelio gatvė 6) on your left as you exit the train station.

Vilniaus Bankas (☎ 268 2093; Gedimino prospektas 12 • ☎ 268 2811; Gedimino prospektas 60 • ☎ 268 1414; Jogailos gatvė 9a) transfers money, takes Thomas Cook and AmEx travellers cheques and has Visa ATMs.

Hansa Bankas (☎ 239 0600; Gedimino prospektas 26 • Pilies gatvė 9 • Vilniaus gatvė 16), which has taken over the Taupomasis Bankas, has MasterCard ATMs, as do the Bankas Snoras kiosks dotted over town.

Post & Communications In the central post office (☎ 262 5468; Gedimino prospektas 7; open 7am-7pm Mon-Fri, 9am-4pm Sat) there's a pizza joint and Internet section as well as stamps, fax and telegram service and the **Express Mail Service** (EMS; ☎ 261 6759).

Email & Internet Access The Internet café **VOO2** (☎ 279 1866; e ianplinka@post.5ci .lt; Ašmenos gatvė 8) boasts a resident iguana.

Bazė (☎ 249 7701; e info@base.lt; Gedimino prospektas 50/2) is speedy, cheap and filled with boys playing games with guns.

Travel Agencies For countryside farmstays, inquire at **Baltic Travel Service** (☎ 212 0220, fax 212 2196; e lcc@bts.lt; Subačiaus gatvė 2; open 8am-6pm Mon-Fri, 10am-4pm Sat).

Lithuanian Student & Youth Travel (☎ 239 7397; e info@jaunimas.lt; Basanavičiaus gatvė 30/13) does cheap fares for ISIC cardholders, while **West Express** (☎ 212 2500, fax 261 9436; e office@westexpress.lt; Stulginskio gatvė 5) offers good all-round service.

Bookshops You will find contemporary and foreign-language stock at **Knygas Vaga** (☎ 249 8392; Gedimino prospektas 50).

Littera (☎ 268 7258; Šv Jono gatvė 12), the university bookshop, has a superb selection of foreign-language books.

Laundry West of the city centre is **Palūstrė** (☎ 634 567; Savanorių prospektas 11a; open 7am-7pm Mon-Fri, 7am-2pm Sat).

Left Luggage Deposit bags at left-luggage rooms (bagažinė) inside the **bus station mall** (open 5.30am-9pm Mon-Fri, 7am-9pm Sat) for 3 Lt per day per bag or in the **train station basement** (open 5.30am-9pm Mon-Fri, 7am-9pm Sat) for 2 Lt per bag per day.

Medical & Emergency Services The **Baltic-American Medical and Surgical Clinic** (☎ 234 2020; e bak@takas.lt; Antakalnio gatvė 124; open 24hr), inside Vilnius University Antakalnis hospital, and the **Medical Diagnostic Centre** (☎ 270 9120; Grybo gatvė 32; open 8am-7pm Mon-Fri, 9am-3pm Sat) both offer an English-speaking, Western-style service.

There's a **24-hour pharmacy** (☎ 261 0135; Gedimino prospektas 27) as well.

Katedros aikštė & Around

Gedimino Tower is at the top of the 48m **Gedimino kalnas** (Gedimino Hill) behind the cathedral. Inside the red-brick tower is a **museum** (open 11am-5pm Tues-Sun Nov-Apr, 10am-7pm Tues-Sun May-Oct). Katedros aikštė is where the human chain between Tallinn and Vilnius, protesting Soviet occupation, ended in 1989.

Gedimino Hill is dominated by the **Vilnius Cathedral**, which was reconsecrated in 1989 after being used as a gallery during the Soviet period. The tall belfry was once part of the castle's defences.

The cathedral was built on an ancient pagan site – the remains and a centuries-old **ritual stone** were discovered when the foundations were dug. The first wooden cathedral was built here in the 13th century, and rebuilt during the 15th century in Gothic style. The outside was completely redone in today's classical form between 1783 and 1801. The 5m **bronze statues** of St Helene, St Stanislav and St Casimir on top of the cathedral were levelled in 1956 but resurrected following restoration work. The interior showpiece is the **Chapel of St Casimir** created from 1623 to 1636, which boasts a bizarre laughing Madonna, a baroque cupola with coloured marble and white stucco sculptures.

Further along Arsenalo gatvė are the **National Museum** (262 9426; Arsenalo gatvė 1; adult/concession 4/2 Lt; open 10am-5pm Wed-Sun) and **Applied Arts Museum** (☎ 262 8080; Arsenalo gatvė 3; admission 8 Lt; open 11am-6pm Tues-Sat, to 4pm Sun), which is showing a fantastic exhibition of jewels discovered hidden in the cathedral walls in 1985. This exhibition will continue until at least the end of 2003.

East of Gediminas Hill

The white **Three Crosses** atop Three Crosses Hill are old Vilnius landmarks said to have stood here since the 17th century in memory of three monks who were crucified at this spot. The crosses, erected in 1989, are replicas of three knocked down and buried by the Soviet authorities.

LITHUANIA

CENTRAL VILNIUS

PLACES TO STAY
1 Victoria
3 Reval Hotel Lietuva (under renovation until 2003)
4 Holiday Inn
13 Ambassador
17 Scandic Hotel Neringa
44 Litinterp
48 Mabre Residence Hotel
54 Stikliai
60 Telecom Guest House
61 E-Guest House
72 AAA Guest House; Mano Liza
73 Radisson SAS Astorija
77 Ida Basar
81 Old Town Youth Hostel
82 Elektros Tinklų Hostel
83 Statybos Guest House; Hotel Gintaras

PLACES TO EAT
2 Ritos Slėptuvė
5 Kuba
16 Čili Picerija
19 Presto Arbata
22 Prie Parlamento; Ministerija
37 Sue's Indian Raja/ Sue Ka Thai
50 Užupio Kavinė
53 The PUB
55 Balti Drambliai
64 La Provence
65 Amatininkų Užeiga
69 Savas Kampas

EMBASSIES & CONSULATES
27 Canada
29 Estonia
32 Latvia
33 Germany
34 USA
38 Australia
57 Finland
62 Belarus

OTHER
6 Applied Arts Museum
7 Gedimino Tower
8 Vilnius Cathedral
9 National Museum
10 Men's Factory
11 Central Post Office
12 Vilniaus Bankas
14 City Hall
15 Lithuanian Opera & Ballet Theatre
18 24-hour Pharmacy
20 West Express
21 Museum of Genocide Victims
23 Bazė Internet
24 Knygos Vaga
25 National Library
26 Seimas
28 Church of the Saint Virgin's Apparition
30 Angaras
31 Gravity
35 Frank Zappa Memorial
36 The Holocaust Museum
39 Lithuanian State Jewish Museum of Vilna Gaon
40 Tourist Information Centre (TIC)
41 President's Palace
42 Vilnius University; Littera
43 St John's Church
45 Mickiewicz Museum
46 St Anne's Church
47 St Michael's Church
49 Angel of Užupis Statue
51 Church of the Holy Mother of God
52 Gero Viskio Baras
56 British Council
58 Lithuanian Student & Youth Travel
59 Paliūstrė
63 Lietuva Cinema
66 St Casimir's Church
67 Old Town Hall; TIC Branch
68 Contemporary Art Centre
70 Brodvėjus
71 VO02
74 Bix
75 Baltic Travel Services
76 National Philharmonic Concert Hall
78 Holy Spirit Church
79 St Teresa's Church
80 Gates of Dawn
84 Bus Station
85 24-hour Currency Exchange
86 Kelvita Tourist Information

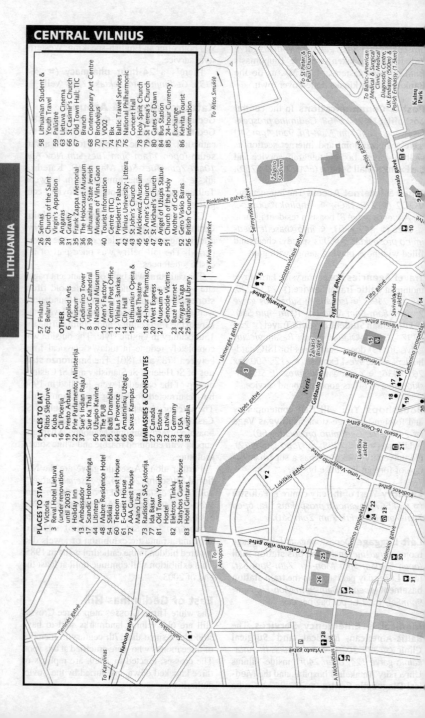

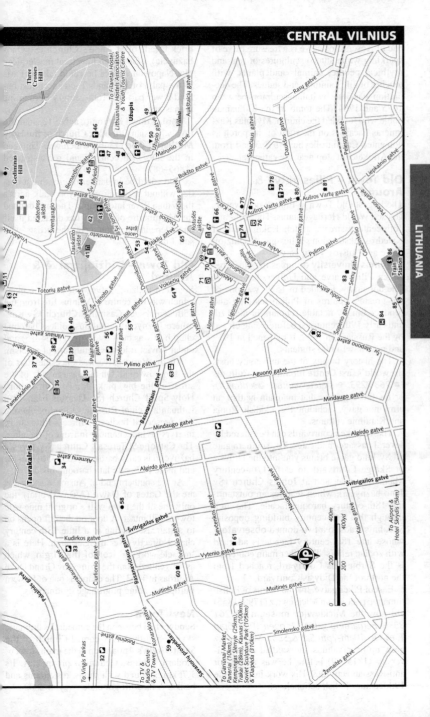

Inside **St Peter & Paul Church** at the far end of Kosciuškos gatvė is a treasure trove of sparkling white stucco sculptures of real and mythical people, animals and plants, with touches of gilt, paintings and statues. The decoration was done by Italian sculptors between 1675 and 1704. The tomb of the Lithuanian noble who founded the church, Mykolas Kazimieras Pacas, is on the right of the porch as you enter. Catch trolleybus No 2, 3 or 4 from the Arkikatedra stop near the cathedral.

Old Town – Pilies gatvė & Around

The largest Old Town in Europe deserves its Unesco World Heritage status. The 15th- and 16th-century streets stretch 1.5km south of Katedros aikštė. along Pilies gatvė, Didžioji gatvė and Aušros Vartų gatvė.

Vilnius University occupies the block between Pilies gatvė and Universiteto gatvė. The university, founded in 1579, was one of the greatest centres of Polish learning and produced many notable scholars in the 17th and early 19th centuries, before being closed by the Russians in 1832. It reopened in 1919 and now has 14,000 students.

The history faculty of the university hosts the world's first **Centre for Stateless Cultures** (☎ 268 7293; e statelesscultures@centras.lt), or for those groups that maintain neither an army nor navy, including the Yiddish, Roma and Karaimic cultures.

The 12 linked courtyards can be entered by several passages and gates. The southern gate on Šv Jono gatvė brings you into the Didysis or Skarga Courtyard, in early 17th-century Mannerist style, and **St John's Church** (Šv Jono bažnyčia), which features an outstanding 18th-century baroque facade. The arch through the 16th-century building opposite St John's leads to a two-domed **observatory** whose late 18th-century facade is adorned with zodiac reliefs. The other main courtyard is the Sarbievijus Courtyard, reached from the north of the Didysis Courtyard.

East of Pilies gatvė, the old rooms of Polish romantic poet Adam Mickiewicz (1798–1855) are now the **Mickiewicz museum** (☎ 261 8836; Bernardinų gatvė 11; open 10am-5pm Tues-Fri, 10am-2pm Sat & Sun). Mickiewicz grew up near Vilnius and studied at its university (1815–19) before he was exiled for anti-Russian activities. His work inspired the 19th-century Polish nationalists.

Across Maironio gatvė is the fine 1581 brick facade of **St Anne's Church** (Šv Onos bažnyčia), a Gothic architectural masterpiece that Napoleon wished he could take to Paris in the palm of his hand. The church just behind it was part of a 16th-century Bernardine monastery.

Farther down Maironio, at No 12, stands a lovely Russian Orthodox **Church of the Holy Mother of God** (1346), which was damaged in the late 17th century and reconstructed (1865–68).

You could be in danger of crossing a border without realising when you walk across the Vilnia River into Užupis. The area dubbed the Montmartre of Vilnius has declared itself an independent republic by the artists who squat there!

Old Town – Didžioji gatvė & Around

Southern Didžioji gatvė widens into a plaza which was the centre of Vilnius life from the 15th century. **St Casimir's Church** (Šv Kazimiero bažnyčia) is Vilnius' oldest baroque church. It was built by Jesuits (1604–15) and under Soviet rule was a museum of atheism.

Aušros Vartų gatvė was once the start of the Moscow road. On the eastern side of the street, is the big, pink, domed 17th-century **Holy Spirit Church** (Šv Dvasios bažnyčia), Lithuania's chief Russian Orthodox church. The preserved bodies of three 14th-century martyrs lie in a chamber in front of the altar. The Catholic **St Teresa's Church** (Šv Teresės bažnyčia) is early baroque (1635–50) outside and more elaborate late baroque inside.

At the southern end of Aušros Vartų gatvė are the **Gates of Dawn** (Aušros Vartai), the only one of the town wall's original nine gate towers still intact. A door on the left opens on to a staircase leading to a little 18th-century chapel directly over the gate arch. Here is a 'miracle-working' **icon of the Virgin**, which as souvenired from the Crimea by Grand Duke Algirdas in 1363. The chapel is one of Eastern Europe's leading pilgrimage destinations.

New Town

Sandwiched between the cathedral's dramatic skyline and the silver-domed **Church of the Saint Virgin's Apparition** is the main street of modern Vilnius, Gedimino prospektas. Its 1.75km is dotted with shops, restaurants and banks. A face-lift got under way in 2002.

A statue of Lenin once towered over Vilnius from Lukiškių aikštė. The building facing the square was the KGB headquarters and prison and is now the **Museum of Genocide Victims** (Genocido Aukų Muziejus; ☎ 249 6264; admission 2 Lt; open 10am-6pm Tues-Sun 15 May-14 Sept, 10am-4pm Tues-Sun 15 Sept-14 May). The museum guide is a former inmate and will show you around the gruesome torture cells. North of Gedimino prospektas is the **Seimas** (parliament) building where the remains of barricades erected there in January 1991 to halt Soviet tanks lie.

The **Holocaust Museum** (☎ 262 0730; Pamėnkalnio gatvė 12; open 9am-5pm Mon-Thur, 9am-4pm Fri) and the **Lithuanian State Jewish Museum of Vilna Gaon** (Lietuvos valstybinis Vilniaus Gaono žydų muziejus; ☎ 261 7907; w www.litjews.org; Pylimo gatvė 4; open 10am-5pm Mon-Fri) are both sobering reminders of how 94% of Lithuania's Jews were massacred.

At Kalinuasko gatvė 1, is the world's only memorial to American rock 'n' roll legend **Frank Zappa**, who died in 1993. The bust was erected by the Lithuanian Frank Zappa fan club in 1995.

Just over 1km southwest of the parliament, at the western end of Čiurlionio gatvė, is pleasant **Vingis parkas**, whose huge stage is the setting for the Lithuanian Song Festival.

The 326m **TV tower** (where Soviet tanks and troops killed 14 people and injured many more as they fought through the crowd that encircled it on 13 January 1991) is in the suburb of Karoliniškes, which is across the river from Vingis parkas. Carved wooden crosses stand as memorials to the victims. Trolleybus No 16 from the train station and No 11 from Lukiškių aikštė go to the Televizijos Bokstas stop. More crosses stand outside the **TV & Radio Centre**, which was also stormed by Soviet troops that same night, 2.5km west of the city centre.

The neglected area north of the Neris is being transformed into an IT business district, dubbed 'Sunrise Valley'.

Places to Stay

Camping Five kilometres from Trakai, the campng ground **Kempingas Slėnyje** (☎/fax 528-51 387; Totoriškes village; doubles 60 Lt, triples 70-80 Lt, suites 130 Lt) has a sauna, sandy beach, paddleboat, boat rental and hot-air balloon rides.

Hostels & Colleges The **Old Town Hostel** (☎ 262 5357, fax 268 5967; e oldtown hostels@delfi.lt; Aušros Vartų gatvė 20/15; beds 32 Lt) has doubled in size but its 25 beds go fast. It's a two-minute walk from the train and bus stations.

Filaretai Hostel (☎ 215 4627, fax 212 0149; e filaretai@post.omnitel.net; Filaretų gatvė 17; beds in 6–8-bed dorms 24 Lt, beds in doubles/triples 32/28 Lt, plus 5 Lt extra 1st night) has 13 rooms, washing machine and satellite TV. Take bus No 34 from outside the bus and train stations to the seventh stop. Both hostels are affiliated to the Lithuanian Hostels Association and can arrange saunas and canoeing trips.

Youth Tourist Centre (Jaunyjų turistų centras; ☎ 261 1547, fax 262 7742; Polocko gatvė 7; beds in triples or quads 24 Lt), near the Filaretai Hostel, has 16 fairly cheap but cheerful rooms.

Private Homes & Flats The accommodation agency **Litinterp** (☎ 212 3850, fax 212 3559; w www.litinterp.lt; Bernardinų gatvė 7-2; singles/doubles from 80/120 Lt; open 8.30am-5.30pm Mon-Fri, 9am-3pm Sat) arranges B&Bs in the Old Town area and in the regional cities of Klaipėda, Nida, Palanga and Kaunas.

Tourist information centres can also book accommodation in private homes in the Old Town area.

Hotels – Budget Proving the old adage of location, location, location, **Hotel Gintaras** (☎ 273 8011; w www.hotelgintaras.lt; Sodų gatvė 14; singles/doubles/quads 80/110/200 Lt) has nothing else going for it except being slap bang in front of the train station.

Run down but friendly **Elektros Tinklų Statybos Guest House** (☎ 216 0254; Šv Stepono 11; beds 24 Lt) has 55 beds and shared bathroom and kitchen. Reception is open 8am to 3pm weekdays.

Hotels – Mid-Range & Top End If you want a good position, **Ambassador** (☎ 261 5460; e info@ambassador.lt; Gedimino prospektas 12; singles/doubles/suites 240/280/360 Lt) is in a prime spot.

The **Telecom Guest House** (☎ 236 7150; e hotel@telecom.lt; Vivulskio gatvė 13a; singles/doubles/suites 250/300/430 Lt) is one of Vilnius' best kept secrets.

LITHUANIA

The modern **E-Guest House** (☎ 266 0730; **w** www.e-guesthouse.lt; Ševčenkos gatvė 16; doubles/apartments 180/240 Lt) is a quirky hi-tech hotel that also offers its guests free Internet connection.

The Lietuva, which was Vilnius' ugliest hotel/landmark, is undergoing a €25 million face-lift to become the **Reval Hotel Lietuva** (Ukmergės gatvė 20) in 2003.

Victoria (☎ 272 4013; **e** hotel@victoria.lt; Saltoniškių gatvė 56; singles/doubles/quads 192/232/320 Lt) has comfortable rooms.

AAA Guest House Mano Liza (☎ 212 2225, fax 212 2608; **e** hotel@aaa.lt; Ligoninės gatvė 5; doubles/luxury suites from 320/560 Lt) is an elegant, romantic hideaway.

Similar to the Mano Liza, is the **Ida Basar** (☎/fax 262 2909; **e** hotel@idabasar.lt; Subačiaus gatvė 1; doubles from 320 Lt).

The **Scandic Hotel Neringa** (☎ 261 0516; **e** neringa@scandic-hotels.com; Gedimino prospektas 23; singles 375-570 Lt, doubles 550-670 Lt) boasts a sauna, airport shuttle bus and conference hall. Its restaurant is a blast from the Soviet past.

Mabre Residence Hotel (☎ 212 2195, fax 212 2240; **e** mabre@mabre.lt; Maironio gatvė 13; singles/doubles/suites from 320/460/580 Lt) is an enchanting choice in a former Orthodox monastery.

The **Radisson SAS Astorija** (☎ 212 0110; **e** reservations.vilnius@radissonSAS.com; Didžioji gatvė 35/2; singles/doubles from 784/880 Lt) is a mint-green classical wonder overlooking the St Casimir's Church.

Holiday Inn (☎ 263 6244; **e** holiday-inn@ibc.lt; Šeimyniškių 1; singles/doubles/suites 483/587/656 Lt) is brand new and well positioned in the city's newest business district.

The cream of the crop of hotels is **Stikliai** (☎ 262 7971, fax 212 3870; **e** stikliai@mail.iti.lt; Gaono gatvė 7; singles/doubles/suites from 600/660/840 Lt).

Places to Eat

Whether it's curry, *kepta duona* or *cepelinai* you want, Vilnius has international and local cuisine. Traditional food survived the Western takeover bid and it's still the cheapest place for a Baltic blow-out with budget binges for about 20 Lt.

Restaurants In the Old Town, **Savas Kampas** (☎ 212 3203; Vokiečių gatvė 4; lunch 10 Lt) has lively night-time dining.

Try **Balti Drambliai** (☎ 262 0875; Vilniaus gatvė 41; meals 20 Lt; open 11am-midnight), for vegetarian heaven. Sue's **Indian Raja/Sue Ka Tai** (☎ 262 3802; Jogailos gatvė 11/2; 40-70 Lt; open noon-11pm) is also good.

Who says the English can't cook? These two British-run places will satisfy the heartiest appetites. They both are open until at least midnight weekdays and later on weekends. **The PUB** (☎ 261 8393; Dominikonų gatvė 9; meals 13-20 Lt; open to 5am Fri & Sat) serves good old shepherd's pie and fish and chips.

Prie Parlamento (☎ 249 6606; Gedimino prospektas 46; meals 25-35 Lt; open to 5am Fri & Sat) is a more upmarket, expat haunt. Its divine chocolate brownies, juicy steaks and full English breakfasts cure all homesickness.

Ritos Slėptuvė (☎ 262 6117; Gostauto gatvė 8; meals 25-40 Lt; open from 7.30am Sun-Thur, 7.30am-4am Fri & Sat) is an underground, all-American diner serving tortillas, steaks and burgers with as much coffee as you can drink. Sister restaurant **Ritos Smuklė** (Rita's Tavern; ☎ 277 0786; Žirmūnų gatvė 68; meals 30-40 Lt; open 10am-midnight daily) is a Lithuanian institution north of the city centre. Hog down on smoked pigs ears (9.60 Lt) while the spit roast turns.

Užupio kavinė (☎ 212 2138; Užupio gatvė 2; meals 30 Lt; open 11am-10pm daily) has a riverside terrace, artsy clientele and good food.

Amatininkų Užeiga (☎ 261 7968; Didžioji gatvė 19/2; meals 30 Lt; open 8am-5am Mon-Fri, 11am-5pm Sat & Sun) serves hearty Lithuanian stews and creamy pancakes all night until dawn.

La Provence (☎ 261 6573; Vokiečių gatvė 24; meals 45-100 Lt; open 11am-midnight daily) has an elegant French menu with such delights as snails.

Cafés & Fast Food For light meals, **Presto Arbata** (☎ 262 1967; Gedimino prospektas 32a; snacks 3.60-8 Lt; open 7am-10pm Mon-Thur, 7am-midnight Fri & Sat) has salads, frothy coffee and blackcurrant cheesecake.

Čili Picerija (☎ 231 2462; Didžioji 5; Gedimino prospektas 23; pizzas 15 Lt; open 8am-midnight daily) has 21 varieties of the staple. **Kuba** (☎ 279 0526; Šeimyniškių 3a; meals 10 Lt) is a classy canteen where you can also buy dishes by weight.

The big-name fast-food companies have a presence along Gedimino prospektas and near transport stations.

Self-Catering Fresh milk straight from the cow's udder, honey and smoked eels are just some of the culinary delights to be found at **Kalvarijų market** *(open 7am-noon Tues-Sun)*.

Entertainment

Bars & Clubs Nightlife begins in Vokiečių gatvė, which, come summer, is awash with young, trendy things enjoying a beer. Aside from Prie Parlamento, which has popular club **Ministerija**, and **The PUB**, try hanging out at **Bix** *(Etmonų gatvė 6)*, a favourite among the city's young and fun crowd, or **Gero Viskio Baras** *(Pilies gatvė 28)*.

The **Contemporary Art Centre** *(Vokiečių 2)* has a smoky hide-out bar filled with arty Lithuanian luvvies!

Or get your dancing gear on for some clubbing.

Gravity *(Jasinskio gatvė 16; admission 25 Lt)* has happening DJs, exotic cocktails and thumping house music until 6am Thursday, Friday and Saturday nights. But forget your smelly combat trousers, dress up as there's a London-style door policy.

Angaras *(Jasinskio gatvė 14)* moves with live bands and a loud crowd that continues on until 6am at weekends.

Two bars, local DJs and live music make **Brodvėjus** *(Mėsinių 4; admission 10 Lt)* a relaxed place.

Trendy clubbers head to the gay club **Men's Factory** *(Žygimantų gatvė 2)*.

Classical Music, Opera & Ballet The State Symphony and Lithuania Chamber Orchestras have prestigious reputations, as does the Lithuanian Philharmonic. Concert halls include the sublime **National Philharmonic** *(☎ 262 6802; Aušros Vartų gatvė 5)*.

The **Lithuanian Opera & Ballet Theatre** *(☎ 262 0636; Vienuolio gatvė 1)* performs classical productions for bargain tickets from 12 to 30 Lt.

Getting There & Away

See the introductory Getting There & Away section earlier in this chapter for international connections to/from Vilnius.

Air If you are buying international air tickets in Vilnius, shop around for the cheapest fare. Under 26s can try **Lithuanian Student and Youth Travel** *(☎ 239 7397; Basanavičiaus gatvė 30/13)*. Most major airlines – including

Estonian Air *(☎ 273 9022)*, **LAL** *(☎ 213 3345; ⓦ www.lal.lt)*, **SAS** *(☎ 239 5500)*, **Lufthansa** *(☎ 230 6031)* and **Finnair** *(☎ 233 0810)* – have an office at the airport. **LOT** *(☎ 273 9020)* is at Room 104, Hotel Skrydis at the airport, while **Austrian Airlines** *(☎ 231 3137)* is at Basanavičiaus 11/1.

In town, **West Express** and **Baltic Travel Service** travel agencies arrange flights and check prices.

Check the airport *(oro uostas)* on ☎ 230 6666 for departures and arrivals.

Bus The bus station *(Autobusų Stotis; ☎ 216 2977; Sodų gatvė 22)* is south of the Old Town next to the train station. Windows 1 to 6 are open between 5.30am and 5.30pm. Timetables for local and international buses are displayed on a large board. If you're still confused head to the **information centre** *(open 6am-9pm)*, which has English-speaking staff, in the ticket hall.

Eurolines *(☎ 215 1377; ⓦ www.eurolines .lt; open 5.30am-9.30pm, Mon-Sat, 5.30am-11am & 2pm-9.30pm Sun)* is based inside the main hall. It sells tickets for international destinations and for ferries.

Bus timetables change frequently so check ⓦ www.autobusai.lt. Buses to destinations within the Baltics include:

Druskininkai 14.50 Lt, two hours, 125km, four direct buses daily,
Kaunas 11.50 Lt, two hours, 100km, about 20 daily (also regular microbuses)
Klaipėda 38 Lt, five to seven hours, 310km, eight daily
Palanga 41 Lt, six hours, 340km, about nine daily
Šiauliai 23 to 27 Lt, 4½ hours, 220km, 12 daily
Trakai 3 Lt, 45 minutes, 28km, about 30 daily

Train The train station *(Geležinkelio Stotis; ☎ 233 0087, 233 0086; Geležinkelio 16)* is next to the bus station. There are 13 to 16 daily trains to Kaunas (9.80 Lt, 1¼ to two hours), three to Klaipėda (25.40 Lt, five hours), five to Šiauliai (24.10 Lt, four hours) and seven to Trakai (2.80 Lt, 40 minutes).

Car & Motorcycle Numerous 24-hour petrol stations selling Western-grade fuel are dotted at strategic points over the city. Most Western car manufacturers have representation in Vilnius, and there are repair services.

Litinterp *(☎ 212 3850; Bernardinų gatvė 7/2)* rents chauffeured or self-drive cars and

LITHUANIA

minibuses in Vilnius, Kaunas and Klaipėda from 210 Lt a day. **Rimas** *(☎/fax 277 6213; e rimas.cars@is.lt)* has the cheapest self-drive cars to rent – from about 80 Lt a day. Both **Avis** *(☎ 230 6820; e avis@avis.lt; Dariaus ir Girėno 32a)* and **Hertz** *(☎ 272 6940; e hertz@hertz.lt; Kalvarijų 14)* have offices at the airport.

Getting Around

To/From the Airport Vilnius airport is 5km south of the city at Rodūnė skelias 2. Bus No 1 runs between the airport and train station; bus No 2 runs between the airport and Lukiškių aikštė. A taxi from the airport to the city centre should cost 15 Lt.

Bus & Trolleybus Trolleybuses run daily from 5.30am to midnight. Bus and trolleybus tickets cost 0.80 Lt from kiosks, 1 Lt when bought from the driver. Validate your ticket by punching it in a machine on the bus or trolleybus. Unpunched tickets warrant a 20 Lt on-the-spot fine. Minibuses shadow most routes; expect to pay about 2 Lt. Check the website **w** www.vilniustransport.lt in English, Lithuanian and Russian.

Taxis Taxis officially charge 1 to 1.30 Lt/km. Cars with meters offer the least chance of being ripped off.

There are ranks outside the train station; in front of the Old Town Hall on Didžioji gatvė and outside the Radisson SAS Astorija hotel.

The cheapest type of taxis are those you call by telephone (☎ 215 0505, 261 6161).

AROUND VILNIUS

Paneriai

Lithuania's brutal history is starkly portrayed at this site of Jewish mass murder. Between July 1941 and July 1944, 100,000 people were killed in the Nazi death camp at Paneriai, 10km southwest of central Vilnius. From the entrance a path leads to the small **Paneriai Museum** *(☎ 264 1847; Agrastų gatvė 15; open 11am-6pm Wed-Sat)*. Paths lead to grassed-over pits where the Nazis burnt the exhumed bodies of their victims to hide the evidence of their crimes.

Getting There & Away There are about 20 suburban trains daily (some terminating in Trakai or Kaunas) from Vilnius to Paneriai station (0.90 Lt, 20 minutes). From the sta-

tion, it is a 1km walk southwest along Agrastų gatvė straight to the site.

Trakai
☎ 528 • pop 6111

Gediminas reputedly made Trakai, 28km west of Vilnius, his capital in 1321. Its two lakeside castles were built over the next 100 years to fend off the German knights. Today the spot on a north-pointing peninsula between two vast lakes is a popular weekend or day trip. From the train station in Trakai, take Vytauto gatvė north to the bus station, then continue north to Karaimų gatvė and the castles.

One peculiarity of the area is the presence of the Karaites or Karaimai, a mixed Judaic and Hebrew sect originating in Baghdad, who adhere to the Torah (rejecting the rabbinic Talmud) and who were known for their awesome physical stature. Some Karaites were brought to Trakai from the Crimea by Vytautas around 1400 to serve as bodyguards. Of the 10,000 Karaites left in the world, 200 live in Lithuania (12 families in Trakai).

The **Tourist Information Centre** *(☎/fax 51 934; e trakaiTIC@is.lt; Vytauto gatvė 69; open 9am-6pm Mon-Fri, 10am-3pm Sat)* sells maps, and books accommodation.

Trakai National Park Information Bureau *(☎ 55 776; Karaimų 5; open 8am-5pm Mon-Thur, 8am-3.45pm Fri)* arranges guided tours of the park and the surrounding area, and also issues fishing permits.

Things to See Among the wooden cottages along Karaimų gatvė, at No 30 is an early 19th-century **Kenessa** (prayer house) of the Karaites. Check out the **Karaite Ethnographic Exhibition** *(Karaimų gatvė 22; open 10am-6pm Wed-Sun)*.

The remains of Trakai's **Peninsula Castle** are towards the northern end of town, in a park close to the shore of Lake Luka. The castle is thought to have been built between 1362 and 1382 by Vytautas' father, Kęstutis.

The painstakingly restored, Gothic, red-brick **Island Castle** *(open 10am-6pm daily)* probably dates from around 1400 when Vytautas found he needed stronger defences. It stands east of the northern end of the peninsula, linked to the shore by footbridges. The moated main tower has a cavernous central court and a range of galleries, halls and rooms, some housing **Trakai History Museum** *(adult/child 8/3.50 Lt)*.

Places to Stay On the northern side of Lake Galvė, **Slėnje Hostel & Camping** (☎/fax 51 387; 2/4-person tent sites 5/7 Lt, dorm beds 20 Lt, rooms 60-220 Lt) is 4km out of Trakai. You can pitch your tent by the lake, stay in wooden cabins or the hostel, which has a sauna and a diving club, and rents boats.

Galvė (☎ 51 345; Karaimų gatvė 41; beds 24-28 Lt) is a wooden home in Trakai with lake views.

Getting There & Away More than 30 buses daily, between 6.55am and 10pm, run from Vilnius bus station to Trakai and back (3 Lt, 45 minutes). There are seven trains daily (2.80 Lt, 40 minutes).

Druskininkai
☎ 313 • pop 21,700
Spa town Druskininkai, 130km south of Vilnius, is the most famous health resort in Lithuania, but it's the nearby **Soviet Sculpture Park** (Grūto Parkas; ☎ 55 511; e hesona@druskininkai.omnitel.net; adult/child 5/2 Lt; open 9am-sunset daily) that draws visitors. Open since 2000, the theme park, which is 7km from Druskininkai, with its defunct Lenins and Stalins and Soviet observation towers, has provoked accusations of trivialising Lithuanian history.

There are four direct buses (14.50 Lt, two hours, 125km) daily between Vilnius and Druskininkai. You can ask to be let off at the village and walk the 1.5km to the park.

Druskininkai town's **tourist information centre** (☎/fax 52 198; e druskininkutib@post.omnitel.net; M-K Čiurlionio gatvė 65; open 10am-6.45pm Mon, Tues, Fri & Sat, 10am-5pm Sun) has a sister branch above the bus station (open Wed & Thur).

Central Lithuania

KAUNAS
☎ 37 • pop 415,800
Kaunas has a reputation as a sprawling urban city and a hotbed of post-Soviet mafia. Think again. It's a thriving cultural and industrial centre with a big student population, a historic Old Town and fine museums and galleries. Lithuania's second city, 100km west of Vilnius at the confluence of the Nemunas and Neris Rivers, is 90% ethnic Lithuanian. Founded in the 13th century, it was reduced to ashes 13 times before WWII, when it received yet another battering.

Kaunas was an important river-trade town in the 15th and 16th centuries, and Lithuania's capital between WWI and WWII.

Orientation
The most attractive part of Kaunas is its historic heart, Rotušės aikštė (City Hall Square), between the two rivers at the western end of the city centre. The new town is focused on the pedestrianised Laisvės alėja, which is farther east. Here you'll find the major shops, hotels, restaurants, galleries and museums. The bus and train stations are about 1km south of the eastern end of Laisvės alėja, down Vytauto prospektas.

Information
The **tourist information centre** (☎ 323 436; e turizmas@takas.lt; Laisvės alėja 36; open 9am-6pm Mon-Fri, 9am-3pm Sat Apr-Sept, 9am-6pm Mon-Fri Oct-Mar) can also help with accommodation.

There's a 24-hour currency exchange at **Lietuvos Taupomasis Bankas** (☎ 322 460; Laisvės alėja 79).

The **central post office** (☎ 401 368; Laisvės alėja 102; open 7.30am-6.30pm Mon-Fri, 7.30am-4.30pm Sat) can help with telecommunications.

Kavinė Internetas (☎ 225 364; Vilniaus gatvė 26; open 10am-10pm) charges 5 Lt per hour before noon (7 Lt after) for Internet.

Humanitas (☎ 209 581; Vilniaus gatvė 11) and **Central Bookstore** (☎ 229 572; Laisvės alėja 81) are excellent bookshops.

Museums cost 2 to 4 Lt and are generally closed Monday (some on Tuesday also).

Rotušės aikštė
The old central square is surrounded by 15th- and 16th-century German **merchants' houses**. The 18th-century white, baroque **former city hall** is now the Palace of Weddings and a ceramics museum.

In the southwestern corner of Rotušės aikštė stands a **statue of Maironis**, or Jonas Maculevičiaus, the Kaunas priest and writer whose works were banned by Stalin but who is now Lithuania's national poet. The **Lithuanian Literary Museum** is behind, in the building where Maironis lived from 1910 to 1932. The southern side of the square is dominated by an 18th-century twin-towered **Jesuit church**.

LITHUANIA

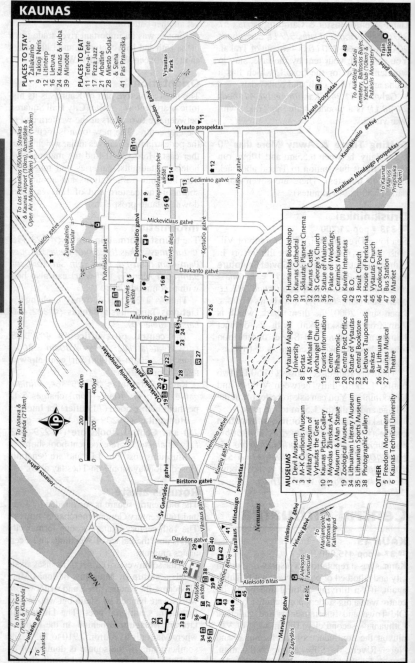

KAUNAS

PLACES TO STAY
1 Žaliakalnio
9 Takioji Neris
12 Litinterp
16 Lietuva
24 Kaunas & Kuba
39 Minotel

PLACES TO EAT
11 Tete-a-Tete
17 Pizza Jazz
21 Arbatinė
28 Miesto Sodas
   & Siena
41 Pas Pranciška

MUSEUMS
2 Devil Museum
3 M-K Ciurlionis Museum
4 Military Museum of
   Vytautas the Great
10 Kaunas Picture Gallery
13 Mykolas Žilinskas Art
   Museum & Man Statue
19 Zoological Museum
34 Lithuanian Literary Museum
35 Lithuanian Sports Museum
38 Photographic Gallery

OTHER
5 Freedom Monument
6 Kaunas Technical University
7 Vytautas Magnas
   University
8 Fortas
14 St Michael the
   Archangel Church
15 Tourist Information
   Centre
18 Philharmonic
20 Central Post Office
22 Statue of Vytautas
23 Central Bookstore
25 Lietuvos Taupomasis
   Bankas
26 Air Lithuania
27 Kaunas Musical
   Theatre
29 Humanitas Bookshop
30 Kaunas Cathedral
31 Skilautai; Planeta Cinema
32 Kaunas Castle
33 St George's Church
36 Statue of Maironis
37 Palace of Weddings;
   Ceramics Museum
40 Kavinė Internetas
42 B.O.
43 Jesuit Church
44 House of Perkūnas
45 Vytautas Church
46 Lookout Point
47 Bus Station
48 Market

Nearby is the **Lithuanian Sports Museum** (*Muziejaus gatvė 7*).

Just off the southeastern corner of the square is the intriguing 16th-century brick **Perkūno namas** (*House of Perkūnas; Aleksotas gatvė 6*), built as offices on the site of a temple to Perkūnas, the Lithuanian god of thunder. Backing onto the river is Lithuania's biggest church, **Vytautas church** (Vytauto bažnyčia), built by the leader in 1402.

Kaunas Cathedral, which is on the northeastern corner of the square, owes much to baroque reconstruction, but the early 15th-century Gothic shape of its windows remain. **Maironis' tomb** is outside the south wall of the cathedral. A reconstructed tower is all that remains of the 13th-century **Kaunas Castle**.

The **Photographic Gallery** (*Rotušės aikštė 1*) has contemporary exhibits.

New Town
The 2km pedestrian Laisvės alėja (Freedom Avenue) is the main artery of Kaunas. At its western end stands a **statue of Vytautas**. In 1972, in the park opposite, student Romas Kalanta burnt himself to death as a protest against Soviet occupation. A memorial to him was unveiled here in 2002. The **Zoological Museum** (*Laisvės alėja 106*) contains 13,000 stuffed animals. The blue, neo-Byzantine **St Michael the Archangel Church** (1893), Nepriklausomybės aikštė (Independence Square), dominates the eastern end of Laisvės alėja.

Worshippers leaving the church are met with the infamous **Man statue**, in front of the **Mykolas Žilinskas Art Museum** (*Nepriklausomybės aikštė 12*). Modelled on Nike the Greek god of victory, he caused a storm of controversy when his glorious pose exposing his manhood was unveiled.

Straddling Donelaičio gatvė, just one block north of Laisvės alėja, is Vienybės aikštė (Unity Square) containing the main buildings of the Kaunas Technical University and the smaller Vytautas Magnus University. The **Freedom Monument** (*Vienybes aikštė*), dated 16 February 1918 (the day Lithuania declared independence), was erected in 1928, hidden during the Stalin era, and put back in place on 16 February 1989.

Nearby, the **Military Museum of Vytautas the Great** (*Donelaičio gatvė 64*) recounts Lithuania's history from prehistoric times to the present day. Of particular interest is the wreck of the aircraft in which two of Lithuania's greatest modern heroes, Darius and Girėnas (pictured on the 10 Lt note), attempted to fly non-stop from New York to Kaunas in 1933. The heroes are buried in the **Aukštieji Šančiai Cemetery** (*Ašmenos gatvė 1*).

Next door is the **M-K Čiurlionis Museum** (*Putvinskio gatvė 55*), with an extensive collection of the romantic symbolic paintings of Čiurlionis (1875–1911), Lithuania's greatest artist and composer. Its second branch is the **Kaunas Picture Gallery** (*Donelaičio gatvė 16*). The fascinating **Devil Museum** (*Velnių Muziejus; Putvinskio gatvė 64*) has a bizarre collection of 2000 devil statuettes gathered by landscape artist Antanas Žmuidzinavičius (1876–1966).

Ninth Fort
Built in the late 19th century, the Ninth Fort (☎ 377 750; admission 4 Lt; open 10am-4pm Wed-Sun winter, 10am-6pm Wed-Mon rest of year) 7km from Kaunas, was used by the Russians in WWI to defend their western frontier against Germany. During WWII the Nazis used it as a death camp. An estimated 80,000 people, mostly Kaunas' Jewish population, were murdered here. The site of the mass grave is marked by stark, monumental sculptures. Take bus No 35 or 23 from the bus station.

Places to Stay
The tourist information centre can save you 30% on hotel prices – handy as there are no hostels in Kaunas.

Litinterp (☎ 228 718; e kaunas@litinterp .lt; Gedimino prospektas 28; singles/doubles/triples from 70/120/180 Lt; open 8.30am-5.30pm Mon-Fri, 9am-3pm Sat) comes to the rescue with B&B.

Lietuva (☎ 205 992; e metropol@takas.lt; Daukanto gatvė 21; singles/doubles with breakfast 120/160 Lt) is a former-Soviet dream of a hotel.

At the Yacht Club is **Baltosios Bure** (☎ 370 422; e jachtklubas@takas.lt; Gimbutienės gatvė 35; rooms 50-180 Lt). Take trolleybus 5 to the end of the route then walk the 1.5km to the lakeside.

Takioji Neris (☎ 306 100; e takneris@ takas.lt; Donelaičio gatvė 27; singles/doubles from 180/220 Lt) has more upmarket rooms.

Kaunas (☎ 750 850; e hotel.kaunas@ takas.lt; Laisvės alėja 79; doubles/suites from 320/500 Lt) is a swanky pillow parlour boasting glass-walled bathrooms!

LITHUANIA

Minotel (☎ 229 981; e minotel@kaunas
.omnitel.net; Kuzmos gatvė 8) is tucked away
in a nice Old Town spot.

Žaliakalnio (☎ 321 412; e reception@
greenhillhotel.lt; Savanorių prospektas 66;
doubles/suites 300/500 Lt) is the new kid on
the hotel block.

Places to Eat

Kuba (☎ 209 932; Laisvės alėja 79; meals
10-15 Lt; open 9am-midnight) is a split-level
canteen and bar.

Miesto Sodas (☎ 424 424; Laisvės alėja
No 93; meals 20-30 Lt; open till midnight) is
trendy with cool club Siena (open to 4am Sat
& Sun) in the basement.

Pas Pranciška (☎ 203 875; Zamenhofo
gatvė 11; meals 15-25 Lt) serves delicious
Lithuanian dishes in a traditional setting.

Arbatinė (☎ 323 732; Laisvės alėja 100;
dishes 15 Lt; open 8.30am-7.30pm Mon-Fri,
10am-6pm Sat) will set vegan pulses racing
with its dairy/meat-free policy.

Pizza Jazz (☎ 204 335; Laisves alėja 68)
has pizza for 9 to 17 Lt.

Tete-a-Tete (☎ 220 462; Vytauto prospektas 56; meals 50-100 Lt) is a good place for
splashing out.

Pubs & Clubs

Cool hang-outs include Fortas (Donelaičio
gatvė 65), an Irish bar open to the wee hours
and the studenty bar B.O. (Muitinės gatvė 9).
Skliautai (Rotušės aikštė 26) has a tiny courtyard filled with local bohemians.

Los Petrankos nightclub (Savanorių
prospektas 124) has a state-of-the-art sound
system for 1500 clubbers. You can have a
beer while bowling at Straikas (☎ 409 000;
Draugystės gatvė 6a).

Getting There & Away

Air The airport (☎ 399 307; Savanorių
prospektas) is 10km north of the Old Town in
the suburb of Karmėlava. International flights
are operated by Air Lithuania (Aviakompan-
ija Lietuva; ☎ 228 176, airport office ☎ 541
400; Kęstučio 69). It flies to Hamburg, Oslo,
Billund and Kristianstad via Palanga.

Bus From Kaunas' long-distance bus station (☎ 409 060; Vytauto prospektas 24),
Kautra bus company (☎ 409 060) runs buses
to Paris, Minsk, St Petersburg, Kaliningrad,
Rīga, Tallinn, Berlin and other destinations in

Germany. Other buses travel to Vienna, Warsaw, Prague and Amsterdam. There are many
domestic connections every day to Vilnius,
Klaipėda and Palanga.

Train From Kaunas train station (☎ 372 260;
Čiurlionio gatvė 16) about 14 trains make the
trip to/from Vilnius daily (9.80 Lt, two hours).
Four daily Kaunas-Šeštokai trains connect
with the Šeštokai-Suwałki train into Poland.
There's also one Moscow train, and two daily
trains to/from Klaipėda (23.40 Lt, six hours),
one to/from Rīga (22 Lt, five hours) and three
to/from Šiauliai (14.10 Lt, three hours).

Boat There's a summer cruise (between 15
May and 1 October) along the Nemunas
River to the Open Air Museum (☎ 346-47
392) at Rumšiškės. The boat leaves Kaunas
Sea Terminal (Kaunas Marios Prieplauka) at
11am, returning at 4pm (12 Lt for adults,
children under the age of seven go free).

The Kaunas-Nida hydrofoil is no more.

ŠIAULIAI & AROUND
☎ 41 • 147,000

Lithuania's fourth-largest city is overshadowed by the legendary Hill of Crosses. But
despite this – and plague, fires and battles –
Šiauliai has survived its troubled history to
become an eccentric city 140km north of
Kaunas and main centre of the northwestern
region of Žemaitija (or Samogitia).

Orientation & Information

The main north-south street is Tilžės gatvė,
with the bus station to the south and SS Peter
& Paul's Church northwards. The main east-
west axis is Vilniaus gatvė.

The Tourist Information Centre (☎ 523
110; e tourinfo@siauliai.sav.lt; Vilniaus
gatvė 213; open 9am-6pm Mon-Fri, 10am-
3pm Sat) arranges trips to the Hill of Crosses.

Vilniaus Bankas and Šiaulių Bankas offer
currency exchange on Tilžės gatvė. A Bankas
Snoras ATM is at the bus station. The post
office is at Aušros alėja 42. West Express
(☎ 523 333, fax 524 978; Vasario 16-osios
gatvė 48) sells train and plane tickets.

Hill of Crosses

About 10km north of Šiauliai, 2km east off
the road to Joniškis and Rīga, the strange
Kryžių kalnas has become a place of national
pilgrimage. It is a two-hump hillock blanketed

by thousands of crosses. Some are devotional, others are memorials (many for people deported to Siberia) and some are finely carved folk-art masterpieces.

Legend says the tradition of planting crosses began in the 14th century. The crosses were bulldozed by the Soviets, only to spring up again.

You can get to the hill from Šiauliai by taxi or bus. There are about 16 buses daily from Šiauliai bus station. Get off at the Domantai stop and walk the 2km track to the hill. Look for the sign 'Kryžių kalnas 2'. A one-way taxi costs about 25 Lt.

Other Attractions
Šiauliai boasts some of the country's stranger museums, including the **Cat Museum** (☎ 523 883; Žuvininkų gatvė 18) – one of only two in the world! – and the **Water Supply Museum** (☎ 525 571; Vytauto gatvė 103).

Places to Stay
Jaunųjų Turistų Centro Nakvynės Namai hostel (☎ 523 992; Rygos gatvė 36; dorm beds 15 Lt) offers hostel accommodation.

Šiauliai (☎ 434 5549; Draugystės prospektas 25; singles/doubles 60/80 Lt) is another spectacularly ugly Soviet masterpiece.

Getting There & Away
Bus Daily services include: Kaunas (17.50 Lt, three hours, about 20 buses), Klaipėda, (20 Lt, 2½ hours, six buses), Rīga (14.50 Lt, three hours, eight buses), Tallinn (8½ hours, one bus) and Vilnius (24 to 27 Lt, four hours, about 12 buses).

Train From the **train station** (Dubijos gatvė 44) each day there are six trains to Vilnius (24.10 Lt, four hours), six to Klaipėda (14.50 Lt, four hours), three to Kaunas (14.10 Lt, four hours) and one to three trains to/from Rīga (2½ hours).

Western Lithuania

KLAIPĖDA
☎ 46 • pop 202,500
Sea port Klaipėda is the gateway to the lush natural beauty of the Curonian Spit. However, Lithuania's third-largest city has some little gems of its own. Most notably it was once the German town of Memel, and some

of the Germanic architecture remains including the famous bell tower

Hitler annexed the town in 1939 and towards the end of WWII it was wrecked when the Red Army invaded. The city celebrates its nautical heritage with a flamboyant Sea Festival each year in July.

Orientation & Information
The Danės River flows west across the city centre to the Curonian (Kuršių) Lagoon, 4km from the open Baltic Sea. The main street, running roughly north-south, is Manto gatvė, which becomes Tiltų gatvė south of the river. The Old Town is centred on Tiltų gatvė. Most hotels, restaurants, banks and the train and bus stations are north of the river.

The **tourist information centre** (☎ 412 186, 412 181; e kltic@takas.lt; Tomo gatvė 2; open 8.30am-5.30pm Mon-Fri, 9am-2pm Sat) is the traveller's saviour. It's closed on Saturday in winter.

Taupomasis Bankas (Manto gatvė 4) offers currency exchange and has an ATM overlooking Teatro aikštė.

The **post office** (☎ 315 014; Liepų gatvė 16; open 8am-7pm Mon-Fri, 9am-4pm Sat) and **telephone & fax centre** (☎ 411 033; Manto gatvė 2; open 9am-10pm) are on the northern side of the river.

Get surfing at **Bitas Internet** (☎ 411 049; Šaulių gatvė 4), which charges 2 Lt per hour.

Things to See
An important landmark on Teatro aikštė (Theatre Square), off Turgaus gatvė, south of the river, is the 1818 **Klaipėda Theatre**. Hitler stood on the balcony of this theatre in 1939 to announce the incorporation of Memel into Germany. Here too stands Klaipėda's much-loved statue of Ännchen von Tharau, unveiled in 1989 in dedication to the 17th-century German poet Simon Dach.

North of the river, there's a **riverside park**, immediately east of Manto gatvė bridge. Klaipėda **Picture Gallery** (☎ 213 319; Liepų gatvė 33; adult/child 3/1.50 Lt; open noon-6pm Tues-Sun) has a sculpture garden.

The quite quirky **Clock & Watch Museum** (☎ 410 415; Liepų gatvė 12; adult/child 4/2 Lt; open noon-6pm Tues-Sat, noon-5pm Sun) has clocks from Gothic to nuclear.

The nearby **post office** (1893) has a unique 48-bell carillon inside its bell tower, making it the largest musical instrument in Lithuania.

LITHUANIA

LITHUANIA

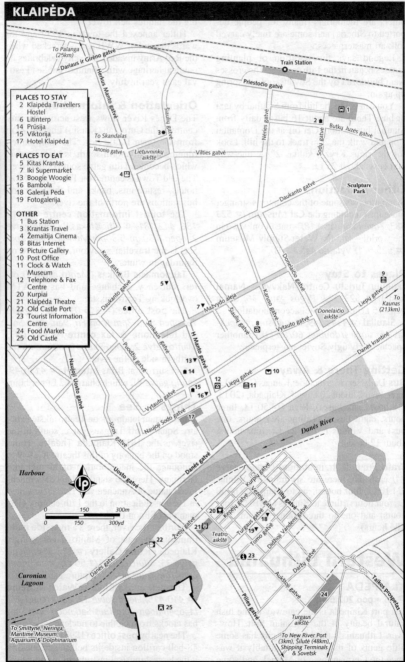

KLAIPĖDA

PLACES TO STAY
2 Klaipėda Travellers Hostel
6 Litinterp
14 Prūsija
15 Viktorija
17 Hotel Klaipėda

PLACES TO EAT
5 Kitas Krantas
7 Iki Supermarket
13 Boogie Woogie
16 Bambola
18 Galerija Peda
19 Fotogalerija

OTHER
1 Bus Station
3 Krantas Travel
4 Žemaitija Cinema
8 Bitas Internet
9 Picture Gallery
10 Post Office
11 Clock & Watch Museum
12 Telephone & Fax Centre
20 Kurpiai
21 Klaipėda Theatre
22 Old Castle Port
23 Tourist Information Centre
24 Food Market
25 Old Castle

To Palanga (25km)

Dariaus ir Girėno gatvė

Train Station

Priestočio gatvė

Nėries gatvė

Butkų Juzės gatvė

Herkus Manto gatvė

Šaulių gatvė

Sodų gatvė

To Skandalas

Janonio gatvė

Lietuvninkų aikštė

Vilties gatvė

Sculpture Park

Daukanto gatvė

Kanto gatvė

Daukanto gatvė

Donelaičio gatvė

Kauno gatvė

Liepų gatvė

To Kaunas (213km)

Mažvydo alėja

Šaulių gatvė

Donelaičio aikštė

Sinkaus gatvė

H Manto gatvė

Vytauto gatvė

Danės krantinė

Puodžių gatvė

Naujoji Uosto gatvė

Jūros gatvė

Vytauto gatvė

Naujoji Sodo gatvė

Liepų gatvė

Danės River

Harbour

Uosto gatvė

Danės gatvė

Kurpių gatvė

Tiltų gatvė

Kepėjų gatvė

Vežėjų gatvė

Turgaus gatvė

Didžioji Vandens gatvė

Teatro aikštė

Tomo gatvė

Žvejų gatvė

Danės gatvė

Curonian Lagoon

Pilies gatvė

Aukštoji gatvė

Daržų gatvė

Taikos prospektas

Turgaus aikštė

To Smiltynė, Neringa, Maritime Museum, Aquarium & Dolphinarium

To New River Port (3km), Šilutė (48km), Shipping Terminals & Sovetsk

0 150 300m
0 150 300yd

Smiltynė

Smiltynė is just across the thin strait that divides Klaipėda from its achingly beautiful coastal sister, Neringa. It has one of nature's best playgrounds to explore with beaches, high dunes and pine forests. The more adventurous can have a traditional sauna (5 Lt) on the Baltic coast.

Smiltynė's biggest crowd-pleaser (after the nudist beaches) is the combined attraction of the extensive **Maritime Museum, Aquarium & Dolphinarium** (☎ 490 751; e olga@ juru.muziejus.lt; museum & aquarium adult/ student 6/3 Lt; open 10.30am-6.30pm Tues-Sun June-Aug, 10.30am-5.30pm Wed-Sun May & Sept, 10.30am-4.30pm Sat & Sun Oct-Apr). Sea lion performances (admission 4 Lt) are at 11.15am and 1.15pm, and dolphin shows (adult/child 10/5 Lt) are at noon and 3pm. Free ferries run every half hour from the old castle port.

Places to Stay

The **Klaipėda Travellers Hostel** (☎ 211 879; e jskuodaite@yahoo.com; Butkų Juzés gatvé 7/4; beds 32 Lt) is a budget option.

Litinterp (☎ 411 814; e klaipeda@litinterp .lt; Šimkaus gatvé 21/4; singles/doubles from 70/140 Lt; open 8.30am-5.30pm Mon-Fri, 10am-3pm Sat) arranges B&B accommodation in private homes.

Viktorija (☎ 400 055; Šimkaus gatvé 2; singles/doubles/triples/quads with shared bathroom 40/60/80/85 Lt, doubles with private bathroom 120 Lt) is shabby.

Up the street from Viktorija, **Prūsija** (☎ 412 081; Šimkaus gatvé 6; singles/doubles 160/ 180 Lt) is a cosier option.

Hotel Klaipėda (☎ 394 372; e hotel@ klaipeda.omnitel.net; Naujoji Sodo gatvé 1; singles/doubles/suites from 180/260/350 Lt) has comfortable renovated rooms.

Places to Eat & Drink

Fotogalerija (Tomo gatvé 7; meals 15-25 Lt), in the heart of the Old Town, serves up light Lithuanian pancakes.

Galerija Peda (☎ 410 710; Turgaus gatvé 10; meals 8-18 Lt) is a stylish option.

On Manto gatvé there are several eating places. **Bambola** (☎ 312 213; Manto gatvé 1; open to midnight Fri & Sat) is a fantastic pizzeria, while **Boogie Woogie** (☎ 411 844; Manto gatvé 5; meals 30 Lt; open to 2am daily) is hugely popular and serves European

fodder. **Kitas Krantas** (☎ 217 365; Manto gatvé 11; meals 25 Lt) is the place where the trendy young things sip cocktails.

Kurpiai (☎ 410 555; Kurpių gatvé 1a; meals 35-60 Lt; open noon-3am) is Lithuania's best bar with good food and live jazz every night.

Skandalas (☎ 411 585; Kanto gatvé 44; meals 40 Lt; open noon-2am) is pretty much a brash American dream, part Wild West, part Mae West.

Iki (Mažvydo aléja 7/11; open 8am-10pm) is a Western-run supermarket.

Getting There & Away

Find international ferry connection information in the Getting There & Away section at the start of this chapter. Daily, there are eight buses to Vilnius, 10 to Kaunas, two to Rīga and two to Nida. From Smiltynė one bus travels down the Curonian Spit to Kaliningrad. There are frequent Smiltynė-Nida buses.

PALANGA

☎ 460 • pop 19,550

Pensioners paradise in winter, party mecca in summer, Palanga seaside resort is 25km north of Klaipėda.

Vytauto gatvé, the main street, runs parallel to the coast about 1km inland. The Catholic church at Vytauto gatvé 51 marks roughly the middle of town. From here Basanavičiaus gatvé, lined with bars and restaurants, runs to the pier.

The **Tourist Information Centre** (☎ 48 822; e palangaturinfo@is.lt; Kretingos gatvé 1; open 8am-8pm May-Oct, 9am-1pm & 2pm-6pm Nov-Apr) adjoins the tiny bus station. The **post, telephone & fax centre** (Vytauto gatvé 53) is opposite. The botanical park is at the southern end of Vytauto gatvé, with an excellent amber museum in the former palace of the noble Polish Tyszkiewicz family.

Palangos Kempingas (☎ 51 676; camping 5 Lt, cabins 10-15 Lt), 2km out of Palanga on the Klaipėda-Palanga highway (A13), has basic wooden cabins or you can pitch a tent. **Litinterp** in Klaipėda can arrange B&Bs in Palanga.

Meguva (☎ 48 839; Valančiaus gatvé 1; singles/doubles/triples from 40/50/45 Lt) is tucked behind the red brick church.

Vila Ramybé (☎/fax 54 124; Vytauto gatvé 54; doubles 100-200 Lt) is a stand-out from the crowd.

LITHUANIA

There are plenty of dining options along Basanavičiaus gatvė including **Monika** (☎ 52 560; *Basanavičiaus gatvė 12; meals 25 Lt),* which serves hearty pancakes in a wooden cabin, **Aitvaras** (☎ 52 042; *Basanavičiaus gatvė 17; meals 30 Lt),* a classy glasshouse with posh pizzas, and **Sachmatinė** (☎ 48 296, *fax 51 655; Basanavičiaus gatvė 45; meals 20-30 Lt),* which has pride of place in Palanga's party territory.

For summer Palanga-Vilnius flights see the introductory Getting Around section earlier in this chapter. The nearest train station is 10km away at Kretinga but there are regular daily buses to Kaunas, Klaipėda, Rīga, Šiauliai and Vilnius.

NERINGA
☎ 469 • pop 2528

The scent of ozone and pine are at their headiest on this thin tongue of sand, much of which is a 4km-wide national park. Waves from the Baltic Sea pound one side, the Curonian Lagoon laps the other. The winds and tree-felling have sculpted the dunes on the fragile Curonian Spit (Kuršių Nerija), which was made a Unesco World Heritage landscape in December 2000. The northern half is Lithuanian, the southern Russian, and a road runs the full 97km length into the Kaliningrad Region.

The main settlement is **Nida** (Nidden), a popular resort near the Russian border where amber is washed up on the shores after storms. German writer Thomas Mann had a house – now a **museum** (☎ 52 260; *admission 2 Lt; Skruzdynės gatvė 17)* – here in the 1930s. Head up Naglių gatvė and climb up **Parnidis Dune** (52m) to the sundial and take in the stupendous views of the 'Lithuanian Sahara'.

North of Nida is **Juodkrantė** (Schwarzort) where the **Witches' Hill** is not to be missed – the fairytale Lithuanian wooden sculptures scattered throughout a wonderful stretch of elk-inhabited forest.

There's a **tourist information bureau** in Nida (☎ 52 345; e *agilainfo@is.lt; open 9am-8pm Mon-Sat, 9am-3pm Sun June-Aug, 10am-6pm Mon-Fri 1 Sept-1 May)* and one in Smiltynė (☎ 391 177; e *kinfo@takas.lt; Smiltynės plentas 11; open 8am-4pm Mon-Fri Sept-May, 8am-4pm Mon-Fri, 10am-4pm Sat June-Aug).*

Places to Stay & Eat
In Nida, **Medikas** (☎ 52 985; *Kuverto gatvė 14; beds per person winter 25 Lt, doubles/triples 120/130 Lt)* is a good option for bargain hunters.

The **Linėja** (☎ 52 390; *Taikos gatvė 18;* e *lineja@pajuris.lt; singles/doubles from 120/150 Lt)* has all mod cons in a package-holiday style concrete block.

In Juodkrantė, **Santauta** (☎ 53 167; *Kalno gatvė 36; singles/doubles/triples 60/90/150 Lt)* has minimalist rooms and **Kurena** (☎ 53 101; *Liudviko Rėzos 10; doubles from 250 Lt)* is a new, tasteful haven.

Seklyčia (☎ 52 945; *Lotmiškio gatvė 1; meals 50-70 Lt; open 9am-midnight)* has views of the dunes of Nida and the best *kepta duona* in Lithuania.

Or try the **smoked fish outlets** near the bus station. They line the main street, Liudviko Rėzos, in Juodkrantė.

Getting There & Away
A passenger ferry departs every half hour from the Old Castle Port in Klaipėda for the northern tip of Neringa. Motorists use the vehicle ferry at the **New River Port** (*Nemuno gatvė 8),* 3km south.

From Smiltynė buses and microbuses run throughout the day to/from Nida, stopping at the main villages along the way.

Macedonia Македонија

The Former Yugoslav Republic of Macedonia (FYROM) is in the south of what was once the Yugoslav Federation. Known widely by its shortened name – Macedonia – its position in the mountainous centre of the Balkan Peninsula between Albania, Bulgaria, Yugoslavia and Greece often made it a political powder keg. The mix of Islamic and Orthodox influences tells of a long struggle ending in 1913 when the Treaty of Bucharest divided Macedonia among three of its neighbours. The then Serbia got the northern part, the southern half went to Greece, and Bulgaria received a much smaller slice. Only in 1992 did ex-Yugoslav Macedonia become totally independent and the country has emerged without being drawn into the wars that have plagued other former Yugoslav republics.

For travellers, Macedonia is a land of contrasts, ranging from Skopje with its time-worn Turkish bazaar and lively cafés to the many medieval monasteries around Ohrid. With its fascinating blend of Orthodox mystery and the exotic Orient, together with Lake Ohrid's world-class beauty, Macedonia offers the traveller an unexpected variety of opportunities for relaxation and exploration.

Despite military confrontations between Albanian Macedonian militants and Slav Macedonian security forces in the summer of 2001, the situation has eased and the country is quite safe to travel in once more.

Facts about Macedonia

HISTORY

Historical Macedonia (from where Alexander the Great set out to conquer the ancient world in the 4th century BC) is mostly contained in present-day Greece, a point Greeks are always quick to make when discussing contemporary Macedonia's use of the name. Romans subjugated the Greeks of ancient Macedonia and the area to the north during the mid-2nd century BC. When the empire was divided in the 4th century AD, this region came under the Eastern Roman Empire ruled from Constantinople. Settlement by Slav tribes in the 7th century changed the ethnic character of the area.

In the 9th century the region was conquered by the Bulgarian tsar Simeon (r. 893–927) and later, under Car Samoil (r. 980–1014), Macedonia was the centre of a powerful Bulgarian state. Samoil's defeat by Byzantium in 1014 ushered in a long period when Macedonia passed back and forth between Byzantium, Bulgaria and Serbia. After the crushing defeat of Serbia by the Turks in 1389, the Balkans became a part of the Ottoman Empire and the region's cultural character again changed.

In 1878 Russia defeated Turkey, and Macedonia was ceded to Bulgaria by the Treaty of San Stefano. The western powers, fearing the creation of a powerful Russian satellite in the heart of the Balkans, forced Bulgaria to give Macedonia back to Turkey.

In 1893 Macedonian nationalists formed the Internal Macedonian Revolutionary Organization (VMRO) to fight for independence from Turkey, culminating in the Ilinden uprising of August 1903, which was brutally suppressed by October. Although the nationalist leader Goce Delčev died before the revolt, he has become the symbol of Macedonian nationalism.

The First Balkan War in 1912 saw Greece, Serbia, Bulgaria and Montenegro together against Turkey. In the Second Balkan War in 1913, Greece and Serbia ousted the Bulgarians and shared Macedonia. Frustrated by this, IMRO continued the struggle against royalist Serbia; the interwar government in Belgrade responded by banning the Macedonian language and even the name Macedonia. Though some IMRO elements supported Bulgarian occupation during WWII, many more joined Josip Broz Tito's partisans, and in 1943 it was agreed that postwar Macedonia would have full republic status in future Yugoslavia. Tito led the communist resistance to German occupation in WWII and later became prime minister, then president of Yugoslavia.

The end of WWII brought Macedonians hopes of unifying their peoples; and this was encouraged by the Greek communist party and Bulgaria's recognition of its Macedonian minorities. However, the Stalin-Tito split of 1948 and the end of the Greek civil war in 1949 put an end to such hopes. Nonetheless, the first Macedonian grammar was published in 1952 and an independent Macedonian Orthodox Church was allowed to form.

Over the subsequent 40 years Yugoslavia as a state 'prospered' in comparison with the other socialist (ie, communist) Eastern European states. There was a relative freedom of movement of Yugoslavs to and from Yugoslavia and the country was quite open as a tourist destination.

On 8 September 1991 a referendum on independence was held in Macedonia and 74% voted in favour. In January 1992 the country declared its full independence from the former Yugoslavia. Belgrade cooperated by ordering all federal troops present to withdraw and, because the split was peaceful, road and rail links were never broken.

Greece delayed diplomatic recognition of Macedonia by demanding that the country find another name, alleging that the term Macedonia implied territorial claims on northern

Greece. At the insistence of Greece, Macedonia was forced to use the 'temporary' title FYROM (the Former Yugoslav Republic of Macedonia) in order to be admitted to the UN in April 1993. When the USA (following six EU countries) recognised FYROM in February 1994, Greece then declared an economic embargo against Macedonia and closed the port of Thessaloniki to trade. The embargo was lifted in November 1995 after Macedonia changed its flag and agreed to discuss its name with Greece. To date, there's been no resolution of this thorny issue, though relations with Greece on the trade front are looking healthy.

In August 2001 fighting broke out between Macedonian security forces and Albanian would-be separatists in the western segment of the country. The fighting stopped when both sides agreed to talks that would allow a greater participation by minority groups in the political life of the country. Steps to achieve this aim were implemented by May 2002 and tensions have since eased.

GEOGRAPHY
Much of Macedonia's 25,713 sq km is a plateau between 600m and 900m altitude. The Vardar River crosses the middle of the country, passing the capital, Skopje, on its way to the Aegean Sea near Thessaloniki. Ohrid and Prespa Lakes in the southwest drain into the Adriatic Sea via Albania; at 294m, Lake Ohrid is the deepest lake on the Balkan Peninsula. In the northwest the Šar Planina marks the border with Kosovo; Titov Vrv (2748m) is the coutnry's highest peak. Macedonia's three national parks are Pelister (near Bitola), Galičica (between Lakes Ohrid and Prespa) and Mavrovo (between Ohrid and Tetovo).

CLIMATE
Macedonia's summers are hot and dry. In winter, warm Aegean winds blow up the Vardar Valley to moderate the continental conditions further north. However, the openness of the Aegean Sea river basin influences this climate, resulting in a generally insufficient rainfall through the region (about 500mm to 700mm annually) that is unevenly distributed across the country. The yearly precipitation also varies, ranging from 490mm in the Ovcepole Ravine to 760mm in the Prespa Ravine. Snow falls on all the mountainous areas from November to April, but in the higher mountains the snow can stay until the end of May.

The temperature range varies widely; summer temperatures can reach 40°C, while in winter it can drop as low as -30°C. The average annual temperatures are above +10°C almost everywhere, which is a characteristic of semi-arid areas. Demir Kapija is the hottest town in the country where temperatures regularly reach 40°C.

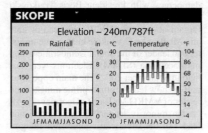

FLORA & FAUNA
Macedonia belongs to the eastern Mediterranean and Euro-Siberian vegetation region and is home to a large number of plant species in a relatively small geographical area. The high mountains are dominated by pines while on the lower mountains beech and oak dominate. On the mountain slopes of the Šar Planina and on Mt Bistra the poppy grows in abundance, the juice of which is considered the best-quality opium juice in the world.

Macedonia is a boundary area between two different zoological zones – the high mountain region and the low Mediterranean valley region. The fauna of the forests is abundant, and includes bears, wild boars, wolves, foxes, squirrels, chamois and deer. The lynx is found, although very rarely, in the mountains of western Macedonia, particularly on Šar Planina, while deer inhabit the region of Demir Kapija. Forest birds include the blackcap, the grouse, the black grouse, the imperial eagle and the forest owl.

The Yugoslav shepherd dog, *sharplaninec*, from the Šar Planina, is known worldwide. It stands some 60cm tall and is a brave, fierce fighter in guarding and defending flocks from bears or wolf packs.

Lakes Ohrid, Prespa and Dojran are separate fauna zones, a result of territorial and temporal isolation. Lake Ohrid's fauna is a relic of an earlier era. The lake is known for letnica trout, lake whitefish, gudgeon and roach, as well as certain species of snails of a genus older than 30 million years. It is also home to the mysterious European eel, which comes to Lake Ohrid from the distant Sargasso Sea to live for up to 10 years. It makes the trip back to the Sargasso Sea to breed, dies and its offspring start the cycle anew.

GOVERNMENT & POLITICS

Macedonia has a presidential parliamentary democracy with President Boris Trajkovski of the Macedonian Internal Revolutionary Organisation party (VMRO) as head of state and Mr Branko Crvenkovski as prime minister and leader of the Social Democratic Union of Macedonia (SDSM). Elections were last held in September 2002. The main opposition party is now led by former prime minister and leader of VMRO Mr Ljubčo Georgievski. Albanian minority leader Mr Ali Ahmeti and leader of the Democratic Union for Integration also polled well in the elections and will now lead the challenge for greater political participation of Albanians in Macedonia.

ECONOMY

Macedonia is a rich agricultural area that feeds itself and exports tomatoes and cucumbers to Western Europe. Cereals, rice, cotton and tobacco are also grown and Macedonian mines yield chromium, manganese, tungsten, lead and zinc. The main north-south trade route from Western Europe to Greece via the valleys of the Danube, Morava and Vardar Rivers passes through the country. Tourism is concentrated around Lake Ohrid.

The collapse of trade with Serbia in the wake of the Kosovo war has undercut Macedonia's main export market, and helped to generate around 32% unemployment.

POPULATION & PEOPLE

Of the republic's two million-plus population, 66.6% are Macedonian Slavs. As the Macedonian language has a close affinity with the Bulgarian language, many ethnographers in the early part of last century considered the Macedonians to be ethnic Bulgarians. Most Slav-speakers now consider themselves to be Macedonians, not Bulgarians.

The largest minority groups are ethnic Albanians (22.7%), Turks (4%), Roma (2.2%), Serbs (2.1%) and others (2.4%). The tensions between ethnic Albanians and Macedonians run fairly high on occasions due in part to the growing population and increasing influence of this large ethnic minority group.

ARTS

Music

The oldest form of Macedonian folk music involves the *gajda* (bagpipes). This is played solo or is accompanied by the *tapan* (two-sided drum), each side of which is played with a different stick to obtain a different tone. These are often augmented by *kaval* (flute) and/or *tambura* (small lute with two pairs of strings). Macedonia has also inherited (from a long period of Turkish influence) the *zurla* (double-reed horn), also accompanied by the *tapan*, and the *Čalgija* music form, involving clarinet, violin, *darabuk* (hour-glass shaped drum) and *đoumbuš* (banjo-like instrument).

Bands playing these instruments may be heard and enjoyed at festivals such as the folklore festival in Ohrid in mid-July or the Ilinden festival in Bitola in early August. Nearly all Macedonian traditional music is accompanied by dancing.

The Macedonian rock band Leb i Sol is well known and singers Biljana Gočevska and Eurovision representative Kalliopi are very popular within the country.

Folk Dancing

The most famous Macedonian folk dance is probably *Teškoto* (The Difficult One). Music for this male dance is provided by the *tapan* and *zurla*. This beautiful dance, performed in traditional Macedonian costume, is often included in festivals or concerts.

Other dances include *Komitsko*, symbolising the struggle of Macedonian freedom fighters against the Turks, and *Tresenica*, a women's dance from the Mavrovo region.

Cinema

Before the Rain, Milcho Manchevski's visually stunning vision of how interethnic war in Macedonia might begin, was filmed mainly in Ohrid in the southwest. *The Peacemaker* was shot in Bitola, to simulate prewar Sarajevo.

SOCIETY & CONDUCT

Macedonians are a very proud and hospitable people and welcome visitors. Show respect to your hosts by learning a few words of Macedonian. Be aware that churches and mosques are not built for tourists, but are working places of worship. Dress and behave accordingly. Be careful when talking politics: The Greek name issue and the Albanian minority question are sensitive topics.

RELIGION

Most of the Albanians and Turks are Muslim, while most Slavs are Orthodox. Both religions coexist harmoniously for the most part.

LANGUAGE

Macedonian is a South Slavic language divided into two large groups, the western and eastern Macedonian dialects. The Macedonian literary language is based on the central dialects of Veles, Prilep and Bitola. Macedonian shares all the characteristics that separate Bulgarian from other Slavic languages, evidence that it's closely related to Bulgarian.

The Cyrillic alphabet is based on the one developed by two Thessaloniki brothers, St Cyril and St Methodius, in the 9th century. It was taught by their disciples at a monastery in Ohrid, from where it spread across the eastern Slavic world.

The Cyrillic alphabet is used almost exclusively in Macedonia. Street names are printed in Cyrillic script only, so it's a good idea to learn the Cyrillic alphabet before you travel to the country. Road signs use both Cyrillic and Latin scripts. Many commercial signs are written in the Cyrillic cursive style, which is unlike the printed Cyrillic script normally seen. Be prepared for confusion.

For a quick introduction to useful Macedonian words and phrases, see the Language chapter at the end of this book.

Facts for the Visitor

HIGHLIGHTS

The Byzantine monasteries of Ohrid, particularly Sveti Sofija and Sveti Kliment, are worth a visit. Lake Ohrid is simply beautiful and the Čaršija (old Turkish bazaar) in Skopje is very colourful.

SUGGESTED ITINERARIES

Depending on the length of your stay, you might want to see and do the following:

Two days
   Visit Ohrid (if your entry point is Skopje, take a bus)
One week
   Visit Ohrid and Skopje
Two weeks
   As above, plus a quick visit to the Heraclea ruins in Bitola and some skiing or hiking in the national parks

PLANNING
When to Go

The best time to enjoy Macedonia is any time between May and September, though the peak season of mid-July to mid-August could be avoided as most Macedonians take their holidays then. Winters can be cold and wet, though there will always be accommodation in both Ohrid and Skopje.

Maps

The best commercial map of the country is the 1:260,000 *Republic of Macedonia* map published by GiziMapis. It is only available in Macedonia. You can find it at Kultura Bookshop in central Skopje. *Baedeker's Greece* map also covers Macedonia.

The tourist office in Skopje has a free road and tourist map of the Republic of Macedonia.

What to Bring

You can find most travel items and consumer goods in Macedonia, but bring along a plug converter and power adaptor (for US visitors) if you plan to use electrical appliances. Slide film is hard to find and is expensive.

TOURIST OFFICES

Only Skopje has an official tourist office (see Skopje later in this chapter for details).

VISAS & DOCUMENTS

Citizens of EU countries and New Zealanders do not need visas to in order to enter Macedonia, but visas are required of citizens of most countries. For nationals of the USA and Australia, the visa is issued free of charge at your port of entry. Canadians and South Africans must buy visas for approximately US$12; these are obtainable either before you go or at the border.

EMBASSIES & CONSULATES
Macedonian Embassies & Consulates

Macedonian embassies are found in the following countries. There are no embassies as yet in Australia or New Zealand.

Albania (☎ 042-330 36, fax 325 14) Rruga Lek Dukagjini, Vila 2, Tirana
Canada (☎ 613-234 3882, fax 233 1852) 130 Albert St, Suite 1006, Ottawa, Ontario K1P 5G4
Turkey (☎ 012-446 9204, fax 446 9206) Filistin sokak 30-2/3, Gaziosman Paşa, Ankara

MACEDONIA

UK (☎ 020-7499 5152, fax 499 2864) 19a
Cavendish Square, London, W1M 9AD
USA (☎ 202-337 3063, fax 337 3093) 3050
K St NW, Washington DC, 20007
Yugoslavia (☎ 011-633 348, fax 182 287)
Gospodar Jevremova 34, 11000 Belgrade

Embassies & Consulates in Macedonia

The following countries have diplomatic representation in Skopje (area code ☎ 02):

Albania (☎ 614 636, fax 614 200) ul H T Karpoš 94a
Australia (☎ 361 114, fax 361 834) ul Londonska 11b
Bulgaria (☎ 116 320, fax 116 139) ul Zlatko Šnajder 3
Canada (☎ 125 228, fax 122 681) ul Mitropolit Teodosie Gologanov 104
Germany (☎ 110 507, fax 117 713) ul Dimitri Čupovski 26
Greece (☎ 130 198, fax 115 718) ul Borka Talevski 6
Turkey (☎ 113 270, fax 117 024) ul Slavej Planina bb
UK (☎ 116 772, fax 117 005) ul Dimitri Čupovski 28
USA (☎ 116 180, fax 117 103) Bulevar Ilindenska
Yugoslavia (☎ 129 298, fax 129 427) Pitu Guli 8

CUSTOMS

Customs checks are generally cursory, though travellers with private cars may attract more attention at land borders.

MONEY
Currency

Colourful Macedonian denar (MKD) banknotes come in denominations of 10, 50, 100, 500, 1000 and 5000 and there are coins of one, two and five denar. Though it is stable, the denar is nonconvertible outside Macedonia. Restaurants, hotels and some shops will accept payment in euros (usually) and US dollars (sometimes); prices are often quoted in these currencies. Most prices in this chapter have been converted to denars from euros or US dollars, so the listed price may not be exact.

Exchange Rates

Conversion rates for major currencies at the time of publication were:

country	unit		denar
Australia	A$1	=	37MKD
Canada	C$1	=	43.30MKD
Euro Zone	€1	=	61MKD
Japan	¥100	=	52MKD
NZ	NZ$1	=	27.15MKD
UK	UK£1	=	99.20MKD
USA	US$1	=	69MKD

For the most recent exchange rates for the denar, see **w** www.xe.net/ucc/full.shtml.

Exchanging Money

Small, private exchange offices in central Skopje and Ohrid change money (cash only) for a rate only slightly better than the banks, but the banks also change travellers cheques. A handful of ATMs can be found in central Skopje; these offer the best exchange rates.

Costs

Except for accommodation in Skopje, Macedonia is not an expensive country. If you stay in a private room in Skopje, you might keep costs to 1800MKD to 2100MKD a day; outside Skopje, frugal travellers may spend 1200MKD to 1500MKD per day.

Tipping

It is common practice in Macedonia to round up restaurant bills and taxi fares to the nearest convenient figure.

POST & COMMUNICATIONS
Post

Mail services to and from Macedonia are efficient and reasonably fast. Letters to the USA cost 38MKD, to Australia 40MKD and to Europe 35MKD. There are poste-restante services available at major post offices.

Telephone & Fax

Macedonia's country code is ☎ 389. A long-distance call costs less at main post offices than in hotels. Drop the initial zero in the city codes when calling Macedonia from abroad. For outgoing calls the international access code in Macedonia is ☎ 99. Buy phonecards in units of 100 (200MKD), 200 (300MKD), 500 (650MKD) or 1000 (1250MKD) from post offices. Some of the larger kiosks also sell the 100-unit cards. You can often make a cheap international phone call at Internet cafés for around 15MKD per minute for all countries.

Macedonia has a digital mobile phone network (MOBIMAK); numbers are preceded by 070. Your provider may have a global-roaming agreement with Macedonia's domestic network. Check before you leave home.

Fax services are available at the main post offices in Skopje and Ohrid.

Email & Internet Access

Skopje and Ohrid both have numerous Internet cafés so that you can keep connected to your real world.

DIGITAL RESOURCES

The good website **w** www.b-info.com/places/Macedonia/republic/ presents a potpourri of data on the country.

BOOKS

The Lonely Planet *Mediterranean Europe phrasebook* will help you with the language. Zoë Brân's *After Yugoslavia*, part of Lonely Planet's Journeys series, retraces the author's 1978 trip through the now much-changed former Serbia & Montenegro. Brân travels in Croatia, Slovenia, Bosnia-Hercegovina and Yugoslavia in an attempt to make sense of what has happened in the intervening years.

Good background books include *Who Are the Macedonians?* by Hugh Poulton, a political and cultural history, Rebecca West's *Black Lamb & Grey Falcon*, a between-the-wars Balkan travelogue, and Robert Kaplan's *Balkan Ghosts*. A recent study is *The New Macedonian Question* edited by James Pettifer – academic essays on this complex issue.

NEWSPAPERS & MAGAZINES

English-language newspapers and magazines can only be found in Skopje. See that section for details.

RADIO & TV

You have a choice of three state Macedonian TV stations and any number of private and satellite channels, including CBC, Eurosport and Euronews. The BBC World Service is found on 9.41 MHz on the Short Wave, and the Voice of America on 107.5 FM.

TIME

Macedonia is one hour ahead of GMT/UTC and goes on daylight-saving time at the end of March, when clocks are turned forward one hour. On the last Sunday of September they're turned back an hour.

LAUNDRY

Macedonia currently has no self-wash laundry services, but your hotel might do a load for a

---

> **Emergency Services**
>
> In case of emergencies telephone ☎ 92 for police, ☎ 93 for fire and ☎ 94 for ambulance.
> The emergency highway assistance number is ☎ 987.

fee. *Chemisko chistenye* (dry cleaning) is available in larger towns. There's a dry cleaner in the basement of the Gradksi Trgovski Centar in Skopje and one in central Ohrid.

TOILETS

Public toilets are invariably of the grotty 'squattie' type. Take toilet paper with you if you must use them, but make use of hotel and restaurant toilets whenever you can.

WOMEN TRAVELLERS

Women travellers should feel no particular concern about travel in Macedonia. Other than possible cursory interest from men, travel is hassle-free and easy.

GAY & LESBIAN TRAVELLERS

Homosexuality in Macedonia is technically legal. Given its tenuous social acceptability, however, it's probably best for visitors to maintain a low profile.

DISABLED TRAVELLERS

Few public buildings or streets have facilities for wheelchairs, but some newer buildings provide wheelchair ramps.

DANGERS & ANNOYANCES

Macedonia is a safe country in general. However, travellers should be on the look out for pickpockets in bus and train stations and exercise common sense in looking after their belongings.

BUSINESS HOURS

Businesses tend to stay open late in Macedonia. Travellers will generally find that most businesses will be open 8am to 8pm weekdays and 8am to 2pm on Saturday.

PUBLIC HOLIDAYS & SPECIAL EVENTS

Public holidays celebrated in Macedonia include New Year (1 and 2 January), Orthodox Christmas (7 January), International Woman's Day (8 March), Easter Monday and Tuesday

MACEDONIA

(March/April), Labour Day (1 to 2 May), Sts Cyril and Methodius Day (24 May), Ilinden or Day of the 1903 Rebellion (2 August), Republic Day (8 September) and 1941 Partisan Day (11 October).

ACTIVITIES

Macedonia's top ski resort is Popova Šapka (1845m), on the southern slopes of Šar Planina west of Tetovo near the border with Kosovo. Mavrovo, in western Macedonia, is a close second. Hiking in any of the three national parks (Galičica and Pelister in the south, and Mavrovo) is a good way to discover the country. Pelister has a nice lodge from which you can base hiking activities.

ACCOMMODATION

Skopje's hotels are very expensive but there are also camping grounds and private-room agencies in Ohrid and Skopje. Skopje's convenient HI hostel is open throughout the year. Beds are available at student dormitories in Skopje in summer. Prices in more expensive hotels are usually quoted in US dollars (US$) or euros.

FOOD & DRINKS

Turkish-style grilled mincemeat is available almost everywhere and there are self-service cafeterias in most towns for the less adventurous. Balkan *burek* (cheese or meat pie) and yogurt makes for a cheap breakfast. Look out for a sign sporting *burekdžilnica (burek* shop). Watch for Macedonian *tavče gravče* (beans in a skillet) and Ohrid trout, which is priced according to weight.

Other dishes to try are *teleška čorba* (veal soup), *riblja čorba* (fish soup), *čevapčinja* (kebabs), *mešena salata* (mixed salad) and the *šopska salata* (mixed salad with grated white cheese).

Skopsko Pivo is the local beer. It's strong and reasonably cheap. DAB is a German brew now made locally under licence. Brand-name European beers are also available. There are a good number of commercially produced wines of average to better quality and the national firewater is *rakija,* a strong distilled spirit made from grapes. *Mastika,* an ouzo-like spirit, is also popular.

ENTERTAINMENT

Entertainment for Macedonia's youth consists of mainly of hanging out in the smart, smoky cafés and bars. Live traditional Macedonian music can often be heard in the restaurants and Skopje has some fine jazz and rock bars to choose from.

SHOPPING

Macedonian mementoes include rugs and small textiles, paintings, traditional costumes, antique coins, handmade dolls and, from Ohrid, wood carvings.

Getting There & Away

AIR

A host of airlines service Skopje's **Petrovac Airport** (☎ *02-235 156).* JAT-Yugoslavia Airlines, Macedonian Airlines (MAT), Adria Airways, Croatia Airlines, Olympic Airways, Malév-Hungarian Airlines, Turkish Airlines, Swiss and Austrian Airlines offer flights from Skopje to a number of European destinations. Some sample one-way prices (but not including airport taxes) are: Amsterdam (€255); Athens (US$120); Belgrade (US$70); İstanbul (US$200); London (US$200); Rome (€200); Zagreb (US$190); and Zürich (320 Sfr). Remember that return prices are always a much better deal.

It may be cheaper to fly into Thessaloniki in northern Greece. Bear in mind, however, that Greece's transport links with Macedonia are poor, consisting of just two trains a day from Thessaloniki.

It might be worth contacting Skopje taxi driver Sašo Trajkovski (see under Taxi later in this section) to pick you up in Thessaloniki and bring you to Skopje.

Some airline phone numbers in Skopje (area code ☎ 02) are:

Adria Airways	☎ 117 009
Alitalia	☎ 118 602
Croatian Airlines	☎ 115 858
JAT-Yugoslavia	☎ 116 532
Macedonian Airlines (MAT)	☎ 116 333
Malév-Hungarian Airlines	☎ 111 214
Olympic Airways	☎ 127 127
Turkish Airlines	☎ 117 214

Any of the innumerable travel agencies in Skopje or Ohrid can book flights with these airlines.

LAND
Macedonia is surrounded by land borders with Greece, Albania, Bulgaria and Yugoslavia and one UN-monitored territory – Kosovo. Access to/from all neighbouring states is generally trouble-free and unrestricted, though there may still be some tension at the Debar crossing with Albania. The Lake Ohrid crossings with Albania are no problem.

Visas are not necessary for travel to Kosovo, and it is quite easy to get there; the border crossing is just a 20-minute trip north from Skopje.

Bus
There are two international bus stations in Skopje: next to the City Museum and on Kej 13 Noemvri beside the river. Check the departure points when you buy a ticket. Buses go to Sofia (640MKD, six hours, three times daily), İstanbul (1860MKD, 14 hours, three to four daily), Belgrade (800MKD, six hours, three times daily), Frankfurt (6100MKD, 24 hours, once a week) and Zagreb (2560MKD, 15 hours, four a week). Buses also travel to Budapest, Vienna and Sarajevo.

Buses between Skopje and Prishtina, the capital of Kosovo, are fairly frequent. To/from Albania you can travel between Tetovo and Tirana by bus (five to six hours, two daily), or walk across the border at Sveti Naum or Kafa San (see the Ohrid section for information).

Train
From Skopje's grim and dim train station trains run between Skopje and Belgrade via Niš (1209MKD, eight to nine hours, twice daily). Sleepers are available. One train goes daily to Ljubljana in Slovenia (2690MKD, 12 hours). Two trains runs daily between Skopje and Thessaloniki (700MKD, six hours), one at 7.15am and the other at 5.18pm. Note that Thessaloniki in Macedonian is 'Solun'.

All the timetables and arrivals/departures boards at Skopje train station are in Cyrillic script only. You'll have to understand Cyrillic to make any sense of them. The staff at the Information desk will be of limited use to you so come prepared with your phrasebook.

Car & Motorcycle
There are several main highway border crossings into Macedonia from the neighbouring countries. You will need a green card endorsed for Macedonia to bring a car into the country.

Albania The crossings are Sveti Naum (29km south of Ohrid), Kafa San (12km southwest of Struga) and Blato (5km northwest of Debar).

Bulgaria The main crossings are just east of Kriva Palanka (between Sofia and Skopje), and east of Delčevo (26km west of Blagoevgrad) and also Novo Selo (that's between Kulata and Strumica).

Greece There are crossings at Gevgelija (between Skopje and Thessaloniki), Dojran (just east of Gevgelija) and Medžitlija (16km south of Bitola).

Kosovo You can cross into Kosovo at Blace between Skopje and Uroševac and also at Jažince between Tetovo and Uroševac.

Yugoslavia Entry to Yugoslavia is via Tabanovce (10km north of Kumanovo). Local trains go as far as Tabanovce.

Taxi
There is at least one enterprising international taxi driver who offers transport to Thessaloniki (€120, up to four persons) and Sofia (€85, up to four persons) from Skopje or the Kosovo border. Get in touch with **Sašo Trajkovski** (☎ 070-279 449; e saso_taxi@yahoo .com). The Thessaloniki service is a through run, while the Sofia service involves a prearranged change of taxi at the border.

DEPARTURE TAX
The airport departure tax at Skopje and Ohrid is about US$18; this is normally included in your ticket.

Getting Around

BUS
Bus travel is well developed in Macedonia with fairly frequent services from Skopje to Ohrid and Bitola. The domestic bus fleet is now getting rather old and creaky, but it is still serviceable.

TRAIN
Macedonia has a limited network of domestic destinations. Possibly the only one of any real interest is the four-hour, three times daily service to Bitola from Skopje. Other destinations

are: Kičevo in the west of the country; Veles, south of Skopje; Tabanovce on the border with Yugoslavia; and Gevgelija on the Greek border, north of Thessaloniki.

CAR & MOTORCYCLE

Skopje is awash with rental-car agencies, from the large ones (Hertz and Avis) to smaller local companies. The tourist office in Skopje has a complete listing. Unleaded and regular petrol is widely available, but is relatively expensive at 80MKD per litre.

Speed limits for cars and motorcycles are 120km/h on motorways, 80km/h on the open road and 50km/h to 60km/h in towns. Speeding fines start from around 1500MKD. It is compulsory to wear a seat belt, though you'll probably find that few people do.

The Macedonia-wide number for emergency highway assistance is ☎ 987.

LOCAL TRANSPORT

A quick way of getting around the country if the buses are not convenient is by taxi, especially if there are two or more of you to share the cost. A half-hour trip, from Skopje to Lake Matka for example, should cost around 350MKD. Taxis are a convenient way to get to Kosovo; 640MKD will get you to the Macedonia-Kosovo border, where taxis are waiting on the other side to whisk you off to Prishtina. Note that these taxis are more expensive and will probably cost €18 and up, depending on your negotiating skills.

Skopje Скопје

☎ 02 • pop 600,000

You'd be hard pressed to claim that Skopje, the capital of Macedonia, is a particularly attractive place, but that is as much the result of a devastating earthquake that destroyed most of the city in the early 1960s as it is due to the fact that a small regional town of the former Yugoslavia has since 1990 been forced to wear the mantle of a nation's number one city. Still, it does have a flourishing restaurant and nightlife, a busy bazaar and two of the icons of Western material commercialism – McDonald's and an Irish pub. Skopje is fine for a short stay of one or two days and there are plenty of semipermanent Westerners on hand to share a kebab or a pint with if you get starved for company.

Following the earthquake in July 1963, which killed 1066 people and virtually demolished the entire town, aid poured in from all over the world to create the modern urban landscape that exists today. It's evident that the planners got carried away by the money being thrown their way, erecting oversized, irrelevant structures, which are now crumbling due to lack of maintenance. Fortunately, much of the old town survived the earthquake, along with the fortress atop the hill, preserving Skopje's historic beauty.

Skopje is strategically set on the Vardar River at a crossroads of Balkan routes close to midway between Tirana and Sofia, the capitals of neighbouring Albania and Bulgaria. Thessaloniki, Greece, is 260km southeast, near the point where the Vardar flows into the Aegean. The Romans recognised the location's importance long ago when they made Scupi the centre of Dardania Province. Later on conquerors included the Slavs, Byzantines, Bulgarians, Normans and Serbs, until the Turks arrived in 1392 and managed to hold onto Uskub (Skopje) until 1912.

Orientation

Most of central Skopje is a pedestrian zone, with the 15th-century Turkish Kamen Most (stone bridge) over the Vardar River linking the old and new towns. South of the bridge is Ploštad Makedonija (Macedonia Square), which leads into ul Makedonija running south. The train station is a 15-minute walk southeast of the stone bridge. The domestic bus station is just north of the stone bridge. Farther north is Čaršija, the old Turkish bazaar.

Detailed maps of Skopje are sold at the tourist information office. The best maps can be found at the Kultura bookshop on Ploštad Makedonija.

Information

Tourist Offices The poorly equipped **tourist information office** (☎ 116 854; open 9am-7pm Mon-Fri, 9am-4pm Sat) has rather indifferent staff who may or who may not be able to speak English. The tourist office usually closes one hour earlier in winter.

Money There are many private exchange offices scattered throughout the old and new towns where you can change your cash at a good rate. The rate at the banks tends to be only slightly lower.

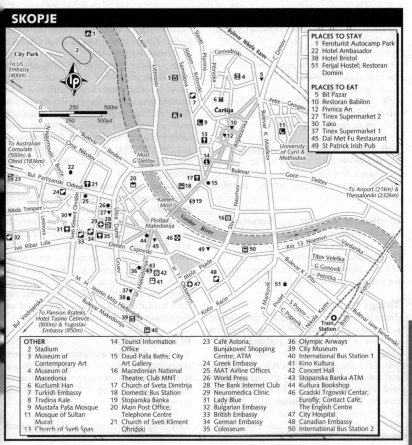

SKOPJE

PLACES TO STAY
1 Feroturist Autocamp Park
22 Hotel Ambasador
38 Hotel Bristol
51 Ferijal Hostel; Restoran Domini

PLACES TO EAT
5 Bit Pazar
10 Restoran Babilon
12 Pivnica An
27 Tinex Supermarket 2
30 Tako
37 Tinex Supermarket 1
45 Dal Met Fu Restaurant
49 St Patrick Irish Pub

OTHER
2 Stadium
3 Museum of Contemporary Art
4 Museum of Macedonia
6 Kuršumli Han
7 Turkish Embassy
8 Trvdina Kale
9 Mustafa Paša Mosque
11 Mosque of Sultan Murat
13 Church of Sveti Spas
14 Tourist Information Office
15 Daud Paša Baths; City Art Gallery
16 Macedonian National Theatre; Club MNT
17 Church of Sveta Dimitrija
18 Domestic Bus Station
19 Stopanska Banka
20 Main Post Office; Telephone Centre
21 Church of Sveti Kliment Ohridski
23 Café Astoria; Bunjakoveć Shopping Centre; ATM
24 Greek Embassy
25 MAT Airline Offices
26 World Press
28 The Bank Internet Club
29 Neuromedica Clinic
31 Lady Blue
32 Bulgarian Embassy
33 British Embassy
35 German Embassy
35 Colosseum
36 Olympic Airways
39 City Museum
40 International Bus Station 1
41 Kino Kultura
42 Concert Hall
43 Stopanska Banka ATM
44 Kultura Bookshop
46 Gradski Trgovski Centar; Eurofly; Contact Café; The English Centre
47 City Hospital
48 Canadian Embassy
50 International Bus Station 2

MACEDONIA

Skopje has a limited number of ATMs, although they can be hard to find and they are not proliferating in numbers as they tend to elsewhere. There is one in the Bunjakoveć Shopping Centre, two in the Gradski Trgovski Centar off Ploštad Makedonija, and another at the Stopanska Banka on ul Makedonija.

Post & Communications The **telephone centre** (*open 24hr*) can be found in the **main post office** (☎ 141 141; *ul Orce Nikolov 1; open 7am-7.30pm Mon-Sat, 7.30am-2.30pm Sun*), 75m north of Ploštad Makedonija, along the river.

Email & Internet Access There are at least three Internet cafés that vie for business in the city's central business district. The newest is **Contact Café** (☎ 296 365; *2nd Floor, Gradksi Trgovski Centar*), but it is the most expensive at 120MKD per hour. It is however a smoke-free zone. **Bank Internet Club** (☎ 221 133; *ul Dame Gruev 9*) is quite modern and efficient and charges 60MKD per hour. Oldest of the bunch and more a café than an Internet centre is **Café Astoria** (*Bunjakoveć Centar; Bul Partizanski Odredi 27a*), charging 100MKD per hour. Scanning, faxing and printing services are available at all cafés.

Newspapers & Magazines On the corner of ul Dame Gruev and Bul Partizanski Odredi in Skopje, **World Press** has quite a wide selection of foreign publications. You can find some English-language newspapers at the **St Patrick Irish Pub** in Skopje. **The English**

Centre (☎ 118 256; e angliski-centar@mt .net.mk), in the Gradski Trgovski Centar, sells English-language books.

Travel Agencies Skopje abounds with travel agencies. A good bet for airline tickets is the modern **Eurofly** (☎ 136 619, fax 136 320; 1st Floor, Gradksi Trgovski Centar), where airline ticket prices are listed boldly by the door in euros and US dollars.

Left Luggage There's a **left-luggage office** (open 24hr) at the train station. The domestic bus station also has a left-luggage area, open 6am to 9pm and charging 40MKD per piece of luggage.

Medical & Emergency Services For medical attention, try the **city hospital** (☎ 130 111; cnr ul 11 Oktomvri & Moše Pijade) or the **Neuromedica private clinic** (☎ 222 170; ul Partizanski 3-1-4). The emergency number for ambulance is ☎ 94 and police ☎ 92.

Things to See
There is very little of historical interest to see in the new city, with the bizarre exception perhaps of the **old train station**, with its **clock** frozen at 5.17 on the morning of 27 July 1963, the moment the earthquake struck and now left as a testimony to that great, yet still recent tragedy. The old train station is now home to the **City Museum** (☎ 114 742; ul MH Jasmin bb; admission 100MKD; open 9am-5pm Tues-Sun, 9am-1pm Sun), with a permanent exhibition portraying the history of the city and seasonal exhibitions of sculpture, photographs and other art media.

Walk north from the Turkish bridge into the old city and you'll see the **Daud Paša Baths** (1466) on the right, once the largest Turkish baths in the Balkans. The **City Art Gallery** (☎ 133 102; open 9am-3pm Tues-Sun) now occupies its six domed rooms. Almost opposite this building is the functioning Orthodox church of **Sveta Dimitrija**.

North again is Čaršija, the old market area, which is well worth exploring. Steps up on the left lead to the tiny **Church of Sveti Spas** (☎ 163 812; admission 60MKD; open 9am-4pm Tues-Fri, 9am-1pm Sat & Sun), with a finely carved iconostasis created in 1824. It's half buried because when it was constructed in the 17th century no church was allowed to be higher than a mosque. In the courtyard at

Sveti Spas is the **Tomb and Museum o Goce Delčev**, a moustached IMRO freedom fighter killed by the Turks in 1903. The ticke gives you access to both.

Beyond the church is the 1492 **Mustafa Paša Mosque** (☎ 117 412), with an earth quake-cracked dome. In the park across the street are the ruins of the city fort the **Tvrdina Kale**, with an 11th-century Cyclopean wal and good views of Skopje. Higher up on the same hill is the **Museum of Contemporary Art** (☎ 117 735; Samoiliva bb; admission 100MKD; open 9am-3pm Tues-Sun), with temporary exhibits.

The lane on the north side of Mustafa Paša Mosque leads back down to Čaršija and the **Museum of Macedonia** (☎ 116 044; Čurčiska 86; admission 100MKD; open 9am-3pm). Its large collection covers the history of the re gion fairly well, but explanations are only ir Macedonian. The museum is in the modern white building behind the **Kuršumli Han** (1550), a caravanserai or inn used by traders during the Turkish period. Skopje's old Ori ental bazaar district is among the largest and most colourful of its kind left in Europe.

Places to Stay
Skopje's prices for accommodation are gen erally high because of the large number of transient foreign missions stationed in the country. There is no real budget-traveller scene to speak of.

Camping You can pitch a tent at the **Fero turist Autocamp Park** (☎ 228 246, fax 162 677; sites per tent & adult around 200MKD, open Apr–mid-Oct). The camping ground is between the river and the stadium, just a 15-minute walk upstream from the Turkish stone bridge along the right (southern) bank.

Hostels Not far from the train station, the **HI Ferijal Hostel** (☎ 114 849, fax 165 029; ul Prolet 25; singles members/nonmembers 1280/1590MKD, doubles per person 935/ 1280MKD; open 24hr year-round) has very tidy and clean, air-conditioned individual rooms. Breakfast is included in the price.

Private Rooms & Pensions The tourist information office (☎ 116 854) can theoret ically arrange single/double rooms in private homes starting at 1150MKD per person, but in practice it is not all that helpful. Insist on something near the centre or you may find yourself some distance from the train station.

Tidy, clean **Pansion Brateks** (☎ 176 606, 070-243 232; ul Aco Karomanov 3; singles/ doubles 1920/3200MKD), in a pleasant area near the Yugoslav embassy, is a reasonable choice if you don't mind a 20-minute walk to the centre.

Hotels The **Hotel Ambasador** (☎ 215 510, fax 121 383; ul Pirinska 36; singles/doubles 2800/4340MKD), beside the Russian embassy, has simple but pleasant rooms (a double bed may mean two single beds put together); breakfast is included.

The ageing but comfortable B-class **Hotel Bristol** (☎ 237 502, fax 166 556; ul Makedonija 15; singles/doubles €42/69) is one more mid-priced option right in the centre of the city worth considering.

The expansive **Hotel Tasino Češmiče** (☎/fax 177 333, ☎/fax 178 329; ul Belgradska 28; singles/doubles 4400/6300MKD) is south of the centre. It has decent, if small, rooms with fridge, TV and phone, and rates include breakfast.

Places to Eat

An excellent choice for travellers is the smart but budget-priced **Restoran Domini** (☎ 115 519; ul Prolet 5; snacks 120MKD), in the basement of the Ferijal Hostel (see Places to Stay earlier in this section).

St Patrick Irish Pub (☎ 220 431; Kej 13 Noemvri; mains 280MKD) is a wood-clad, plush establishment serving full Irish breakfasts from 7.30am onwards and lunches and dinners such as beef in Guinness or Gaelic steak. A pint of very passable Irish ale goes for 180MKD.

From the bridge, **Dal Met Fu Restaurant** (☎ 112 482; Ploštad Makedonija) is fairly obvious on the southern side of the main square, on the left at the start of ul Makedonija. This place is good for pizza and pasta.

Tako (☎ 114 808; Sveti Kliment Ohridski; meals 45-75MKD) is a small smoke-free spot for burritos, fajitas and other Mexican delicacies. It's popular with expats, fast, cheap and has an English-language menu.

Inside the colourful Čaršija try **Restoran Babilon** (☎ 228 408; Čaršija), a restaurant on a little square with a fountain. The grills are good (240MKD) and the atmosphere is very relaxing.

Pivnica An (☎ 212 111; Čaršija; mains 270-300MKD) nearby is a beer house with a range of traditional Macedonian dishes. It is an atmospheric place for a relaxing evening meal and is popular with the expat crowd.

Bit Pazar, next to the Čaršija, is a colourful and lively outdoor market where you can buy salad ingredients. There are two well-stocked **Tinex Supermarkets** (ul Dame Gruev), near the intersection with ul Makedonija, and another close by at ul Makedonija 3.

Entertainment

Check the **Concert Hall** (ul Makedonija 12) for performances. **Club MNT** (☎ 220 767), downstairs below the Macedonian National Theatre, cranks up at around 10pm. The kingpin of the disco scene is **Colosseum** (Dimitri Čupovski). Live jazz, blues and rock music can be heard at **Lady Blue** (cnr Ivo Ribar Lola & Sveti Kliment Ohridski).

Recent English-language movies can be enjoyed at **Kino Kultura** (ul Makedonija), where tickets cost from 60MKD to 120MKD, depending on the viewing time. The liveliest expat bar, at the time of research, was without doubt **St Patrick Irish Pub** (see Places to Eat earlier).

Getting There & Away

Bus The slightly chaotic domestic **bus station** (☎ 236 254) is on the northern side of the river close to the walls of the Trvdina Kale. Buses to all domestic destinations as well as Kosovo depart from here.

There are two bus routes from Skopje to Lake Ohrid: the 167km route through Tetovo (300MKD, three hours) is much faster and more direct than the 261km route that goes via Veles and Bitola. Book a seat to Ohrid the day before if you're travelling in high season (May to August).

Buses to international destinations leave from one of two separate departure points. See the Getting There & Away section earlier in this chapter.

Train See the Getting There & Away section earlier in this chapter for details about international train travel to/from Skopje.

Getting Around

To/From the Airport There are no buses to the airport so unless you arrange transport in advance, you'll be at the mercy of the airport

MACEDONIA

'taxi mafia', which charges 1290MKD to 2200MKD for a ride into town. Do not get into a taxi that has no official taxi sign. It's better to request the place you're staying to help arrange pick-up in advance. Taxis to the airport from the centre cost about 660MKD.

Bus Inner-suburban city buses in Skopje cost 15MKD to 30MKD per trip, depending on what kind of bus and whether you buy your ticket on the bus or in advance.

Taxi Skopje's taxi system is excellent, once you get beyond the unofficial taxis at the airport. All taxis have meters and they always turn them on without prompting. The first few kilometres are a flat 50MKD, and then it's 15MKD per kilometre.

Southern Macedonia

OHRID ОХРНД
☎ 046 • pop 50,000

The Unesco-designated town of Ohrid is the Macedonian tourist mecca and is popular with domestic visitors and visitors from neighbouring countries. Some 30 'cultural monuments' in the area keep visitors busy. The steep, narrow, cobbled streets of the old town make for some pleasant, if occasionally strenuous walking, while the long lakeside promenade is popular with both walkers and joggers alike.

The oldest ruins readily seen today are Roman. A Roman amphitheatre has been restored in the old town while a scattering of Byzantine churches, most with some vivid frescoes, make for a couple of days of fascinating sightseeing.

Under Byzantium, Ohrid became the episcopal centre of Macedonia. The first Slavic university was founded here in 893 by Bishop (Saint) Kliment of Ohrid, a disciple of St Cyril and St Methodius, and from the 10th century until 1767 the patriarchate of Ohrid held sway. The revival of the archbishopric of Ohrid in 1958 and its independence from the Serbian Orthodox Church in 1967 were important steps on the road to modern nationhood.

Lake Ohrid, a natural tectonic lake in the southwestern corner of Macedonia, is the deepest lake in the Balkans (294m) and one

of the world's oldest. One-third of its 450-sq-km surface area belongs to Albania. Nestled amid mountains at an altitude of 695m, the Macedonian section of the lake is the more beautiful, with striking vistas of the water from the beach and hills.

Orientation
The old town of Ohrid is compact and easy to get around on foot and almost everything of interest is here. The bus station is close to the post office, 300m east of the old town. To the south of the old town is Lake Ohrid.

Information
Tourist Offices There's no official tourist office in Ohrid, but travel agencies (there are several small ones in town) can provide local information and offer assorted guided tours. **Generalturist** (☎ 261 071, fax 260 415; ul Partizanska 6) is a good place to start; it sells train and plane tickets. Those needing a personal guide might try voluble **Jana Poposka** (☎ 263 875), who speaks good English and knows Ohrid thoroughly. She can usually be found at the church of Sveti Kliment.

Money The **Ohridska Banka** (ul Sveti Kliment Ohridski) changes travellers cheques and cash and offers Visa advances without commission. Exchange bureaus for cash have proliferated, though few post exchange rates. You can also exchange money at the **post office**. There is one ATM at the **Balkanska Banka** (ul Dimitar Vlahov).

Post & Communications The **telephone centre** (open 7am-8pm Mon-Sat, 9am-noon & 6pm-8pm Sun) is around the corner from the modern post office. Cardphones are outside the post office and dotted around town. You can make cheap overseas phone calls for 15MKD per minute at Cybercity (see Email & Internet Access following).

Email & Internet Access There are currently three Internet centres in town, all close to each other. Ultramodern **Cybercity** (☎ 231 620; w www.cybercity.com.mk; 3rd storey, ul Sveti Kliment Ohridski) charges 60MKD per hour and is probably the best choice. In the same building and on the same floor is **Pal Net** while 50m away is **Asteroida** (ul Dimitar Vlahov bb), where access rates are similarly inexpensive.

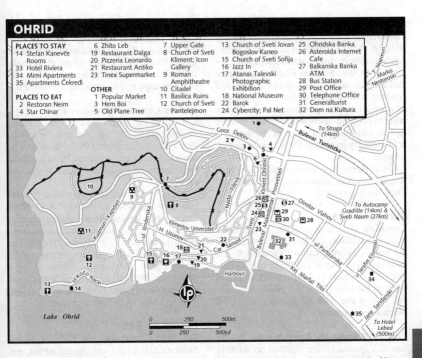

OHRID

PLACES TO STAY
14 Stefan Kanevče Rooms
33 Hotel Riviera
34 Mimi Apartments
35 Apartments Čekredi

PLACES TO EAT
2 Restoran Neim
4 Star Chinar

6 Zhito Leb
19 Restaurant Dalga
20 Pizzeria Leonardo
21 Restaurant Antiko
23 Tinex Supermarket

OTHER
1 Popular Market
3 Hem Boi
5 Old Plane Tree

7 Upper Gate
8 Church of Sveti Kliment; Icon Gallery
9 Roman Amphitheatre
10 Citadel
11 Basilica Ruins
12 Church of Sveti Pantelejmon

13 Church of Sveti Jovan Bogoslov Kaneo
15 Church of Sveti Sofija
16 Jazz In
17 Atanas Talevski Photographic Exhibition
18 National Museum
22 Barok
24 Cybercity; Pal Net

25 Ohridska Banka
26 Asteroida Internet Cafe
27 Balkanska Banka ATM
28 Bus Station
29 Post Office
30 Telephone Office
31 Generalturist
32 Dom na Kultura

Laundry There are no self-service laundrettes in Ohrid, but you can dry clean your grubby gear at **Hem Boi** *(ul Goce Delčev 21)*. Each item will cost around 100MKD.

Things to See

The picturesque old town of Ohrid rises from ul Sveti Kliment Ohridski, the main pedestrian mall. A gnarled 900-year-old **plane tree** stands guard at the northern end of this street. A medieval town wall still isolates the Old Town from the surrounding valley. Head into the Old Town along Car Samoil as far as the **National Museum** (☎ 267 173; *Car Samoil 62; adult/student 100/50MKD; open 10am-3pm Tues-Sun)* in the four-storey dwelling of the Robevi family (1827).

Further along the same street is the 11th-century **Church of Sveti Sofija** *(adult/student 100/30MKD)*, well worth the cost of admission. Apart from the frescoes there is a quite unusual Turkish *mimbar* (pulpit) remaining from the days when this church was operating as a mosque, and an upstairs portico with a photo display of the extensive restoration work. An English-speaking guide is usually on hand.

Nearby, ul Ilindenska climbs to the **Upper Gate** (Gorna Porta); to the right is the 13th-century **Church of Sveti Kliment** *(admission 100MKD; open 9am-5pm)*, almost covered inside with vividly restored frescoes of biblical scenes painted by the Thessaloniki artists Mihail Astrapas and Eftyhios about 1295. In the same area is an **icon gallery** *(open 9am-3pm)* with a fine view from the terrace. The restored walls of the 10th-century **citadel** to the west offer more splendid views.

In the park below the citadel are the ruins of an early Christian **basilica** with 5th-century mosaics covered by protective sand. Nearby is the shell of **Sveti Pantelejmon**, Ohrid's oldest church, which is being refurbished and may reclaim the remains of St Kliment, once held there but later moved to Sveti Kliment where they currently lay.

The tiny 13th-century **Church of Sveti Jovan Bogoslov Kaneo**, on a point overlooking the lake, occupies a very impressive site. Architecturally it displays Armenian as well as Byzantine elements. There's a rocky beach at the foot of the cliffs and in summer young men perform death-defying leaps into the water from the cliff top above the lake.

MACEDONIA

Special Events

The five-day Balkan Festival of Folk Dances & Songs, held at Ohrid in early July, draws folkloric groups from around the Balkan region. The Ohrid Summer Festival, held from mid-July to mid-August, features classical concerts in the Church of Sveti Sofija as well as open-air theatre performances and many other events. An international poetry festival replete with food and drink in the streets is held annually in nearby Struga on 25 and 26 August.

Ohrid hosts a swimming marathon each August, when swimmers race the 30km from Sveti Naum to Ohrid.

Places to Stay

Camping There is no camping ground in the immediate vicinity of Ohrid. The nearest and the best is the **Autocamp Gradište** (☎ 285 945; tent & 2 people 720MKD; open May–mid-Sept), which is 14km south of Ohrid right on the lakeside. It is a pleasant, grassy and shaded site with a long, narrow, gravel beach for swimmers.

Private Rooms & Apartments Private rooms or apartments are your best bet at Ohrid as the camping ground is far from town and the hotels can be pricey. Private rooms can be organised through **Generalturist** or other local travel agencies. They cost on average from 400MKD to 600MKD per person per night. Rooms in the old town are more expensive than those in the newer part of town.

One of the best options and popular with the diplomatic community is **Mimi Apartments** (☎/fax 250 103; e mimioh@mail.com .mk; ul Strašo Pinđur 2; rooms 800MKD). Affable owner Mimi Apostolov has eight comfortable, heated rooms with fridge and satellite TV. Rates include breakfast. He also has a separate, small, two-person apartment for 1500MKD.

For rustic flavour, generous hospitality and real Macedonian home cooking, it's hard to beat the rooms of **Stefan Kanevče** (☎ 070-212 352, 234 813; rooms 600MKD) in Kaneo (the small lakeside settlement you'll see below on the way to the Church of Sveti Jovan Boroslov Kaneo). Stefan's friendly wife Anita (or mama) will cook a hearty breakfast for 160MKD and pan-fried 'small fish' (sardines) from the lake go very well with beer.

A bit more upmarket and roomier is **Apartments Čekređi** (☎ 261 733, 070-570 717; Kej Maršal Tito 27; doubles/triples 1500/2700MKD). The spacious rooms close to the lake are immaculate and are good for a stay of a few days as you can cater for yourself.

Hotels Close to the town centre and overlooking the lake is modern and friendly **Hotel Riviera** (☎ 268 735, fax 254 155; Kej Maršal Tito 4; singles/doubles 1680/2640MKD). The rooms are very comfortable. There are three large apartments with lake views, if you feel expansive.

For extra comfort and some luxury, **Hotel Lebed** (☎ 250 004, fax 263 607; e tani@mt .net.mk; Kej Maršal Tito bb; singles/doubles 2170/3410MKD), about 1km east of town along the lakeside, is an excellent choice. The secluded hotel has eight comfortable rooms with pleasant wood decor. All rooms have phone, satellite TV, and central heating and air-conditioning, and rates include breakfast. Visa and MasterCard are accepted.

Places to Eat

The **Star Chinar** (☎ 260 890; ul Sedmi Noemvri 1) is a neat, modern restaurant near the old plane tree and offers some tasty local specialities. Ask for the English-language menu to see what's on offer.

On the lakefront, **Restaurant Dalga** (☎ 31 948; Kosta Abrash bb) is very popular with travellers, has a glorious lake view from its outdoor patio and offers the now rather rare lake letnica trout (approximately 2000MKD for a good-sized portion of two trout).

One of Ohrid's most atmospheric, though pricier, eating places is the **Restaurant Antiko** (☎ 265 523; Car Samoil 30), in an old house in the old town.

Any number of fast-food and pizza joints speckle the old town area. Try the cosy **Pizzeria Leonardo** (☎ 260 359; Car Samoil 31). An individual pizza and half litre of draft wine costs around 250MKD.

About 100m west of the old plane tree is the traditional and budget-priced **Restoran Neim** (☎ 254 504; Goce Delčev 71), which serves some good musaka or polneti piperki (stuffed peppers).

Picnic-minded travellers can stock up on fresh vegetables at the busy **Popular Market** just north of the old plane tree. Monday is the busiest day. Buy fresh bread and croissants at

Zhito Leb (ul Kliment Ohridski bb) near the old plane tree. There is a **Tinex Supermarket** (Bulevar Makedonski Prosvetiteli bb) for meat and dairy produce as well as most food items.

Entertainment
The mellow **Jazz In**, just towards the water from Sveti Sofija, dominates the after-hours scene. Ohrid's movie theatre is **Dom Na Kultura** (Grigor Prličev), facing the lakeside park. Cultural events are also held here.

Shopping
Pick up some good woodcarvings at **Barok** (☎ 263 151; e barokohrid@yahoo.com; Car Samoil 24; open 10am-2pm & 5-8pm), or some excellent prints of photographs of rural Macedonia by photographer **Atanas Talevski** (☎ 254 059; Kosta Abrash bb; open 9am-9pm). Small prints cost 200MKD and large prints 900MKD.

Getting There & Away
Air Only two airlines currently serve Ohrid. Adria Airways flies to Ljubljana on Wednesday, Saturday and Sunday at 5.45am (€116 one way). Odette Airways flies to Zürich on Saturday (SFR235 one way).

Bus No less than 10 buses a day run between Ohrid and Skopje (300MKD, three hours, 167km), via Kičevo. Another three go via Bitola. The first route is shorter, faster, more scenic and cheaper, so try to take it. During the summer rush, it pays to book a seat the day before.

There are nine buses a day that travel to Bitola (150MKD, 1¼ hours). Buses to Struga (14km) leave about every 15 minutes (5am to 9pm) from stand No 1 at the bus station. Enter through the back doors and pay the conductor (30MKD).

Bulgaria There is one daily bus to Sofia from Ohrid (900MKD, 10 to 12 hours). It departs from Ohrid at 7am.

Yugoslavia There are two buses each day at 5am and 3.30pm from Ohrid to Belgrade (1220MKD, 14 hours), via Bitola.

Albania To go to Albania catch a bus or boat to Sveti Naum monastery, which is very near the border crossing. In summer there are six buses every day from Ohrid to Sveti Naum (80MKD, 29km), in winter three daily. The bus continues on to the border post. From Albanian customs it's 6km to Pogradec; taxis are waiting and should charge only US$6 to US$10 for the ride.

Greece Ohrid has no direct transport links to Greece. Take a bus to Bitola and a taxi from there to the Greek border at Medžitlija/Niki (see also Bitola later in this chapter).

AROUND OHRID
Sveti Naum
Свети Наум
The better part of a second day at Ohrid could be spent on a pilgrimage to Sveti Naum, on the Albanian border 2km south of Ohrid by bus. There you will see the impressive 17th-century **Church of Sveti Naum** rising on a hill above the lake, surrounded by a monastery. The original church was built here in 900, and St Naum was buried here in 910. The graphic frescoes inside the church are mostly 19th century, though fragments of 16th- and 17th-century work remain. You can probably find an English-speaker on hand to act as a guide. The monastery grounds offer a view of the Albanian town of Pogradec across the lake.

Six buses a day run from Ohrid to Sveti Naum; it's 70MKD one way, payable on the bus. Buses generally return 40 minutes after they set out. The bus makes a stop going both ways at the Albanian border.

In summer you can also come by boat but it only leaves when a group is present; ask about times at the wharf or at the travel agencies in town. The fare should be about 150/200MKD one way/return.

BITOLA БИТОЛА
☎ 097 • Pop 90,000
Bitola, the southernmost city of the former Yugoslavia and second largest in Macedonia, sits on a 660m-high plateau between mountains 16km north of the Greek border. The colourful old bazaar area (Stara Čaršija) serves as a reminder that, during a part of the later Ottoman period, the town housed foreign consulates. The busy market days on Tuesday and Friday liven things up somewhat. Otherwise it is a rather drab and uninspiring town and only important to the traveller as a staging post for connections to and from Greece. It's probably best to treat Bitola as a day trip or a stopover between Skopje and Ohrid, as the facilities for

travellers are poor. There are no private rooms, the one hotel is dark and overpriced, and no left-luggage office is available.

The dingy bus and train stations are adjacent to each other, about 1km south of the town centre. To get to the border, you must take a taxi from the bus station (350MKD to 450MKD) and then look for a taxi on the Greek side to the nearest town, Florina.

Heraclea

The main attraction of Bitola city is the magnificent Heraclea ruins *(admission 50MKD, photos 500MKD)*, beyond the old cemetery, 1km south of the bus and train stations. Founded in the 4th century BC by Philip II of Macedonia, Heraclea was conquered by the Romans two centuries later and became an important stage on the Via Egnatia. From the 4th to 6th centuries AD it was an episcopal seat. Excavations of the site are continuing, but the Roman baths, portico and theatre are now visible. More interesting attractions in Bitola are the two early Christian basilicas and the episcopal palace, which is complete with some splendid mosaics.

Moldova

Roughly bounded by the Prut and Nistru (Dniestr in Russian) Rivers, Moldova is a thin sliver of land jammed between Romania and Ukraine. The country, which has been independent since 1991, includes part of historic Bessarabia and has been heavily Russified and Sovietised over the past century.

Still largely unexplored, Moldova today produces some extraordinary wines and shelters what many dub 'the last bastion of Soviet socialism' in Europe – the self-styled republic of Transdniestr created by Russian-speaking separatists.

Facts about Moldova

HISTORY
Bessarabia & Transdniestr
Moldova today straddles two historic regions divided by the Nistru River. Historic Romanian Bessarabia incorporated the region west of the Nistru, while tsarist Russia governed the territory east of the river (Transdniestr). Bessarabia, part of the Romanian principality of Moldavia, was annexed in 1812 by the Russian empire. In 1918, after the October Revolution, Bessarabia declared its independence. Two months later the newly formed Democratic Moldavian Republic united with Romania. Russia never recognised this union.

Then in 1924 the Soviet Union created the Moldavian Autonomous Oblast on the eastern banks of the Nistru River, and incorporated Transdniestr into the Ukrainian Soviet Socialist Republic (SSR). A few months later the Soviet government renamed the oblast the Moldavian Autonomous Soviet Socialist Republic (Moldavian ASSR). During 1929 the capital was moved to Tiraspol from Balta (in present-day Ukraine).

WWII
In June 1940 the Soviet army, in accordance with the terms of the secret protocol associated with the Molotov-Ribbentrop Pact, occupied Romanian Bessarabia. The Soviet government immediately joined Bessarabia with the southern part of the Moldavian ASSR – specifically, Transdniestr – naming it the Moldavian Soviet

Socialist Republic (Moldavian SSR). The remaining northern part of the Moldavian ASSR was returned to the Ukrainian SSR (present-day Ukraine). Bessarabia suffered terrifying Sovietisation, marked by the deportation of 300,000 Romanians.

During 1941 allied Romanian and German troops attacked the Soviet Union. Bessarabia and Transdniestr fell into Romanian hands. Consequently, thousands of Bessarabian Jews were sent to labour camps and then deported to Auschwitz.

In August 1944 the Soviet army reoccupied Transdniestr and Bessarabia. Under the terms of the Paris Peace Treaty of 1947, Romania

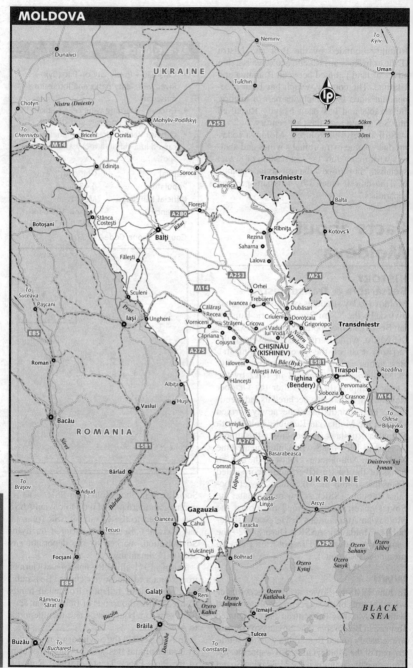

had to relinquish the region and Soviet power was restored in the Moldavian SSR.

Sovietisation & Nationalism

Once in control again the Soviets immediately enforced a Sovietisation programme on the Moldavian SSR. The Cyrillic alphabet was imposed on the Moldovan language (a dialect of Romanian) and Russian became the official state language. Street names were changed to honour Soviet communist heroes, and Russian-style patronymics were included in people's names.

In July 1949, 25,000 Moldovans were deported to Siberia and Kazakhstan. And in 1950–52 Leonid Brezhnev, then first secretary of the central committee of the Moldovan Communist Party, is said to have personally supervised the deportation of a quarter of a million Moldovans. In order to dilute the Moldovan population further, ethnic Russians and Ukrainians were encouraged to settle in the region.

Mikhail Gorbachev's policies of *glasnost* (openness) and *perestroika* (restructuring) from 1986 paved the way for the creation of the nationalist Moldovan Popular Front in 1989. Under the leadership of communist Mircea Snegur as chairman of Moldova's Supreme Soviet, Moldovan written in the Latin alphabet was reintroduced as the official language in August 1989. In February-March 1990 the first democratic elections to the Supreme Soviet (parliament) were won by the Popular Front. Then in April 1990 the Moldovan national flag (the Romanian tricolour with the Moldavian coat of arms in its centre) was reinstated. Transdniestr, however, refused to adopt the new state symbols and stuck to the red banner.

In June 1990 the Moldovan Supreme Soviet passed a declaration of sovereignty. After the failed coup attempt against Gorbachev in Moscow in August 1991, Moldova declared its full independence.

Romania was the first country, quickly followed by the USA, to recognise Moldova's independence.

In December 1991 Mircea Snegur became the democratically elected president. The same month he signed the Alma-Ata Declaration to join the newly established Commonwealth of Independent States (CIS). Moldova's full CIS membership was ratified by the Moldovan parliament only in April 1994.

Moldova was granted 'most-favoured nation' status by the USA in 1992, qualifying for International Monetary Fund (IMF) and World Bank loans the same year. In March 1994 Snegur signed NATO's Partnership for Peace agreement. Moldova's neutrality is inscribed in its constitution, meaning it cannot join NATO and is not a signatory to the CIS collective security agreements.

In August 1999, eight years after the collapse of the Soviet Union, a treaty was finally signed between Moldova and Ukraine, which confirmed their borders. The treaty in effect sticks to the Soviet division of territory. Under the agreement, Moldova gained control of a 100m strip of land along the Danube River.

Moldova took a step forward in its bid for a place in the European Union (EU) when Deputy Prime Minister Ion Sturza signed a Partnership & Cooperation Agreement with the EU in May 1999. But while Moldova is keen to join the ranks of the EU, two major obstacles still block its path: the country's mounting foreign debt and its inadequate economic growth.

Ethnic Tensions

Moldova's race on the road to independence in the late 1980s sparked nationalist sentiments among ethnic minority groups. In the Russian stronghold of Transdniestr, the Yedinstvo-Unitatea (Unity) movement formed in 1988 to represent the interests of the Slavic minorities. In November 1989 the Gagauz Halki political party was created in the south of Moldova, home to the Turkic-speaking Gagauz minority. Both groups' major fear was that Moldova would reunite with Romania.

Following the pursuit of nationalist policies by the Supreme Soviet from early 1990, the Gagauz went on to declare a separate Gagauz Soviet Socialist Republic in August 1991. A month later the Transdniestrans also declared independence from Moldova, establishing the Dniestr Moldovan Republic on the eastern banks of the Nistru River.

Both self-declared republics went on to hold presidential elections in December 1991. Igor Smirnov was elected as head of Transdniestr, Stepan Topal of Gagauzia.

Sporadic outbursts of violence ensued as the Moldovan government refused to accept separatists' claims. In March 1992 President Mircea Snegur declared a state of emergency. Two months later full-scale civil war broke

MOLDOVA

out in Transdniestr when Moldovan police clashed with Transdniestran militia in Tighina (Bendery), on the western bank of the Nistru. Transdniestran troops, with help from Russia, fought their way across Tighina Bridge to take control of Tighina. An estimated 500 to 700 people were killed and thousands wounded.

A cease-fire was signed by Moldova and Russia in July 1992. Provisions were made for a Russian-led, tripartite peacekeeping force comprising Russian, Moldovan and Transdniestran troops to be stationed in the region. Troops remain here today.

Russia continues to play a pivotal role in the Moldovan-Transdniestran conflict. Its 14th army, headquartered in Tiraspol since 1956, covertly supplied Transdniestran rebels with weapons. The continued presence of Russian troops in Transdniestr today is seen by local Russian-speakers as a guarantee of their security.

In 1997 Moldova and Transdniestr signed a Memorandum of Understanding, which guaranteed Transdniestr a degree of autonomy. This agreement has yet to become a reality and subsequent negotiations between the two republics have ended without any results.

At the 1999 Organization for Security and Co-operation in Europe summit in İstanbul, Russia agreed to withdraw its troops from the region by the end of 2002. But Transdniestr, keen to keep the Russians close by, has continually blocked the army's withdrawal.

After coming to power in 2001, Moldova's new communist president, Vladimir Voronin, visited Moscow, where he called for Russian assistance in ending the dispute. Voronin, who is pro-Russian, has also called for Moldova to join Belarus and Russia in their Union Treaty for further economic and political integration and ruled out the possibility of Moldova joining NATO.

GEOGRAPHY

Covering an area of 33,700 sq km, Moldova is the second smallest, after Armenia, of the former Soviet states. Landlocked, it consists almost entirely of gently rolling, partially wooded plains cut through with rivers and streams. The centre of the country is forested and home to Moldova's highest mountain, Mount Balaneşti (430m).

The Prut River marks Moldova's western boundary with Romania and the Nistru River, which crosses the country from north to south,

parallels its eastern border with Ukraine. Moldova also shares northern and southern borders with Ukraine.

CLIMATE

Moldova has a continental climate, with four distinct seasons. Summers are long and hot, with moderate rainfall, and winters are short and mild.

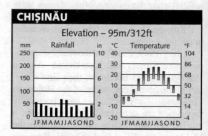

GOVERNMENT & POLITICS

Moldova is a parliamentary republic headed by a president. Its legislature consists of a 101-seat national assembly whose members are elected by proportional representation to four-year terms. In June 2000 the parliament passed a new constitutional law ending the countrywide popular vote for the president. The president is now elected by the parliament for a four-year term and, in turn, with the parliament's approval, appoints the prime minister and the council of ministers.

In the most recent parliamentary elections, held in February 2001, the Partidul Comuniştilor din Republica Moldova (Party of the Communists of the Republic of Moldova) swept to power with more than 50% of the vote, making Moldova the first former Soviet state to return the communists to power since the fall of the Soviet Union. Party leader Vladimir Voronin, a former Soviet era official, was elected president, and Vasile Tarlev appointed prime minister.

The main opposition parties are the Blocul Electoral 'Alianţa Braghiş' (Electoral Bloc Braghis Alliance) and Partidul Popular Creştin Democrat (Christian-Democratic Peoples Party). Elections are next due in 2005.

ECONOMY

Moldova's economy depends heavily on agriculture, representing 31% of GDP. Fruits, vegetables, wine and tobacco are the principal crops. With few natural resources, Moldova relies almost exclusively on external sources for its supplies of oil, coal and natural gas.

After gaining its independence Moldova launched a series of ambitious economic reforms, including the introduction of a stable convertible currency and real interest rates, the end of price fixing, the privatisation of land and the cessation of preferential deals for state enterprises, and the removal of export controls. Yet, despite these efforts, the 1998 economic crisis in Russia impacted severely on the economy, causing an 8.6% drop in GDP. In 1999 GDP fell again by 4.4% and then declined slightly in 2000 following a severe drought.

One of Europe's poorest nations, Moldova owes approximataly US$800 million to international lending organisations, as well as an additional US$600 million in unpaid gas and electricity bills to Russia.

POPULATION & PEOPLE

Moldova is the most densely populated region in the former Soviet Union. Moldovans make up 64.5% of the total population, Ukrainians 13.8%, Russians 13%, Gagauz 3.5%, Bulgarians 2%, Jews 1.5%, and other nationalities such as Belarusians, Poles and Roma 1.7%.

Most Gagauz and Bulgarians live in southern Moldova. In Transdniestr, Ukrainians and Russians total 53% of the region's population; Moldovans make up 40%.

ARTS

There is a wealth of traditional folk art in Moldova, with carpet making, pottery, weaving and carving predominating.

Traditionally, brides made offerings of carpets made by their own hands as their dowry. Today, carpet making continues to be popular throughout the country. Pottery, which is used in everyday life, is decorated with a variety of colourful motifs.

Traditional dancing in Moldova is similar to the traditional dances of other Eastern European countries. Couples dance in a circle, a semicircle or a line to the sounds of bagpipes, flutes, panpipes and violins.

SOCIETY & CONDUCT

Despite their turbulent past, Moldovans have managed to maintain their rich cultural traditions and strong family values. They are proud and hospitable people, and readily welcome visitors into their homes. If you receive such an invitation, take flowers or a small gift for your host.

When entering a home or an apartment, you should remove your shoes at the door and put on slippers. If you have room in your bag, take a pair with you; if not, a thick pair of socks will suffice.

RELIGION

Just over 98% of the population is Orthodox. The Moldovan Orthodox Church, subordinated to the Moscow Patriarchate, is the only officially recognised church.

An increasing number of believers want to switch sides to the breakaway Bessarabian Orthodox Church, which, set up by dissident priests from the Moldovan Church in 1992, looks to the Romanian Orthodox Patriarchate in Bucharest for guidance. The Moldovan government, however, has persistently refused to register the church, citing 'unresolved property claims' as the major reason.

LANGUAGE

Moldovan is essentially Romanian. It was manufactured by the Soviet regime during 1924 in an attempt to create a 'new' language for its newly created Moldavian ASSR and to pave the way for the incorporation of Bessarabia in 1940.

The introduction of the Cyrillic alphabet created a distinction from Romanian and Russified the language. New words were invented, lists of Romanian words 'polluting Moldovan' were drawn up and all words of Latin origin were scrapped.

Today, Moldovan is the principal language except in Transdniestr, where Russian predominates and where Moldovan is written in the Cyrillic script.

Facts for the Visitor

HIGHLIGHTS

Moldova, despite its size, is an intriguing bundle of surprises. Chişinău, the country's charming capital since independence in 1991, is surrounded by fertile plains, and is well known as a rich wine-producing region. North of the city lie two of Moldova's most unique treasures – the underground wine kingdom at Cricova and the fabulous 13th-century monastery carved in a cliff face at Orheiul Vechi. To the southeast is the self-proclaimed republic of Transdniestr and to the south the autonomous republic of Gagauzia.

SUGGESTED ITINERARIES

Allow yourself at least three days to explore Chişinău and the surrounding wine estates; one week if you include Orhei, Orheiul Vechi and Soroca; and two weeks if you venture to Transdniestr and Gagauzia.

PLANNING

The best time to visit is in spring (May to June), when the snow has thawed and the countryside turns into a sea of wildflowers.

The 1:650,000 *Moldova Harta rutieră* (1999), produced by Amco Press, is the only road map available locally. It includes a place name index and costs $1.50.

VISAS & DOCUMENTS

All Western travellers need a visa to enter Moldova.

To get a visa, everyone (except citizens of the EU, USA, Canada and Israel) needs an invitation authorised by the Minister of Tourism from a company, organisation or individual. Unless you already have contacts in Moldova it is *very* difficult to get an invitation.

When you are applying for a visa, you must have a passport and a photo and complete an application form.

Only passport-holders from the EU, USA or Canada can buy visas on arrival at Chişinău airport or at the Albiţa border crossing when travelling by car or bus into Moldova. No invitation is required.

Types of Visa & Costs

A single/double transit visa is valid for three days on entry and costs $35/55. Single-entry tourist visas costing $60 are valid for one month from the date of issue. Multiple-entry visas valid for one/two/three months cost $85/115/135.

Visas can be processed within a day at the **Moldovan consulate** (*Blvd Eroilor 8, Bucharest; applications 9.30am-1pm, collection 3pm-4pm Mon-Fri*) in Romania (*not* at the embassy on Aleea Alexandru).

EMBASSIES & CONSULATES
Moldovan Embassies & Consulates

Moldova has diplomatic representation worldwide, including:

Belgium (☎ 02 732 9659, fax 02 732 9660, e moldova@scynet.be) Ave Emil Max 175, 140 Brussels
Bulgaria (☎ 02-981 7370, fax 02-981 8553, e moldova@www1.infotel.bg) Blvd Patriarh Evtimii 17, 1000 Sofia
Germany (☎ 0446 52 970, fax 0446 52 972, e 113145.334@compusrve.com) Gotland-strasse nr. 16, Berlin 10439
Consulate: (☎ 4969 52 7808, fax 4969 53 1007, e mongenmold@aol.com) Adelheid-strasse nr. 8, Frankfurt am Main
Hungary (☎ 1-209 1191, fax 209 1195, e armrung@mail.elender.hu) Str Karinthy Fr ut 17, fsz 5-6, Budapest
Romania (☎ 01-230 0474, 312 9790, fax 230 7790, e moldova@customers.digiro.net) Aleea Alexandru 40, RO-71273 Bucharest
Russia (☎ 095-924 5353, fax 924 9590, e moldemb@online.ru) 18 Kuznetskii most, RUS-103031 Moscow
Turkey (☎ 312-446 5527, fax 446 5816) Kaptanpasa Sok 49, 06700 GOP/Ankara
Ukraine (☎ 044-290 7721, fax 290 7722, e moldovak@sovam.com) Str Kutuzov 8, UA-252011 Kyiv
USA (☎ 202-667 1130/1137, fax 667 1204, e moldova@dgs.dgsys.com) 2101 S Street NW, Washington, DC 20008

Embassies & Consulates in Moldova

Countries with embassies or consulates in Chişinău (phone code ☎ 2) include:

Bulgaria (☎ 237 983, fax 237 978) Str 31 August 125
France (☎ 234 510, 237 234, fax 237 283) Str Sfatul Ţării 18
Germany (☎ 232 869, 234 672, fax 234 680) Str Maria Cibotari 37
Hungary (☎ 223 404, 227 786, fax 224 513) Blvd Ştefan cel Mare 131
Romania (☎ 237 583, 233 434, fax 233 469) Str Bucureşti 66/1
Russia (☎ 248 286/225, fax 248 288, 547 751) Blvd Ştefan cel Mare 151
Turkey (☎ 245 292, 242 608, fax 225 528) Str A Mateevici 57
Ukraine (☎ 232 563, 234 876, fax 232 562) Str Sfatul Ţării 55
USA (☎ 233 772/266, fax 233 044) Str A Mateevici 103

CUSTOMS

All currency should be declared on arrival in the country, as you are allowed to export only what you have declared. Do not lose this declaration form! You must show it when you leave the country. Exiting Moldova, you are allowed to take out only 200 cigarettes and 1L of hard liquor or wine.

MONEY
Prices listed in this chapter are in US dollars. In-country, however, you will have to pay for everything in Moldovan lei. One leu is divided into 100 bani.

Note that the Transdniestran republic uses its own separate currency (see under Money in the Transdniestr section).

Exchange Rates
At the time of publication, the Moldovan leu was worth:

country	unit		Lei
Australia	A$1	=	7.18 Lei
Canada	C$1	=	8.53 Lei
Euro Zone	€1	=	12.18 Lei
Ireland	IR£1	=	14.95 Lei
Japan	¥100	=	10.49 Lei
Netherlands	f1	=	5.34 Lei
New Zealand	NZ$1	=	5.98 Lei
Romania	10,000 Lei	=	4.24 Lei
UK	UK£1	=	19.57 Lei
Ukraine	1 hv	=	2.52 Lei
USA	US$1	=	13.34 Lei

Exchanging Money
Travellers cheques and credit cards (Visa and MasterCard) are accepted at most banks in Chişinău. Banks charge around 4% commission to cash cheques or give cash advances. In recent years ATMs giving 24-hour advances have sprouted up all over Chişinău.

Keep all receipts when changing money to prove you obtained it legally.

Costs
Most hotels still adhere to the old Soviet three-tier pricing system, meaning foreigners pay twice as much as CIS citizens and three times as much as Moldovans for the same room. Still, Moldova remains fairly inexpensive for foreigners. On average you'll pay around $20 per night for budget accommodation and less than $10 per day for meals and drinks.

Tipping is uncommon in Chişinău and unheard of elsewhere in the country.

POST & COMMUNICATIONS
Avoid mailing letters from Moldova; the post is wildly erratic and letters invariably get lost.

It costs $0.30 to send a postcard or letter under 20g to Western Europe, Australia and the USA.

In Chişinău there are public cardphones from which international calls can be made. Phonecards are sold in units of 50 ($2), 100 ($3.30) and 200 ($5.90) and are available from post and telephone offices.

To make an international call, dial ☎ 8, wait for a dial tone, then dial ☎ 10, followed by the country code, city code and number. Outside of Chişinău, you have to book international calls via an operator from telephone centres.

To call Moldova from abroad dial the international country code ☎ 373, followed by the city code and then followed by the six-digit telephone number.

Cellular phone service is provided by Chişinău-based **Voxtel** (☎ 753 809, 575 757; ⓦ www.voxtel.md; Str Alba Iulia 75). If you bring your own mobile it must be registered at a cost of around $300. Roaming service outside the capital is limited.

Email & Internet Access
Email is available in Internet cafés in Chişinău for around $1 an hour (see that section for locations). For local connections the popular choice is **Relsoft** (☎ 245 580; ⓦ www.relsoft .md; St Alexandru cel Bun 51A).

DIGITAL RESOURCES
For some good general information in English log on to ⓦ www.moldova.md, Moldova's official website. Other excellent sources of information are ⓦ www.ournet.md and ⓦ www .moldova.org, which both have news and tourist links, and ⓦ www.inyourpocket.com, which posts the entire contents of its city guide *Chişinău in Your Pocket* for free.

BOOKS
A good reference is the *Historical Dictionary of the Republic of Moldova* (2000) by Andrei Brezianu.

In *Moldova and the Transdniestr Republic* (2001) author Nicholas Dima examines Russia's involvement in the conflict between the two territories.

The Moldovans: Romania, Russia, and the Politics of Culture (Studies of Nationalities) by Charles King (1999) takes an in-depth look at the national identity versus the cultural traditions of the peoples of Moldova, including a section on Bessarabia and Transdniestr.

MOLDOVA

The witty *Playing the Moldovans at Tennis* follows the exploits of British comedian/author Tony Hawks as he pursues members of the Moldovan football team for a game of tennis – all to win a bet!

MEDIA

Locally, very little is published in foreign languages. The English-language magazine *Welcome* provides updated local news. It's published fortnightly and is available online at [w] www.welcome-moldova.com or from most bookshops and kiosks for $0.75.

Radio France International (RFI) can be picked up on 102.3FM, and the BBC World Service on 68.48FM. Sun TV is a Moldovan-American joint venture that utilises the best of all the cable channels, including CNN, Euronews and the popular private Romanian channel Pro TV.

Since Transdniestran militia took over the Moldovan radio transmitter at Grigoriopol, Radio Moldova International has to broadcast from transmitters in Galbeni. The Grigoriopol transmitter remains under the control of the separatists.

PHOTOGRAPHY & VIDEO

Both Fuji and Kodak film are readily available in Chişinău; a roll of 24/36-exposure print film costs around $2.60/2.85. Several shops in the city offer one-hour processing. While processing quality is good, the costs can mount up, as you must first pay for the film's development then for the printing of each individual frame.

TIME

Moldovan time is GMT/UTC plus two hours. Daylight saving time starts in late March, when clocks are turned forward an hour, and ends in late October, when the clocks are turned back again.

ELECTRICITY

Moldova runs on 220V, 50Hz AC. Most appliances that are set up for 240V will handle this happily. Sockets require two-pin Russian plugs, identical to European plugs except the pins are thinner. Some sockets you can jam a European plug into.

TOILETS

In Moldova most toilets bear Russian signs: Ж for women and M for men. The hygiene

---

Emergency Services

In case of emergency, telephone ☎ 901 for fire, ☎ 902 for police and ☎ 903 for ambulance. The number for gas leaks is ☎ 904. These numbers are valid nationwide.

---

standards are low and toilet paper is scarce, so come prepared.

WOMEN TRAVELLERS

Travelling in Moldova presents few problems for women. But, as with anywhere else in the world use common sense – don't wander around alone at night.

GAY & LESBIAN TRAVELLERS

Moldova repealed its Soviet antigay law in 1995, thereby legalising homosexuality. But it is still not a good idea to be too 'out' in Moldova. **Gender Doc** (220 201 or 276 094; [e] generdoc_m@hotmail.com, genderdoc mail.md; PO Box 422 MD 2004) is a nonprofit organisation that takes care of issues of sexual minorities discrimination in Moldova.

DANGERS & ANNOYANCES

Getting an invitation to visit Moldova is a major hassle. In-country, Soviet bureaucracy can be a trial.

Simply getting around is a pain in the neck. Patience, tolerance and a low expectation of service are key factors in keeping down stress levels. Don't flash your wealth about, beware of pickpockets and stick to the same street rules as in any city.

Travelling in the self-declared republic of Transdniestr is safe providing you stay away from military objects and installations. If in doubt, check with the Moldovan consulate in Bucharest or abroad, or with the OCSE.

PUBLIC HOLIDAYS & SPECIAL EVENTS

National holidays celebrated in Moldova include New Year's Day (1 January), Orthodox Christmas (7 January), International Women's Day (8 March), Orthodox Easter (March/April/May), Victory (1945) Day (9 May), Independence Day (27 August) and National Language Day (31 August).

Transdniestrans boycott the Moldovan independence day and celebrate their own independence day on 2 September.

ACCOMMODATION

Chişinău has a good range of hotels. Most towns have small hotels that have survived from communist days. Basic singles/doubles with a shared bathroom cost about $11/15, while more comfortable rooms with a private bathroom cost upwards of $15/25. In addition, hotels also charge a tourist registration tax of around $1.

FOOD & DRINKS

As Moldova is principally an agriculture-based country there is a profusion of fresh produce available on which local meals are based. Typical dishes include *mămăligă* (cornmeal polenta), *sarmale* (cabbage stuffed with meat or rice), a wide variety of *ciorbăs* (soups), fried meat, baked chicken, *brânza* (salty sheep or goat cheese), fried potatoes and boiled vegetables.

Naturally, all meals are accompanied by a variety of Moldovan wines and champagnes.

ENTERTAINMENT

Plays in theatres are in Moldovan or Russian and films in cinemas are dubbed in Russian. Schedules are displayed in front of theatres and are also listed in newspapers. Tickets should be purchased in advance.

Chişinău has heaps of groovy bars and hip clubs and discos where you can boogie the night away. Outside of the capital you can usually find a good bar or two in most towns and villages where you can while away a few hours drinking with the locals and sampling the Moldovan vintages.

Getting There & Away

Moldova is quite a way off the beaten tourist track. Not many trains and even fewer buses come here, while most of the flights from the Western countries are routed via other Eastern Europe destinations.

AIR

All international flights to Moldova use Chişinău (Kishinev) airport. The only direct flights into Moldova from the West are from Frankfurt, Paris and Rome.

Moldova has three national air carriers: **Moldavian Airlines** (w *www.mdv.md*) offers a direct daily service to Budapest ($180/310 one way/return) with connections to other European cities, including Athens, Frankfurt, Milan, Moscow, Prague and Rome.

Air Moldova International (w *www.ami .md*) flies direct to Frankfurt ($350/237, daily), Kyiv ($137/237, three times a week) and Odesa ($70/121, four times a week).

Air Moldova (w *www.airmoldova.md*), the national carrier for Moldova, has flights daily to Moscow ($170/300); twice weekly to Rome ($258/517), Bucharest ($77/154) and Paris ($491/879); four times weekly to Prague ($257/434); and six times weekly to İstanbul ($200/390).

LAND

Train

Moldova's main train line heads east from Chişinău into Ukraine and then north through Belarus into Russia. Another line originates in Tiraspol, passing through Chişinău on its northbound route to Chernivtsi (Cernăuţi) and Ivano-Frankivsk in Ukraine. There are numerous trains from Chişinău to Ukraine, Belarus and on to Russia. Westbound, there are nightly trains to Romania and beyond.

Bus

From Chişinău's central bus station (Autogară Chişinău), behind the market, buses make regular journeys across the Romanian border to Iaşi ($3.40). There are also daily services to Kyiv ($8) in Ukraine. Be warned; the buses are overcrowded, slow and do not have any air-conditioning.

Border Crossings

Romania To get to/from Romania, cross the border at Albiţa (65km southeast of Iaşi) or Sculeni (24km north of Ungheni).

Ukraine The bridge along the main east-bound road (M21) from Chişinău to Dubăsari (and to Kyiv) is closed to all vehicles. To get to Kyiv from Chişinău you have to follow a minor road east to Vadul lui Vodă, where the bridge across the Nistru was open at the time of research. From Doroţcaia, bear north to Dubăsari and the M21. Before embarking on this route, it is a good idea to check in Chişinău if this is still possible. If you are crossing into Ukraine at the Pervomaisc border, you have to drive through the republic of Transdniestr. See the boxed text on the next page.

MOLDOVA

Getting Around

TRAIN

There are two daily local trains from Chişinău to Odesa, which stop at Tighina (listed by its Russian name Bendery on timetables) and Tiraspol. There are four local trains to Ungheni on the Moldova-Romania border.

BUS & MICROBUS

Moldova has a good network of buses running to most towns and villages. Microbuses, which follow the same routes as the buses, are quicker and more reliable.

CAR & MOTORCYCLE

It is now possible for foreigners to hire and drive a car in Moldova. Be wary, however, as the roads are in a poor condition. If you plan on driving, you'll need an International Driving Permit. The national speed limit is 100km/h and the speed limit in towns and villages is 60km/h. A-95 octane petrol (best for Western vehicles) is $0.42 a litre. Lower grade A-92 (OK for Ladas) is $0.40.

Chişinău

☎ 2 • pop 800,000

Moldova's capital, Chişinău (pronounced 'kish-i-now' in Moldovan and 'kish-i-nev' in Russian), is a surprisingly green city on the banks of the Bâc (Byk) River. Circled by a ring of parks and lakes, it bears more resemblance to a provincial town than a nation's capital. Chişinău was first chronicled in 1420. It became a hotbed of anti-Semitism in the early 20th century; in 1903 the murder of 49 Jews sparked protests from Jewish communities worldwide, and in 1941 during WWII the notorious Chişinău pogrom was executed.

Chişinău was the headquarters base of the USSR's southwestern theatre of military operations during Soviet rule. Between 1944 and 1990 the city was called Kishinev, its Russian name still used by the few travel agencies abroad who actually know where it is.

Orientation

Chişinău's street layout is a typically Soviet grid system of straight streets.

Gara feroviară *(train station; Aleea Gării)* is a five-minute walk from the centre. Exit

---

Border Crossings in Moldova

Since the 1992 civil war, many army control posts have been set up on the Nistru, which marks the 'unofficial' border between Moldova and the self-declared republic of Transdniestr. These posts are set up by the Moldovan army, Transdniestr's border guards and a Russian-led tripartite peacekeeping force.

Before entering Tighina from Chişinău, you have to stop at a control post. Vehicles are searched by the Transdniestrans. Spot checks on your car papers and driving licence by all three forces are frequent.

---

the station, turn right along Aleea Gării to Piaţa Negruzzi, then walk up the hill along Blvd Negruzzi to Piaţa Libertăţii. From here the main street, Blvd Ştefan cel Mare, crosses the town from southeast to northwest.

Autogară Chişinău *(central bus station; Str Mitropolit Varlaam)* is behind the central market.

Maps The the best city map is the *Chişinău Schema Turistică* ($1.35), which is published by STRIH. It lists hotels, museums and theatres and is available from most bookshops.

Information

Tourist Offices Moldova's state tourist office, **Moldova Tur** *(☎ 540 301, fax 540 494;* w *www.moldovatur.travels.ro; Blvd Ştefan cel Mare 4)* sells maps, arranges expensive city tours, organises day trips to Cricova ($20 per person, plus $20/15 for the car/guide) and can get train or plane tickets.

Money For cash advances on MasterCard and Visa and to cash travellers cheques, go to **Moldindconbank** *(Str Armeneasca 38; open 8am-1pm & 2pm-6pm Mon-Fri).*

Banca de Export Import a Moldovei *(Blvd Ştefan cel Mare 6)* gives cash advances in US dollars on Visa or MasterCard. There is also a 24-hour currency exchange here.

Victoria Bank *(Blvd Ştefan cel Mare; open 9am-5pm Mon-Fri, 9am-2pm Sat),* next to Green Hills Nistru Café, gives cash advances on Visa and MasterCard, cashes American Express travellers cheques and has an ATM.

Post & Communications The oficiul poştal *(main post office; ☎ 222 639; Blvd Ştefan* el Mare 134; open 8am-7pm Mon-Sat, 8am-5pm Sun) is on Str Vlaicu Picalab.

For telecommunications, go to **Moldtelecom** (Blvd Ștefan cel Mare; open 24hr). Here you can book international calls, send faxes and telegrams, and purchase phonecards. Its second office is on the corner of Str Tighina and Blvd Ștefan cel Mare 12.

Email & Internet Access By far the most popular place in Chișinău to log on is at the **Univers Internet Café** (Blvd Ștefan cel Mare; open 24hr), above McDonald's; access costs $0.75 per hour.

Another good option is **E Internet Café** (Str Mitropolit G Bănulescu Bodoni 10; open 24hr), near the Cinema Club; access costs $0.50 per hour.

Travel Agencies Chișinău's most customer-friendly agency is **Voiaj** (☎ 546 464, 543 944, fax 272 741; w www.voiaj.net.md; Blvd Negruzzi 8), which sells plane tickets and also organises wine-tasting tours.

Incom Travel Agency (☎ 546 252, fax 274 645; e incom–travel@mdl.net; Str 31 August 49) runs private buses to Western Europe and also organises local tours.

Bookshops Some English-language books – mainly dictionaries and textbooks – can be found at the **Educational Centre** (☎ 228 987; Str Mihai Eminescu 64, Apt 5; open 10am-6pm Mon-Fri, 10am-3pm Sat).

Cartea Academica (Blvd Ștefan cel Mare 148) sells local maps.

Cultural Centres The **Alliance Française** (French Cultural Centre; ☎ 234 510, 237 236, fax 234 781; e alfrmd@mdearn.cri.md; 3rd floor, Str Sfatul Țării 18) screens French films, holds French language courses, has an extensive library and hosts regular cultural events.

Deutscher Lesesaal (☎ 247 906; 2nd floor, Biblioteca Hasdeu, Blvd Ștefan cel Mare 148; open 9am-6pm Mon-Thur, 9am-5pm Sat & Sun) is a small German-language library.

Medical & Emergency Services If you need a doctor or a dentist, contact the US embassy for a list of English-speaking doctors. For emergencies go to the **Emergency Hospital** (☎ 248 435; Toma Ciorbă 1).

To call for an ambulance dial ☎ 903, for police ☎ 902 and for the fire brigade ☎ 901.

Medicor Farm (Blvd Ștefan cel Mare; open 24hr) is opposite Grădina Publică Ștefan cel Mare și Sfînt.

Things to See & Do
Chișinău was heavily bombed during WWII and little remains of its historic heart. Walk northwest along Blvd Ștefan cel Mare to the **Arcul de Triumf** (1841). To its east is **Parcul Catedralei** (Cathedral Park), home to the Orthodox **Catedrala Nașterea Domnului** (Birth of Christ Cathedral; 1830–36). On the park's northwest is a colourful 24-hour **flower market**. The area immediately west of the Arcul de Triumf on Blvd Ștefan cel Mare is dominated by the **Guvernul** (Government House), where cabinet meets. The parliament convenes in the **Parlamentul** (Blvd Ștefan cel Mare 123).

Grădina Publică Ștefan cel Mare și Sfînt (Ștefan the Great and the Saint Public Garden) occupies the western flank of Blvd Ștefan cel Mare. The entrance is guarded by a **statue** of Ștefan himself. This medieval prince is Moldova's greatest hero, bearing testimony to the country's pre-Soviet roots.

From the Arcul de Triumf, bear southwest along Str Pușkin. The **Muzeul Național de Arte Plastice** (National Art Museum; ☎ 241 730; admission $0.75; open 9am-5pm Tues-Sun) is on the corner of Str 31 August. The **Muzeul Național de Istorie a Moldavei** (National History Museum of Moldova; ☎ 244 325; Str 31 August 121a; admission $0.75; open 10am-6pm Tues-Sun) is not far away. A **statue** of Lupoaica Romei (the wolf of Rome) and the abandoned children, Romulus and Remus, stands in front of the museum.

Further along Str Pușkin is **Universitatea Națională din Moldova** (National University of Moldova; ☎ 577 422; Str Mateevici 6). Outside the main entrance is the 1882 **Castelul de apă** (water tower), which is home to the small **Muzeul orașului** (Museum of the City; ☎ 226 037; admission $0.10; open 10am-4pm Mon-Fri). While the museum is uninspiring, climb to the top of the tower and you will be rewarded with a panoramic view of Chișinău.

Walk northwest along Str A Mateevici, then take a turn to the right down Str Sfatul Țării to visit the excellent exhibits at the **Muzeul Național de Etnografie și Istorie Naturală** (National Natural History & Ethnographic Museum; ☎ 244 002; w www.muzee .dnt.md; Str M Kogălniceanu 82; admission

MOLDOVA

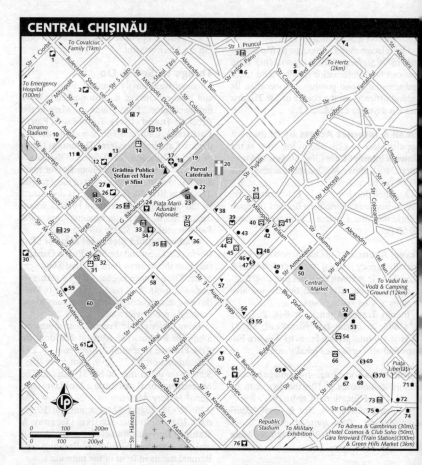

CENTRAL CHIŞINĂU

$0.75; open 10am-6pm Tues-Sun). The highlights include a life-size reconstruction of a mammal skeleton, which was discovered in the Rezine region in 1966.

The extensive **Muzeul de Arheologie şi Etnografie** *(Archaeology & Ethnographic Museum; ☎ 222 574; Str Mitropolit G Bănulescu Bodoni 35; admission $0.10; open 10am-1pm & 2pm-6pm Tues-Sat)* displays reconstructions of traditional houses from Moldova's different regions and has a colourful exhibition of traditional handwoven rugs, carpets and wall hangings.

North of the city centre is the **Muzeul Puşkin** *(Puskin Museum; ☎ 214 138; cnr Str Anton Pann & Str I Pruncul; admission $0.75; open 10am-6pm Tues-Sun),* which is housed in a cottage where Russian poet Alexander Pushkin (1799–1837) spent an exiled three months in the 1820s.

Places to Stay

Camping The closest **camping ground** *(open summer)* is 12km northeast of Chişinău in Vadul lui Vodă forest. It is a popular weekend spot for locals. Take bus No 31 from Autogară Chişinău.

The **Covalciuc Family** *(☎ 758 429; e acov alciuc@yahoo.com; St Primiaverii 4; singles/ doubles $20/30),* the unsuspecting family with whom Tony Hawks stayed while he researched *Playing the Moldovans at Tennis,* has private rooms with self-catering facilities. This charming family will truly make you feel at home and with a little coaxing will give you the low-down on Tony's Moldovan exploits.

CENTRAL CHIŞINĂU

PLACES TO STAY
5 Hotel Turist
6 Hotel Zarea
11 Hotel Dacia
13 Hotel Moldova Jolly Alon
27 Hotel Codru
53 Hotel Meridian
71 Hotel Naţional;
   Moldova Tur
74 Hotel Chişinău

PLACES TO EAT
4 Sănătate
10 Belde Company
36 Cantină
38 McDonald's;
   Univers Internet Café
46 Green Hills Nistru Café
56 Cactus Café & Bar
57 La Brunel
58 La Taifas
62 El Paso
63 Oraşul Vechi; Cafenea &
   Sala Estivala

OTHER
1 Russian Embassy
2 Hungarian Embassy
3 Muzeul Puşkin
7 Preşedinţia Republicii
   Moldova
8 Parlamentul (Parliament
   House)
9 Alliance Française
12 German Embassy

14 Cinema Patria; Pizza Pazza
15 Teatrul Naţional Operă şi
   Balet
16 Statue of Ştefan cel Mare
17 Medicor Farm
18 Cartea Academica;
   Deutscher Lesesaal
19 24-Hour Flower Market
20 Catedrala Naşterea Domnului
21 Teatrul Dramatic Rus A
   Cehov
22 Arcul de Triumf
23 Guvernul
   (Government House)
24 Black Elephant: The
   Underground Club; Internet
25 Muzeul de Arheologie şi
   Etnografie
26 Bulgarian Embassy
28 Palatul Republicii
29 Muzeul Naţional de
   Etnografie şi Istorie Naturală
30 US Embassy
31 Cinema Club
32 E Internet Café
33 Muzeul Naţional de Istorie a
   Moldavei
34 Studio 01
35 Muzeul Naţional de Arte
   Plastice; Pani Pit - Museum
   Café
37 Palatul Naţional
39 Oficiul Poştal
40 Teatrul Municipal Satiricus
41 Filarmonica Naţional

42 Educational Centre
43 Nr.1 Supermarket
44 Sala cu Orgă (Organ Hall)
45 Teatrul Naţional Mihai
   Eminescu
47 Victoria Bank
48 Ialoveni Sherry Factory Shop
   & Bar
49 Magazinul de Firm Cricova
50 Main Entrance to Market
51 Autogara Chişinău (Central
   Bus Station)
52 Main Entrance to Market
54 Moldtelecom
55 Moldindconbank
59 Castelul de apă (Water
   Tower); Muzeul oraşului
   (Museum of the City)
60 Universitatea Naţională din
   Moldova
61 Turkish Embassy
64 Dublin Bar & Restaurant
65 Incom Travel Agency
66 Moldtelecom
67 Tarom Airlines
68 Moldavian Airlines
69 Banca de Export Import a
   Moldovei
70 24-Hour Currency Exchange
72 Air Moldova;
   Voiaj Travel Agency
73 Exhibition Hall
75 Transaero
76 University Cultural House;
   Disco

Private Rooms The best bet for budget travellers is **Adresa** (☎ 544 392, fax 272 096; Blvd Negruzzi 1; 1–2-person apartments from $15 per night). It rents out clean apartments and rooms in and around the city centre. You must pay in advance and discounts are available for long-term stays.

Hotels – Budget Opposite the city's bus station is the surprisingly clean **Hotel Meridian** (☎ 270 620; e meridian@moldovacc .md; Str Tighina 42; singles/doubles with shared bathroom $11/15, with TV & shower $13/19). The entrance is through the Foto Express kiosk.

Hotel Zarea (☎ 227 625; Str Anton Pann 4; singles/doubles with shared bathroom $11/24) has modest rooms, a bar and a billiard club to while away the hours.

Hotel Chişinău (☎ 578 506, fax 578 510; Blvd Negruzzi 7; singles/doubles with bathroom $15/24) is quite an attractive hotel with

pleasant rooms. Its restaurant is reputed for its good traditional Moldovan cuisine.

Hotels – Mid-Range Overlooking the giant Soviet memorial to communist youth, **Hotel Turist** (☎ 229 512/639; Blvd Renaşterii 13a; doubles $35, suite $72) has reasonable rooms with private shower (hot water is unreliable).

Hotel Naţional (☎ 540 305, fax 540 492; Blvd Ştefan cel Mare 2; singles/doubles $40/43) is a towering 17-storey hotel run by Moldova Tur. The hotel has a café, restaurant and casino.

Hotels – Top End Just 250m from the train station, **Hotel Cosmos** (☎ 572 724, fax 542 747; w www.hotel-cosmos.com; Piaţa Negruzzi 2; unrenovated singles/doubles $48/50, renovated singles/doubles $81/100, 2-/3-room apartments $125/195) is an unsightly concrete block. Its renovated rooms have all mod cons, but are pricey – unrenovated rooms

MOLDOVA

are better value. There is a 24-hour bar and a handy left-luggage room.

The **Hotel Codru** (☎ 225 506, fax 237 948; e reservation@codru.dnt.md; Str 31 August 127; singles/doubles $80/120) is quite dark and gloomy, but it is possible to negotiate a cheaper rate for long stays.

The large three-star **Hotel Dacia** (☎ 232 251, fax 234 647; w www.hotel-dacia.com; Str 31 August 135; standard singles/doubles $100/130, business singles/doubles $120/155) is close to parliament in the heart of the city's 'embassy land'.

Next to the German embassy, **Hotel Moldova Jolly Alon** (☎ 232 875/896, fax 232 870; e reservation@ja.moldline.net; Str Maria Cibotari 37; singles/doubles $140/160, junior/deluxe/executive suites $180/250/295) has been considered Chişinău's swankiest hotel for a long time. Perks of staying here include an indoor swimming pool, a sauna and a casino.

Places to Eat

Restaurants The best place to sample authentic Moldovan cuisine is **La Taifas** (☎ 227 692/693; Str Bucureşti 67; meals $1.50-6). Here you can watch as bread is cooked in the old-fashioned way in a wood-fired oven at the back of the restaurant while you're serenaded by a panpipe player. The menu includes the delicious *ciulama* (chicken in wine sauce) with *mămăligă* (Romanian polenta).

Sănătate (☎ 244 116; Blvd Renaşterii 24; meals $1.50-6), once Chişinău's most popular restaurant, still serves excellent Moldovan cuisine, including a huge variety of *mămăligă* dishes. On weekends Moldovan folk singers perform on the adjoining terrace bar.

La Bunel (☎ 222 219; Str Mihai Eminescu 50; sandwiches $0.55-2, meals $2.25-5), meaning 'at Grandpa's', is a good-value Jewish restaurant. In summertime you can enjoy speciality dishes such as *Friptura evereiască* (Jewish stew) sitting under a sea of grape vines in the outside courtyard.

Belde Company (☎ 233 451; Str Lazo 139; meals $2-6), close to the Dinamo Stadium, serves tasty Turkish delights like the iskender kebab ($3) and baklava ($1).

Gambrinus (☎ 504 067; Blvd Negruzzi 4/2; meals $2-7), next to the Seiga store, is a modern restaurant serving Moldovan and international dishes. It has a well-stocked bar and a bright outside terrace.

Three of the city's coolest restaurants – in decor and cuisine – are on Str Armenească. **Cactus Café** (☎ 504 094, 224 257; cnr Str 31 August & Str Armenească; salads $1.65-5.60, meals $3-6) is kitted out 'Wild West' style with swinging saloon doors and chairs suspended from the ceiling. Its mind-boggling menu includes tasty dishes such as spicy pork with chicken liver and cheese sauce ($2.90).

El Paso (☎ 504 100; Str Armenească 10; meals $3-6) serves excellent Mexican cuisine. Don't miss the fried pork with its chocolate-almond sauce! Book in advance to guarantee a table – especially under the arches on the candlelit terrace.

The third place in the line is the elegant **Oraşul Vechi** (Old City; ☎ 225 063, 262 035; Str Armenească 24). Don't be intimidated by the overdressed doormen – the prices are reasonable and the mix of classical and traditional folk music played is top-notch. Adjoining the restaurant is the cheaper and less exclusive **Oraşul Vechi Cafenea** and the **Sala Estivala** (Summer Hall).

Cafés When the sun shines, outdoor cafés sprout like mushrooms. The most popular spot is the terrace outside the Teatrul Naţional Operă şi Ballet.

Pizza Pazza (☎ 232 320; Blvd Ştefan cel Mare 103; small pizzas $1.80-2.95, large $2.25-3.20), behind Cinema Patria, is a funky new café-restaurant with a great outdoor terrace overlooking the park.

Pani Pit – Museum Café (☎ 240 127; Str 31 August; snacks $1.15-3.70, meals $3.35-8) is the perfect place to relax after browsing in the adjoining Muzeul Naţional de Arte Plastice. Italian and Moldovan dishes are served, including *Brizoli Moldova* (veal with garlic) for $2.60.

Green Hills Nistru Café (☎ 226 274; Blvd Ştefan cel Mare 77; pizzas $1.80-3.40, pasta $2.15-4.10, mains $2.70-9), next to the Victoria Bank, has an extensive menu of pizzas, salads, pancakes and coffee.

Fast Food The ever-popular **McDonald's** has three outlets in Chişinău: near to the Kodak Express outlet at Blvd Ştefan cel Mare 134–36, north of the city centre at Str Alco Russo plaza 2 and south of the centre at Blvd Dacia 21.

A more humble experience is a meal in one of the city's Soviet-style canteens. The best of the bunch is the cheap and cheerful **Cantină** *(Str Puşkin; meals less than $1.50)* opposite the Palatul Naţional.

Self-Catering The **central market** *(piaţa centrală; open 7am-5pm daily)* is well worth a visit for its glorious choice of fresh food.

The most central supermarket is **Nr. 1** *(Blvd Ştefan cel Mare; open 9am-10pm daily)*. Also in the centre is **Fidesco** *(Blvd Ştefan cel Mare; open 24hr)*, next to Hotel Naţional.

Green Hills Market *(Blvd Decebal 139; open 9am-9pm Mon-Sat, 9am-8pm Sun)*, southeast of the centre, sells an excellent range of locally produced wines, champagnes and cognacs.

Entertainment

Posters listing 'what's on' are displayed on boards outside the city's various theatres.

Bars & Discos A must is the rustic drinking hole in the basement of **Ialoveni** *(cnr Blvd Ştefan cel Mare & Str Hânceşti)*, which is a sherry factory shop. Swill a tumbler of Moldovan sherry with drunken locals for less than $0.20. Staff speak no English but given they only serve one thing it is easy to make yourself understood!

Black Elephant: The Underground Club *(☎ 234 715; Str 31 August 78a)* is the highlight of Chişinău's nightlife. Its network of blacked-out, tunnelled rooms play host to jazz nights, live bands and discos. The club also has an Internet café and billiard tables.

Dublin *(Str Bulgară 27)* is an expensive but popular Irish-inspired bar-restaurant. A pint of Guinness at this place will set you back around $3.30.

Studio 01 *(☎ 8292 53042; Str 31 August)*, Chişinău's coolest disco, is packed every weekend – if you want a table you'll have to book ahead ($11).

Club Soho *(☎ 275 800; Blvd D.Cantemir; admission $3)* is on the ground floor of the Grand Hall. It is an energetic but expensive disco where a table costs a staggering $14.85.

Theatres Chişinău hosts numerous theatres, although performances are in Russian and Romanian only.

Plays are staged at the **Teatrul Municipal Satiricus** *(Municipal Satirical Theatre; ☎ 224 034; cnr Str Mitropolit Varlaam & Str Mihai Eminescu)* and the **Teatrul Dramatic Rus A**

Cehov *(Chekhov Russian Dramatic Theatre; ☎ 223 362; cnr Str Mitropolit Varlaam & Str Pircaleb)*, sited where Chişinău's choral synagogue was until WWII.

Teatrul Naţional Mihai Eminescu *(Mihai Eminescu National Theatre; ☎ 221 177; Blvd Ştefan cel Mare 79; box office open 10am-1pm & 3pm-6pm daily)* stages contemporary Romanian productions.

Teatrul Naţional Operă şi Balet *(National Theatre of Opera & Ballet; ☎ 245 104; Blvd Ştefan cel Mare; box office open 10am-2pm & 5pm-7pm daily)* is home to the Moldovan national opera and ballet company.

Palatul Naţional *(National Palace; Str Puşkin 24; box office open 11am-5pm daily)* hosts various cabarets, musicals and local theatre group productions.

Classical Music Classical concerts and organ recitals are held at the **Sala cu Orgă** *(Organ Hall; ☎ 228 222; Blvd Ştefan cel Mare 79)* next to the Teatrul Naţional Mihai Eminescu. Tickets are sold at the box office in the Eminescu theatre.

Filarmonica Naţional *(National Philharmonic; ☎ 224 016; Str Mitropolit Varlaam 78)* holds regular concerts.

Cinemas The latest Hollywood blockbuster movies, although dubbed in Russian, are screened at **Cinema Patria** *(☎ 232 905; Blvd Ştefan cel Mare)*. Tickets cost between $0.75 and $3.75.

Cinema Club *(☎ 212 730; Str Mitropolit G Bănulescu Bodoni 8/1)* is Chişinău's only English-language cinema. Tickets for its not-so-recent movies cost between $0.40 and $1.50. Its terrace bar is a popular watering spot for local students.

Shopping

Do not leave Chişinău without visiting the **Magazinul de Firm Cricova** *(☎ 222 775; Blvd Ştefan cel Mare; open 10am-7pm daily)*, the commercial outlet for the Cricova wine factory. **Ialoveni** sherry factory outlet is close by (see Entertainment).

Local artists and craftspeople sell their wares in the small plaza next to the Teatrul Naţional Mihai Eminescu.

Getting There & Away

Air The Chişinău **areoport** *(airport; ☎ 525 412)*, 14.5km southeast of the centre, only

MOLDOVA

handles international flights. Airline offices selling tickets include:

Air Moldova (☎ 546 464, 274 009) Blvd Negruzzi 8
Air Moldova International (☎ 529 791, fax 526 414; e info@ami.md) Chişinău airport
Moldavian Airlines (☎/fax 525 064, ☎ 529 365) Chişinău airport; (☎ 549 339/340, fax 549 341) Blvd Ştefan cel Mare 3
Tarom (☎ 542 154) Blvd Ştefan cel Mare 3 (entrance on Str Ismail)
Transaero (☎ 525 413) Chişinău airport; (☎ 542 454, fax 542 461) Str Ciuflea

Train From **Gara feroviară** (☎ 252 733; Aleea Gării) there are two local trains daily to Ungheni (2½ hours, 108km) on the Moldova-Romania border and to Odesa (4½ hours, 191km) that stop at Tighina (Bendery) and Tiraspol. International trains include a daily service to Bucharest (14 hours, 528km) and a thrice daily service to Moscow (20 hours, 1562km) passing through Kyiv.

Tickets for international trains are sold at the 2nd-floor ticket office, signposted 'Casă Internationale'. The ticket hall for local trains is on the 1st floor.

Bus Most buses within Moldova depart from the **Autogară Chişinău** (☎ 542 185; Str Mitropolit Varlaam), behind the central market. Local services include one every hour to Tiraspol ($1.30, 70km) via Tighina ($1.15); and one every half-hour to Orhei ($0.50, 45km) and Orheiul Vechi ($0.60, 50km). There are also daily services across the border to Romania, including one to Braşov ($10, 8am), Bucharest ($11.20, 6pm) and Constanţia ($9.25, 7.30am) and six to Iaşi ($3.50).

Bus services to south, including to Comrat, use **Autogară Sud-Vest** (☎ 542 185, 723 983; cnr Str Şoseaua Hânceşti & Str Spicului), 2km from the city centre.

Buses to Turkey depart from the train station. **EKIM Tur** (☎ 545 498; Aleea Gării) runs a weekly service to İstanbul ($50, departs 5pm Monday). **Essel** (☎ 276 854, fax 276 912; Aleea Gării) also has a weekly bus to İstanbul ($50, departs 6pm Monday).

Getting Around
To/From the Airport Bus No 65 departs every 30 minutes between 5am and 10pm from the central bus station to the airport. Microbus No 165 departs every 20 minutes

from Str Ismail, near the corner of Blvd Ştefan cel Mare ($0.20).

Bus & Trolleybus Bus No 45 (and microbus No 145) runs from the central bus station to the southwestern bus station. Bus No 1 goes from the train station to Blvd Ştefan cel Mare.

Trolleybus Nos 1, 4, 5, 8, 18 and 22 go to the train station from the city centre. Bus Nos 2, 10 and 16 go to Autogară Sud-vest. Tickets cost $0.08 for buses and $0.05 for trolleybuses and can be purchased at kiosks or directly from the driver.

Most bus routes in town and to many outlying villages are served by nippy microbuses. These small buses are faster and more expensive than regular buses ($0.15 per trip, pay the driver). Route numbers are displayed on the front and side windows.

Car & Motorcycle The only car-rental company in Chişinău is **Hertz** (☎/fax 491 365; e hertz@hertz.mldnet.com; Str Miron Costin), 2km north of the centre in Rîşcani. It also has a **booth** (☎ 526 379) at the airport. A Renault Clio hatchback costs $13 per day plus $0.07 per kilometre.

Taxi The main taxi stand is in front of Hotel Naţional. Drivers here will rip you off. Calling a **taxi** (☎ 746 565, or dial ☎ 705, 706 or 707) is cheaper. The official rate is $0.20 per kilometre.

Around Chişinău

CRICOVA
The village of Cricova, 15km north of Chişinău, boasts an underground wine 'town'. The vast cellars are accessed by a labyrinth of underground streets, well-named Str Pinot, Str Cabernet etc, and stretch over 60km. More than one million bottles of fine white wines are stored in the cellars at a constant 12°C. In Soviet times, Cricova wines and champagnes were considered among the top wines of the USSR. Its sparkling white wine was sold under the label 'Soviet Champagne'. Today, demand for its dry white sauvignon, muscadet and sweeter muscats remains high.

The entrance to the **wine factory** (☎ 2-444 035, fax 2-573 725; w www.cricova-wine .com; Str Ungureanu 1) is uphill along Str 31 August from the bus station, then right.

Tours can be arranged directly through the factory but must be booked in advance (minimum of five people, $27 per person). Travel agencies in Chişinău organise tours including transport to and from Chişinău and wine tasting, as well as souvenir bottles of wine and champagne.

Buy Cricova wine cheaply at the **factory outlet shop** *(open 9am-10pm daily)*, opposite the main bus stop in the centre of the village.

Bus No 2 from Str Hânceşti in Chişinău runs every 15 minutes to Cricova ($0.15).

COJUŞNA

Cricova's competitors operate 25km northwest of Chişinău in the village of Cojuşna. Mainstays include 13 different red and white table wines, including cabernet, sauvignon and Riesling. Cojuşna also produces vodka for Moldova's die-hards as well as heavier port wines.

Cojuşna is geared for tourists. Take in the cellars and various wine-tasting halls decked out in different themes. The winery has no land, having reaped the harvests of smaller wineries for the past 30 years. You can buy wines from the **Cojuşna shop** on the complex.

Phone the **Fabrica de Vinuri Cojuşna** *(Cojuşna Wine Factory;* ☎ *2-715 329, 715 312; open 8am-6pm Mon-Fri)* in advance to book a tour ($24 per person). Tours include a two-hour tasting session of six collection wines.

In Chişinău, don't let travel agencies con you into paying for an expensive tour to Cojuşna. Expensive perks include transport to Cojuşna from Chişinău, plus souvenir bottles of wine.

Bus No 2 runs every 15 minutes from Str Hânceşti (Str Vasile Alecsandri) in Chişinău to Cricova. Get off at the Cojuşna stop. Ignore the turning on the left marked Cojuşna and walk or hitch the remaining 2km along the main road to the winery entrance, marked by a tall, totem-pole-style pillar.

ORHEI

☎ 235 • pop 37,500

The modern town of Orhei, not to be confused with Orheiul Vechi (Old Orhei), is 45km north of Chişinău. It is Moldova's sixth-largest city and was settled on the ruins of 14th-century Orheiul Vechi. Almost decimated during WWII, Orhei has little to offer tourists but serves as a good stepping stone if you want to visit Orheiul Vechi.

The **telephone office** *(Str Vasile Mahu 121)* is close to the former Catholic church. The **central post office** *(Str Vasile Mahu 129)* is a few doors down. You can change money at the **Real Currency Exchange** *(Str Vasile Lupu 33)*.

Things to See

A **statue of Vasile Lupu**, reigning prince of Moldavia (r. 1634–53), stands majestically at the entrance to the city in front of the **Biserica Sfântu Dimitru** (St Dimitru's Church), built in 1637. The main street, Blvd Ştefan cel Mare, is dominated by **Biserica Sfântu Nicolae** (St Nicholas' Church).

Behind the Catholic church is a **monument** to the soldiers killed during the 1992 Moldovan-Transdniestran conflict in Tighina (Bendery) and Dubăsari.

Exhibits at the excellent **Muzeul de Istorie şi Etnografie** *(History & Ethnographic Museum; Str Renaşterii Naţionale 23; admission $0.10; open 9am-5pm Tues-Sun)* trace the city's history down from Vasile Lupu's reign through to Moldova's declaration of independence on 31 August 1989.

Places to Stay & Eat

Hotel Codru *(☎ 24 821; Str Vasile Lupu 36; basic singles/doubles $3.50/5.50)* has basic, unheated rooms with shared bathroom and no hot water. Cold water is available only from 6am to 9am and 7pm to 9pm. Its **restaurant** is next door.

Getting There & Away

Daily buses depart every half-hour from Chişinău to Orhei ($0.50, two hours). From Orhei there is one daily bus at 12.45pm to Orheiul Vechi.

ORHEIUL VECHI

Ten kilometres southeast of Orhei is Orheiul Vechi ('Old Orhei'; usually marked on maps as Trebujeni). Ştefan cel Mare built a fortress here in the 14th century but it was later destroyed by Tatars.

The superb **Complexul Muzeistic Orheiul Vechi** *(Orheiul Vechi Monastery;* ☎ *235-34 242; admission $0.20; open 9am-5pm Tues-Sun)*, carved into a cliff in this wild, rocky, remote spot, is what draws most visitors here. The **Mănăstire în Peşteră** (Cave Monastery), inside a limestone cliff overlooking the Răut River, was dug by Orthodox monks in the

13th century. It remained inhabited until the 18th century, and in 1996 a handful of monks returned to this unique place of worship and are slowly restoring it to its original use.

The central hall of the underground monastery is open to visitors. This served as the main church in the 13th century. Until the 17th century, the monks slept in stone bunks *(keilies)* in an adjacent cave. An earthquake in the 17th century forced them to retreat from these stone cells to smaller caves farther south along the cliff.

In the 18th century the cave-church was taken over by villagers from neighbouring Butceni. In 1905 they built a church above ground dedicated to the Ascension of St Mary. The church was shut down by the Soviets in 1944 and remained abandoned throughout the communist regime. Services resumed in 1996.

A well-presented **village museum** is also included in the monastery complex. The ethnographic exhibits include a traditional 14th-century Moldovan house.

The 1½-hour guided tour is in Moldovan or Russian only. The ticket office is at the foot of the cliff. Shorts are forbidden and women must cover their heads.

Getting There & Away

Daily buses depart every 30 minutes from Chişinău for Orheiul Vechi ($0.60). From Orhei, a bus departs daily for Trebujeni at 12.45pm. Ask to be dropped off by the signposted entrance to the complex. There is a daily afternoon bus that returns to Orhei from Orheiul Vechi.

A taxi from Orhei to Orheiul Vechi costs around $6.

SOROCA

Soroca fortress was part of a medieval chain of military fortresses built by Moldavian princes between the 14th and 16th centuries to defend Moldavia's boundaries. Only its ruins remain.

Strategically placed at (then) Moldavia's most northeastern tip on the banks of the Dniestr River, Soroca was one of the key military strongholds. The ruins today are from a fortress built by Petru Rareş (1527–38) on the site of an older one.

Moldova Tur in Chişinău arranges tours to the fortress (see Information under Chişinău earlier this chapter).

Gagauzia

Gagauzia (Gagauz Yeri) is a self-governed republic covering 3000 sq km in southern Moldova. It has its own legislature, which is autonomous in regional affairs. On a national level, Gagauzia (population 169,300) is represented by the assembly's elected *başkan* (head), who is a member of the Gagauz Halkı political party and holds a safe seat in the Moldovan parliament.

Comrat is Gagauzia's capital. The republic is divided into three districts – Ceadăr-Linga, Comrat and Vulcăneşti. Wedged between these last two is the predominantly Bulgarian-populated district of Taraclia, which is not part of Gagauzia. Gagauz territory is further broken up by three Bulgarian villages in Ceadăr-Linga and a predominantly Moldovan village in Comrat district, all of which are part of 'mainland' Moldova too.

The Gagauz are a Turkic-speaking, Christian ethnic minority whose Muslim antecedents fled the Russo-Turkish wars during the 18th century. They were permitted to settle in the region in exchange for their conversion to Christianity. The language is a dialect of Turkish, with vocabulary influenced by Russian Orthodoxy as opposed to Islamic influences that are inherent in Turkish. Unlike Moldovans, Gagauz lay no claim to any Latin roots or influences, but rather look to Turkey for cultural inspiration and heritage.

The republic has its own flag, its own police force, its own weekly journals, and its own university partly funded by the Turkish government. Students are taught in Gagauzi, Moldovan and Russian – the official languages of the republic.

Gagauz autonomy was officially recognised by the Moldovan government in December 1994. Unlike the more militant separatists in Transdniestr, the Gagauz forfeited independence in preference for large-scale autonomy. Theirs is a predominantly agricultural region with little industry to sustain an independent economy.

COMRAT

☎ 238 • pop 32,000

Gagauzia's capital, 92km south of Chişinău, is no more than a dusty, provincial town. In 1990 it was the scene of clashes between Gagauz nationalists and Moldovan armed forces, pre-empted by calls from local leaders for the Moldovan government to hold a referendum on the issue of Gagauz sovereignty.

Most street signs are in Russian; some older ones are in Gagauzi but in the Cyrillic script. Since 1989, Gagauzi, alongside Moldovan, has used the Latin alphabet.

Orientation & Information
From the bus station, walk south along the main street, ul Pobedy, past the market to ploshchad Pobedy (Victory Square). St John's Church stands on the western side of the square, behind which lies the central park. Prospekt Lenina runs parallel to ul Pobedy, west of the park.

Change money at the **Moldova Agrobank** *(ul Pobedy 52; open 8am-1pm Mon-Fri)*. A small currency exchange is inside the entrance to the market. The **post office** *(ul Pobedy 55; open 8am-6pm Mon-Fri, 8am-5pm Sat)* is next to the bank.

Things to See
Visit the regional **başkani** *(assembly; prospekt Lenina)*. A Gagauzi flag, officially adopted in 1995, and a Moldovan flag fly from the roof.

Next to the assembly is the **Gagauz Culture House**, in front of which stands a statue of Lenin. West of prospekt Lenina is the **Komrat Devlet Üniversitesi** *(Gagauz University; ul Galatsăna 17)*, founded in 1990, the world's only Gagauz university.

Places to Stay & Eat
Hotel Medelean *(☎ 22 572; ul Pobedy 117; singles/doubles $9/13)*, on the eastern side of ploshchad Pobedy, is a fairly modern hotel with a good bar.

Getting There & Away
There are five daily return buses between Chişinău and Comrat ($0.95). From Comrat there are two buses each day via Tighina to Tiraspol, and one only as far as Tighina.

Transdniestr

The self-declared republic of Transdniestr (population 666,800) incorporates the narrow strip of land on the eastern bank of the Nistru River. A predominantly Russian-populated region, it declared independence from Moldova in 1991, sparking off a bloody civil war. An independent state in all but name, it has its own currency, police force and army, and its own (unofficial) borders, which are controlled by Transdniestran border guards.

Its two main towns are Tiraspol, the capital, and Tighina. Tighina is a security zone where the peacekeeping forces are headquartered. The Transdniestran and Russian armies are based in Tiraspol. Westerners can freely travel in the region; Russian is the main language, which can make getting around tough. The police and military in Tighina carry out frequent patrols to insure public safety at night.

Despite all this, visiting Transdniestr provides visitors with a unique opportunity to witness the harsh realities of one of the world's few surviving Soviet bastions.

Government & Politics
Igor Smirnov was elected president of Transdniestr in 1991 after the region's declaration of independence four months previously. In 1994 the Moldovan parliament ratified a new constitution providing substantial autonomy to Transdniestr in regional affairs.

Two main political organisations dominate the Transdniestran parliament and district administrations. The Working Transdniestr (WTD) emerged from the United Council of Workers' Collectives (OSTK) political party, which was responsible for organising the armed uprising against Chişinău in 1992. The Bloc of Left Wing Forces (BLWF) backs a centrally planned economy and revival of the USSR, and is opposed to all market reforms.

In the most recent presidential elections in December 2001 Smirnov was overwhelmingly returned to power, gaining over 80% of the vote. His nearest opponent, Tom Zenovich, the former head of the administration of the city of Tighina, received only 7% of the vote.

Neither Smirnov's presidency nor the Transdniestran parliament is recognised by the Moldovan government.

Economy
As a self-declared republic, Transdniestr's economy is disastrous, despite a third of Moldova's total potential industrial output being concentrated in Tiraspol. When the Russian economy collapsed, so did Transdniestr's industrial production. Inflation is rampant and the local currency is next to worthless. For the average person, economic conditions are abysmal – wages are low and poverty is rife.

Population & People

Two-thirds of Transdniestr's population is elderly and impoverished and yearns for a return to the Soviet Union, under which they had a better quality of life. Russians make up 28.8% of the population, Moldovans 33.8% and Ukrainians 28.8%.

Language

The official state languages in Transdniestr are Russian, Moldovan and Ukrainian. Students in schools and universities are taught in Russian, and the local government and most official institutions operate almost solely in Russian. All street signs are written in Russian, Moldovan in the Cyrillic alphabet and sometimes Ukrainian.

Money

The only legal tender is the Transdniestran rouble (NH). Officially introduced in 1994, it quickly dissolved into an oblivion of zeros. To keep up with inflation, monetary reforms introduced in January 2001 slashed six zeros from the currency, with a new NH1 banknote worth one million roubles in old money. There are now five, 10, 20, 25, 50 and 100 rouble banknotes. One rouble equals 100 kopecks.

Black Market Avoid changing money on the black market, even though this is the standard practice of locals and expats alike. If you are caught, you run the risk of being fined or even imprisoned.

Exchange Rates At the time of publication, the exchange rates were:

country	unit		rouble
European Union	€1	=	NH5.55
Moldova	10 Lei	=	NH4.65
Russia	R10	=	NH1.98
UK	UK£1	=	NH9.01
Ukraine	1 hv	=	NH1.13
USA	US$1	=	NH6.28

Post

Transdniestran stamps featuring local hero General Suvorov can only be used for letters sent within the Transdniestran republic and are not recognised anywhere else. For letters to Moldova, Romania and the West, you have to use Moldovan stamps (available here but less conveniently than in Moldova).

Media

The predominantly Russian Transdniestran TV is broadcast in the republic between 9am and midnight. Transdniestran Radio is on air during the same hours.

The two local newspapers, the *Transdniestr* and *N Pravda*, are in Russian.

TIRASPOL

☎ 233 • pop 194,000

Tiraspol, the second-largest city in Moldova, is 70km east of Chişinău. The city was founded in 1792 following Russian domination of the region. In 1929, Tiraspol was made the capital of the Moldovan Autonomous Soviet Socialist Republic. The MASSR capital was previously located in Balta in present-day Ukraine. Today Tiraspol is the capital of Transdniestr republic.

Registering

All foreign visitors to Tiraspol (but not Tighina) are required to register with the **Tiraspol Militia Passport office** (☎ 34 169; ul Rosa Luxembourg 2). You have to state which hotel you are staying at, how many nights you are intending to stay and the purpose of your visit.

If you intend staying in Tiraspol longer than three hours, you also have to register with **OVIR** (Otdel Viz i Registratsii, or Department of Visas & Registration; ☎ 61 200; pereulok Rayevskaya 10). If you fail to do so, getting out of Transdniestr could be a costly exercise.

Orientation & Information

The train and bus stations are next to each other at the end of ul Lenina. Exit the train station and walk up ul Lenina, past Kirov Park, to ul 25 Oktober (the main street).

Send your mail from the **post office** (ul Lenina; open 8am-7pm Mon-Fri). International calls can be booked at the **central telephone centre** (ul 25 Oktober; open 7am-8.30pm daily). Exchange money next door at **Prisbank** (ul 25 Oktober; open 8am-1pm & 2pm-4.30pm Mon-Fri).

Note that from 1 April to 30 October there is no heating or hot water in Tiraspol.

Things to See

Tiraspol has no history museum but the illustrated panels outside the city administration building, the **House of Soviets** (Dom Sovetov), trace the city's history from 1792, when

A traditional Estonian home in Pärnu

Raekoja plats and its café scene, Tallinn, Estonia

Lake Balaton in Hungary is one of Europe's largest freshwater lakes and a favourite for yachting

The old section of Buda with Matthias Church and Fishermen's Bastion, across the Danube, Budapest

Outdoor swimmers in the warm waters of Széchenyi Baths in City Park, Budapest

Versailles-style Esterhazý Palace, Fertőd, Hungary

Snow clings to the rooftops of Old Rīga, Latvia

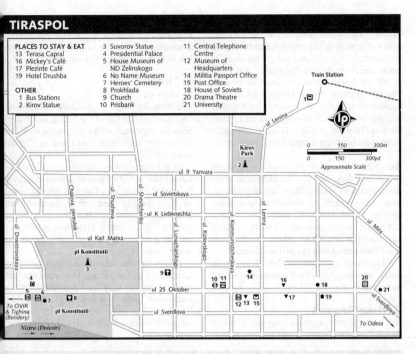

TIRASPOL

PLACES TO STAY & EAT
13 Terasa Capral
16 Mickey's Café
17 Plezinte Café
19 Hotel Drushba

OTHER
1 Bus Stations
2 Kirov Statue

3 Suvorov Statue
4 Presidential Palace
5 House Museum of
 ND Zelinskogo
6 No Name Museum
7 Heroes' Cemetery
8 Prokhlada
9 Church
10 Prisbank

11 Central Telephone
 Centre
12 Museum of
 Headquarters
14 Militia Passport Office
15 Post Office
18 House of Soviets
20 Drama Theatre
21 University

it became part of the Russian empire, through to the 1990s.

A **statue of Lenin** is in front of the House of Soviets. Inside the building is a **memorial** to those who died in the 1992 military conflict. Close to the **Museum of Headquarters** (☎ 35 382; ul Kommunisticheskaya 34; admission $0.15; open 9am-5pm Mon-Sat).

On ul 25 Oktober stands a Soviet armoured **tank** from which the Transdniestran flag flies today. Behind is the **Tomb of the Unknown Soldier**, flanked by an eternal flame in memory of those who died on 3 March 1992 in the first outbreak of fighting. The inscription in Russian reads 'You don't have a name but your deeds are eternal'.

The **house museum** (ul 25 Oktober 42; open 9am-5pm Mon-Sat) of Nikolai Dimitriovich Zelinskogo (1866–1953), the poet who founded the first Soviet school of chemistry, is opposite the **Presidential Palace**, from where Igor Smirnov rules his self-proclaimed republic.

Nearby is a small **no name museum** (ul 25 Oktober 46; admission $0.15; open 9am-5pm Mon-Sat) containing memorabilia from the Trandneistran war.

In front of the **university** (ul Sverdlova), dating from 1930, is a **statue of Chmelnistki**.

Places to Stay & Eat
Hotel Drushba (☎ 34 266; ul 25 Oktober 118; doubles $30), close to the House of Soviets, is the best place to stay in Transdniestr. The rooms have private bath, TV and fridge. Breakfast is not included.

Plezinte Café (ul 25 Oktober 116; snacks $0.20-1.30) serves a small selection of hot snacks, including placinta (pies) and mămăligă. Close by is **Mickey's Café** (☎ 36 291; ul 25 Oktober; burgers $0.70-1.10; pizzas $1.75-2.55), Transdniestr's version of McDonald's. For a quick drink try the **Terasa Capral** (ul 25 Oktober), easily identifiable by its huge Caribbean-style Sprite and Coke umbrellas outside.

Entertainment
Prokhlada (☎ 34 642; ul 25 Oktober 50; open 4pm-3am daily), not far from the Presidential Palace, is a popular underground bar/disco. According to the sign outside you are not allowed to take in hand grenades, guns, gas bottles or alcohol.

MOLDOVA

Getting There & Away

Train Tickets for same-day departures are sold in the main ticket hall of the **train station** (*ul Lenina*). Get advance tickets (at least 24 hours ahead) in the 2nd-floor ticket office.

All Bucharest–Moscow and Chişinău–St Petersburg trains stop in Tiraspol. Most other eastbound trains from Chişinău to Ukraine and Russia stop in Tiraspol too (see Chişinău Getting There & Away). There is one daily local train between Tiraspol and Chişinău.

Bus Tickets for all buses are sold in the main ticket hall. You can pay for tickets to other destinations in Transdniestr only in local currency. Bus tickets to Moldova/Ukraine are only sold in Moldovan lei and local currency.

From Tiraspol there are 12 daily buses to Chişinău ($1.30, 70km). There are also four daily buses to Odesa ($1.80) in Ukraine.

Microbuses to Chişinău ($1.45) leave every hour – or when they're full – from outside the train station. Pay the driver.

Getting Around

Bus No 1 ($0.05; pay the driver) runs between the bus and train stations and the city centre.

Trolleybus Nos 1 and 19 cross the bridge over the Nistru (Dniestr) to Tighina. Several microbuses also make the 20-minute journey but tickets are more expensive.

TIGHINA

☎ 233 • pop 143,800

Traditionally Tighina (Bendery in Russian), on the western banks of the Nistru, has always been an important military stronghold. Russian troops have been stationed at Tighina since 1992.

In the 16th century, Moldavian prince Ştefan cel Mare built a massive defensive fortress here on the ruins of a fortified Roman camp. In 1538 the Ottoman sultan, Suleiman the Magnificent, conquered the fortress and transformed Tighina into a Turkish *raia* (colony), renaming the city Bender, meaning 'belonging to the Turks'.

Following the decisive Russian defeat of Sweden's Charles XII and Ukrainian Cossack leader Ivan Mazepa by Peter the Great at Poltava in 1709, it was to Tighina that the Swedish king and Cossack leader fled for refuge. Mazepa subsequently died in the fortress here.

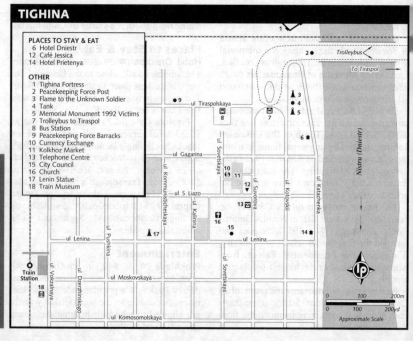

TIGHINA

PLACES TO STAY & EAT
6 Hotel Dniestr
12 Café Jessica
14 Hotel Prietenya

OTHER
1 Tighina Fortress
2 Peacekeeping Force Post
3 Flame to the Unknown Soldier
4 Tank
5 Memorial Monument 1992 Victims
7 Trolleybus to Tiraspol
8 Bus Station
9 Peacekeeping Force Barracks
10 Currency Exchange
11 Kolkhoz Market
13 Telephone Centre
15 City Council
16 Church
17 Lenin Statue
18 Train Museum

Trolleybus

To Tiraspol

ul Tiraspolskaya

Nistru (Dniestr)

ul Gagarina

ul Sovetskaya

ul S Liazo

ul Kommunisticheskaya

ul Kalinina

ul Suvorova

ul Kotovskii

ul Katachenka

ul Lenina

ul Pushkina

ul Lenina

ul Sovetskaya

Train Station

ul Volzalnaya

ul Dzerzhinskogo

ul Moskovskaya

ul Komosomolskaya

0   100   200m
0   100   200yd
Approximate Scale

During the Russo-Turkish wars in the 18th century, Tighina was seized from the Turks by Russian troops who then massacred Turkish Muslims in the city. In 1812 Tighina fell permanently into Russian hands and the fortress was occupied by Russian troops. USSR forces remained stationed here until 1992, when Tighina was made off-limits to armed forces. Theoretically the fortress has been empty since. Nevertheless it is not open to visitors.

The bloodiest fighting during the 1992 military conflict took place in Tighina and many walls of the buildings in the city centre remain badly bullet-pocked. Today the Tighina is protected as a security zone by peacekeeping forces who have various military installations and camouflaged personnel carriers positioned at strategic points in the town. Police and military carry out patrols at night-time to insure public safety.

Information
Change money at the **currency exchange** (ul Sovetskaya) next to the Kolkhoz Market. International telephone calls can be booked from the **telephone office** (ul Suvorova; open 24hr), next door to the **post office** (ul Suvorova; open 8am-12pm & 1pm-6pm Mon-Fri, 8am-12pm & 1pm-4pm Sat).

Tighina's special security zone status means foreign tourists can stay in the city without having to register with the local militia.

Things to See
At the entrance to the city, close to the infamous **Tighina-Tiraspol bridge**, is a **memorial park**, opened in 1996, dedicated to Tighina's 1992 war victims. An eternal flame burns in front of an armoured tank, from which flies the Transdniestran flag.

Haunting **memorials** to those shot dead during the civil war are evident throughout many of the main streets in the centre, including the **City Council building** (ul Lenina 17).

Next to the train station is a **Train Museum**, inside an old Russian CY 06-71 steam locomotive. The museum was closed at the time of research. Alongside Tighina's only museum is a typically Soviet, oversized granite mural in memory of the train workers who died in the 1918 revolution.

Places to Stay & Eat
Hotel Dniestr (☎ 29 478; ul Katachenka 10; singles/doubles $8.20/12.50) overlooking the Dniestr River, has dreary rooms with TV, fridge, private bath and no hot water. Marginally better are the rooms at **Hotel Prietenya** (☎ 29 660; ul Katachenka; doubles $8.20-16), which has a pleasant terrace **restaurant** overlooking the river.

Café Jessica (ul Liazo; salads $0.20-0.55, mains $0.80-1.75), opposite the telephone office, is the best place to eat in town. Statues of penguins stand outside.

Getting There & Away
For rail matters, go to the **train station** (Privokzalnaya ploshchad). The **information desk** (open 8am-noon & 2pm-6pm daily) is in the ticket hall. Questions cost $0.05 each.

There are 16 buses each dat to Chişinău ($1.15) and one daily to Comrat ($2). Tickets can be purchased with both Moldovan lei and local currency.

Trolleybus No 19 for Tiraspol ($0.05) goes from the bus stop next to the main roundabout at the entrance to Tighina. Microbuses clearly marked with their destinations on the front also make the 20-minute journey but cost $0.15.

Moscow & St Petersburg

Russia, the world's largest country, remains a fascinating and rewarding destination and is more accessible today than at any other time in its turbulent history. Russia's principal cities, Moscow and St Petersburg, both fall within the European part of the Russia – all the country west of the Ural Mountains – and are the main centres of international tourism. While these two historical capitals have very different atmospheres – Moscow is bold, brash and mercantile while St Petersburg is cultured and elegant – they represent the best of what Russia has to offer in terms of the country's economic, political, cultural and social life.

Despite the Western media's tendency to emphasise Russia's problems (of which there are plenty), travellers should not encounter any special difficulties here. Crime is comparable to other large European cities and, while patience is needed for dealing with ever-present bureaucracy, visitors will be more than compensated for by Moscow and St Petersburg's architectural splendour and larger-than-life sense of history, as well as by the open-hearted spirit of the locals.

Facts about Russia

HISTORY
European Russia's earliest-known people inhabited the basin of the Don River about 20,000 BC. By 2000 BC a basic form of agriculture had spread from the Danube region as far east as the Moscow area.

These areas fell under the control of various groups, but the migrants who were to give Russia its dominant character were the Slavs. There is some disagreement about where the Slavs originated, but in the first few centuries AD they expanded rapidly to the east, west and south from the vicinity of present-day northern Ukraine and also southern Belarus.

The founding of Novgorod in 862 by Rurik of Jutland is traditionally taken as the birth of the Russian nation, but the development of a cohesive state was set back by the Tatar invasions. Until 1480, these Mongolian warlords – Genghis Khan, his grandson Batu Khan and their Golden Horde successors – controlled the largest land empire the world has ever seen from their base at Saray on the Volga.

At a Glance

- **Moscow** – bustling capital, featuring the Kremlin, Red Square, the Bolshoi Ballet and the timeless All-Russia Exhibition Centre
- **Suzdal** – peaceful town outside Moscow with many old monasteries and churches
- **St Petersburg** – Imperial capital built by Peter the Great boasting Venice-style canals and the art-packed Hermitage
- **Petrodvorets** – Russia's 'Versailles' just a stone's throw from St Petersburg

Population	Moscow: 9 million
	St Petersburg:
	4.6 million
Official Language	Russian
Currency	1 rouble (R)
	= 100 kopecks
Time	GMT/UTC+0300
Country Phone Code	☎ 7

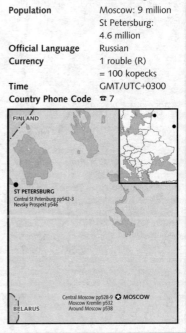

FINLAND

ST PETERSBURG
Central St Petersburg pp542-3
Nevsky Prospekt p546

Central Moscow pp528-9 ✪ MOSCOW
Moscow Kremlin p532
Around Moscow p538

BELARUS

The beginning of the Romanov dynasty in 1613 saw a huge expansion of Russian territory and under the rule of Peter the Great (1696–1725), the founding of a navy and a new capital city, St Petersburg, in 1703.

A workers' revolution in 1905 was an omen for future unrest, which saw the abdication and eventual murder of the last tsar, Nicholas II, in 1917, and the two revolutions resulting

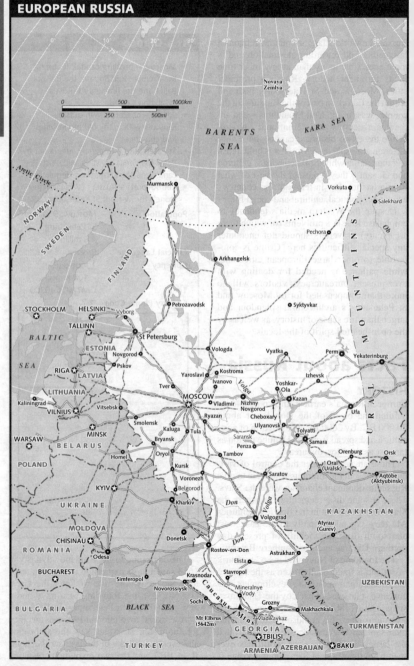

EUROPEAN RUSSIA

in the Bolshevik party (headed by Vladimir Lenin) taking control. After a devastating civil war, the communists managed a one-party system and established the Union of Soviet Socialist Republics (USSR) in 1922.

After the barbarous reign of Josef Stalin, WWII (in which an estimated 26 million Russians died) and the decades-long Cold War, the communist experiment that was the USSR was on the brink of collapse. Mikhail Gorbachev's *glasnost* ushered in Boris Yeltsin's moderately democratic government of the 1990s. Free-market reforms created much upheaval and economic disparity: Russians were now free to travel and to buy anything they liked, but the vast majority hadn't the means to do so. They suffered even more from the fall-out of the 1998 crash of the rouble.

In April 2000, with the economy on a sounder footing, Vladimir Putin was elected president. Despite the ongoing grizzly conflict in renegade Chechnya, government interference with the media and national unease over the sinking of the Kursk submarine in 2001, Putin remains popular. Russia continues to experience healthy economic growth and, post-September 11, 2001, a more respected international reputation with regard to its stance on fighting terrorism alongside its former Cold War foe, the USA.

GEOGRAPHY
Russia takes up 17 million sq km of land from its western borders with the Baltic countries (and the Baltic Sea in the Kaliningrad region), to the Pacific Ocean. Mainly flat, the country rises slightly in the Ural Mountains, marking the border between European Russia and Siberia, and more dramatically in the south (Mt Elbrus, along the border with Georgia, rises to 5642m, Europe's highest peak).

CLIMATE
Moscow and St Petersburg are warm from about mid-May to early September, but both drag themselves through dreary, dark and long winters.

GOVERNMENT & POLITICS
Russia is governed by an executive president with broad powers and the two-house parliament (Duma). All government ministers are appointed by the president (but approved of by the lower house of the Duma), including the premier who is number two in command.

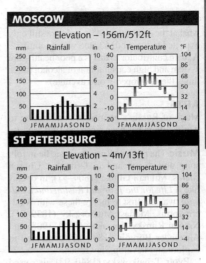

The Duma's upper house, the Federation Council, has 178 seats, occupied by two representatives from each of Russia's 89 administrative districts. It legislates the relationship between central government and the regions. The lower house, the State Duma, oversees all legislation and has 450 members.

ECONOMY
Russia was left an economic shambles on the disintegration of the Soviet Union, but now, over a decade on, its economy is looking more healthy. Growth has been steady (8% in 2000), and inflation – rampant in the 1990s – is under control with a consequent stabilisation of the rouble. Three-quarters of state enterprises have been fully or partly privatised (albeit with much corruption along the way).

In Moscow and St Petersburg you'll notice a burgeoning middle class, but not all have prospered. The boom-and-bust period of the 1990s, as well as the abandonment of the social safety net provided by communism, has left many people worse off; an estimated 20 million Russians live below the official poverty line of US$31 a month.

POPULATION & PEOPLE
Much of Russia's population is ethnic Russian, with dozens of smaller ethnic groups, mainly scattered across Siberia and the north, all with their own languages, traditions and religions. Many of these groups, however, have adopted Russian language, dress and culture.

Though average life expectancy rose somewhat at the end of the 1990s, men are still only expected to live until 62, and women until 72. A main contributor to this is a poor health-care system and high consumption of alcohol (three times the developed-world average).

ARTS

Much of Russia's enormous contribution to world culture has been since the 19th century.

Music The roots of Russian music lie in folk song and dance and in Orthodox Church chants. Mikhail Glinka (1804–57), in operas like *A Life for the Tsar* and *Ruslan and Lyudmila*, was the first to merge these with Western forms. Modest Mussorgsky (1839–81), Nikolai Rimsky-Korsakov (1844–1908) and Alexander Borodin (1833–87) continued to explore and develop Slav roots.

Pyotr Tchaikovsky (1840–93) also used folk motifs but was closer to the Western tradition. His *1812 Overture*, his ballets *Swan Lake* and *The Nutcracker*, and his opera *Yevgeny Onegin* are still some of the world's most popular works. Sergey Rachmaninov (1873–1943), Igor Stravinsky (1882–1971) and Dmitry Shostakovich (1906–75) are other influential composers of the 20th century.

Literature Alexander Pushkin (1799–1837) is revered as the father of Russian literature, and almost every Russian of any age is able to recite some of his verses, likely from his most famous work, *Yevgeny Onegin*. Mikhail Lermontov (1814–41) is another major figure. His first important work, the poem *On the Death of Pushkin*, circulated widely despite its censure. In it, he railed against a society that let such a genius die in a senseless duel. He himself was to be killed in a duel at an early age.

Nicholas Gogol (1809–52) was a master of the romantic realism that became a hallmark of Russian literature. His classics include the mordantly satiric *Dead Souls* and *The Inspector General*. Fyodor Dostoevsky (1821–81) is the Russia's most internationally known author for *Crime and Punishment*, *The Idiot* and *The Brothers Karamazov*. Other giants of Russian literature include Leo Tolstoy *(War and Peace)*, Anton Chekhov and Boris Pasternak *(Dr Zhivago)*. A contemporary Russian writer who has had his books translated and gained international acclaim is Victor Pelevin, a kind of Russian Will Self; try *Babylon*.

SOCIETY & CONDUCT

Russian hospitality is a delightful tradition. If you are invited into someone's home, you can expect to be regaled with stories, to receive many vodka toasts and to be stuffed with food. Take along a gift and remove your shoes indoors.

Gender roles are what Westerners would term 'traditional'; men are expected to open doors for women, who are encouraged to follow lady-like behaviour. Despite this you'll notice, in Moscow and St Petersburg at least, an uninhibited approach to sexual titillation with strip shows, both male and female, happening in many clubs and even restaurants in front of mixed audiences.

RELIGION

The Russian constitution enshrines religious freedom. A law passed in 1997 recognises the Russian Orthodox Church as the leading faith and promises to respect Islam, Judaism and Buddhism. A clause gives courts the power to ban groups inciting hatred or intolerance.

LANGUAGE

Russian is an Indo-European language, with its alphabet adapted from the Greek by Cyril (now St Cyril) in the 9th century. It has gone through several revisions and mutations since. Almost everyone in Russia speaks Russian, even the national minorities, and English is seldom heard or understood outside (and sometimes even in) major cities. Your visit will be much richer if you take the time to learn a little Russian. For pronunciation guidelines and useful words and phrases, see the Language chapter at the back of this book.

In this chapter we will also use: ul for *ulitsa* (street), pr for *prospekt* (avenue), per for *pereulok* (lane), nab for *naberezhnaya* (embankment) and pl for *ploshchad* (square). *Vokzal* is a train station.

Facts for the Visitor

HIGHLIGHTS

Russia's highlights range from ancient architecture to Soviet anachronisms to classical arts. One can't visit Moscow without taking in the Kremlin, but the city offers a host of other uniquely Russian experiences. Paying your respects to Vladimir Ilych in Red Square will be among the most bizarre and memorable parts of your trip. The classical arts are the last incredible bargain in this city; don't miss your chance to hear them hit the high notes at a Tchaikovsky opera or to watch them spin till you are dizzy at the ballet. If you have a chance to leave the city, wander through the Russian fairy-tale landscape of Suzdal.

In St Petersburg, lose yourself amid the artistic riches of the Hermitage and Russian Museum or cruise the canals to admire the city's elegant architecture. Watch the bridges rise over the Neva during summer's White Nights and definitely make time for an opera or ballet at the Mariinksy Theatre. Around St Petersburg explore the country estates of Petrodvorets and Tsarkoe Selo.

SUGGESTED ITINERARIES
Depending on the length of your stay, you could do the following:

Two days
   Visit either Moscow or St Petersburg
One week
   Visit both Moscow and St Petersburg, with a day or two to explore some of the ancient 'Golden Ring' towns northeast of Moscow

PLANNING
When to Go
July and August are the warmest months and the main holiday season (which means securing train tickets can sometimes be a problem). Most theatres close during these months. Early summer features White Nights, when the sun never sets completely and it stays light all night long. The highlight of early autumn is the colourful foliage. Winter, if you're prepared, can be an adventure: furs and vodka keep people warm, and snow-covered landscapes are picturesque.

What Kind of Trip
With sufficient planning and patience, independent travel is an exciting way to experience Russia. The important factor to note is that your ease of travel will be directly in proportion to your knowledge of Russian. Group travel is worth considering for trips out of the city to hard-to-reach destinations.

Maps
Maps of Moscow and St Petersburg are available from many sources in those two cities and outside Russia. Country maps of Russia are also readily available.

What to Bring
Even in the summer, you will need at least a light jacket or sweater for cool evenings. Strong mosquito repellent is a must for St Petersburg summers. By all means carry toilet paper with you, but don't bring a lot from home as adequate brands (meaning soft) are widely sold. Western toiletries, tampons and condoms are also readily available.

TOURIST OFFICES
Tourist offices of the kind that you may be used to in the West do not exist in Russia (St Petersburg is an exception and even that's not great). Instead you're dependent for information mainly on the moods of hotel receptionists/administrators, service bureaus and travel firms. See Travel Agencies under Information in the Moscow and St Petersburg sections.

VISAS & DOCUMENTS
All visitors to Russia need visas, which are obtainable outside Russia only. It's an exit permit too, so if you lose it (or overstay), leaving the country can be harder than getting in.

All Russian visas must be registered with OVIR (Otdel Viz i Registratsii; Department of Visas & Registration), within three business days of your arrival in Russia. Usually your hotel or hostel will take care of it, but you can also register it yourself at a local OVIR office (see Visas & Documents under Moscow and St Petersburg). Some hotels will also register your visa for the fee of one night in their cheapest room. In Moscow it is known as UVIR (Upravlenia Viz i Registratsii).

Types of Visas
Of the six types of visa available, the most common are single- or multi-entry tourist and business visas. Tourist visas, valid for three months, are issued if you have a confirmed booking in a hotel or hostel. More flexible business visas, valid for up to a year, are available with an invitation from a registered Russian company. Some travel agencies can arrange this as well. See Travel Agencies in the Moscow and St Petersburg sections.

Since February 2002, Russia has run a trial scheme where tourists from Schengen countries, as well as from Britain, Japan, and Switzerland, wishing to visit Moscow and St Petersburg for less than 72 hours, can get their visas directly upon entry. Travellers must apply at one of 29 authorised tour operators in

MOSCOW & ST PETERSBURG

their home country 48 hours before departure. Check with your local Russian consulate.

EMBASSIES & CONSULATES
Russian Embassies & Consulates
Check **w** wwww.russianembassy.net for all your Russian embassy requirements.

Australia
Embassy: (☎ 02-6295 9033/9474, fax 6295 1847, **e** rusemb@dynamite.com.au) 78 Canberra Ave, Griffith, ACT 2603
Consulate: (☎ 02-9326 1188, fax 9327 5065, **e** russcon@ozemail.com.au) 7 Fullerton St, Woollahra, NSW 2025

Canada
Embassy: (☎ 613-235 4341, fax 236 6342, **e** rusemb@intranet.ca) 285 Charlotte St, Ottawa; Visa Department (☎ 613-336 7220, fax 238 6158)
Consulate: (☎ 514-843 5901, 842 5343, fax 842 2012, **e** consulat@dsuper.net) 3685 Ave Du Musée, Montreal, Quebec, H3G 2EI

Finland
Embassy: (☎ 09-66 14 49, fax 66 18 12, **e** rusembassy@co.inet.fi) Tehtaankatu 1B, FIN-00140 Helsinki

Germany
Embassy: (☎ 030-220 2821, 226 6320, fax 229 9397, **e** russembassyg@trionet.de) Unter den Linden 63-65, 10117 Berlin
Consulate: (☎ 0228-312 085, fax 312 164, **e** bonn@russische-botschaft.de) Waldstrasse 42, 53177 Bonn
There are also consulates in Hamburg, Leipzig, Munich & Rostok

UK
Embassy: (☎ 020-7229 3628, fax 7727 8625, **w** www.russialink.couk.com/embassy) 13 Kensington Palace Gardens, London W8 4QX
Consular Section: (☎ 020-7229 8027, visa information message ☎ 0891-171 271, fax 020-7229 3215) 5 Kensington Palace Gardens, London W8 4QS
Consulate: (☎ 0131-225 7121, fax 225 9587, **e** visa@edconsul.demon.co.uk) 58 Melville St, Edinburgh E13 7HL

USA
Embassy: (☎ 202-239 8907, fax 483 7579, **w** www.russianembassy.gov) 2641 Tunlaw Rd, NW, Washington DC 20007.
Visa Department: (☎ 202-939 8907, fax 939 8909) 1825 Phelps Place NW, Washington DC 20008
Consulate: (☎ 212-348 0926, fax 831 9162) 9 East 91 St, New York, NY 10128
Consulate: (☎ 415-928 6878, fax 929 0306) 2790 Green St, San Francisco, CA 94103
Consulate: (☎ 206-728 1910, fax 728 1871, **w** www.ruscon.com) 2323 Westin Building, 2001 Sixth Ave, Seattle, WA 98121-2617

Embassies & Consulates in Russia
Many countries maintain embassies in Moscow and consulates in St Petersburg. See the website **w** www.themoscowtimes.ru/travel/facts/embassies.html for a full list.

Embassies in Moscow The area code for the following is ☎ 095.

Australia (☎ 956 60 70, fax 956 61 70, **w** www.australianembassy.ru) Kropotkinsky per 2
Canada (☎ 956 66 66, fax 232 99 48) Starokonyushenny per 23
France (☎ 937 15 00, fax 937 15 77, **w** www.ambafrance.ru) ul Bol Yakimanka 45
Germany (☎ 937 95 00, fax 936 21 43, **w** www.germany.org.ru) ul Mosfilmovskaya 56; *Consular section:* (☎ 936 24 01) Leninsky pr 95A
Poland (☎ 255 00 17, visa section ☎ 254 36 21) ul Klimashkina 4
UK (☎ 956 72 00, fax 956 72 01, **w** www.britemb.msk.ru) Smolenskaya nab 10
Ukraine (☎ 229 10 79, fax 924 84 69) Leontyevsky per 18
USA (☎ 728 50 00, fax 728 50 90, **w** www.usembassy.state.gov/moscow) Novinsky bul 19/23

Consulates in St Petersburg The area code for St Petersburg is ☎ 812.

Canada (☎ 325 84 48, 316 72 22, fax 316 72 22) Malodetskoselsky pr 32
France (☎ 312 11 30, fax 311 72 83) nab reki Moyki 15
Germany (☎ 327 24 00, 327 31 17) Furshtadtskaya ul 39
Poland (☎ 274 41 70, fax 274 43 18) 5-ya Sovetskaya ul 12
UK (☎ 320 32 00, fax 325 31 11) pl Proletarskoy Diktatury 5
USA (☎ 275 17 01, fax 110-70-22) Furshtadtskaya ul 15

CUSTOMS
You may be asked to fill in a declaration form (*deklaratsia*) upon arrival and you should keep this form until your departure from Russia. If the total value of what you've listed is US$1500 or more you must go through a red lane and have the form stamped by a customs official, who may also check your luggage.

When leaving the country, anything that is vaguely 'arty', such as manuscripts, instruments, coins, jewellery or antiques must be submitted for assessment by the **Ministry of**

Culture in Moscow *(ul Neglinnaya 8/10, room 298)* or in St Petersburg *(☎ 311 51 96; Malaya Morskaya ul 17)*.

MONEY
Currency & Exchanging Money
The official currency is the rouble. Roubles come in denominations of 10, 50, 100 and 500. There are 100 kopecks in a rouble. Prices in this chapter are listed in roubles, with the exception of hotels and restaurants that tie their prices to the US dollar.

US dollars and euros are by far the easiest currencies to exchange. Automated teller machines (ATMs), known as *bankomat* in Russian, are now quite common in Moscow and in St Petersburg.

Exchange Rates
At the time of publication, the rouble (R) was officially worth:

country	unit		rouble
Australia	A$1	=	R17.04
Canada	C$1	=	R19.92
Euro Zone	€1	=	R31.16
Japan	¥100	=	R26.53
NZ	NZ$1	=	R14.63
UK	UK£1	=	R49.51
USA	US$1	=	R31.56

Costs
Moscow and St Petersburg are the two most expensive cities in Russia. With serious economising (self-catering, staying in hostels) you could scrape by on US$30 a day. But if you visit museums, take excursions and indulge in nightlife you could easily head towards US$100 a day. There are usually different prices for foreigners and Russian citizens. In this book we list the prices that are charged to foreigners.

Tipping & Bargaining
Tipping is not widespread in Russia. In the better restaurants, count on leaving 10%; elsewhere 5% to 10% of the total is fine. Tipping or offering a small gift to your guide is the accepted practice.

Prices in stores are usually firm and so you cannot bargain. In markets and souvenir stalls, however, you might make a lower counter bid, but Russia is not a place where you can expect protracted haggling.

POST & COMMUNICATIONS
Moscow and St Petersburg have all the services travellers are used to for both regular and express mail, and all modes of telecommunication. The country code for Russia is ☎ 7. To call internationally from Russia, dial ☎ 8, wait for the second tone, then dial ☎ 10 plus the country, city codes, and number. Omit any zeroes from the city code.

Internet & Email Access
Internet facilities are readily available around Moscow and St Petersburg at Internet cafés and at some postal facilities (see those sections for details). Prices are usually about 30R for one hour of access on good, fast machines.

DIGITAL RESOURCES
A good starting place for links about Russia is w www.lonelyplanet.com. Bucknell University's huge, award-winning website w www .departments.bucknell.edu/russian has links to just about any Russian topic you can imagine. An encyclopaedia of tourism-related sites can be found at w russia-tourism.com, with links on a myriad subjects, including travel agents, hotels and much more.

NEWSPAPERS
Be sure to pick up the *Moscow Times* and its sister publication the *St Petersburg Times* for excellent journalism and comprehensive, up-to-date listings. Go to w www.moscowtimes .com and w www.sptimesrussia.com for online versions.

TIME
Moscow and St Petersburg are on GMT/UTC time plus three hours. From the last Sunday in March to the last Sunday in September, clocks are put forward an hour so the time is GMT/UTC plus four hours.

TOILETS
Pay toilets are identified by the words платный туалет *(platny tualet)*, but these are generally unclean. Most tourists opt for toilets in restaurants or luxury hotel lobbies. In any toilet Ж stands for women's *(zhenskiy)*, while M stands for men's *(muzhskoy)*.

WOMEN TRAVELLERS
Although sexual harassment on the streets is rare, it is common in the workplace, in the home and in personal relations. Generally it

has only been young, university-educated women who have been able to take advantage of opportunities offered by the new economy. Discrimination and domestic violence are hard facts of life for many Russian women. Foreign women are likely to be propositioned on the streets, although this interest is rarely dangerous. Women should certainly avoid taking private taxis alone at night.

GAY & LESBIAN TRAVELLERS

While girls walking hand in hand and drunken men being affectionate are common sights throughout Russia, open displays of same-sex love are not condoned. Still, newspapers such as the *Moscow Times* and the *St Petersburg Times* feature articles and listings on the gay and lesbian scene. See also W www.gay.ru/english/ which has up-to-date information, good links and can put you in touch with personal guides for Moscow and St Petersburg.

DISABLED TRAVELLERS

Inaccessible transport, lack of ramps and lifts and no centralised policy for people with physical limitations make Russia a challenging destination for wheelchair-bound visitors.

SENIOR TRAVELLERS

Travellers over the age of 60 can expect to get senior-citizen discounts and good treatment from Russian ticket agencies.

DANGERS & ANNOYANCES

The streets of Moscow and St Petersburg are about as safe, or as dangerous, as those of New York, London or Amsterdam. On crowded transport, beware of pickpockets, who often work in gangs. The media-touted Russian mafia should be of no concern to tourists.

Frightening reports of racial violence against Jewish and darker-skinned people appear from time to time in the media. It's a sure thing that if you look vaguely Caucasian (from the Caucasus) or have dark skin that you'll be targeted with suspicion by many people (and in particular the police). Police

are likely to stop passers-by (seemingly for no reason) and demand to see documents. In case of any trouble, you will probably not be given the benefit of the doubt.

When officials, such as police, ask to see your papers they may be looking for a bribe; they will suggest there is something wrong with your documents and demand a 'fine'. Besides making sure your *dokumenty* are in order, you should ask to see the officer's identification and note the seven-digit number before handing over any of your documents. Show the officer a photocopy of your passport and visa (made after you arrive in Moscow, so that your visa registration is visible). Do not give up your passport and insist on paying your 'fine' at the station, not directly to the officer.

BUSINESS HOURS

Government offices and banks are usually open 9am to 5pm or 6pm Monday to Saturday, with a one- hour break for lunch. Shops often stay open until 7pm or 8pm without a lunch break. Most restaurants are open from noon to midnight daily, although 24-hour (*kruglosutochno*) food shops and restaurants are not uncommon.

Museum hours vary widely and change often, as do their weekly days off. Most shut entrance doors an hour before closing time.

PUBLIC HOLIDAYS & SPECIAL EVENTS

The main public holidays are New Year's Day (1 January), Russian Orthodox Christmas Day (7 January), International Women's Day (8 March), International Labour Day/Spring Festival (1 and 2 May), Victory –1945 – Day (9 May), Russian Independence Day (12 June) and Day of Reconciliation and Accord (the rebranded Revolution Day, 7 November).

Other days that are widely celebrated are Defenders of the Motherland Day (23 February), Easter Monday and Constitution Day (12 December). Much of Russia shuts down for the first half of May and its wealth of holidays.

ACTIVITIES

Camping, hiking, skiing, canoeing and other outdoor activities are all popular with Russians, although the infrastructure for most is rudimentary when compared with Western countries. The best strategy for obtaining information about outdoor activities is to inquire locally at tour agencies and sports stores.

Emergency Services

In the event of an emergency call ☎ 02 for police, ☎ 01 for fire and ☎ 03 for ambulance.

These numbers can be dialled nationwide but have Russian-speaking operators only.

A highlight of any visit to Russia is the bathhouse *(banya)*. The steamy atmosphere and fragrant birch-branch beatings, followed by a cold dip in a plunge pool (or a roll in the snow) and a table laden with goodies, are all part of a quintessential Russian experience.

ACCOMMODATION
Moscow and St Petersburg each have several youth or backpackers' hostels, all more or less in the international mould and able to offer visa support. For information check **W** www .hostelling-russia.ru. With hotels in Moscow or St Petersburg you tend to get what you pay for. Cheap hotels are likely to have peeling wallpaper, broken appliances, uncomfortable furniture and/or dodgy toilets. On an up note, they are usually acceptably clean. There is not really any seasonal variation in price.

FOOD & DRINKS
These days, Russian food – especially in Moscow and St Petersburg – is not nearly as bad as you may fear. The local cuisine is on the heavy side favouring fat-loaded, but delicious, pancakes *(blini)*, creams and hearty meat dishes. The highlight of Russian cuisine is its unique soups such as *borshch* (beetroot), *solyanka* (salty cucumber) and *ukha* (fish). In both cities there are also plenty of good restaurants and cafés that serve international cuisines.

If you think you can get by in Russia without downing a shot or two of vodka, you are fooling yourself.

ENTERTAINMENT
Nightlife is a top attraction in both Moscow and St Petersburg; bars and nightclubs can be just about as wild as you are willing to go. These cultural capitals also offer amazing bargains on classical music, opera and ballet. Usually, the theatres themselves are gorgeous, the performances are spectacular and tickets (except for the tourist-trap Bolshoi) downright cheap.

SHOPPING
Traditional souvenirs include wooden dolls *(matryoshka)*, painted enamel boxes *(palekh)*, ornamental ceramics, floral *'babushka'* and amber products. Russian linens are high quality and, when compared with Western prices, are extremely affordable. If you live in a northern clime, don't go home without a fur hat *(shapka)*. Commemorative stamps and Soviet paraphernalia can be found at markets.

Getting There & Away

AIR
You are most likely fly into Sheremetevo-2 airport in Moscow, but there are also services from several European cities to St Petersburg every day. There are many domestic connections from both cities. Two Russian airlines are Aeroflot and Transaero. The international carriers such as British Airways, Delta, KLM and SAS offer direct flights to Moscow and/ or St Petersburg.

If you shop around you can find good deals, eg, Moscow to London return for about UK£200 or St Petersburg to New York return for US$550.

LAND
Train
The Baltic Countries There are trains between St Petersburg and Tallinn (R710, eight hours, odd-numbered days), Rīga (R968, 13 hours, daily), and Vilnius (R630, 14 hours, odd days). From Moscow to Tallinn there are nightly trains (R1260, 16 hours), Rīga (R3000, 15 hours) and Vilnius (R3000, 15 hours).

Finland There are two daily trains from Helsinki to St Petersburg (R2500, five hours) and one to Moscow (R3450, 16 hours).

Other Destinations From St Petersburg, there are direct trains to Warsaw (30 hours), Berlin (39 hours), Kiev (24 hours) and Minsk (16 hours). Moscow also has direct connections with Warsaw (21 hours), Prague (35 hours), Vienna (34 hours), Budapest (40 hours), Kyiv (14 hours) and Minsk (10 hours).

Bus
The Baltic Countries From St Petersburg, Eurolines (☎ 168 27 48; **W** www.eurolines.ru; *ul Shkapina 10)* runs four or five daily buses to Tallinn (R270 to R330, eight hours), Tartu (R300, eight hours) and Rīga (R500, 11 hours).

Finland Buses going from St Petersburg to Helsinki via Vyborg and Lahti depart from Finnord (☎ 314 89 51; *Italyanskaya ul 37)*. A one-way ticket costs R1050. **Sovavto** (☎ 123 51 25; **w** www.pohjolanliikenne.fi) has daily coaches to Helsinki (R1200) and Turku via Lappeenranta, as well as a Vyborg to Lappeenranta service.

Other Destinations Twice-weekly buses to Germany run from **Stat Express** (☎ 168 20 03, fax 316 24 31; ul Shkapina 10), inside Warsaw station in St Petersburg, stopping in 20 cities and towns. Eurolines has some additional routes to Germany.

Car & Motorcycle

The generally poor condition of Russian roads and the frequency of traffic police pullovers should make any motorist pause before deciding to drive to and through Russia. If you do drive there, make sure you have a valid International Driving Permit and your passport handy, as well as legal and insurance documents for your vehicle.

The Baltic Countries The main border crossings between Estonia and Russia are at Narva/Ivangorod, which is efficient but can also sometimes have long lines, and Koidula/ Pechory, a quiet alternative for driving to Moscow. The M9 Rīga-Moscow road crosses the border east of Rēzekne (Latvia). From Lithuania, it's best to drive up through Latvia first to avoid Belarus.

Finland Highways cross at the border posts of Nuijamaa and Vaalimaa (Brusnichnoe and Torfyanovka respectively on the Russian side). It's best to make this drive for the first time during daylight hours.

Getting Around

TRAIN

Russia is crisscrossed with an extensive rail network that makes the train a viable means of going practically anywhere. Trains can also be a great way to meet Russians from all walks of life, especially since most trains are slow or run overnight, providing plenty of opportunities to strike up conversations.

Suburban or short-distance trains are called *elektrichkas* and do not require advance booking – you can buy your ticket at the suburban train ticket offices (*prigorodny poezd kassas*) at train stations.

The regular long-distance service is a fast train (*skory poezd*). First (*myagki*) class will get you a place in a two-person sleeping carriage, while 2nd (*kupeyny*) class will get you a place in a four-person car.

Platskartny compartments, while cheaper, have open bunk accommodations and are not great for those who value privacy. *Obshchiy* (general) class simply has bench or aeroplane-style seating.

BUS

Buses are a cheap and reliable (though sometimes very slow) way of getting around or between cities. For medium-distance travel (up to 150km), suburban trains are usually best, with some exceptions: from St Petersburg, the buses and taxi buses that travel to Petrodvorets, Pushkin and Pavlovsk are actually quicker and more convenient than the train (see Around St Petersburg).

CAR & MOTORCYCLE

Driving in Russia has its problems (canyon-sized potholes and the dreaded traffic police, or GAI, being some), but if you've got a sense of humour, it can be an adventurous way to see the countryside. Driving in the bigger cities is more trouble than it's worth. Petrol is relatively cheap by Western standards.

HITCHING

Hitching is never entirely safe in any country in the world, and Lonely Planet doesn't recommend it. In Russian cities, hitching rides is called hailing a cab, no matter what type of vehicle stops. In the countryside, hitching is common. Rides are hailed by flagging passing vehicles with a low, up-and-down wave (not an extended thumb). You're expected to pitch in for petrol.

LOCAL TRANSPORT

Both Moscow and St Petersburg have impressive metro systems, and a network of buses, trams, trolleybuses, express buses and taxi buses. Fares range from R5 to R10, with multitrip cards being available for the metro, maing it even cheaper. Public transport usually operates from about 5.30am to 12.30am.

ORGANISED TOURS

Once you're in Russia, you'll find many travel agencies that specialise in city tours and excursions throughout the country. Sometimes these are the best way to visit out-of-the-way sights. See the travel agencies listed under the relevant city sections.

Moscow Москва

☎ 095

Some people love Moscow. Some hate it. Most do both. It's glittering, it's grey. It's friendly, it's surly. It's beautiful, it's bleak. It's pious, it's hedonistic. It's the epicentre of the new Russia, with shops, restaurants and nightlife that most provincial Russians still only dream about. It also epitomises the seamier side of postcommunist Russia: it suffers from growing street crime and rising prices, is riddled with corruption and spattered with beggars. But Moscow is a city of excitement and opportunity where anything can happen.

In the 10th century, Slavic tribes began migrating eastward from the Dnieper River to settle the forest region of the upper Volga. These small agrarian communities grew into fortified towns, ruled by the offspring of Prince Vsevolod, of the Kievan Rurik dynasty. Sometimes allies and sometimes rivals, these medieval princedoms formed a ring of fort-cities, now known as the Golden Ring.

The founding of Moscow is attributed to the prince of Vladimir-Suzdal, Yury Dolgoruky, who hosted a great feast here in 1147. Little did Yury know that the village would become one of the world's major metropolises, a heady mix of business, political intrigue, high culture, history – and fun.

Orientation

Picture Moscow as four road rings that spread out from the centre. Radial roads spoke out across the rings, and the Moscow River meanders across everything from northwest to southeast. The Kremlin, a north-pointing triangle with 750m sides, is at Moscow's heart in every way. Red Square lies along its eastern side, the Moscow River flows to the south.

Information

Money Among the more established banks in Moscow, **Alfa Bank** (open 8.30am-8pm Mon-Sat) has locations all over the city, including ul Arbat 4/1, Kuznetsky Most 7 and the Marriott Grand Hotel at Tverskaya ul 26. Alfa Bank ATMs at these locations dispense both roubles and dollars. **American Express** (☎ 933 66 36,

fax 933 66 35; ul Usacheva 33) is the most reliable place to cash AmEx travellers cheques.

Post & Communications The convenient **Central Telegraph** (Tsentralny Telegraf; Tverskaya ul 7; postal counters open 8am-10pm daily, telephone office open 24hr) offers telephone, fax and Internet services.

Pay phones in Moscow operate with phonecards that are widely available in shops, kiosks and metro stations. To access your Western calling-card account from Moscow dial the following provider numbers: **MCI** (☎ 747 3322, 960 2222), **AT&T** (☎ 755 5042) and **Sprint** (☎ 747 3324).

Email & Internet Access On the lower level of the Okhotny Ryad shopping mall near Red Square, **Time Online** (☎ 363 0060; w www.timeonline.ru; open 24hr) claims to be the largest Internet café in Eastern Europe. After hours, enter from the Kuznetsky Most underground station. Rates range from R30 to R60 per hour.

Drinks and competitive rates are also available at the equally central **Internet Klub** (☎ 924 21 40; Kuznetsky Most 12; open 9am-midnight daily), which charges R60 per hour.

Digital Resources The official Moscow government website, w www.moscow-guide.ru, is frequently updated with information on a range of topics from transport to culture.

Travel Agencies Affiliated with the Travellers Guest House, **Infinity Travel** (☎ 234 6555, fax 234 6556; e info@infinity.ru; Komsomolsky prosp 13) is a great source for cheap airline tickets and other services.

Inside the interesting old Gostiny Dvor building, **Capital Tours** (☎ 232 2442; w www.capitaltours.ru; ul Ilyinka 4) offers a Moscow city tour twice daily (adults/children US$18/10) and Kremlin/Armoury tour (US$30/20), which are recommended.

Medical & Emergency Services Several expensive, foreign-run health services are available in Moscow, including the **American Medical Center** (☎ 933 7700, fax 933 7701; Grokholsky per 1), which has an English-speaking **pharmacy** (open 8am-8pm Mon-Fri, 9am-5pm Sat & Sun). The best Russian facility is **Botkin Hospital** (☎ 945 0045; 2-y Botkinsky proezd 5).

MOSCOW & ST PETERSBURG

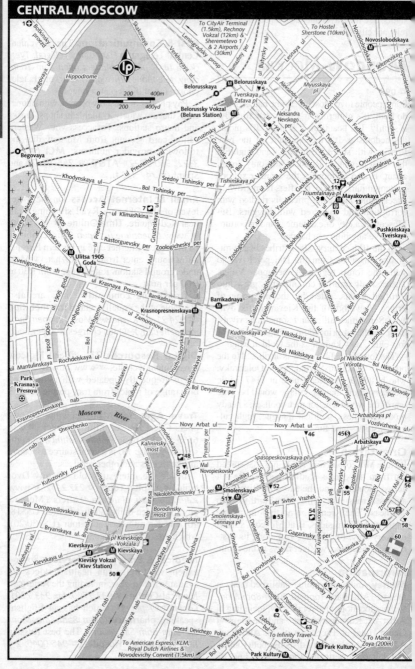

CENTRAL MOSCOW

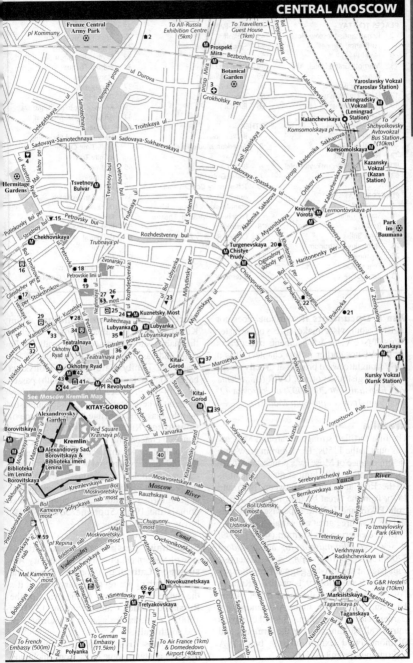

CENTRAL MOSCOW

CENTRAL MOSCOW

PLACES TO STAY
2 Renaissance Moscow Hotel;
   Lufthansa; Airlines
9 Hotel Pekin
13 Marriott Grand Hotel; Alfa
   Bank
14 Hotel Minsk
17 Hotel Tsentralnaya
19 Hotel Budapest
22 Galina's Flat
30 East-West Hotel
35 Hotel Savoy
40 Hotel Rossiya
42 Hotel Moskva
50 Radisson Slavyanskaya Hotel
53 Hotel Arbat

PLACES TO EAT
5 Zen Coffee
8 Starlite Diner
11 Rostiks
15 Taras Bulba
23 Tsentralny Gastronom
26 Jagannat
28 Pelmeshka
33 Zen Coffee

46 Yolki-Palki
49 Tinkoff
51 Smolensky Gastronom
52 Moo-Moo
58 Patio Pizza
59 Spets-Bufet No 7
61 Mama Zoya
65 Yolki-Palki
66 PirOGI

OTHER
1 Botkin Hospital
3 American Medical Centre
4 BB King
6 British Airways
7 Polish Embassy
10 Tchaikovsky Concert Hall
12 American Bar & Grill
16 Stanislavsky & Nemirovich-
   Danchenko Musical Theatre
18 Aeroflot
20 Central Railway Agency
   Ticket Office
21 UVIR
24 Duck
25 Internet Klub

27 Alfa Bank
29 Chekhov Art Theatre
31 Ukrainian Embassy
32 Central Telegraph
34 Bolshoi Theatre
36 Starye Polya
37 Propaganda
38 Proekt OGI
39 Kitaysky Lyotchik Dzhao-Da
41 Archaeological Museum
43 Transaero
44 Okhotny Ryad Shopping
   Mall; Time Online;
   Infinity Travel
45 Alfa Bank
47 US Embassy
48 UK Embassy
54 Canadian Embassy
55 Delta Air Lines
56 Rosie O'Grady's
57 Pushkin Fine Arts Museum
60 Cathedral of Christ the
   Saviour
62 Finnair
63 Australian Embassy
64 State Tretyakov Gallery

Visa & Documents If your hotel does not register your visa, make sure you register yourself (see Visas & Documents under Facts for the Visitor earlier in this chapter). It is a fairly straightforward process at the city's central visa registration office, **UVIR** (*Upravlenia Viz i Registratsii;* ☎ 200 8497; *ul Pokrovka 42; open 9am-1pm & 2pm-6pm Mon-Fri*).

Kremlin

The first fortified stronghold around Moscow was built in the 1150s. The Kremlin grew with the importance of Moscow's princes and in the 1320s it replaced Vladimir as the headquarters of the Russian Church. Between 1475 and 1516, Ivan the Great brought master builders from Pskov and Italy to supervise new walls and towers, three great cathedrals and more.

Before entering the **Kremlin** (☎ 203 0349; **w** *www.kremlin.museum.ru; adult/student R200/100; open 10am-6pm Fri-Wed*) deposit your bags at the **left-luggage office** (*R60 per bag; open 9am-6.30pm*), beneath the Kutafya Tower, just north of the main ticket office. The main ticket office, in the Aleksandrovsky Garden, closes at 4.30pm. The ticket covers entry to all buildings except the Armoury and Diamond Fund Exhibition (see below). A photography permit is R50.

Northern & Western Buildings From Kutafya Tower (Kutafya bashnya), which is the main visitors entrance today, walk up the ramp and pass through the Kremlin walls beneath the **Trinity Gate Tower** (Troitskaya bashnya). The lane to the right (south) passes the 17th-century **Poteshny Palace** (Poteshny dvorets) where Stalin lived. The bombastic marble, glass and concrete **Kremlin Palace of Congresses** (Kremlyovksy Dvorets Syezdov) houses a concert and ballet auditorium.

North of the Kremlin Palace of Congresses, the 18th-century **Arsenal** is ringed with 800 captured Napoleonic cannons. The offices of the president of Russia are in the yellow, triangular former **Senate** (Senat) building. Next door is the 1930s **Supreme Soviet** (Verkhovny Soviet) building.

Sobornaya ploshchad On the northern side of Sobornaya pl is the 15th-century **Assumption Cathedral** (Uspensky sobor), the focal church of pre-revolutionary Russia. It's the burial place of most of the heads of the Russian Orthodox Church from the 1320s to 1700. The tombs are against the north, west and south walls.

The iconostasis dates from 1652 but its lowest level contains some older icons, including the *Virgin of Vladimir* (Vladimirskaya Bogo-mater), an early 15th-century Rublev school copy of Russia's most revered image. The 12th-century original, now in the Tretyakov Gallery, stood in the Assumption Cathedral from the 1480s to 1930. One of the oldest Russian icons, the 12th-century, red-clothed *St George* (Svyatoy Georgy) from Novgorod, is positioned by the north wall.

With its two golden domes rising above the eastern side of Sobornaya pl, the 16th-century **Ivan the Great Bell Tower** (Kolokolnya Ivana Velikogo) is the Kremlin's tallest struc-ture, visible 30km away. Beside the bell tower stands the world's biggest bell, the **Tsar Bell** (Tsar-kolokol), a 202-tonne monster that cracked before it ever rang. North of the bell tower is the mammoth **Tsar Cannon** (Tsar-pushka), cast in 1586, but never shot.

Back on Sobornaya pl, the 1508 **Archangel Cathedral** (Arkhangelsky sobor) at the square's southeastern corner was for centuries the coronation, wedding and burial church of tsars. The tombs of Moscow's rulers from the 1320s to the 1690s are here bar one (Boris Godunov, buried at Sergiev Posad).

Dating from 1489, the **Annunciation Cathedral** (Blagoveshchensky sobor), at the southwestern corner of Sobornaya pl, contains the celebrated icons of the master painter Theophanes the Greek. He probably painted the six icons at the right-hand end of the deesis row, the biggest of the six tiers of the iconostasis. *Archangel Michael* (the third icon from the left on the deesis row) and the adja-cent *St Peter* are ascribed to Andrey Rublev.

Armoury & Diamond Fund In the south-western corner of the Kremlin, the **Armoury** (*Oruzheynaya palata; adult/student R300/ 175*) is a numbingly opulent collection of treasures accumulated over centuries by the Russian State and Church. Your ticket will specify a time of entry. Highlights include the Fabergé eggs in room 2 and the reams of royal regalia in rooms 6 and 9.

If the Armoury hasn't sated your diamond lust, there are more in the separate **Diamond Fund Exhibition** (*Vystavka almaznogo fonda; admission adult/student R300/175; closed for lunch 1pm-2pm*) in the same building.

Alexandrovsky Garden The first public park in Moscow, Alexandrovsky Garden (Alexandrovsky Sad) sits along the Kremlin's

western wall. Colourful flower beds and im-pressive Kremlin views make it a favourite spot for Muscovites and tourists alike to stroll.

The **Tomb of the Unknown Soldier** (Mogila neizvestnogo soldata) at its northern end is a kind of national pilgrimage spot, where newlyweds bring flowers and have their pictures taken. The tomb contains the remains of one soldier who died in December 1941 at Km 41 of Leningradskoe shosse – the nearest the Nazis came to Moscow. Changing of the guard happens every hour.

Red Square

Red Square (Krasnaya pl; from the old Russ-ian word for 'beautiful') lies immediately outside the Kremlin's northeastern wall. As you step on to the square, feast your eyes on the building that, more than any other, says 'Russia' – St Basil's Cathedral, which rises from the slope at the square's southern end.

No picture can prepare you for the crazy confusion of colours and shapes that is **St Basil's Cathedral** (Sobor Vasilia Blazhennogo; ☎ 298 3304; admission R100; open 11am-5pm Wed-Mon). This ultimate symbol of Russia was created between 1555 and 1561 to cele-brate Ivan the Terrible's capture of the Tatar stronghold Kazan. Its design is the culmin-ation of a wholly Russian style that had been developed building wooden churches. The cathedral owes its name to the barefoot holy fool Vasily (Basil) the Blessed, who predicted Ivan's damnation and added (correctly) that Ivan would murder a son.

The granite **Lenin's tomb** (Mavzoley VI Lenina; ☎ 923 5527; admission free; open 10am-1pm Tues-Thur, Sat & Sun), at the foot of the Kremlin wall, is one of Red Square's must-sees, especially since (if some people get their way) the former leader may eventu-ally end up beside his mum in St Petersburg.

Before joining the queue at the northwest-ern corner of Red Square, drop your camera at the left-luggage office beneath the Kutafya Tower, as you will not be allowed to take it with you. Humourless guards ensure that visit-ors remain respectful. After trouping past the embalmed, oddly waxy figure, emerge from the mausoleum and inspect where Stalin, Brezhnev and other communist heavy hitters are buried along the Kremlin wall.

The **GUM** State Department Store, which lines the northeastern side of Red Square, was built in the 19th century to house over 1000

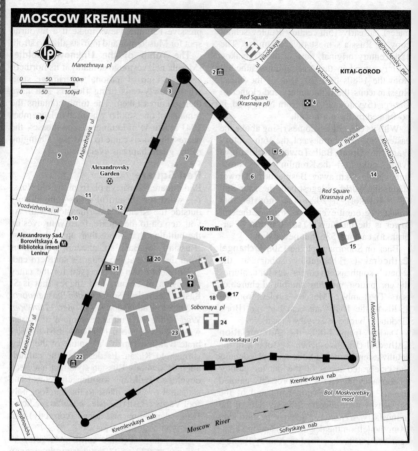

MOSCOW KREMLIN

shops. The tiny **Kazan Cathedral** (*Kazansky sobor; ul Nikolskaya 3; admission free; open 8am-7pm daily, evening service 8pm Mon*), opposite the northern end of GUM, is a 1993 replica of the original.

The **State History Museum** (*Gosudarstvenny Istorichesky Muzey;* ☎ *292 4019; Red Square; adult/student R150/75; open 11am-7pm Wed-Mon*) at the northern end of the square has an enormous collection with coverage of the whole Russian empire from the Stone Age on.

Around Red Square

Manezhnaya pl, at the northern end of Red Square, has been transformed into the vast underground **Okhotny Ryad shopping mall** (☎ *737 8409*). The long, low building on the

southwestern side of the square is the **Manezh Central Exhibition Hall** (*Tsentralny vystavochny zal Manezh;* ☎ *202 8976; open 11am-8pm daily*), home to some of Moscow's most popular art exhibitions. On the northwestern side of the square is the fine edifice of **Moscow State University** (Moskovsky gosudarstvenny universitet), built in 1793.

The 1930s **Hotel Moskva**, fronting the northeastern side of the square, is half constructivist, half Stalinist. The story goes that Stalin was shown two possible designs for the hotel. Not realising they were alternatives, he approved both of them. The builders didn't dare point out his error and built half in each style, with predictably incongruous results.

The entrance to the brand new **Archaeological Museum** (☎ *292 4171; Manezhnaya*

MOSCOW KREMLIN

MOSCOW KREMLIN
3	Tomb of the Unknown Soldier
6	Senate
7	Arsenal
10	Kremlin Ticket Office
11	Kutafya Tower
12	Trinity Gate Tower
13	Supreme Soviet
16	Tsar Cannon
17	Tsar Bell
18	Ivan the Great Bell Tower
19	Assumption Cathedral
20	Kremlin Palace of Congresses
21	Poteshny Palace
22	Armoury & Diamond Fund Exhibition
23	Annunciation Cathedral
24	Archangel Cathedral

RED SQUARE
1	Kazan Cathedral
2	State History Museum
4	GUM State Department Store
5	Lenin's Tomb
15	St Basil's Cathedral

OTHER
8	Moscow State University
9	Manezh Central Exhibition Hall
14	Gostiny Dvor; Capital Tours

pl 1; admission R30; open 10am-6pm Tues-Sun) is at the base of the hotel on the square.

Teatralnaya pl opens out on both sides of Okhotny Ryad, near Manezhnaya pl. The northern half is dominated by the **Bolshoi Theatre** where Tchaikovsky's *Swan Lake* was premiered (unsuccessfully) in 1877.

The narrow old streets to the east of Red Square are known as Kitai-Gorod, which literally means 'Chinatown', but actually has nothing to do with China. The name derives from *kitai*, which means wattle, after the palisades that reinforced the earthen ramp erected around this early Kremlin suburb. Along Teatralny proezd at **Starye Polya** (Old Fields), archaeologists uncovered parts of the 16th-century fortified wall that used to surround Kitai-Gorod, as well as the foundations of the 1493 Trinity Church. Kitai-Gorod is one of the oldest parts of Moscow, settled since the 13th century. There are loads of tiny churches hidden amongst its narrow alleyways.

Pushkin Fine Arts Museum & Around

Moscow's premier foreign art museum is only just a skip from the southwestern corner of the Kremlin. The Pushkin Fine Arts Museum (☎ 203 7412; ul Volkhonka 12; adult/student R160/60, audio guide R100; open 10am-6pm Tues-Sun), which is near Kropotkinskaya metro, is famous for its impressionist and postimpressionist paintings. It also has a broad selection of European works from the Renaissance onward, which were mostly appropriated from private collections after the revolution.

Nearby is the gigantic **Cathedral of Christ the Saviour** (Khram Khrista Spasitelya; ☎ 201 3847; open 10am-5pm daily), rebuilt at an estimated cost of US$360m by Mayor Luzhkov on the site of the original that was destroyed by Stalin, and in place of what was the world's largest swimming pool.

State Tretyakov Gallery

The State Tretyakov Gallery (Gosudarstvennaya Tretyakovskaya galereya; ☎ 951 1362; Lavrushinsky pereulok 10; adult/student R220/110, audio tour R120; open 10am-6.30pm Tues-Sun) has the world's best collection of Russian icons and an outstanding collection of other prerevolutionary Russian art, particularly from the 19th-century Peredvizhniki movement.

Novodevichy Convent

A cluster of sparkling domes behind turreted walls on the Moscow River, Novodevichy Convent (Novodevichy monastyr; ☎ 246 8526; admission R30; open 10am-5pm Wed-Mon) is rich with history and treasures. Founded in 1524 to celebrate the re-taking of Smolensk from Lithuania, it is notorious as the place where Peter the Great imprisoned his half-sister Sofia for her part in the Streltsy Rebellion. Sofia was joined in her retirement by Yevdokia Lopukhina, Peter's first wife, whom he considered a nag.

You enter the convent under the red and white Moscow baroque **Transfiguration Gate-Church**. The oldest and most dominant building is the white **Smolensk Cathedral** (1524–25). **Sofia's tomb** lies among others in the south nave. The **bell tower** against the convent's east wall, completed in 1690, is generally regarded as Moscow's finest. The adjacent **Novodevichy Cemetery** contains the tombs of Khrushchev, Chekhov, Gogol, Mayakovsky, Stanislavsky, Prokofiev, Eisenstein, Gromyko, Raisa Gorbachev and other Russian and Soviet notables.

All-Russia Exhibition Centre

No other place in the country seems to sum up the rise and fall of the Soviet dream quite so well as the All-Russia Exhibition Centre (Vserossiysky Vystavochry Tsentr; VVTs). The old initials by which it is still commonly known, VDNKh, stand for Vystavka Dostizheny Narodnogo Khozyaystva SSSR – USSR Economic Achievements Exhibition.

The centre was created in the 1950s and 60s to impress upon one and all the success of the Soviet economic system. Two kilometres long and 1km wide, it is composed of wide pedestrian avenues and grandiose pavilions, glorifying every aspect of socialist construction. The pavilions represent a huge variety of architectural styles, symbolic of the contributions from many diverse ethnic and artistic movements to the common goal. Here you'll find kitschy socialist realism, the most inspiring socialist optimism and – now – also the tackiest of capitalist consumerism. The centre was an early casualty when those in power finally admitted that the Soviet economy had become a disaster – funds were cut off by 1990. Today, the VVTs is a commercial centre, its pavilions given over to sales of the very imported goods that were supposed to be inferior.

The soaring 100m titanium obelisk beside VDNKh metro is a monument to Soviet space flight. In its base is the **Cosmonautics Museum** (Muzey kosmonavtiki; ☎ 283 7914; admission R30; open 10am-7pm Tues-Sun), a series of displays from the glory days of the Soviet space programme.

Places to Stay – Budget

Guesthouses You will find that **Galina's Flat** (☎ 921 6038; e galinas.flat@mtu-net.ru; ul Chaplygina 8, no 35; dorm beds/singles/doubles US$8/15/20) is just that – a private flat with a few extra rooms that Galina rents out. She has a total of six beds; kitchen and Internet facilities are available.

G&R Hostel Asia (☎ 378 00 01, fax 378 28 66; w www.hostels.ru; Hotel Asia; ul Zelenodolskaya 2/3; dorm beds/singles/doubles with breakfast US$16/30/44), on the top floors of an old hotel 10km southeast of the centre, is one of the best budget options. The management is clued up and runs a travel agency that can book train tickets and the like. Leave Ryazansky Prospekt metro from the end of the train and look for the tallest building around – that's the hostel.

Ten kilometres north of the centre is the **Hostel Sherstone** (☎/fax 797 8075; w www.sherstone.ru; Gostinichny proezd 8/1; dorm beds/singles/doubles US$14/25/40), a branch of the G&R. Services include visa support, free transfers from the railway station and discounts for IYHF cards. It is a 10-minute walk from Vladykino metro.

Travellers Guest House (☎ 951 4059, fax 280 7686; e tgh@glasnet.ru; Bol Pereyaslavskaya ul 50, floor 10; dorm beds US$18, rooms with private/shared bathroom US$48/55) calls itself Moscow's 'first and only' budget accommodation. Perhaps the first, but it is certainly no longer the only, this lacklustre place is a 10-minute walk north of Prospekt Mira metro.

Hotels The **Hotel Tsentralnaya** (☎ 229 8957, fax 292 1221; Tverskaya ul 10; singles/doubles R1150/1750) is pretty crummy, but you can't beat the location. Prices are not bad either, but they won't win you a smile from the surly staff.

Hotel Minsk (☎ 299 1213, fax 299 0362; Tverskaya ul 22; singles/doubles R700/1050) is plagued by the same symptoms as the Tsentralnaya, shabby rooms and disagreeable staff, but it shares a similar prime location. The ticket office in the lobby is useful for train and air tickets.

Places to Stay – Mid-Range

Hotel Moskva (☎ 960 2020, fax 960 5938; Okhotny ryad ul 2; singles/doubles R1600/2500) occupies the block between Manezhnaya pl and Teatralnaya pl. Rooms are tolerable and some also have marvellous views of the Kremlin.

The **Hotel Rossiya** (☎ 232 6046, 232 6248; ul Varvarka 6; singles/doubles from R1500/1600) has – literally – thousands of rooms (some are better than others, but you'll pay more for them). The Rossiya gets a bad rap because it is just so big and ugly, but some swear by the place for its unbeatable location and reasonable prices. Besides, you can't see it if you are inside.

The **Hotel Pekin** (☎ 209 2215, fax 200 1420; w hotelpekin.ringnet.ru; ul Bolshaya Sadovaya 5/1; doubles from US$62) is better than it looks, with its cheesy Oriental decor and noisy casino. However, the staff are very helpful, the rooms are comfortable, and the location is convenient.

East-West Hotel (☎ 290 04 04, fax 291 46 06; **w** www.col.ru/east-west; Tverskoy bul 14/4; singles/doubles with breakfast from US$100/130) is a kitsch but rather charming small hotel on one of central Moscow's most pleasant streets.

Hotel Budapest (☎ 923 2356, fax 921 1266; **w** www.hotel-budapest.ru; Petrovskie linii ul 2/18; singles/doubles with breakfast US$105/147) is the top pick in the mid-range. This elegant central hotel has friendly management and 125 stylish rooms.

Places to Stay – Top End

Just off the Arbat, **Hotel Arbat** (☎ 244 7628, fax 244 0093; **e** hotelarbat@hotmail.com; Plotnikov per 12; singles/doubles with breakfast from US$120/135) has a prime location on a quiet street. This comfortable, 105-room hotel has a decent restaurant as well as a lovely courtyard.

Hotel Savoy (☎ 929 8500/8558, fax 230 2186; ul Rozhdestvenka 3; singles/doubles with breakfast from US$180/230) was the first of Moscow's new-wave luxury hotels when it reopened in 1989. The gilt, murals and chandeliers maintain the atmosphere of prerevolutionary privilege.

Marriott Grand Hotel (☎ 937 0000, fax 937 0001; **w** www.marriott.com; Tverskaya ul 26; singles/doubles with breakfast US$295/305) has a large atrium and roof-top patio with excellent views. This is where President Bush stayed when he visited in 2002, so security must be OK.

Radisson Slavyanskaya Hotel (☎ 941 8020, fax 240 6915; **w** www.radisson.com; Berezhkovskaya nab 2; singles/doubles from US$180/210), 3.5km west of the Kremlin by Kiev station is almost a village in itself with a large business centre, its own shopping mall, a host of cafés and restaurants, a big pool and a movie theatre.

Places to Eat

Restaurants The **Yolki-Palki** (☎ 953 9130; Klimentovsky per 14 Ď ☎ 291 6888; Novy Arbat ul 11; both open 11am-midnight) is a chain of country-cottage-style Russian outlets, specialising in simple, traditional dishes (R150). The beer is cheap and there's a blessed salad bar (R120).

With a number of branches dotted around the city, **Taras Bulba** (☎ 200 6082; ul Petrovka 30/7; meals R600; open noon-midnight) is

the Ukrainian version of Yolki-Palki. There's no salad bar, but the food is good and the atmosphere homy.

Spets-Bufet No 7 (☎ 959 3135; ul Serafimovicha 2; meal R300; open noon-6am) is in the basement of a once-prestigious apartment block that was home to many Communist Party apparatchiks. This 'Special Buffet' recreates the forum where the bigwigs may have eaten. The food is decidedly mediocre (thus making the place more authentic).

The good Georgian restaurant **Mama Zoya** (☎ 201 7743; Sechenovsky per 8 Ď ☎ 242 85 50; Frunzenskaya nab 16; both open noon-11pm) now has two branches offering meals for R200. The latter is on a boat, where fleet-footed dancers and musicians accompany the delicious shashlik and khachi puri (rich cheesy bread).

If you need your vitamins, **Jagannat** (☎ 928 3580, Kuznetsky most 11; mains R150; open noon-midnight daily) is a funky, vegetarian café, restaurant and store. Service is slow but sublime. The food is worth the wait.

Tinkoff (☎ 777 3300; Protochny per 11; beers R120, meals R600; open noon-2am) is Moscow's first microbrewery, featuring live sports on TV, lagers and pilsners on draught, and a metre-long sausage on the menu (yikes).

The original **Starlite Diner** (☎ 290 9638; Bolshaya Sadovaya ul 16; open 24hr) – the quintessential burger and milkshake diner – has a wonderful, leafy outdoor seating area.

Cafés If you are looking for a coffee fix, **Zen Coffee** (☎ 234 17 84; Lesnaya ul 1/2 Ď ☎ 292 51 14; Kamergersky per 6; both open 9am-11pm) has two outlets. The first of these modern, pleasant cafés is opposite Belorussky Vokzal; the second is on the popular pedestrian boulevard leading off from Tverskaya ul to Kuznetsky most.

PirOGI (☎ 951 7596; Pyatnitskaya ul 29/8; open 24hr) is a low-key, bohemian place, that serves coffee, beers and even has books, which you can buy to keep or just peruse while you have a drink.

Cafeterias Dig that spotted cow decor at **Moo-Moo** (☎ 241 1364; ul Arbat 45/23 • ☎ 245 78 20; Komsomolsky prosp 26; both open 10am-11pm), which offers an easy serve-yourself approach to Russian standards. For R150, get borshch, pelmeni (meat-filled dumplings) and a violently coloured dessert.

Pelmeshka (☎ 292 8392; Kuznetsky most 4/3; meals R100; open 11am-midnight), clean and modern, serves the most filling of Russian favourites pelmeni.

Fast Food An omnipresent local chain, **Russkoe Bistro**, is endorsed and, coincidentally, co-owned, by Mayor Luzhkov. It serves cheap, traditional goodies such as pirozhki (pies) and blini. McDonald's also has many locations and all have the same allure: familiar fare and clean toilets.

Rostik's (☎ 251 4950; ul 1-ya Tverskaya-Yamskaya 2/1; open 9am-9pm daily; meals R100) is another chain serving American food (burgers, fried chicken). **Patio Pizza** (w 201 56 26; ul Volkhonka 13a; pizzas from R200) also has branches all over town. Often you'll find Patio Pizza and Rostiks next to each other, as they are run by the same company.

Self-Catering If you want to eat like a Muscovite, you'll buy your food, take it home and cook it there. **Sedmoy Kontinent** supermarket chain (open 24hr) carries mainly local brands but some Western ones as well. The most central locations of the branches are **Smolensky Gastronom** (☎ 241 3581; ul Arbat 54/2) and **Tsentralny Gastronom** (☎ 928 9577; ul Bolshaya Lubyanka 12/1).

Entertainment
The key to finding out what's on is the comprehensive weekly entertainment section in the Thursday *Moscow Times*. For a laugh, you can also try *The Exile*.

Classical Music, Opera & Ballet The
largest concert venue is **Tchaikovsky Concert Hall** (☎ 299 0378; Triumfalnaya pl 4/31), which seats over 1600 and is the home of the famous State Symphony Orchestra.

Spending an evening at the **Bolshoi** (☎ 292 0050; w www.bolshoi.ru; Teatralnaya pl 1) is still one of the most romantic things to do in Moscow. Tickets are hard to come by unless you hang around the theatre before the performance and buy them from a tout.

Another gorgeous theatre is the **Stanislavsky & Nemirovich-Danchenko Musical Theatre** (☎ 229 0649; w www.stanislavsky .ru; ul Bolshaya Dmitrovka 17) with a similar classical repertoire and high-quality performances. The tickets are readily available and relatively cheap.

Theatre Also known as MkhAT, the
Chekhov Art Theatre (☎ 229 8760; w www .art.theatre.ru; Kamergersky per 3) is where method acting was founded over 100 years ago. Watch for English-language versions of Russian classics performed here by the American Studio (☎ 292 0941).

Bars & Clubs In a basement close to Kitai-
Gorod metro is **Kitaysky Lyotchik Dzhao-Da** (☎ 924 5611; w www.jao-da.ru; Lubyansky proezd 25; admission R150), one of the city's best and most relaxed club/restaurants, often with live music.

Proekt OGI (☎ 229 5489; w proekt.ogi.ru; Potapovsky per 8/12; admission R50-80; 8am-11pm) is a vaguely hippy, but definitely hip, place for student types. Enter through the unmarked door in the corner of the courtyard. There is live music most nights.

Every Thursday, **Propaganda** (☎ 924 5732; w www.propagandamoscow.com; Bol Zlatoustinsky per 7) is happening; DJs spin a cool mix for the beautiful people to dance to.

Duck (☎ 923 6158; Pushechnaya ul 9/6; admission varies; open noon-6am daily) is a successor to the Hungry Duck, a bar that was often described as the wildest in Europe.

BB King (☎ 299 8206; ul Sadovaya-Samotechnaya 4/2; noon-2am) is the best venue for live jazz and blues. Concerts and jam sessions go into the wee hours.

As for expat bars, you can't go far wrong at either **American Bar and Grill** (☎ 250 9525; ul 1-ya Tverskaya-Yamskaya 2/1; open 24hr) or **Rosie O'Grady's** (☎ 203 9087; ul Znamenka 9/12; open noon-1am), both of which are pretty self-explanatory.

Shopping
The weekend **Vernisazh market** at the Izmaylovsky Park is a sprawling area packed with art and handmade crafts. Moscow's biggest original range of handicrafts is here and dozens of artists sell their own work. The market is two minutes' walk from Izmaylovksy Park metro.

Getting There & Away
Air Of Moscow's five airports, the most-often used are Sheremetevo 1 and 2 and Domodedovo. You can buy domestic airline tickets at most travel agencies and Aeroflot offices all over town, including the convenient **Aeroflot office** (☎ 753 5555; ul Petrovka 20/1; open 9am-7pm Mon-Sat, 9am-3.30pm Sun).

Transaero airlines also has several ticket offices, including a very convenient one at the corner of Hotel Moskva (☎ 241 4800; Okhotny ryad ul 2; open 9am-9pm daily). International airline offices in Moscow include:

Air France (☎ 937 3839) ul Korovy Val 7
British Airways (☎ 363 2525) Business Centre Parus, ul 1-ya Tverskaya-Yamskaya 23
Delta Air Lines (☎ 937 9090) Gogolevsky bul 11
Finnair (☎ 933 0056) Kropotinsky per 7
KLM-Royal Dutch Airlines (☎ 258 3600) ul Usacheva 33/2
Lufthansa Airlines (☎ 737 6400) Renaissance Moscow Hotel, Olimpiysky prosp 18

Train If all roads lead to Moscow, so then do the railways. There are daily connections with most parts of Russia and the CIS countries, as well as numerous countries in Eastern and Western Europe, and China and Mongolia. There are nine train stations in Moscow, each serving specific destinations.

Besides the train stations proper, tickets are sold throughout the city at **Central Railway Agency ticket offices**, such as (Tsentralnoe Zheleznodorozhnoe Agentstvo; ☎ 262 2566; Maly Kharitonevsky per 6; open 8am-1pm & 2pm-7pm daily). Alternatively, travel agencies and other ticket offices (kassa zheleznoy dorogi) also sell tickets, sometimes for a small commission, but frankly it's worth it.

Bus Buses run to a number of towns and cities within about 700km of Moscow, but they tend to be crowded. However, they are usually faster than the suburban (prigorodny) trains, and are convenient to some destinations. To book a seat you have to go 15km east of the city to the long-distance bus station (Shchyolkovsky Avtovokzal) beside Shchyolkovskaya metro.

Boat The Moscow terminus for cruises to St Petersburg is 10km northeast of the centre at the **Northern River station** (Severny Rechnoy Vokzal; ☎ 459 7476; Leningradskoe shosse 51). Take the metro to Rechnoy Vokzal stop, then walk 15 minutes due west, passing under Leningradskoe shosse and through a nice park.

Getting Around
To/From the Airports There are minibuses that go from both Sheremetevo-1 and Sheremetevo-2 to metro Rechnoy Vokzal. Minibuses also link the Domodedovo airport

to the metro Domodedovskaya, and Vnukovo airport to metro Yugo-Zapadnaya. Suburban trains run between Bykovo station, 400m from the Bykovo airport, and Kazan station.

To book a taxi to/from the airport, call **Logus 88** (☎ 911 9747), which charges R500/800 to/from the Sheremetevo airports, or **Taxi Bistro** (☎ 324 9974, 324 5144) that costs R450 to Sheremetevo.

Metro The metro is the easiest, quickest and cheapest way of getting around Moscow. Nine million people ride the metro every day. The 150-plus stations are marked outside with big 'M' signs. Magnetic tickets are sold at ticket booths for one, two or more rides. Each ride costs R5, unless you buy in bulk (10 rides for R35, 20 for R70, 60 for R150).

Taxi To book a taxi in advance, call the **Central Taxi Reservation Office** (☎ 927 0000; open 24hr).

Around Moscow
Подмосковье

The Golden Ring (Zolotoe Koltso) is a modern name for a loop of very old towns that are northeast of Moscow that preceded the present capital as the political and cultural heart of Russia. The towns' churches, monasteries, kremlins (city forts) and museums make a picturesque portfolio of early Russian art, architecture and history.

VLADIMIR ВЛАДИМИР
☎ 09222 • pop 360,000
Little remains in Vladimir, 178km northeast of Moscow, from its medieval heyday when it was Russia's capital. However, what does remain – several examples of Russia's most ancient and formative architecture – is worth pausing to see en route to/from the more charming town of Suzdal.

Begun in 1158, **Assumption Cathedral** (Uspensky sobor; admission R30; open about 1.30pm-5pm daily) is a white-stone version of Kyiv's brick Byzantine churches, which contains magnificent frescoes by Andrey Rublev and others. Nearby, the **Cathedral of St Dmitry** (Dmitrievsky sobor), built from 1193 to 1197, is where the art of Vladimir-Suzdal stone carving reached its pinnacle.

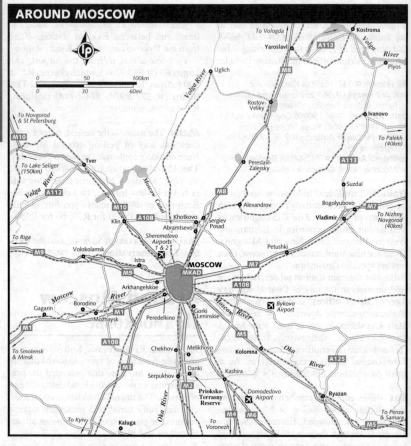

AROUND MOSCOW

From Moscow's Kursky Vokzal (Kursk station), there are numerous suburban trains and buses to Vladimir. There are also bus services to/from Moscow, Nizhny Novgorod, Kostroma, Ivanovo, Suzdal and Kazan.

SUZDAL СУЗДАЛЬ
☎ 09231 • pop 12,000

You have to pinch yourself in Suzdal, 35km north of Vladimir, to be reminded that you've not slipped back in time to ancient Russia. Such is the enchantment spun by this architecturally protected town with its profusion of old monasteries, convents and churches and intricately decorated wooden cottages (izbas) dotted in green fields around the meandering Kamenka River. Green fields reach right into the centre.

Things to See & Do

At the eastern end of ul Kremlyovskaya, the 1.4km-long earth rampart of Suzdal's kremlin encloses the 13th-century **Nativity of the Virgin Cathedral** (Rozhdestvensky sobor), the 1635 bell tower and the **Archbishop's Chambers** (Arkhiyereyskie palati). The latter houses the **Suzdal History Exhibition** (☎ 204 44; admission R30; open 10am-5pm Wed-Mon). The exhibition includes the original 13th-century door from the cathedral, photos of its interior and a visit to the 18th-century **Cross Hall** (Krestovaya palata).

Founded in the 14th century to protect the town's northern entrance, the **Saviour Monastery of St Euthymius** (Spaso-Yevfimievsky monastyr; admission R150, photos R50; open 10am-6pm Tues-Sun) is at the northern end of ul Lenina. Inside, standing before the seven-domed, 12th- and 13th-century **Cathedral of the Transfiguration of the Saviour**, a tall bell tower chimes a lovely 10-minute concert every hour. The old monastery **prison**, set up in 1764 for religious dissidents, now houses a fascinating exhibit on the monastery's military history and prison life, including displays about some of the better-known prisoners who stayed here.

Places to Stay & Eat
Hotel Rizopolozhenskaya (☎ 205 53; ul Lenina; singles/doubles from R250/300) is housed in the decrepit 19-century Monastery of the Deposition, but the rooms are renovated.

Likhoninsky Dom (☎ 219 01, fax 0922-32 70 10; e aksenova-museum@rnt.vladimir.ru; ul Slobodskaya 34; doubles R630), the nicest place to stay, is on a quiet street near the town centre.

Restoran Trapeznaya (☎ 217 63; mains R100-200; open 11am-11pm daily) is in the Archbishop's Chambers in the kremlin. The food is traditional and the atmosphere lively. Be sure to sample the local *medovukha*, a lightly alcoholic, honey-flavoured mead drink that is simply heavenly.

Getting There & Away
Only buses serve Suzdal. There is a direct connection each day with Moscow's Shchyol-kovsky Avtovokzal, two buses each day to Kostroma, five to Ivanovo, and regular services throughout the day to Vladimir.

ROSTOV-VELIKY
РОСТОВ-ВЕЛИКИЙ
☎ 08536 • pop 40,000
This town is one of Russia's oldest, first chronicled in 862. Much less touristy than Suzdal, Rostov is a rustic, charming place with a magnificent kremlin beside shimmering Lake Nero.

Things to See & Do
The unashamedly photogenic **Kremlin** (☎ 317 17; admission R100; open 10am-5pm) is 1.5km south of the train and bus stations. Although founded in the 12th century, nearly all the buildings date from the 1670s and 1680s.

The west and north entrances are gate-churches richly decorated with 17th-century frescoes. The metropolitan's own chapel, the **Church of the Saviour-over-the-Galleries**

(Tserkov Spasa-na-Senyakh), has the most beautiful interior of all. There are **museums** in the metropolitan's house as well as the **White Chamber**.

Places to Stay & Eat
Dom na Pogrebakh (☎ 3 12 44; rooms from R300), right inside the kremlin, has clean, wood-panelled rooms with shared bathrooms that vary somewhat in size and view. **Trapeznaya** (☎ 328 71; meals R200; open 8am-8pm) is a nearby restaurant.

Getting There & Away
The fastest train from Moscow is the express service from Yaroslavsky Vokzal (Yaroslavl station; three hours). Buses from Rostov to Yaroslavl go roughly every hour. Other transit buses go to Moscow (four to five hours, three daily) through Pereslavl-Zalessky and Sergiev Posad.

SERGIEV POSAD
СЕРГИЕВ ПОСАД
☎ 254 • pop 100,000
This town, 60km from Moscow on the Yaroslavl road, was founded around the Trinity Monastery of St Sergius, a place of national spiritual pilgrimage. For its concentrated artistry and its unique role in the interrelated histories of the Russian Church and State, it is well worth a day trip from Moscow.

Trinity Monastery of St Sergius
The monastery (Troitse-Sergieva Lavra; ☎ 4 53 56; admission free, photos R100; grounds open 10am-6pm daily) has additional charges to visit the museums inside.

Built in the 1420s, the dark yet beautiful **Trinity Cathedral** (Troitsky sobor) is the heart of the Trinity Monastery. A memorial service for St Sergius (whose tomb stands in the southeastern corner) goes on all day, every day. The icon-festooned interior is largely the work of the great medieval painter Andrey Rublyov and his students.

Assumption Cathedral (Uspensky sobor), with its star-spangled domes, was modelled on the cathedral of the same name in the Moscow Kremlin. Outside the west door is the **grave** of Boris Godunov.

The **Vestry** (Riznitsa; admission R150; open 10am-5.30pm Tues-Sun), which is behind the Trinity Cathedral, displays the monastery's extraordinarily rich treasury.

Places to Stay & Eat

A short walk east of the monastery, **Russky Dvorik** (☎ 7 53 92, fax 7 53 91; e rus_dvorik@ conternet.ru; ul Mitkina 14/2; singles/doubles with breakfast from US$50/70) is a delightful small hotel.

It also has a separate **restaurant** (☎ 4 51 14; Krasnoy Armii 134; meals R500), that does get overrun with the tour groups at lunch, but it's otherwise pleasant.

Getting There & Away

From Moscow's Yaroslavsky Vokzal, buses and suburban trains to Sergiev Posad leave every half hour or so, taking 75 to 90 minutes.

St Petersburg
Санкт Петербург

☎ 812 pop

Such is the visual power of this handsome city, created by Peter the Great as his 'window on the West', that it's almost impossible to believe that just three centuries ago St Petersburg was little more than a giant swamp. Now it has a history and European savoir-faire that is unique in Russia.

Apart from the seamless architectural ensemble at the heart of St Petersburg, which is threaded with languorous canals, you will find world-class museums and many stunningly opulent palaces.

Piter, as it's affectionately known to residents, also has a lively club and music scene and prides itself on the quality of its performing arts. It's a city to be savoured.

Orientation

St Petersburg sprawls across and around the delta of the Neva River, at the end of the easternmost arm of the Baltic Sea, known as the Gulf of Finland.

The heart of St Petersburg spreads south and east from the Winter Palace and the Admiralty on the Neva's south bank. Nevsky pr, stretching east-southeast from the Admiralty, is the main street.

The north side of the city has three main areas – the westernmost is Vasilevsky Island, at whose eastern end, the Strelka, many of the city's fine early buildings still stand; the middle is the Petrograd Side; and the eastern is the Vyborg Side.

Information

Tourist Offices The official **tourist office** (☎ 311-28 43; e info@ctic.spb.ru; Nevsky pr 41) can help with individual queries, but it does not book accommodation and there's nothing in the way of official literature. A city walking tour from here is US$25.

More helpful are the staff at either the International Holiday Hostel or the HI St Petersburg Hostel (see Places to Stay later in this chapter).

Money There are many **currency-exchange offices** along Nevsky pr – shop around since some offer better rates to foreigners. A reliable one is **Ligovsky** (Ligovsky per 2).

ATM machines are inside every metro station, in hotels and department stores, main post offices and along major streets.

American Express (☎ 326 4500, fax 326 4501; Malaya Morskaya ul 23) only offers travel services. It's open 9am to 5pm and you can pick up forwarded mail here, but correspondents should send mail care of American Express, PO Box 87, SF53501, Lappeenranta, Finland, from where it is forwarded to St Petersburg.

Post & Communications For your mail, the **central post office** (glavpochtamt; ☎ 312 83 02; Pochtamtskaya ul 9) is open 9am to 8pm Monday to Saturday and 10am to 6pm Sunday. For courier service, try Express Mail Service inside the central post office, or the pricey **Westpost** (☎ 275 07 84; Nevsky pr 86), which mails letters and parcels via Finland reliably.

The **Central Telephone Office** (Bolshaya Morskaya ul 3/5) was closed indefinitely when we last checked; other nearby offices where you can prepay the operator to connect you include Nevsky pr 27 and 88. You can also call direct from any of the card-operated phone booths all over the city (Peterstar ones are the cheapest, SPT the most common, BCL the most expensive). Cards can be purchased from metro stations and telephone offices. Rouble coin-operated phones are found inside every metro station.

Email & Internet Access There are Internet cafés all over the city, one of the most prominent is **Quo Vadis?** (Nevsky pr 24), which is open 24 hours, charges R60 per hour, has 65 terminals and a free library with foreign newspapers and magazines to browse. **Kro Magnon** *(Nevsky pr 81)* is cheaper at R40 per hour; its office is on the right-hand side of the courtyard and on the 2nd floor.

Digital Resources Start with w www.spb .ru, which includes links to the English-language biweekly newspaper *St Petersburg Times* and much more.

Travel Agencies A student and discount air-ticket office is **Sindbad Travel** *(☎ 327 83 84;* e *sindbad@sindbad.ru; 3-ya Sovietskaya ul 28),* at the HI St Petersburg Hostel. **Ost-West Kontaktservice** *(☎ 327 34 16;* e *info@ ostwest.com; Nevsky pr 105)* can also help with any travel needs.

Medical & Emergency Services Treatment of Western quality is available at the **American Medical Center** *(AMC; ☎ 326 17 30; Serpukhovskaya ul 10),* with 24-hour emergency care. Consultations cost at least US$100, often more. **Poliklinika No 2** *(☎ 316 62 72; Moskovsky pr 22)* is also recommended – and much cheaper. Two pharmacies that are open 24 hours are **Apteka Petrofarm** *(Nevsky pr 22)* and **Apteka** *(Liteyny pr 56).*

Health Under no circumstances should you drink unboiled tap water, which contains *Giardia lamblia,* a nasty parasite that can cause nausea and diarrhoea. Recommended treatments for giardia are Metronidazole (Flagyl) and Tinidazole (Fasigyn).

Visas & Documents If your hotel does not register your visa, make sure you register yourself (see Visas & Documents under Facts for the Visitor earlier in this chapter). Go to the central office of **OVIR** *(Otdel Viz i Registratsii; ☎ 278 24 81; Kirochnaya ul 4; open 9am-5pm Mon-Fri)* for registration.

The Historic Heart

Foreigner admission prices are listed in roubles for all the following attractions; foreign students get in for half price unless otherwise stated, children the same or less.

The western end of Nevsky pr begins with a knockout: **Dvortsovaya pl** (Palace Square), where the baroque/rococo **Winter Palace** (Zimny dvorets), painted green, white and gold, appears like a mirage under the archway at the start of ul Bolshaya Morskaya. The

palace was commissioned from Bartolomeo Rastrelli in 1754 by Empress Elizabeth and some of its 1057 rooms now house part of the outstanding **Hermitage** *(☎ 311 34 65;* w *www.hermitagemuseum.org; adult/child & student R300/free; open 10.30am-6pm Tues-Sat, 10.30am-5pm Sun),* one of the world's great art museums. The ticket hall is inside the main entrance on the river side of the Winter Palace.

If you plan to visit the Hermitage's other venues – the **General Staff Building** on the opposite side of the square from the Winter Palace, and the **Menshikov Palace**, which is on Vasilevsky Island – in the same day, consider purchasing a combined ticket (adult/ student & child R500/45).

In the middle of the square, the 47.5m **Alexander Column** commemorates the 1812 victory over Napoleon. To the west across the road is the gilded spire of the **Admiralty**, the former headquarters of the Russian navy between 1711 and 1917. West of the Admiralty is **ploshchad Dekabristov** (Decembrists' Square), named after the Decembrists' Uprising of 14 December 1825.

The most famous statue of Peter the Great, the **Bronze Horseman**, stands at the end of the square towards the river. Behind the statue looms the splendid golden dome of **St Isaac's Cathedral** *(☎ 315 97 32; Isaakievskaya pl; admission to cathedral R250, to colonnade R100; open 11am-6pm Thur-Tues),* built between 1818 and 1858. It is currently a museum but used for church services on major religious holidays. Don't miss the panoramic city views from the colonnade around the drum of the dome.

Nevsky Prospekt

The inner 2.5km part of Nevsky pr from the Admiralty to Moscovsky Vokzal (Moscow station) is St Petersburg's main shopping thoroughfare. The most impressive sight along it – apart from the bustling crowd – is the great colonnaded arms of the awesome **Kazan Cathedral**, built between 1801 and 1811 and open for daily services at 9am and 6pm.

At the end of Nevsky pr is the working **Alexandr Nevsky Monastery** *(larva; ☎ 274 04 09; adult/student R50/30),* where you'll find the **Tikhvin Cemetery** *(admission R50),* last resting place of some of Russia's most famous artistic figures, including Tchaikovsky and Dostoevsky.

CENTRAL ST PETERSBURG

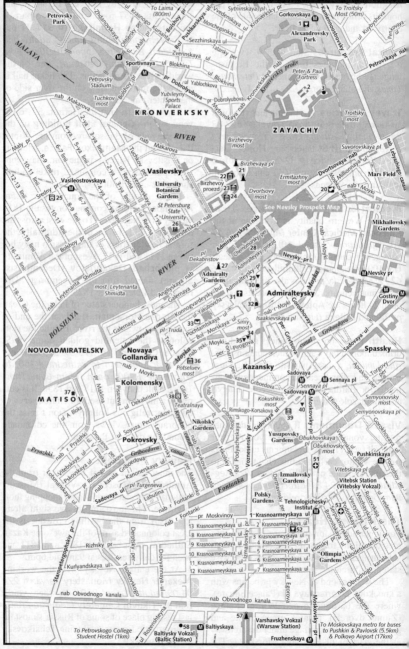

To Laima (800m)

Petrovsky Park

ul Krasnogo Kursanta

Zhdanovskaya nab

Oranienbaumskaya ul

Bol Pushkarskaya ul

Vvedenskaya ul

Sytninskaya pl

Monchegorskaya ul

Gorkovskaya

To Troitsky Most (50m)

ul Kuybysheva

Alexandrovsky Park

Sezzhinskaya ul

Tatarsky per

Kamennoostrovsky pr

ul Krasnogo Kursanta

Olegsky per

Maly pr

Zverinskaya ul

Blokhina

Sportivnaya

ul Blokhina

Petrovsky Stadium

Petrovskaya nab

Bolshoy pr

pr Dobrolyubova

ul Yablochkina

pr Dobrolyubova

Kronverkskaya nab

Peter & Paul Fortress

KRONVERKSKY

Yubileyny Sports Palace

Mytninskaya nab

Kronverksky proliv

nab Makarova

Tuchkov most

RIVER

ZAYACHY

Troitsky most

Birzhevoy most

Suvorovskaya pl

Lebyazhy canala

Maly pr

2-ya l 3-ya linii

4-ya l 5-ya linii

6-7 linii

8-9 linii

10-11 linii

Sredny pr

Tuchkov pereulok

Sredny pr

Birzhevaya pl

Ermitazhny most

Dvortsovaya nab

Millionnaya ul

Mars Field

Vasilevsky

12-13 linii

Vasileostrovskaya

University Botanical Gardens

Birzhevoy proezd

Dvortsovy most

nab Makarova

nab Makarova

See Nevsky Prospekt Map

Mikhailovsky Gardens

14-15 linii

16-17 linii

18-19 linii

St Petersburg State University

Universitetskaya nab

Admiralteyskaya nab

Chernomorsky per

Nevsky pr

Nevsky pr

Gostiny Dvor

RIVER

pl Dekabristov

Admiralteysky proezd

Admiralty Gardens

Admiralteysky

most Leytenanta Shmidta

Angliyskaya nab

Galernaya ul

Konnogvardeysky bul

Admiralteysky

Admiralteysky pr

Gorokhovaya ul

Isaakievskaya pl

Griboedova canal

Sadovaya ul

BOLSHAYA

ul Yakubovicha

Konnogvardeysky per

Siniy most

Spassky

NOVOADMIRATELSKY

Galernaya ul

Admiralteysky canal

pl Truda

Pochtamtskaya ul

Bol Morskaya ul

Pirogova

nab reki Moyki

Sennaya pl

Novaya Gollandiya

nab r Moyki

Potseluev most

Kazansky

Sadovaya

Sennaya pl

Apraksin Torgovy per

Kolomensky

pl Truda

ul Dekabristov

Klinik

nab kanala Griboedova

Kokushkin most

Sadovaya ul

Semyonovsky most

MATISOV

ul A Bloka

Teatralnaya pl

Rimskogo-Korsakova ul

Moskovsky pr

Semyonovskaya pl

nab r Pryazhki

ul Soyuza Pechatnikov

Nikolsky Gardens

Voznesensky pr

Yusupovsky Gardens

Obukhovskogo most

Pushkinskaya

Pryazhka

Pokrovsky

Lermontovsky pr

Kryukov canal

Kanonersky

Griboedova canal

Kryukov canal

Podyacheskaya

Izmailovsky Gardens

Obukhovskogo pl

Vitebskaya pl

Vitebsk Station (Vitebsky Vokzal)

Vitebskovsky pr

nab r Pryazhki

nab Rimskogo-Korsakova Griboedova

Kanonerskaya ul

Labutina

pl Turgeneva

Fontanka

Polsky Gardens

Tehnologichesky Institut

"Olimpia" Gardens

Sadovaya ul

nab r Fontanki

Derzhavinsky per

pr Moskvinoy

1 Krasnoarmeyskaya ul

Staropetergofsky pr

Rizhsky pr

Drovyanaya ul

Tsiolkovskogo

nab r Fontanki

13 Krasnoarmeyskaya ul

8 Krasnoarmeyskaya ul

9 Krasnoarmeyskaya ul

10 Krasnoarmeyskaya ul

11 Krasnoarmeyskaya ul

12 Krasnoarmeyskaya ul

2 Krasnoarmeyskaya ul

3 Krasnoarmeyskaya ul

4 Krasnoarmeyskaya ul

5 Krasnoarmeyskaya ul

6 Krasnoarmeyskaya ul

7 Krasnoarmeyskaya ul

Izmailovsky pr

Egorova

Moskovsky pr

Serpukhovskaya ul

Bronnitskaya ul

Podolskaya ul

Verejskaya ul

Mozhayskaya ul

Ruzovskaya ul

Vvedensky canal

Klimsky pr

Maly pr

Malodetskoselsky pr

Kurlyandskaya ul

Derptsky per

nab Obvodnogo kanala

nab Obvodnogo kanala

To Petrovskogo College Student Hostel (1km)

Baltiysky Vokzal (Baltic Station)

Baltiyskaya

Varshavsky Vokzal (Warsaw Station)

Fruzhenskaya

To Moskovskaya metro for buses to Pushkin & Pavlovsk (5.5km) & Polkovo Airport (17km)

CENTRAL ST PETERSBURG

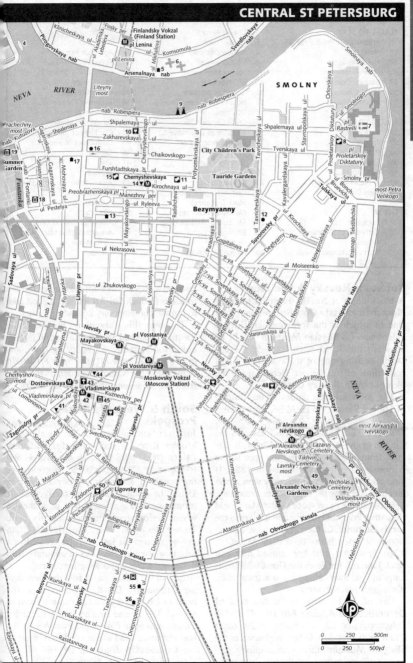

CENTRAL ST PETERSBURG

PLACES TO STAY		4	Cruiser Aurora	27	The Bronze Horseman
5	International Holiday Hostel	6	Kresty Prison	28	Admiralty
13	Hotel Rus	7	Smolny Cathedral	30	American Express
17	Hotel Neva	8	UK Consulate	31	St Isaac's Cathedral
32	Hotel Astoria	9	Sphinx Monuments	33	Central Post Office; Express
37	Matisov Domik	10	JFC Jazz Club		Mail Service
55	Hotel Kievskaya	11	German Consulate	36	Yusupov Palace
56	Kievsky Filial	12	Host Families Association	38	Mariinsky Theatre
		15	US Consulate	39	Railway Museum
PLACES TO EAT		16	OVIR Central Office	42	Kuznechny Market
14	Kafe Marko	18	Musuem of Decorative &	43	Our Lady of Vladimir Church
29	Tandoor		Applied Arts; Sol-Art	45	Dostoevsky Museum
34	Popugay		Gallery	46	Time Out
35	Café Idiot	19	Summer Palace	47	Che
40	Kafe Adzhika	20	French Consulate	48	Moloko
41	U Tyoshi Na Blinakh	21	Rostral Columns	49	Alexandr Nevsky Monastery
44	Bliny Domik	22	Central Naval Museum (Old	50	Griboedov
			Stock Exchange)	51	Poliklinika No 2
OTHER		23	Museum of Zoology	52	69 Club
1	Par.spb	24	Museum of Anthropology &	53	American Medical Center
2	Cathedral of SS Peter		Ethnography	54	Avtovokzal (Bus Station)
	& Paul	25	Teatr Satiry	57	Lenin Statue
3	Start of Battlements walk	26	Menshikov Palace	58	Eurolines

Between Nevsky & the Neva

A block north of Nevsky Prospekt metro is **Ploshchad Iskusstv** (Arts Square) on the far side of which is the former Mikhailovsky Palace now the **Russian Museum** (☎ 311 14 65; admission R240; open 10am-5pm Wed-Mon), housing one of the country's finest collections of Russian art. Behind it are the pleasant **Mikhailovsky Gardens**.

The polychromatic domes of the **Church of Spilled Blood** (☎ 315 16 36, Konyushen-naya pl; admission R240; open 11am-6pm Thur-Tues) are close by. Also known as the Church of the Resurrection of Christ, it was built from 1887 to 1907 on the spot where Alexander II was assassinated in 1881. If your budget is tight, you certainly won't miss much by admiring the elaborate exterior only.

Between the open space of the Mars Field (Marsovo Pole) and the Fontanka River is the lovely **Summer Garden** (Letny sad; admission R10; open 9am-10pm daily May-Oct, 10am-6pm Oct–mid-Apr, closed mid-mid Apr). Laid out for Peter the Great with fountains and pavilions along a geometrical plan, it's a great place to relax.

East of the Fontanka is the **Museum of Decorative and Applied Arts** (☎ 273 32 58; Solyarnoy per 13; admission R150; open 11am-5pm Tues-Sat). Otherwise known as the **Stieglitz Museum**, there's an exquisite collection of objects here, but the real draw is the restored halls, each in a different style. The entrance is through **Sol-Art** gallery, a good spot to browse contemporary art and souvenirs.

The best thing about the unmistakable Rastrelli-designed **Smolny Cathedral** (Smol-enksy sobor; ☎ 278 55 96; pl Rastrelli; admission R100; open 11am-5pm Fri-Wed), 3km east of the Summer Garden, is the view from the top of one of its 63m-tall belfries.

South & West of Nevsky Prospekt

Just over 1km southwest of Nevsky along the Moyka River is the delightful **Yusupov Palace** (☎ 314 98 83; nab reki Moyki 94; R150; open 11am-4pm daily). Notorious as the scene of Rasputin's grisly murder in 1916, the palace has an attractive set of rooms including a jewel box of a theatre where performances are occasionally held. To see the cellar where the Machiavellian mystic supped his last meal (re-created in a kitsch waxwork tableaux), a separate R90 ticket and advance booking is required.

East of the palace and across the meandering Griboedova Canal, is Sennaya pl, the heart of Dostoevskyville; the author lived in several flats around here and many of the locations turn up in *Crime and Punishment*. To find out more head to the small but interesting **Dostoevsky Museum** (☎ 164 69 50; Kuznechny per 5/2; admission R30; open

Trakai's medieval Island Castle fortification, Lithuania

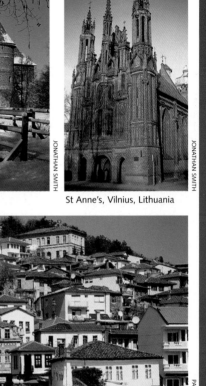

St Anne's, Vilnius, Lithuania

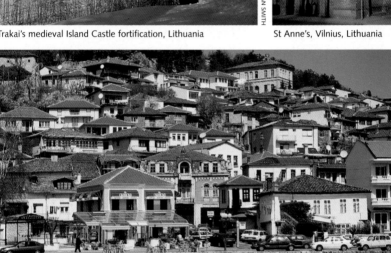

The historical Unesco heritage town of Ohrid, Macedonia, birthplace of the Cyrillic alphabet

The 15th-century Soroca Fortress was once part of a medieval chain of defences in Moldova

Modern spires in Poland's Carpathian Mountains

Autumn colour in Łazienki Park, Warsaw

Late afternoon on Mikołajska St, Kraków

Time passes slowly in Warsaw's Old Town

Snow-carpeted forest, Tatra Mountains, Poland

Burgher houses in Salt Square, Wrocław, Poland

11am-5.30pm Tues-Sun), in the house where the writer died in 1881.

Southwest of Sennaya pl, train buffs and kids will be enchanted by the large collection of models at the **Railway Museum** *(Zhelez-naya Doroga muzey; ☎ 168 80 05; Sadovaya ul 50; admission R20; open 11am-5pm Sun-Thur)*. This is one of the oldest collections of its type in the world; in fact, the museum was established in 1809, 28 years before Russia had its first working train!

Vasilevsky Island

Stand on the Strelka (Tongue of Land), beside the **Rostral Columns** (elaborate oil-fired navigation beacons, now only lit on special occasions) and admire one of the best views across the Neva. The old Stock Exchange is now the grand **Central Naval Museum** *(☎ 218 25 02l, Birzhevaya pl 4; adult/student R90/ 30; open 11am-5.15pm Wed-Sun)*, a tribute to Russia's naval muscle.

A short distance south is the **Museum of Zoology** *(☎ 218 01 12, Universitetskaya nab 1/3; adult/student R30/10, admission free Thur; open 11am-5pm Sat-Thur)*, said to be one of the biggest and best in the world. Amid all those stuffed animals you'll find a 44,000-year-old Siberian mammoth and a live insect zoo.

One block west, in the pale blue and white building with the steeple, is the **Museum of Anthropology & Ethnography** *(Kunstkam-mer; ☎ 218 14 12; Universitetskaya nab 3, entrance around the corner on Tamozhyonny per; admission R100; open 10.30am-5.30pm Tues-Sat, 10.30am-4.30pm Sun)*. Founded by Peter himself in 1714 it contains his personal collection of 'curiosities' (eg, jarred mutant fetuses and the like – bring the kids!).

Petrograd Side

Petrograd Side refers to the cluster of delta islands between the Malaya Neva and Bolshaya Neva channels. The principal attraction here is the **Peter & Paul Fortress** *(Petropavlovskaya krepost; ☎ 238 45 50; admission to all buildings R120, admission to grounds free; open 10am-5pm Thur-Mon, 10am-4pm Tues)*. Founded in 1703, its main use up to 1917 was as a political prison; famous residents include Peter's own son Alexey, Dostoevsky, Gorky and Trotsky. At noon every day a cannon is fired from the **Naryshkin Bastion**, scaring the daylights out of tourists. It's fun to walk the

battlements *(adult/student R50/30; open 10am-10pm daily)*. Most spectacular of all is the **Cathedral of SS Peter & Paul**, with its landmark needle-thin spire and magnificent baroque interior.

East along Petrovskaya nab you'll come to the cruiser **Aurora** *(admission free; open 10.30am-4pm Tues-Thur, Sat & Sun)*, which fired the (blank) shot that signalled the start of the 1917 revolution.

Places to Stay

Homestays & Private Flats The Host Families Association *(HOFA; ☎/fax 275 19 92; e alexei@hofak.hop.stu.neva.ru; Tavri-cheskaya ul 5/25)* is a reliable agency for finding private accommodation. It has four programmes, starting with the basic B&B (singles/doubles from US$25/40) for flats in the centre.

Ost-West Kontaktservice *(☎ 327 34 16; e info@ostwest.com; ul Mayakovskogo 7)* can also arrange homestays and apartment rentals from about $30 a day. Cheaper still are the private flats offered by old women to travellers arriving off major trains at Moscow station. Use your judgment about who to trust (many really are genuine folks in need of extra cash) and check how far from the city centre their place is before accompanying them (ask to see it on a map).

Hostels The long-running **HI St Petersburg Hostel** *(☎ 329 80 18, fax 329 90 19; e ryh@ ryh.ru; 3-ya Sovetskaya ul 28; dorm beds/ doubles US$19/48)*, five minutes' walk from Moscow station, remains popular. Spotless dorms have three to six beds and there's one double, all slightly cheaper in the winter and for ISIC and HI card-holders. All rates include breakfast.

Some people prefer **International Holiday Hostel** *(☎/fax 327 10 70, 327 10 33; e info@ hostel.spb.ru; nab reki Arsenalnaya 9; dorm beds/singles/doubles US$14/37/38)*, a convivial place just south of Finland station. It's quiet and a little out of the way, but does have the advantage of a terrace overlooking the Neva. Rates include breakfast.

St Petersburg Puppet Hostel *(☎ 272 54 01, fax 272 8361; e puppet@ryh.ru; ul Nekrasova 12; dorm beds/doubles US$16/ 42)* is a great option if you can get a place – central, friendly, cosy and clean. Breakfast is included in the price.

NEVSKY PROSPEKT

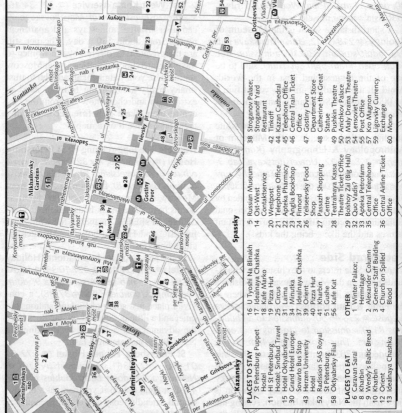

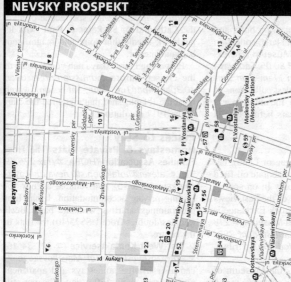

PLACES TO STAY
7 St Petersburg Puppet Hostel
11 HI St Petersburg Hostel; Sindbad Travel
15 Hotel Oktyabrskaya
30 Grand Hotel Europe; Herzen University
43 Radisson SAS Royal St Petersburg
52 Radisson SAS Royal St Petersburg
58 Oktyabrsky Filial

PLACES TO EAT
6 Caravan Sarai
8 Kharbin
9 Wendy's Baltic Bread
10 Khabin
12 Orient
13 Idealnaya Chashka
16 U Tyoshi Na Blinakh
17 Idealnaya Chashka
18 Kafe Marko
19 Pizza Hut
25 Circus
31 Laima
34 Minutka
37 Idealnaya Chashka
39 Orient
40 Pizza Hut
41 Kharbin
51 Gushe
56 Kafe Kat

OTHER
1 Winter Palace; Hermitage
2 Alexander Column
3 General Staff Building
4 Church on Spilled Blood
5 Russian Museum
14 Ost-West; Contaktservice
20 Westpost
21 Telephone Office
22 Apteka Pharmacy
23 Anglia Bookshop
24 Finnord
26 Yeliseevsky Food Shop
27 Passazh Shopping Centre
28 Teatralnaya Kassa Theatre Ticket Office
29 Bolshoy Zal (Big Hall)
32 Quo Vadis?
33 Apteka Petrofarm
35 Central Telephone Office
36 Central Airline Ticket Office
38 Stroganov Palace; Stroganoff Yard Restaurant
42 Tinkoff
44 Kazan Cathedral
45 Telephone Office
46 Central Train Ticket Office
47 Gostiny Dvor Department Store
48 Catherine the Great Statue
49 Pushkin Theatre
50 Anichkov Palace
53 Maly Drama Theatre
54 Lensoviet Theatre
55 Post Office
57 Kro Magnon
59 Ligovsky Currency Exchange
60 Mono

The cheapest deal, but not at all central, is the basic **Petrovskogo College Student Hostel** (☎ 252 75 63, fax 252 65 12; ul Baltiyskaya 26; doubles/triples US$4/6). Reserve in advance, though, as it's often full. From Narskaya metro walk left (south) down pr Stachek away from the Narva Arch to ul Baltiyskaya, where you turn left and continue for another 500m.

Hotels – Budget The best option is **Herzen University Hotel** (☎ 314 74 72, fax 314 76 59; Kazanskaya ul 6; singles/doubles US$42/96), 120m behind the Kazan Cathedral, an ideal location. The old-fashioned rooms are fine, with TV and fridge. Availability is tight, especially in summer, so make a reservation for which there will be a 25% extra charge for the first night.

Hotel Kievskaya (☎ 166 82 50, fax 166 56 93; e info@kievskaia.spb.ru; Dnepropetrovskaya ul 49; singles/doubles/triples US$17/22/24, singles/doubles with private facilities from US$28/60), and its stable mate around the corner, which features the same prices, the **Kievsky Filial** (☎ 166 58 11, fax 166 56 98; Kurskaya ul 40), are both a little grubby and out of the way in a boring neighbourhood.

More central, but only slightly more upmarket, is **Hotel Rus** (☎ 273 46 83, fax 279 36 00; ul Artilleryskaya 1; singles/doubles including breakfast US$44/63). **Hotel Neva** (☎ 278 05 04, fax 273 25 93; ul Chaikovskogo 17; singles/doubles US$36/52) might have once been a fancy bordello, but the cheapest rooms are pretty basic and drab. Still, travellers seldom make bad reports about it and it's only a short bus or trolleybus ride from Nevsky.

Hotels – Mid-Range & Top End Bang opposite the Moscow station, **Hotel Oktyabrskaya** (☎ 118 15 15, fax 315 75 01; Ligovsky pr 10; singles/doubles including breakfast US$80/110) has done plenty of upgrading in recent years. It's a sprawling place, but the new rooms are fine and the staff are pleasant. Of a similar standard and just as convenient is its sister establishment nearby, the smaller **Oktyabrsky Filial** (☎ 277 72 81, fax 315 75 01; Ligovsky pr 4/5; singles/doubles with breakfast US$60/92).

Matisov Domik (☎ 318 54 45, fax 318 74 19; nab reki Pryazhki 3/1; singles/doubles including breakfast US$60/100) about 10 minutes' walk west of the Mariinsky Theatre, is an excellent choice.

Luxurious, and with price tags that match (expect to pay at least US$350/500 for single/double rooms), are the old-world **Hotel Astoria** (☎ 313 57 57, fax 313 50 59; w www.roccofortehotels.com; Bol Morskaya ul 39) in front of St Isaac's Cathedral; the elegant **Grand Hotel Europe** (☎ 329 60 00, fax 329 60 01; w www.grand-hotel-europe.com; Mikhailovskaya ul 1/7); and the **Radisson SAS Royal St Petersburg** (☎ 322 5000, fax 322 5001; w www.radissonsas.com; Nevsky pr 49/2), which is more business oriented.

Places to Eat

Restaurants & Cafés For good-quality, keenly priced Russian cuisine you won't go wrong at the blissful **Bliny Domik** (☎ 315 99 15; Kolokolnaya ul). It has an English menu, as does **Circus** (☎ 310 1077; 4 Malaya Sadovaya ul), an imaginatively decorated basement space, where you're likely to be treated to a complimentary shot of vodka.

The fine Chinese restaurant **Kharbin** has three branches (ul Nekrasova 58 • ul Zhukovskogo 34/2 • nab reki Moyki 48) but locals swear the last one is the best. If you fancy Uzbek cuisine, **Caravan Sarai** (☎ 272 7129; ul Nekrasova 3) does it well in an atmospheric setting with a side order of belly dancing. For authentic Indian dishes (at a price) try **Tandoor** (☎ 312 38 86; Voznesensky pr 2).

A cosy Georgian restaurant with a good reputation is **Kafe Kat** (☎ 311 33 77; Stremyannaya ul 22). Also worth checking out is the friendly and colourful **Kafe Adzhika** (☎ 310 26 27; Moskovsky pr 7; open 24hr).

The Stroganoff Yard (☎ 315 2315; Nevsky pr 17), which is in the courtyard of the Stroganov Palace, has telephones on each table so you can call up strangers while grazing on the good-value US$5 lunch buffet (US$8 at night), which includes some tasty traditional Russian dishes.

Vegetarians will be delighted by both the centrally located **Gushe** (☎ 113 24 05; Vladimirsky pr 5) and **Troitsky Most** (☎ 326 82 21; Mal Posadskaya ul 2 • ☎ 232 66 93 Konversky pr 9/2), with both branches on the Petrograd Side not far from each other.

Practically every traveller drops by **Café Idiot** (☎ 315 16 75; nab reki Moyki 82), and with good reason: the vegetarian food and atmosphere are great, although the prices are on the high side. Nearby is the cheaper **Popugay** (☎ 311 5971; 1 Fornary per), a new hang-out with a laid-back reggae vibe that's popular with overseas students.

Coffee bars are dotted all over the city with **Idealnaya Chaska**, the local equivalent of Starbucks, having the most locations, mainly along Nevsky pr. **Kafe Marko** (Nevsky pr 108 • pr Chernyshevskogo 26) is another good chain with a better selection of food and alcoholic drinks.

Fast Food The following three self-service Russian operations are open 24 hours and a meal at one of them won't cost much over R100. **Laima** (☎ 232 44 28; kanala Griboedova 14 • ☎ 315 55 45; Bolshoy pr 88, Petrograd Side) has a vast menu (there's an English one available) including oodles of salads, soups, main dishes and drinks. Similar places are **Orient** (☎ 277 57 15; Suvorovsky pr 1/8 • ☎ 314 64 43; Bol Morskaya ul 25; dishes under US$3; both open 24hr) and **U Tyoshi Na Blinakh** (Zagorodny pr 18 • Ligovsky pr 25), which specialises in blinis.

If only Western-style fast food will do, there's always **Pizza Hut** (nab reki Moyki 71/76 • Nevsky pr 96), plenty of McDonald's, and **Minutka** (Nevsky pr 20), the Russian version of Subway.

Self-Catering For fresh produce head to the city's liveliest food market **Kuznechny** (Kuznechny per 3) next to Vladirmiskaya metro. There's a well-stocked supermarket in the basement of the **Passazh** shopping centre (Nevsky pr 48; open 10am-10pm daily).

For breakfast supplies and bakery items try **Wendy's Baltic Bread** (Grechesky pr 25).

Entertainment

Check the St Petersburg Times and Pulse for listings of what's on.

Ballet, Opera, Theatre & Classical Music September to the end of June is the main performing season. Most theatres and concert halls are closed Monday.

The Kirov Ballet and Opera are at the **Mariinsky Theatre** (☎ 114 52 64; w www .kirovballet.com; Teatralnaya pl 1). Tickets can be bought at the theatre or any Teatralnaya Kassa, for instance at Nevsky pr 42, but be aware that the eagle-eyed babushkas on the door can spot a foreigner at 20 paces and

will demand you pay the foreigner price, which is 10 times the Russian price.

The internationally renown **Maly Drama Theatre** (☎ 113 20 49; ul Rubinshteyna 18) often stages experimental and frequently unforgettable pieces. Also worth checking out is whatever's playing at the **Lensoviet Theatre** (☎ 113 21 91; Vladimirsky pr 12) and the clever, off-beat plays at **Teatr Satiry** (☎ 314 70 60; Sredny pr 48; Vasilevsky Island).

For classical music, St Petersburg Philarmonia plays at **Bolshoy Zal** (☎ 110 42 57; ul Mikhailovskaya 2), also known as the Shostakovich Academic Philharmonic Big Hall.

Bars & Clubs Microbrewery **Tinkoff** (☎ 314 8485; Kazanskaya ul 7) serves very drinkable ales in a hip beer hall where you'll also find a sushi bar. Despite its Cuban-associated name **Che** (☎ 277 76 00; Poltavskaya ul 3) is a Euro-trendy space and serves some good coffee and wine.

Time Out (☎ 113 24 42; ul Marata 36) is your average sports bar, with pool table and satellite TV, but it also has a foreign book exchange, good pizza and a happy hour from 5pm to 8pm.

For the following clubs expect admission of at least R150 on the weekend.

JFC Jazz Club (☎ 272 98 50; Shpalernaya ul 33) is a cosy, New York-style space with some of the city's best jazz and blues – book on weekends.

Moloko (☎ 274 94 67; Perekupnoy per 12; open 7pm-midnight Thurs-Sun) is in a dimly lit cellar and is the best bet for live rock bands. It's also one of the few places to work up an atmosphere earlier in the evening.

Griboedov (☎ 164 43 55; Voronezhkaya ul 2A) is in an artfully converted bomb shelter and has a no-pop-music policy. Weekends get stiflingly crowded here – the best nights are Wednesday and Thursday.

Par.spb (☎ 233 3374; w www.icc.sp.ru; Alexandrovsky Park 5B) is the hip club of the moment, with different music each night and a strict door policy. Check its website because it may move location.

A gay-friendly place is **Mono** (☎ 164 36 78, Kolomenskaya ul 4; cover charge for men R20-50, women R100; open 10pm-6am daily). The dance floor is tiny, but it's pleasantly decorated and has reasonably priced drinks. Thursday is for women when the cover charges are reversed.

Getting There & Away

Air St Petersburg has direct air links with most major European capitals and major airlines are well represented in the city.

You can also fly jto ust about anywhere you want within Russia and the surrounding republics. Tickets can be purchased at the **Central Airline Ticket Office** (☎ 311 80 93; Nevsky pr 7) and at travel agencies such as Sindbad Travel.

Train St Petersburg has three major long-distance train stations. **Finland station** (Finlyandsky Vokzal; ☎ 168 76 87; pl Lenina, Vyborg Side) has two daily trains to Helsinki. **Moscow station** (Moskovsky Vokzal; ☎ 168 43 74; pl Vosstaniya, Nevsky pr) handles trains to/from Moscow (at least 11 daily), the far north, the Urals, Siberia, Crimea and the Caucasus. **Vitebsk station** (Vitebsky Vokzal; ☎ 055; Zagorodny pr 52) deals with the Baltic countries, Eastern Europe, Ukraine and Belarus. **Baltic station** (Baltiysky Vokzal; ☎ 168 28 59) is for suburban trains.

Tickets can be purchased at the train stations, the **Central Train Ticket Office** (☎ 162 33 44; nab kanala Griboedova 24), the Central Airline Ticket Office, Sindbad Travel and, at a huge mark-up, from any luxury hotel.

Bus The bus station, **Avtovokzal** (☎ 166 57 77; nab Obvodnogo Kanala 36) is 1km from Ligovsky Prospekt metro. It serves Tampere, Vyborg, Pskov, Novgorod, Moscow and other smaller destinations. For buses to Central and Eastern Europe, **Eurolines** (☎ 168 27 40; ul Shkapina 10), 50m west of Baltisky Vokzal, runs several daily buses to Tallin, Tartu, Rīga and has weekly services to Germany. For service to/from Finland, **Finnord** (☎ 314 89 51) and **Sovavto** (☎ 123 51 25) have daily buses. A one-way ticket to Helsinki costs about US$40.

Getting Around

Local Transport Tokens (zhetony) for the metro cost R6, and a variety of magnetic-strip cards for multiple trips are also available from the booths in the stations, which open around 5.30am and close just after midnight every day. Tickets for buses, trolleybuses and tramways (R5 to R10 depending on the service) are bought inside from controllers. To order a taxi, call **New Service** (☎ 327 42 00) or **Taxi na Zakaz** (☎ 100 00 00).

Around St Petersburg

PETRODVORETS
ПЕТРОДВОРЕЦ
☎ 812

Russia's 'Versailles' is Petrodvorets (☎ 427 95 27; admission to grounds adult/student R120/60; open 9am-9pm year-round), the grandiose estate built by Peter the Great, 29km west of St Petersburg. It was badly damaged by the Germans in WWII (many say it was further trashed by the Soviets after the war) and is largely a reconstruction, but still mightily impressive – even when swarming with tourists, as it frequently is.

The centrepiece is the **Grand Cascade & Water Avenue**, a symphony of over 64 fountains and 37 bronze statues, which operates from the end of May to the end of September. Between the cascade and the **Upper Garden** is the **Grand Palace** (adult/student R240/120; open 10am-6pm Tues-Sun). Amid all the eye-boggling interiors, many find the finest room is the simplest – Peter's study, apparently the only one to survive the Germans. The estate features several other buildings of interest – all with their own admission charges and separate opening hours – and can easily take half a day to tour fully.

Getting There & Away

The simplest option is to take the regularly departing double-deck buses from outside Baltic station (R30, 40 minutes); get off at the main entrance on Sankt Peterburgsky pr. In summer, the Meteor hydrofoil (R300, 30 minutes) leaves from St Petersburg's Hermitage every 20 to 30 minutes from 9.30am to at least 7pm.

PUSHKIN & PAVLOVSK
ПУШКИН И ПАВЛОВСК
☎ 812

Brace yourself for crowds again at Pushkin, 25km south of St Petersburg, where you'll find **Tsarkoe Selo**, the estate created by Empresses Elizabeth and Catherine the Great between 1744 and 1796. The big drawcard here is the Rastrelli-designed, baroque **Catherine Palace** (☎ 466 66 69; adult/student R300/150; open 11am-5pm Wed-Mon), built between 1752 and 1756, but practically destroyed in WWII. The exterior and 20-odd rooms have since been expertly restored; the gilt-adorned and mirrored Great Hall is particularly dazzling.

Just wandering around **Catherine Park** (adult/student R60/30; open 9am-5.30pm daily) surrounding the palace is a pleasure. In the outer section of the park is the **Great Pond**, fringed by an intriguing array of structures including a Chinese Pavilion, purposely Ruined Tower and Pyramid where Catherine the Great buried her dogs.

To escape the masses, head 4km further south to Pavlovsk (admission to grounds R40; open daily 9am-6pm), the park and palace designed by Charles Cameron between 1781 and 1786, and one of the most exquisite in Russia. Pavlovsk's **Great Palace** (☎ 470 21 55; adult/student R240/120; open 11am-5pm Sat-Thur), also partly restored after a trashing in WWII, has some delightful rooms, but it's the sprawling, peaceful park that's the real attraction.

Getting There & Away

The most convenient way of getting to both Pushkin and Pavlovsk is to hop on one of the frequent taxi-buses (R15, 30 minutes) that leave from outside metro Moskovskaya, 8km south of the city centre; the buses stop within walking distance of Tsarskoe Selo and outside Pavlovsk.

Trains leave from Vitebsk station's platform 1 to Detskoe Selo station (zone 3 ticket) for Pushkin, and to Pavlovsk station (zone 4) for Pavlovsk (a 30-minute trip to either). Note that while there are several trains prior to 9am, there are far fewer later in the day.

From Detskoe Selo station, a five-minute ride on bus No 370, 371, 378 or 381 takes you to within two minutes' walk of Catherine Palace. From Pavlovsk station, you can either cross the road and walk through the park to the palace, or take bus No 370, 383, 383A or 493 (under 10 minutes).

Poland

Travellers to Poland will delight in its heroic past, urban vitality and natural beauty.

The enduring character of Poland's cities is displayed in the old-world splendour of regal Kraków, in the modern clamour of ambitious Warsaw and in the resilient spirit of maritime Gdańsk. Outdoor enthusiasts will surely be impressed by the undeveloped coastline and intricate waterways in the north, as well as the rugged mountains in the south.

Poland may not be as cheap as it used to be, but it remains excellent value and tourist facilities are often very good. And unlike some countries in Eastern Europe, foreigners are charged the same as locals for everything.

In rural areas, you will certainly still see horse-drawn ploughs and carts, but the cities are as dynamic and cosmopolitan as those found in Western Europe. Over the past decade, Poland has developed into a modern, vibrant and progressive state, yet it has maintained its traditional culture. Poland is now reasserting itself after centuries of occupation and subversion, so now is a great time to visit.

At a Glance

- **Warsaw** – Poland's cosmopolitan melting pot, with a rebuilt Old Town and Chopin's house
- **Kraków** – incredible royal capital packed with untouched centuries-old architecture
- **Auschwitz** – a shocking, emotional and essential visit
- **Zakopane & the Tatra Mountains** – amazing alpine location, offering outdoor fun for all seasons
- **Toruń** – historic city of narrow back lanes, burgher mansions and Gothic churches

Capital	Warsaw
Population	39 million
Official Language	Polish
Currency	1 złoty (zł)
	= 100 groszy
Time	GMT/UTC+0100
Country Phone Code	☎ 48

Facts about Poland

HISTORY

The region now known as Poland was first settled in the Neolithic period (4000 to 2000 BC) and later invaded by such diverse groups as the Celts, Balts and Huns, as well as various Germanic tribes.

In the early Middle Ages, Western Slavs moved into the flatlands between the Vistula and Odra Rivers, and became known as Polanians, or 'people of the plains'. When the ambitions of a local tribal chief converged with those of Roman missionaries, Poland as a political entity was born. In AD 966 Mieszko I, Duke of the Polanians, adopted Christianity in exchange for official recognition from Rome of his status as regional overlord. The Church formally expanded into the area in 1000, when bishoprics were established in Kołobrzeg (Pomerania), Kraków and Wrocław. Mieszko founded the Piast dynasty, which ruled Poland for over 400 years. His son Bolesław Chrobry (Boleslaus the Brave) was crowned Poland's first king by a papal edict in 1025.

Following the battlefield exploits of Mieszko and Bolesław, the Polish kingdom in the early 11th century comprised Wielkopolska, the original Polanian core near Poznań; Pomerania to the north; Silesia to the south; and Małopolska, east of the Vistula. (While Poland subsequently underwent innumerable territorial reconfigurations, its contemporary

POLAND

POLAND

To Ystad, Rønne & Copenhagen	To Karlskrona To Nynäshamn To Vilnius & St Petersburg Kaunas

BALTIC SEA

RUSSIA

LITHUANIA

SŁOWIŃSKI NP Łeba

Ustka Lębork Hel Gulf of Gdańsk Kaliningrad

Słupsk Gdynia Sopot

Kołobrzeg Koszalin Gdańsk

Międzyzdroje WOLIN NP Frombork Lidzbark Suwałki

Świnoujście Elbląg Warmiński Giżycko

Malbork Elbląg-Ostróda Canal Mikołajki Augustów

Szczecinek Ostróda Olsztyn Great Masurian Lake District Hrodna

Szczecin Grudziądz

Piła Chełmno Łomża Białystok

Bydgoszcz Toruń Ostrołęka BIAŁOWIEŻA NP

Gorzów Wielkopolski Inowrocław Ciechanów Hajnówka Białowieża

Frankfurt/Oder Warta Wisła Płock Bug BELARUS

To Berlin Poznań Gniezno Włocławek WARSAW To Minsk

Odra Rogalin Kórnik Konin Kutno Wisła Siedlce Brest

Zielona Góra Leszno Kalisz Łowicz

Cottbus Sieradz Łódź Radom Puławy Lublin

GERMANY Zgorzelec Piotrków Trybunalski Kazimierz Dolny Chełm

To Dresden Jelenia Góra Wrocław Wieluń Kielce Sandomierz Zamość

Sudeten Mountains Brzeg Częstochowa

Wałbrzych Opole Tarnobrzeg San

Kłodzko Nysa Gliwice Katowice Rzeszów Łańcut

Hradec Králové Kraków Tarnów Przemyśl Lviv

PRAGUE Cieszyn Oświęcim Nowy Sącz Sanok To Kyiv & Odesa

Ostrava Bielsko-Biała Rabka Carpathian Mountains UKRAINE

Olomouc Zakopane Tatra Mountains Rysy (2499m) Prešov

CZECH REPUBLIC Poprad

To Vienna & Bratislava SLOVAKIA Košice To Budapest

0 50 100km
0 30 60mi

borders, drawn by Stalin at the end of WWII, closely resemble those of a millennium ago.)

Poland's early success as a regional power was short-lived. German encroachment in the west led to the relocation of the royal capital from Poznań to Kraków in 1038. In the absence of a strong king, rapacious nobles split the realm into four principalities in the mid-12th century. Things did not improve in 1226 when the Prince of Mazovia invited a band of Germanic crusaders to help convert the pagan tribes still living in the north. Subsequently, the Teutonic Knights quickly slashed their way to a sizable swathe of the Baltic coast, and the pagans and Poles were harshly dealt with. The south had its own problems to contend with as marauding Tatars overran Kraków twice in the mid-13th century.

The kingdom was finally reconstituted under Kazimierz III Wielki (the Great), who reigned from 1333 to 1370. Reunified and reinvigorated, Poland prospered. Scores of new towns sprang up, while Kraków blossomed into one of the leading cultural centres in Europe. Unfortunately, his legacy remained etched in stone, not blood: Kazimierz failed to produce a legitimate male heir, so the Piast dynasty reached the end of the line.

Lithuania at this time was a formidable political force and the last pagan stronghold in Eastern Europe, so Poland's nobles decided that Jadwiga, the 10-year-old daughter of Kazimierz's nephew, should marry the Grand Duke of Lithuania, Jagiełło. The union of Poland and Lithuania created a great continental power. It encompassed a vast territory, which stretched from the Baltic to the Black Sea, and assembled a fearsome army, which defeated the Teutonic Knights in 1410.

During the 16th century, the enlightened King Zygmunt I ushered in the Renaissance, lavishly patronising the arts and sciences. Nicolaus Copernicus was busy revolutionising the field of astronomy and, in so doing, reordering the cosmos. In 1569 Poland and Lithuania formally merged into a single state, with Poland acting as senior partner, and both countries remained politically entwined until the late 18th century.

The Jagiellonian dynasty at last expired with the death of Zygmunt II in 1572. The nobility reasserted its dominance over the throne by making the king an elected official of the parliament, known as the *Sejm*. In the absence of a serious Polish contender for king, the Sejm's aristocratic members considered foreigners (over whom the nobles could wield more control). Consequently, seven of Poland's 11 kings in the 17th and 18th centuries were foreigners. Zygmunt's imported Swedish successor, Zygmunt III, moved the capital to Warsaw in 1596.

Throughout the 17th century, the regional rivals of Sweden and Russia marched back and forth across Polish territory, whittling away at the northern and eastern possessions. In the late 18th century, Russia, Prussia and Austria greedily conspired to carve up the politically inept and militarily weak Polish state. In a series of three partitions between 1773 and 1795, Poland was systematically removed from the map of Europe.

From the late 18th to the mid-19th century, Poland, now subject to three empires, experienced a nationalist revival. The romantic movement in the arts preserved folk traditions, recounted past glories and lamented independence lost. National revolutionaries plotted insurrections. Fresh from the American War of Independence, Tadeusz Kościuszko led patriotic forces in an unsuccessful armed rebellion against Russia in 1794. The oppressed Poles fought alongside Napoleon, who in 1807 established a duchy in Warsaw, from where he led his Grand Army to Moscow. Napoleon was eventually crushed by the Russians, as were Polish uprisings in 1831 and 1863.

In the early 20th century the empires of Eastern Europe were finally dismembered after five exhausting years of war and revolution. In 1919 the Treaty of Versailles declared Poland once again to be a recognised sovereign state. No sooner restored, Poland was again at war. Under the command of Marshal Jozef Piłsudski, Poland sought to reclaim its eastern territories from long-time nemesis Russia, now under the Bolsheviks. After two years of inconclusive fighting, the exhausted combatants agreed on a compromise, which returned Vilnius and Lviv to Poland.

But peace didn't last long. On 1 September 1939, a Nazi blitzkrieg poured down on the Polish city of Gdańsk and WWII started. Hitler used Poland as a headquarters and staging ground for the Nazi offensive against the Soviet Union. When the German advance finally stalled and the Red Army's counteroffensive began, Poland became host to a relentlessly grinding campaign of utter devastation. And the Soviets did not come as liberators, but as occupiers of another sort.

Six million Polish inhabitants (roughly 20% of the population) died during WWII. Nazi Germany relegated the Slavic Poles to the role of slave labourers, while Poland's three million Jews were brutally annihilated in death camps. Finally, Poland's borders were redrawn yet again. The Soviet Union claimed the eastern territories and extended the western boundary at the expense of Germany. These border changes were accompanied by the forced resettlement of more than a million Poles, Germans and Ukrainians.

Poland's four decades of Soviet-dominated communist rule were punctuated by waves of protests to which the regime responded with a mix of coercion and concessions. Each round left the communists in power, but more isolated, and the opposition beaten, but more confident. This cycle culminated in the paralysing strikes of 1980–81, led by the Solidarity trade union. This time the regime survived only by imposing martial law.

In the late 1980s, Soviet leader, Mikhail Gorbachev, authorised the Polish communist leader, General Wojciech Jaruzelski, to explore a compromise solution to the political stalemate. In 1989 the communists, Solidarity and the Church held round-table negotiations, which yielded new parliamentary elections. The communists failed to win one seat in open competition, while Solidarity became the political embodiment of Polish nationalism.

The Polish elections of June 1989 triggered a succession of events that soon brought about the collapse of communism across

POLAND

POLAND

Eastern Europe. In 1990, the communist party in Poland disbanded and Solidarity leader, Lech Wałęsa, became Poland's first democratically elected president.

However, the exultations over the demise of communism were soon tempered by the uncertainties of the road ahead. The post-communist transition brought radical changes, which induced new social hardships and political crises. But within a decade Poland appeared to have successfully consolidated a democratic polity, built the foundations for a market economy, and reoriented its foreign relations towards the West. In March 1999, Poland was granted full membership of NATO. Poland is also focussed on joining the EU in the next expansion.

GEOGRAPHY

Bordered by seven states and one sea, Poland covers an area of 312,677 sq km. It is approximately as large as the UK and Ireland put together and less than half as big as Texas.

The northern edge of Poland meets the Baltic Sea. This broad, 524km-long coastline is spotted with sand dunes and seaside lakes. Also concentrated in the northeast are many postglacial lakes – more than any country in Europe except Finland.

The southern border is defined by the mountain ranges of the Sudetes and Carpathians. Poland's highest mountains are the rocky Tatras, a section of the Carpathian Range it shares with Slovakia. The highest peak of the Polish Tatras is Mt Rysy (2499m).

The area in between is a vast plain, sectioned by wide north-flowing rivers. Poland's longest river is the Vistula (Wisła), which winds 1047km from the Tatras to the Baltic.

CLIMATE

Poland has a moderate continental climate with considerable maritime influence along the Baltic coast. As a result, the weather can be unpredictable. Summer is usually warm and sunny, with July the hottest month, but it's the season with the highest rainfall. Spring and autumn are pleasantly warm but can also be rainy. You can expect snow anywhere in Poland between December and March, lingering until April or even May in the mountains.

FLORA & FAUNA

Forests cover about 28% of Poland and, admirably, up to 130 sq km of new forest is planted each year. Some 60% of the forests are pine trees, but the share of deciduous species, such as oak, beech and birch, is increasing.

Poland's fauna includes hare, red deer, wild boar and, less abundant, elk, brown bear and wildcat. European bison, which once inhabited Europe in large numbers, were brought to the brink of extinction early in the 20th century and a few hundred now live in Białowieża National Park. The Great Masurian Lakes district attracts a vast array of bird life, such as storks and cormorants. The eagle, though rarely seen today, is Poland's national bird and appears on the Polish emblem.

Poland has 23 national parks, but they cover less than 1% of the country. No permit is necessary to visit these parks, but most have admission fees (about 5zł per person). Camping in the parks is sometimes allowed, but only in specified sites. Poland also has a network of not-so-strictly preserved areas called 'landscape parks'. About 105 of these parks, covering 6% of Poland, are scattered throughout the country.

GOVERNMENT & POLITICS

The political left, repackaged as Social Democrats, made a startling comeback in parliamentary elections held only three years after the fall of the communists in Poland. In 1995, Lech Wałęsa was narrowly defeated by Aleksander Kwaśniewski of the Democratic Left Alliance (SLD). In October 2000, Kwaśniewski was re-elected as president, while Wałęsa collected just 1% of the vote. In the parliamentary elections a year later, the SLD again won and Solidarity failed to win a even one seat. Leszek Miller, a former senior Communist Party official, became prime minister.

The president is directly elected for a five-year term and nominates the prime minister. The parliament consists of two houses: a 460-seat lower house (the Sejm) and a 100-seat upper house (the Senat). With the imposition

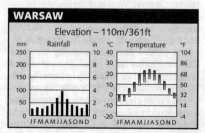

WARSAW

Elevation – 110m/361ft

of a 5% threshold for parliamentary representation, Poland's splintered political groupings have realigned into a relatively coherent multiparty system.

ECONOMY

The economic legacy of the communists included burdensome nanational debt and stagnant production. In 1990 the new government launched a radical 'shock therapy' campaign to build a market economy. Initially the reforms caused hyperinflation and a sharp fall in production, but the economy finally stabilised by the mid-1990s and has since experienced positive growth.

Over 60% of the workforce is in the private sector, with small businesses leading the way. Poland's numerous small farms keep food shelves well stocked, though trade barriers have limited export potential. Many of the mammoth communist-era industries, such as coal and steel, remain under state tutelage.

In mid-2002, the annual inflation rate was only 3.3%, but the GDP growth rate was still alarmingly low (1.1%) and unemployment was unacceptably high (18%). Poland remains desperate to join the EU, and to be part of its monetary union (unlikely until at least 2007).

POPULATION & PEOPLE

Poland was for centuries a multinational country and home to large Jewish, German and Ukrainian communities. However, because of ethnic cleansing and forced resettlements after WWII, Poland became an ethnically homogeneous country – about 98% of the population are now Poles. Poland's Jewish population once numbered more than three million but today it's between 5000 and 10,000.

Over 60% of the citizens live in towns and cities. Warsaw is by far the largest city, followed by Łódź, Kraków, Wrocław, Poznań and Gdańsk. Upper Silesia (around Katowice) is the most densely inhabited area while the northeastern border regions remain the least populated.

Between five and 10 million Poles live outside Poland. This emigre community, known as 'Polonia', is located mainly in the USA (particularly Chicago).

ARTS

Poland's rich literary tradition dates from the 15th century and claims four Nobel laureates. Its modern voice was shaped during the 19th

century during the period of foreign subjugation. Nationalist-inspired writers thrived, including the poet Adam Mickiewicz (1798–1855), and Henryk Sienkiewicz (1846–1916), who won a Nobel Prize in 1905 for *Quo Vadis?*. This nationalist tradition was again revived during the communist period when Czesław Miłosz was awarded the Nobel Prize in 1980 for *The Captive Mind*.

At the turn of the 20th century, the avantgarde 'Young Poland' movement in art and literature developed in Kraków. The most notable representatives of this movement were the writer Stanisław Wyspiański (1869–1907), also famous for his stained-glass work; the playwright, Stanisław Ignacy Witkiewicz (1885–1939), commonly known as Witkacy; and the Nobel laureate Władisław Reymont (1867–1925). In 1996, Wisława Szymborska (1923–) also received a Nobel Prize for her ironic poetry.

Unquestionably, Poland's most famous musician was Frédéric Chopin (1810–49), whose music displays the melancholy and nostalgia that became hallmarks of the Polish national style. Stanisław Moniuszko (1819–72) 'nationalised' 19th-century Italian opera music by introducing Polish folk songs and dances onto the stage. His *Halka* (1858), about a peasant girl abandoned by a young noble, is a staple of the national opera houses.

Jan Matejko (1838–93) is Poland's best-known painter. His monumental historical paintings hang in galleries throughout the country. Wojciech Kossak (1857–1942) is another who documented Polish history; he is best remembered for the colossal *Panorama of Racławicka*, on display in Wrocław.

Poland claims several world-renowned film directors. The most notable is Andrzej Wajda, who received an Honorary Award at the 1999 Academy Awards. Western audiences are probably more familiar with the work of Roman Polański, who directed critically acclaimed films such as *Rosemary's Baby* and *Chinatown*. The late Krzysztof Kieślowski is best known for the trilogy *Three Colours: Blue/White/Red*.

SOCIETY & CONDUCT

Poles are friendly and polite, but not overly formal. The way of life in large urban centres increasingly mimics Western styles and manners. In the countryside, however, a more conservative culture dominates, evidenced by

POLAND

traditional gender roles and strong family ties. In both urban and rural settings, Poles are devoutly religious.

The Poles' sense of personal space may be a bit cosier than you are accustomed to – you may notice this trait when queuing for tickets or manoeuvring along city streets. When greeting each other, Polish men are passionate about shaking hands. Polish women, too, often shake hands with men, but the man should always wait for the woman to extend her hand first.

RELIGION

Over 80% of Poles are practising Roman Catholics. The Orthodox church exists along a narrow strip on the eastern frontier and its adherents constitute about 1% of the population.

The election of Karol Wojtyła, the archbishop of Kraków, as Pope John Paul II in 1978, and his triumphal visit to his homeland a year later, significantly enhanced the status of the church in Poland. The country is proud of its 'Polish Pope': his image is prominently displayed in public places and private homes throughout the country.

The overthrow of communism was as much a victory for the Church as it was for democracy. The fine line between the Church and the state is often blurred in Poland. The Church today is a powerful lobby on social issues. Legislation has been passed that mandates Catholic religious instruction in public schools and 'Christian values' in broadcasting. Some Poles have recently grown wary of the Church's increasing influence in society and politics.

LANGUAGE

Polish is a western variant of the group of Slavonic languages (which includes Czech and Slovak). Visually, Polish looks daunting (how do you possibly pronounce Wrzeszcz, a suburb near Gdańsk?) and is not an easy language to master. However, it is phonetic and there are few dialects or variations.

While Polish is overwhelmingly the major language, some older Poles, especially in the west, speak German, while many of the younger set speak English. Most tourist offices and upmarket hotels have at least one English-speaker, but visitors will do well to learn a few key phrases in Polish. To, umm, polish up on your Polish, see the Language chapter at the back of this book.

Facts for the Visitor

HIGHLIGHTS

Nature buffs will love Poland's pristine Baltic beaches, majestic snowcapped peaks and secluded forest-lined lakes. The beaches of Łeba, perhaps the most inspiring on the coast, are surrounded by miles of unending, desertlike sand dunes. Mikołajki is a charming town that provides access to the Great Masurian Lakes, ideal for biking, sailing and kayaking. Zakopane is the base for hiking and skiing in the Tatras, Poland's most magnificent mountain range. And the Unesco-listed Białowieża National Park is a gorgeous pocket of forest with a bison reserve.

Poland's rich history is recounted by its imposing medieval castles and charming old town squares. Many of them, such as those in Gdańsk and Wrocław, were lovingly rebuilt after WWII. The royal grandeur of Poland's past is best preserved in Kraków's Old Town, which was virtually undamaged during WWII. Visitors can also imagine medieval life at Malbork Castle, the largest Gothic castle in Europe.

Auschwitz is the most vivid reminder of the atrocities that occurred during WWII, while the Nazis left haunting reminders, such as Hitler's former bunker at Wolf's Lair, not far from Olsztyn.

SUGGESTED ITINERARIES

Your itinerary obviously depends on the amount of time available, your interests, where you will arrive and/or depart, and the season, but you may wish to use the list below as a guide:

One Week
Warsaw (two days), Kraków (two), Oświęcim (one), Wrocław (one) & Toruń (one)

Two Weeks
Follow the suggestions above, but add more days to each place. With any extra time, visit Zakopane and the Tatra Mountains (two to three days), Gdańsk and around (two to three), the Great Masurian Lakes (two to three) or Białowieża National Park (one to two).

One Month
Spend longer at the places listed for 'Two Weeks' and include Łódź (one), Częstochowa (one), Poznań and around (three to four), Olsztyn and around (one to two), and places in the southeast such as Lublin and around (three to four) and Zamość (two).

Two Months

All of the above, plus maybe a trek in the Tatras or Sudeten Mountains, or spend more time exploring the Great Masurian Lakes or Białowieża National Park.

PLANNING
When to Go

The tourist season runs roughly from May to September and peaks in July and August. Many Poles – and their children – go on holidays during these two months, so transport is crowded and accommodation is often limited. Most theatres and concert halls are also closed at this time.

The best time to visit Poland is either spring (late April to late June) or early autumn (September to mid-October). These periods are pleasantly warm and ideal for general sightseeing and outdoor activities. Many cultural events still take place in both periods.

Mid-autumn to mid-spring is colder, darker and perhaps less attractive for most visitors. However, it's not a bad time to visit city sights and enjoy the cultural life. Except for skiing (from December to March), outdoor activities are less prominent in this period and many camping grounds and youth hostels are closed.

Maps

Maps of all cities, towns and tourist attractions in Poland are easy to buy throughout the country. Three of the best publishers of maps are Copernicus, Eurocity and Shell, but few are translated into English. Copernicus' *Polska Atlas Samochodowy* (1:200,000) is the most detailed for driving and cycling, but it's bulky.

What to Bring

The days when shelves in Poland were empty is happily long over. You can now buy almost anything, including clothes, toiletries, stationery, sports and camping equipment, and prices are lower than in Western Europe.

RESPONSIBLE TOURISM

In some popular places (such as Kraków and Zakopane), the summer influx of tourists puts a real strain on local infrastructure and the environment. One way to minimise your own impact – and perhaps enjoy yourself more – is to avoid visiting in the high season. Also, spending money in less-visited areas is another way to even out the inequitable financial input caused by tourism while simultaneously broadening your enjoyment and understanding of the country.

TOURIST OFFICES
Local Tourist Offices

Almost everywhere of interest in Poland has a regional tourist office. These offices are usually more helpful, and often open longer hours, than those of the Polish Tourists Association (PTTK), which are more like organisations of travel agencies offering tours, guides and car hire. However, in some places PTTK offices act as de facto regional tourist offices. Staff at both usually speak English (and often German) and sell maps and guidebooks.

Orbis Travel, the largest travel agency in Poland, has offices and operates upmarket hotels throughout the country. It is often the best place to buy tickets for domestic and international trains and airlines, and for international ferries. Orbis does not focus on providing free information to travellers, but staff are helpful and often speak English.

Tourist Offices Abroad

Polish National Tourist Offices in other countries include:

France (☎ 01 47 42 07 42, **W** www.tourisme .pologne.net) 49 ave de l'Opéra, 75002 Paris
Germany (☎ 030-21 00 92 11, **W** www.polen -info.de) Marburger Strasse 1, 10789 Berlin
Netherlands (☎ 020-625 35 70) Leidsestraat 64, 1017 PD Amsterdam
UK (☎ 020-7580 8811, **W** www.pnto.dial.pipex .com) 1st floor, Remo House, 310-312 Regent St, London W1R 5AJ
USA (☎ 212-338 9412, **W** www.polandtour.org) 275 Madison Ave, Suite 1711, New York, NY 10016

VISAS & DOCUMENTS

Citizens of the European Union, Switzerland, Japan, the UK and the USA can receive a visa for up to 90 days (Britons up to 180 days) at all major borders, and international airports and sea ports. Citizens of Australia, Canada, New Zealand, South Africa and Israel must obtain a tourist visa from a Polish embassy or consulate before coming to Poland.

Tourist visas from Polish embassies or consulates are issued for up to 180 days. The price varies between countries, but is usually about US$50. You can obtain a 48-hour transit visa (onward visa required) if you need to pass through Poland. Visas are generally issued in a few days, but an 'express same-day service' is available at some embassies/consulates if you hand over an additional 50% fee.

If you apply for a visa outside your own country (eg, if you're Aussie and received your visa from the Polish embassy in London), keep all documentation – particularly a copy of your visa application form if possible – to show the immigration officials in Poland.

All visas for Poland – whether obtained at a border, airport, sea port, embassy or consulate – are only valid for the period specified and normally *cannot* be extended. If you want to extend your visa, simply leave the country and get another one.

Student Cards

ISIC cards provide discounts on almost all museums (up to 50%), local transport (50%) in Warsaw (but nowhere else), Polferries services (20%), domestic flights on LOT (10%), PKS buses (30%) from Tuesday to Thursday, and some buses run by Polski Express (30%). ISIC cards, however, *cannot* be used for domestic or international train tickets bought in Poland. ISIC cards are available (with the correct documentation) from Almatur, which has offices in every city in Poland.

EMBASSIES & CONSULATES
Polish Embassies & Consulates

For details about Polish diplomatic missions in other East European countries, refer to the relevant chapters elsewhere in this book.

Australia
  Embassy: (☎ 02-6273 1208) 7 Turrana St, Yarralumla, ACT 2600
  Consulate: (☎ 02-9363 9816) 10 Trelawney St, Woollahra, NSW 2025
Canada
  Embassy: (☎ 613-789 0468) 443 Daly Ave, Ottawa 2, Ontario K1N 6H3
  Consulate: (☎ 514-937 9481) 1500 Ave des Pins Ouest, Montreal, Quebec PQ H3G 1B4
  Consulate: (☎ 416-252 5471) 2603 Lakeshore Blvd West, Toronto, Ontario M8V 1G5
  Consulate: (☎ 604-688 3530) 1177 West Hastings St, Suite 1600, Vancouver, BC V6E 2K3
France
  Embassy: (☎ 01 43 17 34 22) 5 rue de Talleyrand, 75007 Paris
  Consulates in Lille and Lyons
Germany
  Embassy: (☎ 030-22 31 30) Lassenstrasse 19–21, 14193 Berlin
  Consulates in Cologne, Hamburg and Leipzig

Netherlands
  Embassy: (☎ 070-360 28 06) Alexanderstraat 25, 2514 JM The Hague
Russia
  Embassy: (☎ 095-231 15 00) ul Klimashkina 4, 123447 Moscow
  Consulate: (☎ 812-274 41 70) ul 5 Sovietskaya 12/14, 193130 St Petersburg
  Consulate: (☎ 0112-27 33 77) ul Kashtanova 51, 236000 Kaliningrad
UK
  Embassy: (☎ 020-7580 0475) 73 New Cavendish St, London W1N 7RB
  Consulate in Edinburgh
USA
  Embassy: (☎ 202-234 3800) 2640 16th St NW, Washington, DC 20009
  Consulates in New York, Chicago and Los Angeles

Embassies & Consulates in Poland

All diplomatic missions that are listed below are in Warsaw (☎ area code 022) unless stated otherwise.

Australia (☎ 521 34 44, W www.australia.pl) ul Nowogrodzka 11
Belarus (☎/fax 617 84 11) ul Ateńska 67
  Consulate-General: (☎/fax 058-341 00 26) ul Jaśkowa Dolina 50, Gdańsk
Canada (☎ 584 31 00, e wsaw@dfait.maeci.gc.ca) Al Jerozolimskie 123
Czech Republic (☎ 628 72 21, e warsaw@embassy.mzv.cz) ul Koszykowa 18
France (☎ 529 30 00, e ambassade@sunik.pagi.pl) ul Puławska 17
  Consulate-General: (☎ 012-424 53 00) ul Stolarska 15, Kraków
Germany (☎ 617 30 11, W www.ambasadaniemiec.pl) ul Dąbrowiecka 30
  Consulate-General: (☎ 012-421 84 73, fax 421 76 28) ul Stolarska 7, Kraków
  Consulate-General: (☎ 058-341 43 66) Al Zwycięstwa 23, Gdańsk
Ireland (☎ 849 66 55, W www.irlandia.pl) ul Humańska 10
Lithuania (☎ 625 33 68, e litwa.amb@waw.pdi.net) Al Szucha 5
Netherlands (☎ 849 23 51, fax 849 83 45) ul Chocimska 6
Russia (☎ 621 34 53, fax 625 30 16) ul Belwederska 49
  Consulate: (☎ 012-422 26 47, fax 422 90 66) ul Biskupia 7, Kraków
Slovakia (☎ 525 81 10, e slovakia@waw.pdi.net) ul Litewska 6
UK (☎ 628 10 01, W www.britishembassy.pl) Al Róż 1
Ukraine (☎ 625 01 27, e emb_pl@mfa.gov.ua) Al Szucha 7

POLAND

Consulate: (☎ 012-429 60 66, fax 429 29 36) ul Krakowska 41, Kraków
USA (☎ 628 30 41, **w** www.usinfo.pl) Al Ujazdowskie 29/31
Consulate: (☎ 012-424 51 00) ul Stolarska 9, Kraków

CUSTOMS

Customs procedures are usually a formality when both entering and leaving Poland, and your luggage will probably only receive a cursory glance.

When entering Poland, you're allowed to bring duty-free articles for personal use. Every foreigner can bring in or take out of Poland the equivalent (in any currency) of up to €5000. If you wish to leave the country with more than €5000 (in any currency), complete a Currency Declaration form on arrival and have it stamped by customs officials. In practice, it is unlikely anyone will ask you how much money you have.

When leaving the country, you may take out duty-free gifts and souvenirs to a total value of up to €90. Note that the export of items manufactured before 9 May 1945 is prohibited.

MONEY
Currency

The official Polish currency is the złoty ('zwo-ti'), abbreviated to zł. (For reasons unclear, the currency is often abbreviated to PLN in English-language publications and documents.) The złoty is divided into 100 groszy, abbreviated to gr. Denominations of notes are 10, 20, 50, 100 and 200 zł (rare), and coins come in one, two five, 10, 20 and 50 gr, and one, two and five zł. Polish currency is convertible so the black market for currency exchange has all but disappeared.

Exchange Rates

At the time of writing, the approximate exchange rates were:

country	unit		złoty
Australia	A$1	=	2.21zł
Canada	C$1	=	2.60zł
Czech Republic	1 Kč	=	0.12zł
Euro Zone	€1	=	3.70zł
Japan	¥100	=	3.15zł
NZ	NZ$1	=	1.89zł
Russia	R1	=	0.11zł
Slovakia	10 Sk	=	0.85zł
UK	UK£1	=	5.85zł
Ukraine	1 hrn	=	0.74zł
USA	US$1	=	4.03zł

Exchanging Money

For maximum flexibility, travellers should bring cash and one or two credit cards. Cash is easy to change and convenient, especially since Poland is a relatively low-crime destination. Private foreign-exchange offices – called *kantor* – are *everywhere*; in fact, there are often so many that we don't need to show them on our maps. Kantors require no paperwork and charge no commission. Exchange rates rarely vary, but rates at kantors in the midst of major tourist attractions, in top-end hotels and at airports are generally poor.

The most widely accepted currencies are the US dollar, the euro and the pound sterling (in that order). Foreign banknotes should be in perfect condition or kantors may refuse to accept them.

Travellers cheques are obviously more secure than cash, but they're also less convenient. Kantors very rarely change travellers cheques. Not all banks do either and most also charge a commission of 2% to 3%. The best place to change travellers cheques are branches of Bank Pekao or PKO Bank. In a remote region, finding an open bank that cashes travellers cheques may be tricky, especially on weekends.

Ask your local bank about the possibility of cashing Eurocheques while in Poland, because some readers have recently had success.

Automated teller machines (ATMs) – called a *bankomat* – are a convenient way of obtaining local currency. ATMs, which accept up to 17 different international credit cards, are now strategically located in the centre of all cities and most smaller towns. Banks without an ATM may provide cash advances over the counter on credit cards, especially Visa. Bank Pekao will give cash advances with Visa and MasterCard; rates are set and charged by your own bank. Credit cards are increasingly useful for buying goods and services, though their use is still limited to upmarket establishments.

Costs

Travellers must pay for everything in Poland (except visas and international airfares) in the local currency, even if prices are quoted to you (and listed in this chapter) in US dollars and euros. Happily, foreigners pay the same price as Poles for everything.

If you use camping grounds and/or youth hostels, and self-cater or eat at cheap cafeterias, it's possible manage on the złoty equivalent of US$15 per person per day. Increase this to $30/25 per person per day travelling as a single/double if you want to stay in decent budget accommodation and eat meals in acceptable restaurants. To add in some cultural events, a few beers, a taxi or two and some 1st-class train travel, allow US$40/35.

Tipping & Bargaining

If a 'service charge' is added to the restaurant bill there is no obligation to tip. In budget-priced restaurants guests rarely leave a tip; in upmarket establishments it is customary to tip 10% of the bill. Tipping taxi drivers is not necessary unless the driver has been particularly helpful – the driver may reward himself with a 'tip' anyway by not giving you the correct change. Bargaining is rare; perhaps only in outdoor markets in smaller towns.

Taxes & Refunds

A Value Added Tax (VAT) of 3% to 22% is added to most goods and services. It is always included in the prices quoted to you and the prices listed in this chapter.

Visitors not from Poland or an EU country are entitled to a refund of VAT paid on goods taken home if they spend more than 200zł in one day at any shop displaying the sign 'Global Refund' (w www.globalrefund.pl). Ask staff at any of the shops about the complicated (but worthwhile) procedures, so you can claim tax reimbursements at international airports, sea ports and borders when you leave.

POST & COMMUNICATIONS
Post

Postal services are operated by Poczta Polska. Most cities have a dozen or more post offices, of which the Poczta Główna (main post office) has the widest range of facilities, including poste restante, fax and, sometimes, Internet.

Letters and postcards sent by air from Poland take about one week to reach a European destination and up to two weeks if sent to anywhere else. Receiving mail via the poste restante system only reliable in large cities such as Warsaw, Kraków and Gdańsk. Poste-restante mail is held for 14 working days, then returned to the sender.

The cost of sending a normal-sized letter (up to 20g) or a postcard to just about anywhere outside Poland is 2zł, plus a surcharge up to 60g for the 'airmail express' service.

Telephone

Major telecommunications facilities in Poland are provided by Telekomunikacja Polska (TP), which usually has a telephone centre near or inside the main post office. Most of the public telephones now use magnetic phonecards, which are available at post offices, kiosks and grocery stores. Phonecards are available in units of 25 (11.30zł), 50 (20.40zł) and 100 (37.20zł) – one unit represents one three-minute local call. The cards can be used for domestic and international calls. Make sure you tear off the perforated corner before placing it into the telephone.

Not long ago, TP upgraded the telephone system so that all numbers throughout Poland have seven digits. (Numbers included in this chapter are currently correct.) If you ring a six-digit number, the new number should be provided in English (eventually) by the operator. Otherwise, if the number starts with:

1 or 2 – add 4 to the beginning
3, 4 or 5 – add 6
6, 7, 81, 82, 83, 84 or 85 – add 2
86, 87, 88 or 89 – add 3

When calling a number from another telephone district within Poland you must add a prefix of 0; then an 'operator code' of 1033, 1044, 1055 or 1066 depending on which telephone operator you choose to use; then the area code (which is listed in the destination sections later); and, eventually, the actual number. It doesn't matter which operator (and code) you use, and operator codes are not used for international calls.

The three mobile (cell) telephone providers are Idea (w www.idea.pl), Era and Plus GSM. Mobile phones are extremely popular as a status symbol and a more reliable alternative to the jammed land lines and occasionally inoperable public phones.

Direct dialling is possible to just about anywhere in the world. Collect calls are also possible to most countries. Inquire at any TP office for the toll-free number to the operator in the country you want to call. These numbers include:

Australia	☎ 00 800 61 111 61
Canada	☎ 00 800 11 141 18
France	☎ 00 800 33 111 33
Germany	☎ 00 800 49 111 49
UK	☎ 00 800 44 111 44
USA (AT&T)	☎ 00 800 11 111 11

To call Poland from abroad, dial the country code (☎ 48), then the two-digit area code (drop the initial '0' and don't use an operator code), and then the seven-digit local number. The Polish international access code for overseas calls from Poland is 00. If you need help, try the operators for local numbers (☎ 913), national numbers and codes (☎ 912) and international codes (☎ 908), but don't expect anyone to speak English.

The cost of a call from a telephone booth using a phonecard to Europe and the UK is about 3zł per minute, about 6zł to North America, and about 9zł to Australia and New Zealand. If you want to use an international operator (☎ 901), you must pay for at least three minutes.

Fax
Faxes can be sent and received at any main post office for the cost of the equivalent telephone call (minimum of three minutes), but with the advent of mobile phones and the Internet, the old-fashioned fax machine is fast becoming obsolete.

Email & Internet Access
Poland is now truly part of the 'cyber world' and several Polish Internet service providers compete for the growing market. Internet centres can be found all over Poland; smaller towns often have a couple of computers in the main post office, while cities offer a wide choice of trendy cyberpubs and Internet cafés. Sending/receiving emails and/or surfing the Net usually costs about 10zł per hour.

DIGITAL RESOURCES
Before you travel – or while you're in Poland – you may wish to access one of the following websites.

W **www.poland.pl** – excellent place to start surfing
W **www.polishpages.com.pl** – best for anything business-related
W **www.insidepoland.com** – current affairs & reasonable links
W **www.polishworld.com** – directories & travel bookings

BOOKS
Jews in Poland by Iwo Cyprian Pogonowski provides a comprehensive record of half a millennium of Polish-Jewish relations in Poland.

God's Playground: A History of Poland by Norman Davies offers an in-depth analysis of Polish history. The condensed version, *The Heart of Europe: A Short History of Poland*, also by Davies, has greater emphasis on the 20th century. *The Polish Way: A Thousand-Year History of the Poles and their Culture* by Adam Zamoyski is a superb cultural overview of Poland. It's crammed with maps and illustrations that bring the past 1000 years to life. *The Polish Revolution: Solidarity 1980–82* by Timothy Garton Ash is entertaining and thoroughly researched.

NEWSPAPERS & MAGAZINES
Warsaw's major English-language publication *The Warsaw Voice* (W www.warsawvoice.pl) is a well-edited but rather too serious weekly providing a useful insight into national politics and business.

The excellent *Welcome to...* series of magazines covers Poznań, Wrocław, Kraków, Gdańsk and Warsaw individually. Just as good are the *What, Where, When* magazines covering (individually) Warsaw, Kraków and Gdańsk. These publications are free.

Recent copies of newspapers and magazines from the UK, the USA, Germany and France are readily available in the cities. Look for them at EMPiK bookshops, which are *everywhere*, and at newsstands in the lobbies of upmarket hotels.

RADIO & TV
The state-run Polish Radio (Polskie Radio) is the main broadcaster, while Warsaw-based Radio Zet and Kraków-based RFM are two nationwide private broadcasters. Plenty of other private competitors operate locally on FM. Almost every word spoken on radio is in Polish, but most music is in English. Major stations in Warsaw include Radio Kolor (103FM) and Radio Pagoda (100.1FM).

Poland has several private TV channels, including PolSat, and two state-owned countrywide channels, but none of them provides any regular foreign-language programmes. Many programmes are so badly overdubbed – with one male voice covering all actors (including children and women) – that you can often still hear the original language. Most

POLAND

major hotels have satellite dishes that allow access to various European and US channels.

TIME

All of Poland lies within the same time zone, ie, GMT/UTC+1 hour. Poland puts its clocks forward one hour in late March and turns them back again in late September.

LAUNDRY

Do-it-yourself laundrettes are rare, but dry-cleaners *(pralnia)* can be found in larger cities. Expect to pay 5zł to 8zł per garment. Top-class hotels offer a faster – but more expensive – dry-cleaning service for guests.

TOILETS

Toilets are labelled *toaleta* or simply 'WC'. Gentlemen should use the door labelled *męski* and/or marked with an inverted pyramid, and the ladies should look for the door labelled *damski* and/or marked with a circle. Public toilets can be found inside all transport terminals and tourist attractions, and cost the user about 1zł. Restaurants often allow nonpatrons to use their facilities for about the same price.

WOMEN TRAVELLERS

Travel for women in Poland is hassle-free except for occasional encounters with drunks. Harassment of this kind is almost never dangerous, but can be annoying. Simply take the usual precautions.

Women travellers may wish to contact the **International Professional Women of Poland** organisation *(☎/fax 022-606 03 14)* or the **International Women's Group** *(☎ 022-630 72 21)*, both based in Warsaw.

GAY & LESBIAN TRAVELLERS

The Polish gay and lesbian movement is less underground than it used to be. Warsaw and Kraków have the most open scene and are the easiest places to make contacts.

The best sources of information in Warsaw are the **Pride Society** *(e pridesociety@yahoo .com)* and the monthly *Warsaw Insider* magazine, which lists current gay and lesbian clubs in the capital. The website **w** www.gej .net is also a useful source of information.

DISABLED TRAVELLERS

Poland is not well set up for people with disabilities, although there have been significant improvements over recent years. Wheelchair ramps are only available at some upmarket hotels and public transport will be a real challenge for anyone with mobility problems.

SENIOR TRAVELLERS

Travelling around Poland causes few problems for mobile senior travellers, especially if you choose upmarket hotels and travel 1st class on trains.

Senior visitors (with the appropriate cards) can receive discounts on domestic flights with LOT (20%), buses operated by PKS (30%) from Tuesday to Thursday and, possibly, all of the three international ferry services.

TRAVEL WITH CHILDREN

Parents travelling with children in Poland should not have any particular problems. Children (under 14) often receive discounts to museums and can usually sleep in the same hotel room as adults for little extra cost. Any of the endless things required by children of all ages are readily available throughout Poland.

USEFUL ORGANISATIONS

You may wish to contact one or more of the following organisations before or during your visit to Poland. Each of these is based in Warsaw (☎ area code 022).

American Friends in Warsaw (☎ 816 70 94)
British Council (☎ 695 59 00, fax 621 99 55) Al Jerozolimskie 59
French Institute (☎ 827 76 40) ul Senatorska 38
Goethe Institute (☎ 656 60 50) 10th floor, Palace of Culture & Science
Polish Community (☎ 826 20 41) ul Krakowskie Przedmieście – for Polish expats
UNICEF (☎/fax 628 03 01) Al Szucha 16/15

DANGERS & ANNOYANCES

Poland is a relatively safe country, though crime has increased steadily since the fall of

---

Emergency Services

The nationwide, toll-free, 24-hour emergency telephone numbers are ☎ 911 for a pharmacy, ☎ 998 for the fire brigade and ☎ 999 for ambulance.

For the police dial ☎ 997 – but call ☎ 112 from a mobile (cell) phone.

Roadside Assistance is available on ☎ 981.

Don't expect the operators for any of these services to speak English, however.

communism. Take care when walking alone at night, especially in the city centre and in the suburb of Praga. Be particularly alert at any time in the Warszawa Centralna (central) train station, the favourite playground for thieves and pickpockets. Theft from cars is becoming a plague, so keep your vehicle in a guarded car park whenever possible. Heavy drinking is common and drunks can be disturbing, though rarely dangerous. Smoking is common in all public places, especially on public transport.

Poland is an ethnically homogeneous nation. Travellers who look racially different may attract some stares from locals, but this is more likely to be curiosity than anything hostile or ostensibly racist. Football (soccer) hooligans are not uncommon, so avoid travelling on public transport with them (especially if their team has lost!).

LEGAL MATTERS

Foreigners are, of course, subject to the laws of Poland, but there are no laws specific to Poland or not obvious to visitors.

BUSINESS HOURS

Most grocery shops are open weekdays (Monday to Friday) 7am or 8am to 6pm or 7pm and until about 2pm on Saturday. Larger stores stay open for a few hours longer. Banks in larger cities are open from about 8am to 5pm weekdays (sometimes until 2pm on Saturday), but open for fewer hours in smaller towns. Kantors generally operate from 9am to 6pm on weekdays and until about 2pm on Saturday.

Larger post offices are normally open 8am to 8pm weekdays, and one post office in the larger cities will often stay open for 24 hours. Government departments operate about 8am to 4pm on weekdays.

The opening hours of museums and other tourist attractions vary greatly. They tend to open any time between 9am and 11am and close some time from 3pm to 6pm. Most museums are open on weekends, but many close on Monday and also stay closed on the day following a public holiday. Most museums also shut their doors one or two hours earlier in the low season (October to April).

PUBLIC HOLIDAYS & SPECIAL EVENTS

Poland's public holidays include New Year's Day (1 January), Easter Monday (March or April), Labour Day (1 May), Constitution Day (3 May), Corpus Christi (one Thursday in May or June), Assumption Day (15 August), All Saints' Day (1 November), Independence Day (11 November) and Christmas (25 and 26 December).

Cultural, musical and religious events are held regularly in Warsaw, Wrocław, Kraków, Częstochowa, Poznań and Gdańsk – refer to the relevant sections later for details.

ACTIVITIES

Hikers and long-distance trekkers can enjoy any of the thousands of kilometres of marked trails across the Tatra and Sudeten Mountains, around Białowieża National Park and the Great Masurian Lakes district, and at places near Poznań and Świnoujście – refer to the relevant sections later for details. Trails are easy to follow and detailed maps are available at most larger bookshops.

Poland is fairly flat and ideal for cyclists. Bicycle routes along the banks of the Vistula River are popular in Warsaw, Toruń and Kraków. Many of the national parks – including Tatra (near Zakopane), Wolin (near Świnoujście) and Słowinski (near Łeba) – offer bicycle trails, as does the Great Masurian Lakes district. Bikes can be rented at most resort towns and larger cities. (Also see Cycling in the Getting Around section later.)

Zakopane will delight skiers from December to March. Facilities tend to be significantly cheaper – though not as developed – as the ski resorts in Western Europe.

Throngs of yachties, canoeists and kayakers enjoy the network of waterways in the Great Masurian Lakes district every summer; boats are available for rent from all lakeside towns. Windsurfers can head to the wind-swept beaches of the Hel Peninsula.

COURSES

Polish-language courses are available in most major cities, but some only operate in summer. In Kraków, look for posters plastered around major tourist attractions; in Warsaw, check out *The Warsaw Voice*. Otherwise, contact one of the following organisations before you leave home.

The Centre for Polish Studies (☎ 058-550 68 59, **W** www.learnpolish.edu.pl) ul Podgorna 8, Sopot

Polonia Institute of the Jagiellonian University (☎ 012-429 76 32, fax 429 93 51) ul Jodłowa 13, Kraków

POLAND

'Polonicum' Institute of Polish Language &
Culture for Foreigners (☎/fax 022-826 54
16), Warsaw University, ul Krakowskie
Przedmieście 26/28
Schola Polonica (☎ 022-625 26 52, **W** www
.schola.pl) ul Jaracza 3 m 19, Warsaw

WORK

Travellers hoping to find paid work in Poland
will probably be sorely disappointed. The
complex paperwork required for a working
visa is enough to put most people off the idea.
Also, wages are low and you'll probably have
to compete for casual work with other Eastern Europeans, who may be willing to work
for a relative pittance.

ACCOMMODATION
Camping
Poland has hundreds of camping grounds and
many offer good-value cabins and bungalows.
Theoretically, most are open from May to
September, but some really only bother open-
ing their gates between June and August.

Hostels
Youth hostels (schroniska młodzieżowe) in
Poland are operated by Polskie Towarzystwo
Schronisk Młodzieżowych (PTSM), a member
of Hostelling International. Currently Poland
has about 130 hostels open all year and about
450 only open in July and August. The all-year
hostels are more reliable and have more facilities, such as a kitchen and dining room. The
seasonal hostels are usually installed in suburban schools (while the students are off for their
holidays) and amenities can be basic. Annoyingly, many hostels have no actual names or
use names that are ambiguous.

Many previously strict hostel rules have
been relaxed or abandoned. Youth hostels are
now open to all, members and nonmembers
alike, with no age limit. Curfew is often 10pm,
but some hostel staff may be flexible. Most
hostels are closed between 10am and 5pm.

A bed in a hostel dormitory costs about
20zł to 25zł per person per night. Single and
double rooms, if available, cost about 45/
70zł. The youth hostel card gives a 10% to
25% discount on these prices for nationals
and, sometimes, for foreigners. Hostels can
also provide sheets for about 5zł per person.

Given the low prices, hostels are popular
and often full. A particularly busy time is
early May to mid-June, when the hostels are

often crowded with groups of rowdy Polish
school kids.

In most major cities, a few student dorms
open as hostels in summer, though they're
often in the suburbs. Regional tourist offices
are the best places to find out which student
hostels are available and how to get there.

Mountain Refuges
PTTK (see the Tourist Offices section earlier)
runs a chain of mountain refuges (schroniska
górskie) for trekkers. They are usually simple,
but the price is right and the atmosphere is
welcoming. They also serve cheap, hot meals.
The more isolated refuges are obliged to accept everyone, regardless of how crowded
they get. As a result, in the high season even a
space on the floor can be hard to find. Refuges
are normally open all year, but confirm with
the nearest PTTK office before setting off.

Hotels
Most cities and towns offer a variety of old
and new hotels ranging from ultrabasic to
extraplush. Rooms with a private bathroom
can be considerably more expensive than
those with shared facilities, sometimes twice
as much. Hotel prices often vary according to
the season and are usually posted (but rarely
in English) at hotel reception desks. Rates
quoted in this chapter include all taxes.

If possible, check the room before accepting. Don't be fooled by the hotel reception
areas, which may look great in contrast to the
rest of the establishment.

Two reliable companies can that can
arrange accommodation over the Internet are
W www.poland4u.com and **W** www.hotels
poland.com. These sometimes have substantial discount offers.

Private Rooms & Apartments
Some cities and tourist-oriented towns have
agencies – usually called a biuro zakwaterowania or biuro kwater prywatnych –
which arrange accommodation in private
homes. Rooms cost about 55/90zł for singles/
doubles depending on the season, amenities
provided and distance from the city centre.
The most important factor to consider is location; if the home is in the suburbs, find out
how far it is from residential public transport.

During the high season, home owners also
directly approach tourists. Prices are often
lower (and open to bargaining), but you're

more likely to be offered somewhere out in the sticks. Also, private homes in smaller resorts and villages often have signs outside their gates or doors offering a *pokoje* (room) or *noclegi* (lodging).

In Warsaw and Kraków a few agencies offer self-contained apartments (with a kitchen and, sometimes, a laundry). Discounts for more than five days are often attractive so they're an affordable alternative to mid-range and top-end hotels. And the price is per apartment, so you can squeeze in as many people as you want (within reason!).

FOOD
Poles start off their day with breakfast *(śniadanie)*, which is roughly similar to its Western counterpart. The most important and substantial meal of the day, *obiad*, is normally eaten between 2pm and 5pm. *Obiad* usually includes a hearty soup as well as a main course. The third meal is supper *(kolacja)*, which is often similar to breakfast.

Etiquette and table manners are much the same as in the West. When beginning a meal, whether it's in a restaurant or at home, wish your fellow diners *smacznego* ('bon appetit'). When drinking a toast, the Polish equivalent of 'cheers' is *na zdrowie* ('to the health').

Regional Dishes
Polish cuisine has been influenced by various cultures, including Jewish, Ukrainian, Russian, Hungarian and German. Polish food is hearty and filling, abundant in potatoes and dumplings, and rich in meat but not vegetables.

Poland's most famous dishes are *bigos* (sauerkraut with a variety of meats), *pierogi* (ravioli-like dumplings stuffed with cottage cheese or minced meat or cabbage and wild mushrooms) and *barszcz* (red beetroot soup originating from Russian *borshch*).

Hearty soups such as *żurek* (sour soup with sausage and hard-boiled eggs) are a highlight of Polish cuisine. Main dishes are often made with pork, including *golonka* (boiled pig's knuckle served with horseradish) and *schab pieczony* (roast loin of pork seasoned with prunes and herbs). *Gołąbki* (cabbage leaves stuffed with minced beef and rice) is a tasty alternative.

Potato pancakes *(placki ziemniaczane)* and crepes *(naleśniki)* are popular snacks. The favourite Polish summer dessert is fresh berries with cream.

Places to Eat
The gastronomic scene in Poland has developed dramatically over the last decade. A constellation of Western-style eating outlets – almost nonexistent in communist Poland – have sprung up to serve culinary delights that were previously unobtainable. Most of the famous international fast-food chains have already conquered all Polish cities and a myriad of Polish imitations has settled in.

The cheapest place to eat is a milk bar *(bar mleczny)*, a no-frills, self-service cafeteria. They're open at around 7am to 8am (for breakfast) and close between 6pm and 8pm (earlier on Saturday); only a handful are open on Sunday. Milk bars are normally self-serve, so it means that you can see what's cooking, and point, pay and enjoy without speaking a word of Polish.

Most top-class restaurants have menus in English and/or German, but don't expect any foreign-language menus or English-speaking waiters in cheaper eateries. Most staff don't speak English, so we haven't included telephone numbers for restaurants in this chapter.

Menus are usually have several sections: soups *(zupy)*, main courses *(dania drugie)* and accompaniments *(dodatki)*. The price of the main course may not include a side dish – such as potatoes, French fries and salads – which you choose separately (and pay extra for) from the *dodatki* section. Also note that the price for some dishes (particularly fish and poultry) is often listed per 100g, so the price will depend on the *total* weight of the fish/meat.

DRINKS
Wódka (vodka) is the national drink, which the Poles claim was invented in their country. In Poland, vodka is usually drunk neat and comes in a number of colours and flavours, including *myśliwska* (flavoured with juniper berries), *wiśniówka* (with cherries) and *jarzębiak* (with rowanberries). The most famous variety is *żubrówka* (bison vodka), flavoured with grass from the Białowieża Forest and often drunk with apple juice. Other notable spirits include *krupnik* (honey liqueur), *śliwowica* (plum brandy) and *winiak* (grape brandy).

Poles also appreciate the taste of a cold beer *(zimne piwo)*. Polish beer is cheap and palatable and particularly enjoyable while sitting at an outdoor café in a city's old town. The top brands found throughout the country (and a lot of research was done on this topic!) include

POLAND

Żywiec, Okocim and EB, while the regional brands are available in every city. Imported beers can be bought at upmarket establishments, particularly any of the plethora of Irish pubs in the cities.

The quantity and quality of Polish wine is nothing to get excited about, but Hungarian and Bulgarian wines are acceptable and cheap. Wines from elsewhere will be expensive.

ENTERTAINMENT

Every city and town has several cinemas offering recently released films. Thankfully, all films are screened with the original soundtrack (normally English) and Polish subtitles (unlike Polish television). Tickets cost from 6zł to 13zł depending on the city, film shown, session time and comfort of the cinema.

Polish theatre continues to impress foreign audiences. Language is obviously an obstacle for foreigners, but theatre buffs may want to visit some of the better theatres just to watch the acting. Most theatres are closed on Monday and every day in July and August. Tickets cost about 15zł to 25zł. If possible, try to get rid of the jeans and sneakers for the evening or you'll definitely be 'frowned upon' by the other patrons.

Some of the largest cities have opera houses and those in Warsaw and Łódź arguably offer the best productions. For classical music, the Filharmonia Narodowa (National Philharmonic) usually holds concerts on Friday and Saturday nights in most major cities. Again, tickets are very cheap.

Warsaw and Kraków have lively jazz scenes. Discos are popular and usually open from 9pm to late on Thursday, Friday and Saturday. And there's no shortage of places for a drink at any time of the day or night.

SPECTATOR SPORTS

Poland's most popular sport is football (soccer). Although the Polish national team did qualify for the World Cup in 2002, it didn't fare as well as the long-suffering Polish fans had hoped. The most prominent teams in the Polish Football Federation are Legia Warszawa, Widzew Łódź and Wisła Kraków.

The most prestigious international sporting event in Poland is the Tour de Pologne, a long-distance cycling race that takes place every September. Other popular sports include basketball and boxing (Poland boasts the WBO light-heavyweight world champion).

SHOPPING

Amber is a fossil resin of vegetable origin that comes primarily from the Baltic region and appears in a variety of colours from pale yellow to reddish brown. The best places to buy jewellery made from amber are Gdańsk, Kraków and Warsaw.

Polish contemporary paintings, original prints and sculptures are sold by private commercial art galleries, especially in Warsaw and Kraków. Polish poster art has received international recognition; the best selection of poster galleries is also in Warsaw and Kraków.

Other ideas for mementoes include crystal glass, handmade pottery (especially from the villages within an hour's drive from Wrocław), chessboards (from shops at the main square in Kraków), and original paintings of Kraków and other picturesque old towns.

Getting There & Away

AIR

The national carrier, **LOT** (w *www.lot.com*), flies to all major European cities, as well as almost everywhere in Germany. LOT and other regional airlines also link Warsaw with Kyiv, Odesa and Lviv (Ukraine), Rīga (Latvia), Minsk (Belarus), Tallinn (Estonia), Vilnius (Lithuania) and Moscow. Warsaw is also serviced by most major European carriers, such as Air France, Alitalia, British Airways, KLM-Royal Dutch Airlines and Lufthansa Airlines. Other regional airlines with flights to/from Warsaw include Aeroflot, Aerosvit, Czech Airlines, Malév Hungarian Airlines, Tarom (from Romania) and Turkish Airlines.

A few flights from Europe also regularly go to/from Gdańsk, Kraków, Poznań, Szczecin and Wrocław – see the relevant sections later in this chapter for details.

From the USA, LOT offers frequent direct flights to Warsaw from Chicago and New York and has a code-share agreement with American Airlines for other US cities. In summer, there are also direct flights on LOT to Kraków from Chicago (April to September) and New York (June to September). For Canadians, LOT flies several days a week directly from Toronto to Warsaw.

From Australia (and New Zealand), the cheapest and most direct way to Poland is by

Qantas to Bangkok, and from there to Warsaw on LOT.

Regular fares to Warsaw are not cheap. However, advance-purchase excursion fares can be good value if you can be flexible and work around the restrictions. Bucket shops in Europe and Asia sell LOT tickets at large discounts, usually from Asia to Western Europe or vice versa with a free stopover in Warsaw. Ask around the budget agencies in Singapore, Penang, Bangkok, London or Amsterdam. Also, an increasing number of travel agencies in Poland try to offer competitive fares. Warsaw is the best place to shop around.

LAND
Border Crossings
Below is a list of major road border crossings that accept foreigners and are open 24 hours.

Belarus – south to north Terespol & Kuźnica Białostocka

Czech Republic – west to east Porajów, Zawidów, Jakuszyce, Lubawka, Kudowa-Słone, Boboszów, Głuchołazy, Pietrowice, Chałupki & Cieszyn

Germany – north to south Lubieszyn, Kołbaskowo, Krajnik Dolny, Osinów Dolny, Kostrzyn, Słubice, Świecko, Gubin, Olszyna, Łęknica, Zgorzelec & Sieniawka

Lithuania – east to west Ogrodniki & Budzisko

Russia – east to west Bezledy & Gronowo

Slovakia – west to east Chyżne, Chochołów, Łysa Polana, Niedzica, Piwniczna, Konieczna & Barwinek

Ukraine – south to north Medyka, Hrebenne, Dorohusk & Zosin

Train
Every day, dozens of trains link Poland with every neighbouring country and beyond. International train travel is not cheap, however, especially for longer routes. To save money on train fares, look into the choice of special train tickets and rail passes – refer to the Getting Around chapter at the beginning of this book. Domestic trains in Poland are significantly cheaper than international ones, so you'll save money if you buy a ticket to the first city you arrive at inside Poland and then take a local train. The official website **w** www .wars.pl has information and you can also buy tickets for some services online.

Please note that some international trains to/from Poland have recently become notorious for theft. Some Poles are now too afraid to take any overnight train to/from Poland.

Keep a grip on your bags, particularly on the Berlin-Warsaw, Prague-Warsaw and Prague-Kraków overnight trains, and on *any* train travelling to/from Gdańsk. Several readers have been gassed while in their compartments and have had everything stolen while they 'slept'. Always reinforce your carriage and, if possible, sleep in a compartment with others. First-class trains, in theory, should be safer.

UK & Germany Train travel from London to Warsaw is either via the Channel Tunnel or Ostend. Tickets can be bought from British Rail ticket offices or travel centres. You may find a cheaper fare from an agency that specialises in travel and tours to Poland, such as **Fregata Travel** (☎ 020-7247 8484; **w** www .fregata travel.co.uk; 83 White Chapel High St, London E1 7QX) or **Polorbis** (☎ 020-7636 4701; **w** www.polorbis.co.uk; Suite 530-2 Walmar House, 288/300 Regent St, London W1B 3AL).

The Warsaw-Berlin route (via Frankfurt/ Oder and Poznań) is serviced by several trains a day, including three EuroCity express trains (€33 2nd class, 6½ hours). There are also numerous connections between Warsaw and Cologne, Dresden, Frankfurt-am-Main and Leipzig; between Kraków and Berlin, via Wrocław; and between Gdańsk and Berlin, via Szczecin.

Czech Republic & Austria Four trains a day travel between Prague and Warsaw (10 to 12 hours) via either Wrocław or Katowice. Every day, four trains also travel between Prague and Wrocław (seven hours) and one plies the route between Prague and Kraków (nine hours).

Two trains a day travel between Vienna and Warsaw (about 10 hours) and one goes between Vienna and Kraków (seven hours).

Slovakia & Hungary Two trains travel daily between Budapest and Warsaw (12 hours), via Bratislava. These trains are routed through a short stretch of the Czech Republic, so get a Czech visa if necessary. The daily train that runs between Budapest and Kraków (11 hours) follows a different route through Košice in eastern Slovakia.

Elsewhere in Eastern Europe Warsaw has direct train links with Kyiv (Ukraine), Minsk (Belarus), Vilnius (Lithuania), and

Moscow and St Petersburg. (These trains only have sleeping cars.) There are also daily trains between Gdańsk and Kaliningrad (five hours) in Russia.

Remember that you may need transit visas for the countries you'll be passing through en route. For example, the Warsaw–Vilnius–St Petersburg train line goes via Hrodna in Belarus. The Belarus border guards will awaken ignorant travellers and demand a US$30 visa fee – or may even send you back from whence you came. You can avoid this by taking a direct bus between Poland and Lithuania.

Bus

International bus services throughout Western and Eastern Europe are offered by dozens of Polish and international companies. Prices for international buses are generally cheaper than for trains, but you will undoubtedly find it more comfortable, and probably quicker, to travel to/from Poland by train.

One of the major bus operators is Eurolines, a consortium of affiliated European bus companies including the Polish national bus company **PKS** (W *www.pekaesbus.com.pl*).

Western Europe PKS operates dozens of buses each week to all major cities in Germany, as well as to Copenhagen on Sunday, from the Dworzec Zachodnia (Western Bus Station) in Warsaw.

Three or four days every week (and daily during summer), **Eurolines** (☎ *0990-808 080;* W *www.gobycoach.com*) has services from London (Victoria) to Zamość, via Poznań, Łódź, Warsaw (Zachodnia) and Lublin; and from London to Kraków, via Wrocław and Częstochowa.

Three times a week, Eurolines goes from Paris (place de la Concorde) to Białystok, via Poznań and Warsaw; from Paris to Kraków, via Wrocław and Częstochowa; and Paris to Gdynia, via Poznań, Toruń and Gdańsk. Book at **Polka Service** (☎ *01 49 72 51 51; 28 vve du Général de Gaulle, Bagnolet*).

Eurolines also has regular buses from Hamburg to Częstochowa, via Wrocław; and from Cologne to Warsaw, via Poznań and Łódź.

Elsewhere in Eastern Europe PKS has regular buses from Warsaw to Rīga (Friday), to Minsk (Tuesday, Friday and Sunday), to Kyiv (Tuesday, Thursday and Saturday) and to Vilnius (daily). These routes should not

normally take more than 12 to 15 hours each, though the actual time depends on traffic lines at the border and customs.

Also, PKS buses run six times a day between Przemyśl and Lviv (three hours), weekly between Suwałki and Vilnius (five hours), regularly between Zakopane and Budapest (nine hours), and twice a day between Gdańsk and Kaliningrad (five hours).

To Kraków, a few buses a week depart from Budapest (10 hours), and one a week makes the long haul from St Petersburg, via Minsk, Warsaw (Dworzec Zachodnia) and Częstochowa.

Car & Motorcycle

To drive a car into Poland you will first need your driving licence from home – you can use this for six months after arrival in Poland, but then you'll have to apply for a local licence. Also required are vehicle registration papers and liability insurance ('green card'). If your insurance is not valid for Poland you must buy an additional policy at the border. The car registration number will be entered in your passport.

SEA

Three companies operate passenger and car ferries all year.

Polferries (W *www.polferries.pl*) offers services between Gdańsk and Nynäshamn (19 hours) in Sweden every day in summer (three times a week in the low season). It also has daily services from Świnoujście to Ystad (9½ hours) in Sweden, to Rønne (five hours) in Denmark on Saturday, and to Copenhagen (10½ hours) five times a week.

Stena Line (W *www.stenaline.com*) operates between Gdynia and Karlskrona (11 hours) in Sweden at least six times a week.

Unity Line runs ferries between Świnoujście and Ystad (eight hours) every day.

Deck tickets normally do not need to be booked in advance. Cabins, which range in standard and therefore price, should be reserved in the high season. Cars should also be booked in advance at any time. Bicycles go free. A return ticket costs about 20% less than two singles and is valid for six months. Any travel agency in Scandinavia will sell tickets. In Poland, inquire at any Orbis Travel office. Orbis can also book tickets for other European ferries, eg, between Italy and Greece.

In summer, passenger boats ply the Baltic coast from Świnoujście to Ahlbeck, Heringsdorf, Bansin and Sassnitz in Germany.

ORGANISED TOURS

A number of tours to Poland can be arranged from abroad.

USA
Affordable Poland (☎ 800 497 9929, **W** www .s-traveler.com) 1600 Saratoga Ave, Suite 609, San Jose, CA 95129

Pat Tours (☎ 413-747 7702, 800 388 0988, **W** www.polandtours.com) 1285 Riverdale St, West Springfield, MA 01089

UK
Polorbis (☎ 020-7636 4701, **W** www.polorbis .co.uk) Suite 530-532 Walmar House, 288/300 Regent St, London W1B 3AL

Martin Randall Travel (☎ 020-8742 3355, **W** www.martinrandall.com) 10 Barley Mow Passage, Chiswick, London W4 4PH

DEPARTURE TAX

International departure tax for flights from Warsaw is US$10 and approximately $8 for departures from other Polish airports. The tax is automatically added to the cost of the ticket whether you buy it in or outside Poland.

Getting Around

AIR

The only domestic carrier, LOT, operates flights several times a day from Warsaw to Gdańsk, Kraków, Łódź, Poznań, Szczecin and Wrocław. So, flying between, for example, Kraków and Gdańsk means a connection in Warsaw and connections are not necessarily convenient. All flights to/from Warsaw cost 171/268zł one way/return – except between Warsaw and Szczecin, which costs about 30% more – but must be booked and paid for at least two weeks in advance. Tickets can be bought at LOT offices and most travel agencies, including the nationwide Orbis Travel.

Promotional fares (eg, early or late flights, weekend flights etc) are often worth looking out for – check the English-language newspapers and magazines.

TRAIN

Trains will be your main means of transport, especially for long distances. They are cheap, fairly reliable and rarely overcrowded (except

for peak times in July and August). The Polish State Railways (PKP) operates more than 27,000km of railway lines and almost every place listed in this chapter (and many, many more) is accessible by train.

Express trains *(pociąg ekspresowy)* are a faster but more expensive way to travel, while fast trains *(pociąg pospieszny)* are a bit slower and maybe more crowded. Slow passenger trains *(pociąg osobowy)* stop at every tree at the side of the track and should be used only for short trips. Express and fast trains do not normally require seat reservations except at peak times; seats on passenger trains cannot be reserved.

InterCity trains operate on some major routes out of Warsaw, including Gdańsk, Kraków, Poznań and Szczecin. They only stop at major cities en route and are faster than express trains (averaging about 100km/h). These trains require seat reservations and a light meal is included in the fare.

Almost all trains carry two classes: 2nd class *(druga klasa)* and 1st class *(pierwsza klasa)*, which is 50% more expensive. The carriages on long-distance trains are usually divided into compartments: 1st-class compartments have six seats and 2nd-class ones contain eight seats. There is often little difference in the standard between the two classes except that fewer people travel in 1st class so you'll always have more room.

In a couchette on an overnight train, compartments have four/six beds in 1st/2nd class. Sleepers have two/three people (1st/2nd class) in a compartment which is fitted with a washbasin, sheets and blankets. Most 2nd-class and all 1st-class carriages have nonsmoking compartments.

Train Stations

Most train stations in the cities are reasonably modern and convenient. The main train station in every city is often identified by the name 'Główny' ('main') – don't make the mistake of getting off at a suburban station if you don't want to.

Large train stations have left-luggage rooms *(przechowalnia bagażu)*, which are usually secure. They operate 24 hours, but generally close once or twice a day for an hour or so. The daily storage charge per item is about 4zł per day or 'part thereof', though some rooms demand that you also pay a percentage (about 1%) of the 'declared value of your baggage' for some unspecified 'insurance' purposes.

Timetables

Train departures *(odjazdy)* are listed on a yellow board and arrivals *(przyjazdy)* on a white board. Ordinary trains are marked in black print; fast trains in red. An additional 'Ex' indicates an express train and InterCity trains are identified by the letters 'IC'. The letter 'R' in a square indicates the train has compulsory seat reservation. The timetables clearly show the time of the train's arrival and departure and which platform *(peron)* it's using.

Timetables for services to/from Warsaw (7zł) and for all of Poland (45zł) are available from major train stations. Although written in Polish, these timetables are useful and easy to use. The same information is available on the PKP's official website **w** www.pkp.pl, but it's in Polish.

Train stations in the larger cities normally have an information desk, but it's rarely staffed with anyone who speaks English.

Tickets

Most large train stations are now computerised, so buying a ticket *(bilety)* is now less of a hassle than it used to be. However, be at the station at least half an hour before the departure time of your train and make sure you're queuing at the right ticket window *(kasa)*. Better still, buy a ticket up to 30 days in advance (for no extra charge) from the train station or (for any trip more than 100km) from any larger Orbis Travel office. (Orbis has offices in the city centres and can issue a ticket in less than a minute.) Sleepers *(miejsca sypialne)* and couchettes *(kuszetki)* can be booked at special counters in larger train stations or from Orbis; advance reservations are advisable.

If a seat reservation is compulsory on your train, you will automatically be sold a reserved seat ticket *(miejscówka)*. It's important to note that if you do not make a seat reservation, you can travel on *any* train (of the type requested, ie, passenger, fast or express) to the destination indicated on your ticket and on the date specified.

Your ticket will list the class *(klasa)*; the type of train *(poc)*; the places the train is travelling from *(od)* and to *(do)*; the major town or junction the train is travelling through *(prez)*; and the total price *(cena)*. If more than one place is listed under the heading

prez (via), find out from the conductor *early* if you have to change trains at the junction listed or be in a specific carriage (the train may separate later).

If you get on a train without a ticket, you can buy one directly from the conductor for a small supplement – but do it right away. If the conductor finds you first, you'll be fined for travelling without a ticket. You can always upgrade from 2nd to 1st class for a small extra fee (about 5zł), plus the additional fare.

Fares

Tickets for fast trains are 50% to 60% more expensive than those for passenger trains, and tickets for express trains are 33% to 50% more than for fast trains. Only 2nd-class fares are listed in this book – for 1st-class fares, add another 50%. A reserved seat, which costs an additional 7zł to 12zł, may be useful for 2nd-class carriages on busy routes at peak times, but is not necessary for 1st-class carriages where a seat is guaranteed. A 1st-/2nd-class couchette costs an extra 50/65zł and a sleeper is an additional 90/140zł.

Note: PKP does not offer discounts on domestic and international trains to foreign students, ISIC card-holders or senior travellers.

Polrail Pass

This pass provides unlimited travel on trains throughout Poland. It is valid for all domestic passenger, fast and express trains, but you'll have to pay a surcharge to use the InterCity and EuroCity services. Passes come in durations of eight days (€162/108 for 1st/2nd class), 15 days (€192/128), 21 days (€216/144) and one month (€273/182). Persons aged under 26 on the first day of travel can buy a 'Junior' pass for 25% to 30% less. Seat reservation fees (when required) are included.

The pass is available from North American travel agencies through Rail Europe and travel agencies in Western Europe. It can also be bought at the **Wasteels** office (☎ *022-620 21 49*) in the underground mezzanine level at the Warszawa Centralna train station in the capital, and at **Orbis Travel** (☎ *022-827 72 65, fax 827 76 05; ul Bracka 16, Warsaw*).

BUS & MINIBUS

Sometimes buses are convenient, especially on short routes and around the mountains in southern Poland. However, trains are almost always quicker and more comfortable for longer distances, and minibuses are far quicker and more direct for short trips. If you can, avoid using buses altogether because they can be frustratingly slow and indirect.

Most buses are operated by the state bus company, PKS, which has bus terminals (*dworzec autobusowy PKS*) in all cities and towns. PKS provides two kinds of service: ordinary buses (marked in black on timetables), which cover mostly regional routes and stop anywhere and everywhere along the way; and fast buses (marked in red), which cover mainly long-distance routes and ignore minor stops.

Timetables are posted on boards either inside or outside PKS bus terminals. Always check any additional symbols next to the departure time of your bus; these symbols often indicate that the bus runs only on certain days or in certain seasons. Terminals in the larger cities normally have an information desk, but it's rarely staffed with anyone who speaks English.

The largest private bus operator is Polski Express, a joint venture with Eurolines National Express based in the UK. Polski Express operates several major long-distance routes to/from Warsaw (see that section later for details) and is faster, more comfortable and often cheaper than PKS buses. Polski Express buses normally arrive at/depart from or near the PKS bus terminals – exceptions are mentioned in the relevant Getting There & Away sections.

Tickets for PKS buses must be bought at the terminal. On long routes serviced by fast buses tickets can be bought up to 30 days in advance, but for short local routes tickets are only available on the same day. Tickets for Polski Express buses can be bought up to 14 days in advance at the terminals or stops where they arrive/depart.

For shorter trips, minibuses usually provide a better alternative to PKS buses. Minibuses always travel faster than buses, usually leave more frequently (normally at set times and not when the minibus is full) and stop *far* less often. The cost of travelling on a minibus is almost the same as on a bus.

CAR & MOTORCYCLE

Poland's 220,000km of sealed roads are in an acceptable condition for leisurely driving. Over the next 15 years Poland had planned to build a 2600km network of toll motorways stretching from the Baltic coast to the Czech border and from Germany to Ukraine, but this has been stalled indefinitely through a lack of funds.

Petrol is readily available at petrol stations, which have mushroomed throughout the country. These places sell several kinds and grades of petrol, including 94-octane leaded, 95-octane unleaded, 98-octane unleaded and diesel. Most petrol stations are open 6am to 10pm (7am to 3pm Sunday), though some operate around the clock.

Car theft is a problem in Poland, so always try to park your vehicle at a guarded car park (*parking strzeżony*). Otherwise, hide or remove your bags so the car looks empty. The radio/cassette player in the car is usually the first thing that attracts thieves' attention.

Also see under Car & Motorcycle in the Getting There & Away section earlier in this chapter.

Road Rules

The speed limit is 130km/h on motorways, 100km/h or 110km/h on two- or four-lane highways, 90km/h on other open roads and 60km/h in built-up areas (50km/h in Warsaw). If the background of the sign bearing the town's name is white you must reduce speed to 60km/h; if the background is green there's no need to reduce speed (unless road signs indicate otherwise). Radar-equipped police are very active, especially in villages with white signs. (Approaching cars often flash their lights in warning.)

Unless signs state otherwise, cars may park on pavements as long as a minimum 1.5m-wide walkway is left for pedestrians. Parking in the opposite direction to the flow of traffic is allowed. The permitted blood alcohol level is 0.02%, so it's best not to drink at all if you're driving.

Seat belts are compulsory in the front seats, but most Polish drivers think its actually safer to drive *without* a belt! Motorbike helmets are also compulsory. Between 1 October and the end of February, all drivers must use their car (and motorbike) headlights during the day (and night!)

Rental

Most of the major international car rental companies, like **Avis** (Ⓦ *www.avis.pl*), **Hertz** (Ⓦ *www.hertz.pl*) and **Europcar** (Ⓦ *www .europcar.com.pl*), are represented in larger cities and have smaller offices at the airports. The rates offered by these companies are not cheap: the prices are comparable to, or even higher than, full-price rental in Western Europe, and promotional discounts are not very often available.

The increasing number of local operators, such as **Payless Car Rental** (**w** *www.payless carrental.pl*), provide a reliable and more affordable alternative. It charges about €55 per day (for one to five days with unlimited kilometres) or €44 per day (eight to 13 days with unlimited kilometres), plus petrol and insurance (from €14 per day).

Some companies offer one-way rentals, but almost all will insist on keeping the car within Poland. And no agency will allow you to drive their precious vehicle into Russia, Ukraine or Belarus. There is nowhere in Poland to rent a motorcycle.

Rental agencies will need to see your passport, your local driving licence (which must be held for at least one year) and a credit card (for the deposit). You need to be at least 21 or 23 years of age to rent a car; sometimes 25 for a more expensive car.

It's usually cheaper to prebook a car in Poland from abroad rather than to front up at an agency inside Poland. It would be even cheaper to rent a car in Western Europe, eg, Berlin or Geneva, and drive it into Poland, but few rental companies will allow this. If they do, special insurance is required.

HITCHING

Lonely Planet does not recommend hitchhiking, but it does take place in Poland. Car drivers rarely stop to pick up hitchhikers, and large commercial vehicles (which are easier to wave down) expect to be paid the equivalent of a bus fare.

BOAT

Sadly, no passenger-boat services regularly travel along the major rivers or the Baltic, despite Poland's long coastline. Several places, such as Kraków and Kazimierz Dolny, offer local river cruises, and from Gdańsk and other ports nearby boats take tourists along the Baltic coast, but these only operate during the peak summer season.

On the Great Masurian Lakes, excursion boats operate in summer between Giżycko, Mikołajki, Węgorzewo and Ruciane-Nida. The most unusual boat trip is the full-day cruise along the Elbląg-Ostróda Canal. There is also rafting in the Dunajec Gorge.

CYCLING

Cycling is not great for getting around cities, but is often a perfect way to travel between villages. Major roads are busy but generally flat, while minor roads can be bumpy. If you get tired, or want to avoid the mountains in the south or travel a long distance in a short time, it's easy to place your bike in the special luggage compartment of a train. These compartments are at the front or rear of slow passenger trains, but rarely found on fast or express trains, and never on InterCity or EuroCity services. You'll need a special ticket for your bike from the railway luggage office.

LOCAL TRANSPORT

Most cities have buses (*autobus*) and trams (*tramwaj*), and some have trolleybuses (*trolejbus*). Public transport throughout Poland runs daily from around 5am to 11pm, and may be crowded during rush hours. Larger cities also have night-time services on buses and trams. Timetables are usually posted at the stops, but don't expect the times to be too accurate.

Most cities and towns have a flat-rate fare of about 2zł for local transport, but if you change trams, buses or trolleybuses you'll need another ticket. Passes for unlimited travel on all public transport for one day, one week or one month are often available but only valid in that particular town or city. For bulky luggage, buy an additional ordinary ticket.

Tickets should be bought beforehand from nearby kiosks – often marked RUCH – and *must* be punched or stamped in a machine upon boarding. You can usually buy tickets on board the bus, tram or trolleybus for a small extra charge, but if the driver doesn't have any tickets or change, you'll have to get off at the next stop and buy a ticket at a kiosk.

Plain-clothed inspectors check tickets more often than they used to and backpackers are their favourite prey. If you're caught without a ticket, pay the fine straight away – but ask for identification and a receipt. *Never* give an inspector your passport; if they threaten you with police intervention, volunteer to accompany them to the nearest police station.

At long last, Warsaw has installed a metro system. However, it's of minimal interest or use to travellers.

Taxi

Taxis in Poland are plentiful and not too expensive by Western standards. Legitimate taxis are usually recognisable by large boards on the roof with the company's name and telephone number. And by law these taxis must display a sign on the window with their fares.

Pirate taxis (called the 'Mafia' by Poles) do not have a sign on top with a name and phone number, nor do they list their fares. (To add to the confusion, some legitimate taxis may have no name or telephone on top of the vehicle, in which case check that the fares are listed on the windows.) For some 'convenient' reason, these illegal taxis often have prime positions outside major tourist haunts, transport terminals and top-end hotels. They tend to charge several times more than the normal fare and should be avoided.

Legitimate taxis can be waved down from along the street or taken from a taxi stand *(postój taksówek)*. Your hotel will happily order a taxi for you; you won't be charged for this by the hotel or taxi.

All legitimate taxis have meters. When you get into a taxi, make sure the driver turns on the meter (and keeps it on) at the correct fare:

tariff 1 – the day time rate (6am-10pm), which is about 2zł per kilometre plus a flag fall (which includes the first kilometre) of about 5zł
tariff 2 – the rate for night-time, Sunday and public holidays (about 50% more)
tariff 3 – the long-distance daytime rate
tariff 4 – the long-distance night-time rate

ORGANISED TOURS

A new breed of travel agencies based in Poland focuses on Western tourists and happily sells tours abroad (often through other agencies). The three listed below are reliable, offer interesting alternatives to the predictable 'cultural tours around Kraków' and other essential services. Some foreign travel agencies are included in the Getting There & Away section earlier, and a few local agencies are also included in the sections later for Warsaw, Kraków and the Great Masurian Lakes district.

Almatur – has offices in most Polish cities. It offers budget-priced sailing, kayaking and horse-riding holidays (mainly July and August). It also operates student hostels in summer, sells tickets on international buses and issues ISIC cards (see the relevant section under Visas & Documents earlier).
Kampio (☎ 022-823 70 70, fax 823 71 44, **e** kampio@it.com.pl) ul Maszynowa 9 m 2, Warsaw – focuses on ecotourism, eg, kayaking, biking and bird-watching trips, around the interesting

regions, such as Białowieża National Park and the Great Masurian Lakes. Guides speak English and German.
Orbis Travel (**w** www.orbis.pl) – the previously government-run dinosaur, which is now privatised. This competent organisation has offices in all cities and towns in Poland, operates 56 hotels around the country and offers package tours to Poles and foreigners in and outside Poland. Major Orbis offices also sell advance tickets for domestic and international trains, and tickets for international ferries and all domestic and international airlines.

Warsaw

☎ 022 • pop 1.75 million

Warsaw, or Warszawa ('vah-SHAH-vah') in Polish, is the geographical, political and economic heart of the country. It's a large, cosmopolitan and modern city, which was mostly rebuilt after WWII, and certainly has enough museums and other attractions to keep most visitors happy for several days.

Warsaw began its life in the 14th century as a stronghold of the Mazovian dukes. When Poland and Lithuania were unified in 1569, Warsaw's strategic central location came to the fore and the capital was transferred here from Kraków. Paradoxically, the 18th century – a period of catastrophic decline for the Polish state – witnessed Warsaw's greatest prosperity. A wealth of splendid churches, palaces and parks were built and cultural and artistic life flourished. The first constitution in Europe, however short-lived, was instituted in Warsaw in 1791.

The 19th century was a period of decay for Warsaw, which became a mere provincial town in the Russian empire. After WWI Warsaw was reinstated as the capital of a newly independent Poland and began to thrive once more. In WWII, however, 700,000 residents perished (over half of the city's population) and 85% of its buildings were destroyed. Very few of the 350,000 Jews living in Warsaw in 1939 escaped the death camps. No other city in Eastern European suffered such immense loss of life or devastation.

Immediately after the war the gigantic task of restoration began and Warsaw re-emerged like a phoenix from the ashes. Parts of the historic city, most notably the Old Town, have been meticulously rebuilt to their previous condition.

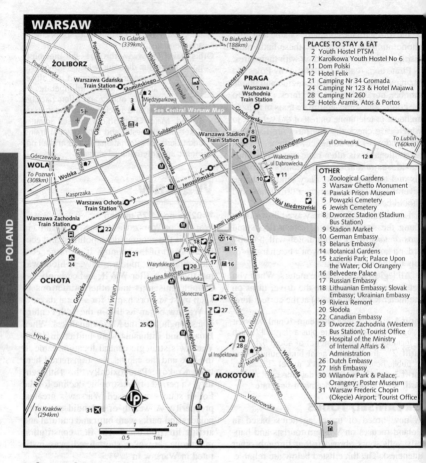

WARSAW

To Gdańsk (339km)
To Białystok (188km)

ŻOLIBORZ

Warszawa Gdańska Train Station

See Central Warsaw Map

PRAGA
Warszawa Wschodnia Train Station

Warszawa Stadion Train Station

To Lublin (160km)

WOLA
To Poznań (308km)

Warszawa Ochota Train Station

Warszawa Zachodnia Train Station

OCHOTA

MOKOTÓW

To Kraków (294km)

PLACES TO STAY & EAT
2   Youth Hostel PTSM
7   Karolkowa Youth Hostel No 6
11 Dom Polski
12 Hotel Felix
21 Camping Nr 34 Gromada
24 Camping Nr 123 & Hotel Majawa
28 Camping Nr 260
29 Hotels Aramis, Atos & Portos

OTHER
1   Zoological Gardens
3   Warsaw Ghetto Monument
4   Pawiak Prison Museum
5   Powązki Cemetery
6   Jewish Cemetery
8   Dworzec Stadion (Stadium Bus Station)
9   Stadion Market
10 German Embassy
13 Belarus Embassy
14 Botanical Gardens
15 Łazienki Park; Palace Upon the Water; Old Orangery
16 Belvedere Palace
17 Russian Embassy
18 Lithuanian Embassy; Slovak Embassy; Ukrainian Embassy
19 Riviera Remont
20 Słodoła
22 Canadian Embassy
23 Dworzec Zachodnia (Western Bus Station); Tourist Office
25 Hospital of the Ministry of Internal Affairs & Administration
26 Dutch Embassy
27 Irish Embassy
30 Wilanów Park & Palace; Orangery; Poster Museum
31 Warsaw Frederic Chopin (Okęcie) Airport; Tourist Office

0   1   2km
0   0.5   1mi

Information

Tourist Offices The official **tourist organisation** (☎ 9431, ⓦ *www.warsawtour.pl*) has several branches: opposite the Royal Castle at Plac Zamkowy *(open 9am-5pm daily)*; in the arrivals hall of the airport *(open 8am-8pm daily May-Oct, 8am-6pm Nov-Apr)*; next to the ticket office at the Dworzec Zachodnia *(Western Bus Station; open 6am-9.30pm daily)*; and in the main hall of the Warszawa Centralna train station *(open 8am-6pm daily)*. Each can provide free city maps of Warsaw, sell maps of other Polish cities, and help you book a hotel room (but not a room in a private home).

Another state-run tourist office, **Warsaw Tourist & Cultural Information** (☎ 656 68 54; *Plac Defilad; open 9am-6pm daily*) is on the ground floor of the Palace of Culture & Science building.

These official tourist offices should not be confused with the many offices signposted 'Warsaw Center of Tourist Information' (one of which is also in the Old Town). These private agencies are helpful, but rarely keen to freely dispense independent information.

Books & Magazines If you're staying here a few days, pick up a copy of the free monthly magazines *Warszawa: What, Where, When* and *Welcome to Warsaw*. Both are a mine of information about cultural events and provide reviews of new restaurants, bars and nightclubs. They're available in the lobbies of most top-end hotels – most reliably, the Hotel Gromada Centrum and Hotel MDM (see Places to Stay later). The comprehensive monthly *Warsaw Insider* (9zł), and the free bimonthly *The Visitor*, are also both published in English and worth finding.

Money Foreign-exchange offices, known as kantors, and ATMs are easy to find around the city centre. Kantors open 24 hours can be found at the Warszawa Centralna train station, and either side of the immigration counters at the airport, but exchange rates at these places are about 10% lower than in the city centre. Avoid changing money in the Old Town where the rates are even lower.

Bank Pekao has a dozen branches in the city, including one along ul Krakowskie Przedmieście, next to the Church of the Holy Cross. Also, useful is the **PBK Bank** *(ground floor, Palace of Culture & Science bldg)* and the **PKO Bank** *(Plac Bankowy 2)*. These banks change major-brand travellers cheques, offer cash advances on Visa and MasterCard and have ATMs that take just about every known credit card. Another place to cash major travellers cheques is **American Express** *(Marriott Hotel, Al Jerozolimskie 65/79)*.

Post & Communications The best place to send and receive letters and faxes is the **main post office** *(ul Świętokrzyska 31/33; open 24hr)*. The poste restante is at window No 12. Letters should be addressed to Poste Restante, Poczta Główna, ul Świętokrzyska 31/33, 00-001 Warszawa 1.

For telephone calls, use a phonecard at any of the plethora of telephone booths around the city or inside the main post office.

Email & Internet Access Internet centres and cafés are springing up all around Warsaw. The most atmospheric places are **Casablanca** *(ul Krakowskie Przedmieście 4/6)* and **Studio.tpi** *(ul Świętokrzyska 3)*.

Several very convenient but dingy **Internet centres** are also found along the underground mezzanine level of the Warszawa Centralna train station.

Travel Agencies Refer to Organised Tours later in this section for information about travel agencies based in Warsaw.

Bookshops The **American Bookstore** *(ul Nowy Świat 61)* offers a wide selection of Lonely Planet titles, English publications and

maps. The largest array of foreign newspapers and magazines is in the **EMPiK Megastore** *(ul Marszałkowska 116/122)*. For trashy novels in English, visit **Co-Liber** bookshop *(cnr Marszałkowska & ul Widok)*, next to Max Bar restaurant.

Laundry Take your dirty clothes to **Alba Dry Cleaning** *(ul Chmielna 26)*.

Medical Services Some of the many pharmacies throughout the city stay open all night, including one in the Warszawa Centralna train station.

The **Hospital of the Ministry of Internal Affairs & Administration** *(☎ 602 15 78; ul Wołoska 137)* is a private hospital preferred by important government officials and diplomats. **CM Medical Center** *(☎ 458 70 00; 3rd floor, Marriott Hotel, Al Jerozolimskie 65/79)* offers specialist doctors, carries out laboratory tests and makes house calls. Otherwise, ring your embassy for other recommendations.

Things to See & Do

Old Town All places listed below – and many more – are detailed (in English and on a map) in the free pamphlet *Warsaw: The Old Town*, available from the official tourist offices.

The main gateway to the Old Town is **Plac Zamkowy** (Castle Square). Amazingly, all of the 17th- and 18th-century buildings around this square were completely rebuilt from their foundations after WWII. (Compare the square now with photos taken immediately after WWII; these photos are on postcards today.) The reconstruction was so superb that the Old Town has been included on Unesco's World Heritage List. In the centre of the square is the **Monument to Sigismund III Vasa**, who moved the capital from Kraków to Warsaw.

The square is dominated by the massive 13th-century **Royal Castle** *(admission free to the courtyards; open 10am-4pm Mon-Sat, 11am-4pm Sun, closed Mon 1 Oct-15 Apr)*. The castle developed over the centuries as successive Polish kings added wings and redecorated the interior, but it was nothing more than a pile of rubble in 1945. The castle was completely rebuilt between 1971 and 1984.

The highlights of the castle's interior are the **King's Apartments** *(admission 14zł)* and the **Art Gallery** *(admission 9zł)*. Both can only be visited on a guided tour (in Polish); a

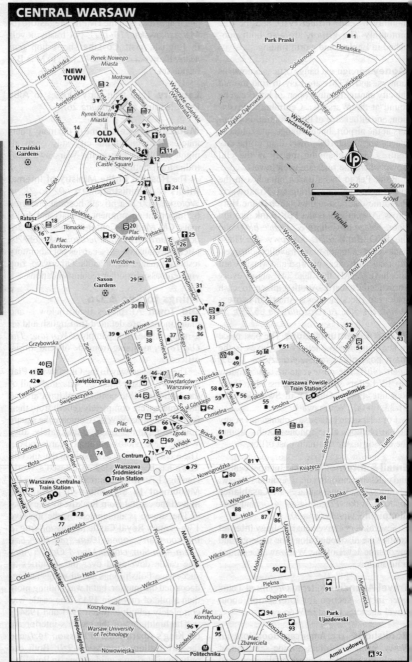

CENTRAL WARSAW

CENTRAL WARSAW

PLACES TO STAY
1 Hotel Praski
21 Old Town Apartments
28 Hotel Orbis Europejski
32 Hotel Harenda; Pub
Harenda
37 Hotel Mazowiecki
47 Hiotel Warszawa
52 Hotel Belfer
53 Hotel Na Wodzie
55 Smolna Youth Hostel No 2
63 Hotel Gromada Centrum
78 Marriott Hotel; CM Medical
Centre; American Express
84 Hotel Powiśle
88 City Apartments
89 Biuro Podróy Syrena (Private
Rooms)
95 Hotel MDM

PLACES TO EAT
3 Restauracja Pod Samsonem
5 Bar Mleczny Pod
Barbakanem
8 Karczma Gessler
9 Restauracja Bazyliszek
17 Salad Bar Tukan
23 Restauracja Siedem
Grzechow
34 Bar Mleczny Uniwersytecki
43 McDonald's; Grocery Shop
46 Restaurant Varsovia
51 Salad Bar Tukan
56 Restaurancja Wegetariańska;
Bar Co Tu
57 Mata Hari
59 Bar Mleczny Familijny
60 Restaurant Polska
65 Bar Turecki; Bar Krokiecik
70 Pizza Hut; KFC

71 Max Bar; Co-Liber Bookshop
73 MarcPol Supermarket
81 Bar Mleczny Szwajcarski
86 Café Ejlat
87 Adler Bar & Restaurant
96 Bar Hoa Lan

OTHER
2 Marie Skłodowska-Curie
Museum
4 Barbican
6 Warsaw Historical Museum
7 Adam Mickiewicz Museum
of Literature
10 St John's Cathedral
11 Royal Castle
12 Monument to Sigismund III
Vasa
13 Tourist Office
14 Monument to the Warsaw
Uprising
15 State Archaeological
Museum
16 PKO Bank
18 Jewish Historical Institute
19 Barbados
20 Teatr Wielki
22 Irish Pub
24 St Anne's Church
25 Carmelite Church (Seminary
Church)
26 Radziwiłł Palace
27 Połocki Palace
29 Tomb of the Unknown
Soldier
30 Zachęta Contemporary Art
Gallery
31 Warsaw University
33 Casablanca
35 Church of the Holy Cross

36 Bank Pekao
38 Ethnographic Museum
39 Trakt
40 Jewish Theatre
41 Nożyk Synagogue
42 Our Roots
44 Filharmonia Narodowa
45 Main Post Office
48 Studio.tpi
49 Almatur
50 Chopin Museum; Morgan's
Irish Pub
54 Teatr Ateneum
58 American Bookstore
61 Orbis Travel
62 Pub Krista
64 Cepelia
66 Alba Dry Cleaning
67 Kino Relax
68 Hybrydy
69 Kino Atlantic
72 EMPiK Megastore
74 Palace of Culture & Science;
Warsaw Tourist & Cultural
Information Office; PBK
Bank; Centrum Sztuki Studio
75 Polski Express Bus Stop
76 Tourist Office
77 LOT Head Office
79 ZASP Kasy Teatralne
80 Australian Embassy
82 National Museum
83 Museum of the Polish Army
85 St Alexander's Church
90 US Embassy
91 French Embassy
92 Ujazdów Castle; Center of
Contemporary Art
93 British Embassy
94 Czech Embassy

POLAND

tour in English, German or French costs an extra 75zł per group. Entry to the whole complex is free on Sunday, when no guides are available in any language, but you still need to line up for (free) tickets to the apartments and/or gallery. On any day in summer, arrive at the castle early and be prepared to wait.

From the Castle head down ul Świętojańska to the 15th-century Gothic **St John's Cathedral** (*ul Świętojańska 8; admission free; open 10am-1pm & 3pm-5.30pm Mon-Sat*), the oldest church in Warsaw. This road continues to the magnificent **Rynek Starego Miasta** (Old Town Square).

Alongside this square is the **Warsaw Historical Museum** (*Rynek Starego Miasta 42; admission 5zł, free Sun; open 11am-6pm Tues & Thur, 10.30am-4pm Wed, Fri, Sat &*

Sun). Make sure you're there at midday to see the English-language film (included in the admission fee), which unforgettably depicts the wartime destruction of the city. Nearby is the **Adam Mickiewicz Museum of Literature** (*Rynek Starego Miasta 20; admission 5zł; open 10am-3pm Mon, Tues & Fri, 11am-6pm Wed, Thur & Sun*). It features displays about the history of Polish literature and exhibits about this revered Polish writer.

Walk west for one block to the **Barbican**, part of a medieval wall that encircled Warsaw and was built on a bridge over a moat. To the north along ul Freta is the **Rynek Nowego Miasta** (New Town Square). On the way, perhaps pop into the **Marie Skłodowska-Curie Museum** (*ul Freta 16; admission 5zł; open 10am-4pm Tues-Sat, 10am-2pm Sun*).

It features modest displays about the great lady in the house where she was born. Many Polish streets are named after Marie Curie, but she has been given the Polish-French name, Marie Skłodowska-Curie.

Marie Curie laid the foundations for radiography, nuclear physics and cancer therapy. She was born in Warsaw, then part of Russia, in 1867. Curie lived in Poland for 24 years before being forced (under Russian law) to leave Poland (because she was a woman) to further her studies.

In Paris, she and her French husband Pierre Curie discovered two new radioactive chemical elements: radium and polonium (named after her homeland). She won numerous awards and distinctions, including two Nobel Prizes. Tragically, she died at the age of 67 from leukaemia caused by prolonged exposure to radiation.

If you're interested, take a detour to the **State Archaeological Museum** (ul Długa 52; admission 6zł; open 9am-4pm Mon-Fri, 10am-4pm Sun), based in a 17th-century former arsenal. It houses some unremarkable bits and pieces excavated from all over Poland.

The Royal Way (Szlak Królewski) This 4km route links the Royal Castle with Łazienki Park (see the next section) via ul Krakowskie Przedmieście, ul Nowy Świat and Al Ujazdowskie. The places mentioned here (and numerous others) are detailed in English and on a map in the free pamphlet, *Warsaw: The Royal Route*, available from the official tourist offices. If you want to save time and energy, jump on and off bus No 180, which stops at most places along this route and continues to Wilanów Park (see the later section).

Just south of the Royal Castle is the 15th-century **St Anne's Church** (ul Krakowskie Przedmieście 68; admission free; open daylight hours), one of the most ornate churches in the city. You can climb the **tower** (admission 3.50zł; open 10am-6pm Tues-Sun) for views of Plac Zamkowy and the castle. About 300m further south is the former **Carmelite Church** (ul Krakowskie Przedmieście 52/54; admission free; open daylight hours), also known as the Seminary Church. Nearby, the **Radziwiłł Palace** (not open to the public) is occupied by the Polish president. Opposite, **Połocki Palace** (ul Krakowskie Przedmieście 15/17; admission free; open 10am-6pm Tues-Sun) houses a modern art gallery.

To the west of the neoclassical Hotel Orbis Europejski are the **Saxon Gardens** (admission free; permanently open). At the entrance is the small but poignant **Tomb of the Unknown Soldier** (admission free; permanently open), which occupies a fragment of an 18th-century royal palace destroyed in WWII. The ceremonial changing of the guard takes place here on Sunday at noon.

South of the tomb, the **Zachęta Contemporary Art Gallery** (ul Królewska; admission 10zł, free Fri; open 10am-6pm Tues-Sun) features modern painting, photography and sculpture, and many excellent special exhibits. About 200m further south is the **Ethnographic Museum** (ul Kredytowa 1; admission 5zł, open 9am-4pm Tues, Thur & Fri, 11am-7pm Wed, 10am-5pm Sat & Sun). This large building displays various traditional Polish costumes, crafts and folk art.

Back on the Royal Way is the 17th-century **Church of the Holy Cross** (ul Krakowskie Przedmieście 3; admission free; open most afternoons). This is where Chopin's heart is preserved (in the second pillar on the left-hand side of the main nave). It was brought from Paris, where Chopin died of tuberculosis aged only 39, in accordance with his will. If you want to know more, head along ul Tamka towards the river to the small **Chopin Museum** (ul Okólnik 1; admission 7zł; open about 10am-4pm Mon-Sat), which features, among other things, the great man's last piano and a collection of his manuscripts.

Return to the Royal Way and head south along ul Nowy Świat to the roundabout at the junction of Al Jerozolimskie. On the way to the river is the enormous **National Museum** (Al Jerozolimskie 3; museum admission 11zł, temporary exhibitions 15zł, free Sat; open 10am-4pm Tues, Wed & Fri, noon-5pm Thur, 10am-5pm Sat & Sun). It houses a magnificent collection of Polish sculptures and art from the medieval period to the present. Next door, and in the same massive complex, is the **Museum of the Polish Army** (Al Jerozolimskie 3; admission 8zł, free Fri; open about 11am-5pm Wed-Sun). The huge collection of weapons, medals and so on is probably only of interest to military buffs.

Continue south along Al Ujazdowskie and cross busy ul Armii Ludowej. Over the road is the cutting-edge **Center of Contemporary Art** (Al Ujazdowskie 6; admission 10zł, free Thur; open about 11am-6pm Tues-Sun). It's housed in the reconstructed **Ujazdów Castle**, built during the 1620s. Further down (towards the south) is the small **Botanical Gardens** (admission 4zł; open 9am-7pm Mon-Fri, 10am-8pm Sat & Sun).

Łazienki Park This park (admission free; open daylight hours) is large (74 hectares), shady and popular. It's best known for the 18th-century **Palace upon the Water** (admission 11zł, free Thur; open 9am-3.30pm Tues-Sun). It was the summer residence of Stanisław August Poniatowski, the last king of Poland, who was deposed by a Russian army and confederation of Polish magnates in 1792. The park was once a royal hunting ground attached to Ujazdów Castle.

The **Old Orangery** (admission 6zł, free Tues; open 9am-4pm Tues-Sun) contains a gallery of sculpture and also an 18th-century theatre. Between noon and 4pm every Sunday in summer (May to September) piano recitals are held here among the rose gardens.

Wilanów Park This equally splendid park (ul Wisłostrada; admission free; open 9.30am-dusk daily) is about 6km southeast of Łazienki Park. The centrepiece is the magnificent **Wilanów Palace** (admission 18zł, free Thur; open 9.30am-4.30pm Wed-Mon). The palace was the summer residence of King Jan III Sobieski who defeated the Turks at Vienna in 1683, thereby ending the Turkish threat to Central Europe. In summer, arrive early and be prepared to wait. The last tickets are sold two hours before closing time.

In the well-kept park behind the palace is the **Orangery** (admission free; open 9.30am-4.30pm Wed-Mon), which houses an art gallery. The **Poster Museum** (admission 8zł, free Wed; open 10am-4pm Tues-Sun), in the former royal stables, is one of the best places to see Poland's world-renowned poster art.

To reach Wilanów, take bus No 180 from anywhere along the Royal Way (see earlier section).

Palace of Culture & Science This giant eyesore (Plac Defilad; open 8am-8pm daily) is an apocalyptic piece of Stalinesque architecture. This 'gift of friendship' from the Soviet Union to the Polish nation was built in the early 1950s and is still Poland's largest and tallest (234m) building. It has a huge congress hall, three theatres and a cinema.

The **observation terrace** (admission 15zł; open 9am-6pm daily) on the 30th floor provides a panoramic view, which is perhaps best appreciated at the coffee shop. Poles often joke that this is the best view of Warsaw because it's the only one that doesn't include the Palace of Culture & Science itself!

Jewish Heritage

The vast suburbs northwest of the Palace of Culture & Science were once predominantly inhabited by Polish Jews. During WWII the Nazis established a Jewish ghetto in the area but razed it to the ground after crushing the Warsaw Ghetto Uprising in April 1943. This tragic event is immortalised by the **Monument to the Warsaw Uprising** (cnr ul Długa & ul Miodowa).

The **Warsaw Ghetto Monument** (cnr ul Anielewicza & ul Zamenhofa) also commemorates victims using pictorial plaques. The nearby **Pawiak Prison Museum** (ul Dzielna 24/26; admission free; open about 10am-4pm Wed-Sun) occupies the former building used as a Gestapo prison during the Nazi occupation. Moving exhibits include letters and other personal items.

Arguably the most dramatic remnant of the Jewish legacy is the vast **Jewish Cemetery** (ul Okopowa 49/51; admission free; open 9am-4pm Sun-Fri May-Sept, 9am-3pm Sun-Fri Oct-Apr). Founded in 1806, it still has over 100,000 gravestones and is the largest collection of its kind in Europe. Visitors must wear a head covering before entering the cemetery, which is accessible from the Old Town on tram Nos 22, 27 and 29.

The **Jewish Historical Institute** (ul Tłomackie 3/5; admission 10zł; open 9am-4pm Mon-Wed & Fri, 11am-6pm Thur) features permanent exhibits about the Warsaw Ghetto, as well as art and photographs relating to local Jewish history. Tucked away behind the **Jewish Theatre** is the neo-Romanesque **Nożyk Synagogue** (ul Twarda; admission 3.50zł; open 10am-8pm Sun-Thur, 10am-4pm Fri). Warsaw's only synagogue that managed to survive WWII, albeit in a sorry state. It has subsequently been restored and is still used today for religious services.

A walking tour of these – and around 20 other – Jewish sites are detailed (in English and with a map) in the free pamphlet, Historical Sites of Jewish Warsaw, available from the official tourist offices.

POLAND

Organised Tours

The following companies offer tours around Warsaw.

Almatur (☎/fax 826 26 39, e dot@almatur.pl) ul Kopernika 23 – see Organised Tours in the Getting Around section earlier.

Orbis Travel (☎ 827 72 65, fax 827 76 05) ul Bracka 16 – has branches all over Warsaw, as well as at the airport. See Organised Tours in the Getting Around section earlier.

Our Roots (☎/fax 620 05 56) ul Twarda 6 – Warsaw's primary agency for anyone interested in tours about local Jewish heritage.

Trakt (☎ 827 80 68, w www.trakt.com.pl) ul Kredytowa 6 – guided tours of Warsaw in English and 21 other languages. Walking tours cost about 40zł per group per hour.

Special Events

Warsaw's major annual events include the International Book Fair (May), the Warsaw Summer Jazz Days (late June/early July), the Mozart Festival (June-July), 'Art of the Street' International Festival (July) and the 'Warsaw Autumn' Festival of Contemporary Music (September).

Places to Stay

Warsaw is the most expensive city in Poland for accommodation. The number of upmarket hotels is rising, while trying to find anywhere cheap within 30 minutes of the city centre by tram is increasingly difficult. If you're having trouble finding a room anywhere, one of the official tourist offices will help you (see the Information section earlier).

Camping The largest and most central camping ground in Warsaw is **Camping Nr 34 Gromada** (☎ 825 43 91; ul Żwirki i Wigury 32; camping per tent 11zł, electricity 9zł, cabins per person 20zł; open Apr-Oct). Staff are friendly and helpful, and the camping ground is clean and popular. It's accessible from the airport on bus Nos 175 and 188, and from Warszawa Centralna train station on bus Nos 136 and 175.

Set in extensive and secure grounds, **Camping Nr 123** (☎/fax 823 37 48, e camp123@ friko6.onet.pl; ul Warszawskiej 1920r 15/17; camping per person/tent 10/10zł; open year-round) features bungalows and hotel rooms and is close to the Dworzec Zachodnia bus station. The complex also features indoor tennis courts and an outdoor swimming pool (all open to the public).

Camping Nr 260 (☎ 842 27 68; ul Inspektowa 1; camping per person/tent 12/5zł; open May-Sept) is a lifeless and treeless place, accessible on any bus heading towards Wilanów Park from the Old Town.

Hostels Each hostel listed below closes between at least 10am and 4pm each day.

Smolna Youth Hostel No 2 (☎/fax 827 89 52; ul Smolna 30; dorm beds 33zł; singles/ doubles with TV & shared bathroom 60/ 110zł; open year-round) is the best and most central. For singles or doubles, book in advance and book dorm beds in summer. The three-night maximum is often waived when it's not so busy.

Karolkowa Youth Hostel No 6 (☎/fax 632 97 46; ul Karolkowa 53a; dorm beds from 35zł; open year-round) is in the Wola suburb and accessible by tram No 12, 22 or 24 from the Warszawa Centralna train station. This well-established and friendly place has laundry and Internet facilities. It also offers rooms and apartments comparable to the hotels that charge twice as much, ie, singles without/with bathroom for 80/130zł, doubles with TV and shared bathroom from 130zł and apartments for two with kitchen, TV and bathroom for 160zł.

Youth Hostel PTSM (☎ 831 17 66; ul Międzyparkowa 4/6; dorm beds 35zł; open Apr-Oct) is in parkland in the northern suburbs. The rates are cheaper, but the standards are far lower than the other two hostels, and there are no single or double rooms. Take bus No 175 from the central train station or airport.

Private Rooms & Apartments Rooms in private homes can be arranged through **Biuro Podróży Syrena** (☎/fax 629 49 78; e office@ syrena-pl.com; ul Krucza 17). Singles/doubles with shared bathroom in the city centre cost 79/110zł for one or two nights and as little as 68/96zł for three or more nights. Apartments with a double bed, kitchen, bathroom and TV are available for 250zł to 320zł per night.

If you're going to stay in Warsaw for a while a private apartment may end up being cheaper than a mid-range hotel. Apartments are furnished with a kitchen, bathroom, laundry and (usually) cable TV, and fit as many people as you can squeeze in.

Old Town Apartments (☎/fax 826 78 63; ul Kozia 3/5) offers, well, apartments in the Old Town. The 'studios' cost US$70/350 per day/week and apartments from US$95/475 (one bedroom) to US$110/550 (two bedrooms).

The agency **City Apartments** (*☎/fax 628 76 11;* **e** *info@hotelinwarsaw.com; ul Hoża 38)* offers large apartments (mostly in the Old Town) for less: 'studios' cost US$60/300 per day/week and apartments US$85/425 (one bedroom) and US$100/500 (two bedrooms).

Hotels – Budget The best value in the capital can be found at **Hotel Majawa** (*☎/fax 823 37 48;* **e** *camp123@friko6.onet.pl; ul Warszawskiej 1920r 15/17; hotel singles/ doubles with shared bathroom 80/109zł; double bungalows without/with bath from 79/109zł).* The bungalows at this camping ground are private and clean, while the hotel rooms are quiet, spotless and bright.

Hotel Na Wodzie (*☎/fax 628 58 83; ul Wybrzeże Kościuszkowskie; single/double cabins with shared bathroom 65/85zł; open Apr-Nov)* is actually in two boats – the *Aldona* and *Anita* – both anchored along the Vistula River between the railway and Poniatowski bridges. The living quarters are adequate, but the location leaves something to be desired.

The best choice of budget accommodation is along ul Mangalia, where three one-star hotels are virtually next door to each other – perhaps check out all three and then decide. They all belong to Hotel Felix (see next section) and information is available on its website. Singles/doubles with bath at all three cost 120/150zł, and they are accessible by bus Nos 118, 403, 503 and 513 along ul Sobieskiego.

Hotel Aramis (*☎ 842 09 74;* **e** *aramis@ felix.com.pl; ul Mangalia 3b)* is the largest and best equipped. **Hotel Atos** (*☎ 841 43 95;* **e** *atos@felix.com.pl; ul Mangalia 1)* only has nine rooms, but is cosy. **Hotel Portos** (*☎ 842 68 51;* **e** *portos@felix.com.pl; ul Mangalia 3a)* is also fairly good value for the price.

Hotels – Mid-Range All hotels listed in this section include breakfast in the room rates.

A former army dorm, **Hotel Mazowiecki** (*☎ 827 23 65;* **w** *www.mazowiecki.com.pl; ul Mazowiecka 10; singles/doubles from 150/ 200zł, with bath 210/270zł)* was once reserved for military officers. The classy foyer belies the ordinary rooms, but it's pleasant enough and convenient.

Hotel Praski (*☎/fax 818 49 89;* **w** *www .praski.pl; Al Solidarności 61; singles/doubles with shared bathroom from 150/200zł)* is on the other side of the river, but little more than 1km from the Old Town. It has been renovated in recent years and is one of the best two-star places in the capital.

Hotel Powiśle (*☎ 628 00 14, fax 621 66 57; ul Szara 10a; singles/doubles from 180/ 250zł)* is a quiet and friendly place, but a little out of the way of the better bars and restaurants. The rooms are large and feature new bathrooms, TVs and some have fridges.

Hotel Belfer (*☎/fax 625 51 85; ul Wybrzeże Kościuszkowskie 31/33; singles/ doubles 110/246zł, with bath 169/250zł)* was formerly a teachers hotel. Rooms on the upper floors provide good views of the Vistula River, but the place is run down and the rooms are generally small and poorly furnished. A last resort.

Hotel Warszawa (*☎ 826 94 21;* **e** *hotel .warszawa@syrena.com.pl; Plac Powstańców Warszawy 9; singles/doubles 170/250zł, with bath 250/360zł)* is a multistorey Stalinesque monstrosity. Although stuck in the 1960s, it's comfortable and convenient and staff are pleasingly friendly. The buffet breakfast will probably fill you up until dinnertime.

Hotel Felix (*☎ 810 06 91;* **w** *www.felix .com.pl; ul Omulewska 24; singles/doubles from 200/235zł)* is an unexciting Soviet-style block, but is spotlessly clean and good value. Take tram No 9, 24 or 44 from the Warszawa Centralna train station.

Hotels – Top End Places listed below offer all the amenities you would expect for these prices, including breakfast. It's worth asking about 'weekend rates' (ie, Friday, Saturday and Sunday nights), which are often 20% to 30% less.

Hotel Harenda (*☎ 826 00 71, fax 826 26 25; ul Krakowskie Przedmieście 4/6; singles/ doubles 320/370zł)* boasts a pleasant location in the Old Town and an appealing ambience. The singles are remarkably small, however, but all the bathrooms are spotless. It's far nicer than the communist-era throwbacks still operating elsewhere.

The **Hotel Orbis Europejski** (*☎ 826 50 51;* **e** *europej@orbis.pl; ul Krakowskie Przed-mieście 13; singles/doubles €120/150)* is in a charming location near the Saxon Gardens. Most rooms are uninspiring, but the place just oozes charm and history.

Hotel Gromada Centrum (*☎ 625 15 45, fax 625 21 40; Plac Powstańców Warszawy 2;*

POLAND

singles/doubles 400/480zł) has an excellent location and efficient and friendly staff. The bathrooms are outstanding.

Hotel MDM (☎ *621 62 11, fax 621 41 73; Plac Konstytucji 1; singles/doubles 415/ 545zł)* is large and unremarkable, but convenient and staffed with friendly folk.

Places to Eat

Warsaw has a wider range of eating places than any other Polish city. There's been a virtual explosion of modern bistros, pizzerias, snack bars and international fast-food chains in recent years, yet a number of genuine milk bars still exist and have the cheapest food in town.

The free booklet *Warszawa Restaurants*, available from the official tourist offices, lists hundreds of restaurants serving every conceivable cuisine, while the English-language newspapers and magazines (see Information section earlier) provide reviews of what's currently in vogue.

Polish Restaurants The Old Town boasts some of Warsaw's best restaurants specialising in Polish cuisine, but prices are predictably high. Each is likely to offer a menu in English.

Karczma Gessler *(Rynek Starego Miasta 21/21a; mains from 45zł)* continues to be recommended by satisfied patrons. The food and decor in this romantic cellar are spectacular, though it's not cheap and vegetarians will not find much to satisfy their taste buds.

Restauracja Bazyliszek *(Rynek Starego Miasta 3/9; mains 38-75zł)* is one of the longest standing Polish restaurants in the capital and continues to maintain high standards. It serves hearty, traditional fare (including lots of meaty game) in old-world surroundings.

Restauracja Siedem Grzechów *(ul Krakowskie Przedmieście 45; mains 35-55zł)* is a quaint downstairs place decorated with 1920s memorabilia. It's a lively place and ideal for an evening meal and/or drink.

Restaurant Polska *(ul Nowy Świat 21; mains from 35zł)* is another favourite situated in an elegant basement. The Polish dishes are more for tourist palates, but still authentic, and the choice is mouthwatering. Enter gate No 21 and walk straight ahead for 100m.

Dom Polski *(ul Francuska 11; mains from 30zł)* is perennially popular with tour groups and out-of-towners looking for tasty food and reasonable prices. It's worth the pleasant walk over the bridge.

Restaurant Varsovia *(ul Świętokrzyska 15; meals about 15zł)* is a reasonably classy place with a range of Polish and Western meals listed on a menu in English. It's just around the corner from Hotel Warszawa.

Bar Krokiecik *(ul Zgoda 1; meals 8-10zł),* near Bar Turecki, is a central option for more affordable Polish meals.

Other Restaurants Offering a large array of tasty Chinese meals and a menu in English, **Bar Co Tu** *(just off ul Nowy Świat; most meals under 10zł)* is a small but popular eatery. It's not far down (south) from the Restauracja Wegetariańska

Bar Hoa Lan *(ul Śniadeckich 12; mains 8-15zł)* is much like the Co Tu – small, cosy, friendly and cheap – but it leans more to Vietnamese and doesn't have a menu in English.

Adler Bar & Restaurant *(ul Mokotowska 69; starters 15zł, mains about 35zł)* is a tiny oasis among the concrete jungle. It's worth a splurge for impeccable service and the variety of Polish and Bavarian *nouvelle cuisine.*

Café Ejlat *(Al Ujazdowskie 47; mains 24-42zł)* offers large portions of authentic Jewish food, as well as live music (mostly on Saturday and Sunday nights).

Restauracja Pod Samsonem *(ul Freta 3/5; mains 19-27zł),* which is opposite the Marie Skłodowska-Curie Museum, is frequented by locals for inexpensive and tasty meals with a combined Polish and Jewish flavour. Daily specials are listed in crayon on the side of the wooden door.

Vegetarian For adventurous vegetarians **Mata Hari** *(ul Nowy Świat 52; soups 5zł & mains 7-12zł)* is a superb option offering delicious and cheap Indian food.

Restauracja Wegetariańska *(just off Nowy Świat; soups & salads from 5zł)* is another enticing place for healthy, meat-free food.

Salad Bar Tukan *(sandwiches about 3zł, salads from 5zł)* has several outlets around the capital, including Plac Bankowy 2 (in the blue skyscraper) and ul Tamka 37. The Tukan probably offers the widest choice of salads in Poland.

Cafeterias Opposite the Barbican, **Bar Mleczny Pod Barbakanem** *(ul Mostowa 27/29; mains 8-12zł)* is a popular milk bar that has survived the fall of the Iron Curtain and continues to serve cheap, unpretentious food. It's position would be the envy of many upmarket eateries.

Three milk bars along the Royal Way are at comfortably short walking intervals.

Bar Mleczny Uniwersytecki (*ul Krakowskie Przedmieście 20; mains 8-12zł*) is packed with students – probably there for the cheap prices rather than the food itself.

Bar Mleczny Familijny (*ul Nowy Świat 39; soups 3-4zł, mains 6-11zł*) is incongruously in the fashionable shopping district.

Bar Mleczny Szwajcarski (*ul Nowy Świat 5; mains 7-12zł*) is another rock-bottom, no-frills eatery.

Fast Food Junk-food junkies will not suffer withdrawal symptoms while in Warsaw.

Pizza Hut (*ul Widok*) offers the normal array of pizzas and a salad bar, and has a menu in English and German. Next door, the smiling face of Colonel Sanders looms large over an outlet of **KFC**. The golden arches of **McDonald's** are *everywhere* – most noticeably on the corner of ul Świętokrzyska and ul Marszałkowska.

Turkish food is increasingly popular and reasonably cheap and healthy. **Bar Turecki** (*ul Zgoda 3; meals 8-13zł*) is one of the best – seek out the tempting aroma wafting across the street.

For more choice, try one of the self-serve cafeterias around town – ideal for seeing what you want and pointing at it without a word of Polish. **Max Bar** (*cnr Marszałkowska & ul Widok; lunch specials 7.50zł*) offers a wide array of food and is popular.

Self-Catering The most convenient places to shop for groceries are the **MarcPol Supermarket**, in front of the Palace of Culture & Science building, and the **grocery shop** (*cnr ul Świętokrzyska & ul Marszałkowska*) downstairs and next to McDonald's.

Entertainment
For more information about what to do, and where and when to go, check out *The Buzz* section of *The Warsaw Voice* and the informative *Warszawa: What, Where, When*.

Pubs & Bars Warsaw is now flooded with all sorts of pubs and bars. The most charming places for a drink are around Rynek Starego Miasta in the Old Town, but the prices are predictably high.

Two authentic Irish pubs are great spots to meet expats and enjoy a Guinness (or three). **Irish Pub** (*ul 3 Miodowa*) is popular and near the Old Town, with live music most nights. **Morgan's Irish Pub** (*ul Tamka 40*), under the Chopin Museum, is busy, especially with sports nuts glued to the large-screen TVs.

Pub Harenda (*ul Krakowskie Przedmieście 4/6*), at the back of Hotel Harenda, is often crowded. It provides an appealing beer garden and equally appealing happy hours. Live jazz music is performed here during the week and there's dance music on weekends.

Pub Krista (*ul Górskiego 8*), along the extension of ul Złota, has been recommended by some of our readers for its fine ales and cellar atmosphere.

Nightclubs The following two student clubs are popular and cheap, but only open from June to September. **Riviera Remont** (*ul Waryńskiego 12*) has live music (often jazz) on Thursday and Saturday nights. **Słodoła** (*ul Batorego 10*) is another popular student club which pulsates with techno music most nights.

Hybrydy (*ul Złota 7/9*) has been going for some 45 years and is still trendy! It features all sorts of taped and live music most nights.

Barbados (*ul Wierzbowa 9; open Wed-Sat*), over the road from the Teatr Wielki, is where the 'beautiful people' of Warsaw come.

The official tourist offices have updated lists of what's hot and what's not, and the *Warsaw Insider* is always a great source.

Cinemas To fill in a rainy afternoon, or to avoid watching Polish TV in your hotel room, try catching a film at one of the 40 cinemas across the city. Two central options are **Kino Atlantic** (*ul Chmielna 33*) and **Kino Relax** (*ul Złota 8*).

Theatre, Opera & Ballet Advance tickets for most events at most theatres can be bought at **ZASP Kasy Teatralne** (*Al Jerozolimskie 25; open 11am-6pm Mon-Fri, 11am-2pm Sat*) or at the **EMPiK Megastore** (*ul Marszałkowska 116/122*). Otherwise, same-day tickets may be available at the box offices. Remember, most theatres close in July and August.

Centrum Sztuki Studio (*Palace of Culture & Science building*) and **Teatr Ateneum** (*ul Jaracza 2*) lean towards contemporary Polish-language productions. **Teatr Wielki** (*Grand Theatre; Plac Teatralny 1*) is the main venue for opera and ballet. **Filharmonia Narodowa** *(ul Jasna 5)* has concert and chamber halls.

In **Łazienki Park**, piano recitals are held every Sunday from May to September and chamber concerts are staged there in summer at the **Old Orangery**.

Shopping

An impressive display of Poland's relatively new free-market enthusiasm is the huge bazaar at the **Stadion Market** *(Al Jerozolimskie)* in the suburb of Praga. It's open daily from dawn until around noon and busiest on weekends. Beware of pickpockets.

Reasonably priced handicrafts are available from several outlets of the nationwide **Cepelia** chain, including one at ul Chmielna 8. Stalls in and around Rynek Starego Miasta sell charming mementos, such as paintings of the Old Town, jewellery and traditional dolls.

Getting There & Away

Air The Warsaw Frederic Chopin Airport is more commonly called the Okęcie Airport, after the suburb, 10km southwest of the city centre, where it's based. This small and barely functional airport has international arrivals downstairs and departures upstairs. Domestic arrivals and departures occupy a small separate part of the same complex.

The useful tourist office is on the arrivals level of the international section. It sells city maps and can help find a place to stay. At the arrivals level, there are also a few ATMs that accept major international credit cards, and several kantors. Avoid the Orbis Travel office because of its astronomical fees and low exchange rates. There are also several car-rental companies, a left-luggage room and a newsagent where you can buy public transport tickets. Buses and taxis depart from this level.

Domestic and international flights on LOT can be booked at the **LOT** head office (☎ 657 80 11, *Al Jerozolimskie 65/79)* in the Marriott Hotel complex or at any travel agency, including the Orbis Travel. Other airline offices are listed in the *Warszawa: What, Where, When* and *Welcome to Warsaw* magazines.

Information about international and domestic flights to/from Warsaw is included in the introductory Getting There & Away and Getting Around sections earlier.

Bus Warsaw has two major bus terminals for PKS buses.

Dworzec Zachodnia *(Western Bus Station; Al Jerozolimskie 144)* handles all domestic buses heading south, north and west of the capital, including Częstochowa (31zł), Gdańsk (55zł), Kazimierz Dolny (17zł), Kraków (36zł), Olsztyn (30zł), Toruń (31zł), Wrocław (41zł) and Zakopane (49zł). This complex is southwest of the city centre and adjoins the Warszawa Zachodnia train station. Take the commuter train that leaves from Warszawa Śródmieście station.

Dworzec Stadion *(Stadium Bus Station; ul Sokola 1)* adjoins the Warszawa Stadion train station. It is also easily accessible by commuter train from Warszawa Śródmieście. Dworzec Stadion handles a few domestic buses to the east and southeast, eg, Lublin (24zł), Białystok (20zł) and Zamość (35zł), as well as Kazimierz Dolny.

Polski Express (☎ 620 03 26) operates coaches from the airport, but passengers can get on/off and buy tickets at the obvious stall along Al Jana Pawła II, next to the Warszawa Centralna train station. Polski Express buses travel daily to Białystok (30zł); Częstochowa (34zł); Gdynia, via Sopot and Gdańsk (53zł); Kraków (54zł); Lublin (31zł); Toruń (35zł); and Wrocław (35zł).

International buses depart from and arrive at Dworzec Zachodnia or, occasionally, outside the Warszawa Centralna train station. Tickets for the international buses are available from the bus offices at Dworzec Zachodnia, from agencies at Warszawa Centralna or from any of the major travel agencies in the city, including Almatur.

Train Warsaw has several train stations, but the one that most travellers will use almost exclusively is **Warszawa Centralna** *(Warsaw Central; Al Jerozolimskie 54)*; it handles the overwhelming majority of domestic trains and all international services. Refer to the Getting There & Away section earlier for details about international trains to/from Warsaw, and to the relevant Getting There & Away sections later in this chapter for information about domestic services to/from Warsaw.

Remember, Warszawa Centralna is often *not* where domestic and international trains start or finish, so make sure you get on or off the train at this station in the few minutes allotted. And watch your belongings closely at all times, because pickpocketing and theft is an increasing problem.

On the street level of the central station, the spacious main hall houses ticket counters, ATMs and snack bars, as well as a post office, a newsagent (for public-transport tickets) and also a tourist office. Along the underground mezzanine level leading to the tracks and platforms are a dozen kantors (one of which is open 24 hours), a **left-luggage office** *(open 7am-9pm daily)*, lockers, eateries, several other places to buy tickets for local public transport, Internet centres and bookshops.

Tickets for domestic and international trains are available from counters at the station (but allow at least an hour for possible queuing) or, in advance, from any major Orbis Travel office (see under Organised Tours earlier). Tickets for immediate departures on domestic and international trains are also available from numerous, well-signed booths in the underpasses leading to Warszawa Centralna.

Some domestic trains also stop at Warszawa Śródmieście station, 300m east of Warszawa Centralna, and Warszawa Zachodnia, next to Dworzec Zachodnia bus station.

Getting Around

To/From the Airport The cheapest way of getting from the airport to the city centre (and vice versa) is on bus No 175. This bus leaves every 10 to 15 minutes for the Old Town, via ul Nowy Świat and the Warszawa Centralna train station. It operates daily from 5am to 11pm. If you arrive in the wee hours, night bus No 611 links the airport with Warszawa Centralna every 30 minutes.

The taxi fare between the airport and the city centre is about 25zł. Make sure you take one of the official taxis with a name and telephone number on top and fares listed on the window; you can arrange this at one of the three official taxi counters on the arrivals level of the international section of the terminal. The 'Mafia' cabs still operate at the airport and charge astronomical rates.

Public Transport Warsaw's public transport is frequent, cheap and operates daily from 5am to 11pm. The fare (2.40zł) is a flat rate for any bus, tram, trolleybus or metro train anywhere in the city – ie, one 2.40zł fare is valid for one ride on one form of transport. Warsaw is the only place in Poland where students with an ISIC card get a discount (50%). Bulky luggage (anything that exceeds 60cm x 40cm x 20cm) costs an extra 2.40zł.

Tickets (valid on all forms of public transport) for 60/90 minutes are 3.60/4.50zł, and passes (for all public transport) are available for one day (7.20zł), three days (12zł), one week (26zł) and one month (66zł). Daily tickets are actually valid for 24 hours and start from the time you first use it. Tickets should be purchased before boarding from kiosks (including those marked RUCH) and punched in one of the small machines on-board. Ticket inspectors are not uncommon and fines are high.

One very useful bus is the 'sightseeing route' No 180, which links Powązki Cemetery with Wilanów Park. It stops at most attractions listed in the Royal Way section earlier, as well as Łazienki Park, and travels via ul Krakowskie Przedmieście and ul Nowy Świat.

A metro line operates from the Ursynów suburb (Kabaty station) at the southern city limits to Ratusz (Town Hall), via the city centre (Centrum), but is of limited use to visitors. Local commuter trains head out to the suburbs from the Warszawa Śródieście station.

Taxi Taxis are a quick and easy way to get around – as long as you use official taxis and drivers use their meters. Beware of 'Mafia' taxis parked in front of top-end hotels, at the airport, outside Warszawa Centralna train station and in the vicinity of most tourist sights.

Car Rental There is little incentive to drive a rented car through Warsaw's horrific traffic and confusing streets, and you're likely to get serious migraines looking for car parks anyway. But there are lots of good reasons to hire a car in Warsaw for jaunts around the countryside. Offices for major car-rental companies are listed in the local English-language newspapers and magazines, and these companies also have counters at the airport. Alternatively, book through a travel agency. More details about car rental is under Car & Motorcycle in the Getting Around section earlier.

Mazovia & Podlasie

Mazovia only came to the fore when the capital was transferred to Warsaw in 1596. It has never been a fertile region, so there are few historic towns – the notable exception is Poland's second largest city, Łódź. To the east along the Belarus border is Podlasie, which literally means 'land close to the forest'. The highlight of the region is the magnificent Białowieża National Park.

ŁÓDŹ
☎ 042 • pop 840,000

Łódź ('Woodge') is slowly cleaning up its dull image and pollution-stained buildings. It offers several elegant malls and plenty of parklands, and is worth a visit if you're getting sick of the tourist hordes in Kraków.

Many of the attractions – and most of the life-support systems, such as banks, kantors and ATMs – are along, or just off, the backbone of ul Piotrkowska. The **tourist office** (☎/fax 633 71 69, ul Traugutta 18) is 300m east of the main street.

The **Historical Museum of Łódź** (ul Ogrodowa 15; admission 6zł; open 10am-2pm Tues & Thur-Sun, 2pm-6pm Wed) is 200m northwest of Plac Wolności, which is at the northern end of the main drag. Also worthwhile is the **Museum of Ethnography & Archaeology** (Plac Wolności 14; admission 6zł; open about 10am-4pm Tues-Sun).

Herbst Palace (ul Przędalniana 72; admission 6zł; open about noon-4pm Tues-Sun) has been converted into an appealing museum. It's accessible by bus No 55 heading east from the cathedral at the southern end of ul Piotrkowska. The **Jewish Cemetery** (ul Bracka 40; admission 2zł; open 9am-5pm Sun-Thur, 9am-3pm Fri; enter from ul Zmienna) is one of the largest in Europe. It's 3km northeast of the city centre and accessible by tram No 1 or 6 from near Plac Wolności.

The tourist office can provide information about camping grounds and private rooms. The **youth hostel** (☎ 630 66 80, fax 630 66 83, ul Legionów 27; dorm beds 30-60zł) is one of the best in Poland, so book ahead. It's only 250m west of Plac Wolności.

Hotel Urzędu Miasta (☎ 640 66 09, fax 640 66 45, ul Bojowników Getta Warszawskiego 9; singles/doubles with bathroom 110/145zł) is good value and only 500m north of Plac Wolności.

LOT (☎ 633 48 15; ul Piotrkowska 122) flies to Warsaw four times a week. From the Łódź Kaliska train station, 1.2km southwest of central Łódź, trains go regularly to Wrocław, Poznań, Toruń and Gdańsk. For Warsaw and Częstochowa, use the Łódź Fabryczna station, 400m east of the city centre. Buses go in all directions from the bus terminal, next to the Fabryczna train station.

BIAŁOWIEŻA NATIONAL PARK
☎ 085

Białowieża ('Byah-wo-VYEH-zhah') is Poland's oldest national park and the only one registered by Unesco as a Biosphere Reserve and a World Heritage Site. The 5346 hectares protect the primeval forest, as well as 120 species of birds. Animal life includes elk, wild boar, wolf and, the uncontested king of the forest, the rare European bison (which was once thought to be extinct).

The ideal base is the charming village of Białowieża. The main road to Białowieża from Hajnówka leads to the southern end of Palace Park; alternatively, a slight detour around the park leads to the village's main street, ul Waszkiewicza. Along this street is a **post office** and **Internet centre**, but there's nowhere to change money. (The nearest kantor is in Hajnówka.)

You'll find the **PTTK office** (☎/fax 681 26 24, ⓦ www.pttk.sitech.pl; open 8am-4pm daily) is at the southern end of Palace Park. Serious hikers should contact the **National Park Office** (☎ 681 29 01; open 9am-4pm daily) inside Palace Park. Most maps of the national park (especially the one published by PTOP) details several enticing **hiking trails**.

Things to See & Do
A combined ticket (12zł) allows you entry to the museum, the bison reserve and the nature reserve. Alternatively, you can pay for each attraction separately.

The elegant and compact **Palace Park** (admission free; open daylight hours) is only accessible on foot, bicycle or horse-drawn cart across the bridge from the PTTK office. Over the river is the excellent **Natural & Forestry Museum** (admission 5zł; open 9am-4pm Tues-Sun June-Sept, 9am-3pm Oct-May), one of the best of its kind in the country. Unfortunately, the adjacent **lookout tower** isn't tall enough to get any decent views of the surrounding national park.

The **European Bison Reserve** (admission 5zł; open 9am-5pm daily) is a small park containing many of these mighty beasts, as well as wolves, strange horse-like tarpans and mammoth żubrońs (hybrids of bisons and cows). Entrance to the reserve is just north of the Hajnówka-Białowieża road, about 4.5km west of the PTTK office – look for the signs along the żebra żubra trail or follow the green or yellow marked trails.

The main attraction is the **Strict Nature Reserve** *(admission 5zł; open 9am-5pm daily)*, which starts about 1km north of the Palace Park. It can only be visited on a three-hour (Polish-language) tour with a licensed guide along a 6km trail. If you want a guide who speaks English or German you'll be slugged 150zł per group. Licensed guides (in any language) can be arranged at the PTTK office or any travel agency in the village. Note that the reserve does close sometimes due to inclement weather.

A more comfortable way to visit the nature reserve is by horse-drawn cart (with a guide), which costs 100zł (three hours) and holds four people. Otherwise, it may be possible (with permission from the PTTK office) to visit the reserve by bicycle (with a guide).

The PTTK office and **Zimorodek** *(☎ 681 26 09, ul Waszkiewicza 2)*, opposite the post office, rent bikes. Contact Wejmutka (see Places to Stay & Eat) about hiring a **canoe** for a leisurely paddle along the river.

Places to Stay & Eat
Plenty of homes along the road from Hajnówka offer private rooms for about 30/50zł for singles/doubles.

Youth Hostel *(☎/fax 681 25 60; ul Waszkiewicza 6; dorm beds 17zł, rooms per person 25zł; open year-round)* is one of the best in the region. The bathrooms are clean and the kitchen is excellent.

Dom Wycieczkowy PTTK *(☎/fax 681 25 05; singles from 50zł, doubles with bath 80zł)* boasts a serene location inside the Palace Park. It has seen better days, but the position and rates are hard to beat. It has a **restaurant**.

Pension Gawra *(☎ 681 28 04, fax 681 24 84, ul Poludnlowa 2; rooms without/with bath 60/100zł)* is excellent value. This quiet, homely place with large rooms overlooking a typically pretty garden is just off the main road from Hajnówka, about 400m southwest of Palace Park.

Pensjonacik Unikat *(☎/fax 681 27 74, ul Waszkiewicza 39; singles/doubles from 40/80zł)* is charmingly decorated (complete with bison hides on the wall) and good value. The **restaurant** offers traditional food at reasonable prices and has a menu in both German and English.

Wejmutka *(meals 7-12zł)*, alongside the river opposite the PTTK office, has one of the nicest settings in eastern Poland.

Getting There & Away
From Warsaw, take the express train (at 2.07pm) from Warszawa Centralna to Siedlce (1½ hours), wait for a connection on the slow train to Hajnówka (two hours), and then catch one of the nine daily buses to Białowieża. Back to Warsaw, the only sensible option is the 11.06am train from Hajnówka to Siedlce, with an immediate connection to Warszawa Centralna.

Five buses a day travel from the Dworzec Stadion station in Warsaw to Białystok (four hours), from where buses regularly go to Białowieża (2½ hours) – but you may need to stay overnight in Białystok. To Warsaw, a bus leaves Białowieża for Białystok at 5.55am.

Małopolska

Małopolska (literally 'little Poland') encompasses the whole of southeastern Poland, from the Lublin Uplands in the north down to the Carpathian Mountains along the borders with Slovakia and Ukraine. Kraków became the royal capital of Małopolska in 1038 and remained so for over 500 years. Visitors to the region can admire the royal dignity of Kraków, explore the rugged beauty of the Tatra Mountains and witness the tragic remnants of the Jewish heritage.

KRAKÓW
☎ 012 • pop 770,000

Kraków is Poland's third-largest city and one of its oldest, dating from the 7th century. The city was founded by Prince Krak, who, according to legend, secured its prime location overlooking the Vistula River after outwitting the resident dragon.

In 1000 the bishopric of Kraków was established here. By 1038 the city became the capital of the Piast kingdom, and the kings ruled from Wawel Castle until 1596. Even after the capital was moved to Warsaw, Polish royalty continued to be crowned and buried at the Wawel Cathedral.

At this crossing of trade routes from Western Europe to Byzantium and from southern Europe to the Baltic sea, a large medieval city developed. Particularly good times came with the reign of King Kazimierz the Great, a generous patron of the arts.

Kraków is the only large city in Poland whose old architecture survived WWII intact.

KRAKÓW

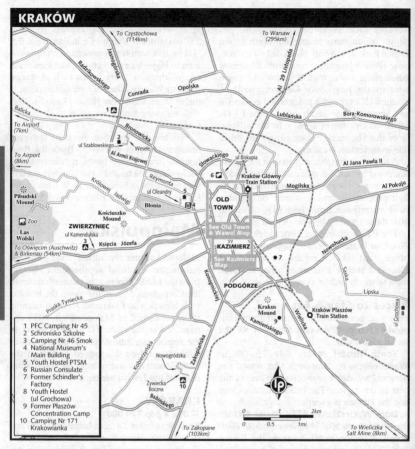

To Częstochowa (114km)
To Warsaw (295km)

Radzikowskiego
Jasnogórska
Conrada
Opolska
Al 29 Listopada
Lublańska
Bora-Komorowskiego
Balicka
1
Bronowicka
To Airport (7km)
2 ul Szablowskiego
Wesele
Al Armii Krajowej
Słowackiego
ul Biskupia
To Airport (8km)
Reymonta
Królowej Jadwigi
6 Kraków Główny Train Station
Al Jana Pawła II
Piłsudski Mound
ul Oleandry
5
Mogilska
Al Pokoju
Kościuszko Mound
Błonia
4 OLD TOWN
Zoo
Las Wolski
ZWIERZYNIEC
ul Kamendulska
See Old Town & Wawel Map
Nowohucka
To Oświęcim (Auschwitz) & Birkenau (54km)
3 Księcia Józefa
KAZIMIERZ
See Kazimierz Map
7
Vistula
Praska Tyniecka
Konopnickiej
PODGÓRZE
Lipska
Krakus Mound
Kraków Płaszów Train Station
Kamieńskiego
Wielicka
ul Grochowa
8
Kobierzyńska
Zakopiańska
Nowogródzka
9
Żywiecka Boczna
10
Babińskiego
To Zakopane (103km)
To Wieliczka Salt Mine (8km)

1 PFC Camping Nr 45
2 Schronisko Szkolne
3 Camping Nr 46 Smok
4 National Museum's Main Building
5 Youth Hostel PTSM
6 Russian Consulate
7 Former Schindler's Factory
8 Youth Hostel (ul Grochowa)
9 Former Płaszów Concentration Camp
10 Camping Nr 171 Krakowianka

0   1   2km
0   0.5   1mi

In January 1945 a sudden encircling man-oeuvre by the Soviet Red Army forced the Germans to evacuate the city, so Kraków was saved from destruction.

No other city in Poland better captures its intriguing history: the Old Town harbours towering Gothic churches and the splendid Wawel Castle, while Kazimierz, the now-silent Jewish quarter, recounts a more tragic story. Kraków is also home to world-class museums and a lively cultural scene. In 1978 Unesco included the Old Town of Kraków on its first World Heritage list. This historic core has changed little.

Information
Tourist Offices & Publications There is a confusing array of tourist offices in Kraków.

Kraków's **Municipal Tourism Information Centre** (*Rynek Główny 1/3; ☎ 428 36 00; open 8am-6pm Mon-Fri, 9am-3pm Sat & Sun*) is the major office. There is also a smaller and less busy **tourist office** (*☎ 432 01 10, e it-krakow@wp.pl; open 8am-8pm Mon-Fri, 9am-5pm Sat & Sun*) along the path between ul Szpitalna and the main train station. Another **tourist counter** (*☎ 421 50 31, e ap2info@interia.pl; open about 6am-10am & 3pm-8pm daily*) is at the far end of the main train station building.

The Kazimierz **tourist office** (*☎ 432 08 40, e biuro@kazimierzbiuro.kraknet.pl; ul Józefa 7; open 10am-4pm Mon-Fri*) provides information about Jewish heritage in that area.

The **Culture Information Centre** (*☎ 421 77 87, w www.karnet.krakow2000.pl; ul Św*

Jana 2; open 10am-6pm Mon-Fri, 10am-4pm Sat) is the best place to get information about (and tickets for) the plethora of cultural events in the city.

Two free monthly magazines, *Welcome to Craców & Małopolska* and *Kraków: What, Where, When* (the latter also in German), are available at the tourist offices and some travel agencies and upmarket hotels. The *Kraków Insider* booklet (6.50zł) is also very useful.

The tourist offices, as well as some hotels and travel agencies, sell the 'Craców Tourist Card' (45/65zł for two/three days). This card provides free admission to all museums and attractions in Kraków and access on all public buses and trams, as well as various discounts (up to 40%) for organised tours and at selected restaurants.

Money Kantors and ATMs can be found all over the city centre. It's worth noting, however, that most kantors close on Sunday and areas near Rynek Główny square and the main train station offer terrible exchange rates. There are also exchange facilities at the airport. For travellers cheques, try **Bank Pekao** *(Rynek Główny 31)*, which also provides cash advances on MasterCard and Visa.

Post & Communications The **main post office** *(ul Westerplatte 20; open 8am-8pm Mon-Fri, 8am-2pm Sat, 9am-noon Sun)* has a poste-restante bureau. Mail addressed to Poste Restante, Poczta Główna, ul Westerplatte 20, 31-045 Kraków 1, Poland, can be collected at window No 1. Telephone calls can be made at the **telephone centre** *(ul Wielopole; open 24hr)*, next to the Main Post Office, or from the **post & telephone office** *(ul Lubicz 4; open 24hr)*, conveniently opposite the main train station building.

Email & Internet Access The most atmospheric place to check emails is downstairs at **Cyber Café U Luisa** *(Rynek Główny 13)*. Otherwise, try **Centrum Internetowe** *(Rynek Główny 9)*, where views of the square from the window are so exceptional that it's hard to concentrate on the computer screen, or **Looz Internet Café** *(ul Mikołajska 13)*, a dingy Internet café-cum-pub.

Bookshops The widest selection of regional and city maps, as well as Lonely Planet titles, is in **Sklep Podróżnika** *(ul Jagiellońska 6)*. As usual, the **EMPiK Megastore** *(Rynek Główny 5)* sells foreign newspapers and magazines. For literature and trashy novels (in English and German), check the **Columbus Bookshop** *(ul Grodzka 60)* or **Księgarnia Językowa** *(Plac Matejki 5)*. For publications related to Jewish issues visit the **Jarden Jewish Bookshop** *(ul Szeroka 2)* in Kazimierz.

Things to See & Do

Old Town The magnificent **Rynek Główny** is the largest (roughly 800m wide and 1200m long) medieval town square in the whole of Europe. Dominating the square is the 16th-century Renaissance **Cloth Hall** (Sukiennice). On the ground floor is a large **craft market** and upstairs is the **Gallery of 19th-Century Polish Painting** *(admission 5zł, free Sun; open 10am-3.30pm Tues, Wed, Fri-Sun, 10am-6pm Thur)*, which includes several famous works by Jan Matejko.

The ostentatious 14th-century **St Mary's Church** *(Rynek Główny 4; admission 2.50zł; open noon-6pm Mon-Sat)* fills the north-eastern corner of the square. The huge main altarpiece by Wit Stwosz (Veit Stoss) of Nuremberg is the finest Gothic sculpture in Poland. Every hour a *hejnał* (bugle call) is played from the highest tower of the Church. Today, it's a musical symbol of the city; the melody based on five notes was played in medieval times as a warning call. It breaks off abruptly to symbolise when, according to legend, the throat of a 13th-century trumpeter was pierced by a Tatar arrow.

West of the Cloth Hall is the 15th-century **Town Hall Tower** *(admission 3zł; open 10am-5pm Wed-Fri, 10am-4pm Sat & Sun)*, which you can climb. Also worth a visit is the **Historical Museum of Kraków** *(Rynek Główny 35; admission 5zł; open 9am-3.30pm Tues, Wed & Fri, 11am-6pm Thur)*.

From St Mary's Church, walk up (northeast) ul Floriańska to the 14th-century **Florian Gate**, the only one of the original eight gates. Behind the gate is the **Barbican** *(admission 5zł; open 9am-5pm daily May-Sept)*, a defensive bastion built in 1498. Nearby, the **Czartoryski Museum** *(ul Św Jana 19; admission 5zł; open about 10am-3.30pm Tues-Sun)* features an impressive collection of European art, including some works by Leonardo da Vinci and Rembrandt.

South of Rynek Główny, Plac Wszystkich Świętych is dominated by two 13th-century

KRAKÓW – OLD TOWN & WAWEL

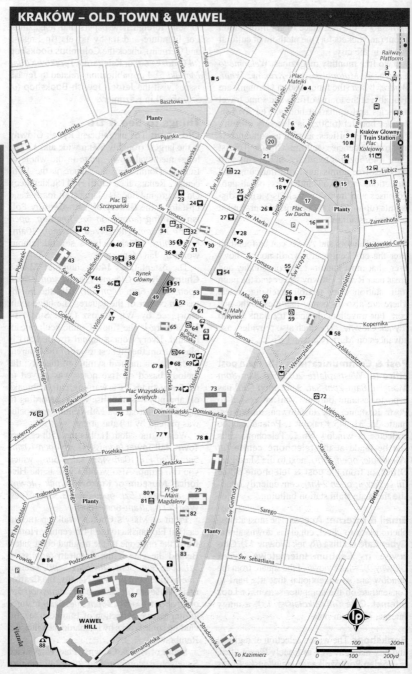

KRAKÓW – OLD TOWN & WAWEL

PLACES TO STAY	OTHER		
5 Pokoje Gościnne Jordan; Jordan (Travel Agency)	1 Underground Passage to Buses to Oświecim (Auschwitz & Birkenau)	46	Police Station
9 Biuro Turystyki i Zakwaterowania Waweltur (Private Rooms)	2 Bus No 208 to Airport	48	Town Hall Tower
	3 Minibuses to Wieliczka	49	Cloth Hall; Craft Market
10 Jordan Tourist Information & Accommodation Center	4 Księgarnia Językowa Bookshop	50	Gallery of 19th-Century Polish Painting
13 Hotel Europejski	6 LOT Office	51	Municipal Tourism Information Centre
14 Hotel Polonia	7 Bus Terminal	52	Statue of Adam Mieckiewicz
26 Hotel Pollera	8 Private Buses to Zakopane	53	St Mary's Church
34 Hotel Saski	11 Post & Telephone Office	54	Jazz Club U Muniaka
57 Hotel Wit Stwosz	12 Bus B to Airport	56	Black Gallery
58 Hotel Wyspiański	15 Tourist Office	59	Looz Internet Café
67 Hotel Rezydent	16 Church of the Holy Cross	61	EMPiK Megastore
78 Hotel Wawel Tourist	17 Teatr im Słowackiego	63	Pub Bastylia
84 Pensjonat Rycerski	20 Barbican	64	Centrum Internetowe
	21 Florian Gate	65	St Adalbert's Church
PLACES TO EAT	22 Czartoryski Museum	66	Cyber Café U Luisa
18 Bistro Rożowy Słoń	23 Equinox	68	Almatur
19 Restauracja Sąsiedzi	24 Irish Pub Pod Papugami	69	US Consulate
28 Restaurant Orient Lychee	25 Piwnica Pod Złotą Pipą	70	German Consulate-General
29 Bar Mleczny Dworzanin	27 Indigo Jazz Club	71	Main Post Office
30 Café Camelot	32 Kino Sztuka	72	Telephone Centre
31 Restauracja Chłopskie Jadło	33 Kino Apollo	73	Dominican Church
44 Jadłodajnia Kuchcik	35 Culture Information Centre	74	French Consulate-General
45 Salad Bar Chimera	36 Orbis Travel	75	Franciscan Church
47 Restauracja Sphinx	37 Historical Museum of Kraków	76	Filharmonia Krakówska
55 Ipanema	38 Bank Pekao	79	Church of SS Peter & Paul
60 Green Way Bar Wegetariański; Jadłodajnia U Stasi	39 Klub Pasja	81	Wyspiański Museum
	40 Sklep Podróżnika Bookshop	82	St Andrew's Church
62 Bistro Rożowy Słon	41 Stary Teatr	83	Columbus Bookshop
77 Pod Aniolami	42 Klub Kulturalny	85	Cathedral Museum
80 Restauracja U Literatów	43 St Anne's Church	86	Wawel Cathedral
		87	Wawel Castle
		88	Dragon's Cave

monastic churches: the **Dominican Church** *(ul Stolarska 12; admission free; open 9am-6pm daily)* to the east and the **Franciscan Church** *(Plac Wszystkich Świętych 5; admission free; open 9am-5pm daily)* to the west. The latter is noted for its stained-glass windows.

South along ul Grodzka is the early-17th-century Jesuit **Church of SS Peter & Paul** *(ul Grodzka 64; admission free; open dawn-dusk daily)*, the first baroque church built in Poland. The Romanesque 11th-century **St Andrew's Church** *(ul Grodzka 56; admission free; open 9am-6pm Mon-Fri)* was the only building in Kraków to withstand the Tatars' attack of 1241.

Along ul Kanonicza – probably Kraków's most picturesque street – is the **Wyspiański Museum** *(ul Kanonicza 9; admission 5zł, free Sun; open 11am-6pm Tues-Thur, 9am-3.30pm Wed & Fri, 10am-3.30pm Sat & Sun)*. It is dedicated to Poland's renowned poet, painter, playwright and stained-glass designer.

Wawel Hill South of the Old Town is the dominant Wawel Hill *(admission to grounds free; open 6am-8pm daily May-Sept, 6am-5pm Oct-Apr)*. This hill is crowned with a castle and cathedral, both of which are the very symbols of Poland and the guardians of its national history.

Inside the extensive grounds are several worthwhile attractions; all are open from about 9.30am to 3pm Tuesday to Friday and from 10am to 3pm on Saturday and Sunday. Each place has different opening hours on Monday (as indicated below). Currently, entry to the Treasury & Armoury and Lost Wawel is free on Monday, but check this at the ticket office because the allocated days with free entry (and regulations about it) change regularly.

Allow at least three hours to explore the castle and cathedral and come early, especially in summer. As soon as you arrive, stop at the *kasa* (ticket office) in the grounds; entry to most attractions is limited and only available by ticket (even when admission is free you'll still need a ticket).

Inside the magnificent **Wawel Castle**, the largest and most popular exhibits are the **Royal Chambers** *(admission 15zł; closed Mon)* and the **Royal Private Apartments** *(admission 15zł; closed Mon)*. Entry to the latter is only allowed on a guided tour (included in the admission fee), but if you want a guide who speaks English, French or German contact the **guides office** *(☎ 422 09 04)* along the laneway up to the hill.

Dominating the hill is the 14th-century **Wawel Cathedral** *(admission free, but total of 6zł admission to tombs & bell tower; open 9am-5pm Mon)*. For four centuries it was the coronation and burial place of Polish royalty, as evidenced by the **Royal Tombs** where 100 kings and queens have been buried. The golden-domed **Sigismund Chapel** (1539), on the southern side of the cathedral, is considered to be the finest Renaissance construction in Poland, and the **bell tower** houses the country's largest bell (11 tonnes). More exhibits about the cathedral are in the **Cathedral Museum** *(admission 5zł; closed Mon)*.

Other attractions in the complex include the **Museum of Oriental Art** *(admission 6zł; closed Mon)*; the **Treasury & Armoury** *(admission 12zł; open 9.30am-1pm Mon)*; the **Lost Wawel** *(admission 6zł; open 9.30am-noon Mon)*, which has some archaeological exhibits; and the quirky **Dragon's Cave** *(admission 3zł; open 9am-5pm Mon)*.

Kazimierz Founded by King Kazimierz the Great in 1335, Kazimierz was until the 1820s an independent town with its own municipal charter and laws. In the 15th century, Jews were expelled from Kraków and forced to re-settle in a small prescribed area in Kazimierz, separated by a wall from the larger Christian quarter. The Jewish quarter later became home to Jews fleeing persecution from all corners of Europe.

By the outbreak of WWII there were 65,000 Jews in Kraków (around 30% of the city's population), and most lived in Kazimierz. During the war the Nazis relocated Jews to a walled ghetto in Podgórze, just south of the Vistula River. They were exterminated in the nearby **Płaszów Concentration Camp**, as portrayed in Steven Spielberg's haunting film *Schindler's List*. The current Jewish population in Kraków is about 100.

These days Kazimierz is undergoing a renaissance as citizens of all creeds and religions realise the benefit of living in such a charming place so close to the city centre.

Kazimierz has two historically determined sectors. Its western Catholic quarter is dotted with churches. The 14th-century Gothic **St Catherine's Church** *(ul Augustian 7; admission free; open only during services)* boasts a

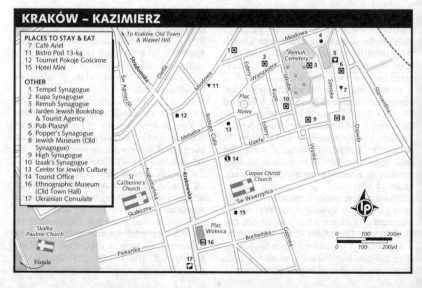

KRAKÓW – KAZIMIERZ

PLACES TO STAY & EAT
7 Café Ariel
11 Bistro Pod 13-ką
12 Tournet Pokoje Gościnne
15 Hotel Mini

OTHER
1 Tempel Synagogue
2 Kupa Synagogue
3 Remuh Synagogue
4 Jarden Jewish Bookshop & Tourist Agency
5 Pub Ptaszyl
6 Popper's Synagogue
8 Jewish Museum (Old Synagogue)
9 High Synagogue
10 Izaak's Synagogue
13 Center for Jewish Culture
14 Tourist Office
16 Ethnographic Museum (Old Town Hall)
17 Ukrainian Consulate

singularly imposing 17th-century gilded high altar, while the 14th-century **Corpus Christi Church** *(ul Bożego Ciała 26; admission free; open 9am-5pm Mon-Sat)* is crammed with baroque fittings. The **Ethnographic Museum** *(Plac Wolnica; admission 4zł; open 10am-6pm Mon & Wed-Sat, 10am-2pm Sun)* in the Old Town Hall has a reasonably interesting collection of regional crafts and costumes.

The eastern Jewish quarter is dotted with synagogues, many of which miraculously survived the war. The most important is the 15th-century **Old Synagogue**, the oldest Jewish religious building in Poland. It now houses the **Jewish Museum** *(ul Szeroka 24; admission 6zł; open 9am-3pm Wed-Thur, 11am-7pm Fri, 9am-4pm Sat & Sun)*.

A short walk north is the small 16th-century **Remuh Synagogue** *(ul Szeroka 40; admission 5zł; open 9am-4pm Mon-Fri)*, the only one still used for religious services. Behind it, the **Remuh Cemetery** *(admission free; open 9am-4pm Mon-Fri)* boasts some extraordinary Renaissance gravestones. Nearby, the restored **Izaak's Synagogue** *(ul Jakuba 25; admission 6zł; open 9am-7pm Sun-Fri)* shows documentary films about life in the Jewish ghetto.

It's easy to take a self-guided walking tour around Kazimierz (and other parts of Kraków) with the booklet *Retracing Schindler's List* (in German or English). It contains a map and plenty of explanations and is available from the **Jarden Jewish Bookshop** *(ul Szeroka 2, Kazimierz)*.

Wieliczka Salt Mine Wieliczka ('Vyeh-LEECH-kah'), 15km southeast of the city centre, is famous for the **Wieliczka Salt Mine** *(www.kopalnia.pl; ul Daniłowicza 10; admission 29zł; camera permit 13zł, 20% discount Nov-Feb; open 8am-8pm daily Apr-Oct, 8am-4pm Nov-March)*. Remarkably, this eerie world of pits and chambers is all hewn out by hand from solid salt, and every single element, from chandeliers to altarpieces, is made of salt. Appropriately, the mine is included on Unesco's World Heritage list.

The highlight of a mine visit is the richly ornamented **Chapel of the Blessed Kinga**, which is actually a church measuring 54m by 17m and is 12m high. Construction of this underground temple took more than 30 years (1895–1927), resulting in the removal of 20,000 tonnes of rock salt. The **museum** *(admission 12zł)* is on the 3rd floor of the mine.

The obligatory guided tour (included in the admission fee) through the mine takes about two hours (a 2km walk). Tours in English operate at 10am, 12.30pm and 3pm, but only between June and August; one or two tours a day (June to August) also run in German (depending on demand). If you're visiting independently, you must wait for a tour to start, but the management guarantees that you'll wait no more than one hour. If you join a Polish-language tour, buy an English-language booklet (7zł) at the mine. Otherwise, prebook a private tour (about 85zł for a small group) in English or German. Last admission to the mine is about three hours before closing time.

Minibuses to Wieliczka town depart every 15 minutes between 6am and 8pm from near the bus terminal in Kraków and drop passengers outside the salt mine (but ask the driver to do this). Trains between Kraków and Wieliczka leave every 45 minutes throughout the day, but the train station in Wieliczka is a fair walk from the mine.

Organised Tours

The following companies operate tours of Kraków and surrounding areas.

Almatur (☎ 422 09 02, ul Grodzka 2) – all sorts of interesting outdoor activities in and around Kraków during summer.

Jordan (☎ 421 21 35, **W** www.jordan.krakow.pl) ul Długa 9 – tours to Auschwitz and Wieliczka

Jarden Tourist Agency (☎/fax 421 71 66, **W** www.jarden.pl) ul Szeroka 2 – the best agency for tours of Jewish heritage. Guided walking tours around Kazimierz cost 25/30zł per person (two/three hours). It's showpiece – 'Retracing Schindler's List' – (two hours by car) costs 45zł per person. All tours require a minimum of three and must be arranged in advance. All tours are in English, but French- and German-speaking guides can be organised.

Orbis Travel (☎ 422 40 35, **W** www.orbis.travel.krakow.pl) Rynek Główny 41 – with a number of agencies around town including one at the Old Town square

Zeluga Krakowska (☎ 422 08 55) – boat trips along the Vistula between May and September from near Wawel Hill.

Special Events

Kraków boasts one of the richest cycles of annual events in Poland. Major cultural festivals include the Jewish Culture Festival (June/July) and International Festival of Street Theatre (July). Major musical events include the

POLAND

Organ Music Festival (March/ April) and the Summer Jazz Festival (July). Contact the helpful Culture Information Centre (see under Tourist Offices earlier) for full programme details and bookings.

Seven days after Corpus Christi (a Thursday in May or June), Kraków has a colourful pageant headed by Lajkonik, a legendary figure disguised as a Tatar riding a hobbyhorse.

Places to Stay

Kraków is unquestionably Poland's premier tourist destination, so booking any form of accommodation between April and October is strongly recommended – and *essential* in July and August. If you can't find any accommodation anywhere, contact the tourist offices in the main train station building and along the path near ul Szpitalna.

Camping   Four kilometres west of the Old Town is **Camping Nr 46 Smok** (☎ 429 72 66; *ul Kamedulska 18; camping per person/tent 15/10zł; open June-Sept).* It's small, quiet and pleasantly located. To get here frrom outside the Kraków Główny train station building, take tram No 2 to the end of the line in Zwierzyniec and change for any westbound bus (except No 100).

Camping Nr 171 Krakowianka (☎ 266 41 91; *ul Żywiecka Boczna 4; camping per person/tent 15/10zł; open May-Sept)* is on the road to Zakopane 5km south of the Old Town. Take tram No 19 or bus No 119 from the main train station.

PFC Camping Nr 45 (☎ 637 21 22; *ul Radzikowskiego 99; camping per person/tent 15/14zł; open June–mid-Sept)* is beside the Motel Krak on the Katowice road about 4km northwest of the Old Town. It's large and well equipped, but the traffic noise can be considerable. To get here, take bus No 501 from the main train station.

Hostels   The largest hostel in Poland, **Youth Hostel PTSM** (☎ 633 88 22, e smkrakow .pro.onet.pl; *ul Oleandry 4; dorm beds 14-24zł; open year-round)* is only 1km west of the Old Town. Although it has 380 beds, it's sometimes full – and always noisy. Take tram No 15 from outside the main train station building and get off just past Hotel Cracovia.

Another **Youth Hostel** (☎/fax 653 24 32; *ul Grochowa 21; dorm beds 15-25zł; doubles with shared bathroom per person 50zł;*

open year-round) is on the 3rd floor of a student dormitory. It's in a quiet suburb 5km southeast of the Old Town and quite remote. Take bus No 115 from the train station.

Schronisko Szkolne (☎ 637 24 41; *ul Szablowskiego 1c; dorm beds 15-25zł; open year-round)* is 3.5km northwest of the Old Town. This place is not too convenient either, but it's more likely to have space in July and August (when some 200 extra beds become available). Take tram No 4 or 13 from the train station.

The tourist offices will have information about the current availability of accommodation in **student hostels** during the summer months (July to September), though some hostels offer a few rooms all year. Singles/ doubles with a shared bathroom are cheap – from 60/80zł – but the hostels are invariably far from the Old Town.

Private Rooms   In summer, you may be accosted by intimidating old ladies offering private rooms. As always, check the location before making any decision.

Biuro Turystyki i Zakwaterowania Waweltur (☎/fax 422 16 40; *ul Pawia 8; open 8am-8pm Mon-Fri, 8am-2pm Sat)* arranges private rooms. Singles cost from 64zł to 75zł and doubles from 96zł to 128zł. The rates are cheaper the further away you stay from the Old Town.

Jordan Tourist Information & Accommodation Centre (☎ 422 60 91; w www.jordan .krakow.pl; *ul Pawia 12; open 8am-6pm Mon-Fri, 9am-1pm Sat-Sun)* is next door. It offers slightly better rooms for higher prices: about 90/110zł for singles/doubles.

The tourist counter in the main train station building can arrange double rooms (no singles) in the Old Town for about 100zł and well-appointed single/double apartments (with bathroom and kitchen) close to the Old Town for 110/130zł. The tourist office in Kazimierz can also arrange **private rooms** in that area.

Hotels – Budget   Note that one of the youth hostels, and most student hostels, have individual rooms and that private rooms and apartments are often better value than hotels. See the sections earlier for details.

Kazimierz is only a short walk from the Old Town and almost feels like a separate village. Most places in Kazimierz are expensive, but a couple of cheapies can be found.

Tournet Pokoje Gościnne (☎ 292 00 88; W www.nocleg.krakow.pl; ul Miodowa 7; singles/doubles 140/180zł) is a new place offering simple but comfortable and quiet rooms. The bathrooms are tiny, however.

Hotel Mini (☎ 430 61 00, fax 430 59 88; Plac Wolnica 7; singles/doubles 130/220zł) is central but quiet, just back from the Ethnographic Museum. The singles are small, but the doubles are large and attic-style and contain some lounge furniture. All are spotlessly clean. Your leg muscles will get a workout going up and down the stairs.

Hotels – Mid-Range & Top End Unless stated otherwise, all rooms listed below contain a TV and rates include breakfast.

Near the bus and train stations, **Hotel Polonia** (☎ 422 12 33; e polonia@bci.krakow .pl; ul Basztowa 25; singles/doubles 99/ 119zł, with bath 250/285zł) is in a grand old building. The newer rooms are not great value and face the noisy main road, but the ones with a shared bathroom are excellent value – but book ahead.

The **Pokoje Gościnne Jordan** (☎ 421 21 25; W www.jordan.krakow.pl; ul Długa 9; singles/doubles from 140/210zł) is about the best value within walking distance of the Old Town, so book ahead. The rooms are modern but unremarkable. The reception is in the travel agency next door.

Pensjonat Rycerski (☎ 422 60 82, fax 422 33 99; Plac Na Groblach 22; doubles without/ with bath from 195/270zł) is one of the surprisingly few places close to Wawel Hill – and it charges accordingly. Still it's popular and often booked out.

Hotel Saski (☎ 421 42 22, fax 421 48 30; ul Sławkowska 3; singles/doubles 160/170zł, with bath 200/260zł) is ideally located in an historic house just off Rynek Główny. It's comparatively good value and the rooms feature ornate furniture, but readers have complained about late-night noise from nearby cinemas and cafés. Breakfast is additional to the room rate.

Formerly the drab Dom Turysty PTTK hostel, the **Hotel Wyspiański** (☎ 422 95 66; e wyspianski@janpol.com.pl; ul Westerplatte 15; singles/doubles Mon-Thur from 250/310zł, Fri-Sun from 220/260zł) has now been completely renovated. It's no longer the bargain it was, but prices are marginally acceptable on weekends.

Hotel Pollera (☎ 422 10 44; W www .pollera.com.pl; ul Szpitalna 30; singles/ doubles 295/345zł) is a classy place with large rooms crammed with elegant furniture. The singles are unexciting, but the doubles are far nicer. It's central and quiet (except for the squeaky floors). Substantial discounts are available between October and March.

Near the main square, **Hotel Wawel Tourist** (☎ 424 13 00; W www.wawel-tourist.com .pl; ul Poselska 22; doubles 190zł, singles/ doubles with bath from 195/280zł) is in a recently renovated 16th-century building. It's quiet and well furnished (though some rooms are small) and staff are friendly.

Hotel Rezydent (☎ 429 54 95, fax 429 55 76; ul Grodzka 9; singles/doubles US$85/ 120) is a newish place with modern facilities only a stone's throw from the main square.

Hotel Wit Stwosz (☎ 429 60 26; W www .wit-stwosz.hotel.krakow.pl, ul Mikołajska 28; singles/doubles 320/360zł) is in a historic town house along a quiet street. It's comfortable, stylish and remarkably good value for a top-end hotel.

Places to Eat

By Polish standards, Kraków is a food paradise. The Old Town is tightly packed with good gastronomic venues, ranging from rock-bottom to top-notch. Privatisation has pretty much eliminated the dirt-cheap proletarian milk bars, but many excellent affordable alternatives have popped up in their place.

One local speciality is *obwarzanki*, a ring-shaped pretzel powdered with poppy seeds, and available from vendors dozing next to their pushcarts.

Almost every proper restaurant that is listed below can provide menus in English and, possibly, German.

Polish Restaurants Recommended by several readers, **Restauracja Chłopskie Jadło** (ul Św Jana 3; mains 18-35zł) is arranged as an old country inn and serves scrumptious Polish food from the 'Peasant's Kitchen'.

Restauracja U Literatów (ul Kanonicza 7; mains from 12zł) may look uninviting with the plastic tables but it's a tiny oasis of greenery with a courtyard setting (hidden from the main street).

Jadłodajnia Kuchcik (ul Jagiellońska 12; mains 8-15zł) offers substantial portions of home-cooked Polish food in unpretentious

POLAND

surroundings. You may have to wait for a table between noon and 2pm.

Bistro Pod 13-ką (*ul Miodowa 13; mains 10-15zł*) is arguably the best place in Kazimierz to try tasty authentic Polish cooking at affordable prices.

Restauracja Sąsiedzi (*ul Szpitalna 40; mains from 10zł*) is a popular split-level place with cafeteria-style food at sensible prices.

Pod Aniolami (*ul Grodzka 35; mains from 30zł*) delighted at least one reader who says this restaurant serves the 'best meals in Kraków'. There are plenty of meat dishes and the surroundings are cosy, if a little smoky.

Other Restaurants For large helpings (with the obligatory dollop of sliced Polish cabbage), **Restaurant Orient Lychee** (*ul Floriańska 27; meals with rice about 10zł*) is one of several Chinese-cum-Vietnamese eateries located in the Old Town. The service is quick and informal.

Café Camelot (*ul Św Tomasza 17; salads about 8zł, mains from 12zł*) has a cosy interior, but if the weather's fine or it's too smoky indoors some tables are set up among the ferns outside. It's perfect for enjoying a sandwich, salad and/or decent coffee while perusing a few day-old English-language newspapers.

Ipanema (*ul Św Tomasza 28; mains about 16zł*) is a newish place that has been recommended by readers for its authentic Brazilian cuisine at reasonable prices.

Café Ariel (*ul Szeroka 18; mains 18-25zł*) is a quaint place in the heart of Kazimierz, which offers a mouthwatering array of authentic Jewish meals.

Restauracja Sphinx (*Rynek Główny 26; mains from 15zł*) is one of several identical places found throughout Poland. As usual, the portions are large, the service is quick and the restaurant is located in a prime position. It's one of the few places around the main square with reasonably priced drinks.

Vegetarian In an attractive cellar along an arcade, **Salad Bar Chimera** (*ul Św Anny 3; salads from 5zł*) offers some of the best salads in Kraków – all listed alphabetically (in Polish) from 'A to Z'.

Green Way Bar Wegetariański (*ul Mikołajska 16; snacks from 6zł, mains from 10zł*) has outlets in several Polish cities. It rarely fails to satisfy anyone looking for something healthy and/or meat-free.

Fast Food Undoubtedly the cheapest place in the middle of the Old Town is **Bar Mleczny Dworzanin** (*ul Floriańska 19; mains from 8zł*). It's often standing room only and the lines of hungry patrons are long.

Bistro Różowy Słoń (*ul Sienna 1 & ul Szpitalna 38; meals about 6zł*) is recognisable by the bright pink chairs and cartoon-painted walls. The 'Pink Elephant' offers, among other tasty treats, a huge selection of pancakes (about 20 types!) and a salad bar – all at remarkably low prices.

Jadłodajnia U Stasi (*ul Mikołajska 16; mains 6-12zł*), near the Green Way Bar Wegetariański, is one of the oldest and best-known eateries. This unpretentious place is very popular for its *pierogi* (stuffed dumplings), but it's only open at lunchtime.

Self-Catering There are no supermarkets or even major grocery shops in the Old Town, so the best place for self-catering is any of the number of **delikatessy** found along the streets.

Entertainment

The comprehensive (free) English-language booklet, *Karnet*, published by the Culture Information Centre (see Tourist Offices earlier), lists almost every event in the city.

Pubs & Bars There are more than 100 pubs and bars in the Old Town alone. Many are housed in ancient vaulted cellars, but non-smokers beware: all have poor ventilation and most patrons seem to take delight in chain-smoking. Some of the best places to relax with a drink are any of the plethora of places around Rynek Główny, but prices are high.

Irish Pub Pod Papugami (*ul Św Jana 18*) was recently refurbished and is now a charming underground watering hole decorated with old motorcycles (among other strange items).

Klub Kulturalny (*ul Szewska 25*) is set in a labyrinthine array of beautiful medieval brick vaults. It's long established and popular, with good music and pleasant atmosphere.

Piwnica Pod Złotą Pipą (*ul Floriańska 30*) is another place located that's inside an inviting cellar. It's more suited to conversation than listening to music.

Pub Bastylia (*ul Stolarska 3*) is a bizarre place on five levels with some floors decorated like a French jail!

Pub Ptaszyl (*ul Szeroka 10*) is an artsy place to check out if you're in Kazimierz.

Nightclubs For foot-tapping jazz head to **Jazz Club u Muniaka** (ul Floriańska 3) or the **Indigo Jazz Club** (ul Floriańska 26).

Black Gallery (ul Mikołajska 24) is a crowded underground pub-cum-nightclub that only gets going after midnight and stays open *really* late.

Klub Pasja (ul Szewska 5) occupies vast brick cellars. It's trendy and attractive and popular with foreigners for its Western music and billiard tables.

Equinox (ul Sławkowska 13/15) has long been one of the most popular haunts in the Old Town. Discos are held most nights.

Cinemas Two of the better and more convenient cinemas showing recent films are **Kino Apollo** (ul Św Tomasza 11a) and **Kino Sztuka** (cnr Św Tomasza & Św Jana).

Theatre The best-known venue, **Stary Teatr** (ul Jagiellońska 1), consistently offers quality productions. **Teatr im Słowackiego** (Plac Św Ducha 1), built in 1893, focuses on Polish classics and large-scale productions. It was totally renovated in 1991 and its interior is spectacular. **Filharmonia Krakówska** (ul Zwierzyniecka 1) boasts one of the best orchestras in the country; concerts are usually held on Friday and Saturday.

Getting There & Away

For information about travelling from Kraków to Zakopane, Częstochowa or Oświęcim (for Auschwitz), refer to the relevant Getting There & Away sections later.

Also see the Getting There & Away section earlier in this chapter for information about the international bus and train services to and from Kraków.

Air The John Paul II International Airport is more often called the Balice Airport, after the suburb in which it's located about 15km west of the Old Town. LOT flies between Kraków and Warsaw six times a day, and offers direct flights from Kraków to Frankfurt, London, Paris, Rome and Zurich.

In summer, LOT also flies directly from Chicago (April-Sept) and New York (June to September). In addition, Austrian Airlines flies directly between Kraków and Vienna several times a week. Bookings for all flights can be made at the **LOT** office (☎ 422 4215; ul Basztowa 15).

Bus The main **bus terminal** (Plac Kolejowy) is conveniently opposite the main train station building and only minutes on foot from the Old Town. However, trains are more frequent and faster so bus services are limited to the regional centres of minimal interest to travellers, as well as Lublin (three a day), Zamość (two), Warsaw (four), Wrocław (two) and Cieszyn (eight) on the Czech border.

Polski Express buses to Warsaw depart from a spot opposite the bus terminal.

Train The lovely old **Kraków Główny** train station (Plac Dworcowy), on the northeastern outskirts of the Old Town, handles all international trains and almost all domestic rail services. (Note that the railway platforms are about 150m north of the station building.)

Each day from Kraków, five InterCity trains speed to Warsaw (2¾ hours) and about four express (46zł in 2nd class) and five fast trains also travel to the capital. Also every day from Kraków there are three trains to Wrocław, two to Poznań, two to Lublin and six to Gdynia, via Gdańsk.

Advance tickets for international and domestic trains can be booked directly at the Kraków Główny station building or from **Orbis Travel** (see Organised Tours earlier).

Getting Around

The airport is accessible on Bus No 208, which leaves from a spot just north of the bus terminal in Kraków every 30 to 40 minutes. More frequent and faster is 'Bus B', which leaves from a stop along ul Lubicz and opposite Hotel Europejski. A taxi to or from the airport will cost about 50zł.

Any of the numerous travel agencies in Kraków can arrange car rental. Alternatively, most companies, like **Payless** (☎ 639 32 62, fax 639 32 63), have counters at the airport.

Kraków is ideal for cycling. The bike paths along both sides of the Vistula River from Wawel Hill are very pleasant (if a little crowded on summer weekends). If you want to escape the city, head out to the **Kościuszko Mound** in Zwierzyniec, where the hilly roads are less busy and more pleasant. Bikes can be rented from the **Jordan Tourist Information & Accommodation Centre** (ul Pawia 12).

AB City Tour offers tours on tiny, train-like electric cars around Rynek Główny (5zł per person) and Kazimierz (20zł). They leave hourly from the main square.

OŚWIĘCIM

☎ 033 • pop 48,000

The name of Oświęcim ('Osh-FYEN-cheem'), about 60km west of Kraków, may be unfamiliar to outsiders, but the German name, Auschwitz, is not. This was the scene of the most extensive experiment in genocide in the history of humankind.

The Auschwitz camp was established in April 1940 in the prewar Polish army barracks on the outskirts of Oświęcim. Originally intended to hold Polish political prisoners, the camp eventually developed into the largest centre for the extermination of European Jews. Towards this end, two additional camps were subsequently established: the much larger Birkenau (Brzezinka), or Auschwitz II, 3km west of Auschwitz; and Monowitz (Monowice), several kilometres west of Oświęcim. These death factories eliminated 1.5 to two million people of 27 nationalities – about 90% of whom were Jews.

Auschwitz

Auschwitz was only partially destroyed by the fleeing Nazis, so many of the original buildings remain as a bleak document of the camp's history. A dozen of the 30 surviving prison blocks house sections of the **State Museum Auschwitz-Birkenau** (admission free; open 8am-7pm daily June-Aug, 8am-6pm May & Sept, 8am-5pm Apr & Oct, 8am-4pm March & 1 Nov-15 Dec, 8am-3pm Dec 16-end Feb).

About every half-hour, the cinema in the **Visitors' Centre** at the entrance to Auschwitz shows a 15-minute documentary film (admission 2zł) about the liberation of the camp by Soviet troops on 27 January 1945. It's shown in several different languages throughout the day; check the schedule at the information desk as soon as you arrive at the camp. The film is not recommended for children under 14 years old. The Visitors' Centre also has a cafeteria, kantor and left-luggage room, and several bookshops.

Some basic explanations in Polish, English and Hebrew are provided on site, but you'll understand more if you buy the small Auschwitz Birkenau Guide Book (translated into about 15 languages) from the bookshops at the Visitors' Centre. English-language tours (3½ hours; 25zł per person) of Auschwitz and Birkenau are guaranteed to leave daily at 11.30am, while another starts at 1pm if there's enough demand. Tours in German commence

when a group of seven or eight can be found. But make sure that you receive your allotted time; some guides tell you to wander around Birkenau by yourself and to make your own way back to Auschwitz.

Birkenau

It was actually at Birkenau (admission free; same opening hours), not Auschwitz, where the extermination of huge numbers of Jews took place. This vast (175 hectares), purpose-built and efficient camp had over 300 prison barracks and four huge gas chambers complete with crematoria. Each gas chamber held 2000 people, and electric lifts raised the bodies to the ovens. The camp could hold 200,000 inmates at one time.

Although much of the camp was destroyed by retreating Nazis, the size of the place, fenced off with barbed wire stretching almost as far as the eye can see, provides some idea of the scale of this heinous crime. The viewing platform above the entrance also provides further perspective. In some ways, Birkenau is even more shocking than Auschwitz and there are far fewer tourists.

Places to Stay & Eat

For most visitors, Auschwitz and Birkenau is an easy day trip from Kraków.

The **cafeteria** in the Visitors' Centre is sufficient for a quick lunch.

Centrum Dialogu i Modlitwy (☎ 843 10 00, fax 843 10 01; ul Kolbego 1; camping/rooms with breakfast per person 20/65zł) is 700m southwest of Auschwitz. It's comfortable and quiet, and most rooms have a private bathroom.

Hotel Glob (☎/fax 843 06 43; ul Powstańców Śląskich 16; singles/doubles with breakfast 100/150zł) is an ugly building about 100m from the train station in Oświęcim. The rooms are decent enough but a little noisy.

Getting There & Away

From Kraków Główny station, eleven trains go to Oświęcim (two hours) each day, though more depart from Kraków Płaszów station. Check the schedules the day before so you can plan your visit properly. The most convenient departure from Kraków Płaszów is at 7.20am, and at 7.45am from Kraków Główny.

Far more convenient are the 12 buses (10zł, 90 minutes) per day to Oświęcim which depart from the small bus stop on ul Bosacka in

Kraków; the stop is at the end of the underpass below the railway platforms. Get off at the final stop (outside the PKS bus maintenance building), 200m from the entrance to Auschwitz. The return bus timetable to Kraków is displayed at the Birkenau Visitors' Centre.

Every hour on the hour from 11am to 4pm (inclusive) between 15 April and 31 October buses shuttle passengers between the visitors' centres at Auschwitz and Birkenau. Otherwise, between both places follow the signs for an easy walk (3km) or take a taxi. Auschwitz is also linked to central Oświęcim and the town's train station by bus Nos 19 and 24-29 every 30 to 40 minutes.

Most travel agencies in Kraków offer organised tours of Auschwitz (including Birkenau). However, some tours do not provide private transport, so it's often easier (and far cheaper) to use the public transport system and join an official tour from the Visitors' Centre in Auschwitz.

CZĘSTOCHOWA
☎ 034 • pop 260,000

Częstochowa ('Chen-sto-HO-vah'), 114km northwest of Kraków, is the spiritual heart of Poland. This likeable town owes its fame to the miraculous Black Madonna kept in the Jasna Góra monastery. The Paulites of Hungary founded the Jasna Góra monastery in 1382 and received the Black Madonna shortly thereafter. In 1430 the holy icon was stolen by the Hussites, who slashed the face of the Madonna. The wounds began to bleed, so the frightened thieves abandoned the icon and ran off. The monks who found the panel wanted to clean it, and a spring miraculously bubbled from the ground. The spring exists to this day, and St Barbara's Church was founded on the site. The picture was restored and repainted, but the scars on the face of the Virgin Mary were left as a reminder of the miracle.

Early in the 17th century the monastery was fortified, and it was one of the few places in the country to withstand the Swedish sieges of the 1650s. This miracle was again attributed to the Black Madonna. In 1717 the Black Madonna was crowned 'Queen of Poland'.

From the train station, and adjacent bus terminal, turn right (north) up Al Wolności – along which there are several Internet centres – to the main thoroughfare, Al Najświętszej Marii Panny (sensibly simplified to Al NMP). At the western end of this broad avenue is the monastery and at the eastern end is Plac Daszyńskiego. Between both is the **tourist office** (☎/fax 368 22 60; Al NMP 65; open 9am-5pm Mon-Fri, 10am-2pm Sat), several banks, kantors and travel agencies, including **Orbis Travel** (Al NMP 40/42).

Things to See
The **Paulite Monastery on Jasna Góra** (admission free; open dawn-dusk daily) retains the appearance of a hill-top fortress. Inside the grounds are three **museums** (admission free but donations welcome; all open 9am-5pm daily): **The Arsenal**, with a variety of old weapons; the **600th-Anniversary Museum** (Muzeum Sześćsetlecia), which contains Lech Wałęsa's 1983 Nobel Peace Prize; and **The Treasury** (Skarbiec), featuring offerings presented by the faithful.

The **tower** (open 8am-4pm daily Apr-Nov) is the tallest (106m) historic church tower in Poland. The baroque church is beautifully decorated. The image of the Black Madonna on the high altar of the adjacent chapel is hard to see, so a copy is on display in the **Knights' Hall** (Sala Rycerska) in the monastery.

On weekends and in holidays expect long queues for all three museums. The crowds in the chapel may be so thick that you're almost unable to enter, much less get near the icon.

In the Town Hall the **Częstochowa Museum** (Plac Biegańskiego 45; admission 2.50zł; open 8.30am-4pm Wed-Sat, 10am-4pm Sun) features an ethnographic collection and modern Polish paintings.

Special Events
The major Marian feasts at Jasna Góra are 3 May, 16 July, 15 August (especially), 26 August, 8 September, 12 September and 8 December. On these days the monastery is *packed* with pilgrims.

Places to Stay & Eat
Camping Oleńka (☎/fax 324 74 95; ul Oleńki 10/30; camping per person/tent 15/10zł, 3-/4-bed rooms with shared bathroom 25/50zł, bungalows with bath 80/100zł; open year-round) is only 100m west of the monastery. It would get unbearably noisy here in midsummer and when there's a pilgrimage.

The **youth hostel** (☎ 324 31 21; ul Jasnogórska 84/90; open July-Aug; dorm beds about 18zł), two blocks north of the tourist office, has modest facilities.

Dom Pielgrzyma (☎ *324 70 11; ul Wyszyńskiego 1/31; singles/doubles from 70/90zł)* is a huge place behind the monastery. It offers numerous quiet and comfortable rooms, and is remarkably good value.

Plenty of **eateries** can be found near the Dom Pielgrzyma. Better restaurants are dotted along Al NMP, such as the classy **Restaurant Polonus** *(Al NMP 75; mains from 14zł)* near the path up to the monastery. **Bar Viking** *(cnr Waszyngtona & ul Nowowiejskiego; mains from 11zł)*, about 200m south of the Częstochowa Museum, is cheap and cheerful.

Getting There & Away

Every day from the **bus terminal** *(Al Wolności 45)* three buses go to Kraków, three travel to Wrocław, one heads for Zakopane and three speed off to Warsaw. International buses also often pass through Częstochowa – see the Getting There & Away section earlier in this chapter.

From the impressive **train station** *(Al Wolności 21)*, eleven trains a day go to Warsaw (51zł 2nd-class express). There are also four to five daily trains to Gdynia, via Gdańsk, Łódź, Olsztyn and Zakopane; six to Kraków; and nine to Wrocław.

ZAKOPANE

☎ 018 • pop 30,000

Nestled at the foot of the Tatra Mountains, Zakopane is the most famous resort in Poland and the major winter-sports capital. Although essentially a base for skiing and hiking in the Tatras, Zakopane itself has an enjoyable, laid-back atmosphere, even if it is overbuilt, overpriced and commercialised.

In the late 19th century, Zakopane became popular with artists, many of whom came to settle and work here. The best known are the composer Karol Szymanowski and the writer and painter, Witkacy. The father of the latter, Stanisław Witkiewicz (1851–1915), was inspired by traditional local architecture and experimented with the so-called Zakopane style. Some buildings he designed still remain.

Information

The **Tourist Information Centre** (☎ *201 22 11; ul Kościuszki 17; open 8am-8pm Mon-Sat, 9am-7pm Sun May-Sept, 8am-5pm daily Oct-Apr)* is helpful. The knowledgable English-speaking staff can arrange private rooms, inquire on your behalf about hotel vacancies, organise car rental and sell hiking and city maps. The centre can also arrange rafting trips down the Dunajec River (see the Dunajec Gorge section later) and guides for the Tatra Mountains (see later), as well as one-day trips to Slovakia (60zł per person).

Dozens of **kantors** can be found along the main streets. Several banks along the pedestrian mall, such as **PKO Bank** *(ul Krupówki 19)*, handle foreign exchange, as does **Bank Pekao** *(cnr ul Staszica & Al 3 Maja)*. The combined **main post office** and **telephone centre** *(ul Krupówki)* is along the mall. **GraNet Internet Café** *(ul Krupówki 2)* is a convenient place to surf the Net.

Centrum Przewodnictwa Tatrzańskiego *(Tatra Guide Centre;* ☎ *206 37 99; ul Chałubińskiego 42/44)* and **Biuro Usług Turystycznych PTTK** (☎ *201 58 48; ul Krupówki 12)* can arrange English- and German-speaking mountain guides with advance notice. **Orbis Travel** (☎ *201 48 12; ul Krupówki 22)* offers the usual services, as well as accommodation in private homes.

Księgarnia Górska, in the reception area of the Dom Turysty PTTK (see later), is by far the best place for regional hiking maps.

Things to See & Do

The **Tatra Museum** *(ul Krupówki 10; admission 4zł; open 9am-5pm Tues-Sat, 9am-3pm Sun)* has exhibits about regional history, ethnography and geology, and plenty of displays about the flora and fauna of the Tatras.

Head southwest on ul Kościeliska to **Villa Koliba** *(ul Kościeliska 18)*, the first design (1892) by Witkiewicz in the Zakopane style. Predictably, it now houses the **Museum of Zakopane Style** *(admission 4zł; open 9am-5pm Wed-Sat, 9am-3pm Sun)*. About 350m southeast is **Villa Atma** *(ul Kasprusie 19)*. Inside is **Szymanowksi Museum** *(admission 4zł; open about 10am-4pm Tues-Sun)*, dedicated to the great musician who once lived there. There are piano recitals in summer.

The **Tatra National Park Natural Museum** *(ul Chałubińskiego 42a; admission 4zł; open 9am-2pm Mon-Sat)*, near the Rondo en route to the national park, has some mildly interesting exhibits about the park's natural history.

A short walk northeast up the hill leads to **Villa Pod Jedlami** *(ul Koziniec 1)*, another splendid house in the Zakopane style (the interior cannot be visited). Perhaps Witkiewicz's greatest achievement is the **Jaszczurówka**

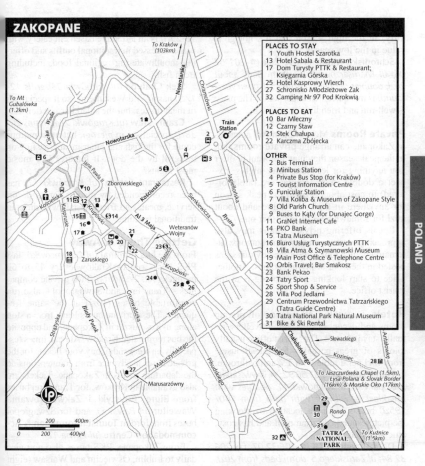

ZAKOPANE

PLACES TO STAY
1 Youth Hostel Szarotka
13 Hotel Sabala & Restaurant
17 Dom Turysty PTTK & Restaurant;
    Księgarnia Górska
25 Hotel Kasprowy Wierch
27 Schronisko Młodzieżowe Żak
32 Camping Nr 97 Pod Krokwią

PLACES TO EAT
10 Bar Mleczny
12 Czarny Staw
21 Stek Chałupa
22 Karczma Zbójecka

OTHER
2 Bus Terminal
3 Minibus Station
4 Private Bus Stop (for Kraków)
5 Tourist Information Centre
6 Funicular Station
7 Villa Koliba & Museum of Zakopane Style
8 Old Parish Church
9 Buses to Kąty (for Dunajec Gorge)
11 GraNet Internet Cafe
14 PKO Bank
15 Tatra Museum
16 Biuro Usług Turystycznych PTTK
18 Villa Atma & Szymanowski Museum
19 Main Post Office & Telephone Centre
20 Orbis Travel; Bar Smakosz
23 Bank Pekao
24 Tatry Sport
26 Sport Shop & Service
28 Villa Pod Jedlami
29 Centrum Przewodnictwa Tatrzańskiego
    (Tatra Guide Centre)
30 Tatra National Park Natural Museum
31 Bike & Ski Rental

POLAND

Chapel, about 1.5km further east along the road to Morskie Oko.

Mt Gubałówka (1120m) offers excellent views over the Tatras and is a favourite destination for tourists who don't feel like *too* much exercise. The **funicular** (one way/return 8/14zł) covers the 1388m-long route in less than five minutes and climbs 300m from the funicular station just north of ul Krupówki. It operates between 9am and 9pm from 1 May to 30 September, but at other times it only runs on weekends. An all-day pass for skiers costs 70zł; a one-day pass at other times for 10 rides costs 50zł.

Places to Stay

Like all seasonal resorts, accommodation prices fluctuate considerably between the low season and high season (December to February and July to August). It is always wise to book accommodation in advance at these peak times, especially on weekends. Rates for the high seasons are listed below.

Camping You'll find that **Camping Nr 97 Pod Krokwią** (☎ 201 22 56; ul Żeromskiego 34; camping per person 15zł, bungalows per person 35-45zł; open year-round) is convenient and clean. Take any bus or minibus to Kuźnice and get off at the Rondo.

Hostels The friendly and homely **Youth Hostel Szarotka** (☎ 206 62 03; ul Nowotarska 45; dorm beds 35-50zł; doubles 140zł; open year-round) is along a noisy road about a 10-minute walk from the town centre. It does get packed (and untidy and sometimes dirty) in the high season and it's not great value in the low season.

Schronisko Młodzieżowe Żak (☎ 201 57 06; ul Marusarzówny 15; dorm beds about 20zł; doubles per person from 35zł; open year-round) is in a quiet area to the south. The place is well-run and friendly.

Private Rooms Most of the travel agencies in Zakopane can arrange **private rooms**, but in the peak season they may not want to offer you anything for less than three nights. Expect a double room (singles are rarely offered) to cost about 50zł in the peak season for anywhere in the town centre and about 40zł for somewhere a little further out.

Locals offering private rooms may also approach you at the bus or train stations; alternatively, just look out for the obvious signs posted in the front of private homes. Another place to start looking and booking is at the tourist office.

Hotels Given the abundance of private rooms and decent hostels, few travellers actually stay in hotels. The tourist office usually knows of great bargains for guesthouses: from 40zł per double with TV and bathroom.

Hotel Sabala (☎ 201 50 92; w www.sabala .zakopane.pl; ul Krupówki 11; doubles with breakfast & without/with bath from 140/195zł) boasts a superb location overlooking the picturesque pedestrian mall and has cosy, attic-style rooms.

Dom Turysty PTTK (☎ 206 32 07, fax 206 32 84; ul Zaruskiego 5; dorm beds from 20zł, doubles 80zł; singles/doubles with bath from 70/120zł) is a renovated former hostel. It offers heaps of different types of rooms, so check a few out first. The **restaurant** on the ground floor is open early for breakfast.

Hotel Kasprowy Wierch (☎/fax 201 27 38; ul Krupówki 50b; doubles with TV & breakfast 200zł) is comfortable, central and cosy.

Places to Eat

The central pedestrian mall, ul Krupówki, is lined with all sorts of eateries. **Bar Mleczny** (ul Krupówki 1; mains from 6zł) is about the only milk bar in town these days.

Downstairs from the Orbis Travel office, **Bar Smakosz** (ul Krupówki 22; mains 8-10zł) offers some outdoor tables and reasonable prices in a central location.

Karczma Zbójecka (ul Krupówki 28; mains 18-25zł) is an attractive basement eatery with waiters dressed in traditional outfits and offering mouthwatering regional food, including fresh fish.

Stek Chałupa (ul Krupówki 33; grills 12-17zł) has a Wild West theme, so it specialises in meat dishes, but the salad bar is extensive.

Czarny Staw (ul Krupówki 2/4; mains 20-38zł) specialises in pierogi, but most patrons come for the fish and other meats roasting on the grill by the door. It features live music most nights.

Restaurant Sabala (ul Krupówki 11) has been recommended by readers for its decor, service, meals and friendly staff who dress in traditional costume.

Getting There & Away

From the **bus terminal** (ul Chramcówki), fast PKS buses run to Kraków every 45 to 60 minutes (9zł, 2½ hours). Two private companies – Trans Frej and Szwagropol – also run comfortable buses (10zł) at the same frequency. These private buses leave from a stop along ul Kościuszki in Zakopane, and opposite the bus terminal in Kraków. At peak times (especially on weekends), buy your tickets for the private buses in advance from counters outside the departure points in Zakopane. Tickets are also available in Kraków: for Trans Frej buses from **Biuro Turystyki i Zakwaterowania Waweltur** (ul Pawia 8); and for Szwagropol buses from **Jordan Tourist Information & Accommodation Centre** (ul Pawia 12).

From Zakopane, PKS buses also go twice daily to Lublin, Oświęcim and Warsaw (eight hours) and once to Przemyśl and Sanok. A couple of buses per week (daily in summer) also go to Budapest (nine hours) in Hungary.

PKS buses – and minibuses from opposite the bus terminal – regularly travel to Lake Morskie Oko (see next section) and on to Polana Palenica. To cross into Slovakia, get off this bus/minibus at Łysa Polana, cross the border on foot and take another bus to Tatranská Lomnica in Slovakia. Buses and minibuses to Kuźnice also leave every 20 minutes.

From the **train station** (ul Chramcówki), trains for Kraków (42zł 2nd-class express, 3½ hours) leave every two hours or so, but avoid the passenger train, which takes up to five hours. Between one and three trains a day go to Częstochowa, Gdynia via Gdańsk, Lublin, Łódź and Poznań, and five head to Warsaw.

THE TATRA MOUNTAINS

☎ 018

The Tatras, 100km south of Kraków, is the highest range of the Carpathian Mountains. Roughly 60km long and about 15km wide, this mountain range stretches across the Polish-Slovak border. A quarter is in Poland and is now mostly part of the Tatra National Park (about 212 sq km). The Polish Tatras contain more than 20 peaks over 2000m, the highest of which is Mt Rysy (2499m).

Cable Car to Mt Kasprowy Wierch

Almost every Polish tourist has made the cable car trip (return 28zł; open 7.30am-8pm daily in summer, 7.30am-4pm in winter) from Kuźnice (3km south of central Zakopane) to the summit of Mt Kasprowy Wierch (1985m). At the end of the trip, you can get off and stand with one foot in Poland and the other in Slovakia. The one-way journey takes 20 minutes and climbs 936m. The cable car normally shuts down for a few weeks in May, June and November, and won't operate if the snow and, particularly, the winds are dangerous.

The view from the top is spectacular (clouds permitting). Two chair lifts transport skiers to and from various slopes between December and April. A small **cafeteria** serves skiers and hikers alike. In the summer, many people return to Zakopane on foot down the Gąsienicowa Valley, and the most intrepid walk the ridges all the way across to Lake Morskie Oko via Pięciu Stawów, a strenuous hike taking a full day in good weather.

If you buy a return ticket, your trip back is automatically reserved for two hours after your departure, so buy a one-way ticket to the top (18zł) and another one down (10zł) if you want to stay longer. Mt Kasprowy Wierch is popular, so the lines for tickets are long; in summer, arrive early and expect to wait. PKS buses and minibuses to Kuźnice frequently leave from Zakopane.

Lake Morskie Oko

One of the most popular destinations in the Tatras is the emerald-green Lake Morskie Oko (Eye of the Sea), among the loveliest in the Tatras. The easiest way to reach the lake is by road from Zakopane. PKS buses and minibuses regularly depart from Zakopane for Polana Palenica (30 minutes), from where a road (9km) continues uphill to the lake. Cars,

bikes and buses are not allowed up this road, so you'll have to walk, but it's not steep (allow about two hours one way). Alternatively, take a horse-drawn carriage (32/15zł uphill/downhill, but very negotiable) to within 2km of the lake. In winter, transport is by horse-drawn four-seater sledge, which is more expensive. The last minibus to Zakopane returns between 5pm and 6pm.

Hiking

If you're doing any hiking in the Tatras get a copy of the *Tatrzański Park Narodowy* map (1:25,000), which shows all hiking trails in the area. Better still, buy one or more of the 14 sheets of *Tatry Polskie* (available at the bookshop in the Dom Turysty PTTK in Zakopane). In July and August these trails can be overrun by tourists, so late spring and early autumn are the best times. Theoretically you can expect better weather in autumn (September to October) when rainfall is lower.

Like all alpine regions, the Tatras can be dangerous, particularly during the snowy time (November to May). Always use common sense and remember that the weather can be unpredictable. Bring proper hiking boots, warm clothing and waterproof rain gear – and be prepared to use occasional ropes and chains (provided along the trails) to get up and down some rocky slopes. Guides are not necessary because many of the trails are marked, but guides can be arranged in Zakopane (see that section for details) for about 180zł per day.

Several picturesque valleys south of Zakopane include the **Dolina Strążyska**. You can continue from the Strążyska by the red trail up to **Mt Giewont** (1909m), 3½ hours from Zakopane, and then walk down the blue trail to Kuźnice in two hours.

Two long and beautiful forested valleys, the **Dolina Chochołowska** and the **Dolina Kościeliska**, are in the western part of the park, known as the Tatry Zachodnie (West Tatras). These valleys are also ideal for cycling. Both valleys are accessible by PKS buses and private minibuses from Zakopane.

The Tatry Wysokie (High Tatras) to the east offer quite different scenery: bare granite peaks and glacial lakes. One great way to get there is to take the cable car to **Mt Kasprowy Wierch** (see earlier) and then hike eastward along the red trail to Mt Świnica (2301m) and on to the Zawrat pass (2159m) – a toughish three to four hours from Mt Kasprowy. From

POLAND

Zawrat, descend northwards to the Dolina Gąsienicowa along the blue trail and then back to Zakopane.

Alternatively, head south (also along the blue trail) to the wonderful **Dolina Pięciu Stawów** (Five Lakes Valley) where there is a mountain refuge 1¼ hours from Zawrat. The blue trail heading west from the refuge passes **Lake Morskie Oko**, 1½ hours from the refuge.

Skiing

Zakopane boasts four major ski areas (and several smaller ones) with over 50 ski lifts. **Mt Kasprowy Wierch** and **Mt Gubałówka** offer the best conditions and most challenging slopes in the area, with the ski season extending until early May. Lift tickets cost about 7zł per ride. Alternatively, you can buy an all-day pass (70zł), which is expensive but allows you to skip the queues. Take the funicular or cable car (see earlier) and purchase your lift tickets on the mountain.

Ski equipment rental is available at all facilities except Mt Kasprowy Wierch. Otherwise, stop off on your way to Kuźnice at the **ski rental** place near the Rondo in Zakopane. Other places in Zakopane, such as **Tatry Sport** (*ul Piłsudskiego 4*) and **Sport Shop & Service** (*ul Krupówki 52a*), also rent ski gear.

Cycling

Cycling is a pleasant way to get around Zakopane and to see some of the less steep parts of the Tatras. Bicycles can be rented at several places in Zakopane, particularly near the Rondo. The **Dolina Chochołowska** and **Dolina Kościeliska**, in the Tatry Zachodnie, are the best places in the park for cycling. The service road, which marks the northern boundary of the park, Droga pod Reglami, also offers a pleasant and picturesque ride.

Places to Stay

Tourists are not allowed to take their own cars into the park; you must walk in, take the cable car or use an official vehicle owned by the park or a hotel/hostel.

Camping is also not allowed in the park, but eight PTTK mountain refuges/hostels provide simple accommodation. Most refuges are small and fill up fast; in midsummer and midwinter they're invariably packed beyond capacity. No one is ever turned away, however, though you may have to crash on the floor if all the beds are taken. Do not arrive

too late, and bring along your own bed mat and sleeping bag. All refuges serve simple hot meals, but the kitchens and dining rooms close early (sometimes at 7pm).

The refuges listed here are open all year, but some may be temporarily closed for renovations or because of inclement weather. Check the current situation at the Dom Turysty PTTK in Zakopane or the regional **PTTK headquarters** (*☎/fax 018-438 610*) in Nowy Sącz.

The easiest refuge to reach from Zakopane is the large and decent **Kalatówki Hostel** (*☎/fax 206 36 44; dorm beds 35zł, doubles with bathroom & breakfast about 145zł*), a 40-minute walk from the Kuźnice cable-car station. About 30 minutes beyond Kalatówki on the trail to Giewont is **Hala Kondratowa Hostel** (*☎ 201 52 14; dorm beds 20-22zł*). It's in a great location and has a great atmosphere, but it is small.

Hikers wishing to traverse the park might begin at the **Roztoka Hostel** (*☎ 207 74 42; dorm beds 22-30zł*), accessible by the bus/minibus to Morskie Oko. An early start from Zakopane, however, would allow you to visit Morskie Oko in the morning and stay at the **Morskie Oko Hostel** (*☎ 207 76 09; dorm beds from 35zł*), or continue through to the **Dolina Pięciu Stawów Hostel** (*☎ 207 76 07; dorm beds from 25zł*). This is the highest (1700m) and most scenically located refuge in the Polish Tatras.

A leisurely day's walk northwest of Pięciu Stawów is the **Murowaniec Hala Gąsienicowa Hostel** (*☎ 201 26 33; dorms 20-30zł*), from where you can return to Zakopane.

Getting There & Away

Refer to the Zakopane section earlier for details about travelling to the national park.

DUNAJEC GORGE

An entertaining and leisurely way to explore the Pieniny Mountains is to go **rafting** on the Dunajec River, which winds its way along the Polish-Slovak border through a spectacular and deep gorge. Adrenalin junkies may be disappointed, however, because this is *not* a white-water rafting experience. In recent years, the course of the river has changed so it now cuts through Slovakia for a few kilometres, but Polish and Slovak immigration officials don't wait on rafts to check passports.

The trip starts at the wharf (Przystan Flisacka) in Kąty, 46km northeast of Zakopane, and finishes at the spa town at Szczawnica. The 17km (2½-hour) raft trip operates between May and October, but only starts when there's a minimum of 10 passengers.

The gorge is an easy day trip from Zakopane. In summer, 10 PKS buses to Kąty leave from a spot along ul Kościeliska. Alternatively, catch a regular bus to Nowy Targ (30 minutes) from Zakopane and one of six daily buses (one hour) to Kąty. From Szczawnica, take the bus back to Zakopane or change at Nowy Targ. Each day, five buses also travel between Szczawnica and Kraków.

To avoid waiting around in Kąty for a raft to fill up, organise a trip at any travel agency in Zakopane or at the tourist office. The cost is about 60zł per person, and includes transport, equipment and guides, as well as a visit to the timber Gothic church in **Debno Podhalanskie** and the ruined castle at **Czorsztyn**.

SANOK
☎ 013 • pop 40,000

Sanok is noted for its unique **Museum of Folk Architecture** (ul Rybickiego 3; admission 8zł; open about 9am-4pm daily), which features architecture from regional ethnic groups. Walk north from the town centre for 1.5km along ul Mickiewicza. The **Historical Museum** (ul Zamkowa 2; admission 6zł; open 9am-3pm daily) is housed in an obvious 16th-century castle and contains Poland's most impressive collection of Ruthenian icons.

Sanok is also an excellent base to explore surrounding villages, many of which have some lovely old churches. The best way to get around is along the marked **Icon Trail**. This **hiking** or **cycling** trail commences in Sanok and completes a 70km loop, passing by 10 village churches as well as picturesque and pristine mountain countryside. More information and maps (in English) are available from the **PTTK office** (☎ 463 21 71; ul 3 Maja 2), near the main square, Plac Św Michała.

Convenient budget accommodation is available at **Hotel Pod Trzema Różami** (☎/fax 463 09 22; ul Jagiellońska 13; singles/doubles with bathroom 85/120zł), about 200m south of the main square. Further south (about 400m) and up the scale is **Hotel Jagielloński** (☎/fax 463 12 08; ul Jagiellońska 49; singles/doubles with bathroom from 85/110zł). Both have an attached **restaurant**.

The **bus terminal** and adjacent **train station** are about 1km southeast of the main

square. Four buses go daily to Przemyśl, and buses and fast trains go regularly to Kraków and Warsaw.

PRZEMYŚL
☎ 016 • pop 70,000

Perched on a hillside overlooking the San River and dominated by four mighty historic churches, Przemyśl ('PSHEH-mishl') is a picturesque town with a sloping and well-preserved **Rynek** (town square). The **tourist office** (☎/fax 675 16 64; ul Ratuszowa) is one block north of the Rynek.

About 350m southwest of the Rynek are the ruins of a 14th-century **castle** (ul Zamkowa), built by Kazimierz Wielki. The **Regional Museum** (Plac Czackiego 3; admission 5zł; open 10.30am-5.30pm Tues & Fri; 10am-2pm Wed, Thur, Sat & Sun) houses a splendid collection of Ruthenian icons. It's about 150m southeast of the Rynek.

Przemyśl has a wide selection of inexpensive accommodation, including the well-kept **Youth Hostel Matecznik** (☎/fax 670 61 45; ul Lelewela 6; dorm beds 18-22zł; open year-round). It's a 20-minute walk northwest down ul Kościuszki from the Rynek or take one of the city buses. **Hotelik Pod Basztą** (☎ 678 82 68; ul Królowej Jadwigi 4; singles/doubles with shared bathroom 60/78zł) is just below the castle.

Bar Rubin (ul Kazimierza Wielkiego 19; mains 9-15zł), 250m east from the Rynek, is inexpensive and friendly.

From Przemyśl, buses run to Lviv (95km) in Ukraine six times a day and regularly to all towns in southeastern Poland. Trains run regularly from Przemyśl to Lublin, Kraków and Warsaw and stop here on the way to/from Lviv. The bus terminal and adjacent train station in Przemyśl are about 1km northeast of the Rynek.

LUBLIN
☎ 081 • pop 360,000

Throughout its history, Lublin has seen repeated invasions by Swedes, Austrians, Russians and Germans. During WWII the Nazis established a death camp at nearby Majdanek, but Lublin does boast happier remnants of its Jewish heritage. The city didn't experience significant wartime damage so the Old Town has retained much of its historic architectural fabric – though parts are in serious need of restoration.

POLAND

POLAND

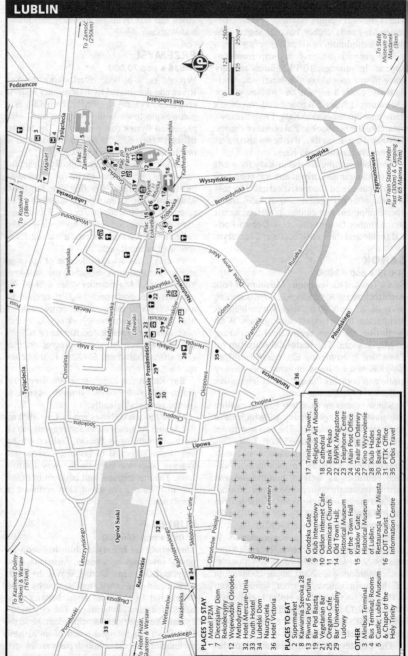

LUBLIN

PLACES TO STAY
1 Motel PZM
7 Diecezjalny Dom
   Rekolekcyjny
12 Wojewódzki Ośrodek
   Metodyczny
32 Hotel Mercure-Unia
33 Youth Hostel
34 Lubelski Dom
   Nauczyciela
36 Hotel Victoria

PLACES TO EAT
2 Supermarket
8 Kawiarnia Szeroka 28
13 Piwnica Pod Fortuną
19 Bar Pod Basztą
25 Vegetarian Bar
29 Oregano Cafe
   Bar Uniwersalny
   Ludowy

OTHER
3 Minibus Terminal
4 Bus Terminal; Rooms
5 Castle; Lublin Museum
   & Chapel of the
   Holy Trinity
6 Grodzka Gate
9 Klub Internetowy
10 Odilon Internet Cafe
11 Dominican Church
14 Old Town Hall;
   Historical Museum
   of the Town Hall
15 Kraków Gate;
   Historical Museum
   of Lublin;
   Restauracja Ulice Miasta
16 LOIT Tourist
   Information Centre
17 Trinitarian Tower;
   Religious Art Museum
18 Cathedral
20 Bank Pekao
23 Telephone Centre
24 EMPiK Megastore
26 Main Post Office
27 Teatr im Osterwy
28 Kino Wyzwolenie
30 Klub Hades
31 Bank Pekao
35 Orbis Travel
   PTTK Office

Information

The **LOIT Tourist Information Centre** (☎ 532 44 12, e loit@inetia.pl; ul Jezuicka 1/3; open 10am-6pm Mon-Sat, 10am-3pm Sun) has helpful English-speaking staff. It's also a good place to pick up maps of Lublin and other Polish and Ukrainian cities. The **PTTK office** (☎ 532 96 54; ul Krakowskie Przedmieście 78; open 9am-4pm Mon-Fri) can help with guides, car rental and organised tours. Both offices sell the handy *Lublin: A Tourist Guidebook* (10zł), ideal if you're going to explore the Old Town in depth.

Bank Pekao (ul Królewska 1 • ul Krakowskie Przedmieście 64) changes travellers cheques and gives cash advances on Visa and MasterCard. Plenty of ATMs can be found on ul Krakowskie Przedmieście, but most kantors seem to be along ul Peowiaków.

The **main post office** (ul Krakowskie Przedmieście 50) is easy to find, but the adjacent **telephone centre** is back from the main road. For cybermail, try **Klub Internetowy** (ul Swietoduska 16), at the back of a small laneway off ul Wodopojna, or **Odilon Internet Café** (Plac po Farze) in the Old Town. Maps and books are available from the **EMPiK Megastore** (ul Krakowskie Przedmieście 16).

Things to See

Old Town The compact historic quarter is centred around the **Rynek**, the irregularly shaped main square surrounding the oversized neoclassical **Old Town Hall** (1781). Downstairs, the **Historical Museum of the Town Hall** (admission 5zł; open 9am-4pm Wed-Sat, 9am-5pm Sun) is about as unexciting as it sounds.

The more enticing **Historical Museum of Lublin** (Plac Łokietka 3; admission 3zł; open 9am-4pm Wed-Sat, 9am-5pm Sun) is inside the 14th-century **Kraków Gate**, the only significant remnant of the medieval fortifications. At noon every day, a bugler comes from nowhere and plays a special tune from on top of the gate. (If you just love bugling, come here for the annual **National Bugle Contest** on 15 August.)

For an expansive **view** of the Old Town, climb the **Trinitarian Tower** (1819), which houses the **Religious Art Museum** (Plac Kathedralny; admission 8zł; open 10am-5pm daily Apr-Oct). According to legend, the metal rooster on top of the tower will crow when a virgin walks past! Next to the tower is the

16th-century **cathedral** (Plac Kathedralny; admission free; open dawn-dusk daily) with its impressive baroque frescoes all over its interior. The painting of the Virgin Mary is said to have shed tears in 1945 so it's a source of pride and reverence for local believers.

Castle Built on a hill northeast of the Old Town is a magnificent 14th-century castle (admission free; open dawn-dusk daily). It was mostly destroyed, so what remains was rebuilt as a prison during the 1820s and remained as such until 1944. During the Nazi occupation, more than 100,000 people passed through this prison before being deported to the death camps. Most of the edifice is now occupied by the **Lublin Museum** (w www.zamek-lublin .pl; admission 6zł; open 9am-4pm Wed-Sat, 9am-5pm Sun). This extensive museum contains a number of sections realting to archaeology, ethnography, decorative art, paintings, arms and coins.

At the eastern end of the castle – but only accessible through the museum entrance – is the exquisite 14th-century **Chapel of the Holy Trinity** (admission 10zł; open 9am-4pm Mon-Sat, 9am-5pm Sun). Its interior is entirely covered with amazing Russo-Byzantine frescoes painted in 1418 – possibly the finest medieval wall paintings in Poland. Admittance to the chapel is restricted, so tickets (which also allow you entry to the museum) must be bought in advance at the museum entrance.

Majdanek About 4km southeast from the Old Town is the **State Museum of Majdanek** (w www.majdanek.pl; admission free; open 8am-6pm daily May-Sept, 8am-3pm Oct-Apr). It commemorates one of the largest death camps in Europe, and was the first such memorial in the world. About 235,000 people, representing 51 nationalities from 26 countries (including over 100,000 Jews), were exterminated here. Barracks, guard towers and barbed wire fences remain as they were more than 50 years ago; even more chilling are the crematorium and gas chambers.

At the entrance to the site is a **Visitors' Centre** (admission free; open 8am-4pm daily May-Sept, 8am-3pm Oct-Apr), where a short film (admission 2zł) can be seen. From the Centre, the marked 'visiting route' (5km) passes the massive stone **Monument of Fight & Martyrdom** and finishes at the domed **mausoleum** holding the ashes of many victims.

This is a vast area so allow at least two hours. And note that children under 14 years old are *not* permitted anywhere in the camp. Trolleybus No 156 from near the Bank Pekao along ul Królewska goes to the entrance of Majdanek.

Pick up the free *Heritage Trail of the Lublin Jews* pamphlet (in English) from the tourist office if you want to walk along the marked **Jewish Heritage Trail** around Lublin.

Places to Stay

Camping Lublin's only camping ground is **Camping Nr 65 Marina** (*☎/fax 744 10 70; ul Krężnicka 6; camping per person/tent 10/10zł, cabins from 65zł; open May-Sept)*. It's serenely located on a lake about 8km south of the Old Town – take Bus No 17, 20 or 21 from the train station to Stadion Sygnał and then catch bus No 25.

Hostels The **Youth Hostel** (*☎/fax 533 06 28; ul Długosza 6; dorm beds 20-32zł; open year-round)* is modest but well run. It's 50m up a lane off ul Długosza and in the heart of the university district.

The **Wojewódzki Ośrodek Metodyczny** (*☎ 532 92 41, fax 534 46 34; ul Dominikańska 5; dorm beds about 40zł)* is good value and often busy, so book ahead. Look for the sign 'Wojewódzki Ośrodek Doskonalenia Nauczycieli' outside.

Diecezjalny Dom Rekolekcyjny (*☎ 532 41 38; ul Podwale 15; dorm beds about 30zł)* is a Catholic institution, so please behave appropriately. There is a 10pm curfew.

Hotels Opposite the train station, **Hotel Piast** (*☎ 532 16 46; ul Pocztowa 2; dorm beds 25zł, singles/doubles with shared bathroom 50/75zł)* is ideal for a late-night arrival or an early-morning departure. However, it's a long way from anywhere else and not in a pleasant part of town. Similarly unappealing are the musty and noisy **rooms** *(singles/doubles 43/60zł)* at the bus terminal (see under Getting There & Away later).

Lubelski Dom Nauczyciela (*☎ 533 82 85, fax 533 03 66; ul Akademicka 4; singles/doubles from 80/83zł, doubles with bath 150zł)* is a teachers hostel. Most of the rooms are tiny, but clean and perfectly acceptable, while the renovated rooms have a bathroom.

The **Motel PZM** (*☎ 533 42 32; ul Prusa 8; singles/doubles with bathroom & breakfast

150/190zł)* is probably the best value in the mid-range. The rooms are modern and the hotel is handy to the castle and bus terminal.

Hotel Victoria (*☎ 532 70 11, fax 532 90 26; ul Narutowicza 58/60; singles with toilet & sink 80zł, singles/doubles with bath & TV 200/300zł)* has been renovated, despite its outward appearances, and is convenient and comfortable. You can probably find better value than the rooms with bath, but it's ideal for the single traveller who can live without a shower. (There is no communal shower either.)

Hotel Mercure-Unia (*☎ 533 72 12; **e** mer .unia@orbis.pl; Al Racławickie 12; singles/doubles with bath, TV & breakfast 376/450zł)* is modern and convenient.

Places to Eat

Patronised by city workers and university students, **Bar Uniwersalny Ludowy** *(ul Krakowskie Przedmieście 60; mains 8-12zł)* is a long-established milk bar.

Bar Pod Basztą *(ul Królewska 6; meals from 8zł)* is a clean and modern place, which is ideal for a budget-priced lunch of hamburgers or *pierogi ruskie*.

A few **takeaway joints** along Plac Zamkowy have set up outdoor (plastic) tables, but more appealing are the atmospheric bars and restaurants lining the Rynek. **Piwnica Pod Fortuna** *(Rynek 8; mains from 28zł)* is one of several charming places to enjoy Polish and Western food, but like most others in this area prices are high.

Restauracja Ulice Miasta *(Plac Łokietka 2; mains from 12zł)* has a great position adjoining the Kraków Gate. Enjoy one of its daily three-course specials (about 20zł) or just relax with a drink after traipsing around the Old Town.

Kawiarnia Szeroka 28 *(ul Grodzka 21; mains about 20zł)* offers artistic charm, Jewish cuisine and economical dining if you stick to soups (6zł) and salads (8zł). Other attractions are the terrace views and live Jewish music on summer weekends.

Oregano Café *(ul Kościuszki; main meals from 14zł)* has a menu in English. Most main courses are pricey, but soups (8zł) and pasta dishes (14zł to 19zł) are great value and tasty.

Vegetarian Bar *(ul Narutowicza 3)* is downstairs along a courtyard off the main road. It's a popular place with young locals who want cheap, meatless food. There is a **supermarket** and **market** near the bus terminal.

Entertainment

The main venue for drama is **Teatr im Osterwy** (ul Narutowicza 17), which features mostly classical plays with some emphasis on national drama. **Klub Hades** (ul Hempla) features live music (including rock and jazz) most nights and a disco on Friday. Ask around the hostels about the best **student nightclubs**. The quaint but unpronounceable **Kino Wyzwolenie** (ul Peowiaków 6) shows recent English-language films.

Getting There & Away

The **bus terminal** (Al Tysiąclecia), opposite the castle, handles most of the traffic. At least one bus a day heads to Białystok, Kraków, Łódź, Olsztyn, Toruń and Zakopane. Each day, six buses also go to Przemyśl, nine head to Zamość and 12 to 15 travel to Warsaw (three hours). From the same terminal, Polski Express offers eight daily buses to Warsaw.

The **Lublin Główny** train station (Plac Dworcowy) is 1.2km south of the Old Town and accessible by trolleybus No 160. At least six trains go daily to Warsaw (45zł 2nd-class express, 2½ hours) and two fast trains travel to Kraków (four hours). Tickets can be purchased at the station or from **Orbis Travel** (☎ 532 22 56; e orbis.lublin@pbp.com.pl; ul Narutowicza 33a).

For more information about transport to places near Lublin, see the Around Lublin section next.

AROUND LUBLIN

Kozłówka

The hamlet of Kozłówka ('Koz-WOOF-kah'), 38km north of Lublin, is famous for its sumptuous late-baroque **palace**, which now houses the **Museum of the Zamoyski Family** (admission 12.50zł; open 10am-4pm Tues, Thur & Fri, 10am-5pm Wed, Sat & Sun Mar-Nov). It featrues original furnishings, ceramic stoves and an unusually large collection of paintings.

The palace is also noted for its **Socialist-Realist Art Gallery** (admission 4zł; same opening hours). It has an overwhelming number of portraits and busts of the revolutionary communist leaders, and also features scenes of farmers, factory workers and family members building communism, as well as communist political and satirical posters.

You can stay in the **palace rooms** (☎ 081-852 83 10, fax 852 83 50), but contact staff ahead about availability and current costs.

From Lublin, two buses head to Kozłówka each morning, usually on the way to Michóv. Only a few buses return directly to Lublin in the afternoon, so check the timetable before visiting the museum. Alternatively, you can catch one of the frequent buses to/from Lubartów, which is regularly connected by bus and minibus to Lublin.

Kazimierz Dolny

☎ 081 • pop 4000

Set on the bank of the Vistula River at the foot of wooded hills, Kazimierz Dolny (usually just known locally as Kazimierz) is a charming village with fine historic architecture and museums. During the week, Kazimierz is a lethargic place, but it has become a fashionable destination and does get unreasonably crowded on summer weekends. (It attracts about 1.5 million visitors each year!) For some, the highlight is the annual **National Festival of Folk Bands & Singers** in June.

From the **bus stop** follow ul Tyszkiewicza (and the crowds) southwest for 100m. Then turn left at the post office to the Rynek town square (about two minutes' walk) or continue straight ahead and over the creek to ul Senatorska. From the Rynek, ul Nadwiślańska heads northwest towards the Vistula and ul Klasztorna heads southwest over the creek to ul Krakowska.

The **PTTK tourist office** (☎/fax 881 00 46; Rynek 27) has local bus timetables posted on the window. It also sells the useful Mapa Turystyczna 2001, which details (in English) the main attractions, and arranges accommodation in private rooms. The small **PKO Bank** (ul Senatorska) may change money; otherwise, try the **post office** (ul Tyszkiewicza 2), which has a foreign-exchange counter.

Things to See & Do All museums listed below are open 10am and 4pm Tuesday to Sunday from May to September and 10am and 3pm from October to April).

The elegant 15th-century **Rynek** is lined with merchants homes. The finest example is the **House of the Celej Family** (ul Senatorska 11/13), which accommodates the **Town Museum** (admission 5zł).

Obvious cobblestoned laneways from the Rynek lead up to the ruins of the 14th-century **castle**, the 13th-century **watch tower** and several abandoned **granaries**. All provide fine **panoramas** of the town and river.

POLAND

Several marked **walking trails** originate at the Rynek. The *Mapa Turystyczna 2001*, available at the tourist office, has details.

At the end of ul Nadwiślańska, there are motorised 'gondolas' offering **boat trips** (7zł, 45 minutes) on the Vistula. From the same point, a boat regularly crosses the river to **Janowiec** from May to September. Otherwise, from a point about 10 minutes' further southwest along the river (also accessible from ul Krakowska), a car/passenger ferry also crosses the river to Janowiec all year. Janowiec is home to an elegant 16th-century castle and the **Castle Museum** *(admission 6zł)*.

About 600m northeast along the river from the end of ul Nadwiślańska is the **Natural Museum** *(ul Puławska 54; admission 5.50zł)*. It's easy to spot along the road from Lublin.

Places to Stay & Eat Although Kazimierz has many places to stay, you may face a shortage on summer weekends. Look for signs outside homes and in shop windows, and expect to pay about 30/50zł per person in low/high season. The tourist office can also help.

Strażnica Youth Hostel *(☎ 881 04 27; ul Senatorska 25; dorm beds with breakfast 28-35zł; open year-round)* boasts a position and building the envy of many other expensive pensions. It's clean and friendly, and should be booked ahead at all times.

Pensjonat Pod Wietrzną Górą *(☎/fax 881 05 43; ul Krakowska 1; singles/doubles with bathroom & breakfast from 85/175zł)* is one of several charming pensions within a stone's throw of the Rynek.

Dziunia *(☎ 0603-635 746; accommodation per person about 50zł; open May-Sept)* offers something a little different – cabins in a boat moored along the river at the end of ul Nadwiślańska. Facilities are shared and basic, however. It's one of several other adjacent boats with a **bar** and **restaurant**.

Piekarnia Artystyczna *(ul Nadrzeczna 6)*, along the southeastern extension of ul Senatorska, sells delicious bread and pastries. It's also an ideal place for a hot drink or ice cream.

Tables and chairs spill out into the village square from several enticing English-style pubs. **Bistro Mars** *(Rynek 11; meals from 10zł)* sells cold beers, tasty *pierogi* and pizzas.

Getting There & Away Kazimierz is an easy day trip from Lublin. Buses to Puławy, via Kazimierz Dolny, leave Lublin every 90

minutes or so, but the hourly minibuses from near the bus terminal in Lublin are quicker and cheaper. From Kazimierz, six buses go directly to Warsaw Stadion station (three hours) and two for Warsaw Zachodnia station.

ZAMOŚĆ
☎ 084 ● pop 65,000

Zamość ('ZAH-moshch') was founded in 1580 by Jan Zamoyski, the chancellor and commander-in-chief of Renaissance Poland, who intended to create an ideal urban settlement and impregnable barrier against Cossack and Tatar raids from the east. During WWII, the Nazis renamed the town 'Himmlerstadt' and imported German colonists to create what Hitler had hoped would become an eastern bulwark for the Third Reich. The Polish inhabitants were expelled from the town and its environs, and most of the Jewish population was exterminated.

Fortunately, the Old Town of Zamość escaped war destruction. Restoration work, which has been inching along for decades, has returned the central square to its former splendour and the Old Town was added to Unesco's World Heritage list in 1992.

Information
The **Tourist Information Centre** *(☎ 639 22 93; e zoit@zamosc.um.gov.pl; Rynek Wielki 13; open 8am-6pm Mon-Fri, 10am-3pm Sat & Sun May-Sept, 8am-4pm Mon-Fri Oct-Apr)* is in the town hall. It sells the handy *Along The Streets of Zamość* (5zł), in English and French, and international bus tickets.

Bank Pekao *(ul Grodzka 2)* has an ATM, cashes travellers cheques and gives advances on Visa and MasterCard. There's a 24-hour **foreign-exchange counter** in Hotel Zamojski. There's also a **kantor** in the Market Hall. The quaint **main post office** *(ul Kościuszki)* is near the cathedral. If you find an Internet centre in the Old Town, please send us an email and let us know! The unnamed **bookshop** *(cnr ul Staszica & ul Bazyliańska)* sells maps.

Things to See
Rynek Wielki is an impressive Renaissance square (exactly 100m by 100m) dominated by the lofty **Town Hall** and surrounded by arcaded burghers' houses. Many of these houses have preserved the fancy stucco design on their interiors and exteriors. The **Museum of Zamość** *(admission 5.50zł; open 9am-2pm*

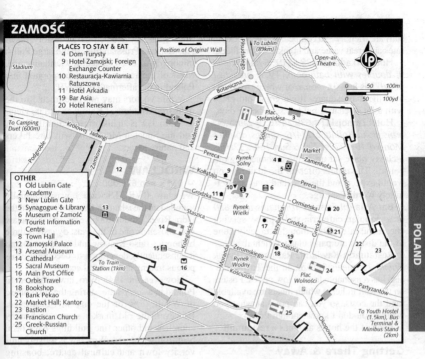

ZAMOŚĆ

PLACES TO STAY & EAT
4 Dom Turysty
9 Hotel Zamojski; Foreign Exchange Counter
10 Restauracja-Kawiarnia Ratuszowa
11 Hotel Arkadia
19 Bar Asia
20 Hotel Renesans

OTHER
1 Old Lublin Gate
2 Academy
3 New Lublin Gate
5 Synagogue & Library
6 Museum of Zamość
7 Tourist Information Centre
8 Town Hall
12 Zamoyski Palace
13 Arsenal Museum
14 Cathedral
15 Sacral Museum
16 Main Post Office
17 Orbis Travel
18 Bookshop
21 Bank Pekao
22 Market Hall; Kantor
23 Bastion
24 Franciscan Church
25 Greek-Russian Church

POLAND

Mon-Fri) is based in two of the loveliest buildings at Rynek Nos 24 and 26.

Southwest of the square is the mighty 16th-century **cathedral** *(ul Kolegiacka; admission free; open dawn-dusk daily)*, which holds the tomb of Zamoyski in the chapel to the right of the high altar. In the grounds, the **Sacral Museum** *(admission 2.50zł; open 10am-4pm Mon-Fri, 10am-1pm Sat & Sun May-Sept, 10am-1pm Sat & Sun only Oct-Apr)* features various robes, paintings and sculptures.

Zamoyski Palace (not open to the public) lost much of its character when it was converted into a military hospital in the 1830s. Nearby, the **Arsenal Museum** *(ul Zamkowa 2; admission 5.50zł; open 9am-4pm Mon-Fri)* is an unremarkable military museum. To the north of the palace stretches a beautifully landscaped **park**.

Before WWII, Jews accounted for 45% of the town's population (of 12,000) and most lived in the area north and east of the palace. The most significant Jewish architectural relic is the Renaissance **synagogue** *(cnr ul Zamenhofa & ul Bazyliańska)*, built in the 1610s. It's now used as a public library, so you can go inside and see the decorative walls.

On the eastern edge of the Old Town is the antiquated **Market Hall**. Behind it is the best surviving **bastion** from the original wall that encircled Zamość.

Places to Stay & Eat

Camping Duet *(☎/fax 639 24 99; ul Królewej Jadwigi 14; camping per person/tent 6.50/10zł, single/double bungalow 75/93zł; open year-round)* is about 1km west of the Old Town. It also has tennis courts, and a **restaurant**, swimming pool, sauna and Jacuzzi.

The **Youth Hostel** *(☎ 627 91 25; ul Zamoyskiego 4; dorm beds 22-30zł; open July & Aug)* is in a school about 1.5km east of the Old Town and not far from the bus terminal. It's basic but adequate.

Dom Turysty *(☎ 639 26 39; ul Zamenhofa 11; doubles with shared bathroom 45zł)* can't quite decide which of several alternative names to use, but everyone knows it as simply Dom Turysty. The rooms are unexceptional but the price and location are attractive.

Hotel Renesans *(☎ 639 20 01, fax 638 51 74; ul Grecka 6; singles/doubles Mon-Fri 128/183zł, Sat & Sun 105/152zł)* offers spacious, modern rooms with a fridge, desk and separate seating area. It's in a top location and staff are friendly and competent. The weekend rates are great value and breakfast is included.

Hotel Arkadia (☎ 638 65 07; Rynek Wielki 9; doubles with bathroom, TV & breakfast 100zł) has just six rooms, of which two overlook the main square. It's a grand old place with a lot of charm, but has seen better days.

Hotel Zamojski (☎ 639 25 16; e zamosc@ orbis.pl; ul Kołłątaja 2/4/6; singles/doubles Mon-Fri 192/272zł, Sat & Sun 164/232zł) is a classy place set up in three connecting old houses. The rooms offer all the luxuries you would expect, and the weekend rates are definitely worth a splurge.

Bar Asia (ul Staszica 10; mains from 8zł) is a popular cafeteria-style place serving cheap and tasty food, though strangely none of the dishes are particularly Oriental.

Restauracja-Kawiarnia Ratuszowa (Rynek Wielki 13; meals 9-10zł), in the Town Hall, also has reasonable food at low prices. Posters on the wall indicate which meals are available (and the cost), so you can point at what you want if you don't know enough Polish.

Each of the hotels also has a **restaurant**.

Getting There & Away

Buses are normally more convenient and quicker than trains. The **bus terminal** (ul Hrubieszowska) is 2km east of the Old Town and linked by frequent city buses. Daily, two fast buses go to Kraków, four or five to Warsaw (five hours) and nine to Lublin (two hours).

Far quicker, and surprisingly cheaper, are the minibuses that travel every 30 minutes between Lublin and Zamość. They leave from the minibus stand across the road from the bus terminal in Zamość and from a disorganised corner northwest of the bus terminal in Lublin.

From the **train station**, about 1km southwest of the Old Town, several slow trains head to Lublin (about four hours) every day and three slow trains plod along to Warsaw (six hours). **Orbis Travel** (☎ 639 30 01; ul Grodzka 18) sells train tickets.

Silesia

Silesia in southwestern Poland includes Upper Silesia, the industrial heart of the country; Lower Silesia, a fertile farming region with a cultural and economic centre in Wrocław; and the Sudeten Mountains, a forested range that runs for over 250km along the Czech border. Silesia has spent much of its history under Austrian and Prussian rule, so the large Polish minority was often subject to Germanisation. Most of the region was reincorporated into Poland in the aftermath of WWII.

While visitors may not be attracted to the industrial wonders of Katowice and its vicinity, Wrocław is an historic and dignified city, and the Sudeten Mountains will lure hikers and nature lovers.

WROCŁAW
☎ 071 • pop 675,000

Wrocław ('VROTS-wahf') was originally founded on the island of Ostrów Tumski in the Odra River. About 1000 years ago, Wrocław was chosen as one of the Piast dynasty's three bishoprics (also Kraków and Kołobrzeg) and it subsequently developed to become a prosperous trading and cultural centre.

However, in 1945 Wrocław returned to Poland in a sorry state; during the final phase of WWII, 70% of the city was destroyed. However, the old market square and many churches and other fine buildings have been beautifully restored. Wrocław is a lively university town and cultural centre, boasting many theatres, museums and annual festivals.

Information

The **Tourist Information Centre** (☎ 344 11 11; W www.wroclaw.pl; Rynek 14; open 9am-7pm Mon-Fri, 9am-5pm Sat) is helpful and sells some souvenirs. A **tourist information counter** (☎ 369 54 97) is in the Wrocław Główny train station. The practical *Welcome to Wrocław* magazine (in English or German) is available free from the tourist offices, as well as travel agencies and upmarket hotels.

Bank Pekao (ul Oławska 2) cashes travellers cheques and gives advances on Visa and MasterCard. There are kantors *all* over the city centre and a number in the bus and train stations. ATMs are also plentiful, including at the train station.

The **main post office** (Rynek) conveniently overlooks the main square. The **Cyber & Tea Tavern** (ul Kuźnicza 29) offers visitors the chance to surf the Net while indulging in a drink or two. Alternatively, try the busy little **W Sercu Miasta** down a laneway in the middle of the Rynek.

The best place for maps and guidebooks is **Księgarnia Podróżnika** (ul Wita Stwosza

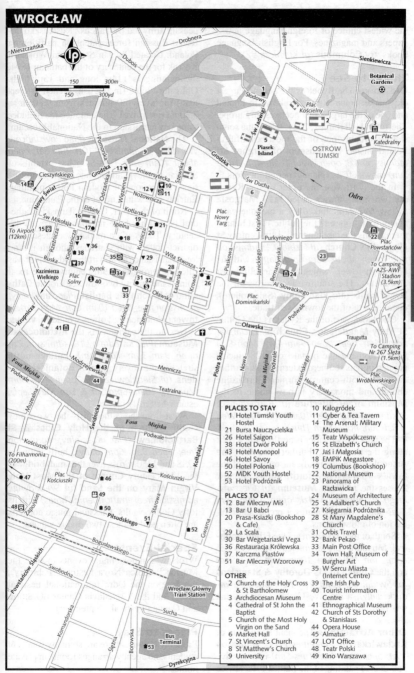

WROCŁAW

PLACES TO STAY
1 Hotel Tumski Youth Hostel
21 Bursa Nauczycielska
26 Hotel Saigon
38 Hotel Dwór Polski
43 Hotel Monopol
46 Hotel Savoy
50 Hotel Polonia
52 MDK Youth Hostel
53 Hotel Podróżnik

PLACES TO EAT
12 Bar Mleczny Miś
13 Bar U Babci
20 Prasa-Ksiazki (Bookshop & Cafe)
29 La Scala
30 Bar Wegetariaski Vega
36 Restauracja Królewska
37 Karczma Piastów
51 Bar Mleczny Wzorcowy

OTHER
2 Church of the Holy Cross & St Bartholomew
3 Archdiocesan Museum
4 Cathedral of St John the Baptist
5 Church of the Most Holy Virgin on the Sand
6 Market Hall
7 St Vincent's Church
8 St Matthew's Church
9 University

10 Kalogródek
11 Cyber & Tea Tavern
14 The Arsenal; Military Museum
15 Teatr Współczesny
16 St Elizabeth's Church
17 Jaś i Małgosia
18 EMPiK Megastore
19 Columbus (Bookshop)
22 National Museum
23 Panorama of Racławicka
24 Museum of Architecture
25 St Adalbert's Church
27 Ksiegarnia Podróżnika
28 St Mary Magdalene's Church
31 Orbis Travel
32 Bank Pekao
33 Main Post Office
34 Town Hall; Museum of Burgher Art
35 W Sercu Miasta (Internet Centre)
39 The Irish Pub
40 Tourist Information Centre
41 Ethnographical Museum
42 Church of Sts Dorothy & Stanislaus
44 Opera House
45 Almatur
47 LOT Office
48 Teatr Polski
49 Kino Warszawa

POLAND

19/20). **EMPiK Megastore** *(Rynek 50)* offers the widest choice of foreign-language newspapers and magazines. For English-language books, try **Columbus** *(ul Kuźnicza 57)*.

Things to See

Old Town The **Rynek** is the second-largest old market square (after Kraków) in Poland and one of the largest (3.7 hectares) in Europe. The **Town Hall** (built 1327–1504) on the south side is certainly one of the most beautiful in Poland. Inside, the **Museum of Burgher Art** *(admission 4zł; open about 10am-4pm Tues-Sun)* shows off its splendid period interiors.

In the northwestern corner of the Rynek are two small houses called **Jaś i Małgosia** *(ul Św Mikołaja)* linked by a baroque gate. (They're not open to the public.) Just behind them looms the monumental, 14th-century **St Elizabeth's Church** *(ul Elżbiety 1; admission free; open about 8am-6pm daily)* with its 83m-high tower, which you can climb for city **views**. The southwestern corner of the Rynek spills into **Plac Solny** (Salt Square), once the site of the town's salt trade.

One block east of the Rynek is the Gothic **St Mary Magdalene's Church** *(ul Łaciarska; admission free; open 9am-4pm Mon-Sat)* with a Romanesque portal from 1280 incorporated into its southern external wall. Further east, the 15th-century former Bernardine church and monastery is now home to the **Museum of Architecture** *(ul Bernardyńska 5; admission 5zł; open 10am-4pm Tues, Wed & Sat-Sun, noon-6pm Thur)*.

The university quarter is north of the Rynek along the river bank. Further around is **The Arsenal**, the most significant remnant of the town's 15th-century fortifications. It now houses the **Military Museum** *(ul Cieszyńskiego 9; admission 4zł; open 10am-4pm Tues-Sun)*, which features a predictable collection of old weapons.

South of the Old Town are the **Ethnographical Museum** *(ul Kazimierza Wielkiego 35; admission 4zł; open 10am-4pm Tues-Sun)* and the **Church of Sts Dorothy & Stanislaus** *(ul Świdnicka; admission free; open dawn-dusk daily)*, a massive Gothic complex that was built in 1351.

Other Attractions The giant **Panorama of Racławicka** *(ul Purkyniego 11; admission 19zł; open 9am-4pm Tues-Sun)* is a massive 360-degree painting of the Battle of Racławice

(1794). In this battle near Kraków the Polish peasant army led by Tadeusz Kościuszko defeated Russian forces intent on partitioning Poland. Created by Jan Styka and Wojciech Kossak for the centenary of the battle in 1894, the painting is 114m long and 15m high. Obligatory tours (in English, French or German) run every 30 minutes from 9.30am to 3.30pm (inclusive). The entrance fee includes same-day admission to the National Museum.

The **National Museum** *(Plac Powstańców Warszawy 5; admission 10zł, free Sat; open about 10am-4pm Tues-Sun)* has exhibits of Silesian medieval art and one of the country's finest collections of modern Polish painting. Entry is free with a ticket to the Panorama.

North of the river, Ostrów Tumski (Cathedral Island) has been inhabited since the 8th century. Today it's a markedly ecclesiastical district dotted with churches, though it's no longer an island (an arm of the Odra River was filled in during the 19th century). The focal point is the mighty two-towered Gothic **Cathedral of St John the Baptist** *(Plac Katedralny; admission free; open 10am-6pm Mon-Sat)*. A **tower** (admission 5zł) offers wonderful **views**.

Next to the cathedral is the **Archdiocesan Museum** *(Plac Katedralny 16; admission 2zł; open 9am-3pm Tues-Sun)*. Further north stretches the lovely, restful **Botanical Gardens** *(ul Sienkiewicza 23; open 8am-6pm Mon-Fri, 10am-6pm Sat & Sun May-Sept)*, established in 1811.

West from the cathedral is the two-storey Gothic **Church of the Holy Cross & St Bartholomew** *(Plac Kościelny; admission free; open 9am-6pm daily)*, built between 1288 and 1350. Cross over the small bridge to the 14th-century **Church of the Most Holy Virgin Mary on the Sand** *(ul Św Jadwigi; admission free; erratic opening hours)* with its lofty Gothic vaults. Classical music concerts are often held in these two divine venues.

Special Events

Wrocław's major annual events include the Musica Polonica Nova Festival (February), the Jazz on the Odra International Festival (May) and the Wratislavia Cantans Oratorio and Cantata Festival (September).

Places to Stay

Probably because there are so many transient students, no agency arranges rooms in private homes.

Camping Camping Nr 267 Ślęża *(☎/fax 343 44 42; ul Na Grobli 16/18; camping per person/tent 14/3zł, double bungalows with shared/private bathroom 75/150zł; open year-round)* is on the bank of the Odra, 2km east of the Old Town. No local transport goes all the way, so take tram No 4 to Plac Wróblewskiego from the train station and walk about 1km further east.

Camping AZS-AWF Stadion *(☎ 348 46 51; ul Paderewskiego 35; camping per person/ tent 10/4zł, double bungalows with shared bathroom 41zł; open May-Sept)* is near the Olympic stadium in Park Szczytnicki, 4km east of the Old Town. Take tram No 9 from the train station.

Hostels Not far from the train station, **MDK Youth Hostel** *(☎ 343 88 56;* **e** *mdk .kopernik.wp.pl; ul Kołłątaja 20; dorm beds about 25zł)* is in a grand (but poorly signed) mustard-coloured building. It's almost always full, so book ahead.

Hotel Tumski Youth Hostel *(☎ 322 60 99;* **w** *www.hotel-tumski.com.pl; ul Słodowy 10; dorm beds from 25zł)* is convenient and staff are friendly. It's good value, but some rooms are cramped. It's attached to the bright orange Hotel Tumski.

Bursa Nauczycielska *(☎ 344 37 81; ul Kotlarska 42; singles/doubles with shared bathroom 55/90zł)* is a teachers hostel ideally located just one block northeast of the Rynek. Rooms are clean and well kept.

Hotels Unless stated otherwise, all hotels listed below offer rooms with a bathroom and TV, and rates include breakfast. Many places offer substantial discounts for weekends (Saturday and Sunday night) and some may offer the same discount on Friday night if requested.

Hotel Podróżnik *(☎ 373 28 45; ul Sucha 1; singles/doubles 90/130zł)* is on the 1st floor of the bus terminal. It's obviously convenient and noisy, yet surprisingly pleasant.

Hotel Polonia *(☎ 343 10 21;* **e** *polonia@ odratourist.pl; ul Piłsudskiego 66; singles/ doubles Mon-Fri from 155/188zł, Sat & Sun from 116/142zł)* is handy to the train and bus stations. It's a bit musty and old-fashioned but good value.

Hotel Savoy *(☎/fax 372 53 79; Plac Kościuszki 19; singles/doubles Mon-Fri about 110/130zł, Sat & Sun about 90/110zł)* is in an excellent spot midway between the train station and Old Town. It's good value, especially on weekends. Breakfast is an extra 10zł.

Hotel Saigon *(☎/fax 344 28 81; ul Wita Stwosza 22/23; singles/doubles Mon-Fri 155/188zł, Sat & Sun 139/169zł)* has some bizarre Chinese-style decorations in the foyer, but the rooms are bland and unexciting. It's convenient but a little noisy. The highlight is the outstanding breakfast.

Beside the Opera House, **Hotel Monopol** *(☎ 343 70 41;* **e** *monopol@orbis.pl; ul Modrzejewskiej 2; singles/doubles from 115/150zł, with bath from 180/260zł)* is particularly good value and guests have the dubious honour of staying in the same hotel that was once frequented by the infamous Austrian former house painter with the funny moustache.

Hotel Dwór Polski *(☎/fax 372 34 15, ul Kiełbaśnicza 2; singles/doubles Mon-Fri 300/ 360zł, Sat & Sun 220/280zł)* is worth a splurge – but book ahead. This gorgeous place set back from the road is nicely furnished with old-fashioned beds. Guests can luxuriate in the large bathrooms or the (free) sauna.

Places to Eat

For hearty, hot dishes at cheap prices, **Bar Mleczny Wzorcowy** *(ul Piłsudskiego 86; mains from 8zł)* is a typical milk bar with a long menu (in Polish).

Bar Mleczny Miś *(ul Kuźnicza 45-47; mains 8-12zł)*, in the university area, is basic but popular with frugal university students.

Bar U Babci *(ul Więzienna 16; meals about 12zł)* is a cosy, family-run place serving honest Polish food at prices that suit students. Only four or five dishes are offered every day, but each is delicious.

Bar Wegetariański Vega *(Rynek 1/2; snacks from 5zł, meals about 12zł)* is in the centre of the Rynek and offers the best value in the Old Town. It doesn't have any outdoor tables, but the healthy treats that are on offer are excellent value. It's open from 8am for a breakfast of muesli or omelettes.

Most places around the Rynek are classy, with outdoor tables and impeccably dressed waiters, but expect to pay *at least* 20zł for a main course.

Restauracja Królewska *(Rynek 5; mains from 28zł)*, in the gastronomic complex of the Dwór Polski (Polish Court), continues to be Wrocław's top spot for traditional Polish cuisine in a historic setting. **Karczma Piastów** *(ul Kiełbaśnicza; mains from 18zł)*, at the back of

POLAND

the same complex, also serves authentic Polish food, but is cheaper and less formal.

La Scala *(Rynek 38; mains from 25zł)* offers authentic Italian food and, according to those in the know, the best cappuccino in town. It's pricey, but worth a splurge.

Prasa-Ksiaźki *(ul Kuźnicza; open 10am-7pm Mon-Fri, 10am-2pm Sat)* is a bookshop-cum-café. It's ideal for meeting locals while getting a caffeine fix.

Entertainment

Wrocław is an important cultural centre, so there's always something going on somewhere. Check out the (free) bimonthly *Wrocław Cultural Guide* for details (in English) of what's on and where. It's available from the tourist offices and upmarket hotels.

The Irish Pub *(Plac Solny 5)* is certainly one of the more authentic Celtic-style drinking establishments in Poland, but like most places around the Rynek it's expensive. There's live music most nights.

Kalogródek *(ul Kuźnicza 29)* is a poky beer garden in a concrete jungle, but popular among students. The surrounding streets are packed with other cheap and friendly haunts.

Teatr Polski *(ul Zapolskiej 3)* is the major mainstream city venue and stages classic Polish and foreign drama. **Teatr Współczesny** *(ul Rzeźnica 12)* tends more towards contemporary productions.

Filharmonia *(ul Piłsudskiego 19)* hosts concerts of classical music, mostly on Friday and Saturday night.

Kino Warszawa, at the back of a laneway off ul Piłsudskiego, shows recent English-language films.

Getting There & Away

Orbis Travel *(☎ 343 26 65; Rynek 29)* and **Almatur** *(☎ 344 47 28; ul Kościuszki 34)* offer the usual services. If you're travelling to/from Wrocław on Friday, Saturday or Sunday, book your bus or train ticket as soon as possible because thousands of itinerant university students travel to/from the city most weekends.

Refer to the Getting There & Away section earlier in this chapter for information about international buses and trains to/from Wrocław.

Air Every day, LOT flies about eight times between Wrocław and Warsaw and once between Wrocław and Frankfurt-am-Main. Most days, SAS also flies to Copenhagen

(April to October only) and Eurowings goes to Munich (all year). Tickets for all airlines can be bought at the **LOT office** *(☎ 343 90 31; ul Piłsudskiego 36)*.

The airport is in Strachowice, about 12km west of the Old Town. Bus No 406 links the airport with Wrocław Główny train station and bus terminal, via the Rynek.

Bus The **bus terminal** *(ul Sucha 11)* is just south of the main train station. Several PKS buses a day go to Warsaw, Poznań, Częstochowa and Białystok (seven hours). Polski Express also offers several buses a day to Warsaw. For most travel, however, the train is more convenient.

Train The **Wrocław Główny** station *(ul Piłsudskiego 105)* was built in 1856 and is a historical monument in itself. Every day, fast trains to Kraków depart every one or two hours, and several InterCity and express trains (62zł 2nd class) go to Warsaw (six hours), usually via Łódź. Wrocław is also regularly linked by train to Poznań, Częstochowa, Szczecin and Lublin.

SUDETEN MOUNTAINS

The Sudeten Mountains (Sudety) run for over 250km along the Czech-Polish border. The Sudetes feature dense forests, amazing rock formations and deposits of semiprecious stones, all of which can be explored along any of the extensive network of trails for **hiking** or **mountain biking**. The highest part of this old and eroded chain is Mt Śnieżka (1602m). Both the following towns offer the normal tourist facilities.

Szklarska Poréba in the northwestern end of the Sudetes offers superior facilities for **hiking** and **skiing**. It's at the base of Mt Szrenica (1362m), and the town centre is at the upper end along ul Jedności Narodowej. The small **tourist office** *(☎/fax 075-717 24 49; [w] szklarskaporeba.pl; ul Jedności Narodowej 3)* has accommodation information and maps. Nearby, several trails begins at the intersection of ul Jedności Narodowej and ul Wielki Sikorskiego. The red trail goes to Mt Szrenica (two hours) and offers a peek at Wodospad Kamieńczyka, a spectacular waterfall.

Karpacz to the southeast has a bit more to offer in terms of nightlife, though it attracts fewer serious mountaineers. It's loosely clustered along a 3km road winding through

Łomnica Valley at the base of Mt Śnieżka. The **tourist office** (*☎/fax 075-761 97 16; ul Konstytucji 3 Maja 25A*) should be your first point of call. To reach the peak of Mt Śnieżka on foot, take one of the trails (three to four hours) from Hotel Biały Jar. Some of the trails pass by one of two splendid postglacial lakes, Mały Staw and Wielki Staw.

The bus is the fastest way of getting around the region. Every day from Szklarska Poręba, about four buses head to Wrocław and one slow train plods along to Warsaw. From Karpacz, get a bus to Jelenia Góra, where plenty of buses and trains go in all directions.

For the Czech Republic, take a bus from Szklarska Poręba to Jakuszyce, cross the border on foot to Harrachov (on the Czech side) and take another bus from there.

Wielkopolska

Wielkopolska ('Great Poland') is the cradle of the Polish nation. In the 6th and 7th centuries AD, Slavic tribes settled the flatlands in this region, from which they eventually derived the name Polanians, or 'inhabitants of the plain'. Despite the royal seat moving to Kraków in 1038, Wielkopolska remained as Poland's most important province until the second partition in 1793, when it was annexed to Prussia. The region then passed back and forth between Polish and German hands several times, culminating in the liberation battles of 1945, which devastated the area. Today, Poznań has been rebuilt and is the region's major commercial and cultural centre.

POZNAŃ
☎ 061 ● pop 610,000

Poznań, midway between Berlin and Warsaw, is the focal point of early Polish history. In the 9th century the Polanian tribes built a wooden fort on the island of Ostrów Tumski, and from 968 to 1038 Poznań was the de facto capital of Poland. By the 15th century Poznań was already a trading centre and famous for its fairs. This commercial tradition was reinstituted in 1925, and today the fairs – held for a few days each month – dominate the economic and cultural life of the city.

Information
The **Tourist Information Centre** (*☎/fax 855 33 79; Stary Rynek 59/60; open 9am-5pm Mon-Fri, 10am-2pm Sat*) is helpful. The **City Information Centre** (*☎ 851 96 45; ul Ratajczaka 44; open 10am-7pm Mon-Fri, 10am-5pm Sat & Sun*) handles bookings for cultural events. The free bi-monthly *Welcome to Poznań* magazine is available at most of the decent hotels.

Bank Pekao (*ul Św Marcin 52/56 ● ul 23 Lutego*) is probably the best place for travellers cheques and credit cards. A few of the kantors in the city centre are shown on the map; there's also one in the bus terminal and another (open 24 hours) in the train station.

For old-fashioned communication visit the **main post office** (*ul Kościuszki 77*) or the **telephone centre** (*Stary Rynek*). Check your emails at the **Internet Café** (*Plac Wolności 8*) or at **Klik** (*ul Szkolna – enter from off ul Jaskółcza*), a funky pub-café-Internet centre that offers some pleasing privacy.

EMPiK Megastore (*Plac Wolności*) offers the largest choice of foreign magazines and newspapers. For maps and Lonely Planet guidebooks, visit the excellent **Turystyczna Globtrotter** (*ul Żydowska*) or **Glob-Tour** inside the train station.

Things to See
Old Town The Old Market Square, **Stary Rynek**, has been beautifully restored to its historic shape. The focal point is the Renaissance **Town Hall** (built 1550–60) with its decorative facade facing east. In accordance with a strange custom, every day at noon two metal goats high above the clock butt their horns together 12 times. Inside the building, the **Poznań Historical Museum** (*admission 5.50zł, free Sat; open about 10am-4pm Mon-Tues, Fri & Sun, noon-6pm Wed*) reveals the city's past through splendid period interiors.

The square also features the **Wielkopolska Military Museum** (*Stary Rynek 9; admission 5.50zł; open about 10am-3pm Tues-Sun*) and the unique **Museum of Musical Instruments** (*Stary Rynek; 45/47; admission 5.50zł; open 11am-5pm Tues-Sun*). The **Archaeological Museum** (*ul Wodna 27; admission 3zł; open about 10am-4pm Tues-Sun*) features displays about the ancient history of the region, as well as some Egyptian artefacts.

The 17th-century **Franciscan Church** (*ul Franciszkańska 2; admission free; open about 8am-8pm daily*), one block west of the Rynek, has an ornate baroque interior, complete with wall paintings and rich stucco work. On a hill

POLAND

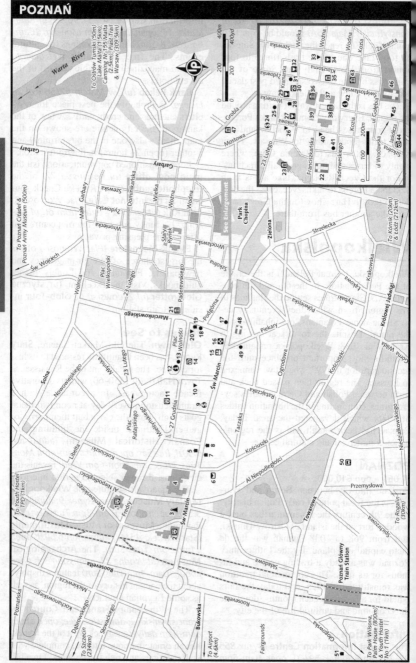

POZNAŃ

POZNAŃ

PLACES TO STAY		4	Palace of Culture	31	Turystyczna Globtrotter
5	Hotel Lech	6	Main Post Office		(Bookshop)
7	Hotel Royal	9	Bank Pekao	32	O'Morgan's Irish Pub
8	Hotel Wielkopolska	11	Teatr Polski	34	Deja Vu
19	Hotel Rzymski	12	City Information Centre	35	Museum of Musical
28	Dom Turysty	13	EMPiK Megastoreq		Instruments
51	Biuro Zakwaterowania	14	Internet Cafe	36	Town Hall; Poznań Historical
	Przemysław (Private Rooms)	15	Kino Muza		Museum
		16	Shopping Centre Pasaz	37	Souvenir Stalls
PLACES TO EAT		17	Kantor	38	Wielkopolska Military
10	Spaghetti Bar Piccolo	18	Orbis Travel		Museum
20	Bar Caritas	21	National Museum:	39	Weigh House
26	Spaghetti Bar Piccolo		Paintings & Sculpture	41	Kantor
33	Pizzeria di Luigi		Gallery	42	Tourist Information Centre
40	Restauracja Sphinx	22	Franciscan Church	43	Archaeological Museum
45	Bar Wegetariański; Bar	23	Museum of Applied Arts	44	Klik (Internet Cafe)
	Pasibruzch	24	Bank Pekao	46	Parish Church of St
		25	Kantor		Stanislaus
OTHER		27	Galaxy Klub; Bee Jay's	47	Wielkopolska Ethnographic
1	Teatr Wielki	29	El Otro Muchos Patatos		Museum
2	Filharmonia	30	Telephone Centre;	48	St Martin's Church
3	Monument to the Victims		Gospoda Pod	49	LOT Office
	of June 1956		Koziołkami	50	Bus Terminal

POLAND

above the church is the **Museum of Applied Arts** (admission 3zł; open about 10am-4pm Tues, Wed, Fri-Sun).

The nearby **National Museum: Paintings & Sculpture Gallery** (Al Marcinkowskiego 9; admission 10zł, free Sat; open about 10am-5pm Tues-Sun) holds a typical collection of art, including medieval church woodcarving and Polish paintings.

Two blocks south of Stary Rynek is the large, pink baroque **Parish Church of St Stanislaus** (ul Gołębia 1; admission free; open erratic hours) with a three-naved interior with monumental altars built in the mid-17th century. A short stroll to the southeast is the **Wielkopolska Ethnographic Museum** (ul Grobla 25; admission 5.50zł; open about 10am-4pm Tues, Wed, Fri-Sun), which features a worthwhile collection of woodcarving and traditional costumes of the area.

Other Attractions About 1.3km north of the Old Town is the 19th-century Prussian **Poznań Citadel**, where 20,000 German troops held out for a month in February 1945. The fortress was destroyed by artillery fire but a park was laid out on the site, which incorporates the **Poznań Army Museum** (Al Armii Poznań; admission 4zł; open 9am-4pm Tues-Sat, 10am-4pm Sun).

The massive 1956 strike by the city's industrial workers was the first major popular upheaval in communist Poland. The strike was cruelly crushed by tanks, leaving 76 dead and over 600 wounded. In a park in the new city centre, the moving **Monument to the Victims of June 1956** commemorates the event.

In **Park Wilsona**, less then 1km southwest of the train station, is the **Palm House** (ul Matejki 18; admission 5.50zł; open about 9am-4pm Tues-Sun). This huge greenhouse (built in 1910) contains 19,000 species of tropical and subtropical plants, including a remarkable collection of giant cacti and towering bamboo trees.

Ostrów Tumski is 1km east of the Old Town (take any eastbound tram from Plac Wielkopolski). This river island is dominated by the monumental, double-towered **Poznań Cathedral** (ul Ostrów Tumski), originally built in 968 but rebuilt several times since. The Byzantine-style **Golden Chapel** (1841), and the **mausoleums** of Mieszko I and Bolesłaus the Brave, are behind the high altar. Opposite the cathedral is the 15th-century **Church of the Virgin Mary** (ul Panny Marii 1/3), possibly the purest Gothic building in the city.

Further out from Ostrów Tumski and about 2.5km east of the Old Town is **Lake Malta**. This 64-hectare artificial lake is a favourite weekend destination for Poles, and holds sailing regattas, outdoor concerts and other events in summer. The carnival atmosphere is enhanced by games, food and souvenir stands.

To get to the lake hop on tram No 1, 4 or 8 from Plac Wielkopolski.

Special Events
Poznań's trade fairs are its pride. The largest take place in January, June, September and October. A dozen additional smaller fairs also occur throughout the year. Major cultural events include the St John's Fair (June) and the Malta International Theatre Festival (late June).

Places to Stay
During trade fairs, the rates of Poznań's hotels and private rooms tend to increase (and in some cases double) and accommodation may be difficult to find. (The hard part is knowing when a fair is actually taking place.) The tourist office will help you find a room if you're having trouble; otherwise, it pays to book ahead. Prices given in this section are for off-fair periods.

Camping On the northeastern shore of Lake Malta, **Camping Nr 155 Malta** (☎ 876 62 03, fax 867 62 83; ul Krańcowa 98; camping per person/tent 7/5zł, single/double bungalows 150/180zł; open year-round) is 3.5km east of the Old Town. One reader claimed that this was the 'most beautiful camping ground in Poland', but it's not accessible by public transport (so take a taxi).

Hostels A 15-minute walk southwest of the train station along ul Głogowska, **Youth Hostel No 1** (☎/fax 866 40 40; ul Berwińskiego 2/3; dorm beds 16zł; open year-round) is adjacent to Park Wilsona. It's small and basic, but fills up fast.

Youth Hostel TPD (☎/fax 848 58 36; ul Drzymały 3; dorm beds 16-28zł; open year-round) is newer and more comfortable. It's 3km north of the train station (take tram No 11), and 3km northwest of the Old Town (tram No 9).

The tourist office should know which **student hostels** and **worker hostels** are open, but most of these are in the outer suburbs.

Private Rooms In the main hall of the train station, **Glob-Tour** (☎/fax 866 06 67) offers cheap singles from 40zł to 50zł and doubles from 50zł to 60zł. The agency is open 24 hours, but private rooms can only be arranged between 7am and 10pm daily.

Not too far from the train station is **Biuro Zakwaterowania Przemysław** (☎ 866 35 60; W www.przemyslaw.com.pl; ul Głogowska 16; open 8am-6pm Mon-Fri, 10am-2pm Sat) who can organise singles/doubles starting from 55/75zł.

Hotels The rates for each hotel listed below include breakfast. Many places offer substantial discounts on weekends, but not during trade fairs.

Dom Turysty (☎/fax 852 88 93; W www .domturysty-hotel.com.pl; Stary Rynek 91; dorm beds about 60zł, singles/doubles 125/182zł, with bath 190/310zł) is set in an 18th-century former palace. It's a bit musty and old-fashioned, but boasts the best location in Poznań. The breakfast is hardly worth getting up for, however.

Hotel Lech (☎/fax 853 01 51; ul Św Marcin 74; singles/doubles Mon-Fri 181/270zł, Sat & Sun 122/220zł) is stuck in the 1960s, but the bathrooms are modern and spotless.

Hotel Wielkopolska (☎ 852 76 31, fax 851 54 92; ul Św Marcin 67; singles/doubles 130/170zł, with bath & TV 180/230zł) is better value. The rooms are overdue for some renovation, but it's quiet and comfortable.

The **Hotel Royal** (☎ 858 23 00; W www .hotel-royal.com.pl; ul Św Marcin 71; singles/doubles Mon-Fri 290/370zł Sat & Sun, 232/296zł) has been extensively renovated. This gorgeous place set back from the main road offers rooms with a huge bed and excellent bathroom. It's certainly worth a splurge, especially on weekends.

Hotel Rzymski (☎ 852 81 21, fax 852 89 83; Al Marcinkowskiego 22; singles/doubles Mon-Fri 182/246zł, Sat & Sun 164/221zł) doesn't look like too much from the outside, but it offers large, comfortable rooms in a good central location.

Places to Eat
You can point at what you want without resorting to your phrasebook at **Bar Caritas** (Plac Wolności 1; mains 8-12zł), a cheap and convenient milk bar.

Bar Pasibruzch (ul Wrocławska 23; lunch specials 8zł) is another cafeteria with plenty of tasty, hot food waiting to be dolloped onto your plate.

Bar Wegetariański (ul Wrocławska 21; meals from 10zł), a funky vegetarian place in a cellar off the main road. Staff are happy to recommend one or more of their delicious healthy wonders.

Gospoda Pod Koziołkami (*Stary Rynek 95; main meals from 20zł*) is worth a splurge. If you don't want any of the typically heavy grills, try the salad bar and lighter meals offered upstairs.

Spaghetti Bar Piccolo (*ul Rynkowa 1 • ul Ratajczaka 37; meals about 4zł*) is the best of several similar places offering plastic dishes of pasta and a modest choice of salads at remarkably cheap prices.

Pizzeria di Luigi (*ul Woźna; pizzas 10zł, pasta 10-12zł*) serves some of the tastiest pasta northeast of Italy. The owners may not be Italian, but the food is authentic and the setting is cosy.

Bee Jay's (*Stary Rynek 87; meals from 15zł*), next to the Galaxy Klub, is one of the more reasonably priced eateries around the main square. It offers passable Indian meals and pricey Mexican fare, among other items – all listed on a menu in English. There's live music on weekends.

Restaurant Sphinx (*Stary Rynek 77; mains about 15zł*) is part of a nationwide chain that offers grills with the trimmings, and a menu in English. The line for the colossal takeaway burgers is predictably long.

Entertainment

O'Morgan's Irish Pub (*ul Wielka 7*) is *the* place to go for a beer or two, but beware: any drinking or eating establishment around or near the Rynek is way overpriced.

Déjà Vu (*ul Woźna 21*) is a very small but cosy bar, popular with students who take advantage of discounted drinks.

Galaxy Klub (*Stary Rynek 85*) is a well-frequented place to let your hair down (if you have any). **El Otro Muchos Patatos** (*Stary Rynek 92; entrance opposite Dom Turysty*) features taped and live Latin music (sometimes even performed by the Polish owners!) most nights.

Teatr Polski (*ul 27 Grudnia 8/10*) is the major centre for plays and dances, while **Teatr Wielki** (*ul Fredry 9*) is where opera and ballet are more likely to be held. **Filharmonia** (*ul Św Marcin 81*) offers classical concerts at least every Friday night.

Kino Muza (*Św Marcin 30*) is one of several cinemas offering current films in comfortable surroundings.

Getting There & Away

LOT flies five times a day between Warsaw and Poznań. Also, LOT has flights from Poznań to Hanover and Düsseldorf most days; LOT and SAS fly daily to Copenhagen; and Austrian Airlines goes regularly to Vienna. Tickets for all airlines are available from the **LOT** office (☎ *858 55 00; ul Piekary 6*) or from **Orbis Travel** (☎ *853 20 52, Al Marcinkowskiego 21*). The airport is in the western suburb of Ławica, 7km from the Old Town and accessible by bus Nos 59 and 78.

The **bus terminal** (*ul Towarowa 17*) is a 10-minute walk east of the train station. Bus services are poor, however, and really only useful for regional towns, such as Kórnik and Rogalin (see Around Poznań next). Buses travel from Poznań four or five times a day to Łódź, once to Toruń and thrice to Wrocław, but the trains are better.

The busy **train station** (*ul Dworcowa 1*) is well set up. Every day, it offers nine trains to Kraków (74zł 2nd-class express, 6½ hours), a dozen to Szczecin (half of which continue to Świnoujście), seven to Gdańsk, four to Toruń and seven to Wrocław. About 15 trains a day also head to Warsaw (46zł 2nd-class express, five hours), including several Inter-City services (three hours).

For information about international buses and trains to/from Poznań, refer to the Getting There & Away section earlier in this chapter.

AROUND POZNAŃ

Kórnik, about 20km southeast of Poznań, is noted for the **Castle of Kórnik**. Inside, the **museum** (*ul Zamkowa 5; admission 8zł; open about 9am-4pm Tues-Sun*) displays fabulous 19th-century furnishings and interiors. Behind the castle is the large, English-style **Arboretum** (*admission 5zł; open 9am-5pm daily May-Sept, 9am-3pm Oct-Apr*), with some 3000 plant species. Buses connect Poznań with Kórnik every 30 minutes or so.

The popular and well-established **Trasa Kornicka** (Kornik Route) is an 80-km **hiking** and **cycling** trail from Poznań to Szreniawy via Kórnik, Rogalin and the Wielkopolska National Park. Details are available from the tourist office in Poznań.

Rogalin, about 30km south of Poznań, boasts the large 18th-century baroque **Palace of Rogalin**, which houses an extensive **museum** (*admission 6.50zł; open 10am-4pm*

Tues-Sun). Some visitors come just to wander around the **gardens** surrounding the castle. Buses travel about every two hours between Poznań and Rogalin, but use several different routes. Buses between Kórnik and Rogalin are infrequent, however, so check the timetables if you plan to visit both destinations in one day from Poznań.

THE PIAST TRAIL

A popular tourist route winding east from Poznań to Inowrocław is the Piast Trail (Szlak Piastowski), which includes places and monuments relating to early Polish history.

Lake Lednica

Lake Lednica is 30km east of Poznań on the road to Gniezno. The **Museum of the First Piasts** *(admission 5.50zł; open about 10am-5pm Tues-Sun; closed 16 Nov-14 Feb)* is on the lakeshore. From the museum, the island of **Ostrów Lednicki**, which was the site of a stronghold built by the first Piasts in the 10th century, is accessible by boat between mid-April and early November. Visitors can see the remains of a church and a stone palace, where researchers claim Duke Mieszko I was probably baptised in 966.

About 2km south of the museum, and 500m north of the Poznań-Gniezno road is the **Wielkopolska Ethnographic Park** *(admission 6.50zł; open about 9am-5pm Tues-Sun; closed 16 Nov-14 Feb)*. It features some 19th-century rural architecture from the region.

From Poznań, take one of the eight daily buses (fewer on weekends) to Gniezno via Pobiedziska – *not* via Kostrzyn. Buy your ticket for Lednogóra, which is the closest village on this road, and ask the driver to let you off.

Gniezno

Gniezno ('GNYEZ-no'), 50km east of Poznań, is commonly considered the first capital of the Polish nation. About 1000 years ago an archbishopric was established here, and in 1025 Boleslaus the Brave was crowned in the local cathedral to become the first Polish king.

The first stop for all visitors should be the **tourist office** *(☎ 428 41 00; ul Tumska 12)*, which is one block northwest of the Rynek (old town square).

Gniezno's pride and joy is the **cathedral** *(ul Tumska; admission free; open about 9am-5.30pm Mon-Sat, 1pm-5.30pm Sun)*, a large, twin-towered Gothic structure rebuilt in the

14th century. The **Museum of the Origins of the Polish State** *(ul Kostrzewskiego 1; admission 5.50zł; open 10am-5pm Tues-Sun)*, on the western side of Lake Jelonek from the Rynek, recounts some regional history.

Internat Medycznego Studium Zawodowego *(☎ 426 34 09; ul Mieszka I 27; singles/doubles with shared bathroom 35/ 70zł)* is excellent value. It's located approximately 200m south of the southeastern end of the mall (ul Tumska).

The **City Hotel** *(☎ 425 35 35; Rynek 15; doubles without/with bathroom 85/122zł)* is in a prime location. The rooms are cramped, but it's good value.

The train and bus stations are both 1km southeast of the Rynek and accessible from along the extension of ul Tumska. Trains run regularly to Poznań and Toruń, and buses travel to Poznań via Lake Lednica.

Pomerania

Pomerania (Pomorze) stretches along the Baltic coast from the German frontier to the lower Vistula Valley in the east. The region rests on two large urban pillars: Szczecin at its western end and Gdańsk to the east. Between them stretches the sandy coastline dotted with beach resorts. Further inland is a wide belt of rugged, forested lakeland sprinkled with medieval castles and towns, and the charming city of Toruń.

TORUŃ

☎ 056 • pop 208,000

Toruń is a historic city, characterised by its narrow streets, burgher mansions and mighty Gothic churches. The compact Old Town was built on the slopes of the wide Vistula and is one of the most appealing in central Poland. Toruń is famous as the birthplace of Nicolaus Copernicus, who spent his youth here and after whom the local university is named.

In 1233 the Teutonic Knights established an outpost in Toruń. Following the Thirteen Years' War (1454–66), the Teutonic Order and Poland signed a peace treaty here, which returned to Poland a large area of land stretching from Toruń to Gdańsk. In the following centuries, Toruń suffered a fate similar to that of the surrounding region: Swedish invasions and Prussian domination until the early 20th century.

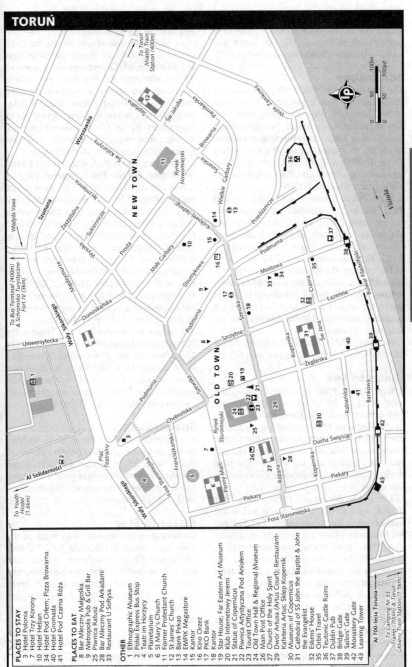

TORUŃ

To Toruń
Miasto Train
Station (600m)

NEW TOWN

Rynek
Nowomiejski

OLD TOWN

Rynek
Staromiejski

Vistula

To Youth
Hostel
(1.6km)

To Bus Terminal (400m)
& Schronisko Turystyczne
Fort IV (3km)

To Camping Nr 33
Tramp (700m) & Toruń
Główny Train Station (1.5km)

Al 700-lecia Torunia

0   50   100m
0   50   100yd

PLACES TO STAY
1 Hotel Polonia
7 Hotel Trzy Korony
10 Hotel Heban
34 Hotel Pod Orłem; Pizza Browarna
40 Hotel Gromada
41 Hotel Pod Czarną Różą

PLACES TO EAT
8 Bar Mleczny Małgoska
9 Metropolis Pub & Grill Bar
25 Piwnica Ratusz
28 Bar Mleczny Pod Arkadami
33 Restaurant U Sołtysa

OTHER
1 Ethnographic Museum
2 Polski Express Bus Stop
4 Teatr im Horzycy
5 Planetarium
6 St Mary's Church
11 Former Protestant Church
12 St James' Church
13 Bank Pekao
14 EMPIK Megastore
15 Kantor
16 Kino Orzeł
17 PKO Bank
18 Kantor
19 Star House; Far Eastern Art Museum
20 Klub Internetowy Jeremi
21 Statue of Copernicus
22 Piwnica Artystyczna Pod Aniołem
23 Tourist Office
24 Old Town Hall & Regional Museum
26 Main Post Office
27 Church of the Holy Spirit
29 Dwór Artusa (Artus Court); Restauracja-
   Kafeteria Artus; Sklep Kopernik
30 Museum of Copernicus
31 Cathedral of SS John the Baptist & John
   the Evangelist
32 Eskens' House
35 Orbis Travel
36 Teutonic Castle Ruins
37 Dublin Pub
38 Bridge Gate
39 Sailors' Gate
42 Monastery Gate
43 Leaning Tower

Fortunately, the city suffered little damage during WWII, so Toruń is the best-preserved Gothic town in Poland. The Old Town was added to Unesco's World Heritage list in 1997.

Information

The **tourist office** (☎ 621 09 31; ⓦ *www.it .torun.com.pl; Rynek Staromiejski 1; open about 9am-4pm Mon-Sat, also 9am-1pm Sun May-Sept)* is certainly worth a visit. There's also a **tourist information counter** inside the main train station. The free, glossy *Toruń Tourist & Business Guide*, available from most decent hotels, lists a few worthwhile eateries and nightclubs.

Bank Pekao *(ul Wielkie Garbary 11)* and **PKO Bank** *(ul Szeroka)* cash travellers cheques and give cash advances on Visa and MasterCard. A couple of handy **kantors** are shown on the map. There's no shortage of ATMs along ul Różana and ul Szeroka.

The **main post office** *(Rynek Staromiejski)* overlooks the main square, while **Klub Inter-netowy Jeremi** *(Rynek Staromiejski 33)* is above the Irish Pub. Books and maps are available from the **EMPiK Megastore** *(ul Królowej-Jadwigi)*.

As usual, **Orbis Travel** (☎ 655 48 63; *ul Mostowa 7)* can help with air and train tickets.

Things to See

Rynek Staromiejski is unquestionably the focal point of the Old Town. The massive 14th-century brick **Old Town Hall** now shelters the **Regional Museum** *(admission 8.50zł; open 10am-4pm Tues-Sun)*. It features some historical exhibits and regional artwork, and you can climb to the top of the 40m-high **tower** (from May to September only) for the fine **views**.

The richly decorated, 15th-century **Star House**, with its Baroque facade and spiral wooden staircase, contains the **Far Eastern Art Museum** *(Rynek Staromiejski 35; admission 5.50zł; open 10am-4pm Tues-Sun)*.

Just off the northwestern corner of the square is the late-13th-century **St Mary's Church** *(ul Panny Marii; admission free; open dawn-dusk daily)*, a Gothic building with magnificent 15th-century stalls. Behind the church is the **Planetarium** *(ul Franciszkańska 15; admission 8zł; open 9am-6pm Tues-Fri, 11am-5pm Sat & Sun)*. Rather dated presentations take place six times a day from Monday to Friday and three times on both Saturday and

Sunday. A few shows are offered in English and German during the summer.

In 1473, Copernicus was born in the brick Gothic house that now houses the disappointing **Museum of Copernicus** *(ul Kopernika 15/17; admission 9zł, free Sun; open 10am-4pm Tues-Sun)* stretched over two adjoining buildings. A short audiovisual 'sound & light' presentation (included in the ticket) about Copernicus' life in Toruń is shown every 30 minutes. A soundtrack in English – and even Esperanto! – is available during summer.

One block east is the **Cathedral of SS John the Baptist & John the Evangelist** *(ul Żeglarska; admission free; open 8am-6pm daily)*, started around 1260 but not completed until over 200 years later. Its massive **tower** houses Poland's second-largest bell (after the Wawel Cathedral in Kraków). Behind the church, **Eskens' House** *(ul Ciasna 4/6; admission 4.50zł; open 10am-4pm Wed-Sun)* has old weapons and modern Polish paintings. Further east are the ruins of the **Teutonic Castle** *(ul Przedzamcze; admission free; permanently open)*, destroyed in 1454 by angry townsfolk protesting against the oppressive regime.

In a park just north of the Old Town is the **Ethnographic Museum** *(ul Wały Sikorskiego 19; admission 8zł; open about 10am-4pm daily, closed Mon Oct-Mar)*. It showcases many traditional customs, costumes and weapons. An English-speaking guide will cost an extra 30zł per small group.

Special Events

Toruń breaks out of its comparative slumber during the Probaltica Music & Art Festival of Baltic States (May), the Contact International Theatre Festival (May/June) and the Music and Architecture International Summer Festival (July and August).

Places to Stay

Camping A five-minute walk west of the main train station is **Camping Nr 33 Tramp** *(☎/fax 654 71 87; ul Kujawska 14; camping per person/tent 10/15zł, doubles/4-person cabins with shared bathroom from 71/95zł; open mid-May–mid-Sept)*. The cabins and rooms are simple and it's alarmingly close to the train line.

Hostels The **Youth Hostel** (☎ 654 45 80; *ul Św Józefa 22/24; dorm beds 15-25zł; open year-round)* is 2km northwest of the Rynek.

It's accessible on bus No 11 from the main train station and the Old Town.

Schronisko Turystyczne Fort IV (☎ 655 82 36, fax 655 81 34; ul Chrobrego; dorm beds from 20zł; open year-round) is charmingly located in an old Prussian fort. Although not convenient, it's relatively easy to reach on bus No 14 leaving from the bus terminal and main train station.

Hotels All hotels listed (except the Polonia) are charming, old-fashioned pensions, which are both convenient and quiet. Unless stated otherwise, each offers rooms with a bathroom and TV, and rates include breakfast.

Hotel Polonia (☎ 622 30 28; Plac Teatralny 5; singles/doubles 150/180zł) has been recently renovated (at last!), but is no longer a bargain. It is, however, still a good mid-range option.

Hotel Trzy Korony (☎/fax 622 60 31; Rynek Staromiejski 21; singles/doubles 90/110zł, with bath 150/190zł) is not quite as nice as the outside would suggest. It does boast a superb location, however, overlooking the main square so ask for a room with a view.

For good value try the **Hotel Pod Orłem** (☎/fax 622 50 24; W www.hotel.torun.pl; ul Mostowa 17; singles/doubles 110/140zł, breakfast per person 15zł). The rooms are smallish and have squeaky wooden floors, and some contain poky bathrooms, but the service is good and the scrumptious breakfast will take your mind off its other (minor) faults.

Hotel Pod Czarna Róża (☎/fax 621 96 37; ul Rabiańska 11; singles/doubles 170/210zł) is extremely cosy. The rooms feature lovely antique-style furniture, and staff are pleasingly friendly and helpful.

The **Hotel Heban** (☎ 652 15 55; W www.hotel-heban.com.pl; ul Małe Garbary 7; doubles 250zł) is over a classy restaurant of the same name. Rooms are lovingly furnished and have a modern bathroom. It's worth a splurge, but not if you're travelling alone.

Hotel Gromada (☎ 622 60 60; ul Żeglarska 10/14; singles/doubles Mon-Thur 185/240zł, Fri-Sun 150/195zł) is not great value compared to the others, except on weekends. Dinner in the classy restaurant attached costs a reasonable 30zł (guests only).

Places to Eat

Bar Mleczny Małgośka (ul Szczytna 10/12; meals from 7zł) is a clean and convenient milk bar that also offers passable hamburgers and pizzas.

Bar Mleczny Pod Arkadami (ul Różana 1; meals from 8zł), just off Rynek Staromiejski, is much the same.

Several decent Italian restaurants are along ul Mostowa. **Pizza Browarna** (ul Mostowa 17; mains 10-12zł), under Hotel Pod Orłem, is very popular with locals. Nearby, **Restaurant u Sołtysa** (ul Mostowa; mains from 15zł) serves traditional Polish food.

Metropolis Pub & Grill Bar (ul Podmurna 28; mains 9-12zł) is a dark but inviting place (complete with indoor waterfall!) that serves pasta, pizza and Polish food. Daily specials (from 6zł) are advertised on sandwich boards along ul Szeroka.

Piwnica Ratusz (Rynek Staromiejski; mains about 12zł) is probably the best-value eatery around the main square. Look out for the daily specials (5zł to 8zł).

Restaurant-Kafeteria Artus (Rynek Staromiejski 6; soups 5zł, mains 9-12zł), inside Dwór Artusa (Artus Court), is the most charming place in Toruń. Set up inside an elegant indoor courtyard, the prices are not as high as the setting would suggest. The menu is in English and German.

Toruń is famous for its gingerbread (pierniki), produced here since, well, forever. It comes in a variety of shapes, including figures of local hero Copernicus, and can be bought at **Sklep Kopernik** (Rynek Staromiejski 6) in Dwór Artusa.

Entertainment

Piwnica Artystyczna Pod Aniołem (Rynek Staromiejski 1), set in a splendid spacious cellar in the Old Town Hall, offers live music some nights. Other great places for a drink include the quasi-Irish **Dublin Pub** (ul Mostowa) and **Piwnica Ratusz** (see Places to Eat), which offers a few outdoor tables in the square and a huge cavernous area downstairs.

Teatr im Horzycy (Plac Teatralny 1) is the main stage for theatre performances, while **Dwór Artusa** (Artus Court; Rynek Staromiejski 6) often presents classical music.

Kino Orzez (ul Strumykowa 3) shows recent films.

Getting There & Away

The **bus terminal** (ul Dąbrowskiego) is a about a 10-minute walk north of the Old Town. It offers regular services to regional

POLAND

villages of minimal interest to travellers and surprisingly few long-distance buses. **Polski Express** *(Al Solidarności)* has hourly services to Warsaw (four hours) and two a day to Szczecin. Refer to the Getting There & Away section earlier in this chapter for information about international buses to/from Toruń.

The main **Toruń Główny** train station *(Al Podgórska)* is on the opposite side of the Vistula River and linked to the Old Town by bus Nos 22 and 27. Some (but not all) trains stop and finish at the more convenient **Toruń Miasto** train station, about 500m east of the New Town.

From the Toruń Główny station, there are services to Poznań (three a day), Gdańsk (six), Kraków (three), Łódź (seven), Olsztyn (nine), Szczecin (one) and Wrocław (two). Five trains a day head towards Warsaw (51zł 2nd-class express, four hours). Trains travelling between Toruń and Gdańsk often change at Bydgoszcz, and between Toruń and Kraków you may need to get another connection at Inowrocław.

GDAŃSK

☎ 058 • pop 475,000

Gdańsk is an important port and shipbuilding centre along the Baltic coast. In existence since the 9th century, Gdańsk came to the fore after the Teutonic Knights seized it in 1308. Within half a century it became a thriving medieval town known as Danzig.

In 1454, many inhabitants staged an armed protest against economic restrictions imposed by the rulers and destroyed the Teutonic Knights' castle and pledged loyalty to the Polish monarch. In return, Gdańsk was given numerous privileges by the Poles, including a monopoly over the grain trade and a degree of political independence. So, by the mid-16th century, Gdańsk controlled three-quarters of Poland's foreign trade; it was then the country's largest city and the Baltic's greatest port.

In 1793 Gdańsk fell under Prussian dominion and this lasted until the 20th century, when, in the aftermath of WWI, it became the virtually autonomous Free City of Danzig. The importance of this strategic port was emphasised when the Nazis bombarded Westerplatte and, thereby, started WWII. The war devastated most of Gdańsk, but the historic quarters have been almost completely rebuilt.

Today, Gdańsk is most famous as the birthplace (in 1980) of the Solidarity trade union, which was the catalyst for the fall of communism in Poland and in the rest of the former Soviet bloc.

Information

The helpful **PTTK office** *(☎/fax 301 13 43; e pttkgda@gdansk.com.pl; ul Długa 45; open 10am-6pm daily)* is conveniently opposite the Main Town Hall. The free monthly magazines *Welcome to Gdańsk, Sopot, Gdynia* and *Gdańsk, Gdynia, Sopot: What, Where, When* are annoyingly hard to find; try the top-end hotels in the city centre.

Bank Gdański *(Wały Jagiellońskie 14/16 • Długi Targ 14/16)* also has other offices at central locations. **Bank Pekao** *(ul Garncarska 23)* will provide cash advances on Visa and MasterCard. Some **kantors** are located on the map; one is open 24 hours in the main train station. There are plenty of ATMs all over the city centre.

For snail mail, go to the **main post office** *(ul Długa 22)*. The poste restante is in the same building but the entrance is through the back door from ul Pocztowa. Mail should be addressed to: Your Name, Poste Restante, ul Długa 22/28, 80-801 Gdańsk 50, Poland. Next to the main entrance of the post office is the **telephone centre** *(ul Długa 26)*.

The most convenient place to check your emails is **Rudy Kot** *(ul Garncarska 18/20)*. It's also a decent pub that offers inexpensive meals and occasionally features live music. Otherwise, try **Jazz 'n' Java** *(ul Tkacka)*, which also offers music and drinks.

Almatur *(☎ 301 24 24; Długi Targ 11)* and **Orbis Travel** *(☎ 301 45 44; ul Podwale Staromiejskie 96/97)* both provide the usual services to travellers. The PTTK office also offers (expensive) walking tours around the Old Town, and tours of Oliwa, Westerplatte, Gdynia and Sopot.

English Books Unlimited *(ul Podmłyńska 10)* has the best choice of English-language books and dictionaries. The widest selection of foreign-language press is in the **EMPiK Megastore** *(ul Podwale Grodzkie 8)*, across the road from the main train station; a smaller **EMPiK** *(Długi Targ)* is in the Main Town.

Things to See

Main Town The richest architecture and most thorough restoration are found in this historic quarter. Ul Długa (Long Street) and Długi Targ (Long Market) form the city's main thoroughfare; both are now pedestrian malls. They are known collectively as the **Royal Way**, along which Polish kings traditionally paraded during their periodic visits. They entered the Main Town through the **Upland Gate** (built in the 1770s on a 15th-century gate), passed through the **Golden Gate** (1614) and proceeded east to the Renaissance **Green Gate** (1568). This gate was intended to be the kings' residence though none of them stayed here (they preferred the cosier houses nearby).

Inside the towering Gothic **Main Town Hall** (ul Długa 47) is the **Gdańsk History Museum** (admission 5zł, free Wed; open about 10am-4pm Tues-Sun). It, well, provides a history of Gdańsk, including photos of the damage caused during WWII.

Near the Town Hall is **Neptune's Fountain** (1615), behind which stands the **Artus Court Museum** (ul Długi Targ 43/44; admission 5zł, free Wed; open 10am-4pm Tues-Sat, 11am-4pm Sun) where local merchants used to congregate. The adjacent **Golden House** (1618) has perhaps the richest facade in town. A little further west, the 18th-century **Dom Uphagena** (ul Długa 12; admission 5zł, free Sun; open about 10am-4pm Tues-Sun) features the sort of ornate furniture typical of the houses along this old street.

Two blocks north of Green Gate along the waterfront is the 14th-century **St Mary's Gate**, which houses the **Archaeological Museum** (ul Mariacka 25/26; admission 5.50zł, free Sat; open about 10am-4pm Tues-Sun). It features plenty of displays about amber, and offers **river views** from the adjacent tower. Through this gate, the most picturesque street in Gdańsk – **ul Mariacka** (St Mary's St) – is lined with 17th-century burgher houses.

At the end of ul Mariacka is the gigantic 14th-century **St Mary's Church** (admission free; open about 8am-8pm daily), possibly the largest old brick church in the world. Inside, the 14m-high astronomical clock is certainly unique: its maker had his eyes gouged out to prevent him from creating a rival. The fabulous **panorama** from the 82m tower is well worth the climb (405 steps). West along ul Piwna (Beer St) is the Dutch Renaissance **Arsenal** (1609), now occupied by a market.

Further north along the waterfront is the 15th-century **Gdańsk Crane**, the largest of its kind in medieval Europe and capable of hoisting loads of up to 2000kg. It's now part of the

Central Maritime Museum (ul Szeroka 67/68 & ul Ołowianka 9; open 10am-4pm Tues-Sun). The museum has several sections either side of the river, including the obvious **Sołdek Museum Ship**. A ticket to each of the three sections costs 5zł or 12zł to the entire museum complex.

Old Town Almost totally destroyed in 1945, the Old Town has never been completely rebuilt apart from a handful of churches. The largest and most remarkable of these is **St Catherine's Church** (ul Wielke Młyny; admission free; open about 8am-6pm Mon-Sat), Gdańsk's oldest church (begun in the 1220s). Opposite, the **Great Mill** (ul Wielke Młyny) was built by the Teutonic Knights in around 1350. It used to produce 200 tonnes of flour per day and continued to operate until 1945. More recently, it has been converted into a modern shopping complex.

Right behind St Catherine's is **St Bridget's Church** (ul Profesorska 17; admission free; open about 10am-6pm Mon-Sat). Formerly Lech Wałęsa's place of worship, the church was a strong supporter of the shipyard workers and its priest often spoke about political issues during his sermons in the 1980s.

At the entrance to the Gdańsk Shipyards to the north stands the **Monument to the Shipyard Workers** (Plac Solidarności). It was erected in late 1980 in memory of 44 workers killed during the riots of December 1970. Down the street is the evocative **Roads to Freedom Exhibition** (ul Doki 1; admission 5zł, free Wed; open 10am-4pm Tues-Sun), also known as the **Solidarity Museum**.

Old Suburb This section of Gdańsk was also reduced to rubble in 1945. Little of the former urban fabric has been reconstructed, except for the former Franciscan monastery that now houses the **National Museum** (ul Toruńska 1; admission 12zł, free Sat; open 10am-5pm Tues-Sun). The museum is famous for its Dutch and Flemish paintings, especially Hans Memling's 15th-century Last Judgement. If the museum looks deserted, open the gate yourself; a member of staff will soon find you and demand a ticket.

Adjoining the museum is the former Franciscan **Church of the Holy Trinity** (ul Św Trójcy; admission free; open about 10am-8pm Mon-Sat), which was built at the end of the 15th century.

POLAND

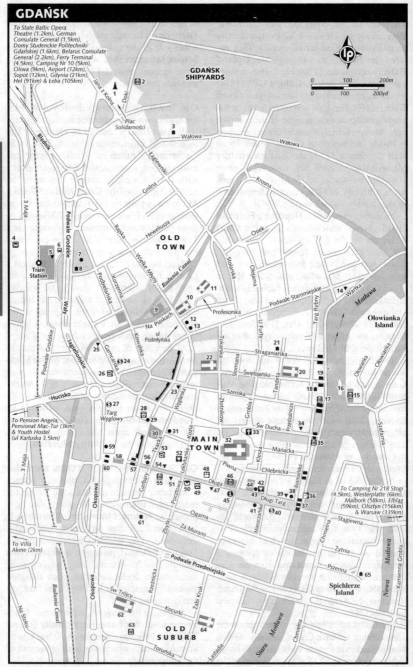

GDAŃSK

PLACES TO STAY		6	Bus to Westerplatte	36	Dock (for Excursion
3	Youth Hostel	7	EMPiK Megastore		Boats)
8	Grand Tourist (Private	9	Great Mill	37	Green Gate
	Rooms)	10	St Catherine's Church	38	EMPiK
18	Hotel Hanza	11	St Bridget's Church	40	Bank Gdański
21	Dom Aktora	12	English Books Unlimited	41	Almatur
61	Dom Harcerza	13	Orbis Travel	42	Jazz Club
65	Hotel Novotel Gdańsk	15	Central Maritime	43	Golden House
			Museum	44	Artus Court Museum;
PLACES TO EAT		16	Sołdek Museum Ship		Neptune's Fountain
5	McDonald's	17	Central Maritime Museum;	45	PTTK Office
14	Restauracja Kubicki		Gdańsk Crane	46	Main Town Hall; Gdańsk
23	Bar Mleczny Turystyczny	19	St John's Gate		History Museum
25	Green Way	20	St John's Church	48	Kino Helikon; Kino Neptun
34	Pub Duszek	22	St Nicholas' Church	49	Telephone Centre
39	Restaurant Sphinx	24	Bank Pekao	50	Main Post Office
47	Bar Mleczny Neptun	26	Rudy Kot	52	Celtic Pub
51	Karzcma Hevelius	27	Bank Gdański	53	Jazz 'n' Java
54	Pizza Hut; KFC	28	Teatr WybrzeAe	55	Dom Uphagena
		29	Kantors	56	Kantors
OTHER		30	Arsenal; Market	57	Golden Gate
1	Monument to the	31	Kantors	58	Foregate
	Shipyard Workers	32	St Mary's Church	59	LOT Office
2	Roads to Freedom	33	Royal Chapel	60	Upland Gate
	Exhibition (Solidarity	35	State Archaeological	62	Church of the Holy Trinity
	Museum)		Museum; St Mary's	63	National Museum
4	Bus Terminal		Gate	64	Church of SS Peter & Paul

Oliwa About 9km northwest of the Main Town in the suburb of Oliwa is **Park Oliwski** *(ul Cystersów)*. This lovely piece of greenery surrounds the soaring **Oliwa Cathedral** *(admission free; open about 8am-8pm daily)*, built in the 13th century with a Gothic facade and a long, narrow central nave. The famous Baroque organ is used for recitals each hour between 10am and 3pm Monday to Saturday in June, July and August. Elsewhere in the park is the **Ethnographic Museum** *(admission 4zł; open about 10am-4pm Tues-Sun)* in the Old Granary, and the **Modern Art Gallery** *(admission 8zł; open about 9am-4pm Tues-Sun)* in the former Abbots' Palace.

To reach the park, take the commuter train to the Gdańsk Oliwa station. From there, it's a 10-minute walk; head (west) up ul Poczty Gdańsk, turn right (north) along the highway and look for the signs (in English) to 'Ethnographic Museum' and 'Cathedral'.

Westerplatte When the German battleship *Schleswig-Holstein* began shelling the Polish naval post at Westerplatte at 4.45am on 1 September 1939, World War II had officially started. The 182-man Polish garrison held out against ferocious attacks for seven days before surrendering.

A park at Westerplatte, 7km north of the Main Town, now features a hill-top **memorial** *(admission free; permanently open)*, a small **museum** *(ul Sucharskiego; admission 2zł; open about 10am-4pm Tues-Sun May-Sept)* and plenty of other **ruins** caused by the Nazi bombardment. The café at the bus stop serves light meals and drinks.

Bus No 106 (25 minutes) goes to the park every 15 minutes from a stop outside the main train station in Gdańsk. Alternatively, excursion boats (33/46zł one way/return) to and around Westerplatte leave from a dock near the Green Gate in Gdańsk between 1 April and 30 October.

Special Events
The Dominican Fair (first two weeks in August) is an annual shopping fair dating back to 1260. Organ recitals are held at the Oliwa Cathedral twice a week (mid-June-late Aug) as part of the International Organ Music Festival. St Nicholas' and St Bridget's Churches also host organ recitals.

St Mary's Church is the stage for the International Organ, Choir & Chamber Music Festival (every Friday in July and August). Also popular is the International Street & Open-Air Theatre Festival (July).

POLAND

Places to Stay

If you're having trouble finding accommodation, the PTTK Office (see the Information section earlier) is happy to ring around a few hotels and hostels (for no charge). Also refer to the Around Gdańsk section later for details of a few (of the many) places to stay in nearby Sopot and Gdynia.

Camping About 5.5km northeast of the Main Town, **Camping Nr 218 Stogi** (☎ 307 39 15, fax 343 55 47; ul Wydmy 9; camping per person/tent sites 10/10zł, beds in cabins from 23zł; open May-Sept) is only 200m from the excellent beach in the seaside holiday centre of Stogi. Take tram No 8 from the main train station in Gdańsk.

Camping Nr 10 (☎/fax 343 55 31; ul Hallera 234; camping per person/tent 10/ 11.50zł, beds in cabins about 30zł; open May-Sept) is in the suburb of Brzeźno, about 1km from the beach. It's accessible by tram No 13 from the main train station in Gdańsk and by tram No 15 from the ferry terminal in Westerplatte.

Hostels The main **Youth Hostel** (☎/fax 301 23 13; ul Wałowa 21; dorm beds 15zł; singles/doubles with shared bathroom from 25/50zł; open year-round) is only five minutes' walk northeast of the main train station. It's in a quiet, old building back from the road. It's often full, particularly in summer, so book ahead. The noticeboard next to the reception is a mine of local information.

Another **Youth Hostel** (☎ 302 60 44, fax 302 41 87; ul Kartuska 245b; dorm beds 17-33zł; open year-round) is 3.5km west of the main train station; take bus No 161 or 167 along ul 3 Maja from the back of the station.

Domy Studenckie Politechniki Gdańskiej (☎ 347 25 47; ul Wyspiańskiego 7a; singles/ doubles from 30/48zł) opens about 10 of its student dorms as travellers' hostels between early July and late September. A bed will vary in price depending on the facilities and standards (some even have private bathrooms). All are in the suburb of Gdańsk Wrzeszcz and accessible by public transport.

Private Rooms Opposite the main train station, **Grand Tourist** (☎ 301 26 34, e tourist@ gt.com.pl; ul Podwale Grodzkie 8; open 8am-7pm Mon-Fri, 8am-2pm Sat) is below the street level. It offers private singles/doubles in

the city centre for 55/90zł and rooms in the suburbs from 43/75zł. The apartments with a kitchen, bathroom and double bed are good value for 180zł per night. When making your choice, work out the distance from the house to the frequent and inexpensive local commuter train line.

Hotels The rooms are small but cosy, and the bathrooms are clean at **Dom Harcerza** (☎ 301 36 21; e domharcerza@go2.pl; ul Za Murami 2/10; doubles with shared bathroom 60zł), which offers the best value and location for any budget-priced hotel. It's popular (so get there early or book ahead) and it can get noisy when large groups are staying there.

Three charming, family-run pensions offering comfortable rooms with a bathroom and breakfast are located 3km or less west of the city centre.

Pension Angela (☎/fax 302 23 15; ul Beethowena 12; doubles about 100zł) is cosy and the breakfasts are admirably large. It's accessible by bus No 130 or 184 from the main train station.

Another friendly place is **Pensionat Mac-Tur** (☎/fax 302 41 70; w www.mactur.gda .pl; ul Beethowena 8; rooms per person 70-120zł). It is located only just a few metres from Angela's.

Villa Akme (☎/fax 302 40 21; w www .akme.gda.pl; ul Drwęcka 1; singles/doubles about 110/150zł) has been renovated and is very nice. It's 2km southwest of the main train station and accessible by bus No 118, 155 or 208.

Dom Aktora (☎/fax 301 61 93; ul Straganiarska 55/56; singles/doubles with shared bathroom 200/250zł, apartments from 300zł) is a quaint place offering seven apartments (with TV, sitting room and bathroom) but only two rooms. It's always popular, so be sure to book ahead.

Hotel Hanza (☎ 305 34 27; w www.hanza -hotel.com.pl; ul Tokarska 6; singles/doubles with bathroom & breakfast from 580/650zł) is attractively perched along the waterfront near the Gdańsk Crane. Some rooms have views and all are comfortable and quiet, but you would hope so for this sort of price.

On Spichlerze Island, the **Hotel Novotel Gdańsk** (☎ 300 27 50; e ngdansk@orbis.pl; ul Pszenna 1; singles/doubles with breakfast from 292/366zł), is popular with businessmen and families and offers affordable luxury.

Places to Eat

Bar Mleczny Neptun *(ul Długa 33/34; meals about 12zł)* is classier than your run-of-the-mill milk bar. It's open at 7am for breakfast, but closes at 6pm.

Bar Mleczny Turystyczny *(ul Węglarska 1/4; meals about 10zł)* is more basic than the Neptun, but food is displayed cafeteria-style so it's easier to point at what you want without speaking Polish.

Karzcma Hevelius *(ul Długa 18; soups 5zł, mains from 12zł)* is a favourite: it's cosy and friendly, and you can choose hearty Polish food from a menu in German and English. The lunch specials (from 8zł) are worth looking out for.

Restauracja Kubicki *(ul Wartka 5; mains from 20zł)* is a decent mid-priced place to try Polish food from an English menu. It claims to be one of the oldest places in Gdańsk (established 1918), and offers appropriately old-fashioned decor and service.

Pub Duszek *(ul Św Ducha 119/121; soups 7zł, mains from 12zł)* is one of several similarly quaint and quiet eateries in the back streets offering tasty food. It has a tiny basement and a few tables outside. The menu is in English.

Restaurant Sphinx *(ul Długi Targ 31/32; mains about 14zł)* serves pizzas, as well as large grills with all the trimmings. The long line of people next door are queuing for a 'Sphinx Burger' (5zł), which is so big that a plastic fork is also provided to help you shovel the salads into your mouth.

Green Way *(ul Garncarska 4/6; meals 7-10zł)* is always popular with local vegetarians for sandwiches, crepes and salads.

Pizza Hut and **KFC** are joint tenants at ul Długa 75/76. **McDonald's** *(ul Podwale Grodzkie 1)* is inside the main train station. For self-catering, visit the **supermarket** inside the former Arsenal facing Targ Węglowy.

Entertainment

State Baltic Opera Theatre *(Al Zwycięstwa 15)* is in the suburb of Wrzeszcz, not very far from the commuter train station at the Gdańsk Politechnika.

Teatr Wybrzeże *(Targ Węglowy 1)*, next to the Arsenal, is the main city theatre. Both Polish and foreign classics (all in the Polish language) are often part of the repertoire.

Jazz Club *(Długi Targ 39/40)* is the main jazz venue and has live music on weekends.

Celtic Pub *(ul Lektykarska 3)* is authentic, popular and doesn't try too hard to be too Irish.

Kino Helikon and **Kino Neptun** *(ul Długa 57)*, which share the same premises, both offer newish films in relatively comfortable surroundings.

Getting There & Away

Refer to the Getting There & Away section earlier in this chapter for information about international bus and train services to/from Gdańsk, and international ferry services to/from Gdańsk and Gdynia. For travel to surrounding places, see Around Gdańsk next.

Air From Gdańsk, LOT flies to Warsaw about eight times a day and once a day to Frankfurt and Hamburg. SAS also flies daily to Copenhagen. Tickets for all airlines can be bought at the **LOT** office (☎ 301 28 21; ul Wały Jagiellońskie 2/4).

Bus The **bus terminal** *(ul 3 Maja 12)* handles all domestic and international services. It's behind (west of) the main train station and connected to ul Podwale Grodzkie by an underground passageway. Every day, there are four buses to Olsztyn, four to Toruń, six to Warsaw (50zł, six hours) and one or two to Białystok and Świnoujście. Polski Express also offers daily buses to Warsaw from this bus terminal.

Train The city's main train station, **Gdańsk Główny** *(ul Podwale Grodzkie 1)*, is conveniently located on the western outskirts of the Old Town. Most long-distance trains actually start or finish at Gdynia, so make sure you get on/off quickly at the Gdańsk Główny station.

Each day about 18 trains head to Warsaw, including 10 express trains (59zł 2nd class, five hours) and five InterCity services (3½ hours). Also each day, there are six trains to Olsztyn, 10 to Kraków, five to Wrocław via Poznań, seven to Toruń and four to Szczecin. Trains also head to Białystok and Lublin once or twice a day.

Boat Polferries uses the **ferry terminal** *(ul Przemysłowa)* in Nowy Port, about 5km north of the Main Town but only a short walk from the local commuter train station at Gdańsk Brzeżno. Orbis Travel and the PTTK Office in Gdańsk can provide information and sell tickets.

Between 1 May and 30 September, excursion boats leave regularly each day from the dock near the Green Gate in Gdańsk for Sopot (33/46zł one way/return) and Gdynia (39/54zł) – and you can even go to Hel (46/59zł)! From the same dock, boats also head out to Westerplatte (33/46zł) between 1 April and 30 October.

Getting Around

The airport is in Rębiechowo, about 12km northwest of Gdańsk. It's accessible by bus No 110 from the Gdańsk Wrzeszcz local commuter train station or less frequently by Bus B from outside the Gdańsk Główny train station. Taxis will cost about 30zł one-way.

The local commuter train, known as the SKM, runs every 15 minutes almost all day and night between the Gdańsk Główny and Gdynia Główna Osobowa train stations, via the Sopot and Gdańsk Oliwa stations. (Note: the line to Gdańsk Nowy Port, via Gdańsk Brzeżno, is a separate branch line that leaves less regularly from Gdańsk Główny.) Buy tickets at any station and validate them in the machines at the platform entrance.

Cars can be rented from a number of agencies at the airport or organised at any travel agency in Gdańsk.

AROUND GDAŃSK

Gdańsk is part of the so-called Tri-City Area, which stretches 30km along the coast from Gdańsk to Gdynia and includes Sopot. Gdynia and Sopot are easy day trips from Gdańsk and both provide cheaper and nicer accommodation options.

Sopot
☎ 058 • pop 43,000

Sopot, 12km north of Gdańsk, has been one of Poland's most fashionable seaside resorts since the 19th century. It has an easy-going atmosphere and there are long tidy stretches of sandy **beach**.

From the train station, turn left (north) and walk about 200m to the **tourist office** (☎ 550 37 83; ul Dworcowa 4; open 8am-7pm Mon-Fri, 10am-6pm Sat-Sun May-Sept, 8am-4pm Mon-Fri Oct-Apr). From there, head down ul Bohaterów Monte Cassino, one of Poland's most attractive pedestrian malls, past the church to Poland's longest **pier** (515m). Signposted from along this mall is an Internet centre, **www.c@fe** (ul Chmielewskiego 5a).

Opposite Pension Wanda (see below), the **Museum Sopotu** was being renovated at the time of research.

Places to Stay & Eat There is little in the way of budget options, but the tourist office can arrange **private rooms** from 50/100zł for singles/doubles.

Camping Nr 19 (☎ 550 04 45; ul Zamkowa Góra 25; camping per person/tent 15/15zł, 3-bed cabins about 100zł; open May-Sept) is the largest and best camping ground in Sopot. It's at the north end of town near the Sopot Kamienny Potok commuter train station, which is one stop north of the Sopot station.

Pension Wanda (☎ 550 30 37, fax 551 57 25; ul Poniatowskiego 7; singles/doubles with bathroom & breakfast from 150/210zł) has a handy location (about 500m southeast of the pier) and some rooms with views.

Hotel Eden (☎/fax 551 15 03; ul Kordeckiego 4/6; doubles without/with bathroom from 120/180zł) is a quiet pension overlooking the town park one street from the beach.

Grand Hotel Orbis (☎ 551 00 41; e sogrand@orbis.pl; ul Powstańców Warszawy 12/14; singles/doubles with bathroom & breakfast 330/450zł) is next to the pier overlooking the beach. It has just been renovated and is worth a splurge. The elegant **restaurant** offers marvellous views and impeccable service.

Bistros and **cafés** serving almost every conceivable cuisine sprout up in summer along the mall and the promenades. **Restaurant Irena** (ul Chopina 36; mains from 12zł), two blocks south of the tourist office, continues to be popular among holiday-makers for its hearty Polish food and friendly service.

Getting There & Away From the Sopot **train station** (ul Dworcowa 7), local commuter trains run every 15 minutes to Gdańsk Główny and Gdynia Główna Osobowa stations. Excursion boats leave several times a day (May to September) from the Sopot pier to Gdańsk, Gdynia and Hel.

Gdynia
☎ 058 • pop 260,000

Gdynia, 9km north of Sopot, is the third part of the Tri-City Area. It has nothing of the historic splendour of Gdańsk, nor relaxed beach ambience of Sopot; it's just a busy, young city with an omnipresent port atmosphere.

From the main Gdynia Główna Osobowa train station – where there is a **tourist office** – follow ul 10 Lutego east for about 1.5km to the pier. At the end of the pier is the recommended **Oceanographic Museum & Aquarium** *(admission 8.50zł; open 10am-5pm daily)*, which houses a vast array of sea creatures, both alive and embalmed.

A 20-minute walk uphill (follow the signs) from Teatr Muzyczny on Plac Grunwaldzki (about 300m southwest of the start of the pier) leads to **Kamienna Góra**. This hill offers wonderful **views**, best enjoyed while sipping a drink at the **Major Restaurant**.

Places to Stay & Eat To be honest, no hotel in central Gdynia is worth recommending. Those on a budget can try the **Youth Hostel** *(☎ 627 10 05, ul Energetyków 13a; dorm beds about 20zł; open year-round)*. It's about 3km northwest of the city centre and accessible by bus Nos 104 or 150 from ul Jana z Kolna near the bus terminal.

Alternatively, contact **Biuro Zakwaterowań Turus** *(☎ 621 82 65; ul Starowiejska 47; entrance from ul Dworcowa)*, opposite the train station, about a private room. Singles/doubles cost from 65/95zł, but a minimum booking of three nights is often required.

There are plenty of **milk bars** in the city centre and several upmarket **fish restaurants** along the pier. **Bistro Kwadrans** *(Skwer Kościuszki 20; mains 8-12zł)*, one block north of the median strip along ul 10 Lutego, is recommended for tasty Polish food.

Getting There & Away Local commuter trains link the **Gdynia Główna Osobowa** station *(Plac Konstytucji)* with Sopot and Gdańsk every 15 minutes. From the same station, trains regularly go each day to Hel (in summer) and Lębork (for Łeba). From the small **bus terminal** outside this train station, minibuses also go to Hel and Łeba, and two buses run daily to Świnoujście.

Stena Line uses the **Terminal Promowy** *(ul Kwiatkowskiego 60)*, about 5km northwest of Gdynia. Ask about the free shuttle central bus between Gdańsk and here, via Gdynia and Sopot, when you book your ticket, or take bus No 150 from outside the main train station.

Between May and September, excursion boats leave regularly throughout the day to Gdańsk, Sopot and Hel from a point halfway along the pier in Gdynia.

Hel
This old fishing village at the tip of the, umm, phallic Hel Peninsula north of Gdańsk is now a popular beach resort. The pristine, wind-swept **beach** on the Baltic side stretches the length of the peninsula. On the other (southern) side the sea is popular for **windsurfing**; equipment can be rented at the villages of Władysławowo and Jastarnia. Hel is a popular day trip from Gdańsk and worth visiting – if only to say that you've 'been to Hel and back'!

The odd-sounding **Fokarium** *(ul Morska 2)*, along the main road, is home to many endangered Baltic grey seals. The 15th-century **Gothic church** *(bul Nadmorksi 2)*, along the esplanade near the Fokarium, houses the **Museum of Fishery** *(admission 5.50zł; open about 10am-4pm Tues-Sun)*.

The best places to stay are any of the numerous **private rooms** offered in local houses (mostly from May to September). Expect to pay about 75zł per double.

To Hel, minibuses leave every hour or so from outside the main train station in Gdynia and several slow trains depart from Gdańsk and Gdynia daily from May to September. Hel is also accessible by excursion boat from Gdańsk, Sopot and Gdynia – see those sections earlier for details.

Łeba
☎ 059 ● pop 4100
Łeba ('WEH-bah') is a sleepy fishing village that turns into a popular seaside resort between May and September. The wide sandy **beach** stretches in both directions and the water is reputedly the cleanest along the Polish coast – ideal if you're looking for a beach resort.

From the train station, and adjacent bus stop, head east along ul 11 Listopada as far as the main street, ul Kościuszko. Then turn left (north) and walk about 1.5km to the better eastern beach via the esplanade (ul Nadmorska); if in doubt, follow the signs to the beachside Hotel Neptune.

The **tourist office** *(☎ 866 25 65; open 8am-4pm Mon-Fri May-Sept)* is inside the train station. There are several **kantors** along ul 11 Listopada.

Słowiński National Park This 186-sq-km park begins just west of Łeba and stretches along the coast for 33km. It contains a diversity of habitats, including forests, lakes, bogs and beaches, but the main attraction is the huge number of massive (and shifting) **sand dunes** that create a desert landscape. The wildlife and birdlife is also remarkably rich.

From Łeba to the sand dunes, follow the signs from near the train station northwest along ul Turystyczna and take the road west to the park entrance in the hamlet of Rąbka. Minibuses ply this road in summer from Łeba; alternatively, it's a pleasant walk or bike ride (8km). No cars or buses are allowed beyond the park entrance.

Places to Stay & Eat Many houses offering **private rooms** open their doors all year, but finding a room during the summer tourist season can be tricky.

Camping grounds include the **Intercamp 84** (☎ 866 12 06; ul Turystyczna 10) and **Camping Nr 41 Ambré** (☎ 866 24 72, ul Nadmorska 9a) – but bring mosquito repellent if you don't want to be eaten alive.

Biuro Wczasów Przymorze (☎ 866 13 60; ul Dworcowa 1), diagonally opposite the train station, also arranges private rooms.

Hotel Wodnik (☎ 866 13 66; **W** www .wodnik.leba.pl; ul Nadmorska 10; singles/ doubles with bathroom & breakfast from 120/150zł) is one of several pensions along the esplanade on the eastern side of the beach.

There are plenty of decent **eateries** in the town centre and along ul Nadmorska.

Getting There & Away The usual transit point is Lębork, 29km south of Łeba. To Lębork, slow trains run every hour or two from Gdańsk, via Gdynia, and there are buses every hour from Gdynia. Between Lębork and Łeba, you have a choice of four trains or eight buses a day. In summer (June to August), two buses and two trains run directly between Gdynia and Łeba and one train a day travels to/from Warsaw (eight hours).

Malbork
☎ 055 • pop 42,000
Malbork, 58km southeast of Gdańsk, boasts the **Malbork Castle** (admission 15.50zł; grounds open 9am-4pm, rooms 9am-3pm Tues-Sun), the largest Gothic castle in Europe. It was built by the Teutonic Knights in 1276 and became capital of the Grand Master of Teutonic Knights in 1309. It was badly damaged during WWII, but has been almost completely rebuilt since. It was placed on the Unesco World Heritage list in 1997.

Admission includes a compulsory three-hour tour (in Polish). Tours in English, French or German are available for an additional 126zł per group, but should be arranged in advance. The last tickets are sold at 2.30pm.

The **Youth Hostel** (☎ 272 24 08; ul Żeromskiego 45; dorms beds about 25zł; open year-round) is in a local school about 500m south of the castle.

Hotel & Restaurant Zbyszko (☎ 272 26 40, fax 272 33 95; ul Kościuszki 43; singles/ doubles with bathroom & breakfast 120/ 170zł) is conveniently located along the road to the castle. The rooms are fairly unremarkable but serviceable for one night.

Hotel & Restaurant Zamek (☎/fax 272 33 67; singles/doubles with bathroom, TV & breakfast 190/210zł) is inside a restored medieval building in the Lower Castle. The rooms are a bit old-fashioned, but the bathrooms are new.

The train and bus stations are about 1km southeast of the castle. As you leave the train station, turn right, cut across the highway, head down ul Kościuszki and follow the signs to the castle. Malbork is on the busy Gdańsk-Warsaw railway line, so it's an easy day trip from Gdańsk. There are buses every hour to Malbork from Gdynia and five daily from Gdańsk. From Malbork, trains also regularly go to Elbląg, Toruń and Olsztyn.

ŚWINOUJŚCIE
☎ 091 • pop 45,000
In a remote northwestern corner of Poland, Świnoujście ('Shvee-no-OOYSH-cheh') is quite a detour from other major destinations in Poland. However, if you're passing through on your way to/from Germany or Scandinavia, it's an enjoyable stopover.

Świnoujście sits on two islands at the mouth of the Świna River. Wolin Island on the southeastern side of the river has the port and bus and trains stations, while the town centre is across the river to the northwest on Uznam Island. A free ferry connects both sides every 15 minutes.

The **Tourist Information Centre** (☎/fax 322 49 99, **e** cit@fornet.com.pl; open 9am-5pm daily) is inside one of the two adjacent townside ferry terminals on Uznam Island. From either townside terminal, walk 400m west along the waterfront and then continue 300m northwest on ul Armii Krajowej to Plac Wolności. Here are the **post office**, **kantors** and **Internet centres**. From the square, the **beach** is 700m north along ul Piłsudskiego.

Things to See & Do

The self-explanatory **Museum of Seafishing** (Plac Rybaka 1; admission 4.50zł; open 9am-4pm Tues-Fri, 11am-4pm Sat-Sun) is about 400m west of the ferry terminals in town.

Locally available maps indicate pleasant **cycling** paths all around the town and countryside. Bikes can be rented from around the two ferry terminals in town.

About 15km east of Świnoujście, **Międzyzdroje** is a popular seaside resort with a lovely **beach** surrounded by the thickly forested **Wolin National Park**. This park features many lakes, including the horseshoe-shaped **Lake Czajcze** and the aptly named **Lake Turkusowe** (Turquoise). There's a small **bison reserve** (admission 5zł; open 10am-6pm Tues-Sun June-Sept) 2km east of Międzyzdroje.

Places to Stay & Eat

The rates given below are for the very busy high season.

Camping Nr 44 Relax (☎/fax 321 39 12; ul Słowackiego 1; camping per person/tent 10/5zł, 3-bed cabins about 135zł; open June-Sept) enjoys an excellent location along a secluded piece of the beach. Turn right (east) from along ul Piłsudskiego.

The **Youth Hostel** (☎/fax 327 06 13; ul Gdyńska 26; dorm beds 22zł; open all year) is a long way from the beach – to get there follow the signs along ul Grunwaldzka from Plac Wolności.

Dom Rybaka (☎/fax 321 29 43; ul Wybrzeże Władysława IV 22; singles/doubles 36/66zł, doubles with bathroom 110zł) is pleasantly located about 500m west of the townside ferry terminals.

The best places to eat and drink in Świnoujście are the two **food centres** along the promenade, ul Żeromskiego.

Getting There & Away

The border crossing for Germany is 2km northwest along ul Konstytucji 3 Maja from Plac Wolności.

From Świnoujście, buses regularly go to Gdynia and Międzyzdroje, but trains are more frequent. Every day, slow trains go every two hours to Szczecin (2¼ hours), via Międzyzdroje, and fast trains go to Warsaw (summer only), Kraków, Poznań and Wrocław.

International ferries depart from the **ferry terminal** near Świnoujście Port train station, one stop beyond the main Świnoujście station. **Morskie Biuro Podróży PŻB** (☎ 322 43 96; ul Brema 9/2) sells tickets for Polferries; **Biuro Podróży Partner** (☎ 322 43 97; ul Bohaterów Września 83/14) handles tickets for Unity Line. Both are only a few paces from the post office. See the Getting There & Away section earlier in this chapter for information about ferries from Denmark and Sweden to Świnoujście, and boats from there to Germany.

SZCZECIN

☎ 091 ● pop 425,000

Szczecin ('SHCHEH-cheen') is the main urban centre and port in northwestern Poland. It has a colourful and stormy history, but sadly most remnants were destroyed during WWII. Therefore, Szczecin has none of the charm of Toruń or Poznań, but it's a worthwhile stopover if you're travelling to/from Germany.

The **tourist information office** (☎ 434 04 40, Al Niepodległości 1) is helpful but the **tourist office** (☎ 434 02 86; open 10am-6pm daily) in the castle is better set up. The **post office** and most **kantors** and **Internet centres** are along the main street, Al Niepodległości.

The city's major attraction is undoubtedly the huge and rather austere **Castle of the Pomeranian Princess** (ul Korsazy 34; admission free; open dawn-dusk daily), 500m northeast of the tourist office. Originally built in the mid-14th century, it was enlarged in 1577 and rebuilt after WWII. Inside the grounds, the **Castle Museum** (admission 8zł; open about 10am-4pm Tues-Sun) features displays about the bizarre history of the castle.

A short walk down (south) from the castle is the 15th-century **Old Town Hall** (Plac Rzepichy), which contains the **Historical Museum of Szczecin** (admission 6zł; open about 10-4pm Tues-Sun). Nearby is the charmingly rebuilt 'old town' with cafés and bars. Three blocks northwest of the castle is the **National Museum** (ul Staromłyńska 27; admission 5.50zł; open about 10am-4pm Tues-Sun).

Places to Stay & Eat

Camping PTTK Marina (☎/fax 460 11 65, ul Przestrzenna 23; camping per person/tent 10/5zł, double cabins from 85zł; open May-Sept) is on the shore of Lake Dąbie – get off at the Szczecin Dąbie train station and ask for directions (2km).

POLAND

POLAND

Youth Hostel PTSM (☎ 422 47 61; ul Monte Cassino 19a; dorm beds 10-35zł; open year-round) is located 2km northwest of the tourist office.

Hotel Promorski (☎ 433 61 51; Plac Brama Portowa 4; singles/doubles with shared bathroom from 60/64zł) is fairly basic but it is perfectly adequate. It's central (200m west of Al Niepodległości), but a little noisy.

Hotel Podzamcze (☎/fax 812 14 04; ul Sienna 1/3; singles/doubles with bathroom & breakfast 180/230zł) is in a charming location near the Old Town Hall.

Two restaurants about 200m west along ul Obrońców Stalingradu from the northern end of Al Niepodległości are popular: **Bar Turysta**, at No 6a, is a standard milk bar, while **Bar Rybarex**, at No 6 next door, is ideal for fresh fish with salad and chips.

Dublin Pub (ul Kaszubska 57), around the corner from the Promorski, is popular and offers a limited range of meals.

Getting There & Away

LOT flies between Szczecin and Warsaw about seven times a day and most days to Copenhagen. Book at the **LOT** office (☎ 433 50 58; ul Wyzwolenia 17), about 200m up from the northern end of Al Niepodległości.

The **bus terminal** (Plac Grodnicki), and the nearby **Szczecin Główny** train station (ul Kolumba), are 600m southeast of the tourist office. Two buses a day head for Gdynia, but there's little else of use to travellers. Express and fast trains travel regularly to Poznań, Gdańsk and Warsaw (34zł 2nd-class express, seven hours), and slow trains plod along every two hours to Świnoujście.

Advance tickets for trains and ferries are available from **Orbis Travel** (☎ 434 26 18; Plac Zwycięstwa 1), about 200m west of the main post office.

Warmia & Masuria

Warmia and Masuria are in northeastern Poland, to the east of the lower Vistula Valley. Here the Scandinavian glacier left behind a typical postglacial landscape characterised by some 3000 lakes, many linked by rivers and canals, creating a system of waterways enjoyed by yachties and canoeists. The winding shorelines are surrounded by hills and forests, making this picturesque lake district one of the most attractive areas in the country. There's little industry and so little pollution.

OLSZTYN
☎ 089 • pop 165,000

Olsztyn ('OL-shtin') is a likeable transport hub with an attractive old town of cobblestoned streets, art galleries, cafés, bars and restaurants. It's also the obvious base from where to explore the region, including the Great Masurian Lakes district (see later).

Olsztyn's history has been a successive overlapping of Prussian and Polish influences. From 1466 to 1773 the town belonged to the kingdom of Poland. Nicolaus Copernicus, administrator of Warmia, commanded Olsztyn Castle from 1516 to 1520. With the first partition of Poland, Olsztyn became Prussian Allenstein and remained so until 1945. The city was badly damaged during WWII, but has been mostly rebuilt.

Everyone should stop at the helpful **tourist office** (☎/fax 535 35 65; e oldtur@praca.gov.pl; ul Staromiejska 1; open 8am-3.30pm Mon-Fri). The few **kantors** around town are marked on the map; otherwise, try the **PKO Bank** (cnr ul 1 Maja & ul 11 Listopada).

For snail mail, go to the **main post office** (ul Pieniężnego); for 'cybermail', try the **Internet centre** inside the **telephone office** (ul Pieniężnego) opposite. Books and maps are sold at **EMPiK** (ul 1 Maja) and the quaint little **Ambassador Bookshop** in the Gazeta Olsztyńska Museum.

Things to See

The **High Gate** (or Upper Gate) is all that remains of the 14th-century city walls. A little further west, the 14th-century **Castle of the Chapter of Warmia** (ul Zamkowa 2) contains the **Museum of Warmia & Mazury** (admission 6zł; open 9am-5pm Tues-Sun May-Sept, 10am-4pm Tues-Sun Oct-Apr). It features plenty of exhibits about Copernicus, who made some astronomical observations here in the early 16th century, as well as some coins and art.

The **Rynek** (Market Square) was destroyed during WWII and rebuilt in a style only superficially reverting to the past. To the east, the red-brick Gothic **Cathedral of Św Jakuba Większego** (ul Długosza) dates from the 14th century. Its 60m tower was added in 1596. **Gazeta Olsztyńska Museum** (ul Targ Rybny 1; admission 5zł; open 9am-4pm Tues-Sun)

POLAND

OLSZTYN

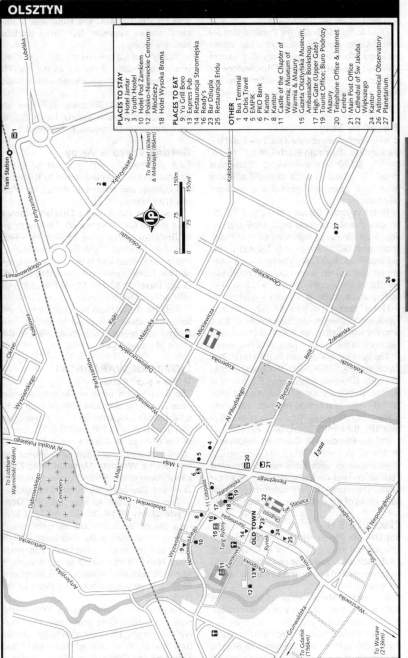

PLACES TO STAY
2 Hotel Jantar
3 Youth Hostel
10 Hotel Pod Zamkiem
12 Polsko-Niemieckie Centrum Młodzieży
18 Hotel Wysoka Brama

PLACES TO EAT
9 Yu Grill Boro
13 Express Pub
14 Restauracja Staromiejska
16 Ready's
23 Bar Dziupla
25 Restauracja Eridu

OTHER
1 Bus Terminal
4 Orbis Travel
5 EMPIK
6 PKO Bank
7 Kantor
8 Kantor
11 Castle of the Chapter of Warmia; Museum of Warmia & Mazury
15 Gazeta Olsztyńska Museum; Ambassador Bookshop
17 High Gate (Upper Gate)
19 Tourist Office; Biuro Podróży Mazury
20 Telephone Office & Internet Centre
21 Main Post Office
22 Cathedral of Sw Jakuba Większego
24 Kantor
26 Astronomical Observatory
27 Planetarium

is a town museum housed in a building once occupied by the local newspaper.

Outside the Old Town, the **Planetarium** (Al Piłsudskiego 38; admission 7zł) has shows between 10am and 4pm every day except Monday. The **Astronomical Observatory** (ul Żołnierska 13; admission 7zł) offers tours between 9am and 3.30pm every day but Monday – get tickets from the Planetarium.

Places to Stay

Conveniently between the Old Town and the train station, the **Youth Hostel** (☎ 527 66 50, fax 527 68 70; ul Kopernika 45; dorm beds from 24zł, doubles with shared bathroom from 56zł; open year-round) is a well-run place and tidy.

Hotel Wysoka Brama (☎/fax 527 36 75, ul Staromiejska 1; dorm beds 16zł, singles/doubles with shared bathroom from 45/58zł, apartment 160zł) is superbly located in the old section of High Gate. The dorms are nothing special and the rooms are unremarkable, but the large apartment (with kitchen, TV, seating and bathroom) is worth a splurge.

Hotel Jantar (☎ 533 54 52; ul Kętrzyńskiego 5; singles/doubles from 50/80zł, doubles with bath from 100zł) is convenient but stuck in the 1960s – perhaps a last resort.

The best option in town is the **Hotel Pod Zamkiem** (☎ 535 12 87; e hotel@olsztyn.com.pl; ul Nowowiejskiego 10; singles/doubles with bathroom, TV & breakfast 130/180zł) is the best option in town. This cosy pension has charming rooms in a convenient spot near the castle. Breakfast is excellent.

Polsko-Niemieckie Centrum Młodzieży (☎ 534 07 80, fax 527 69 33; ul Okopowa 25; singles/doubles with bathroom & breakfast 160/180zł) is also ideally situated next to the castle. The rooms are very comfortable (some have views of the castle) and staff are friendly.

Places to Eat

Bar Dziupla (Rynek 9/10; mains from 10zł) is renowned among locals for its tasty Polish food, such as pierogi. The restaurant is small so you may need to order takeaway and eat in the square.

Restauracja Staromiejska (ul Staromiejska 4/6; mains about 18zł) is one of several appealing cafés facing the tiny town square.

Restauracja Eridu (ul Prosta 3/4; mains from 12zł) offers some inexpensive Middle Eastern choices.

Yu Grill Boro (ul Nowowiejskiego; grills about 15zł), opposite the Hotel Pod Zamkiem, serves Yugoslav fare in an outdoor parkside setting.

Ready's (ul Staromiejska; grills from 12zł) is a popular place at the top of the mall. It serves mainly grills, smothered with various sauces and salads.

Express Pub (ul Okopowa; daily specials about 8zł) is popular among locals for its cosy interior and authentic Polish food.

Getting There & Away

Each day from the **bus terminal** (ul Partyzantów) four or five buses travel to Białystok and Gdańsk, and another 10 depart for Warsaw (five hours).

Also every day from the **Olsztyn Główny** train station (ul Partyzantów), four trains go to Białystok, three head to Warsaw (33zł 2nd-class express), eight leave for Gdańsk, two go to Poznań and Wrocław, and six depart for Toruń (a route not covered by buses). **Orbis Travel** (☎ 527 44 55; Al Piłsudskiego) sells advance train tickets.

Refer to the relevant sections later for information about buses and trains between Olsztyn and regional attractions, such as the Great Masurian Lakes district.

LIDZBARK WARMIŃSKI
☎ 089 • pop 18,000

This town, 46km north of Olsztyn, was the main seat of the Warmian bishops from 1350 until Prussia took over in 1773. Copernicus also lived here from 1503 to 1510. The **Castle of the Bishops of Warmia** miraculously survived numerous wars and now houses the entertaining **Warmian Museum** (Plac Zamkowy; admission 8.50zł; open 9am-5pm Tues-Sun May-Sept, 10am-4pm Oct-Apr).

The best places to stay are the **Dom Wycieczkowy PTTK** (☎ 767 25 21; ul Wysoka Brama 2; singles/doubles with shared bathroom 42/65zł) in the 15th-century **High Gate**; and the charming, but small, **Pensjonat Pizza Hotel** (☎ 767 52 59; ul Konstytucji 3 Maja 26; doubles without/with bathroom 98/132zł), only about 500m northeast of the High Gate.

From the bus terminal, about 500m northwest of the High Gate, buses travel to Olsztyn every hour. There are also regular buses travelling between Lidzbark Warmiński and Frombork and Gdańsk.

FROMBORK

☎ 055 • pop 2600

This small, sleepy town on the shore of the Vistula Lagoon was founded in the 13th century. A fortified ecclesiastical township was later erected on Cathedral Hill overlooking the lagoon. Frombork is most famous, however, as the place where Copernicus wrote his astounding *On the Revolutions of the Celestial Spheres*.

Cathedral Hill is now occupied by the extensive **Nicolaus Copernicus Museum**, with several sections requiring separate tickets. Perhaps the highlight is a red-brick Gothic **cathedral** *(admission 5zł; open 9.30am-5pm Mon-Sat May-Sept, 9am-4pm Oct-Apr)* built in the 14th century.

Youth Hostel Copernicus *(☎ 243 74 53; ul Elbląska 11; dorm beds about 15zł; open year-round)* also allows camping. It's 500m west of Cathedral Hill on the road to Elbląg.

Dom Wycieczkowy PTTK *(☎ 243 72 52; ul Krasickiego 2; dorm beds from 25zł; singles/ doubles with bathroom from 45/65zł)* is large and only 80m west of Cathedral Hill.

The bus and train stations are along the riverfront about 300m northwest of the castle. Frombork can be directly reached by bus from Elbląg (hourly), Gdańsk, Lidzbark Warmiński and Malbork. From Olsztyn, get a connection in Elbląg.

ELBLĄG-OSTRÓDA CANAL

This 82km waterway between Elbląg and Ostróda is the longest navigable canal still used in Poland. Built between 1848 and 1876, it was used for transporting timber from the rich inland forests to the Baltic Sea. To resolve the 99.5m difference in water levels, the canal utilises an unusual system of five water-powered slipways so that boats are actually sometimes carried across dry land on rail-mounted trolleys.

Normally, **excursion boats** (mid-May to late September) depart from both Elbląg and Ostróda daily at 8am (80zł, 11 hours), but actual departures depend on the number of willing passengers. For information, call the **boat operators** *(in Elbląg ☎ 055-232 43 07, in Ostróda 089-646 38 71)*.

In Elbląg, **Camping Nr 61** *(☎/fax 055-232 43 07; ul Panieńska 14; cabins 75zł; open May-Sept)*, right at the boat dock, is pleasant. **Hotel Galeona** *(☎/fax 055-232 48 08; ul Krótka 5; singles/doubles without bathroom*

52/65zł) in the city centre is good value. In Ostróda, try **Dom Wycieczkowy Drwęcki** *(☎/fax 646 30 35, ul Mickiewicza 7; singles/ doubles with shared bathroom 55/65zł)*, 500m east of the bus and train stations.

Elbląg is easily accessible by train and bus from any of the cities of Gdańsk, Malbork, Frombork and Olsztyn. Ostróda is also regularly connected by train to Olsztyn and Toruń and by bus to Olsztyn and Elbląg.

THE GREAT MASURIAN LAKES

The Great Masurian Lakes district east of Olsztyn is a verdant land of rolling hills interspersed with glacial lakes, peaceful farms and dense forests. The district has over 2000 lakes, the largest of which is **Lake Śniardwy** (110 sq km), Poland's largest lake. About 200km of canals connect these lakes, so the area is a prime destination for yachties and canoeists, as well as those who prefer to hike, fish and mountain-bike.

The detailed *Wielkie Jeziora Mazurskie* map (1:100,000) is essential for anyone exploring the region by boat, canoe, bike, car or foot. The *Warmia i Mazury* map (1:300,000), published by Vicon and available at regional tourist offices, is perfect for anyone using private or public transport, and has explanations in English.

Getting Around

Yachties can sail the larger lakes all the way from Węgorzewo to Ruciane-Nida. Expect to pay between $25 and $100 per day for a boat for four to five people with mattresses.

Canoeists will perhaps prefer the more intimate surroundings along rivers and smaller lakes. The most popular kayak route takes about 10 days (106km) and follows rivers, canals and lakes from Sorkwity to Ruciane-Nida with places to stay and eat along the way. Brochures explaining this route are available at regional tourist offices. There's also an extensive network of trails – ideal for **hiking** and **mountain biking** – around the lakes.

Most travellers prefer to enjoy the lakes in comfort on the **excursion boats**. Boats run daily (May to September) between Giżycko and Ruciane-Nida, via Mikołajki; and daily (June to August) between Węgorzewo and Ruciane-Nida, via Giżycko and Mikołajki. In practice, however, services are more reliable from late June to late August. Schedules and fares are clearly posted at the lake ports.

POLAND

THE GREAT MASURIAN LAKES

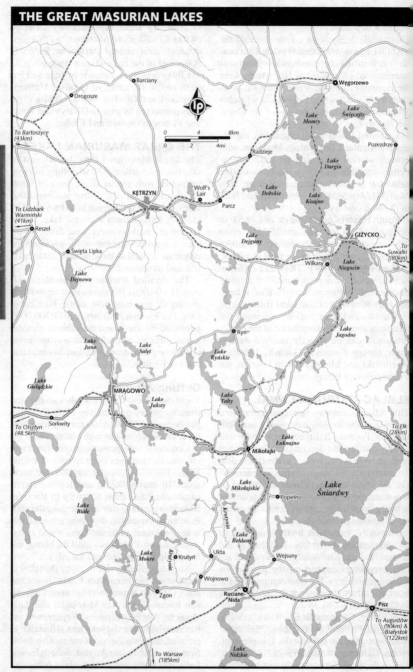

Travelling around the lakes district by train and bus is not very convenient, so allow plenty of time. Otherwise, you can organise a tour with **Diuna** (☎/fax 087-423 02 09; e diuna@post.pl; Pisz), or **Biuro Podróży Mazury** (☎/fax 089-527 40 59; e postmaster@ottkmazury.pl; ul Staromiejska 1, Olsztyn).

Reszel

Reszel, about 60km northeast of Olsztyn, has an old town dominated by the massive 14th-century **Reszel Castle** (admission 1zł; open dawn-dusk daily). It has been partially converted into an **art gallery** and **restaurant**. It also houses the **Zamek Reszel Kreativ Hotel** (☎ 089-755 01 09, fax 755 15 97; singles/doubles with bathroom & breakfast 180/230zł), which offers nicely furnished rooms with lovely views. Plenty of buses link Reszel with Kętrzyn, Święta Lipka and Olsztyn.

Święta Lipka

This hamlet boasts an exquisite 17th-century **church** (admission free; open 7am-7pm daily), considered one of the purest examples of late-baroque architecture in Poland. One highlight of the interior is the lavishly decorated organ. The angels adorning the 5000 pipes play their instruments and dance to the music when the organ is sounded. This mechanism is demonstrated several times daily from May to September and recitals are held Friday nights from June to August.

Ask any of the regional tourist offices for a list of homes in Święta Lipka offering **private rooms**. There are several places to eat and drink near the church.

Buses run to Kętrzyn and Reszel every hour or so, but less often to Olsztyn and Lidzbark Warmiński.

Kętrzyn

The 14th-century **castle** (admission free; permanently open) in this charming village houses the worthwhile **Regional Museum** (admission 3zł; open about 9am-4pm Mon-Fri, 9am-3pm Sat & Sun).

Hotel Koch (☎ 089-752 20 58, fax 752 23 90; ul Traugutta 3; singles/doubles 125/180zł), in the centre, is the best place to stay.

Zajazd Pod Zamkiem (☎ 089-752 31 17, fax 752 20 41; ul Struga 3) is a classy restaurant next to the castle. It also offers a few sumptuous singles/doubles with bathroom and breakfast for 90/130zł.

Buses leave regularly for most places in the lake district, as well as Olsztyn. A few trains a day go to Gdańsk, via Elbląg, and Olsztyn.

Wolf's Lair

Hitler's wartime headquarters was at Gierłoż, 8km east of Kętrzyn, in Wolf's Lair (admission 7zł; open 8am-dusk daily). Hitler arrived here on 26 June 1941 (four days after the invasion of the Soviet Union) and stayed until 20 November 1944, except for a few short trips to the outside world.

In July 1944 a group of pragmatic, high-ranking German officers tried to assassinate Hitler. The leader of the plot, Claus von Stauffenberg, arrived from Berlin on 20 July on the pretext of informing Hitler of the newly formed reserve army. As a frequent guest he had no problems entering the meeting with a bomb in his briefcase. He placed his briefcase a few feet from Hitler and left to take a pre-arranged phone call. The explosion killed two staff members and wounded half a dozen others, but Hitler suffered only minor injuries. Stauffenberg and some 5000 people involved in the plot were subsequently executed.

On 24 January 1945, as the Red Army approached, the Germans blew up Wolfsschanze (as it was known in German), so most bunkers were destroyed. However, cement slabs – some 8.5m thick – and twisted metal remain, giving this hideous place an eerie feel.

A large map is posted at the entrance and the remaining bunkers are clearly labelled in English. Guides speaking English and German also wait at the entrance and charge about 65zł per group for a 90-minute tour of the site. Booklets allowing a self-guided walking tour are available in English and German at the kiosk in the car park.

Hotel Wilcze Gniazdo (☎ 089-752 44 29, fax 752 44 92; singles/doubles with bathroom & breakfast 60/80zł) is charmless but functional. A **restaurant** is attached.

Catch one of several daily buses from Kętrzyn to Węgorzewo and get off at the entrance. Between May and September, bus No 1 from the train station in Kętrzyn also goes to the site.

Giżycko
☎ 087

Set on the northern shore of Lake Niegocin, Giżycko ('Ghee-ZHITS-ko') is the largest lakeside centre in the region. There are some

POLAND

significant ruins of the **Boyen Fortress** *(admission free; permanently open)*, built by the Prussians between 1844 and 1855 to protect the border with Russia.

Near the main square (Plac Grunwaldzki) are the **tourist information office** (☎ *428 52 65,* e *infoturyst@wp.pl; ul Warszawska 17, enter from ul Kętrzyńskiego)* and **Bank Pekao** *(ul Olsztyńska 17)*. There are some **kantors** in the town centre, including one at **Orbis Travel** *(ul Dąbrowskiego 3)*, about 250m east of the main square.

Sailing boats are available from **Almatur** (☎ *428 33 88; ul Moniuszki 24)*, 700m west of the fortress, **Centrum Mazur** at Camping Nr 1 **Zamek** and **Orbis Travel**.

Hotel Wodnik (see next) rents out bicycles and kayaks, sell tickets for the excursion boats and arranges car rental.

Places to Stay & Eat Just west of the canal, **Camping Nr 1 Zamek** (☎ *428 34 10; ul Moniuszki 1; camping per person/tent 15/10zł, cabins about 22zł per person; open mid-June–early Sept)* is simple but central. **Motel Zamek** (☎ *428 24 19; doubles 120zł; open May-Sept)* is part of the same complex.

The **Youth Hostel** (☎ *428 29 59; dorm beds 18zł; open year-round)* is in the Boyen Fortress.

Hotel Wodnik (☎ *428 38 72, fax 428 39 58; ul 3 Maja 2; singles/doubles with bathroom & breakfast from 88/129zł)*, just off the main square, is good value.

Café Bar Ekran *(Plac Grunwaldzki; mains from 12zł)* serves some very tasty home-made Polish food.

Getting There & Away From the train station, on the southern edge of town near the lake, around eight trains run daily to Kętrzyn and Olsztyn, and two head to Gdańsk.

From the adjacent bus terminal, buses travel regularly to Węgorzewo, Mikołajki, Kętrzyn and Olsztyn. Also, one or two buses go daily to Lidzbark Warmiński and six head to Warsaw.

Mikołajki
☎ 087

Mikołajki ('Mee-ko-WAHY-kee'), 86km east of Olsztyn, is a picturesque little village

and probably the best base for exploring the lakes. The **tourist office** (☎ */fax 421 68 50; Plac Wolności 3)* is in the town centre. There are several **kantors** nearby, but there is nowhere to change travellers cheques or get cash advances.

Sailing boats – and often **canoes** – can be hired from **Wioska Żeglarska** (☎ *421 60 40, ul Kowalska 3)* at the waterfront, and also from the **Hotel Wałkuski** (☎ *421 64 70; ul 3 Maja 13a)*.

Lake Śniardwy and Lake Łuknajno are ideal for **cycling**. The tourist office can provide details and maps, and bikes can be rented from **Hotel Wałkuski** or **Pensjonat Mikołajki** (☎ *421 64 37, ul Kajki 18)*.

Places to Stay & Eat Across the bridge, **Camping Nr 2 Wagabunda** (☎ *421 60 18; ul Leśna 2; camping per person/tent 15/12zł, cabins about 75zł; open May-Sept)* is a 10-minute walk southwest of the town centre.

The **Youth Hostel** (☎ *421 64 34; ul Łabędzia 1; dorm beds about 16zł; open July-Aug)* is next to the stadium about 500m from the main square on the Łuknajno road.

Several charming pensions and homes that offering **private rooms** are dotted all along ul Kajki, the main street leading around Lake Mikołajskie; another collection of pensions can be found along the roads to Ruciane-Nida and Ełk.

Hotel & Restaurant Mazur (☎ *421 69 41; Plac Wolności; singles/doubles with bathroom & breakfast 150/200zł)* is an enticing place overlooking the town square.

Plenty of **eateries** spring up in summer along the waterfront and around the town square to cater for peak-season visitors.

Getting There & Away From the bus terminal, next to the train station on the southern edge of the town near the lake, four buses go to Olsztyn each morning. Otherwise, get a bus (hourly) to Mrągowo and change there for Olsztyn and Kętrzyn. Several buses also go daily to Giżycko and two or three depart in summer for Warsaw.

From the sleepy train station, a few slow trains shuttle along daily to Olsztyn and Kętrzyn, and two fast trains head to Gdańsk and Białystok.

Romania

A country where mass tourism means you, a horse and cart and a handful of farmers, Romania *is* the Wild West of Eastern Europe. Straddling the rugged Carpathian Mountains, with rich green valleys and farms spread throughout the countryside, it offers an extraordinary kaleidoscope of cultures to discover and sights to see. Transylvania's colourful old cities are straight out of medieval Hungary or Germany, while the exotic painted Orthodox monasteries of Moldavia evoke Byzantium. Western Romania bears the imprint of the Austro-Hungarian Empire, while Roman and Turkish influences colour Constanța. Bucharest – seen by travellers as everything from 'the Paris of the East' to 'Hell on Earth' – has a Franco-Romanian charm all of its own.

The secret to exploring this surprise package of unexpected delights – declared by many readers as Eastern Europe's most exciting, best-value destination for adventurous travellers – is balance. Romania's historical cities are fascinating, but explore the countryside too. Your most memorable times could be spent amid the humble grace of the rural population or atop a horse and cart.

Facts about Romania

HISTORY

Thracian tribes, more commonly known as Dacians, inhabited ancient Romania. From the 7th century BC the Greeks established trading colonies along the Black Sea at Callatis (Mangalia), Tomis (Constanța) and Histria. In the 1st century BC, a Dacian state was established to counter the advance of Roman legions north of the Danube. The last king, Decebalus, consolidated this state but was unable to prevent the Roman conquest in AD 105–06.

The slave-owning Romans brought a superior civilisation and mixed with the conquered tribes to form a Daco-Roman people who spoke Latin. A noted visitor during the Roman period was the Latin poet Ovid, exiled to Constanța by Roman Emperor Augustus.

Faced with Goth attacks in AD 271, Emperor Aurelian withdrew the Roman legions south of the Danube, but the Romanised

At a Glance

- **Bucharest** – bombastic architecture and Dracula's tomb
- **The Prahova Valley** – Saxon fortresses; stunning castle at Bran; mountain resorts
- **Sighişoara** – beautiful medieval town surrounded by hills
- **Southern Bucovina** – a World Heritage Site of painted monasteries
- **Maramureş** – untouched valleys and remote forests, perfect for hiking

Capital	Bucharest
Population	22.4 million
Official Language	Romanian
Currency	1 leu = 100 bani
Time	GMT/UTC+0200
Country Phone Code	☎ 40

Vlach peasants remained in Dacia. Waves of migrating peoples, including the Goths, Huns, Avars, Slavs, Bulgars and Magyars (Hungarians), swept across this territory from the 4th to the 10th centuries.

From the 10th century the Magyars expanded into Transylvania and by the 13th century all of Transylvania was under the Hungarian crown. German Saxons first came to Transylvania after the devastating Tatar raids of 1241 and 1242, when King Bela IV of Hungary offered the Saxons free land and tax

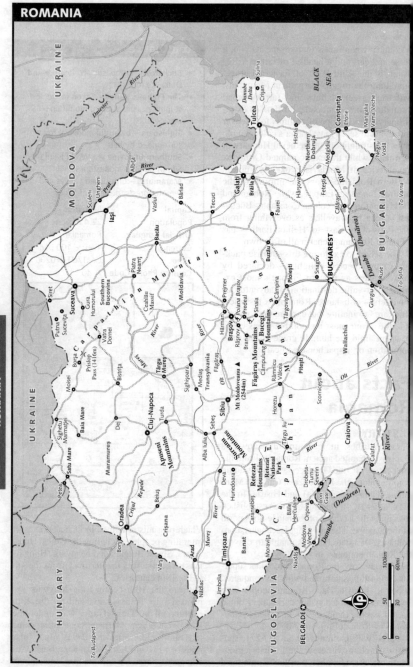

incentives to settle and defend the crown's southeastern flank.

The Romanian-speaking principalities of Wallachia and Moldavia offered strong resistance to the Ottomans' northern expansion in the 14th and 15th centuries. Mircea the Old, Vlad Ţepeş and Steven the Great (Ştefan cel Mare) were legendary figures in this struggle.

Vlad Ţepeş, ruling prince of Wallachia in 1456–62 and 1476–77, gained the name Ţepeş (Impaler) after the primary form of capital punishment he used to punish his enemies – impaling. A wooden stake was carefully driven through the victim's backbone without touching any vital nerve, ensuring at least 48 hours of conscious suffering before death. He is perhaps more legendary as the inspiration for 19th-century novelist Bram Stoker's Count Dracula. (Vlad was called Dracula, meaning 'son of the dragon', after his father, Vlad Dracul, a knight of the Order of the Dragon.

When the Turks conquered Hungary in the 16th century, Transylvania became a vassal of the Ottoman Empire. In 1600 the three Romanian states – Transylvania, Wallachia and Moldavia – were briefly united under Michael the Brave (Mihai Viteazul). In 1687 Transylvania fell under Habsburg rule. Turkish suzerainty, however, persisted in Wallachia and Moldavia well into the 19th century.

After the Russian defeat in the Crimean War (1853–56), Romanian nationalism grew. In 1859 Alexandru Ioan Cuza was elected to the thrones of Moldavia and Wallachia, creating a national state, taking the name Romania in 1862. The reformist Cuza was forced to abdicate in 1866 and his place was taken by the Prussian prince Karl of Hohenzollern, who took the name Carol I. Romania then declared independence from the Ottoman Empire in 1877 and, after the 1877–78 War of Independence, Dobruja became part of Romania.

In 1916 Romania entered WWI on the side of the Triple Entente (Britain, France and Russia) with the objective of taking Transylvania – where 60% of the population was Romanian – from Austria-Hungary. The Central Powers (Germany and Austria-Hungary) occupied Wallachia, but Moldavia was defended by Romanian and Russian troops. With the defeat of Austria-Hungary in 1918, the unification of Banat, Transylvania and Bucovina with Romania was finally achieved.

In the years leading to WWII, Romania, under foreign minister Nicolae Titulescu, sought security in an alliance with France. After the fall of France in May 1940 Romania became isolated and in June the USSR occupied Bessarabia (taken from Russia after WWI). On 30 August 1940 Romania was forced to cede northern Transylvania to Hungary by order of Nazi Germany and Fascist Italy. In September southern Dobruja was given to Bulgaria.

To defend the interests of the ruling classes, General Ion Antonescu forced King Carol II to abdicate in favour of his son Michael. Then Antonescu imposed a fascist dictatorship. In June 1941 he joined Hitler's anti-Soviet war. The results were gruesome: 400,000 Romanian Jews and 36,000 Roma (Gypsies) were murdered at Auschwitz and other camps.

On 23 August 1944 Romania suddenly changed sides, captured 53,159 German soldiers and declared war on Nazi Germany. By this act, Romania salvaged its independence and shortened the war.

After the war, the Soviet-engineered return of Transylvania enhanced the prestige of the left-wing parties, which won the parliamentary elections of November 1946. A year later the monarchy was abolished and the Romanian People's Republic was proclaimed.

Soviet troops withdrew in 1958 and after 1960 Romania adopted an independent foreign policy under two leaders, Gheorghe Gheorghiu-Dej (1952–1965) and his protege Nicolae Ceauşescu (1965–89), both imprisoned during WWII.

Ceauşescu's domestic policy was chaotic and megalomaniac. In 1974 the post of president was created for him. He placed his wife Elena, son Nicu and three brothers in important political positions during the 1980s. Some of Ceauşescu's expensive follies were projects such as the Danube Canal from Agigea to Cernavo, the disruptive redevelopment of southern Bucharest in 1983–89, and the 'systemisation' of agriculture by the resettlement of rural villagers into concrete apartment blocks.

By the late 1980s the USA withdrew Romania's most-favoured-nation trading status. Undaunted, Ceauşescu continued spending millions of dollars. His great blunder was the decision to export Romania's food to help finance his projects. In November 1987 workers rioted in Braşov and in the winter of 1988–89 the country suffered its worst food shortages in decades.

ROMANIA

The spark that ignited Romania came on 15 December 1989, when Father Lászlo Tökés publicly condemned the dictator from his Hungarian church in Timişoara, prompting the Reformed Church of Romania to remove him from his post. Police attempts to arrest demonstrating parishioners failed and civil unrest quickly spread, prompting Ceauşescu to proclaim martial law in Timiş County and dispatch troops to crush the rebellion.

On 21 December in Bucharest, an address made by Ceauşescu during a mass rally was cut short by anti-Ceauşescu demonstrators. They booed the dictator, then retreated to the boulevard between Piaţa Universităţii and Piaţa Romană, only to be crushed hours later by police gunfire and armoured cars. The next morning, thousands more demonstrators took to the streets, and a state of emergency was quickly announced. At midday Ceauşescu reappeared with his wife on the balcony of the Central Committee building to speak, only to be forced to flee by helicopter from the roof of the building. The couple were arrested in Târgovişte, taken to a military base and, on 25 December executed by a firing squad.

The National Salvation Front (FSN) took immediate control of the country. In May 1990, it won the country's first democratic elections, placing Ion Iliescu at the helm as president and Petre Roman as prime minister. In Bucharest, student protests against this former communist rule were ruthlessly squashed by 20,000 coal miners shipped to the capital courtesy of Iliescu. Ironically, when the miners returned in September 1991, it was to force the resignation of Petre Roman whose free-market economic reforms, it was believed, had led to worsening living conditions.

In 1996 Emil Constantinescu, leader of the reform-minded Democratic Convention of Romania (CDR), was elected as president.

Romania Today
Promised economic reforms were hampered by internal party bickering. After 15 months of office, Prime Minister Victor Ciorba was forced to step down and, in March 1998, President Constantinescu appointed Radul Vasile as the prime minister. A series of harsh free-market reforms ensued. Unlike mid-1997 the when miners agreed to pit closures in return for lucrative redundancy packages, in early 1999, 10,000 striking miners threatened to storm Bucharest in response to government attempts to close 37 less-profitable pits. The militant miners were eventually stopped when Prime Minister Radul Vasile agreed to a 35% wage hike and stalled the closure of two mines.

Romania joined the Council of Europe in 1993. It applied for full NATO membership in 1996, was rejected, but hoped to be admitted into the defensive alliance in November 2002. The EU started accession talks with Romania in March 2000; full EU membership is slated for 2007–10.

In December 1999 Constantinescu dismissed Radul Vasile and replaced him with former National Bank of Romania governor Mugur Isărescu. But by mid-2000 Isărescu was fighting for his political life after the opposition accused him of mismanagement of the State Property Fund. This was followed in May 2000 by the collapse of the National Fund for Investment (NFI) which saw thousands of investors lose their savings.

Scandal and corruption surrounded the November/December 2000 electoral race. The opposition Party of Social Democracy (PDSR) candidate and former president, Ion Iliescu, was almost forced to pull out after allegations that his 1996 presidential campaign had been funded illegally. Meanwhile, incumbent president Constantinescu withdrew from the race in July announcing that he would not run for office in such a 'Mafia-type system'.

The final shockwave came in late November when a disquieting 28.3% of Romania's disgruntled electorate backed extreme-right politician Cornelui Vadim Tudor from the Greater Romania Party (PRM). But run-off elections in mid-December saw the notoriously xenophobic politician crushed by Ion Iliescu's leftist PDSR.

The 70-year-old Iliescu, who won 36.4% of the first round-vote, secured 66% of nationwide votes and secured another term in office – he had served as president between 1990 and 1996.

Since taking power, Romania's integration into Europe and economic reform have topped Iliescu's political agenda.

GEOGRAPHY
Covering 237,500 sq km, oval-shaped Romania is larger than Hungary and Bulgaria combined. The Danube River drains the entire country (except the Black Sea coast) and completes its 2850km course in Romania's Danube Delta.

Central and northern Romania is taken up by the U-shaped Carpathian Mountains. The highest point is Mt Moldoveanu (2544m) in the Făgăraş range southeast of Sibiu. The Transylvanian Plain, a plateau with valleys and hills, occupies the centre of the U; the Moldavian plateau is to the east. Earthquakes are quite common in the south and southwest.

The Carpathian Mountains account for approximately one-third of the country's area, with alpine pastures above and thick fir, spruce and oak forests below. Another third of Romania is covered by hills and tablelands full of orchards and vineyards. The final third is a fertile plain where cereals, vegetables, herbs and other crops are grown.

CLIMATE

The average annual temperature is 11°C in the south and on the coast, but only 2°C in the mountains. Romanian winters can be extremely cold and foggy with lots of snow from mid-December to mid-April. In summer there's usually hot, sunny weather on the Black Sea coast.

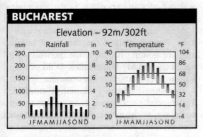

FLORA & FAUNA

Rural Romania has thriving animal populations, which include chamois, lynx, fox, deer, wolf, bear and badger. The birdlife is most varied in the Danube Delta, though you'll see eagles, hawks and vultures almost everywhere in the country.

GOVERNMENT & POLITICS

Romania has a constitutional republic government with a multiparty parliamentary system consisting of the Chamber of Deputies and the Senate. The president is elected by the people; his nominations for prime minister and the cabinet must be approved by parliament. The current president is Ion Iliescu and the prime minister is Adrian Natase. Both belong to the Party of Social Democracy (PDSR).

The main political parties are the ruling leftist PDSR, the centrists Democratic Convention of Romania (CDR) and the extreme-right Greater Romania Party (PRM).

The next parliamentary and presidential elections, held every four years, are slated for November 2004.

ECONOMY

Romania's postcommunist shift from a centrally planned to a market economy continues to haunt much of the populace. Poverty is widespread – an estimated 44.5% of the population live below the poverty line – and the average monthly salary remains at an inadequate US$100. Meanwhile unemployment, having decreased slightly from 11.4% in 1999 to 10.1% in 2001, remains high.

The end of 2000 saw the country's economy finally emerge from a gruelling recession that had lasted three years. GDP increased by 1.6% in 2000, the first positive growth recorded since 1996, then again by 3.9% in 2001. Inflation, too, while still alarmingly high, dropped from 45.9% in 1999 to 34% in 2001.

Despite the promise of future EU membership, the next few years leading up to it are expected to be as economically painful as the past, as the government continues to shut down oversized, loss-making state enterprises and privatise others. With Romania currently ranked last among EU expansion candidates and the European Bank for Reconstruction and Development (EBRD) rating the country's economic progress as 'the region's worst', the new government has vowed to promote economic reform.

Romania's largest foreign-trade partners are Italy, Germany, France, Turkey and the UK. Investment confidence, however, is low. Over the last 11 years Romania has only been able to secure US$6 billion of foreign investment, a mere drop in the ocean considering US$2 billion of this was EBRD investment.

POPULATION & PEOPLE

Fifty-three per cent of Romania's population live in towns and cities. Bucharest is the largest city, then Constanţa, Iaşi, Timişoara, Galaţi, Braşov, Cluj-Napoca and Craiova.

Ethnic Romanians comprise 89.5% of the population, Hungarians 7.1%, Roma 1.8%, Germans 0.5%, Ukrainians 0.3% and other nationalities 0.8%. While the government estimates that 400,000 Roma live in Romania, a more accurate figure would be two million, making it the world's largest Roma community. Unfortunately anti-Roma sentiment in the country remains strong.

ARTS

Painter Nicolae Grigorescu (1838–1907) absorbed French impressionism and created canvases alive with the colour of the Romanian peasantry. His work is displayed in Bucharest, Iaşi and Constanţa.

Abstract sculptor Constantin Brâncuşi (1876–1957), a native of Târgu Jiu who later moved to France, revolutionised sculpture by emphasising form and the beauty of the material itself.

Romantic poet Mihai Eminescu (1850–89) captured the spirituality of the Romanian people. The satirist Ion Luca Caragiale (1852–1912) decried the impact of precipitous modernisation on city life in his plays through comic irony. Playwright Eugene Ionesco (1912–94) was an exponent of the 'theatre of the absurd'. Former dissident Paul Goma, born in 1935, and Andrei Codrescu who moved to the USA in 1966, are noted contemporary voices. Poetic works by Romanian-born Paul Celan (1920–70), who wrote mainly in German, have been translated into English.

Music

Traditional Romanian folk instruments include the *bucium* (alphorn), *cimpoi* (bagpipes), *cobză* (a pear-shaped lute) and *nai* (a panpipe of about 20 cane tubes). There are many kinds of flute, including the *ocarina* (a ceramic flute) and the *tilinca* (a flute without finger holes). The violin is the most common folk instrument in contemporary Romania. Famous composer, George Enescu (1881–1955), was a virtuoso violinist who utilised Romanian folk themes in his work.

The *doină* is an improvised love song, a sort of Romanian blues with a romantic or social theme. The *baladă*, on the other hand, is a collective narrative song steeped with feeling.

Couples dance in a circle, a semicircle or line. In the *sârbă* males and females dance quickly in a closed circle with hands on each other's shoulders. The *horă* is another circle dance. In the *brâu* (belt dance), dancers form a chain by grasping their neighbour's belt.

Modern Romani (Tzigane) music has absorbed many influences. Professional *lăutari* (musicians) circulate through villages inviting neighbours to join in weddings, births, baptisms, funerals and harvest festivals. *Cântec* (improvised songs) are directed at a specific individual and designed to elicit an emotional response. To appeal to older people, *lăutari* sing *baladă* or *cântece epice* (epic songs) in verse, often recounting the exploits of Robin Hood-style *haiduci* (outlaws) who apply justice through their actions.

SOCIETY & CONDUCT

Postcommunist Romania is a jigsaw of economics and attitude as much as of ethnicity. Many of the older generation hark back with nostalgia to communist days when prices were low, pensions high and state-benefits abundant. By contrast, Romania's younger generation is full of beans. A small chunk already drives big fast cars, while the remaining chunk is driven by the dream of it.

Romanians are typically strong-minded, stubbornly proud and egocentric. They are staunchly aware of their roots and take great pride in their country's rich natural heritage and folk culture. Befriend any Romanian and within hours an expedition to the mountains will be mapped out for you.

Men and women greet each other with a kiss. Women walk down the street linking arms or holding hands, while menfolk offer each other hearty handshakes. Wild gesticulations in conversation are common.

Romanian hospitality is equally formidable. These people spill their hearts to you, welcome you with open arms into their homes, feed you until you burst, and expect *nothing* in return except friendship. Don't rebuff it.

RELIGION

Most people (87% of the total population) are Romanian Orthodox, 5% Roman Catholic, 6% Protestant and 1% Greek Orthodox. There are small Muslim and Jewish communities as well (less than 1% combined).

LANGUAGE

Romanian is closer to classical Latin than other Romance languages. Some Slavic words were incorporated in the 7th to 10th centuries as the Romanian language took definite shape. English and French are the first foreign languages taught in Romanian schools; German is useful in Transylvania. Speakers of Italian, Spanish and French should be able to understand some Romanian. This is one Eastern

European country where Russian won't get you very far.

A few useful terms are *bloc* (building), *bulevardul* (boulevard), *calea* (avenue), *intrarea* (entrance), *piaţa* (square), *scara* (stairway), *şoseaua* (highway) and *strada* (street). In Romania, you can use the French *merci* to say 'thank you'.

See the Language chapter at the back of the book for pronunciation guidelines and useful words and phrases.

Facts for the Visitor

HIGHLIGHTS

Romania's most valuable asset is its diversity, offering as much to do and see to tourists who want to stray off the beaten tourist track as those who want to stay well and truly on it.

Most people's 'must-see' list includes Bucharest's Palace of Parliament and Village Museum; Bran Castle near Braşov (Count Dracula never actually slept there); Peleş Castle in Sinaia (among Eastern Europe's finest royal pads); the painted monasteries of Southern Bucovina; and the well-preserved medieval towns of Cluj-Napoca, Braşov, Sighişoara and Sibiu.

Things generally not on any list but which should be part of any trip include: a few nights in a rural Romanian home around Bran (the more remote the better); a mountain hike to 2000m in Sinaia (there is a cable car); Maramureş' villages (with home-made cheese); a boat ride through the Danube Delta's wild waterways (watching birds and fish); and a shot-slamming session of fiery *ţuică* with new-found friends.

SUGGESTED ITINERARIES

Depending on the length of your stay, you could do the following things:

Two days
  Visit Braşov and Sinaia.
One week
  Visit Braşov, Sinaia, Bran (not missing Râşnov Castle), Sighişoara and perhaps Cluj-Napoca. Southbound travellers to Bulgaria should add a day in Bucharest.
Two weeks
  Visit Bucharest, Braşov, Sinaia, Bran/Râşnov, Sighişoara, Sibiu and Cluj-Napoca with at least one mountain hike – or skip Cluj-Napoca and visit Bucovina's monasteries.

One month
  Concentrate on Bucharest, Transylvania, Bucovina, Maramureş and the Danube Delta.

PLANNING
When to Go

May and June are the best months to visit, followed by September and early October. Spring in Romania is a pastiche of wildflowers, melodious bird song and rivers flowing with melted snow. At higher elevations snow lingers as late as early May and the hiking season doesn't begin in earnest until mid-June. Along the Black Sea coast, resorts start filling up in June and stay packed until the end of August. Romania is famous for its harsh winters, which can be extremely cold, foggy and snowy from mid-December to mid-April. Tourism during this time focuses on ski resorts such as Poiana Braşov and Sinaia.

Maps

The best country map of Romania available abroad is Marco Polo's 2000 edition of *România* (1:750,000). In the country, the Bucharest-based **Amco Press** (☎/fax 021-340 31 09; **e** amco@mail.kappa.ro; Blvd Nicolae Grigorescu 29A) publishes a good range of country and city maps, which are available in bookshops in Bucharest, Braşov and other larger cities.

Those intent on exploring Transylvania in any depth should invest in the truly outstanding map *Erdély-Transilvania-Siebenbürgen* (1:500,000), which features nearly every forest road, dirt track and village in Transylvania, Crişan, Banat and Maramureş. Published by Dimap it is sold in selected bookshops in Bucharest and Transylvania (US$1.85).

Be aware that street names in Romania are prone to change.

What to Bring

Don't bring too much. Most forgotten items can easily be picked up in Bucharest or other larger cities. If you intend travelling around, take a backpack. A light daypack is handy.

Necessities everyone should bring include a first-aid kit, water bottle, a Swiss army knife and a small torch (flashlight). A universal sink plug is also handy. Bring your own gear if you plan to hike or camp. Binoculars and insect repellent are essential for travellers heading into the Danube Delta. Indestructible footwear is also recommended.

ROMANIA

Bring spare tapes for your camcorder, contact lens solution and any special medicines you might need. In Bucharest and larger cities, tampons, sanitary towels and condoms are widely available; elsewhere they're not.

An 'emergency' stash of Western currency in cash is also handy. While banks and ATMs are widespread in cities, they are virtually nonexistent in villages and small towns.

TOURIST OFFICES
Local Tourist Offices
Romania does not have a national tourist office, prompting a handful of privately run tourist offices and dozens of travel agencies to mushroom. The services and information they offer range from the superb to the useless.

Touring ACR, the travel agency arm of the Automobil Clubul Român (Romanian Automobile Club), has desks in several hotels around Romania which provide general information for visiting motorists (and others).

Tourist Offices Abroad
Contrary to the disheartening lack of information in-country, Romania runs a string of efficient tourist offices abroad, coordinated by the **National Authority for Tourism** (☎ 021-410 12 62; w www.turism.ro; Str Apolodor 17, RO-70663 Bucharest).

France (☎ 01 40 20 99 33, fax 01 40 20 99 43,
  e roumanie@office-tourisme-roumanie.com)
  12 rue des Pyramides, F-75001 Paris
UK (☎ 020-7224 3692, fax 7935 6435,
  e uktourff@romania.freeserve.co.uk) 22
  New Cavendish Street, London W1M 7LH
USA (☎ 212-545 84 84, fax 251 04 29,
  e ronto@erols.com) 14 East 38th St, 12th
  Floor, New York, NY 10016

VISAS & DOCUMENTS
Passport
Your number one document is your passport. Its validity must extend to at least six months beyond the date you enter the country in order to obtain a visa. Never *ever* part with your passport (see Street Scams under Dangers & Annoyances later in this chapter).

Visas
Citizens of the EU, Canada, Switzerland and Japan may travel visa-free in Romania for up to 90 days. Citizens of Turkey can stay for up to 60 days and Americans for 30 days without a visa. All other Western visitors, including

Israelis, require a visa which must be bought from a Romanian embassy or consulate outside Romania.

Visa costs vary dramatically between embassies. A single-entry transit visa (US$35 to $38) is valid for three days and allows you to enter Romania once. Double-entry transit visas (US$35 to $50) allow you to enter the country twice and stay for three days each time. Transit visas must be used within one month of the issue date.

A regular, single-entry visa (US$35 to $50) is valid for 30 days from the day you enter the country; the visa must be used within three months of the date it was issued. Multiple-entry visas (US$70 to $90) are valid for six months and allow you to stay up to 30 days at a time. Overstaying your visa will result in a US$34 fine.

Visa Extensions You can extend your stay by reporting to a passport office, such as the **Visa Extensions Office** (☎ 012-650 30 50; Str Luigi Cazzavillian 11; open 9am-1pm Mon, Tues, Thur & Fri) in Bucharest. A visa extension costs US$30.

EMBASSIES & CONSULATES
Romanian Embassies & Consulates
Romanian embassies and consulates worldwide include:

Australia (☎ 02-6286 2343, fax 6286 2433,
  e roembcbr@cyberone.com.au) 4 Dalman
  Crescent, O'Malley, ACT 2606 Canberra
Canada (☎ 613-789 5345, fax 789 4365,
  e romania@cyberus.ca) 655 Rideau St,
  Ottawa, Ontario K1N 6A3
France (☎ 01 40 62 22 02/4, fax 01 45 56 97
  47, e ambparis.roumanie@francophonie.org)
  3–5 Rue de l'Exposition, F-75007 Paris
Germany (☎ 030-803 30 18/19, fax 803 16 84,
  e ro.amb.berlin@t-online.de)
  Matterhornstrasse 79, D14129 Berlin
Netherlands (☎ 070-354 37 96, fax 354 15 87,
  e ambrom@tip.nl) Catsheuvel 55, NL-2517
  KA, The Hague
UK (☎ 020-7937 9666, fax 7937 8069,
  ☎/fax 7937 4675, e romania@roemb.demon
  .co.uk) 4 Palace Green, London W8 4QD
USA (☎ 202-387 6902, 332 4846, fax 232
  4748, e consular@roembus.org) 1607 23rd
  St NW, Washington DC 20008
  Consulate in New York: (☎ 212-682 9120,
  fax 972 8463, e mail@romconsny.org) 200
  East 38th St, New York, NY 10016

ROMANIA

Consulate in Los Angeles: (☎ 310-444 0043, fax 445 0043, |e| consulat.la@roconla.org) 11766 Wilshire Blvd, Suite 560, Los Angeles, CA 90025

Embassies & Consulates in Romania

The following embassies and consulates are in Bucharest (area code ☎ 021):

Australia (☎ 320 98 26, |W| www.romania australia.ro) Blvd Unirii 74
Bulgaria (☎ 230 21 50, |e| bulebassy@pcnet.ro) Str Vasile Lascăr 32
Canada (☎ 307 50 00, |W| www.dfait-maeci.gc .ca/bucharest) Str Nicolae Iorga 36
France (☎ 312 02 17, |W| www.ambafrance-ro .org) Str Biserica Amzei 13–15
Germany (☎ 230 25 80, |e| germanembassy -bucharest@ines.ro) Str Rabat 21
Hungary (☎ 312 00 73, |e| hunembro@ines.ro) Str Jean Louis Calderon 63–65
   Consulate: (☎ 312 04 68) Str Henri Coandă 5
Moldova (☎ 230 04 74, |e| moldova@customers .digiro.net) Aleea Alexandru 40
   Consulate: (☎ 410 98 27) Blvd Eroilor 8
UK (☎ 312 03 03, |W| www.britain.ro) Str Jules Michelet 24
Ukraine (☎ 211 69 86, |e| emb-ukr@itcnet.ro) Calea Dorbanţilor 16
   Consulate: (☎ 223 27 02) Str Tuberozelor 5
USA (☎ 210 40 42, |W| www.usembassy.ro) Str Nicolae Filipescu 26
Yugoslavia (☎ 211 98 71) Calea Dorobanţilor 34

CUSTOMS

Romanian customs regulations are complicated but they are not often enforced. Gifts that are worth up to a total of US$100 may be imported duty free. For foreigners, duty-free allowances are 4L of wine, 1L of spirits and 200 cigarettes.

Officially, you're allowed to import hard currency up to a maximum of US$10,000. Valuable goods and foreign currency over US$1000 should be declared upon arrival.

MONEY

All prices are listed in this chapter in US dollars (abbreviated to $). In the country however, you have to pay for all your purchases and services in Romanian lei (singular leu).

Currency

There are coins of 50, 100 and 500 lei and banknotes of 1000, 5000, 10,000, 50,000 and 100,000 lei.

Exchange Rates

At the time of publication, the Romanian leu (plural: lei) was officially worth:

country	unit		leu
Australia	A$1	=	17,622 lei
Canada	C$1	=	20,610 lei
Euro Zone	€1	=	32,205 lei
Japan	¥100	=	27,312 lei
NZ	NZ$1	=	15,382 lei
UK	UK£1	=	50,091 lei
USA	US$1	=	31,838 lei

Exchanging Money

Currency exchanges dot almost every street corner in Bucharest and major cities. By contrast, changing your foreign currency in the countryside can present huge challenges (always keep a secret stash of cash at hand).

You can change travellers cheques (into dollars or lei) and get Visa or MasterCard cash advances (in lei only) for 3% to 5% commission at most branches of Banca Comercială Română and Banca Ion Ţiriac. American Express has a representative in Bucharest (see Money in the Bucharest section later).

ATM machines that give 24-hour advances (Cirrus, Plus, Visa, MasterCard, Eurocard) have mushroomed in recent years, particularly in the capital and major cities. There's a couple of ATMs at Otopeni airport and Gara de Nord in Bucharest.

Whether you change money at a bank or currency exchange, you need your passport. It is illegal for foreigners to change lei back into foreign currencies, however, this law is rarely enforced

Black Market Changing money on the street is illegal, risky and the quickest way to get ripped off. Black marketeers who offer to change money on the street are professional thieves. Counting out a roll of money in front of you, then switching it with a dud roll at the last instant is common. Another trick is for the moneychanger to take your dollars and give you the correct amount, only to shout 'not good, not good' as you leave and insist on giving 'your' money back in exchange for theirs.

Costs

Romania is a relatively inexpensive country for foreigners. Restaurant meals, drinks, public transport, museum admissions, theatre

ROMANIA

tickets and private rooms are less expensive here than in many other European countries. On average you'll pay US$20 to US$35 per night for budget accommodation and less than $10 per day for meals and drinks.

Tipping & Bargaining

In flashier restaurants in Bucharest, waiters will not hesitate to ask where their tip is if you fail to leave one. Elsewhere, tipping remains a rarity – and often undeserved. Tips (alias bribes) should not be offered to officials, including train conductors.

Some bargaining, but not much, goes on in flea markets. Countrywide, taxi drivers drive the hardest bargain. *Always* haggle.

POST & COMMUNICATIONS
Post

Mail boxes in Bucharest are red and labelled *Poştă Romană*; elsewhere they may be yellow. Stamps *(timbre)* are sold at post offices.

Main post offices are open until 8pm Monday to Saturday, and until noon on Sunday. When mailing purchases home from Romania, you may be asked to pay an export duty equivalent to 20% of their value. The Romanian postal service is improving, but is still slow and unreliable.

Your post-restante mail (c/o Poste Restante, Poştă Romană Oficiul Bucureşti 1, Str Matei Millo 10, RO-70700 Bucureşti, ROMANIA) can be collected from the main post office in Bucharest at Str Matei Millo 10. Times for the

collection of mail are 7.30am to 8pm on weekdays and 7.30am to 1pm on Saturday. Mail will be held for one month.

Postcards/letters (20g) to the UK or elsewhere in Europe cost $0.40/0.55 and $0.60/0.75 to North America.

Telephone

Romania's telephone system is – in cities and towns at least – pretty reliable. In the countryside however, a telephone can be something of a luxury. Public phones are rare or nonexistent, while many places to stay and/or eat only have a mobile phone (cellphone) – or no phone at all.

In towns and cities, making a local, regional or international call from one of the many orange-coloured cardphones is simple. You can purchase a magnetic phonecard *(cartela telefonică)* at the telephone building in Bucharest or any telex-fax office or post office.

Only phonecards worth 50,000 lei ($1.60) and 100,000 lei ($3.10) are available. To exchange a spent card midway through a call, press the button on the telephone labelled 'K'. This allows your remaining credit to be stored, giving you enough time to insert a new card without being rudely cut off. Incoming calls (limited to three minutes) can also be received on these cardphones.

Romania's international operator is reached by dialling ☎ 971. To call an English-speaking operator abroad dial ☎ 021-800 4444 for British Telecom, ☎ 021-800 4288 for AT&T USA

Area Code Changes

In 2002 all telephone area codes throughout Romania expanded by one digit. The changes, which were implemented in June, affected the geographic area codes for fixed telephones, mobile access codes and codes for toll-free services.

Geographic area codes were modified by adding a '2' to the existing codes. Thus, Bucharest's area code changed from 01 to 021 and Braşov's from 068 to 0268. The access code for the Republic of Moldova has also changed from 02 to 099.

Mobile area codes were changed from three-digit area codes to four-digit codes. The '9' in the old codes was exchanged for a '7' and an additional digit was added to indicate the mobile carrier ('2' indicates Mobifon). Hence, 091 became 0721; 092 became 0722; 093 became 0723; 090 became 0740; 094 became 0744; 095 became 0745; 096 became 0766; and, 098 became 0788.

Non-geographic service numbers beginning with 08, such as the 0800 toll-free numbers, were also expanded by adding '0' immediately after the area code. Thus, the number 0800 12345 changed to 0800 012345.

While plans exist to standardise all emergency short codes with that of the rest of Europe, at the time of writing no date had been set. Telephone numbers following the area codes remain unchanged.

See Romtelecom's website at ⓦ www.romtelecom.ro for more information on the changes.

Direct, ☎ 021-800 1800 for MCI Worldwide or ☎ 021-800 0877 for Sprint.

To call other cities in Romania, dial the area code (given in the relevant sections of this chapter), followed by the recipient's number. To call a mobile/cellphone, likewise dial the respective area code (listed as part of the telephone number) and subscriber's number. To call Romania from abroad dial the international access code, Romania's country code (☎ 40), the area code (minus the first 0) and the number.

Fax

Sending an international fax from any telex-fax office in Bucharest or main post office elsewhere in Romania is easy and costs around $2 per A4 page; to receive a fax should cost no more than $1 a page.

Email & Internet Access

In Bucharest there are literally dozens of Internet cafés and places providing public Internet access, a couple of which are open 24 hours. Count on paying around $1 per hour in the capital. Outside the capital, there are Internet cafes in every city and most smaller towns.

DIGITAL RESOURCES

Among the many online Romanian information resources, find the latest breaking news, views and local press digests on Ⓦ www .centraleurope.com/romaniatoday, the website of Central Europe Online. A more hands-on approach is taken by locally published city guide Bucharest In Your Pocket (Ⓦ www .inyourpocket.com), which posts its entire contents free of charge on its website. The Romania Travel Guide (Ⓦ www.rotravel .com) is another useful site, covering all aspects of travel around Romania.

BOOKS & CD-ROMS

A History of Romania, edited by Kurt Treptow and also available on CD-ROM, is the most comprehensive history book around, combining a clear account of events with biographies, photos and maps. Another essential read is Athene Palace by RG Waldeck, a memoir of Bucharest's grand hotel and the political intrigues that filled its atmospheric lobby prior to WWII. Romania at the outbreak of WWII is also portrayed in Olivia Manning's The Balkan Trilogy, while it is Dacian, Byzantine and Saxon Romania eras that are beautifully evoked in Alan Ogden's Romania Revisited: On the Trail of English Travellers 1601–1941.

Kiss the Hand You Cannot Bite: The Rise and Fall of the Ceauşescus, by Edward Behr, provides fascinating background on the 1989 revolution. Dracula fiends should indulge in Vlad III Dracula: The Life and Times of the Historical Dracula, also by Kurt Treptow.

Many of these, plus numerous other titles, are published by the Iaşi-based **Center for Romanian Studies** (Ⓦ www.romanianstudies .ro) which has an online catalogue.

NEWSPAPERS & MAGAZINES

The most popular Romanian daily papers are Adevărul (The Truth) which favours the PDSR, România Libera, an opposition voice, and Evenimentul Zilei (Daily Events), a popular mainstream paper.

Nine O'Clock (Ⓦ www.nineoclock.ro) is Bucharest's free, English-language daily, found stacked in neat piles on hotel reception desks and online. The leading business newspapers in English are the weekly Bucharest Business Week (Ⓦ www.bbw.ro) and rival The Business Review (Ⓦ www.bbw.ro).

Bucharest In Your Pocket is a locally produced city guide, published every two months and sold in news kiosks and bookshops.

Newsstands and hotels in larger cities sell Newsweek, Time, The Economist, International Herald Tribune, Wall Street Journal and other international papers.

TIME

Romanian time is GMT/UTC plus two hours, which means there's a one-hour difference between Romania and Hungary and Yugoslavia. Romania starts daylight-saving time at the end of March, when clocks are turned forward an hour. At the end of October, they're turned back an hour.

LAUNDRY

Self-service laundrettes simply do not exist in Romania, with the exception of Nuf Nuf in Bucharest where you can wash your socks and smocks for $1.40 a load. Failing that, make use of the washing machine at Bucharest's Villa Helga and Elvis' Villa Bucharest (free to guests) – or hand-wash.

TOILETS

The cleanest toilet is behind a bush – not that bush squatting is allowed in towns and cities where you'll be arrested if you pull down your pants in public. Women's toilets are marked with the letter *F (femei)* or with an *s*. Men's are marked *B (bărbaţi)* or *t*.

WOMEN TRAVELLERS

Romania is generally a safe place for women to travel in, although the usual rules apply: do not wander alone late at night and avoid sitting in empty compartments on long-distance and overnight trains etc. If you should encounter offensive behaviour, a few strong words – such as shouting *poliţia!* – is usually sufficient to ward off trouble.

GAY & LESBIAN TRAVELLERS

In late 2001, article 200 of Romania's penal code was scrapped decriminalising homosexual relations. Showing affection in public, however, remains a criminal offence for gays and lesbians in Romania, who can still be thrown in jail for five years for so much as holding hands. The Orthodox Church considers homosexuality a sin, and a surprising number of young Romanians feel that gay and lesbian relationships are 'unnatural'. Hotel managers might turn away openly gay couples, so be discreet if you're travelling with a same-sex partner.

Bucharest has an active gay and lesbian community, which is represented by **Accept** (☎ 021-252 16 37, fax 252 56 20; **w** www .accept-romania.ro; CP 34-56, Bucharest). In Cluj-Napoca there's **Association Attitude** (**e** attitude@rdslink.ro) for the gay and lesbian community in Transylvania.

DISABLED TRAVELLERS

Disabled travellers will find it difficult – in fact, impossible – to conquer Romania alone. Street surfaces are woefully uneven, while ramps and specially equipped toilets and hotel rooms are virtually unheard of. There is not a single wheelchair-accessible train or bus in the country. Consider joining a package tour.

Emergency Services

For nationwide emergency assistance phone ☎ 055 for police and ☎ 061 for ambulance.

While plans exist to standardise all emergency short codes with those used in the rest of Europe, at the time of research no date had been set.

DANGERS & ANNOYANCES

Bucharest has a serious stray-dog problem – a bizarre legacy of systemisation in the 1980s when scores of city-centre homes were demolished, forcing dog-owners to let their pets loose on the streets. These dogs have since multiplied – and continue to multiply, despite sporadic attempts by the authorities to rid the city of its unnerving canine presence. Most dogs roaming the city centre are harmless if left alone, but bitches with puppies can be snappy. Keep well clear.

Other annoyances include heavy pollen (spring is murder for allergy sufferers), year-round pollution in larger cities and swarms of mosquitoes in summer. Beware of theft. If you have a car, never leave anything of any value inside it, and take care in hotels by locking valuables in your pack or suitcase when you go out.

Street Scams

Tourist Police A man stops you in the street and asks if you want to change money. You refuse. Seconds later, another man appears, arrests the first man, and demands to see your passport, explaining that he is from the tourist police. Simply walk away. If he flashes an ID badge, still do not hand over your passport. As a last resort, insist on being accompanied to the nearest police station – on foot. Taking a taxi with a thief is not a good idea.

Stupid Tourist A man stops you on the street, explains that he is from a foreign country, explains that he has never seen a 100,000 lei banknote before, and asks you to show him one. If you pull out your wallet, it – and the stupid tourist – will be gone before you can say Jack Robinson.

Fake Taxi Driver A man greets you as you get off the train at Gara de Nord station, explains that he is from Villa Helga hostel, and offers to drive you there. Anyone who says they are from the hostel is a dud. Staff *never* meet guests at the station. Insist on making your own way there. The same scenario has been used for the new Elvis' Villa Bucharest.

BUSINESS HOURS

Banking hours are 9am to 2pm or 3pm weekdays. Most shops and markets are closed on Sunday. Many museums close on Monday. Theatrical performances and concerts usually begin at 7pm, except on Monday and in summer when most theatres are closed.

PUBLIC HOLIDAYS & SPECIAL EVENTS

Public holidays are New Year (1 and 2 January), Easter Monday (March/April), National Unity Day (1 December) and Christmas (25 and 26 December).

Many festivals take place in summer, including the three-day Bucharest Carnival in June and the Golden Stag international pop music festival in Braşov in July. Folklore festivals include Hora la Prislop in Maramureş in July and the International Festival of Danubian Folklore in Tulcea in August.

In September there's Sibiu's Cibinium music festival and, the next month, Cluj-Napoca's Musical Autumn. In December the Days of Bihor Culture takes place in Oradea, and Sighetu Marmaţiei celebrates its Christmas festival.

ACTIVITIES
Skiing & Snowboarding

Romania's ski resorts are Sinaia, Predeal and Poiana Braşov, all in the Carpathian Mountains between Bucharest and Braşov.

Although incomparable to Alpine ski resorts, Poiana Braşov and Predeal offer a range of green to black slopes, suitable for skiers and snowboarders of all abilities. Poiana Braşov – the largest resort – has 15km of runs (level differences of 32m to 765m), served by two cable cars, a gondola and a handful of draglifts. Predeal has 6km of ski runs (level differences of 30m to 390m), a couple of chairlifts and four draglifts.

Sinaia's slopes are more limited and best-suited to day skiers. But, atop Bucegi Plateau above Sinaia, there is an 8km cross-country route and a 13-bend bobsled track.

The ski season runs from December to mid-March. You can hire gear at the main hotels for $9 to $12 per day. There are ski schools in Poiana Braşov and Predeal.

Hiking

Romania's Carpathian Mountains offer endless opportunities for hikers; the most popular areas are the Bucegi and Făgăraş ranges, south and west of Braşov. Other Carpathian hiking zones include the Retezat National Park, northwest of Târgu Jiu; the Şureanu Mountains, between Alba Iulia and Târgu Jiu; the Apuseni Mountains, southwest of Cluj-Napoca; and the Ceahlău Massif, between Braşov and Suceava.

COURSES

The **Romanian Cultural Foundation** (*Fundaţia Culturală Română;* ☎ *021-230 28 54, fax 230 75 59;* ⓦ *www.fcr.ro; Aleea Alexandru 38, 71273 Sector 1 Bucharest)* organises summer workshops in Baia Mare in Maramureş. Course subjects range from Romanian language to folk art, cuisine, and traditional song and dance.

ACCOMMODATION
Camping

There are dozens of camping grounds around Romania; those with bungalows are called *popas truistic*. Sites vary enormously, many without toilets and/or showers. Most grounds open from around May to September.

Wild camping is prohibited in cities and in the Danube Delta, but not necessarily elsewhere, particularly on the coast where it is fairly common. If anyone hints there could be a problem about camping somewhere, believe them and go elsewhere. Wherever you camp, take care of your gear.

Mountain Huts

In most mountain areas there's a network of cabins or chalets *(cabana)* with restaurants and dormitories. These are much cheaper than hotels. No reservations are required, but arrive early if the cabana is in a popular location, for example next to a cable-car terminus. Count on good companionship rather than cleanliness or comfort at these places. Many open year-round and in winter cater for skiers.

Hostels

In the last couple of years a number of new hostels have sprouted around the country. Hostels charge around $10 a night for a bed in a two- to 10-bed room, most not including breakfast. Check on Romania's **Youth Hostel Association** (☎/*fax 064-186 616;* ⓦ *www .dntcj.ro/yhr; headquarters: Str Clăbucet 2/69, RO-3400 Cluj-Napoca)*. Some of its accredited hostels are, in fact, hotels or cabanas, which also tout dorm beds.

Hotels

Rooms in a good, modern hotel only cost about $10 more than you'd pay for a flea pit.

ROMANIA

So, it may be better value in the long run to take a room with a private bathroom.

All accommodation prices in this chapter are listed in US dollars ($), calculated at the official rate. Payment is required in Romanian lei in cash in low-budget hotels and by credit card or cash in better hotels.

Romanian hotels are rated by the government on a star system. The zero- and one-star hotels, while generally clean, almost always have a shared bathroom and toilet; ask to be sure. They charge from $12 to $25. Most two-star hotels are good value with clean rooms with TV and private bath for between $20 and $40. Three-star places charge $50 to $100 for a double with in-room phone and cable TV. At some hotels breakfast *(mic dejun)* is often included in the price.

Private Rooms

Homestays are abundant in most major towns and cities where, chances are, you will be approached by someone offering you a room *(cameră)* the moment you step off the train. Always verify the exact location of the room you are being offered on a map and insist on seeing it before parting with any cash. Count on paying between $10 and $25 per person.

Agrotourism (B&B in the countryside) is popular in many rural areas. The leading organisations in this field are **ANTREC** *(Asociaţia Naţională de Turism Rural, Ecologi şi Cultural; head office:* ☎/fax 021-223 70 24; Ⓦ *www.antrec.ro; Str Maica Alexandra 7, Bucharest)* which has properties countrywide; and **Fundaţia OVR Agro-Tur-Art** *(Opération Villages Roumains;* ☎/fax 330 171; Ⓦ *www.vaduizei.ovr.ro; house No 161; Vadu Izei)* which works with families in Maramureş and Moldavia.

Count on paying between $15 and $30 for a double room, plus $5 per person per meal. An excellent independent website is Ⓦ www .ruraltourism.ro, which provides contact details, prices and even pictures of many of the rural homes throughout the country.

FOOD

Romanian restaurants are affordable; outside Bucharest, it is difficult to spend more than $15 per day on food. On the other hand, you can happily spend $35 or more a day in the capital, including wine. Restaurants can be hard to find and/or very basic in more rural areas, offering the same things with unnerving consistency: grilled pork, grilled chicken, fried cheese and French fries. Always look carefully at the menu; dishes priced per 100g should be treated with caution.

Romanian favourites include *ciorbă de peri-şoare* (a spicy soup made with meatballs and vegetables), *ciorbă de burtă* (tripe soup), *ghiveci* (vegetable stew), *tocană* (onion and meat stew) and *ciorbă de legumă* (vegetable soup often cooked with meat stock). Restaurants and beer gardens often offer *mititei* or *mici* (pronounced 'meech'; grilled meatballs). Other common dishes are *muşchi de vacă/porc/miel* (cutlet of beef/pork/lamb), *ficat* (liver), *piept de pui* (chicken breast) and *cabanos prăjit* (fried sausages). Vegetarians should opt for a non-meaty *caşcaval pane* (breaded fried cheese) or *castraveţi* (tomatoes and cucumber salad). Cooking styles include *la grătar* (grilled), *prăjit* (fried), *fiert* (boiled) and *la frigare* (roasted on a spit). Almost every dish comes with *cartofi* (potatoes) or *orez* (rice).

Folk dishes are harder to find but they're delicious, especially *ardei umpluţi* (stuffed peppers) and *sarmale* (cabbage or vine leaves stuffed with spiced meat and rice). *Mămăligă* is cornmeal polenta that goes well with everything. Typical desserts are *paturi cu brinză* (cheese pastries), *plăcintă* (turnovers), *clătite* (pancakes) and *papănaşi* (a curd tartlet).

DRINKS

Romania is noted for its excellent wine, while the local beer is notable mostly for its low price (about $0.75 for a half-litre). Imported Hungarian and German beers are available but more expensive. Among the best Romanian wines are Cotnari, Murfatlar, Odobeşti, Târnave and Valea Călugărească. Red wines are called *negru* and *roşu*, while white wine is *vin alb*. *Vin de masă* is table wine. A bottle of decent Romanian wine shouldn't cost more than $4 ($10 in Bucharest).

Must is a fresh unfermented wine available during the wine harvest. *Ţuică* (plum brandy) is a strong liqueur drunk at the start of a meal. *Crama* refers to a wine cellar and a *berarie* is a beer hall. A couple of toasts are *poftă bună* (bon appétit) and *noroc!* (cheers!).

Beware of *Ness*, an awful instant coffee made from vegetable extracts. It's always served super sweet and tepid. Proper cafés serve *cafea filtru* (filtered coffee) and espresso (but don't get your hopes up). Unless you specifically ask, coffee and *ceai* (tea) are not often served *cu lapte* (with milk). *Apă minerală* (mineral water) is quite cheap and also widely available.

ENTERTAINMENT

Ask about local events at the main theatre and concert hall and visit any theatre ticket offices you can find. Opera companies exist in Bucharest, Cluj-Napoca, Iaşi and Timişoara. In large towns buy the local paper and try to decipher the entertainment listings.

Bucharest is loaded with hip bars to drink in and hot clubs to boogie the night away. Most other larger towns are graced with at least one groovy joint.

SHOPPING

Traditional purchases in Romania include plum brandy, embroidered blouses and handicrafts. The latter is easiest to find at major tourist sights, such as at the craft stalls which fill the square at the foot of Bran Castle or around Bucovina's painted monasteries.

Getting There & Away

AIR

Romania's national airline **Tarom** (**w** www
.tarom.digiro.net; UK: ☎ 020-7935 3600, fax
7487 2913; 27 New Cavendish Street, London, W1M 7RL • USA: ☎ 212-687 6014, fax
661 6056; 342 Madison Ave, Suite 168, New
York 10173) has weekly flights between Bucharest's Otopeni airport and most European capitals – including Amsterdam ($259), Berlin ($310), Budapest ($225), Chişinău ($154), Düsseldorf ($310), Frankfurt ($310), Prague ($210), Sofia ($145) and Warsaw ($260) – and to/from New York ($500) and Tel Aviv ($500).

It also operates a handful of international flights between airports in Constanţa to/from İstanbul ($187) and Munich ($388); and Timişoara to/from Düsseldorf ($239), Frankfurt ($239), London ($350) and New York ($500). All prices listed are for return flights and exclude airport taxes.

Tarom offers special youth fares to people aged up to 25 on its European and transatlantic flights, and aged up to 24 on its weekly flights to/from Tel Aviv. Youth tickets are valid for one year and there are no restrictions.

Students aged 24 to 31 years are eligible for youth fares too. Children aged two to 12 years pay 50% of the standard fare.

Numerous other airlines fly to/from Romania, including Air France, Air Ukraine, Alitalia, Austrian Airlines, British Airways, Czech Airlines, KLM, LOT, Lufthansa, Malév Hungarian Airlines, Olympic Airways, Swiss International Airlines and Turkish Airlines.

LAND
Train

In Romania, international train tickets are sold at CFR offices – look for the 'Agenţie de Voiaj CFR'. Most international trains require advance seat reservations ($2 to $4), even if you're travelling on an Inter-Rail pass. (Seat reservations are automatically included in tickets purchased in Romania.) If you already have a ticket, you may be able to make reservations at the station an hour before departure, but at least one day in advance is preferable.

Hungary & Beyond There are six trains daily between Bucharest's Gara de Nord and Budapest-Keleti ($30/58 2nd-class single/return, 12 hours, 873km). The *Pannonia Expres* arrives from Munich, via Vienna, Prague, Bratislava and Budapest; and the *Dacia Expres* comes from Vienna through Budapest to Bucharest.

A cheaper alternative is to hop aboard one of the two daily local Hungarian trains that shuttle between the towns of Oradea and Budapest-Nyugati ($20, five hours). Seat reservations aren't required. Local trains also depart from Békéscsaba, Hungary, for Oradea (90km) three times daily.

The *Carpaţi* makes its way from Warsaw through Kraków, Sibiu and Braşov on to Bucharest (2nd-class single/return $58/117, 27 hours, 1645km).

The *Bulgaria Expres* runs between Bucharest and Moscow (42 hours), stopping in Kyiv (2nd-class single $26, 28 hours, 806km), and the *Pretenia* travels to Chişinău (2nd-class single/return $13/25, 13 hours, 637km), in Moldova.

Yugoslavia The daily *Bucureşti* train shuttles from Bucharest's Gara de Nord to Belgrade-Dunav (2nd-class single $15 plus $10/15 for a couchette/sleeper, 13 hours, 693km), stopping in Drobeta–Turnu Severin and Timişoara on the way.

ROMANIA

Bulgaria & Turkey Trains from Romania to Bulgaria are slow and crowded. Between Sofia and Bucharest (1st/2nd-class single seat $30/21, bed $38/26, 12 hours) there are two trains, both of which stop in Ruse.

The overnight Bucharest-İstanbul *Bosor* express travels through eastern Bulgaria (2nd-class single/return $21/42, 17 hours, 803km) and stops in Ruse en route.

Bus

There's little reason to go to Romania by bus with such good train services available. The public bus system is terrible and private companies can be expensive. The exception is the bus to İstanbul ($27/51 single/return, 11 to 14 hours), which is faster than the train.

Numerous private bus companies operate daily buses between Germany and Romania. Tickets are sold from ticketing agencies in Romania's larger cities; these are listed in the relevant Getting There & Away sections.

Car & Motorcycle

Drivers need vehicle registration papers, liability insurance and a driving licence. Make sure your car is in good condition and carry a petrol can, oil and basic spares. Car rental is expensive. See the Getting Around section later for road rules.

When crossing the border by car, expect long queues at Romanian checkpoints, particularly on weekends. Carry food and water for the wait. Don't even consider trying to bribe a Romanian official and beware of unauthorised people charging dubious 'ecology', 'disinfectant' or other dodgy taxes at the border. (Ask for a receipt.)

Hungary There are border crossings at Petea (11km northwest of Satu Mare), Borş (14km northwest of Oradea), Vărş (66km north of Arad) and Nădlac (between Szeged and Arad).

Yugoslavia Cross at Jimbolia (45km west of Timişoara), Moraviţa (between Timişoara and Belgrade), Naidăş (120km east of Belgrade) and Porţile de Fier (Iron Gate; 10km west of Drobeta–Turnu Severin).

Bulgaria Cross at Calafat (opposite Vidin, Bulgaria), Giurgiu (opposite Ruse), Călăraşi (opposite Silistra), Negru Vodă (37km northeast of Tolbuhin) or Vama Veche (10km south of Mangalia).

The Giurgiu bridge toll across the Danube is $10/3 for cars/motorcycles (payable only in US$). A one-way fare for the main ferry costs $25/5 per car/passenger, or $10/1 per car and driver/passenger on the smaller BAC ferry. The Calafat ferry is $13/2 per car/passenger and the Călăraşi ferry is $3/0.30 per car and passengers/foot passenger. All crossings command an additional $6 ecological tax (payable in Romanian lei).

Moldova To get to/from Moldova, cross the border at Albiţa (65km southeast of Iaşi) or Sculeni (24km north of Ungheni).

Ukraine Use Siret, 45km north of Suceava on the road to Chernivtsi (Cernăuţi), to travel to Ukraine.

Walking

You can walk in or out of Romania at most of its border crossings, except those with Moldova and Ukraine. Hitch a ride instead. Pedestrians are not permitted to use the so-called 'Friendship Bridge' to or from Ruse, Bulgaria, but you can go by taxi ($30) or ferry.

DEPARTURE TAX

There is no departure tax in Romania.

Getting Around

AIR

The state-owned carrier Tarom has an extensive network of domestic flights from Bucharest. Many flights to Constanţa only run in July and August, but you can fly out of Bucharest's Băneasa domestic airport to most other parts of the country year-round.

Airfares are expensive. A one-way fare from Bucharest to Cluj-Napoca/Constanţa is around $90/67. Return fares are double. Children aged two to 12 years get a 50% reduction. Only 10kg of luggage is carried free, and you pay 1% of your airfare for every kilogram over the weight allowance.

TRAIN

Căile Ferate Române *(CFR; Romanian State Railways;* **w** *www.cfr.ro)* runs trains over 11,106km of track across Romania. The national train timetable *(mersul trenurilor)* is published in book form each May and is sold for $1.60 in CFR offices.

There are four types of trains in Romania: *personal* (slow) and *inter-city* (IC), *accelerat* and *rapid* (all speedier). On express trains you pay a supplement of $0.50 to $3 for the required seat reservation. At major stations there are separate ticket windows for 1st and 2nd class. Irrespective of the class you choose, fares are low: it costs about $0.85 to travel 100km in 1st class on a local train and $2.95 to travel in 2nd class on an express.

If you're caught riding in the wrong class you pay a $6 penalty. If you board a train without a ticket you could face a penalty of $8 to $11.

If possible, buy tickets for express trains a day in advance at a CFR office; remember most are closed on Sunday. CFR offices do not sell tickets for express trains leaving the same day; you must buy a ticket at the station *no more than one hour* before departure.

Your ticket will give the code number of your train along with your assigned carriage (*vagon*) and seat (*locul*).

If you have an international ticket right through Romania, you're allowed to make stops along the route but must purchase a reservation ticket each time you reboard an *accelerat* or *rapid* train. If the international ticket was issued in Romania, you must also pay the express train supplement each time.

Sleepers (*vagons de dormit*) are available between Bucharest and Cluj-Napoca, Oradea, Suceava, Timişoara, Tulcea and other large cities, and are a good way to cut down on your accommodation expenses. First-class sleeping compartments have two berths; 2nd-class sleepers have three berths; and 2nd-class couchettes have six berths. Book these well in advance at a CFR office in town.

Train Passes

Inter-Rail passes (sold to European residents only) and Balkan Flexipasses (available to everyone) are accepted in Romania, but Eurail passes are not. Even with a pass you must buy a reservation in the station every time you reboard an express. No supplements or fees are required for local trains.

BUS

Buses are less reliable and more crowded than trains. On rural routes only one or two buses run daily. Schedules posted in bus stations are often out of date, so always check at the ticket window. Purchase your ticket at a bus station (*autogară*) before boarding to avoid potential problems with the driver. If the bus is the only way to get to/from somewhere, try to reserve a seat by buying a ticket the day before.

CAR & MOTORCYCLE

Don't attempt to drive in Romania unless your car is in good shape and has been serviced. Repair shops are common, but unless you're driving a Renault (the same as Romania's Dacia) or a Citroën (the basis for the Oltcit model in Romania), parts are hard to come by.

Romania has two short stretches of motorway (*autostradă*): between Bucharest and Ploieşti (114km) and between Cernavodă and Fiteşti (15km). The latter is a toll road, so you have to pay a small fee. Some major roads (*drum naţional*) have been resurfaced but most are in a poor, pot-holed condition. Secondary roads (*drum judeţean*) can become dirt tracks, and mountain and forestry roads (*drum forestier*) can be impassable after heavy rain. Check the pressure of your tyres before entering Romania because it's often impossible to do so at Romanian petrol stations. Punctures can be repaired at shops labelled *vulcanizare*.

More hazardous than the dire state of roads are the obstacles moving about on them. Many drivers are aggressive and lack discipline. Horse-drawn carts piled high with hay, cows, pigs, drunks, children and other moving contraptions dart in, out and along roads without warning (it's illegal to honk at them lest you scare the horses). Some roads have no markings and are unlit – as are many vehicles.

Members of foreign automobile clubs (such as AA and AAA) are covered by Romania's **Automobil Clubul Român** (*ACR; 24hr emergencies:* ☎ 927). Of course, you must still pay: emergency road service costs upwards of $10 to $13, and towing is $0.57 per kilometre.

Petrol is widely available in Romania, with Shell, Lukoil, Petrom and Agip operating sparkling, Western-style stations across the country, with at least one 24-hour station in every major city. Most accept Visa and/or MasterCard. Western-grade petrol (*benzină*) and diesel (*motorină*) are the norm, including unleaded 95-octane (*fără plumb* or *benzină verde*), premium and super (96–98 octane).

Road Rules

The speed limit for cars is 60km/h in built-up areas and 80km/h on the open road. Motorcyclists are limited to 40km/h in built-up areas and 50km/h on the open road. Drink driving is severely punished in Romania; the blood alcohol limit is 0.01%.

If you are fined for a traffic violation, insist on a receipt before parting with cash. Don't accept a written statement that doesn't specify the exact amount, otherwise the money may go straight into the police officer's pocket.

Rental
Avis, Budget, Hertz and Europcar have offices in most cities. Car rental is expensive. If coming from abroad, it is often cheaper to book (and pay) for a car in advance through offices overseas, and collect it upon arrival at Bucharest's Otopeni airport. To hire a car in Romania costs upwards of $47, unlimited kilometres. Check if prices quoted include the required 19% VAT.

HITCHING
Hitching is never entirely safe in any country in the world, and we don't recommend it. Travellers who decide to hitch should understand that they take a small, but potentially serious, risk. People who do choose to hitch will be safer if they travel in pairs and let someone know where they are planning to go.

Hitching in Romania is variable. Small cars are usually full and there isn't much traffic on secondary roads, where you may really need a ride. It's common practice to pay the equivalent of the bus fare to the driver. Occasionally drivers solicit business at bus and train stations as a way of covering their fuel costs.

BOAT
Navrom offers a regular passenger boat service between Tulcea and Sulina on the Black Sea year-round ($3.50). In summer hydrofoils speed from Tulcea to Crişan ($4.30) and Sulina ($4.60); see the Danube Delta section for details.

LOCAL TRANSPORT
Public Transport
Public transport is good, but overcrowded. Tram, bus and trolleybus services usually run from 5am to 11pm or midnight. Purchase tickets at kiosks marked *bilete* or *casă de bilete* before boarding, and validate them once aboard. Some tickets are good for one trip (*călătorie*); others are for two trips, each end of the ticket being valid for one ride. Tickets cost less than $0.20.

Taxi
Taxi drivers can be as shockingly corrupt or as surprisingly honest as anywhere else in the world. In Bucharest, Braşov and other larger cities, taxis tout meters which work. Count on paying around $0.45 per kilometre. If there's no meter, bargain for a price beforehand. It's always cheaper to phone for a taxi.

ORGANISED TOURS
Numerous travel agencies both locally and abroad offer group tours around Romania, enabling you to see the country's prime sights in a minimum of time.

In Romania, the group **Aventours & Roving România** (☎ 0268-326 271, fax 472 718, 0744-212 065; ⓦ www.discoveromania.ro; Str Paul Richter 1 apt1, Braşov) can organise anything from mountain hikes to minibus and Land Rover tours.

In the UK try **Footloose Adventure Travel** (☎ 01943-604 030, fax 604 070; ⓔ footrv@ globalnet.co.uk; 3 Springs Pavement, Ilkley, West Yorkshire, LS29 8HD), which organises walking tours throughout Transylvania and the Carpathians.

Bucharest

☎ 021 • pop 2.2 million

Tree-lined boulevards, park-girdled lakes and pompous public monuments give Bucharest (Bucureşti) a smooth Parisian flavour. Founded by a legendary shepherd named Bucur on the plains between the Carpathian foothills and the Danube River, Bucharest became the capital of Wallachia in 1459, during the reign of Vlad Ţepeş. The national capital since 1862, it is contemporary Romania's largest and wealthiest metropolis, which many travellers either love or hate.

During the 1980s the city was transformed by Nicolae Ceauşescu's attempt to recast Bucharest as a grandiloquent socialist capital, with the behemoth House of the People as its centrepiece. The revolution of December 1989 put an end to its Stalinist makeover, yet reminders of the Ceauşescu era remain – from ugly bloc-style apartments to neglected buildings and stray dogs. Yet, on a fast-track to recovery since the mid-1990s, Bucharest's greatest and grandest old edifices have been restored and fashionable new shops, restaurants and nightspots abound. The city is at its best in spring and summer, when relaxed crowds fill the beer gardens and parks.

Orientation

Bucharest's main train station, **Gara de Nord**, is a few kilometres northwest of Bucharest's centre. The station is connected by the metro to the centre at Piaţa Victoriei on the northern side or to Piaţa Unirii to the south. Bus Nos 79, 86 and 133 will take you mid-centre to Piaţa Romană. The main boulevard (and the north-south metro line) runs between Piaţa Victoriei, Piaţa Romană, Piaţa Universităţii and Piaţa Unirii, and changes its name three times.

Maps The Librăria Noi (see Bookshops later in this section) sells the well-detailed *Planul Oraşului Bucureşti* (AGC; 1:20,000; $1.85) and a host of other road and city maps.

Information

Tourist Offices Thanks to the friendly team at Elvis' Villa Bucharest (see Places to Stay), Bucharest finally has an official **tourist information office** *(end of Line 2, Gara de Nord; open 7am-10pm daily)*. The staff, who speak English, Italian and Japanese, can make hotel reservations, call taxis and will happily provide detailed information on the city and surrounding sights.

Motoring information is available from **Automobil Clubul Român** *(ACR;* ☎ *222 15 53, fax 222 15 52;* e *acr@acr.ro; Str Tache Ionescu 27)*.

Money Currency exchanges are dotted all over the city, including along Blvd General Magheru and Blvd Nicolae Bălcescu. **Alliance Exchange** *(Blvd Nicolae Bălcescu 30)* and **OK Exchange Nonstop** *(Str George Enescu)*, around the corner from McDonald's, both open 24 hours.

There are numerous ATMs around town accepting Visa and MasterCard, including at Otopeni airport and next to **IDM Exchange** *(open 5.30am-11pm daily)* at Gara de Nord.

The **Banca Comercială Română** *(Blvd Regina Elisabeta 5; open 9am-5.30pm Mon-Fri, 9am-12.30pm Sat)*, opposite Bucharest University, cashes travellers cheques and gives cash advances on credit cards. It has two ATMs outside, as does its **branch office** *(Calea Victoriei 155)*.

Lost AmEx cards/cheques can be replaced at the local American Express representative,

Marshal Turism *(*☎ *223 12 04, fax 223 12 03;* w *www.marshal.ro; Blvd General Magheru 43; open 9am-7pm Mon-Fri, 9am-1pm Sat)*.

Post & Communications The **Poştă Română Oficiul Bucureşti 1** *(central post office; Str Matei Millo 10; open 7.30am-8pm Mon-Fri, 8m-2pm Sat)* is off Calea Victoriei. Poste-restante mail, kept for one month, can be collected here. Branch post offices can be found at Str Tache Ionescu 5, at Str Ion Câmpineanu 23, and near Gara de Nord at Str Gării de Nord 6–8.

Card-operated public phones are abundant on the streets and in hotel lobbies. RomTelecom phonecards are sold at post offices or at a **telex-fax office** like the one on Str Tache Ionescu. Alternatively, feed a 50,000 lei note into the phonecard dispensers at the airport and train station. There's a **telephone office** *(cnr Calea Victoriei & Str Matei Millo; open 24hr)*.

Email & Internet Access Logging-on is no problem in Bucharest. **PC-Net Internet Café** *(*☎ *650 42 14; Calea Victoriei 136)* sports a genuine café as well as several computers. There's another *(Blvd Carol I 25)* just off Piaţa Rosetti. Both are open 24 hours and charge around $1.25 an hour.

PC-Net *(*☎ *208 04 00, fax 208 04 30; Blvd Mircea Eliade 18)* is Bucharest's most reliable and fastest Internet service provider charging $1/2/4/8 for 5/10/20/50 hours.

Travel Agencies Bucharest touts numerous travel agencies that take bookings for hotels, run city tours and can arrange various trips into the countryside.

Nova Tours *(*☎ *315 13 57/8, fax 312 10 41;* e *nova.tour@snmail.softnet.ro; Blvd Nicolae Bălcescu 21)* organise both sightseeing tours of Bucharest and fishing trips into the Danube Delta.

The local STA Travel representative is **ZIP International** *(*☎*/fax 212 35 22;* w *www .ziptravel.ro; Str A Phillippide 9)* and caters mostly to students.

The **Company of Mysterious Journeys** *(*☎*/fax 231 40 22, 092-599 099;* e *cdt@ art.ro; Str George Călinescu 20)* is the official operator for the Transylvanian Society of Dracula's spooky tours.

Bookshops For English-language novels, dictionaries and guidebooks about Romania,

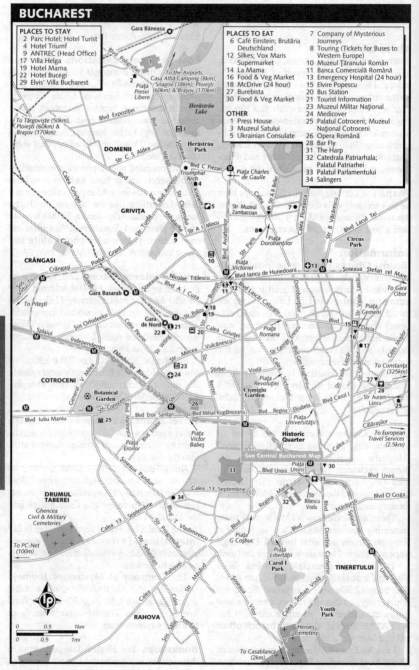

BUCHAREST

PLACES TO STAY
2 Parc Hotel; Hotel Turist
4 Hotel Triumf
9 ANTREC (Head Office)
17 Villa Helga
19 Hotel Marna
22 Hotel Bucegi
29 Elvis' Villa Bucharest

PLACES TO EAT
6 Café Einstein; Brutăria Deutschland
12 Silkes; Vox Maris Supermarket
14 La Mama
16 Food & Veg Market
18 McDrive (24 hour)
27 Burebista
30 Food & Veg Market

OTHER
1 Press House
3 Muzeul Satului
5 Ukrainian Consulate
7 Company of Mysterious Journeys
8 Touring (Tickets for Buses to Western Europe)
10 Muzeul Ţăranului Român
11 Banca Comercială Română
13 Emergency Hospital (24 hour)
15 Elvire Popescu
20 Bus Station
21 Tourist Information
23 Muzeul Militar Naţional
24 Medicover
25 Palatul Cotroceni; Muzeul Naţional Cotroceni
26 Opera Română
28 Bar Fly
31 The Harp
32 Catedrala Patriarhală; Palatul Patriarhei
33 Palatul Parlamentului
34 Salingers

the outstanding **Librăria Noi** (☎ *311 07 00; Blvd Nicolae Bălcescu 18; open 10am-8pm Mon-Sat, 11am-7pm Sun*) is best. English-language books are also available at **Salingers** (☎ *403 35 34;* e *info@salingers-bookstore .com; Calea 13 Septembrie 90*). **Librăria din Fundul Curții** (☎ *659 44 30; Calea Victoriei 120*) sells art and history books.

Laundry At **Nuf Nuf** (☎ *335 01 68; Calea Șerban Vodă 76-78; open 24hr*) a 5kg load costs around $1.40/1.55 to wash/dry. Have a coffee and watch TV while you wait. Guests staying at Villa Helga and Elvis' Villa hostels can machine-wash their clothes for free.

Left Luggage The **left-luggage counter** (*open 24hr*) at Gara de Nord, on the right-hand side of the central hall if your back is facing the tracks, charges around $0.50/1 per day to leave a small/big bag.

Medical & Emergency Services A good private clinic with English-speaking staff and a 24-hour emergency service is **Medicover** (☎ *310 44 10; emergencies ☎ 310 40 40; Calea Plevnei 96*).

For emergencies go to the **Emergency Hospital** (*Spitalul de Urgență;* ☎ *230 01 06; Calea Floreasca 8; open 24hr*).

There is a **24-hour pharmacy** (*cnr Calea Victoriei & Str Stravropoleos*). **Farmacia Magheru** (*cnr Blvd General Magheru & Str Pictor Verona; open 8am-8pm daily*) has a list of other pharmacies open late and/or on Sunday posted in its window.

To call (Romanian-speaking only) an ambulance ☎ 961, the police ☎ 955 and the fire brigade ☎ 981.

Dangers & Annoyances Scams and snarling street dogs are rife in Bucharest. To safeguard both your wallet and ankles, see Dangers & Annoyances and the Street Scams under Dangers & Annoyances in Facts for the Visitor section earlier in this chapter.

Things to See & Do
Central Bucharest From the northwestern corner of Piața Unirii, across the river and a little west along Splaiul Independenței, find narrow Str Șelari. Enter the old city on this street and to your right view the ruins of Vlad Țepeș' **Old Princely Court** (*Str Franceză*) from 1462. Cross Str Franceză and drink a

quick beer in the interior courtyard of **Hanul lui Manuc** (☎ *313 14 15; open 10am-10.30pm daily*), an inn dating from 1808.

Walk west on Str Franceză a few blocks and, when you see a large white church, turn right onto Str Poștei and continue to the **Biserica Stavropoleos** (Stavropoleos Church; 1724), a Unesco-protected building built by a Greek monk in a typical Brâncoveanu style.

Bear west to Calea Victoriei and one of Bucharest's most important museums, the **Muzeul Național de Istorie** (*National History Museum;* ☎ *315 70 56; admission $0.45; open 10am-6pm Wed-Sun*) is in the former Post Office Palace (1899). Its 41 rooms and 600,000 exhibits tell the story of the country from prehistoric times to WWI. The highlight is its fabulous basement treasury crammed with gold objects and precious stones.

Proceeding north on Calea Victoriei, you'll come to **Str Lipscani**, the old trading bazaar street that runs through to Blvd Brătianu. Continue north and a short detour west at Blvd Regina Elisabeta brings you to lovely **Grădina Cișmigiu**, the city's oldest park with a rowing-boat lake and pleasant beer garden.

Resuming the walk north on Calea Victoriei, after about four blocks, you'll arrive at Piața Revoluției and **Biserica Crețulescu** (Crețulescu Church; 1722), a red-brick structure badly damaged in the 1989 revolution and currently under renovation. To its north, and dominating the entire western side of the square, is the massive **Palatul Regal** (Royal Palace), an official royal residence from 1834 (its current facade dates from 1937). The palace displays an extensive collection of Romanian and European art in the four-storey **Muzeul Național de Artă** (*National Art Museum;* ☎ *313 30 30;* e *national.art@ art.museum.ro; Calea Victoriei 49-53; admission $1.25; open 10am-6pm Wed-Sun*).

Ceaușescu made his last speech from the balcony of the former **Central Committee of the Communist Party** building, the long, white-stone edifice opposite Biserica Crețulescu. It houses the Senate today. The **Central University Library** (1895) was gutted by fire during the 1989 revolution but has since been restored to house a European Union information centre, a new university library and an Austrian bank. The skeletal building behind this is another revolution victim, and will be left charred and bullet-riddled to honour those who died in 1989.

ROMANIA

Just north of the library is the city's main concert hall, the neoclassical **Ateneul Român** (*Romanian Athenaeum;* ☎ 315 87 98; *Str Franklin 1*), built by French architect Albert Galleron in 1888. Its interior decoration is magnificent. Check the box office here for performance schedules.

North again is the excellent **Muzeul Cotecţiilor de Artă** (*Art Collection Museum;* ☎ 659 66 93; *Calea Victoriei 111; adult/ concession $0.95/0.30; open 10am-6pm Wed-Sun*). Note the many fine works by the 19th-century painter Nicolae Grigorescu.

Turn right onto Str Piaţa Amzei to find the city's bustling open **food market** tucked between Bucharest's two main boulevards – it's the place to buy fresh fruit and vegetables.

The centre's other main artery has multiple names – Blvd Lascăr Catargiu/Blvd General Magheru/Blvd Nicolae Bălcescu/Blvd Brătianu – and is parallel to Calea Victoriei. On the southwestern corner of Piaţa Universităţii is **Muzeul de Istorie şi Artă al Municipiului Bucureşti/Palatul Şuţu** (*Municipal History & Art Museum;* ☎ 313 85 15; e mistorie@ sunu.rnc.ro; *Blvd Brătianu 2; admission $0.30; open 9am-5pm Wed-Sun*), inside neo-Gothic Şuţu Palace (1832–34) with displays on Bucharest 100 years ago.

Southern Bucharest In the last years of the Ceauşescus' reign, the southern section of Bucharest around **Piaţa Unirii** was redesigned to create the new civic centre. From Piaţa Unirii metro station, walk over to the large ornamental **fountain** (dry for years) in the middle of the square to get your bearings.

Walk southwest from the fountain, across Blvd Unirii and up Blvd Regina Maria for 200m to the **Catedrala Patriarhala** (Patriarchal Cathedral; 1658) and **Palatul Patriarhei** (Patriarch's Palace; 1875). West from the fountain, Blvd Unirii runs straight towards the enormous **Palatul Parlamentului** (*Palace of Parliament;* ☎ 311 36 11; e cic@camera .ro; *Calea 13 Septembrie 1; admission $1.90; open 10am-4pm daily*), Ceauşescu's House of the People. It's an incredible Stalinist structure that was still unfinished when Ceauşescu was overthrown in 1989. Three shifts of 20,000 workers and 700 architects toiled for over five years on this massive palace, using almost exclusively Romanian materials. At 330,000 sq metres in area, it is the second-largest building in the world after the US Pentagon. Numerous historic structures were demolished in order to accommodate it. Today it houses Romania's parliament and a conference centre.

Northern Bucharest Exiting from Piaţa Victoriei metro station, you see the **Muzeul Ţăranului Român** (*Museum of the Romanian Peasant;* ☎ 650 53 60; w www.itcnet.ro/mtr; *Şoseaua Kiseleff 3; adult/concession $0.60/ 0.15, guide $1.55 per hour; open 10am-6pm Tues-Sun*), a fantastic museum displaying Romania's largest collection of folklore treasures. From here, walk up tree-lined **Şoseaua Kiseleff**, Bucharest's most prestigious residential area during the communist era, to the **Arcul de Triumf** (Triumphal Arch, 1936), built to commemorate the reunification of Romania in 1918. Its resemblance to the Arc de Triomphe in Paris was intentional.

A short walk north is one of Bucharest's best sights, the **Muzeul Satului** (*Village Museum;* ☎ 222 91 10; *adult/student $1.25/ 0.45, camera/video $1.55/9.40; open 9am-6pm Tues-Sun, 9am-5pm Mon*) with full-scale displays of nearly 300 churches, wooden houses and farm buildings, first assembled here in 1936. It is surrounded by beautiful **Herăstrău Park**, with lush gardens and a lake filled with all manner of boats in summer. To get here by bus, take No 131 or 331 from Blvd General Magheru or Piaţa Romană to the 'Muzeul Satului' stop.

Western Bucharest To explore this area take the M3 metro from Piaţa Unirii west to Eroilor stop, or walk west on Splaiul Independenţii along the Dâmboviţa River. You could also walk west along Blvd Kogălniceanu, past Cişmigiu Garden, to **Opera Română** (*Opera House;* ☎ 314 69 80; w www.onrbucuresti .fx.ro; *Blvd Kogălniceanu 70-72*), then cross the road. From Piaţa Eroilor head west along Blvd Eroii Sanitari to Blvd Marinescu and the wall of **Palatul Cotroceni** (Cotroceni Palace; 1893), which was built for Queen Marie. It now serves as the president's residence and holds the **Muzeul Naţional Cotroceni** (*Cotroceni Museum;* ☎ 222 12 00; *Blvd Geniului 1; admission $1.55; open 9.30am-4.30pm Tues-Sun*) with exhibitions of 17th- and 18th-century art. Visits are only possible by prearranged appointment only.

North on Blvd Marinescu is Bucharest's **Grădina Botanică** (*Botanical Garden;* ☎ 410 91 39; *Şoseaua Cotroceni 32; open 8am-8pm*

CENTRAL BUCHAREST

PLACES TO STAY
30 Hotel Carpaţi
34 Hotel Muntenia
35 Hotel Inter-Continental
59 Hanul lui Manuc

PLACES TO EAT
3 Gregory's
4 Food & Veg Market; Unic & Vox Maris Supermarkets
10 Pâtisserie Parisienne Valerie
14 Nicoreşti
15 Menuet
16 Bistro Atheneu
24 Burebista Vâătorescu
33 Cofetăria Continental
46 Springtime
48 Count Dracula Club
54 Caru cu Bere
54 Mes Amis
56 Amsterdam Grand Café

OTHER
1 ZIP International (STA Travel Representative)
2 Marshal Turism
4 Automobil Clubul Român
5 OK Exchange Nonstop
7 Telex-Fax Office
8 Muzel Cotecţiilor de Artă
9 Fiatest Centre Educationnel (Language School)
11 Librăria din Fundul Curţii
12 Planter's Club
16 Farmacia Magheru
17 Salsa 2
18 Ateneul Român
19 Muzeul Naţional de Artă
20 Central University Library
21 Alliance Exchange
22 US Embassy
23 US Consulate
25 Librăria Noi
26 Nova Tours
27 Senate
28 Biserica Creţulescu
29 Branch Post Office
31 Central Post Office
32 Telephone Office
36 Teatrul Naţional Ion Luca Caragiale; Lăptăria Enache
37 PC-Net Internet Café
38 Muzel de Istorie şi Artă al Municipiului Bucureşti/Palatul Şuţu
39 University
40 Banca Comercială Română
41 PC-Net Internet Café
42 Cinemateca Română
43 Police Station
44 CFR Train Ticket Office
45 Tipsy
47 Tarom
49 Muzeul Naţional de Istorie
50 24-hour Pharmacy
52 Biserica Stavropoleos
53 Club A
55 Backstage
57 Double T (Buses to Western Europe)
58 Old Princely Court
60 Twice

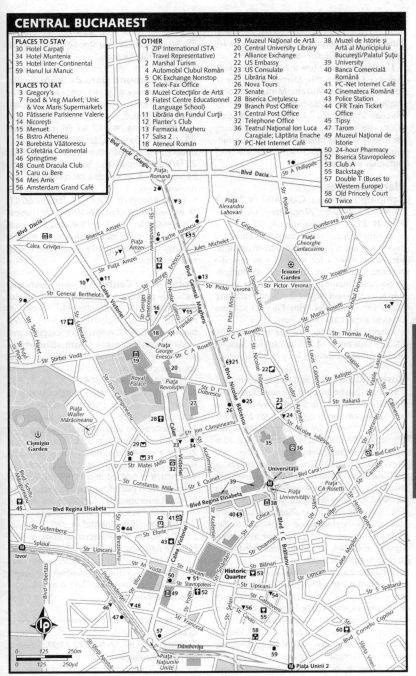

ROMANIA

0   125   250m
0   125   250yd

daily). The garden has approximately 10,000 plant species. You can also visit the **Botanical Museum & Greenhouse** *(admission $0.10; open 9am-1pm Tues, Thur & Sun)*.

Heading back east towards the centre along Şoseaua Cotroceni/Str Mircea Vulcănescu, you will pass the **Muzeul Militar Naţional** *(National Military Museum; ☎ 638 76 30; Str Mircea Vulcănescu 125-127; admission $0.95; open 9am-5pm Tues-Sun)*, recounting the history of the Romanian army. The exhibition dealing with the 1989 revolution is of particular interest.

Places to Stay

Camping In Băneasa, **Casa Albă** *(☎ 230 52 03, ☎/fax 230 62 55; Aleea Privighetorilor 1-3; huts $11-14; open mid-Apr–Oct)* is a restaurant with adjoining camp site. There are two-bed wooden huts on the well-maintained site, or negotiate a fee to pitch your tent. To get here, take bus No 301 from Piaţa Romană to Şoseaua Bucureşti-Ploieşti; get off at the stop after Băneasa airport and head east along Aleea Privighetorilor. Bus No 783 to/from Otopeni airport also stops here.

Alternatively, you can camp at Snagov Lake, 38km north of Bucharest (see Snagov in the Wallachia section, later in this chapter).

Hostels Elvis is alive and well in Bucharest! The 'king' can be found at the new **Elvis' Villa Bucharest** *(☎ 312 16 53; w www.elvisvilla .ro; Str Avram Iancu 5; dorm beds from $8, discounts for long-term stays)*, close to the centre, just off Piaţa Pache Protopopescu. Run by a dynamic Australian couple, it offers free breakfast, washing, Romanian cigarettes, a half-litre of beer and one hour of Internet use every day. Take trolleybus No 85 from Gara de Nord to Calea Morşilor stop; or No 783 from Otopeni airport to Piaţa Universităţii, then any trolleybus three stops east to the Calea Morşilor stop. Elvis has also been sighted in Braşov and Sighişoara, see Places to Stay in those sections later.

Villa Helga *(☎/fax 610 22 14; w www .rotravel.com/hotels/helga; Str Salcâmilor 2; dorm beds $9.90; discounts for long-term stays)* provides a dorm bed, breakfast, kitchen facilities, free laundry and locally produced Carpaţi cigarettes. It's conveniently close to the centre od the city, east of Piaţa Romană, past Piaţa Gemeni. Take bus No 79 or 133 from Gara de Nord for six stops to Piaţa

Gemeni or bus No 783 from Otopeni airport to Piaţa Română, then walk or take bus No 79, 86, 133 or 126 two stops east along Blvd Dacia to Piaţa Gemeni.

Hotels – Around Gara de Nord Bucharest touts plenty of grotty, one- and two-star hotels, clustered around the train station and in the city centre.

Hotel Marna *(☎ 212 83 66, fax 312 94 55; e marna@xnet.ro; Str Buzeşti 3; singles/ doubles/triples with shared bathroom $12/ 20/30)* is perhaps the best of this station bunch, with a welcoming reception and renovated rooms.

Hotel Bucegi *(☎ 212 71 54, fax 212 66 41; w www.stalingrad.ro; Str Witing 2; singles/ doubles/triples/quads with shared bathroom $16/25/30/40)*, 30m from the train station, is a noisy but surprisingly clean hotel with cramped rooms.

Hotels – City Centre Bucharest's most aesthetically pleasing budget option is the **Hotel Carpaţi** *(☎ 315 01 40, fax 312 18 57; Str Matei Millo 16; singles/doubles with shared bathroom $12/28)*. A sparkling reception area leads to pleasant singles with shared bathroom. Doubles with private shower *or* toilet are more expensive.

Hotel Muntenia *(☎ 314 60 10, fax 313 68 19; Str Academiei 19-21; singles/doubles/ triples with shared bathroom $16/25/33, suite $50)* is large and noisy but has a great location near the university.

Hanul lui Manuc *(☎ 313 14 15, fax 312 28 11; w www.hanulmanuc.ro; Str Franceză 62-64; singles/doubles with bath from $22/ 42)*, which is housed in a 19th-century merchants' inn, is one of the most historic places to stay. Unfortunately, the rooms are shabby, its restaurant pricey and its staff surly.

Hotel Inter-Continental *(☎ 310 20 20, fax 312 04 86; w www.interconti.com; 4 Blvd Nicolae Bălcescu; singles $173-283, doubles $190-307)* is an ugly concrete monstrosity that towers over the surrounding cityscape. That aside, the rooms are lavish and the service impeccable.

Hotels – North of Centre Heading north towards the Arcul de Triumf is elegant **Hotel Triumf** *(☎ 222 31 72, fax 223 24 11; Şoseaua Kiseleff 12; singles/doubles $46/61, apartments $92)*. The hotel grounds are superb.

Southwest of the Press House is the **Parc Hotel** (☎ 224 44 00, 224 29 84; **e** bestwest@ parch.ro; **w** www.parch.ro; Blvd Poligrafiei 3-5; singles $99-109, doubles $119-125, apartments $159), a smart, three-star Best Western hotel with large, modern rooms.

Hotel Turist (☎ 224 20 00, ☎/fax 224 23 17; **e** dht@parch.ro; Blvd Poligrafiei 3-5; singles $38-50, doubles $50-66), the large grey hotel immediately behind the Parc, has modest rooms.

Places to Eat

Restaurants With a rash of flashy restaurants serving expensive international cuisine, dining out in Bucharest can be expensive. However, it is still easy to track down traditional Romanian dishes in cheap and cheerful restaurants.

La Mama (☎ 212 40 86; Str Barbu Văcărescu 3; mains around $2.50), a convivial contemporary spot a little north of the centre, dishes up hearty portions of munch-worthy Romanian cuisine for a delicious price. Advance reservations are essential.

Burebista (☎ 210 97 04; Calea Moşilor 26; mains $1.40-4) has live music and excellent service – the caşcaval pâine is a little rubbery but the papanaşi (a cheese doughnut with sour cream and jam) is divine.

Nicoreşti (☎ 211 24 80; Str Maria Rosetti 40; mains $1.50-4) is a popular place with good-sized portions.

The ghoulish **Count Dracula Club** (☎ 312 13 53; **e** romantic@fx.ro; Splaiul Independenţei 8a; mains $1.70-5) is a restaurant where human skulls, pickled bats and blood-dripping walls enliven the dining experience. For the full house-of-horror effect, eat in the coffin-clad chapel.

Caru cu Bere (☎ 313 75 60; Str Stavropoleos 3; dishes around $3.50), a beer hall dating back to 1875, is worth a visit for its lavish, Gothic-style decor. Traditional Romanian dishes appear dirt cheap – until you realise prices are listed per 100g.

Burebista Vââtorescu (☎ 211 89 29; Str Batiştei 14; mains $2-6) touts a menu that is devoted almost entirely to such carnivorous delights as bear steaks and wild boar – vegetarians take heed!

Menuet (☎ 312 0143; Str Nicolae Golescu 14; mains $2-6), despite its heavy, old-style furnishings, dishes up excellent Romanian cuisine in a semi-French setting.

Bistro Atheneu (☎ 313 49 00; Str Episcopiei 3; mains $2.50-6), opposite the Romanian Athenaeum, is an old favourite. Its high-quality food, French-inspired atmosphere and serenading musicians draw large crowds.

Silkes (☎ 312 69 70; Piaţa Victoriei; breakfast $2.65-6, meals $4.5-6), previously the Sydney Bar & Grill, is an overpriced bar/restaurant – the Big Burrito is $5.95 – popular with expats.

Cafés Bucharest is riddled with cofetării specialising in Turkish coffee and freshly made cakes, pastries and other sweet-tooth temptations.

Cofetăria Continental (☎ 638 50 22; Calea Victoriei 56), adjoining Hotel Continental, is a great place for sampling rich, gooey cakes in a smoke-free environment.

Café Einstein (☎ 230 43 84; Str Beller 1), overlooking Piaţa Dorobanţilor, is connected to Brutăria Deutschland, a German-style bakery that bakes the best bread in town.

Amsterdam Grand Café (☎ 313 75 80; Str Covaci 6), one block north of the Old Princely Court, is Bucharest's hot new spot to unwind over a frothy cappuccino. With comfy leather chairs, well-stocked bar, scrumptious snacks, and a soon-to-be opened upstairs restaurant its longevity is assured.

Fast Food Bucharest is plastered with fast-food outlets and 24-hour kiosks selling hot dogs, burgers, popcorn, covrigi (rings of hard bread speckled with salt crystals) and other munch-while-you-walk snacks.

Gregory's (☎ 461 08 53; Blvd General Magheru 32-34 • Piaţa Universităţii; open 24hr) serves delicious, filling sandwiches made fresh before your eyes.

Springtime (Splaiul Independenţei 7; Piaţa Universităţii • Piaţa Victoriei), which has several outlets across the city, is always packed.

McDonald's has countless branches in central Bucharest; its **McDrive** (cnr Str Buzeşti & Str Polizu; open 24hr) is a five-minute walk from Gara de Nord.

Self Catering Three **open-air markets** have fresh fruit and vegies: one at Piaţa Amzei between Calea Victoriei and Blvd General Magheru; another on Piaţa Gemeni; and a third east of Piaţa Unirii.

Unic and **Vox Maris** (open 24hr) supermarkets have branches on Piaţa Amzei; Vox

ROMANIA

Maris has a second branch on Piaţa Victoriei. **Pâtisserie Parisienne Valerie**, at the northern end of Calea Victoriei, sells delicious cakes and pastries. For nutty German breads, try **Brutăria Deutschland** *(Str Edgar Quinet 5, Piaţa Dorobanţilor)*.

Entertainment

For a weekly what's on listing, pick up a copy of *Şapte Seri* (Seven Evenings), a free entertainment magazine, widely distributed across town.

Bars & Discos Painted a vivid orange, the **Bar Fly** *(☎ 252 02 93; Blvd Ferdinand I 3)*, near Elvis' Villa Bucharest, is a genial cellar bar playing a thoroughly eclectic mix of music covering everything ranging from the Beatles to Christmas carols (it was actually April when we visited).

The Harp *(☎ 335 65 08; Str Bibescu Voda 1)* is the quintessential Irish pub abroad with plenty of Guinness and good pub grub.

One of Bucharest's most popular, mainstream drinking holes, the **Planter's Club** *(☎ 659 76 06; Str Mendeleev 35)* is crammed with an English-speaking crowd most nights until 5am.

Tipsy *(Blvd Schitu Măugureanu 13)* is a simple but soulful bar, which markets itself as the capital's only plub (pub-cum-club). Its outside terrace buzzes until 4am in summer.

Backstage *(☎ 312 39 45; Str Gabroveni 14)* is the top joint for jigging to the beat of live bands. There's also trendy **Lăptăria Enache** *(Ⓦ www.laptaria.totalnet.ro; Blvd Nicolae Bălcescu 2)*, a rooftop bar on the 4th floor of the National Theatre (enter via the unmarked entrance on the theatre's northern side).

Club A *(☎ 315 68 53; Str Blănari 4)*, run by university students from the architecture faculty, teems with students seeking cheap drinks most weekends.

Salsa 2 *(Str Luterană)*, a large nightclub behind Hotel Bucureşti, is filled with bongos, steel drums and body-beat dancers.

Twice *(Str Sf Vineri)*, a hot new spot in the centre, pumps nightly to the techno beat (downstairs) and grooves to trashy 80s and 90s disco tunes (upstairs).

Gay & Lesbian Venues Situated in Tineretului Park, **Casablanca** *(☎ 330 12 06; Sala Polivalentă)* is the best gay-friendly club in Bucharest.

Classical Music Attending a performance at the **Ateneul Român** *(Romanian Athenaeum; ☎ 315 87 98; box office: ☎ 315 68 75; Str Benjamin Franklin 1; tickets $1.25-3; box office open noon-7pm)*, home to the George Enescu philharmonic orchestra, is a must. Performances start at 6.30pm or 7pm.

Theatres Bucharest has countless theatres, offering a lively mix of comedy, farce, satire and straight contemporary plays. Tickets cost about $3. Theatres close in July and August.

The most sought-after tickets are those for performances at the **Teatrul Naţional Ion Luca Caragiale** *(Ion Luca Caragiale National Theatre; ☎ 614 71 71, 615 47 46; Blvd Nicolae Bălcescu 2)*, across from the Hotel Inter-Continental. The box office is on the southern side of the building facing Blvd Carol I.

Cinemas Bucharest's cinemas show current films in their original language with Romanian subtitles for about $1 a ticket. Mainstream cinemas are on the section of Blvd Nicolae Bălcescu between Hotel Inter-Continental and Piaţa Romană, and on Blvd Regina Elisabeta. Alternative films are screened at **Cinemateca Română** *(☎ 313 04 83; Str Eforie 2)* and at **Elvire Popescu** *(☎ 210 02 24; Blvd Dacia 77)* adjoining the French Institute.

Getting There & Away

Air International flights use **Otopeni airport** *(☎ 230 16 02)*, 17km north of Bucharest. Domestic flights use **Băneasa airport** *(Şoseaua Bucureşti-Ploieşti 42)*, 8km north.

Tarom *(main office: ☎ 337 20 37, fax 337 20 36; Ⓦ www.tarom.ro; Splaiul Independenţei 17 • ☎ 314 25 20, fax 314 05 28; Str Buzeşti 59-61)* operates flights several times a week to Cluj-Napoca, Constanţa, Iaşi, Oradea, Timişoara, Sibiu and Suceava. The fares for these flights are quoted in the relevant sections of this chapter.

Numerous international airlines have an office on Blvd Nicolae Bălcescu or Blvd General Magheru.

Train Most express trains and many local trains use **Gara de Nord** *(☎ 223 08 80; Blvd Gării de Nord 2)*, Bucharest's central train station. To enter the station, flash your valid train ticket or buy a platform ticket ($0.10) at the entrance. Some trains to/from Snagov and Tulcea depart from **Gara Obor** *(☎ 252 02 04;*

Blvd Gării Obor) and some to Constanţa use **Gara Băneasa** *(☎ 222 48 56; Piaţa Gării)*.

At Gara de Nord there are separate ticket halls for 1st and 2nd class; tickets for international destinations are sold in the 1st-class ticket hall marked *casele de bilete Cl 1*. Express train tickets are only sold at the station one hour before departure. Timetables are posted in the main hall. If you plan to roam the country buy a timetable *Mersul Trenurilor* at the information desk.

Wasteels *(☎ 222 78 44;* w *www.wasteels travel.ro)*, which sells discounted tickets to Western Europe for under 26s, is on the right as you enter the main building.

Advance ticket purchases can be made from a **CFR office** *(main office: Str Domniţa Anastasia 10-14)*.

International trains to/from Bucharest include services to Belgrade, Bratislava, Budapest, İstanbul, Kyiv, Kraków, Moscow, Munich, Prague, Sofia, Vienna and Warsaw.

Bus Bucharest's central bus station – a stop rather than a fully fledged station – is outside Hotel Ibis on Calea Griviţei. Domestic services are poor and ever-changing timetables are stuck on lamp posts at the stop; drivers sell tickets.

Several private bus companies on and around Piaţa Gara de Nord, such as **Ortadoğu Tur** *(☎ 312 24 23, 637 67 78; Piaţa Gara de Nord 1)*, run daily buses to İstanbul ($27/51 single/return). Tickets for buses to Chişinău ($10/20 single/return) in Moldova are sold at **Autotrans** *(☎ 312 22 11, 335 32 90)* in the next door building.

Tickets for daily buses to Germany are sold by **Double T** *(☎ 313 36 42;* e *doublet@fx.ro; Calea Victoriei 2)* or **Touring** *(☎ 230 36 61;* e *touring.rez@eurolines.ro; Str Sofia 26)*.

Getting Around
To/From the Airports Going to the city centre from Otopeni, catch bus No 783 from outside the main terminal; buy a magnetic ticket (double-journey tickets only, $0.90) at the kiosk to the right or direct from the bus driver. From Băneasa, exit the terminal and cross to the opposite side of the busy Bucharest-Piteşti road. Every 15 minutes from 6.30am to 9pm you can take bus No 783 to Otopeni and Băneasa from Piaţa Unirii and various bus stops on the eastern side of Blvd Brătianu, Blvd Nicolae Bălcescu and Blvd General

Magheru. It takes 20 minutes to reach Băneasa (ask someone to point out the stop) and 30 minutes to Otopeni (the end of the line).

Avoid using taxi drivers waiting at both airports at all costs, unless you are happy to pay an outrageous $25 to $40 for the 20- to 35-minute ride.

Public Transport Public transport runs from around 5am to midnight, with a reduced service on Sunday.

For buses, trams and trolleybuses, buy your tickets ($0.17) at streetside RATB kiosks marked *casă de bilete* or *bilete*. Validate the ticket on board or risk a $5 fine. One-day/weekly passes ($0.60/2.10) entitle you to unlimited travel on buses, trams and trolleybuses.

The metro has three lines, which are handy for getting around the centre. Trains run every five to seven minutes. Buy a magnetic-strip card for two/10 rides ($0.30/1.50) at a subterranean kiosk.

Taxi Opt for a cab with a meter and honest driver: both **Cristaxi** *(☎ 9461/6)* and **Meridian** *(☎ 9444)* are reputable. Flag one down on the street (identifiable by the yellow pyramid fixed to their roofs) or call one from any phone on the street. The fixed metered rate usually works out at $0.20 per kilometre.

Most taxi drivers that hang around the airports and Gara de Nord are unscrupulous; caution is advised.

Wallachia

Wallachia, home of the nation's capital, is a flat, tranquil region of farms and small-scale industrial complexes that stretches across the Danube plain north to the crest of the Carpathian Mountains. Although the Danube River flows right along the southern edge of Wallachia, it is best seen between Moldova Veche and Drobeta–Turnu Severin in the west, where it breaks through the Carpathians at the legendary Iron Gate, a gorge of the Danube River on the Romanian-Yugoslav border.

Founded by Radu Negru in 1290, this principality was subject to Hungarian rule until 1330, when Basarab I defeated the Hungarian king Charles I and declared Wallachia to be independent. The Wallachian princes established their first capitals – Câmpulung, Curtea de Argeş and Târgovişte – near the mountains, but in the 15th century Bucharest gained the ascendancy.

After the fall of Bulgaria to the Turks in 1396, Wallachia faced a new threat and in 1417 Mircea the Old was forced to acknowledge Turkish suzerainty. Other Wallachian princes like Vlad Țepeș and Michael the Brave (Mihai Viteazul) became national heroes by defying the Turks and refusing to pay tribute. In 1859 Wallachia was united with Moldavia, paving the way for the modern Romanian state.

SNAGOV
☎ 018 • pop 8000

Snagov, 38km north of Bucharest, is a favourite picnic spot for city dwellers, with a famous 16th-century **church** tucked away on a small island on Snagov Lake. The first monastery was built on the island during the 11th century, and in 1456 Vlad Țepeș built fortifications and a prison near the church. The present church dates from 1521. The body of the infamous Vlad Țepeș is reputedly buried below the dome. You can **hire a boat** ($1.50 per hour) to row to the island from **Complex Astoria** (☎ 314 83 20), a lakeside leisure complex.

The early 20th-century **Palatul Snagov**, just across the lake from the island, was built by Prince Nicolae, brother of King Carol II. During the Ceaușescu era it was used for meetings of high-level government officials and today houses the Snagov Complex restaurant. Ceaușescu had a summer home on Snagov Lake, **Villa No 10**, which is now rented out to rich and famous tourists.

There are a handful of camp sites in the lakeside oak forest plus a few beer gardens and food stands.

From June to September two trains daily run from Bucharest's Gara de Nord to Snagov Plajă (one hour) which is a 10-minute walk from Complex Astoria. In winter these trains only run at weekends.

Villa Helga and Elvis' Villa in Bucharest (see Places to Stay in that section) arrange informal tours to Snagov.

CALAFAT
☎ 0251

The small town of Calafat on the Danube opposite Vidin in Bulgaria is a convenient entry/exit point to/from Bulgaria. Car ferries cross the Danube hourly year-round ($13 plus $2 per person in hard currency only, 30 minutes).

There are frequent local trains to/from Craiova (2½ hours, 107km), from where you can catch an express train to Bucharest or Timișoara. The ferry landing is right in the centre of Calafat, about four blocks from the train station.

DROBETA–TURNU SEVERIN
☎ 0252 • pop 118,114

Drobeta-Turnu Severin is on the Danube, bordering Yugoslavia. Though of ancient origin, the present town was laid out in the 19th century and has a pleasant series of parks in the centre of town.

From the train station follow Blvd Republicii east for 1.5km to the Hotel Parc at the intersection of Str Bibiescu. From here walk one block north, then turn right onto Str Decebal, where you'll find the post, CFR and telephone offices.

West of Drobeta-Turnu Severin, the train runs along the northern bank of the Danube through the famous **Iron Gate**, passing a huge, concrete hydroelectric power station (1972). On top of this is a road that links Romania to Yugoslavia.

The cheapest rooms can be found at **Tinertului Hotel** (☎/fax 317 99; Str Crişan 25; singles/doubles/triples $17/34/50). However, the 170-room **Hotel Traian** (☎ 311 760, fax 310 290; Blvd Vladimirescu 74; singles/doubles $26/37) is better value.

All express trains between Bucharest and Timișoara stop here.

Transylvania

To most people, the name Transylvania conjures images of haunted castles, werewolves and vampires. The 14th-century castles at Râsnov and Bran certainly appear ready-made for a Count Dracula movie.

Yet the charms of Transylvania are far more diverse – mountain scenery, some of Romania's best hiking and skiing, and rural villages that haven't changed much since the 18th century. For lovers of medieval art and history, it's an unparalleled chance to escape the tourist hordes in Budapest and Prague and see an overlooked corner of the old Austro-Hungarian empire.

For 1000 years, up until WWI, Transylvania was associated with Hungary. In the 10th century a Magyar tribe, the Szeklers, settled in what they called Erdély (Beyond the Forest). Saxon merchant-knights, who were invited in to help defend the eastern frontiers of Hungary, followed them in the 12th century.

The seven towns the Saxons founded – Bistriţa (Bistritz), Braşov (Kronstadt), Cluj-Napoca (Klausenburg), Mediaş (Mediasch), Sebeş (Muhlbach), Sibiu (Hermannstadt) and Sighişoara (Schässburg) – gave Transylvania its name in German, Siebenbürgen (Seven Cities). Before 1989 there were an estimated 370,000 ethnic Germans living in Romania, mostly in Transylvania. After the revolution huge numbers migrated to Germany and by 1995 less than 62,000 remained. They've left behind many small villages around Sibiu and Sighişoara that seem to have been lifted directly out of 19th-century Germany.

Medieval Transylvania was an autonomous unit ruled by a prince responsible to the Hungarian crown. After the defeat of Hungary by the Turks in 1526 the region became semi-independent.

In 1683 Turkish power was broken and Transylvania came under Habsburg rule in 1687. In 1848, when the Hungarians revolted against the Habsburgs, Romania sided with the Austrians. After 1867 Transylvania was fully absorbed into Hungary. In 1918 the Romanians massed at Alba Iulia to demand Transylvania's union with Romania.

This was never fully accepted by Hungary and from 1940 to 1944 it re-annexed much of the region. After the war, Romanian communists quashed nationalist sentiments. Today, feelings of resentment have been quelled and Romania's relations with its western neighbour continue to strengthen.

SINAIA
☎ 0244

This popular ski resort snuggles at an altitude of 800m to 930m in the narrow Prahova Valley, at the foot of the Bucegi Mountains. Sinaia is a convenient day trip from Bucharest or Braşov. Although its monastery has existed since the 17th century, Sinaia developed into a major resort only after King Carol I decided to build his summer residence, the magnificent Peleş Castle, there in 1870.

A train line from Bucharest followed in 1879 and the local elite soon arrived en masse. Until 1920 the Hungarian-Romanian border ran along Predeal Pass just north of Sinaia. For convenience this area has been included in the Transylvania section, even though, strictly speaking, it is in Wallachia.

Orientation & Information
The train station is directly below the centre of town. From the station climb up the stairway across the street to busy Blvd Carol I. The Hotel Montana and cable car are to the left, the monastery and palace are uphill to the right.

Surmont Sports *(Str Cuza Vodă)*, at the base of the cable-car station, sells hiking maps, skis, tents and imported outdoor gear.

There are currency exchanges inside Hotels International and Montana along Blvd Carol I. **Banca Comercială Română** *(open 8am-5.30pm Mon-Fri, 8.30am-12.30pm Sat)*, just past the Hotel Montana, gives cash advances on Visa/MasterCard; it also has an ATM.

There's a **left-luggage office** *(open 24hr)* at the train station.

Things to See & Do
From the train station walk up the stairway to town, turn left and make a quick right onto Str Octavian Goga, then curve left at the old *cazino*. There's a stairway here, at the top of which is **Mănăstirea Sinaia** (Sinaia Monastery), named after Mt Sinai. The large Orthodox church dates from 1846 and an older church (1695), with its original frescoes, is in the compound to the left. Beside the newer church is a small **Muzeul de Istorie** *(history museum; open 10am-6pm daily)*.

Just past the monastery begins the road to **Peleş Castle** *(admission $3)*, the former royal palace, dating from 1883. It is one of the country's finest castles, built in the German-Renaissance style for Prussian prince Carol I, first king of Romania (r. 1866–1914). The queue can be long on weekends, but it's worth waiting as the interior rooms are magnificent.

A few hundred metres uphill from the main palace is the smaller **Pelişor Palace** *(admission $2)*, in mock-medieval style. Pelişor was built for Carol I's son, Ferdinand, and was decorated in the Art Nouveau style by Queen Marie. Tours for both are given between 9.15am and 3.15pm Wednesday to Sunday.

Sinaia is a great base for **hiking** in the Bucegi Mountains. Nonhikers should take the **cable car** *(☎ 311 674; Str Telecabinei; return $2.75; open 8am-4pm Tues-Sun)* from Hotel Montana to Cota 1400 (a station near Hotel Alpin) and continue on the cable car or ski lift up to Cota 2000 (near Cabana Mioriţa).

ROMANIA

Sinaia's big attraction is **skiing**. It has 10 downhill tracts, three cross-country trails, three sleigh slopes and a bobsled slope. The **Snow ski school and gear shop** (☎ 311 198; *Str Cuza Vodă 2a*), at the foot of the cable-car station behind Hotel Montana, rents complete snowboard and ski equipment for $7 a day.

Places to Stay

Private Rooms Hang around at the train station for a few minutes and you'll undoubtedly be offered a private room. The going rate is $8 to $10 per person.

Cabanas By the cable car station is **Hotel Alpin** (☎ 312 351; *Cota 1400*). Just below it at 1300m is **Cabana Brădet** (☎ 311 551; *beds in shared rooms year-round $6*). Prices are similar for shared rooms at **Cabana Valea cu Brazi** (☎ 313 635) above the cable car at 1500m; a path leads up from Hotel Alpin.

Hotels The cheapest option is **Pensiunea Parc** (☎ 314 821; *Blvd Carol I; doubles $10*). It has 12 doubles with shared bathroom.

Hotel Sinaia (☎ 311 551; Ⓦ www.mmc.ro/sinaia; *Blvd Carol I, 8; 2-star singles/doubles $20/30, 3-star $27/42*), across from the Pensiunea Parc, has pleasant well-priced rooms.

Hotel Montana (☎ 312 751; *Blvd Carol I, 24; singles/doubles $25/40*), near the cable car, is another affordable option.

Hotel Palace (☎ 310 625; *Str Octavian Goga 4; singles/doubles from $44/66*), a large stately hotel founded in 1911, is an elegant splurge.

Holiday Inn Resort Sinaia (☎ 310 440, fax 310 551; Ⓔ sales@holiday–inn.ro; *Str Toporaşilor 1A; singles/doubles/triples $96/122/140; suites $210-340*), about 3km south of the centre, is the resort's top hotel. Attractions include a heated swimming pool, restaurant, disco and bar.

Places to Eat

Taverna Sârbului (☎ 314 400; *Calea Codrulu I; dishes $1-4*) is a new traditional Romanian restaurant, considered by some to be the region's best. Speciality dishes include steaming bowls of *ciorbă de burtă* and the delicious plump *samarle*.

Mont Blanc (☎ 310 105; *Str Octavian Goga 33; dishes around $4*), opposite the Hotel Palace, offers a not-so-authentic touch of France.

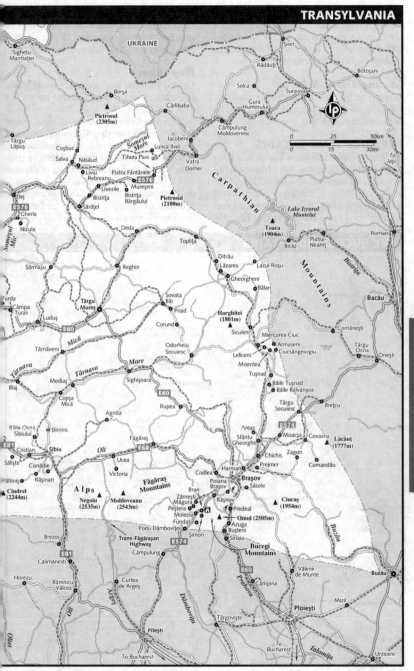

ROMANIA

Brutăria Deutschland (☎ 312 552; Blvd Carol I 8; snacks $0.50-3; dishes $1-4) is a good, cheap place to fill up on doughnuts, coffee and beer in between ski runs. It also doubles as a German restaurant.

Getting There & Away
Sinaia is on the Bucharest-Braşov train line – 126km from the former and 45km from the latter. All express trains stop here.

THE BUCEGI MOUNTAINS
The Bucegi Mountains are Romania's best-kept secret, rivalling the Tatra Mountains of Slovakia and even the Alps for trekking. Getting lost is difficult, thanks to a network of marked trails, while cabanas are open all year for hikers and cross-country skiers. The only

danger is the weather; winter is severe, waist-deep snow can linger to May and summer thunderstorms are common. If you sleep in cabanas, it's a good idea to bring extra food.

Day Hikes
Catch a morning train from Braşov or Sinaia to Buşteni, then the Buşteni **cable car** (☎ 314 532; one way $1.85; open 9am-4pm Wed-Mon) up to **Cabana Babele** (2206m). From Babele you hike south to **Cabana Piatra Arsă** (1950m), where you pick up a blue trail that descends to Sinaia via **Poiana Stănii** (a five-hour walk in total). The beginning of the blue trail is poorly marked at Piatra Arsă, so study the large map on the cabana's wall carefully. This trip across alpine pastures and through the forest is varied and downhill all the way.

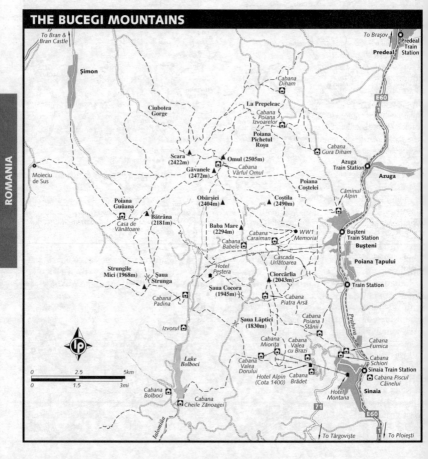

THE BUCEGI MOUNTAINS

A variation on this route involves taking the Sinaia cable car up to **Cabana Mioriţa** (1957m), near the crest. You then walk north to **Cabana Piatra Arsă** (1½ hours) and on to **Cabana Babele** (another hour), where you can catch the Buşteni cable car down the mountain. This hike is uphill (350m) and you must take two cable cars.

Longer Hikes

A more ambitious expedition involves taking one of the two cable cars already mentioned and hiking northwest across the mountains to **Bran Castle**. You can do this in one strenuous day if you get an early start from Babele, but it's preferable to take two days and camp freelance or spend a night at **Cabana Vârfu Omul**.

As you look north from Babele, you'll see a red-and-white TV transmitter on a hill. To the left is a yellow-marked trail that leads to Cabana Vârfu Omul (two hours) on the summit (2505m). North of Babele the scenery gets dramatic, with dizzying drops into valleys.

From Omul to Bran Castle takes another six hours, following the yellow-triangle trail. Begin by crossing Mt Scara (2422m) before dropping into Ciubotea Gorge. Once you clear the tree-line the trail descends through thick forest. Eventually you come out on a logging road beside a river, which you follow for 2½ hours to Bran Castle.

Places to Stay & Eat

Cabana Babele (☎ 315 304), **Cabana Caraiman** and **Cabana Piatra Arsă** (☎ 311 911) all charge $3 to $9 per person, depending on whether you want a bed in a double room or a mattress in the dormitory. All of these cabanas (as well as **Cabana Mioriţa** farther south) serve inexpensive meals and drinks and are open year-round.

Cabana Vârfu Omul (mattresses per person $3; open May-Sept) is small and basic, with 35 mattresses in a dormitory. Meals (soup, bread and omelette) are served only occasionally, so bring your own food.

It's always best to check with the local tourist office about which cabanas are open.

BRAŞOV

☎ 0268 • pop 319,908

Braşov (Brassó in Hungarian) is one of the most visited cities in Romania – and for good reason. Piaţa Sfatului, the central square, is the finest in the country, and is lined with baroque facades and pleasant outdoor cafés. The ski resorts of Sinaia and Poiana Braşov, the castles of Bran and Râşnov, and trails into the dramatic Bucegi Mountains are within easy reach.

A charming medieval town flanked by verdant hills on both sides, Braşov started out as a German mercantile colony named Kronstadt. At the border of three principalities it became a major medieval trading centre. The Saxons built some ornate churches and town houses, protected by a massive wall that still remains. The Romanians lived at Scheii, just outside the walls to the southwest.

Contemporary Braşov is the sixth-largest city in Romania.

Orientation

The train station (gara) is a long way from the city centre. Take bus No 4 (buy tickets at a kiosk) to Central Park or Str Mureşenilor. Strada Republicii, Braşov's pedestrian-only promenade, is crowded with shops and cafés from Central Park to Piaţa Sfatului.

Braşov has two main bus stations: Autogară 1, next to the train station, and Autogară 2, west of the train station near the Stadion Tineretului stop (local bus No 12 or 22 go to/from the centre).

Information

Tourist Offices At long last Braşov has an official **tourist information office** (main hall at the train station; open 8am-noon & 3.15pm-9.15pm daily, reduced winter hours). The office, operated by Elvis' Villa Braşov (see Places to Stay), can book accommodation and provides detailed information on Braşov and the surrounding areas.

Money Numerous currency exchange outlets are scattered around the city. **Banca Comercială Română** (BCR; Piaţa Sfatului 14; open 8.30am-5pm Mon-Fri, 8.30am-noon Sat) changes travellers cheques, gives cash advances on Visa/MasterCard and has an ATM, as does **Banca Comercial Ion Ţiriac** (BCIT; Str Michael Weiss 20; open 9am-3.30pm).

There are also ATMs located outside the Aro Palace restaurant on Blvd Eroilor and opposite McDonald's on Str Republicii.

Post & Communications Braşov's **central post office** (Str Iorga 1; open 7am-8pm Mon-Fri, 8am-1pm Sat) is opposite the Heroes Cemetery.

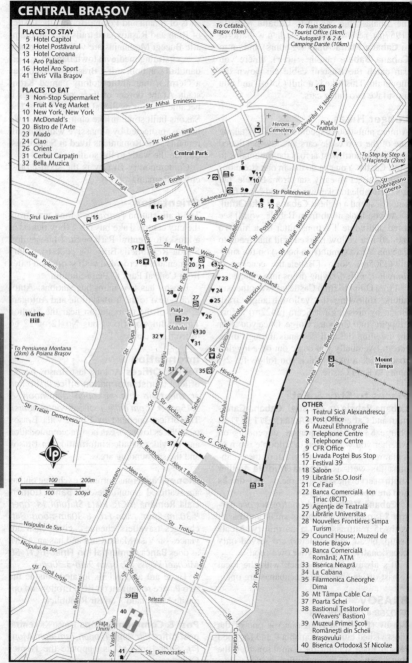

CENTRAL BRAŞOV

To Cetatea
Braşov (1km)

To Train Station &
Tourist Office (3km),
Autogară 1 & 2 &
Camping Darste (10km)

PLACES TO STAY
5 Hotel Capitol
12 Hotel Postăvarul
13 Hotel Coroana
14 Aro Palace
16 Hotel Aro Sport
41 Elvis' Villa Braşov

PLACES TO EAT
3 Non-Stop Supermarket
4 Fruit & Veg Market
10 New York, New York
11 McDonald's
20 Bistro de l'Arte
23 Mado
24 Ciao
26 Orient
31 Cerbul Carpaţin
32 Bella Muzica

Str Mihai Eminescu

Heroes
Cemetery

Piaţa
Teatrului

Str Nicolae Iorga

Central Park

Str Lungă

Blvd Eroilor

Şirul Livezii

Str Sadoveanu

Str Politechnicii

Calea Poienii

Str Sf Ioan

Str Muresenilor

Str Michael
Weiss

Str Republicii

Str Poştavului

Str Nicolae Bălcescu

Str Castelului

Str Dobrogeanu
Gherea

To Step by Step &
Hacienda (2km)

Warthe
Hill

Str Piaţa Enescu

Str Amata Română

Str Dupa Ziduri

Piaţa
Sfatului

Str Nicolae Bălcescu

To Pensiunea Montana
(2km) & Poiana Braşov

Str G Dimai

Str Gheorghe Barţiu

Str Richter

Str Porta Schei

Str Cerbului

Str Castelului

Hirscher

Str Traian Demetrescu

Str Beethoven

Aleea T Brediceanu

Str G Coşbuc

Str Tiberiu Brediceanu

Mount
Tâmpa

0   100   200m
0   100   200yd

Brâncoveanu

Aleea Saguna

Nisipulni de Sus

Str Trotuş

Nisipului de Jos

Str Dupa Iniste

Brâncoveanu

Str Prundului

Str Reteat

Str Lacea

Str Petőfi

Str Curcanilor

Retezat

Piaţa
Unirii

Str Vasile Sartu

Str Democratiei

OTHER
1 Teatrul Sică Alexandrescu
2 Post Office
6 Muzeul Ethnografie
7 Telephone Centre
8 Telephone Centre
9 CFR Office
15 Livada Poştei Bus Stop
17 Festival 39
18 Saloon
19 Librărie St.O.Iosif
21 Ce Faci
22 Banca Comercială Ion
     Ţiriac (BCIT)
25 Agenţie de Teatrală
27 Librărie Universitas
28 Nouvelles Frontiéres Simpa
     Turism
29 Council House; Muzeul de
     Istorie Braşov
30 Banca Comercială
     Română; ATM
33 Biserica Neagră
34 La Cabana
35 Filarmonica Gheorghe
     Dima
36 Mt Tâmpa Cable Car
37 Poarta Schei
38 Bastionul Ţesătorilor
     (Weavers' Bastion)
39 Muzeul Primei Şcoli
     Românești din Scheii
     Braşovului
40 Biserica Ortodoxă Sf Nicolae

The **central telephone centre** *(Blvd Eroilor 23; open 7am-10pm Mon-Sat)* is between the Capitol and Aro Palace Hotels. There is a second centre on Str Mihail Sadoveanu.

Email & Internet Access Braşov's most user-friendly Internet café, **Ce Faci** *(Str Michael Weiss 18; open 24hr)*, charges \$0.50 per hour for access.

Travel Agencies For good deals on international plane tickets get in contact with **Nouvelles Frontières Simpa Turism** *(☎ 476 948; e simpabv@simpaturism.ro; Piaţa Sfatului; open 9am-5pm Mon-Fri)*, which also has an exchange office.

Bookshops The best places for maps, postcards and guidebooks are **Librărie St.O.Iosif** *(☎ 477 799; Str Mureşenilor 14)* and **Librărie Universitas** *(☎ 142 306; Piaţa Sfatului 5)*.

Left Luggage The **left-luggage office** *(open 24hr)* in the train station is in the underpass leading from the tracks.

Things to See

In the middle of Piaţa Sfatului is the Council House (1420), now the **Muzeul de Istorie Braşov** (Braşov History Museum), which was closed at the time of writing). The 58m Trumpeter's Tower above the building dates from 1582.

The Gothic **Biserica Neagră** *(Black Church; ☎ 144 143; Curtea Johannes Honterus 2; adult/concession \$0.65/0.30; open 10am-3.30pm Mon-Sat)*, built between 1384 and 1477, looms just south of the square. The church's name comes from its appearance after a fire in 1689. As you walk around the building to the entrance, you'll see statues on the exterior of the apse. The originals are now inside and Turkish rugs hang from every balcony. During July and August, recitals are given on the 1839 organ at 6pm on Tuesday, Thursday and Saturday (\$2).

Go south a little to the neoclassical **Poarta Schei** (Schei Gate; 1828), then walk 500m up Str Prundului to Piaţa Unirii. Through the gate the sober rows of Teutonic houses change to the small, simpler houses of the former Romanian settlement.

On Piaţa Unirii you'll find the black-spired 1595 Orthodox **Biserica Ortodoxă Sf. Nicolae** *(Piaţa Unirii 2)*. Beside the church is the

Muzeul Primei Şcoli Româneşti din Scheii Braşovului *(First Romanian School Museum; ☎ 143 879; Piaţa Unirii 2-3; adult/concession \$0.30/0.15; open 9am-5pm Tues-Sun)*, which houses a collection of icons, paintings on glass and old manuscripts. The clock tower (1751) was financed by Elizabeth, empress of Russia.

Go back the way you came and turn right just before the Schei Gate to reach the 16th-century **Bastionul Ţesătorilor** *(Weavers' Bastion; ☎ 310 919; Str Coşbuc; admission \$0.30; open 9am-5.30pm Tues-Sun)*, slightly hidden above the sports field. This corner fort on the old city walls has a museum with a fascinating scale model of Braşov in the 17th century, created in 1896.

Above the bastion is a pleasant promenade through the forest overlooking Braşov. Halfway along you'll come to the **Telecabina Tâmpa** *(cable car; Str Brediceanu; one way/return \$0.65/1; open 9.30am-5pm Mon-Fri, 9.30am-6pm Sat & Sun)*. The cable car rises from 640m to 960m and offers stunning views. The hike to the top, following a series of zigzagging trails, takes 45 minutes and is well worth the effort.

The art gallery that is inside the **Muzeul Etnografic** *(Ethnographic Museum; ☎ 475 562, e etnobv@deltanet.ro; Blvd Eroilor 21; admission \$0.30; open 10am-6pm Tues-Sun summer, 9am-5pm winter)*, next to the Hotel Capitol, has a good Romanian collection on the upper floor.

Cetatea Braşov, a whitewashed fort on a hill overlooking the old town, was built in 1580 to defend Kronstadt's Saxon merchants from marauding Turks. Today it houses an expensive restaurant.

Activities

Braşov is a good base for hiking and climbing in the Carpathians. **Step by Step** *(☎/fax 315 756; w www.sbstours.com; Str Molidului 9)* can organise small hikes to major expeditions, as well as paragliding and bungee jumping. All staff are accredited members of the Romanian Mountain Guide Association.

Places to Stay

Camping Braşov's only camping ground, **Camping Darste** *(☎ 339 967, fax 339 462; Calea Bucureşti 285; camping \$5, doubles per person \$5)*, is inconveniently 10km northeast of the centre. It has small, two-bed wooden huts and plenty of space to pitch a tent.

Private Rooms You will have no problem finding a private room in Braşov. While the infamous **Maria and Grig Bolea** *(☎ 311 962; $7-10 per person)* might seem a bit pushy, their rooms are fine. Beware of fake Marias trying to trade off her good name.

Hostel The city's only hostel is the new **Elvis' Villa Braşov** *(Kismet Dao Villa; ☎ 478 930, 0721-844 940; w www.elvisvilla.com; Str Democratiei 2B; dorm beds from $8)* in the heart of Schei district. Here you'll not only get a comfy dorm bed but also breakfast, Internet access, laundry service, beer and cigarettes. Staff can also arrange ski hire and lessons as well as informal tours to Bran and Râşnov. To get here from the train station catch bus No 4 to the end of the line at Piaţa Unirii.

Hotels The cheapest option in this category is **Hotel Aro Sport** *(☎ 478 800, fax 475 228; w www.aro-palace.ro; Str Sf Ioan 3; singles/ doubles with shared bathroom $11/14)* behind the Aro Palace Hotel. It has spartan and well-worn rooms.

Hotel Postăvarul *(☎ 144 330, fax 141 505; Str Politechnicii 2; singles/doubles/ triples with shared bathroom $14/20/30)*, smack-bang in the city's medieval centre, is in a separate wing of the overpriced **Hotel Coroana**. Rooms are exceptionally clean and excellent value.

Painted a shocking lime green, **Pensiunea Montana** *(☎ 472 731; e dinuc@hip.ro; Str Stejăriş, singles $37-40, doubles $45-50)* is a tranquil retreat with bright, airy rooms, just off the road to Poiana Braşov.

Hotel Capitol *(☎ 418 920, fax 472 999; Blvd Eroilor 19; singles/doubles $60/80)*, despite its unappealing facade, has surprisingly spacious, modern rooms.

A somewhat beleaguered four-star hotel facing Central Park, **Aro Palace** *(☎ 478 800, fax 475 228; w www.aro-palace.ro; Blvd Eroilor 27; singles/doubles $70/85)* has plush rooms, with heavy wall panelling, cable TV, phone and fridge.

Places to Eat
A small cellar restaurant with great ambiance, **Bella Muzica** *(☎ 476 946; Str Gheorghe Bar-itiu 2; mains $1.50-4)* is the place to go for the city's best Hungarian, Mexican and Romanian fare. Try the bean soup served in a hollowed out loaf of bread ($1.60) – it's superb!

New York, New York *(☎ 478 548; Str Re-publicii 55; mains $1.50-5)*, tucked away in an alley beside McDonald's, touts a menu of American, European and Oriental dishes. It also has a good selection of vegetarian dishes such as *clătite cu ciuperci albe* (crepe with white mushrooms).

Cerbul Carpaţin *(☎ 143 981; Piaţa Sfatu-lui 12; mains $1.50-5)*, once Braşov's most famous restaurant, serves typical Romanian fare. Some nights there's live folk music.

Mado *(☎ 475 385; Str Republicii 10; menu specials $2-3, mains $2-5)* is a welcoming place, popular with locals. The upstairs restaurant has excellent menu specials includ-ing a main, salad and drink deal available until 8pm. Its downstairs café serves delicious Turkish ice creams.

Coffee lingerers will love **Orient** *(Str Re-publicii 2)* which serves traditional-style Turkish coffee, and **Bistro de l'Arte** *(☎ 473 994; Piaţa Enescu)*, a cosy café with an ever-changing art exhibition adorning its walls.

You can get your sugar high at **Ciao** *(Str Republicii)*, with one of the many decadent cakes and pastries.

Braşov's **fruit and vegetable market** is at the northern end of Str N Bălcescu. Nearby in Duplex '91 is the **Non-Stop Supermarket**.

Entertainment
To find out what's on in Braşov, pick up a copy of *Zile şi Nopţi* (Day and Night), a free fortnightly entertainment magazine, available throughout town.

Bars & Discos The three hippest bars in Braşov are **Saloon** *(☎ 141 611; Str Mure-şenilor 11-13)*, a pub-cum-restaurant with a cellar bar; **La Cabana** *(Str Hirsher 1)*, a trad-itional dimly lit, smoke-filled bar; and the trendy **Festival 39** *(☎ 0754-415 991; Str Mureşenilor 23)*, with its cosy decor and de-lightful staff.

Haçienda *(☎ 413 971; Str Carpaţilor 17)* is a large disco in an old factory in the east.

Cinemas Braşov has four cinemas showing films in their original language with Roman-ian subtitles. The most central one is the **Astra** *(☎ 419 621; Str Lunga 1; admission $0.65)*.

Theatre & Classical Music The Teatrul Sică Alexandrescu *(☎ 418 850; Piaţa Teatru-lui 1)* has plays, recitals and opera throughout the year, or catch performances at the **Filarmonica Gheorghe Dima** *(☎ 143 113; Str Hirscher 10)*. Get information about both at the **Agenţie de Teatrală** *(Str Republicii 4)*, just off Piaţa Sfatului.

Getting There & Around

Train Advance tickets are sold at the **CFR office** *(☎ 142 912; Str Republicii 53; open 8am-7pm Mon-Fri, 9am-1pm Sat)*. International tickets can also be purchased in advance from **Wasteels** *(☎ 424 313)*, located in the train station hall.

Braşov is well connected to Sighişoara (128km), Cluj-Napoca (331km) and Oradea (484km) by fast trains. Local trains to/from Sinaia (45km) run frequently. Local trains from Braşov to Sibiu (223km) drop off hikers headed for the Făgăraş Mountains. The international trains *Dacia*, *Traianus* and *Ister* go to Budapest (707km). The *Pannonia Expres* runs to Budapest (707km), Bratislava (922km) and Prague (1323km). The *Carpati* goes to Warsaw (1499km) and Kraków.

Bus To get to Poiana Braşov ($0.50, every 30 minutes, 13km), catch bus No 20 from the Livada Poştei stop on Blvd Eroilor.

Braşov has two main bus stations. **Autogară 1** is next to the train station; international buses arrive/depart from here, as do buses to other Romanian towns. Every Thursday there's a 7am bus to Budapest ($13, 17 hours). Local travel agencies have information on private buses to Germany, Hungary, Poland and Bulgaria.

Autogară 2 *(Str Avram Iancu 114)*, west of the train station, has buses to Bran/Râşnov every half hour ($0.50, pay the driver). Daily buses also leave here for Făgăraş. Take local bus No 12 or 22 from the centre to the Stadion Tineretului stop on Str Stadionului.

BRAN & RÂŞNOV
☎ 0268

It's hard to visit Romania without seeing **Bran Castle** *(☎ 238 332; Str Principală 498; adult/concession $2/0.65, camera/video $1.70/4.70)*, dating from 1378, in travel brochures or on postcards. Though this fairy-tale castle is impressive in itself, don't be taken in by tales that Bran is Count Dracula's castle – it's unlikely the real Vlad Ţepeş ever set foot here. It was, however, a favourite summer retreat of Queen Marie in the 1920s.

Still, it's fun to run through the castle's 57 rooms. Beside the entrance to the castle is a **Muzeul Satului** (Village Museum) with a collection of Transylvanian farm buildings. Your ticket admits you to the farmhouses, castle and the **Muzeul Vama Bran** (Vama Bran Museum) below the castle. They all open 9am to 4pm Tuesday to Sunday.

Râşnov offers the dual attraction of a convenient camping ground and the ruins of the 13th-century **Râşnov Castle** *(☎ 230 255; adult/concession $0.80/0.50; open Tues-Sun)*. Everyone who makes the trip agrees that Râşnov's hill-top fortress is more dramatic and much less touristy than the castle at Bran.

Places to Stay & Eat
Wild camping is not permitted around Bran Castle. A good alternative is the **Hanul Bran** *(☎ 236 404; Str Principală 363; doubles/triples $8/12)*, a rustic old inn near the castle with tired rooms.

ANTREC *(☎/fax 236 884; Str Lucian Bologa 10)* arranges inexpensive accommodation in 250 private homes in Bran and the surrounding villages.

Popasul Reginei *(☎ 236 834; Str Aurel Stoian 398; doubles/triples $12.50/15.50)* is a clean, modern motel with pleasant rooms and a restaurant.

Vila Bran *(☎ 236 886; Str Principală 271; doubles/triples with shared bathroom $16/24)* is superbly positioned in a picturesque orchard. Breakfast costs $1.25.

In Râşnov, **Camping Valea Cetaţii** *(camping $2.50, two-bed cabins $8; open June-Aug)* and **Hotel Cetate** *(☎ 230 266; doubles/triples $16/22; open year-round)* are side by side, directly below the castle on the road to Poiana Braşov, less than 1km from Piaţa Unirii or about 2km from the bus stop to/from Braşov. The hotel has five double rooms and two triples with private bath.

Getting There & Away
Buses to Bran and Râşnov ($0.50) leave half-hourly from Braşov's Autogară 2. It's best to visit Bran first and then stop at Râşnov on the way back. Return buses leave Bran every hour between 5.30am and 7.30pm.

From the bus stop in Bran the castle is easy to spot. From the stop in Râsnov, walk 100m east towards the mountains, turn right at Piaţa Unirii and watch for the hillside stairs in the courtyard of the unmarked Casa de Cultură (on your left). The castle is a 15-minute walk up the hill.

POIANA BRAŞOV
☎ 0268

Poiana Braşov (1020m), nestled in the mountains of the southern Carpathians, is Romania's premier ski resort. Poiana has six chair lifts, one gondola, and two cable cars (telecabina). A few of these operate services year-round to the summit of Postăvarul Massif (1799m), where there's a splendid view of Braşov and the surrounding Carpathians.

A large map by the bus stop indicates where the cable cars and hotels are.

Activities

Telecabina B is near Hotel Sport. Telecabina A and the adjacent gondola are near the Hotel Teleferic. All three drop you high on the mountain near Cabana Cristianul Mare, and are open 9am to 4pm daily ($2.80 return).

From Cabana Cristianul Mare it's possible to **hike** down to Timişu de Jos (on the rail line from Sinaia to Braşov) in four hours. Otherwise hike back down to Poiana Braşov via Cabana Postăvarul in less than two hours. A direct 9km road links Poiana Braşov to Râsnov, a pleasant downhill walk.

The **Centrul de Echitaţie** (☎ 262 161), 300m down the road to Braşov, has **horse riding** for $9 per hour between 10am and 5pm. The trails here are stunning. Winter **sleigh rides** are $5 an hour.

You can use the sauna and swimming pool at Hotel Alpin for $8.

If you want to go **skiing**, lift tickets are sold on a point system; a 10/20/30/60 point ticket costs $2.90/5.50/7.90/14.70. Lessons cost around $10 per hour. Rent snowboards, skis, boots and poles from the hotels for $9 per day.

Places to Stay & Eat

Cabana Cristianul Mare (open year-round except part Nov), at 1690m, is a large wooden chalet with an attached restaurant. Fifteen minutes downhill from Cristianul Mare is the quieter **Cabana Postăvarul** (☎ 312 448), at 1585m. Both offer beds in shared rooms for $5.50 per person.

Next door to the tourist village, the **Hotel Poiana Ursului** (☎ 262 216; doubles/triples with shared bathroom $17/20) is the resort's cheapest hotel.

Hotel Caraiman (☎/fax 262 420; singles/doubles $18/22) has 66 rooms. Next door is the **Hotel Piatra Mare** (☎ 262 226; singles/doubles $34/55). The three-star **Hotel Sport** (☎ 262 313, fax 262 130; doubles $60) is one of the more flashy hotels.

Most travel agencies in Braşov take bookings for hotels in Poiana Braşov.

Getting There & Away

From Braşov, bus No 20 from the Livada Poştei stop runs to Poiana Braşov ($0.50, every 30 minutes, 13km).

SIGHIŞOARA
☎ 0265

Sighişoara (Schässburg in German, Segesvár in Hungarian), birthplace of Vlad Ţepeş, is a perfectly preserved medieval town in beautiful hilly countryside. Eleven towers stand along Sighişoara's intact city walls; inside are cobblestoned streets lined with 16th-century burgher houses and untouched churches. All trains between Bucharest and Budapest (via Oradea), and several trains a day from Braşov, pass through here. Many readers have named Sighişoara their favourite town in Romania.

Sighişoara has most recently gained fame as the soon-to-be home of the new multimillion dollar Dracula Park, being built on the plateau above the city. The Romanian government plans to give new life to the country's ailing tourism industry by promoting its most notorious son, Vlad Ţepeş, widely believed to be the inspiration for Bram Stoker's fictitious Count Dracula. The government hopes the park, expected to open in 2003, will create 3000 much-needed new jobs and generate $20 million revenue per year. Not everyone is supportive; critics include Lutheran clergymen, Britain's Prince Charles and Greenpeace.

Orientation

Follow Str Gării south from the train station to the Soviet war memorial, where you turn left to the large Orthodox church. Cross the Târnava Mare River on the footbridge here and take Str Morii to the left, then keep going all the way up to Piaţa Hermann Oberth and the old town. Many of the facilities you'll want to use are found along Str 1 Decembrie 1918.

Information

Tourist Offices Elvis' Villa Sighişoara (see Places to Stay) operates a **tourist information**

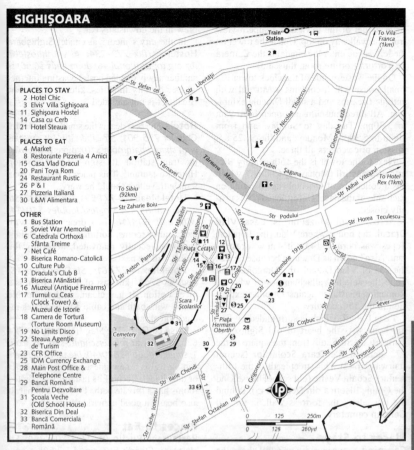

SIGHIŞOARA

PLACES TO STAY
2 Hotel Chic
3 Elvis' Villa Sighişoara
11 Sighişoara Hostel
14 Casa cu Cerb
21 Hotel Steaua

PLACES TO EAT
4 Market
8 Restorante Pizzeria 4 Amici
15 Casa Vlad Dracul
20 Pani Toya Rom
24 Restaurant Rustic
26 P & I
27 Pizzeria Italiană
30 L&M Alimentara

OTHER
1 Bus Station
5 Soviet War Memorial
6 Catedrala Orthoxă
   Sfânta Treime
7 Net Café
9 Biserica Romano-Catolică
10 Culture Pub
12 Dracula's Club B
13 Biserica Mănăstirii
16 Muzeul (Antique Firearms)
17 Turnul cu Ceas
   (Clock Tower) &
   Muzeul de Istorie
18 Camera de Tortură
   (Torture Room Museum)
19 No Limits Disco
22 Steaua Agenţie
   de Turism
23 CFR Office
25 IDM Currency Exchange
28 Main Post Office &
   Telephone Centre
29 Bancă Română
   Pentru Dezvoltare
31 Şcoala Veche
   (Old School House)
32 Biserica Din Deal
33 Bancă Comerciala
   Română

Train Station
To Vila Franca (1km)
To Hotel Rex (1km)
To Sibiu (92km)

ROMANIA

booth *(open 8am-10pm daily)* at the train station. **Steaua Agenţie de Turism** (☎ 771 932; *Str 1 Decembrie 10; open 9am-5pm Mon-Fri, 9am-1pm Sat)* arranges rooms and has information on buses to Hungary and Germany.

Money Change travellers cheques and get Visa/MasterCard cash advances at **Banca Comerciala Română** *(Str 1 Mai 12; open 8.30am-noon Mon-Fri)* or at **Banca Româna Pentru Dezvoltare** *(Piaţa Hermann Oberth; open 8am-2pm Mon-Fri)*. Both have ATMs.

There's a **currency exchange** *(open 9am-5pm Mon-Fri, 9am-1pm Sat)* inside the Steaua Agenţie de Turism office. The **IDM exchange** *(Piaţa Hermann Oberth; open 8am-8pm Mon-Fri, 8am-1pm Sat)* will give cash advances on both Visa and MasterCard.

Post & Communications The **telephone centre** *(open 7am-9pm Mon-Fri, 8am-1pm & 5pm-8pm Sat)* is in the **main post office** *(Piaţa Hermann Oberth 17)*.

Net Café *(Str Nicolae Iorga; open 10am-11pm daily)* charges $0.50 per hour to access the Internet.

Left Luggage The **left-luggage office** *(open 24hr)* is located on the main platform at the train station.

Things to See
The first tower you reach above Piaţa Hermann Oberth is the massive **Turnul cu Ceas** *(clock tower; Piaţa Muzeului)* – the 1648 clock still keeps time. The 14th-century tower is now the **Muzeul de Istorie**, with a

good collection of WWI-era photographs, a scale model of the town and a superb view from the walkway on top. Under the tower on the left as you enter the citadel is the **Camera de Tortură** (torture room museum).

On the western side of the clock tower is a small house which contains a **Muzeul** with antique firearms and a small Dracula exhibition. All three museums are open from 9am to 5.30pm Tuesday to Sunday, and from 10am to 5.30pm Monday, and the $1.25 admission price covers all three.

Next to the tower is the 15th-century **Biserica Mănăstirii** (Monastery Church), which has a collection of Oriental rugs hanging on each side of the nave. Unfortunately, it is usually closed.

Across Piaţa Muzeului is **Casa Vlad Dracul**, the house where Vlad (the Impaler) Ţepeş was born in 1431; it's now a restaurant. Also known as Draculea because he was the son of Vlad Dracul (the Dragon), Vlad Ţepeş became a Wallachian prince who led Romanian resistance against Ottoman expansion in the 15th century.

Piaţa Cetăţii, which is surrounded by fine old houses, is the heart of old Sighişoara. Turn left up Str Şcolii from the square to the 172 steps of the **Scara Şcolarilor** (school stairway; 1642). This street leads to the 14th-century **Şcoala Veche** (old school house) and the Gothic **Biserica din Deal** (1345). Behind the hill, along the fortress wall, is the old **German cemetery**.

Places to Stay

Camping You can camp on a hill above the town, but it's a stiff half-hour hike up from the train station. Walk east along the train tracks to a bridge, then cross the tracks and turn left onto a road leading up. At the end of this road is the **Vila Franca** (☎ 771 046; Str Dealul Gării; camping per tent $3, 2-bed bungalows $10) camping ground and restaurant. The bungalows are OK, but facilities for campers in tents are poor to nonexistent.

Hostels The third in the Elvis hostel chain is the friendly **Elvis' Villa Sighişoara** (☎ 772 546; w www.elvisvilla.com; Str Libertăţii 10; dorm beds from $8). As well as the standard free breakfast, laundry service, Internet, beer and cigarettes, your host Nathan, Sighişoara's unofficial tour guide, will happily introduce you to the local hiking trails and make sure

you relax at the end of the day with a cold brew in the downstairs bar.

In the city's medieval citadel **Sighişoara Hostel** (☎/fax 772 234; e youthhostel@ ibz.org.ro; Bastionul 46; dorm beds $6.50) is another newly opened hostel boasting Internet access, laundry facilities, kitchen and a bar. Breakfast is not included.

Hotels The best deal is the small, clean **Hotel Chic** (☎ 775 901; Str Libertăţii 44; doubles with shared bathroom $10), directly opposite the train station. Its sign reads 'Non-Stop Hotel Restaurant'. This place is rough – lone female travellers should be wary.

Hotel Steaua (☎ 771 594, fax 771 932; Str 1 Decembrie 12; singles/doubles $10/14, with bath $14/18) is a dreary place with dark, musty rooms. Fortunately its restaurant has been recently renovated; hopefully the rooms will be next.

Hotel Rex (☎ 777 615; Str Dumbravel 18; doubles $25), 1km east of the old town, is a nicer option. It has clean, modern double rooms with bath and cable TV, and rates include breakfast.

Casa cu Cerb (The Stag House; ☎/fax 774 625; w www.ar-messerschmitt-s.ro; Str Şcolii 1; singles/doubles $20/40; breakfast per person $2.65) is a new guest house in the heart of the citadel. Each of its tastefully decorated rooms has a private bath, TV and mini bar. It also boasts a good upmarket restaurant.

Places to Eat

Restaurant Rustic (☎ 0723-805 355; Str Hermann Oberth 5; mains $2-3.50), a new restaurant sporting a 'rustic', heavy wooden interior, serves hearty portions of traditional Romanian dishes.

Casa Vlad Dracul (☎ 518 108; Str Cositorarilor 5; mains $2.40-3.70), inside Vlad Dracul's former house in the citadel, is a must for any Dracula freaks. There's a good restaurant in the upstairs area and a berarie (pub) downstairs

Pizzeria Italiană (☎ 775 450; Piaţa Hermann Oberth 1; meals around $2) has a decent selection of pizza, pasta and soups.

Ristorante Pizzeria 4 Amici (☎ 772 652; Str Octavian Goga 12; pizzas $1.20-1.55; pasta $1-2.45) has outside tables. Scrumptious pizzas are priced from $1.20.

Pani Toya Rom (Str O Goga) is a tasty patisserie and fast-food shop serving kebabs for $0.50 and mouthwatering baklava for $2.90 per kilogram.

P & I *(Piaţa Hermann Oberth)* is a large, terrace patisserie and café above the park.

The daily **market** off Str Tîrnavei has a good selection of fruit, vegetables and cheeses. **L&M Alimentara** *(Str Ilarie Chendi)* is a well-stocked supermarket.

Entertainment

Two popular drinking holes in the citadel are: the **Culture Pub** *(Str Bastionul)*, a casual pub-cum-club serving cheap snacks and cold beers, and **Dracula's Club B**, on the southern side of the Primăria, which has pool tables and dart boards. Both also have Internet access.

No Limits *(☎ cell 0722-593 791; Str Turnu-lui 1; open 10pm-4am)* is a chic disco, on the right of the arched entry into the citadel.

Getting There & Away

The **CFR office** *(☎ 771 820; Str 1 Decembrie 2; open 7.30am-7.30pm Mon-Fri)* sells domestic and international train tickets. All trains between Bucharest (via Braşov) and Cluj-Napoca stop at Sighişoara. For Sibiu (95km) you must change trains at Mediaş or Copşa Mică.

Buses leaving from the **bus station** *(auto-gară; ☎ 771 260)*, adjacent to the train station, include two to Sibiu ($2.60, 92km) and one to Făgăraş ($1.90, 86km). Steaua Agenţie de Turism has information on weekly buses to Hungary and Germany.

SIBIU
☎ 0269 • pop 169,460

Beautiful Sibiu is just far enough off the beaten track to be spared the tourist tide that occasionally engulfs Braşov. Founded in the 12th century on the site of the former Roman village of Cibinium, Sibiu (Hermannstadt to the German Saxons, Nagyszében to Hungarians) has always been one of the leading cities of Transylvania. Destroyed by the Tatars in 1241, the town was later surrounded by strong walls that enabled the citizens to resist the Turks. Under the Habsburgs from 1703 to 1791 and again from 1849 to 1867, Sibiu served as the seat of the Austrian governors of Transylvania. Much remains from this colourful history, especially in the old town, which is one of the largest and best preserved in Romania. Sibiu is also a gateway to the spectacular Făgăraş Mountains.

Orientation

The adjacent bus and train stations are near the centre of town. Exit the station and stroll up Str General Magheru four blocks to Piaţa Mare, the historic centre.

Information

Tourist Offices Sibiu has a **tourist information office** *(☎/fax 211 110; w www .primsb.ro; Str Nicolae Bălcescu 7; open 9am-5pm Mon-Fri, 10am-1pm Sat)* right in the centre of town. Its friendly English speaking staff will happily answer all your questions.

Money There are **IDM exchanges** giving cash advances on Visa/MasterCard at Piaţa Mică 9, Str Papiu Ilarian 12, and Parcul Tineretului 20; all are open 8am to 8pm weekdays, and 9am to 2pm Saturday. There are also currency exchanges inside Hotels Bulevard and Impăratul Romanilor.

Banca Comercială Romănă *(Str Nicolae Bălcescu 11)* cashes travellers cheques, gives cash advances and has an outside ATM.

Post & Communications The **main post office** *(Str Mitropoliei 14; open 7am-8pm Mon-Fri, 8am-1pm Sat)* can help with postal requirements. Make phone calls at Sibiu's **telephone centre** *(Str N Bălcescu 13; open 7am-7pm daily)*.

You can send email and access the Internet at **Internet Café Împăratul Romanilor** *(☎ 216 500; Str N Bălcescu 4; open 6am-midnight daily)*. Access costs around $0.50 an hour.

Bookshops The **Librărie Dacia Traian** *(Piaţa Mare 7)* has English-language novels, postcards and some maps. **Librărie Noica** *(Str Nicolae Bălcescu 16)* also has English books and guides.

Left Luggage The **left-luggage office** *(open 24hr)* at the train station is at the western end of the main platform near track 1.

Things to See & Do

Central Sibiu is a perfectly preserved medieval monument and the best way to begin your visit is by strolling along Str Nicolae Bălcescu and Piaţa Mare, the main square. The 1588 **Turnul Sfatului** *(council tower; admission $0.85; open Tues-Sun)*, overlooks the colourful houses and guild halls of the square. Climb to the top for a superb view.

SIBIU

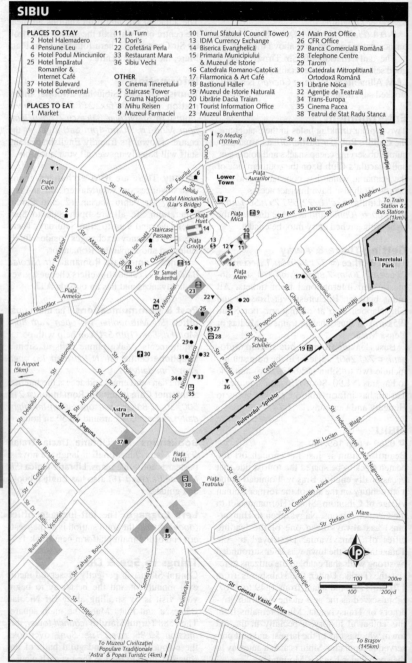

Walk through Piaţa Mare past the baroque **Catedrala Romano-Catolică** (Catholic Cathedral) to the **Muzeul Brukenthal** (Brukenthal Museum; ☎ 217 691; Piaţa Mare 4-5; admission $1; open 9am-5pm Tues-Sun), the oldest and finest art gallery in Romania. Founded in 1817, the museum is in the palace (1785) of Baron Samuel Brukenthal, former governor of Transylvania. Along with the paintings, it contains excellent archaeological and folk-art collections.

West along Str Samuel Brukenthal is the **Muzeul de Istorie** (History Museum; ☎ 218 143; Str Mitropoliei 2; admission $1; open 9am-5pm Tues-Sun), dating from 1470, which was once the **Primaria Municipiului** (town hall).

Nearby is the Gothic **Biserica Evanghelică** (Evangelical church; Piaţa Huet), built between 1300 and 1520, its great five-pointed tower visible from afar. Note the four magnificent baroque funerary monuments on the upper nave and the organ with 6002 pipes (1772). The **tomb** of Mihnea Vodă cel Rău (Prince Mihnea the Bad), son of Vlad Ţepeş, is in the closed-off section behind the organ. This prince (r. Wallachia 1507–10) was murdered in the church square after a service in March 1510. Don't miss the splendid fresco of the Crucifixion (1445) in the sanctuary.

To reach the lower town from here, walk down the 13th-century **Staircase Passage** on the opposite side of the church from where you entered, or cross the photogenic **Podul Minciunilor** (Liars' Bridge; 1859) on nearby Piaţa Mică to reach the steep stairway. The bridge gained its nickname because it's believed that it will collapse if anyone tells a lie while standing on it.

Also on Piaţa Mică is the **Muzeul Farmaciei** (Pharmaceutical Museum; ☎ 218 191; Piaţa Mica 26; admission $1; open 9am-5pm Tues-Sun), with its collection of antique drug jars and medical tools.

Walk southwest from Piaţa Mică, along Str Mitropoliei to the **Catedrala Mitroplitiană Ortodoxă Română** (Orthodox Cathedral; 1906), a monumental building styled after the Hagia Sofia in İstanbul. Next, turn left onto Strada Tribunei and follow it across Piaţa Unirii to Str Cetăţii, turning left to begin a pleasant walk northeast along a narrow park and the 16th-century **city walls** and watch towers. At the far end is the **Bastionul Haller** (Haller Bastion; 1551) and before that the

Muzeul de Istorie Naturală (Natural History Museum; 1849; ☎ 436 868; Str Cetăţii 1; admission $1; open 9am-5pm Tues-Mon). Take a narrow street on your left-hand side to return to Piaţa Mare.

If you have an extra afternoon, take in the **Muzeul Civilizaţiei Populare Tradiţionale 'Astra'** (Astra Museum of Traditional Folk Civilisation; ☎ 420 340; admission $1; open 10am-6pm Tues-Sun April-Nov, shorter winter hours) open-air ethnographic museum in Dumbrava Park, south of the city centre (take trolleybus No T1 from the train station).

Places to Stay

Camping The closest camping ground is **Popas Turistic** (☎ 214 022; trolleybus No T1 from train station; camping per tent $5; 2-bed cabins $12; open June-Sept), beside the Hanul Dumbrava Restaurant 4km southwest of the town centre. There are rooms in worn-out cabins, or pitch your tent on the shady lawn.

Private Rooms Rooms in private houses can be arranged by **ANTREC** (☎/fax 233 503; e tht@rdslink.ro) from $10 per person, which includes breakfast.

Hotels West of Piaţa Huet, just off Str Turnului is the insalubrious **Pensiune Leu** (☎ 218 392; Str Moş Ion Roată 6; accommodation per person $6), with very simple rooms. Better quality is the four-room **Hotel Halemadero** (☎ 212 509; Str Măsarilor 10; accommodation per room $20), which overlooks a very pleasant garden and patio. The rooms are austere, the bathroom shared, and the adjacent bar is a friendly hangout.

Hotel Podul Minciunilor (☎ 217 259; Str Azilului 1; accommodation per room $15) is a small hotel operated by a friendly German/Romanian couple. Its decent-sized rooms have a private bathroom and TV (one station only).

Hotel Bulevard (☎ 412 121, fax 210 158; Piaţa Unirii 10; singles/doubles with breakfast $25/35) is an excellent-value, two-star hotel close to the centre.

Hotel Împăratul Romanilor (☎ 216 500, fax 213 278; Str N Bălcescu 4; singles/doubles $32/40, apartments $70) is Sibiu's most colourful hotel. Founded in 1555, it took its name in 1773 after a visit by Habsburg emperor Josef II. Its pleasant renovated rooms each have a private shower/bath and colour TV. Breakfast is included in the room rate.

ROMANIA

Hotel Continental (☎ 218 100, fax 210 125; Calea Dumbrăvii 2-4; singles/doubles with breakfast $50/80), an upmarket 15-storey hotel, has plush rooms with direct-dial phone and colour TV.

Places to Eat
La Turn (☎ 213 985; Piaţa Mare 1; mains $1.40-4, 3-course menu $4.80), next to the old council tower, has a terrace overlooking the square and serves traditional Romanian cuisine. If your stomach can take it try the schnitzel stuffed with brains ($2).

Restaurant Mara (☎ 217 025; Str N Bălcescu 21; mains $1.50-5) is a small, quiet bistro with an English-language menu and excellent service.

Împăratul Romanilor (☎ 218 086; Str N Bălcescu 4; mains $2-5), in the hotel of the same name, is rather stuffy but the food is top-notch.

Sibiu Vechi (☎ 431 971; Str Papiu Ilarian 3; mains $2-5) is a well-known traditional Romanian restaurant serving typical local specialities.

Dori's (☎ 217 697; Piaţa Mica 14) is an inexpensive patisserie serving freshly baked breads and yogurt.

Cofetăria Perla (☎ 217 115; Piaţa Mare 6) has a great selection of rich cakes and pastries, and excellent Turkish coffee.

Stock up on vegetables and fruit at the **market** (Piaţa Cibin), northeast of Str Măsarilor near Hotel Halemadero.

Entertainment
Performances at the **Filarmonica** (Str Filarmonicii 2), off Str General Magheru, and the **Teatrul de Stat Radu Stanca** (☎ 413 114; Blvd Spitelor 2-4), just off Piaţa Unirii, are worth seeing. Buy tickets at the **Agenţie de Teatrală** (☎ 217 575; Str N Bălcescu 17; open 10am-5pm Tues-Fri, 10am-1pm Sat). Tickets for most performances cost around $1.

Art Café (Str Filarmonicii 2; open 8am-2am daily), inside the Filarmonica building, is a trendy cellar club attracting an older bohemian crowd with blues and funky jazz.

Crama Naţional (☎ 232 135; Piaţa Mica 18; open 5pm-1am daily) is a less sophisticated dark cellar bar.

Cinema Tineretului (Youth Theatre; ☎ 211 420; Str Alexandru Odobescu; admission $0.50) is an ageing auditorium-cum-bar with coffee tables and sofas from which you can

watch your favourite Hollywood film while enjoying a beer.

Cinema Pacea (☎ 217 021; Str N Bălcescu 29; admission $0.80) also shows American films with Romanian subtitles; the entrance is via a side alley off the main street.

Getting There & Away
Air The national carrier **Tarom** (☎ 211 157; Str N Bălcescu 10) has three flights weekly to Bucharest ($68/83 single/return). Tarom's shuttle bus goes to/from the airport, 5km west of the centre.

Train There's a **CFR office** (☎ 216 441; Blvd Nicolae Bălcescu 6; open 7.30am-7.30pm Mon-Fri). The train station (gara) is at the eastern end of Str General Magheru on Piaţa 1 Decembrie. From Sibiu there are seven daily trains to Braşov (223km), one express train daily to Cluj-Napoca (198km) and Timişoara, seven local trains to Copşa Mică (45km), and four express trains to Bucharest (389km). For Sighişoara, you have to change at Copşa Mică or Mediaş.

Bus The bus station (autogară) is opposite the train station. There's a daily service to Cluj-Napoca ($4, 230km) and two daily to Sighişoara ($2.60, 92km).

Mihu Reisen (☎ 211 744; Str 9 Mai 52) operates private buses to Germany as well as Bucharest, Braşov and Cluj-Napoca. **Trans-Europa** (☎ 211 296; w www.transeuropa; Str N Bălcescu 41) sells bus tickets to countries in Western Europe.

THE FĂGĂRAŞ MOUNTAINS
In summer a small but steady stream of backpackers descends on the Făgăraş Mountains, a section of the Carpathian Mountains in the centre of Romania. They soon get lost in the alpine glory of Făgăraş, the most dramatic hiking area in the country.

The main drawback is getting there: from train stations along the Sibiu-Braşov line, most trailheads are 8km to 15km south, poorly serviced by bus and difficult to hitch to.

To hike the Făgăraş you must be in good physical shape and have warm clothing and sturdy boots. The trails are well marked, but keep the altitude in mind and be prepared for cold and rain at any time.

From November to early May these mountains are snow covered; August and September

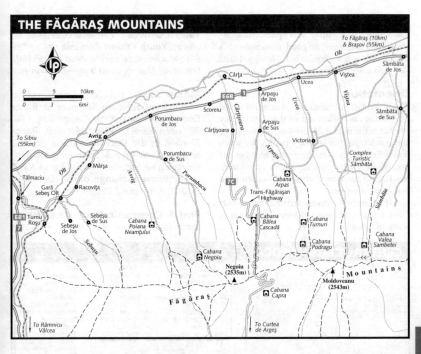

THE FĂGĂRAŞ MOUNTAINS

are the best months. Basic food is available at the cabanas but carry a supply of biscuits and your water bottle. You'll meet lots of other hikers eager to tell you of their adventures, and with a good map (available in bookshops in Sibiu) you'll soon know exactly where to go.

Routes & Places to Stay

The easiest access is from Sibiu, and local trains on the Făgăraş line to Braşov pass many starting points.

One of the best places to get off the train is Ucea (59km from Sibiu), from where you can catch one of the seven daily buses to **Victoria**. From Victoria you can hike to **Cabana Turnuri** (1520m; 20 beds) in approximately six hours. The first leg is rather boring, but the scenery becomes stunning once you start the ascent. The next morning head for **Cabana Podragu** (2136m; 68 beds), which is four hours south of Cabana Turnuri.

Cabana Podragu makes a good base if you want to climb Mt Moldoveanu (2543m), which is Romania's highest peak. It's a pretty tough uphill climb, but the views from the summit are unbeatable. Otherwise, hike eight hours east, passing by Mt Moldoveanu on the

way, to **Cabana Valea Sambetei** (1407m; 100 beds).

From Cabana Valea Sambetei you can descend to the railway in Ucea, via Victoria, in a day.

CLUJ-NAPOCA
☎ 0264 • pop 332,297

Cut in two by the Someşul Mic River, Cluj-Napoca is as Hungarian as it is Romanian; known as Klausenburg to the Germans and Kolozsvár to the Hungarians. The old Roman name of Napoca was added to the city's official title to emphasise its Daco-Roman origin, but it is simply referred to as Cluj.

The history of Cluj-Napoca goes back to Dacian times. In AD 124, during the reign of Emperor Hadrian, Napoca attained municipal status and Emperor Marcus Aurelius elevated it to a colony. Documented references to the medieval town date back to 1183. German merchants arrived in the 12th century and after the Tatar invasion of 1241 the medieval earthen walls of *castrenses de Clus* were rebuilt in stone. From 1791 to 1848 and again after the union with Hungary in 1867, Cluj-Napoca served as the capital of Transylvania.

Because Cluj is a major university town it has a relaxed, inviting atmosphere, fine architecture and several good museums. It's well worth a few days' visit. Nearby Turda Gorge is also worth a look.

Orientation

The train station *(gara)* is 1.5km north of the city centre. Walk left out of the station, buy a ticket at the red L&M kiosk across the street and catch tram No 101 or a trolleybus south down Str Horea. On the trolleybus get off immediately after crossing the river; on tram No 101 go two stops, then walk south until you cross the river.

All major bus services arrive at and depart from the bus station *(autogară)*, which is north of town.

Information

Tourist Offices For hostel accommodation, contact **Youth Hostels România** *(☎/fax 186 616;* **W** *www.dntcj.ro/yhr; head office: Piaţa Ştefan cel Mare 5; open 9am-4am Mon-Fri).*

Money Change travellers cheques and get Visa/MasterCard cash advances at **Banca Comercială Română** *(Str George Barţiu 10-12; open 8am-12.30pm Mon-Fri).* **Banca Română Pentru Dezvoltare** *(Piaţa Unirii 7; open 8.30am-1pm & 2pm-4pm Mon-Fri)* gives cash advances on Visa and has an ATM.

The **Prima Exchange office** *(Str Bolyai János 2-4)* is open 24 hours.

Post & Communications The **telephone centre** *(open 7.30am-8pm Mon-Fri, 8am-1pm*

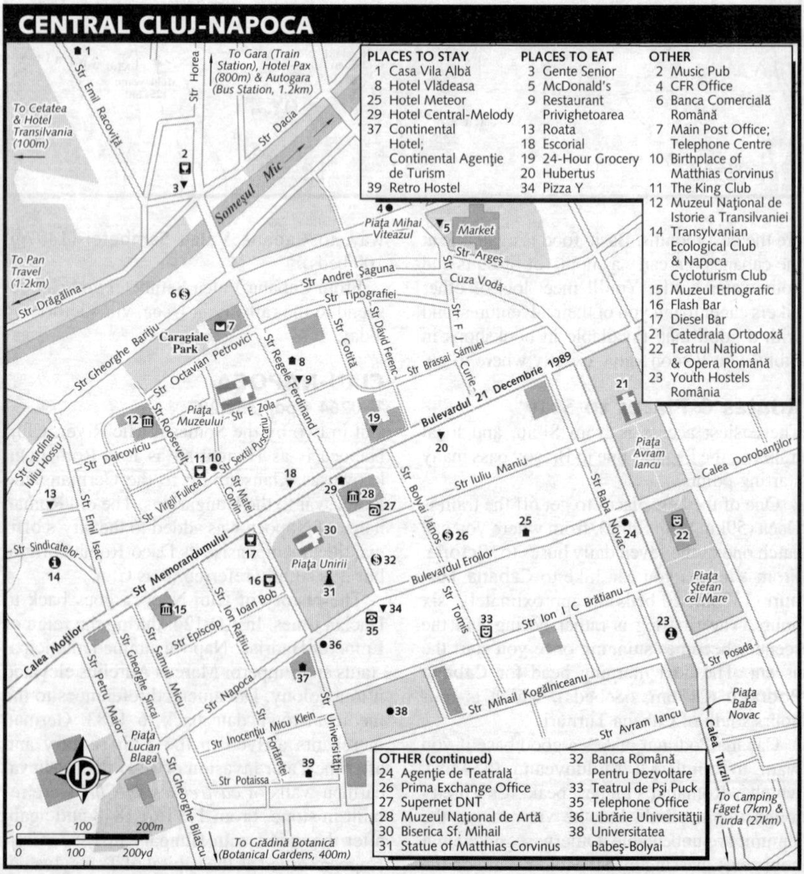
CENTRAL CLUJ-NAPOCA
PLACES TO STAY
1 Casa Vila Albă
8 Hotel Vlădeasa
25 Hotel Meteor
29 Hotel Central-Melody
37 Continental Hotel; Continental Agenţie de Turism
39 Retro Hostel
PLACES TO EAT
3 Gente Senior
5 McDonald's
9 Restaurant Privighetoarea
13 Roata
18 Escorial
19 24-Hour Grocery
20 Hubertus
34 Pizza Y
OTHER
2 Music Pub
4 CFR Office
6 Banca Comercială Română
7 Main Post Office; Telephone Centre
10 Birthplace of Matthias Corvinus
11 The King Club
12 Muzeul Naţional de Istorie a Transilvaniei
14 Transylvanian Ecological Club & Napoca Cycloturism Club
15 Muzeul Etnografic
16 Flash Bar
17 Diesel Bar
21 Catedrala Ortodoxă
22 Teatrul Naţional & Opera Română
23 Youth Hostels România
OTHER (continued)
24 Agenţie de Teatrală
26 Prima Exchange Office
27 Supernet DNT
28 Muzeul Naţional de Artă
30 Biserica Sf. Mihail
31 Statue of Matthias Corvinus
32 Banca Română Pentru Dezvoltare
33 Teatrul de Pşi Puck
35 Telephone Office
36 Librărie Universităţii
38 Universitatea Babeş-Bolyai
To Gara (Train Station), Hotel Pax (800m) & Autogara (Bus Station, 1.2km)
To Cetatea & Hotel Transilvania (100m)
To Pan Travel (1.2km)
To Camping Făget (7km) & Turda (27km)
To Grădină Botanică (Botanical Gardens, 400m)
Someşul Mic
Str Horea
Str Emil Racoviţă
Str Dacia
Piaţa Mihai Viteazul
Market
Str Argeş
Str Andrei Şaguna
Str Tipografiei
Str Cuza Vodă
Str Drăgălina
Caragiale Park
Str Gheorghe Barţiu
Str Octavian Petrovici
Str Regele Ferdinand I
Str Cotită
Str Dávid Ferenc
Str Brassai Sámuel
Str F Curie
Bulevardul 21 Decembrie 1989
Piaţa Muzeului
Str E Zola
Str Roosevelt
Str Sextil Puşcariu
Str Cardinal Iuliu Hossu
Str Daicoviciu
Str Virgil Fulicea
Str Matei Corvin
Str Emil Isac
Str Sindicatelor
Str Memorandumului
Piaţa Unirii
Str Iuliu Maniu
Str Bolyai János
Bulevardul Eroilor
Str Baba Novac
Piaţa Avram Iancu
Calea Dorobanţilor
Str Tomis
Str Ion I C Brătianu
Piaţa Ştefan cel Mare
Str Posada
Calea Moţilor
Str Episcop
Str Ioan Bob
Str Ion Raţiu
Str Gheorghe Şincai
Str Samuil Micu
Str Petru Maior
Str Napoca
Str Mihail Kogălniceanu
Str Avram Iancu
Piaţa Baba Novac
Calea Turzii
Str Universităţii
Str Inocenţiu Micu Klein
Str Fortăreţei
Piaţa Lucian Blaga
Str Gheorghe Bilascu
Str Potaissa
0 100 200m
0 100 200yd

Sat) is located behind the **post office** *(Str Regele Ferdinand 33; open 7am-8pm Mon-Fri, 7am-1pm Sat)*. There's another **telephone office** *(Piaţa Unirii 5; open 7am-10pm daily)*. **Supernet DNT** (☎ 430 425; e setsala@ supernet.dntcj.ro; Str Iuliu Maniu 1; open 24hr) charges $0.80 per hour for you to check emails or surf the Internet.

Travel Agencies At the Continental Hotel, **Continental Agenţie de Turism** (☎ 195 405, fax 193 977; e conticj@codec.ro; Str Napoca 1; open 9am-5pm Mon-Fri) books hotel rooms and arranges car rental.

Pan Travel (☎/fax 420 516; w www .pantravel.ro; Str Grozavescu 13) provides top-notch travellers' advice, has a variety of regional tours and arranges private accommodation and car rental.

Bookshops The **Librărie Universităţii** *(Piaţa Unirii)*, opposite the Continental Hotel, stocks English-language novels.

Left Luggage The **left-luggage office** *(open 24hr)* is inside the train station near the restaurant.

Things to See

A 15th-century Gothic hall church with a neo-Gothic tower (1859), **Biserica Sfântul Mihail** (St Michael's Church) stands impressively above Piaţa Unirii. Flanking it to the south is a huge equestrian statue (1902) of the famous Hungarian king Matthias Corvinus (r. 1458–90). On the eastern side of the square is the excellent **Muzeul Naţional de Artă** *(National Art Museum; ☎ 196 953; Piaţa Unirii 30; admission $0.50; open 10am-4.30pm Wed-Sun)* in the baroque Banffy Palace (1785). Strada Matei Corvin leads from the northwestern corner of the square on to **Corvinus' birthplace** (in 1440), which is at No 6 (closed to the public).

To the west on Piaţa Muzeului is the interesting **Muzeul Naţional de Istorie a Transilvaniei** *(History Museum of Transylvania; ☎ 191 718; admission $0.25; open Tues-Sun)*, open since 1859. None of the captions is in English but it's still worth walking through. There's also the **Muzeul Etnografic** *(Ethnographic Museum; ☎ 192 344; Str Memorandumului 21; admission $1; open 9am-5pm Tues-Sun)*, which displays Transylvanian folk costumes.

South is the fragrant **Grădina Botanică** *(Botanical Gardens; Str Gheorghe Bilaşcu 42; admission $0.25; open 9am-8pm daily)*, which features greenhouses, a museum and a Japanese garden. In summer you'll need to allow several hours to explore it.

For an overall view of Cluj-Napoca, climb up the steps behind Hotel Astoria to the **cetatea** (citadel; 1715), which sounds more impressive than it is. After climbing all those steps, stop for a beer on the terrace at Hotel Transilvania.

Activities

Cluj is a major centre for **mountain biking**, **hiking** and **caving** enthusiasts. For details on the caves and hiking routes contact the **Transylvanian Ecological Club** *(☎/fax 431 626; w www.greenagenda.org/cet; Apt 6, Str Sindicatelor 3; open 11am-5pm Mon-Fri)*.

In the apartment next door is the **Napoca Cycloturism Club** (☎ 450 013; w www .ccn.ro; Apt 8, Str Sindicatelor 3), who can organise bike rental and guides.

Places to Stay

Camping Up in the hills, 7km south of Cluj-Napoca is **Camping Făget** (☎ 196 234; camping per person $1.50, 2-bed bungalows $9; open mid-May–mid-Oct), with 143 bungalows. To reach the camping ground take bus No 35 from Piaţa Mihai Viteazul south down Calea Turzii to the end of the line. From here it's a marked 2km hike to the site.

Private Rooms Rooms in private houses around Cluj can be booked through **ANTREC** (☎ 198 135, 424 536; Piaţa Avram Iancu 15; from $5 per person).

Hostels The new **Retro Hostel** (☎/fax 450 452; w www.retro.ro; Str Potaissa 13; dorm beds $9, bed per person in doubles or triples $13) has opened near the old city wall. From Piaţa Unirii turn south down Str Universităţii. Str Potaissa is the second street on the right.

Hotels Opposite the train station, the **Hotel Pax** (☎/fax 433 729; e hotelpax@yahoo .com; Piaţa Gării 2; singles/doubles/triples with shared bathroom $13/17/22) is noisy but clean.

Hotel Vlădeasa (☎ 194 429; Str Regele Ferdinand 20; singles/doubles/triples $14/22/29) is the cheapest option in the centre of

ROMANIA

the city. Its spotless rooms are good value. The reception is through an archway adjacent to the Restaurant Vlădeasa.

Hotel Central-Melody (☎ 197 465, fax 197 468; e melody@codec.ro; Piaţa Unirii 29; singles/doubles from $23/27), overlooking the square, has rooms at an OK price.

Hotel Meteor (☎/fax 191 060; w www .hotelmeteor.ro; Blvd Eroilor 29; singles/ doubles/triples with breakfast $24/30/36) is a good mid-range option offering clean, comfortable rooms. It also has an excellent cheap restaurant.

Also on the square, the **Continental Hotel** (☎/fax 193 977; e conticj@codec.ro; Str Napoca 1; singles/doubles $27/36, with bath $44/57) is a stately hotel with pleasant rooms. It is also a member of Youth Hostels Romania and has 20 'hostel' doubles (bed in 2-bed room with shared bathroom $9). Bookings can be made in advance through the hotel's tourist office (see Tourist Offices).

Casa Vila Albă (☎/fax 432 277; Str Emil Racoviţă 22; doubles $70), near the base of the Citadel, has luxurious, classy doubles and is well-worth the splurge. The hotel's restaurant is one of the best in the city.

Places to Eat

Restaurant Privighetoarea (☎ 193 480; Str Regele Ferdinand 16; dishes $1-3), near Hotel Vlădeasu, doles out hearty portions of meat, potatoes and soups, spicy meatballs and breaded cheese.

Escorial (☎ 196 909; Piaţa Unirii 23; mains $2-3, side dishes $1-2), an upmarket cellar restaurant and club with a distinct old-worldly air, serves traditional Hungarian cuisine.

Roata (☎ 192 022; Str Alexandru Ciura 6a; dishes $1.25-3) offers good, filling Romanian dishes such as the Taci şi înghite (close your eyes and swallow) mămăligă for $1.50.

Hubertus (☎ 196 743; Blvd 21 Decembrie 1989, 22), a local culinary mainstay, is the place to head for game or quail (seasonal). It has a small courtyard decorated with hunting motifs. Cognac is the traditional start to a meal here.

Pizza Y (Piaţa Unirii 1; pizzas & pastas $1-2) offers 34 types of pizza as well as fresh salads and pasta.

Gente Senior (☎ 432 807; Str Horea 5; pizzas & pastas $1.50-2.50), with its refreshingly green interior, serves the largest and most delicious pizzas in Cluj by far.

For fresh produce, the **central market** is behind McDonald's on Piaţa Mihai Viteazul. Strada Regele Ferdinand is lined with pastry and snack vendors. For self-caterers, there's a small **grocery** (cnr Str Memorandumului & Str David Ferenc; open 24hr).

Entertainment

Bars & Discos
The ever-popular **Music Pub** (☎ 432 517; Str Horea 5), not far from the train station, hosts live folk, jazz and rock bands most weekends.

The **Diesel Club** (☎ 198 441; Piaţa Unirii 17) and the **Flash Bar** (Piaţa Unirii 10) attract a more stylish, young crowd.

The King Club (☎ 408 392; Str Roosevelt 2; admission $0.65; open 24hr) is a fun bar with a nightly disco. The club draws its large student following with its infamous 'Beer Belly' nights (Wednesday), where for $2.20 you can drink as much as your 'belly' can stomach.

Theatre & Classical Music
The neo-baroque **Teatrul Naţional & Opera Română** (National Theatre & Opera House; ☎ 191 799; Piaţa Ştefan cel Mare 24) was designed by the famous Viennese architects Fellner and Hellmer (1906).

Look out for performances at the **Teatrul de Pşi Puck** (Puck Puppet Theatre; ☎ 195 992; Str Ion IC Brătianu). The **Agenţie de Teatrală** (☎ 195 363; Blvd Eroilor 36) sells tickets for most events.

Getting There & Away

Train
Advance train tickets are sold at the **CFR office** (☎ 432 001; Piaţa Mihai Viteazul 20; open 7am-7pm Mon-Fri). There are express trains running from Cluj to Oradea (2½ hours, 153km), Sighişoara (three hours, 203km), Braşov (five hours, 331km), Timişoara (six hours, 337km) and Bucharest (eight hours, 497km).

Through trains travel to Iaşi via Gura Humorului and Suceava. To reach Sibiu you may have to change at Copşa Mică. Sleepers are available to Bucharest.

Bus
A bus to Budapest ($6.50, 399km, once a week) leaves from the bus station, across the bridge from the train station. Other services include one a day to Sibiu ($4, 166km) and Sighetu Marmaţiei ($5, 217km), and three a day to Turda ($1, 27km).

AROUND CLUJ-NAPOCA

Thirty kilometres southeast of Cluj-Napoca is **Turda**, which was the seat of the Transylvanian *diet* in the mid-16th century. The reason to visit Turda is strictly practical – to hike or catch a bus to **Cheile Turzii** (Turda Gorge), a short but stunning break in the limestone mountains 9km southwest.

You can hike the gorge's length in under an hour, but you can camp for a night or two to explore the surrounding network of marked trails – the map outside the cabana's restaurant details half a dozen different routes.

A good two-hour trek is to follow the red-cross trail through the gorge, then the steep red-dot trail up and over the peak before you return to the cabana.

It's also possible to go all the way from Turda Gorge to Cluj, along the vertical red-stripe trail via Turni and Camping Făget (on the outskirts of Cluj). This 29km hike will take 10 to 12 hours.

Places to Stay & Eat

You can **freelance camp** in the grassy valley at the gorge's northern end. Otherwise, try the noisy **Cabana Cheile Turzii** (☎ *0745-599 031; camping per tent $1, singles/doubles/ triples $6/10/16*), at the southern foot of the gorge. An **restaurant** at the cabana serves simple meals.

Potaissa Hotel (☎ *311 691; Piaţa Republicii 6; singles & doubles with/without bath $25/16)* is a modest two-star hotel with decent rooms in the centre of Turda.

Castelul Prinţul Vânător (*The Hunter Prince Castle;* ☎ *316 850;* **w** *www.abline.ro/ huntercastle; Str Suluţiu 4-6; doubles $35)* is a kitsch, over-the-top, Dracula-inspired hotel not far from the Potaissa Hotel. In the hotel's restaurant you can sink your teeth into a bear steak ($12.50).

Getting There & Away

There are three daily buses from Cluj to Turda ($1, reduced service on weekends). The last bus back from Turda to Cluj leaves about 5pm.

From Turda you can hike to the gorge in 2½ hours. Starting at Piaţa Republicii follow signs for Cîmpeni and, 1km past the village of Mihai Viteazu, turn right at the 'Cheile Turzii' sign. From here it's another 5km. Follow the paved road uphill past the quarry and go left at the fork. If you're driving, do not attempt this steep road after heavy rains.

Crişana & Banat

The plains of Crişana and Banat, divided by the Mureş River, merge imperceptibly into Yugoslavia's Vojvodina and Hungary's Great Plain. From the late 9th century until the Ottoman conquest in 1552, the territory was under Hungarian rule. In 1699 the Turks relinquished Hungary to Austria, but held Banat until their defeat by the Habsburgs in 1716. In 1718 Banat became part of the Austro-Hungarian Empire, after which Swabians from southwestern Germany arrived to colonise the region. Until 1918 all these regions were governed jointly as part of the Habsburg Empire. The Treaty of Trianon in 1920 split the territory among Romania, Hungary and Yugoslavia, setting their current borders.

Crişana and Banat are the door to Romania, and all trains travelling from Hungary and Yugoslavia pass through one of the gateway cities: Timişoara, Arad and Oradea; all good places to stop and get your bearings.

ORADEA

☎ 0259 • pop 223,680

Of the cities of the old Austro-Hungarian empire, Oradea (Nagyvárad in Hungarian, Grosswardein in German) is probably the one that has best retained its 19th-century elegance. When Oradea was ceded to Romania in 1920, this example of Habsburg majesty became the backwater it is today – a time capsule for romantics in search of a simpler world.

Orientation & Information

The train station is a few kilometres north of town; tram Nos 1 and 4 run south from Piaţa Bucureşti (across from the station) to Piaţa Unirii. The main square north of the river is Piaţa Regele Ferdinand, just across the bridge from Piaţa Unirii.

For motoring inquiries, get in contact with the **Automobil Clubul Român** (☎ *130 725; Piaţa Independenţei 31; open 8.30am-4.30pm Mon-Fri, 10am-1pm Sat)*.

Banca Comercială Română (*open 8.30am-1pm Mon-Fri)*, at the southern end of Piaţa Independenţei, cashes travellers cheques, gives cash advances on Visa/MasterCard and has an ATM. The bank's Calea Republicii office also has an ATM.

The **post office** (*Str Roman Ciorogariu; open 7am-8.30pm Mon-Fri, 8am-1pm Sat)*

ROMANIA

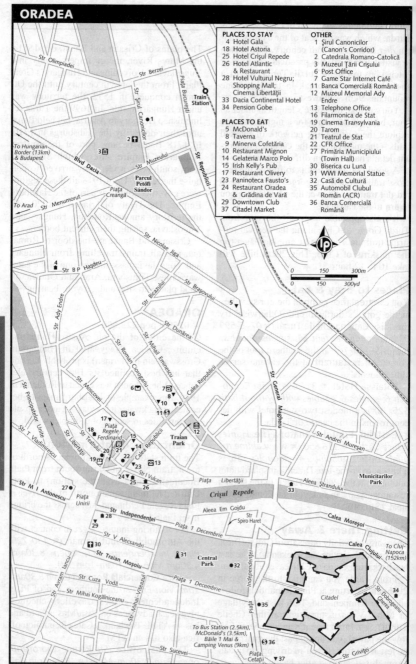

ORADEA

PLACES TO STAY
- 4 Hotel Gala
- 18 Hotel Astoria
- 25 Hotel Crişul Repede
- 26 Hotel Atlantic & Restaurant
- 28 Hotel Vulturul Negru; Shopping Mall; Cinema Libertăţii
- 33 Dacia Continental Hotel
- 34 Pension Gobe

PLACES TO EAT
- 5 McDonald's
- 8 Taverna
- 9 Minerva Cofetăria
- 10 Restaurant Mignon
- 14 Gelateria Marco Polo
- 15 Irish Kelly's Pub
- 17 Restaurant Olivery
- 23 Paninoteca Fausto's
- 24 Restaurant Oradea & Grădina de Vară
- 29 Downtown Club
- 37 Citadel Market

OTHER
- 1 Şirul Canonicilor (Canon's Corridor)
- 2 Catedrala Romano-Catolică
- 3 Muzeul Ţării Crişului
- 6 Post Office
- 7 Game Star Internet Café
- 11 Banca Comercială Română
- 12 Muzeul Memorial Ady Endre
- 13 Telephone Office
- 16 Filarmonica de Stat
- 19 Cinema Transylvania
- 20 Tarom
- 21 Teatrul de Stat
- 22 CFR Office
- 27 Primăria Municipiului (Town Hall)
- 30 Biserica cu Lună
- 31 WWI Memorial Statue
- 32 Casă de Cultură
- 35 Automobil Clubul Român (ACR)
- 36 Banca Comercială Română

can help with postal requirements, while the **telephone office** *(Calea Republicii 5; open 7am-9pm daily)* is down the alleyway near Liberty Bingo.

Game Star Internet Café *(Str Mihai Eminescu 4; open 24hr)*, next to the Taverna Bar & Restaurant, charges about $0.50 per hour for Internet access.

The **left-luggage office** *(open 24hr)* at the train station is beside the restaurant on the main platform.

Things to See

Oradea's most imposing sights are on Piaţas Unirii and Regele Ferdinand. Overlooking the Crişul Repede River, is the magnificent **Vulturul Negru** *(Black Vulture; Piaţa Unirii)* hotel and shopping mall, built in 1908. The mall, with its fabulous stained-glass ceiling, links Piaţa Unirii with Str Independenţei. The Orthodox church on the piaţa is known as the **Biserica cu Lună** (Moon Church; 1784) for a 3m sphere on the tower which shows the phases of the moon. Listen for the trumpet tune playing from the **Primăria Municipiului** (Town Hall) every hour.

Just east of Piaţa Unirii is **Central Park** with the **Casă de Cultură** at its eastern end. Farther east is the **Cetatea Oradiei**, built in the 13th century, which has been converted into government offices and is not really worth seeing.

Across the bridge from Piaţa Unirii, the green neoclassical **Teatrul de Stat** (State Theatre; 1900), designed by Viennese architects Fellner and Hellmer, dominates Piaţa Regele Ferdinand. To its right begins the long, pedestrianised Calea Republicii, lined with bookshops, and cafés. Nearby, in the centre of **Traian Park**, is the small **Muzeul Memorial Ady Endre** *(Ady Endre Memorial Museum; open Tues-Sun)* dedicated to the Hungarian left-wing poet.

Oradea's other worthy buildings are in a park a block southwest of the train station. Across the road is **Şirul Canonicilor** (Canon's Corridor), a series of archways that date back to the 18th century. The **Catedrala Romano-Catolică** (Catholic Cathedral; 1780) is the largest in Romania.

The **Palatul Episcopia Ortodoxă** (Episcopal Palace; 1770), with 100 fresco-adorned rooms and 365 windows, was modelled after Belvedere Palace in Vienna. Now it's the **Muzeul Ţării Crişului** *(Museum of the Land of the Criş Rivers; open Tues-Sun)*, with some of the best history and art exhibits in Romania.

Places to Stay

Camping You can camp at **Băile 1 Mai** *(May-mid–Sept; camping per person $2, cabins per person $5)*, 9km southeast of Oradea. If it's full, walk 500m along the road past the bus terminus to **Camping Venus**. Take southbound tram No 4 (black number) from the train station or an eastbound tram No 4 (red number) from Piaţa Unirii to the end of the line, then bus No 15 to the last stop. There's a large thermal swimming pool nearby.

Hostel The new **Pension Gobe** *(☎/fax 414 845; Str Dobrogeanu Gherea 26; accommodation per person with breakfast from $10-12)*, on the eastern side of the citadel, is the city's best budget option. A member of Youth Hostels România, it offers beds in either of its cosy three- or four-bed rooms. There is also a small restaurant and bar, and kitchen facilities are available for self-caterers.

Hotels The 1908 Art Nouveau **Hotel Vulturul Negru** *(☎ 135 417; Str Independenţei 1; singles/doubles $7/14, doubles with bath $17)* is musty and worn, but otherwise OK.

Hotel Crişul Repede *(☎ 132 509; Str Libertăţii 8; singles/doubles $13/16)* has tired rooms with less-than-hygienic bathrooms. Some rooms overlook the river; all are noisy.

Hotel Astoria *(☎ 130 508; Str Teatrului 1; singles/doubles $9/14, doubles with shower $18)* has more appealing two-star rooms. Its singles, however, are cramped. Room rates include breakfast.

Hotel Atlantic *(☎ 426 911, fax 410 788; e wpd@comser.ro, Str I Vulcan 9; singles/doubles with breakfast $33/41)* is a classy hotel with four spacious, modern rooms – each with its own private bar – and there is also an excellent restaurant.

Hotel Gala *(☎/fax 467 177; Str BP Haşdeu 20; singles/doubles $46/68)* has clean, comfortable rooms and rates include breakfast. The hotel also arranges free transfers for hotel guests.

Dacia Continental Hotel *(☎ 418 655, fax 411 280; Aleea Ştrandului 1; singles/doubles $70/107)* is an ultramodern nine-storey hotel catering mostly to business travellers. Rates include breakfast. It has a night bar and swimming pool and accepts Visa/MasterCard.

ROMANIA

Places to Eat

Restaurant Oradea & Grădina de Vară
(Calea Republicii 5-7; dishes $2-5) still
draws a crowd with its lovely outdoor terrace
and occasional live music.

Restaurant Olivery (☎ 432 959; Str
Moscovei 12; meals $3-5) is an unpretentious
cellar restaurant with quality food at pretty
reasonable prices.

Restaurant Mignon (☎ 419 518; Str
Roman Ciorogariu; meals $5-7) is the city's
most elegant – and expensive – choice. It
serves excellent continental cuisine.

Irish Kelly's Pub *(Calea Republicii; pasta
$0.80-1.25, pizzas $1.50-2.25, mains $1.10-
3.50)*, with its large outdoor terrace, is a popular spot to enjoy a beer and a not-so-authentic
Irish meal.

Taverna *(Str Mihai Eminescu 2; 2-course
daily specials around $2.15)* is a pleasant bar-
cum-restaurant with good-value, two-course
specials such as *supă de legume* (vegetable
soup) followed by some *Tocăniţă de Porc*
(pork stew).

Calea Republicii is lined with inexpensive
cafés and eateries. Three of the most popular
include: **Paninoteca Fausto's**, serving a good
selection of sandwiches and pizza slices;
Minerva Cofetăria, which has delicious pastries; and **Gelateria Marco Polo**, the place
for yummy Italian ice cream.

Further afield try **Downtown Club** *(Piaţa
Unirii)* a smart café/bar where you can get a
croissant and cappuccino for a paltry $0.50.

Stock up on fresh fruit and vegetables at
the **Citadel Market** *(Piaţa Independenţei)*.
McDonald's two outlets are at Calea Republicii 30 and south of the centre on the corner
of Str Nufărului and Ciheiului.

Entertainment

Theatre & Classical Music Tickets for
performances at the **Filarmonica de Stat**
*(State Philharmonic; ☎ 130 853; Str Mos-
covei 5)* can be purchased from the **ticket
office** inside the Philharmonic. There's a
ticket office inside the **Teatrul de Stat** *(State
Theatre; ☎ 130 835; Str Madach Imre 3-5)*.

Cinema Films are shown in their original
language at **Cinema Libertăţii** (☎ 134 097;
Str Independenţei 1), in the Vulturul Negru
building, and **Cinema Transylvania** (☎ 131
171; Piaţa Regele Ferdinand). Tickets to the
shows cost $0.65.

Getting There & Away

Air Tickets for the daily flights to Bucharest
($85/123 single/return) are sold by **Tarom**
(☎/fax 131 918; Piaţa Regel Ferdinand 2).

Train For rail inquiries, contact the **CFR office** *(☎ 130 578; Calea Republicii 2; open
7am-7pm Mon-Fri)*. International tickets must
be purchased at the CFR office in advance.

Express trains run east to Cluj-Napoca
daily (2½ hours, 153km). Four trains run
each day from Oradea to Budapest-Nyugati
station (four hours): the *Claudiopolis*, *Corona* and *Ady Endre* express trains and one
local train, the *Partium*.

Bus From Oradea bus station there are daily
services to Deva and Satu Mare, and three to
Beiuş. A daily bus to Budapest ($6/10 single/
return, 10 hours, pay the driver) departs from
outside the train station at 7.30am.

Most of the travel agencies can arrange
buses to Budapest, Kraków and cities throughout Austria and Germany.

TIMIŞOARA
☎ 0256 • pop 332,277

Timişoara (Temesvár in Hungarian, Tem-
eschburg in German) is the fourth-largest city
in Romania, and has outdoor cafés and regal,
Habsburg-era buildings fronting its three
main squares. It was also the centre of the
protests in December 1989, igniting the countrywide protests that was to eventually topple
Ceauşescu.

Timiş County, of which Timişoara is the
administrative centre, is the richest agricultural area in Romania. The Banat plain around
Timişoara is an eastward extension of Yugoslavia's Vojvodina, and the Bega Canal,
which curves through the city, leads into the
Tisa River in Yugoslavia.

Orientation

Timişoara Nord train station is just west of
the city centre. Walk east on Blvd Republicii
to the Opera House and Piaţa Victoriei. A
block north is the verdant Piaţa Libertăţii.
Piaţa Unirii, the old town square, is two
blocks farther north. Otherwise, trolleybus
Nos 11 and 14 travel from the station eastward down Blvd Republicii, then they turn
north onto Str 1 Mai.

Timişoara's bus station *(autogară)* is beside the Idsefin Market, three blocks from the

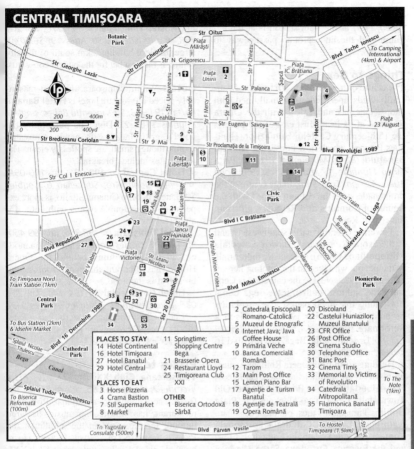

CENTRAL TIMIŞOARA

PLACES TO STAY
14 Hotel Continental
16 Hotel Timişoara
27 Hotel Banatul
29 Hotel Central

PLACES TO EAT
3 Horse Pizzeria
4 Crama Bastion
7 Stil Supermarket
8 Market

11 Springtime;
Shopping Centre
Bega
21 Brasserie Opera
24 Restaurant Lloyd
25 Timişoreana Club
XXI

OTHER
1 Biserica Ortodoxă
Sârbă

2 Catedrala Episcopală
Romano-Catolică
5 Muzeul de Etnografic
6 Internat Java; Java
Coffee House
10 Banca Comercială
Română
12 Tarom
15 Main Post Office
17 Agenţie de Turism
Banatul
18 Agenţie de Teatrală
19 Opera Română

20 Discoland
22 Castelui Huniazilor;
Muzeul Banatului
23 CFR Office
26 Post Office
28 Cinema Studio
30 Telephone Office
31 Banc Post
32 Cinema Timiş
33 Memorial to Victims
of Revolution
34 Catedrala
Mitropolitană
35 Filarmonica Banatul
Timişoara

train station. Take Blvd General Dragalina south to the canal, which you cross and follow northeast to the next bridge.

Information
Tourist Offices The friendly office **Agenţie de Turism Banatul** (☎ 198 862, fax 191 913; ⓦ www.turismbanatul.ro; Str 1 Mai 2) sells town maps.

Foreign Consulates The **Yugoslav consulate** (☎ 190 334, fax 190 425; Str Remus 4; open 9am-noon Mon-Thur) is two blocks west of the Technical University.

Money You can cash travellers cheques and get Visa or MasterCard cash advances at the **Banca Comercială Română** (Str 9 Mai; open

8.30am-12.30pm Mon-Fri), just off Piaţa Libertaţii. Just off Piaţa Victoriei, the **Banc Post** (Blvd Mihai Eminescu; open 8.30am-2.30pm Mon-Fri) also has an ATM. There are also lots of currency-exchange offices dotted throughout the city.

Post & Communications The **telephone office** (Blvd Mihai Eminescu; open 7am-9pm daily) is off Piaţa Victoriei. The **main post office** (Blvd Revoluţiei 1989; open 7am-8pm Mon-Fri, 8am-noon Sat) is two blocks east of the Hotel Continental.

Have a coffee while you email friends at **Internet Java** (Str Pacha 6; open 24hr), inside the Java Coffee House (see Places to Eat). It will cost $0.60 per hour to check your emails or surf the Web.

Left Luggage The left-luggage office *(open 24hr)* at the train station is at the beginning of the underground passageway to the tracks.

Things to See

The centre of town is **Piaţa Victoriei**, a beautifully landscaped pedestrian mall lined with shops, cinemas and cafés, with the **Opera Română** at its head. Just east of the piaţa is the 15th-century **Castelui Huniazilor** (Huniades Palace), which now houses the **Muzeul Banatului** *(Banat Museum; ☎ 191 339; Piaţa Iancu Huniade 1; admission $0.95; open 10am-4.30pm Tues-Sun)*. In the centre of the promenade, note the column topped with the figures of **Romulus and Remus**, a gift from the city of Rome.

Towering over the mall's southwestern end is the exotic Romanian Orthodox **Catedrala Mitropolitană** (1946); in front are **memorials** to the people who died in the fighting here in December 1989. Next to the cathedral is **Central Park**, and just south of it the **Bega Canal** runs along tree-lined banks. The revolution began on 15 December 1989 at the **Biserica Reformată** *(Reformed Church; Str Timotei Cipariu 1)*, south of the Bega, just off Blvd 16 Decembrie 1989.

Heading north from Opera Română, pedestrianised Str Alba Iulia leads to the gardens of **Piaţa Libertăţii** and the **Primăria Veche** (Old Town Hall; 1734). Two blocks north, **Piaţa Unirii** is Timişoara's most picturesque square featuring a baroque **Catedrala Episcopală Romano-Catolică** (Catholic Cathedral; 1754) and the **Biserica Ortodoxă Sârbă** (Serbian cathedral; 1754). Walk east for the **Muzeul de Etnografic** *(Ethnographic Museum; Str Popa Şapcă 8; admission $0.60; open 10am-4.30pm Tues-Sun)*, which has Banat folk costumes and crafts.

Places to Stay

Camping The well-maintained **Camping International** *(☎ 225 596; Aleea Pădurea Verde 6; camping for 2 people around $2, 2-/4-bed bungalows $15/30; open year-round)* is in the Green Forest north of town. From the train station catch trolleybus No 11 to the end of the line. The bus stops less than 50m from the camp's main entrance on Calea Dorobanţilor. The camping ground has bungalows with central heating and tent space. A small restaurant is also on the premises.

Hostel Previously known as Casă Tineretului, **Hostel Timişoara** *(☎ 191 170, fax 201 238; e fitt@xnet.ro; Str Arieş 19; $6.50)*, a large, modern building 2km south of the city centre, is the best bet for the budget conscious.

Hotels Within Timişoara, the most reasonably priced city-centre hotel is **Hotel Banatul** *(☎/fax 191 903; Str Vincenţiu Babes; singles/doubles $16/22)*. Don't be put off by the hotel's grim facade; its newly renovated rooms, though small, are spotlessly clean. The room rates include breakfast.

Hotel Central *(☎ 190 091, fax 190 096; e central@online.ro; Str Lenau 6; doubles $28)*, next door to Cinema Studio, is more expensive. It has double rooms with bath, TV and breakfast.

Hotel Timişoara *(☎ 198 854, fax 199 450; Str 1 Mai 2; singles/doubles $40/55)*, a modern 11-storey building behind the Opera House, has pleasant three-star rooms, and breakfast is included.

Hotel Continental *(☎ 194 144, fax 204 038; Blvd Revoluţiei 3; singles/doubles $49/60)* near Civic Park has recently had a facelift. Its three-star rooms are good value and the hotel accepts credit cards.

Places to Eat

Timişoreana Club XXI *(☎ 122 822; Piaţa Victoriei 2; mains $1-2.85, side dishes $0.30-0.70)*, a contemporary, 'traditional' Romanian restaurant, has loud techno music. Its large outdoor terrace, right in the middle of the Piaţa, is the perfect place to quaff down a local brew of – what else? – Timişoreana Club XXI.

Restaurant Lloyd *(☎ 0721-935 397; Piaţa Victoriei 2; mains $3-9)* is Timişoara's classiest restaurant. Its Romanian and international dishes are expensive – the Black Caviar is a pocket-pinching $20 – and portions, though well presented, are small.

Crama Bastion *(☎ 221 199; Str Hector 1; mains $2-5)*, in a section of the city's 18th-century fortifications, is a wine cellar with a small menu of Romanian dishes.

Brasserie Opera *(Piaţa Iancu Huniade; mains $0.75-1.90)*, close to the opera house, serves mostly pizzas, pastries and beer.

Horse Pizzeria *(☎ 229 666; Str Popa Şapcă; pizzas $0.75-2.50)* offers a mouth-watering array of pizzas in two sizes – regular and mini. A good bet is the salami and *caşcaval* (cheese) pizza ($2).

Springtime *(Str Proclamaţia de la Timi-şoara)*, in the Shopping Centre Bega, serves the usual hamburgers, fries and cakes as well as ice cream.

Java Coffee House *(☎ 432 495; Str Pacha 6; open 24hr)* is a great spot for that early morning pick-me-up or for a late night snack after the theatre.

For self-caterers, there's the **Stil Supermarket** *(Str Mărăşeşti 10; open 24hr)* and a colourful **produce market** *(Str Brediceanu Coriolan)* near the intersection of Str 1 Mai.

Entertainment

Discos & Bars Increasingly popular is **The Note** *(☎ 294 719; Str Mehadia; open 2pm-3am Tues-Sun)*, which has a DJ on Friday nights playing a cool mix of rock/pop music and hosts regular live concerts.

Lemon Piano Bar *(Str Alba Iulia)* is a fancy underground piano/cocktail bar where you can listen to live performances from 7pm to 10pm daily.

Discoland *(☎ 190 008; Piaţa Iancu Huni-ade 1; open 10pm-4am daily)* is the place to go if you want to groove the night away.

Theatre & Classical Music The **Agenţie de Teatrală** *(Theatre Ticket Office; ☎ 195 012; Str Mărăşeşti 2)* is across from Hotel Timişoara. There are professional and student-directed performances year-round at the **Opera Română** *(☎ 201 284)* and also at the **Filarmonica Banatul Timişoara** *(☎ 192 521; Blvd CD Loga 2)*.

Cinemas Films in their original language are screened at **Cinema Studio** *(Str Leanu Nicolaus; adult/concession $0.95/0.65)*, next to Hotel Central, and **Cinema Timiş** *(Piaţa Victoriei; adult/concession $1.10/0.80)* near the telephone centre.

Getting There & Away

Air The national airline **Tarom** *(☎/fax 190 150; Blvd Revoluţiei 3-5)*, opposite Hotel Continental, has flights to Bucharest from Monday to Saturday ($90/125 single/return).

Train Direct express trains link Timişoara to Iaşi via Cluj-Napoca and Suceava. The service to Bucharest (eight hours) is fairly frequent via Băile Herculane, Drobeta-Turnu Severin and Craiova; sleepers are available to/from Bucharest.

Timişoara is connected with Belgrade by the one daily express train: the *Bucureşti* (8½ hours, 175km). Advance reservations are required. International tickets must be bought at the **CFR office** *(☎ 191 889; Piaţa Victoriei 2; open 8am-8pm Mon-Fri)*.

Bus Twice-weekly buses connect Timişoara to Békéscsaba (138km) and Szeged (257km). There's a weekly service to Budapest ($9, eight hours). The international ticket window is open 9am to 5pm weekdays, otherwise you can usually pay the driver.

Maramureş

A visit to the valleys of Maramureş is like stepping back in time. Cut off by a natural fortress of mountains, it has remained largely untouched by the 20th century.

Maramureş was never conquered by the Romans, earning the region the title 'land of the free Dacians'. Social activities revolve around the tall-steepled, wooden village churches dating from the 15th and 16th centuries. Traditional folk costumes are donned in villages on special holidays. The colourful costumes bear motifs typical of each village. Horse carts share the roads with automobiles. Maramureş is practically impossible to explore without private transport.

The region was first attested in 1199. Hungary gradually exerted its rule over the region from the 13th century onwards. Tatar invasions of the Hungarian-dominated region continued well into the 17th and 18th centuries, the last battle being documented on the Prislop Pass in 1717. Many churches sprang up in Maramureş around this time to mark the Tatars' final withdrawal from the region.

Maramureş was annexed by Transylvania in the mid-16th century. In 1699 the Turks ceded Transylvania to the Austrian empire and it was not until 1918 that Maramureş, along with the rest of Transylvania, was returned to Romania.

Between 1940 and 1944 the Maramureş region – along with the rest of northern Transylvania – fell under pro-Nazi Hungarian rule.

SIGHETU MARMAŢIEI
☎ 0262 • pop 40,000

Sighetu Marmaţiei is the northernmost town in Romania, lying at the confluence of the

ROMANIA

Tisa, Izei and Ronişoara Rivers, 2km from the Ukrainian border.

Sighet (as it's called locally) is a farming town, famed for its vibrant winter festival and peasant costumes.

Information

The **tourist office** *(Piaţa Libertăţii 21; open 8am-4pm Mon-Fri, 9am-1pm Sat)* runs a currency exchange and rents cars.

The **post and telephone office** *(Str Ioan Mihaly de Apşa)* is opposite the Muzeul Maramureş.

The **Banca Comercială Română** *(Str Iuliu Maniu; open 8.30am-2.30pm Mon-Fri)* gives cash advances on Visa and has an ATM. There is also an ATM outside Hotel Tisa on Piaţa Libertăţii.

Things to See

Piaţa Libertăţii & Around Sighet, first documented in 1328, was a strong cultural and political centre. On Piaţa Libertăţii is the **Biserica Reformată** (Hungarian Reformed Church), built during the 15th century. Close by is the 16th century **Biserica Romano-Catolică** (Roman Catholic Church).

On Piaţa Libertăţii is the **Muzeul Maramureş** *(Maramureş Museum; ☎ 311 512; Piaţa Libertăţii 15; admission $0.35; open 10am-6pm Tues-Sun)*, an ethnographic museum where colourful folk costumes, rugs and carnival masks are displayed.

Just off the square is Sighet's only remaining **synagogue** *(Str Bessarabia 10)*. Before WWII there were eight synagogues serving a large Jewish community, which comprised 40% of the town's population.

The Jewish writer and 1986 Nobel Peace Prize winner, Elie Wiesel, who coined the term 'Holocaust' was born in and was later deported from Sighet. His **house** is on the corner of Str Dragoş Vodă and Str Tudor Vladimirescu.

Along Str Gheorghe Doja, there is a **monument** *(Str Mureşan)* to the victims of the Holocaust.

Serious art lovers should also visit the private collection displayed in the **Muzeul Pipaş** *(Pipaş Museum; ☎ 319 330)*, 2km east of Sighet in Tisa village.

The traditional peasant houses from the Maramureş region have been reassembled in Sighet's outstanding open-air **Muzeul Satului** *(Village Museum; ☎ 314 229; Str Doboies*

40; admission $0.30; open 10am-5pm Tues-Sun), on the right as you approach the town from the south.

Sighet Prison Sighet's former maximum-security prison is now a museum, although little evidence remains of the horror it once housed. During May 1947 the communists embarked on a reign of terror, imprisoning, torturing, killing and deporting thousands of people. Between 1948 and 1952, 180 of Romania's academic and government elite were imprisoned here.

Today four white marble plaques covering the barred windows of the prison list the 51 prisoners who died in the Sighet cells. Eight more plaques list those prisoners who survived the torture.

The prison, inside the old courthouse, was closed down in 1974. In 1989 it was reopened as a **Memorialul Victimelor Comunismului şi al Rezistenţei** *(The Memorial Museum of the Victims of Communism and of the Resistance; Str Corneliu Coposu 4; ☎ 316 848; e Memorialul.Sighet@mail.multinet.ro; admission $1; open 10am-6pm Tues-Sun)*. It was open to the public in 1997. Photographs

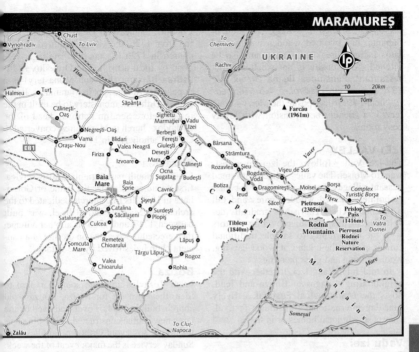

MARAMUREŞ

are displayed and you can visit the torture chambers and cells.

Places to Stay & Eat

Sighet's one central hotel, **Hotel Tisa** (☎ 312 645; Piaţa Libertăţii 8; singles/doubles $17/22) has 43 rooms, most with private bathroom, TV and telephone (that mysteriously don't work). Water is only available for limited periods throughout the day.

Motel Buţi (☎/fax 311 035; Str Simion Bărnuţiu 6; singles/doubles with shared bathroom $13/20) is excellent value. Its rooms, though a little claustrophobic, are squeaky clean and rates include breakfast.

Motel Perla Sigheteana (☎ 310 613, fax 310 268; w www.sighetumarmatiei.alphanet .ro; Str Avram Iancu 65A; doubles $22), just out of town on the road to Săpânţa, has up-market doubles with private bath, TV and telephone, and rates include breakfast.

All the hotels have **restaurants**.

Getting There & Away

Train The **CFR office** (☎ 312 666; Piaţa Libertăţii 25; open 7am-2pm Mon-Fri) is near the tourist office. There are two trains daily to Cluj-Napoca (six hours, 223km) and one to Bucharest (12 hours, 720km).

The **bus station** (Str Gării) is opposite the train station. Local buses include six daily to Baia Mare ($1.45, 65km); two daily to Satu Mare ($1.90, 122km); and one daily to Bârsana, Botiza, Ieud and Săpânţa.

SĂPÂNŢA
☎ 0262 • pop 5000

Săpânţa, which is 12km northwest of Sighetu Marmaţiei, is famous for its **Merry Cemetery**, known for the colourfully painted wooden markers above the tombstones. The cemetery was the creation of Ioan Stan Pătraş, a simple wood sculptor who, in 1935, began carving crosses to mark graves in the church cemetery. Each cross depicts the deceased person at their trade with humorous epitaphs that are inscribed below. Since Pătraş' death, Dumitru Pop, his apprentice, has carried on the master's tradition.

Săpânţa's crosses attract coachloads of tourists every year. Villagers sit outside their cottages, their fenceposts strung with colourful rugs and hand-woven bags for sale. Buses run daily trips to/from Sighet.

ROMANIA

Camping Poieni (☎ 322 228; cabins per person $2.50; open June-Aug), 3km south of Săpânţa, has two-bed wooden cabins, and rates include breakfast. Tents can also be pitched. Also onsite is an excellent trout **restaurant**. **Pensiunea Ileana** (☎/fax 372 137; e pens.sapanta@rol.ro; No 656; bed/full board $9/15), opposite the Merry Cemetery, is a friendly new pension with lovely cosy rooms.

IZEI VALLEY

The Izei Valley follows the Izei River eastward to Moisei. The valley is lined with small peasant villages that are renowned for their elaborately carved wooden gates and tall wooden churches. Tourism is gradually developing in this region, providing visitors with the opportunity to sample traditional cuisine or try their hand at wood carving, wool weaving and glass painting.

In mid-July, Vadu Izei, together with the neighbouring villages of Botiza and Ieud, hosts the **Maramuzical Festival**, a lively four-day international folk music festival. Guests stay in local homes or in tents.

Vadu Izei

☎ 0262 • pop 3000

Vadu Izei is at the confluence of the Izei and Mara Rivers, 6km south of Sighetu Marmaţiei. Its museum is in the oldest house in the village (1750).

The **Fundaţia OVR Agro-Tur-Art** (☎/fax 330 171; w www.vaduizei.ovr.ro; house No 161) sells maps and guides of the region and can arrange for a French- or English-speaking guide for $12/20 a half/full day. It also sells local crafts. Its office is at the northern end of the village. If it's closed, contact **Ramona Ardelean** (☎ 330 348) or **Nicolae Prisăcaru** (☎ 330 093; e prisnic@conseco.ro; house No 343). Agro-Tur-Art will arrange guided tours of Maramureş' wooden churches; wood carving, icon painting and wool weaving workshops; traditional folk evenings; and fishing trips.

Agro-Tur-Art arranges accommodation in **private homes**. Some 20 families offer beds for $10 a night (breakfast $2, lunch $2, dinner $3). Bookings can be made through the Agro-Tur-Art office or directly at the homes involved. Some homes are signposted and their owners welcome guests knocking at their door.

Bârsana

Continue southeast for 12km to Bârsana. Dating from 1326, the village acquired its first church in 1720 (its interior paintings were done by local artists). The Orthodox **Mănăstirea Bârsana** (Bârsana Monastery) is a popular pilgrimage spot in Maramureş. It was the last Orthodox monastery to be built in the region before Serafim Petrovai, head of the Orthodox church in Maramureş, converted to Greco-Catholicism in 1711.

Rozavlea

Continue south past Strâmtura to Rozavlea, first documented under the name of Gorzohaza in 1374. Its fine church, dedicated to the archangels Michael and Gabriel, was built between 1717 and 1720 in another village, then erected in Rozavlea on the site of an ancient church destroyed by the Tatars.

Botiza

From Rozavlea continue south for 3km to Sieu, then turn off for Botiza. Botiza's old church, built in 1694, is overshadowed by the large new church constructed in 1974 to serve the 500 or so devout Orthodox families. The Sunday service is the major event of the week.

Opération Villages Roumains runs an efficient agrotourism scheme in Botiza. Half/full board in a local home is $14/16.50 a night; camping $4.50. Bookings can be made with local representative **George Iurca** (☎/fax 334 233; e botizavr@sintec.ro) at No 742. George, who speaks French, English and German, guides for $13.50 a day, rents mountain bikes for $4.50/day and organises fishing trips.

Ieud

The oldest wooden church in Maramureş, dating from 1364, is in Ieud, 6km south of the main road. Ieud was first documented in 1365. Its fabulous Orthodox 'Church on the Hill' was built from fir wood and housed the first document known to be written in Romanian (1391–92), in which the catechism and church laws pertaining to Ieud were coded.

The church was restored in 1958 and in 1997. It is generally locked but the key is available from the porter's house, which is distinguishable by a simple wooden gate opposite the *textile incaltaminte* in the centre of the village.

Ieud's second church, Greco-Catholic, was built in 1717. It is unique to the region as it has no porch. At the southern end of the village it houses one of the largest collections of icons on glass found in Maramureş.

Opération Villages Roumains runs a small agrotourism scheme in Ieud. You can make advance bookings through the office in Vadu Izei or go straight to the local representative, **Chindriş Dumitru** (✆/fax 336 100). A bed for the night starts at $13, including breakfast.

Moisei

Moisei lies 7km northeast of Săcel, at the junction of route 17C and route 18. A small town at the foot of the Rodna Massif, known for its traditional crafts and customs, Moisei gained fame in 1944 when retreating Hungarian (Horthyst) troops gunned down 31 people before setting fire to the village.

In 1944, following the news that the front was approaching Moisei, villagers started to flee, including those forced-labour detachments stationed in the village. Occupying Hungarian forces organised a manhunt to track down the deserters. Thirty-one were captured and detained in a small camp in Vişeu de Sus without food or water for three weeks. On 14 October 1944 Hungarian troops brought the 31 prisoners to a house in Moisei, locked them inside, then shot them through the windows. Before abandoning the village, the troops set it on fire, leaving all 125 remaining families homeless.

Only one house in Moisei survived the blaze: the one in which the prisoners were shot. Today, it houses a small **muzeul** (admission $0.35) of tribute to those who died in the massacre. Opposite, on a hillock above the road and railway line, is a circular **monument** to the victims. The 12 upright columns symbolise sun and light. Each column is decorated with a traditional carnival mask, except for two that bear human faces based on the features of the two survivors.

The museum and monument are at the eastern end of the village. If the museum is locked, knock at the house next door and ask for the key.

Borşa

Ore has been mined at Borşa, 12km east of Moisei, since the mid-14th century. The area was colonised in 1777 by German miners from Slovakia; later, Bavarian-Austrian miners moved to Baia Borşa, 2km northeast of the town, to mine copper, lead and silver.

The **Complex Turistic Borşa**, a small ski resort and tourist complex 10km east of Borşa town, is a main entrance to the **Rodna Mountains**, part of which form the **Pietrosul Rodnei Nature Reservation** (5900 hectares). For useful information on the hiking trails leading into the massif talk to staff at the two-star **Hotel Cerbal** (✆ 0262-344 199; Str Fântâna; singles/doubles/triples $18/22/30). Rates include breakfast.

In winter, you can ski down the 2030m-long ski run in the complex. There's a **ski lift** (Str Brâdet 10; open 7am-6pm daily), but ski hire is not available.

PRISLOP PASS

Prislop Pass is the main route from Maramureş into Moldavia. Hikers can trek from Borşa to the east across the Prislop Pass. From Moldavia you can bear northeast to Câmpulung Moldovenesc and on to the monasteries of Bucovina.

At 1416m, a roadside monument honours the site of the last Tatar invasion before their flight from the region in 1717. Nearby is **Hanul Prislop**, site of the **Hora de la Prislop festival**, held every August. The festival has its origins in a traditional sheep market. Today it's just for merrymaking with friends from the surrounding villages.

Moldavia

With its forest-clad hills and tranquil valleys, Moldavia rivals Transylvania when it comes to natural beauty, rich folklore and turbulent history. Prince Bogdan won Moldavian independence from Hungary in 1349, after which the centre of the medieval principality, tucked away in the easily defended Carpathian foothills, became known as Bucovina (meaning 'beech wood').

From Suceava, Ştefan cel Mare (Ştefan the Great), called the 'Athlete of Christ' by Pope Pius VI, led the resistance against the Turks from 1457 to 1504. He and his son, Petru Rareş, erected fortified monasteries throughout Bucovina. Many have survived centuries of war and weather, with their stunning exterior frescoes intact. Only with the defeat of Petru Rareş by the Turks in 1538 did Moldavia's golden age wane. Moldavia regained a measure of its former glory after it was united with the principality of Wallachia by Prince

Alexandru Ioan Cuza in 1859 – a date marking the birth of the modern Romanian state.

Medieval Moldavia, however, was much larger than the portion incorporated into Romania in 1859. Bessarabia, the portion east of the Prut River, was conquered and claimed by Russia in 1812. Despite being recovered by Romania from 1918 to 1940 and again from 1941 to 1944, Bessarabia is now split between Ukraine and the Republic of Moldova. Northern Bucovina was annexed by the Soviets in 1940 and is now part of Ukraine.

IAŞI
☎ 0232 ● pop 347,000

Iaşi ('yash'), the capital of Moldavia from 1565, is a university city steeped in history. From 1859, Iaşi served as the national capital until it was replaced by Bucharest in 1862. This illustrious history accounts for the city's great monasteries, bust-lined streets and parks, churches and museums. During WWI the seat of the Romanian government was briefly moved back to Iaşi.

Modern Iaşi is Romania's third-largest city and its streets bustle with student life, restaurants, bars and hot night spots.

Orientation

To reach Piaţa Unirii from Iaşi train station, walk northeast along Str Gării two blocks, then turn right onto Str Arcu. From Piaţa Unirii, Blvd Ştefan cel Mare şi Sfânt runs southeast past the Mitropolia Moldovei (Moldavian Metropolitan Cathedral) to the Palatul Culturii (Palace of Culture).

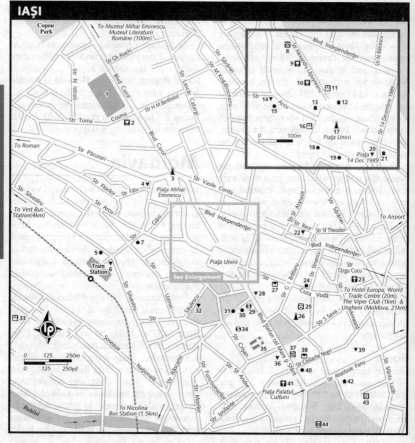

Information

Tourist Offices Iaşi has no official tourist office; your best bet is **Icar Tours** (see Travel Agencies), whose friendly staff speak English and French.

The **Automobil Clubul Român** *(Str Gării 13–15)*, assists motorists and sells a small selection of road maps of the region.

Money The **Banca Comercială Română** *(Blvd Ştefan cel Mare şi Sfânt 6)* cashes travellers cheques, gives cash advances on Visa/MasterCard and has an ATM. **BCIT** *(Blvd Ştefan cel Mare şi Sfânt 12)* offers identical services. Currency exchanges can be found all over the city.

Post & Telephone You can send mail from the **main post office** *(Str Cuza Vodă; open 7am-8pm Mon-Fri, 7am-1pm Sat)* near the Hotel Continental, or the **post office** *(Str Costache Negri)*, which is opposite the Civic Centre. Phonecards for use in public telephones are sold at the **telephone centre** *(Str Alexandru Lăpuşneanu; open 8am-8pm Mon-Fri, 8am-3pm Sat)*.

One of the best and largest Internet centres in Iaşi is **Discovery Internet Café** *(Blvd Ştefan cel Mare şi Sfânt; open 24hr)*, which charges $0.50 per hour for you to check emails or surf the Web.

Left Luggage The **left-luggage office** *(open 24hr)*, is on platform 1, to the right as you enter the station.

Travel Agencies For bus tickets to Western Europe and for car rental contact **Icar Tours** *(☎ 216 319, fax 217 160, e icar@icar.ro; Blvd Stefan Cel Mare)*, on the ground floor of the Galeriile Comerciale Centre.

Bookshops The top bookshop is **Junimea** *(Piaţa Unirii 4)* which stocks an excellent range of maps, dictionaries and novels in English and French.

Things to See & Do

From Piaţa Unirii the broad, tree-lined Blvd Ştefan cel Mare şi Sfânt stems east. Along this way is the giant **Mitropolia Moldovei**. With a cavernous interior painted by Gheorghe Tattarescu, it was built between 1833 and 1839. In mid-October thousands of pilgrims flock here to celebrate the day of St Paraschiva, the patron saint of the cathedral and of Moldavia. Inside the cathedral lies a coffin said to contain the bones of St Friday.

Opposite is a park where local artists sell their masterpieces. At the park's northeastern end is the **Teatrul Naţional** (National Theatre; 1894–96). In front of it is a **statue** of its founder Vasile Alecsandri (1821–90), a poet who single-handedly created the theatre's first repertoire with his Romanian adaptation of a French farce.

Continuing along the boulevard you pass the fabulous **Biserica Trei Ierarhi** (Church of the Three Hierarchs; 1637–39), unique for its rich exterior which is covered in a wealth of intricate patterns in stone. In its original form,

ROMANIA

the exterior was covered in gold. Built by Prince Vasile Lupu, the church was badly damaged by Tartar attacks in 1650 but later restored. Inside are the marble tombs of the Prince Vasile Lupu and his family, Prince Alexandru Ioan Cuza and Moldavian prince Dimitrie Cantemir.

At the southern end of Blvd Ştefan cel Mare şi Sfânt stands the giant neo-Gothic **Palatul Culturii** (☎ 218 383; admission $2/1 adults/concession; open 10am-5pm Tues-Sun), built between 1906 and 1925 on the ruins of the **old princely court**, founded by Prince Alexandru cel Bun (r. 1400–32) in the early 15th century.

The main attraction of the 365-room building today is the four first-class museums it houses: the **Muzeul de Etnografic** (Ethnographic Museum), which has exhibits ranging from agriculture, fishing and hunting to wine making, as well as traditional costumes and rugs; the **Muzeul de Artă** (Art Museum), containing works by Romanian artists including Nicolae Grigorescu and Moldavian-born Petre Achiţemie; the **Muzeul de Istorie** (History Museum), where the exhibits include portraits of all of Romania's rulers from AD 81; and the **Muzeul Politehnic** (Technical Museum), which displays various mechanical creations and musical instruments.

A few blocks north, past the central market, is the fortified **Mănăstirea Golia** (Golia Monastery; Str Cuza Vodă), which was built in a late-Renaissance style. The monastery's walls and the 30m Golia tower at the entrance shelter a 17th-century church, noted for its vibrant Byzantine frescoes and intricately carved doorways.

To get to **Copou Park** (1834–48) catch the No 1 or 13 tram north from Piaţa Unirii. The park, which was established during the princely reign of Mihail Sturza, is famed as being a favourite haunt of poet Mihai Eminescu (1850–89), who allegedly wrote some of his best works beneath his favourite **linden tree** in this park.

The tree is still standing, behind a 13m-tall **monument of lions**, opposite the main entrance to the park. A bronze bust of Eminescu stands in front of it. To the right of the lion monument is the **Muzeul Mihai Eminescu – Muzeul Literaturii Române** (Mihai Eminescu Museum of Literature; admission $0.20; open 10am-5pm Tues-Sun), which recalls the life of the poet.

Places to Stay

Hotels The best budget option is the **Hotel Continental** (☎ 211 846; Piaţa 14 Decembrie 1989; Cat A singles/doubles $18/26, Cat B singles/doubles $13/22), which has passable rooms with shared bathroom. Rooms facing the street are noisy and vibrate when trams pass. The hotel has a small café and currency exchange on the ground floor.

Hotel Traian (☎ 143 330, fax 212 187; Piaţa Unirii 1; Cat A singles/doubles $24/36; Cat B singles/doubles/triples $18/24/40), on the central square, has decent well-priced rooms. But staff will offer you the most expensive room if you're a foreigner.

The **Hotel Unirea** (☎ 240 404, fax 212 864; e chunirea@email.ro; Piaţa Unirii 5; singles/doubles $19/25) is a characterless three-star hotel with a restaurant and panoramic café on the 13th floor.

Hotel Moldova (☎ 142 304, fax 212 862; Piaţa Palatului 31; doubles $38) boasts an indoor swimming pool, sauna and tennis court, open to nonguests too.

Hotel Europa (☎ 242 000, fax 242 001; e hotel@europa.ro; Str Anastasie Panu 26; singles/doubles $165/195, apartments $325) is a gleaming new high-rise adjoining the World Trade Centre. Each of its luxurious rooms has a private bath, mini bar, Internet connection and cable TV.

Places to Eat

Casa Bolta Rece (☎ 212 255; Str Rece 10; mains $2-5), dating from 1799, serves delicious traditional Romanian food. Try the house speciality, feteasca neagră (black pudding) served with mămăligă and topped with salty sheep's cheese.

GinGer Ale (☎ 276 017; Str Săulescu 23; mains $1.50-5) is a fun Irish-inspired restaurant and bar, which bizarrely enough serves Indian curry soup. On weekends there are lunchtime discounts.

Club RS (☎ 213 060; Str Fătu 2; mains $0.65-3, 4-course set menu $4) favoured by Iaşi's student community, is a friendly Greek café-restaurant-bar and nightclub all rolled into one. Student discounts available.

Metro Pizza (Blvd Ştefan cel Mare şi Sfânt 18; pizzas $1.15-2) serves excellent, 26cm-round pizzas and also has a takeaway counter for those on the go.

Restaurant Select (☎ 210 715; Piaţa 14 Decembrie 1989; mains $2-5), opposite the

Summer sun along Poland's Baltic coast

Rural peace in the Pieniny region of Poland

Bucharest's Romanian Athenaeum concert hall

Bistriţa, Romania – the heart of 'Dracula Land'

Scaling the heights of Romania's Carpathians

A fisherman checks the results of his efforts – dawn on the Danube Delta, Romania

All-Russia Exhibition Centre fountain, Moscow

So much to see, The Hermitage, St Petersburg

Colour abounds at Moscow's St Basil's Cathedral

Truly a Winter Palace, home of the Hermitage, on the banks of the Neva, St Petersburg

Hotel Continental, is favoured mainly for its bingo hall and casino.

Self-caterers should head to the **central market**, great for fresh fruit and vegetables (*entrances Str Anastasie Panu & Str C Negri*).

The **Central Supermarket** (*Blvd Ştefan cel Mare şi Sfânt; open 8am-8pm Mon-Sat*) has an excellent range of imported and local products as does the **Adda Supermarket** (*Str Arcu; open 24hr*).

Entertainment

Bars & Discos Iaşi has an abundance of outdoor cafés-cum-bars-cum-discos. The terraces at **Salon Vânătoresc** and **Corsu**, both on Str Alexandru Lăpuşneanu, are hot spots on sunny days. The terrace at the popular **Casa Universatarilor** (*☎ 140 029, Blvd Carol 9*) is packed from June onwards, if only for the wonderful scent of its many lime trees.

Iaşi's best student disco is **Disco Ecstasy** (*☎ 258 425*) at the Complexul Studenţească 'Tudor Vladimirescu' east of town (five stops from Piaţa Unirii on tram No 8).

The **Viper Club** (*☎ 0721-218 823; Iulius Mall*), southeast of the centre, is the current *in* spot to dance the night away.

Theatre & Classical Music The Teatrul Naţional Vasile Alecsandri (*☎ 116 778; Str Agatha Bârsecu*) has plays and opera recitals throughout the year. For advance bookings contact the **Agenţia de Opera** (*☎ 255 999, Blvd Ştefan cel Mare şi Sfânt 8; open 10am-1pm Mon-Fri*). Also popular are the concerts held inside the **Filarmonica** (*☎ 114 601, Str Cuza Vodă 29*).

Cinemas The latest box-office hits are screened in English at the **Victoria** (*☎ 112 502, Piaţa Unirii 4*) and **Republica** (*☎ 114 327, Str Alexandru Lăpuşneanu 12*). Tickets cost around $1.

Getting There & Away

Air The national carrier **Tarom** (*☎ 115 239; Str Arcu 3–5*) operates a daily flight on weekdays between Iaşi and Bucharest ($73/132 single/return).

Train Iaşi is on the main train line between Bucharest and Kyiv, which passes via Chişinău. The Ungheni border crossing is only 21km away. International trains depart from **Nicolina train station**, 1.5km south of the

centre; tickets must be purchased in advance from the **CFR Office** (*☎ 147 673; Piaţa Unirii 9-11*). Reservations are required for the daily train from Iaşi to Chişinău.

If you are planning to visit the monasteries in southern Bucovina take a train to Suceava then change trains there.

Bus From **Vest bus station** (*Str Cantacuzino*) there are five daily buses to Chişinău ($4.70) in the Republic of Moldova. Tickets for the daily private bus to İstanbul ($31, 8am) are sold at **Toros Excursii** (*☎ 276 339; Str Gării*).

Southern Bucovina

The painted churches of southern Bucovina are among the greatest artistic monuments of Europe – in 1993 they were collectively designated a World Heritage site by Unesco. Erected at a time when northern Moldavia was threatened by Turkish invaders, the monasteries were surrounded by strong defensive walls. Great popular armies would gather inside these fortifications, waiting to do battle. To educate the illiterate peasants who were unable to understand the liturgy, biblical stories were portrayed on the church walls in colourful pictures. The exteriors of many of the churches are completely covered with these magnificent 16th-century frescoes. Remarkably, most of the intense colours have been preserved despite five centuries of rain and wind.

Bucovina's monasteries are generally open 9am to 5pm or 6pm daily. Admission is about $0.70. If your time is limited, Voroneţ, Humor and Moldoviţa monasteries, all accessible by bus and train, provide a representative sample of what Bucovina has to offer.

SUCEAVA
☎ 0230 ● pop 117,571

Suceava, the capital of Moldavia from 1388 to 1565, was a thriving commercial centre on the Lviv-İstanbul trading route. Today it's the seat of Suceava County and gateway to the painted churches of Bucovina. Its few old churches and historic fortress are easily seen in a day.

Orientation

Piaţa 22 Decembrie is the centre of town. Suceava has two train stations, Suceava and Suceava Nord, both north of the city centre and easily reached by trolleybus.

ROMANIA

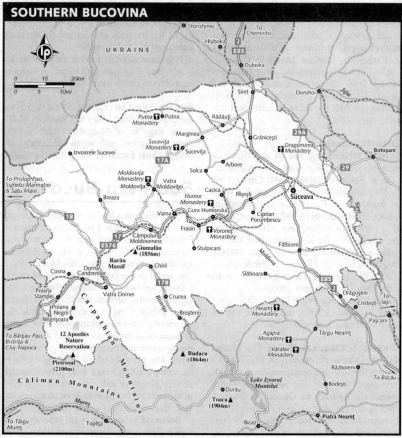

SOUTHERN BUCOVINA

From Suceava station, cross the street, buy a ticket at a kiosk and take trolleybus No 2 or 3 to the centre of town. From Suceava Nord take trolleybus No 5.

Information
Tourist Offices There are no official tourist offices, but staff at **Bucovina Estur** (see Travel Agencies), on the main square, speak English and have the best information.

Money The **Platinum** currency exchange (*open 9am-5pm Mon-Fri, 9am-1pm Sat*) is inside Bucovina Estur.

The **Banca Comercială Ion Ţiriac** (*BCIT; Piaţa 22 Decembrie; open 9am-4pm Mon-Fri*), exchanges travellers cheques and gives Visa and MasterCard cash advances. **Banca**

Comercială Română (*Str Ştefan cel Mare 31; exchange open 8.30am-1.30pm Mon-Fri*), cashes travellers cheques. Both of these banks have ATMs.

Post & Communications The **telephone centre** (*cnr Str Nicolae Bălcescu & Str Firmu; open 7am-9pm Mon-Fri, 8am-4pm Sat*) is near the **post office** (*Str Dimitrie Onciu*), which has the same opening hours.

The **Assist Internet Café & Computer Shop** (*Str Ana Ipătescu 7; open 9am-1am daily*), opposite McDonald's, charges \$0.50 per hour for Internet access.

Travel Agencies A good option is **Bucovina Estur** (*☎/fax 522 694; e bestur@assist.ro; Str Ştefan cel Mare 24; open 9am-6pm Mon-Fri,*

9am-1pm Sat) which arranges private rooms, has a variety of monastery tours and rents cars.

Left Luggage The **left-luggage office** *(open 24hr)* at Suceava train station is at the information window on the main platform.

Things to See
The **Casă de Cultură** is at the western end of Piaţa 22 Decembrie. North of the bus stop along Blvd Ana Ipătescu lie the foundations of the 15th-century **Princely Palace**. To the west is **Biserica Sfântul Dumitru** (St Dimitru's church; 1535) built by Petru Rareş.

West of Piaţa 22 Decembrie, behind Casă de Cultură, is **Hanul Domnesc** *(Str Ciprian Porumbescu 5)*, a princely 16th-century guesthouse that now houses a **Muzeul Etnografic** *(Ethnographic Museum; ☎ 213 775; admission $0.35; open 10am-6pm Tues-Sun)* with a good collection of folk costumes.

Return to Piaţa 22 Decembrie and follow Str Ştefan cel Mare south past **Central Park** to the surprisingly informative **Muzeul de Istorie al Bucovinei** *(Bucovina History Museum; admission $0.50; open 10am-6pm Tues-Sun)*, at No 33. The presentation comes to an abrupt end at 1945 and old paintings now hang in rooms that formerly glorified the communist era.

Backtrack a little to the park and take Str Mitropoliei southeast to the **Mănătirea Sfântul Ioan cel Nou** (Monastery of Saint John the New; 1522). The paintings on the outside of the church are badly faded, but they give you an idea of the painted churches that Bucovina is famous for.

Continue on Str Mitropoliei, keeping left on the main road out of town, until you see a large wooden gate marked 'Parcul Cetatii' on the left. Go through it and, when the path divides, follow the footpath with the park benches around to the left to the huge **equestrian statue** (1966) of the Moldavian leader, Ştefan cel Mare. Twenty metres back on the access road to the monument is another footpath on the left, which descends towards the **Cetatea de Scaun** (1388), a fortress that held off Mehmed II, conqueror of Constantinople (İstanbul) in 1476.

Places to Stay
Camping If you are desperate, try **Camping Suceava** *(☎ 214 958; Str Cernăuţi; 2-bed hut $4)*, a filthy camping ground by the Suceava River, between Suceava Nord and Suceava train stations.

Private Rooms Bucovina Estur (see Travel Agencies earlier in this section) arranges rooms in **private homes** for $15 per person in Suceava and surrounding villages.

Hotels The best-value is the central **Hotel Gloria** *(☎ 521 209, fax 520 005; Str Mihai Vasile Bumbac 4; singles $7; singles/doubles with bath $15/19)*. Breakfast is included.

Vila Alice *(☎ 522 254; Str Simeon Florea Marian; singles/doubles $18/20)* is a tranquil place with decent rooms and congenial, helpful staff. Breakfast, however, is an overpriced $3.15 extra.

Hotel Suceava *(☎ 521 079, fax 521 080; W www.suceava.iiruc.ro/central-turism; Str N Bălcescu 4; singles/doubles/triples $22/29/43)* is a drab four-storey hotel in the centre of town. Breakfast is included.

Continental Arcaşul Hotel *(☎ 520 785, fax 227 598; Str Mihai Viteazul 4-6; singles/doubles $37/49)* offers the stock-standard Continental chain rooms – modern, clean and expensive. Rates include breakfast.

Hotel Balada *(☎ 223 198, fax 520 087; Str Mitropoliei 3; W www.balada.ro; singles/doubles $48/52)* has well-appointed rooms with direct-dial phones and cable TV.

Places to Eat
Eating options in Suceava are limited.

Barul de zi Arcaşul *(Str Mihai Viteazul 4-6; breakfast $1-2; lunch & dinner special $2.50)*, part of the Continental Arcaşul Hotel, specialises in delicious *pui la rotisor* (roast chicken) and offers good meal deals. There's also a billiard table and two computers with Internet access ($0.50 per hour).

Markiz *(☎ 520 219; Str Alecsandri; burgers $0.65-1, pizzas $1-2.50, mains $2.50-4)*, opposite the bus station, serves up heavenly cakes and pastries as well as hamburgers, kebabs and pizzas.

Latino *(☎ 523 627; Str Curea Domnească 9; pasta $2-3, pizzas $1.70-2.50, meals $3-4.50)*, with its flavoursome selection of Italian and international dishes, is a refreshing new addition to Suceava's otherwise moribund restaurant scene.

McDonald's *(Blvd Ana Ipătescu; open 7am-midnight daily)* is across from the Assist Internet Café.

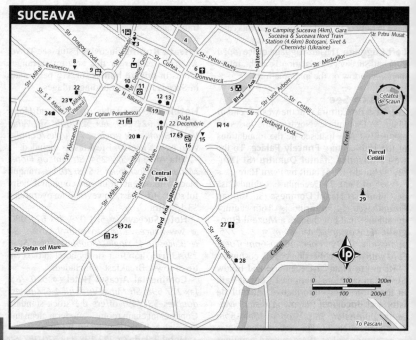

SUCEAVA

PLACES TO STAY
13 Hotel Suceava &
    Restaurant Suceava
20 Hotel Gloria
22 Continental Arcaşul
    Hotel
24 Vila Alice
28 Hotel Balada

PLACES TO EAT
2 Markiz
3 Latino
4 Vegetable Market
8 Eurostela 24-hour Shop
15 McDonald's
23 Barul de zi Arcaşul

OTHER
1 Autogara
5 Princely Palace
    Ruins
6 Biserica Sfântul
    Dumitru
7 Post Office
9 Cinema Modern
10 Automobil Clubul
    Român (ACR) Office
11 Telephone Centre
12 CFR Office
14 Buses to/from Train
    Station
16 Assist Internet Café &
    Computer Shop

17 Banca Comercială Ion
    Ţiriac (BCIT)
18 Bucovina Estur &
    Platinum Currency
    Exchange
19 Casă de Cultură &
    Cinema
21 Hanul Domnesc &
    Muzeul Etnografic
25 Muzeul de Istorie al
    Bucovinei
26 Banca Comercial
    Română
27 Mânăstirea Sfantul Ioan
    cel Nou
29 Statue of Ştefan cel Mare

Not far from Biserica Sfântul Dumitru is Suceava's main **vegetable market**. **Eurostela** *(Str Mihai Eminescu 2A; open 24hr)* is a well-stocked supermarket that is close to the Cinema Modern.

Entertainment
Cinema Modern, facing the roundabout at the western end of Str N Bălcescu, screens films in their original language. There's also

a small cinema inside the **Casă de Cultură** *(Piaţa 22 Decembrie)*.

Getting There & Away
Train Express trains run Bucharest (seven hours), Iaşi (1½ hours) and Cluj-Napoca (6½ hours) are fairly regular.

The local trains (slower) travel to Gura Humorului, Putna, Câmpulung Moldovenesc and Vatra Dornei.

For reservations, contact the **CFR office** (☎ 214 335; Str N Bălcescu 8; open 7am-8pm Mon-Fri).

Bus The **bus station** (autogară; Str Armenească) is in the centre of town. Tickets for international destinations are sold at window No 4. Six buses run daily (except Monday) between Suceava and Chernivtsi (Cernăuţi) in Ukraine ($4, 90km).

Buses to Romanian destinations include nine daily to Gura Humorului ($1.20, 37km), seven to Botoşani ($1.30, 42km) and one to Iaşi ($2.80, 141km).

GURA HUMORULUI
☎ 0230
This small logging town, 37km west of Suceava, is an ideal centre for visiting the monasteries. Most trains stop here and the adjacent train and bus stations are seven minutes' walk from the centre of town. Voroneţ and Humor monasteries are the main reasons to visit Gura Humorului (see these sections later in the chapter).

The **post office** (cnr Str Bucovinei & Str 9 Mai) handles postal requirements.

You can **camp** for free by the Moldovan River 1km south of town at the foot of the wooded hills. Otherwise, your best bet is one of the numerous private **villas** that have sprung up all over town in recent years. A good option is the friendly **Vila Ramona** (☎ 232 996; **w** www.ramona.ro; Str Oborului 6; singles & doubles $14), 200m off the main road, which has cosy rooms with shared bathroom.

Getting There & Away
Gura Humorului is on the main train line between Suceava and Cluj-Napoca.

Buses from Gura Humorului's **bus station** (Str Ştefan cel Mare 37) include seven daily to Humor and Suceava, and three to Voroneţ. Weekend services are greatly reduced.

You can also walk the 4km south to Voroneţ through beautiful farmland. It's a 6km hike north to Humor monastery from the town centre. If you have limited time, bargain with taxi drivers for tours to the monasteries.

VORONEŢ
The *Last Judgment*, which fills the western wall at Mănătirea Voroneţ is perhaps the most marvellous of Bucovina's frescoes. At the top, angels roll up the signs of the zodiac to indicate the end of time. The middle fresco shows humanity being brought to judgment. On the left St Paul escorts the believers, while on the right Moses brings forward the nonbelievers. Below is the Resurrection. Even the wild animals give back body pieces to complete those rising from the graves.

The northern wall depicts the book of Genesis. The southern wall features the Tree of Jesse with the genealogy of biblical personalities. Inside, facing the iconostasis, is the famous portrait of Ştefan the Great offering the Voroneţ Church to Christ. The vibrant blue pigment used throughout the frescoes here is known worldwide as 'Voroneţ blue'.

If you arrive early in the day, you may be able to attend a service and hear the nuns perform a traditional board-tapping ritual dating from the days when church bells were banned.

Places to Stay
Casa Elena (☎ 230 651; fax 230 968; **w** www.casaelena.ro; singles/doubles $22/30), 2km from Gura Humorului on the main road to Voroneţ Monastery, has 10 rooms, and rates do not include breakfast. The hotel also has a billiard room and a 24-hour restaurant.

HUMOR
At Humor, an active monastery run by kindly nuns, the predominant colour is deep red. On the church's southern exterior wall (AD 1530) the 1453 siege of Constantinople is depicted, with the parable of the return of the prodigal son beside it. On the porch is the *Last Judgment* and, in the first chamber inside the church, scenes of martyrdom. Humor has the most impressive interior frescoes of all the monasteries.

MOLDOVIŢA
Mănătirea Moldoviţa (1532) is in the middle of a quaint Romanian farming village, and has a life of its own. Moldoviţa consists of a strong fortified enclosure with towers and brawny gates, and a magnificent painted church at its centre. The monastery has undergone careful restoration in recent years.

The fortifications here are actually more impressive than the frescoes. On the church's southern exterior wall is a depiction of the defence of Constantinople in AD 626 against Persians dressed as Turks, while on the porch is a representation of the *Last Judgment*, all on a background of blue. Inside the sanctuary,

ROMANIA

on a wall facing the original carved iconostasis, is a portrait of Prince Petru Rareş (Moldovița's founder) and his family offering the church to Christ. All these works date from 1537. In the monastery's small museum is Petru Rareş' original throne.

Places to Stay & Eat

Mărul de Aur (☎ 030 336 180; doubles & triples $7), between the train station and the monastery, has tired rooms. Downstairs is a smoke-filled restaurant serving basic meals and beer 24 hours a day. The hotel also operates a **camping ground** (camping free, cabins $4), 3km out of town on the road to Sucevița.

Getting There & Away

Moldovița Monastery is right above Vatra Moldoviței's train station (be sure to get off at Vatra Moldoviței, not Moldovița). From Suceava there are eight daily trains to Vama (1½ hours). From Vama three trains daily leave for Vatra Moldoviței (50 minutes).

SUCEVIȚA

Mănăstirea Sucevița is the largest and finest of Bucovina's monasteries. The church inside the fortified quadrangular enclosure (built between 1582 and 1601) is almost completely covered in frescoes. Green and red colours dominate. As you enter you first see the *Virtuous Ladder* fresco covering most of the northern exterior wall, which depicts the 30 steps from hell to paradise. On the southern exterior wall is a tree symbolising the continuity of the Old and New Testaments. The tree grows from the reclining figure of Jesse, who is flanked by a row of ancient philosophers. To the left is the Virgin as a Byzantine princess, with angels holding a red veil over her head. Mysteriously, the western wall remains blank. Legend has it that the artist fell off his scaffolding and died, thus the wall was left unfinished. Apart from the church, there's a small museum at Sucevița Monastery.

Places to Stay & Eat

It's worth spending a night here and doing a little hiking in the surrounding hills, which are forest-clad and offer sweeping views. Freelance **camping** is possible in the field across the stream from the monastery. Otherwise, try **Popas Turistic Bucovinean** (☎/fax 565 389; huts $10, singles/doubles with bath $22/27), 5km south of Sucevița on the road to Vatra

Moldoviței. It has two charming villas and an excellent Moldavian restaurant. Rates include a breakfast of ham and eggs. There are also wooden two-bed huts.

Getting There & Away

Sucevița is the most difficult monastery to reach by public transport. The road connecting Sucevița and Moldovița monasteries (36km) winds up and over a high mountain pass (1100m), through forests and small alpine villages. The road is stunning and offers unlimited freelance camping opportunities, but you need a car to explore it fully (hiking up would be madness). It's possible to hike the 20km north to Putna in about five hours.

PUTNA

Mănăstirea Putna (1466), built by Ştefan cel Mare, is still home to an active religious community with groups of monks chanting mass just before sunset. Ştefan and his family are buried in the church, to the right as you enter. The large building that is behind the monastery contains a small **museum** of medieval manuscripts, rare 15th-century textiles and the holy book of the great prince. The monks living at Putna practise icon painting, shepherding and wood sculpture. Putna is easy to reach by train and makes a good day trip from Suceava.

Places to Stay & Eat

Cabana Putna (cabins per person $5), which is signposted 50m off the main road through the village leading to the monastery, has three- and four-bed cabins with shared bathrooms, and rates include breakfast.

Some people **camp** freelance in the field opposite the rock-hewn Daniel the Hermit's cave at Chilia, 2km from the train station. To get there, follow the river upstream to a wooden bridge, cross over the river and continue straight ahead.

Getting There & Away

Local trains travel to Putna from Suceava five times a day (two hours). The monastery is at the end of the road, just under 2km from the train station.

You can hike the 20km from Putna to Sucevița monastery in about five hours. Follow the trail marked with blue crosses in white squares that starts near the hermit's cave. About 4km down the road turn off to the left.

ROMANIA

Dobruja

Dobruja, the land between the Danube River and the Black Sea, was joined to Romania in 1878 when a combined Russo-Romanian army drove the Turks from Bulgaria. In antiquity the region was colonised first by the Greeks and then by the Romans, both of whom left behind a great deal for visitors to admire. Histria, 70km north of Constanţa, is the oldest settlement in Romania, founded by Greek merchants in 657 BC. From AD 46, Dobruja was the Roman province of Moesia Inferior. At Adamclisi the Romans scored a decisive victory over the Geto-Dacian tribes, which made possible their expansion north of the Danube. Dobruja later fell under Byzantium and in 1418 was conquered by the Turks.

Today the soft, sandy beaches along the 245km southern half of Romania's tideless Black Sea coast are the country's main tourist spots. Each summer trains are jammed with Romanians in search of fine white sand, warm water and sunshine; in midsummer the Black Sea coast resembles a massive outdoor party, with beachfront barbecues and plenty of beer.

The high season runs from mid-May to late September. From October to late April, the beaches are quiet and the weather is cold. During the low season only a few hotels remain open to house the trickle of tourists and spa clients.

There are nine main resorts lining the sea coast: Mamaia, Eforie Nord, Eforie Sud, Costineşti, Neptun-Olimp, Jupiter, Venus-Aurora, Saturn and Mangalia. Mamaia, on the northern fringe of Constanţa, has many sporting facilities and a freshwater lake for sailing and water skiing.

Cheap accommodation is scarce. Expect to pay $30 and up for a comfortable hotel room; advance reservations are advisable from mid-June to August.

CONSTANŢA
☎ 0241 • pop 346,830

Constanţa is Romania's largest port and its second-largest city. In the 6th century BC, Constanţa was the Greek merchant town of Tomis, which the Romans later renamed after emperor Constantin, who developed the city in the 4th century AD. By the 8th century, the city had been destroyed by invading Avars. After it was taken by Romania in 1877, King

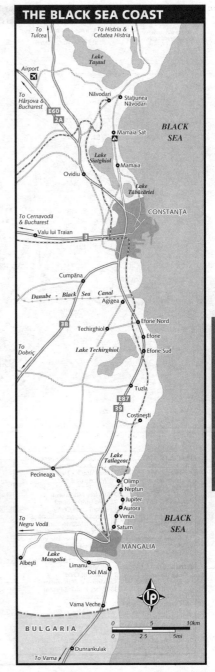

THE BLACK SEA COAST

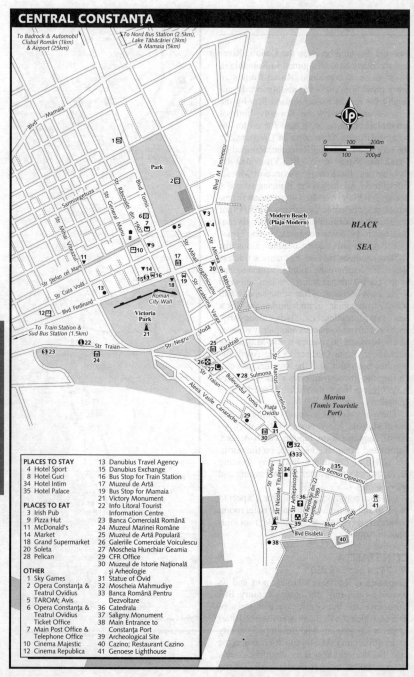

CENTRAL CONSTANŢA

To Badrock & Automobil
Clubul Român (1km)
& Airport (25km)

To Nord Bus Station (2.5km),
Lake Tăbăcăriei (3km)
& Mamaia (5km)

Blvd Mamaia

Park

Str Răscoalei din 1907

Str General Manu

Sarmisegetuza

Str Mihai Viteazul

Blvd Tomis

Blvd M Eminescu

Str Ştefan cel Mare

Str Cuza Vodă

Str Mihai

Str Mircea cel Bătrân

Blvd Ferdinand

Str Ecaterina Varga

To Train Station &
Sud Bus Station (1.5km)

Roman
City Wall

Victoria Park

Str Traian

Str Negru Vodă

Karatzali

Str Traian

Bulevardul Tomis

Aleea Vasile Canarache

Sulmona

Marcus Aurelius

Str

Piaţa
Ovidiu

Modern Beach
(Plaja Modern)

BLACK

SEA

Marina
(Tomis Touristic
Port)

Blvd Revoluţie din 22
Decembrie 1989

Str Arhiepiscopiei

Str Ovidiu

Str Nicolae Titulescu

Str Remus Opreanu

Blvd Carpaţi

Blvd Elisabeta

0   100   200m
0   100   200yd

PLACES TO STAY
4   Hotel Sport
8   Hotel Guci
34 Hotel Intim
35 Hotel Palace

PLACES TO EAT
3   Irish Pub
9   Pizza Hut
11 McDonald's
14 Market
18 Grand Supermarket
20 Soleta
28 Pelican

OTHER
1   Sky Games
2   Opera Constanţa &
    Teatrul Ovidius
5   TAROM; Avis
6   Opera Constanţa &
    Teatrul Ovidius
    Ticket Office
7   Main Post Office &
    Telephone Office
10 Cinema Majestic
12 Cinema Republica

13 Danubius Travel Agency
15 Danubius Exchange
16 Bus Stop for Train Station
17 Muzeul de Artă
19 Bus Stop for Mamaia
21 Victory Monument
22 Info Litoral Tourist
    Information Centre
23 Banca Comercială Română
24 Muzeul Marinei Române
25 Muzeul de Artă Populară
26 Galeriile Comerciale Voiculescu
27 Moscheia Hunchiar Geamia
29 CFR Office
30 Muzeul de Istorie Naţională
    şi Arheologie
31 Statue of Ovid
32 Moscheia Mahmudiye
33 Banca Română Pentru
    Dezvoltare
36 Catedrala
37 Saligny Monument
38 Main Entrance to
    Constanţa Port
39 Archeological Site
40 Cazino; Restaurant Cazino
41 Genoese Lighthouse

ROMANIA

Carol I turned it into an active port and seaside resort with a railway line to Bucharest.

Much remains from every period of Constanţa's colourful history, despite industrial development to the north and west. The picturesque old town has a peaceful Mediterranean air and a few excellent museums that you can easily see in an afternoon. Constanţa's city beaches are crowded and a bit dirty; instead, sun-worshippers could head to the nearby resort of Mamaia, 20 minutes away by bus.

Orientation

Constanţa's train station is about 2km west of the old town. To reach old Constanţa, exit the station, buy a ticket ($0.20) from the kiosk to the right and take trolleybus No 40, 41 or 43 down Blvd Ferdinand to Victoria Park (Parcul Victoriei) four stops from the station; or just walk along Blvd Ferdinand.

North of Blvd Ferdinand is Constanţa's business district. The area around Str Ştefan cel Mare is lined with shops and restaurants as well as theatres.

Information

Tourist Offices Staff at Constanţa's **Info Litoral Tourist Information Centre** (☎ 555 000, fax 555 111; **w** www.infolitoral.ro; Str Traian 36, Scara C, Apt 31) are friendly and well informed.

Money The **Banca Comercială Română** (Str Traian 1; open 8.30am-noon Mon-Fri) cashes travellers cheques, gives cash advances on Visa/MasterCard and has an ATM. **Banca Română Pentru Dezvoltare** (Str Arhiepiscopiei 9; open 9am-2pm Mon-Fri) offers the same services. **Danubius Exchange** (Blvd Ferdinand 44) changes money at good rates.

Post & Communications The telephone centre (open 7am-10pm daily) is in the **main post office** (Blvd Tomis 79; open 7am-8pm Mon-Fri, 8am-1pm Sat).

Sky Games (☎ 614 765; Blvd Tomis 129; open 24hr) charges $0.50 per hour to access the Internet.

Travel Agencies Staff at **Danubius Travel Agency** (☎ 615 836, fax 618 010; **w** www .rotravel.com/agencies/danubius; Blvd Ferdinand 36; 9am-7pm Mon-Fri, 9am-2pm Sat) speak English and can arrange day trips to the Danube Delta and Murfatlar winery.

Left Luggage The left-luggage office (open 24hr) in the train station is downstairs inside the passageway from the main hall to the tracks.

Dangers & Annoyances Constanţa is plagued with street hustlers and thieves. Don't change money on the streets and beware of friendly boys crowding around you.

Things to See & Do

The first place you'll notice in the centre of town is **Victoria Park** (Blvd Ferdinand), which has remains of the 3rd-century **Roman city wall**, pieces of Roman sculpture and a modern **Victory monument**. On the corner of Blvd Tomis is the **Muzeul de Artă** (Art Museum; ☎ 617 012; **e** arta@cjc.ro; Blvd Tomis 82-84; admission $0.60; open 9am-5pm Wed-Sun), and the adjoining **small gallery** where contemporary art exhibits are held. As you walk south on Blvd Tomis you come to the worthwhile **Muzeul de Artă Populară** (Folk Art Museum; ☎ 616 133; Blvd Tomis 32; admission $0.60; open 9am-5pm Wed-Sun) in an ornate building on the left.

The **Muzeul Marinei Române** (Naval History Museum; ☎ 619 035; Str Traian 53; admission $0.55; open 9am-5pm Tues-Sun), has detailed exhibits on early Romanian history. The captions are in Romanian, but the illustrations are informative. Back on Blvd Tomis heading south you will also pass by the **Moscheia Hunchiar Geamia** (Geamia Hunchiar Mosque; 1868), which was built with stones from the old gate of the former Ottoman fortress.

Constanţa's most renowned attraction is the **Muzeul de Istorie Naţională şi Arheologie** (History & Archaeological Museum; ☎ 618 763; Piaţa Ovidiu 12; admission $0.60; open 9am-5pm Tues-Sun), with exhibits on three floors. It includes 24 Roman statues from the 2nd-century, discovered under the old train station in 1962. The most unusual objects are kept in the treasury downstairs. Don't miss the 2nd-century AD sculpture of Glykon, a serpent with the muzzle of an antelope and the eyes, ears and hair of a human. Most cases have captions in English and German.

The archaeological fragments of Roman Tomis spill over onto the surrounding square. Facing these is a glass museum, which shelters a gigantic 3rd-century **Roman mosaic** discovered in 1959. The **statue of Ovid**, erected on

ROMANIA

Piaţa Ovidiu in 1887, commemorates the Latin poet exiled to Constanţa in AD 8.

A block south is **Moscheia Mahmudiye** *(Mahmudiye Mosque; Str Arhiepiscopiei)*, dating from 1910, with a 140-step minaret you can climb when the gate is unlocked. Two blocks farther down the same street is an Orthodox **Catedrala** (1885). One block to the right is the **Saligny monument**, overlooking the modern harbour.

From the monument, a peaceful promenade meanders along the waterfront, offering sweeping views of the Black Sea. On summer evenings this is a popular hangout for kids, entwined couples and old men playing chess. Have a beer or coffee on the terrace of Constanţa's French baroque **cazino** (1910). Further along the promenade is the **Genoese lighthouse** (1860) and pier, with a fine view of old Constanţa.

Places to Stay

Camping The nearest camping ground is in Mamaia, but an easy 20-minute trolleybus ride will take you there.

Hotels North of Blvd Ferdinand is the **Hotel Sport** *(☎ 617 558, fax 611 009; Str Cuza Vodă 2; singles/doubles/triples with breakfast $28/35/45)*, which is a nice modern hotel by the beach. The triple has a bunk bed and some rooms have balconies overlooking the beach. The hotel is usually fully booked out with athletic groups.

Hotel Palace *(☎ 614 696; Str Remus Opreanu 7; 2-star singles/doubles $20/28, 3-star $59/79)*, in the old town, is in a beautiful location that overlooks the sea. Room rates include breakfast.

Hotel Intim *(☎/fax 617 814; Str Nicolae Titulescu 9; singles/doubles with breakfast $34/39)* is an elegant 21-room hotel close to the port.

Hotel Guci *(☎/fax 638 426; Str Răscoalei 23; singles/doubles $99/123)* is Constanţa's top hotel, with luxurious rooms with all the mod-cons. Perks of staying here include a Jacuzzi, sauna and gym.

Places to Eat

Restaurant Cazino *(☎ 617 416; Blvd Elisabeta 2; meals $1.50-3)* is worth a look, if only for the large outdoor terrace overlooking the Black Sea. In summer live music plays on the terrace.

Soleta *(☎ 614 511; Str Mircea cel Bătrân 49-51; meals $1.50-3)* offers inexpensive, authentic Lebanese dishes.

Pelican *(☎ 615 976; Str Sulmona 9; mains $1.50-4)* serves good, well-priced Romanian cuisine. It also has a fine terrace and serves up cocktails.

Badrock *(☎ 0721-204 000; Str Călăraşi 1; rice dishes $1.50-4, curries $2.90-4)*, opposite the ACR office, is a kitsch Flintstone-theme restaurant that confusingly serves Indian dishes. Check it out!

Irish Pub *(☎ 550 400; Str Ştefan cel Mare 1; mains $3-5)* is a friendly, but expensive, restaurant with a vast drinks list and pleasant outdoor terrace overlooking the sea. Highly recommend is the Irish beef pie cooked with Guinness ($3.05).

There are plenty of fast-food outlets at the modern **Galeriile Comerciale Voiculescu** *(Blvd Tomis)*. **McDonald's** has an outlet at Str Ştefan cel Mare, beside the Tomis department store, and north of the centre at Blvd Mamaia. There's also a **Pizza Hut** *(Str Răscoalei 1907, 10)*.

Stock up on fruit, cheese and vegies at the **market** off Str Răscoalei 1907, behind the bus stop. The **Grand Supermarket** *(Blvd Tomis 57; open 24hr)* has good cakes and sweets.

Entertainment

The **Opera Constanţa** *(☎ 615 268, box office 611 536; e operaconstanta@acasa.ro; Str Mircea cel Bătrân 97)* is in a park. The **Teatrul Ovidius** *(☎ 611 744, box office 520 426; e teatrul.ovidiu@rdsct.ro; Str Mircea cel Bătran 97)* is also based here.

Films are presented in their original language at the **Cinema Majestic** *(☎ 664 411; Str Ştefan cel Mare 33)* and **Cinema Republica** *(☎ 616 287; Blvd Ferdinand 58)*.

Getting There & Away

Air In summer there are international flights to/from Constanţa's airport, 25km from the city centre (see the introductory Getting There & Away section earlier in this chapter for more details).

Tarom *(☎ 662 632, fax 614 066; Str Ştefan cel Mare 15)* runs one flight on Wednesday, Friday, Saturday and Sunday, from Constanţa to Bucharest ($50/100 single/return). Tarom runs a free shuttle for customers from its office to the airport that leaves 1½ hours before flight departures.

Train Constanţa's train and bus stations are at the western end of Blvd Ferdinand. The **CFR office** (☎ 617 930; Aleea Vasile Canarache 4; open 7.30am-7pm Mon-Fri, 7.30am-1pm Sat) is behind the archaeological museum.

Constanţa is well connected to Bucharest's Gara de Nord by express train (three hours). There are also direct services to Braşov and Iaşi and during summer to Timişoara and Suceava; the Ovidius express train runs overnight between Constanţa and Budapest-Keleti (17 hours) via Bucharest.

Local trains run north to Tulcea (179km, via Medgidia), south to Mangalia (43km) and west to Bucureşti-Obor. For northern Romania, take a Bucharest-bound train west to Feteşti (79km) and change for Făurei (for Iaşi) or Buzău (for Suceava).

Bus If you're travelling south down the Black Sea coast, buses are more convenient than trains. Exit Constanţa's train station and walk 50m to the right, to the queue of buses. Private minibuses leave every 30 minutes for Mangalia ($0.90), stopping at Eforie Nord, Eforie Sud, Neptun-Olimp, Venus and Saturn; pay the driver.

Trolleybus Nos 40, 41 and 43 go to Constanţa's town centre; No 41 continues north stopping at the southern end of Mamaia's 8km strip ($0.20). Bus No 23 travels north to Năvodari making several stops in Mamaia en route ($0.30).

There is a daily bus to İstanbul ($25/50 single/return, 17½ hours) via Bulgaria, departing from the Sud (southern) bus station, next to the train station, at noon.

From the Nord (northern) bus station, private minibuses run every hour to Tulcea ($2.45, 125km).

MAMAIA
☎ 0241

Just north of Constanţa, Mamaia, an 8km strip of beach between Lake Siutghiol and the Black Sea, is Romania's most popular resort. The main activities here are swimming and sunbathing, drinking beer and strolling along the boardwalk that runs along the beach following the main road. Best of all, Constanţa is just a bus ride away (No 41).

Information
The **Agenţia de Turism** (☎ 831 168, fax 831 052; open 7am-4pm Mon-Thur, 7am-1pm Fri), on the highway side of Hotel Riviera, north of the Cazino, arranges car rentals and accommodation.

Every hotel has a currency exchange, but to change travellers cheques or get a cash advance you must go to Constanţa. Most of the large hotels accept credit cards.

The **telephone centre** and **post office** (both open 8am-8pm Mon-Fri June-Sept) share an office on the boardwalk, 200m south of the Cazino complex.

Things to See & Do
In summer a boat ferries tourists across freshwater Lake Mamaia to **Ovidiu Island** every hour ($3 return). The boat leaves from the wharf near **Mamaia Cazino**, on the lake side of the strip, behind the Cazino Bazar.

All kinds of **water sports**, such as sailboarding, water-skiing, yachting, rowing and pedal boating, are available on Lake Mamaia.

The **tennis courts** at Grăvina Boema, on the highway running between the Doina and Victoria hotels, cost $7 per hour including equipment rental.

Places to Stay
Camping The large **Popas Mamaia** (☎ 831 357; camping per tent $2, bed in hut $6) is 2km from the northern end of Mamaia's 8km strip. Take bus No 23 from the train station. It stops outside the site.

One kilometre farther is **Popas Hanul Piraţilor** (☎/fax 831 702; bus No 23; double huts $10, 2-room villas $20) between the main road and the beach.

Beach Chalets The **Cazino Delta Pensiune** (☎ 831 665), inside the Cazino complex on the southern side, and the **Mini-Hotel** (☎ 831 878), on the northern side of the Cazino, rent out chalets (basic rooms with mattresses). Both have double chalets with shared bathroom and cold water for around $7.

Hotels Mamaia is lined with about 60 hotels of varying standards.

Pensiune Victory (☎ 831 153, fax 831 253; doubles $25), smack-bang on the beach, is a modest pension with bright, airy rooms (half overlook the beach).

Parc Hotel (☎ 831 720; singles/doubles/triples $30/44/61), at the southern end of the boardwalk near the Pescărie bus stop, has well-priced standard rooms.

Hotel Albatros (☎ 831 381, fax 831 346; low season singles/doubles $26/35, high season $61/87), 20m left of the Statia Cazino bus stop, is a convivial place with decent rooms. The two-star **Hotel Condor** (☎ 831 142, fax 831 906), next door, has similar prices.

Best Western Savoy Hotel (☎ 831 426, fax 831 266; e hotel.savoy@impromex.ro; w www.bestwestern.com; low/high season doubles $72/144), a bright and cheery hotel at the resort's northern end, has first-class three-star rooms with all mod-cons.

Places to Eat

Almost every hotel has an adjoining restaurant serving the usual pork and grilled meatballs.

Terasa Panalba (mains $0.60-2.60), opposite the Cazino, serves delicious traditional Romanian dishes. Also good is the Cazino's **Delta Restaurant**.

Fast-food stands along the boardwalk suffice for lunch and hot snacks.

Getting There & Away

Bus No 23 ($0.30) runs north from the train station to Năvodari past the major hotels in Mamaia. Alternatively, catch trolleybus No 40 to the Pescărie bus stop near Hotel Parc, then change to trolley bus No 47. In summertime a shuttle bus operates up and down Mamaia's 5km boardwalk.

EFORIE NORD

☎ 041 • pop 9351

Eforie Nord, 17km from Constanţa, is the first large resort south of the city. The beach lies below 20m cliffs on the eastern side of the town.

The train station is only a few minutes' walk from the post office and main street, Blvd Republicii. Exit the station and turn left; turn left again after Hotel Belvedere and then right onto Blvd Republicii.

Most hotels and restaurants are on Str Tudor Vladimirescu, which runs parallel to Blvd Republicii along the beach.

There are currency exchanges at nearly every hotel, supermarket and street corner. The **telephone centre** (open 7am-10pm daily) is at the **main post office** (Blvd Republicii 119; open 9am-6pm Mon-Fri).

Tiny **Lake Belona**, just behind the southern end of the beach, is a popular bathing spot, as its water is warmer than the Black Sea. Because Eforie Nord is close to Constanţa it tends to be overcrowded; the beaches are better and cleaner further south.

Southwest of Eforie Nord is **Techirghiol Lake**, a former river mouth famous for its black sapropel mud, effective against rheumatism. The cold mud baths are the only place in Romania where nudism is allowed (separate areas are designated for women and men). **Popas Şincai** (mud baths open 8am-8pm daily mid-June–early Sept; see Places to Stay) offers the cheapest baths in town ($0.60). The lake is 2m below sea level, and its waters are four times as salty as the sea.

Places to Stay & Eat

The best camping facilities are at **Camping Meduza** (☎/fax 742 385; camping per person $2, 2-bed bungalows $5), behind the Minerva at the northern end of the beach. Walk north along Str Tudor Vladimirescu and turn immediately left after Club Maxim. There are tent spaces and clean bungalows.

Popas Şincai (☎ 741 401; huts per person $5), a few hundred metres west of Eforie Nord's train station, has camping space and two-room huts. Walk west to the far end of the railway platform, cross the tracks and follow a path to a breach in the wall.

Delfinul Hotel, Meduza Hotel and **Steaua de Mare Hotel** (☎ 704 125, fax 704 124; Str Tudor Vladimirescu 39-43) stand side by side at the northern end of the beach. Owned by the same company they specialise in natural cures and mud baths. Single/double rooms in all three start from $27/47 in the low season.

Getting There & Away

The **CFR office** (☎ 617 930; Str Republicii 11), next to the post office, sells tickets for express trains. All trains between Bucharest and Mangalia stop at Eforie Nord, but you're better off on a private minibus (see Getting There & Away under Constanţa).

NEPTUN-OLIMP

☎ 041

Before the 1989 revolution, Neptun-Olimp was the exclusive tourist complex of Romania's Communist Party. Neptun-Olimp in fact two resorts in one. Olimp, a huge complex of hotels facing the beach, is the party place. Neptun, 1km south, is separated from the Black Sea by two small lakes amid some lush greenery. Together they form a vast expanse of hotels and discos.

The resort complex offers a reasonable range of **activities**: tennis, windsurfing, jet-skiing, sailing, mini-golf, billiards, bowling and discos. Neptun-Olimp is perhaps the nicest and most chic of the Romanian Black Sea resorts.

The **Dispecerat Cazare** (room dispatcher; ☎ 701 300; open 24hr June-Sept) can give you information on hotels and take bookings. The office is inside the Levent Market on the main street.

The **Banca Comercială Română** (open 8.30am-11.30am Mon-Fri) is in the centre of the resort on the main street in Neptun. It cashes travellers cheques and gives cash advances on Visa/MasterCard. There's also the **exchange office** (open 9am-5pm Mon-Fri June-Sept), attached to the Levent Market on the main street.

The **post office** and **telephone centre** are a block north of Hotel Decebal on the main road in Neptun.

Places to Stay & Eat

Holiday Village Neptun (☎ 701 224; camping per person $2, double brick cottages $9, double hut with running water per person $6 July & August; open year-round) is at the southern end of Lake Neptun II.

Camping Olimp (☎ 731 314), at the northern end of Olimp's tourist strip, charges similar prices for its 140 basic wooden huts. Both the Neptun and the Olimp are packed out in summer.

Neptun-Olimp's hotels are not for budget travellers, charging from $36 for a double room without breakfast. Without reservations you'll pay more.

There are numerous **fast-food** joints, but a nicer place to eat is **Calul Bălan** (☎ 731 912; mains $2-5), on the left as you enter Neptun's main street from the south, which is renown for its local cuisine and folklore shows.

Getting There & Away

Halta Neptun station is within walking distance of the Neptun-Olimp hotels, midway between the two resorts. All trains travelling from Bucharest or Constanța to Mangalia stop at Halta Neptun.

The **CFR office** (Str Plopilor) is inside Neptun's Hotel Apollo, northwest of Lake Neptun II.

Private minibuses run between the resort towns and Mangalia ($0.30).

MANGALIA
☎ 041 • pop 44,110

Formerly ancient Greek Callatis, Mangalia, founded in the 6th century BC, contains several minor archaeological sites. It is a quiet town, not a place for partying, and attracts many elderly European tour groups.

Orientation & Information

Mangalia's train station is 1km north of the centre. Turn right as you exit and follow Şoseaua Constanţei (the main road) south. At the roundabout, turn left for Hotel Mangalia and the beach or go straight ahead for the pedestrianised section of Şoseaua Constanţei, for most facilities. Private and city buses stop in front of the train station and **Staţia Stadion** (Şoseaua Constanţei), south of the roundabout.

Most hotels have their own currency exchanges. The **Banca Comercială Română** (Şoseaua Constanţei 25; open 8am-noon Mon-Fri) cashes travellers cheques, gives cash advances on Visa and MasterCard and has an ATM. **Banca Agricolă** (Str Teilor 7; open 8am-11.30am Mon-Fri) is on the beachfront.

The **telephone centre** (open 7am-10pm daily) and **post office** (open 7am-8pm Mon-Fri) are both at Ştefan cel Mare 16.

Graphity Club Internet & Games (☎ 758 284; Str Ştefan cel Mare 5; open 24hr) has email access for $0.50 per hour.

Things to See & Do

At the roundabout, a street runs left straight down to Hotel Mangalia and the beach, with the ruins of a 6th-century **Palaeo-Christian basilica** and a fountain dispensing sulphurous mineral water. Return to the roundabout and continue south on Şoseaua Constanţei. You'll soon reach the **Muzeul Arheologie Callatis** (Callatis Archaeological Museum; ☎ 752 872; admission $0.75; open 9am-8pm daily June-Aug) on the left, with a good collection of Roman sculpture. Just past the high-rise building next to the museum are some remnants of a 4th-century necropolis.

Continue south on Şoseaua Constanţei for another 500m to the town centre. On most summer evenings cultural events take place in **Casă de Cultură**, which has a large mural on its facade. Further ahead is the Turkish **Moscheia Esmahan Sultan** (Sultan Esmahan Mosque; 1460; ☎ 754 250; admission $0.15; open 10am-5pm daily). All these sights can easily be seen in two hours.

ROMANIA

Places to Stay & Eat

ANTREC (☎ 759 473, fax 757 400; Str George Murnu 13, Block D, Apt 21) arranges rooms in private homes in Mangalia and other coastal resorts from $15 a night.

Three two-star hotels on the promenade, the **Hotel Zenit** (☎ 751 646, fax 752 052; Str Teilor 7), **Hotel Astra** (☎ 751 673, fax 752 052; Str Teilor 9) and **Hotel Orion** (☎/fax 751 156; Str Teilor 11) are quite pleasant and charge $29/44 low/high season a night for a double with private bath.

Hotel Mangalia (☎ 752 052, fax 753 510; Str Rozelor 35; single/doubles low season $20/31, high season $27/50) is a popular choice with tour groups for its spa treatments.

Hotel **restaurants** are the main dinner option. Otherwise your best bet is **Captain Mondy's Irish Pub** (☎ 753 168; Blvd 1 Decembrie 1918; small pizzas $0.90-1.70, large pizzas $1.25-2.10, mains $1.85-3.35), a small pub/restaurant close to the port. Its dishes, while not very *Irish*, are good and filling.

Getting There & Away

From Constanţa there are 21 trains daily in summer (1¼ hours) but only five daily during winter. Many of these trains are direct to/from Bucharest's Gară de Nord (4½ hours). In summer there are express trains to/from Iaşi, Oradea, Suceava and Timişoara.

The **CFR office** (☎ 752 818; Str Ştefan cel Mare 16; open 9am-5pm Mon-Fri) adjoins the **post office**.

Private minibuses from Constanţa stop throughout the day at Mangalia's train station and near the roundabout (see Getting There & Away under Constanţa).

The Danube Delta

At the end of its long journey across Europe the mighty Danube River empties into the Black Sea just south of the Ukrainian border. At this point the Danube splits into three separate channels – the Chilia, Sulina and Sfântu Gheorghe – creating a 5800-sq-km wetland of marshes, floating reed islets and sandbars, which is a sanctuary for 300 species of birds and 160 species of fish. Reed marshes cover 156,300 hectares, constituting one of the largest single expanses of reed beds existing in the world.

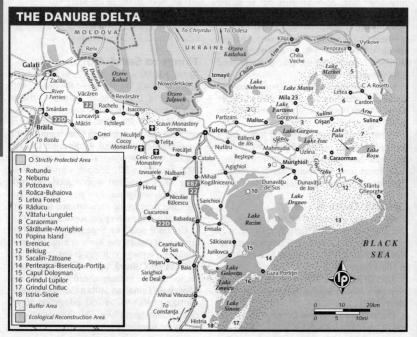

THE DANUBE DELTA

☐ Strictly Protected Area

1 Rotundu
2 Nebunu
3 Potcoava
4 Roãca-Buhaiova
5 Letea Forest
6 Rãducu
7 Vãtafu-Lungulet
8 Caraorman
9 Sãrãturile-Murighiol
10 Popina Island
11 Erenciuc
12 Belciug
13 Sacalin-Zãtoane
14 Periteaşca-Bisericuţa-Portiţa
15 Capul Doloşman
16 Grindul Lupilor
17 Grindul Chituc
18 Istria-Sinoie

☐ Buffer Area
☐ Ecological Reconstruction Area

The Danube Delta (Delta Dunarii) is under the protection of the Administration of the Danube Delta Biosphere Reserve Authority (DDBRA), set up in response to the ecological disaster that befell the Delta region during Ceauşescu's attempt to transform it into an agricultural region. Now there are 18 protected reserves (50,000 hectares) that are off limits to tourists or anglers, including the 500-year-old Leţea Forest and Europe's largest pelican colony. The Delta is also included in Unesco's World Heritage list.

The part of the Delta most accessible to foreigners is the middle arm, which cuts directly across from Tulcea to Crişan and Sulina (71km). Most river traffic uses the Sulina arm, including the ferries and touring boats from Tulcea.

Getting Around

Most hotels and travel agencies in Tulcea arrange day trips through the Delta on small motorboats. You can also approach local boat operators directly and arrange a private trip for an agreed price.

The government-subsidised Navrom operates passenger ferries to several towns and villages in the Delta. However, you'll need small boats to see the most interesting wildlife, as commercial traffic and passenger ferries have driven the birds deeper into the Delta. It's easy to hire rowing boats (around $15 to $20 for a few hours) from village anglers and this is the only way to penetrate the more exotic backwaters.

All visitors need a permit to travel in the Delta. As a tourist, you're fined $200 if you enter a protected area without a permit. Permits cost $1 and are sold in Tulcea's travel agencies and at hotel receptions in Crişan, Sulina and Murighiol. Permits are automatically included in organised tour prices. You need a special permit to fish or camp.

Be sure to take some food and water and lots of mosquito repellent on any expedition into the Delta. Warning: do not drink Danube water!

Hydrofoils Hydrofoils sail daily from Tulcea to Sulina ($4.60, 1½ hours) via Crişan ($4.30, one hour). The hydrofoil departs from the AFDJ Galaţi terminal, opposite the DDBRA office, at 2pm daily. Return hydrofoils depart from Sulina at 7am daily. Purchase tickets when boarding the hydrofoil.

Ferries The Sulina ferry leaves Tulcea at 1.30pm Monday to Friday. The return ferry departs from Sulina 7am Tuesday to Saturday ($3.50). It stops at Partizani, Maliuc, Gorgova and Crişan. To get to Mila 23 and Caraorman disembark at Crişan and catch a local boat onward.

Ferry tickets are sold at Tulcea's **Navrom terminal** (☎ 511 553, fax 512 443; Str Gării 30) from 11.30am to 1.30pm. In summer the queues are long, so get in the correct line early (each window sells tickets to a different destination).

Organised Tours Tulcea's hotels and travel agencies offer day trips on the Delta from mid-May to September (see Information under Tulcea).

Ibis Tours (☎/fax 040-511 261; w www .ibis-tours.ro; Str Grivitei 1, Block C1, Apt 9, Tulcea) arranges bird-watching tours in the Delta and Dobruja led by professional ornithologists for around $25 a day. A longer day trip includes the journey from Tulcea to Murighiol by bus, followed by two to three hours on a small boat touring bird colonies.

TULCEA
☎ 040 • pop 97,038

Tulcea, a modern industrial city, is an important port and gateway to the Danube Delta paradise. It was settled by Dacians and Romans from the 7th to 1st centuries BC. The city has a broad riverfront promenade but offers few other attractions, so tourists usually arrange to catch the first ferry into the Delta.

Tulcea hosts the International Folk Festival of Danubian Countries each year in August.

Orientation

Tulcea's bus and train stations, and the Navrom ferry terminal, are adjacent, overlooking the Danube at the western end of the riverfront promenade, which stretches east along the river to Hotel Delta. Lake Ciuperca is west of the stations. Inland two blocks, between Str Păcii and Str Babadag, is Piaţa Unirii, the centre of Tulcea. Str Babadag is a long commercial and residential street leading up to the Banca Comercială Română.

Information

Tourist Offices The **DDBRA** (☎ 550 344, fax 550 498; e deltainfo@ns.tim.ro; Str Portului; open 8am-4pm Mon-Fri) has a central tourist information centre right on the riverfront opposite the AFDJ Galaţi terminal. It sells maps of the Delta and travel permits.

Fishing and hunting permits are sold at the **Fishing & Hunting Association** (☎ *511 404; Str Isaccea 10; open 7am-2pm Mon-Fri, 5pm-8pm Wed & Fri, 7am-1pm Sat)*. A map in the window highlights the areas where tourists are allowed to fish and hunt. Next door is a **fishing tackle shop** *(open 10am-6pm Mon-Fri, 7am-1pm Sat)* that sells camping gear.

Money The hotels have currency exchanges. **Banca Comercială Română** *(Str Toamnei; open 8am-11am Mon-Fri)* cashes travellers cheques, gives cash advances on Visa and MasterCard and has an ATM.

Post & Communications The **post office** *(open 7am-8pm Mon-Fri, 8am-noon Sat)* and **telephone centre** *(open 7am-8pm daily)* are at Str Păcii 6.

Future Games Internet (☎ *518 372; Str Isaccea; open 24hr)* charges $0.60 per hour for Internet access.

Travel Agencies The **Danubius Travel Agency** (☎*/fax 516 649; Str Păcii; open 8.30am-6.30pm Mon-Fri, 9am-1pm Sat)*, in Hotel Europolis, arranges boat trips to Crişan. **Nouvelles Frontières/Simpa Turism** (☎*/fax 515 753;* W *www.simpaturism.ro)*, in the Hotel Delta, arranges day trips along the Sulina arm to Crişan and back along the Old Danube via Mila 23 for $25 per person.

Left Luggage The **left-luggage office** *(open 24hr)* is at the train station.

Things to See

As you stroll along the river you'll see the **Independence Monument** (1904) on Citadel Hill, at the far eastern end of town. You can reach this by following Str Gloriei from behind the Egreta Hotel to its end; the views are superb. The **Muzeul de Arheologie şi Istorie** (History & Archaeology Museum) is just below the monument. On your way back, look for the minaret of **Moscheia Azizie** (Azizie Mosque; 1863) down Str Independenţei.

At the southern end of Str Gloriei, turn left onto Str 9 Mai; the **Muzeul Etnografic** (Ethnographic Museum) at No 2 has traditional costumes, fishing gear and carpets among its exhibits.

The **Muzeul Naţional de Istorie** *(Natural History Museum; Str Progresului 32)* has a good collection of Danube fish and detailed exhibits on the Delta's wildlife.

In front of the Greek Orthodox church opposite the museum is a **memorial** to the local victims of the 1989 revolution.

Tulcea's museums are open 8am to 4pm daily, except Monday ($0.50).

Places to Stay

Camping A no-camping regulation within Tulcea's city limits is strictly enforced by the local police.

Private Rooms Accommodation in private homes throughout the Delta can be booked through **ANTREC** (☎*/fax 511 279, 0744-294 217;* W *www.antrec-tulcea.go.ro; Str Portului)*, which has a small office in the DDBRA building on the riverfront. Bed and breakfast is $9, an extra meal is an additional $3.50. Staff also arrange local guides and boat hire.

Hotels Rooms in Tulcea are expensive, with little choice.

Hotel Egreta (☎ *517 103, fax 517 105; Str Păcii 3; singles/doubles $17/25)*, which includes breakfast in its rates, is the city's cheapest option.

Hotel Europolis (☎ *512 443; Str Păcii 20; singles/doubles $20/26)* has reasonable two-star rooms with private bath and cable TV.

Hotel Delta (☎ *514 721; Str Isaccea 2; singles/doubles $45/55)* is a bland concrete high-rise with overpriced rooms.

Houseboats Moored opposite Hotel Delta is the *Navitur* **House Boat** (☎ *518 894, fax 518 953; double cabins with shared bathroom $12)*. There's no hot water but there's a small bar-café aboard.

Top of the range are the three-star *Delta 3* and the four-star *Delta 2* run by the travel agency **ATBAD** (☎ *514 114;* W *atbad.hypermart.net; St Babadag 11)*. Nightly rates on board start at $120 per person for a group of six, dropping to $68 for a group of 16. Rates include full board and transfers.

Places to Eat

Restaurant Comandor (meals $2-5), moored at the riverfront promenade, is a large air-conditioned floating restaurant specialising in fresh seafood.

Restaurant Select (Str Păcii 6; meals $2-5) has an extensive menu (in six languages) and great food.

The outside terrace of **Carul cu Bere**, next to Restaurant Select, is a fun place to enjoy a beer and people watch. There are beer gardens along the riverfront promenade, too.

Fast Food Trident (Str Babadag; snacks $0.50-2), opposite the Diana Department Store, is an excellent spot for cheesy pizzas and pasta.

Union Visa Café (☎ 515 163; Str Unirii; breakfast $0.30-1, mains $1-2) is OK for a drink and a quick bite; its adjoining grocery has all the basics.

Stock up on cheese, fruit and vegies at the **produce market** at the end of Str Păcii, 100m past Hotel Europolis next to the small park.

Getting There & Around

There are three trains daily to/from Constanţa via Medgidia (four hours, 179km). The daily express train from Bucharest's Gară de Nord takes around five hours (334km). The local train to/from Bucharest is bearable if you go 1st class. Advance train tickets are sold at the **CFR office** (☎ 513 360; Str Babadag 4; open 9am-4pm Mon-Fri), opposite Piaţa Unirii.

Private minibuses run daily from the bus station to Bucharest ($5.80, 263km) and Constanţa ($2.45, 123km).

TULCEA TO SULINA

The Tulcea-Sulina ferry's first stop is at **Partizani**, a small fishing village. Next stop is **Maliuc**, a popular stop for tour groups. From Maliuc you can hire fishing boats for tours of smaller waterways to the north for $10 to $15 per hour. North of Maliuc is **Lake Furtuna**, great for bird-watchers.

The ferry's next stop is **Crişan**, at the junction with the Old Danube. At the junction's tip is the DDBRA's **Ecological Information Centre** (open 8am-4pm Tues-Sun), featuring wildlife displays and a video room. At the main Crişan ferry dock, ask about side trips to **Mila 23** or **Caraorman** (you'll need a permit), and about renting a rowboat.

Sulina, the final stop, is a romantic spot on the eastern edge of Europe. Approximately

5500 people live here – half the Delta's population. Sulina is not connected to the European road network so there are few vehicles.

A canal dug between 1880 and 1902 shortened the length of the Tulcea-Sulina channel from 83.3km to 62.6km, ensuring Sulina's future as the Danube Delta's main commercial port. After WWI Sulina was declared a 'free port' and trade boomed. Greek merchants dominated business here until their expulsion in 1951. The Sulina channel has been extended 8km out into the Black Sea by two lateral dykes.

Although not as good a base as Maliuc or Crişan for seeing Delta wildlife, Sulina is a pleasant place with a **beach**, a 19th-century **lighthouse** and an old **cemetery** with Romanian, Ukrainian, Turkish, Greek, Jewish and British graves, testimony to the colourful ethnic mix that once passed through the town's docks. The **DDBRA office** (open 10am-6pm Tues-Sun) is at No 1.

Places to Stay

You can **camp** along the beach in Sulina.

As you're getting off the ferry, watch out for people offering private rooms. The going rate is about $6 per person. ANTREC operates an efficient **agrotourism scheme** in the Delta. Half-board (bed and breakfast) is $9 per person. Bookings can be made through the local representatives. In Crişan contact Petre Vasiliu (☎ 0744-957 148), who speaks English and French, and in Sulina contact Mihai Călin (☎ 0740-052 349).

Hotel Astir (☎ 543 379; Sulina; rooms with shared bathroom per person $6) is a small two-star hotel a few hundred metres west along the riverfront from the Sulina Cinema. The entrance is from the rear.

Hotel Jean Bart (☎ 543 123; Sulina; rooms per person $8) is a quick 10-minute walk from the ferry landing; turn right as you exit the harbour. It has doubles, triples or four-bed rooms.

Getting There & Away

For information on ferries and hydrofoils, see the Danube Delta Getting Around section earlier in this section.

Slovakia

Slovakia's rugged High Tatra mountains, the gentler natural beauty of the Malá Fatra hills, and the canyons of the Slovenský raj offer some of the best terrain in Europe for outdoor activities. Best of all, these places are off the beaten track as most visitors don't get further than Bratislava.

Slovakia is also rich in architecture, arts and folk culture. Bratislava is a lively, cosmopolitan city with a rich cultural life, while East Slovakia boasts a treasury of unspoiled medieval towns. There are about 180 castles in Slovakia, the largest and most photogenic being Spišský hrad, east of Levoča.

Rural Slovaks still preserve their peasant traditions, evident in the colourful crafts and folk costumes you'll see in remote Slovak villages. The majority of Slovaks are warm and friendly people prepared to go out of their way to help you enjoy their country.

Facts about Slovakia

HISTORY

Slavic tribes first occupied what is now Slovakia in the 5th century AD. In 833, the prince of Moravia captured Nitra and formed the Great Moravian Empire, which included all of present Central and West Slovakia, the Czech Republic and parts of neighbouring Poland, Hungary and Germany. The empire converted to Christianity with the arrival of the missionaries, Cyril and Methodius, in 863.

In 907, the Great Moravian Empire collapsed as a result of the political intrigues of its rulers, and invasion by Hungary. By 1018 the whole of Slovakia was annexed to Hungary and remained so for the next 900 years (although the Spiš region of East Slovakia belonged to Poland from 1412 to 1772).

The Hungarians developed mining (silver, copper and gold) and trade (gold, amber and furs). After a Tatar invasion in the 13th century, the Hungarian king invited the Saxon Germans to settle the depopulated northeastern borderlands.

When the Turks overran Hungary in the early 16th century, the capital moved from Buda to Bratislava. After the creation of the

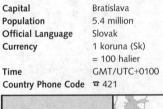

dual Austro-Hungarian monarchy in 1867, a policy of enforced Magyarisation was instituted in Slovakia. In 1907 Hungarian became the sole language of elementary education.

As a reaction to this, Slovak intellectuals cultivated increasingly closer cultural ties with the Czechs, who were themselves dominated by the Austrians. The concept of a single Czecho-Slovakian political entity was born

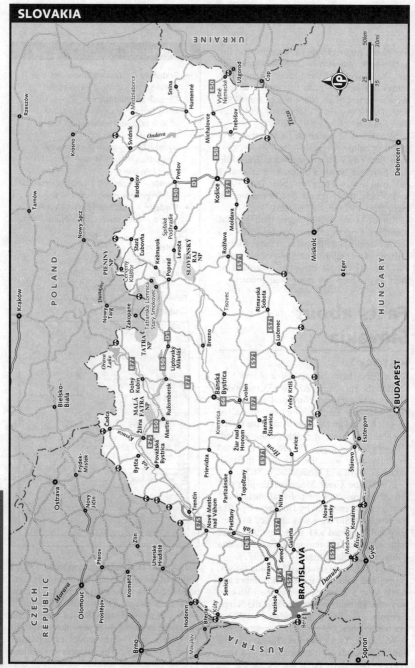

and, after the Austro-Hungarian defeat in WWI, Slovakia, Ruthenia, Bohemia and Moravia were united as Czechoslovakia.

The centralising tendencies of the sophisticated Czechs alienated many Slovaks. After the 1938 Munich Pact that forced Czechoslovakia to cede territory to Germany, Slovakia declared autonomy within a federal state. Hungary took advantage of this instability to annex a strip of southern Slovakia including Košice and Komárno. The day before Hitler's troops invaded Czech territory in March 1939, a fascist puppet state headed by Jozef Tiso (executed in 1947 as a war criminal) was set up, and Slovakia became a German ally.

In August 1944 Slovak partisans instigated the Slovak National Uprising (Slovenské národné povstanie, or SNP) against the Tiso regime, an event that is now a source of national pride. It took the Germans several months to crush the uprising. In the wake of Soviet advances in early 1945, a Czechoslovak government was established at Košice two months before the liberation of Prague.

The Czechoslovakia established after the war was to have been a federal state, but after the communist takeover in February 1948 power once again became centralised in Prague. Many of those who resisted the new communist dictatorship were ruthlessly eliminated by execution, torture and starvation in labour camps.

Although the 1960 constitution granted Czechs and Slovaks equal rights, only the 1968 'Prague Spring' reforms introduced by Alexander Dubček (a rehabilitated Slovak communist) implemented this concept. In August 1968, Soviet troops quashed democratic reform, and although the Czech and Slovak Republics theoretically became equal partners in a federal Czechoslovakia in 1969, the real power remained in Prague.

The Velvet Revolution of 1989 led to a resurgence of Slovak nationalism. In February 1992 the Slovak parliament rejected a treaty that would have perpetuated a federal Czechoslovakia.

The rift deepened with the June 1992 elections, which brought to power the nationalist Movement for a Democratic Slovakia (HZDS) headed by Vladimír Mečiar. In July the Slovak parliament voted to declare sovereignty. Mečiar held negotiations with his Czech counterpart Václav Klaus, but they could not reach a compromise. They subsequently agreed that the federation would peacefully dissolve on 1 January 1993.

Mečiar dominated Slovak politics for the next five years. His authoritarian rule gained control of most of the media, and the passing of antidemocratic laws (and the mistreatment of Slovakia's Hungarian and Roma minorities) attracted criticism from human rights groups, the EU and the US government.

Mečiar's controversial reign ended when Mikuláš Džurinda, leader of the right-leaning Slovak Democratic Coalition (SDK), was elected prime minister in 1998. Yet Slovak society remains deeply polarised. There is still strong support for Mečiar, who took 43% of the vote in the 1999 presidential election, narrowly losing to former communist Rudolf Schuster. Parliamentary elections held in September 2002 returned the ruling coalition of centre-right parties. Mr Mečiar's HZDS party gained the largest single vote at 19.5%, its poorest showing in a decade, but could not form a majority government.

The centre-right coalition, led by Džurinda, includes a new pro-business party ANO (New Citizens Alliance) headed by media mogul Pavol Rusko. The new government is expected to boost ties with the West and the path appears clear for Slovakia's entry into NATO by 2003 and the EU in 2004 or 2005.

GEOGRAPHY

Slovakia sits in the heart of Europe, straddling the northwestern end of the Carpathian Mountains. This hilly 49,035 sq km country forms a clear physical barrier between the plains of Poland and Hungary. Almost 80% of Slovakia is more than 750m above sea level, and forests, mainly beech and spruce, cover 40% of the country.

Southwestern Slovakia is a fertile lowland stretching from the foothills of the Carpathians down to the Danube (Dunaj in Slovak), which forms the border with Hungary from Bratislava to Štúrovo.

Central Slovakia is dominated by the Vysoké Tatry (High Tatras) mountains along the Polish border, Gerlachovský štít (2654m), the highest peak in the Carpathians, and the forested ridges of the Nízke Tatry, the Malá Fatra and the Veľká Fatra. South are the limestone ridges and caves of Slovenský raj and Slovenský kras. The longest river, the Váh, rises in the Tatras and flows 390km west and south to join the Danube at Komárno.

SLOVAKIA

CLIMATE

Slovakia generally experiences hot summers and cold winters. The warmest, driest and sunniest area is the Danube lowland, which is east of Bratislava.

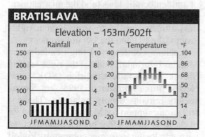

ECOLOGY & ENVIRONMENT

The Slovak environment is not as badly polluted as other European countries. The larger towns that have seen rapid industrialisation since WWII suffer most, especially Bratislava and Košice, but also Žilina and Trenčín. According to government figures, pollution has decreased since 1996.

Slovakia's first (Soviet-designed) nuclear power station was built at Bohunice nearby Trnava in the 1970s and supplies about a third of the country's electricity; the government has agreed to close it down by 2008. A second plant at Mochovce, east of Nitra, came online in June 1998, attracting protest from Austria.

The Gabčíkovo hydroelectric project on the Danube west of Komárno became highly controversial after Hungary backed out of the joint project in 1989 due to environmental considerations. Both countries are still negotiating on the project. Gabčíkovo produces enough electricity to cover the needs of every home in Slovakia and its canal allows the largest river vessels to reach Bratislava all year.

NATIONAL PARKS

Slovakia's national parks contain bears, marmots, wolves, lynxes, chamois, otters and minks. Deer, pheasants, partridges, ducks, wild geese, storks, grouse, eagles and other birds of prey can be seen across the country.

There are five national parks: Malá Fatra (east of Žilina), Nízke Tatry (between Banská Bystrica and Poprad), Tatra National Park (north of Poprad), Pieniny (along the Dunajec River) and Slovenský raj (near Spišská Nová Ves). In this chapter we cover all of these except Nízke Tatry.

GOVERNMENT & POLITICS

Slovakia is a parliamentary republic headed by the president (currently Rudolf Schuster), who is elected for a five-year term by the National Council; the next presidential election is in 2004. The president appoints and dismisses ministers. The cabinet is headed by the prime minister. The single-chamber National Council has 150 members, elected every four years by proportional representation.

ECONOMY

Since the break-up of Czechoslovakia in 1993 the Slovak economy has lagged behind its neighbour's. Following a slump from 1998 to 2001, growth was projected at 4% for 2002 and 2003. Unemployment remains very high at 18% (but up to 90% among the Roma), and the average monthly salary is just US$400.

Slovakia's manufacturing sector produces ceramics, chemicals, machinery, petroleum products, steel, textiles and weapons, and agriculture remains an important part of the economy with over one-third of the country under cultivation. Slovakia's main trading partners are Germany, the Czech Republic, Russia and Italy.

POPULATION & PEOPLE

Slovakia has a population of 5.4 million, of which 86% are Slovaks, 10% Hungarians and 1% Czechs. The 600,000 ethnic Hungarians live mostly in southern and eastern Slovakia. Official census figures from 1999 put the Roma population at just 1.7% (90,000), but the true figure is thought to be between 200,000 and 400,000.

The nomadic culture of the Roma has been destroyed by its assimilation into mainstream Slovak life under communist rule. Recently, as heavy industrial jobs have disappeared, many Slovak Roma have moved abroad. As elsewhere in Eastern Europe, there is much prejudice against Roma.

The largest cities are Bratislava (population 441,500), Košice (235,000), Prešov (92,000), Nitra (86,500) and Žilina (84,000).

ARTS

Slovakia has many outstanding buildings, paintings and sculptures by both foreign and local artists. Some of the most notable Gothic masterpieces can be found in St James' Church in Levoča, and there are magnificent Renaissance buildings in Bardejov.

SLOVAKIA

Slovak cinema first made its mark as part of the Czechoslovak 'New Wave' of the 1960s, with classic films like *Smrt si rika Engelchen* (Death Calls Itself Engelchen; 1963) directed by Ján Kádar and *Obchod na korze* (The Shop on the Main Street; 1965) by Elmar Klos. The Czechoslovak film industry stagnated after the 1968 Soviet invasion, and lack of funding has meant that little serious movie-making has been done since 1993. Martin Sulík is Slovakia's most promising new director, winning an Oscar nomination for *Všetko, čo mám rád* (Everything I Like, 1992), and receiving international acclaim for *Záhrada* (The Garden; 1995) and *Krajinka* (The Landscape; 2000).

Music

Traditional Slovak folk instruments include the *fujara* (a 2m-long flute), the *gajdy* (bagpipes) and the *konkovka* (a strident shepherd's flute). Folk songs helped preserve the Slovak language during Hungarian rule, and in East Slovakia ancient folk traditions are a living part of village life.

In classical music, the 19th-century works of Ján L Bela and the symphonies of Alexander Moyzes receive world recognition. A small rock and pop scene has produced the young singer-songwriter Jana Kirschner, whose second album *V Cudzom Meste* (In A Strange Town; 1999) went platinum.

SOCIETY & CONDUCT

Despite the surliness that Slovaks sometimes show to each other in service industries, they are generally friendly and hospitable. It is customary to say 'good day' (*dobrý den*) when you enter a shop, hotel or restaurant, and 'goodbye' (*do videnia*) when you leave. On public transport, younger people will readily give up their seats to the elderly and infirm.

If you are invited to someone's home, bring flowers for your hosts (an odd number – even numbers are for funerals!). If your hosts remove their shoes you should do the same. For a classical concert or theatre, men wear a suit and tie, while women wear a dinner dress. Casual dress is fine in contemporary venues, such as theatre or rock/jazz concerts.

RELIGION

Religion is taken seriously, with Roman Catholics forming the majority and Evangelicals also numerous; East Slovakia has many Greek Catholics and Orthodox believers.

LANGUAGE

Although many people working in tourism have a good knowledge of English, in rural Slovakia very few people speak anything other than Slovak. German is probably the most useful non-Slavic language. Any effort to communicate in Slovak will be appreciated.

Slovak is a West Slavic language, very closely related to Czech – the two languages are mutually comprehensible. See the Language chapter at the end of this book for details on Slovak pronunciation and some useful words and phrases. Lonely Planet's *Eastern Europe phrasebook* has a complete chapter on Slovak.

Facts for the Visitor

HIGHLIGHTS

Bratislava's old town and castle are worth exploring, as are the picturesque, historic towns of Bardejov, Levoča and Košice. Spišský hrad, towering above Spišské Podhradie, is the largest castle in the country.

The rocky peaks of the Vysoké Tatry and the wooded hills of the Slovenský raj offer excellent hiking and mountaineering, while the Malá Fatra has good hiking and skiing.

SUGGESTED ITINERARIES

Depending on the length of your stay, you could do the following things:

Two days
  Visit Bratislava and Devín Castle
One week
  Visit Bratislava, the Vysoké Tatry, Levoča and Košice

PLANNING
When to Go

Locals take their holidays in July and August, when the mountain areas like the Tatras and Malá Fatra are at their most crowded, but cities like Bratislava have lower hotel prices and cheap student dorm beds available. The accommodation options in the mountain resorts is cheapest from May to June and again from September to October.

Maps

The Austrian publisher Freytag & Berndt has a good map of Slovakia (*Slovenská republika*, 1:500,000). The whole country is covered by excellent 1:50,000 hiking maps published by

Vojenský kartografický ústav (VKÚ), which also produces more detailed skiing and hiking maps (1:25,000) and plans of major towns and cities.

TOURIST OFFICES
Local Tourist Offices

Slovakia has quite an extensive network of municipal information centres *(Mestské informačné centrum; ☎ 16 186)* belonging to the Association of Information Centres of Slovakia (AiCES). The staff speak English, organise sightseeing tours and guides, and can also assist with accommodation. Offices are normally open 8am to 6pm weekdays and to noon Saturday during summer (June to August), 9am to 5pm weekdays only the rest of the year.

Branches of the commercial agency Satur can also help with accommodation, and ISIC, Euro<26 and IYTC cards are available from some major offices.

Tourist Offices Abroad

The Slovak Tourist Board *(☎/fax 224 94 60 82; Purkyňova 4)* has an office in central Prague, but there is no representation of the Board in other countries.

VISAS & DOCUMENTS

Nationals of Canada, New Zealand and most European countries do not need a visa for tourist visits of up to 90 days (UK citizens up to 180 days; US, Italian and South African citizens up to 30 days). At the time of research, Australians *do* need a visa.

EMBASSIES & CONSULATES
Slovak Embassies

Slovak embassies abroad include:

Australia (☎ 02-6290 1516) 47 Culgoa Circuit, O'Malley, ACT 2606
Austria (☎ 01-318 90 55211) Armbrustergasse 24, 1-1190 Wien
Canada (☎ 613-749 4442) 50 Rideau Terrace, Ottawa, Ontario K1M 2A1
Czech Republic (☎ 233 32 54 43) Pod Hradbami 1, 160 00 Praha 6
France (☎ 01 45 20 78 75) 125 rue de Ranelagh, 75016 Paris
Germany (☎ 030-889 26 20) Pariser Strasse 44, Berlin 107 07 Berlin
Hungary (☎ 01-273 35 00) Stefania ut 22-24, H-1143 Budapest XIV
Netherlands (☎ 070-416 7773) Parkweg 1, 2585 JG The Hague

Poland (☎ 022-525 81 10) Litevska 6, 00-581 Warszawa
UK (☎ 020-7313 6490) 25 Kensington Palace Gardens, London W8 4QY
Ukraine (☎ 044-229 79 22) Jaroslavov val 34, 252 034 Kyiv
USA (☎ 202-237 1054) 3523 International Court NW, Washington, DC 20008

Embassies & Consulates in Slovakia

Australia and New Zealand do not have embassies in Slovakia; the nearest are in Vienna and Berlin respectively. The following are all in Bratislava (area code ☎ 02).

Austria (☎ 54 43 29 85) Ventúrska 10
Czech Republic (☎ 59 20 33 03) Hviezdoslavovo 8
France (☎ 59 34 71 11) Hlavné nám 7
Germany (☎ 54 41 96 40) Hviezdoslavovo nám 10
Hungary (☎ 54 43 05 41) Sedlárska 3
Poland (☎ 54 41 31 96) Hummelova 4
UK (☎ 54 41 96 32) Panská 16
Ukraine (☎ 59 20 28 16) Radvanská 35
USA (☎ 54 43 08 61) Hviezdoslavovo nám 4

CUSTOMS

If you're over 18 years of age, you can bring in 2L of wine, 1L of spirits and 250 cigarettes, along with reasonable personal effects and up to 3000 Sk worth of gifts and other noncommercial goods.

You cannot export genuine antiques. The customs officers are very strict and will readily confiscate goods that are even slightly suspect. If you have any doubts about what you are planning to take out of the country, check with the curatorial staff at the National Museum in Bratislava.

Arriving visitors may be asked to prove they have at least US$50 a day for each day of their stay (or a credit card), but this is rarely enforced. You may also be asked for proof of medical insurance.

MONEY
Currency

Slovakia's currency is the Slovak crown *(Slovenská koruna;* Sk), containing 100 hellers *(halier)*. There are coins of 10, 20 and 50 hellers, and one, two, five and 10 crowns (Sk). Banknotes come in denominations of 20, 50, 100, 200, 500, 1000 and 5000 crowns.

Exchange Rates

As this book went to print, the Slovenská koruna (Sk) was officially worth:

country	unit		koruna
Australia	A$1	=	24.55 Sk
Canada	C$1	=	28.86 Sk
Euro Zone	€1	=	44.52 Sk
Japan	¥100	=	37.91 Sk
NZ	NZ$1	=	21.31 Sk
UK	UK£1	=	70.93 Sk
USA	US$1	=	45.38 Sk

Exchanging Money

The easiest place to change cash and travellers cheques is at a branch of the Všeobecná úverová banka (VÚB; General Credit Bank), Slovenská sporiteľňa (Slovak Savings Bank) or Investičná banka (Investment Bank) where there's a standard 1% commission. Satur offices and the post office exchange windows charge 2% commission. Banks often give a slightly better rate for travellers cheques than for cash. Most banks are open 8am or 9am to 4pm or 5pm weekdays (some close for 30 minutes noon and 1.30pm).

Credit cards (Visa, MasterCard, Eurocard and AmEx) can be used in most major hotels, restaurants and shops. Some of the larger branches of major banks give cash advances on credit cards. ATMs (bankomat) are easily found in most towns, and most accept Visa, MasterCard, Eurocard, Plus and Cirrus.

Some exchange places may not accept damaged US dollar notes.

Costs

Slovakia is still a bargain compared to the Czech Republic. You'll find food, admissions and transport are cheap and accommodation is manageable, except in Bratislava. If you camp or stay in hostels, eat in local pubs and take local transport, expect to spend about US$15 to US$20 a day. Students usually get 50% off the entry price at museums and galleries.

POST & COMMUNICATIONS
Post

Airmail is fairly reliable, but don't post anything valuable. Express Mail Services are available from most post offices, but if you are mailing a parcel over 2kg from Slovakia, it has to be sent from a customs office (colnica; open 8am to 3pm weekdays); post office staff will direct you to the nearest one. Poste restante mail can be sent to major post offices in larger cities and will be kept for one month; it should be addressed to Poste Restante, Pošta 1.

A postcard/letter (20g) to European countries is 10/14 Sk and elsewhere 14/18 Sk by airmail). A 2kg parcel to most European countries costs 650 Sk airmail. Most post offices are open 7am or 8am to 5pm or 8pm weekdays and to noon Saturday. In large cities and towns they also open 8am to noon Sunday.

Telephone

Slovakia's telephone system has been overhauled and modernised in the last few years. All the area codes were changed in July 2001; the old codes (beginning with ☎ 07 to 09) no longer work, but still appear on some signs and publicity materials. For directory inquiries call ☎ 120 (for the region you are calling from) or ☎ 121 (for numbers elsewhere in Slovakia). For international enquiries call ☎ 0149.

Direct-dial international calls can be made at post offices, telephone centres and most public phones on the street (look for the green or blue sticker saying 'international'). Most public telephones now accept phonecards only, though a few still take coins. Phonecards (telefónna karta) costing 60 Sk, 100 Sk, 140 Sk, 180 Sk or 350 Sk are available from post offices and any shop displaying the phonecard logo. A peak-rate (7am to 7pm weekdays), three-minute direct-dial call from Slovakia will cost about 30 Sk to the UK, France, Canada and USA; 30 Sk to South Africa; 38 Sk to Australia; and 90 Sk to New Zealand.

To call Slovakia from abroad, dial the international access code, then dial ☎ 421 (the country code for Slovakia), then the area code (minus the initial zero) and the number. The international access code in Slovakia is ☎ 00. For further information and a list of country and access codes see 'Appendix – Telephones' at the back of this book.

The Country Direct service is available in Slovakia (get a full list of countries and numbers from any telephone office or directory). Useful numbers include:

Australia Direct	☎ 0800 006101
Canada Direct	☎ 0800 000151
Canada (AT&T)	☎ 0800 000152
Deutschland Direct	☎ 0800 004949
France Direct	☎ 0800 003301
Netherlands	☎ 0800 003101
UK Direct (BT)	☎ 0800 004401
USA (AT&T)	☎ 0800 000101
USA (MCI)	☎ 0800 000112
USA (Sprint)	☎ 0800 087187

SLOVAKIA

Fax & Telegram

Telegrams can be sent from most post offices, while faxes can only be sent from certain major post offices.

Email & Internet Access

There are Internet cafés in most large towns and tourist centres.

DIGITAL RESOURCES

The Slovakia Document Store at **w** slovakia .eunet.sk contains links to a wealth of information on Slovakia. For up-to-date news and current affairs check out the websites of The Slovak Spectator (**w** www.slovakspectator .sk) and Slovakia.org (**w** www.slovakia.org). Most Slovak towns maintain a website; eg, **w** www.kosice.sk for Košice's.

BOOKS

For a very readable history try Stanislav J Kirschbaum's *A History of Slovakia – The Struggle for Survival*. William Shawcross' *Dubček & Czechoslovakia* is a biography of the late leader and an account of the 1968 Prague Spring. One of the few fictional works readily available in English translation is *The Year of the Frog* by Martin Šimečka, a story about a young intellectual who is made a social outcast by the communist government for his political views.

Lonely Planet's *Czech & Slovak Republics* by Richard Nebeský & Neil Wilson gives extensive information on the nuts and bolts of travelling in Slovakia.

NEWSPAPERS & MAGAZINES

The Slovak Spectator (35 Sk) is a weekly Bratislava-based, English-language paper that includes the latest information on what's happening in the city. In Bratislava and most major tourist centres the main European and US newspapers and magazines are available.

RADIO & TV

BBC English-language programmes are available 24 hours in Bratislava on FM 93.8 and in Košice on FM 103.2. Hotel room TVs with satellite connections can receive English-language channels such as Sky News, Eurosport and BBC World.

TIME

The time in Slovakia is GMT/UTC plus one hour. At the end of March Slovakia goes on summer time and clocks are set forward an hour. At the end of October they're turned back an hour.

WOMEN TRAVELLERS

Slovakia's rate of sexual violence is low in comparison to that of Western countries and assaults on solo female travellers are rare.

GAY & LESBIAN TRAVELLERS

Homosexuality has been legal since the 1960s and the age of consent is 16, but gay or lesbian partners do not have the same legal status as heterosexual partners.

There is a gay-support organisation called **Ganymedes** (☎ *02-52 49 57 96; PO Box 4, 830 00 Bratislava*). The lesbian organisation is **Museion** (e *vamo@ba.psg.sk; Saratovská 3, 841 02 Bratislava for postal inquiries only*).

DISABLED TRAVELLERS

There are very few facilities for disabled people. Transport is a major problem as buses and trams have no wheelchair access. KFC and McDonald's entrances and toilets are wheelchair friendly. For more information contact the **Alliance of Organisations of Disabled People in Slovakia** (*Asociácia organizácií zdravotne postihnutých občanov SR*; ☎ *02-52 44 41 19*; **w** *www.zutom.sk/ aozpo; Žabotova 2, 811 04 Bratislava*).

DANGERS & ANNOYANCES

Crime is low compared with the West. Some Bratislava taxi drivers have been known to overcharge foreigners and in touristy places some waiters occasionally overcharge. Another problem is the increasing number of robberies on international trains passing through the country. Sometimes the passengers are gassed to sleep in their compartments and then relieved of their valuables.

Bad driving – especially dangerous overtaking – is a widespread problem.

Confusingly, buildings on some streets have two sets of numbers. The blue number is the actual street number while the red number

---

Emergency Services

In the event of an emergency call ☎ 158 for state police, ☎ 150 for fire, ☎ 155 for ambulance, ☎ 154 for car breakdown assistance. These numbers can be dialled nationwide.

is the old registration number. The streets themselves are sometimes poorly labelled.

Recent years have seen a rise in violent racist attacks by skinhead gangs on Roma people, and also on dark-skinned tourists.

BUSINESS HOURS

On weekdays, shops open at around 8am or 9am and close at 5pm or 6pm. Many small shops, particularly those in country areas, close for up to an hour for lunch between noon and 2pm, and almost everything closes on Saturday afternoon and all day Sunday. Major department stores open on weekends and stay open until 7pm on Thursday and Friday. Most restaurants are open every day but smaller ones often close by 9pm or even earlier.

Most museums and castles are closed on Monday and the day following a public holiday. Many tourist attractions are closed from November to March and open on weekends only in April and October. Staff at some isolated sights take an hour off for lunch. The main town museums stay open all year.

PUBLIC HOLIDAYS & SPECIAL EVENTS

Public holidays are New Year's and Independence Day (1 January), Three Kings Day (6 January), Good Friday and Easter Monday (March/April), Labour Day (1 May), Cyril and Methodius Day (5 July), SNP Day (29 August), Constitution Day (1 September), Our Lady of Sorrows Day (15 September), All Saints' Day (1 November) and Christmas (24 to 26 December).

During late June or early July folk dancers from all over Slovakia meet at the Východná Folklore Festival, 32km west of Poprad. There are folk festivals in June in Červený Kláštor and Kežmarok, and in many other towns from June to August. The two-week Bratislava Music Festival is held from late September to early October, and the Bratislava Jazz Days weekend is in late October.

ACTIVITIES

Slovakia is one of Eastern Europe's best areas for hiking (see the Malá Fatra, Vysoké Tatry and Slovenský raj sections for details). There is excellent rock climbing and mountaineering in the Vysoké Tatry, and paragliding is also becoming popular. Contact the **Mountain Guide** (Horský Vodca; ☎ 052-442 22 60) office in Starý Smokovec for more information.

Slovakia offers some of the best cycling terrain in Central Europe, with uncrowded roads and beautiful scenery. East Slovakia especially is prime cycling territory. Mountain biking in the Vysoké Tatry and Slovenský raj is excellent. **Tatrasport** (☎ 055-442 52 41) has branches in Starý Smokovec, Štrbské Pleso and Tatranská Lomnica and rents out mountain bikes for 299 Sk a day.

Slovakia has some of Europe's cheapest ski resorts, but the skiable areas are small and few lifts are linked. The season runs from December to April in the Vysoké Tatry, Nízke Tatry and Malá Fatra. There is good downhill and cross-country skiing in the Vysoké Tatry and the Malá Fatra. Ski and snowboard gear is available for hire at very competitive rates, but the waits at uplift can be excruciatingly long during the peak season.

Some of Slovakia's major rivers such as the Váh, Hron and Nitra offer good canoeing and kayaking. **T-Ski** (☎ 055-442 32 00) in Starý Smokovec can arrange rafting trips (from 580 Sk per person). For information on rafting on the Dunajec River in Pieniny National Park, see the Dunajec Gorge section.

WORK

The unemployment rate in Slovakia is high and there are not many job opportunities for non-Slovak speakers. Your best bet is to find a job teaching English. The **British Council** (☎ 02-54 43 17 93; Panská 17, Bratislava) has a teaching centre in Bratislava, or try the **Berlitz Language Centre** (☎ 02-54 43 37 96; Na vŕšku 6, Bratislava).

ACCOMMODATION

Foreigners can often pay 30% to 100% more for accommodation than Slovaks. Unless otherwise stated, all prices quoted for rooms are for a single/double/triple/quad.

Accommodation in the mountain resorts can be up to 50% cheaper in the low season (usually May to June and October to November); prices quoted in this chapter are for the high season.

Camping

There are several hundred camping grounds around the country, usually open from May to September. They're often accessible on public transport, but there's usually no hot water. Most have a small snack bar and many have small cabins for rent that are cheaper than a hotel room. Camping wild in national parks is prohibited.

Hostels

The Hostelling International (HI) handbook lists an impressive network of hostels, but they're mostly open in July and August only, and usually full. In July and August many student dormitories become temporary hostels. Satur and municipal information offices usually have information on hostels and can make advance bookings for you.

Tourist hostels *(Turistické ubytovňy)*, which provide very basic and cheap dormitory accommodation, are not connected to the HI network. You should ask about them at information offices.

Private Rooms & Pensions

Private rooms (look for signs reading *'privát'* or *'Zimmer frei'*) are usually available in tourist areas (from 200 Sk per person). AiCES tourist information offices and travel agencies like Satur can book them. Some have a three-night minimum-stay requirement.

Many small pensions (often just glorified private rooms) exist in tourist regions, and these offer more personalised service and cheaper rates than hotels.

Hotels

Hotels in Bratislava are considerably more expensive than in the rest of the country. There are five categories, from one star (budget) to five star (luxury). Two-star rooms are typically US$15/20, three-star around US$25/40 (but up to US$60 in Bratislava).

FOOD

The cheapest eateries are the self-service restaurants called *jedáleň* or *bistro*, which sometimes have tasty dishes like barbecued chicken or hot German-style sausage. Train station buffets and busy beer halls are also cheap. If the place is crowded with locals, is noisy and looks chaotic, chances are it will have great lunch specials at low prices.

Lunches are generally bigger and cheaper than dinners. Dinner is usually eaten early, between 6pm and 7pm. Don't expect to be served at any restaurant if you arrive within half an hour of closing time.

The Slovak for menu is *jedálny lístok*. The main categories are *predjedlá* (starters), *polievky* (soups), *hotová jedlá* (ready-to-serve

dishes), *jedlá na objednávku* (dishes prepared as they are ordered), *mäsité jedlá* (meat dishes), *ryby* (fish), *zelenina* (vegetables), *šaláty* (salads), *ovoce* (fruit), *zákusok* (dessert) and *nápoje* (drinks). Anything that comes with *knedle* (dumplings) will be a hearty meal.

Vegetarians are catered for at a small but increasing number of restaurants and health-food shops, although in small towns you might be restricted to salads and *vysmážaný syr* (deep-fried cheese). Note that many of the innocent-looking vegetable-based soups may use a ham or beef stock, and dishes advertised as 'vegetarian' *(bezmasa)* may actually contain meat!

Tipping is optional. If you were happy with the service, you could round up the bill to the next 5 Sk (or to the next 10 Sk if the bill is over 100 Sk).

Cafés (*kaviáreň* or *cukráreň*) offer cakes, puddings and coffee as good as anything you'll find in neighbouring Austria at a fraction of the price.

Local Specialities

Soups include *cesnaková polievka* (garlic soup), a treat that is not to be missed. Slovakia's traditional dish is *bryndžové halušky* (dumplings baked with sheep's-milk cheese and bits of bacon).

Meat dishes come with potatoes – either boiled, fried or as chips. Goulash or *segedín* (also known as *kološárska kapusta* – a beef goulash with sauerkraut in cream sauce) comes with *knedle*. *Kapor* (carp) or *pstruh* (trout) can be crumbed and fried or baked. *Ovocné knedle* or *guľky* (fruit dumplings), with whole fruit inside, come with cottage cheese or crushed poppy seeds, as well as melted butter.

DRINKS

Slovak wine is good and cheap. Well-known brands include Tokaj from southern Slovakia, and Kláštorné (a red) and Venušíno čáro (a white), both from the Modra region north of Bratislava.

Slovak *pivo* (beer) is as good as Czech – try Zlatý Bažant from Hurbanovo or Martiner from Martin.

Coffee is usually served Turkish-style *(turecká káva)* with sludgy grounds in the cup. For ordinary black/white coffee order *espresso/espresso s mliekom*. Tea *(čaj)* can be enjoyed in a tearoom *(čajovná)*.

SHOPPING
Good buys include china, Bohemian crystal, jewellery, folk ceramics, garnets, fancy leather goods, special textiles, lace, embroidery, shoes, colour-photography books and souvenirs. Antiques and valuable-looking artworks are closely scrutinised by customs.

Getting There & Away

AIR
Bratislava's MR Štefanik airport receives only a small number of flights from continental Europe. Vienna's Schwechat airport is just 60km from Bratislava, and is served by a vast range of much cheaper international flights.

Czech Airlines (ČSA) flies between Bratislava and Prague several times every day with connections to major European cities, New York, Montreal and Toronto. Return flights from New York to Bratislava (via Prague) can cost as little as US$600, and London to Bratislava (via Prague) from £225. See also Air under Getting There & Away in the Bratislava section.

LAND
Bus
Seven buses a day (four at the weekend) link Bratislava to Schwechat airport in Vienna (€7.20, one hour) and central Mitte Busbahnhof (€10.90, 1½ hours). See also Getting There & Away in the Bratislava section.

Train
There are trains from Bratislava to Vienna (Südbahnhof) five times daily (one hour). From Vienna there are connections to most Western European cities and there are several express trains daily from Bratislava to Budapest (three hours). See Getting There & Away in the Bratislava section. Daily sleeper services travel to Kyiv, Ukraine, changing at Košice (30 hours, 1443km), and to Moscow, changing at Warsaw (33 hours, 1991km).

There are three expresses a day between Košice and Muszyna (1¼ hours) in Poland. From Muszyna trains travel to Nowy Sącz and (less frequently) to Kraków. There's also a daily train from Košice to Bucharest (15½ hours). See also the Košice Getting There & Away section in this chapter.

Car & Motorcycle
There is only one border crossing to/from Austria (at Berg, southwest of Bratislava) and to/from Ukraine (at Vyšne nemecké), but there are plenty of options to/from the Czech Republic, Hungary and Poland.

RIVER
See Boat under Getting There & Away in the Bratislava section.

Getting Around

BUS
Intercity bus travel, operated by the various branches of Slovenská autobusová doprava (SAD), is generally slower and less comfortable than the train, and not much cheaper. Departures are less frequent, and weekend services are more sharply reduced than rail services. One-way bus tickets cost around 24/46/96/190 Sk for 25/50/100/200km. It is advisable to arrive at least 10 minutes before departure time.

When trying to decipher bus schedules beware of departure times bearing footnotes you don't completely understand. Check the time at the information window whenever possible. It is helpful to know that *premáva* means 'it operates' and *nepremáva* means 'it doesn't operate'.

TRAIN
Slovak Republic Railways (*Železnice Slovenskej republiky* or *ŽSR*) provides a cheap and efficient service. One-way fares (2nd class) are 24/48/98/196 Sk for 25/50/100/200km; the surcharge for express services is around 20 Sk to 70 Sk. Most of the places covered in this chapter are on or near the main railway line between Bratislava and Košice.

By express train from Bratislava it's 1¾ hours to Trenčín, almost three hours to Žilina, five hours to Poprad, 5½ hours to Spišská Nová Ves, and 6½ hours to Košice.

Most train stations in Slovakia have a left-luggage office (*úschovňa*) where you can leave your bag for 10 Sk to 20 Sk, and/or lockers for 5 Sk. When using lockers, remember to set the combination dial inside the door *before* you close it.

The Czech website **W** www.vlak-bus.cz has Slovakia's national railway and bus timetables online.

SLOVAKIA

CAR & MOTORCYCLE

There are plenty of petrol stations. Leaded petrol is available as *special* (91 octane) and *super* (96 octane), unleaded as *natural* (95 octane) or *natural plus* (98 octane); diesel is *nafta* or just *diesel*. Natural 95 costs around 33 Sk a litre, diesel 30 Sk.

Road Rules

You can drive in Slovakia using your own licence. Speed limits are 40km/h to 60km/h in built-up areas, 90km/h on open roads and 130km/h on motorways; motorbikes are limited to 90km/h. At level crossings over railway lines the speed limit is 30km/h. Beware of speed traps (usually just outside the city limits) as the police can levy on-the-spot fines of up to 2000 Sk.

In order to use the motorways in Slovakia (which are denoted by green signs), all drivers must purchase a motorway sticker (*nálepka*), which should be displayed in the windscreen. You can buy stickers at border crossings, petrol stations or Satur offices (100 Sk for 15 days, 600 Sk for a year, for vehicles up to 1.5 tonnes). You can be fined 5000 Sk if you don't have a sticker.

Rental

Avis has offices in Bratislava and Košice. Its cheapest cars cost around 1650 Sk a day including unlimited kilometres and Collision Damage Waiver. There are much cheaper local companies (see Getting Around in the Bratislava section). Cars hired in the Czech Republic can usually be driven into Slovakia without extra insurance, but not vice versa – check with the rental company.

BICYCLE

Cyclists should be aware that roads are often narrow and potholed, and in towns the cobblestones and tram tracks can be a dangerous combination, especially when it has been raining. Theft is a problem in large cities, so a good chain and lock are a must.

It's fairly easy to transport bikes on trains. First purchase your train ticket and then take it with your bicycle to the railway luggage office. There you fill out a card, which will be attached to your bike. You will be given a receipt that should list all the accessories on your bike, such as lights and dynamo. The cost of transporting a bicycle is usually 10% of the train ticket.

HITCHING

Slovakia is no safer than other European countries when it comes to hitching: many hitchers are assaulted and/or raped, and each year a few are killed. Despite these dangers many Slovaks, including young women travelling alone, choose to hitch.

LOCAL TRANSPORT

City buses and trams operate from around 4.30am to 11.30pm daily. Tickets are sold at public transport offices, from ticket machines and newsstands and must be validated once you're aboard.

Bratislava

☎ 02 • pop 441,500

Bratislava is Slovakia's capital and largest city. Here the Carpathian Mountains, which stretch 1200km from the Iron Gate of Romania, finally slope down to the Danube. The Austrian border is almost within sight of the city and Hungary is just 16km away.

Founded in AD 907, Bratislava was already a large city in the 12th century. Commerce developed in the 14th and 15th centuries, and in 1467 the Hungarian Renaissance monarch Matthias Corvinus founded a university here, the Academia Istropolitana. The city became Hungary's capital in 1541, after the Turks captured Buda, and remained so from 1563 to 1830. In St Martin's Cathedral 11 Hungarian kings and seven queens were crowned. Bratislava flourished during the reign of Maria Teresa of Austria (1740–80) when some imposing baroque palaces were built. In 1918 the city was included in the newly formed Republic of Czechoslovakia, in 1969 it became the state capital of a federal Slovak Republic, and in 1993 it was named the capital of an independent Slovakia.

Many beautiful monuments survive in the old town to tell of its past under Hungarian rule, and Bratislava's numerous museums are surprisingly rich. The opera productions of the Slovak National Theatre rival anything in Europe. Bratislava isn't as swamped by Western tourism as are Budapest and Prague (except on weekends when the Austrians invade).

Orientation

Hviezdoslavova nám is a convenient reference point, with the old town to the north, the

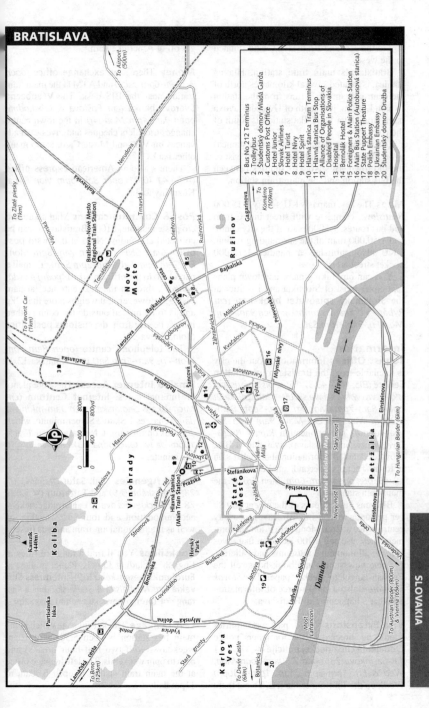

BRATISLAVA

1	Bus No 212 Terminus
2	Trolleybus
3	Študentský domov Mladá Garda
4	Customs Post Office
5	Slovak Airlines
6	Hotel Junior
7	Hotel Turist
8	Hotel Nivy
9	Hotel Spirit
10	Hlavná stanica Tram Terminus
11	Hlavná stanica Bus Stop
12	Alliance of Organisations of Disabled People in Slovakia
13	Hospital
14	Bernolák Hostel
15	Foreigners & Main Police Station
16	Main Bus Station (Autobusová stanica)
17	State Puppet Theatre
18	Polish Embassy
19	Ukrainian Embassy
20	Študentský domov Družba

SLOVAKIA

Danube to the south, the Slovak National Theatre to the east and Bratislava Castle siutated to the west.

Bratislava's main train station, Hlavná stanica, is located several kilometres north of the centre. Tram No 1 runs from the station to nám L Štúra, just south of Hviezdoslavova nám. Bratislava-Petržalka station is south of the river.

The main bus station (autobusová stanica) is on Mlynské nivy, a little over 1km east of the old town. Bus No 210 shuttles between the bus station and the main train station.

Maps The best map is VKÚ's hefty 1:15,000 *Bratislava*, complete with street index, tram and bus routes, 1:5000 plan of the city centre and 1:50,000 map of the surrounding region. VKÚ also publishes a handier 1:15,000 pocket street atlas.

You can buy hiking maps and town plans that cover most of Slovakia and its cities at the **Slovenský spisovatel bookshop** *(cnr Rybárska brána & Laurinská; open 9am-6pm Mon-Fri, 9am-1pm Sat)*.

Information
Tourist Offices Information about the city is available from the **Bratislava Information Service** *(BIS; ☎ 54 43 37 15; e bis@bratislava .sk; w www.bratislava.sk/bis; Klobučnícka 2; open 8am-7pm Mon-Fri June-Sept, 9am-5.30pm Mon-Fri Oct-May, 9am-1pm Sat year-round)*. The publication *Kam v Bratislave* (Where in Bratislava), available at BIS, provides detailed information about what's on in town. There is a second, smaller **BIS** *(☎ 52 49 59 06; open 9am-6pm Mon-Fri)* at the main train station.

BIS runs guided tours of the city at 300 Sk per person; a tour in English leaves their city centre office at 2pm Monday to Friday in summer. They also sell a 100 Sk ticket that gives entry to all municipal museums and galleries.

Some newsstands and bookshops sell the English-language weekly paper *The Slovak Spectator*, also a good source of information on what's happening in Bratislava.

Visa Extensions Visa or passport inquiries should be directed to the foreigners police **Oddelenie cudzineckej polície** *(☎ 61 01 11 11; Sasinkova 23; open 7.30am-noon Mon, Wed & Fri, 1pm-3pm Mon, 1pm-5.30pm Wed)*, on the 1st floor to the left. To get there

take tram No 4, 6, 7 or 11 from Špitalská and get off at Americké nám.

Money There's an **exchange office** *(open 7.30am-6pm daily)* and ATM at the main train station near the BIS desk. The **Všeobecná úverová banka** *(cnr Poštová & Obchodná; open 9am-4pm Mon-Fri)* in the town centre changes travellers cheques and gives cash advances on Visa and MasterCard, as do many other banks.

There's also an **American Express office** *(☎ 54 41 40 01; open 8am-5pm Mon-Fri)* at Kuzmányho 8.

Post & Communications Mail addressed c/o poste restante, 81000 Bratislava 1, can be collected at window No 6 at the **main post office** *(nám SNP 34; open 7am-8pm Mon-Fri, 7am-6pm Sat, 9am-2pm Sun)*. To mail a parcel, go to the office marked '*podaj a výdaj balíkov*', through the next entrance, at nám SNP 35. However, if it weighs more than 2kg and is to be mailed outside the country then it must be sent from the **customs post office** *(Tomášikova 54)*.

The **telephone centre** *(open 8am-7pm Mon-Fri, 9am-1pm Sat)* is at Kolárska 12.

Email & Internet Access There are plenty of Internet cafés. **Internet Centrum** *(cnr Michalská & Sedlárska; open 9am-midnight daily)* charges 1 Sk to 2 Sk per minute, which depends on time used. **Netcafe** *(open 10am-10pm daily; Obchodná 53)* charges 1.5 Sk per minute.

Travel Agencies Both **Satur** *(☎ 55 41 01 28; Jesenského 5-9)* and **Tatratour** *(☎ 52 92 78 88; Mickiewiczova 2)* can arrange tickets, accommodation and tours in Slovakia, as well as international air, train and bus tickets.

Bookshops You'll find a range of titles in English, including Lonely Planet guides, at **Eurobooks** *(Jesenského 5-9)*. **Interpress Slovakia** *(cnr Michalská & Sedlárska)* has a vast range of foreign newspapers and magazines.

Left Luggage The left-luggage office at the main bus station is open 5.30am to 10pm weekdays (with two half-hour breaks) and 6am to 6pm weekends. The left-luggage office at the main train station is open 6.30am to 11pm daily.

Ascending the barren Lomnický štít, High Tatras, Slovakia

Levoča, Slovakia

Enjoy autumn's artistry around the alpine lake of Štrbské pleso in the High Tatras, Slovakia

Street café, Ljubljana, Slovenia

Hire a gondola to visit the island church in Lake Bled, Slovenia

Cossack musician, Ukraine

The bustle of modern life along the old streets of Lviv, Ukraine

Historic buildings and parklands roll down the hill to meet the port on Kyiv's waterfront, Ukraine

The rounded Meded rises above alpine Black Lake, Montenegro

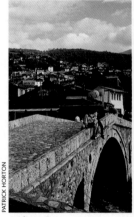

Bridging Prizren, Kosovo

Medical & Emergency Services For medical emergencies call ☎ 155. The main outpatient clinic is at the **hospital** on Mýtna 5. There's a 24-hour pharmacy *(lekáreň)* at nám SNP 20.

The main police station *(polícia)* is located at Sasinkova 23.

Things to See & Do

You could begin your exploring at the **Slovak National Museum** *(adult/child 20/10 Sk, free last Sun of month; open 9am-5pm Tues-Sun)*, built in 1928, opposite the hydrofoil terminal on the river. The museum features anthropology, archaeology, natural history and geology exhibits, with a large relief map of Slovakia.

Further west along the riverfront is the overhanging facade of the **Slovak National Gallery** *(Rázusovo nábrežie 2; adult/child 20/10 Sk; open 10am-6pm Tues-Sun)*, which houses Bratislava's major art collection. The controversial modern building daringly incorporates an 18th-century palace.

Backtrack slightly to nám L Štúra where you'll find the neobaroque **Reduta Palace** (1914), which is now Bratislava's main concert hall. Go north up Mostová to the recently renovated Hviezdoslavovo nám, a broad, tree-lined space dominated by the flamboyant **Slovak National Theatre** (1886) on the right, with Ganymede's Fountain (1888) in front.

Crowded, narrow Rybárska brána runs through the old town to Hlavné nám; at the centre is Roland's Fountain (1572). To one side is the old town hall (1421), now the **Municipal Museum** *(admission 25 Sk; open 10am-5pm Tues-Sun)*, with torture chambers in the cellar and an extensive historical collection housed in finely decorated rooms. You enter the museum from the picturesque inner courtyard, where concerts are held in summer.

Leave the courtyard through the east gate and you'll be on the square in front of the **Primate's Palace** (1781). Enter to see the Hall of Mirrors where Napoleon and the Austrian emperor Franz I signed a peace treaty in 1805. In the municipal gallery on the 2nd floor are rare English tapestries (1632). St George's Fountain stands in the courtyard. On Saturday, the palace is crowded with couples being married, but it's still open to visitors.

Return through the old town hall courtyard and turn left into Radničná 1 to find the **Museum of Wine Production** *(adult/child 20/10 Sk; open 9.30am-4.30pm Wed-Mon)* in

the Apponyi Palace (1762). You can buy a museum guidebook in English. Next, head north on Františkánske nám to the **Franciscan Church** (1297). The original Gothic chapel, with the skeleton of a saint enclosed in glass, is accessible through a door on the left near the front. Opposite this church is the **Mirbach Palace** *(Františkánske nám 11; adult/child 40/20 Sk, free 1st Sat of month; open 10am-5pm Tues-Sun)*, built in 1770, which is a beautiful rococo building that now houses a good collection of art.

From the palace continue along narrow Zámočnícka to the **Michael Tower** *(adult/child 20/10; open 10am-5pm Tues-Fri, 11am-6pm Sat & Sun May-Sept, 9.30am-4.30pm Tues-Sun Oct-Apr)*, with a collection of antique arms and a great view from the top. Stroll south down Michalská to the **Palace of the Royal Chamber** *(Michalská 1)*, built in 1756. Now the university library, this building was once the seat of the Hungarian parliament. In 1848 serfdom was abolished here.

Take the passage west through the palace to the Gothic **Church of the Clarissine Order**, which has a pentagonal tower (1360) supported by buttresses. Continue west on Farská, then turn left into Kapitulská and go straight ahead to the 15th-century coronation church, **St Martin's Cathedral**. Inside is a bronze statue (1734) of St Martin cutting off half his robe for a beggar.

The busy motorway in front of St Martin's follows the moat of the former city walls. Construction of this route and the adjacent bridge was controversial as several of the city's historic structures had to be pulled down and vibrations from the traffic have structurally weakened the cathedral. Find the passage under the motorway and head up towards **Bratislava Castle**, built above the Danube on the southernmost spur of the Little Carpathian Mountains.

From the 1st to the 5th centuries, Bratislava Castle was a frontier post of the Roman Empire. Since the 9th century the castle has been rebuilt several times; it was the seat of Hungarian royalty until it burnt down in 1811.

Reconstructed between 1953 and 1962, the castle now has a large **Historical Museum** *(adult/child 40/20 Sk; open 9am-5pm Tues-Sun)* in the main building, and the interesting **Museum of Folk Music** *(adult/child 40/20 Sk; open 9am-5pm Tues-Sun)* in a northern wing. Climb up to the castle grounds for a

SLOVAKIA

CENTRAL BRATISLAVA

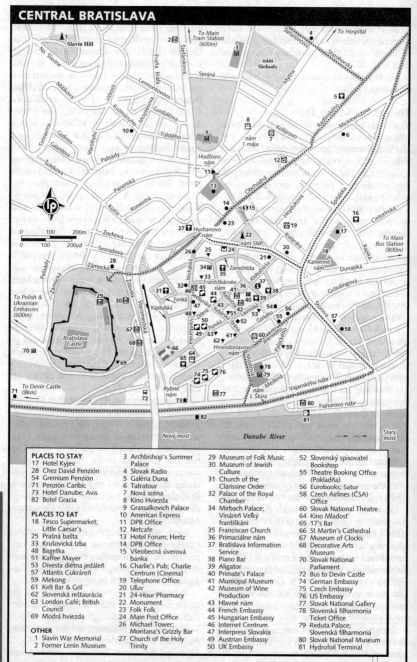

PLACES TO STAY
17 Hotel Kyjev
28 Chez David Penzión
54 Gremium Penzión
71 Penzión Caribic
73 Hotel Danube; Avis
82 Botel Gracia

PLACES TO EAT
18 Tesco Supermarket;
   Little Caesar's
25 Prašná bašta
33 Krušovická Izba
48 Bagetka
51 Kaffee Mayer
53 Divesta diétna jedáleň
57 Atlantis Cukráreň
59 Mekong
61 Kelt Bar & Gril
62 Slovenská reštaurácia
63 London Café; British
   Council
69 Modrá hviezda

OTHER
1 Slavín War Memorial
2 Former Lenin Museum

3 Archbishop's Summer
   Palace
4 Slovak Radio
5 Galéria Duna
6 Tatratour
7 Nová scéna
8 Kino Hviezda
9 Grassalkovich Palace
10 American Express
11 DPB Office
12 Netcafe
13 Hotel Forum; Hertz
14 DPB Office
15 Všeobecná úverová
   banka
16 Charlie's Pub; Charlie
   Centrum (Cinema)
19 Telephone Office
20 Uľuv
21 24-Hour Pharmacy
22 Monument
24 Main Post Office
26 Michael Tower;
   Montana's Grizzly Bar
27 Church of the Holy
   Trinity

29 Museum of Folk Music
30 Museum of Jewish
   Culture
31 Church of the
   Clarissine Order
32 Palace of the Royal
   Chamber
34 Mirbach Palace;
   Vináreň Veľký
   františkáni
35 Franciscan Church
36 Primaciálne nám
37 Bratislava Information
   Service
38 Piano Bar
39 Aligator
40 Primate's Palace
41 Municipal Museum
42 Museum of Wine
   Production
43 Hlavné nám
44 French Embassy
45 Hungarian Embassy
46 Internet Centrum
47 Interpress Slovakia
49 Austrian Embassy
50 UK Embassy

52 Slovenský spisovateľ
   Bookshop
55 Theatre Booking Office
   (Pokladňa)
56 Eurobooks; Satur
58 Czech Airlines (ČSA)
   Office
60 Slovak National Theatre
64 Kino Mladosť
65 17's Bar
66 St Martin's Cathedral
67 Museum of Clocks
68 Decorative Arts
   Museum
70 Slovak National
   Parliament
72 Bus to Devín Castle
74 German Embassy
75 Czech Embassy
76 US Embassy
77 Slovak National Gallery
78 Slovenská filharmonia
   Ticket Office
79 Reduta Palace;
   Slovenská filharmonia
80 Slovak National Museum
81 Hydrofoil Terminal

great view. The **Slovak National Parliament** meets in the modern complex that overlooks the river just beyond the castle.

At the foot of the hill is the **Decorative Arts Museum** *(adult/child 20/10 Sk; open 11am-5pm Wed-Mon)* and almost opposite is the **Museum of Clocks** *(adult/child 20/10 Sk; open 9.30am-4.30pm Wed-Mon)*. Further north is the **Museum of Jewish Culture** *(Židovská 17; adult/child 30/15 Sk; open 10am-5pm Sun-Fri)*.

As you return from the castle, take a stroll across the Danube on one of the pedestrian walkways on the sweeping **Nový most** (New Bridge), built in 1972. On the far side you can take a lift up one of the pylons to an expensive café that sits 80m above the river.

Communist Bratislava From nám SNP, where there is a monument to the heroes of the Slovak National Uprising, head north to Hodžovo nám and along Mýtna to the corner with Štefanovičova, where the chunky **Slovak Radio** (Slovenský rozhlas) building, like an upside-down stepped pyramid, sits among the housing estates.

West from nám Slobody along Spojná and north up Štefánikova, you will come to the former **Lenin Museum**, now an art gallery. Continue north a little, then west up the steps of Puškinova towards the **Slavín War Memorial** (1965). This is where 6847 Soviet soldiers who died in the battle for Bratislava in 1945 are buried. There's a good view of modern Bratislava from here, especially of the prefabricated suburb of Petržalka to the south.

Hiking

To get out of the city and up into the forested Little Carpathian Mountains, take trolleybus No 203 northeast from Hodžovo nám to the end of the line at Koliba, then walk up the road for about 20 minutes to the **TV tower** on Kamzík hill (440m). There is a viewing platform and a revolving café at the top.

Maps posted at the tower outline the many hiking possibilities in the area, including a 6km walk that goes down the Vydrica Valley to Partisan Meadow. Continue down the road to Vojenská hospital from where bus No 212 runs back to Hodžovo nám.

Places to Stay

Satur can book private rooms (from 400 Sk per person), pensions and hotels. BIS can assist in finding accommodation in private rooms, student dormitories (open during summer only, from 200 Sk per person), hostels, pensions (from about 1200 Sk a double) and hotels. Reservations are recommended year-round.

Camping A lake resort that's 7km northeast of Bratislava – Zlaté piesky (Golden Sands) – has bungalows, a motel, a hotel and a camping ground. Tram Nos 2 (from the main train station) and 4 (from the city centre) terminate here. You can hire rowing boats and sailboards in summer and there are also tennis courts.

As you cross the pedestrian bridge from the tram stop you'll see the Hotel Flora (see Hotels – Suburbs, following) just to your left. Bear left past the hotel to find the lakeside **Intercamp Zlaté piesky** *(☎/fax 44 25 73 73; e kempi@netax.sk; camp sites 40-60 Sk, plus per person 70 Sk, per car 70 Sk; 4-bed bungalows 830 Sk; open mid-Apr–mid-Oct)*.

Hostels The following places offer accommodation in July and August only; the BIS desk at the train station will help you arrange hostel accommodation, if you can resist their attempts to sell you a private room, which are often a long way from the city centre and no cheaper than hostels.

The 12-storey **Bernolák Hostel** *(☎ 52 49 71 84, fax 52 49 77 24; Bernolákova 1; beds per person from 130 Sk)*, about five blocks east of the main train station, is closest to the city centre. There's a swimming pool and disco (audible throughout the building).

Študentský domov Mladá Garda *(☎ 44 25 30 20, fax 44 45 96 90; e ubytovacie@ garda.sk; Račianska 103; beds per person 140-200 Sk; open mid-July–end Aug)* is 4km northeast of town; take tram No 3, 5, 7 or 11. The 24-hour reception has both English- and German-speaking staff.

Študentský domov Družba *(☎ 65 42 00 65; Botanická 25; singles/doubles 500/900 Sk)* is 20 minutes west of the city centre near the Danube (take tram No 1 from the train station, No 4 or 12 from nám L Štúra). It has comfortable, well-equipped rooms with bathroom and TV.

Hotels & Pensions – Centre The best deal near the centre of Bratislava is **Penzión Caribic** *(☎ 54 41 83 34, fax 54 41 83 33; Žižkova 1/A; singles/doubles 800/1500 Sk)*, beneath the castle.

SLOVAKIA

A good place in the heart of town is **Gremium Penzión** (☎ 54 13 10 26, fax 54 43 06 53; Gorkého 11; singles/doubles 890/1600 Sk), with rooms that include breakfast. You'll need to book ahead to get one of the few rooms available.

The friendly, welcoming **Hotel Spirit** (☎ 54 77 75 61, fax 54 77 78 17; e univ@stonline .sk; Vančurova 1; singles/doubles/triples 900/1300/1600 Sk) is ... well, colourful. Descend the steps behind the tram terminus at the train station, turn left under the railway bridge, then left again. You can't miss it; in fact, wear your sunglasses.

Botel Gracia (☎ 54 43 21 32, fax 54 43 21 31; singles/doubles 1750/2400 Sk) has comfy en suite cabins in a former cruise boat moored near the Hotel Danube on Rázusovo nábrežie.

Hotel Kyjev (☎ 52 96 10 82, fax 52 92 68 20; e rezervacia@kyjev-hotel.sk; singles/doubles 2200/2400 Sk) is a graceless tower block overlooking the Tesco department store on Špitálska, but it's central. Rooms with bathroom and TV are reasonable value and include breakfast.

In the splurge category is **Chez David Penzión** (☎ 54 41 38 24, fax 54 41 26 42; Zámocká 13; doubles 4700 Sk), a modern hotel built on the site of the old Jewish ghetto below the castle.

If you feel like really splashing out, the luxury **Hotel Danube** (☎ 59 34 08 33, fax 54 41 43 11; e danube@internet.sk; Rybné nám 1; singles/doubles €146/166) has a swimming pool and riverside location.

Hotels – Suburbs There is lots of soulless but perfectly acceptable accommodation in modern hotels a short bus or tram ride away from the centre.

Friendly **Hotel Turist** (☎ 55 57 27 89, fax 55 57 31 80; e hotel@turist.sk; Ondavská 5; singles/doubles/triples 1020/1250/1500 Sk) has dated but functional rooms with bathroom and balcony. Take bus No 61 or 74 from the main train station to the Zimný štadión stop; Ondavská is the third street on the right after the stop. **Hotel Nivy** (☎ 55 41 03 90, fax 55 41 03 89; e hotel@hotelnivy.sk; Líščie nivy 3; doubles/quads 1300/2400 Sk) is a bigger place with slightly nicer accommodation just two blocks past the Turist.

Hotel Junior (☎ 43 33 80 00, fax 43 33 80 65; e recepcia@juniorhotel.sk; Drieňová 14; singles/doubles 1970/2480 Sk) overlooks a small lake in the eastern suburbs (take tram No 8, 9 or 12, or bus No 34, 38 or 54).

The slightly seedy **Hotel Flora** (☎ 44 25 79 26, fax 44 25 79 45; Zlaté piesky; doubles from 620 Sk) is next to the camping ground (see Camping earlier) at Zlaté piesky. While the Flora is cheap and clean, it's not recommended for lone females.

Places to Eat

Restaurants – Budget If you fancy a cheap and filling sandwich, try **Bagetka** (sandwiches 30-95 Sk; open 9am-9pm Mon-Sat, 2pm-9pm Sun), in a passage between Zelená and Venturská. Busy **Divesta diétna jedáleň** (Laurinská 8; mains 54-64 Sk; open 11am-3pm Mon-Fri) provides low-calorie and vegetarian lunches.

Two good inexpensive pubs serving typical Slovak food for lunch and dinner are **Prašná bašta** (Zámočnícka 11; mains 105-185 Sk; open 11am-11pm daily) and the **Krušovická Izba** (Biela 5; mains 80-130 Sk; open 9am-midnight Mon-Fri, 10am-10pm Sat & Sun).

Little Caesar's on the ground floor in Tesco (see Self-Catering following) does great pizza by the slice, to eat in or take away.

Restaurants – Mid-Range The **Kelt Bar & Gril** (Hviezdoslavovo nám 26; mains 95-250 Sk; open 11am-11pm daily) serves an international menu that ranges from pasta to nachos to New York steaks.

The delicious Thai dishes served at the elegant **Mekong** (Palackého 18; mains 90-220 Sk; open 11am-11pm Mon-Sat, 11am-10pm Sun) make a welcome change from pork and dumpling meals.

Also worth trying is the wine restaurant **Vináreň Veľký františkáni** (Františkánske nám 10; mains 100-200 Sk; open 11am-11pm daily) in the old monastery beside the Mirbach Palace, where Romani musicians often perform.

Modrá hviezda (Beblavého 14; mains 80-150 Sk; open 11.30am-11pm Mon-Sat), on the way up to the castle, is a wine bar and restaurant that features Slovak cuisine.

Restaurants – Top End The master chef in **Slovenská reštaurácia** (Hviezdoslavovo nám 20; mains 95-295 Sk; open 11am-11pm daily) serves gourmet Slovak cuisine; wash it down with a bottle of Slovakian Modrá or Tokaj wine.

Cafés The streets of central Bratislava have been taken over by countless cafés in the last few years. The classy **Kaffee Mayer** *(Hlavné nám 4; open 9am-1am daily)* has excellent but pricey coffee, cakes and light meals. For a cheaper cappuccino, try the **London Café** *(Panská 17; open 10am-9pm Mon-Fri)* in the British Council's courtyard.

Atlantis Cukráreň *(Štúrova 13; open 9am-9pm Mon & Wed-Fri, 10am-7pm Sat & Sun)* sells Bratislava's best ice cream for just 6 Sk a scoop; on Sunday afternoon the queue runs out the door and along the street.

Self-Catering There is a good **supermarket** *(open 8am-9pm Mon-Fri, 8am-7pm Sat, 9am-7pm Sun)* in the basement of Tesco on the square Kamenné nám.

Entertainment

Opera and ballet are presented at the **Slovak National Theatre** *(Hviezdoslavovo nám)*, except during August. The local opera and ballet companies are outstanding. Tickets are sold at the **booking office** *(pokladňa; cnr Jesenského & Komenského; open 8am-5.30pm Mon-Fri, 9am-noon Sat)* behind the theatre. Tickets are sold in the theatre itself an hour before the performance, but they're usually sold out *(vypredané)* by then, especially on weekends.

Nová scéna *(Kollárovo nám 20)* presents operettas, musicals and drama (the latter in Slovak). The ticket office is open 12.30pm to 7pm weekdays and an hour before performances (by when they're usually sold out).

The **Slovenská filharmonia** *(cnr nám L Štúra & Medená)* is based in the Reduta Palace, across the park from the National Theatre. The **ticket office** *(Palackého 2; open 1pm-7pm Mon, Tues, Thur & Fri, 8am-2pm Wed)* is inside the building.

Štátne Bábkové divadlo *(State Puppet Theatre; Dunajská 36)* puts on puppet shows for kids, usually at 9am or 10am and sometimes again at 1.30pm or 2.30pm.

Bars & Clubs For loud music and a young crowd, try **Charlie's Pub** *(Špitálska 4; open 6pm-4am Sun-Thur, 6pm-6am Fri & Sat)*, one of the city's most popular drinking places.

Montana's Grizzly Bar *(Michalská 19; open 11am-midnight daily)*, at the base of the Michael Tower, is the meeting place for English-speaking expats. It has an attractive beer garden.

Two bars that have live jazz several times a week are **17's Bar** *(Hviezdoslavovo nám 17; open 11.30am-1am Mon-Thur, 11.30am-2am Fri & Sat, 4pm-11pm Sun)* and **Aligator** *(Laurinská 7; open 4pm-3am Mon-Sat)*. The **Piano Bar** *(Laurinská 11)* is the place for a pleasant and quiet drink.

Galéria Duna (**W** www.duna.sk; *Radlinského 11)* is a club that hosts rock bands, dance music or whatever the alternative scene has to offer – coming events are posted on its website (in Czech, but usable).

Cinemas In the same complex as Charlie's Pub is the four-screen **Charlie Centrum** cinema, which shows the films in their original language. Other cinemas in the city centre are **Kino Mladosť** *(Hviezdoslavovo nám 17)* and **Kino Hviezda** *(nám 1.mája 9)*.

Shopping

For folk handicrafts head to **Uľuv** *(nám SNP)* or **Folk Folk** *(Obchodná 10)*.

Getting There & Away

Air There are daily flights from Bratislava to Prague with **ČSA** *(☎ 52 96 13 25; Štúrova 13)* and to Košice with **Slovak Airlines** *(☎ 44 45 00 96; Trnavská cesta 56)*. The best prices out of Bratislava are available by booking online with the no-frills **SkyEurope Airlines** *(☎ 48 50 48 50;* **W** *www.skyeurope.com)*, which flies to Košice (740 Sk one way), Prague (from 1525 Sk) and Split (2525 Sk) in Croatia.

Bus Buy your ticket from the ticket windows, not the driver at Bratislava's **main bus station** *(SAD/Eurolines information ☎ 0984-222 222, international lines ☎ 55 56 73 49; Mlynské nivy)*, east of the city centre. Reservations for the buses marked 'R' on the posted timetable can be bought from the AMS counter. The footnotes on the timetables in this station are in English.

Seven buses a day connect Bratislava to Vienna (Mitte Busbahnhof; €10.90, 1½ hours). Ten express buses a day run to Prague (4¾ hours). Other buses leaving Bratislava daily include nine to Košice (334 Sk, seven hours), three to Bardejov (468 Sk, 9½ hours) and one to Starý Smokovec (336 Sk, 7¾ hours). There's a weekly bus to Győr (200 Sk, 2½ hours), Hungary.

Eurolines buses to Bratislava include five a week from Brussels (€122 one way, 16 hours) via Vienna, one daily from Zürich (65 Sfr, 13 hours) and three every week (five in summer) from London (UK£78, 22 hours). The Zürich bus continues to Košice twice a week (21 hours, 94 Sfr).

There are also buses from Bratislava to Belgrade (9½ hours) on Monday and Friday, Budapest (four hours, daily), and Kraków (eight hours, weekly). Tickets can be bought either at the international ticket window in the bus station or at the adjacent Eurolines office, depending on the destination. Beware of buses that transit the Czech Republic, as you could be put off at the border if you need a visa and don't have one.

Train All express trains between Budapest (380 Sk, 2¾ hours) and Prague (528 Sk, 4½ hours) call at Bratislava. There are frequent trains from Bratislava to Košice (414 Sk, six hours) via Trenčín, Žilina and Poprad.

There are hourly trains between Vienna (Südbahnhof) and Bratislava's main train station (1½ hours). One nightly train departs for Moscow (33 hours).

Boat An interesting way to enter or leave Slovakia is on the hydrofoils that ply the Danube between Bratislava and Vienna once a day Wednesday to Sunday from mid-April to October (twice daily on Friday and Saturday in May to September and on Thursday in July and August). These 1¾-hour trips cost €19/29 one way/return. Buy tickets at the **hydrofoil terminal** (Fajnorovo nábrežie 2). In late summer the service can be interrupted because of low water levels.

There is also a daily (twice daily in August) hydrofoil service between Bratislava and Budapest from mid-April to October. The trip downstream to Budapest takes four hours (40 minutes longer upstream to Bratislava), and costs €59/83 one way/return (10% off for ISIC holders).

Getting Around

To/From the Airport Bratislava's airport (Letisko MR Štefánika) is 7km northeast of the city centre. The only way to get there is on city bus No 61 from the train station or by taxi (around 280 Sk).

Tram & Bus Bratislava's public transport (Dopravný podnik Bratislava or DPB) is based on an extensive tram network complemented by bus and trolleybus. You can buy tickets (12/14/20 Sk for 10/30/60 minutes) at DPB offices and from machines at main tram and bus stops – validate the ticket in the little red machines on the bus or tram when you board.

Tourist tickets (turistické cestovné lístky) valid for one/two/three/seven days (75/140/170/255 Sk) are sold at DPB offices at the train and bus stations, in the underground passageway below Hodžovo nám (open 6am to 7pm weekdays) and on Obchodná near the Hotel Forum (open 9.30am to 5.30pm weekdays). The one- and two-day tickets can also be bought from ticket machines.

Note that bags larger than 30cm x 40cm x 60cm need a half-fare ticket. Travellers have reported being fined up to 1200 Sk for not having a ticket for their backpacks.

Taxi Bratislava's taxis all have meters and drivers are far less likely to try to overcharge you than those in Prague. To order one call **Fun Taxi** (☎ 16 777) or **Otto Taxi** (☎ 16 322).

Car There are several inexpensive local car-rental companies (contact BIS or Satur for others), such as **Favorit Car** (☎ 44 88 41 52; Pri vinohradoch 275), that rent out a Škoda Felicie for around 580 Sk per day plus 3 Sk per kilometre; weekly rates with unlimited kilometres begin at around 7000 Sk including collision-damage waiver, but the office is 8km out of town. **Avis** (☎ 53 41 61 11) has a desk in the Hotel Danube, while **Hertz** (☎ 43 63 66 62) has a desk in the lobby of the Hotel Forum; both have desks at Bratislava's airport, but renting from these outlets costs two to three times more than a local agency.

AROUND BRATISLAVA

From the 1st to the 5th centuries AD, **Devín Castle** (open Tues-Sun May-Oct) was a frontier post of the Roman Empire. During the 9th century the castle was a major stronghold of the Great Moravian Empire. The castle withstood the Turks but was blown up in 1809 by the French. Today it is regarded as a symbol of the Slovaks who maintained their identity despite a millennium of foreign rule. The Gothic ruins contain an exhibit of artefacts found on site. Austria is just across the river.

Getting There & Away

Catch bus No 29 (two an hour) from the Nový most bus terminal to the castle, on a hill where the Morava and Danube Rivers meet. Stay on the bus to the end of the line and walk back to the castle. Remember to take a bus ticket for the journey back; there's no ticket machine at the Devín stop.

West Slovakia

TRENČÍN
☎ 032 • pop 57,000

For many centuries, where the Váh River valley begins to grow narrow between the White Carpathians and the Strážov Hills, Trenčín Castle guarded one of the main trade routes between the Danube River and the Baltic Sea. Laugaricio, a Roman military post (the northernmost Roman camp in Eastern Europe) was set up here in the 2nd century AD; a rock inscription that is dated AD 179 mentions the Roman 2nd Legion and its victory over the Germanic Kvad tribes.

The mighty castle that now towers above the town was first noted in a Viennese chronicle in 1069. In the 13th century the castle's master Matúš Čák held sway over much of Slovakia, and in 1412 Trenčín obtained the rights of a free royal city. The present castle dates from that period, and although both the castle and town were destroyed by fire in 1790, much has been restored. Today Trenčín is a centre of Slovakia's textile industry.

Orientation & Information

From the adjacent bus and train stations walk west through the city park and underneath the highway to the Tatra Hotel, from which a street bears left uphill to Mierové nám, the main square.

The helpful, well-informed staff at the **AiCES information centre** (☎ 743 35 05; *Štúrovo nám 10; open 8am-6pm Mon-Fri, 8am-1pm Sat*) can assist you to find accommodation; during the summer months ask about the student dormitories.

The **Všeobecná úverová banka** (*Mierové nám 48*) cashes travellers cheques, and there is an ATM at another VÚB branch across the street at No 37.

The telephone centre is in the **main post office** (*Mierové nám*). Check your email at the **Internet Klub Modra Linka** (*open 10am-10pm daily*), next to the information centre, for 1 Sk per minute.

TRENČÍN

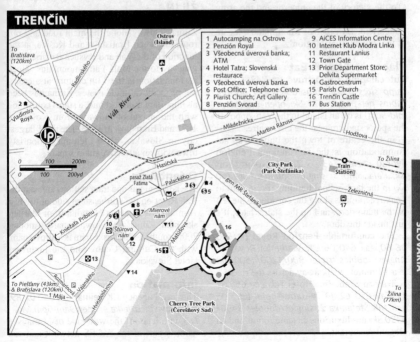

1	Autocamping na Ostrove
2	Penzión Royal
3	Všeobecná úverová banka; ATM
4	Hotel Tatra; Slovenská restaurace
5	Všeobecná úverová banka
6	Post Office; Telephone Centre
7	Piarist Church; Art Gallery
8	Penzión Svorad
9	AiCES Information Centre
10	Internet Klub Modra Linka
11	Restaurant Lanius
12	Town Gate
13	Prior Department Store; Delvita Supermarket
14	Gastrocentrum
15	Parish Church
16	Trenčín Castle
17	Bus Station

SLOVAKIA

Things to See

At the western end of Mierové nám are the baroque **Piarist Church** and the 16th-century **town gate**, which contains a clock that plays old-fashioned tunes on the hour. The **art gallery** *(admission 10 Sk; open 9am-5pm Tues-Sun)*, in the former Piarist convent next to the church, features works by local artists, notably the realist painter MA Bazovský.

A covered stairway from the corner of the square opposite Piarist Church leads to the Gothic **parish church** and the entrance to **Trenčín Castle** *(admission 80 Sk; open 9am-5pm daily Apr-Sept)*. The highlight of the tour (no English) – mostly dreary 18th-century paintings of the ruling family – is the view from the tower. The so-called Well of Love on the first terrace is 70m deep. At night-time the castle is lit with green and purple fairy lights. The two-hour Medieval Days show includes sword fighting and ghosts (9pm every second Friday or Saturday from May to September).

The famous **Roman inscription** of AD 179 is on the cliff behind the Hotel Tatra and can only be seen through a viewing window on the hotel's staircase – ask at reception for permission to see it. The translation reads: 'To the victory of the emperor and the army which, numbering 855 soldiers, resided at Laugaricio. By order of Maximianus, legate of the 2nd auxiliary legion'.

Places to Stay & Eat

Autocamping na Ostrove *(☎ 743 40 13; camp sites 65 Sk, plus 65 Sk per person; cabins per person 120 Sk; open mid-May–mid-Sept)* is on an island in the Váh, opposite the sports stadium near the city centre.

In the centre of town the only cheap accommodation is the nonsmoking **Penzión Svorad** *(☎/fax 743 03 22; e svorad@host .sk; Palackého 4; singles/doubles 500/750 Sk)* in the high school building. From 7am to 4pm, reception is along the corridor to the left of the main door, and up the stairs; later, it's just inside the door.

The comfortable **Penzión Royal** *(☎ 640 06 60, fax 640 06 61; Vladimíra Roya 19; singles/doubles/triples 900/1200/1500 Sk)* is a 10-minute walk away across the river.

The top-of-the-line **Hotel Tatra** *(☎ 650 61 11, fax 650 62 13; e tatra@hotel-tatra.sk; gen MR Štefánika 2; singles/doubles 3490/4490 Sk)* has luxurious en suite rooms and an elegant restaurant.

Gastrocentrum *(mains 35-65 Sk; open 7am-5pm Mon-Fri)* is a self-service cafeteria serving filling hot meals. You'll find better, but pricier, food and a pleasant atmosphere at **Restaurant Lanius** *(Mierové nám 22; mains 65-110 Sk; open 10am-10pm Sun-Thur, 10am-11pm Fri & Sat)*.

Slovenská restaurace *(mains 80-120 Sk; open 11am-midnight daily)*, in the basement of the Tatra Hotel, serves traditional Slovak food, though you run the risk of being serenaded at your table by a violinist.

There's a **Delvita supermarket** *(open 8am-6pm Mon-Wed, 8am-7pm Thur & Fri, 8am-1pm Sat)* in the Prior department store, two blocks west of the square.

Getting There & Away

All express trains on the main railway line from Bratislava (142 Sk, 1¾ hours) to Košice via Žilina stop here. There are six buses a day to Bratislava, Žilina and Košice, and several to Brno in the Czech Republic.

Central Slovakia

ŽILINA

☎ 41 • pop 84,000

Žilina, midway along the main road and rail routes between Bratislava and Košice, at the junction of the Váh and Kysuca Rivers, is the gateway to the Malá Fatra mountains. Since its foundation in the 13th century at a crossing of medieval trade routes, Žilina has been an important transport hub, a status confirmed with the arrival of railways from Košice in 1871 and Bratislava in 1883. The third-largest city in Slovakia, it's a pleasant, untouristy town with an attractive main square.

Orientation

The adjacent bus and train stations are near the Váh River on the northeastern side of town, a 10-minute walk along Národná from Mariánské nám, Žilina's old town square. Another 200m south of Mariánské nám is Štúrovo nám, with the Cultural Centre and the luxurious Hotel Slovakia.

Information

The travel agency **CK Selinan** *(☎ 562 07 89; Burianova medzierka 4; open 9am-5pm Mon-Fri)*, in a lane off the west side of Mariánské nám, is part of the AiCES network and can provide information about Žilina and the Malá Fatra area.

The **Všeobecná úverová banka** *(Na bráne 1; open 7.30am-4.30pm Mon-Wed & Fri, 7.30am-noon Thur)*, two blocks south from Mariánské nám changes travellers cheques and has an ATM.

The **post office** *(Sladkovičova 1)* is three blocks north of Mariánské nám. There's an **Internet Klub** *(open 10am-10pm daily)* in the south end of the Dom Kultúry on Šturovo nám, which charges 1 Sk a minute.

Things to See

Apart from the renovated old town square, with its picturesque church and covered arcade, the only sight worth seeking out is the collection of naive art figures made of metal and wire at the dilapidated **Regional Museum** *(admission 30 Sk; open 8am-4pm open Tues-Sun)*, in the Renaissance castle across the river in Budatín, a 15-minute walk northwest from the train station.

Places to Stay & Eat

Pension GMK Centrum *(☎ 562 21 36; Mariánské nám 3; singles/doubles from 790/1290 Sk)* has smallish rooms, and is tucked away in an upstairs passage off the square. **Penzión Majovey** *(☎ 562 41 52, fax 562 52 39; Jána Milca 3; singles/doubles 700/900 Sk)* is nicer.

If these places are full, you can always resort to the comfortable if slightly run-down **Hotel Polom** *(☎ 562 11 51; Hviezdoslavova 22; singles/doubles 820/1050 Sk)* opposite the train station, where the renovated rooms come with en suite bathroom and TV. Older rooms with no frills cost 390/530 Sk.

Bageteria *(Jána Milca 1)* on the corner of Národná is a good place for hefty sandwiches and inexpensive buffet food.

Radničná vináreň *(Mariánské nám 28; mains 100-140 Sk; open 10am-midnight Mon-Sat, noon-midnight Sun)* has outdoor tables and a cellar restaurant serving good, inexpensive Slovak dishes.

Campari Pizza *(Zaymusova 4; pizza 50-100 Sk; open 11am-9pm Mon-Fri)*, on the north side of Štúrovo nám, has a nice back terrace where you can down pseudo-pizza and cheap red wine.

Getting There & Away

Žilina is on the main railway line from Bratislava to Košice via Trenčín and Poprad, and is served by frequent express trains. Most trains between Prague and Košice also stop at Žilina. Express trains from Žilina take 6¼ hours to Prague (466km), 1¼ hours to Trenčín (92 Sk), 2¾ hours to Bratislava (212 Sk), two hours to Poprad (158 Sk) and three hours to Košice (250 Sk).

There are also daily direct trains to Kraków in Poland (provided you don't need a visa to transit the Czech Republic). You can avoid Czech territory by going through Poprad and the Javorina/-ysa Polana border crossing on to Zakopane.

There are several buses a day to Brno (134km) and Prague.

MALÁ FATRA
☎ 041

The Malá Fatra (Little Fatra) mountain range stretches 50km across northwestern Slovakia; Veľký Kriváň (1709m) is the highest peak. Two hundred square kilometres of this scenic range, north of the Váh River and east of Žilina, are included in Malá Fatra National Park. At the heart of the park is the Vrátna dolina, a beautiful mountain valley with forested slopes on all sides.

Noted for its rich flora, Vrátna dolina has something for everyone. The hiking possibilities vary from easy tourist tracks through the forest to scenic ridge walks, and in winter there is downhill and cross-country skiing and snowboarding. There are plenty of places to stay and eat, though in midsummer and winter accommodation is tight. The valley is an easy day trip from Žilina. The mountains are accessible by road, trail and chairlift for anyone with the urge to enjoy their beauty.

Information

There's an **AiCES Information Centre** *(☎ 599 31 00; e ztt@terchova.sk; 10am-3.45pm Mon-Fri, open 10am-4pm Sat, 10am-2pm Sun)* in the Obecni úrad (regional offices) in Terchová. The **Slovenská sporiteľňa** bank next door has an exchange counter and an ATM. The **post office** is 100m further east on the main road.

The **Mountain Rescue Service** *(Horská služba; ☎ 569 52 32)*, on the access road to Hotel Boboty, can provide detailed information on the national park.

If you plan to hike, you should get the VKÚ's 1:50,000 *Malá Fatra – Vrátna* map (sheet No 110).

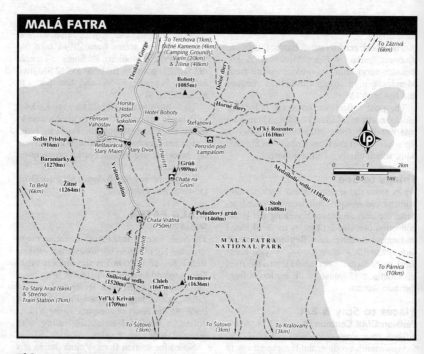

MALÁ FATRA

Things to See & Do

The road enters the Vrátna dolina just south of Terchová, where it runs through the **Tiesňavy Gorge** with rocky crags on both sides. One rock resembles a person praying (turn and look back after you've passed through the gorge).

From **Chata Vrátna** (750m) at the head of the valley, a two-seater chairlift (110/140 Sk one way/return) climbs 770m to Snilovské sedlo (1520m), a saddle midway between Chleb (1647m) and Veľký Kriváň (1709m). Take along warm clothes as it will be a lot cooler on top.

From Snilovské sedlo you can follow the red trail southeast along the mountain ridges past Hromové (1636m), then northeast to Poludňový grúň (1460m) and Stoh (1608m) to Medziholie sedlo (1185m), below the rocky summit of Veľký Rozsutec (1610m). An orange trail skirting the side of Stoh avoids a 200m climb.

From Medziholie it's easy to descend via another green trail to **Štefanová**, a picturesque village of log houses. You can do the hike from Snilovské sedlo to Štefanová via Medziholie in about four hours. Other possible hikes from Snilovské sedlo are the blue trail to Starý

Dvor via Baraniarky (1270m; three hours) and the red trail west to Strečno train station via the Starý hrad ruins (6½ hours).

Skiing There is good downhill skiing and snowboarding for all levels, with some 20 inexpensive lifts at various places in the valley (few are linked, though). Reasonable skis, boots and snowboards are available for hire. The best time is from late December to March.

Places to Stay & Eat

No camping is allowed in the Vrátna dolina. The nearest **camping grounds** are at Nižné Kamence, 3.5km west of Terchová, and at Varín, another 11km towards Žilina.

There are lots of **private rooms** in Terchová from 200 Sk per person.

The friendly **Hotel Terchová** (☎ 569 56 25, fax 569 56 30; e vratna@hotel-terchova.sk; singles/doubles 720/1440 Sk), at the Vrátna junction in Terchová, is new and comfortable.

Horsky Hotel pod Sokolím (☎/fax 569 53 26), on the hill above the good **Reštaurácia Starý Majer**, and **Pension Vahostav** (☎ 569 53 06), about 1km further up the valley, have beds for 200 Sk to 300 Sk per person.

Chata Vrátna (☎ 569 57 39, fax 569 57 31; e chatavratna@icos.sk; dorm beds 150 Sk, double/triple/quads 460/590/690 Sk), a large wooden chalet at the head of the valley, is usually full with hikers in summer and skiers in winter. In spring and late autumn, groups of school children pack the dormitories. There are regular hotel rooms as well as dorm beds.

There's a big **potraviny** (grocery; open 6am-6pm Mon-Fri, 6am-2pm Sat, 8am-noon Sun) beside the Hotel Terchová.

Štefanová Friendly **Chata vo Vyhnana** (☎/fax 569 51 24; e chatavyhnana@stonline .sk; half/full board per person 160/300 Sk) in Štefanová has good dorm accommodation. A few minutes' walk up the green trail in Štefanová village is **Chata pod Skalným mestom** (☎ 569 53 63; beds per person 300 Sk). A few hundred metres beyond is the slightly posher **Penzión pod Lampášom** (☎ 569 53 92; full board per person 700 Sk). There are also several private rooms (privaty) around the village – look for the 'zimmer frei' signs.

The comfortable **Hotel Boboty** (☎ 569 52 28, fax 569 57 37; singles/doubles 800/1000 Sk) is a five-minute walk up from the bus stop near Štefanová. The hotel, with a sauna, swimming pool and restaurant, was being renovated and extended at the time of research.

Getting There & Around

The bus from Žilina to Chata Vrátna (one hour, 32km) leaves from platform No 10 at Žilina bus station nine times a day. If you come on a day trip, check the times of return trips at the information counter at Žilina bus station before setting out.

You can hire bicycles in Terchová – ask at the information centre for details.

East Slovakia

East Slovakia is one of the most attractive touring areas in Central Europe. In one compact region you can enjoy superb hiking in the Vysoké Tatry (High Tatra) mountains, rafting on the Dunajec River, historic towns such as Levoča and Bardejov, the great medieval castle at Spišské Podhradie, the charming spa of Bardejovské Kúpele and city life in Košice. Getting around is easy, with frequent trains and buses to all these sights plus easy access to Poland and Hungary. In spite of all these attractions, the region still feels somewhat off the beaten track.

VYSOKÉ TATRY
☎ 0969

The Vysoké Tatry (High Tatras) are the only truly alpine mountains in Central Europe. This 27km-long granite massif covers 260 sq km, forming the northernmost portion of the Carpathian Mountains. The narrow, rocky crests soar above wide glacial valleys with precipitous walls. At 2654m, Gerlachovský štít (Mt Gerlach) is the highest mountain in the entire 1200km Carpathian range, and several other peaks exceed 2500m.

Enhancing the natural beauty packed into this relatively small area are clear mountain lakes, thundering waterfalls and dazzling snowfields. The lower slopes are covered by dense forest; from 1500m to 1800m lies a belt of shrubs and dwarf pines, and above are alpine flora, bare rock and snow.

Since 1949, most of the Slovak part of this jagged range has been included in the Tatra National Park (Tanap), the first national park to be created in former Czechoslovakia, complementing a similar park in Poland. A 600km network of hiking trails reaches all the alpine valleys and many peaks. The red-marked Tatranská magistrála trail follows the southern slopes of the Vysoké Tatry for 65km through a variety of striking landscapes. Other routes are also colour-coded and easy to follow. Park regulations require you to keep to the marked trails and to refrain from picking flowers.

Climate & When to Go

When planning your trip, keep in mind that the higher trails are closed from November to mid-June, to protect the delicate environment. There's snow by November (on the highest passes as early as September), and many snowfields linger until May or even June. Beware of sudden thunderstorms, especially on ridges and peaks where there's no protection. Always wear hiking boots and carry warm clothing. Remember that the assistance of the Mountain Rescue Service is not free. July and August are the warmest (and most crowded) months, while August and September are the best for high-altitude hiking. Hotel prices are lowest from April to mid-June.

The **Tanap Mountain Rescue Service office** next to Satur in Starý Smokovec can give you a weather report for the next day.

VYSOKÉ TATRY

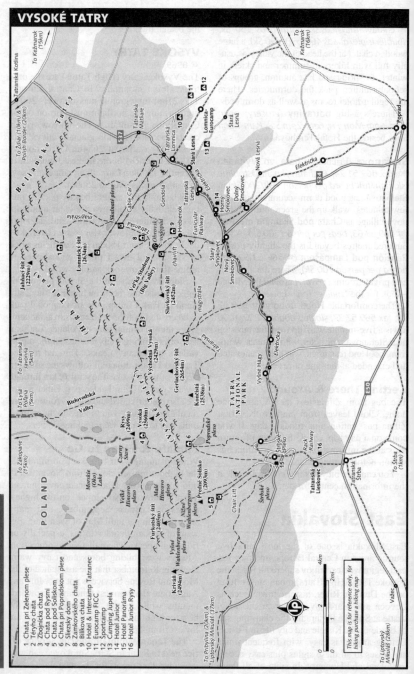

1 Chata pri Zelenom plese
2 Teryho chata
3 Zbojnícka chata
4 Chata pod Rysmi
5 Chata pod Soliskom
6 Chata pri Popradskom plese
7 Sliezsky dom
8 Zamkovského chata
9 Bilíkova chata
10 Hotel & Intercamp Tatranec
11 Eurocamp FICC
12 Sportcamp
13 Camping Jupela
14 Hotel Junior
15 Hotel Panoráma
16 Hotel Junior Rysy

To Kežmarok (15km)
Tatranská Kotlina
To Ždiar (10km) & Polish Border (20km)
Belianske Tatry
To Kežmarok (16km)
Poprad
Tatranská Matliare
E537
Tatranská Lomnica
Lomnica-Eurocamp
Stará Lesná
Nová Lesná
Električka
E534
Jahňací štít (2229m)
Skalnaté pleso
Cable Car
magistrála
Pyšenská
Tatranská
Ohrovský
Gondola
Skalnaté pleso
Hrebienok
Tatranská Lesná
Električka
Horný Smokovec
Dolný Smokovec
Lomnický štít (2634m)
Veľká Studená (Big Valley)
vodopád
chairlift
Funicular Railway
Starý Smokovec
Nový Smokovec
Slavkovský štít (2452m)
magistrála
High Tatry (Vysoké Tatry)
Vysoká (2560m)
Východná Vysoká (2429m)
Gerlachovský štít (2654m)
Končistá (2538m)
Popradské pleso
Vyšné Hágy
Električka
To Tatranská Javorina (5km)
To Tatranská Polana (5km)
To Lysá Polana (5km)
Bielovodská Valley
Rysy (2499m)
POLAND
Czarny Staw
Morskie (Oko) Lake
To Zakopane (15km)
Veľké Hincovo pleso
Malé Hincovo pleso
Furkotský štít (2405m)
Nížné Wahlenbergovo pleso
Vyšné Wahlenbergovo pleso
Predné Solisko (2093m)
Chair Lift
Kriváň (2494m)
To Pribylina (20km) & Liptovský Mikuláš (27km)
TATRA NATIONAL PARK
Štrbské Pleso
Rack Railway
Tatranská Lieskovec
Štrba
Tatranská Štrba
To Štrba (1km)
To Liptovský Mikuláš (28km)
Važec
E50

This map is for reference only, for hiking purchase a hiking map

0   1   2   2mi
0   2   4km

Orientation

Starý Smokovec, an early 20th-century resort that is well connected to the rest of the country by road and rail, makes a pleasant base camp. Small electric trains trundle frequently between here and Štrbské Pleso, Tatranská Lomnica and Poprad, where they link up with the national railway system. Buses also run frequently between the resorts. Cable cars, chairlifts and a funicular railway carry you up the slopes to hiking trails that soon lead you away from the throng. During winter, skiers flock to the area. All three main train stations have left-luggage offices.

Maps Our Vysoké Tatry map is intended for initial orientation only. Buy a proper VKÚ 1:25,000 or 1:50,000 *Vysoké Tatry* hiking map when you arrive. Good maps are usually available at hotels, shops and newsstands inside the park. When buying your map, make sure you get a green one with summer hiking trails and not a blue one with winter ski routes.

Information
Tourist Offices The main AiCES Tatra information centre (☎ 442 34 40; e tik .vysoketatry@sinet.sk; open 8am-6pm daily Dec–mid-Apr, 8am-4.30pm Mon-Sat rest of year) in the Dom služieb shopping centre, northwest of Starý Smokovec train station, has plenty of information on the region but does not book accommodation. There's another office (☎ 449 23 91; open 8.30am-6pm daily Dec–mid-Apr, 8.30am-11.30am & noon-4pm Mon-Fri rest of year) next to Obchodný dom Toliar department store, opposite the Štrbské Pleso train station.

The helpful staff at the **Satur office** (☎ 442 24 97; e smokovec@satur.sk; open 8am-4pm Mon-Fri), just above the train station at Starý Smokovec, provide general advice, mountain guides and tours, and can book beds in local hotels, pensions and mountain huts.

Check out the website maintained by the **Tatra National Park** (w www.tanap.sk) as it is packed with useful information on accommodation, mountain guides, equipment rental and trail conditions.

Money The **Všeobecná úverová banka** (open 8am-noon & 1pm-4pm Mon-Wed & Fri, 8am-noon Thur), in the commercial centre above the bus station in Starý Smokovec, changes travellers cheques and has an ATM.

Post & Communications The post office (open 7.30am-noon & 1am-4pm Mon-Fri, 8am-10am Sat), near Starý Smokovec train station, has coin and cardphones, and sells phonecards. You can check email at the café next door to Starý Smokovec information centre, and in Hotel Toliar in Štrbské Pleso.

Things to See & Do
Above Starý Smokovec From Starý Smokovec a funicular railway, built in 1908, takes you up to **Hrebienok** (1280m; 60 Sk one way), a ski resort with a view into the Veľká Studená (Big Valley). Alternatively, it takes less than an hour to walk up to Hrebienok (green trail). If you catch the funicular railway, a 20-minute walk north from the top station along the red Tatranská magistrála trail takes you to the **Obrovský vodopád** (waterfall).

For great scenery, fork left before the waterfall on the blue trail that leads to Zbojnícka chata in the Veľká Studená (three hours). Beyond Zbojnícka, the blue trail climbs over a 2373m pass and descends the long Bielovodská valley towards the Polish border.

Zamkovského chata is just off the Magistrála, less than an hour north from Hrebienok. From here a green trail leads northwest to Téryho chata in the Malá Studená (three hours). The round trip from Hrebienok to Zamkovského, Téryho and Zbojnícka and back to Hrebienok takes about eight hours. The trail from Téryho to Zbojnícka is one-way only, in that direction, and involves some steep ascents with the aid of chains and ladders.

Štrbské Pleso From the modern ski resort of Štrbské Pleso with its glacial lake (1346m), take the red-marked Magistrála trail for about an hour up to **Popradské pleso**, an idyllic lake at 1494m. The Magistrála runs along the south shore of Štrbské pleso lake – just head uphill from the train station to find it. From Popradské pleso the Magistrála zigzags steeply up the mountainside then traverses east towards Sliezský dom and Hrebienok (four hours). A shorter option is to hike up the blue trail from Popradské pleso to the Hincovo lakes (1½ hours).

Tatranská Lomnica In 1937 a 30-person cable car (lanová dráha) opened from Tatranská Lomnica to the mountain lake of **Skalnaté pleso** (1751m). The **cable car** (120 Sk one way; open Wed-Mon) is very popular with the tourists, so during the peak seasons of July to September and December to April get to the ticket office early. Note that it's often closed for maintenance in November and May.

A modern gondola with four-seat cabins *(120 Sk one way; closed 1st Mon June-Aug)* also runs to Skalnaté pleso via Štart, leaving from above the Horec Hotel in Tatranská Lomnica – it is faster and has shorter queues than the cable car.

There's a big observatory at Skalnaté pleso, where a smaller 15-person **cable car** carries you to the summit of **Lomnický štít** at 2632m *(300 Sk one way)* for a sweeping view of the entire Vysoké Tatry range. You're only allowed 30 minutes at the top, and if you miss your car down, you'll have to wait until another car has room for you. From Skalnaté pleso it's two hours' walk down Magistrála trail to Hrebienok and the funicular railway down to Starý Smokovec.

The **Tatra National Park Museum** *(open 8am-noon & 1pm-4.30pm Mon-Fri, 8am-noon Sat & Sun)*, a few hundred metres from the bus station, has an exhibition on the area's natural and human histories.

Activities

Mountain Climbing You can reach the summit of Slavkovský štít (2452m) via the blue trail from Starý Smokovec (seven to eight hours return). Mt Rysy (2499m), right on the Polish border, is a nine-hour return trip from Štrbské pleso (via Popradské pleso and chata pod Rysmi). You can do these routes on your own, but to scale the peaks without marked hiking trails (Gerlachovský štít included) you must hire a mountain guide. Members of recognised climbing clubs are exempt from this requirement.

Satur in Starý Smokovec books guides from the Tanap Mountain Rescue Service office for 4000 Sk to 5000 Sk per day for a guide for up to five people.

Skiing & Snowboarding Štrbské Pleso, Starý Smokovec and Tatranská Lomnica all have lifts offering fairly average downhill skiing and snowboarding, as well as good cross-country skiing trails. Štrbské Pleso and Starý Smokovec are much better suited to beginners and intermediates, while Tatranská Lomnica is more suitable for intermediates and experts. Ski/snowboard hire costs from 249/390 Sk a day.

Places to Stay

Camping No wild camping is permitted within Tatra National Park. **Camping Jupela** (☎ 446 74 93; camp sites 80 Sk, plus 90 Sk per person; open May-Sept) is 10 minutes' walk downhill from Stará Lesná train station.

There are three camping grounds 2km from Tatranská Lomnica (near Tatranská Lomnica-Eurocamp train station on the line to Studený potok). The largest is **Eurocamp FICC** (☎ 446 77 41, fax 446 73 46; camp sites 90 Sk, plus 120 Sk per person, bungalows 1050-1500 Sk; open year-round), five minutes' walk from the train station, with four-person luxury bungalows with private bath. The Eurocamp has restaurants (which include the good folkloric Koliba Restaurant), bars, shops, a supermarket, a swimming pool, tennis, sauna, disco, hot water and row upon row of parked caravans.

An eight-minute walk south of Eurocamp is the less-expensive **Športcamp** (☎ 446 72 88; open June-Sept) where there are also four- or five-person bungalows that must be booked ahead in summer. A 10-minute walk north of Eurocamp, towards Tatranská Lomnica, is the **Hotel & Intercamp Tatranec** (☎ 446 70 92).

Chaty Up on the hiking trails are nine mountain chalets *(chaty)*, but given their limited capacity and the popularity of the area, they may all be full in midsummer. Many of the chalets close for maintenance in November and May. Although food is available at the chalets, you should bring some of your own supplies. A stay in a chata is one of the best mountain experiences the Tatras have to offer.

Satur in Starý Smokovec can reserve beds at most of the chalets. High-season prices are around 300 Sk to 500 Sk per person.

The following are the main chalets on the upper trails, from west to east:

Chata pod Soliskom (1800m) At the top of the Štrbské Pleso chairlift, it is small and very busy.

Chata pri Popradskom plese (1500m; ☎ 449 21 77) Eight-bed, six-bed and double rooms with restaurant

Chata pod Rysmi (2250m) Open June to October. This chata was destroyed by an avalanche in winter 1999 to 2000, and again in February 2001, and was being rebuilt – in a safer location! – at the time of writing.

Sliezský dom (1670m; ☎ 442 52 02; [e] gotravel@neta.sk) Large mountain hotel with restaurant and cafeteria

Zbojnícka chata (1960m; ☎ 0903-619 000) Alpine bunks and restaurant

Téryho chata (2015m; ☎ 442 52 45) Alpine bunks and restaurant
Zamkovského chata (1475m; ☎ 442 26 30) Alpine bunks and restaurant
Bilíkova chata (1220m; ☎ 442 24 39) Attractive wooden chalet with double rooms
Chata pri Zelenom plese (1540m; ☎ 446 74 20) Dorm accommodation with restaurant

Private Rooms Satur can help out with private rooms (250 Sk to 500 Sk per person) and apartments. You can also check out the website for the **Tatra National Park** (ⓦ www .tanap.sk/homes.html).

Hotels In the high seasons (mid-December to February and mid-June to September), hotel prices almost double compared with the low seasons (March to mid-June and October to mid-December). Most prices quoted in this section are high season.

The Satur office at Starý Smokovec can help you to find a room in all categories, from budget to deluxe. They do not always know about last-minute cancellations in hotels so if they can't direct you to any accommodation, then tramp around to see what you can find.

Starý Smokovec & Around One of the best deals at Starý Smokovec is the friendly, family-run **Pension Vesna** (☎ 442 27 74, fax 442 31 09; ⓔ vesna@sinet.sk; apartments per person 700 Sk), behind the large sanatorium below Nový Smokovec train station. Spacious three-bed apartments with private bath are available, and the owner speaks English. You can take a short cut through the sanatorium grounds to get there (ask), or follow the red signs west from the train station.

Hotel Smokovec (☎ 442 51 91, fax 442 51 94; ⓔ smokovec@tatry.net; doubles/quads 1980/3560 Sk), located immediately above Starý Smokovec train station, has spacious rooms including a bath and TV; breakfast is 130 Sk extra. It also has a swimming pool.

The majestic and century-old **Grand Hotel** (☎ 442 21 54, fax 442 21 57; singles/doubles 1700/2900 Sk), opposite Hotel Smokovec, has a certain old-fashioned elegance. Use of the indoor swimming pool is included.

The cheapest place to stay if you have an HI or ISIC card is **Hotel Junior** (☎ 442 26 61, fax 442 24 93; singles/doubles/triples/quads 350/680/840/1010 Sk), just below the Horný Smokovec train station. The hotel is often full of noisy school groups.

The 96-room **Park Hotel** (☎ 442 23 42, fax 442 23 04; singles/doubles 550/1100 Sk) above Nový Smokovec train station, and the **Hotel MS 70** (☎ 442 29 72, fax 442 29 70; doubles/triples 920/1330 Sk), west of the Park Hotel, are good mid-range choices.

Tatranská Lomnica The best value in town is the **Penzión Bělín** (☎/fax 446 77 78; ⓔ belin@tatry.sk; rooms per person 240 Sk), on the main road just a few minutes' walk north of the train station.

The squat, monolithic **Hotel Slovan** (☎ 446 78 51, fax 446 76 27; ⓔ slovan@tatry.sk; singles/doubles 950/1420 Sk) is five minutes' uphill behind Hotel Slovakia. It lacks character, but is not bad value for rooms with private bath and satellite TV.

One of Slovakia's most romantic hotels is the 89-room **Grandhotel Praha** (☎ 446 79 41/5, fax 446 78 91; ⓔ grandpraha@ tatry.sk; singles/doubles 2100/3100 Sk), built in 1905 and hidden in the forest up the hill beside the cable-car terminal.

Štrbské Pleso The 11-storey **Hotel Panoráma** (☎ 449 21 11, fax 449 28 10; ⓔ hotel@ hotelpanorama.sk; singles/doubles 985/ 1770 Sk) is the pyramidal eyesore next to the shopping centre above the Štrbské Pleso train station. The rooms are good, all have baths, and the view is much nicer looking out.

You'll find some cheaper options down the hill in Tatranská Štrba, including **Hotel Junior Rysy** (☎ 4484 845, fax 448 42 96; ⓔ hotel .rysy@ke.telecom.sk; singles/doubles 700/ 900 Sk), just a few minutes' walk from the Tatranská Lieskovec stop on the rack-railway between Tatranská Štrba and Štrbské Pleso.

Places to Eat
Almost all the hotels and chalets in this region have their own restaurants. Just above the bus station at Starý Smokovec is **Bistro-Fast Food Tatra** (open 10am-7pm daily), but the self-service **bistro** (open 8am-7pm daily) in Hotel Smokovec is better.

For typical Slovak food with a Roma band, head for the mid-range **Restaurant Koliba** (open 5pm-midnight), just southwest of the train station.

The friendly **restaurant** (mains 130-190 Sk; open 11.30am-11pm daily), above the Tatrasport shop opposite the bus station, is the nicest place in town.

SLOVAKIA

There's a good self-service restaurant in the **Obchodný dom Toliar** (open 8am-7pm daily) next to Štrbské Pleso train station.

There are **supermarkets** in Starý Smokovec, Tatranská Lomnica and Štrbské Pleso, all open 7.45am to 5.45pm Monday to Friday, and 8am to noon Saturday and Sunday; the *potraviny* (grocery), just east of the Hotel Smokovec, is open noon to 6pm on Saturday.

Getting There & Away

Bus There are regular express buses from Bratislava to Starý Smokovec (seven hours) and Tatranská Lomnica. From Starý Smokovec there are eight buses a day to -ysa Polana; six to Levoča; two to Bardejov; four to Žilina (125 Sk, 3¼ hours); three to Trenčín; and one to Brno and Prague (11 hours) in the Czech Republic. The Hungarian Volánbusz bus from Budapest to Tatranská Lomnica runs twice a week (seven hours).

Train To reach Vysoké Tatry, take any of the express trains running between Prague, Bratislava and Košice, and change at Poprad. There are frequent narrow-gauge electric trains between Poprad and Starý Smokovec.

Alternatively, get off the express at Tatranská Štrba, a main-line station west of Poprad, and take the rack-railway up to Štrbské Pleso.

The booking offices in Starý Smokovec and Tatranská Lomnica train stations can reserve sleepers and couchettes from Poprad to Bratislava and to Prague, Karlovy Vary and Brno in the Czech Republic.

Walking into Poland For anyone who is interested in walking between Slovakia and Poland, there's a highway border crossing near Javorina, an hour from Starý Smokovec by bus (46 Sk). The bus is occasionally crowded and the bus stop is 100m from the border (bus times posted). On the Polish side, buses can fill up with people on excursions between Morskie Oko Lake and Zakopane, so it's easier southbound than northbound.

You'll find a bank where you can change money at -ysa Polana on the Polish side, but there's no Slovak bank at Javorina. The rate offered at the border is about 10% worse than in Zakopane. Southbound travellers should buy a few dollars worth of Slovak crowns at an exchange office in Poland to pay the onward bus fare to Starý Smokovec or Poprad, as this may not be possible at the border.

A bus direct from Poprad to Zakopane, Poland, leaves Starý Smokovec bus station at 6.15am on Thursday and Saturday (two hours). Also ask Satur about its excursion buses to Zakopane and Kraków.

Getting Around

Electric trains travel from Poprad to Starý Smokovec (16 Sk, 30 minutes) and Štrbské Pleso (26 Sk, one hour) about every half-hour, and from Starý Smokovec to Tatranská Lomnica (11 Sk, 15 minutes) about every 30 to 60 minutes. These trains make frequent stops along their routes; when there isn't a ticket window at the station, go immediately to the conductor on boarding to buy your ticket.

A rack-railway connects Štrba (on the main Žilina-Poprad road and train line) with Štrbské Pleso (22 Sk, 5km). A two-/six-day ticket giving unlimited travel on the Tatra trains costs 136/262 Sk.

You can hire **mountain bikes** from Tatrasport in Starý Smokovec for 299 Sk a day.

POPRAD

☎ 052 • pop 53,000

Poprad is a modern industrial city with little to interest visitors; however, it's an important transportation hub. The electric railway from here to Starý Smokovec was built in 1908 and extended to Štrbské Pleso in 1912.

The **AiCES information centre** (☎ 772 17 00; nám Sv Egídia 2950/114; open 8.30am-noon & 1pm-5pm Mon-Fri, 9am-1pm Sat) covers the whole Tatry region, and rents bicycles for 200 Sk a day.

There's a 24-hour left-luggage desk at the Poprad train station.

Places to Stay & Eat

If you arrive late, you could stay at the rundown **Hotel Európa** (☎ 772 18 83; singles/doubles/triples 250/400/550 Sk) just outside of the Poprad train station.

In town, **Tatratour** (☎ 776 37 12; nám Sv Egídia 9) can arrange smarter pension accommodation from 350 Sk per person.

Ulica 1.mája, north of the main square, has several good eateries including **Slovenská reštaurácia** (mains 45-65 Sk; open 11am-11pm daily) and a cheap **pizzeria** (open 9.30am-7pm Mon-Sat).

There's also a **supermarket** above the Prior department store at the western end of the town square.

Getting There & Away

Bus There are buses to almost everywhere in Slovakia departing from the large bus station next to the train station, including Bratislava (336 Sk, four hours), Košice (158 Sk, two hours), Červený Kláštor (62 Sk, 1¾ hours), Levoča (26km), Spišské Podhradie (41km) and Bardejov (125km).

Train Poprad is a major junction on the main train line from Prague and Bratislava to Košice. Express trains run to Žilina (two hours) and Košice (1½ hours) every couple of hours. Electric trains climb 13km to Starý Smokovec, the main Vysoké Tatry resort, every hour or so. A branch line runs to Plaveč (two hours by local train), where you can get a connection to Muszyna, five times a day.

KEŽMAROK

☎ 052 • pop 21,100

Over the centuries this fiercely independent town, its northwestern skyline dominated by the mighty Vysoké Tatry range, was the second most important in the region after Levoča. In the 13th century it was colonised by the Germans and was granted royal status in 1380. The citizens of Kežmarok declared an independent republic in 1918 but almost immediately the town was incorporated into Czechoslovakia. These days Kežmarok has a well-preserved old town with a castle and three interesting churches to admire.

If you can make it to Kežmarok on the second weekend in July, don't miss the Festival of European Folk Crafts, with exhibits of craft making, folk dancing and singing.

Orientation & Information

The bus and train stations are side by side northwest of the old town, just across the Poprad River.

There's a useful **AiCES information office** (☎ 452 40 47; open 8.30am-noon & 1.30pm-5pm Mon-Fri, 9am-2pm Sat year-round, 9am-2pm Sun June-Sept) located at Hlavné nám 46 for tourist help.

Things to See

The **New Evangelical Church** (cnr Toporcerova & Hviezdoslavova; open 9am-noon & 2pm-5pm daily May-Sept), built in 1894, is a huge red and green pseudo-Moorish structure housing the mausoleum of Imre Thököly, who fought with Ferenc Rákóczi against the Habsburg takeover of Hungary. Next door, the **Wooden Articulated Church** (open 9am-noon & 2pm-5pm daily May-Sept) was built in 1717 without a single iron nail and has an amazing cross-shaped interior of carved and painted wood.

North of Hlavné nám is the 15th-century Gothic **Church of the Holy Cross** (nám Požárnikov), with its beautifully carved wooden altars supposedly crafted by students of Master Pavol of Levoča.

The **Kežmarok Museum** (admission 50 Sk; open 9am-4pm Tues-Sun), inside the 15th-century Kežmarok Castle, features history, archaeology and period-furniture.

Places to Stay & Eat

The basic **Karpaty Camping** (☎ 452 24 90) is about 4km southwest of the town centre on the road to Poprad. **Private rooms** through AiCES cost from 200 Sk per person.

Beneath the castle walls is **Penzión Hubert** (☎ 0905-248 460; Hradská cesta 8; rooms per person 300 Sk), while **Hotel Štart** (☎ 452 29 15; rooms per person from 290 Sk) is 10 minutes' walk north of the castle.

The **Kežmarská Restaurant** (Hradné nám 5; mains 60-120 Sk; open 9am-10pm daily) opposite the castle is reasonable, or try **Pizza Palermo** (Hlavné nám 8; mains 60-100 Sk; open 10am-10pm daily) for pizza and pasta.

Getting There & Away

Buses are faster and more plentiful than trains – they run about hourly from Poprad, and there are eight daily from Starý Smokovec. There are also five daily buses to Červený Kláštor.

DUNAJEC GORGE

☎ 052

The Pieniny National Park (21 sq km), created in 1967, combines with a similar park in Poland to protect the 9km Dunajec Gorge between the Slovak village of Červený Kláštor and Szczawnica, Poland. The river here, flowing between 500m limestone cliffs, forms the international boundary.

At the mouth of the gorge is a 14th-century fortified **Carthusian monastery** (admission 25 Sk; open 9am-5pm daily May-Sept, 9am-4pm Tues-Sat Oct-Apr), now used as a park administrative centre and museum with a good collection of statuary and old prints of the area. Near the monastery is an **information centre** (open 9am-5pm daily May-Sept).

From May to October, river trips (200 Sk per person) on wooden rafts depart from two locations at Červený Kláštor: opposite the monastery, and 1km upriver west of the village. A raft will set out only when enough passengers appear. When business is slow you may have to wait. Note that this is not white-water rafting – the Dunajec is a rather sedate experience.

From the downriver terminus you can hike back to the monastery in a little over an hour. The rafting operation on the Polish side is larger and better organised (see Dunajec Gorge in the Poland chapter for details), and the Slovak raft trip is much shorter than the Polish one.

Even if you don't go rafting, it's still worth hiking along the riverside trail through the gorge on the Slovak side (no such trail exists on the Polish side).

Places to Stay

Across a small stream from the monastery is a **camping ground** (open mid-June–mid-Sept). No bungalows are available.

There are several pensions in Červený Kláštor plus the **Hotel Pltník** (☎ 482 25 25; beds per person 500 Sk), which can often be booked out in summer.

One kilometre up the road to Veľký Lipník from the monastery is **Hotel Dunajec** (☎ 482 20 27), with some inexpensive bungalows across the road.

Close to Lesnica, which is just 2km east of Cerveny Klastor, near the downstream end of the rafting trip, is the inexpensive **Pieniny chata** (☎/fax 439 75 30; beds 150 Sk, doubles with breakfast 430 Sk), which is often full during the summer.

Getting There & Away

Direct buses run between Červený Kláštor and both Poprad and Stara Ľubovňa, and there are buses from Stará Ľubovňa to Bardejov, Prešov and Košice.

Although Poland is just across the river, there's no official border crossing here. You can take a bus to Stará Ľubovňa and then a train to Plaveč, where a local train departs three times daily for Muszyna in Poland, 16km away. Alternatively, you can use the -ysa Polana crossing (see Getting There & Away in the Vysoké Tatry section) to make your way to Zakopane.

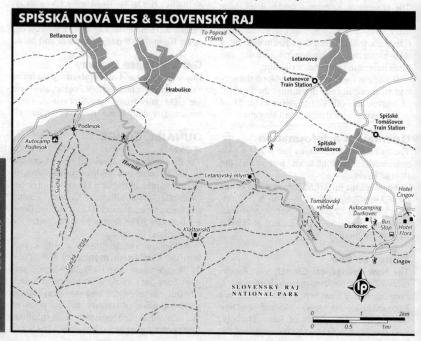

SPIŠSKÁ NOVÁ VES & SLOVENSKÝ RAJ

SLOVENSKÝ RAJ

☎ 053

South of Poprad lies the Slovenský raj (Slovak Paradise), a national park created in 1988. This mountainous karst area features forests, cliffs, caves, canyons, waterfalls and 1896 species of butterfly, and is prime hiking territory.

Orientation & Information

The nearest town is **Spišská Nová Ves**, 23km southeast of Poprad. The main trailheads on the northern edge of the national park are at Čingov, 5km west of Spišská Nová Ves, and Podlesok, 1km southwest of Hrabušice.

The **AiCES information centre** (☎ 442 82 92; Ⓦ *www.slovenskyraj.sk; Letná 49; open 8.30am-5.30pm Mon-Fri, 9.30am-1pm Sat June-Sept; 9.30am-4pm Mon-Fri Oct-May*) in Spišská Nová Ves can help with accommodation and national park information. You can buy VKÚ's 1:25,000 *Slovenský raj* hiking map (sheet No 4) here.

You can cash travellers cheques or use the 24-hour ATM at the **Slovenská sporiteľňa** (*nám MR Štefánika*). The telephone centre is in the **main post office** (*nám MR Štefánika 7; open 7am-7pm Mon-Fri, 7am-11am Sat*).

Things to See & Do

From Čingov a blue trail leads up the **Hornád River gorge**, passing below Tomášovský výhľad, to Letanovský mlýn. The trail up the river is narrow and there are several ladders and ramps where hikers can only pass one by one. During peak periods hikers are allowed to travel only in an upstream direction from Čingov, returning over Tomášovský výhľad.

One kilometre beyond Letanovský mlýn, a green trail leaves the river and climbs sharply up to **Kláštorisko**, where there's a **restaurant** (☎ 449 33 07; *cabins per person 200 Sk; open daily year-round*), with chalet *(chaty)* accommodation. To stay here in midsummer, you should call ahead to check availability. From Kláštorisko you can follow another blue trail back down the ridge towards Čingov. You'll need around six hours to do the entire circuit, lunch at Kláštorisko included.

From Podlesok, an excellent day's hike heads up the **Suchá Belá gorge** (with several steep ladders), then east to Kláštorisko on a yellow then red trail. From here, take the blue trail down to the Hornád River, then follow the river gorge upstream to return to Podlesok. Allow six to seven hours.

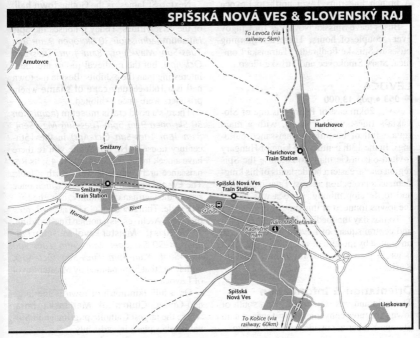

SPIŠSKÁ NOVÁ VES & SLOVENSKÝ RAJ

Places to Stay

You can camp at the **Autocamping Ďurkovec** (☎ 429 71 05, fax 429 71 06; e durkovec@ durkovec.sk; camp sites 40 Sk, plus per person 50 Sk, dorm beds 150 Sk, bungalows 1800 Sk), about 20 minutes' walk west from Čingov bus stop, and at **Autocamp Podlesok** (☎ 449 02 81; e slovrajbela@globtelnet.sk; camp sites 100 Sk, huts per person 300 Sk).

The family-oriented **Hotel Flora** (☎ 449 11 31, fax 449 11 30; singles/doubles with bath 550/800 Sk) is just east of Čingov. Nearby is the comfortable, chalet-style **Hotel Čingov** (☎ 443 36 33, fax 443 36 30; e hotelcingov@ slovanet.sk; singles/doubles 750/900 Sk).

Getting There & Away

Slovenský raj trailheads are accessible by bus from Spišská Nová Ves at Čingov, and by car at Podlesok. The closest train station is Spišské Tomášovce, an hour's walk from Letanovský mlýn on a green-marked trail. Only local trains stop at this station (about nine a day between Poprad and Spišská Nová Ves).

Spišská Nová Ves is on the main railway line from Žilina to Košice, with trains from Poprad every hour or so. All trains stop here. A branch line runs 13km north to Levoča with services every two hours or so.

Buses leave Spišská Nová Ves for Čingov every couple of hours. There are morning buses to Spišské Podhradie, Tatranská Lomnica, Starý Smokovec and Štrbské Pleso.

LEVOČA
☎ 053 • pop 13,000

Levoča, 26km east of Poprad, is one of Slovakia's finest walled towns, with a main square full of beautiful Renaissance buildings. In the 13th century the king of Hungary invited Saxon Germans to colonise the Spiš region on the eastern borderlands of his kingdom, as a protection against Tatar incursions and to develop mining. Levoča was one of the towns founded at this time.

To this day the medieval walls, street plan and central square of Levoča have survived, unspoiled by modern development. The town is an easy stop on the way from Poprad to Košice.

Orientation & Information

The train and bus stations are 1km south of town. The most convenient bus stop is at nám Štefana Kluberta, outside the Košice Gate.

The **AiCES information centre** (☎ 451 37 63; nám Majstra Pavla 58; open 9am-5pm Mon-Fri, 9.30am-2pm Sat) is at the top of the square. **Slovenská sporiteľňa** (nám Majstra Pavla 56; open 8am-3pm Mon-Fri, 8am-4pm Wed) changes travellers cheques and also has an ATM.

The **telephone centre** is in the **post office** (nám Majstra Pavla 42; open 8am-noon & 1pm-4.30pm Mon-Fri, 8am-11.30am Sat). You can check email at **System House** (Košická 3; open 8am-11.30am & 12.30pm-4.30pm Mon-Fri) for 1.50 Sk per minute.

Things to See

Nám Majstra Pavla, Levoča's central square, is filled with superb Gothic and Renaissance buildings. The 15th-century **St James' Church** (admission 40 Sk; open 2pm-5pm Mon, 9am-5pm Tues-Sat, 1pm-5pm Sun June-Sept; 8am-4pm Tues-Sat Oct-May) contains a towering Gothic altar (1517) by Majster Pavol (Master Paul) of Levoča, one of the largest and finest of its kind in Europe. The Madonna on this altar appears on the 100 Sk banknote. Buy tickets in the Municipal Weights House opposite the north door.

Next to St James' is the Gothic **town hall**, enlivened by Renaissance arcades and murals of the civic virtues. Today it houses the **Spiš Museum** (admission 30 Sk; open 9am-5pm Tues-Sun May-Sept, 8am-4pm Tues-Sun Oct-Apr), but the medieval rooms are more interesting than the exhibits. Beside the town hall is a 16th-century **cage of shame** where prisoners were once exhibited.

There's a good **crafts museum** (admission 30 Sk; open 9am-5pm Tues-Sun May-Sept, 8am-4pm Tues-Sun Oct-Apr) in the 15th-century house at No 40. While you're there have a peek in the courtyard of No 43; its Renaissance architecture is well worth a look. The **Evangelical church** (1837), which once served the German community, is in the Empire style. **Thurzov dom** (1532) at No 7, now the State Archives, is another fine building. At No 20 is the **Majster Pavol Museum** (admission 30 Sk; open 9am-5pm Tues-Sun May-Sept, 8am-4pm Tues-Sun Oct-Apr), with icons that were painted by Majster Pavol of Levoča.

On a hill 2km north of town is the large neo-Gothic **Church of Mariánska hora**, where the largest Catholic pilgrimage in Slovakia takes place in early July.

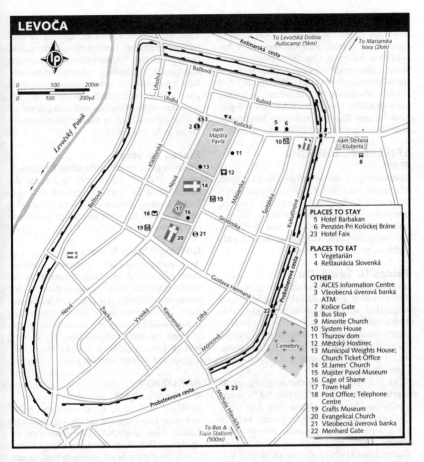

LEVOČA

PLACES TO STAY
5 Hotel Barbakan
6 Penzión Pri Košickej Bráne
23 Hotel Faix

PLACES TO EAT
1 Vegetarián
4 Reštaurácia Slovenká

OTHER
2 AiCES Information Centre
3 Všeobecná úverová banka ATM
7 Košice Gate
8 Bus Stop
9 Minorite Church
10 System House
11 Thurzov dom
12 Mestský Hostinec
13 Municipal Weights House; Church Ticket Office
14 St James' Church
15 Majster Pavol Museum
16 Cage of Shame
17 Town Hall
18 Post Office; Telephone Centre
19 Crafts Museum
20 Evangelical Church
21 Všeobecná úverová banka
22 Menhard Gate

Places to Stay

The **Levočská Dolina Autocamp** (☎ 451 27 05; open mid-June–Aug) is 5km north of nám Štefana Kluberta on the road to Závada. Bungalows are available.

AiCES can book accommodation for travellers, including **private rooms** from 250 Sk per person. Most of the rooms are outside the old town; those inside are more expensive, around 300 Sk to 400 Sk.

The slightly run-down, 25-room **Hotel Faix** (☎ 451 23 35; Probstnerova cesta 22; doubles 700 Sk), which is between the train station and the old town, has basic doubles with a shower or toilet.

Penzión Pri Košickej Bráne (☎ 451 28 79; Košická 16; 450 Sk per person) is just inside the Košice Gate.

The best-value hotel within the city walls is the charmingly old-fashioned **Hotel Barbakan** (☎ 451 4310, fax 451 3609; e recepcia.hot@barbakan.sk; Košická 15; singles/doubles 1150/1450 Sk). The rates include breakfast and the rooms have an en suite bathroom, TV and minibar.

Places to Eat

The best place for a meal is the homely and inexpensive **Reštaurácia Slovenká** (nám Majstra Pavla 62; mains 70-110 Sk; open 9am-10pm daily). The popular **Vegetarián** (Uhoľná 137; mains 30-70 Sk; open 10am-3.15pm Mon-Fri), is off the northwest corner of the main square. For a beer, try the Slovenká or the lively **Mestský hostinec** (nám Majstra Pavla 11).

Getting There & Away

Levoča is connected by hourly local trains to Spišská Nová Ves (15 Sk, 20 minutes), 13km south on the main line from Bratislava to Košice. Bus travel is more practical with frequent services to Poprad (30 minutes) and Spišské Podhradie (20 minutes) and eight daily to Košice (two hours). All buses stop at nám Štefana Kluberta and some local buses stop at the train station in the south of town.

SPIŠSKÉ PODHRADIE
☎ 053

Considering its nearness to the tourist magnet of Spišský hrad (Spiš Castle), the small town of Spišské Podhradie, 15km east of Levoča, is surprisingly dismal and run down. There's no reason to linger in the town itself, but nearby Spišský hrad and Spišská Kapitula are sights of prime importance.

Things to See & Do

If you're arriving by bus from Levoča, ask the driver to drop you at **Spišská Kapitula**, on a ridge 1km west of Spišské Podhradie. This 13th-century ecclesiastical settlement is completely encircled by a 16th-century wall, and the single street running between the two medieval gates is lined with some picturesque Gothic houses.

At the upper end is the magnificent **St Martin's Cathedral** (admission 30 Sk; open 10am-5pm Mon-Sat, 11am-4pm Sun May-Oct, 1pm-3pm Mon-Fri Nov-Apr), built in 1273, with twin Romanesque towers and a Gothic sanctuary. Inside are three folding Gothic altars (1499) and, near the door, a Romanesque white lion. On either side of the cathedral are the seminary and the Renaissance bishop's palace (1652).

Crowning a ridge on the far side of Spišské Podhradie is the 180m-long **Spišský hrad** (admission 50 Sk; open 9am-6pm daily May-Sept, 9am-3pm daily Nov-Apr), the largest castle in Slovakia. In 1993 it was added to Unesco's world heritage list. The castle is directly above the train station, 1km south of Spišské Podhradie's bus stop. Cross at the tracks near the station and follow the yellow markers up to the castle. The first gate is always locked, so carry on to the second one higher up. (If you're driving or cycling, the access road is off the Prešov highway east of town.)

The castle was founded in 1209 – the defenders of Spišský are said to have repulsed the Tatars in 1241 – and reconstructed in the 15th century. Until 1710 the Spiš region was administered from here. Although the castle burnt down in 1780, the ruins and the site are spectacular. The highest castle enclosure contains a round Gothic tower, a cistern, a chapel and a rectangular Romanesque palace perched over the abyss. Weapons and instruments of torture are exhibited in the dungeon (explanations in Slovak only).

Places to Stay

The only place to stay is **Penzión Podzámok** (☎/fax 454 17 55; e sykora@sn.psg.sk; Podzámková 28; beds per person 350 Sk), with a friendly, English-speaking owner. To get there, turn left after the bridge just south of Mariánské nám.

Getting There & Away

A branch train line connects Spišské Podhradie to Spišské Vlachy (9km), a station on the main line from Poprad to Košice. Departures are scheduled to connect with Košice trains. You can use at the left-luggage office in the Spišské Podhradie train station.

There are frequent buses from Košice (1½ hours), Levoča (15km), Spišská Nová Ves (25km) and Poprad (45 minutes).

BARDEJOV
☎ 054 • pop 32,200

Bardejov received its royal charter in 1376, and grew rich on trade between Poland and Russia. After an abortive 17th-century revolt against the Habsburgs, Bardejov's fortunes declined, but the medieval town survived. In late 1944 heavy fighting took place at the Dukla Pass on the Polish border, 54km northeast of Bardejov on the road to Rzeszów (preserved WWII Soviet tanks can be seen from the road).

The sloping central square lined with the Gothic-Renaissance houses built by wealthy merchants has been carefully preserved. Much of the town's walls, including the moat, towers and bastions, remain intact. The town hosts several festivals, one of the liveliest being The Market (jarmok), when Radničné nám turns into one big market with lots of food, drink and good times included.

Orientation

The bus and train station (left-luggage office open 7am to 6.30pm Monday to Saturday, 11am to 8pm Sunday) is a five-minute walk northeast from Radničné nám, the main square in Bardejov.

Information
The helpful **AiCES information centre** (☎ 472 62 73; Radničné nám 21; open 9am-4.30pm Mon-Fri) can assist with accommodation and guided tours.

The **Investičná banka** (Radničné nám; open 8am-4.30pm Mon, Tues, Thur & Fri, 8am-2pm Wed) changes travellers cheques and has an ATM.

The **telephone centre** is in the **main post office** (Dlhý rad 14).

Things to See
The 14th-century **Church of St Egídius** is one of the most remarkable buildings in the country, with no less than 11 tall Gothic altarpieces, built from 1460 to 1510, all with their own original paintings and sculptures. The structural purity of the parish church and the 15th-century bronze baptismal font are very striking.

There are four branches of the **Šariš Museum** (admission 25 Sk; open 8.30am-noon & 12.30pm-5pm daily May-Sept) on the main square. In the centre is the **old town hall** (1509), the first Renaissance building in Slovakia, now a museum with more altarpieces and a historical collection. Two museums face one another on Rhodyho at the southern end of the square: one has an excellent natural history exhibit, the other a collection of icons. A fourth branch at Radničné nám 13 has temporary art exhibits.

Places to Stay
There's not a lot to choose from. First choice is the excellent **Penzión Semafór** (☎ 474 44 33, 0905-830 984; e semafor@stonline.sk; cnr Kellerova & BS Timravy; singles/doubles 500/1000 Sk) is a few minutes' walk north of the old town.

Šport Hotel (☎ 472 49 49; Kutuzovova 31; rooms per person 500 Sk), a slightly worn out, two-storey block overlooking the Topľa River, is aimed mainly at Slovak families, but may take you in if they have room.

If you have some cash to spare, the flashy **Hotel Bellevue** (☎ 472 84 04, fax 472 84 09; Mihalov; singles/doubles 1800/2200 Sk) sits on a hilltop 3km southwest of the centre; take bus No 8 westbound from Dlhý rad.

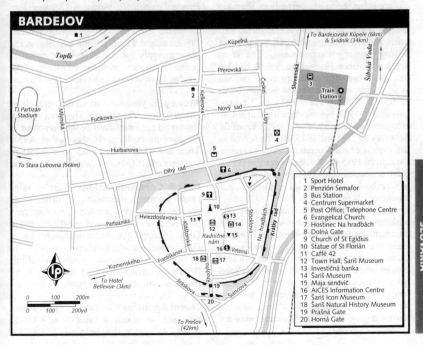

BARDEJOV

1 Sport Hotel
2 Penzión Semafor
3 Bus Station
4 Centrum Supermarket
5 Post Office; Telephone Centre
6 Evangelical Church
7 Hostinec Na hradbách
8 Dolná Gate
9 Church of St Egídius
10 Statue of St Florián
11 Caffé 42
12 Town Hall; Šariš Museum
13 Investičná banka
14 Šariš Museum
15 Maja sendvič
16 AiCES Information Centre
17 Šariš Icon Museum
18 Šariš Natural History Museum
19 Prašná Gate
20 Horná Gate

SLOVAKIA

Places to Eat

Again, there is not much choice. Apart from a few pizza restaurants there is the beer hall **Hostinec Na hradbách** (Stöcklova 16; mains 50-90 Sk; open 10am-10pm Mon-Fri, 11am-3pm Sat & Sun).

Maja sendvič (Radničné nám 15; open 8am-9pm Mon-Thur, 8am-11pm Fri, 3pm-11pm Sat, 3pm-8pm Sun) sells huge baguette sandwiches for around 30 Sk. Popular cafés on and around the square include **Caffé 42** at the corner of Hviezdoslava.

There's a supermarket at **Centrum** (cnr Slovenská & Dlhý rad; open 6am-6pm Mon-Thur, 6am-8pm Fri, 6am-4pm Sat).

Getting There & Away

There are frequent buses from Bardejov to Košice (79 Sk, 1¾ hours). If you want to go to the Vysoké Tatry, there are hourly buses to Poprad (120 Sk, two hours); there are also two buses daily direct to Starý Smokovec (three hours), six to Bratislava (10 hours) and six to Žilina (five hours).

KOŠICE

☎ 055 • pop 235,000

Košice is the second-largest city in Slovakia and capital of the eastern part of the country. Before WWI, Košice had a Hungarian majority and the historic and ethnic influence of nearby Hungary remains strong. The Transylvanian prince Ferenc Rákóczi II had his headquarters at Košice during the Hungarian War of Independence against the Habsburgs (1703–11). The town became part of Czechoslovakia in 1918 but was again occupied by Hungary between 1938 and 1945. From 21 February to 21 April 1945, Košice served as the capital of the liberated Czechoslovakia. On 5 April 1945 the Košice Government Program – which made communist dictatorship in Czechoslovakia a virtual certainty – was announced here.

Although now a major steel-making city with vast new residential districts built during communist rule, there is a great deal in the revamped old town that is of interest to visitors. Churches and museums abound, and there's also an active state theatre. The city is a good base for excursions on to other East Slovak towns. The daily trains travelling between Kraków and Budapest stop here, making Košice a good arrival or departure point for visitors to Slovakia.

Orientation

The adjacent bus and train stations are just east of the old town. A five-minute walk along Mlynská will bring you into Hlavná (Main Street), which broadens to accommodate the squares of Hlavné nám and nám Slobody.

The left-luggage office in the train station is open 24 hours a day, except for three 45-minute breaks.

Information

Tourist Offices The AiCES information centre (☎ 16 168; e mic@pangea.sk; open 8am-5pm Mon-Fri, 9am-1pm Sat), in the Dargov department store, opposite the Hotel Slovan sells maps, guidebooks and concert tickets, and also provides information about accommodation.

The **municipal information centre** (☎ 625 88 88; Hlavná 59; open 9am-6pm Mon-Fri, 9am-1pm Sat) in the town hall provides much the same services, and also sells parking tickets.

Visa Extensions The police and passport office (Úradovňa cudzineckej polície a pasovej služby; trieda Slovenského Národného Povstania; open 10am-noon & 12.30pm-6pm Mon & Wed, 7am-noon Tues, Thur & Fri), across the street from the huge Košice/Mestský municipal administration building, is the place to apply for visa extensions, complete police registration or report a lost visa. Take bus No 19 west from Štúrova.

Money If you need to change travellers cheques try **Všeobecná úverová banka** (Hlavná 112; open 8am-5pm Mon-Wed & Fri, 8am-noon Thur). It also has an ATM. There are many other banks with exchange counters and ATMs on Hlavná and Mlynská.

Post & Communications There's a **telephone centre** in the **main post office** (Poštová 2; open 7am-7pm Mon-Fri, 7am-2pm Sat). A more convenient post office is at the Dargov shopping centre, at the corner of nám Osvoboditeľov and Mojmirova.

You can check your email at **NetClub** (Hlavná 9; open 9am-10pm daily) for 50 Sk per hour with a 10 Sk minimum.

Travel Agencies You can buy international train and bus tickets at **Satur** (☎ 622 31 22; Hlavná 1), next to Hotel Slovan.

KOŠICE

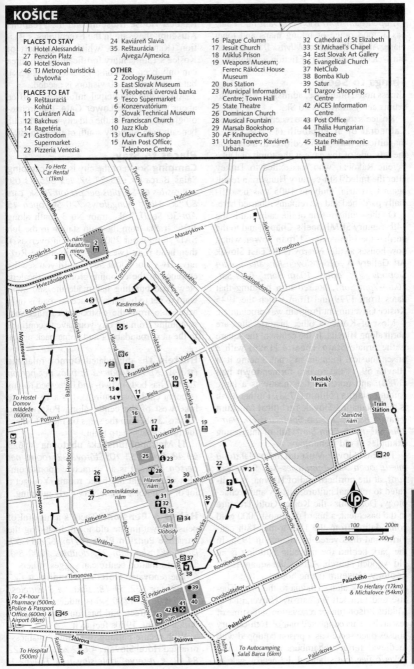

PLACES TO STAY
1 Hotel Alessandria
27 Penzión Platz
40 Hotel Slovan
46 TJ Metropol turistická ubytovňa

PLACES TO EAT
9 Reštaurciá Kohút
11 Cukráreň Aida
14 Bakchus
14 Bagetéria
21 Gastrodom Supermarket
22 Pizzeria Venezia

24 Kaviáreň Slavia
35 Reštaurácia Ajvega/Ajmexica

OTHER
2 Zoology Museum
3 East Slovak Museum
4 Všeobecná úverová banka
5 Tesco Supermarket
6 Konzervatórium
7 Slovak Technical Museum
8 Franciscan Church
10 Jazz Klub
13 Uľuv Crafts Shop
15 Main Post Office; Telephone Centre

16 Plague Column
17 Jesuit Church
18 Mikluš Prison
19 Weapons Museum; Ferenc Rákóczi House Museum
20 Bus Station
23 Municipal Information Centre; Town Hall
25 State Theatre
26 Dominican Church
28 Musical Fountain
29 Marsab Bookshop
30 AF Kníhupectvo
31 Urban Tower; Kaviáreň Urbana

32 Cathedral of St Elizabeth
33 St Michael's Chapel
34 East Slovak Art Gallery
36 Evangelical Church
37 NetClub
38 Bomba Klub
39 Satur
41 Dargov Shopping Centre
42 AiCES Information Centre
43 Post Office
44 Thália Hungarian Theatre
45 State Philharmonic Hall

SLOVAKIA

Bookshops The **Marsab Bookshop** *(Hlavná 41; open 8am-6pm Mon-Fri, 9am-noon Sat)* has a good range of hiking maps and town plans. **AF Kníhupectvo** *(Mlynská)* has a small but welcome selection of fiction in English.

Things to See

Unless noted otherwise, admission to the museums and galleries is 20 Sk.

Košice's top sight is the recently renovated **Cathedral of St Elizabeth** (1345–1508), a magnificent late-Gothic edifice. In a crypt on the left side of the nave is the tomb of Duke Ferenc Rákóczi, who was exiled to Turkey after the failed 18th-century Hungarian revolt against Austria. Only in 1905 was he officially pardoned and his remains reburied here.

On the southern side of the cathedral is the 14th-century **St Michael's Chapel**, and to the north is the 14th-century **Urban Tower**, which now houses a café. Nearby is the **East Slovak Art Gallery** *(Východoslovenská galéria; nám Slobody 27; open 10am-6pm Tues-Sat, 10am-2pm Sun)*, housed in a building that dates from 1779 and from which the 1945 Košice Government Program was proclaimed.

Most of Košice's other historic sites are north along Hlavná. In the centre of the square is the ornate **State Theatre** (1899) with a kitsch musical fountain in front. Facing it at Hlavná 59, is the rococo former **town hall** (1780), and north of the theatre is a large baroque **plague column** (1723). Further north is the fascinating **Slovak Technical Museum** *(Hlavná 88; open 8am-5pm Tues-Fri, 9am-2pm Sat, noon-5pm Sun)*, full of interesting examples of old technology.

The **East Slovak Museum** *(nám Maratónu mieru; open 9am-5pm Tues-Sat, 9am-1pm Sun)*, at the northern end of Hlavná, is dedicated to regional culture, history and archaeology. Don't miss the Košice Gold Treasure in the basement, a hoard of almost 3000 gold coins dating from the 15th to the 18th centuries and discovered by chance in 1935. In the park behind the museum building is an old wooden church. Across the square is the **Zoology Museum** (same hours).

Walk back along Hlavná to the State Theatre and turn left on narrow Univerzitná to **Mikluš Prison** (under renovation at the time of research). This connected pair of 16th-century houses once served as a prison equipped with medieval torture chambers and cells. The ticket office that's behind the nearby gate at Hrnčiarska 7 also sells tickets for **Ferenc Rákóczi House Museum** and the **Weapons Museum**; these are in the Executioner's Bastion (Katova bašta), which was a part of Košice's 15th-century fortifications. All three can only been seen on a guided tour (20 Sk), but a minimum of 10 visitors is needed.

Ask at the municipal information office about tours of the **Lower Gate**, the archaeological remnants of the old city walls that lie beneath nám Slobody south of the cathedral.

Places to Stay

Camping South of the city is **Autocamping Salaš Barca** *(☎ 623 33 97, fax 625 83 09; camp sites 60 Sk, plus per person 70 Sk, cars 80 Sk, 3-bed bungalows 720 Sk; open 15 Apr-30 Sept)*. Take tram No 3 south along Južná trieda from the train station to the Juh SAD stop (about 200m before an overpass), then head right (west) on Alejová (the Rožňava Hwy) for about 500m until you see the entrance to the camping ground on the left. New road building has made the site awkward to get to by car – the access road is only accessible from the eastbound carriageway, so coming from the city you have to continue to the next roundabout and come back again.

Hostels The dilapidated **Domov mládeže** *(☎ 642 90 52; Medická 2; beds per person 150 Sk)* has beds in two- and three-bed rooms (student card not required). It's a 15-minute hike west of the centre along Poštová and Vojenská, then up the steps on the left where the road bends sharp right.

TJ Metropol turistická ubytovňa *(☎ 625 59 48, fax 76 31 10; Štúrova 32; rooms per person 300 Sk)* is an attractive sports complex with bright but basic rooms. You get a lot of tram noise in the very early morning.

Hotels & Pensions There's a handful of pensions within the old town, including the attractive **Penzión Platz** *(☎/fax 622 34 50; Dominikánske nám 23; doubles 1200 Sk)*. The information centre can suggest others.

The renovated **Hotel Alessandria** *(☎ 622 59 03, fax 622 59 18; Jiskrova 3; singles/ doubles 1150/1790 Sk)* is hidden away on a quiet back street, and has four-star facilities with a quaint, 1970s feel to it.

With secure parking, luxurious, business-oriented **Hotel Slovan** *(☎ 622 73 78, fax 622 84 13; e reserve@hotelslovan.sk; Hlavná 1;*

singles/doubles from 2250/3100 Sk) is the best and priciest place in town, with an elegant restaurant.

Places to Eat
A popular place to eat on the main square is the inexpensive **Bakchus** *(Hlavná 8; mains 55-90 Sk; open 9am-11pm Mon-Fri, 10am-midnight Sat & Sun)*, with an international menu and an open courtyard in summer.

Reštaurácia Ajvega/Ajmexica *(Orlia 10; mains 90-135 Sk; open 11am-10pm daily)* combines a tasty vegetarian menu with carnivorous Mexican fare. **Reštauraciá Kohút** *(Hrnčiarska 23; mains 100-180 Sk; open 11.30-midnight daily)* serves chicken dishes and kebabs, and has a nice summer garden out back.

Pizzeria Venezia *(Mlynská; mains 80-110 Sk; open 11am-10pm daily)* with pleasant outdoor tables, has good pizzas and pasta.

Elegant **Kaviáreň Slavia** *(Hlavná 59)*, all dark wood and art-nouveau detailing, is a good place for coffee and cakes, while **Cukráreň Aida** *(cnr Hlavná & Biela)*, has the best ice cream in town. **Kaviáreň Urbana** *(open Mon-Fr)* is set in the 14th-century Gothic Urban Tower and serves coffee, drinks and cakes.

You can get cheap baguette sandwiches at **Bagetéria** *(Hlavná 74; open 8.30am-9pm Mon-Thur, 8.30am-10pm Fri, 9am-9pm Sat, 10am-8pm Sun)*.

There are supermarkets at **Tesco** *(Hlavná; open 8am-8pm Mon-Wed, 8am-9pm Thur & Fri, 8am-6pm Sat & Sun)* and **Gastrodom** *(Mlynská; open 6am-7pm Mon-Fri, 6am-1pm Sat)*.

Entertainment
The renovated **State Theatre** *(Hlavné nám)* stages regular performances. The **Thália Hungarian Theatre** and **State Philharmonic** are in the southwestern corner of the old town; performances are held once or twice a week. Recitals are sometimes given at the **Konzervatórium** *(Hlavná 89)*.

Bars & Clubs The cellar bar **Bomba klub** *(Hlavná 5; open 10am-midnight Mon-Thur, 10am-1am Fri, 11am-midnight Sat, noon-midnight Sun)* is a popular bar with both locals and English-speaking visitors. **Jazz Klub** *(Kováčska 39; open 4pm-2am daily)* has live

jazz twice a week; the café-bar is open from 11am Monday to Friday.

Shopping
Uľuv *(Hlavná 76)* has a good selection of local handicrafts.

Getting There & Away
Train A sleeper train leaves Košice daily at 7.10am for Kyiv (22 hours, 998km). Overnight trains with sleepers and couchettes are also available between Košice and Bratislava (seven hours, 445km) and Prague (11 hours, 708km), Plzeň (896km), Brno (493km) and Karlovy Vary (897km) in the Czech Republic. Daytime express trains connect Košice to Poprad (122 Sk, two hours), Žilina (250 Sk, three hours), Bratislava and Prague.

The daily *Cracovia* express train between Budapest (four hours) and Kraków (five hours) passes through Košice (reservations are required). Northbound, the *Cracovia* departs Košice at 1.05am, and southbound at 5.38am.

Bus For shorter trips to Levoča (two hours), Bardejov (1½ hours) and Spišské Podhradie (1½ hours), you're better off taking a bus. A bus to Užgorod, Ukraine (2½ hours), leaves Košice every afternoon. There's also a daily bus to Prague (12 hours).

Heading for Poland, there's a bus from Košice to Nowy Targ (four hours) at 5.45am every Thursday and Saturday, and to Krosno every Wednesday, Friday and Saturday. In both cases the fare is paid to the driver.

There's a bus from Košice to Miskolc (Hungary) at 6.30am on Wednesday, Friday and Saturday (two hours), and at 5.40pm Monday to Thursday. You should book your ticket the day before at window No 1 in the bus station. On Wednesday this bus continues to Budapest (five hours).

Car You will find **Hertz** *(☎ 633 06 56)* has offices at Watsonova 5, while **Avis** *(☎ 632 58 63)* is at Prešovská 69; both have desks at Košice airport. Satur can suggest cheaper local agencies.

Getting Around
Bus and tram tickets are available for 8 Sk from tobacconists, newsstands and public transport kiosks.

Slovenia

Slovenia (Slovenija) is one of the most over-looked gems in all of Europe. The wealthiest nation of former Yugoslavia, Slovenia – an Alpine country – has much more in common with its Central European neighbours than with the Balkan countries it split from in a 10-day war in 1991. The two million Slovenes were economically the most well-off among the peoples of what was once Yugoslavia, and the relative affluence and orderliness of this nation is immediately apparent. Many of its cities and towns bear the imprint of the Habsburg Empire and the Venetian Republic, and the Julian Alps are reminiscent of Switzerland.

Fairy-tale Bled Castle, breathtaking Lake Bohinj, the scenic caves at Postojna and Škocjan, the lush Soča Valley, the coastal towns of Piran and Koper and thriving Ljubljana are great attractions. All are accessible at much less than the cost of similar places in Western Europe. The amazing variety that is packed into one small area makes this country truly a 'Europe in miniature'. An added bonus is that Slovenia is a nation of polyglots, and communicating with these friendly, helpful people is never difficult.

Facts about Slovenia

HISTORY

The early Slovenes settled in the river valleys of the Danube Basin and the eastern Alps during the 6th century AD. Slovenia was brought under Germanic rule in 748, initially by the Frankish empire of the Carolingians, who converted the population to Christianity, and then as part of the Holy Roman Empire in the 9th century. The Austro-German monarchy took over control in the early 14th century and ruled (as the Habsburg Empire from 1804) right up until the end of WWI in 1918 – with only one brief interruption.

Over those six centuries, the upper classes became totally Germanised, though the peasantry retained their Slovenian identity. The Bible was translated into the vernacular during the Reformation in 1584, but Slovene did not come into common usage as a written language until the early 19th century.

At a Glance

- **Ljubljana** – historic riverside centre; panoramic views from Ljubljana Castle
- **Bled** – fashionable resort town in shadow of Julian Alps on an emerald-green lake
- **Lake Bohinj** – beautiful glacial lake with secluded swimming beaches
- **Škocjan & Postjna Caves** – karst formations; awesome Predjama Castle
- **Piran** – pretty coastal town with Venetian Gothic architecture

Capital	Ljubljana
Population	1.97 million
Official Language	Slovene
Currency	1 tolar (SIT) = 100 stotinov
Time	GMT/UTC+0100
Country Phone Code	☎ 386

In 1809, in a bid to isolate the Habsburg Empire from the Adriatic, Napoleon set up the Illyrian Provinces (Slovenia, Dalmatia and part of Croatia) with Ljubljana as the capital. Though the Habsburgs returned in 1814, French reforms in education, law and public administration endured. The democratic revolution that swept Europe in 1848 also brought increased political and national consciousness among Slovenes and, following WWI and the dissolution of the Austro-Hungarian Empire,

SLOVENIA

To Salzburg · To Graz & Vienna · HUNGARY · AUSTRIA · Klagenfurt · Villach · Mura · Murska Sobota · Beltinci · Lenti · Redics · Lendava · Karavanke Tunnel · Dravograd · Drava · Maribor · Drava River · Kranjska Gora · Jesenice · Slovenj Gradec · Slovenska Bistrica · Ptuj · Ormož · Čakovec · Vršič Pass · Triglav (2864m) · Lesce · Velenje · Bovec · Triglav National Park · Bled · Krvavec (1970m) · Rogaška Slatina · Varaždin · Julian Alps · Kobarid · Vogel (1922m) · Bohinjska Bistrica · Kranj · Brnik Airport · Kamnik · Celje · Krapina · ITALY · Tolmin · Cerkno · Škofja Loka · LJUBLJANA · Sava River · Zidani Most · Sevnica · Gorizia · Idrija · Nova Gorica · Vrhnika · Ivančna Gorica · Krško · Brežice · CROATIA · Soča · Logatec · ZAGREB · Karst · Postojna · Cerknica · Novo Mesto · Sežana · Ribnica · Trieste · Divača · Pivka · Kočevje · Metlika · ADRIATIC SEA · Izola · Škocjan Caves · Ilirska Bistrica · Črnomelj · Piran · Koper · Portorož · CROATIA · Delnice · Karlovac · Umag · Buje · Buzet · Novigrad · Opatija · Rijeka · 0 25 50km · 0 15 30mi

Slovenia was included in the Kingdom of Serbs, Croats and Slovenes.

During WWII much of Slovenia was annexed by Germany, with Italy and Hungary taking smaller bits of territory. The Slovenian Partisans fought courageously from mountain bases against the invaders, and Slovenia joined the Socialist Federal Republic of Yugoslavia in 1945.

Moves by Serbia in the late 1980s to assert its leading role culturally and economically among the Yugoslav republics was a big concern to Slovenes. When Belgrade abruptly ended the autonomy of Kosovo (where 90% of the population is ethnically Albanian) in late 1988, Slovenes feared the same could happen to them. For some years, Slovenia's interests had been shifting to the capitalist west and north; the Yugoslav connection, on the other hand, had become not only an economic burden but a political threat as well.

In the spring of 1990, Slovenia became the first Yugoslav republic to hold free elections and shed 45 years of communist rule; in December the electorate voted by 88% in favour of independence. The Slovenian government began stockpiling weapons, and on 25 June

1991 it pulled the republic out of the Yugoslav Federation. Slovenia took control of the border crossings and a 10-day war ensued. Resistance from the Slovenian militia was determined and, as no territorial claims or minority issues were involved, the Yugoslav government agreed to a truce brokered by the European Community (EC).

Slovenia got a new constitution in late December 1991, and on 15 January 1992 the EC formally recognised the country. Slovenia was admitted to the UN in May 1992 and is currently negotiating to become a member of the EU. Accession is expected to be granted in January 2004.

GEOGRAPHY

Slovenia is wedged between Austria and Croatia and shares much shorter borders with Italy and Hungary. With an area of just 20,256 sq km, Slovenia is the smallest country in Eastern Europe, about the size of Wales or Israel. Much of the country is mountainous, culminating in the northwest with the Julian Alps and the nation's highest peak, Mt Triglav (2864m). From this jagged knot, the main Alpine chain continues east along the Austrian border, while the Dinaric Range runs southeast along the coast into Croatia.

Below the limestone plateau of the Karst region lying between Ljubljana and Koper is Europe's most extensive network of karst caverns, which gave their name to other such caves around the world.

The coastal range forms a barrier isolating the Istrian Peninsula from Slovenia's corner of the Danube Basin. Much of the interior east of the Alps is drained by the Sava and Drava Rivers, both of which empty into the Danube. The Soča flows through western Slovenia into the Adriatic.

CLIMATE

Slovenia is temperate with four distinct seasons, but topography creates three individual climates. The northwest has an alpine climate with strong influences from the Atlantic as well as abundant precipitation. Temperatures in the Alpine valleys are moderate in summer but cold in winter. The coast and western Slovenia, as far north as the Soča Valley, have a Mediterranean climate with mild, sunny weather much of the year, though the burja, a cold and dry northeasterly wind from the Adriatic, can be fierce at times. Most of eastern Slovenia has a continental climate with hot summers and cold winters.

Most of the rain falls in March and April and again in October and November. January is the coldest month with an average temperature of -2°C and July the warmest (21°C).

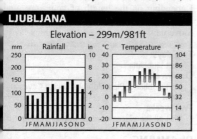

LJUBLJANA
Elevation – 299m/981ft

ECOLOGY & ENVIRONMENT

Slovenia is a very green country – over half its total area is covered in forest – and is home to 2900 plant species; Triglav National Park is particularly rich in indigenous flowering plants. Common European animals (deer, boar, chamois) abound, and rare species include *Proteus anguinus*, the unique 'human fish' that inhabits pools in karst caves.

GOVERNMENT & POLITICS

Slovenia's constitution provides for a parliamentary system of government. The National Assembly, which has exclusive jurisdiction over passing of laws, consists of 90 deputies elected for four years by proportional representation. The 40 members of the advisory Council of State are elected for five-year terms by regions and special-interest groups. The head of state, the president, is elected directly for a maximum of two five-year terms. Executive power is vested in the prime minister and the 15-member cabinet.

In parliamentary elections in November 2000, a centrist alliance of the Liberal Democrats, the People's Party, Social-Democrats and the Democratic Party of Pensioners of Slovenia garnered more than two-thirds of the vote, seating 62 MPs. Liberal Democrat Party leader Janez Drnovšek, prime minister from the first elections in 1992, again was elected head of government. Milan Kučan – a former Communist, elected as Slovenia's first president in November 1992, received a second five-year term in 1997. The most recent presidential elections were held during November 2002.

ECONOMY

Slovenia has emerged as one of the strongest economies of the former socialist countries of Eastern Europe in the years since independence. Inflation has dropped, employment is on the rise and the per-capita GDP has hovered around US$10,000 for the past few years.

For many Slovenes, however, the economic picture remains unclear. Real wages continue to grow – but faster than inflation, which puts Slovenia's international competitiveness at a disadvantage. Inflation rocketed up to 200% after independence and has steadily declined since; it is currently at 8.4%. The official unemployment rate is around 8%.

POPULATION & PEOPLE

Slovenia was the most homogeneous of all the Yugoslav republics; about 88% of the population are Slovenes. About 5% of the population is considered Croat, Serbian or Bosnian (mostly recent immigrants) and small ethnic enclaves of Italians (3000) and Hungarians (8500) still live in border areas. Some towns are officially bilingual; you'll see Italian in Piran, Koper and Portorož, and Magyar (Hungarian) in Murska Sobota and

Lendava. There are some 2300 Roma (Gypsies), mostly in the northeast.

ARTS

Slovenia's best-loved writer is the Romantic poet France Prešeren (1800–49), whose lyric poetry set new standards for Slovenian literature and helped to raise national the consciousness. Disappointed in love, Prešeren wrote sensitive love poems but also satirical verse and epic poetry.

Many notable bridges, squares and buildings in Ljubljana and elsewhere in Slovenia were designed by the architect Jože Plečnik (1872–1957), who studied under Otto Wagner in Vienna.

Postmodernist painting and sculpture has been more or less dominated since the 1980s by the multimedia group Neue Slowenische Kunst (NSK) and the five-member artists' cooperative IRWIN. Avante-garde dance is best exemplified by Betontanc, an NSK dance company that mixes live music and theatrical elements (called 'physical theatre' here) with sharp political comment.

Since WWII, many Slovenian folk traditions have been lost, but compilations by the trio Trutamora Slovenica (available at music shops in Ljubljana) examine the roots of Slovenian folk music. Folk groups – both 'pure' and popular – to watch out for include the Avseniki, Ansambel Lojzeta Slaka, the Alpski Kvintet led by Oto Pestner, and the Roma band Šukar.

Popular music runs the gamut from Slovenian *chanson* (best exemplified by Vita Mavrič) and folk to jazz and techno. Three punk groups from the late 1970s and early 1980s, Pankrti, Borghesia and Laibach, hailed from Slovenia.

Literature is extremely important to Slovenes; the last census marked a 99.6% literacy rate. Popular fiction writers include Drago Jančar and Boris Pahor. *Afterwards: Slovenian Writing 1945–1995*, edited by Andrew Zawacki, showcases the talents of the modern Slovenian *literati* (available in English at all large Ljubljana bookshops).

RELIGION

About 70% of Slovenes consider themselves Roman Catholic, but churches are hardly full on Sunday. Most weddings are now civil ceremonies. Yugoslav immigrants have brought a small Muslim population of about 5%.

LANGUAGE

Slovene is a South Slavic language written in the Roman alphabet and closely related to Croatian and Serbian. It is grammatically complex with lots of cases, genders and tenses and has something that is very rare in linguistics: singular, dual and plural forms. It's one *miza* (table) and three or more *mize* (tables) but two *mizi*.

Virtually everyone in Slovenia is able to speaks at least one other language: Croatian, Serbian, German, English and/or Italian. English is definitely the preferred language of the young.

See the Language section at the end of the book for pronunciation guidelines and useful words and phrases. Lonely Planet's *Eastern Europe phrasebook* contains a chapter on Slovene.

Facts for the Visitor

HIGHLIGHTS

Ljubljana, Piran and Koper have outstanding architecture; the hill-top castles at Bled and Ljubljana are impressive. The Škocjan and Postojna Caves are among the world's foremost underground wonders. The Soča Valley is indescribably beautiful in spring, while the frescoed Church of St John the Baptist is in itself worth the trip to Lake Bohinj.

SUGGESTED ITINERARIES

Depending on the length of your stay, you might want to see and do the following in Slovenia:

Two days
Visit Ljubljana
One week
Visit Ljubljana, Bled, Bohinj, Škocjan Caves and Piran
Two weeks
Visit all the places covered in this chapter

PLANNING
When to Go

Snow can linger in the mountains as late as June, but May and June are great months to be in the lowlands and valleys when everything is fresh and in blossom. (April can be a bit wet though.) In July and August, hotel rates go up and there will be lots of tourists, especially on the coast, but all the youth hostels are open. September is an excellent month to visit as the days are long and the weather still warm, and it's the best time for hiking and climbing. October and November can be quite rainy, and winter (December to March) is definitely for skiers.

Maps

The Geodesic Institute of Slovenia (Geodetski Zavod Slovenije; GZS), the country's principal cartographic agency, produces national (1:300,000), regional (1:50,000) and topographical maps of the entire country (64 sheets at a scale of 1:50,000) as well as city plans. The Alpine Association of Slovenia (Planinska Zveza Slovenije; PZS) has some 30 different hiking maps, with scales as large as 1:25,000.

TOURIST OFFICES
Local Tourist Offices

Located in the World Trade Centre, the **Slovenian Tourist Board** *(STO; ☎ 01-589 18 40, fax 589 18 41; ⓦ www.slovenia-tourism.si; Dunajska cesta 156)* is the umbrella organisation for tourist offices in Slovenia. It handles requests for information in writing or you can check out its excellent website.

The best office for face-to-face information in Slovenia is the **Ljubljana Tourist Information Centre** (TIC). Most of the destinations that are described in this chapter have some form of tourist office but if the place you're visiting doesn't, seek some assistance at a branch of one of the big travel agencies (eg, Kompas or Globtour) or from museum or from hotel staff. You can find comprehensive sites on most towns in this chapter on the Internet by typing in the city name, such as ⓦ www .ljubljana.si or ⓦ www.ptuj.si.

Tourist Offices Abroad

The Slovenian Tourist Board maintains tourist offices in the following countries:

Austria (☎ 01-715 4010, fax 713 8177) Hilton Center, Landstrasser Hauptstrasse 2, 1030 Vienna
Croatia (☎ 01-457 2118, fax 457 7921, ⓔ kompas-zagreb@zg.tel.hr) Hotel Esplanade, Mihanovičeva 1, 10000 Zagreb
Germany (☎ 089-2916 1202, fax 2916 1273, ⓔ slowenien.fva@t-online.de) Maximiliansplatz 12a, 80333 Munich
Hungary (☎ 1-269 6879, fax 268 1454, ⓔ tourism.and.travel@kompas.hu) Rakoczi ut 14, 1072 Budapest

Italy (☎ 022 951 1187, fax 022 951 4071, ⓔ slovenia@tin.it) Galeria Buenos Aires 1, 20124 Milan
Netherlands & Belgium (☎ 010-465 3003, fax 465 7514, ⓔ kompasnl@euronet.nl) Benthuizerstraat 29, 3036 CB Rotterdam
Switzerland (☎ 01-212 6394, fax 212 5266, ⓔ adria.slo@bluewin.ch) Löwenstrasse 54, 8001 Zürich
UK (☎ 020-7287 7133, fax 7287 5476, ⓔ slovenia@cpts.fsbusiness.co.uk) 49 Conduit St, London W1S 2YS
USA (☎ 212-358 9686, 358 9025, ⓔ slotouristboard@sloveniatravel.com) 345 East 12th St, New York, NY 10003

In addition, the Kompas travel agency has representative offices in many cities around the world, including:

Canada (☎ 514-938 4041) 4060 Ste-Catherine St West, Suite 535, Montreal, Que H3Z 2Z3
France (☎ 01-53 92 27 80) 14 Rue de la Source, 75016 Paris
USA (☎ 954-771 9200) 2929 East Commercial Blvd, Suite 201, Ft Lauderdale, FL 33306

VISAS & DOCUMENTS

Passport-holders from Australia, Canada, Israel, Japan, New Zealand, Switzerland, USA and EU countries do not require visas for stays in Slovenia of up to 90 days; those from the EU as well as Switzerland can also enter on a national identity card for a stay of up to 30 days. Citizens of other countries requiring visas (including South Africans) can get them at any Slovenian embassy or consulate. They cost the equivalent of €20 for a single entry and €40 for multiple entries.

EMBASSIES & CONSULATES
Slovenian Embassies & Consulates

Slovenia has diplomatic representation in the following countries; the website ⓦ www.gov .si/mzz/eng contains further listings.

Australia (☎ 02-6243 4830) Advance Bank Centre, Level 6, 60 Marcus Clark St, Canberra, ACT 2601
Austria (☎ 01-586 1309) Nibelungengasse 13, 1010 Vienna
Canada (☎ 613-565 5781) 150 Metcalfe St, Suite 2101, Ottawa, Ontario K2P 1P1
Croatia (☎ 01-631 1000) Savska cesta 41/IX, 10000 Zagreb
Germany (☎ 030-206 1450) Hausvogteiplatz 3-4, 10117 Berlin

Hungary (☎ 1-438 5600) Cseppkő ut 68, 1025 Budapest
Italy (☎ 068 091 4310) Via Leonardo Pisano 10, 00197 Rome
UK (☎ 020-7495 7775) Suite 1, Cavendish Court, 11-15 Wigmore St, London W1H 9LA
USA (☎ 202-667 5363) 1525 New Hampshire Ave NW, Washington, DC 20036

Embassies & Consulates in Slovenia

Selected countries that have representation in Ljubljana (area code ☎ 01) appear in the following list. Citizens of countries not listed here should contact their embassies in Vienna or Budapest.

Albania (☎ 432 23 24) Ob Ljubljanici 12
Australia (☎ 425 42 52) Trg Republike 3/XII
Austria (☎ 479 07 00) Prešernova cesta 23
Bosnia-Hercegovina (☎ 432 40 42) Kolarjeva 26
Canada (☎ 430 35 70) Miklošičeva cesta 19
Croatia (☎ 425 62 20) Gruberjevo nab 6
France (☎ 426 45 25) Barjanska 1
Germany (☎ 251 61 66) Prešernova cesta 27
Hungary (☎ 512 18 82) ul Konrada Babnika 5
Ireland (☎ 308 12 34) temporary office at Grand Hotel Union, Miklošičeva cesta 1
Netherlands (☎ 420 14 61) Palača Kapitelj, Poljanski nasip 6
Romania (☎ 505 82 94) Podlimbarskega 43
Slovakia (☎ 425 54 25) Tivolska cesta 4
South Africa (☎ 200 63 00) Pražakova ul 4
UK (☎ 200 39 10) Trg Republike 3/IV
USA (☎ 200 55 00) Prešernova cesta 31

CUSTOMS

Travellers are allowed to bring in the usual personal effects, a couple of cameras and electronic goods for their own use, as well as 200 cigarettes, a generous 4L of spirits and 1L of wine.

MONEY
Currency

Slovenia's currency, the tolar, is abbreviated as SIT. Prices in shops and restaurants, and train and bus fares are always in tolars, but because of inflation, a few hotels, guesthouses and even camping grounds use the euro. For that reason, some accommodation and a few other items are listed in this book in euros. You are always welcome to pay in tolars, though.

Money includes coins of one, two, five and 10 tolars and the banknotes are in denominations of 10, 20, 50, 100, 200, 500, 1000, 5000 and 10,000 tolars.

Exchange Rates

Conversion rates for major currencies at the time of publication are listed below:

country	unit		tolar
Australia	A$1	=	135.65 SIT
Canada	C$1	=	155.21 SIT
Euro Zone	€1	=	228.88 SIT
Japan	¥100	=	192.05 SIT
NZ	NZ$1	=	116.81 SIT
UK	UK£1	=	355.39 SIT
USA	US$1	=	237.10 SIT

Exchanging Money

Cash & Travellers Cheques It is simple to change cash at banks, travel agencies, any *menjalnica* (private exchange bureau) and certain post offices. Slovenia recently had a problem with travellers-cheque fraud, so it's difficult to exchange them, even at banks, but restaurants and hotels will still accept them.

There's no black market and exchange rates vary little, but watch out for a commission (*provizija*) of up to 3% tacked on by some tourist offices, hotels and travel agencies.

ATMs & Credit Cards Visa, MasterCard/Eurocard and American Express credit cards are widely accepted at most restaurants, shops, hotels, car-rental firms and travel agencies; Diners Club less so.

Automated teller machines (ATMs) linked to Cirrus or Plus now blanket Slovenia; their locations are noted in the Information sections of the individual destinations. Clients of Visa can get cash advances in tolars from any A Banka branch; MasterCard and Eurocard can be used any branch of **Nova Ljubljanska Banka** (☎ *01-425 01 55; Trg Republike 2, Ljubljana*); and **American Express** (☎ *01-431 90 20; Trubarjeva, Ljubljana*).

Costs

Slovenia remains much cheaper than neighbouring Italy and Austria, but don't expect the low prices you'd see in Eastern European countries like Hungary or Bulgaria.

If you stay in private rooms or at guesthouses, eat at medium-priced restaurants and travel 2nd class on the train or by bus, you should get by for under US$40 a day. Staying at hostels or college dormitories, eating takeaway at lunch and at self-service restaurants at night will cut costs considerably.

Travelling in a little more style and comfort – occasional restaurant splurges with bottles of wine, an active nightlife, staying at small hotels or guesthouses with 'character' – will cost about US$65 a day.

Tipping & Bargaining

Tipping isn't customary in Slovenia, but no-one's going to complain if you leave your change at the table in a restaurant.

Unlike some of its Eastern European neighbours, bargaining is not commonplace in Slovenia. You can try it at street markets, but you run the risk of offending someone.

Taxes & Refunds

A 'circulation tax' (prometni davek) not unlike Value-Added Tax (VAT) applies to the purchase of most goods and services here. Visitors can claim refunds on total purchases of 15,000 SIT or more (certain tobacco products and spirits are exempt) through Kompas MTS, which has offices at Brnik airport and some two dozen border crossings. Ask for a DDV-VP form at the time of purchase.

Most towns and cities levy a 'tourist tax' on overnight visitors of between 150 SIT and 300 SIT per person per night (less at camping grounds), which is included in the prices listed in this chapter.

POST & COMMUNICATIONS
Post

Poste restante is sent to the main post office in a city or town (in the capital, it goes to the branch at Slovenska cesta 32, 1101 Ljubljana) where it is held for 30 days. American Express card-holders can have their mail addressed c/o Atlas Express, Trubarjeva cesta 50, 1000 Ljubljana.

Domestic mail costs 31 SIT for up to 20g and 56 SIT for up to 100g. Postcards are 31 SIT. For international mail, the base rate is 95 SIT for 20g or less, 221 SIT for up to 100g and 83 SIT to 107 SIT for a postcard, depending on the size. Then you have to add on the airmail charge: 30 SIT for every 10g. An aerogramme is 125 SIT.

Telephone

The easiest place to make long-distance calls and send faxes and telegrams is from a post office or telephone centre; the one at Trg Osvobodilne Fronte (Trg OF) near the train and bus stations in Ljubljana is open 24 hours.

Public telephones on the street do not accept coins; they require a phonecard (telefonska kartica) available at all post offices and some newsstands.

Phonecards cost 700/1000/1700/3500 SIT for 25/50/100/300 pulses. A local one-minute call absorbs one pulse, and a three-minute call from Slovenia will cost about 126 SIT to most of Western Europe, the USA, Canada and Croatia; 162 SIT to Eastern Europe; 342 SIT to Australia; and 486 SIT to Japan, South Africa and New Zealand. International rates are 20% cheaper between 7pm and 7am Monday to Saturday, and all day Sunday.

The international access code in Slovenia is ☎ 00. The international operator or directory inquiries can be reached on ☎ 115. To call Slovenia from abroad dial the international access code, ☎ 386 (Slovenia's country code), the area code (without the initial zero, eg, 1 in Ljubljana) followed by the number.

Email & Internet Access

There is now an Internet café in almost every town in Slovenia. Ljubljana has 11 places to check your email. If you can't find an Internet café (in Ptuj, for example), try the local university or library. They will usually let travellers log on to the Internet for free or at little cost.

DIGITAL RESOURCES

The official Slovenian tourist information website is ⓦ www.slovenia-tourism.si. You can find information on accommodation, traffic conditions, the different regions etc.

The site ⓦ www.matkurja.com is a comprehensive overview of Slovenian websites, including resources for travellers. Many sites are in English.

See the Digital Resources section in the Ljubljana section for more useful websites.

BOOKS

Books can be expensive in Slovenia. Lonely Planet's Slovenia is the only complete and independent English-language guide to this country. Discover Slovenia, published annually by the Cankarjeva Založba bookshop in Ljubljana (3500 SIT), is a colourful and easy introduction available in seven languages, including English, German, and French, and Zoë Brân's After Yugoslavia, part of the Lonely Planet Journeys series, retraces the author's 1978 trip through the former Yugoslavia.

NEWSPAPERS & MAGAZINES

Slovenia publishes four daily newspapers, the most widely read being *Delo* (Work), *Večer* (Evening) and *Slovenske Novice* (a tabloid with Slovenian news). The entertainment and culture magazine *Ljubljana Life* is published monthly and is available in hotels and at the TIC. There are no local English-language newspapers, though the *International Herald Tribune*, *Guardian International*, *Financial Times* and *USA Today* are available in the afternoon on the day of publication at hotels and department stores in Ljubljana.

RADIO & TV

News, weather, traffic and tourist information in English, German and Italian follows the Slovene-language news, on Radio Slovenija 2 during the weekends in July and August. Also in July and August, Radio Slovenija 1 and 2 broadcast a report on the weather, including conditions on the sea and in the mountains, in the same languages. There's a nightly news bulletin in English and German at 10.30pm throughout the year on Radio 1. Most Slovene hotels have English- or German-language cable channels.

TIME

Slovenia is one hour ahead of GMT/UTC. The country goes onto summer time (GMT/UTC plus two hours) on the last Sunday in March when clocks are advanced by one hour. On the last Sunday in October they're turned back one hour.

LAUNDRY

Commercial laundrettes are rare in Slovenia. The best places to look for do-it-yourself washers and dryers are hostels, college dormitories and camping grounds, and there are a couple of places in Ljubljana that will do your laundry reasonably quickly (see Laundry under Information in the Ljubljana section).

PHOTOGRAPHY

Film is plentiful and fairly inexpensive in Slovenia. A roll of 24 exposures costs about 900 SIT.

WOMEN TRAVELLERS

Women are unlikely to encounter problems while travelling in Slovenia. Crime is low and harassment is rare. There is a **women's crisis helpline** (☎ 080 11 55) for emergencies.

Emergency Services

In the event of an emergency call ☎ 113 for the police and ☎ 112 for the fire, first aid or ambulance services.

The automobile assistance (AMZS) information number is ☎ 530 53 00. For road emergency and towing services ring ☎ 1987. These numbers can be dialled nationwide.

GAY & LESBIAN TRAVELLERS

The gay association **Roza Klub** (☎ 01-430 47 40; Kersnikova ul 4, Ljubljana), organises a disco every Sunday night at Klub K4 in Ljubljana. Roza Klub is made up of a gay branch of the Š/vKUC (Student Cultural Centre), Magnus, as well as a lesbian branch, LL (the same contact details as Roza Klub).

The **GALfon** (☎ 01-432 40 89) is a hotline and source of general information for gays and lesbians. It operates daily from 7pm to 10pm. The **Slovenian Queer Resources Directory** (W www.ljudmila.org/siqrd) leaves no stone unturned.

Gay and lesbian travellers should encounter no major problems in Slovenia.

DISABLED TRAVELLERS

Slovenia's government is currently working on making public spaces more accessible to the disabled, but it's still a pretty tough go. A group that looks after the interests and special needs of physically challenged people is the **Zveza Paraplegikov Republike Slovenije** (ZPRS; ☎ 01-432 71 38) in Ljubljana.

SENIOR TRAVELLERS

Senior citizens may be entitled to discounts in Slovenia on things like museum admission fees, provided they show proof of age.

DANGERS & ANNOYANCES

Slovenia is hardly a violent or dangerous place. Police say that 90% of all crimes reported involve theft so travellers should take the usual precautions. Bike theft is fairly common in Ljubljana.

BUSINESS HOURS

Shops, groceries and department stores open 7.30am or 8am to 7pm on weekdays and to 1pm on Saturday. Bank hours are generally 8am to 4.30pm or 5pm on weekdays (often with a lunch break) and till noon on Saturday.

Main post offices are open 7am to 8pm on weekdays, till 1pm on Saturday and occasionally 9am to 11am on Sunday.

PUBLIC HOLIDAYS & SPECIAL EVENTS

Public holidays in Slovenia include two days at New Year (1 and 2 January), National Culture Day (8 February), Easter Sunday and Monday (March/April), Insurrection Day (27 April), two days for Labour Day (1 and 2 May), National Day (25 June), Assumption Day (15 August), Reformation Day (31 October), All Saints' Day (1 November), Christmas (25 December) and Independence Day (26 December).

Though cultural events are scheduled throughout the year, the highlights of the Slovenian summer season (July and August) are the International Summer Festival in Ljubljana; the Piran Musical Evenings; the Primorska Summer Festival at Piran, Koper, Izola and Portorož in July; and Summer in the Old Town in Ljubljana, with three or four cultural events a week taking place.

ACTIVITIES
Skiing

Skiing is by far the most popular sport in Slovenia, and every fourth Slovene is an active skier. The country has many well-equipped ski resorts in the Julian Alps, especially Vogel (skiing up to 1840m) above Lake Bohinj, Kranjska Gora (1600m), Kanin (2300m) above Bovec, and Krvavec (1970m), northeast of Kranj.

All these resorts have multiple chairlifts, cable cars, ski schools, equipment rentals and large resort hotels.

Hiking

Hiking is almost as popular as skiing in Slovenia, and there are approximately 7000km of marked trails and 165 mountain huts. Visitors can experience the full grandeur of the Julian Alps in the Triglav National Park at Lake Bohinj, and for the veteran mountaineer there's the Slovenian Alpine Trail, which crosses all the highest peaks in the country.

Kayaking, Canoeing & Rafting

The best white-water rafting is on the Soča, one of only half a dozen rivers in the European Alps whose upper waters are still unspoiled. The centre is at Bovec.

Fishing

Slovenia's rivers and Alpine lakes and streams are teeming with trout, grayling, pike and other fish. The best rivers for angling are the Soča, the Krka, the Kolpa and the Sava Bohinjka near Bohinj. Lake fishing is good at Bled and Bohinj.

Cycling

Mountain bikes are available for hire at Bled and Bohinj. You can also rent bikes on the coast and in Ljubljana.

WORK

Employment of foreigners in Slovenia is among the most restricted in Europe. Even foreign businesses have difficulty obtaining working visas for their employees. This is likely to change when Slovenia is accepted into the EU, expected 1 January 2004. Legislation will be changed to reflect that in the more liberalized EU countries.

ACCOMMODATION
Camping

In summer, camping is the cheapest way to go, and you'll find there are convenient camping grounds all over the country. You don't always need a tent as some camping grounds have inexpensive bungalows or caravans. Two of the best camping grounds are Zlatorog on Lake Bohinj and Jezero Fiesa near Piran, though they can be very crowded in summer. It is forbidden to camp 'rough' in Slovenia.

Hostels & Student Dormitories

Slovenia has only a handful of 'official' hostels, including two in Ljubljana and excellent ones in Bled and Piran, but many others aren't open year-round. You'll find that some college dormitories accept travellers in the summer months.

Private Rooms & Apartments

Private rooms arranged by tourist offices and travel agencies can be inexpensive, but a surcharge of up to 50% is often levied on stays of less than three nights. You can often bargain for rooms without the surcharge by going directly to any house with a sign reading 'sobe' (rooms).

Pensions & Guesthouses

A small guesthouse (called a *penzion* or *gostišče*) can be good value, though in July and

SLOVENIA

August you may be required to take at least one meal and the rates are higher.

Farmhouses

The agricultural cooperatives of Slovenia have organised a unique program to accommodate visitors on working farms. Prices are about 3500 SIT per night for bed and breakfast (30% more if less than a two-night stay) to about 5000 SIT per night with full-board during high season (July, August and around Christmas). Contact the **Association of Tourist Farms of Slovenia** (☎ 03-491 64 80; ⓔ ztks@siol.net). Bookings can be made through **ABC Farm & Countryside Holidays** (☎ 01-507 61 27, fax 519 98 76; Ul Jožeta Jame 16, Ljubljana).

Hotels

Hotel rates vary according to the time of year, with July and August the peak season and May/June and September/October the shoulder seasons. In Ljubljana, prices are constant all year. Many hotels in Slovenia includes breakfast in the price, and many offer free admission or discounts to the spa in town.

FOOD

Slovenian cuisine is heavily influenced by the food of its neighbours. From Austria, there's *klobasa* (sausage), *zavitek* (strudel) and *Dunajski zrezek* (Wiener schnitzel). *Njoki* (potato dumplings), *rižota* (risotto) and the ravioli-like *žlikrofi* are obviously Italian, and Hungary has contributed *golaž* (goulash), *paprikaš* (chicken or beef 'stew') and *palačinke* (thin pancakes filled with jam or nuts and topped with chocolate). And then there's that old Balkan stand-by, *burek*, a greasy, layered cheese, meat or even apple pie served at takeaway places everywhere.

No Slovenian meal can be considered complete without soup, be it the very simple *goveja juha z rezanci* (beef broth with little egg noodles), *zelenjavna juha* (vegetable soup) or *gobova juha* (mushroom soup). There are several types of Slovenian dumplings called *štruklji* that are made with various types of local cheese.

Also try the baked delicacies, including *potica* (walnut roll) and *gibanica* (pastry filled with poppy seeds, walnuts, apple and/or sultanas and cottage cheese and topped with cream). Traditional dishes are best tried at an inn (*gostilna* or *gostišče*).

Many restaurants have set lunches for 900 to 1600 SIT. These can be great value, as some are upmarket restaurants where dinner can cost three or four times as much.

DRINKS

Wine-growing regions of Slovenia are Podravje in the east, noted for such white wines as Renski Rizling (a true German Riesling), Beli Pinot (Pinot Blanc) and Traminec (Traminer); Posavje in the southeast (try the distinctly Slovenian light-red Cviček); and the area around the coast, which produces a hearty red called Teran made from Refošk grapes. *Vinska cesta* means 'wine road', and wherever you see one of these signs, you'll find wineries and vineyards open for tasting. They cover the area around Maribor, where it's said that every house has its own vineyard.

Žganje is a strong brandy or *eau de vie* that is distilled from a variety of fruits, but most commonly plums. The finest brandy is Pleterska Hruška, made from pears.

SPECTATOR SPORTS

For skiing enthusiasts, World Cup slalom and giant slalom events are held at Kranjska Gora in late December. In early January, women's World Cup skiing takes place in Maribor.

SHOPPING

Slovenia isn't famous for its handicrafts, but there are some beautiful things available, especially antiques. Every Sunday, the **antique flea market** takes place along the Ljubljanica River. You'll find furniture, stamps, art, knick-knacks and every imaginable item. Most of the best craft stores, including **Dom** and **365**, and the best antique shops can be found on Mestni trg (square) near the Town Hall.

Getting There & Away

AIR

Slovenia's national air carrier, **Adria Airways** (in Ljubljana ☎ 01-231 33 12, at Brnik airport ☎ 04-202 51 11; ⓦ www.adria.si) has non-stop flights to Ljubljana from cities including Amsterdam, Brussels, Copenhagen, Frankfurt, Istanbul, London, Moscow, Munich, Ohrid, Paris, Sarajevo, Skopje, Split, Tirana, Vienna and Zürich. You can check out the website for the schedules. From May to October, Adria flies to Dublin, Manchester and Tel Aviv.

Lufthansa flies from Frankfurt and Munich and Swiss from Zürich.

LAND

Bus

Buses from Ljubljana serve a number of international destinations, including the following cities and towns: Belgrade (7100 to 7400 SIT, three daily); Frankfurt (17,550 SIT, daily at 7.30pm); Munich (7900 SIT, daily at 7.30pm); Rijeka (2880 SIT, daily at 7.40pm); Split (7140 SIT, daily at 7.40pm); Trieste (2110 SIT, daily at 6.25am) and Zagreb (2570 SIT, three daily).

Italy Nova Gorica is the easiest departure point from Slovenia to Italy, as you can catch up to five buses a day to/from the Italian city of Gorizia or simply walk across the border at Rožna Dolina. Take one of 17 daily buses (2020 SIT). Koper also has good connections with Italy – some 17 buses a day on weekdays go to/from Trieste, 21km to the northeast. There's also a daily bus from Trieste to Ljubljana (2110 SIT, daily at 6.25am).

Hungary There is no direct bus that links Ljubljana to Budapest. Instead, take one of up to five daily buses to Lendava; the Hungarian border is 5km to the north. The first Hungarian train station, Rédics, is only 2km beyond the border.

Train

The main train routes into Slovenia from Austria are Vienna/Graz to Maribor and Ljubljana and Salzburg to Jesenice. Tickets cost 8000 SIT from Ljubljana to Salzburg (four hours) and 11,558 SIT to Vienna (six hours). But it's cheaper to take a local train to Maribor (1380 SIT) and buy your ticket on to Vienna from there. Similarly, from Austria you should only buy a ticket as far as Jesenice or Maribor, as domestic fares are much lower than the international fares.

There are three trains a day between Munich and Ljubljana (12,806 SIT, seven hours). Take the EuroCity *Mimara* via Salzburg or the *Lisinski* express, which leaves at 11.30pm (a sleeping carriage is available). A 1000 SIT supplement is payable on the *Mimara*. Seat reservations (600 SIT) are available on both.

Two trains a day travel from Trieste to Ljubljana (4400 SIT, three hours) via the towns of Divača and Sežana. From Croatia it's Zagreb to Ljubljana (2500 SIT, 2½ hours) via Zidani Most, or Rijeka to Ljubljana (2099 SIT, 2½ hours) via Pivka. The InterCity *Drava* and *Venezia Express* trains link Ljubljana with Budapest (9900 SIT, eight hours, two daily) via northwestern Croatia and Zagreb respectively. Three trains a day go to Belgrade (8000 SIT).

Border Crossings

Slovenia maintains some 150 border crossings with Italy, Austria, Hungary and Croatia, but only 26 are considered international or interstate crossings. The rest are minor crossings only open to Slovenian citizens or others with special permits.

SEA

From late March to November on Friday, Saturday and Sunday, the *Prince of Venice*, a 39m Australian-made catamaran seating some 330 passengers, sails between Izola and Venice (return ticket 15,000/13,500/9500 SIT high/shoulder/off season). The boat departs from Izola at 8am and returns at 5.30pm. There's an additional sailing on Tuesday and Saturday in July and August. The price of the boat trip includes a sightseeing tour in Venice. From Izola there are frequent buses to Portorož, Piran and Koper. Another catamaran, the *Marconi*, links Trieste with Piran (see Cruises in the Piran section).

DEPARTURE TAX

A departure tax of 2700 SIT is levied on all passengers leaving Slovenia by air, though this is almost always included in your airline ticket price.

Getting Around

BUS

Except for long journeys, the bus is preferable to the train in Slovenia. Departures are frequent. In some cases you don't have much of a choice; travelling by bus is the only practical way to get from Ljubljana to Bled and Bohinj, the Julian Alps and much of the coast.

In Ljubljana you can buy your ticket with seat reservation (600 SIT, depending on the destination) the day before, but many people simply pay the driver on boarding. The one time you really might need a reservation is Friday afternoon, when many students travel from Ljubljana to their homes or people leave the city for the weekend. There is a 220 SIT charge for each bag placed underneath the bus.

Useful footnotes that you might see on the Slovenian bus schedules include: *vozi vsak dan* (runs daily); *vozi ob delavnikih* (runs on working days – Monday to Friday); *vozi ob sobotah* (runs on Saturday); and *vozi ob nedeljih in praznikih* (runs only on Sunday and holidays).

TRAIN

Slovenske Železnice (SŽ; Slovenian Railways) operates on just over 1200km of track. The country's most scenic rail routes run along the Soča River from Jesenice to Nova Gorica via Bled (Bled Jezero station) and Bohinjska Bistrica (89km) and from Ljubljana to Zagreb (160km) along the Sava River.

On past timetables in Slovenia, *odhod* or *odhodi vlakov* means 'departures' and *prihod* (or *prihodi vlakov*) is 'arrivals'. If you don't have time to buy a ticket, seek out the conductor who will sell you one for an extra charge of 200 SIT.

CAR & MOTORCYCLE

Even though it's a small country, having your own wheels will help if you're planning some outdoor activities, as the buses don't run frequently off the beaten path. The use of seat belts in the front seats is compulsory in Slovenia, and a new law requires all vehicles to have their headlights on throughout the day outside built-up areas. Speed limits for cars are 50km/h in built-up areas, 90km/h on secondary roads, 100km/h on main highways and 130km/h on motorways.

Tolls are payable on several motorways, but they're not terribly expensive. For example, Ljubljana to Postojna will cost 440 SIT. Petrol remains relatively cheap: 187.00/195.20 SIT per litre for 95/98 octane (both unleaded). Diesel costs 154.60 SIT.

Slovenia's automobile club, the **Avto Moto Zveza Slovenije** (AMZS; ☎ 01-530 53 00), may be a helpful contact.

The permitted blood-alcohol level for motorists is 0.05% or 0.5g/kg of blood (the level is zero for professional drivers) and the law is strictly enforced. Anything over that could earn you a fine of 25,000 SIT and one to three demerit points.

Car Rental

Car rentals from international firms like Avis, National, Budget and Kompas Hertz vary widely in price, but expect to pay from about 14,750/73,920 SIT a day/week with unlimited mileage, collision damage waiver, theft protection and personal accident insurance for a compact (like a Ford Fiesta). Add 20% VAT.

Some car-rental agencies have minimum-age rules (21 or 23 years) and/or require that you've had a valid licence for one or even two years. Three international chains are **Kompas Hertz** (☎ 01-231 12 41; Miklošičeva ul 11), **National** (☎ 01- 588 44 50; Baragova ul 5) and **Avis** (☎ 01- 430 80 10; Čufarjeva ul 2). They also have counters at the airport. Two excellent smaller agencies, with more competitive rates, are **ABC Rent a Car** (☎ 04-236 79 90; open 24hr) at Brnik airport and **Avtoimpex** (☎ 01- 519 72 97; Celovška cesta 252) in Ljubljana.

HITCHING

Hitchhiking is legal everywhere except on motorways and some major highways and is generally easy; even young women do it. But hitching is never a totally safe way of getting around and, although we mention it as an option, we don't recommend it.

Ljubljana

☎ 01 • pop 280,000

Ljubljana (Laibach in German) is by far the largest and most populous city in Slovenia. However, in many ways the city, the name of which almost means 'beloved' *(ljubljena)* in Slovene, doesn't feel like an industrious municipality of national importance but a pleasant, self-contented town with responsibilities only to itself and its citizens. The most beautiful parts of the city are the Old Town below the castle and the embankments designed by Plečnik, along the narrow Ljubljanica River.

Ljubljana began as the Roman town of Emona, and legacies of the Roman presence can still be seen throughout the city. The Habsburgs took control of Ljubljana in the 14th century and later built many of the pale-coloured churches and mansions that earned the city the nickname 'White Ljubljana'. From 1809 to 1814 Ljubljana was the capital of the Illyrian Provinces, Napoleon's short-lived springboard to the Adriatic.

Despite the patina of imperial Austria, contemporary Ljubljana has a vibrant Slavic air all its own. It's like a little Prague without the hordes of tourists but with all the facilities you'll need. Almost 50,000 students attend Ljubljana University's 20 faculties and three art academies, so the city always feels young.

Orientation

The tiny bus station and renovated train station are opposite each other on the square Trg Osvobodilne Fronte (known as Trg OF) at the northern end of the town centre (called Center).

Information

Tourist Offices The Ljubljana **Tourist Information Centre** *(TIC; ☎ 306 12 15, fax 306 12 04; e pcl.tic-lj@ljubljana.si; Stritarjeva ul 2; open 8am-8pm Mon-Fri, 10am-6pm Sat, Sun & holidays in summer; to 6pm daily low season)* is in the historical Kresija building southeast of Triple Bridge. The **branch office** *(☎/fax 433 94 75; open 9am-9pm daily in summer, 10am-5.30pm Mon-Fri Oct-May)* is at the train station. The TIC is worth visiting to pick up free maps and brochures, organise sightseeing trips or inquire about accommodation options.

The main office of the **Alpine Association of Slovenia** *(☎ 434 30 22; w www.pzs.si; Dvoržakova ul 9)* is in a small house set back from the street. It can help plan trekking or hiking trips anywhere in the country, including the Julian Alps.

Money There are more than 50 ATMs in Ljubljana. Many are in the Center, including an **A Banka** *(Trg Osvobodilne Fronte 2)* opposite the train station and another one at Slovenska 58 (where card-holders can get cash advances). There are branches of Banka Koper outside the Globtour agency in the Maximarket passageway connecting Trg Republike with Plečnikov trg and at Cigaletova ul 4.

You can get cash advances on MasterCard at **Nova Ljubljanska Banka** *(Trg Republike 2; open 8am-5pm Mon-Fri, 9am-noon Sat)*. Next to the SKB Banka on Trg Ajdovščina is a currency exchange machine that changes the banknotes of 18 countries into tolar at a good rate. **Hida exchange bureau** *(Pogarčarjev trg 1; open 7am-7pm Mon-Fri, 7am-2pm Sat)* is inside the Seminary building near the open-air market.

Post & Communications Poste-restante mail will only be held for 30 days at the **post office** *(☎ 426 46 68; Slovenska cesta 32; postal code 1101; open 7am-8pm Mon-Fri, 7am-1pm Sat)*. Make international telephone calls or send faxes from here or the **main post office** *(Pražakova ul 3; same hours)*.

To mail a parcel you must go to the **special customs post office** *(Trg OF 5; open 24hr)* opposite the main station. Do not seal your package until after it has been inspected; the maximum weight is about 15kg, depending on the destination.

Email & Internet Access Internet access is free at **Klub K4 Café** *(☎ 431 70 10; Kersnikova ul 4)*. **Cyber Café** *(Slovenska cesta 10)* sells drinks and has five terminals for 200/400/600 SIT for 15/30/60 minutes; students pay half price.

Kavarna Čerin *(☎ 232 09 90, Trubarjeva 52)* is a full-service café with free Internet access (and peanuts) for the purchase of a drink. Hotel Turist (see Places to Stay later in this section) has an Internet connection, free for guests, 220 SIT per 20 minutes for all others (available 24 hours).

Digital Resources Useful websites for Ljubljana include:

W **www.ljubljana.si** City of Ljubljana

W **www.uni-lj.si** Ljubljana University (check out the Welcome page with practical information in English for foreign students)

W **www.geocities.com/ljubljanalife** The English -language magazine for expatriates and visitors

Travel Agencies Backpackers and students should head for the **ZMT Infopoint** *(☎ 438 03 12; Kersnikova ul 6)*, which sells ISIC cards, **Mladi Turist** *(☎ 425 92 60; Salendrova ul 4)*, the office of the Slovenian Youth Hostel Association, or **Erazem Travel Office** *(☎ 433 10 76; Trubarjeva cesta 7)*.

There is also an **American Express** representative *(☎ 431 90 20; Trubarjeva 50)* in the city centre.

Bookshops Ljubljana's largest bookshop is **Mladinska Knjiga** *(Slovenska cesta 29)*. It has an extensive collection of books in English. There's also **DZS** *(☎ 200 80 42; Mestni tri 26)*. **Kod & Kam** *(Trg Francoske Revolucije 7)* is excellent for travel guides and maps, especially if you plan to go hiking.

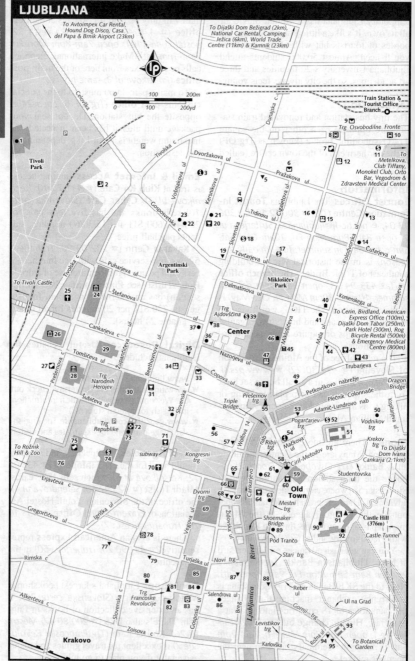

LJUBLJANA

To Avtoimpex Car Rental,
Hound Dog Disco, Casa
del Papa & Brnik Airport (23km)

To Dijaški Dom Bežigrad (2km),
National Car Rental, Camping
Ježica (6km), World Trade
Centre (11km) & Kamnik (23km)

0   100   200m
0   100   200yd

Train Station &
Tourist Office
Branch

Celovška c

Dunajska c

Trg Osvobodilne Fronte

To Metelkova,
Club Tiffany,
Monokel Club, Orto
Bar, Vegodrom &
Zdravstveni Medical Center

Tivoli Park

Tivolska c

Dvoržakova ul

Pražakova ul

Cigaletova ul

Kersnikova c

Vošnjakova ul

Gosposvetska c

Trdinova ul

Slovenska

Kolodvorska ul

Čufarjeva ul

Resljeva c

To Tivoli Castle

Puharjeva ul

Argentinski
Park

Tavčarjeva ul

Dalmatinova ul

Miklošičev
Park

Štefanova

Cankarjeva c

Komenskega c

To Čerin, Birdland, American
Express Office (100m),
Dijaški Dom Tabor (250m),
Park Hotel (300m), Rog
Bicycle Rental (500m) &
Emergency Medical
Centre (800m)

Tomšičeva ul

Trg
Ajdovščina

Center

Nazorjeva ul

Miklošičeva c

Maľa c

Trubarjeva c

Župančičeva

Beethovnova ul

Prešernova

Tomšičeva ul

Trg
Narodnih
Herojev

Šubičeva ul

Čopova ul

Slovenska

Petkovškovo nabrežje

Plečnik Colonnade

Dragon
Bridge

Triple
Bridge

Prešernov
trg

Adamič-Lundrovo nab

Pogačarjev
trg

Vodnikov
trg

To Rožnik
Hill & Zoo

Trg
Republike

subway

Kongresni
trg

Wolfova

Ribji
trg

Mačkova

Krekov
trg

To Dijaški
Dom Ivana
Cankarja (2.1km)

Erjavčeva c

Ciril-Metodov trg

Študentovska
ul

Gregorčičeva ul

Igriška ul

Dvorni
trg

Vegova ul

Cankarjeva

Židovska ul

Old
Town

Mestni
trg

Castle Hill
(376m)

Castle Tunnel

Rimska c

Turjaška ul

Novi trg

Shoemaker
Bridge

Pod Trančo

Stari trg

Reber
ul

Ul na Grad

Aškerčeva c

Trg
Francoske
Revolucije

Salendrova ul

Breg

Ljubljanica

Levstikov
trg

Gornji trg

Reber
ul

Krakovo

Zoisova c

Gosposka ul

Karlovška c

Rožna ul

To Botanical
Garden

LJUBLJANA

PLACES TO STAY
40 Hotel Turist; Klub Central
46 Grand Hotel Union
80 Pri Mraku

PLACES TO EAT
 5 Burek Stand
13 Burek Stand
19 Evropa Café
35 Quick
38 Šestica
44 Napoli
53 Ribca
57 Zvezda Café
65 Žibila
67 Ljubljanski Dvor
68 Burja
77 Prema
79 Foculus
87 Pri Viteza
88 Najboljski Gyros
94 Špajza
95 Pri sv Florianu; Moro

OTHER
 1 Tivoli Recreation Centre &
    Zlati Klub
 2 Ilirija Swimming Pool
 3 Alpine Association of Slovenia
 4 City Bus Ticket Kiosks
 6 Main Post Office
 7 Canadian Consulate
 8 City Airport Buses
 9 Post Office (Customs)
10 Bus Station
11 A Banka

12 Kompas Cinema
14 Avis
15 Kinoteka Cinema
16 Kompas Hertz Car Rental
17 Banka Koper
18 A Banka
20 K4 Café; Roza Klub;
    University Student Centre
21 ZMT Infopoint
22 Adria Airways
23 Lufthansa Ticket Office
24 National Gallery
25 Church of Sts Cyril &
    Methodius
26 Museum of Modern Art
27 US Embassy
28 National Museum
29 Opera House
30 Parliament Building
31 Jazz Club Gajo
32 Mladinska Knjiga Bookshop
33 Post Office (Poste Restante)
34 Komuna Cinema
36 Kompas Travel Agency;
    Holidays' Pub
37 Cankarjeva Založba Bookshop
39 SKB Banka
41 Tour As
42 Patrick's Irish Pub
43 Salon
45 Art Nouveau Bank Buildings
47 Union Cinema
48 Franciscan Church
49 Erazem Travel Office
50 Produce Market
51 Cathedral of St Nicholas

52 Hida Exchange Bureau;
    Seminary
54 Tourist Information Centre (TIC)
55 Prešeren Monument
56 Chemoexpress Laundry
58 Robba Fountain
59 Town Hall
60 Vinoteka Movia
61 DZS Bookshop
62 Bicycle Rentals
63 365
64 Maček
66 Filharmonija
69 Ljubljana University
70 Ursuline Church of the Holy
    Trinity
71 Brewery Pub
72 Maximarket Department Store
    & Supermarket; Banka Koper
73 Globtour Agency
74 Nova Ljubljanska Banka
75 UK Embassy; Australian
    Consulate
76 Cankarjev Dom
78 Cyber Cafe
81 Ilirija Column
82 Križanke Booking Office
83 Križanke Theatre
84 Kod & Kam Bookshop
85 National & University Library
86 Mladi Turist
89 Dom
90 Castle Tower
91 Ljubljana Castle
92 Pentagonal Tower
93 Church of St Florian

The best places to buy English and other foreign-language newspapers and magazines are the newsstands in the lobby of the **Grand Hotel Union** *(Miklošičeva cesta 1)* and in the basement of the **Maximarket department store** *(Trg Republike)*.

Laundry The student dormitory **Dijaški Dom Kam** *(Kardeljeva ploščad 14)*, north of the Center in Bežigrad, has washing machines and dryers that you can use (Building C), as does **Camping Ježica** *(Dunajska cesta 270)*.

Chemoexpress *(Wolfova ul 12; open 7am–6pm Mon-Fri)* near Prešernov trg is an old-style laundry and dry cleaner.

Left Luggage The 24-hour left-luggage office *(garderoba;* 400 SIT per piece) at the train station is on platform No 1. There is a smaller *garderoba* (open 5.30am to 8.15pm) inside the bus station.

Medical Services In a medical emergency, dial ☎ 112, or go to the **emergency medical centre** *(☎ 232 30 60; Bohoričeva 9)*. If you need to see a doctor, try the **Zdravstveni dom Center** *(☎ 472 37 00; Metelkova 9)*.

Things to See & Do

The most picturesque sights of old Ljubljana are along the banks of the Ljubljanica, a tributary of the Sava that curves around the foot of Castle Hill.

Opposite the tourist information centre and the Kresija building is the celebrated **Triple Bridge**. In 1931, Jože Plečnik added the side bridges to the original central span, which dates from 1842. On the northern side of the bridge is Prešernov trg with its pink **Franciscan church** (1660), a **statue** (1905) of poet France Prešeren and some wonderful Art Nouveau buildings. A lively pedestrian street, **Čopova ul**, runs northwest.

On the southern side of the bridge in Mestni trg, the baroque **Robba Fountain** stands in front of the **Town Hall** (Magistrat; 1718). Italian sculptor Francesco Robba designed this fountain in 1751 and modelled it after one in Rome. Enter the town hall to see the double Gothic courtyard. South of Mestni trg is **Stari trg**, full of atmosphere day and night. Northeast are the twin towers of the **Cathedral of St Nicholas** (1708), which contains impressive frescoes. Behind the cathedral is Ljubljana's colourful open-air **produce market** (closed Sunday) and an arch-fronted **colonnade** along the riverside designed by Plečnik.

Ljubljana Castle has finally been renovated, so you can now climb the 19th-century Castle Tower to the west, view the exhibits in the Gothic chapel and the **Pentagonal Tower** (open Tues-Sun). There's a new virtual **museum** (adult/child 700/400 SIT; open 10am-9pm daily). Študentovska ul, opposite the Vodnik statue in the market square, offers a panoramic path to the castle, or try Reber ul between Stari trg 17 and 19. You can take the tram, which leaves Prešernov trg (next to the Triple Bridge) daily during the winter at 20 past the hour from 10am to 3pm, and May to September from 10am to 8pm. The train costs 500/350 SIT for adults/children and students.

Near the now-closed Municipal Museum is the 1941 **National & University Library** (Gosposka ul 14), designed by Plečnik, and north on Gosposka ul is the main building (1902) of **Ljubljana University** (Kongresni trg 12), which was formerly the regional parliament. The elegant **Filharmonija** (Philharmonic Hall), at No 10 on the southeastern corner of the square, is home to the Slovenian Philharmonic Orchestra. The **Ursuline Church of the Holy Trinity** (1726), with an altar by Robba, faces Kongresni trg to the west.

Walk west along Šubičeva ul to several fine museums. The **National Museum** (Muzejska ul 1; adult/child 500/300 SIT; open 10am-6pm Tues-Sun), built in 1885, has prehistory and natural history collections. The highlight is a Celtic *situla*, a kind of pail, from the 6th century BC sporting a fascinating relief.

The **National Gallery** (Prešernova cesta 24; adult/child 700/500 SIT, free Sat afternoon; open 10am-6pm Tues-Sun) displays European portraits and landscapes from the 17th to 19th centuries, as well as copies of medieval frescoes. The gallery's north wing has a permanent collection of European paintings from the Middle Ages to the 20th century and is used for temporary exhibits.

Diagonally opposite the National Gallery is the **Museum of Modern Art** (Cankarjeva ul 15; adult/senior 1000/500 SIT, children free; open 10am-6pm Tues-Sun) where a part of the International Biennial of Graphic Arts is held summers of odd-numbered years.

The Serbian Orthodox **Church of Sts Cyril & Methodius** (open 3pm-6pm Tues-Sat), opposite the Museum of Modern Art, is worth visiting to see the beautiful modern frescoes. The subway from the Museum of Modern Art leads to Ljubljana's green lung, **Tivoli Park**.

Activities

The **Tivoli Recreation Centre** (☎ 431 51 55; Celovška cesta 25) in Tivoli Park has bowling alleys, tennis courts, an indoor swimming pool, a fitness centre and a roller-skating rink. In summer, there's minigolf. The **Zlati Klub** at this centre has several saunas, a steam room, warm and cold splash pools and even a small outside pool surrounded by high walls so you can sunbathe in the nude (mixed sexes, but Friday mornings 9am-1pm are women only).

The outdoor **Ilirija pool** (Celovška cesta 3; open 9am-11am Mon-Fri, 6.30pm-10pm Tues-Thur, 10am-8pm Sat & Sun in summer) is opposite the Tivoli hotel.

Organised Tours

Guided tours (€5.50, half-price for students, pensioners and children) of Ljubljana are available in Slovene and English from in front of the Town Hall at Mestni trg 1. Tours leave at 5pm daily from 1 June to 30 September and at 11am Sunday from 1 October to 31 May.

Places to Stay

Camping Some 6km north of Center on the Sava is **Camping Ježica** (☎ 568 39 13; Dunajska cesta 270; bus No 6 or 8; tent or caravan sites per adult/child low season €6/5, high season €8/6; bungalow singles/doubles/triples €25/40/50), a shady camping area open year-round with a restaurant and swimming pool that accommodates 300 people.

Hostels & Student Dormitories Three student dormitories (dijaški dom) are open to foreign travellers in July and August. Most central is **Dijaški Dom Tabor** (☎ 234 88 40, fax 234 88 55; e ssljddta1s@guest.arnes.si; Vidovdanska ul 7; singles 4000 SIT, doubles or triples per bed 2900/3400 SIT members/ nonmembers) across from the Park Hotel and affiliated with Hostelling International (HI). Rates include breakfast.

Dijaški Dom Bežigrad (☎ 534 28 67; e dd .lj-bezigrad@guest.arnes.si; Kardeljeva pl 28; bus No 6; singles/shared per person 3800/ 3300 SIT, breakfast 460 SIT) another HI member, is in the Bežigrad district 2km north of the train and bus stations. The Bežigrad has 50 rooms available in July and August.

Dijaška Dom Ivana Cankarja (☎ 474 86 00; e dd.lj-ic@guest.arnes.si; Polanski cesta 26; accommodation per person €10-14, including breakfast €12-15) is just east of the town centre (10% less for students).

Private Rooms & Apartments The TIC has about 40 **private rooms** on its list, but just a handful are in Center. Most of the others would require a bus trip up to Bežigrad. Prices range from 3500 SIT for singles and 5000 SIT for doubles. It also has eight apartments and one studio – four of which are central – for one to four people costing from 9700 SIT to 16,700 SIT. Whether you're looking for an apartment for one day or several months, try **Tour As** (☎ 434 26 60; e info@apartmaji.si; Mala ul 8) by Hotel Turist.

Hotels The best deal for location and quality is **Pri Mraku** (☎ 433 40 49; e mrak@daj-dam .si; Rimska cesta 4, singles/doubles 13,950/ 19,200 SIT). For 8450 SIT per person, up to four people can have a 5th-floor room with shared bathroom. The Mraku also has an excellent restaurant.

The 122-room **Park Hotel** (☎ 433 13 06, fax 433 05 46; e hotel.park@siol.net; Tabor 9; singles/doubles from €37/50) is where most people usually end up, as it's the city's only large budget hotel close to Center and the Old Town. It's pretty depressing, but the price is right and rates include breakfast. Students with cards get a 20% discount.

Bit Center Hotel (☎ 548 00 55, fax 548 00 56; w www.bit-center.net; Litijska 57; bus No 9 from the railway station; singles/ doubles or triples 5490/8190 SIT, breakfast 800 SIT), one small step up from a hostel, is also a possibility. Hotel guests get a 50% discount on sauna and health-club services, available in the same building.

A reasonable alternative in the town centre is the three-star **Hotel Turist** (☎ 234 91 30,

fax 234 91 40; e info@hotelturist.si; Dalmatinova; 15 singles/doubles from €66/90).

Places to Eat

Restaurants There are several excellent restaurants in Ljubljana that are relatively good value. **Šestica** (Slovenska cesta 40; lunch menus 1000-1400 SIT, mains 1100-2000 SIT) is a 200-year-old stand-by with a pleasant courtyard.

If you're in the mood to try horse meat, visit **Pri Vitezu** (Breg 4), a pricey but highly rated restaurant along the Ljubljanica.

Pri sv Florijanu (☎ 351 22 14; Gornji trg 20; set lunch 1690 SIT) has creative modern Slovenian food, including a great vegetable soup and leek risotto. The set lunch is good value. **Moro**, the happening new Moroccan themed bar and restaurant, is downstairs.

The capital abounds in Italian restaurants and pizzerias. Among the best in town are **Ljubljanski Dvor** (Dvorni trg 1) on the west bank of the Ljubljanica and **Foculus** (Gregorčičeva ul 3; small/large pizzas 800/1100 SIT) next door to the Glej Theatre. Other pizzapasta places include **Napoli** (Prečna ul 7) off Trubarjeva cesta and **Čerin** (Trubarjeva 52), which also has Internet access in its next-door Kavarna Čerin.

Špajza (Gornji trg 28) is popular with locals. **Casa del Papa** (☎ 434 31 58; Celovška 54) serves Latin-influenced lunch and dinner in a Hemingway-inspired setting.

The delicious vegetarian restaurant **Vegodrom** (☎ 459 17 50, Maistrova 10) also serves Indian cuisine like samosas and paluk paneer.

Cafés For coffee and cakes you might try the elegant **Evropa Café** (Gosposvetska cesta 2) on the corner of Slovenska cesta or the trendy **Zvezda Café** (Wolfova 14).

Self-Service & Fast Food For hamburgers, to-go coffee and other fast food visit **Quick** (Cankarjeva cesta 12; open 6.30am-11pm Mon-Sat, 4pm-10pm Sun), with a play area for kids. For a quick and tasty lunch, try **Ribca** (Pogarčarjev trg), a seafood bar below the Plečnik Colonnade. **Najboljski Gyros** (Stari trg 19; open 9am-1am Mon-Thurs, noon-1am Fri & Sat) sells gyros, pizzas and crepes, all under 1000 SIT.

There are **burek stands** (about 500 SIT) at several locations in Ljubljana. The one at Kolodvorska ul 20 is open 24 hours.

Self-Catering In the basement of the Maxi-market shopping arcade, the **supermarket** (*Trg Republike; open 9am-8pm Mon-Fri, to 3pm Sat & Sun*) has about the largest selection in town. The best places for picnic supplies are the city's many delicatessens, including **Žibila** (*Kongresni trg 9*) and **Burja** (*Kongresni trg 11*). For healthy snacks and vegetarian food, try **Prema** (*Gregorčičeva 9*).

Entertainment

Ask the TIC for its monthly programme of events in English – it is called *Where to? in Ljubljana* – or check out *Ljubljana Life*, the English-language monthly magazine available at the TIC and in hotels and restaurants.

Pubs & Bars A fun place to try Slovenian wine is **Vinoteka Movia** (*Mestni trg 2*), a wine bar next to the Town Hall. Pleasant and congenial places for a *pivo* (beer) or glass of *vino* (wine) include **Salon** (*Trubarjeva cesta 23*), **Patrick's Irish Pub** (*Prečna ul 6*) and **Holidays' Pub** (*Slovenska cesta 36*) next to the Kompas travel agency. Along the river, the most popular bar for locals and tourists is **Maček** (*Cankarjevo nab 19*).

Clubs Two of the most popular conventional clubs are **Klub Central** (*Dalmatinova ul 15*) next to the Turist Hotel and **Hound Dog** (*Trg Prekomorskih Brigad 4*) in the Hotel M, both populated by a young crowd. The student hang-out **K4** (*Kersnikova ul 4*) has a disco every night, open until the wee hours on Friday and Saturday nights and until around midnight on other nights. A popular place is **Metelkova mesto** (along Metelkova cesta near Maistrova ul), where squatters have turned former Yugoslav army barracks into the hippest spot in town, with several nightclubs and bars.

Gay & Lesbian Venues A popular spot for both gays and lesbians on Sunday night is **Roza Klub** (*open 10pm-4am*) at K4. At the Metelkova squat, there's a café/pub for gays called **Club Tiffany**. **Monokel Club** (*open Thur-Mon*) is a popular spot for lesbians in the same building.

Rock & Jazz Ljubljana has a number of excellent rock clubs with canned or live music including **Orto Bar** (*Grablovičeva ul 1*) and the **Brewery Pub** (*Plečnikov trg 1*). For jazz,

you cannott beat the **Jazz Club Gajo** (*Beethovnova ul 8*) near the Parliament building. **Birdland** (*Trubarjeva cesta 50*) also has a jam session on Wednesday night and occasional jazz concerts on the weekend.

Classical Music, Opera & Dance Ljubljana is home to two orchestras. Concerts are held in various locations all over town, but the main venue – with up to 700 cultural events every year – is **Cankarjev Dom** (*Trg Republike*). The **ticket office** (☎ 241 71 00; open 10am-2pm & 4.30pm-8pm Mon-Fri, 10am-1pm Sat & 1hr before performances), is in the basement of the nearby Maximarket mall. Tickets will cost anywhere between 1500 SIT and 3000 SIT with gala performances worth as much as 6000 SIT. Also check for any concerts performed at the beautiful **Filharmonija** (*Kongresni trg 10*).

At the ticket office of the **Opera House** (☎ 425 48 40; Župančičeva ul 1; open 2pm-5pm Mon-Fri, 6pm-7pm Sat & 1hr before performances) you can also buy ballet tickets.

For tickets to the Ljubljana Summer Festival and anything else that is staged at the Križanke, go to the **booking office** (☎ 252 65 44; Trg Francoske Revolucije 1-2; open 10am-2pm & 4.30pm-8pm Mon-Fri, 10am-1pm Sat & 1hr before performances) behind the Ilirija Column.

Cinemas For first-run films, try the **Komuna** (*Cankarjeva cesta 1*), **Kompas** (*Miklošičeva cesta 38*) or **Union** (*Nazorjeva ul 2*). All three generally have three screenings a day. The **Kinoteka** (*Miklošičeva cesta 28*) shows art and classic films. Cinema tickets generally cost around 800 SIT, and there are discounts usually available for the first session on weekday screenings.

Getting There & Away

Bus You can reach virtually anywhere in the country by bus from the capital. The timetable in the shed-like **bus station** (☎ 090 42 30; Trg OF) lists all routes and times.

Some sample destinations and one-way fares are: Bled (1220 SIT, hourly); Bohinj (1730 SIT, hourly); Jesenice (1310 SIT, hourly); Koper (2200 SIT, eight a day); Maribor (2370 SIT, 10 a day); Murska Sobota (3570 SIT, five a day); Novo Mesto (1390 SIT, hourly); Piran (3370 SIT, seven a day); Postojna (1120 SIT, 25 a day) Ptuj (connect in Maribor); and Rogaška Slatina (1950 SIT, daily at 9.30am).

Train All domestic and international trains arrive at and depart from the station (☎ 291 33 32; Trg OF 6). Local trains leave Ljubljana regularly for Bled (680 SIT, 51km); Jesenice (800 SIT, 64km); Koper (1380 SIT, 153km); Maribor (1380 SIT, 156km); Murska Sobota (2100 SIT, 216km); and Novo Mesto (950 SIT, 75km).

There is a 260 SIT surcharge on domestic InterCity train tickets. For more details on international trains to/from Ljubljana, see the introductory Getting There & Away section of this chapter.

Getting Around

To/From the Airport The city bus from lane No 28 leaves every hour for Brnik airport (680 SIT), 23km to the northwest, hourly at 10 minutes past the hour Monday to Friday and weekends on odd hours. There's also an **airport shuttle** (☎ 040-887 766) for about 2500 SIT. A taxi will cost between 5000 SIT and 6500 SIT. Brnik is about 40 to 45 minutes from the city centre.

Bus Ljubljana's bus system (☎ 582 24 60) is excellent and very user-friendly. There are 22 lines; five (Nos 1, 2, 3, 6 and 11) are considered to be main lines. These start to operate at 3.15am and run until midnight, while the rest run from 5am to 10.30pm.

You can either pay on board the bus (230 SIT) or use the tiny yellow plastic tokens (170 SIT) that are available from the bus station, newsstands, tobacconists, post offices and the two kiosks on the pavement in front of Slovenska cesta 55. An all-day ticket is also available for 660 SIT.

Taxi You can call a taxi on one of 10 numbers: ☎ 9700 to 9709. Flag fall is 150 SIT, and rates are 100 to 300 SIT per kilometre, depending on time of day. A taxi from the bus or train station to downtown runs at about 700 SIT, and 2000 SIT to outlying hotels.

Bicycle Visitors can rent bicycles from **Rog** (☎ 520 03 10; open 8am-7pm Mon-Fri, 8am-noon Sat), next to Rozmanova ul 1. From June to the end of September, you can also rent bikes near **Café Maček** (☎ 041-696 515) on Cankarjevo nab.

Julian Alps

Slovenia shares the Julian Alps in the northwestern corner of the country with Italy. The tri-peaked Mt Triglav (2864m), the country's highest summit, is climbed regularly by thousands of weekend warriors, but there are countless less ambitious hikes on offer in the region. Lakes Bled and Bohinj make ideal starting points – Bled with its comfortable resort facilities, Bohinj right beneath the rocky crags themselves. Most of this spectacular area falls within the boundaries of the Triglav National Park, which was established in 1924.

BLED
☎ 04 • pop 5400

Bled, a fashionable resort at just over 500m, is set on an idyllic, 2km-long emerald-green lake with a little island and church in the centre and a dramatic castle towering overhead. Trout and carp proliferate in the clear water, which is surprisingly warm and a pleasure for swimming or boating. To the northeast, the highest peaks of the Karavanke Range form a natural boundary with Austria, and the Julian Alps lie to the west. Bled has been a favourite destination for travellers for decades. All in all, it is beautiful but be warned that it can get very crowded – and pricey – in season.

Orientation

Bled village is at the northeastern end of the lake below Bled Castle. The bus station is also here on Cesta Svobode, but the main Lesce-Bled train station is about 4km to the southeast. In addition there's Bled Jezero, a branch-line train station northwest of the lake, not far from the camping ground.

Information

Tourist Offices Beld **tourist office** (☎ 574 11 22, fax 574 15 55; w www.bled.si; Cesta Svobode 15; open 9am-7pm Mon-Sat, 9am-3pm Sun Apr-Oct; 9am-5pm Mon-Sat, 9am-2pm Sun Nov-Mar) is next to the Park Hotel. In July and August the office stays open till 10pm Monday to Saturday and to 8pm on Sunday. Ask for the useful booklet Bled Tourist Information (300 SIT), available in English or German, which is reproduced on the town's useful website.

In Triglav shopping centre, **Kompas** (☎ 574 15 15; Ljubljanska cesta 4) sells some good

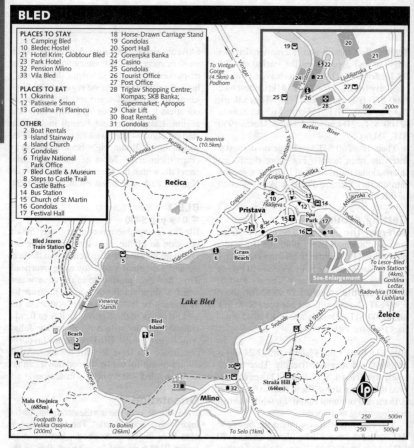

BLED

PLACES TO STAY
1 Camping Bled
10 Bledec Hostel
21 Hotel Krim; Globtour Bled
23 Park Hotel
25 Pension Mlino
33 Vila Bled

PLACES TO EAT
11 Okarina
12 Patisserie Šmon
13 Gostilna Pri Planincu

OTHER
2 Boat Rentals
3 Island Stairway
4 Island Church
5 Gondolas
6 Triglav National
   Park Office
7 Bled Castle & Museum
8 Steps to Castle Trail
9 Castle Baths
14 Bus Station
15 Church of St Martin
16 Gondolas
17 Festival Hall

18 Horse-Drawn Carriage Stand
19 Gondolas
20 Sport Hall
22 Gorenjska Banka
24 Casino
25 Gondolas
26 Tourist Office
27 Post Office
28 Triglav Shopping Centre;
   Kompas; SKB Banka;
   Supermarket; Apropos
29 Chair Lift
30 Boat Rentals
31 Gondolas

hiking maps. The **Triglav National Park office** (☎ 578 02 00; Kidričeva cesta 2; open 7am-3pm Mon-Fri) is located on the lake's northern shore.

Email & Internet Access Internet access is available at the **Bledec Hostel** at a cost of 500 SIT for 30 minutes. In the Triglav shopping centre, **Apropos** (Ljubljanska cesta 4; open 8am-midnight Mon-Sat) charges 1000 SIT for one hour, 500 SIT for 30 minutes.

Money Gorenjska Banka (Cesta Svobode 15; open 9am-11.30am & 2pm-5pm Mon-Fri, 8am-11am Sat), in the Park Hotel shopping complex, has an ATM for MasterCard/Cirrus holders. SKB Banka ATM (Ljubljanska cesta 4; open 8.30am-noon & 2pm-5pm Mon-Fri)

accepts all cards. Kompas and the tourist office change money.

Post & Communications The **post office** (Ljubljanska cesta 10; open 7am-7pm Mon-Fri, to noon Sat) is also in the centre of town.

Things to See

There are several trails to **Bled Castle** (adult/child 700/400 SIT; open 9am-8pm daily May-Sept, 9am-5pm Oct-Apr), the easiest is the one south from behind Bledec Hostel at Grajska cesta 17. The castle was the seat of the Bishops of Brixen (South Tirol) for over 800 years. Atop a steep cliff 100m above the lake, it offers magnificent views in clear weather. The **museum** presents the history of the area and allows a peep into a small 16th-century chapel. The expensive restaurant serves drinks on a terrace with a magnificent view.

Bled's other striking feature is tiny **Bled Island** (Blejski Otok) at the western end of the lake. The tolling 'bell of wishes' echoes across the lake from the tall white belfry rising above the dense vegetation. It's said that all who ring it will get their wish; naturally it chimes constantly. Underneath the present baroque church are the foundations of what was a pre-Romanesque chapel, unique in Slovenia. Most people reach the island on a *pletna*, a large gondola hand-propelled by a boatman. The price (1800 SIT per person) includes a half-hour visit to the island, church and belfry. If there are two or three of you it would be cheaper and more fun to hire a rowing boat (2000 SIT an hour for up to four) from the Castle Baths on the shore below the castle, in Mlino on the southern lakeshore or in front of the **Casino** (*Cesta Svobode 15*).

Hiking

An excellent half-day hike from Bled features a visit to the most impressive **Vintgar Gorge** (*adult/child 500/300 SIT; open daily May-Oct*), 4.5km to the northwest. Head northwest on Prešernova cesta then north on Partizanska cesta to Cesta v Vintgar. This will take you to Podhom, where signs point the way to the gorge entrance. A wooden footbridge hugs the rock wall for 1600m along the Radovna River, crisscrossing the raging torrent four times over rapids, waterfalls and pools before reaching **Šum Waterfall**.

From there a trail leads over Hom Hill (834m) east to the ancient pilgrimage **Church of St Catherine**. The trail then leads due south through Zasip and back to Bled. From late June to mid-September an Alpetour bus makes the run from Bled's bus station to Vintgar daily, or take the hourly Krnica bus to Spodnje Gorje which is 1km from the entrance; in summer there are two daily buses from Spodnje Gorje to the gorge entrance.

Places to Stay

Camping At the western end of the lake **Camping Bled** (*☎ 575 20 00; adult/child low season 1250/875 SIT, high season 1840/1290 SIT; open Apr–mid-Oct*) is in a quiet valley about 2.5km from the bus station. The location is good and there's even a beach, tennis courts, a large restaurant and a supermarket, but it fills up very quickly in summer.

Hostels The **Bledec Hostel** (*☎ 574 52 50; Grajska cesta 17; beds low/high season with ISIC/IYHF card €14/15, without card €17/19*) has a total of 55 beds in 13 rooms. Self-service laundry facilities are available for 800 SIT. Breakfast is included.

Private Rooms Finding a private room in Bled is easy. Travel agencies have extensive lists, and there are lots of houses around the lake with '*sobe*' or '*Zimmer frei*' signs indicating rooms to rent. **Kompas** (*☎ 574 15 15; e kompas.bled@siol.net; Ljubljanska cesta 4 singles €14-21, doubles €18-34, 2-person apartments €24-38*) is a good place to start. Rooms or apartments are also available from the tourist office or **Globtour Bled** (*☎ 574 41 86, fax 574 41 85; Ljubljanska cesta 7*) at Krim Hotel. All charge similar prices.

Hotels Most of Bled's hotels are pretty expensive affairs. Among the cheapest is the 212-bed **Hotel Krim** (*☎ 579 70 00, fax 574 37 29; e hotelkrim@hotel-krim.si; Ljubljanska cesta 7; singles/doubles high season €48/68*) in the town centre.

Central **Park Hotel** (*☎ 579 30 00; e info@gp-hoteli-bled.si; Cesta Svobode 15; singles/doubles €91/98 low season, €107/114 high season*) has attractive rooms, some with a wonderful lake view.

Across from the boat rentals and just a little way out of town, is the attractive **Pension Mlino** (*☎ 574 14 04, fax 574 15 06; Cesta Svobode 45; doubles summer 6600 SIT, off season 4400 SIT*).

For a splurge and a little history, check out **Vila Bled** (*☎ 579 15 00; Cesta Svobode 26; e vilabled@robas.si; singles/doubles low season €95/135, high season €115/155*), a grand resort hotel that was once Tito's summer home. It's been a hotel since the 80s, and includes tennis courts, a private boathouse, and Communist-era artwork.

Places to Eat

Bled's best choice for an affordable meal is the homy **Gostilna Pri Planincu** (*Grajska cesta 8; meals from 2000 SIT*), which is just a stone's throw from the bus station. The menu includes some excellent dishes such as mushroom soup and grilled chicken with fries and salad.

Okarina (*☎ 574 14 58; Riklijeva cesta 9*) has top-rate Indian cuisine with an assortment

SLOVENIA

of vegetarian dishes as well as offering its Slovenian specialities.

Patisserie Šmon *(Grajska 3)* offers scrumptious desserts and coffee.

There's a **supermarket** in the Triglav shopping centre.

A few miles out of town in Radovljica is **Gostilna Lečtar** *(☎ 537 48 00; Linhartov trg 2; closed Tuesday)*. This traditional restaurant is one of the most famous in Slovenia, and Radovljica is a charming small town with frescoed buildings. Take the main highway towards Ljubljana and you'll see signs for Radovljica.

Getting There & Around

If you're coming from Ljubljana, take the bus not the train. The train from Ljubljana will leave you at the Lesce-Bled station, 4km southeast of Bled while the bus takes you to the town centre. There are buses to Ljubljana (hourly), Bohinj (hourly starting at 7.20am), Radovljica (every 30 minutes) and Kranjska Gora via Lesce (eight daily). One bus a day from July to mid-September goes to Bovec via Kranjska Gora and the heart-stopping Vršič Pass.

Lesce-Bled train station handles up to 20 trains a day from Ljubljana (55 minutes). About eight cross the Austrian border, continuing on to Germany. There are six trains daily to Jesenice, six to Nova Gorica, 10 to Bohinj, and one a day at 6.14am during the summer to Skofja Loca.

Kompas *(☎ 574 15 15; Ljubljanska cesta)* rents out bicycles and mountain bikes for 4700/1500/2200 SIT per hour/half-day/day.

BOHINJ
☎ 04

Bohinj is a larger and much less developed glacial lake, 26km southwest of Bled. It is exceedingly beautiful, with high mountains that rise directly from the basin-shaped valley. There are secluded beaches for swimming just off the trail along the northern shore and there are many hiking possibilities, including an ascent of Mt Triglav.

Orientation

There is no town called Bohinj; the name actually refers to the entire valley, its settlements and the lake. The largest town in the Bohinj area is Bohinjska Bistrica (population 3080), 6km east of the lake. The main settlement on

the lake is Ribčev Laz at the southeastern corner. All in a row just up from the bus stop, are the post office, tourist office, a supermarket, a pizzeria and the Alpinum travel agency.

About 1km north across the Sava Bohinjka River and at the mouth of the Mostnica Canyon sits the town of Stara Fužina. The Zlatorog Hotel is situated at Ukanc at the western end of the lake near the camping ground and the cable car, which takes visitors up Mt Vogel and to the ski lifts (1922m).

Information

There's a helpful and very efficient **tourist office** *(☎ 572 33 70, fax 572 33 30; w www .bohinj.si; Ribčev Laz 48; open 7.30am-8pm daily July–mid-Sept, 8am-6pm Mon-Sat, 9am-3pm Sun mid-Sept–Jun)*. Its website contains much useful information.

The tourist office can change money but there's a 3% commission. There's an ATM at the post office next door. There are braches of **Gorenjska Banka** at Trg Svobode 2b and in Bohinjska Bistrica.

The **post office** *(Ribčev Laz 47; open 8am-6pm Mon-Fri, 8am-noon Sat)* is open during the listed hours but with a couple of half-hour breaks during the day.

Alpinum travel agency *(☎ 572 34 41; Ribčev Laz 50)* organises sporting activities in Bohinj and rents rooms.

Things to See & Do

The **Church of St John the Baptist**, on the northern side of the Sava Bohinjka across the stone bridge from Ribčev Laz, has exquisite 15th-century frescoes and can lay claim to being the most beautiful and evocative church in Slovenia. The **Alpine Dairy Museum** *(adult/child 400/300 SIT)*, at house No 181 in Stara Fužina about 1.5km north of Ribčev Laz, has a small but interesting collection related to Alpine dairy farming in the Bohinj Valley, once the most important such centre in Slovenia. If you have time, take a walk over to **Studor**, a village a couple of kilometres to the east renowned for its *kozolci* and *toplarji*, single and double hayracks that are unique to Slovenia.

Sporting equipment is available to rent from **Alpinsport kiosk** *(☎ 572 34 86; Ribčev Laz 53)*, just before the stone bridge to the church. Canoes & kayaks cost from 800/3100 SIT per hour/day. It also organises **guided mountain tours** (4600 SIT) and **canoe trips** (3600 SIT) on the Sava, as well as 'canyoning' through the rapids of the Mostnica Gorge stuffed into a neoprene suit, life jacket and helmet starting at 7900 SIT.

The **Vogel cable car** *(adult/child return 1000/700 SIT)*, above the camping ground at the western end of Lake Bohinj about 5km from Ribčev Laz, will whisk you 1000m up into the mountains. It runs every half-hour year round except in November, from 8am to 6pm (till 8pm in July and August). From the upper station (1540m) you can scale **Mt Vogel** in a couple of hours for a sweeping view of the surrounding region.

Savica Waterfall

An hour's hike west of the Zlatorog Hotel at Ukanc is the **Savica Waterfall** *(adult/child 300/150 SIT)*, the source of the Sava River, which gushes from a limestone cave and falls 60m into a narrow gorge. It costs 500 SIT for the car park, but the receipt can be redeemed for a drink at the restaurant.

Places to Stay

Autocamp Zlatorog *(☎ 572 34 82, fax 572 34 83; camp sites per person 1100-2100 SIT; open year-round)* caters mostly to camper vans, but its location on the lake near the Zlatorog Hotel can't be beaten.

The tourist office can arrange **private rooms** *(singles/doubles with shower low season 1920/3200 SIT, July & August to 2400/4000 SIT)* in neighbouring villages. There is usually a 30% surcharge for if you are staying fewer than three days.

Places to Eat

Pizza Center *(Ribčev Laz 50)*, next to the Alpinum travel agency, is very popular year-round.

For a truly different lunch, try **Planšar** *(Stara Fužina 179)* opposite the Alpine Dairy Museum. It specialises in home-made dairy products, and you can taste a number of local specialities for about 700 SIT.

There's a **Mercator supermarket** *(Ribčev Laz 49; open 7am-7pm Mon-Fri, 7am-5pm Sat)* for self-caterers.

Getting There & Around

There are hourly buses between Ribčev Laz and Ljubljana via Bled, Radovljica, Kranj and Bohinjska Bistrica. There are also about six local buses a day to Bohinjska Bistrica. All of these buses stop near the post office on Triglavska cesta in Bohinjska Bistrica and in Ribčev Laz (500m from the TIC towards Pension Kristal) before carrying on to Zlatorog Hotel in Ukanc. The closest train station is at Bohinjska Bistrica, which is on the Jesenice to Nova Gorica line.

Mountain bikes and helmets can be rented from **Alpinsport kiosk** *(☎ 572 34 86; Ribčev Laz 53)* for 800/3100 SIT per hour/day.

KRANJSKA GORA

☎ 04 • pop 1530

Known primarily for the best skiing in Slovenia, Kranjska Gora is also a worthy summer and off-season sporting ground. Climbing, fishing, ice-skating, hiking, bicycling – it's all here.

The Kranjska Gora **tourist office** *(☎ 588 17 68; e turisticno.drustvo.kg@siol.net; Tičarjeva 2; open 8am-8pm Mon-Sat, 9am-6pm Sun; off-season to 3pm Mon-Fri, to 6pm Sat & 1pm Sun)* has useful handouts and sells maps and guides to surrounding areas.

A good ski school and rental place is **Bernik** *(☎ 588 14 70; e sport@s5.net; Borovška cesta 88a)*.

Places to Stay & Eat

For **private rooms**, you can contact the tourist office. A decent, well-priced hotel that's in the centre of town is the **Hotel Prisank** *(☎ 588 41 70; e info@htp-gorenjka.si; Borovška 93; depending on season singles 5100-9400 SIT, doubles 7200-13,500 SIT)*.

Pizzeria Pino *(☎ 588 15 64; Borovška 75)* sells good meat and vegetarian pizzas for 700 to 1200 SIT.

There is also the **Mercator supermarket** *(Borovška 92)* in the same street.

HIKING MT TRIGLAV

The Julian Alps are among the finest hiking areas in Central and Eastern Europe. None of the 150 mountain huts *(planinska koča or planinski dom)* is more than five hours' walk from the next. The huts in the higher regions are open from July to September, and in the lower regions from June to October. You'll never be turned away if the weather looks bad, but some huts on Triglav get very crowded at weekends, especially in August and September. A bed for the night should cost about 2500 SIT per person. Meals are also available, so you don't need to carry a lot of gear. Leave most of your things below, but warm clothes, sturdy boots and good physical condition are indispensable.

The best months for hiking are August to October, though above 1500m you can encounter winter conditions at any time. Keep to the trails that are well marked with a red circle and a white centre, rest frequently and never *ever* try to trek alone.

For good information about the mountain huts and detailed maps, contact the **Alpine Association of Slovenia** (see the Information section under Ljubljana) or the TICs in Bled, Bohinj, Kranjska Gora (all excellent places to start a mountain-hut hike) or Ljubljana. You will also be able to pick up a copy of the 1:20,000 *Triglav* map or the 1:50,000-scale *Julijske Alpe – Vzhodni Del* (*Julian Alps – Eastern Part*), which is published by the Alpine Association and available at bookshops and tourist offices.

The *Dnevnik S Slovenske Planinske Poti*, a mountain hut 'passport', is a booklet published by the Alpine Association and available at any Triglav area tourist office. Hikers can bring this booklet with them to any of the 150 huts and try to collect as many stamps as possible.

Soča Valley

BOVEC & KOBARID
☎ 05 • pop 1775 & 1460

The Soča Valley, defined by the bluer-than-blue Soča, stretches from the Triglav National Park to Nova Gorica and is one of the most beautiful and peaceful spots in Slovenia. Of course it wasn't always that way. During much of WWI, this was the site of the infamous Soča (or Isonzo) Front, which claimed the lives of an estimated one million people and was immortalised by the American writer Ernest Hemingway in his novel *A Farewell to Arms*. Today visitors flock to the town of Kobarid to relive these events at the award-winning **Kobarid Museum** (☎ 389 00 00; Gregorčičeva ul 10; adult/student & child 700/500 SIT) or, more commonly, head for Bovec, 21km to the north, to take part in some of the best whitewater rafting in Europe. The season lasts from April to October.

In Bovec, the people to see for any sort of water sports are **Soča Rafting** (☎ 389 62 00; e soca.rafting@arctur.si), 100m from the Alp Hotel (across from the post office) or **Bovec**

Rafting Team (☎ 388 61 28; Trg Golobarskih Žrtev) in the small kiosk opposite the Martinov Hram restaurant. Rafting trips on the Soča lasting about 1½ hours start at 7000 SIT (students receive a discount). The cost of the trip includes all necessary safety equipment and gear. A kayak costs from 4500 SIT for four hours including equipment; a two-person canoe is 5500 SIT per person. There are kayaking lessons in summer (eg, a two-day intensive course for beginners costs 24,000 SIT without equipment).

In Kobarid, the **tourist office** in the Kobarid Museum and, in Bovec, the **Avrigo Tours agency** (☎ 388 60 22; Trg Golobarskih Žrtev 47), next to the Alp hotel, can organise **private double rooms** from 2500 SIT per person.

There are four camping grounds in Bovec – the closest is **Polovnik** (☎ 388 60 69) – and there is one in Kobarid – **Koren** (☎ 388 53 12).

Getting There & Away
There are up to six buses between Kobarid and Bovec and to Tolmin daily. Other destinations include Ljubljana (two to five buses daily), Nova Gorica (four to six) and Cerkno (up to five). In July and August there's a daily bus to Ljubljana via the Vršič Pass and Kranjska Gora. From Bled there are three trains every day to Most na Soći (55 minutes) from where you can catch regular buses to Kobarid and Bovec (45 minutes).

Karst Region

POSTOJNA
☎ 05 • pop 8200

Vying with Bled as the top tourist spot in Slovenia, **Postojna Cave** (adult/student & child 2400/1200 SIT) continues to attract the hordes. The electric train ride into the cave (to breeze through the less attractive parts) makes a visit seem a bit like Disneyland. Visitors get to see about 5.7km of the cave's over 20km on a 1½-hour tour in Slovenian, English, German or Italian. About 4km are covered by an electric train that will shuttle you through colourfully lit karst formations along the so-called Old Passage; the remaining 1700m is on foot. The tour ends with a viewing of a tank full of *Proteus anguinus*, the 'human fish' inhabiting Slovenia's karst caves. Dress warmly as the cave is a constant 9.5°C (with 95% humidity) all year.

From May to September, tours leave on the hour between 9am and 6pm daily. In March, April and October there are tours at 10am, noon, 2pm and 4pm with an extra daily one at 5pm in April and additional tours on the weekend in October at 11am, 1pm, 3pm and 5pm. Between November and February, tours leave at 10am and 2pm on weekdays, with extra ones added at noon and 4pm on the weekend and public holidays.

If you have the chance, visit the **Predjama Castle**, an awesome 16th-century fortress perched in the gaping mouth of a hill-top cavern 9km northwest of Postojna. As close as you'll get from Postojna by local bus (and during the school year only), though, is Bukovje, a village about 2km north of Predjama. Visiting the castles and the moderately impressive caves costs 1300/650 SIT for adults/students and children. A taxi from Postojna plus an hour's wait at the castle costs 12,000 SIT.

Orientation & Information

Postojna Cave is about 2km northwest of the town's bus station while the train station is 1km southeast of the centre. The caves are well signposted from the town centre and taxis are available from the bus and train stations.

The **tourist office** (☎ 726 51 83; Jamska cesta 9; e td.tic.postojna@siol.net; open 8am-6pm Mon-Fri, to 7pm in summer, 8am-noon Sat year-round) is in the shopping centre beneath the Hotel Jama.

Kompas (☎ 726 42 81; e info@kompas -postojna.si; Titov trg 2a) can arrange **private rooms** from 2800 SIT per person.

Getting There & Away

Postojna is a day trip from Ljubljana or a stopover on the way to/from the coast or Croatian Istria; almost all buses between the capital and the coast stop here. There are direct trains to Postojna from Ljubljana (one hour, 67km, 21 per day) and Koper (1½ hours, 86km, 13 per day) but the bus station is closer to the caves.

ŠKOCJAN CAVES
☎ 05

Škocjan Caves (adult/student/child 1700/ 1000/800 SIT), which some travellers consider a highlight of their visit, are close to the village of Matavun, 4km southeast of Divača (between Postojna and Koper). They have

been heavily promoted since 1986 when they were first entered on Unesco's World Heritage List. There are seven two-hour tours a day at 10am, and 11.30am and on the hour from 1pm to 5pm from June to September. Tours leave at 10am, 1pm and 3.30pm in April, May and October. There's a daily tour at 10am and an extra one at 3pm on Sunday and holidays from November to March.

These caves are in located in more natural surroundings than the Postojna Cave but are tough to reach without your own transport. From the train station at Divača (there are up to a dozen trains daily to/from Ljubljana), you can follow a path leading southeast through the village of Dolnje Ležeče to Matavun. The driver of any bus heading along the highway to or from the coast will let you off at the access road (there are huge signs announcing the caves) if you ask in advance. From where the bus drops you, walk the remaining 1.5km to the caves' entrance.

LIPICA
☎ 05 • pop 130

The famous Lipizzaner horses of the imperial Spanish Riding School in Vienna have been bred here since the 18th century and now perform at numerous equestrian events around the world. You can tour the 311-hectare **Lipica Stud Farm** (☎ 739 15 80; fax 734 63 70; e lipica@siol.net; adult/student & child €6/2; open year-round); there are between four and nine tours a day, depending on the season. A tour combined with an exhibition (€12/4), in which the snow-white creatures go through their paces is available at 3pm Tuesday, Friday and Sunday from May to October but Friday and Sunday only in April. If you've made prior arrangement, you can ride the horses all year or take a riding lesson (€17 to €60, depending on the season and length).

There are several expensive hotels available on the premises, or try the **Pension Risnik** (☎ 763 00 08; Kraška cesta 24; accommodation per person 2200 SIT) in nearby Divača.

For dinner, try the excellent Italian cuisine at **Gostilna Malovec** (☎ 763 12 25; Kraška cesta 30a).

Lipica is 10km southwest of Divača and 10km south of Sežana, which are both on the main train line from Trieste to Ljubljana. From Monday to Friday there are five buses a day from Sežana to Lipica.

The Coast

KOPER
☎ 05 • pop 24,000

Koper, only 21km south of Trieste, is an industrial port town with a quaint city centre. The town's Italian name, Capodistria, recalls its former status as capital of Istria under the Venetian Republic in the 15th and 16th centuries. After WWII, the port was developed to provide Slovenia with an alternative to Italian Trieste and Croatian Rijeka. Once an island but now firmly connected to the mainland by a causeway, the Old Town's medieval flavour lingers despite the industry, container ports, high-rise buildings and motorways beyond its 'walls'. This administrative centre is the largest town on the Slovene coast and makes a good base for exploring the region.

Orientation

The bus and train stations are combined in a modern structure about a kilometre southeast of the Old Town at the end of Kolodvorska cesta. There's a left luggage facility open 5.30am to 10pm that costs 400 SIT.

Information

Tourist Offices You will find the **tourist office** (☎/fax 627 37 91; Ukmarjev trg 7; open 9am-9pm Mon-Sat, 9am-1pm Sun June-Sept; 9am-2pm & 5pm-7pm Mon-Fri, 9am-1pm Sat Oct-May) opposite the marina.

Money The fairly central **Nova Ljubljanska Banka** (Pristaniška ul 45; open 8.30am-noon, 3.30pm-6pm Mon-Fri) has an ATM. There are also a couple of private exchange offices on Pristaniška ul, including **Maki** (open 8am-7pm Mon-Fri, to 1pm Sat). The ATM on the southeastern corner of Titov trg takes Visa, MasterCard, Maestro and Cirrus. The ATM at the post office accepts MasterCard and Cirrus.

Post & Communications The **post office** (Muzejski trg 3; open 8am-7pm Mon-Fri, 8am-noon Sat) is near the regional museum.

Email & Internet Access Travellers can use the five computers at **PINA** (Gregorčičeva ul 6, 3rd floor), a cultural and educational centre, for free. The computers are available on weekdays 10am to 2pm and 6pm to 10pm, and 6pm to 10 pm on Saturday.

Things to See

From the stations you enter Prešernov trg through the **Muda Gate** (1516). Walk past the bridge-shaped **Da Ponte Fountain** (1666), into Župančičeva ul and then right onto Čevljanka ul. This leads to Titov trg, the medieval central square. Most of the things to see in Koper are clustered here.

The 36m-high **City Tower** (1480), which you can climb daily in summer, stands beside the **Cathedral of St Nazarius**, dating mostly from the 18th-century. The lower portion of the cathedral's facade is Gothic, and the upper part is Renaissance. North is the sublime **Loggia** (1463), now a café and gallery, and to the south is the 1452 **Praetorian Palace** (free guided visits 10.15am and 5pm), both good examples of Venetian Gothic style. On the narrow lane behind the cathedral is a 12th-century Romanesque baptistry called the **Carmine Rotunda**. Trg Brolo to the east of the cathedral contains several more old Venetian buildings, including **Brutti Palace**, now a library, at No 1 and the **Fontico**, a 14th-century granary, at No 4.

The **Koper Regional Museum** (Kidričeva ul 19; adult/student & child 350/250 SIT; open 8am-3pm Mon-Fri, 8am-1pm Sat year-round, 6pm-8pm Mon-Fri in summer) is in the Belgramoni-Tacco Palace. It contains old maps and photos of the port and coast, an Italianate sculpture garden and paintings from the 16th to 18th centuries, and copies of medieval frescoes.

Places to Stay

The closest camping grounds are **Adria** (☎ 652 83 23), at Ankaran about 10km to the north by road, and **Jadranka** (☎ 640 23 00) at Izola 8km to the west.

Both the tourist office and **Kompas** (☎ 627 15 81; Pristaniška ul) opposite the vegetable market have private rooms for about 2700 to 3100 SIT per person, depending on the category and season. Apartments for three/four people start at 10,000/16,000 SIT. Most of the rooms are in the new town beyond the train station.

In July and August the **Dijaški Dom Koper** (☎ 627 32 52; Cankarjeva ul 5; beds per person 3500 SIT), an official hostel in the Old Town east of Trg Brolo, rents out 380 beds in triple rooms. The rest of the year only three beds are available. An HI card will get you a 10% discount.

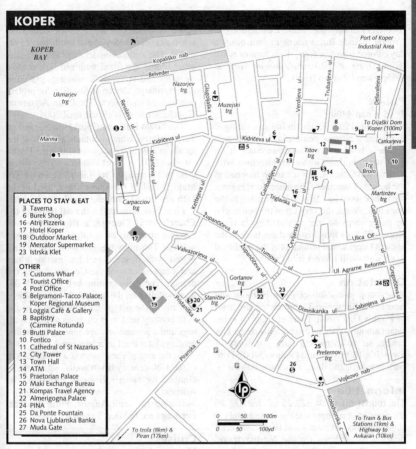

KOPER

KOPER BAY

Port of Koper Industrial Area

Kopališko nab

Belveder

Ukmarjev trg

Marina

●1

PLACES TO STAY & EAT
3 Taverna
6 Burek Shop
16 Atrij Pizzeria
17 Hotel Koper
18 Outdoor Market
19 Mercator Supermarket
23 Istrska Klet

OTHER
1 Customs Wharf
2 Tourist Office
4 Post Office
5 Belgramoni-Tacco Palace;
  Koper Regional Museum
7 Loggia Café & Gallery
8 Baptistry
  (Carmine Rotunda)
9 Brutti Palace
10 Fontico
11 Cathedral of St Nazarius
12 City Tower
13 Town Hall
14 ATM
15 Praetorian Palace
20 Maki Exchange Bureau
21 Kompas Travel Agency
22 Almerigogna Palace
24 PINA
25 Da Ponte Fountain
26 Nova Ljublanska Banka
27 Muda Gate

To Izola (8km) & Piran (17km)

To Dijaški Dom Koper (100m)

To Train & Bus Stations (1km) & Highway to Ankaran (10km)

0   50   100m
0   50   100yd

The only hotel in the Old Town is the renovated **Hotel Koper** (☎ 610 05 00, fax 610 05 94; e koper@terme-catez.si; Pristaniška ul 3; singles/doubles off season 10,700/17,200 SIT, July & Aug 13,000/20,800 SIT), with its business-like facilities.

Places to Eat

For fried dough on the go, head for the **burek shop** (Kidričeva ul 8). **Pizzeria Atrij** (Triglavska ul 2; open to 10pm daily) has a courtyard out the back.

One of the most colourful places for a meal in Koper is **Istrska Klet** (Župančičeva ul 39; mains around 1200 SIT), in an old palace. This is a good place to try Teran, the hearty red (almost purple) wine from the Karst and coastal wine-growing areas.

Taverna (Pristaniška ul 1; lunch 850/1000 SIT), in a 15th-century salt warehouse opposite the marina, has some decent fish dishes and lunch menus.

The large shopping centre and outdoor **market** (Pristaniška ul; open 7am-2pm) is open most days and contains a **Mercator supermarket** and various **food shops**.

Getting There & Away

There are buses almost every 20 minutes on weekdays to Piran (17km) and Portorož via Izola, and every 40 minutes on weekends. Buses also leave every hour or 90 minutes for Ljubljana (2400 SIT, 2¼ hours) via Divača and Postojna. You can also take the train to Ljubljana (1700 SIT, 2¼ hours), which is much more comfortable.

Up to 17 buses a day depart for Trieste (600 SIT) during the week. Destinations in Croatia include Buzet (three or four buses a day), Poreč (three or four), Pula (one or two); Rijeka (one at ˜10.10am), Rovinj (one at 3.55pm) and Zagreb (two).

PIRAN
☎ 05 • pop 4400

Picturesque Piran (Pirano in Italian), sitting at the tip of a narrow peninsula, is everyone's favourite town on the Slovenian coast. It's a gem of Venetian Gothic architecture with narrow little streets, but it can be mobbed at the height of summer. The name derives from the Greek word for 'fire', *pyr*, referring to the ones lit at Punta, the very tip of the peninsula, to guide ships to the port at Aegida (now Koper). Piran's long history dates back to the ancient Greeks, and remnants of the medieval town walls still protect it to the east.

Orientation
Buses stop just south of Piran Harbour and next to the library on Tartinijev trg, the heart of Piran's Old Town. Piran charges an exorbitant amount of money to park inside the city centre, so go to the car park just south of town. It's 1600 SIT for 24 hours (3400 SIT to park in town), and there's a shuttle into Piran.

Information
The **tourist office** (☎ 673 25 07, fax 673 25 09; Stjenkova ul) opposite the Piran Hotel essentially rents out rooms and keeps very brief hours. Instead head for the **Maona travel agency** (☎ 673 12 91; e maona@siol.net; Cankarjevo nab 7; open Apr-Oct), where the helpful and knowledgable staff can organise accommodation, an endless string of activities and boat cruises. During the months when the office is closed, ask at the agency in nearby Portorož (see that section later in the chapter).

Banka Koper (Tartinijev trg 12; open 8.30am-noon & 3pm-5pm Mon-Fri, to noon Sat) changes cash and has an ATM.

There's a **post office** (Cankarjevo nab 5; open 8am-7pm Mon-Fri, 8am-noon Sat) on the harbourfront.

Things to See & Do
The exhibits of Piran's **Maritime Museum** (Cankarjevo nab 3; adult/student 500/400 SIT; open 9am-noon & 3pm-6pm Tues-Sun), in a 17th-century harbourside palace, focus on the three 'Ss' that have shaped Piran's development over the centuries: the sea, sailing and salt-making (at Sečovlje just southeast of Portorož). The antique model ships are first-rate; other rooms are filled with old figureheads, weapons and votive folk paintings placed in the pilgrimage church at Strunjan for protection against shipwreck. The **Piran Aquarium** (Tomšičeva ul 4) is closed until 2004.

The **Town Hall** and **Court House** stand on Tartinijev trg, which contains a statue of the local violinist and composer Giuseppe Tartini (1692–1770). A short distance to the northwest is Prvomajski trg (also known as Trg Maja 1) and its baroque **cistern**, used in the 18th century to store the town's fresh water.

Piran is dominated by the tall tower of the **Church of St George**, a Renaissance and baroque structure on a ridge above the sea north of Tartinijev trg. It's wonderfully decorated with frescoes and has marble altars and a large statue of the George slaying the dragon. The free-standing **bell tower** (1609) was modelled on the campanile of San Marco in Venice; the octagonal **Baptistry** from the 17th century next to it contains altars, paintings and a Roman sarcophagus from the 2nd century, later used as a baptismal font.

To the east of the church is a 200m stretch of the 15th-century **town walls**, which can be climbed for superb views of Piran and the Adriatic.

During July and August, **Piran Musical Evenings** are held on Tartini trg.

Cruises
Maona and other travel agencies in Piran and Portorož can book you on any number of cruises – from a loop that takes in the towns along the coast to day-long excursions to Venice, Trieste, Rovinj or Brioni National Park in Croatia.

From late-May to October, the large catamaran *Marconi* sails down the Istrian Coast in Croatia as far as the Brioni Islands and the national park there. All-day excursions cost €54/29 return for adults/children aged four to 12; lunch is extra. To Rovinj the cost is €27/18. The boat leaves at 10am and returns at about 6.45pm except in September when it departs and returns 20 minutes earlier. At 8.35pm (6.50pm in September) on the same days, the *Marconi* heads for Trieste (35 minutes, one way €16/12 for adults/children) and returns the following morning at 9am.

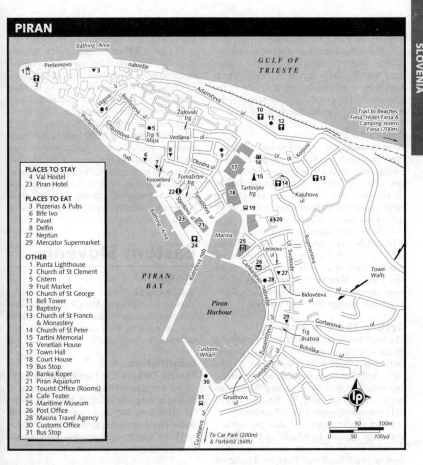

PIRAN

PLACES TO STAY
4 Val Hostel
23 Piran Hotel

PLACES TO EAT
3 Pizzerias & Pubs
6 Bife Ivo
7 Pavel
8 Delfin
27 Neptun
29 Mercator Supermarket

OTHER
1 Punta Lighthouse
2 Church of St Clement
5 Cistern
9 Fruit Market
10 Church of St George
11 Bell Tower
12 Baptistry
13 Church of St Francis & Monastery
14 Church of St Peter
15 Tartini Memorial
16 Venetian House
17 Town Hall
18 Court House
19 Bus Stop
20 Banka Koper
21 Piran Aquarium
22 Tourist Office (Rooms)
24 Cafe Teater
25 Maritime Museum
26 Post Office
28 Maona Travel Agency
30 Customs Office
31 Bus Stop

Places to Stay

Camping The closest camping ground is **Camping Jezero Fiesa** (☎ 674 62 30, fax 674 64 26; open June-Sept) at Fiesa, 4km by road from Piran (but less than a 1km walk on the coastal trail east of the Church of St George). It's in a quiet valley by two small ponds, and close to the beach, but can be crowded.

Private Rooms & Hostels The **tourist offices** (☎ 674 70 15; ⓦ www.portoroz.si) in Piran and Portorož as well as the **Maona travel agency** (☎ 674 64 23; ⓔ maona@ siol.net) can arrange private rooms and apartments throughout the year. Single rooms cost 3100 to 3800 SIT, depending on the category and the season, while doubles are 4600 to 6600 SIT and triples 5800 SIT to 7700 SIT.

Apartments for two are 6200 SIT to 7700 SIT. They usually levy a 50% surcharge for rooms if you stay fewer than three nights.

A very central, relatively cheap place is the **Val Hostel** (☎ 673 25 55, fax 673 25 56; ⓔ yhostel.val@siol.net; Gregorčičeva ul 38a; beds off-season per person €16, summer & holidays €18; open year-round) at Vegova ul. It has 56 beds with shared shower; breakfast is included in the rates.

Hotels Not in Piran itself, but definitely one of the nicest places to stay on the coast is **Fiesa** (☎ 671 22 00, fax 671 22 23; ⓔ hotel.fiesa@ amis.net; singles/doubles €35/52, July & Aug €50/89). The hotel is a pleasant, four-storey, 22-room place overlooking the sea near the Jezero Fiesa camping ground.

With a position right at the edge of the water is the **Piran Hotel** (☎ 676 21 00, fax 676 25 22; e recepcija.piran@hoteli-piran.si; Kidričeva nab 4; singles/doubles low season from €41/66, high season €58/98), which has recently refurbished rooms. Sitting on your private balcony during sunrise makes the higher-priced, sea-view rooms worth it.

Places to Eat
Piran has plenty of seafood restaurants along Prešernovo nab, but you do pay for location. Two good ones are **Bife Ivo** and **Pavel**. You can also try the local favourites: **Delfin** (Kosovelova ul 4) near Prvomajski trg or the more expensive **Neptun** (Župančičeva ul 7) behind Maona travel agency.

Cafe Teater, just south of the Piran Hotel, offers six beers on tap and light snacks. There are also several pizzerias along Prešernovo nab near the Punta lighthouse including **Flora** and **Punta**. Mercator supermarket (open 7am-8pm Mon-Fri, 7am-1pm Sat, 7am-11am Sun) is opposite Trg Bratsva 8.

Getting There & Away
The local bus company I&I links Piran with Portorož and Lucija (bus No 1); with Portorož and Fiesa (bus No 2; mid-June to August only); with Strunjan and Portorož (bus No 3); and with Portorož, Sečovlje and Padna (bus No 4). Schedules vary, but bus No 1 (210 SIT) runs about every 10 to 15 minutes.

Other destinations that can be reached from Piran include Ljubljana via Divača and Postojna (six to 10 a day) and Nova Gorica (one or two). Six buses head for Trieste on weekdays, and there are two daily departures for Zagreb. One bus daily heads south for Croatian Istria at 4.25pm, stopping at the coastal towns of Umag, Poreč and Rovinj.

PORTOROŽ
☎ 05 • pop 2950
The 'Port of Roses' is essentially a solid strip of high-rise hotels, restaurants, bars, travel agencies, shops, discos, beaches with turnstiles, parked cars and tourists. It's not to everyone's taste, but it does have the best beaches in Slovenia and tons of places to stay and eat. The **tourist office** (☎ 674 02 31, fax 674 82 61; w www.portoroz.si; Obala 16; open 9am-9pm high season) is also the TIC for Piran. It has information on the Primorska Summer Festival, a celebration of music and dance that takes place in Portorož, Piran, Koper and Izola throughout July.

The **post office** (K Stari cesta 1; open 8am-7pm Mon-Fri, 8am-noon Sat) is opposite the now empty Palace Hotel (1891).

Try at either the tourist office or **Kompas** (☎ 617 80 00; e portoroz@kompas.si; Obala 41) for private accommodation.

The beaches at Portorož, including the main one accommodating 6000 bodies, are 'managed' so you'll have to pay anywhere from 300 to 800 SIT to use them. They are open 9am to dusk in season. You can rent cabin space, umbrellas and chaise lounges, and there's a variety of activities to spend more money on, including water skiing, paragliding and water bike rentals.

Eastern Slovenia

MARIBOR
☎ 02 • pop 96,900
Maribor straddles the Drava River, but everything you'll want to access is on the northern side, between the train station and 'Lent,' the old town.

Information
Tourist Offices The **tourist office** (☎ 234 66 11, fax 234 66 13; e matic@maribor.si; Partinzanska cesta 47; open 9am-6pm Mon-Fri, 9am-1pm Sat) is across from the train station. It can arrange private accommodation and has a wealth of information on the vinska cestas (wine routes) in the area.

Money There's an ATM in the train station. **Nova KBM Banka** has an ATM opposite Maribor Castle on Slovenska ul. **Ljubljanska Banka** (Ventrinjska 2; open 9am-1pm & 3pm-5pm Mon-Fri) exchanges cash with no commission.

Post & Communications The main **post office** (Partinzanska cesta 54) is next to the train station. The exchange desk is open 7am to 7pm Monday to Saturday and 9am to 1pm Sunday for cash transactions only.

Email & Internet Access If you don't mind the smoke, **Kibla multimedijski center** offers free Internet access. Enter the Narodni Dom building at Kneza Koljca ul 9 and go through the first door on the left.

Things to See and Do

Maribor is the second largest city in Slovenia, industrial but with a charming pedestrian city centre, largely free of tourists. Although not readily available outside the country, some connoisseurs say Slovenian wines equal French or Italian. The 2,400-year-old viticulture tradition in this region is most evident in the hills around Maribor. The city is also the starting point for winery tours of the surrounding area. There's no public transport in these areas, so you'll need a rental car (see the Getting There & Around section later).

The oldest living grapevine, **Stara Trta** (*Vojašniška 8*), has been continuously producing wine for over 400 years. Across from the castle in Trg Svobode is the **Vinag** wine cellar, a 20,000-sq-metre cellar that can store seven million litres of wine.

Enjoy the 'green treasure' Pohorje area on a day trip using local bus No 6, which departs from the train station. The bus drops you at the Pohorje cable car, which will take you to areas for hiking and skiing.

The **Lent Festival** takes over Maribor for two weeks in the end of June and start of July.

Places to Stay

HI hostel **Dijaski Dom 26 Junij** (*☎ 480 17 10; Zeleznikova ul 12; bus No 3; accommodation per person 2700 SIT*) is only open July and August.

A fairly central and inexpensive hotel is **Club VIP** (*☎ 229 62 00, fax 229 62 10; Tomšičeva 10; singles/doubles €36/55*). To take advantage of the free entry into the Fontana spa, try the pleasant, central **Orel Hotel** (*☎ 250 67 00, fax 251 84 97; e orel@ termemb.si; Grajski trg 3a; singles/doubles 12,000/19,000 SIT*).

Places to Eat

Bolarič deli (*Juličeva ul 3; light meals 450-900 SIT open 7am-7pm Mon-Fri, to 1pm Sat*) is the cheapest place around. Decent pizza can be found at **Verdi** (*Dravska ul*), next to the river. Around the corner is **Grill Ranca** (*Vojašniška ul 4*), serving Balkan favourites.

The **Mercator supermarket** (*open 7am-8pm Mon-Fri, 7am-6pm Sat, 8am-11am Sun*) is a few steps away from the bus station.

Getting There & Away

Ten buses a day go to Ljubljana, starting at 5am and ending at 5.50pm. This is the best jump-off point for Rogaška Slatina (three daily) or Ptuj (20 daily). Take local bus No 6 to get to the Pohorje cable car.

Trains link Maribo to many cities in neighbouring countries: Vienna (7489 SIT, four hours, two a day); Graz (2358 SIT, one hour, two a day); and Zagreb (3100 SIT, three hours, two a day at 12.10pm and 7.55pm); Budapest (7000 SIT, seven hours, two daily at 9.10am and 3.20pm; change at Pragersko). Trains also go to Ljubljana (2½ hours, eight daily).

Getting Around

To follow the *vinska cesta*, try **Avis** (*☎ 228 79 10; Partizanska cesta 24; open 8am-4pm Mon-Fri, to noon Sat*).

If you want to get around the area without a car, you can rent bicycles at **Café Promenada** (*☎ 613 13 10; Lackova u 45*).

PTUJ
☎ 02 • pop 19,100

Charming and compact Ptuj is Slovenia's version of an Italian hill town. It's first incarnation was as *Poetovio*, a Roman village. Remnants of its Roman past still dot the town, and there's a hill-top castle with a magnificent museum.

Information

The helpful Ptuj **tourist office** (*☎ 779 60 11; w www.ptuj.si; Slovenski trg 3; open 8am-5pm Mon-Fri, to 1pm Sat*) also opens a branch at No 14 during the summer.

Things to See & Do

The hill-top castle features the **Ptuj Regional Museum** (*adult/child 600/300 SIT; open 9am-5pm winter, to 6pm in summer, to 8pm Sat & Sun July & Aug*), with exhibits on musical instruments, weaponry, the Kurentovanje Festival and Ptuj's history. Call ahead to arrange an English-speaking guide (250 SIT).

About 1.5km from the centre of town is **Terme Ptuj** (*☎ 782 72 11; Pot v Toplice 9; adult/child 1800/1200 SIT*), a giant spa complex with four swimming pools, water slides, massage treatments and eight tennis courts.

The **library** (*Prešernova ul 33-35*) is in the building complex known in the 1700s as the *Small Castle*. You can also check your email for free for up to one hour on the 2nd floor. The ornate **Town Hall** (*Mestni trg 1*) was built in 1907 to resemble the earlier late-Gothic version. The **Town's Tower** (*Slovenski trg*) stands in front of the **Provost's Church**. The tower was mentioned as early as 1376 in city documents, and has been rebuilt many times down through the centuries.

Every February for the 10 days surrounding Mardi Gras, Ptuj hosts the **Kurentovanje Festival**, a district-wide party that attracts visitors from all over the world.

Places to Stay & Eat
The TIC arranges **private accommodation** starting at around 3500 SIT per person.

The **Terme Ptuj camping ground** (☎ 782 72 11; adult/child €8.60/6.10) offers free access to the spa complex. It also has **apartments** (singles/doubles/rooms for up to 6 people €40/65/82).

The central **Garni Hotel Mitra** (☎/fax 774 21 01; e fredi@zerak.com; Prešernova ul 6; singles/doubles/triples 7700/11,000/13,500 SIT) offers pleasant rooms.

A great place to try Slovenian seafood dishes is **Ribič** (☎ 771 46 71; Dravska ul 9). It serves fresh fish for 4000 SIT per kilo and a host of Slovene specialities.

There's an **open-air market** (Novi trg; open 7am to 3pm daily) for self-caterers.

Getting There & Away
Ptuj is on the line to many European destinations. There are trains to Munich (10 hours, two per day), Venice (eight hours, one daily), Zagreb (three hours, five a day) and Ljubljana

(2½ hours, 11 a day). By bus, you can get to Maribor (680 SIT, 40 minutes, at least hourly), Rogaška Slatina (3.10pm daily) and Ljubljana (2½ hours, 11 daily).

THERMAL SPAS
Slovenia was once a Roman protectorate, and this is evident in Slovenian devotion to spa culture. Nearly every town in this chapter boasts a spa, and there are a multitude of spas off the beaten track as well. The famous healing properties of the region's thermal waters have brought visitors to Slovenia for centuries. For information about spas in Slovenia, contact the **Slovenian Spas Community** (☎ 03-544 21 11; w www.terme-giz.si).

Rogaška Slatina
The most famous and oldest spa town in Slovenia, Rogaška Slatina is past its heyday as the premier spot to 'take the waters', but it's in beautiful surroundings and has several good spas.

In the middle of the town there's a **tourist office** (☎ 03-811 50 13; e tic.rogaska@siol .net; Zdraviliški trg 1) near several hotels and spas. A good bet for a bed is the **Zdraviliški Dom** (☎ 03-811 20 00; doubles from €35).

To get to Rogaška Slatina, take either the bus or train to Celje and transfer. The bus drops you off next to the town centre, which is pedestrian-only, and the train stops about 200m away.

Ukraine

Ukraine, which means 'borderland', was the traditional crossroads between the Baltic and Black Seas and the fringe between Europe and Central Asia. This former state of the Soviet Union is slowly adjusting to independence, capitalism and democracy, and these days proudly looks more towards Eastern Europe than to Russia.

Ukraine is a vast, varied and colourful land. In the west, the beautiful city of Lviv is stamped with a Central European elegance, while to the south is the exotic and intriguing port of Odesa. The ancestral Tatar homeland of Crimea is a semi-autonomous peninsula famed for its spectacular palaces, castles, mountains and resorts such as Yalta. The capital, Kyiv, is energetic and cosmopolitan.

Travelling around Ukraine is often not easy; buses and trains are slow and sometimes uncomfortable, and food and accommodation is rarely to the standard expected in the West. However, if you're willing to forego a bit of comfort and convenience, you'll find Ukraine both captivating and hospitable.

Facts About Ukraine

HISTORY

The Scythians dominated the plains north of the Black Sea from the 7th to the 4th century BC, while around the same time the Greeks established colonies along the Black Sea coast. Between the 4th and 2nd centuries BC, the Sarmatians from the east displaced the Scythians everywhere except in Crimea.

During the 2nd century AD, the Ostrogoths, a Germanic people from northern Poland, set up a state covering most of modern Ukraine, but less than 200 years later the Huns invaded. In the 6th and 7th centuries the Slavs spread throughout Ukraine, and in the 8th century most of the country fell under the Khazars, a nomadic group of Turkic and Iranian tribes.

Following trade and settlement expansion into the area by the Scandinavians (Varyagi) from the 6th century, Oleh of Novgorod declared himself ruler of Kyiv in 882. The city grew to be capital of the large, unified Varyagi (or Rus) state that during its peak stretched

At a Glance

- **Kyiv** – many interesting museums, churches and monasteries on the glorious Dnipro River
- **Lviv** – evocative skyline of towers and church spires; Renaissance, baroque and neoclassical buildings
- **Kamyanets-Podilsky** – historic architecture and a dramatic landscape
- **Odesa** – bustling port with ornate baroque architecture
- **Crimea** – charming Sevastopol and Simferopol; hiking the forested Crimean Mountains

Capital	Kyiv
Population	48.8 million
Official Language	Ukrainian
Currency	1 hryvnia (hrn)
	= 100 kopeks
Time	GMT/UTC+0200
Country Phone Code	☎ 380

between the Volga River, Danube River and Baltic Sea. King Svyatoslav later crushed the Khazars, but was eventually defeated by the fierce Turkic Pechenegs. His successor, Volodymyr, later visited Constantinople and accepted Christianity in 988, thereby founding the Russian and Ukrainian Orthodox Church. By the 11th and 12th centuries the Varyagi state began to splinter into 10 rival

UKRAINE

UKRAINE

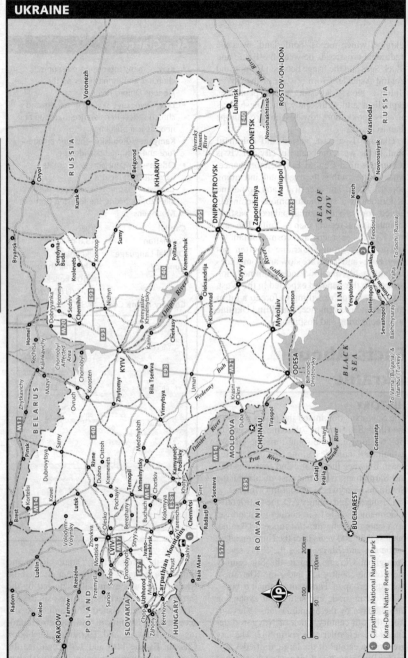

Carpathian National Natural Park

Kara-Dah Nature Reserve

princedoms. When prince of Suzdal Andriy Bogolyubov sacked Kyiv in 1169, followed by the Mongols 70 years later, the end of the Varyagi era was complete.

The regions of present-day western, central and northern Ukraine later united under Prince Roman Mstyslavych, who gained control of Kyiv in 1203. There was a period of relative prosperity under his dynamic son King Danylo and grandson Lev. During this time, much of eastern and southern Ukraine came under the control of the Volga-based Golden Horde. Its empire was emasculated, however, in the 14th century by the Black Death, as well as by the growing military strength of Russian, Polish and Lithuanian rulers.

Cossacks & Russian Control

By the 15th century, the uncontrolled steppe in southern Ukraine began to attract runaway serfs, criminals, Orthodox refugees and other outcasts from Poland and Lithuania. Along with a few semi-independent Tatars, the inhabitants formed self-governing militaristic communities and became known as *kazaks* (Cossacks), from the Turkic word meaning 'outlaw, adventurer or free person'. Ukrainian Cossacks eventually developed the self-ruling Cossack Hetmanate, which to some degree reasserted the concept of Ukrainian self-determination.

In 1648, Hetman Bogdan Khmelnytsky (aided by Tatar cavalry) overcame the Polish rulers at the battle of Pyliavtsi. He was forced to engage in a formal but controversial military alliance with Muscovy in 1654, but in 1660 a war broke out between Poland and Russia over control of Ukraine. This ended with treaties that granted control over Kyiv and northern Ukraine to Russia and territory to the west of the Dnipro River to the Poles.

During the 18th century Russia expanded into southern Ukraine and also gained most of western Ukraine from Poland, except for the far west, which went to the Habsburg Empire. Perpetual occupation fuelled Ukrainian nationalism, which was born in Kyiv during the 1840s and inspired by the prolific writer and poet Taras Shevchenko.

The 20th Century

Following WWI and the collapse of tsarist power, Ukraine had a chance – but failed – to gain independence. Civil war broke out and exploded into anarchy: six different armies vied for power and Kyiv changed hands five times within a year. Eventually, Ukraine was again divided between Poland, Romania, Czechoslovakia and Russia. The Russian part became a founding member of the USSR in 1922, but Stalin looked upon Ukraine as a laboratory for testing Soviet restructuring, while stamping out 'harmful' nationalism. Consequently, he engineered a famine in 1932–33 which killed millions in Ukraine.

The Soviet Red Army rolled into Polish Ukraine in September 1939. The Germans attacked in 1941 and by the end of the year controlled virtually all of Ukraine. Kharkiv and Kyiv were retaken by the Red Army, however, two years later. An estimated six million Ukrainians died in the war, which left most of the country's cities in ruin. After WWII, the USSR kept the territory it had taken from Poland in 1939.

The focus of the *glasnost*-era opposition to Soviet rule developed from the Church in western Ukraine and the disastrous explosion of a nuclear reactor at Chornobyl in 1986 (see Ecology & Environment later). Discontent about the latter was exacerbated by the slow government response and subsequent cover-up. Riots against occupation started during 1988 in Lviv. In July 1990, the Ukrainian parliament did issue a sovereignty declaration, but this was too little for the growing independence movement. In October, a wave of protests in Kyiv forced the resignation of the old-guard prime minister.

Independence

Shortly after a failed Soviet coup in August 1991, the Verkhovna Rada (Supreme Council) of Ukraine adopted a declaration of independence. In a subsequent referendum 84% of the population voted for an independent Ukraine.

Inevitably, factions arose within the new government. Growing dissatisfaction forced the government to resign in September 1992, but difficulties still plagued the second government. Disagreements and tensions with Russia and the West escalated, while skyrocketing hyperinflation, fuel shortages and plummeting consumer power caused further widespread dissatisfaction. Paradoxically, the 1994 presidential elections saw the rise of the re-established Ukrainian Communist Party.

Relative economic stability was achieved during the mid-1990s under pro-Russian reformer Leonid Kuchma, when inflation fell

UKRAINE

from an inconceivable 10,000% in 1993 to 10% in 1997. The hryvnia, Ukraine's new currency, was introduced in 1996 and a process of privatisation kick-started the economy. Despite all this, living conditions declined and the government couldn't pay its workers. After the March 1998 parliamentary elections, the Ukrainian Communist Party again stormed to victory.

Despite Ukraine witnessing its first positive growth in GDP since independence, the fragile economy failed to weather the financial storm that ripped across Russia in 1998. Consumer power in Ukraine plummeted as the hryvnia, in September alone, took a 51% tumble in value.

Presidential elections in October 1999 saw the incorrigible President Kuchma re-elected. International observers believed that the parliamentary elections held in March 2002 were fairer than before, but still far from perfect.

GEOGRAPHY

At 603,700 sq km, Ukraine is the largest country wholly in Europe (discounting European Russia). The topography consists almost entirely of steppe – gently rolling, partially wooded plains – at a mean height of 175m. The only serious altitudes are along a short stretch of the Carpathian Mountains in the west and the Crimean Mountains in the south.

Approximately 3000 rivers flow through Ukraine, including the big four: the Dnister, the Pivdenny Buh, the Dnipro and the Siversky Donets.

CLIMATE

Inland Ukraine enjoys a relatively moderate continental climate. The hottest month, July, averages 23°C, while the coldest, January, is literally freezing. Eastern Ukraine can catch chilling Siberian gales, while the west enjoys the tail end of the warm Mediterranean winds. Along the coast, Yalta and Odesa enjoy a marginally subtropical climate and are much milder in winter. June and July are the wettest months in the interior. While most of Ukraine receives about 114cm of rain a year, Crimea has an annual average of only 40cm.

ECOLOGY & ENVIRONMENT

On 26 April 1986, reactor No 4 at Chornobyl nuclear power station, 100km north of Kyiv, exploded and nearly nine tonnes of radioactive material (90 times as powerful as the Hiroshima bomb) spewed into the sky. An estimated 4.9 million people living in northern Ukraine, southern Belarus and southwestern Russia were affected. Western monitors now conclude that radioactivity levels at Chornobyl are negligible, so organised tours of the site and surrounding 'ghost' villages are possible. Check the English-language press in Kyiv for details about excursions.

Besides the horrors of Chornobyl, acid rain has been reported in much of the Carpathian Mountains, around Kyiv, and along the southern stretches of the Dnipro River. Many rivers have also been polluted by waste runoff from industry due to lax restrictions and minimal controls. Much of the silt carried downstream from Chornobyl is radioactive, but little is known about the potential danger.

GOVERNMENT & POLITICS

The Ukrainian constitution provides for sovereignty as a nonsocialist state. Executive power is in the hands of the president and prime minister, while legislative authority is vested in the 450-member Verkhovna Rada.

Parliamentary elections are held every four years. The president, elected by popular vote for a five-year term, appoints the prime minister and 35 cabinet ministers. All appointments must be approved by the Verkhovna Rada, and a new cabinet has to be formed every time a prime minister is appointed.

The country is divided into 24 administrative divisions (each called an *oblast*), while the Autonomous Republic of Crimea retains some degree of self-government.

ECONOMY

Crucial steps towards privatisation during the 1990s have been slow to have an effect, despite austere economic targets set by the IMF and World Bank. Loans to aid Ukraine's painful transition from a centralised to a market economy were repeatedly suspended as the government dragged its feet on implementing

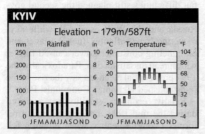

KYIV

Elevation – 179m/587ft

economic reforms. Ukraine remains one of the major recipients of US aid, but attracts very little foreign investment because of widespread corruption and an unattractive legal and tax system. In mid-2002, the average monthly wage was US$61 and average monthly pension was US$30.

POPULATION & PEOPLE

Ukraine's population has steadily declined since independence. About 66% live in urban areas like Kyiv, Kharkiv, Dnipropetrovsk, Odesa and Donetsk. Some 73% are Ukrainian and another 22% are ethnic Russians. The remainder includes Belarusians, Moldovans, Bulgarians, Poles, Hungarians, Romanians and Jews. Almost all of the country's Tatar population (about 250,000) lives in Crimea.

ARTS

Early folk dances that symbolised seasonal rituals were the inspiration for many Ukrainian ballets. They were based on the calendar feasts in peasant life: winter, spring, summer, autumn and the harvest. Combined with incantations and songs, dances also celebrated the rites of birth, marriage and death. The most famous were those of the Cossacks. Peculiar styles (like the 'duck-kick') evolved into unique dances that encapsulate the spirit and legends of these proud people.

Nostalgic fascination for oral traditions handed down between generations led to written anthologies of song and dance. *Bylyny* is an epic narrative poem that tells of the courageous deeds of historic Ukrainian heroes. *Duma* is a lyrical ballad that glorified the exploits of the Cossacks and was performed by a *kobzar* minstrel, while the *chumak* songs recount the tales of the Cossack salt traders.

Many Ukrainians believe that to understand their heritage you must appreciate the significance of Taras Shevchenko, who was punished by exile in 1847 for his satirical poems about Russian oppression. Arguably the most talented and prolific Ukrainian writer of the early 20th century was Ivan Franko, whose scholarly and moving works shed light on the issues plaguing Ukrainian society. He was inevitably imprisoned by the Russians.

SOCIETY & CULTURE

While Ukrainians are generally tolerant of most faux pas done by foreigners, you may want to know that:

- Women should not sit at the corner of a table in a Ukrainian home (because the woman will remain unwed for the next seven years).
- Women should not sit on anything built from concrete (because their ovaries will freeze and they will be unable to bear children).
- No-one should shake hands across the threshold (it brings bad luck).
- No-one should leave an empty bottle on the table during a meal (it will cause a fight).

RELIGION

According to the Ukrainian constitution, the church is separate to the state. Nearly 97% of Ukrainians are Christian. Complex historical reasons mean central and southern Ukraine mostly follow the Moscow-based Orthodox Church, while the rest of the country follows the Kyiv-based Orthodox Church or the Ukrainian Autocephalous Orthodox Church. (The latter is also known as the Ukrainian Greek-Catholic Church and is under the jurisdiction of the Vatican.) There are some small Jewish minorities in all cities, while Muslim communities, primarily Tatars, live in Crimea.

LANGUAGE

Ukrainian was adopted as the sole official language at independence. However, many Ukrainians, especially in the south, prefer to speak Russian. An ugly hybrid of the two languages called Surzhyk is spoken in Kyiv and other major cities.

English is understood by staff at most major hotels but very rarely elsewhere. Consequently, you will have to learn some Russian and/or Ukrainian words and phrases, and be able to decipher the Cyrillic alphabet – refer to the Russian section of the Language chapter at the back of this book. For a more in-depth guide to both languages get a copy of Lonely Planet's *Ukrainian phrasebook* and/or *Russian phrasebook*.

Facts for the Visitor

HIGHLIGHTS

Highlights in Kyiv include the highly evocative cave monastery at the Kyiv-Pechersk National Preserve and the sparkling St Sophia Cathedral. In the west, the old towns of Lviv and Ivano-Frankivsk are elegant and the fortified castle town of Kamyanets-Podilsky is fascinating. To the south, exotic Odesa boasts plenty of history and museums.

UKRAINE

In Crimea, the highlights are the Khans' Palace at Bakhchysaray, the resort of Yalta and the charming port of Sevastopol.

SUGGESTED ITINERARIES

You may wish to use the list below as a guide, but remember that Ukraine is a *huge* country.

One Week
Kyiv (two days), Lviv (two to three) and Chernivtsi and Kamyanets-Podilsky (two to three); or spend the whole week exploring Crimea

Two Weeks
Visit Kyiv and western Ukraine, as described above, and spend one week in Crimea

One Month
Stay longer in the places listed above, as well as visit Uzhhorod (two days), Ivano-Frankivsk (two to three days) and Odesa (three to four). If you have any extra time, hike around the Carpathian National Natural Park and take a boat down the Dnipro River.

PLANNING
When to Go

Ukraine's tourist spots are rarely crowded in the summertime, except those near Odesa and in Crimea. The better hotels in Yalta are often fully booked during July and August, and boat trips along the Dnipro River and Black Sea coast only operate from May to September. Mid-April to early June is the best time to visit the country. In summer, it can be stiflingly hot and horribly dusty, but at the same time also surprisingly wet.

Maps

Freytag & Berndt's *Ukraine* (1:1,200,000) is the best map available outside Ukraine. Inside the country, accurate city maps are readily available but few are in English. The best ones are published (in Cyrillic) by Kartografia and feature bright blue covers.

What to Bring

Everything you could possibly need is readily available in the major cities. Women should pack a scarf to cover their head when visiting monasteries.

TOURIST OFFICES

With the notable exception of Lviv, tourist offices do not exist anywhere in the country. Ukraine also has no tourist offices abroad, but most of its embassies and consulates (see that section later in the chapter) stock some practical information.

VISAS & DOCUMENTS
Visas

Visa regulations are in disarray so the information in this section is likely to be different (hopefully easier) by the time you travel to Ukraine. According to the Ministry of Foreign Affairs – and Ukrainian travel agencies (which obviously financially benefit from the status quo) – anyone wanting a tourist visa must have a 'support letter' (invitation) from someone in Ukraine and prebooked accommodation for at least the first night. However, many readers (including the author) have recently received a tourist visa *without* having an invitation or prebooked accommodation. At the time of research, the Ukrainian government was planning to allow citizens of the EU, the USA, Canada, Switzerland and Japan to obtain an eight-day extendable tourist visa (US$22) on arrival at airports and sea ports in Odesa and Simferopol.

The upshot is that currently most foreigners will need a Ukrainian visa before they travel, so contact a Ukrainian embassy or consulate and ask about what *it* requires. The websites run by the Ukrainian embassy in Washington (**w** www.ukremb.com) and the US Embassy in Kyiv (**w** www.usemb.kiev.ua) detail the current requirements.

One-month, extendable tourist visas from Ukrainian embassies and consulates cost about US$40 – or about US$80 for the 'express' (same-day) service – and are valid for three months. On the application form, you may be asked to list your 'prebooked hotel' for the first night and a 'contact' in Ukraine; in both cases, just add any hotel listed in this chapter.

Transit visas are available for a maximum of 72 hours, but you currently need proof that you're *only* transiting – and do not intend staying in – Ukraine, eg, a train/bus/boat ticket through Ukraine and a visa for the next country of destination. Transit visas are *not* issued on arrival and cannot be extended.

If you do need a 'support letter' and proof of prebooked accommodation, contact one of the travel agencies listed under Organised Tours in the Getting There & Away and Getting Around sections later, or contact **w** www.hotelsukraine.com for help.

Visa Extensions Tourist visas can be extended for a maximum of two months at the **Department of Citizenship, Passport & Immigration** (☎ 044-224 9051; bul Tarasa

Shevchenka 34, Kyiv; open 9am-5pm Mon-Fri). The cost of the extension is about 10 hrn (US$2) per day. If you have applied for a tourist visa through a Ukrainian-based travel agency it should arrange the extension (for an extra fee of about US$30).

Hostel, Student & Seniors Cards

There are no hostels in Ukraine, and discount cards for student and senior travellers are not accepted anywhere.

EMBASSIES & CONSULATES
Ukrainian Embassies & Consulates

For details about Ukrainian diplomatic missions in other Eastern European countries, refer to the relevant chapters elsewhere in this book.

Australia *Consulate-General:* (☎ 02-9328 5429, fax 9328 5164) Level 3, Edgecliff Centre, 203–233 New South Head Rd, NSW 2027
Belgium & The Netherlands (☎ 02 379 21 00, fax 02 379 21 79) ave Albert Lancaster 30, 1180 Brussels
Canada (☎ 613-230 2961, fax 230 2400) 310 Somerset St West, Ottawa, Ontario K2P 0J9; Consulate in Toronto
France (☎ 01 43 06 07 37, fax 01 43 06 02 94) 21 ave de Saxe, 75007 Paris
Germany (☎ 030-2888 7116, fax 2888 7163) Albrechtstrasse 26, 10117 Berlin
Consulate in Munich
Russia (☎ 095-229 1079, fax 924 8469) Leontevsky pereulok 18, Moscow, 103009
Consulate: (☎ 0812-312 1048, fax 312 3210) bul Mala Morska 6, office 5, St Petersburg
UK (☎ 020-7727 6312, fax 7792 1708) 60 Holland Park W11, London W11 3SJ
USA (☎ 202-333 0606, fax 333 0817) 3350 M St NW, Washington, DC 20007
Consulates in New York & Chicago

Embassies & Consulates in Ukraine

All embassies listed below are in Kyiv (area code ☎ 044):

Australia (☎ 246 4223) vul Kominternu 18/137
Belarus (☎ 290 0201, e belarus@visti.com) vul Sichnevoho Povstannya 6
Canada (☎ 464 1144) vul Yaroslaviv val 31; Consulate in Lviv
France (☎ 228 7369) vul Reitarska 39
Germany (☎ 216 7498) vul Honchara 84; Consulate in Lviv
Hungary (☎ 238 6381, fax 212 2090) vul Reitarska 33; Consulate in Uzhhorod

Moldova (☎ 290 7721, fax 290 7722) vul Sichnevoho Povstannya 6
Netherlands (☎ 490 8200) pl Kontraktova 7; Consulate in Lviv
Poland (☎ 230 0700, fax 464 1336) vul Yaroslaviv val 12; Consulate in Lviv
Romania (☎ 224 5261, e romania@iptelecom .net.ua) vul Kotsyubynskoho 8
Consulates in Odesa & Chernivtsi
Russia (☎ 244 0963, fax 246 3469) prosp Povitroflotsky 27
Consulates in Odesa, Lviv & Simferopol
Slovakia (☎ 212 0310, fax 212 3271) vul Yaroslaviv val 34; Consulate in Uzhhorod
UK (☎ 462 0011) vul Desiatynna 9
USA (☎ 490 0000) vul Kotsyubynskoho 10

CUSTOMS

On arrival at Boryspil International Airport (only) in Kyiv, you must complete a Customs Declaration Form. On the reverse side of the form, list all major valuables you're bringing into the country, such as jewellery and video/still cameras. If you have filled in the reverse side, and/or are entering Ukraine (via Kyiv airport) with more than €5000, walk through the red channel upon arrival; only walk through the green channel if you have nothing to declare.

This form is checked, stamped and handed back to you – do *not* lose it. When you leave Ukraine (via Kyiv airport), fill out a second identical form and surrender both to the customs official. If you enter Ukraine at any other point, and so do not receive a form on arrival, you will not be required to follow this procedure. Keep all receipts for cash obtained with credit cards and/or travellers cheques in case you're asked by customs officials. Travellers are also not allowed to take more than 85 hryvnia out of Ukraine.

MONEY
Currency

The hryvnia is divided into 100 units, each called a kopek. Coins come in denominations of one, two, five, 10, 25 and 50 kopeks, while there are one, two, five, 10, 20, 50, 100 and 200 hryvnia notes. Hryvnia is usually abbreviated as 'hrn', though it's sometimes listed in the English-language press as 'UHR'.

Most travel agencies, all international airlines and US dollars (US$). In these cases, we have also listed prices in this chapter in US dollars, though by law payments must be made in hryvnia. The only things you can legally pay for in foreign currency (usually US dollars) are international flights and foreign visas.

Exchange Rates

Exchange rates at the time of publication were:

country	unit		hryvnia
Australia	A$1	=	2.86 hrn
Canada	C$1	=	3.38 hrn
Euro Zone	€1	=	5.10 hrn
Japan	¥100	=	4.40 hrn
New Zealand	NZ$1	=	2.48 hrn
Russia	R10	=	1.63 hrn
UK	UK£1	=	8.00 hrn
USA	US$1	=	5.33 hrn

Exchanging Money

Foreign-exchange offices – signposted as *obmin valyuty* – are on almost every street corner in Ukraine. They all accept US dollars, euros and roubles in cash, but less than half accept UK pounds and Australian or Canadian dollars. Your chances of changing any other currency, especially from neighbouring countries, are remote. Banks offer the same rates for cash as foreign-exchange offices, but the process takes *far* longer. Exchanging money on the black market is unnecessary and illegal.

Travellers Cheques These can be cashed at branches of major banks, but the process is lengthy, confusing and expensive (about 2% commission). Aval Bank, Ukr Exim Bank and Ukrsoubank normally change travellers cheques in US dollars, UK pounds and euros, but only those issued by the major international companies.

ATMs Automated teller machines (ATMs) – known as *bankomat* – accept both Visa and MasterCard/EuroCard. They are more commonly found in the lobbies of major hotels than attached to banks, and most charge about 2.5% commission.

Credit-Card Warning

International monetary agencies rate Ukraine as one of the worst countries in the world for credit-card fraud, whether during business transactions or in ATMs. In fact, the US State Department urges all travellers to use *only* cash while travelling around Ukraine.

Credit Cards Cash advances in hryvnia with major credit cards are possible (with a 3% commission), but the procedure is as confusing and time-consuming as cashing travellers cheques. Aval Bank and Ukr Exim Bank will normally provide cash advances, but the best place to try is Western Union. Most upmarket hotels, restaurants and shops in the cities and larger towns accept major credit cards.

Costs

For budget travel, allow at least US$22/18 per person per day travelling as a single/double, though US$25/22 is more realistic. If you want to stay in mid-priced hotels, travel on 1st-class trains and eat at the Western-style restaurants, allow at least US$40/36. Your daily budget will blow out substantially if you stay in Kyiv for long!

POST & COMMUNICATIONS
Post

Normal-sized letters or postcards cost 2.70 hrn to anywhere outside Ukraine by 'ordinary mail' or 3.50 hrn for 'express' service.

Telephone

When dialling Ukraine from abroad, dial the country code (☎ 380), the area code (but drop the initial 0) and then the relevant number. For interstate calls within Ukraine, dial ☎ 8, the area code (including the initial 0) and then the appropriate number. To call overseas from Ukraine, dial ☎ 810, followed by the country code, area code and number.

Area codes are listed in this book under the relevant sections. If a telephone number has seven digits, use the two-digit area code, but if the telephone number has five/six digits use the four-/three-digit area code – plus the zero if required.

Every city and large town has a telephone centre (many open 24 hours). To make interstate or international calls, pay in advance at the counter inside the telephone centre (you will get change for unused time). Local and interstate calls can also be made from public phones with a phonecard, bought from kiosks and post offices. In addition, international calls can be made at special Utel telephones found in major post offices, telephone centres and upmarket hotels with a Utel phonecard.

The cost of a call per minute from a telephone centre is 6 hrn to the UK and Europe, 11 hrn to Australia and New Zealand, and 9 hrn

Tourist Prices Abolished!

In August 2002, the Ukrainian government introduced legislation to abolish the 'tourist prices' that foreigners were charged for hotel rooms and admission to tourist attractions.

The great news for travellers is that the rates for most hotels in the larger cities and the admission charges for most tourist attractions will be about 50% less than those listed in this chapter.

The standardised price structure will, no doubt, take some months to be accepted; in fact, some hotels and tourist attractions may continue to charge 'tourist prices'. If so, insist on paying the normal local price and remind the proprietors of this welcome legislation.

to the USA and Canada. There are discounts of about 20% between 9pm and 8am Monday to Friday, and most of the weekend.

Your mobile (cell) phone will probably work in Ukraine, but contact your own operator to make sure. Ukrainian mobile phone companies include Kyivstar (W www.kyivstar .net) and UMC.

Fax
Faxes can be sent from any major post office for the cost of the equivalent telephone call. At the Central Post Office in Kyiv, you can also receive faxes for a small fee.

Email & Internet Access
Numerous Internet centres have opened up around Ukraine in recent years. Access may be slow at times, but it's pretty cheap: about 6 hrn per hour.

DIGITAL RESOURCES
You may wish to access one of the following websites before you travel:

W www.brama.com – art, culture and business
W travel.kyiv.org – travel-related information and photos
W www.uazone.net/Ukraine.html – a wide range of details and useful links

BOOKS
Based upon the author's travels around Ukraine in 1993–95, *Borderland – A Journey through the History of Ukraine*, by Anna Reid, is a highly readable account of Ukrainian history.

Ukraine: A History, by Orest Subtelny, presents a concise and easy-to-read, but weighty, account.

For a bleak, but probably accurate, portrayal of corruption in Ukraine, look for the newly published novel *Death and the Penguin* by Andrey Kurkov.

NEWSPAPERS & MAGAZINES
The *Kyiv Post* (W www.kpnews.com) is an enjoyable digest of local and regional politics and business, and includes a useful entertainment lift-out. The colourful *What's On* has plenty of advice about what to see and where to eat and drink in Kyiv. Both are free, published weekly and available at the upmarket hotels in Kyiv. The quarterly *Kyiv Business Directory* (W www.ukrbiz.net) is essential if you're staying in the capital for a while.

All international English- and German-language newspapers and magazines are very expensive and difficult to find.

Ukraine is rated by international media associations as one of the most dangerous places on earth for journalists; several who have been investigating the corrupt activities of the president and his cronies have paid the ultimate price.

RADIO & TV
Top-end hotels offer CNN and some German- and French-language stations via satellite; otherwise, you're stuck with uninspiring Ukrainian channels. Near the borders of Poland and Russia, equally incomprehensible drivel can be watched in these languages.

Popular radio stations in Kyiv include Gala Radio (100FM) and Europa Plus (107FM). Most international radio services – with the exception, these days, of the BBC – can be easily heard on short-wave radio.

TIME
Ukraine is in one time zone, ie, GMT plus two hours. During daylight saving from the first Sunday in April until the last Sunday in October, it's GMT plus three hours.

TOILETS
Pay toilets are common and acceptably clean. Women's toilets are marked Ж (*zhinochy*); men's are marked Ч or М (*cholovichy* or *muzhcheny*). Better hotels provide toilet paper, but it's akin to sandpaper so bring (or buy) your own.

UKRAINE

Emergency Services

The nationwide, toll-free, 24-hour emergency telephone numbers are ☎ 01 for fire, ☎ 02 for police and ☎ 03 for ambulance. However, don't expect anyone to speak English.

HEALTH

Cholera was in near-epidemic proportions in Crimea during 1994. No outbreaks have been reported since, but it's best to drink bottled water (easily obtainable) in Crimea – and, to be safe, anywhere in Ukraine. According to international agencies, Ukraine has an AIDS and HIV infection rate of nearly 1%, the highest in Europe and almost an official pandemic. Criminals released from Russian prisons have spread tuberculosis in some rural areas.

WOMEN TRAVELLERS

Women are not likely to experience sexual harassment on the streets, though sexual stereotyping remains strong. Simply take the usual precautions.

DANGERS & ANNOYANCES

Inherent bureaucracy and apathy are nasty hangovers from the old Soviet days. Corruption is innate in the government and most businesses, but will have little or no obvious impact on travellers. Kyiv, and Ukraine in general, is no more (un)safe than any Western European city/country, but take the usual precautions to protect yourself and your property.

LEGAL MATTERS

Ukrainian police can legally demand to see your passport and visa and detain you for up to three hours while your documents are checked. However, *never* give your passport to any policeman or official on the street. Offer to accompany them to the police station or simply say that your passport is at your hotel; both responses usually dissuade the official(s) from pursuing their inquiries.

BUSINESS HOURS

Official working hours are 9am (or 10am) to 5pm (or 6pm) on weekdays (ie, Monday to Friday). Shops often stay open until about 8pm on weekdays and all day Saturday. Most cafeterias and cafés are open 9am to 7pm daily, while restaurants tend to open from noon until midnight.

Most banks are open 9am to 1pm weekdays, while foreign-exchange offices open from about 9am to 7pm every day (except Sunday). Major post offices are usually open 9am to 7pm weekdays and 9am to 5pm on Saturday; smaller branches close earlier and don't open on Saturday.

Museums and many other tourist attractions operate from about 9am to 5pm, but frustratingly close for one or two days a week. Also, many museums close for one 'sanitary day' during the last week of each month.

PUBLIC HOLIDAYS & SPECIAL EVENTS

The official public holidays are New Year's Day (1 January), Orthodox Christmas (7 January), Orthodox Easter (April/May), International Labour Day (1 May), Victory Day (9 May), Holy Trinity Day (June), Constitution Day (28 June) and Independence Day (24 August).

Some of the larger festivals include the Carnival Humorina in Odesa (1 April); Kyiv Days, a colourful spring festival in honour of the capital city (last weekend of May); Crimean Stars in Yalta, to celebrate Crimean history and culture (August); and the Halba Beer Festival in Lviv (late May).

ACTIVITIES

Hiking, trekking and camping opportunities are richest in the Carpathian National Natural Park and around Crimea – see those sections later for details. Nothing much is organised for tourists, however, and you'll need to bring all your own equipment. Before arrival, try to buy *Hiking Guide to Poland & Ukraine*, by Tim Burford, which describes different hikes around Ukraine. Available in Kyiv are the detailed Topograficheskaya Karta series of maps, though hiking trails are poorly marked on the maps or not at all.

The untouched slopes of the Carpathians are also popular with skiers between November and March. See the Carpathian National Natural Park section later for details.

COURSES

To learn Ukrainian, contact the **ABC Center** in Kyiv (☎ *044-239 1091;* Ⓦ *www.ukrbiz .net/31224; vul Patrisa Lumumby 23/35)*; to learn Russian, try the **Odesa Language Study Centre** (☎ *0482-345 058, fax 347 798;* Ⓦ *www.studyrus.com)* in Odesa.

WORK

The majority of foreigners working in Ukraine are employed by large companies, or are diplomats or journalists – all of whom arranged their jobs *before* arriving. Your chances of picking up seasonal work with an acceptable salary range from slim to nil.

ACCOMMODATION

Camping in the wild is permitted in the Carpathian National Natural Park, where cabins are also available for hikers (see that section later in this chapter). Organised camping grounds are rare anywhere in Ukraine and are usually at least 10km from the city centre. Hostels of any kind are unheard of.

Many hotels are unsightly concrete monstrosities built in the '60s and '70s. Rooms are often well-worn with outdated furniture, but are reasonably comfortable and cheap. Many hotels have cheaper rooms with a shared bathroom – bring your own towel, soap and toilet paper. Some better hotels can be booked in advance through **w** www.hotelsukraine.com – often at a substantial discount.

Private rooms in family homes are an increasingly popular option in Odesa and around Crimea during summer. Look out for older ladies – especially at train stations – with signs around their necks reading кімнати (*kimnaty*, Ukrainian) or комнаты (*komnaty*, Russian) – both of which mean 'rooms'. Before deciding, however, always check the exact location and proximity to public transport. The cost ranges from 40 to 65 hrn per person per night.

If you're staying in Kyiv for more than a few days it's worth booking an apartment (see the Kyiv section for details).

FOOD

Much of Ukraine's cuisine is based on grains and vegetables like potato, cabbage, beet and mushroom. Beef, pork, chicken and fish are widely used, and most dishes are boiled, fried or stewed. Desserts are usually laden with honey and fruit and baked into sweet breads.

Perhaps try *varenyky* (dumplings made with rolled dough), *borshch* (based on a beet and mixed-vegetable broth) or *holubtsi* (delicious cabbage rolls stuffed with seasoned rice, meat or buckwheat). Chicken Kiev (*kotleta po-Kyivsky*), the internationally known chunk of deep-fried boneless chicken stuffed with butter, is disappointingly hard to find in Ukraine. And beware of *salo*, (inedible) slices of pig fat.

DRINKS

Coffee is usually frothy, grind-filled and Turkish-style, or bitter instant Nescafe. Tea is also served black, strong and oversweetened. Crimea produces excellent wines, and champagne from around Odesa is surprisingly palatable. The most popular Ukrainian beer is probably Slavutych and Obolon. Sold on practically every street corner in Kyiv during summer is *kvas*, certainly an acquired taste.

ENTERTAINMENT

Enchanting traditional folk shows can be seen in upmarket restaurants and open-air theatres during summer in the major cities. In Kyiv, Lviv and Odesa, bars feature live jazz and rock music and nightclubs present the latest dance beats. Opera and ballet theatres in these three cities are worth attending even if you don't understand a word. But don't bother going to a cinema anywhere in Ukraine unless you're fluent in Russian.

The *teatralna kasa* (theatre ticket office) sells advance tickets. Same-day tickets are also available at theatre box offices, sometimes in the morning but usually about one hour before the curtain rises.

SPECTATOR SPORTS

Sports lovers should try to see Dynamo Kyiv play at the massive Respublikanskiy Stadium in the capital. One of the few 'sports' in which Ukraine can claim a world champion is chess.

SHOPPING

Beautifully painted eggs known as *pysanky* come in a variety of distinctive patterns, each symbolising a special meaning and ritual. Ukrainian embroidery is steeped in tradition, and popular souvenirs include embroidered towels and woven rugs. Ceramics feature flowery patterns of green and yellow. Carved wooden boxes, plates and candlesticks are equally delightful mementoes.

Getting There & Away

AIR

AeroSvit and Ukraine International Airlines offer direct flights between Kyiv and every major city in Western and Eastern Europe. Most of the major European airlines also fly

UKRAINE

And Then There Was One

At the time of writing, three major Ukrainian airlines – Ukraine International Airlines, Air Ukraine and AeroSvit – planned to merge into one: United Airlines of Ukraine. Therefore, some information about international and domestic flights listed throughout this chapter may be incorrect, but the destinations and frequencies are unlikely to change too much.

regularly to and from Kyiv. Air Ukraine, Aeroflot and AeroSvit also fly to Kyiv from Moscow, St Petersburg and Rīga (Latvia). Elsewhere in Ukraine, LOT flies to Lviv and Odesa from Warsaw; and AeroSvit travels to Odesa from Warsaw and Athens, and to Simferopol from Sofia, İstanbul, Stockholm and Tallinn (Estonia). There are no direct flights between Ukraine and the USA, Canada, Australia or New Zealand, so you'll have to get a connection to elsewhere in Europe.

LAND
Border Crossings
The following major borders are normally open 24 hours and accept foreigners:

Belarus: Dobryyanka between Chernihiv (Ukraine) and Homel (Belarus); and Kortelisi between Kovel and Brest
Hungary: Chop between Uzhhorod and Nyiregyhaza
Moldova: Duba between Krasni Okni and Chişinău
Poland: Mostiska between Lviv and Przemyśl
Romania: Siret between Chernivtsi and Suceava
Russia: between Krolevets and Oryol for Moscow; and between Donetsk and Novoshakhtinsk for the Caucasus region
Slovakia: between Uzhhorod and Michalovce

Bus
Buses are far slower, less frequent and less comfortable than the trains for long-distance travel. Most days, rumbling old public buses leave Kyiv for Athens, Warsaw, Prague, Rīga, Tallinn, Moscow, Belgrade, İstanbul and Vilnius (Lithuania). Lviv is also well connected to both Western and Eastern Europe by public bus.

Two private bus companies offering services to European cities, such as London, Paris and Brussels, are Eastern European Travel and Ecolines. Both operate from the main bus terminals in Kyiv and Lviv.

Train
Russia Each day, twelve trains go to Moscow from Kyiv (15 hours), and others head regularly to the Russian capital from Lviv (19 hours), Odesa (25 hours) and Simferopol (28 hours). Trains also run each day to St Petersburg from Kyiv (25 hours) and Lviv (30 hours), via Vilnius, and from Odesa (35 hours) and Simferopol (37 hours).

Belarus Every day, trains head to Minsk from Kyiv (11 hours), Lviv (17 hours), Odesa (20 hours) and Simferopol (29 hours). To Brest, there are trains from Kyiv (14 hours) on alternate days (ie, odd-numbered dates of the month), and daily services from Chernivtsi (18 hours), Odesa (16 hours) and Lviv (15 hours).

Poland Each day, trains from Lviv to Warsaw (13 hours), Kraków (seven hours) and Lublin (10½ hours) cross at the Ukrainian border of Mostiska. Trains split at Mostiska for Warsaw, via Lublin; for Kraków change trains at Przemyśl. The daily Berlin-Kyiv train also passes through Warsaw (15½ hours to Kyiv). In addition, there are regular trains between Uzhhorod and Przemyśl, and Odesa and Warsaw.

Other Countries There are also daily services from Kyiv to Prague (via Lviv), Sofia, Budapest and Rīga; and from Lviv to Budapest. Between mid-June and late September, extra trains from Kyiv head to Rīga, Belgrade and the Bulgarian cities of Burgas and Varna.

CAR & MOTORCYCLE
To drive a private or rented vehicle to and around Ukraine you'll need an International Driving Permit/Licence. You'll also require appropriate vehicle insurance, which can be obtained at the border (or rental agency) if you don't have a Green Card. See the Getting Around chapter at the beginning of this book for more details.

BOAT
Between May and September, luxury boats cruise to Varna (Bulgaria), İstanbul and Sochi (Russia) from Odesa, Sevastopol and Yalta. More affordable, however, are the *Gloria* and *Kaledonia*, which both sail weekly (May to September) between Odesa, Yalta and İstanbul. Information about, and tickets for, all boats around the Black Sea from Ukraine are

Getting Around – Air 809

Meandering into Moldova

It's essential to note that trains between Chernivtsi and Odesa travel through Moldova, so you'll need a Moldovan visa *before* you get onto the train. Although the train between Kyiv and Chernivtsi briefly crosses into Moldova, Moldovan immigration officials don't seem perturbed if you can prove that you're going back into Ukraine.

available from **Eugenia Travel** (e *janna@ eugen.intes.odessa.ua*) at the boat passenger terminal in Odesa (☎ *0482-218 581*), and next to Hotel Yuzhnaya in Yalta (☎ *0654-328 140; vul Ruzvelta 12*).

ORGANISED TOURS

The foreign-based travel agencies listed here provide packaged tours to Ukraine, as well as visa services and hotel bookings.

Inntel-Moscow Travel (☎ 020-7495 7555, fax 7495 8555, w www.inntel-moscow.co.uk) 70 Piccadilly, London W1J 8HP, UK
RJ's Tours (☎ 780-415 5633, fax 415 5639, w www.rjstours.shawbiz.ca) 11708-135A St, Edmonton AB T5M 1L5, Canada
Scope Travel (☎ 973-378 8998, fax 378 7903, w www.scopetravel.com) 1605 Springfield Ave, Maplewood NJ 07040, USA

DEPARTURE TAX

Departure tax is included in the cost of all international flights from Ukraine whether the ticket is bought inside or outside the country.

Getting Around

AIR

The main domestic airports are at Kyiv, Ivano-Frankivsk, Chernivtsi, Odesa, Dnipropetrovsk, Lviv, Simferopol and Donetsk. Most flights are operated by the three major airlines (see the boxed text 'And Then There Was One' in the Getting There & Away section earlier), though a few are also run by minor regional outfits. Schedules can be confusing, so it makes sense to book tickets with a reputable travel agency such as Kiyavia, which has offices in most major cities. Domestic flights are not cheap – eg, about US$80 one way between Kyiv and Simferopol – and tickets must be bought with hryvnia.

BUS

Travelling around the country by train is often far quicker and more comfortable than by bus, so long-distance bus routes are gradually disappearing throughout Ukraine. Most public buses are decrepit, but a few private bus companies, such as Autolux, offer comfortable services from Kyiv to Odesa and Lviv.

Larger cities often have several bus terminals – called an *avtovokzal* – but only one normally handles long-distance routes of interest to travellers. Tickets can be bought one or two days in advance at the major bus terminal and sometimes at separate ticket offices in the city centres.

TRAIN

Train travel is normally frequent, cheap and efficient. An overnight train is an economical way to get around, and most services are timed to depart at dusk and arrive in the morning (after dawn). The regular long-distance service is called a *skory poyizd* (fast train) though the *expres poyizd* is faster. The passenger train *(pasazhyrsky poyizd)* is very slow and should be avoided.

Generally, there are four classes:

zahalny vagon – an upright, hard-bench seat, only available on day trains
platskart – a hard bunk in an open area, always overcrowded, dirty and smelly
kupe – a sleeper compartment with four berths, approximately twice the price of a *platskart*
spalny vagon (SV) – a sleeper compartment with two berths. Not all trains offer SV, which costs about three times more than a *kupe*

If you need some comfort and privacy, buy a *kupe* or SV compartment for yourself.

Railway employees speak nothing but Ukrainian and Russian so you will have to learn a few key words and phrases in those languages. Also, you should be able to read Cyrillic, though updated and comprehensive timetables for Kyiv are printed in English in the *Kyiv Business Directory* and listed in English at the main train station in the capital.

Tickets can often be bought at special offices in the city centres, as well as at the train stations. A station is called a *zaliznychny vokzal* or simply *vokzal*. Each one has a left-luggage counter, signposted камери схову or камера зберігання.

Your ticket will include the number of your carriage *(vagon)* and bunk or seat *(mesta)*. In

SV and *kupe* class, blankets are provided but clean sheets and pillowcases are available for an extra 7 hrn (in total). And bring your own food, drink and toilet paper.

CAR & MOTORCYCLE

Driving in Ukraine is a nerve-racking experience that any sensible motorist should avoid. Road signs are often frustratingly absent and always in Cyrillic, so be sure you have a good map and can understand this foreign alphabet.

In theory, cars should be driven on the right. Speed limits are normally 60km/h in towns, 90km/h on major roads and 120km/h on highways. It's illegal to drive if you have drunk *anything* beforehand, and drivers and front-seat passengers must wear seat belts. Both laws, however, are commonly flouted by Ukrainians.

Petrol *(benzyn)* is available at octane levels of 76, 92 and 95 and in larger cities at 98. Diesel is common, but unleaded petrol is not.

Rental

Major international car-rental companies, such as Avis, Europcar and Hertz, have offices at the airports in Kyiv and Odesa. They charge from US$42 per day, plus US$0.42 per kilometre, or from US$78 per day for unlimited kilometres – about 40% less for rental periods of seven days or more. Rates include insurance but not petrol. You may need special permission from the rental company to drive outside the Kyiv or Odesa areas.

You can also rent a car with a driver through larger hotels and better travel agencies in Kyiv, Lviv, Ivano-Frankivsk, Yalta and Odesa. For day trips, haggle with a taxi driver, but pay no more than 30 hrn per hour or about 1 hrn per kilometre.

HITCHING

Hitching is never entirely safe in any country in the world, and we don't recommend it. However, hitching is a common method of getting around remote areas of Ukraine, but you'll almost certainly have to pay for the lift.

BOAT

Between May and September, luxury boats regularly cruise up and down the mighty Dnipro River between Kyiv and Odesa. All-inclusive five-day trips between both cities cost from US$250 per person. Book at **Kyiv River Port** *(☎ 044-416 1229, fax 462 5019)*, at the boat passenger terminal in Kyiv, and **Eugenia Travel** *(☎ 0482-218 581; e janna@ eugen.intes.odessa.ua)*, at the boat passenger terminal in Odesa.

Boats also shuttle along the Crimean coast during summer – see the Yalta section later for details.

LOCAL TRANSPORT

Cheap but crowded trolleybuses, trams and buses operate in all cities and major towns. Tickets are often sold at street kiosks – in which case tickets *must* be punched in the machine on board – but in some cities you pay the driver or wait for the conductor. Ticket inspectors are common and mean, and happily issue on-the-spot fines (10 hrn) to ignorant foreigners. Kyiv boasts a decent metro (subway) system; plastic tokens *(zhetony)* are sold inside metro stations.

In most Ukrainian cities, zippy minibuses – known as a *marshrutka* – follow major bus and tram routes. They're slightly more expensive but worth using if you can read the destinations signs (in Cyrillic) on the front window.

Taxis are easy to find, but drivers almost never use their meter – so always set a price beforehand. Private cars often double as unofficial taxis, but hailing a private car is best done by someone who knows what they're doing (ie, a local). And *never* get into a private car-cum-taxi if there's already another passenger inside.

ORGANISED TOURS

These three travel agencies in Ukraine can organise tours, arrange visas and book hotels:

Olymp Travel (☎ 044-253 7108, fax 253 8329, W www.olymp-travel.kiev.ua) vul Shovkovychna 24, Kyiv

Mandry (☎ 0322-971 661, W www.mandry -travel.lviv.ua) pl Rynok 44, Lviv

Ukrzovnishintour Inc (☎ 044-229 8464, fax 226 2049, W www.uit.com.ua) vul Bogdana Khmelnytskoho 26b, Kyiv

Kyiv Київ

☎ 044 • pop 2.6 million

The capital of Ukraine, Kyiv (Kiev in Russian), is considered the mother city for all Eastern Slavic people. It is elegantly situated along the glorious Dnipro River and boasts numerous parks and islands. There are also enough museums, churches and monasteries in Kyiv to keep most travellers busy for several days while planning their assault on the rest of Ukraine.

Information

Money Foreign-exchange offices and banks are all over the city centre; foreign-exchange offices in the arrivals hall at Boryspil International Airport and in Hotel Tourist (see Places to Stay) also accept major travellers cheques. There are ATMs at the Boryspil airport, the Central Post Office building and most major hotels. For cash advances on credit cards, try **Western Union** inside Hotel Lybid (pl Peremohy) and on the ground floor of the TsUM department store (cnr vul Khreshchatyk & vul Bogdana Khmelnytskoho).

Post & Communications At the **Central Post Office** (vul Khreshchatyk 22; open 8am-9pm Mon-Fri, 8am-7pm Sat) you can also send and receive faxes. Next door is the **Telephone Centre** (open 24hr). There are **Internet centres** inside the Central Post Office; at the train ticket office (bul Tarasa Shevchenka 38/40), next to Hotel Ekspres; and on the corner of vul Khreshchatyk and Kruty uzviz.

Bookshops The best selection of topographical hiking maps is offered at **Naukova Dumka** (vul Hrushevskoho 4), while maps of Ukrainian cities are sold at **Medichna Kniha** (vul Chervonoarmiyska 23). The best place for new and second-hand English-language novels is the trendy **Baboon Book Coffee Shop** (vul Bogdana Khmelnytskoho 39).

UKRAINE

KYIV

To Chernihiv (140km)

To Lviv (550km), Chernivtsi (657km) & Ivano-Frankivsk (670km)

To Moscow

To Boryspil International Airport (34km)

To Odesa (489km) & Ivano-Frankivsk (670km)

PLACES TO STAY
1 Prolisok
11 Hotel Tourist;
   Hotel Adria;
   Foreign-Exhange
   Office; Cafeteria
26 Hotel Holoseevskaya

METRO STATIONS
2 Sviatoshyn
3 Beresteiska
5 Petrivka
7 Shuliavska
8 Politekhnichny
   Institut
9 Maydan
   Nezalezhnosti
10 Hidropark
12 Livoberezhna
13 Darnytsia
15 Osokorky
18 Druzhby Narodiv
19 Lybidska
20 Palats Ukraina
21 Palats Sportu;
   Ploshcha Lva
   Tolstoho
22 Vokzalna

OTHER
4 St Cyril's Church
6 American Medical
   Centre
14 Romanian &
   US Embassies
16 Botanical Gardens
17 Vydubytsky
   Monastery
23 Russian Embassy
24 Zhulyany Airport
25 Central Bus
   Terminal
27 Museum of Folk
   Architecture
   & Everyday Life
   in Ukraine

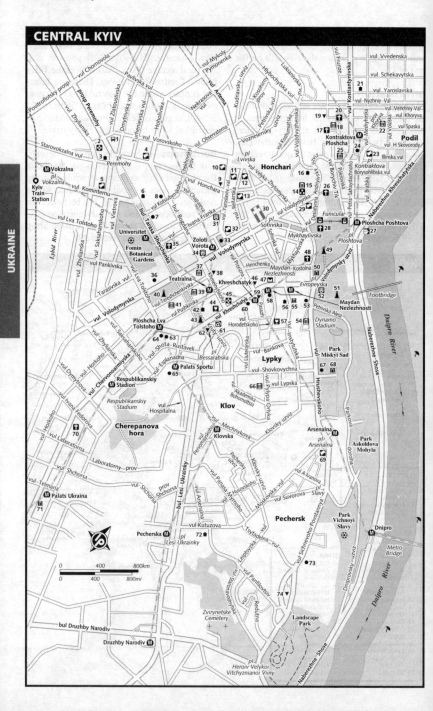

CENTRAL KYIV

CENTRAL KYIV

PLACES TO STAY
3 Hotel Lybid; Western Union; Cocktail Bar 111
6 Hotel Ekspres; Train Ticket Office; Internet Centre
16 Andrew's Hotel
21 Hotel Domus
42 Saint Petersburg Hotel
56 Hotel Ukraina
72 Hotel Service

PLACES TO EAT
9 Bistro Gastronom
19 Podil Market
38 Dom Ashnia
46 Kozak Mamay
59 Apollo
62 Bessarabsky Market
74 Tsarske Selo

OTHER
1 Polit Buses & Minibuses to Boryspil Airport
2 Ukraina (Department Store)
4 German Embassy
5 Australian Embassy
7 Dept of Citizenship, Passport & Immigration (Visa Extensions)
8 Baboon Book Coffee Shop
10 Canadian Embassy
11 Slovak Embassy
12 French Embassy

13 Hungarian Embassy
14 Desiatynna Church
15 Ukraine History Museum
17 Florivsky Monastery
18 Apteka Museum
20 Church of Mykola Prytysko
22 Chornobyl Museum
23 Netherlands Embassy
24 Kontraktova Dim
25 Museum of One Street
26 St Andrew's Church
27 Boat Passenger Terminal; Kyiv River Port Office (Boats to Odesa)
28 St Michael's Monastery
29 UK Embassy
30 St Sophia Cathedral & Monastery
31 Ivan Franko National Drama Theatre
32 Polish Embassy
33 Golden Gate
34 National Opera Theatre
35 St Volodymyr's Cathedral
36 Kyiv University
37 National Museum of Science & Natural History
39 Taras Shevchenko National Museum
40 Shevchenko Statue & Park
41 Russian Art Museum
43 Lenin Statue
44 Art Club 44

45 TsUM (Department Store); Western Union
47 Central Post Office & Internet Centre; Telephone Centre
48 St Alexander Church
49 Prince Volodymyr Statue
50 Ukrainsky Dim
51 Monument to the Unification of Russia & Ukraine
52 Ukrainian National Philharmonic
53 Naukova Dumka (Bookshop)
54 National Art Museum
55 Palace of Culture & Arts
57 Rok Kafe
58 Kiyavia Travel Agency; Mister Snack
60 Teatralna Kasa
61 Internet Centre
63 Ukrainsky Suvenir
64 Medichna Kniha (Bookshop)
65 Sports Palace
66 Kyiv History Museum
67 Parliament Building
68 Mariyinsky Palace
69 Belarusian & Moldavan Embassies
70 St Nicholas' Church
71 Ukraina Palace
73 Kyiv-Pechersk National Preserve

Medical Services If worst comes to worst, contact the **American Medical Centre** *(AMC; ☎ 490 7600; vul Berdychivska 1; open 24hr)*. The English-language press lists several other medical centres, hospitals and dental clinics in Kyiv.

Things to See

City Centre The extensive **Russian Art Museum** *(vul Tereshchenkivska 9; admission 6.50 hrn; open 10am-6pm Fri-Tues)* is as good a place as any to start a walking tour of the capital. Nearby, the **Taras Shevchenko National Museum** *(bul Tarasa Shevchenka 12; admission 2 hrn; open 10am-5pm Tues-Sun)* contains 4000 items that are related to this revered and multitalented 19th-century Ukrainian poet-cum-artist.

One block north is the **National Museum of Science & Natural History** *(vul Bogdana Khmelnytskoho 15; admission 5 hrn; open 10am-5pm Wed-Sun)*, which offers extensive exhibits on archaeology, geology, botany and

zoology. A couple of blocks to the northeast is the **Golden Gate** *(vul Volodymyrska 40a; admission 5 hrn; open 10am-5pm Fri-Wed)*, the historic gateway to the ancient city. It was originally built in 1037, but most of what remains was rebuilt in 1982.

Further along this street is the magnificent 11th-century **St Sophia Cathedral & Monastery** *(vul Volodymyrska 24; admission 10 hrn; open 10am-6pm Fri-Tues, 10am-5pm Wed)*. It's the oldest standing church in Kyiv, though only the basic structure and several of the interior mosaics and frescoes are original. The cathedral was included on Unesco's World Heritage list in 1990.

On the eastern corner of pl Mykhaylivska is the marvellous **St Michael's Monastery** *(admission free; open 10am-4pm Mon-Sat)*, with its seven-cupola cathedral. Inside the reconstructed, three-tiered **bell tower** is a small **museum** *(admission 3.50 hrn; open 10am-4pm Wed-Sun)*, dedicated to the reconstruction of the monastery.

UKRAINE

The 19th-century **St Alexander Church** (vul Kostolna 17; admission free; open dawn-dusk daily), down the road, is recognisable by its large central dome and twin bell towers. Further south is the **National Art Museum** (Museum of Fine Arts; vul Hrushevskoho 6; admission 3 hrn; open 10am-5pm Sat-Thur), which provides an exhausting collection of works from the last 700 years.

Continue south along vul Hrushevskoho to the **Parliament Building** (not open to the public) and the adjacent baroque, 18th-century **Mariyinsky Palace**. Tours of the palace must be prebooked at the **Kyiv History Museum** (vul Pylypa Orlyka 8; admission 2 hrn; open 10am-5pm Sat-Thur), housed in a former palace in a leafy neck of the woods.

Continue to the **Kyiv-Pechersk National Preserve** (see the following section) or backtrack towards St Michael's Monastery. The funicular (50 kopeks one way), open 6.30am to 11pm daily, heads down to the bottom of the charming Podil district. Head north up vul Petra Sahadydachnoho to visit the **Chornobyl Museum** (prov Khoryva 1; admission 5 hrn; open 10am-6pm Mon-Sat), housed in a fawn-coloured building with a tower just off vul Khoryva. Although very little is explained in English, it's a chilling reminder of the worst nuclear accident in history.

West is the 17th-century **Church of Mykola Prytysko** (admission free; open 8am-8pm daily), a lovely example of early Ukrainian baroque. Nearby is the enchanting **Apteka Museum** (vul Prytytsko Mykilska; admission 5 hrn; open 9am-5pm Tues-Sun), housed in Kyiv's first public pharmacy (1728); and the **Florivsky Monastery** (admission free; open dawn-dusk daily), which is a former 15th-century women's convent.

Cobblestoned Andriyivsky uzviz heads uphill past the tiny **Museum of One Street** (Andriyivsky uzviz 2b; admission 6 hrn; open noon-6pm Tues-Sun), which engagingly re-captures some local history. Further uphill are the ruins of the **Desiatynna Church** (admission free; permanently open) in front of the **Ukraine History Museum** (vul Volodymyrska 2; admission 4 hrn; open 10am-5pm Thur-Tues). This museum houses about 600,000 exhibits of archaeological and recent historical interest.

Opposite the museum is the 18th-century **St Andrew's Church** (Andriyivsky uzviz 23; admission 9 hrn; open about 8am-5pm Fri-Wed), an inspired baroque interpretation of the traditional churches of St Petersburg.

Kyiv-Pechersk National Preserve This vast area (vul Sichnevoho Povstannya; admission 16 hrn; open 8am-late evening daily), also known as the **Caves Monastery**, is one of the highlights of Ukraine. Built in 1051 and spread across wooded slopes above the Dnipro, this complex is the spiritual heart of the Ukrainian people. The museums and churches inside the preserve have extra admission fees (3 to 5 hrn each) and are open daily from about 10am to 5pm.

The main entrance is through the striking **Trinity Gate Church**, a well-preserved piece of early-12th-century architecture. Just north is the small, late-17th-century **St Nicholas' Church**. Further along is the unmistakable **Dormition Cathedral** and its 97m-high **Great Belfry** (1731–44), which has wonderful views. Directly south is the **Refectory Church of St Anthony & Theodosius**, which sports the monastery's most famous gold-striped dome. Other highlights include the fascinating **Museum of Microcaricature**, the **Historical Treasures Museum** and the 17th-century **All Saints' Church**.

The **Nearer Caves** are a few minutes' walk southeast of the cathedral and through the southern gate. Inside the caves, dozens of niches contain open, glass-topped coffins with mummified monks' bodies. Women have to cover their head with a scarf, and men are obliged to remove their hats. Wearing shorts and T-shirts, and using a video/still camera, are also forbidden.

The **excursion bureau** (☎ 291 3171) is on the left just past the main entrance of the monastery complex. Three-hour guided tours in just about every conceivable language cost 160 hrn per group (including admission fees), but need to be prebooked. Unofficial guides lingering inside the complex offer two-hour tours in English for about 40 hrn per small group. The main entrance to the complex is a 15-minute walk south along vul Sichnevoho Povstannya from the Arsenalna metro station.

Museum of Folk Architecture & Everyday Life in Ukraine This open-air museum (admission 3 hrn; open 10am-5pm Thur-Tues summer, 10am-4pm Thur-Tues winter) is spread over 160 hectares of scenic rolling hills. It features, among other things, numerous

17th- to 20th-century wooden cottages, churches, farmsteads and windmills. It's about 10km south (by road) from the city centre. Take trolleybus No 4 or 11 from the Lybidska metro station to the VDNKh trolleybus stop and then bus No 24 to the end of the line. A taxi will cost about 35 hrn one way.

Places to Stay

See the boxed text under Money in the Facts for the Visitor section earlier for information about the planned abolition of the two-tiered price system. If 'tourist prices' for hotels in Kyiv have been abolished by the time you get there, rates for most hotels and apartments listed here should be reduced by about 50%.

Camping Twelve kilometres west of the city centre is **Prolisok** (☎ 451 8038; prosp Peremohy 139; tent sites 20 hrn, camping per person 15 hrn; open year-round). It's a hassle to reach by public transport; catch bus No 37 from the Svyatoshyn metro station.

Apartmentsu If you're staying in Kyiv for more than a few days, it's certainly worth booking an apartment. Try **Hotel Service** (☎/fax 295 8832; w www.hotel.kiev.ua; vul Staronavodnytska 4 • airport ☎ 408 4494; 1/2-room apartments US$65/90) or one of the agencies listed in the Kyiv Post and Kyiv Business Directory. Room rates are for fully equipped apartments.

Hotels Unless stated otherwise, all hotels listed here offer rooms with a TV and bathroom, and rates include breakfast.

Hotel Holoseevskaya (☎ 261 4116, fax 263 7835; prosp 40-richchya Zhovtnya 93; singles/doubles 57/107 hrn) is remarkably good value for Kyiv, but don't expect too much for this price (which does not include breakfast). Take trolleybus No 4, 11 or 12 from the Lybidska metro station.

Hotel Ekspres (☎ 221 8995; bul Tarasa Shevchenka 48-50; singles/doubles 120/210 hrn, with bathroom from 340/510 hrn) is a 10-minute walk from the train station. It's a leftover from the 1960s, but reasonably comfortable and convenient.

Hotel Tourist (☎ 517 8832; w www .hotel-tourist.kiev.ua; vul Raisy Okipnaya 2; singles/doubles 278/311 hrn) is so large that it's probably never been full. On the plus side, it's only 100m from the Livoberezhna

metro station; on the down side, staff can be surly and the rooms are dated.

The **Hotel Adria** (☎ 516 2459; w www .adria.kiev.ua; vul Raisy Okipnaya 2; singles/ doubles US$98/117) rather strangely shares the same building as the Hotel Tourist, but has far nicer rooms. It has friendly and competent staff.

Saint Petersburg Hotel (☎/fax 229 7364; bul Tarasa Shevchenka 4; singles/doubles from 261/305 hrn) is central and excellent value. The rooms are large and comfortable, though some are a little noisy.

Andrew's Hotel (☎ 416 2256, fax 416 63651; vul Vozdvyzhenska 60; doubles from US$75) is a nice place in the bohemian neighbourhood of Podil. It's good value and quiet.

Hotel Ukraina (☎ 229 0347, fax 229 8772; vul Instytutska 4; singles/doubles from 381/550 hrn) is the obtrusive Soviet-style monstrosity overlooking the main square in the city centre. It's certainly past its use-by date, but worth considering.

Hotel Domus (☎ 462 5120, fax 462 5145; vul Yaroslavska 19; singles/doubles US$140/ 190) is the closest you will find to a cosy, family-run pension in Kyiv.

Places to Eat

Check the Kyiv Post and What's On to find out which new places are worthwhile. Most restaurants serving non-Ukrainian cuisine are very expensive – with prices at least as high as those in Western Europe.

Dom Ashnia (vul Bogdana Khmelnytskoho 22; mains from 7 hrn) offers authentic and cheap Ukrainian food in a large, modern cafeteria. Just point at what you want, line up (of course), pay and enjoy. The self-serve **cafeteria** on the ground floor of the Hotel Tourist (see Places to Stay) offers similar sorts of meals for the same sort of price.

Tsarske Selo (vul Sichnevoho Povstannya 42/1; mains from 24 hrn) is Kyiv's quintessential Ukrainian restaurant; waiters wear straw hats, a waterfall trickles in the corner and complimentary garlic bread and salo (ugh!) are provided.

Kozak Mamay (vul Prorizna 4; soups from 10 hrn, mains from 20 hrn) is a less-expensive option for tasty Ukrainian food served by traditionally dressed waiters. In summer, most patrons sit around outdoor tables while the folk band plays to nobody inside. It has a menu in English.

UKRAINE

Apollo (vul Khreshchatyk 15; mains from 25 hrn) has been recommended by expats for its authentic and delicious Italian food – and, importantly, for some of the best coffee in Ukraine. Like almost everywhere serving continental cuisine, however, it's very expensive.

Baboon Book Coffee Shop (vul Bogdana Khmelnytskoho 39; mains from 15 hrn) is a trendy place, ideal for meeting other travellers and expats. The two-course 'business lunch' (20 hrn) is recommended. The menu is in English.

McDonald's is found all over Kyiv. For something different, try a tasty sandwich at Mister Snack (vul Horodetskoho 4), next to the Kiyavia office, or take a stroll around Hidropark, on an island in the river, and enjoy a sizzling-hot shashlik.

Bessarabsky Market (pl Bessarabska) is a beautiful market hall, and Podil Market (vul Khoryva) is also reasonably clean and inviting. Bistro Gastronom (vul Yaroslaviv val 21/20) is a small supermarket offering shopping trolleys and delicacies favoured by homesick diplomats.

Entertainment

Comprehensive lists of things to do are featured in What's On and the Kyiv Post, as well as the monthly KyivCult booklet (2 hrn), available at the Baboon Book Coffee Shop (see Places to Eat).

A performance at the lavish National Opera Theatre (vul Volodymyrska 50) is a grandiose affair. Also recommended for a spot of culture are the Ivan Franko National Drama Theatre (vul Ivana Franka) and the Ukrainian National Philharmonic (Volodymyrska uzviz 2). Advance tickets and the schedules for most theatres are available at the Teatralna Kasa (vul Khreshchatyk 21); tickets are also available at the theatres about one hour before the curtain rises.

Rok Kafe (vul Horodetskoho 10) is one of several welcoming watering holes with outdoor tables surrounding a small park. Places to shake your booty include Cocktail Bar 111 (Hotel Lybid, pl Peremohy), complete with revolving bar, and the ultra-trendy Art Club 44 (vul Khreshchatyk 44).

Shopping

The stalls along the cobblestoned Andriyivsky uzviz near St Andrew's Church are the best places to pick up quality souvenirs. Ukrainsky

Suvenir (vul Chervonoarmiyska 23) is also worth a look. Department stores that sell everyday items – and groceries – include the old-style TsUM (cnr vul Khreshchatyk & bul Bogdana Khmelnytskoho) and the massive, newly renovated Ukraina (pl Peremohy).

Getting There & Away

For information about international flights, trains and buses to/from Kyiv, refer to the introductory Getting There & Away section earlier in this chapter.

Air Most international flights use the Boryspil International Airport, while all domestic flights (and a few to/from Moscow and Eastern Europe) use the more convenient Zhulyany Airport. From Kyiv, there are flights daily to Dnipropetrovsk, Donetsk, Odesa, Simferopol and Lviv, and weekly to Ivano-Frankivsk and Chernivtsi.

Because so many domestic airlines fly around Ukraine, it pays to get advice and buy tickets at a travel agency like Kiyavia (☎ 056; vul Horodetskoho 4). Offices of all the major international airlines are listed in the Kyiv Business Directory and What's On (see Newspapers & Magazines earlier in this chapter).

Bus Almost all long-distance buses use the Central Bus Terminal (pl Moskovska 3). To get there, take any minibus, bus or trolleybus, or walk (20 minutes), from the Lybidska metro station – if in doubt, look for the ubiquitous golden arches of McDonald's next to the terminal.

Every day, there are three public buses to Lviv, seven to Odesa and two each to Ivano-Frankivsk, to Kamyanets-Podilsky and to Chernivtsi. Buses for Chernihiv leave every 30 minutes. Schedules for places in southern, eastern and western Ukraine are listed on three different walls in the terminal building.

From the same terminal, the private bus company Autolux (☎ 442 8583) operates comfortable, faster and slightly more expensive buses to Odesa, Lviv and Simferopol (early June to mid-September only).

Train The Kyiv Train Station (pl Vokzalna 2) is next to the Vokzalna metro station. Inside this superbly renovated train station, departure times, and the availability of tickets, for all trains leaving within two to three hours are listed in English on a computer screen. There are six trains a day to Odesa, four each to Lviv, Uzhhorod and Ivano-Frankivsk, two to Sevastopol and one to Kamyanets-Podilsky, Simferopol, Chernihiv and Chernivtsi.

You can buy tickets at the train station, but it's far easier to buy advance tickets (only) at the **train ticket office** (*☎ 050; bul Tarasa Shevchenka 38/40; open 8am-8pm daily*), next to Hotel Ekspres; or at **Kiyavia** (*vul Horodetskoho 4*). To stop black marketeers, you'll need to show your passport when buying any train tickets in Kyiv (only).

Boat All long-distance trips along the Dnipro River start and finish at the **boat passenger terminal** (*pl Ploshtova*). See the introductory Getting Around section earlier in this chapter for more information.

Getting Around

To/From the Airport Every 30 minutes from 5am to 11pm Polit buses run to (and from) the Boryspil International Airport (10 hrn, 45 to 60 minutes). They leave from a stop beside the LukOil petrol station on bul Tarasa Shevchenka, not far from the Hotel Lybid. Around the corner from this stop, minibuses also go (when full) to the airport for the same price. Boryspil is about 40km east of the city centre, so a taxi will set you back about 80 hrn!

To Zhulyany Airport, take trolleybus No 9 (40 minutes) from pl Peremohy or a minibus from outside St Volodymyr's Cathedral on bul Tarasa Shevchenka.

Public Transport Crowded buses, trams and trolleybuses shuttle around Kyiv between 5.30am and midnight every day. Tickets (50 kopeks) are available at street kiosks or directly from the driver or conductor. Many routes are also serviced by nippy minibuses.

The metro is the quickest and most direct form of public transport, so you'll spend less time standing with your face under someone else's armpit. However, stations are poorly marked in any language, so keep the metro map handy.

Taxi The uncommon yellow Daewoos with chequered black-and-white stripes down their sides have meters and charge about 1 hrn per kilometre. Otherwise, flag down an unofficial taxi or private car on the street, but don't pay more than 10 hrn for a short trip within the city centre.

CHERNIHIV ЧЕРНІГІВ
pop 301,200

Chernihiv, 140km northeast of Kyiv, was the capital of one of the most important princedoms within the Varyagi State (see the History section earlier).

The historic centre of Chernihiv is two blocks southeast along prosp Miru from the main square (pl Krasna). It is now part of the extensive Chernihiv State Architectural & Cultural Reserve, better known as **Dytynets**. Highlights include the 11th-century **Spaso-Preobrazhensky Cathedral** (*admission free; open dawn-dusk daily*), the **Boryso-Hlibsky Cathedral** (*admission free; open erratic hours*) and the **Chernihiv History Museum** (*admission 5 hrn; open 10am-6pm Fri-Wed*).

From Dytynets, walk 3km (or take trolleybus No 8) southwest along vul Tolstoho to the **Hill of Glory Monument** (*cnr vul Uspenskoho & vul Tolstoho*). From there, stairs lead to the labyrinthine **Antoniy Caves** (*admission 2 hrn; open 9am-5pm Fri-Wed*). Nearby is the 58m-high bell tower at the **Troyitsko Monastery** (*admission 3.50 hrn; open 9am-6pm daily*), and beyond it is the 17th-century **Trinity Cathedral** (not open to the public).

The crumbling, antiquated **Hotel Hradetsky** (*☎ 04622-450 25; prosp Miru 68; singles/ doubles with bathroom from 61/85 hrn*) is 2km northwest of pl Krasna. The restaurant here is adequate.

The train and bus stations are at pl Vokzalna, about 2.5km west of pl Krasna. From Kyiv, one train (three hours) travels here daily and buses leave every 30 minutes.

Western Ukraine

Western Ukraine has been continuously tossed back and forth between rival states, so its history is littered with sieges, wars, fires and plagues. This region enjoyed more freedom under Polish and Habsburg rulers, and its people were not under the repressive Russian sphere until WWII. Consequently, western Ukraine has a Central European elegance.

LVIV ЛЬВІВ
☎ 0322 • pop 778,900

Lviv (Lvov in Russian) is the largest city in western Ukraine. Because it escaped bombing during WWII, Lviv boasts dozens of original towers, churches and spires, as well as Gothic,

UKRAINE

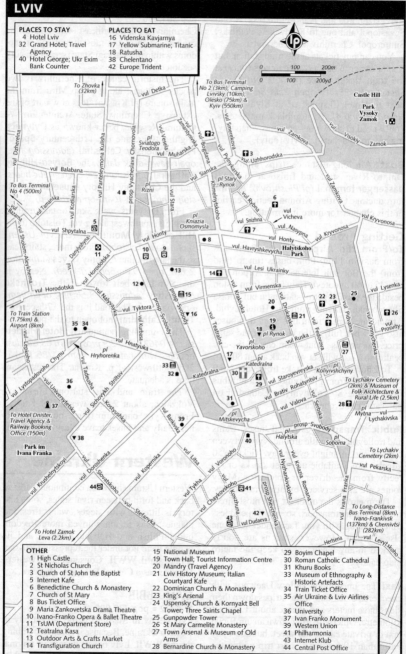

LVIV

PLACES TO STAY	PLACES TO EAT
4 Hotel Lviv	16 Videnska Kavjarnya
32 Grand Hotel; Travel	17 Yellow Submarine; Titanic
Agency	18 Ratusha
40 Hotel George; Ukr Exim	38 Chelentano
Bank Counter	42 Europe Trident

OTHER
1 High Castle
2 St Nicholas Church
3 Church of St John the Baptist
4 Internet Kafe
6 Benedictine Church & Monastery
7 Church of St Mary
8 Bus Ticket Office
9 Maria Zankovetska Drama Theatre
10 Ivano-Franko Opera & Ballet Theatre
11 TsUM (Department Store)
12 Teatralna Kasa
13 Outdoor Arts & Crafts Market
14 Transfiguration Church

15 National Museum
19 Town Hall; Tourist Information Centre
20 Mandry (Travel Agency)
21 Lviv History Museum; Italian
    Courtyard Kafe
22 Dominican Church & Monastery
23 King's Arsenal
24 Uspensky Church & Kornyakt Bell
    Tower; Three Saints Chapel
25 Gunpowder Tower
26 St Mary Carmelite Monastery
27 Town Arsenal & Museum of Old
    Arms
28 Bernardine Church & Monastery

29 Boyim Chapel
30 Roman Catholic Cathedral
31 Khuru Books
33 Museum of Ethnography &
    Historic Artefacts
34 Train Ticket Office
35 Air Ukraine & Lviv Airlines
    Office
36 University
37 Ivan Franko Monument
39 Western Union
41 Philharmonia
43 Internet Klub
44 Central Post Office

Renaissance, baroque and neoclassical buildings. The Old Town, which was included on Unesco's World Heritage List in 1998, is one of the highlights of Ukraine.

Information

The **Tourist Information Centre** (☎/fax 975 767; W www.about.lviv.ua; pl Rynok 1; open 9am-6pm Mon-Fri) is inside the Town Hall. It arranges opera/theatre bookings and guides, dispenses useful (free) brochures and sells the colourful and detailed Lviv Tourist City Map (7 hrn), ideal for an in-depth exploration of the Old Town.

There are dozens of foreign-exchange offices all over central Lviv. **Western Union** (vul Kopernika 4) can provide cash advances and has an ATM, while the **Ukr Exim Bank** counter inside Hotel George (pl Mitskevycha 1) is also useful.

Internet Klub (vul Dudaeva 12) is friendly but a bit cramped, while the **Internet Kafe** (vul Shpytalna 8) is open longer hours. **Mandry** (☎ 971 661; W www.mandry-travel.lviv.ua; pl Rynok 44) can arrange guides and local tours. **Khuru Books** (pl Mitskevycha) has several sections, one of which sells maps and English-language books.

Things to See

City Centre Along the eastern edge of the elegant prosp Svobody is a 100-year-old palace that houses the **National Museum** (prosp Svobody 20; admission 2 hrn; open 10am-6pm Mon-Sat, noon-8pm Sun). It features 15th- to 19th-century icons and works by Ukrainian artists. Down the road, the **Museum of Ethnography & Historic Artefacts** (prosp Svobody 15; admission 3 hrn; open 10am-5.30pm Wed-Sun) features an excellent collection of regional folk art.

Ploshcha Rynok is the best-preserved urban square in the country. The **Lviv History Museum** (pl Rynok 4/6 & 24; admission 1 hrn per building 1 hrn; open 10am-5pm Thur-Tues) contains over 250,000 items about the history of Lviv and western Ukraine in three separate buildings. The lovely **courtyard** (admission 40 kopeks) has been elegantly converted into the Italian Courtyard Kafe.

Overlooking the southwestern corner of Rynok is the 15th-century **Roman Catholic Cathedral** (Latin Metropolitan Cathedral; pl Katedralna; admission free; open 8am-8pm daily). It's a busy working church with a

Gothic feel. Nearby, the 17th-century **Boyim Chapel** (Knyazya Romana; admission free; open 8am-8pm daily) is the burial chapel of a wealthy Hungarian merchant family.

Just east of pl Rynok is the large dome of the 18th-century **Dominican Church & Monastery** (pl Muzeyna; admission free; open 10am-6pm Mon-Sat). Further east is the arched facade of the 17th-century **King's Arsenal**, which is not open to the public.

Immediately to the south is the 16th-century **Uspensky Church** (vul Ruska; admission free; open around 8am-6pm Mon-Sat), which is easily distinguished by the 65m-high, triple-tiered **Kornyakt Bell Tower**. A door to the right of the tower leads into the churchyard and the three-domed, 16th-century **Three Saints Chapel** (admission free; open dawn-dusk daily). This chapel is one of the finest pieces of Renaissance architecture in Lviv.

Further south, the 16th-century **Town Arsenal** houses the **Museum of Old Arms** (vul Pidvalna 5; admission 1 hrn; open 10am-5.45pm Thur-Tues). In a park opposite is the 16th-century **Gunpowder Tower** (not open to the public), part of the old system of walls and bastions that once ran along vul Pidvalna.

Other Attractions For sweeping views head to the **High Castle** (admission free; permanently open), the 14th-century remains of a stone castle that languishes atop Castle Hill amid a manicured hillside park.

About 2km east of the city centre is the **Lychakiv Cemetery** (vul Mechnikova; admission free; open dawn-dusk daily), one of the most beautiful in Eastern Europe. Take tram No 2 or 7 (as for the museum) to the 'Lychakivska Kladovyshche' stop and walk south for 200m.

About 2.5km east is the open-air **Museum of Folk Architecture & Rural Life** (vul Chernecha Hora 1; admission 1 hrn; open 10am-6pm Tues-Sun), where about 100 old wooden buildings dotted 50 hectares. Take tram No 2 or 7 from along vul Lychakivska to the 'vulitsya Mechnikova' stop. Then follow the signs north on foot (1.25km).

Places to Stay

Camping Lvivsky (☎ 721 373; tent sites 10 hrn, camping per person 12 hrn; open May-Sept) is 10km northeast of the city centre. It's along the road to Kyiv and near the village of Dublyany.

Hotel Lviv (☎/fax 792 547; vul Vyach-eslava Chornovola 7; singles/doubles with bathroom from 70/100 hrn) is a massive, ugly throwback to the 1970s with the mandatory grumpy staff. It's only worthwhile if your budget won't stretch to the George.

Hotel George (☎ 725 952; e geoh@mail .lviv.ua; pl Mitskevycha 1; singles/doubles 111/157 hrn, with bathroom 362/382 hrn) is an elegant 100-year-old building. Rates for the rooms with bathrooms are outrageous, but those with shared facilities are excellent value. The breakfast is admirably extensive and included in the price.

Hotel Zamok Leva (Lion's Castle; ☎ 971 563, fax 351 102; vul Hlinki 7; singles 220-380 hrn, doubles 250-410 hrn) is in a leafy suburb 25 minutes' walk southwest of the city centre. The cheaper rooms in the basement have showers but share a communal toilet; dearer rooms feature elegant bathrooms. Rates include breakfast.

Hotel Dnister (☎ 971 017, fax 971 021; vul Mateyko 6; singles/doubles with bathroom 243/276 hrn) is set back from the road overlooking Park im Ivana Franka. The rooms are large, well-furnished and far better value than the expensive rooms at the George. Guests have raved about the breakfast here, which is included in the room price.

Grand Hotel (☎ 727 665; w www.ghgroup .com.ua; prosp Svobody 13; singles/doubles with bathroom & breakfast US$95/120) is a charming and fully restored 100-year-old hotel with professional staff and superb rooms; rates include breakfast.

Places to Eat

The (free) *Where to Eat Out?* pamphlet from the Tourist Information Centre lists many other enticing eateries.

Europe Trident (prosp Shevchenka 14; mains 15-18 hrn) offers imaginative dishes such as 'fiery steak' and 'pork ribs in whisky'. Look for the 'Europa' sign over the door. The menu is in English.

Yellow Submarine (vul Teatralna 4; mains around 15 hrn) was obviously set up by a big fan of the Fab Four. You can watch videos of the Beatles while munching on an 'Abbey Road steak'. The menu is in English.

Titanic (vul Teatralna 4; soups from 5 hrn, mains from 12 hrn), next door to Yellow Submarine, features very impressive nautical decor. It offers self-service salads and tasty

vegetable soups, and staff are all, umm, 'decked' out with appropriate maritime gear.

Chelentano (vul Slovatskoho 16; mains 6-10 hrn) is a small, crowded place that sells pizzas, crepes and salads (2 to 3 hrn). It's often standing room only.

Ratusha (pl Rynok; mains from 6 hrn) is inside the western part of the Town Hall. It offers cheap cafeteria-style Ukrainian food and tastier treats in the accompanying bar.

Videnska Kavjarnya (prosp Svobody 12) has been recommended by readers for tasty coffee and delicious Ukrainian and Austrian food. It also offers a menu in English.

Entertainment

For a perfect evening, enjoy a drink at one of the cafés in the parks and a performance at the **Ivano-Franko Opera & Ballet Theatre** (prosp Svobody 28), the **Philharmonia** (vul Chaykovskoho 7) or the **Maria Zankovetska Drama Theatre** (vul Lesi Ukrainky 1). Advance tickets for each theatre are sold at the **Teatralna Kasa** (prosp Svobody 37).

Getting There & Away

Air Lviv Airlines offers flights every day from Lviv to Kyiv and Moscow, and less regularly to Odesa, Ivano-Frankivsk and Simferopol (May to September only). LOT also flies daily between Lviv and Warsaw. **Air Ukraine** and **Lviv Airlines** have a combined office (☎ 748 5276; vul Hnatyuka 20-22), but staff are predictably unhelpful. Therefore, buy your tickets at Mandry (see Information earlier) or the travel agencies at Hotel Dnister or Grand Hotel (see Places to Stay earlier).

Bus Lviv has eight bus terminals, but only one is of use to most travellers – ie, the **long-distance bus terminal** (vul Stryiska 189), about 8km south of the city centre. Every day from this terminal there are three buses each to Kyiv (46 hrn, 12 hours) and Ivano-Frankivsk, one to Chernivtsi, two to Uzhhorod, and six to Przemyśl in Poland. From the same terminal, Autolux also operates buses regularly to Kyiv (52 hrn, 10 hours).

Advance tickets for public buses within Ukraine, as well as to Rīga, Brest, Warsaw and Prague, are sold at the **bus ticket office** (vul Teatralna 26; open 9am-7pm daily). Mandry (see under Information earlier) sells tickets for international buses run by Eastern European Travel.

Train From the **train station** *(pl Dvirtseva)*, about 1.75km west of the city centre, there are services each day to Uzhhorod, Rakhiv, Kolomyya, Chernivtsi and Ivano-Frankivsk, and handy overnight trains to Odesa (13 hours) and Sevastopol, via Simferopol (30 hours). Trains to Kyiv (52/140 hrn for *kupe*/SV class, 12 hours) run four times a day. There are also regular services from Lviv to Warsaw, Prague, Moscow, St Petersburg and Rīga.

Advance tickets are available from the **train ticket office** *(vul Hnatyuka 20-22; open 8am-8pm Mon-Fri, 8am-6pm Sat & Sun)*. The best-kept secret in Lviv is the **Railway Booking Office** *(open 9am-6pm daily)* on the ground floor of Hotel Dnister (see Places to Stay earlier).

Getting Around

The airport is 8km west of the city centre and accessible by trolleybus No 9 from the university building on vul Universytetska. Tram Nos 1, 6 and 9 link the train station with prosp Svobody and pl Rynok, while trolleybus No 5 connects pl Rynok with the long-distance bus terminal.

AROUND LVIV

The historical town of **Zhovkva** (Жовква) is about 32km north of Lviv. The simplistic Renaissance **palace** *(admission 3 hrn; open 9am-6pm daily)* on the southern side of the town square originally served as a defensive castle. From there, walls lead to the 17th-century **Zvirynetska Gate** *(admission free; permanently open)*. Eight buses a day go to Zhovkva from Bus Terminal No 4 *(vul Bazarna 11)* in Lviv, a 10-minute walk northwest from the TsUM department store.

Olesko (Олесько), 75km east of Lviv, boasts a 13th-century hill-top **castle** *(admission 5 hrn; open 8am-8pm daily)*. Opposite is the 18th-century **Capuchin Church & Monastery**, which houses an **art museum** *(admission 2 hrn; open 10am-6pm Wed-Sun)*. About eight buses a day go to Olesko from Bus Terminal No 2, which is at the end of tram line No 6 from central Lviv.

UZHHOROD УЖГОРОД

☎ 03122 • pop 124,400

This beautiful town is the southern gateway to the Ukrainian section of the Carpathian Mountains. It's an ideal staging post for anyone

travelling to/from Slovakia or Hungary, but probably too far off the beaten track for many other travellers.

Aval Bank *(pl Evhena Fentsika 19)*, on the main square, provides most financial services, though **foreign-exchange offices** can be found around the town centre.

Things to See

The 15th-century **Uzhhorod Castle** *(vul Kapitulna)* is on an obvious hill about 400m northeast of the main square. It features the **Museum of Local Lore & Art Gallery** *(admission 2 hrn; open 9am-5.30pm Tues-Sun)* and the enchanting, open-air **Museum of Folk Architecture & Rural Life** *(admission 1.50 hrn; open 9am-6pm Wed-Mon)*.

Also worth visiting is the 17th-century **cathedral** *(vul Kapitulna; admission free; open dawn-dusk daily)*, along the road to the castle, and the **Art Museum** *(admission 3 hrn; pl Zhupanatska 3; open 9am-5pm Tues-Sun)*, which is about 500m northwest of the main square.

Places to Stay & Eat

Hotel Svitanok *(☎ 34 309, fax 35 268; vul Koshytska 30; singles/doubles from 55/65 hrn)* is a simple, friendly place about 1.5km northwest of the main square.

Hotel Uzhhorod *(☎ 35 060, fax 32 070; pl Khmelnytskoho 2; singles/doubles with bathroom 95/155 hrn)* is a massive hotel south of the river about 1km west of the main square. It's bland but the rooms are comfortable enough.

Pid Zamkom *(vul Ivana Olbrakhta 3; mains from 15 hrn)*, which is about 250m below (southeast of) the castle, specialises in the regional cuisine.

Getting There & Away

The **bus terminal** *(prosp Svobody)* is about 1.5km south of the main square. Every day, one or two buses go to Michalovce and Kos (both in Slovakia), Miskolc and Nyiregyhaza (both in Hungary). There are also daily buses from Uzhhorod to Rakhiv, Ivano-Frankivsk, Odesa, Chernivtsi and Lviv.

From the **train station** *(vul Stantsyina)*, opposite the bus terminal, trains travel daily to Lviv and Kyiv (51/137 hrn for *kupe*/SV class, 21 hours). On even-numbered dates, there are also trains running to Ivano-Frankivsk and to Chernivtsi.

UKRAINE

IVANO-FRANKIVSK
ІВАНО-ФРАНКІВСЬК
☎ 03422 • pop 237,400

Ivano-Frankivsk is traditionally the cultural and economic capital of the Carpathian region. It boasts numerous parks, malls, squares and churches, and is one of the most appealing cities in western Ukraine.

Around the main square (pl Vichevy), you'll find an **Internet Centre** and a **foreign-exchange office**. The **Ukr Exim Bank** (*vul Nezalezhnosti 40*), next to Hotel Ukraina, handles other financial transactions.

Things to See
Ploshcha Rynok is dominated by the **Town Hall**, which houses the appealing **Regional Museum** (*admission 2 hrn; open 10am-5pm*

Tues-Sun). East of the square is the former, 18th-century **Armenian Church** (*admission free; open dawn-dusk daily*), with its attractive baroque facade and rounded bell towers.

Just west of pl Rynok is the elongated pl Sheptytskoho. It's flanked by two churches: the elegant 17th-century **Roman Catholic Church** (*admission free; open 8am-8pm daily*) and the baroque, 18th-century **Ukrainian Greek-Catholic Church** (*admission free; open 9am-3pm Mon-Sat*).

Places to Stay & Eat
Hotel Dnister (*☎ 25 356; vul Sichovykh Striltsiv 12; singles/doubles 58/84 hrn*) is convenient and cheap, but on a busy corner.

In a central location, **Hotel Ukraina** (*☎ 22 609; vul Nezalezhnosti 40; singles/doubles*

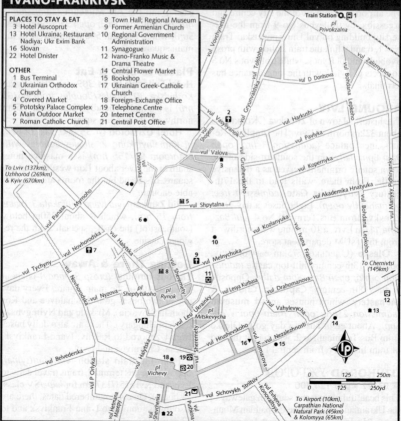

IVANO-FRANKIVSK

PLACES TO STAY & EAT
3 Hotel Auscoprut
13 Hotel Ukraina; Restaurant Nadiya; Ukr Exim Bank
16 Slovan
22 Hotel Dnister

OTHER
1 Bus Terminal
2 Ukrainian Orthodox Church
4 Covered Market
5 Pototsky Palace Complex
6 Main Outdoor Market
7 Roman Catholic Church
8 Town Hall; Regional Museum
9 Former Armenian Church
10 Regional Government Administration
11 Synagogue
12 Ivano-Franko Music & Drama Theatre
14 Central Flower Market
15 Bookshop
17 Ukrainian Greek-Catholic Church
18 Foreign-Exchange Office
19 Telephone Centre
20 Internet Centre
21 Central Post Office

Train Station
pl Privokzalna

vul Vovchynetska
vul Tolstoho
vul Zaliznychna
vul Bohdana Lepkoho
vul D Dontsova
vul Vasylyanok
vul Hryniaivska
vul Harkushi
vul Skopena
vul Pavlyka
vul Valova
vul Kopernyka
vul Grushevskoho
vul Akademika Hnatyuka
vul Shpytalna
vul Kozlanyuka
vul Ivana Franka
vul Bohdana Lepkoho
vul Mariyky Pidhiryanky
vul Dnistrovska
vul Melnychuka
vul Lesya Kurbasa
vul Drahomanova
To Chernivtsi (145km)
vul Vahylevycha
vul Nezalezhnosti
vul Komarova
To Lviv (137km), Uzhhorod (269km) & Kyiv (670km)
vul Panasa Myrnoho
vul Novhorodska
vul Halytska
vul Tychyny
vul Novhorodska
vul Nyzova
pl Sheptytskoho
pl Rynok
vul Sheremety
vul Lesi Ukrainky
pl Mitskevychoho
vul Hrushevskoho
vul Belvederska
vul P Orlyka
vul Halytska
vul Sheremety
pl Vichevy
vul Sichovykh Striltsiv
vul Hetmana Mazepy
vul Shevchenka
vul Poshkina
vul Yevhena Konovaltsa

To Airport (10km), Carpathian National Natural Park (45km) & Kolomyya (65km)

0   125   250m
0   125   250yd

with bathroom 90/135 hrn) offers an huge number of comfortable but unremarkable rooms in a central location. The attached **Restaurant Nadiya** *(mains from 4 hrn)* is a formal place with a menu in English.

Slovan *(vul Komarova 4; mains under 10 hrn)* has an enticing outdoor setting and some of the tastiest pizzas west of Kyiv. Most patrons come for the scrumptious ice-cream sundaes and banana splits.

Getting There & Away

From the airport, 10km south of the city centre, there are weekly flights to Lviv and Kyiv. Bus No 1 or 1A from the train station go to the airport.

The **bus terminal** *(pl Privozksalna)* is in front of the train station. Several buses travel daily to Kyiv, Uzhhorod, Lviv, Chernivtsi, Kolomyya and Rakhiv. Most buses to Chernivtsi continue to Chişinău in Moldova.

Every day from the **train station**, at least two trains travel to Lviv, Chernivtsi, Rakhiv, Kolomyya and Kyiv (43/115 hrn for *kupe/*SV class, 12 hours), and one heads to Odesa (21 hours), Moscow, Minsk and St Petersburg. There's also one train every alternate day to Uzhhorod.

CARPATHIAN NATIONAL NATURAL PARK

About 45km south of Ivano-Frankivsk lies Carpathian National Natural Park (CNNP), Ukraine's largest (503 sq km). The park protects wolves, brown bears, lynx, bison and deer, and features some of the highest peaks along the Ukrainian side of the Carpathians.

The primary downhill **skiing** area is in **Yablunytsia**, a pretty village 30km south of Yaremcha. Equipment can be hired in Yaremcha from the Karpaty Resort Complex (see Places to Stay later). Downhill and cross-country skiing is also possible around **Bogdan** (1500m), 20km east of Rakhiv, where Turbaza Tisa (see Places to Stay) rents gear.

During summer, the park is transformed into a busy **hiking** area. Some of the trails are marked, but most are impossible to follow without the help of a local guide. The few available hiking maps are also not 100% accurate and paradoxically they actually feature few hiking trails.

The useful **CNNP office** (☎ 03434-21 155; e *ecoplay@phantom.pu.if.ua; vul Stussa 6)* in Yaremcha can arrange guides for

around 100 hrn per day. The CNNP office, and the **Carpathian Agency for Agro-Eco Tourism** (☎/fax 03132-21 406; e *office@ card.uzhgorod.ua; vul Myru 1)* in Rakhiv, can both provide information and maps, organise tours and arrange accommodation in private homes (about 25 hrn per person).

The regional centre for the indigenous Hutzuls is **Kolomyya** (Коломия), about 65km south of Ivano-Frankivsk. Traditional arts and crafts are displayed in Kolomyya's **Museum of Hutzul Folk Art** *(vul Teatralna; admission 4 hrn; open 10am-4pm Wed-Sun)*, 500m north of pl Vidrodzhennya (the main square).

Places to Stay

Wild **camping** is allowed in the park. Contact the CNNP office about the hiking **cabins** that are around the park, but bring your own food and bedding.

Turbaza Tisa (☎ 03132-21 027; vul Ivana Franka 4; doubles with bathroom 40 hrn)* in Rakhiv offers grubby rooms.

Turbaza Syniogeriha (☎ 03132-22 413; bed in standard/deluxe rooms per person from 35/50 hrn)*, 8km from Rakhiv, is better than Turbaza Tisa. It's spectacularly located on a mountain top.

Karpaty Resort Complex *(☎/fax 03434-22 134; vul Dachna 30; singles/doubles with full board from US$50/62)* is a luxurious resort sprawling across the hillside above the Yaremcha village.

Getting There & Away

Exploring the park by public transport can be very time-consuming, so arrange a car with a driver in Yaremcha or Rakhiv, or organise a tour with Hotel Auscoprut or Hotel Ukraina in Ivano-Frankivsk. Alternatively, 'eco-tours' can be booked ahead with the **Carpathian Biosphere Reserve** headquarters *(☎/fax 03132-22 193;* w *cbr.nature.org.ua; vul Krasny Pleso 77)*, 3km from central Rakhiv.

From Rakhiv, buses go daily to Chernivtsi, Ivano-Frankivsk and Uzhhorod; and from Kolomyya, five buses travel daily to both Ivano-Frankivsk and Chernivtsi.

Every day, two trains chug along the park between Rakhiv and Kolomyya, via Yaremcha. From Kolomyya, there are trains that head for Chernivtsi, Ivano-Frankivsk and Lviv every day, while from Rakhiv, there are daily trains that operate to Ivano-Frankivsk and Lviv.

CHERNIVTSI ЧЕРНІВЦІ
☎ 0372(2) • pop 254,800

The mixed history of this charming town has resulted in a wide variety of architectural styles, from Byzantine to baroque, along its many elegant streets.

There are a few **foreign-exchange offices** in the city centre and others can be found at the bus terminal and train station. **Aval Bank** (vul Olgi Kobilyanskoi 13) has an ATM and changes travellers cheques. **Infocom Internet Centre** (vul Universytetska) is just back from the road and easy to miss.

Things to See
The **Regional Museum** (pl Tsentralna 10; admission 5 hrn; open 10am-4pm Tues-Sun) was being renovated at the time of research,

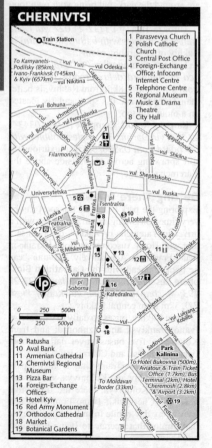

CHERNIVTSI

To Kamyanets-Podilsky (85km), Ivano-Frankivsk (145km) & Kyiv (657km)

1 Parasvevya Church
2 Polish Catholic Church
3 Central Post Office
4 Foreign-Exchange Office; Infocom Internet Centre
5 Telephone Centre
6 Regional Museum
7 Music & Drama Theatre
8 City Hall

9 Ratusha
10 Aval Bank
11 Armenian Cathedral
12 Chernivtsi Regional Museum
13 Pizza Bar
14 Foreign-Exchange Offices
15 Hotel Kyiv
16 Red Army Monument
17 Orthodox Cathedral
18 Market
19 Botanical Gardens

To Hotel Bukovina (500m), Aviatour & Train Ticket Office (1.7km), Bus Terminal (2km), Hotel Cheremosh (2.8km) & Airport (3.2km)

To Moldavan Border (33km)

but the caretaker urges all visitors to come by. At the western end of pl Teatralna is the 100-year-old **Music & Drama Theatre** (vul Kotlyarevskoho), a gift from the Habsburgs.

The **Chernivtsi Regional Museum** (vul Olgi Kobilyanskoi 28; admission 3 hrn; open 9am-4.30pm Thur-Tues) features a worthy collection of books, photos and paintings. One block further northeast, the former 19th-century **Armenian Cathedral** (vul Ukrainska 30; admission free; open 8am-5pm Mon-Sat) houses an organ and concert hall.

Places to Stay & Eat
Hotel Bukovina (☎/fax 585 620; vul Holovna 141; singles/doubles 80/120 hrn) is a charmless, bright-yellow building set off the main road. The staff here grudgingly accept foreigners.

Hotel Kyiv (☎ 22 483; vul Holovna 46; singles/doubles 80/100 hrn) in the city centre has seen *far* better days, but is clean, comfortable and convenient.

Hotel Cheremosh (☎ 48 400, fax 585 588; vul Komarova 13a; singles/doubles US$40/60) is about 3.5km south of the town centre – take a taxi. The rooms are stuck in the 1960s, but the bathrooms were probably updated sometime since.

Pizza Bar (vul Holovna 77; small pizzas 2.50 hrn) sells tasty pizzas and salads, as well as cheap soft drinks and beer.

Ratusha (vul Ivana Franka 3; mains about 15 hrn) is a charming place with old-fashioned (read: slow) service and regional cuisine.

Getting There & Away
Tickets for the weekly flights to Kyiv are available at **Aviatour** (vul Holovna 128), not far from the bus terminal. The airport is only 3.5km southeast of the town centre.

Every day from the **bus terminal** (vul Holovna 219), there are six buses that travel to Ivano-Frankivsk, two to Kyiv (12 hours), one to Lviv, about eight to Kamyanets-Podilsky and Uzhhorod, and several that go to Rakhiv and Kolomyya.

Every day from the **train station** (vul Yuri Gagarina 38), there is one train to Kyiv (42/104 hrn for *kupe*/SV class, 14 hours), two or three to Lviv via Ivano-Frankivsk, and one each to Odesa, Kolomyya and Przemyśl (in Poland). Trains also leave on alternate days for Uzhhorod, Moscow and St Petersburg. The **train ticket office**, next to Aviatour, sells advance tickets. Refer to the Getting There & Away section earlier in this chapter for information about dipping into Moldova while travelling by train to/from western Ukraine.

KAMYANETS-PODILSKY
КАМЯНЕЦЬ-ПОДІЛЬСЬКИЙ
☎ 03849 • pop 103,600

Kamyanets-Podilsky, which is 85km northeast of Chernivtsi, has stood since at least the 11th century on a sheer-walled rock 'island'. The combination of historic architecture and dramatic landscape makes this town one of the highlights of Ukraine.

The fortified old town is accessible by two bridges. The western bridge takes you to the castle and the eastern bridge heads to the 'new town'. The road (partially called vul Starobulvarna) between the two bridges passes the old town square (pl Virmenskyi). **Aval Bank** *(vul Starobulvarna 10)* can handle most financial transactions.

Things to See

The 16th-century **Dominican Monastery & Church** *(pl Virmenskyi; admission free; open dawn-dusk daily)* features a tall, ornately moulded bell tower. In a park just to the north is the 14th-century **Old Town Hall** *(admission 2 hrn; open 9am-5pm Tues-Sun)*, which houses an eclectic collection of local art.

Another 500m further the north is the 16th-century **Cathedral of SS Peter & Paul** *(vul Tatarska; admission free; open 8am-3pm Mon-Sat)*. About two minutes' walk further north is the 16th-century **Porokhovi Gate** *(admission free; permanently open)* and the seven-storey, stone **Kushnir Tower** *(admission free; permanently open)*.

The old **castle** *(vul Zamkova; admission 2.50 hrn; open 9am-5pm daily)* was originally built of wood in the 10th century, but reconstructed of stone some 500 years later. On the north side of the courtyard is the worthwhile **Ethnographic Museum** *(admission 2 hrn; open 9am-5pm daily)*.

Places to Stay & Eat

Hotel Ukraina *(☎ 39 148; vul Lesi Ukrainky 32; doubles with bathroom 144 hrn)* has OK rooms, but has seen better days. It's in the 'new town', 1km northeast of pl Virmenskyi.

Fort-Post Kafe *(vul Vali; mains from 6 hrn)* is a charming spot about 200m east of the Old Town Hall.

Getting There & Away

The **bus terminal** *(vul Koriatovychiv)* is 1km east of the eastern bridge, and the **train station** is 1.3km north of the bus terminal. About eight buses run each day to Chernivtsi and two go to Kyiv. Every evening, one direct overnight train leaves for Kyiv (12 hours).

Southern Ukraine

Despite continual occupation by Russians, Germans and Serbs, southern Ukraine never really seemed worth fighting over – except for the exotic port of Odesa. There is nothing much in this region besides Odesa, which is also an obvious stopover between Lviv or Kyiv and Crimea.

ODESA ОДЕСА
☎ 0482 • pop 990,100

Odesa (Odessa in Russian) is Ukraine's gateway to the Black Sea and the country's largest commercial port. It's a hectic industrial city with polluted seas, but also a popular holiday centre (particularly for Ukrainians, Turks and Russians). Odesa has a proud heritage that is separate to the rest of Ukraine, so most locals prefer to speak Russian.

There are plenty of **foreign-exchange offices** around the city centre and ATMs in the foyers of most major hotels. Otherwise, try **Western Union** *(cnr vul Rishelevskaya & vul Deribasovskaya)*, inside the Teatralna Kasa office. For 'cyber mail', try the **Mouse Club** *(vul Chaykovskoho)*. The **bookshop** *(vul Deribasovskaya 27)* stocks maps as well as some English-language books.

Things to See & Do

City Centre The **Pasazh** *(vul Preobrazhenskaya)* is a lavish shopping mall built in 1897–98 with rows of baroque sculptures. The impressive **Cathedral of the Assumption** *(vul Preobrazhenskaya 70; admission free; open 8am-8pm Mon-Sat)* is six blocks south.

Back towards the port are a gaggle of museums. The **Archaeological Museum** *(vul Lanzheronovskaya 4; admission 6 hrn; open 10am-5pm daily May-Sept, 10am-5pm Sat & Sun Oct-April)* is the first of its kind in the former Russian Empire. Across the road is the crimson-coloured **Sea Fleet Museum** *(vul Lanzheronovskaya 6; admission 2 hrn; open 10am-5pm Fri-Wed)*.

UKRAINE

UKRAINE

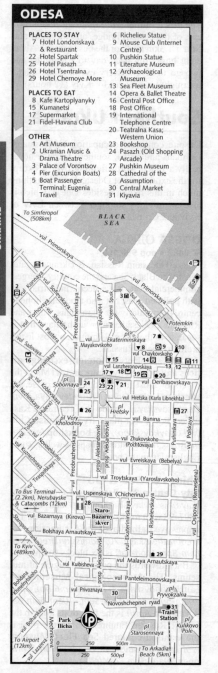

ODESA

PLACES TO STAY
7 Hotel Londonskaya & Restaurant
22 Hotel Spartak
25 Hotel Pasazh
26 Hotel Tsentralna
29 Hotel Chernoye More

PLACES TO EAT
8 Kafe Kartoplyanyky
15 Kumanetsi
17 Supermarket
21 Fidel-Havana Club

OTHER
1 Art Museum
2 Ukranian Music & Drama Theatre
3 Palace of Vorontsov
4 Pier (Excursion Boats)
5 Boat Passenger Terminal; Eugenia Travel
6 Richelieu Statue
9 Mouse Club (Internet Centre)
10 Pushkin Statue
11 Literature Museum
12 Archaeological Museum
13 Sea Fleet Museum
14 Opera & Ballet Theatre
16 Central Post Office
18 Post Office
19 International Telephone Centre
20 Teatralna Kasa; Western Union
23 Bookshop
24 Pasazh (Old Shopping Arcade)
27 Pushkin Museum
28 Cathedral of the Assumption
30 Central Market
31 Kiyavia

The **Literature Museum** *(vul Lanzheronovskaya 2; admission 3 hrn; open 10am-4.30pm Tues-Sun)* features some excellent exhibitions about the lives and works of Pushkin, Chekhov and Tolstoy. Pushkin buffs should also head to the **Pushkin Museum** *(vul Pushkinskaya 13; admission 9 hrn; open 10am-5pm Tues-Sun)*.

At the northwestern end of the elegant bul Primorskiy is the **Palace of Vorontsov** (not open to the public), the decrepit residence of a former governor. The terrace behind the palace offers brilliant views over the port. A footbridge to the west leads to the excellent **Art Museum** *(vul Sofievskaya 5a; admission 2 hrn; open 10am-5pm Wed-Mon)*. It features some marvellous works by Russian and Ukrainian artists. Pay the extra 2 hrn to see the amazing catacombs below the museum.

Catacombs The sandstone below Odesa is riddled with about 1000km of catacombs (so some buildings in the city are literally sinking). One network of tunnels in Nerubayske, 12km northwest of Odesa, sheltered a group of partisans during WWII. This event is explained at the **Museum of Partisan Glory** *(admission 5 hrn; open 9am-4pm Mon-Fri, 9am-2pm Sat)*. Public transport is unreliable, so take a taxi.

Beaches Odesa's beaches get unbelievably crowded in summer. The most popular is **Arkadia Beach**, which is lined with all sorts of eateries and amazing open-air thematic discos. Take tram No 5 along vul Rishelevskaya to the end of the line.

Places to Stay
During summer, it's pretty easy to arrange a **private room** in a home from one of the older ladies hanging around the train station. Expect to pay about 45 hrn per person per day including meals.

Hotel Spartak *(☎ 268 924; vul Deribasovskaya 25; singles/doubles from 52/72 hrn)* is scruffy, but the location is unbeatable. A hot shower costs an extra 3 hrn.

Hotel Pasazh *(☎ 224 849, fax 224 150; vul Preobrazhenskaya 34; doubles from 48 hrn, singles/doubles with bathroom 88/90 hrn)* is adjacent to the beautiful shopping arcade. The rooms are spacious, but most of the furniture (including the TV) dates from about 1955. Every room has a different interior and price.

Hotel Tsentralna *(☎ 268 406, fax 268 689; vul Preobrazhenskaya 40; singles/doubles with bathroom 108/162 hrn)* is the best of the three cheapies and notable because it contains furniture less than 40 years old.

Hotel Chernoye More *(☎ 300 904, fax 300 906; vul Rishelevskaya 59; doubles with bathroom US$40-90)* is a former government-run place, which is slowly being renovated. The cheaper rooms are good value but small, while the dearer ones feature air-conditioning. Breakfast costs an extra 25 hrn per person.

Places to Eat
Kafe Kartoplyanyky *(vul Ekaterininskaya 2; mains from 8 hrn)* is one of a just a handful of small, cheap cafeteria-style eateries that trade in the city centre.

Fidel-Havana Club *(vul Deribasovskaya 23; mains from 15 hrn)* is an American-style joint with a boat-shaped bar at one end. The menu is extensive and in English.

The restaurant at **Hotel Londonskaya** *(bul Primorskiy 11; entrees 10-12 hrn, mains 18-25 hrn)* has a menu (in English) featuring 'new prices' that are surprisingly affordable.

Kumanetsi *(vul Lanzheronovskaya 7; salads 8-12 hrn, mains around 25 hrn)* has some outdoor tables, waiters in traditional costumes, and a menu in English. It's a little pricey but is popular.

Getting There & Away
Tickets for the many daily flights to Kyiv and weekly flights to Lviv are available at the Kiyavia office at the train station. The Airport, 12km southwest of the city centre, is accessible by bus No 129 from the train station.

The **bus terminal** *(vul Kolontaevskaya 58)* is 3km southwest of the city centre. It has buses every day to Uzhhorod, Simferopol, Yalta and Kyiv (57 hrn, 11 hours), but the train is quicker and more comfortable. From the same terminal, Autolux runs fast private buses to Kyiv (59 hrn, 7½ hours) several times each day.

Every day from the **train station** *(pl Pryvokzalna)*, there are six trains to Kyiv (40/106 hrn for *kupe*/SV class, 12 hours), and daily services to Chernivtsi, Lviv, Simferopol, Sevastopol and Ivano-Frankivsk, as well as to Chișinău, Moscow, Minsk, St Petersburg, Rīga and Warsaw (alternate days). Refer to the Getting There & Away section earlier in this chapter for information about dipping into Moldova while travelling by train to/from western Ukraine.

During summer, boats regularly leave the **boat passenger terminal** *(vul Primorskaya)* for trips around the Black Sea and up the Dnipro River as far as Kyiv (see the Getting Around section earlier). More affordable are the short boat trips around the port and beaches near Odesa that leave from the end of the pier throughout the day during summer.

Crimea Крим

Crimea first became a chic leisure spot in the 1860s when Russia's imperial family built a summer pad at Livadia near Yalta. During the Soviet era millions came each year, attracted by the warmth, beauty, beaches and mountain air. Most visitors concentrate on Yalta, though Sevastopol and Simferopol do exude some charm, while the more adventurous take advantage of rare hiking opportunities. *The Sights of the Crimea* (10 hrn) is a worthwhile investment if you're going to spend some time exploring the peninsula.

Hiking
The forested Crimean Mountains make up the highest range between the Caucasus and the Carpathians. Some of the better spots for hiking are the cave cities of **Chufut-Kale** (3km east of Bakhchysaray) and **Manhup-Kale** (22km south of Bakhchysaray); **Bolshoi Canyon**, about 15km northwest of Yalta; Crimea's highest peak, Roman-Cosh (1545m), along the road between Yalta and Alushta; and the **Kara-Dah Nature Reserve** in the northeast. Hiking maps are available from stalls in the train station at Simferopol.

SIMFEROPOL СІМФЕРОПОЛЬ
☎ 0652 • pop 327,000
Simferopol is the capital of the Autonomous Republic of Crimea. It's also the regional transport hub and an ideal base for exploring the peninsula.

There are numerous **foreign-exchange offices** near the major hotels and at the bus and train stations. Otherwise, try **Ukrsoubank** *(prosp Kirova 36)*. The best place in Crimea to check your emails is the **Sky-Net Internet Kafe** *(vul Karla Marksa 7)*. Regional maps and books (in English) about Crimea are available from the **bookshop** *(prosp Kirova 32)*.

UKRAINE

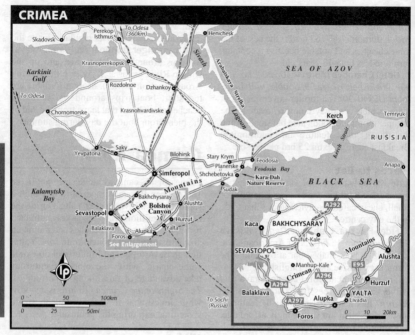

CRIMEA

Things to See

The town's **Crimean Regional Museum** *(vul Pushkina 8; admission 5 hrn; open 9am-5pm Wed-Mon)* features plenty of maps, tombstones and weaponry. One block away is the five-domed **Three Saints Church** *(vul Hoholya; admission 2 hrn; open 8am-6pm Mon-Sat)*. Also worth a look is the **Art Museum** *(vul Libknekhta 35; admission 3.50 hrn; open 10am-4pm Tues-Sun)*, which is in a grand, yellow building.

Towards the east of the town centre is the elegant **Church of SS Peter & Paul** *(vul Oktyabraskaya; admission free; open 10am-4pm Mon-Sat)* and the nearby **Holy Trinity Cathedral** *(vul Odeskaya; admission free; open 8am-8pm daily)*. A bit further east, up the quaint vul Kurchatova, is a restored **mosque** overlooking a colourful neighbourhood repopulated by Tatars.

Places to Stay

Upstairs from the courtyard at the train station are some **rooms** *(singles from 60 hrn, doubles 60-100 hrn)*. They're reasonably comfortable and convenient, but noisy. All rooms are with shared bathroom.

Hotel Ukraina *(☎ 510 165, fax 278 495; vul Rozy Lyuxemburg 7; singles/doubles from 72/100 hrn, with bathroom from 110/160 hrn)* is central and comfortable, and has helpful English-speaking staff. All rates include breakfast.

Hotel Moskva *(☎ 232 012, fax 237 389; vul Kyivskaya 2; singles/doubles with bathroom from 81/138 hrn)* is a massive, former government-run place near the long-distance bus terminal. It's typically faded and worn, but acceptable. Rates include breakfast.

Places to Eat

Eva Kafe *(prosp Kirova; mains from 11 hrn)* is a clean and popular place overlooking a park. It offers all sorts of tasty soups and pancakes, as well as (excellent) pizzas and (fatty) shashliks.

Kiyazha Vtikha *(mains from 18 hrn)* is located in an old-style home surrounded by outdoor tables and located in a shady park. It specialises in Ukrainian cuisine and is worth a stroll from the town centre.

Kafe Amigo *(vul Zhukovskoho; burgers from 3 hrn)* is *the* place for cheap Western delights, such as pizzas, hamburgers and delicious ice cream.

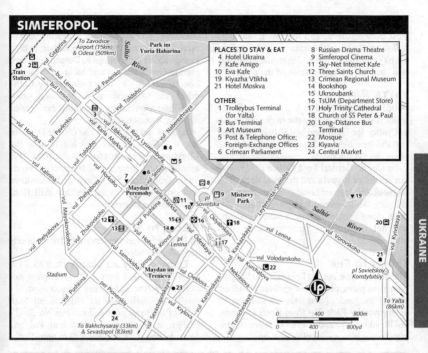

SIMFEROPOL

PLACES TO STAY & EAT		OTHER	
4 Hotel Ukraina		1 Trolleybus Terminal	8 Russian Drama Theatre
7 Kafe Amigo		(for Yalta)	9 Simferopol Cinema
10 Eva Kafe		2 Bus Terminal	11 Sky-Net Internet Kafe
19 Kiyazha Vtikha		3 Art Museum	12 Three Saints Church
21 Hotel Moskva		5 Post & Telephone Office;	13 Crimean Regional Museum
		Foreign-Exchange Offices	14 Bookshop
		6 Crimean Parliament	15 Uksroubank
			16 TsUM (Department Store)
			17 Holy Trinity Cathedral
			18 Church of SS Peter & Paul
			20 Long-Distance Bus
			Terminal
			22 Mosque
			23 Kiyavia
			24 Central Market

Getting There & Away

See the relevant sections later for details about transport around Crimea from Simferopol.

Crimea Air flies daily to Kyiv and weekly to Lviv (from May to September). All sorts of other airlines offer international flights to/from Simferopol (more in summer) – see the Getting There & Away section earlier for details. Tickets for all flights are available at **Kiyavia** (vul Sevastopolskaya 22). **Zavodskoe Airport** is 15km northwest of the town centre and accessible by minibuses Nos 50 and 115 from bul Lenina.

The **bus terminal** (vul Gagarina), next to the train station, offers public buses to all major places in Crimea. The **long-distance bus terminal** (vul Kyivskaya 4) in the eastern suburbs of Simferopol has regular services to eastern Crimea and elsewhere in Ukraine. However, with the exception of the daily public buses to Odesa (10 hours), trains are far more comfortable and often quicker for most long-distance trips.

Autolux runs private buses each day (from early June to mid-September) between Kyiv (100 hrn, 14 hours) and the bus terminal near the train station in Simferopol. Minibus No

64 links the long-distance bus terminal with the train station, via bul Lenina.

From the grand **train station** (vul Gagarina), there is one train a day to Kyiv (75/206 hrn for kupe/SV class, 19 hours), plus an extra five services a week between June and September. In addition, there are daily trains to Lviv (30 hours) and Odesa (13 hours), and others to Moscow, Minsk and St Petersburg. Most trains to/from Simferopol are very busy, so book your tickets as early as possible.

BAKHCHYSARAY БАХЧИСАРАЙ

Bakhchysaray, 33km southwest of Simferopol, boasts the remarkable **Khans' Palace** (vul Lenina 129; admission 6 hrn; open 9am-5pm Thur-Mon). Built by Russian and Ukrainian slaves in the 16th century, it is one of the most magnificent palaces in Ukraine and provides a marvellous insight into the history of Crimea.

Every day, seven trains travel between Simferopol and Sevastopol, via Bakhchysaray. Buses between Simferopol and Sevastopol often do not stop at Bakhchysaray, however, but minibuses to Bakhchysaray that leave from the long-distance bus terminal in Simferopol every one or two hours.

The train station in Bakhchysaray is 3km west of the palace, and the bus terminal is 1.5km northeast of the train station – bus No 4 links the two stations. From the train station, bus No 2 stops in front of the palace.

YALTA ЯЛТА
☎ 0654 • pop 81,500

Yalta is overwhelmingly *the* major attraction in Crimea for Ukrainian and Russian tourists, but the beaches are disappointing and the place can get impossibly crowded in summer.

Inside the **Central Post Office** (*pl Lenina*) is a branch of **Kiyavia** and the **Aval Bank**. The **Ukrsoubank** (*nab im Lenina*) cashes travellers cheques, while several **foreign-exchange offices** along the promenade handle cash. The **Internet Centre** (*vul Ekaterininskaya 3*) is often closed.

Things to See
The **promenade**, nab im Lenina, stretches past numerous piers, palm trees, (pebble) beaches, snack bars, gardens and souvenir stalls as far as **Prymorsky Park**. Up from Hotel Oreanda, vul Pushkinskaya and vul Hoholya are charming thoroughfares with elegant shops.

From vul Kirova look for the path to the chairlift (2.50 hrn one way), operating 9am to 6pm daily from May to September, which swings above the rooftops to **Darsan**, a bizarre pseudo-Greek temple and lookout. Near the bottom station, the **Aleksandr Nevsky Cathedral** (*vul Sadovaya; admission free; open 9am-4pm Mon-Sat*) is a beautiful example of neo-Byzantine architecture.

Anton Chekhov wrote *The Cherry Orchard* and the *Three Sisters* in what is now the **Chekhov House-Museum** (*vul Kirova 112; admission 10 hrn; open 10am-5pm Wed-Sun*). Trolleybus No 1 from pl Sovietskaya will drop you a few blocks downhill from (south of) the museum.

Places to Stay
In July and August reservations for all hotels are recommended.

Camping Polyana Skazok (*☎ 395 219, fax 397 439; tent sites 15 hrn, camping per person 15 hrn, cabins per person from 22 hrn*) is beneath majestic cliffs about 5km west of the town centre. Take bus No 26, 27 or 28 from the main bus terminal to 'Polyana Skazok' and walk another 1.5km uphill.

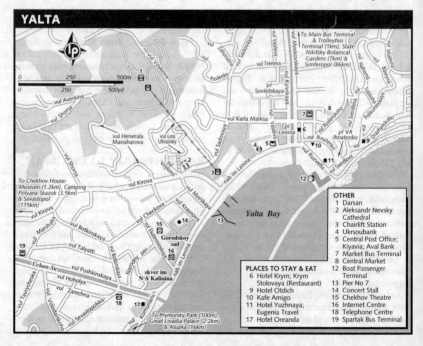

YALTA

OTHER
1 Darsan
2 Aleksandr Nevsky Cathedral
3 Chairlift Station
4 Ukrsoubank
5 Central Post Office; Kiyavia; Aval Bank
7 Market Bus Terminal
8 Central Market
12 Boat Passenger Terminal
13 Pier No 7
14 Concert Stall
15 Chekhov Theatre
16 Internet Centre
18 Telephone Centre
19 Spartak Bus Terminal

PLACES TO STAY & EAT
6 Hotel Krym; Krym Stolovaya (Restaurant)
9 Hotel Otdich
10 Kafe Amigo
11 Hotel Yuzhnaya; Eugenia Travel
17 Hotel Oreanda

During summer, women hang around the main bus terminal offering **private rooms**. Alternatively, look for signs outside homes along vul Ekaterininskaya. Expect to pay about 60 hrn per person per night.

Hotel Krym (*☎ 326 001, fax 322 001; vul Moskovskaya 1; singles/doubles from 35/40 hrn, doubles with bathroom from 100 hrn*) is worn and the rooms are small, but it's central and excellent value.

Hotel Otdich (*☎ 355 079; vul Drazhyn-skoho 14; singles/doubles with bathroom 64/113 hrn*) is a quiet pension along a suburban street. It's clean and comfortable, and some rooms have sea views; rates include breakfast.

Hotel Yuzhnaya (*☎ 271 603; e office@ hotel-bristol.com.ua; vul Ruzvelta 10; singles/ doubles with bathroom from 133/218 hrn*), also called Hotel Bristol, is a classy place opposite the boat passenger terminal. The rooms are thoroughly renovated and exceptional value; rates include breakfast.

Places to Eat

In summer, nab im Lenina is chock-a-block with open-air **cafés** and **bars**. Numerous **fish restaurants** also line the promenade, but all are pretty much the same – and expensive. Most offer menus in English.

Krym Stolovaya (*vul Moskovskaya 1; mains around 5 hrn*), next to Hotel Krym, is a self-service cafeteria serving cheap and hearty Ukrainian food.

Kafe Amigo (*vul Ihnatenko 50*), like its counterpart in Simferopol, serves cheap and tasty burgers, pizzas and ice cream.

Getting There & Away

The world's longest – and slowest! – trolleybuses leave from the **trolleybus terminal** (*vul Gagarina*), near the train station in Simferopol, for Yalta (2½ hours) every 20 minutes. In Yalta, trolleybuses start/finish at the **trolleybus terminal** (*vul Moskovskaya*), opposite the main bus terminal.

Minibuses and buses (1½ to 2 hours) leave every 30 minutes from the bus terminal (*vul Gagarina*) in Simferopol for Yalta. They stop at the **main bus terminal** (*vul Moskovskaya*), a five-minute ride on trolleybus No 1, 2 or 3 along vul Moskovskaya/Kyivskaya from central Yalta. From this terminal, buses also leave regularly for Sevastopol and Bakhchysaray, and once a day for Odesa.

From **Pier No 7** (*nab im Lenina*), boats travel daily (May to September) along the Crimean coast to Alupka, Sudak and Sevastopol. See the Getting There & Away section earlier in the chapter for details about boat trips around the Black Sea. All use the central **boat passenger terminal** (*vul Ruzvelta*).

AROUND YALTA

The 1000-hectare **State Nikitsky Botanical Gardens** (*admission 5 hrn; open around 8am-7pm daily*), 7km northeast of Yalta, are worth visiting for the beautiful landscapes and marvellous views. Take bus No 34 from the **market bus terminal** near the central market in Yalta to the 'Upper Gate' bus stop.

In February 1945 Stalin, Roosevelt and Churchill held their Yalta Conference in the **Great Livadia Palace** (*admission 5 hrn; open 8am-7.30pm Thur-Tues June-Sept, 10am-4.30pm Thur-Tues Oct-May*), 3km southwest of central Yalta. It features photos and memorabilia about this historic event, and displays about the palace's original owner, the last Russian Emperor, Nicholas II. Bus No 5 from the **Spartak Bus Terminal** (*vul Pushkinskaya*) in Yalta stops near the palace.

The magnificent cliff-side **Swallow's Nest** castle (*admission 8 hrn; open 8am-6pm Tues-Sun*) is accessible on foot (1½ hours one way) from Livadia; follow the signs to 'Turbaza Kitkynz & Sanatoria Parus'.

The palace-park complex at **Alupka** (*admission free; open 8am-6pm daily*), 16km southwest of Yalta, boasts a stunning coastal setting and the majestic **Alupkinsky Palace** (*admission 8 hrn; open 8am-9pm Tues-Sun July-Sept, 10am-4pm Tues-Sun Oct-June*). Bus No 27 runs every hour to the palace from the main bus terminal in Yalta.

SEVASTOPOL СЕВАСТОПОЛЬ
☎ 0692 • pop 341,800

As a major Russian naval port Sevastopol was closed to tourists until 1996. These days, however, this appealing town is more charming than Simferopol and considerably less crowded than Yalta.

The **Central Post Office** (*vul Bolshaya Morskaya*) has a branch of the **Aval Bank**. There are also plenty of **foreign-exchange offices** near the port, and **ATMs** inside the Sevastopol and Ukraina hotels. **Internet Salon** (*vul Bolshaya Morskaya 33*) is not far from the post office.

UKRAINE

Things to See

From the train station and adjacent bus terminal, take any minibus or trolleybus up to the first major square, pl Suvorova. Then stroll down vul Lenina to the **Black Sea Fleet Museum** *(vul Lenina 11; admission 5 hrn; open 10am-5pm Wed-Sun)*, which provides colourful displays about the controversial Russian fleet.

At the end of vul Lenina is the mammoth pl Nakhimova. To the north is an elegant seaside **park**. Just off the northern tip of the park, the **Eagle Column** commemorates Russian ships sunk in this harbour during 1854. Further southwest along the esplanade is a **dolphinarium** *(admission 12 hrn; open 10am-4.30pm Tues-Sun)* and to the left is the grand **Lunacharskoho Theatre**.

Walk up past this theatre to prosp Nakhimova, and look for the steps heading up (south) through a park to the **Lenin Statue**. Behind the statue is the golden dome of **St Vladimir's Cathedral** *(admission free; open 9am-3pm Mon-Sat)*. Veer right and walk past the cathedral along leafy vul Suvorova for 200m, and take the steps to the right (west) down vul Serheeva-Tsenskoho to the busy vul Bolshaya Morskaya.

Bolshaya Morskaya continues south past the **Intercession Cathedral** *(admission free; open dawn-dusk daily)* to the busy intersection at pl Ushakova. Continue straight ahead (southeast) through the park for about 300m to the **Panorama** *(admission 12 hrn; open*

9.30am-5.30pm daily), a massive work of art commemorating the defence of Sevastopol in the Crimean War. From here, hike down any path or steps back to the train and bus stations.

Places to Stay & Eat

Hotel Sevastopol *(☎ 523 682, fax 523 671; prosp Nakhimova 8; doubles from 86 hrn, singles/doubles with bathroom 135/188 hrn)* is a historic old building, but the rooms are unremarkable.

Hotel Ukraina *(☎ 522 127; vul Hoholya 2; doubles with bathroom 98-168 hrn)* is another Soviet-style concrete block overlooking pl Ushakova. It's convenient, but typically uninspiring. And readers have complained about noisy cafés nearby.

For fish meals and harbour views, try any of the **cafés** and **restaurants** along the waterfront between the park and Lunacharskoho Theatre. In the peaceful park surrounding the Panorama are several other decent **eateries**.

Getting There & Away

Seven trains and about 10 buses travel daily between Simferopol and Sevastopol, but avoid any bus that takes the laborious detour through Yalta. From the Sevastopol **bus terminal** *(vul Vokzalnaya)*, buses also leave for Yalta every 90 minutes. Every day from the adjacent **train station** *(vul Portovaya)*, there are services to Odesa, Lviv and Kyiv (51/137 hrn for *kupe*/SV class, 20 hours), and several a week to Moscow and St Petersburg.

Yugoslavia Југославија

The Federal Republic of Yugoslavia, which consists of Serbia and Montenegro, occupies the heart of the Balkans astride major land and river routes from Western Europe to Asia Minor. It is a region with a tumultuous history.

Since June 1999 Kosovo, previously part of Serbia, has been a UN-NATO protectorate. The UN still recognises Kosovo as part of Yugoslavia until its future is decided. For this reason it is included in this chapter.

Facts about Yugoslavia

HISTORY

The original inhabitants of the region were the Illyrians, followed by the Celts, who arrived in the 4th century BC. The Roman conquest of Moesia Superior (Serbia) began in the 3rd century BC and under Augustus the empire extended to Singidunum (Belgrade) on the Danube. In AD 395 Theodosius I divided the empire and what is now Serbia passed to the Byzantine Empire, while Croatia remained part of the Western Roman Empire.

During the 6th century, Slavic tribes (Serbs, Croats and Slovenes) crossed the Danube and occupied much of the Balkan Peninsula. In 879 Sts Cyril and Methodius converted the Serbs to the Orthodox religion.

An independent Serbian kingdom appeared in 1217 with a 'Golden Age' during Stefan Dušan's reign (1346–55). After Stefan's death Serbia declined and, at the Battle of Kosovo on 28 June 1389, the Turks defeated Serbia, ushering in 500 years of Islamic rule. A revolt in 1815 led to de facto Serbian independence from the Turks. Autonomy was recognised in 1829 and complete independence was then achieved in 1878.

On 28 June 1914, Austria-Hungary used the assassination of Archduke Ferdinand by a Serb nationalist as a pretext to invade Serbia, sparking WWI. After the war, Croatia, Slovenia, Vojvodina, Serbia, Montenegro and Macedonia formed the Kingdom of Serbs, Croats and Slovenes under the king of Serbia. In 1929 the country became Yugoslavia.

On 25 March 1941 Yugoslavia joined the Tripartite Alliance, a Nazi-supported fascist

military pact. This sparked a military coup. Peter II was installed as king and Yugoslavia abruptly withdrew from the Alliance. Livid, Hitler ordered immediate invasion and Yugoslavia was subsequently carved up between Germany, Italy, Hungary and Bulgaria.

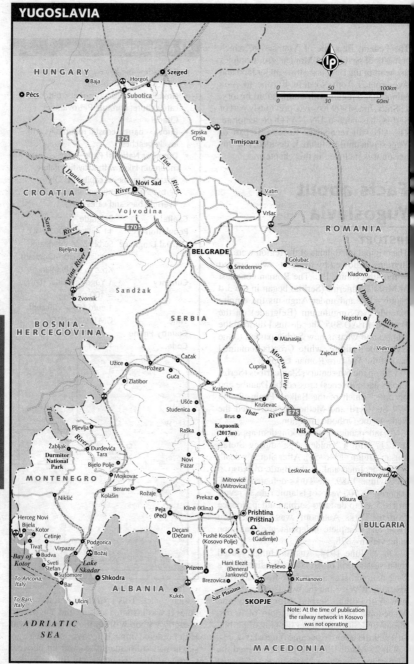

YUGOSLAVIA

HUNGARY

Baja
Horgoš
Szeged
Pécs
Subotica

E75

Srpska Crnja
Timişoara

Tisa River

CROATIA
Danube
Novi Sad
Vojvodina
Vatin

E70
BELGRADE
Vršac

ROMANIA

Bijeljina
Smederevo
Golubac
Kladovo

Sava River
Drina River
Zvornik

Sandžak
SERBIA

Danube River
Negotin
Vidin

BOSNIA-HERCEGOVINA

Manasija
Zaječar

Čačak
Morava River
Ćuprija

Užice
Požega
Guča
Kraljevo

Zlatibor
Ušče
Kruševac
E75

Studenica
Brus
Ibar River
Niš

Tara River
Raška
Kapaonik (2017m)

Pljevlja

Žabljak
Đurđevića Tara
Durmitor National Park
Bijelo Polje
Novi Pazar

MONTENEGRO
Mojkovac
Mitrovicě (Mitrovica)
Leskovac
Dimitrovgrad

Nikšić
Kolašin
Berane
Rožaje
Prekaz
Klisura

Herceg Novi
Bijela
Kotor
Cetinje
Peja (Peč)
Klinë (Klina)
Prishtina (Priština)
BULGARIA

Tivat
Virpazar
Podgorica
Božaj
Deçani (Dečani)
Fushë Kosovë (Kosovo Polje)
Gadimě (Gadimlje)

Bay of Kotor
Sveti Stefan
Budva
Lake Skadar
KOSOVO
Preševo

To Ancona, Italy
Sutomore
Bar
Shkodra
Prizren
Hani Elezit (Deneral Janković)
Kumanovo

To Bari, Italy
Ulcinj
ALBANIA
Brezovica
Sar Planina
SKOPJE

ADRIATIC SEA
Kukës

Note: At the time of publication the railway network in Kosovo was not operating

MACEDONIA

0   50   100km
0   30   60mi

YUGOSLAVIA

Almost immediately the Communist Party, under Josip Broz Tito, declared an armed uprising, laying the basis for a future communist Yugoslavia. In 1945 the Communist Party won control of the national assembly, abolished the monarchy and declared Yugoslavia a federal republic. Serbia's size was reduced with Bosnia-Hercegovina, Montenegro and Macedonia being granted republic status within this 'second' Yugoslavia. Albanians of Kosovo and Hungarians of Vojvodina were denied republic status as their national homelands were outside Yugoslavia.

Tito broke with Stalin in 1948 and, as a reward, received US$2 billion in economic and military aid from the USA and UK between 1950 and 1960. Growing regional inequalities led, however, to increased tension in the area as Slovenia, Croatia and Kosovo demanded greater autonomy.

In 1986 the Serbian Academy of Sciences called on Serbia to reassert its hegemony. When Slobodan Miloševic took over as Communist Party leader in Serbia, he espoused a vision of a 'Greater Serbia' that horrified Slovenia and Croatia. On 25 June 1991 Slovenia and Croatia declared independence, leading to an invasion of Slovenia by the federal army. Consequently the then European Community (EC), imposed a weapons embargo on Yugoslavia.

On 15 January 1992, both Croatian and Slovenian independence was recognised by the EC. This prompted Macedonia and Bosnia-Hercegovina to demand recognition of their own independence. Montenegro alone voted to remain in Yugoslavia. On 27 April 1992 a 'third' Yugoslav federation was declared by Serbia and Montenegro. The new constitution made no mention of 'autonomous provinces', infuriating Albanians in Kosovo, long brutally repressed by Serbia. Violence in Kosovo erupted in January 1998, largely provoked by the federal army and police.

The West provided a storm of protest but little else other than another arms embargo. In March 1999 peace talks in Paris failed when Serbia rejected a US-brokered peace plan. In a reply to resistance in Kosovo, Serbian forces moved to empty the country of its Albanian population. Hundreds of thousands fleeing into Macedonia and Albania galvanised America and NATO into action. Not wishing to enter a potentially disastrous land war, they embarked on a 78-day bombing campaign.

Watch this space

By the time you read this chapter it could be in the wrong part of the book, it should be under 'S' for Serbia and Montenegro. There's still a lot of wrangling and politicking to be done before the parliaments of Serbia and Montenegro agree to dump the name (and constitution) of Yugoslavia. So to be safe, and accurate, we've decided to wait until it's official.

On 12 June 1999 the Serbian forces withdrew from Kosovo.

In the September 2000 federal presidential elections the opposition, led by Vojislav Koštunica, declared victory, a claim denied by Miloševic. Hundreds of thousands of opposition supporters occupied the streets and a general strike was called. In the meantime, Yugoslavia's constitutional court annulled the election and pronounced that Miloševic should remain as president. On 5 October opposition supporters occupied parliament and the state TV station. The following day Russia recognised Koštunica's presidency, a move that persuaded Miloševic that his days had ended.

Koštunica immediately restored ties with Europe, acknowledged Yugoslav atrocities in Kosovo and, in November, Yugoslavia rejoined the UN. In December, Miloševic's party was soundly defeated in Serbian parliamentary elections. In April 2001 Miloševic was arrested for misappropriating state funds and abusing his position. In June he was extradited to the Netherlands to stand trial at the international war crimes tribunal. It's likely that other extraditions will follow.

During April 2002 Serbia and Montenegro agreed to replace the federation with a union of Serbia and Montenegro. The deal was brokered under heavy EU pressure, which sought to prevent further violence in the region. Montenegro also placed a three-year hold on any independence referendum. At the time of research the constitutional detail still had to be written, wrangled over and ratified by parliament. Until then the name Yugoslavia remains.

GEOGRAPHY

Mountains and plateaus account for the lower half of this 102,350-sq-km federation. Serbia covers 77,651 sq km, Montenegro 13,812 sq km, and Kosovo 10,887 sq km. Yugoslavia's interior and southern mountains belong to the Balkan Range while the coastal range is an arm of the Dinaric Alps. Most rivers flow north into the Danube, which runs through Yugoslavia for 588km. Down south, rivers have cut deep canyons into the plateau.

Yugoslavia's only coastline is the scenically superb 150km Montenegrin coast. The Bay of Kotor is southern Europe's only real fjord and Montenegro's Tara Canyon is the largest in Europe.

CLIMATE

The north has a continental climate with cold winters and hot, humid summers. The coastal region has hot, dry summers and relatively cold winters with heavy snowfall inland.

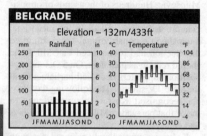

GOVERNMENT & POLITICS

Yugoslavia has a presidential parliamentary system with federal power vested in a parliament headed by prime minister Dragiša Pešić and president Vojislav Koštunica. Serbia and Montenegro also have their own parliaments, prime ministers and presidents who wield political power. In the new union, Serbia and Montenegro will be semi-independent states with foreign affairs, customs and defence controlled federally.

ECONOMY

Conflict, sanctions and disruption of trade links have devastated the economy over 20 years. The old Yugoslav economy was based on the whole federation with states specialising in certain industries. Now each state has to survive on its own.

Hyperinflation, the highest in European history, was a constant problem. At one point, it was cheaper to use banknotes to paper walls than to buy wallpaper. The dinar has now become quite stable. Inflation in 2001 was 40%, 26% is expected for 2002 and 10% is targeted for 2003.

Agricultural production is mainly on the northern plain. Vojvodina and Kosovo have most of the mineral resources, including coal and petroleum, hence the strategic importance of those former autonomous regions to Serbia. Yugoslavia is largely self-sufficient in fuel.

Kosovar economic restructure has been greatly hindered by issues of legal ownership of factories and equipment.

POPULATION & PEOPLE

The last published figures came from the 1991 census with no figures yet released from the April 2002 census. The population is made up of Serbs (62%), Montenegrins (5%), Albanians (estimated at 17%), Hungarians (3%) and Slavic Muslims (3%), plus Croats, Roma, Slovaks, Macedonians, Romanians, Bulgarians, Turks and Ukrainians. War has altered those figures, especially with about 400,000 refugees in Serbia and Montenegro.

About 23% of Vojvodina's population is Hungarian, concentrated around Subotica. There are large Slavic Muslim and Albanian minorities in Montenegro and southern Serbia; Belgrade has an estimated Muslim population of 10,000.

ARTS
Literature

The Bosnian-born Nobel Prize winner Ivo Andric's novel *Bridge on the Drina* foresaw the region's disasters of the early 1990s. The respected writer Milorad Pavic's novel *Dictionary of the Khazars* is a novel written in the form of a dictionary. Other books worthy of the traveller's perusal are *In the Hold* by Vladimir Arsenijević, *Words are Something Else* by David Albahari, *Petrija's Wreath* by Dragoslav Mihailović and *Fear and its Servant* by Mirjana Novaković.

Cinema

The award-winning film *Underground*, by Sarajevo-born director Emil Kusturica, is worth seeing. Told in a chaotic, colourful style, the film deals with Yugoslav history. *Tockovi*, by Djordje Milosavljevic, is a black comedy where the hero wanders into lonely motel on a stormy night and gets stuck with a group of people who think he's a mass murderer. Bosnian director Danis Tanovic's *No Man's Land* superbly deals with an encounter between a Serb and Bosnian soldier stuck in a trench on their own during the Bosnian war.

Music

Serbia's vibrant dances are similar to those of Bulgaria with musicians using bagpipes, flutes and fiddles.

Kosovar music bears the deep imprint of five centuries of Turkish rule with high whine flutes carrying the tune above the beat of a goatskin drum.

Blehmuzika, or brass music influenced by Turkish and Austrian military music, has become the national music of Serbia with an annual festival at Guča in August.

Popular with the younger generation is Momcilo Bajagic whose music fuses traditional elements with street poetry and jazz. Djorde Balaševic appeals to a wider audience, again combining traditional elements with modern motifs. Darkwood Dub, combining fusion and rock with electronic music, and Eyesburn, who blends hard rock with reggae sampling, are two popular current bands.

SOCIETY & CONDUCT

All nationalities are hospitable to visitors despite recent history. Respect should be shown for all religious establishments and customs. Dress appropriately and learning some basic words will open doors and create smiles.

RELIGION

Serbs and Montenegrins are predominantly Orthodox, Hungarians are Roman Catholic and Albanians are predominantly Muslim.

LANGUAGE

Serbian is the common language, with Albanian spoken in Kosovo. Through working abroad, many Yugoslavs have German as a second language and educated people often know English and French.

While, Hungarians in Vojvodina use the Latin alpabet, Montenegrins and Serbians use both Latin and Cyrillic. (See the Macedonian language section at the back of this book for the alphabet.)

Facts for the Visitor

HIGHLIGHTS

There is a wealth of castles, like the baroque Petrovaradin Citadel at Novi Sad, Belgrade's Kalemegdan Citadel and Smederevo. Kosovo has Turkish architecture and street cafés in Prizren, and the old Montenegrin capital of Cetinje will please romantics. Of the beach resorts, Budva is chic but Kotor is more impressive with its fjord and medieval walled town. Montenegro's Tara Canyon and Durmitor National Park stack up to any similar sights in the world.

SUGGESTED ITINERARIES

Depending on time available and where you arrive you might visit the following:

Two days
Visit Serbia (Belgrade and Vojvodina), Montenegro (Budva, Cetinje and Kotor) or Kosovo
One week
Visit two of the regions
Two weeks
Visit all the areas that are covered in this chapter

PLANNING
When to Go

Avoid the Montenegrin coast during July and August when accommodation becomes quite expensive and scarce. The ski season is generally December to March.

Maps

The Freytag & Berndt map *Yugoslavia, Slovenia, Croatia* shows former Yugoslavia with the new countries. The *Savezna Republika Jugoslavija Autokarta* map shows the new borders and some town maps. *Plan Grada Beograd* is a detailed Belgrade city map. The latter two are available free from the Tourist Organization of Belgrade. A Kosovo map is available from bookshops in Prishtina.

TOURIST OFFICES

There are tourist offices in Belgrade, Novi Sad, Niš, Prishtina and Prizren. Elsewhere, travel agencies may help with information.

VISAS & DOCUMENTS

A visa is only required for Serbia, but not for Montenegro or Kosovo. You'll need an initial hotel booking to accompany your visa application. The website of the Ministry of Foreign Affair's (W www.mfa.gov.yu) has details.

Serbia has been trialling granting 30-day visas at Belgrade airport and border posts; this may become permanent. Please note, the crossings between Serbia and Kosovo or Montenegro are not through border posts (see the boxed text 'Border Crossings' in the Getting There & Away section later in this chapter).

EMBASSIES & CONSULATES
Yugoslav Embassies
Yugoslavia has embassies in the following countries:

Australia (☎ 02-6290 2630, fax 6290 2631,
  ⓔ yuembau@ozemail.com.au) 4 Bulwarra
  Close, O'Malley, Canberra, ACT 2606
Canada (☎ 613-233 6289, fax 233 7850,
  ⓦ www.yuemb.ca) 17 Blackburn Ave,
  Ottawa, Ontario, K1A 8A2
France (☎ 01 40 72 24 24, fax 01 40 72 24 11,
  ⓔ pariz@compuserve.com) 54 rue de la
  Faisanderie 75116, Paris
UK (☎ 020-7235 9049, fax 7235 7090,
  ⓦ www.yugoslavembassy.org.uk) 28
  Belgrave Square, London, SW1X 8QB
USA (☎ 202-332 0333, fax 332 3933,
  ⓦ www.yuembusa.org) 2134 Kalorama Rd
  NW, Washington DC, 20008

Embassies & Consulates in Yugoslavia
The following countries have representation in Belgrade:

Albania (☎ 306 5350) Bulevar Mira 25A
Australia (☎ 624 655) Cika Ljubina 13
Bulgaria (☎ 361 3980) Birčaninova 26
Canada (☎ 306 3000) Kneza Miloša 75
France (☎ 302 3500) Pariska 11
Germany (☎ 361 4255) Kneza Miloša 74–6
Hungary (☎ 444 0472) Brigada (Krunska
  Proleterskih) 72
Romania (☎ 361 8327) Kneza Miloša 70
UK (☎ 645 087) Resavska (Generala Ždanova) 46
USA (☎ 361 9344) Kneza Miloša 50

MONEY
Currency
Montenegro and Kosovo have adopted the euro and the dinar is not accepted. Serbia, however, retains the dinar, which is used for most transactions, although some hotels may want payment in euros or US dollars. Some international train journeys may require part payment in dinar and part in euros. The euro is quite readily accepted in Serbia as many Serbians work in Western Europe.

Exchange Rates
Conversion rates for major currencies at the time of publication are listed below:

country	unit		euro		dinar
Australia	A$1	=	€0.61	=	37.81 DIN
Canada	C$1	=	€0.71	=	44.20 DIN
Euro Zone	€1			=	62.43 DIN
Japan	¥100	=	€0.87	=	54.39 DIN
NZ	NZ$1	=	€0.51	=	32.10 DIN
UK	£1	=	€1.58	=	98.73 DIN
USA	US$1	=	€1.09	=	67.83 DIN

Exchanging Money
Until expected global banking agreements are made, few banks handle travellers cheques or credit cards. Come with euros in cash. Many exchange offices in Serbia will readily change these and other hard currencies into dinars and back again when you leave. Look for their large blue diamond signs hanging outside.

Tipping & Bargaining
It's common to round up restaurant bills; taxi drivers will expect the same. Prices are fixed in shops and generally in markets as well, but you might be successful in bargaining.

POST & COMMUNICATIONS
Post
Parcels should be taken unsealed to the main post office for inspection. Allow time to check the repacking and complete the transaction.

You can receive mail, addressed poste restante, in all towns for a small charge.

Telephone & Fax
The international access code for outgoing calls is ☎ 99. To call Yugoslavia from outside, dial the international access code from the country you are in, ☎ 381 (country code), area code (without the initial zero) and the number.

In Serbia you can use a phonecard (100, 300 or 500 DIN) to make a call from a public phone. A phone call to Europe/Australia/North America costs 42/76/76 DIN a minute. In Montenegro the highest-value phonecard (€1.70) doesn't give enough time (Europe/Australia/North America €0.90/1.64/1.64 per minute), so use the post office to call. The same issue applies for Kosovo where a call to Europe/Australia/North America costs €0.56/1.23/1.23 per minute. Press the *i* button on Serbian and Montenegrin public phones for dialling commands in English.

Faxes can be sent from any large hotel or from post offices. In Serbia they charge 172/236/236 DIN per page to Europe/Australia/North America.

Email & Internet Access
Internet cafés are widespread throughout the country and have fast connections.

DIGITAL RESOURCES

Three informative websites for travellers to check out are **W** www.serbia-tourism.org.yu, **W** www.visit-montenegro.com and **W** www.beograd.org.yu.

BOOKS

Rebecca West's *Black Lamb & Grey Falcon* is a classic portrait of prewar Yugoslavia. Former partisan and dissident Milovan Djilas' fascinating books about Yugoslav history and politics are published in English.

Titles dealing with the turbulence of the 1990s include *Yugoslavia: Death of a Nation* by Laura Silber and Allan Little, Misha Glenny's 1998 book *The Fall of Yugoslavia* and *Yugoslavia's Bloody Collapse* by Christopher Bennett (1996). *The Death of Yugoslavia* by Laura Silber (published November 2002) continues the account. Zoë Brân's *After Yugoslavia* retraces the author's 1978 trip through Yugoslavia.

NEWSPAPERS & MAGAZINES

Some foreign-language magazines are available but it can be hard to find newspapers. Try the newsstands in Belgrade's Kneza Mihaila or outside the Sports Complex in Prishtina.

RADIO & TV

The liberalisation of Serbia has permitted an independent media. Studio B, the independent radio and TV station, closed several times under Milošević, is flourishing along with another 13 stations, including three state-owned channels all offering sport, movies, politics, news programmes, debates and foreign-made series. CNN, Eurosport and MTV are also available with the right equipment. Many FM and AM radio stations cater to all tastes.

TOILETS

Restaurant and hotel toilets are a cleaner option than public toilets, which are few and far between.

WOMEN TRAVELLERS

Other than a cursory interest shown by men towards solo women travellers, travelling is hassle-free and easy. Dress more conservatively than usual in Muslim areas of Kosovo.

GAY & LESBIAN TRAVELLERS

Homosexuality has been legal in Yugoslavia since 1932. For more information, contact

---

Emergency Services

In an emergency dial ☎ 92 for police, ☎ 93 for the fire service and ☎ 94 for the ambulance.

If you need motoring assistance in Belgrade call ☎ 987 and in Serbia and Montenegro (ie, outside Belgrade) for motoring assistance the number is ☎ 011 9800.

Arkadia *(Brace Baruh 11, 11000 Belgrade)* or check the website **W** www.gay-serbia.com.

DISABLED TRAVELLERS

There are very few facilities in the region for those with disabilities. Wheelchair access could be problematic in Belgrade with its numerous inclines but most hotels will have lifts.

DANGERS & ANNOYANCES

Travel nearly everywhere is safe but avoid southeastern Serbia and Mitrovica (Mitrovicë) in Kosovo where Serb-Albanian tension still remains. There are some land mines still to be cleared in Kosovo so look out for warnings and if you're going off the beaten track check with the United Nations Interim Administration Mission (UNMIK) or Kosovo Force (KFOR) – see the Kosovo section for contact information.

Many Yugoslavs are chain-smokers who can't imagine that they might inconvenience nonsmokers. 'No smoking' signs are routinely ignored. It's fine to discuss politics if you're also willing to listen. Check with the police before photographing any official building they're guarding.

BUSINESS HOURS

Banks keep long hours, often 7am to 7pm weekdays and 7am to noon Saturday. On weekdays many shops open at 7am, close noon to 4pm but reopen to 8pm. Department stores, supermarkets and some restaurants are open all day. Most government offices close on Saturday; although shops stay open until 2pm many other businesses close at 3pm.

PUBLIC HOLIDAYS & SPECIAL EVENTS

Public holidays in Serbia and Montenegro include New Year (1 and 2 January), Orthodox Christmas (6 and 7 January), Constitution Day, Serbia (28 March), Constitution Day of Federal Republic of Yugoslavia (27 April),

International Labour Days (1 and 2 May), Victory Day (9 May) and Uprising Day, Montenegro (13 July). If 28 March or 13 July fall on a Sunday, the following Monday or Tuesday is a holiday. Orthodox churches celebrate Easter between one and five weeks later than other churches.

In Kosovo, 28 November is Flag Day and Easter Monday is a public holiday.

Belgrade hosts a film festival (FEST) in February, a jazz festival in August, an international theatre festival (BITEF) in September and a festival of classical music in October. Every August Novi Sad hosts the Exit music festival, attracting bands from all over Europe to within the Petrovaradin Citadel. Niš hosts a jazz and blues festival in its citadel in mid-July. There's an annual festival of brass-band music at Guča near Čačak in the last week of August. Budva's summer festival is in July and August and Herceg Novi hosts the Suncale Skale music festival in July.

ACTIVITIES

Serbia's main ski resorts are Zlatibor and Kopaonik, while Montenegro's is Žabljak. Kosovo's resort at Brezovica has reopened. The ski season is from December to March, while resorts are popular for hiking in summer. For white-water rafting the Tara River in Montenegro's Durmitor National Park is the most important river in the country.

ACCOMMODATION

For hostel accommodation contact Ferijalni Savez Beograd (see the Belgrade Places to Stay section for details). Hostels exist in Belgrade, Palić (Subotica), Kladovo (east Serbia), Kopaonik (southern Serbia) and at Sutomore and Bijela (southern Montenegro).

Hotels can be pricey, Belgrade hotels are reasonable for a capital, Montenegrin hotels outside the coast and Žabljak are iniquitously expensive and Kosovo accommodation is scarce and pricey. Private rooms (along the coast, seldom inland and not in Belgrade), organised through travel agencies, are best. In summer you can camp along the Montenegrin coast at a few organised camping grounds. An overnight bus or train will always save you a night's accommodation.

FOOD

This region is a delight for meat eaters but a trial for vegetarians. The cheapest snack is burek, a greasy pie made with *sir* (cheese), *meso* (meat), *krompiruša* (potato) or *pecurke* (mushrooms); with yogurt it makes a good breakfast filler. *Čevapčići* (grilled kebabs of spiced minced meats) are very popular all over, as is the universal pizza. A good midday meal of soup or *čevapčići* should cost about 120 DIN/€2.

Regional Dishes

Yugoslavia's regional cuisines range from spicy Hungarian goulash in Vojvodina to Turkish kebab in Kosovo. A speciality of Vojvodina is *alaska čorba* (fiery riverfish stew). In Montenegro, try *kajmak* (cream from boiled milk which is salted and turned into cheese).

Serbia is famous for grilled meats, such as *čevapčići*, *pljeskavica* (large, spicy hamburger steak) and *ražnjići* (a pork or veal shish kebab with onions and peppers). All together they become a *mešano meso* (mixed grill). *Duveć* is grilled pork cutlets with spiced stewed peppers, zucchini and tomatoes in rice cooked in an oven – delicious.

Other popular dishes to try are *musaka* (aubergine and potato arranged in layers with minced meat), *sarma* (cabbage stuffed with minced meat and rice), *kapama* (stewed lamb, onions and spinach with yogurt) and *punjena tikvica* (zucchini stuffed with minced meat and rice).

For vegetarians there's the ubiquitous pizza or a *Srpska salata* (Serbian salad) of raw peppers, onions and tomatoes, seasoned with oil, vinegar and maybe chilli. Also ask for *gibanica* (cheese pie), *zeljanica* (cheese pie with spinach) or *pasulj prebranac* (a dish of cooked and spiced beans). *Šopska salata* is also very popular, consisting of chopped tomatoes, cucumber and onion, topped with grated soft white cheese.

DRINKS

Pivo (beer) is universally available. Nikšićko *pivo* (both light and dark), brewed at Nikšić in Montenegro, is terribly good. Yugoslav cognac is called *vinjak*, many people distil their own plum brandy and Montenegrin red wine is a good drop.

Coffee is usually served Turkish-style, 'black as hell, strong as death and sweet as love'. Superb espresso and cappuccino, however, can be found in many cafés. If you want anything other than herbal teas (camomile or hibiscus) then ask for Indian tea.

Getting There & Away

You must fill out a currency declaration form on arrival and show it on departure, otherwise you'll have problems.

AIR

JAT (Yugoslav Airlines) operates regional services throughout Europe. Montenegro Airlines flies between Podgorica and Budapest, Frankfurt and Zürich. Other airlines like Lufthansa and Aeroflot fly to Belgrade and Austrian Airlines, Swiss International Air Lines, Adria Airlines, British Airways and Turkish Airlines fly into Prishtina.

LAND
Train

International trains from Belgrade call at Novi Sad and Subotica heading north and west, and at Niš going east. No trains run in Kosovo at present and Montenegro has no international services. Reservations are recommended; presenting a student card will you get a reduction on some trains. Eurail and Inter-Rail passes are accepted and sold at Belgrade train station.

Sample services from Belgrade are:

destination	cost (DIN)	duration (hrs)	frequency
Bucharest	1799	14	daily
Budapest	2311	7	daily
İstanbul	5787	26	daily
Ljubljana	1731	10	daily
Moscow	6423	50	daily
Munich	4940	17	daily
Sofia	1250	11	daily
Thessaloniki	1933	16	daily
Vienna	3518	11	daily
Zagreb	1110	7	daily

Car & Motorcycle

Drivers from Britain, Spain, Germany and some other countries need an international driving licence, otherwise visitors can use their national licences. Vehicles need a third-party insurance recognised in Yugoslavia plus insurance (from €80 a month) bought at the border. For more details contact **Auto-Moto Savez Jugoslavije** (*Yugoslav Automotive Association;* ☎ 011 9800; ⓦ www.amsj.co.yu;

Border Crossings

Visitors flying into Kosovo can only legally first enter Serbia via Macedonia as there are no immigration facilities at the crossings between Kosovo and Serbia or Montenegro. While you can enter Serbia without a check, problems will arise at hotels or leaving the country – there'll be no entry stamp in your passport which means you're there illegally.

Similarly if you are driving into Kosovo from Albania or Macedonia and on to Serbia, you'll have to go via Macedonia to buy the necessary insurance at the border post.

Ruzveltova 18, Belgrade). For travel into Kosovo see the boxed text 'Border Crossings' above. Traffic police are everywhere so drive carefully and stick to speed limits.

SEA

A ferry service operates between Bar and Italy (see Bar in the Montenegro section later).

DEPARTURE TAX

There is a departure tax of 600 DIN when leaving Yugoslavia by air.

Getting Around

AIR

JAT flies from Belgrade to Tivat and Podgorica (Montenegro) several times daily and plans three flights a week to Prishtina. JAT runs inexpensive buses between airports and city centres. Montenegro Airlines also flies daily between Podgorica and Belgrade.

BUS

Buses are necessary for travel in Kosovo and to Rožaje (Montenegro) and Novi Pazar (Serbia), both gateways to Kosovo. You'll also need buses for the Montenegrin coast and getting to Žabljak.

TRAIN

Jugoslovenske Železnice (JŽ) provides adequate railway services from Belgrade serving Novi Sad, Subotica, Niš, and the highly scenic line down to Bar. There are four classes of train: *ekspresni* (express), *poslovni* (rapid), *brzi* (fast) and *putnicki* (slow), so make sure you have the right ticket.

Car Hire

VIP, Hertz, Europcar and Net Rent a Car all have offices at Belgrade airport. The typical cost of a small car is €55 a day.

Serbia Србија

The dominant role of Serbia (Srbija) in Yugoslavia was underlined by its control of two formerly autonomous provinces, Vojvodina and Kosovo, and the capital being Belgrade.

BELGRADE БЕОГРАД

☎ 011 • pop 2 million (est. 2002)

Belgrade (Beograd) is strategically situated on the southern edge of the Carpathian Basin where the Sava River joins the Danube. Destroyed and rebuilt 40 times in its 2300-year history, Belgrade is well on its way to being a European capital. It is a lively, vibrant city with fine restaurants, shops, bars and street cafés, and chic crowds.

History

The Celtic settlement of Singidunum was founded in the 3rd century BC on a bluff overlooking the confluence of the two rivers. The Romans arrived during the 1st century AD and stayed until the 5th century. Much of Kneza Mihaila is built over the main Roman street. The Slavic name Beograd (White City) first appeared in a papal letter in 878.

The Serbs made Belgrade their capital in 1403 after being pushed north by the Turks who captured the city in 1521. In 1842 the city became the Serbian capital and in 1918 the capital of the Kingdom of Serbs, Croats and Slovenes, later Yugoslavia.

Orientation

The train station and the two adjacent bus stations are on the southern side of the city. From the train station, travel east along Milovana Milovanovića and up Balkanska to Terazije, the heart of modern Belgrade. Kneza Mihaila, Belgrade's lively pedestrian boulevard, runs northwest through the old town from Terazije to the Kalemegdan Citadel overlooking the Sava and Danube Rivers.

Information

Tourist Offices The friendly and helpful **Tourist Organization of Belgrade** (☎ 635 622, fax 635 343; Terazije Passage; open 9am-8pm Mon-Fri, 9am-4pm Sat) is in the underpass near Kneza Mihaila. (Note the public toilets here for future reference.) There's a **tourist office** (☎ 601 555; open 8am-8pm daily) at Belgrade airport.

Money You can cash most travellers cheques at **Atlas Bank** (☎ 302 4000; Emilijana Josimovića 4) or AmEx travellers cheques at the **Astral Banka** (cnr Maršala Birjuzova & Pop Lukina). There are numerous private exchange offices in Belgrade, just look out for the large blue diamond sign.

Currently the only ATM machine that accepts foreign-issued cards is in the foyer of the **Hotel InterContinental** (Vladimira Popovića 10), which accepts Visa cards. In the same foyer **Delta Banka** (open 6.30am-10pm daily) cashes travellers cheques.

Post & Communications For phone calls there's the **central post office** (Zmaj Jovina 17; open 7am-8pm daily) and the **telephone centre** (Takovska; open 7am-midnight Mon-Fri, 7am-10pm Sat & Sun) in the **Main Post Office** by Sveti Marko church.

Changes to seven-digit numbers should be completed by 2003 but be aware that some numbers listed may change.

Email & Internet Access Better to use in the daytime, **IPS** (Makedonska 4; open 24hr) charges 80 DIN an hour. At night Belgrade's young commandeer the terminals to play the latest game. **Plato Cyber Club** (Akademski plato 1; open 24hr) charges 35 DIN an hour and has a huge, separate game section.

Travel Agencies The main office for **JAT** (☎ 642 773, fax 642 534; w www.jat.co.yu; Srpskih Vladara 18) deals with just its own services, while **Putnik** (☎ 323 2911, fax 323 4461; w www.putnik.co.yu; Terazije 27) has a wide range of domestic and international transport and tour services.

Bas Turist (☎ 638 555, fax 784 859; BAS bus station) and, across the street, **Turist Biro Lasta** (☎ 641 251, fax 642 473; Milovana Milovanovića 1) and **Putnik** (Milovana Milovanovića; open 7am-7pm) all sell tickets for buses. **KSR Beograd Tours** (☎ 641 258, fax 687 447; Milovana Milovanovića 5; open Mon-Sat) has train information and tickets at train station prices but without the crowds. The helpful staff speak good English.

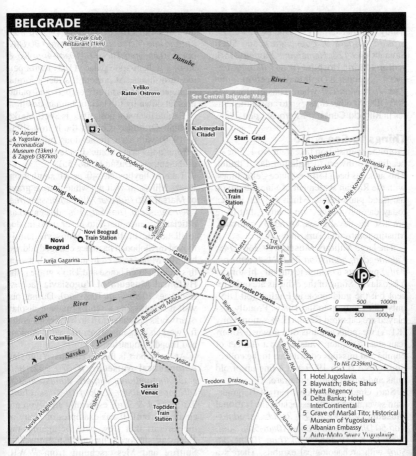

BELGRADE

To Kayak Club
Restaurant (1km)

Danube

River

Veliko
Ratno Ostrovo

See Central Belgrade Map

●1
□2

Kalemegdan
Citadel

Stari Grad

To Airport
& Yugoslav
Aeronautical
Museum (13km)
& Zagreb (387km)

Kej Oslobodenja

Lenjinov Bulevar

29 Novembra

Takovska

Partizanski Put

Mije Kovacevica

Ruzveltova

Drugi Bulevar

3

Central
Train
Station

Spenih

Miloša

Vladara

7

Novi Beograd
Train Station

4

Vladimira
Popovica

Nemanjina

Kneza

Trg
Slavija

Bulevar INA

Novi
Beograd

Jurija Gagarina

Gazela

LP

Vracar

Bulevar Franše D'Eperea

0   500   1000m
0   500   1000yd

River

Sava

Bulevar voj Mišica

Bulevar Mira

5●

Stevana Prvovenčanog

Ada Ciganlija

Savsko
Jezero

Radnicka

Bulevar · Vojvode – Mišica

6□

Vojvode Stepe

Bulevar INA

To Niš (239km)

Savska Magistrala

Požeška

Teodora Draizera

Nemanog Junaka

Savski
Venac

Topčider
Train
Station

1 Hotel Jugoslavia
2 Blaywatch; Bibis; Bahus
3 Hyatt Regency
4 Delta Banka; Hotel
  InterContinental
5 Grave of Maršal Tito; Historical
  Museum of Yugoslavia
6 Albanian Embassy
7 Auto-Moto Savez Yugoslavije

YUGOSLAVIA

Jolly Travel (☎ 323 2393, fax 334 1843; W www.jolly.co.yu; Kneza Miloša 9) offers sightseeing tours of Belgrade from €50 to €55 for two people. It offers car hire and books airline tickets and hotels.

Bookshops There are two good shops for English books and magazines. **Plato Bookshop** (off Kneza Mihaila) is the smaller of the two Plato bookshops. The **International Press Service Bookshop** (IPS; ☎ 328 1859; Trg Republike 5), in the basement of the building, stocks foreign magazines, videos and CDs.

Libraries At the Kalemegdan end of the street, the **City Library** (Kneza Mihaila; open 8am-8pm Mon-Fri, 2pm-8pm Sat), has books in foreign languages. Also of interest are the

foundations of a large Roman atrium in the basement plus a small exhibition of remains.

The British Council (Terazije 8; open 11am-4pm Mon, Wed & Fri, 2pm-7pm Tues & Thur) has quite a good range of newspapers, magazines and books.

Laundry While your hotel laundry will cope with your usual washing, **Express Dry Cleaners** (☎ 322 3479; Majke Jevrosime 53) will charge you 150 DIN to dry-clean trousers or 300 DIN for a jacket.

Left Luggage There is a **left-luggage room** (open 6am-10pm daily) at the BAS bus station, which charges 40 DIN per piece. The train station **left-luggage office** (open 24hr) charges 10 DIN per piece.

Medical & Emergency Services Two handy pharmacies are **Prvi Maj** (☎ 324 0533; *Srpskih Vladara 9; open 24hr*); and **Sveti Sava** (☎ 643 170; *Nemanjina 2; open 24hr*).

Boris Kidrič Hospital (☎ 643 839; *Pasterova 1*), operates a **Diplomatic Section** (*open 7am-7pm Mon-Fri*) where consultations are 300 DIN. At other times, go to any of the clinics in **Klinički Centar** (*Pasterova; open 24hr*).

Things to See & Do

From the train station take tram No 1, 2 or 13 heading northwest to **Kalemegdan Citadel**. This area has been fortified since Celtic times, with the Roman settlement of Singidunum on the flood plain below. Much of what is seen today dates from the 17th century, but there are also medieval gates, Orthodox churches, Muslim tombs and Turkish baths.

The large **Military Museum** (☎ 360 4149; *Kalemegdan; admission 20 DIN; 10am-5pm daily*) presents a complete military history of Yugoslavia. Some of the exhibits are quite recent but the guidebook in English (30 DIN) only takes you up to the 1980s. Proudly displayed are captured Kosovo Liberation Army (KLA) weapons and bits of a downed American stealth fighter. Outside are a number of bombs and missiles contributed to the collection by NATO in 1999 and a line-up of old guns and tanks, some quite rare.

Stari Grad is the oldest part of Belgrade, with several museums, especially the **National Museum** (☎ 624 322; *Trg Republike; admission 50 DIN, free Sun; open 10am-5pm Tues, Wed, Fri & Sat; noon-8pm Thur; 10am-2pm Sun*) with archaeological exhibits. There's a modern art gallery on the 3rd floor displaying just a fraction of a very large collection of national and European art, including some from Pablo Picasso and Claude Monet. Nadežeta Petrović (1873–1915), one of Serbia's first women artists, is well represented.

A few blocks away is the **Ethnographical Museum** (☎ 328 1888; *Studentski Trg 13; admission 40 DIN; open 10am-5pm Tues-Fri, 9am-5pm Sat, 9am-1pm Sun*), with a comprehensive collection of Serbian costumes and folk art. Detailed explanations are in English. Nearby is the **Gallery of Frescoes** (☎ 621 491; *Cara Uroša 20; admission 50 DIN; 10am-5pm Mon-Wed, Fri & Sat, noon-8pm Thur, 10am-2pm Sun*) with full-size replicas (and some originals) of paintings from churches and monasteries.

What could be a memorable museum is the **Palace of Princess Ljubice** (☎ 638 264; *Kneza Sime Markovića 8; admission 30 DIN; open 10am-5pm Tues-Fri, 10am-4pm Sat & Sun*), a Balkan-style palace (1831) with period furnishings. At present it's just a formal arrangement of furniture, carpets and paintings let down by the lack of human detail.

Behind the main post office is **Sveti Marko Serbian Orthodox Church** (built from 1932 to 1939) with four tremendous pillars supporting a towering dome. Inside is the grave of the emperor Dušan (1308–55).

Take trolleybus No 40 or 41 south from Kneza Miloša to visit the white marble **grave of Maršal Tito** (*Bulevar Mira; admission free; open 9am-2pm Tues-Sat*). It's adjacent to an official residence that Tito never lived in, due to ill health. In 1999 the Miloševic family moved in; Slobodan has since changed address but Mrs M has refused to move out. Between this well-guarded house and Tito's grave is the **Historical Museum of Yugoslavia** (*admission free; 10am-5pm Tues-Sun*). During our visit it was hosting a semipermanent display of artworks presented to Tito by various grateful workers' organisations, toadying minions and friendly countries.

At the airport is the exceptional **Yugoslav Aeronautical Museum** (☎ 670 992; *Belgrade International Airport; admission 300 DIN; open 8.30am-2.30pm Tues-Fri, 11am-3.30pm Sat & Sun*), especially so if you are an aircraft buff. It has examples of many of the aircraft that flew with or against the Yugoslav air force, including a Hurricane, Spitfire and Messerschmitt from WWII, Russian MIG fighters and more bits of that infamous American stealth fighter.

Ada Ciganlija, an island park in the Sava River, is just the place to escape the bustle of Belgrade. In summer you can swim in the river (naturists 1km upstream), rent a bicycle or just stroll among the trees. Many small cafés overlooking the beach sell cold beer at reasonable prices.

Places to Stay

Inquiries and bookings for youth hostels should be made through the helpful **Ferijalni Savez Beograd** (☎ 324 8550, fax 322 0762; **w** *www.hostels.org.yu; 2nd floor, Makedonska 22*). You will need to have an HI membership, an international student card or you can join (300 DIN) when booking.

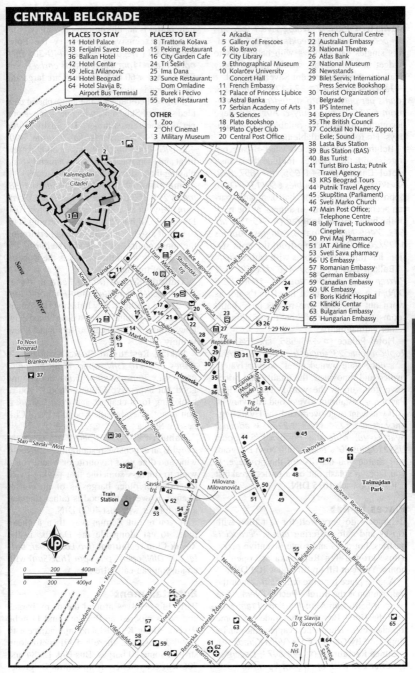

There are two hostels in Belgrade. **Hotel Slavija B** (☎ 450 842; Svetog Save 1-9; rooms per person including breakfast US$11.50) offers singles and doubles with bathrooms to budget travellers. This special price is only available through Ferijalni Savez Beograd.

Jelica Milanovic (☎ 323 1268; Krunska 8; rooms per person with shared/private bathroom €7.50/9; open July & Aug) is college accommodation only available during holidays. No food is available here.

Belgrade is full of state-owned, B-category hotels and their prices include breakfast. **Hotel Centar** (☎ 644 055, fax 657 838; Savski trg 7; singles/doubles 680/1360 DIN), opposite the train station, has basic and spartan accommodation in an annexe at the back of the hotel. **Hotel Beograd** (☎ 645 199, fax 643 746; Nemanjina 6; singles/doubles 1522/2044 DIN), visible from the train station, has time-worn rooms with bathrooms.

Balkan Hotel (☎ 687 466, fax 687 581 Prizrenska 2; singles/doubles 1600/2250 DIN) is a useful central hotel that's not as worn out as some. The rooms have bathrooms, the staff is helpful but the breakfast is rather unimaginative.

Hotel Palace (☎ 185 585, fax 184 458; Topličin venac 23; singles/doubles US$71/92) is a once state-owned hotel. Now privately owned and renovated, the quality and prices have gone up in the world. The top-floor Panorama restaurant gives good city views.

If you want to go overboard, the **Hyatt Regency** (☎ 301 1234, fax 311 2234; e admin@ hyatt.co.yu; Milentija Popovića 5; rooms US$220 plus 20% tax), in dull Novi Beograd, will charge you heavily for the privilege. If you fancy a splash out on a buffet breakfast it'll set you back 1075 DIN.

Places to Eat
Belgraders do very well for fast food with kiosks and cafés offering burek, čevapčići, pastries, hot dogs and some inventive pizza. Those around Trg Republika are open 24 hours. You can fill up for under 100 DIN.

A great place for a breakfast burek near the train station is the **Burek i Pecivo** (Nemanjina 5; open 5am-1pm Mon-Fri, 5am-11am Sat), near the Hotel Beograd. Belgrade has some top-class cafés and the best cappuccino can be sipped at **City Garden Cafe** (Vuka Karadžića).

Sunce Restaurant (☎ 324 8474; Dečanska 1; buffet 249 DIN; open 9am-9pm Mon-Sat)

is a rarity – a vegetarian restaurant. The many-item buffet is an all-you-can-eat variety.

For inexpensive seafood try the **Polet Restaurant** (Njegoševa; meals 140-300 DIN; open 11am-11pm daily) and its corba (spicy fish soup) for 60 DIN. Portions are large and the service is attentive.

For local colour visit the atmospheric cobbled street of Skadarska with open-air evening performances in summer. **Tri Šeširi** (Three Hats; ☎ 324 7501; Skadarska 29; dishes 300-460 DIN; open lunch & dinner daily) offers meat and more meat dishes plus a nightly band playing those stirring Serbian folk songs.

Ima Dana (☎ 323 4422; Skadarska 38; meals 250-350 DIN; open 11am-5pm, 7pm-1am daily) does a lovely pike dish for 1000 DIN a kilo, although the size of serving is up to you. It also has a resident band performing the songs composed in Skadarska during the 19th century when this area was the Bohemian part of the Balkans.

Trattoria Košava (Kralja Petra 6; dishes 300-400 DIN; 9am-1am Mon-Fri, noon-1am Sat & Sun) is a light, airy Italian-style restaurant reportedly doing the best osso bucco ever. Downstairs, a small café offers snacks and yummy cakes.

Peking Restaurant (Vuka Karadžića 2; dishes 275-410 DIN; open 11am-midnight Mon-Sat, 2pm-midnight Sun) does some good but expensive Chinese food if you're hankering for a change, and even kajmak if you're not. There's quite a population of Chinese in Serbia.

Bahus (☎ 602 971; open 10am-midnight daily) is an expensive restaurant where you'd wine and dine your favourite or where you'd want to impress someone that paying twice the price of other barges is of no consequence. However the food is rather fine and a 1kg lobster will cost 4000 DIN.

If you're out Zemun way then a cheap place to eat alongside the Danube is the **Kayak Club restaurant** (Ivo Lola Ribar; buffet 199 DIN; open 2pm-6pm Thur-Sun) with an all-you-can-eat buffet.

Entertainment
Party life revolves around the many barges and boats moored on the Sava and Danube Rivers. Along Kej Oslobođenja, adjacent to Hotel Jugoslavia, there's a kilometre-long strip of some 20 barges. Bus Nos 15, 84 and 706 will get you here from central Belgrade.

Blaywatch *(open 11am-1am daily)* is a play on the TV series *Baywatch* and the Serbian *Blay* which means to do nothing. This is where those with the youth, clothes and money come to flaunt it. **Bibis** *(open 10am-2am daily)* is a much more agreeable place, popular in winter, selling cheaper drinks and also snacks; the beer comes in large pottery mugs decorated with a green kangaroo.

On the western bank of the Sava River is another 1.5km strip of floating bars, restaurants and discos. Here you'll find **Cocktail No Name** playing pop and 80s music, **Zippo** for Serbian folk music, **Exile** pounding out techno and nearby **Sound** playing house and disco. Getting there is by walking over the Brankov Most or by tram No 7, 9 or 11.

Back on land there's the interesting **Oh! Cinema!** *(☎ 328 4000; Kalemegdan Citadel)* café/bar overlooking the Danube and zoo. It's a favourite place to hang out through summer nights with live music, probably giving insomnia to the tigers below.

Rio Bravo *(Kralja Petra 54; open 11am-2am Mon-Fri, 5pm-2am Sat & Sun)* has live bands at the weekend and recorded music other nights. There are four venues offering different music and this is the place for jazz and 1920s Chicago music.

For a mix-and-match evening among the clubs the best place to wander is down Strahinjića Bana, four blocks northeast of Studentski trg.

The **Bilet Servis** *(☎ 625 365; Trg Republike 5; 9am-8pm Mon-Fri, 9am-3pm Sat)* has a counter for event tickets and the English-speaking staff here will happily search for something for you.

During winter there are opera performances at the elegant **National Theatre** *(☎ 620 946; Trg Republike; box office open 10am-2pm Tues-Sun, 10am-3pm performance days)*. **Belgrade Philharmonia** concerts take place in **Kolarčev University** *(☎ 630 550; Studentski trg 5; box office open 10am-noon & 6pm-8pm daily)*, usually on Wednesday and Friday, except in July and August. In October it hosts a festival of classical music.

Concerts also take place in the **Serbian Academy of Arts & Sciences** *(☎ 334 2400; Kneza Mihaila 35; admission free; concerts 6pm Mon & Thur)*, which also presents exhibitions. When we visited there was a display of military and civil uniforms; coal miners even had a dress uniform in communist times. **Dom**

Omladine *(☎ 322 0127; Makedonska 22)* has nonclassical music concerts, film festivals and multimedia events.

The **French Cultural Centre** *(Kneza Mihaila 31; open noon-6pm Mon-Fri, 11am-3pm Sat)* often shows free films and videos.

For the latest Hollywood blockbuster the **Tuckwood Cineplex** *(☎ 323 6517; Kneza Miloša 7; tickets 100-200 DIN)* shows films in either English or with English subtitles.

Getting There & Away

Bus Frequent buses to many places around Yugoslavia leave from both bus stations. Posted destinations are in Cyrillic only and it's easier to buy your ticket from a ticket agency. Sample services are Niš (435 DIN, three hours), Podgorica (850 DIN, nine hours), Budva (900 DIN, 12 hours) and Novi Pazar (275 DIN, three hours) for Kosovo.

Train International trains are covered in more detail in the introductory Getting There & Away section. Overnight trains with couchettes or sleepers travel from Belgrade to Bar (1100 DIN, nine to 11 hours); a sleeper supplement costs 2000 DIN.

There are four trains a day to Novi Sad (120 DIN, two hours), two to Subotica (155 DIN, 3½ hours) and four to Niš (300 DIN, five hours). All trains to Subotica call at Novi Sad and international trains also call at both places.

Train Station Ticket counters are numbered; international tickets are sold at Nos 11 and 12 and regular tickets at Nos 7 to 20. Sleeper and couchette reservations are made at Nos 19 and 20 and information is at Nos 23 and 24. Timetables are in the Latin alphabet. There's a **tourist bureau** *(open 7am-9.30pm daily)*, **exchange bureau** and **sales counter** *(☎/fax 658 868; open 9am-4pm Mon-Sat)* for Eurail passes at the track end of the station.

Getting Around

To/From the Airport Surcin airport is 18km west of Belgrade. Ignore taxi drivers who'll meet you in the airport; they overcharge. Instead go outside and look for a fare from 450 to 600 DIN to Belgrade.

The JAT bus (30 DIN; airport to town hourly 5am to 9pm, town to airport hourly 7am to 8pm) is the best transport between town (Hotel Slavija B, Trg Slavija) and airport via the train station.

Public Transport Private buses and state-owned buses, trams and trolleybuses charge 10 DIN for any journey.

Taxi Belgrade's taxis are in plentiful supply and the flag fall is 40 DIN. A trip around the town centre should cost around 150 DIN. Check that the meter is running. If not, point it out to the driver.

VOJVODINA ВОЈВОДИНА

Until annexed by Serbia in 1990, Vojvodina (21,506 sq km) was an autonomous province. Slavs settled here in the 6th century, Hungarians in the 10th century and Serbs in 1389 after their defeat by the Turks. The region was under Turkish rule from the 16th century until the Habsburgs cleared them out in the late 17th century. Again, it became a refuge for Serbs leaving Turkish-controlled lands farther south. The region remained a part of Hungary until 1918. This low-lying land of many rivers merges imperceptibly into the Great Hungarian Plain and Romania's Banat. Many canals crisscross this fertile plain that provides much of Yugoslavia's wheat, corn and crude oil.

Novi Sad Нови Сад
☎ 021 • pop 270,000 (est. 2002)

Novi Sad, capital of Vojvodina, is a modern city situated at a strategic bend of the Danube. The city developed in the 18th century when a powerful fortress was constructed on a hill top, overlooking the river, to hold the area for the Habsburgs. Novi Sad's attractions are simply wandering the pedestrian streets, such as Dunavska, with their strings of smart boutiques and lively outdoor cafés, and visiting Petrovaradin Citadel.

Orientation & Information The adjacent train and intercity bus stations are at the end of Bulevar Oslobođenja, on the northwestern side. It's a 20-minute walk to the city centre, otherwise catch bus No 11A to the city bus station. Then ask directions to the **tourist office** (☎ 421 811; Dunavska 27) in a quaint old part of town. The **telephone centre** (open 24hr) is next to the **main post office**.

It's easier to buy domestic and international train tickets from **KSR Beograd Tours** (☎ 27 445, fax 27 423; Svetozara Miletića 4) than at the train station. **Atlas Bank** (☎ 421 600; Futoška 2) or the **Micro Finance Bank** (☎ 58 942; Bulevar Cara Lazara 7b) will cash euro or US-dollar travellers cheques.

Novi Sad hosts the Exit Festival in August, attracting music bands from all over Europe.

Things to See & Do The main museum in Novi Sad is **Muzej Vojvodine** (☎ 26 555; Dunavska 35 & 37; admission 20 DIN; open 9am-7pm Tues-Fri, 9am-2pm Sat & Sun) and is housed in two buildings. No 35 covers the

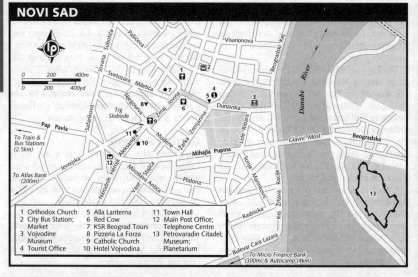

NOVI SAD

1	Orthodox Church	5	Alla Lanterna	11	Town Hall
2	City Bus Station; Market	6	Red Cow	12	Main Post Office; Telephone Centre
3	Vojvodine Museum	7	KSR Beograd Tours	13	Petrovaradin Citadel; Museum; Planetarium
4	Tourist Office	8	Pizzeria La Forza		
		9	Catholic Church		
		10	Hotel Vojvodina		

To Train & Bus Stations (2.5km)

To Atlas Bank (200m)

To Micro Finance Bank (300m) & Autocamp (4km)

history of Vojvodina from Palaeolithic times to the late 19th century; No 37 takes the story to 1945 with emphasis on WWI and WWII. The collection is impressive in its thoroughness and, although captioned in Serbian, the main explanatory panels are in English.

Over the river is the majestic **Petrovaradin Citadel**, the 'Gibraltar of the Danube', built between 1699 and 1780 and designed by the French architect Vauban. Stairs beside the large church in the lower town lead up to the fortress. There's a small **museum** (*☎ 432 055; admission 30 DIN; open 9am-5pm Tues-Sun Apr-June, 9am-5pm July-Mar)* and a **planetarium** (*☎ 433 038; admission 40 DIN; shows 7pm Thur, 5pm Sat & Sun)* in the citadel. The chief pleasure is simply to walk the walls and enjoy the splendid view. Have a close look at the clock tower. The hour hand is the longer one so that the clock would be easy to read from the river.

Places to Stay & Eat On the Danube the large **autocamp** (*☎ 368 400, fax 366 801; Ribarsko Ostrvo; bungalows per double/triple 1400/1745 DIN)* has some basic, well-used bungalow accommodation. Breakfast is not included but there are two restaurants onsite. There's a small zoo, a children's playground and beaches on the Danube. Take bus No 4 from the train station or city centre to Liman and then walk towards the river or take a taxi ride for 80 DIN.

The oldest, most appealing and central of Novi Sad's hotels is **Hotel Vojvodina** (*☎ 622 122, fax 615 445; Trg Slobode 2; singles/ doubles 1600/2200 DIN)*. With an attractive pastel facade, it's convenient but expensive for rooms with bathroom and breakfast.

Alla Lanterna (*☎ 622 002; Dunavska 27; meals 240-290 DIN; open 8am-midnight)* is a pizza/pasta place with bags of atmosphere. Maybe it's something to do with the internal wall decorations that must have taken several truckloads of pebbles. In warm weather the café sprawls onto the pedestrian street.

Pizzeria La Forza (*Katolicka Porta 6; pasta dishes 150-180 DIN; open 8am-11pm Mon-Sat, 3pm-11pm Sun)* is a bright and cheery spot for a quick bite with a good selection of filling pasta.

The **Red Cow** (*cnr Dunavska & Zmaj Jovina)* is a trendy Irish pub that's just the place for a refreshing Guinness or draught Nikšić or an evening out.

Getting There & Away Novi Sad is served by frequent local trains to Belgrade (120 DIN, two hours) and Subotica (112 DIN, 1½ hours), plus international trains.

Subotica Суботица
☎ 024 • pop 150,000 (est. 2002)

At 10km from the border at Kelebija, Subotica is a useful transit point to/from Szeged (Hungary); it's also worth a day trip from Belgrade. The train station is just a short walk from the town centre.

The **Micro Finance Bank** (*Lenjina Park 8)* cashes travellers cheques and there's a **currency exchange office** (*open 8am-7pm Mon-Fri, 8am-1pm Sat)* in the old town hall.

The train station has a **left-luggage office** (*37.50 DIN per item; open 24hr)* and an **exchange office**.

Things to See The imposing Art Nouveau **town hall** (*Trg Republike)*, built in 1910, contains an excellent **historical museum** (*open 9am-2pm Tues-Sat)* on the 1st floor (captions in Serbian and Hungarian) displaying regional life and a mammoth skull. Check whether the exquisitely decorated council chambers are open. The dark varnished wood, green baize cloth and high-backed chairs give a succinct air of petty municipal power.

An equally exquisite piece of architecture is the amazingly beautiful Art Nouveau **Modern Art Gallery** (*Trg Lenina 5; open 7am-1pm Mon, Wed & Fri, 7am-6pm Tues & Thur, 9am-noon Sat)*.

Places to Stay & Eat The only hotel in Subotica is **Hotel Patria** (*☎ 554 500, fax 551 762; Đure Đakovica; singles/doubles 1800/ 2800 DIN)*, where rooms come with bath and breakfast. Avis has a desk here (see also Rental under Car & Motorcycle in the introductory Getting Around chapter) and the hotel can organise local excursions. There's a youth hostel **Zorka** (*☎ 754 418; Palić; per person €6, full board €12)* by the lake at Palić for budget accommodation.

There is a dearth of restaurants in the town centre but the **Pizza Vento** (*Borisa Kidriča 2; pizzas 160-200 DIN; open 7am-midnight)* is a relaxing spot for a decently large pizza and a beer. Go to **Lipa** (*Đure Đakovica 13, burek 60 DIN; open 24hr)*, a bakery and *burek* shop, for an excellent cheese and mushroom *burek* and yogurt for breakfast. **Ravel Nušićeva**

(Trg Republike; open 9am-10pm daily) does the best line in squidgy cakes and some excellent coffee.

Getting There & Away There are two local trains a day to/from Szeged, Hungary (155 DIN, 1¾ hours), and international trains. Trains to Belgrade (155 DIN, 3½ hours) also call at Novi Sad. Five daily buses serve Szeged and Subotica (€2.50, 1½ hours) but the train is more convenient.

SMEDEREVO СМЕДЕРЕВО

Smederevo Fortress *(admission 10 DIN; open daylight hours)* is a triangular fort with 25 towers and a water moat fronting the Danube River. An inner citadel overlooks the river. Built by despot Djuradj Brankovic, it served as his capital from 1428 to 1430. The fortifications were never really tested in battle and the only damage has been wrought by time and the massive explosion of an ammunition train in WWII.

Smederevo Museum *(admission 10 DIN; open 10am-5pm Mon-Fri, 10am-3pm Sat & Sun)* is a 'history of the town' museum with artefacts dating from Roman times and some interesting frescoes. A half-hourly bus service (130 DIN, 1½ hours) from Belgrade makes this a pleasant day trip.

NIŠ НИШ

☎ 018 • pop 300,000 (est. 2002)

Niš lies at the junction of several international road and rail routes. It was first settled in pre-Roman times and flourished during the time of local boy made good, Emperor Constantine (280–337 AD). Turkish rule lasted from 1386 until 1877 despite several Serb revolts, of which the Ćele Kula is a gruesome reminder (for details see its entry in the Things to See section later).

Orientation & Information

Just north of the river is Tvrđava Citadel and to the west is the main market area and the bus station. The train station is to the west on Dimitrija Tucovića.

The very helpful staff at the **Tourist Organisation of Niš** *(☎ 523 455; Gen Milojka Lešjanina 26)* can provide some basic tourist literature in English.

The **Micro Finance Bank** *(☎/fax 547 845; Lole Ribara 19)* will cash euro or US-dollar travellers cheques.

The **Web Caffe** *(Kultur Centre, 3rd floor, Pobede; open 9am-midnight Mon-Sat, noon-midnight Sun)* is a central Internet café charging 90 DIN an hour.

KSR Beograd *(☎ 523 808; Trg Oslobođenja 9)* sells train tickets in a more relaxed and helpful atmosphere than the train station.

Things to See

Tvrđava *(Jadranska; admission free; open 24hr)* is a citadel that was built by the Turks in 1396 on the site of a Roman fortress. It's a large open area, bounded by a defensive stone wall, with nothing within to get wildly excited about; even the small **mosque** seems to be an empty shell.

The macabre **Ćele Kula** *(Tower of Skulls; Brače Taskovića; admission 60 DIN; open 9am-4pm Tues-Sat, 10am-2pm Sun)* was erected by the Turks in 1809 as a warning to would-be Serbian rebels. During 1809 a force under the Duke of Resava trying to liberate Niš, attacked a larger Turkish force. The Serbs suffered heavily. The Duke rushed the Turkish defences and fired his pistol into their powder magazine. The resulting explosion reportedly wiped out 4000 Serbs and 10,000 Turks. When the battle was won all the dead Serbs were beheaded, scalped and their skulls embedded in this short square tower. Only 58 remain.

Mediana *(Sofia rd; admission site free, museum 20 DIN; open 9am-4pm Tues-Sat 10am-2pm Sun)*, on the eastern outskirts of Niš, is the remains of a 4th-century Roman palace complex possibly belonging to the emperor Constantine the Great. Archaeological digging has revealed a palace, forum and a large grain storage area with some large, almost intact, pottery vessels.

Places to Stay & Eat

Niš Hotel *(☎ 24 643, fax 23 779; Voždova 12; singles/doubles 1550/2230 DIN)* is probably the best-value hotel in town. The rooms are large and come with bathrooms.

Casablanca *(☎ 40 750; Jeronimova 26; dishes 180-350 DIN; open noon-1am)* has a varied menu with Mexican, French, Italian and Greek dishes accompanied on most nights with a similar mix in music.

Tramvaj *(Tramway; Pobede 9)* is an intriguing small café in the centre of town that has an Isle of Man (UK) tram as its servery while customers sit on slatted tram benches.

The Tramvaj does a nice aromatic coffee and the staff is very interested in anyone who is keen on trams.

Montenegro
Црна Гора

From an interior with Alpine-type scenery to giddy-deep canyons, coastal fjords, and a sparsely vegetated and highly folded limestone mountain range that plummets down to an azure Adriatic sea, the 13,812-sq-km **Republic of Montenegro** (Crna Gora) has got the works.

North of Podgorica, both the railway and road run through the Moraca Canyon, while 40km west of Mojkovac is the 1.3km-deep Tara Canyon. Other striking features include the winding Bay of Kotor, the largest fjord in southern Europe, and the vast, beautiful and ecologically significant Lake Skadar. Of historical interest are the old towns of Budva, Cetinje and the walled cities of Kotor and Herceg Novi.

Montenegro is a very popular holiday spot; June to September is the high season peaking in July and August. Quoted accommodation prices are for the high season.

History
Only tiny Montenegro was able to keep its head above the Turkish tide that engulfed the Balkans for over four centuries from the 14th century omwards. From 1482 Montenegro was ruled from Cetinje by *vladike* (bishops). With the defeat of the Turks in 1878, Montenegrin independence was assured and was later recognised by the Congress of Berlin. Nicola I Petrovic, Montenegro's ruler, declared himself king in 1910 but was evicted by the Austrians in 1916; after the end of WWI, Montenegro was incorporated into Serbia. During WWII Montenegrins fought valiantly in Tito's partisan army and afterwards the region was rewarded with republic status within Yugoslavia.

Montenegro has been in the Yugoslav federation through its several incarnations, but recently a burgeoning independence movement has developed. Under the proposed new union with Serbia, Milo Đukanović, President of Montenegro has placed any independence moves on hold.

Getting There & Away
You can enter Montenegro by road from Croatia, Serbia, Kosovo and Albania or by ship from Italy. Crossing into Albania at Božaj requires a €20 taxi ride from Podgorica, walking over the border and catching an onward taxi. Similarly it's a €15 taxi ride from Herceg Novi to the Croatian border or catch the one daily bus to the border. For details on crossing into Kosovo see the Rožaje section later in this chapter.

The only international rail connections are through Serbia. A main rail line runs from Belgrade to Bar where ferries connect for Italy.

PODGORICA ПОДГОРИЦА
☎ 081 • pop 170,000 (est. 2002)
Podgorica is a place to arrive in, do your business and leave. Don't bother to stay here. The cheapest hotel charges foreigners €50, twice that for a local. It's far better to go south and stay at the cheaper private rooms and apartments on the coast.

Orientation & Information
The train and bus stations (including a post office branch) are adjacent in the eastern part of the town. The hub of the town centres around Slobode. **Atlas Bank** (☎ 248 870; Stanka Dragojevića 4-6; open 8am-4pm Mon-Fri, 8am-1pm Sat) will cash AmEx and Thomas Cook travellers cheques and the **Podgorica Bank** (Novaka Miloševa 8a; open 7am-8pm Mon-Sat) will give cash advances up to €500 on Visa cards.

You'll find an Internet café, **Internet cg** (Vučedolska 13; open 9am-9pm Mon-Sat), off Slobode, that charges €1.80 an hour.

JAT (☎ 244 248, fax 245 065; Ivana Milutinovica 20) runs an airport transfer bus (€1.50) leaving from its office 1½ hours before every flight and returning following each arrival. **Montenegro Airlines** (☎ 224 406, fax 246 207; e officepg@mgx.cg.yu; Slobode 23) flies to Frankfurt, Zürich and Budapest.

Places to Eat
There are some cheap eating places around the bus and train stations, and some pleasant cafés in Bokeška.

The **Pizzeria Leone** (Njegoševa 42; pizzas €3.15-4.20; open 8am-midnight Mon-Sat, 3pm-midnight Sun) caters for the Montenegrins' love of Italian food and also serves the excellent local Nikšić beer.

Getting There & Away

There are five buses daily to Belgrade (€14, nine hours), five to Žabljak (€6, four hours), 10 to Rožaje (€6, four hours), many to Budva (€3.25, 1½ hours). A bus leaves each Sunday and Wednesday at 7.30am for İstanbul, which costs €100.

You can fly to Belgrade for €46.50 or take the scenic train route (€8 plus €9 sleeper supplement, eight hours). There are frequent trains to Bar and two daily trains to Nikšić (€1.60, two hours).

LAKE SKADAR & VIRPAZAR

A causeway carries road and rail transport from Podgorica to Bar over the western edge of the 44km-long Lake Skadar. The biggest lake in the Balkans, it's one of the largest bird sanctuaries and remaining pelican habitats in Europe. Jutting westward from the causeway is the 400-year old Turkish castle of Lesendro. Check with the **Gorbis travel agency** (☎ 081-230 624; e gorbis@cg.yu; Slobode 47) in Podgorica about trips on the lake.

Alternatively nose around Virpazar, south of the causeway, where in summer there are likely to be sightseeing boats. In Virpazar you'll also find one of the finest restaurants in the whole of Montenegro, the 100-year-old **Pelican Restaurant** (Virpazar; dishes €5-10; open 8am-midnight daily), decorated quite exotically with dried plants and herbs, old photographs and nautical ephemera. However it's really the service that provides the ambience and dessert is always on the house. For starters try dalmatinsko varvo, a potato, onion and spinach pie and follow that with a fish salad of perch, eel or trout – all fresh from the lake. Weekend evenings, May to September, there's live music. The Pelican also has **accommodation** (doubles €20 with shared bathroom).

BAR БАР
☎ 085

Backed by a precipitous coastal range, Bar is a would-be modern city and Yugoslavia's only port. There's little to attract a visitor to Bar except as a convenient transport centre.

The ferry terminal in Bar is 300 metres from town centre but the bus and train stations are about 2km southeast of the centre.

Tourist information is very limited and your best bet is to try **Montenegro Tourist** (☎ 311 133; Obala 13 Jula) by the ferry terminal.

Places to Stay & Eat

Visitors with plenty of time or their own transport will be able to choose from a whole range of places with 'sobe', 'zimmer' or 'private room' signs all along the coast. **Adria Tours** (☎ 313 621; Novo Pristanište 65; full board singles/doubles €15/29), a couple of kilometres northwest at Šušanj, can arrange accommodation.

Hotel Topolica (☎ 311 013, fax 312 731; e htpkorali@cg.yu; B-grade singles/doubles including breakfast €16.85/25.60), a four-storey socialist relic, is the only hotel in town. The B-grade section at the back comes with private bathrooms and shabby furniture. If you ask you can get a room with a sea view.

Places to eat are limited with drinks-only cafés and bars outnumbering restaurants. **Pizeria Bell** (Vladimira Rolovic, Podkovica C; pizza €3, pasta €4-5; open 7am-11pm daily), is just up the street from the ferry terminal. It is a small cosy pizza/pasta joint that's open year-round.

Getting There & Away

Four trains a day travel to and from Belgrade (€8, nine hours). The couchette supplement is €9, making this cheap accommodation plus transport.

There are two buses every day to Ulcinj (€1.80, 1½ hours) and frequent buses daily to Budva (€2, 45 minutes) and Kotor (€3.20, three hours).

Montenegro Lines (☎ 312 336; Obala 13 Jula) sails at 10pm on Tuesday, Thursday and Saturday to Bari (Italy). In summer it's a daily service. Deck passage (10 hours) costs €40 and a bunk from €13. For ferries to Ancona (Italy) chat to **Mecur** (☎ 313 617, fax 313 618; e mercur@eunet.yu; Obala 13 Jula). The Thursday service takes 16 hours and costs €46 for a deck seat.

In midsummer, transport to/from Bar is very crowded as all of Serbia heads for the beach.

ULCINJ УЛЦИЊ
☎ 085

Founded by the Greeks, Ulcinj gained notoriety as a North African pirate base between 1571 and 1878. There was even a market for slaves from whom the few resident black families are descended. The Turks held the area for over 300 years and today there are many Muslim Albanians in Ulcinj. Many Kosovars fled here as refugees in 1999 and come today as holiday makers. The busy season is July and August when Ulcinj bulges at the seams with several thousand extra people.

Orientation & Information
Buses from Bar stop on the edge of town. Walk into town by turning right onto 26 Novembar at the first major junction. Mala Plaža (Small Beach) is below the old town at the end of 26 Novembar. Velika Plaža (Great Beach), Ulcinj's famous 12km stretch of unbroken sand, begins about 5km southeast of the town (take the Ada bus or a minibus in season).

intron cyber caffe (26 Novembar; open 9am-2pm daily) is up a side alley just opposite Caffe Montenegro; one hour costs €2.50.

Things to See
The ancient ramparts of old Ulcinj (Stari Grad) overlook the sea, but most of the buildings inside were shattered by earthquakes in 1979 and later reconstructed. The museum (open 7am-noon Mon-Fri) containing Montenegrin and Turkish artefacts is by the upper gate. You can walk among the houses and along the wall for the view.

Places to Stay
The camping ground Tomi is east of Milena and adjacent to Velika Plaža; it's open May to September. Farther on (100 metres), there's a sign to HTP Velika Plaža (☎ 413 145; Ada Rd), offering a variety of accommodation. Inappropriately named houses (per person with shared bathroom €3) have two beds with just enough walk-around space; bungalows (per person with private bathroom €5) take three people and have more space; and pavilions (per person with private bathroom €8) are larger still and also take three people. Out-of-season prices are 20% less. Restaurants onsite offer breakfast/lunch/dinner cost €3/6/4.

The many private rooms and apartments can be booked through a travel agency like Real Estate Tourist Agency (☎ 421 609, fax 421 612; w www.realestate.cg.yu; 26 Novembar). It can also organise accommodation in private rooms (from €10, no meals) or in a hotel (doubles from €42, breakfast/ half-board/ full board €4/9/12).

Of the several hotels the Albatros (☎ 423 628, fax 423 263; e info@hoteli-albatros .cg.yu; A-category singles/doubles €37.90/ 58.30, B-category €29.30/45.10) is a pleasant modern hotel, 15 minutes' walk up the hill

from Mala Plaža. Rooms all have private bathrooms and the price includes full board. Guests can use the sauna, fitness room and swimming pool.

Places to Eat
There are some chic eating places like the Restaurant Teuta (038 137; Stari Grad; dishes €13-25; open 8am-late daily) in the Old Town if your budget can take it. You're paying for good food and a rooftop view over the town and sea. On the seafront is a string of restaurants specialising in seafood; try the Marinero (Obala Borisa Kidriča; dishes €15; open 7am-late daily) for coffee or a full meal.

There are also numerous inexpensive cafés around town offering čevapčići. Gallo Nero (☎ 315 245; 26 Novembar; dishes €5-12; open 10am-late daily) has the best food in Ulcinj, matched by excellent service. You can come here for a snack or a full-blown meal.

Getting There & Away
Buses to Bar (€1.60, 45 minutes) run every couple of hours in season. There's only one bus, late in the day, to Podgorica so go via Bar. Many minibuses and buses ply the road to Ada (and Velika Plaža) from the market place or the main post office for €1.50 in season.

BUDVA БУДВА
☎ 086
Budva is Yugoslavia's top beach resort. Fine beaches punctuate the coastline all the way to Sveti Stefan, with high barren coastal mountains forming a magnificent backdrop.

The modern bus station (no left-luggage office) is about 1km from the Old Town. The main square is at the end of Mediteranska by the harbour, where JAT (☎ 41 641; Mediteranska 2) has an office. Its bus (€2) travels between Tivat airport and the office, leaving 1½ hours before each flight.

Things to See
Budva's big tourist-puller is its old walled town. Levelled by two earthquakes in 1979, it has since been completely rebuilt as a tourist attraction. It's so picturesque it seems almost contrived. Budva's main beach is pebbly and average. Mogren Beach is better, follow the coastal path northwards for 500m from the Grand Hotel Avala.

About 5km southeast of Budva is the former village of Sveti Stefan, which is an island now linked to the mainland and a luxury hotel complex. Admission is €3.75 so settle for the long-range picture-postcard view.

Places to Stay & Eat

If you are travelling with a tent, try **Autocamp Avala** (☎ 451 205; open June-Sept) at Boreti, 2km on the road to Bar or the manager may help you find a private room nearby.

Again there's a whole string of private rooms, apartments and hotels on this coastal strip, just look out for signs that say *'sobe'*, *'zimmer'* or *'rooms'*. The helpful **Globtour** (☎ 451 020, fax 52 827; e globtourbd@cg .yu; Mediteranska 23) can arrange **private rooms** (half-board/full board €7.50/10).

Pleasant, B-grade **Hotel Mediteran** (☎ 51 423; Bečiči; rooms per person €27), booked by **Maestral Tours** (☎/fax 52 250; Mediteranska 23), is about 2km south along the coast. This rambling holiday hotel has several restaurants, an English pub and a private part of the beach.

The handiest hotel for the old part of the city is the modern **Hotel Mogren** (☎ 452 041, fax 51 750; singles/doubles €40.90/66.40) just outside the northern gate of the Old Town. Rates are very high during the peak season but the rooms are well equipped and quite large; some have balconies overlooking the Old Town.

Budva has no shortage of expensive bars and restaurants in the Old Town or along the harbourside. Probably the best is the **Restaurant Jadran** (☎ 451 028; Slovenska obala 10; dishes €5-10; open 8am-late daily), with some very appetising fish dishes. It's a circular restaurant decked out with nautical junk and with an outside patio overlooking the floodlit Old Town.

Getting There & Away

There are frequent buses to Podgorica (€3.25, 1½ hours) that pass through Cetinje (€2, 35 minutes), Kotor (€1.70, 30 minutes) and Bar (€2, one hour). There are also eight buses daily to Belgrade (€15, 12 hours) and one to Žabljak (€8, four hours).

KOTOR КОТОР
☎ 082

Kotor is a big secret. Not only is the town at the head of southern Europe's deepest fjord, but it also has a walled medieval city that is Unesco listed.

Orientation & Information

Four kilometres of walls encircle the Old Town (another Stari Grad) built over a thousand years from the 9th century. The main access is via an 18th-century gate fronting onto the harbour. Within is an entanglement of small streets and lanes linking squares where the main aristocratic families had mansions. Six Romanesque churches date from the 12th and 13th centuries, St Tripun's Cathedral (1166) being the most important. Also significant is a 6th-century clock tower.

For information on accommodation try **Mercur Intours** (☎ 325 113, fax 325 137; Stari Grad, opposite the main entrance) and **Meridian Travel Agency** (☎ 11 188, fax 11 226; e travel@cg.yu; Stari Grad); both have helpful English-speaking staff.

Within the Old Town **IDK Computers** (Stari Grad; open 2pm-midnight summer, 5pm-midnight rest of year) charges €2 per hour for Internet access.

Things to See & Do

The major attraction by far is wandering around the Old Town, popping into the old churches, dawdling for coffee at the pavement cafés and people-watching. Energetic? Then slog up the steep winding path to the old fortifications on the mountainside above Kotor. You'll be rewarded with stunning views of Kotor fjord.

Kotor has a proud maritime history and the **Maritime Museum** (Stari Grad; admission €1; open 7am-7pm Mon-Sat & 9am-5pm Sun May-Sept, 7am-3pm Mon-Fri & 9am-noon Sat & Sun Oct-Apr) covers much of it over its three storeys of displays. A leaflet in English is available.

If you have transport then travel to Cetinje via a string of hairpin bends over the mountains. The views are marvellous. Alternatively drive around the fjord and see all the little stone harbours cuddling braces of small boats against the waves.

Places to Stay and Eat

For **private rooms** (per person from €8) and **hotels** (doubles half-board €34.60) contact the information booth outside the main entrance to the city or try a travel agency (see Orientation & Information earlier).

Hotel Rendezvous (☎ 16 796; Stari Grad; singles/doubles €20/40) is a private hotel above a small bar. For its price it's the best value within the Old Town. The rooms, although they are small, are quite acceptable and have private bathrooms. It can be a bit noisy at night.

Bastion Restaurant *(Stari Grad; dishes €5-8; open 10am-late)* is a small, almost unannounced, restaurant near St Mary's church in the north-eastern part of the Old Town. It's a very popular lunchtime venue and you may need to wait for a table. Although rather pricey the food is fresh, hot and tasty.

The **Pizzeria Giardino** *(Stari Grad; meals €3.50-5; open 9am-late)* is probably the best value restaurant within the Old Town. The pizza marinara was one of the best we tasted in Montenegro.

Getting There & Away
The bus station is south of the Old Town. Frequent buses ply to Podgorica (€4.50, two hours), Herceg Novi (€2, one hour) and Budva (€1.50, 30 minutes). If you are driving, the shortest way to Herceg Novi is via the ferry at Lepetane (€3.50 per car, every half hour).

AROUND KOTOR
Perast is a small waterside village about 30km from Kotor. The interest here is the small island in the fjord called **Lady of the Rock**. What is remarkable is that this is an artificial island that was created by the locals over 550 years by taking and dropping stones on the site every July 22. An underwater rock helped the work start and a later sinking of 87 captured ships loaded with rocks made island-creation a little easier.

Between mid-May and mid-October boats regularly ply between the island and Perast for €1 return; just ask on the waterfront. A hourly minibus service connects with Kotor for €1.

HERCEG NOVI ХЕРЦЕГ НОВИ
☎ 088
Herceg Novi is another walled town, a day trip from Kotor or Budva, that's also the nearest town to the Croatian border.

Private accommodation *(per person €5-8)* and **hotels** *(singles/doubles including breakfast from €25/36)* can be arranged through **Gorbis** *(☎ 26 085; Njegoševa 64)*, which is also a ticketing agency. There are many small restaurants and bars around the old citadel. The bus station is on the main highway with a frequent bus service to Kotor (€1, one hour).

CETINJE ЦЕТИЊЕ
☎ 086
Cetinje, perched on a high plateau above Budva, is the old capital of Montenegro, and is subject of songs and epic poems. Many remains of old Cetinje, from the museums to palaces, mansions and monasteries. At the start of the 20th century all the large states of Europe had embassies here. Short hikes can be made in the hills behind Cetinje Monastery.

From the bus station turn left and then right and you will find the main square, Balšica Pazar. There is a big wall map in the square to help you get oriented.

There are no banks here for exchanging your money.

Things to See & Do
The most imposing building in Cetinje is the former parliament, which is now the **National Museum of Montenegro** *(Novice Cerovic; admission €1.50; open 9am-5pm daily in season, 9am-2.30pm Mon-Fri off season)*. It houses extensive exhibits showcasing Montenegro from 60,000 BC to the modern day. On display are many old books, some copies of frescoes, 44 captured Turkish flags and the coat (three bullet holes in the back) of Duke Danlo, last prince-bishop, who was killed in Kotor in 1860.

Adjacent to the museum is the 1832 residence of the prince-bishop Petar II Petrovic Njegoš, also a museum and known as **Biljarda Hall** *(admission €1.50; open 9am-5pm in season, 9am-2pm off season)* because of the billiard table installed in 1840. The Hall houses a fascinating relief map of Montenegro, which was created by the Austrians in 1917 for tactical planning purposes.

The **Royal Court** *(admission €2; open 9am-3pm Mon-Fri off season, 9am-5pm daily in season)* is the former residence (1871) of Nicola Petrović I, the last king of Montenegro. Although looted during WWII, sufficient furnishings, many stern portraits and period weapons remain to give a picture of the times.

Twenty kilometres away on the summit of **Mt Lovcen** (1749m), the 'Black Mountain' that gave Montenegro its Italian name, is the mausoleum of Petar II Petrovic Njegoš, a revered poet and ruler. Take a taxi and then climb 461 steps to the mausoleum with its sweeping view of the Bay of Kotor, mountains, coast and, on a clear morning, Italy.

YUGOSLAVIA

Cetinje Monastery Founded in 1484, and rebuilt 1785, Cetinje Monastery (*€0.50; 8am-7pm daily May-Oct, groups only Nov-Apr*) contains a copy of the *Oktoih* or *Octoechos* (Book of the Eight Voices), printed near here in 1494 – it's one of the oldest collections of liturgical songs in a Slavic language. For the curious, or devout, the monastery has a portion of the true cross and the mummified right hand of St John the Baptist. The latter, important as the hand that baptised Christ, is set in a be-jewelled casket with a little glass window. It takes some imagination to conjure it as a hand.

The museum houses a collection of portraits, vestments, ancient hand-written texts and gifts from Russian churches.

Places to Stay & Eat
If you want a **private room** (*€5 per person*) ask at **Alliance Tours** (☎ *31 157;* e *alliance@ cg.yu; Njegoševa 32; open Mon-Sat*) next door to the post office; it also sells airline tickets and has tourist information. **Petar Martinovic** (☎ *31 809; Bajova Pivljanina 19; beds €7.50-10*) offers accommodation without meals. The rooms in this corner house are quite comfortable; the more expensive ones have bathrooms.

Otherwise, the only hotel is the **Grand Hotel** (☎ *31 876, fax 31 213; Njegoševa; singles/doubles €25.57/40.92*), a modern overrated 'five-star' hotel where rooms come with bathroom and breakfast. There's a disco on Friday and Sunday nights and a swimming pool.

There's no glut of eating places in Cetinje. **Restoran Korzo** (*Njegoševa; mains €3-5; open 8am-11pm daily*) next to the post office has a big mixed grill speciality that is popular locally. **Gradska Kafana** (*dishes €4-6; open 7am-11pm daily*), next door to the Royal Court, has an expansive courtyard for some al fresco dining.

Getting There & Away
With a frequent bus services from Kotor (€2, 45 minutes) and Budva (€2, 35 minutes), Cetinje is an easy day trip.

DURMITOR NATIONAL PARK
☎ 0872
Durmitor National Park is a popular hiking and mountaineering area just west of the ski resort **Žabljak**, the highest town in Yugoslavia at 1450m.

Some 18 mountain lakes dot the Durmitor Range and you can walk around the largest, **Crno jezero** (*Black Lake*), which is 3km from Žabljak, in an hour or two and take a swim in summer. The massive rounded hump of Meded (2287m) rises directly behind the lake surrounded by a backdrop of other peaks, including Savin kuk (2313m), which can be climbed in eight hours there and back. The 1.3km-deep **Tara Canyon** that cuts dramatically into the earth for about 80km is best seen from a rock promontory at Curevac, a €4 taxi ride away.

Durmitor enjoys two tourist seasons, June to September and December to March. Be prepared as the weather is very changeable, even in summer.

Orientation & Information
Žabljak town centre is around the junction of the Nikšić road from the south and the Đurdevica Tara bridge road. Here there's a tourist information centre, taxi stand and bus stop. Adjacent is the Hotel Žabljak, Ski Centar Durmitor and a supermarket. The **bus station**, on the Nikšić road, is at the southern end of town.

The **Tourist Information Centre** (☎ *61 659; town centre; open 8am-8pm daily in season, 8am-3pm off season*) has maps and some fine books but the attendant doesn't speak English. For more information go to Sveti Đordije (see its entry in the following Places to Stay & Eat section) where the owner speaks English, German and Italian.

The **Durmitor National Park office** (☎ *61 474, fax 61 346; next to Hotel Durmitor; open 7am-2pm Mon-Fri*) sells good maps of the park and has a small exhibition of local fauna and flora.

Places to Stay & Eat
Sveti Đordije (☎/*fax 61 367; Njegoševa*), just opposite the turn-off to Hotel Jezera, is a tourist agency that can arrange **private rooms** (*per person with shared bathroom from €6.50, 4-person apartment €34*). Out of season there's a 20% discount; half-board costs an extra €7.50 per person.

The Tourist Information Centre arranges accommodation in **private rooms** (*winter/ summer season €5-7.50/4-6*).

Ski Centar Durmitor (☎ *61 144, fax 61 579; town centre*) is quite happy to book hotel accommodation for you.

Planinka (☎ 61 344; singles/doubles half-board €20/30), which is in the town centre, and **Hotel Jezera** (☎ 61 103, fax 61 579; Nje-goševa; singles/doubles €25/40 B&B) are both modern ski hotels with good amenities, restaurants and bars.

The **Hotel Žabljak** (☎ 61 300; town centre; singles/doubles with breakfast €18/26) has quite reasonable rooms with bathrooms. Out of season this may be the only hotel open.

On a hill top five minutes' walk beyond the national park office is **Autocamp Ivan-do**, which is just a fenced-off field. People around here rent **private rooms** (€6 per person) but bring your own sleeping bag. Set right in the middle of the forest, Ivan-do is a perfect base for hikers.

National Restaurant (☎ 61 337; dishes €5-8.50; open 8am-late daily), behind the city council offices; is a new restaurant-bar. Try its kačamak with sour milk (like yogurt) if you're hungry. We had it for lunch, didn't need an evening meal and even next day's breakfast was a struggle. On a cold winter's day a glass or two of loza (grappa) is very warming.

All the hotels have **restaurants** open to nonresidents.

Activities

In winter there's skiing, snowboarding, motor-sledging or having fun with a dog-drawn team. In summer there's rafting trips down the steep forested Tara Gorge and over countless foaming rapids. These begin at Splavište near the Đurdevica Tara bridge. There's also horse riding, hiking, cycling, mountaineering and paragliding.

The **Sports Association** (☎ 069 477 681) rents out motor sledges (from €20/35 per half/one hour). **Ski Centar Durmitor** arranges ski passes (€6.15/35.79 per day/week), ski lessons (€3.07/17.90 for one/seven lessons) and also equipment rental (€3.07/17.90 per day/week).

Rafting is a group activity but individuals can join by prior arrangement. **Sveti Đordije** offers two-/three-day trips for €200/250 per person including transfers, accommodation and food. A one-day trip with food, transfers and accommodation costs €80. The minimum group size is eight. Ski Centar Durmitor organises trips for groups of 25.

Sveti Đordije also organises summer day tours around the Durmitor area. Typically these are for six to eight people (individuals may join) and cost €30 per person. The day trip includes a visit to the **Piva Monastery**, near the Bosnian border, which has remarkable frescoes.

The **Durmitor National Park office** also offers rafting trips for €150 for a group of 10, although individuals can join. It has horses for hire for €25/50 for a half/whole day, including an English-speaking guide.

Getting There & Away

There's a 4.30am and 4pm bus to Belgrade (€12.25, 10 hours) and also services to Pod-gorica (€6.10, 5½ hours), Nikšić (€5, 2½ hours) and Mojkovac (€3.50, 3½ hours). At Mojkovac you can connect with Bar-Belgrade trains. There is one daily direct bus from Bel-grade to Žabljak (750 DIN, 10 hours).

ROŽAJE РОЖАЈЕ

This town is a gateway to Kosovo and if you're forced to stay there's the dreadful **Rožaje Hotel** (☎ 0871-71 335; Maršala Tita 1; singles/doubles with bath €26/47), with its thoroughly abused rooms.

Rožaje is on the Podgorica to Belgrade bus route with five buses to Podgorica (€4.50, four hours) and three to Belgrade (€8.50, six hours) a day. For Kosovo there's the option of a taxi (€20) or minibus (€5) from outside the bus station to Peja. There's also a 2pm bus direct to Peja (€4, two hours).

Kosovo

Since June 1999, Kosovo has been adminis-tered as a UN-NATO protectorate. Before ethnic cleansing, some two million people occupied Kosovo's 10,887 sq km, making it a densely populated region with a high birth rate. Albanian refugees have returned but this divided province still has the remaining Serbs living in ghettos. Many Serbs are refugees in Serbia and Montenegro.

The Albanians adopted Islam after the Turkish conquest and today the region has a definite Muslim air, from food and dress to the ubiquitous mosques.

History

Following their defeat in 1389 by the Turks, the Serbs abandoned the region to the Albani-ans, descendants of the Illyrians, the original inhabitants.

When the Turks left Kosovo in 1913 Serbia regained control. In the ensuing years 500,000 Albanians emigrated and Serbs were brought in to settle the vacated land. In WWII, the territory was incorporated into Italian-controlled Albania, then liberated in October 1944 by Albanian communist partisans.

Tito wanted Albania united with Kosovo in the new Yugoslavia. It never happened. Two decades of pernicious neglect ensued until an autonomous province was created in 1974 and economic aid increased. Little changed and the standard of living in Kosovo remained a quarter of the Yugoslav average. In 1981 demonstrations calling for full republic status were put down by military force; 300 died and 700 were imprisoned.

Trouble began anew in November 1988 with demonstrations against the sacking of local officials and president Azem Vllasi. Further unrest and a coal miners' strike in February 1989 led to the suspension of Kosovo's autonomy and a state of emergency. Serious rioting followed with 24 unarmed Albanian civilians shot dead. In July 1990 the Serbian parliament cancelled Kosovo's autonomy, broadcasts in Albanian ceased, and the only Albanian-language newspaper was banned. Some 115,000 Albanians lost their jobs and were replaced by loyalist Serbs. Despite Serbian opposition, a referendum with a 90% turnout produced a 98% vote for independence.

The Kosovo Liberation Army (KLA) was formed in 1996 out of frustrated attempts to negotiate autonomy. Early in 1998 the Yugoslav army attacked the village of Prekaz in central Kosovo and using heavy armour almost wiped out the Jeshari clan. The Serbs claimed Adem Jeshari, now a Kosovo folk hero, was a terrorist. Fifty-three were killed including women and young children.

This massacre of the Jeshari galvanised international opinion and thousands flocked to join the KLA. Condemned widely by most international governments, the Milošević regime continued its clampdown, attracting a US-led arms embargo.

In March 1999, during talks in Paris a US-backed plan to return Kosovo's autonomy was rejected by Serbia. Stepping up attacks on the KLA, Serbia moved to empty the country of its Albanian population. Nearly 850,000 Albanian Kosovars fled to Albania and Macedonia. Serbia ignored demands to desist and NATO unleashed a bombing campaign on 24 March 1999. On 2 June Milošević acquiesced to a UN settlement, Serb forces withdrew and the Kosovo Force (KFOR), comprising of NATO and Russian forces, took over.

Peace has not been easy. KFOR had to persuade the KLA to demilitarise and the Serb population to return. Potential and real revenge attacks on the remaining Serbs have made them isolated communities protected by KFOR. Many properties have been destroyed and Orthodox churches and monasteries are guarded by KFOR troops.

The elections in November 2001 and subsequent all-party discussions resulted in a coalition government with Ibrahim Rugova as the president of Kosovo. A cabinet seat has been reserved for the Serbs but their requested Ministry (return of refugees) is not within the remit of the new government; it's responsibility still controlled by the UN.

There is a gradual process with the new government in Serbia to normalise relations and this is a key element to Kosovo's future.

Getting There & Away

Serbia & Montenegro There are four direct buses between Prishtina and Novi Pazar in Serbia (€4.50, three hours) with frequent connections to Belgrade (370 DIN, six hours).

From Peja there's an 8am bus to Rožaje (€5, two hours). Alternatively there are minibuses (€5) or taxis (€20) to be found outside the bus station. A 9am daily Podgorica service from Prizren (€14, 11½ hours) calls in at Peja (€11, 9½ hours). A direct bus travels from Prishtina to Ulcinj (€36, 10 hours).

International There are many international bus services, run by a variety of companies and travel agencies, serving much of Europe; following are some sample routes and fares.

Direct buses travel to Skopje (Macedonia) from Prishtina (€4.50, 1½ hours) and Prizren (€9, two hours) although the length of this trip depends on border delays. Tirana (Albania) buses leave from Prishtina (€26, 10 hours), Peja (€25, nine hours), and from Prizren (€20, nine hours) where minibuses and taxis also daily ply the same route for €30. Buses to İstanbul go from Prishtina (€30, 20 hours) and Prizren (€30, 20 hours) and Peja at 4pm Wednesday and 10pm Sunday (€30, 20 hours). A service also runs to Sarajevo from Prishtina (€31, 10 hours).

Air Austrian Airlines, Swiss International Air Lines, Adria Airlines, British Airways and Turkish Airlines all fly into Prishtina airport. Arriving passengers who are carrying more than €10,000 are required to complete a currency declaration form; failure to do so may mean losing 25% of it when you leave. The departure tax is €12.80.

Getting Around
There is an excellent bus service linking all the main towns and villages. Buses between Prishtina and Peja operate half hourly (€3.50, one hour) and every 15 minutes to Prizren (€3.50, two hours); frequent services also link Prishtina and Prizren (€3.00, 1½ hours). There was a stab at resurrecting the railway; it ended after a short trial but services will resume sometime.

PRISHTINA (PRIŠTINA)
☎ 038 • pop 160,000 (est. 2002)
The capital, with all the beauty and grace that Soviet-style excesses in concrete could bestow, has little at present to offer. It's more a jumping-off point to the more interesting Peja and Prizren.

Orientation & Information
Confusion still reigns in Prishtina as street names have yet to be settled; Ramiz Sadiku St has changed names three times. Most of the people navigate by landmarks. The main streets are Mother Theresa and Ramiz Sadiku Sts that run from the south to converge near the National Theatre in the north. UNMIK (United Nations Interim Administration Mission in Kosovo) headquarters are off Mother Theresa, by the Grand Hotel and west of this is the Sports Complex shopping mall with restaurants and a supermarket. The bus station is in the southwestern outskirts and the airport 17km to the southwest.

Maps of Prishtina can sometimes be difficult to find but ask at kiosks or bookshops along Mother Theresa.

A useful source of information on what's going on in Kosovo is **HCIC** (Humanitarian Community Information Centre; ☎ 549 168, fax 549 169; **W** www.reliefweb.int/hcic; UNHCR Bldg). It has a useful atlas on Kosovo, books and press releases. Foreign newspapers are available from outside the Monaco restaurant in the Sports Complex shopping mall; the latest papers arrive at 6pm.

The **Turist Kosova** (☎ 243 688; Nënë Tereza 36) van provides travel information and books flights and international buses.

There's an **exchange office** (open 7am-7pm daily) at the airport at present but **Micro Enterprise Bank** (☎ 548 052, fax 549 625; Rr Skenderbeu; open 9am-4pm Mon-Fri), off Mother Theresa, will cash travellers cheques.

PTK (Post Telephone Kosova; open 8am-9pm Mon-Fri, 8am-3pm Sat) is in the stylish coppered-roof building next to the National Theatre. Alternatively **Premium Internet Cafe** (opposite UNMIK; open 24hr) charge €1 a minute for a call anywhere in the world. Internet access is €2.50 an hour and you can quaff a beer while you surf.

Things to See
At the time of research the **Kosovo Museum** was closed for renovations. Behind it are two mosques: **Sultan Fatih** (the larger) and **Jashar Pasha** with rich internal decorations.

Places to Stay
The **Grand Hotel** (☎ 20 211, fax 548 138; Mother Theresa; singles/doubles €75/110), Prishtina's top-notch hotel, offers all the facilities you'd expect for the price you pay. On the same street is the **Iliria** (☎ 24 042; Mother Theresa; singles/doubles €30/60), the cheapest in town and with very helpful staff. Breakfast comes fast with big cups of coffee and when you drop crumbs the waiter quickly appears with a hand-held vacuum cleaner.

One of the city's newest hotels is **Hotel Baci** (☎ 548 356; Rr Ulpiana 1/1; singles/doubles €76/100), a swish new place with well-furnished rooms. If you go for an apartment (€130 to €180) you get a Jacuzzi.

Places to Eat & Entertainment
There are many places to eat along Mother Theresa and Ramiz Sadiku St. Cafés in side streets abound, selling *burek* and hamburgers for €1 to €1.50. Pasta and pizza cafés charge up to €2.50.

Pëllumbi (☎ 548 713; Rr për Fushë Kosovë; dishes €7-18; open 8am-midnight daily) is Kosovo's top restaurant, on the outskirts of town on the Peja road. You're likely to see top UN, Kosovo government and visiting diplomats wining and dining here. The food is quite superb and you pay for it. Try the hot bread entree, which comes with just-baked bread and a variety of dips and cheeses.

A&A Pizza Restaurant (☎ 044 161 713; Rr Rexhep Mala 39; dishes €2-6; open 11am-11pm daily) is another popular restaurant but way down on the important-people scale. Set in a cosy ambience, its pasta and pizza is as good as any Italian restaurant could offer.

One of the most prominent bars serving the large expat population is **John's Kukri Bar** (open 7am-midnight daily), opposite and north of UNMIK, which offers big breakfasts, snacks and booze throughout the day and evening. There's live music most weekends. **Boom Boom Room** (open 10am-until the last guest buys), behind and west of UNMIK, is a large single room pub that's again popular with the expat crowd and young Kosovars. There's a variety of beers on tap and snacks are available.

Getting Around
Numbered Kombis (minibuses) roam the streets. Bus Nos 1 and 2 go down Kral Petri St, from where it's a short walk through a housing estate to the bus station. The fare is €0.50.

The easiest way between town and the airport is by taxi with a fare that should be between €15 and €20. Otherwise minibuses to Slatina, passing the Russian checkpoint at the airport road entrance, go into town (€1). The disadvantage, if you're luggage-heavy, is the half a kilometre walk to the airport terminal. **Radio Taxi Victory** (☎ 550 889) charges €10 to the airport.

AROUND PRISHTINA
Gadimë Cave
Some 35km south of Prishtina, Gadimë Cave (Marble Cave; admission €2.50; open 9am-6pm daily), the only show cave in Kosovo, is definitely worth a plunge underground. It's renowned for its helictites (thin stalactites growing at strange angles), but the claim that this is the only cave in the world with them isn't true. You'll get a 30-minute tour for the imagination as the guide proudly points out various formations or shadows as the map of Kosovo or the national symbol of Albania – the eagle. Please, despite what everyone else does, don't touch the formations, it only discolours them.

There are two buses (11am and 2pm) each day that go to Gadimë Cave from Prishtina. As it's the end of the bus route you can ask the driver to wait for you to return from your half-hour cave tour.

Memorial Prekaz
This memorial to the slaughter of the Jeshari clan by the Serbs consists of the shelled remains of their two houses and the cemetery where they are buried. It is an extremely popular site with up to 9000 visitors a day. To visit negotiate a deal with a taxi driver in Prishtina for about €50.

BREZOVICA
Kosovo's important ski resort, 60km south of Prishtina, has been recently reopened. There are nine ski runs here going up to 2500m served by seven chairlifts although not all are working. At present there's no public transport to the resort and the KFOR checkpoint on the road to Brezovica will cause some delays.

Ski equipment and snowboards can be hired (€10 per day), ski lifts cost (€0.50 per journey) and lessons are also available (€10 per hour). Even if you're not a skier a trip up the ski lift is worth it to see the stunning snow scenery.

For accommodation, try the **Molika Hotel** (☎ 290-70 452; ski resort; singles/doubles/triples €35/60/75) in the resort, which has a restaurant plus several bars and cafés.

PEJA (PEČ)
☎ 039
Peja was badly damaged by the departing Yugoslav forces and many picturesque buildings remain as shells and rubble. Add to that the removal of all (Serbian) street names and there's a sense of chaos in Peja. However, the backdrop is superb with 2000m-plus mountains towering over the town.

Orientation & Information
Both road and railway from Prishtina run into the northern part of town. Striking south, and into town, is former Maršal Tito St, currently without a name. The bus station is at the intersection of these two routes.

The **UNMIK police station** is on former Maršal Tito St and is a useful source of information. The **Micro Entreprise Bank** (☎ 32 075, fax 33 128; Rr Sheshi i Heronjëve 6) will cash travellers cheques and change money. **Dardania Tours** (☎ 33 030; main square) takes booking for the buses to both İstanbul and Tirana.

In the square south of the bazaar is the **Premium Internet Cafe** (Sheshi i Republikës; open 8am-11pm daily), which charges €2 an hour for Internet access and €0.50 a minute for international telephone calls – anywhere.

Things to See & Do

Peja's mosques have been severely damaged and are unfortuantely locked awaiting restoration. However, the imposing dome of the 15th-century **Bajrakli Mosque** rising above the colourful **bazaar**, gives Peja an authentic Oriental air.

Two kilometres west of Peja is **Patrijaršija Monastery**, seat of the Serbian Orthodox patriarchate. The monastery is closed to visitors but ask KFOR for permission. If you do wangle a pass from KFOR you'll be rewarded with three mid-13th-century churches with glorious medieval frescoes. Two kilometres on is the start of the magnificent **Rugovo Gorge**, which is an excellent hiking area. Although there should be no problem, check with KFOR before doing anything adventurous.

Another site needing KFOR's OK is Peja's most impressive **Visoki Decani Monastery** (1335). It's 15km south, but accessible by frequent local buses and a 2km walk.

Places to Stay & Eat

Hotel Dypon (☎/fax 31 593; Rr Kosovë-Pejë 216/5; singles/doubles/triples €25/35/60), almost opposite the train station, has modern rooms with bathrooms. Service is good and prices include breakfast.

The nearby **Hotel Jusaj** (☎ 34 455, fax 27 631; Rr 254/7; singles/doubles/triples including breakfast €20/40/60) has recently been reopened giving the Dypon some very much needed competition. The cheaper, more basic, rooms don't have bathrooms and those that do cost €10 extra.

Autocamp **Kamp Karagac** (doubles including breakfast €30) is on the southern outskirts of town. It is only open for business between May and September.

There are plenty of cheap burek and hamburger joints near the bus station and many bars and cafés to service the foreign residents.

Nositi (Rr Sheshi i Heronjëve; dishes €5-7.50; open 8am-midnight daily), a favourite with foreigners in Peja, specialises in pizza and pasta dishes. It also provides an American breakfast for €2.50.

Victoria (Rr Sheshi i Heronjëve; meals €5-10; open 7am-11pm daily) next door is another favourite with a similar menu. It does a nice ice-cream sundae.

PRIZREN
☎ 029

Prizren was once the medieval capital of 'Old Serbia' but the architectural influence is Turkish. The place seems like a party town as people throng the many bars and cafés along the river and in the plaza Shadrvan; on Sunday evening in the better weather, groups and families promenade through the area.

One of the delights of visiting Prizren is wandering through the streets looking at the old architecture. There's far more here than in either Prishtina or Peja.

At the time of writing KFOR was experimenting with having no curfew, but check when you get here to see if it's been reinstated.

Orientation & Information

Most of the (Serbian) road names have been removed and until new ones have been conjured up there are very few street names. The town revolves around the river and Shadrvan, a cobblestone plaza with a fountain in the middle. The bus station is on the northwestern side of town. Crossing the river just west of the main bridge is a 'new' medieval bridge built to replace the old one destroyed by floods in 1979. The **bus station** is on the Peja road about 2km from the centre.

The **Tourist Association of Prizren** (☎ 32 843; Sheshi Lidhjës se Prizrenit; open 8am-7.30pm Mon-Sat) provides information. The office, behind MCM Liridona restaurant, has a town (sketch) map and a leaflet in English. **Micro Entreprise Bank** (☎ 42 550, fax 44 338; Rr Shadërvani) will cash your travellers cheques. The **main post office** (open 8am-9pm daily), next to Theranda Hotel, is also the telephone centre.

Private travel agencies in the town also run international buses. **Dardania Tours** (☎ 22 358; Lidhja Prizrenit) has buses that go to İstanbul and Tirana, as does **Gold Tours** (☎/fax 23 149; e goldtours2@hotmail.com; Rr Remzi Ademi 31).

Big Ben Internet Caffe (Seshi i Lidhjës; open 24hr) behind the Theranda Hotel has a satellite connection and charges €2 an hour.

Things to See

The Orthodox **Church of Bogorodica Ljeviška** (1307) and **Sveti Georgi** (1856) are closed and protected by soldiers and barbed wire. It's worth a look at their current fortifications and a chat to the soldiers, they might even let you in for a look. The **Sveti Spas** church above the town is now an observation post with barbed wire blocking access. Similarly the fine castle on top of the hill is out of bounds.

Sinan Pasha Mosque (1561) on the riverside dominates the centre and can be visited for its fine, decorated high-dome ceiling. Up the road from the Theranda Hotel are the newly restored **Gazi Mehmed Pasha Baths** (1563). Check at the tourist office for a visit as it's usually only opened for groups.

You'll find a small **museum** *(admission €0.50; open 9am-noon daily)*, about 200m east of the tourist office, with some local artefacts, but it seems to spend more time closed than open.

Places to Stay & Eat

Accommodation in Prizren is pretty limited. The faded and ill-maintained **Theranda Hotel** *(☎ 22 292; singles/doubles/triples €25/35/45)* in the centre of town has rooms with bathrooms and carpet to trip over.

Hotel Prizren *(☎ 30 106, fax 41 552; Rr Bajram Curri; singles/doubles/triples €25/35/45)* is about a kilometre northwest of the centre and is a better bet. Unusually for this region there are facilities for people with disabilities and wheelchair access. There's a restaurant and nightclub open from 8pm daily.

There are plenty of cafés, bars and restaurants clustered around the river and Shadrvan. Many have menus in German and English. **Holiday** *(Sheshi Shadrvan; dishes €2.50-5.50, fish €5.50-13; open 8am-midnight daily)* is a large, popular-with-families restaurant with a good local reputation down by the 'new' medieval bridge.

MCM Liridona restaurant *(dishes €1.50-4; open 8am-midnight daily)* is an excellent Turkish restaurant near the river. Come here for a fine kebab or just some *mezes* and dips – the hummus comes on the large size and if you're not that hungry it's an adequate filler. Have a glass of *ajran* as well; it's a most refreshing yogurt drink.

If you have transport or are happy to take a taxi then try the extremely popular **Restaurant Liqeni** *(☎ 044 113 245; Vërmicë; fish dishes €9; open 8am-11pm daily)* on the road to the Albanian border; people come here just for the crispy trout. The restaurant's on the edge of a rapid stream; the owner has created a catch pond where you can spot your forthcoming meal.

Appendix – Telephones

Dial Direct

You can dial directly from public telephone boxes from almost anywhere in Europe to almost anywhere in the world. This is usually cheaper than going through the operator. In much of Europe, public telephones accepting phonecards are becoming the norm and in some countries coin-operated phones are difficult to find.

To call abroad simply dial the international access code (IAC) for the country you are calling from (most commonly ☎ 00 in Europe but see the following table), the country code (CC) for the country you are calling, the local area code (usually dropping the leading zero if there is one) and then the number. If, for example, you are in Italy (international access code ☎ 00) and want to make a call to the USA (country code ☎ 1), San Francisco (area code ☎ 415), number ☎ 123 4567, then you dial ☎ 00-1-415-123 4567. To call from the UK (☎ 00) to Australia (☎ 61), Sydney (☎ 02), number ☎ 1234 5678, you dial the following: ☎ 00-61-2-1234 5678.

Home Direct

If you would rather have somebody else pay for the call, you can, from many countries, dial directly to your home country operator and then reverse charges; you can also charge the call to a phone company credit card. To do this, simply dial the relevant 'home direct' or 'country direct' number to be connected to your own operator. For the USA there's a choice of AT&T, MCI or Sprint Global One home direct services. Home direct numbers vary from country to country – check with your telephone company before you leave, or with the international operator in the country you're ringing from. From phone boxes in some countries you may need a coin or local phonecard to be connected with the relevant home direct operator.

In some places (particularly airports), you may find dedicated home direct phones where you simply press the button labelled USA, Australia, Hong Kong or whatever for direct connection to the operator. Note that the home direct service does not operate to and from all countries, and that the call could be charged at operator rates, which makes it expensive for the person paying. Placing a call on your phone credit card is more expensive than paying the local tariff.

Dialling Tones

In some countries, after you have dialled the international access code, you have to wait for a second dial tone before dialling the code for your target country and the number. Often the same applies when you ring from one city to another within these countries: wait for a dialling tone after you've dialled the area code for your target city. If you're not sure what to do, simply wait three or four seconds after dialling a code – if nothing happens, you can probably keep dialling.

Phonecards

In major locations phones may accept credit cards: simply swipe your card through the slot and the call is charged to the card, though rates can be very high. Phone-company credit cards can be used to charge calls via your home country operator.

Stored-value phonecards are now almost standard all over Europe. You usually buy a card from a post office, telephone centre, newsstand or retail outlet and simply insert the card into the phone each time you make a call. The card solves the problem of finding the correct coins for calls (or lots of correct coins for international calls) and generally gives you a small discount.

Call Costs

The cost of international calls varies widely from one country to another: a US$1.20 call from Britain could cost you US$6 from Turkey. The countries shown in the 'Telephone Codes & Costs' table that follows are rated from * (cheap) to *** (expensive), but rates can vary depending on which country you are calling to (for example, from Italy it's relatively cheap to call North America, but more expensive to call Australia). Reduced rates are available at certain times, usually from mid-evening to early morning, though it varies from country to country – check the local phone book or ask the operator for more details. Calling from hotel rooms can be very expensive.

Telephone Codes & Costs

	CC	cost (see text)	IAC	IO
Albania	355	***	00	12
Andorra	376	**	00	821111
Austria	43	*	00	09
Belarus	375	***	8(w)10	(017) 233 2971
Belgium	32	**	00	1224 (private phone)
				1223 (public phone)
Bosnia-Hercegovina	387	**	00	900/901/902
Bulgaria	359	**	00	0123 (calls)
				0124 (inquiries)
Croatia	385	**	00	901
Cyprus	357	***	00	
Cyprus (Turkish)	90+392		00	
Czech Republic	420	*	00	1181/0149
Denmark	45	**	00	141
Estonia	372	***	000	165
Finland	358	**	00, 990, 994, 999	020222
France	33	*	00(w)	12
Germany	49	*	00	11834
Gibraltar	350	***	00	100
Greece	30	*	00	161
Hungary	36	*	00(w)	199
Iceland	354	***	00	5335010
Ireland	353	*	00	114
Northern Ireland	44+28	*	00	155
Italy	39	**	00	15
Latvia	371	***	00	115
Liechtenstein	423	**	00	114
Lithuania	370	***	00	194/195
Luxembourg	352	**	00	0010
Macedonia	389	***	99	901
Malta	356	**	00	194
Moldova	373	***	8(w)10	973
Morocco	212	***	00(w)	12
Netherlands	31	**	00	0800-0410
Norway	47	**	00	181
Poland	48	**	00	901
Portugal	351	**	00	099
Romania	40	***	00	971
Russia	7	**	8(w)10	
Slovakia	421	**	00	0149
Slovenia	386	**	00	115
Spain	34	**	00(w)	025
Sweden	46	**	00	0018
Switzerland	41	**	00	114
Tunisia	216	**	00	
Turkey	90	***	00	115
UK	44	*	00	155
Ukraine	380	**	810	079/073
Yugoslavia	381	***	99	901

CC – Country Code (to call into that country)
IAC – International Access Code (to call abroad from that country)
IO – International Operator (to make inquiries)
(w) – wait for dialling tone

Other country codes include: Australia ☎ 61, Canada ☎ 1, Hong Kong ☎ 852, India ☎ 91, Indonesia ☎ 62, Israel ☎ 972, Japan ☎ 81, Macau ☎ 853, Malaysia ☎ 60, New Zealand ☎ 64, Singapore ☎ 65, South Africa ☎ 27, Thailand ☎ 66, USA ☎ 1

Language

This Language chapter contains pronunciation guidelines and basic vocabulary to help you get around Eastern Europe. For background information about the languages, see the Language sections under Facts for the Visitor in the relevant country chapters.

Some of the languages in this chapter use polite and informal modes of address (indicated by the abbreviations 'pol' and 'inf' respectively). Use the polite form when addressing older people, officials or service staff. For more detailed coverage of all the languages included in this chapter, get a copy of Lonely Planet's *Eastern Europe*, *Baltic* or *Russian phrasebook*.

Albanian

Pronunciation

Written Albanian is phonetically consistent and pronunciation shouldn't pose too many problems for English speakers. The Albanian **rr** is trilled and each vowel in a diphthong is pronounced. However, Albanian possesses certain letters that are present in English but rendered differently. These include:

ë	often silent; at the beginning of a word it's like the 'a' in 'ago'
c	as the 'ts' in 'bits'
ç	as the 'ch' in 'church'
dh	as the 'th' in 'this'
gj	as the 'gy' in 'hogyard'
j	as the 'y' in 'yellow'
q	between 'ch' and 'ky', similar to the 'cu' in 'cure'
th	as in 'thistle'
x	as the 'dz' in 'adze'
xh	as the 'j' in 'jewel'

Basics

Hello.	*Tungjatjeta/Allo.*
Goodbye.	*Lamtumirë.*
	Mirupafshim. (inf)
Yes.	*Po.*
No.	*Jo.*
Please.	*Ju lutem.*
Thank you.	*Ju falem nderit.*
That's fine.	*Eshtë e mirë.*
You're welcome.	*S'ka përse.*
Excuse me.	*Me falni.*
Sorry. (excuse me, forgive me)	*Më vjen keq* or *Më falni, ju lutem.*

Signs – Albanian

Hyrje	**Entrance**
Dalje	**Exit**
Informim	**Information**
Hapur	**Open**
Mbyllur	**Closed**
E Ndaluar	**Prohibited**
Policia	**Police**
Stacioni I Policisë	**Police Station**
Nevojtorja	**Toilets**
Burra	**Men**
Gra	**Women**

Do you speak English?	*A flisni anglisht?*
How much is it?	*Sa kushton?*
What's your name?	*Si quheni ju lutem?*
My name is ...	*Unë quhem ...* or *Mua më quajnë ...*

Getting Around

What time does the ... leave/arrive?	*Në ç'orë niset/ arrin ...?*
boat	*barka/lundra*
bus	*autobusi*
tram	*tramvaji*
train	*treni*
I'd like ...	*Dëshiroj ...*
a one-way ticket	*një biletë vajtje*
a return ticket	*një biletë kthimi*
1st/2nd class	*klas i parë/i dytë*
timetable	*orar*
bus stop	*stacion autobusi*
Where is ...?	*Ku është ...?*
Go straight ahead.	*Shko drejt.*
Turn left.	*Kthehu majtas.*
Turn right.	*Kthehu djathtas.*
near/far	*afër/larg*

Around Town

a bank	*një bankë*
chemist/pharmacy	*farmaci*
the ... embassy	*... ambasadën*
my hotel	*hotelin tim*
the market	*pazarin*
newsagency	*agjensia e lajmeve*
the post office	*postën*
the telephone centre	*centralin telefonik*

Emergencies – Albanian

Help!	Ndihmë!
Call a doctor!	Thirrni doktorin!
Call the police!	Thirrni policinë!
Go away!	Zhduku!/Largohuni!
I'm lost.	Kam humbur rrugë.

the tourist office	zyrën e informimeve turistike
What time does it open/close?	Në ç'ore hapet/ mbyllet?

Accommodation

hotel	hotel
camping ground	kamp pushimi
Do you have any rooms available?	A keni ndonjë dhomë të lirë?
a single room	një dhomë më një krevat
a double room	një dhomë më dy krevat
How much is it per night/per person?	Sa kushton për një natë/ për një njeri?
Does it include breakfast?	A e përfshin edhe mëngjesin?

Time, Days & Numbers

What time is it?	Sa është ora?
today	sot
tomorrow	nesër
yesterday	dje
in the morning	në mëngjes
in the afternoon	pas dreke
Monday	e hënë
Tuesday	e martë
Wednesday	e mërkurë
Thursday	e ënjte
Friday	e premte
Saturday	e shtunë
Sunday	e diel

1	një
2	dy
3	tre
4	katër
5	pesë
6	gjashtë
7	shtatë
8	tetë
9	nëntë
10	dhjetë
100	njëqind
1000	njëmijë

one million	një milion

Bulgarian

Pronunciation

Unlike English, Bulgarian spelling has an almost one-to-one representation between letter and sound. Most Bulgarian sounds occur in the English language as well, so with a little practice you'll have no problem making yourself understood.

Basics

Hello.	zdraveyte	Здравейте.
(inf)	zdrasti	Здрасти.
Goodbye.	dovizhdane	Довиждане.
(inf)	chao	Чао.
Yes.	da	Да.
No.	ne	Не.
Please.	molya	Моля.
Thank you.	blagodarya	Благодаря.
(inf)	mersi	Мерси.
I'm sorry. (forgive me)	sâzhalyavam (prostete)	Съжалявам. (простете)
Excuse me.	izvinete me	Извинете ме.

I don't understand.	
az ne razbiram	Аз не разбирам.
What's it called?	
kak se kazva tova?	Как се казва това?
How much is it?	
kolko struva?	Колко струва?

Getting Around

What time does the ... leave/arrive?	
v kolko chasa zaminava/pristiga ...?	
В колко часа заминава/пристига ...?	
city bus	
gradskiyat avtobus	градският автобус

Signs – Bulgarian

Вход	Entrance
Изход	Exit
Информация	Information
Отворено	Open
Затворено	Closed
Забранено	Prohibited
Полицейско Управление	Police Station
Тоалетни	Toilets
Мъже	Men
Жени	Women

intercity bus
mezhdugrad-   междуградският
  skiyat avtobus   автобус
plane
samolehtât   самолетът
train
vlakât   влакът
tram
tramvayat   трамваят

arrival
pristigane   пристигане
departure
zaminavane   заминаване
timetable
razpisanie   разписание

Where is the bus stop?
  kâde e avtobusnata spirka?
  Къде е автобусната спирка?
Where is the train station?
  kâde e zhelezopâtnata gara?
  Къде е железопътната гара?
Where is the left-luggage room?
  kâde e garderobât?
  Къде е гардеробът?
Please show me on the map.
  molya pokazhete mi na kartata
  Моля покажете ми на картата.

straight ahead   *napravo*   направо
left   *lyavo*   ляво
right   *dyasno*   дясно

Around Town
the bank   *bankata*   банката
the church   *tsârkvata*   църквата
the hospital   *bolnitsata*   болницата
the market   *pazara*   пазара
the museum   *muzeya*   музея
the post office   *poshtata*   пощата

the tourist office
  byuroto za turisticheska informatsiya
  бюрото за туристическа информация

Accommodation
Do you have any rooms available?
  imateh li svobodni stai?
  Имате ли свободни стаи?
How much is it?
  kolko struva?
  Колко струва?
Does it include breakfast?
  zakuskata vklyuchena li e?
  Закуската включена ли е?

Bulgarian Cyrillic Alphabet

Vowels
Cyrillic	Roman	Pronunciation
А а	a	as the 'a' in 'father' (but shorter)
Е е	e	as the 'e' in 'bet'
О о	o	as in 'pot'
И и	i	as in 'bit'
Ъ ъ	â	a characteristic Bulgarian neutral vowel sound; it roughly resembles the 'a' in 'soda' or 'address'
У у	u	as in 'put'

Consonants
Cyrillic	Roman	Pronunciation
Б б	b	as in 'boy'
В в	v	as in 'vice'
Г г	g	as the 'g' in 'go'
Д д	d	as in 'door'
Ж ж	zh	as the 's' in 'pleasure'
З з	z	as in 'zoo'
Й й	y	as the 'y' in 'yes'
К к	k	as in 'king'
Л л	l	as in 'let'
М м	m	as in 'met'
Н н	n	as in 'net'
П п	p	as in 'pen'
Р р	r	as the trilled Scottish 'r'
С с	s	as in 'see'
Т т	t	as in 'tip'
У у	u	as in 'put'
Ф ф	f	as in 'foot'
Х х	kh	as the 'ch' in Scottish *loch*
Ц ц	ts	as in 'lets'
Ч ч	ch	as in 'chip'
Ш ш	sh	as in 'ship'
Щ щ	sht	as the '-shed' in pushed'
Ю ю	yu	as the word 'you' but shorter
Я я	ya	as in 'yard' but shorter

camping ground
  kâmpinguvane   къмпингуване
youth hostel
  obshtezhitie   общежитие
guesthouse
  pansion   пансион
hotel
  khotel   хотел
private room
  stoya v chastna   стоя в частна
  kvartira   квартира

single room
edinichna staya
единична стая
double room
dvoyna staya
двойна стая

Time, Days & Numbers

What time is it?
kolko e chasât?
Колко е часът?

today	*dnes*	днес
tonight	*dovechera*	довечера
tomorrow	*utre*	утре
yesterday	*vchera*	вчера
in the morning	*sutrinta*	сутринта
in the evening	*vecherta*	вечерта

Monday	*ponedelnik*	понеделник
Tuesday	*vtornik*	вторник
Wednesday	*sryada*	сряда
Thursday	*chetvârtâk*	четвъртък
Friday	*petâk*	петък
Saturday	*sâbota*	събота
Sunday	*nedelya*	неделя

1	*edno*	едно
2	*dve*	две
3	*tri*	три
4	*chetiri*	четири
5	*pet*	пет
6	*shest*	шест
7	*sedem*	седем
8	*osem*	осем
9	*devet*	девет
10	*deset*	десет
100	*sto*	сто
1000	*hilyada*	хиляда

| one million | *edin milion* | един милион |

Croatian & Serbian

Pronunciation

The writing systems of Croatian and Serbian are phonetically consistent: every letter is pronounced and its sound will not vary from word to word. With regard to the position of stress, only one rule can be given: the last syllable of a word is never stressed. In most cases the accent falls on the first vowel in the word.

Serbian uses the Cyrillic alphabet so it's worth familiarising yourself with it (see the Macedonian section in this chapter). Croatian uses a Roman alphabet and many letters are pronounced as in English – the following are some specific pronunciations.

c	as the 'ts' in 'cats'
ć	as the 'tch' sound in 'future'
č	as the 'ch' in 'chop'
đ	as the 'dy' sound in 'verdure'
dž	as the 'j' in 'just'
j	as the 'y' in 'young'
lj	as the 'lli' in 'million'
nj	as the 'ny' in 'canyon'
š	as the 'sh' in 'hush'
ž	as the 's' in 'pleasure'

The principal difference between Serbian and Croatian is in the pronunciation of the vowel 'e' in certain words. A long 'e' in Serbian becomes 'ije' in Croatian, eg, *reka/rijeka* (river), and a short 'e' in Serbian becomes 'je' in Croatian, eg, *pesma/pjesma* (song). Sometimes, however, the vowel 'e' is the same in both languages, as in *selo* (village). There are a number of variations in vocabulary between two languages. In the following phrase list these are indicated by 'C/S' for Croatian/Serbian.

Basics

Hello.
Zdravo. Здраво.
Goodbye.
Doviđenja. Довиђења.
Yes.
Da. Да.
No.
Ne. Не.
Please.
Molim. Молим.
Thank you.
Hvala. Хвала.

Signs – Croatian & Serbian

Entrance/Exit
Улаз/Излаз
Ulaz/Izlaz

Open/Closed
Отворено/Затворено
Otvoreno/Zatvoreno

Information
Информације
Informacije

Rooms Available
Слободне Собе
Slobodne Sobe

Full/No Vacancies
Нема Слободне Собе
Nema Slobodne Sobe

Police
Милиција
Milicija (S)/*Policija* (C)

Police Station
Станица Милиције
Stanica Milicije (S)/*Policija* (C)

Prohibited
Забрањено
Zabranjeno

Toilets
Тоалети
Toaleti (S)/*Zahodi* (C)

That's fine/
You're welcome.
| *U redu je/* | У реду је/ |
| *Nema na čemu.* | Нема на чему. |

Excuse me.
| *Oprostite.* | Опростите. |

Sorry. (excuse me, forgive me)
| *Pardon.* | Пардон. |

Do you speak English?
| *Govorite li* | Говорите ли |
| *engleski?* | енглески? |

How much is it ...?
| *Koliko košta ...?* | Колико кошта ...? |

What's your name?
| *Kako se zovete?* | Како се зовете? |

My name is ...
| *Zovem se ...* | Зовем се ... |

Getting Around

What time does the ... leave/arrive?
| *Kada ... polazi/dolazi?* |
| Када ... полази/долази? |

boat	
brod	брод
city bus	
autobus	аутобус
gradski	градски
intercity bus	
autobus	аутобус
međugradski	међуградски
train	
voz (S)/	воз
vlak (C)	
tram	
tramvaj	трамвај

one-way ticket	
kartu u jednom	карту у једном
pravcu	правцу
return ticket	
povratnu kartu	повратну карту
1st class	
prvu klasu	прву класу
2nd class	
drugu klasu	другу класу

Where is the bus/tram stop?
Gde je autobuska/tramvajska stanica? (S)
Gdje je autobuska/tramvajska postaja? (C)
Где је аутобуска/трамвајска станица?

Can you show me (on the map)?
Možete li mi pokazati (na karti)?
Можете ли ми показати (на карти)?

Go straight ahead.
Idite pravo napred (S)/*naprijed.* (C)
Идите право напред.

Turn left.
Skrenite lljevo (C)/*levo.* (S)
Скрените лево.

Turn right.
Skrenite desno.
Скрените десно.

near	
blizu	близу
far	
daleko	далеку

Around Town

I'm looking for ...
| *Tražim ...* | Тражим ... |
a bank
| *banku* | банку |
the ... embassy
| *... ambasadu* | ... амбасаду |
my hotel
| *moj hotel* | мој хотел |

LANGUAGE

the market
pijacu — пијацу
the post office
poštu — пошту
the telephone centre
telefonsku centralu — телефонску централу
the tourist office
turistički biro — туристички биро

Accommodation

hotel
hotel — хотел
guesthouse
privatno — приватно
prenoćište — преноћиште
youth hostel
omladinsko — омладинско
prenoćište — преноћиште
camping ground
kamping — кампинг

Do you have any rooms available?
Imate li slobodne sobe?
Имате ли слободне собе?
How much is it per night/per person?
Koliko košta za jednu noć/po osobi?
Колико кошта за једну ноћ/по особи?
Does it include breakfast?
Dali je u cenu (S)/cijenu (C)
uključen i doručak?
Дали је у цену укључен и доручак?

I'd like ...
Želim ...
Желим ...
a single room
sobu sa jednim krevetom
собу са једним креветом
a double room
sobu sa duplim krevetom
собу са дуплим креветом

Time, Days & Numbers

What time is it?
Koliko je sati? — Колико је сати?
today
danas — данас
tomorrow
sutra — сутра
yesterday
juče (S) — јуче
jučer (C)
in the morning
ujutro — ујутро
in the afternoon
popodne — поподне

Monday
ponedeljak — понедељак
Tuesday
utorak — уторак
Wednesday
sreda (S) — среда
srijeda (C)
Thursday
četvrtak — четвртак
Friday
petak — петак
Saturday
subota — субота
Sunday
nedelja (S) — недеља
nedjelja (C)

1	*jedan*	један
2	*dva*	два
3	*tri*	три
4	*četiri*	четири
5	*pet*	пет
6	*šest*	шест
7	*sedam*	седам
8	*osam*	осам
9	*devet*	девет
10	*deset*	десет
100	*sto*	сто
1000	*hiljada (S)*	хиљада
	tisuću (C)	

one million
jedan milion (S) — један милион
jedan milijun (C)

Czech

Pronunciation

Many Czech letters are pronounced as per their English counterparts. An accent lengthens a vowel and the stress is always on the first syllable. Words are pronounced as written, so if you follow the guidelines below you should have no trouble being understood. When consulting indexes on Czech maps, be aware that ch comes after h. An accent over a vowel indicates that it is lengthened.

c	as the 'ts' in 'bits'
č	as the 'ch' in 'church'
ch	as in Scottish loch
ď	as the 'd' in 'duty'
ě	as the 'ye' in 'yet'
j	as the 'y' in 'you'
ň	as the 'ni' in 'onion'
ř	as the sound 'rzh'
š	as the 'sh' in 'ship'
ť	as the 'te' in 'stew'
ž	as the 's' in 'pleasure'

Basics

Hello/Good day.	Dobrý den. (pol)
Hi.	Ahoj. (inf)
Goodbye.	Na shledanou.
Yes.	Ano.
No.	Ne.
Please.	Prosím.
Thank you.	Děkuji.
That's fine/You're welcome.	Není zač/Prosím.
Sorry. (forgive me)	Promiňte.
I don't understand.	Nerozumím.
What is it called?	Jak se to jmenuje?
How much is it?	Kolik to stojí?

Getting Around

What time does the ... leave/arrive?	Kdy odjíždí/přijíždí ...?
boat	loď
city bus	městský autobus
intercity bus	meziměstský autobus
train	vlak
tram	tramvaj
arrival	příjezdy
departure	odjezdy
timetable	jízdní řád
Where is the bus stop?	Kde je autobusová zastávka?

Signs – Czech

Vchod	Entrance
Východ	Exit
Informace	Information
Otevřeno	Open
Zavřeno	Closed
Zakázáno	Prohibited
Policie	Police Station
Telefon	Telephone
Záchody/WC/ Toalety	Toilets

Where is the station?	Kde je nádraží?
Where is the left-luggage room?	Kde je úschovna zavazadel?
Where is it?	Kde je to?
Please show me on the map.	Prosím, ukažte mi to na mapě.
left	vlevo
right	vpravo
straight ahead	rovně

Around Town

the bank	banka
the chemist	lékárna
the church	kostel
the market	trh
the museum	muzeum
the post office	pošta
the tourist office	turistické informační centrum (středisko)
travel agency	cestovní kancelář

Accommodation

hotel	hotel
guesthouse	penzión
youth hostel	ubytovna
camping ground	kemping
private room	privát
single room	jednolůžkový pokoj
double room	dvoulůžkový pokoj
Do you have any rooms available?	Máte volné pokoje?
How much is it?	Kolik to je?
Does it include breakfast?	Je v tom zahrnuta snídaně?

Time, Days & Numbers

What time is it?	Kolik je hodin?
today	dnes
tonight	dnes večer
tomorrow	zítra
yesterday	včera

Emergencies – Czech

Help!	Pomoc!
Call a doctor/	Zavolejte doktora/
ambulance/police!	sanitku/policii!
Go away!	Běžte pryč!
I'm lost.	Zabloudil jsem. (m)
	Zabloudila jsem. (f)

in the morning	ráno
in the evening	večer

Monday	pondělí
Tuesday	úterý
Wednesday	středa
Thursday	čtvrtek
Friday	pátek
Saturday	sobota
Sunday	neděle

1	jeden
2	dva
3	tři
4	čtyři
5	pět
6	šest
7	sedm
8	osm
9	devět
10	deset
100	sto
1000	tisíc

one million	jeden milión

Estonian

Alphabet & Pronunciation

The letters of the Estonian alphabet are: **a b d
e f g h i j k l m n o p r s š z ž t u v õ ä ö ü**.

a	as the 'u' in 'cut'
b	similar to English 'p'
g	similar to English 'k'
j	as the 'y' in 'yes'
š	as 'sh'
ž	as the 's' in 'pleasure'
õ	somewhere between the 'e' in 'bed' and the 'u' in 'fur'
ä	as the 'a' in 'cat'
ö	as the 'u' in 'fur' but with rounded lips
ü	as a short 'you'
ai	as the 'i' in 'pine'
ei	as in 'vein'
oo	as the 'a' in 'water'
uu	as the 'oo' in 'boot'
öö	as the 'u' in 'fur'

Greetings & Civilities

Hello.	Tere.
Goodbye.	Head aega or Nägemiseni.
Yes.	Jah.
No.	Ei.
Excuse me.	Vabandage.
Please.	Palun.
Thank you.	Tänan or Aitäh. (thanks)
Do you speak English?	Kas te räägite inglise keelt?

Getting Around

airport	lennujaam
bus station	bussijaam
port	sadam
stop (eg, bus stop)	peatus
train station	raudteejaam

bus	buss
taxi	takso
train	rong
tram	tramm
trolleybus	trollibuss

ticket	pilet
ticket office	piletikassa/kassa
soft class/deluxe	luksus
sleeping carriage	magamisvagun
compartment (class)	kupee

Around Town

bank	pank
chemist	apteek
currency exchange	valuutavahetus
market	turg
toilet	tualett

Where?	Kus?
How much?	Kui palju?

Time, Days & Numbers

today	täna
tomorrow	homme
yesterday	eile

Signs – Estonian

Sissepääs	Entrance
Väljapääs	Exit
Avatud/Lahti	Open
Suletud/Kinni	Closed
Mitte Suitsetada	No Smoking
WC	Public Toilet
Meestele	Women
Naistele	Men

Emergencies – Estonian

Help!	Appi!
I'm ill.	Ma olen haige.
I'm lost.	Ma olen eksinud.
Go away!	Minge ära!
Call ...!	Kutsuge ...!
a doctor	arst
an ambulance	kiirabi
the police	politsei

Monday	esmaspäev
Tuesday	teisipäev
Wednesday	kolmapäev
Thursday	neljapäev
Friday	reede
Saturday	laupäev
Sunday	pühapäev

1	üks
2	kaks
3	kolm
4	neli
5	viis
6	kuus
7	seitse
8	kaheksa
9	üheksa
10	kümme
100	sada
1000	tuhat

Hungarian

Pronunciation

The pronunciation of Hungarian consonants can be simplified by pronouncing them more or less as in English; the exceptions are listed below. Double consonants ll, tt and dd aren't pronounced as one letter as in English but lengthened so you can almost hear them as separate letters. Also, cs, zs, gy and sz (consonant clusters) are separate letters in Hungarian and appear that way in telephone books and other alphabetical listings. For example, the word *cukor,* (sugar) appears in the dictionary before *csak* (only).

c	as the 'ts' in 'hats'
cs	as the 'ch' in 'church'
gy	as the 'j' in 'jury'
j	as the 'y' in 'yes'
ly	as the 'y' in 'yes'

ny	as the 'ni' in 'onion'
r	like a slightly trilled Scottish 'r'
s	as the 'sh' in 'ship'
sz	as the 's' in 'set'
ty	as the 'tu' in British English 'tube'
w	as 'v' (found in foreign words only)
zs	as the 's' in 'pleasure'

Vowels are a bit trickier, and the semantic difference between a, e or o with and without an accent mark is great. For example, *hát* means 'back' while *hat* means 'six'.

a	as the 'o' in hot
á	as in 'father'
e	a short 'e' as in 'set'
é	as the 'e' in 'they' with no 'y' sound
i	as in 'hit' but shorter
í	as the 'i' in 'police'
o	as in 'open'
ó	a longer version of o above
ö	as the 'o' in 'worse' with no 'r' sound
ő	a longer version of ö above
u	as in 'pull'
ú	as the 'ue' in 'blue'
ü	similar to the 'u' in 'flute'; purse your lips tightly and say 'ee'
ű	a longer, breathier version of ü above

Basics

Hello.	Jó napot kívánok. (pol)
	Szia/Szervusz. (inf)
Goodbye.	Viszontlátásra. (pol)
	Szia/Szervusz. (inf)
Yes.	Igen.
No.	Nem.
Please.	Kérem.
Thank you.	Köszönöm.
Sorry. (forgive me)	Sajnálom/Elnézést.

Signs – Hungarian

Bejárat	**Entrance**
Kijárat	**Exit**
Információ	**Information**
Nyitva	**Open**
Zárva	**Closed**
Tilos	**Prohibited**
Rendőrőr-	**Police Station**
Kapitányság	
Telefon	**Telephone**
Toalett/WC	**Toilets**
Férfiak	**Men**
Nők	**Women**

Excuse me.	*Bocsánat.*
What's your name?	*Hogy hívják?* (pol)
	Mi a neved? (inf)
My name is ...	*A nevem ...*
I don't understand.	*Nem értem.*
Do you speak English?	*Beszél angolul?*
What is it called?	*Hogy hívják?*
How much is it?	*Mennyibe kerül?*

Getting Around

What time does the ... leave/arrive?	*Mikor indul/érkezik a ...?*
boat/ferry	*hajó/komp*
city bus	*helyi autóbusz*
intercity bus	*távolsági autóbusz*
plane	*repülőgép*
train	*vonat*
tram	*villamos*
arrival	*érkezés*
departure	*indulás*
timetable	*menetrend*
Where is ...?	*Hol van ...?*
the bus stop	*az autóbuszmegálló*
the station	*a pályaudvar*
the left-luggage room	*a csomagmegőrző*
Please show me on the map.	*Kérem, mutassa meg a térképen.*
(Turn) left.	*(Forduljon) balra.*
(Turn) right.	*(Forduljon) jobbra.*
(Go) straight ahead	*(Menyen) egyenesen elore.*
near/far	*közel/messze*

Around Town

Where is ...?	*Hol van ...?*
a bank	*bank*
a chemist	*gyógyszertár*
the market	*a piac*
the museum	*a múzeum*
the post office	*a posta*
a tourist office	*idegenforgalmi iroda*
What time does it open?	*Mikor nyit ki?*
What time does it close?	*Mikor zár be?*

Accommodation

hotel	*szálloda*
guesthouse	*fogadót*
youth hostel	*ifjúsági szálló*

Emergencies – Hungarian

Help!	*Segítség!*
Call a doctor!	*Hívjon egy orvost!*
Call an ambulance!	*Hívja a mentőket!*
Call the police!	*Hívja a rendőrséget!*
Go away!	*Menjen el!*
I'm lost.	*Eltévedtem.*

camping ground	*kemping*
private room	*fizetővendég szoba*
Do you have rooms available?	*Van szabad szobájuk?*
How much is it per night/ per person?	*Mennyibe kerül éjszakánként/ személyenként?*
Does it include breakfast?	*Az ár tartalmazza a reggelit?*
single room	*egyágyas szoba*
double room	*kétágyas szoba*

Time, Days & Numbers

What time is it?	*Hány óra?*
today	*ma*
tonight	*ma este*
tomorrow	*holnap*
yesterday	*tegnap*
in the morning	*reggel*
in the evening	*este*
Monday	*hétfő*
Tuesday	*kedd*
Wednesday	*szerda*
Thursday	*csütörtök*
Friday	*péntek*
Saturday	*szombat*
Sunday	*vasárnap*
1	*egy*
2	*kettő*
3	*három*
4	*négy*
5	*öt*
6	*hat*
7	*hét*
8	*nyolc*
9	*kilenc*
10	*tíz*
100	*száz*
1000	*ezer*
one million	*millió*

Latvian

Alphabet & Pronunciation

The letters of the Latvian alphabet are: **a b c č d e f g ģ (Ǵ) h i j k ķ l ļ m n ņ o p r s š t u v z ž.**

c	as the 'ts' in 'bits'
č	as the 'ch' in 'church'
ģ	as the 'j' in 'jet'
j	as the 'y' in 'yes'
ķ	as 'tu' in 'tune'
ļ	as the 'lli' in 'billiards'
ņ	as the 'ni' in 'onion'
o	as the 'a' in 'water'
š	as the 'sh' in 'ship'
ž	as the 's' in 'pleasure'
ai	as the the 'i' in 'pine'
ei	as in 'vein'
ie	as in 'pier'
ā	as the 'a' in 'barn'
ē	as the 'e' in 'where'
ī	as the 'i' in 'marine'
ū	as the 'oo' in 'boot'

Greetings & Civilities

Hello.	*Labdien* or *Sveiki.*
Goodbye.	*Uz redzēšanos* or *Atā.*
Yes.	*Jā.*
No.	*Nē.*
Excuse me.	*Atvainojiet.*
Please.	*Lūdzu.*
Thank you.	*Paldies.*
Do you speak English?	*Vai jūs runājat angliski?*

Getting Around

airport	*lidosta*
train station	*dzelzceļa stacija*
train	*vilciens*
bus station	*autoosta*
bus	*autobuss*
port	*osta*

taxi	*taksometrs*
tram	*tramvajs*
stop (eg, bus stop)	*pietura*
departure time	*atiešanas laiks*
arrival time	*pienākšanas laiks*
ticket	*biļete*
ticket office	*kase*

Around Town

bank	*banka*
chemist	*aptieka*
currency exchange	*valūtas maiņa*
hotel	*viesnīca*
market	*tirgus*
post office	*pasts*
toilet	*tualete*
Where?	*Kur?*
How much?	*Cik?*

Time, Days & Numbers

today	*šodien*
yesterday	*vakar*
tomorrow	*rīt*
Sunday	*svētdiena*
Monday	*pirmdiena*
Tuesday	*otrdiena*
Wednesday	*trešdiena*
Thursday	*ceturtdiena*
Friday	*piektdiena*
Saturday	*sestdiena*

1	*viens*
2	*divi*
3	*trīs*
4	*četri*
5	*pieci*
6	*seši*
7	*septiņi*
8	*astoņi*
9	*deviņi*
10	*desmit*
100	*simts*
1000	*tūkstots*

Lithuanian

Alphabet & Pronunciation

The letters of the Lithuanian alphabet are: **a b c č d e f g h i/y j k l m n o p r s š t u v z ž**. The **i** and **y** are partly interchangeable.

c	as 'ts'
č	as 'ch'
y	between the 'i' in 'tin' and the 'ee' in 'feet'
j	as the 'y' in 'yes'
š	as 'sh'
ž	as the 's' in 'pleasure'
ei	as the 'ai' in 'pain'
ie	as the 'ye' in 'yet'
ui	as the 'wi' in 'win'

Accent marks above and below vowels (eg, **ā**, **ė** and **į**) all have the general effect of lengthening the vowel:

ā	as the 'a' in 'father'
ę	as the 'ai' in 'air'
į	as the 'ee' in 'feet'
ų	as the 'oo' in 'boot'
ū	as the 'oo' in 'boot'
ė	as the 'a' in 'late'

Greetings & Civilities

Hello.	Labas/Sveikas.
Goodbye.	Sudie or Viso gero.
Yes.	Taip.
No.	Ne.
Excuse me.	Atsiprašau.
Please.	Prašau.
Thank you.	Ačiū.
Do you speak English?	Ar kalbate angliškai?

Getting Around

airport	oro uostas
bus station	autobusų stotis
port	uostas
train station	geležinkelio stotis
stop (eg, bus stop)	stotelė
bus	autobusas

Signs – Lithuanian

Įėjimas	**Entrance**
Išėjimas	**Exit**
Informacija	**Information**
Atidara	**Open**
Uždara	**Closed**
Nerūkoma	**No Smoking**
Patogumai	**Public Toilets**

Emergencies – Lithuanian

Help!	Gelėbkite!
I'm ill.	Aš sergu.
I'm lost.	Aš paklydęs/ paklydusi. (m/f)
Go away!	Eik šalin!
Call ...!	Iššaukite ...!
a doctor	gydytoją
an ambulance	greitąją
the police	policiją

taxi	taksi
train	traukinys
tram	tramvajus
departure time	išvykimo laikas
arrival time	atvykimo laikas
ticket	bilietas
ticket office	kasa

Around Town

bank	bankas
chemist	vaistinė
currency exchange	valiutos keitykla
hotel	viešbutis
market	turgus
post office	paštas
toilet	tualetas

Where?	Kur?
How much?	Kiek?

Times, Days & Numbers

today	šiandien
tomorrow	rytoj
yesterday	vakar

Monday	pirmadienis
Tuesday	antradienis
Wednesday	trečiadienis
Thursday	ketvirtadienis
Friday	penktadienis
Saturday	šeštadienis
Sunday	sekmadienis

1	vienas
2	du
3	trys
4	keturi
5	penki
6	šeši
7	septyni
8	aštuoni
9	devyni
10	dešimt
100	šimtas
1000	tūkstantis

Macedonian

Pronunciation

The spelling of Macedonian is more or less phonetic: almost every word is written exactly the way it's pronounced and every letter is pronounced. With regard to the position of word stress, only one rule can be given: the last syllable of a word is never stressed. There are 31 letters in the Macedonian Cyrillic alphabet (see the boxed text). The pronunciation of the Roman or Cyrillic letter is given to the nearest English equivalent.

Basics

Hello.
Zdravo.   Здраво.
Goodbye.
Priatno.   Приатно.
Yes.
Da.   Да.
No.
Ne.   Не.
Please.
Molam.   Молам.
Thank you.
Blagodaram.   Благодарам.
You're welcome.
Nema zošto/   Нема зошто/
Milo mi e.   Мило ми е.
Excuse me.
Izvinete.   Извинете.
Sorry. (forgive me)
Oprostete ve   Опростете ве молам
molam.

Do you speak
English?
Zboruvate li   Зборувате ли
angliski?   англиски?
What's your name?
Kako se vikate? Како се викате?
My name is ...
Jas se vikam ... Јас се викам ...
How much is it?
Kolku čini toa? Колку чини тоа?

Getting Around

What time does the next ... leave/arrive?
Koga doagja/zaminuva idniot ...?
Кога доаѓа/заминува идниот ...?

boat
brod   брод
city bus
avtobus gradski автобус градски

Cyrillic	Roman	Pronunciation
А а	a	as in 'rather'
Б б	b	as in 'be'
В в	v	as in 'vodka'
Г г	g	as in 'go'
Ѓ ѓ	gj	as the 'gu' in 'legume'
Е е	e	as the 'e' in 'bear'
Ж ж	zh	as the 's' in 'pleasure'
З з	z	as in 'zero'
Ѕ ѕ	zj	as the 'ds' in 'suds'
И и	i	as the 'i' in 'machine'
Ј ј	j	as the 'y' in 'young'
К к	k	as in 'keg'
Л л	l	as in 'let'
Љ љ	lj	as the 'lli' in 'million'
М м	m	as in 'map'
Н н	n	as in 'no'
Њ њ	nj	as the 'ny' in 'canyon'
О о	o	as the 'aw' in 'shawl'
П п	p	as in 'pop'
Р р	r	as in 'rock'
С с	s	as in 'safe'
Т т	t	as in 'too'
Ќ ќ	ć	as the 'cu' in 'cure'
У у	u	as the 'oo' in 'room'
Ф ф	f	as in 'fat'
Х х	h	as in 'hot'
Ц ц	c	as the 'ts' in 'cats'
Ч ч	č	as the 'ch' in 'chop'
Џ џ	dz	as the 'j' in 'judge'
Ш ш	š	as the 'sh' in 'shoe'

Macedonain Cyrillic Alphabet

intercity bus
avtobus   автобус
megjugradski   меѓуградски
train
voz   воз
tram
tramvaj   трамвај

I'd like ...
Sakam ...   Сакам ...
a one-way ticket
bilet vo eden   билет во еден правец
pravec
a return ticket
povraten bilet   повратен билет
1st class
prva klasa   прва класа
2nd class
vtora klasa   втора класа

Signs – Macedonian

Entrance
Влез — *Vlez*
Exit
Излез — *Izlez*
Open
Отворено — *Otvoreno*
Closed
Затворено — *Zatvoreno*
Information
Информации — *Informacii*

Rooms Available
Сози За Издавање
Sobi Za Izdavanje
Full/No Vacancies
Полно/Нема Место
Polno/Nema Mesto
Police
Полиција
Policija
Police Station
Полициска Станица
Policiska Stanica
Prohibited
Забрането
Zabraneto
Toilets (Men/Women)
Клозети (Машки/Женски)
Klozeti (Maški/Zhenski)

timetable
vozen red — возен ред
bus stop
avtobuska stanica — автобуска станица
train station
zheleznička stanica — железничка станица

Where is ...?
Kade je ...? — Каде је ...?
Go straight ahead.
Odete pravo napred. — Одете право напред.
Turn left/right.
Svrtete levo/desno. — Свртете лево/десно.
near/far
blisku/daleku — блиску/далеку

I'd like to hire a car/bicycle.
Sakam da iznajmam kola/točak.
Сакам да изнајмам кола/точак.

Around Town
bank
banka — банка

chemist/pharmacy
apteka — аптека
the embassy
ambasadata — амбасадата
my hotel
mojot hotel — мојот хотел
the market
pazarot — пазарот
newsagency
kiosk za vesnici — киоск за весници
the post office
poštata — поштата
stationers
knižarnica — книжарница
the telephone centre
telefonskata centrala — телефонската централа
the tourist office
turističkoto biro — туристичкото биро

What time does it open/close?
Koga se otvora/zatvora?
Кога се отвора/затвора?

Accommodation
hotel
hotel
хотел
guesthouse
privatno smetuvanje
приватно сметување
youth hostel
mladinsko prenočište
младинско преноќиште
camping ground
kamping
кампинг

Do you have any rooms available?
Dali imate slobodni sobi?
Дали имате слободни соби?
How much is it per night/per person?
Koja e cenata po noč/po osoba?
Која е цената по ноќ/по особа?
Does it include breakfast?
Dali e vključen pojadok?
Дали е вклучен ројадок?

a single room
soba so eden krevet
соба со еден кревет
a double room
soba so bračen krevet
соба со брачен кревет
for one/two nights
za edna/dva večeri
за една/два вечери

Emergencies – Macedonian

Help!
Pomoš! Помош!
Call a doctor!
Povikajte lekar! Повикајте лекар!
Call the police!
Viknete policija! Викнете полиција!
Go away!
Odete si! Одете си!
I'm lost.
Jas zaginav. Јас загинав.

Time, Days & Numbers

What time is it?
Kolku e časot? Колку е часот?
today
denes денес
tomorrow
utre утре
yesterday
včera вчера
morning
utro утро
afternoon
popladne попладне

Monday
ponedelnik понеделник
Tuesday
vtornik вторник
Wednesday
sreda среда
Thursday
četvrtok четврток
Friday
petok петок
Saturday
sabota сабота
Sunday
nedela недела

1	*eden*	еден
2	*dva*	два
3	*tri*	три
4	*četiri*	четири
5	*pet*	пет
6	*šest*	шест
7	*sedum*	седум
8	*osum*	осум
9	*devet*	девет
10	*deset*	десет
100	*sto*	сто

one million *eden milion* еден милион

Polish

Pronunciation

Written Polish is phonetically consistent, which means that the pronunciation of letters or clusters of letters doesn't vary from word to word. The stress almost always goes on the second-last syllable.

Vowels

a   as the 'u' in 'cut'
e   as in 'ten'
i   similar to the 'ee' in 'feet' but shorter
o   as in 'lot'
u   a bit shorter than the 'oo' in 'book'
y   similar to the 'i' in 'bit'

There are three vowels unique to Polish:

ą   a nasal vowel sound like the French *un*, similar to 'own' in 'sown'
ę   also nasalised, like the French <u>un</u>, but pronounced as 'e' when word-final
ó   similar to Polish **u**

Consonants

In Polish, the consonants **b, d, f, k, l, m, n, p, t, v** and **z** are pronounced more or less as they are in English. The following consonants and clusters of consonants sound distinctly different to their English counterparts:

c   as the 'ts' in 'its'
ch   similar to the 'ch' in the Scottish *loch*
cz   as the 'ch' in 'church'
ć   much softer than Polish **c** (as 'tsi' before vowels)
dz   similar to the 'ds' in 'suds' but shorter
dź   as **dz** but softer (as 'dzi' before vowels)
dż   as the 'j' in 'jam'
g   as in 'get'
h   as **ch**
j   as the 'y' in 'yet'
ł   as the 'w' in 'wine'
ń   as the 'ny' in 'canyon' (as 'ni' before vowels)
r   always trilled
rz   as the 's' in 'pleasure'
s   as in 'set'
sz   as the 'sh' in 'show'
ś   as **s** but softer (as 'si' before vowels)
w   as the 'v' in 'van'
ź   softer version of **z** (as 'zi' before vowels)
ż   as **rz**

Basics

Hello. (inf)	*Cześć.*
Hello/ Good morning.	*Dzień dobry.*
Goodbye.	*Do widzenia.*
Yes/No.	*Tak/Nie.*
Please.	*Proszę.*
Thank you.	*Dziękuję.*
Excuse me/ Forgive me.	*Przepraszam.*
I don't understand.	*Nie rozumiem.*
What is it called?	*Jak to się nazywa?*
How much is it?	*Ile to kosztuje?*

Getting Around

What time does the ... leave/arrive?	*O której godzinie przychodzi/odchodzi ...?*
plane	*samolot*
boat	*statek*
bus	*autobus*
train	*pociąg*
tram	*tramwaj*
arrival	*przyjazd*
departure	*odjazd*
timetable	*rozkład jazdy*
Where is the bus stop?	*Gdzie jest przystanek autobusowy?*
Where is the station?	*Gdzie jest stacja kolejowa?*
Where is the left-luggage room?	*Gdzie jest przecho-walnia bagażu?*
Please show me on the map.	*Proszę pokazać mi to na mapie.*
straight ahead	*prosto*
left	*lewo*
right	*prawo*

Around Town

the bank	*bank*
the chemist	*apteka*
the church	*kościół*

the city centre	*centrum miasta*
the market	*targ/bazar*
the museum	*muzeum*
the post office	*poczta*
the tourist office	*informacja turystyczna*
What time does it open/close?	*O której otwierają/ zamykają?*

Accommodation

hotel	*hotel*
youth hostel	*schronisko młodzieżowe*
camping ground	*kemping*
private room	*kwatera prywatna*
Do you have any rooms available?	*Czy są wolne pokoje?*
How much is it?	*Ile to kosztuje?*
Does it include breakfast?	*Czy śniadanie jest wliczone?*
single room	*pokój jednoosobowy*
double room	*pokój dwuosobowy*

Time, Days & Numbers

What time is it?	*Która jest godzina?*
today	*dzisiaj*
tonight	*dzisiaj wieczorem*
tomorrow	*jutro*
yesterday	*wczoraj*
in the morning	*rano*
in the evening	*wieczorem*
Monday	*poniedziałek*
Tuesday	*wtorek*
Wednesday	*środa*
Thursday	*czwartek*
Friday	*piątek*
Saturday	*sobota*
Sunday	*niedziela*
1	*jeden*
2	*dwa*
3	*trzy*
4	*cztery*
5	*pięć*

6	sześć
7	siedem
8	osiem
9	dziewięć
10	dziesięć
20	dwadzieścia
100	sto
1000	tysiąc
one million	milion

Romanian

Pronunciation

Until the mid-19th century, Romanian was written in the Cyrillic script. Today Romanian employs 28 Latin letters, some of which bear accents. At the beginning of a word, **e** and **i** are pronounced 'ye' and 'yi', while at the end of a word **i** is almost silent. At the end of a word **ii** is pronounced 'ee'. The stress is usually on the penultimate syllable.

ă	as the 'er' in 'brother'
î	as the 'i' in 'river'
c	as 'k', except before **e** and **i**, when it's as the 'ch' in 'chip'
ch	always as the 'k' in 'king'
g	as in 'go', except before **e** and **i**, when it's as in 'gentle'
gh	always as the 'g' in 'get'
ş	as 'sh'
ţ	as the 'tz' in 'tzar'

Basics

Hello.	Bună.
Goodbye.	La revedere.
Yes.	Da.
No.	Nu.
Please.	Vă rog.
Thank you.	Mulţumesc.
Sorry. (forgive me)	Iertaţi-mă.
Excuse me.	Scuzaţi-mă.
I don't understand.	Nu înţeleg.
What is it called?	Cum se cheamă?
How much is it?	Cît costă?

Getting Around

What time does the ... leave/arrive?	La ce oră pleacă/soseşte ...?
boat	vaporul
bus	autobusul
train	trenul
tram	tramvaiul
plane	avionul

arrival	sosire
departure	plecare
timetable	mersul/orar

Where is the bus stop?	Unde este staţia de autobuz?
Where is the station?	Unde este gară?
Where is the left-luggage room?	Unde este biroul pentru bagaje de mînă?
Please show me on the map.	Vă rog arătaţi-mi pe hartă.

straight ahead	drept înainte
left	stînga
right	dreapta

Around Town

the bank	banca
the chemist	farmacistul
the church	biserica
the city centre	centrum oraşului
the ... embassy	ambasada ...
the market	piaţa
the museum	muzeu
the post office	poşta
the tourist office	birou de informatii turistice

Accommodation

hotel	hotel
guesthouse	casa de oaspeţi
youth hostel	camin studentesc
camping ground	camping
private room	cameră particulară
single room	o cameră pentru o persoană
double room	o cameră pentru două persoane

Do you have any rooms available?	Aveţi camere libere?
How much is it?	Cît costă?
Does it include breakfast?	Include micul dejun?

Signs – Romanian

Intrare	Entrance
Ieşire	Exit
Informaţii	Information
Deschis	Open
Inchis	Closed
Nu Intraţi	No Entry
Staţie de Poliţie	Police Station
Toaleta	Toilets

Emergencies – Romanian

Help!	*Ajutor!*
Call a doctor!	*Chemaţi un doctor!*
Call the police!	*Chemaţi poliţia!*
Go away!	*Du-te!/Pleacă!*
I'm lost.	*Sînt pierdut.*

Time, Days & Numbers

What time is it?	*Ce oră este?*
today	*azi*
tonight	*deseară*
tomorrow	*mîine*
yesterday	*ieri*
in the morning	*dimineaţa*
in the evening	*seară*
Monday	*luni*
Tuesday	*marţi*
Wednesday	*miercuri*
Thursday	*joi*
Friday	*vineri*
Saturday	*sîmbătă*
Sunday	*duminică*

1	*unu*
2	*doi*
3	*trei*
4	*patru*
5	*cinci*
6	*şase*
7	*şapte*
8	*opt*
9	*nouă*
10	*zece*
100	*o sută*
1000	*o mie*

one million	*milion*

Russian

The Cyrillic Alphabet

The Cyrillic alphabet resembles Greek with some extra characters. Each language that uses Cyrillic has a slightly different variant. The alphabet chart opposite shows the letters used in Russian with their Roman-letter equivalents and common pronunciations.

Pronunciation

The sounds of **a**, **o**, **e** and **я** are 'weaker' when the stress in the word does not fall on them, eg, in вода (*voda*, water) the stress falls on the second syllable, so it's pronounced 'va-DA', with the unstressed pronunciation for

Russian Cyrillic Alphabet

Cyrillic	Roman	Pronunciation
А а	a	as the 'a' in 'father' when stressed; as the 'a' in 'ago' when unstressed
Б б	b	as the 'b' in 'but'
В в	v	as the 'v' in 'van'
Г г	g	as the 'g' in 'god'
Д д	d	as the 'd' in 'dog'
Е е	ye	as the 'ye' in 'yet' when stressed; as the 'ye' in 'yeast' when unstressed
Ё ё	yo	as the 'yo' in 'yore'
Ж ж	zh	as the 's' in 'measure'
З з	z	as the 'z' in 'zoo'
И и	i	as the 'ee' in 'meet'
Й й	y	as the 'y' in 'boy'
К к	k	as the 'k' in 'kind'
Л л	l	as the 'l' in 'lamp'
М м	m	as the 'm' in 'mad'
Н н	n	as the 'n' in 'not'
О о	o	as the 'o' in 'more' when stressed; as the 'a' in 'ago' when unstressed
П п	p	as the 'p' in 'pig'
Р р	r	as the 'r' in 'rub' (but rolled)
С с	s	as the 's' in 'sing'
Т т	t	as the 't' in 'ten'
У у	u	as the 'oo' in 'fool'
Ф ф	f	as the 'f' in 'fan'
Х х	kh	as the 'ch' in 'Bach'
Ц ц	ts	as the 'ts' in 'bits'
Ч ч	ch	as the 'ch' in 'chin'
Ш ш	sh	as the 'sh' in 'shop'
Щ щ	shch	as 'shch' in 'fresh chips'
ъ		'hard' sign
Ы ы	y	as the 'i' in 'ill'
ь		'soft' sign
Э э	e	as the 'e' in 'end'
Ю ю	yu	as 'you'
Я я	ya	as the 'ya' in 'yard'

o and the stressed pronunciation for **a**. The vowel **й** only follows other vowels in so-called diphthongs, eg, ой 'oy', ей 'ey, yey'. Russians usually print **ё** without the dots, a source of confusion in pronunciation.

The 'voiced' consonants б, в, г, д, ж and з are not voiced at the end of words or before voiceless consonants. For example, хлеб (bread) is pronounced 'khlyep'. The г in the common adjective endings -ero and -oro is pronounced 'v'.

Basics

Hello.
zdrastvuyte — Здравствуйте.
Good morning.
dobraye utra — Доброе утро.
Good afternoon.
dobryy den' — Добрый день.
Good evening.
dobryy vecher — Добрый вечер.
Goodbye.
da svidaniya — До свидания.
Bye! (inf)
paka! — Пока!
How are you?
kak dila? — Как дела?
Yes.
dat — Да.
No.
net — Нет.
Please.
pazhalsta — Пожалуйста.

Thank you (very much).
(bal'shoye) spasiba
(Большое) спасибо.
Pardon me.
prastite/pazhalsta
Простите/Пожалуйста.
No problem/Never mind.
nichevo (literally, 'nothing')
Ничего.
Do you speak English?
vy gavarite pa angliyski?
Вы говорите по-английски?
What's your name?
kak vas zavut?
Как вас зовут?
My name is ...
minya zavut ...
Меня зовут ...
How much is it?
skol'ka stoit?
Сколько стоит?

Getting Around

What time does the ... leave?
f katoram chasu pribyvaet ...?
В котором часу прибывает ...?
What time does the ... arrive?
f katoram chasu atpravlyaetsa ...?
В котором часу отправляется ...?

bus
aftobus — автобус
fixed-route minibus
marshrutnaye — маршрутное
taksi — такси

steamship
parakhot — пароход
train
poyezt — поезд
tram
tramvay — трамвай
trolleybus
traleybus — троллейбус

pier/quay
prichal/pristan'
причал/пристань
train station
zhilezna darozhnyy vagzal
железно дорожный (ж. д.) вокзал
stop (bus/trolleybus/tram)
astanofka
остановка

one-way ticket
bilet v adin kanets
билет в один конец
return ticket
bilet v oba kantsa
билет в оба конца
two tickets
dva bilety
два билета
soft or 1st-class (compartment)
myahkiy
мягкий
hard or 2nd-class (compartment)
kupeyny
купейный
reserved-place or 3rd-class (carriage)
platskartny
плацкартный

Where is ...?
gde ...? — Где ...?
to (on) the left
naleva — налево

Ukrainian

Because of Ukraine's history of domination by outside powers, the language was often considered inferior or subservient to the dominant languages of the time – Russian in the east, Polish in the west. Today, the Ukrainian language is slowly being revived, and in 1990 it was adopted as the official language. Russian is understood everywhere by everyone, so although it may be diplomatic and polite to speak Ukrainian (especially in the west), you'll have no problem being understood if you speak Russian.

Alphabet & Pronunciation

Around 70% of the Ukrainian language is identical or similar to Russian and Belarusian. The Cyrillic chart in the Russian section of this chapter covers the majority of letters used in Ukrainian alphabet. Ukrainian has three additional letters not found in Russian, **i**, **ï**, and **є**, all of which are neutral vowel sounds (the Russian letter **o** is often replaced by a Ukrainian **i**). The Ukrainian **г** usually has a soft 'h' sound. The Ukrainian alphabet doesn't include the Russian letters **ё**, **ы** and **э**, and has no hard sign, **ъ**, although it does include the soft sign, **ь**. These differences between the two languages are sometimes quite simple in practice: for example, the town of *Chernigov* in Russian is *Chernihiv* in Ukrainian. Overall, Ukrainian is softer sounding and less guttural than Russian.

The **-я** *(-ya)* ending for nouns and names in Russian (especially street names) is dropped in Ukrainian, and the letter **и** is transliterated as *y* in Ukrainian, whereas in Russian it's transliterated as *i*, eg, a street named *Deribasovskaya* in Russian would be *Derybasivska* in Ukrainian.

to (on) the right
  naprava   направо
straight on
  pryama   прямо

Around Town

bank
  bank   банк
market
  rynak   рынок
newsstand
  gazetnyy kiosk   газетный киоск
pharmacy
  apteka   аптека

post office
  pochta   почтам
telephone booth
  tilifonnaya budka   телефонная будка
open
  otkryta   открыто
closed
  zakryta   закрыто

Accommodation

hotel
  gastinitsa   гостиница
room
  nomer   номер
breakfast
  zaftrak   завтрак

How much is a room?
  skol'ka stoit nomer?
  Сколько стоит номер?

Time, Date & Numbers

What time is it?
  katoryy chas   Который час?
today
  sivodnya   сегодня
yesterday
  vchira   вчера
tomorrow
  zaftra   завтра
am/in the morning
  utra   утра
pm/in the afternoon
  dnya   дня
in the evening
  vechira   вечера

Monday
  panidel'nik   понедельник
Tuesday
  ftornik   вторник
Wednesday
  srida   среда
Thursday
  chitverk   четверг
Friday
  pyatnitsa   пятница
Saturday
  subota   суббота
Sunday
  vaskrisen'e   воскресенье

0	*nol'*	ноль
1	*adin*	один
2	*dva*	два
3	*tri*	три
4	*chityri*	четыре
5	*pyat'*	пять

Emergencies – Russian

Help!	
na pomashch'!/	На помощь!/
pamagite!	Помогите!
I'm sick.	
ya bolen (m)	Я болен.
ya bal'na (f)	Я больна.
I need a doctor.	
mne nuzhin vrach	Мне нужен врач.
hospital	
bal'nitsa	больница
police	
militsiya	милиция
I'm lost.	
ya zabludilsya (m)	Я заблудился.
ya zabludilas' (f)	Я заблудилась.

6	*shest'*	шесть
7	*sem'*	семь
8	*vosim'*	восемь
9	*devit'*	девять
10	*desit'*	десять
11	*adinatsat'*	одиннадцать
100	*sto*	сто
1000	*tysyacha*	тысяча

one million
(adin) milion   (один) миллион

Slovak

Pronunciation

The 43 letters of the Slovak alphabet have similar pronunciation to those of Czech. In words of three syllables or less the stress falls on the first syllable. Longer words generally also have a secondary accent on the third or fifth syllable. There are thirteen vowels (a, á, ä, e, é, i, í, o, ó, u, ú, y, ý), three semi-vowels (l, ľ, r) and five diphthongs (ia, ie, iu, ou, ô). Letters and diphthongs which may be unfamiliar to native English speakers include the following:

c	as the 'ts' in 'its'
č	as the 'ch' in 'church'
dz	as the 'ds' in 'suds'
dž	as the 'j' in 'judge'
ia	as the 'yo' in 'yonder'
ie	as the 'ye' in 'yes'
iu	as the word 'you'
j	as the 'y' in 'yet'
ň	as the 'ni' in 'onion'
ô	as the 'wo' in 'won't'
ou	as the 'ow' in 'know'
š	as the 'sh' in 'show'
y	as the 'i' in 'machine'
ž	as the 'z' in 'azure'

Basics

Hello.	*Ahoj.*
Goodbye.	*Dovidenia.*
Yes.	*Áno.*
No.	*Nie.*
Please.	*Prosím.*
Thank you.	*Ďakujem.*
Excuse me/	*Prepáčte mi/*
Forgive me.	*Odpuste mi.*
I'm sorry.	*Ospravedlňujem sa.*
I don't understand.	*Nerozumiem.*
What is it called?	*Ako sa do volá?*
How much is it?	*Koľko to stojí?*

Getting Around

What time does	*Kedy odchádza/*
the ... leave/arrive?	*prichádza ...?*
boat	*loč*
city bus	*mestský autobus*
intercity bus	*medzimestský autobus*
plane	*lietadlo*
train	*vlak*
tram	*električka*
arrival	*príchod*
departure	*odchod*
timetable	*cestovný poriadok*
Where is the	*Kde je autobusová*
bus stop?	*zastávka?*
Where is the	*Kde je vlaková*
station?	*stanica?*
Where is the left-	*Kde je uschovňa*
luggage room?	*batožín?*
Please show me	*Prosím, ukážte mi*
on the map.	*to na mape.*
left	*vľavo*
right	*vpravo*
straight ahead	*rovno*

Signs – Slovak

Vchod	**Entrance**
Východ	**Exit**
Informácie	**Information**
Otvorené	**Open**
Zatvorené	**Closed**
Zakázané	**Prohibited**
Polícia	**Police Station**
Telefón	**Telephone**
Záchody/WC/	**Toilets**
Toalety	

Help!	*Pomoc!*
Call a doctor!	*Zavolajte doktora/*
	lekára!
Call an ambulance!	*Zavolajte záchranku!*
Call the police!	*Zavolajte políciu!*
Go away!	*Chod preč! (sg)/*
	Chodte preč! (pl)
I'm lost.	*Nevyznám sa tu.*

Around Town

the bank	*banka*
the chemist	*lekárnik*
the church	*kostol*
the city centre	*stred (centrum) mesta*
the market	*trh*
the museum	*múzeum*
the post office	*pošta*
the telephone centre	*telefónnu centrálu*
the tourist office	*turistické informačné centrum*

Accommodation

hotel	*hotel*
guesthouse	*penzión*
youth hostel	*mládežnicka ubytovňa*
camping ground	*kemping*
private room	*privat*
Do you have any rooms available?	*Máte voľné izby?*
How much is it?	*Koľko to stojí?*
Does it include breakfast?	*Sú raňajky zahrnuté v cene?*
single room	*jednolôžková izba*
double room	*dvojlôžková izba*

Time, Days & Numbers

What time is it?	*Koľko je hodín?*
today	*dnes*
tonight	*dnes večer*
tomorrow	*zajtra*
yesterday	*včera*
in the morning	*ráno*
in the evening	*večer*
Monday	*pondelok*
Tuesday	*utorok*
Wednesday	*streda*
Thursday	*štvrtok*
Friday	*piatok*
Saturday	*sobota*
Sunday	*nedeľa*

1	*jeden*
2	*dva*
3	*tri*
4	*štyri*
5	*päť*
6	*šesť*
7	*sedem*
8	*osem*
9	*deväť*
10	*desať*
100	*sto*
1000	*tisíc*
one million	*milión*

Slovene

Pronunciation

Slovene pronunciation isn't difficult. The alphabet consists of 25 letters, most of which are very similar to English. It doesn't have the letters 'q', 'w', 'x' and 'y', but the following letters are added: ê, é, ó, ò, č, š and ž. Each letter represents only one sound, with very few exceptions, and the sounds are pure and not diphthongal. The letters **l** and **v** are both pronounced like the English 'w' when they occur at the end of syllables and before vowels. Though words like *trn* (thorn) look unpronounceable, most Slovenes (depending on dialect) add a short vowel like an 'a' or the German 'ö' in front of the 'r' to give a Scot's pronunciation of 'tern' or 'tarn'. Here is a list of letters specific to Slovene:

c	as the 'ts' in 'its'
č	as the 'ch' in 'church'
ê	as the 'a' in 'apple'
e	as the 'a' in 'ago' (when unstressed)
é	as the 'ay' in 'day'
j	as the 'y' in 'yellow'
ó	as the 'o' in 'more'
ò	as the 'o' in 'soft'
r	a rolled 'r' sound
š	as the 'sh' in 'ship'
u	as the 'oo' in 'good'
ž	as the 's' in 'treasure'

Basics

Hello.	*Pozdravljeni.* (pol)
	Zdravo/Živio. (inf)
Good day.	*Dober dan!*
Goodbye.	*Nasvidenje!*
Yes.	*Da* or *Ja.* (inf)
No.	*Ne.*
Please.	*Prosim.*

Thank you (very much).	*Hvala (lepa).*
You're welcome.	*Prosim/Ni za kaj!*
Excuse me.	*Oprostite.*
What's your name?	*Kako vam je ime?*
My name is ...	*Jaz sem ...*
Where are you from?	*Od kod ste?*
I'm from ...	*Sem iz ...*

Getting Around

What time does ... leave/arrive?	*Kdaj odpelje/ pripelje ...?*
boat/ferry	*ladja/trajekt*
bus	*avtobus*
train	*vlak*
one-way (ticket)	*enosmerna (vozovnica)*
return (ticket)	*povratna (vozovnica)*

Around Town

Where is the/a ...?	*Kje je ...?*
bank/exchange	*banka/menjalnica*
embassy	*konzulat/ambasada*
post office	*pošta*
telephone centre	*telefonska centrala*
tourist office	*turistični informa- cijski urad*

Accommodation

hotel	*hotel*
guesthouse	*gostišče*
camping ground	*kamping*
Do you have a ...?	*Ali imate prosto ...?*
bed	*posteljo*
cheap room	*poceni sobo*

Emergencies – Slovene

Help!	*Na pomoč!*
Call a doctor!	*Pokličite zdravnika!*
Call the police!	*Pokličite policijo!*
Go away!	*Pojdite stran!*

single room	*enoposteljno sobo*
double room	*dvoposteljno sobo*
How much is it per night?	*Koliko stane za eno noč?*
How much is it per person?	*Koliko stane za eno osebo?*
for one/two nights	*za eno noč/za dve noči*
Is breakfast included?	*Ali je zajtrk vključen?*

Time, Days & Numbers

today	*danes*
tonight	*nocoj*
tomorrow	*jutri*
in the morning	*zjutraj*
in the evening	*zvečer*
Monday	*ponedeljek*
Tuesday	*torek*
Wednesday	*sreda*
Thursday	*četrtek*
Friday	*petek*
Saturday	*sobota*
Sunday	*nedelja*

1	*ena*
2	*dve*
3	*tri*
4	*štiri*
5	*pet*
6	*šest*
7	*sedem*
8	*osem*
9	*devet*
10	*deset*
100	*sto*
1000	*tisoč*
one million	*milijon*

Thanks

Many thanks to the travellers who used the last edition and wrote to us with helpful hints, useful advice and interesting anecdotes:

Nick Adlam, Saara Aho, Felicitie Algate, Onur Alver, Carole Amaio, Bashar Amso, Sonja Andreotti, Alan Andrews, Josee Archambault, Philippe Armstrong, Elena Arriero, Saara Arvo, Brian & Mary Ashmore, Sini Asikainen, Becky Askew, Olivier Auber, Kyle Austen, Andrei Avram, Kris Ayre, Jerry Azevedo, Ivan Babiuk, Monika Bailey, Ivna Bajsic, Jordan Bannister, Catherine Barber, Ann Barker, Steve Barnett, Andrew Barton, Georgina Barton, Dobromir Batinkov, Andrew Baynham, Szirti Bea, John Bedford, Fero Bedner, Matt Beks, Kriss Bell, Tony Bellette, Jacob Bendtsen, Martin Bergling, David Bertolotti, Tim J Bertram, Sarah Bevis, Alisa Bieber, Brenda Bierman, Gerry Bierman, Alexandre Billette, John Bisges, Cam Black, Johanna Black, Steve Blair, Louise & Brad Bland, Alexis Blane, Esther Blodau-Konick, Chris Bolger, Mandi Booth, Vincent Borlaug, Bela Borsos, Andy Bramwell, Howard Bramwell, Jean-Claude Branch, Jeanne Brei, Claire Briggs, Dawson Brown, Edmund Brown, Kevin Brown, Marl Allen Brown, Dylan Browne, Andrea Brugnoli, Rod George Bryant, Renay Buchanan, Victoria Burford, Megan Burkholder, Rob Butler, Martin Cahn, Fergy Campbell, Stuart Candy, Donna Capper, Fred Carreon, Andrew Cerchez, Matt Chaffe, Greg Chandler, Rebekka Chaplin, Anthi Charalambous, Dr CW Chen, Julian Chen, Farid Chetouani, Anna Chilton, Eitan D Chitayat, Mark Christian, Ivan Chudomirov, Niko Cimbur, Michael Claes, Jack Clancy, Chrissy & Malcolm Clark, Erica Clarke, Christian Claussen, Joe Clavan, Edward Congdon, Elizabeth Connolly, Martha W Connor, Phil Coote, Andrew Cork, Dermot Corrigan, Brad Costello, Jessika Croizat, Phil Cubbin, Mark Curley, Alix Daley, Paul Dalton, Robert K Daly, Ryan Davidson, Shaun Davidson, Robert Davison, Mike Dean, Michel Delporte, RJ Dempsey, Andy Dennis, Philippe Dennler, Luc Desy, Sante D'Ettorre, Kathleen Diamond, Susan Dilks, Sarah Dillon, Floris Dirks, Elizabeth Dobie-Sarsam, Sarah Dodson, Sadhu Doh, Nicola Doran, Ryan Dougherty, Sasa Drach, Ravit & Sagi Dror, Peter Duffy, Michelle Dumford, Alexandru Dumitru, Loretta Dupuis, Jon Durham, Robin Elliott, Mary Ellis, Mark Emmerson, Gennevene Ensor, Yury Epstein, James Evans, Tim Eyre, Bernard Farjounel, Eli Feiman, Anne Fenerty, Armando Ferra, Rob Ferrara, Leonard Fitzpatrick, Amy Fletcher, Kristine Flora, Kamil Fogel, Karen Forster, Nick Fowler, Helen Frakes, Trudy Fraser, Biff Frederikson, Nicola Freeman, Emma French, Maria French, Tini Frey, Charlotte Froomberg, Ludek Frybort, Benoit Gabory, Jean Galsworthy, Wes Galt, Jane Galvin, Ricardo Gama, Dorin Garofeanu, Sharon Gartenberg, Felicity Gatchell, Elise Gatti, Ryan Gawel, Marietta Georgia, Dave Gibbs, Monique Gijsbrechts, Tim Gilley, Janos Ginstler, Paul W Gioffi, Leonard A Girard, Ian Glennon, Arno Gloeckner, Gerard Godbaz, Alan Godfrey, Roland Goldsack, Irene Gomez, Samantha Gordon, Jono Gourlay, Robert Grammig, Ed Graystone, Carlos Griell, Gabriel Gruss, Kreso Gudelj, Dagmara Gumkowska, Lars Gyllenhaal, Brian Aslak Gylte, Erja Haenninen, Morten Hagedal, Roy F Halvorsen, Clare Hamilton, Leah Hamilton, Kato Martin Hansen, Mariska Hansen, Sue Harrison, Guy Harvey-Samuel, Max Hasse, Jan Havranek, Shona Hawkes, Catherine Hegyi, Sina Helbig, Irene Herrera, Margaret Heuen, Niall Hewitt, Brendan Hickey, Peter Hicks, Coleman Higgins, Paul & Elain Hirsch, Marrianne Hoeyland, Paul Hoffman, Jaap Hoftijzer, Belinda Hogan, Catherine Holland, Adrian Holloway, Ville Holmberg, Diane Hooley, Joe Hooper, Cherrie Hosken, Ivaylo Hristov, Petr Hruska, Silvia Hruskova, Laura Hughes, Gemma Humphrey, Stephen Humphrey, Mark Huntsman, Steuart Hutchinson, Josephine Hutton, Robert Hyman, Bruce & Kay Ikawa, Molnar Ildiko, Jarkko Inkovaara, Dancea Ioana, Becky Ip, Jessica Jacobson, Melissa Jacobson, Tom Jacoby, Martijn & Klaas Jan, Rok Jarc, Prashant Jayaprakash, Janaka Jayasingha, Jentz Jensen, Ida Johansson, John Johnson, Nicky Johnson, Sally Jo Johnson, Andrew Jones, Margaret Jones, Scott L Jones, Thomas Neumark Jones, Maritta Jumppanen, Roman Kaczaj, Judith Kahan, Max Kamenetsky, Nemo Kaufhold, Gerald Kellett, Adam Kightley, John Killick, Rob Kingston, Andrew Kirkup, Dean & John Klinkenberg, Teja Klobucar, David Klur, Timo Knaebe, Heidi Knudsen, Barbara Kocot, Marnix Koets, Denis Koishi, Aleksandar Kolekeski, Samo Kolnik, Nathan Korpela, Igor Korsic, Juraj Kosticky, Eva Kouw, Sead Kozlic, Kazuki Kozuru, Sari Kreitzer, Berit Kreuze, Donna Krupa, Erki Kurrikoff, Doug Lacey, Anne-Mari Laiho, Andrew

Lamont, GWA Lamsvelt, Trevor Landers, Christine Landry, Goss Lauren, San Lauw, Flo Le Corff, Lee Leatham, Brian Lema, Desmond Leow, Juha Levo, Ralf Liebau, Rich Lillywhite, Ajasja Ljubertic, Ian Lockett, Sabine Loebbe, Lisa Long, Thomas Loos, Alicia López-Miedes, Don Lowman, Oliver Lyttelton, Deirdre MacBean, Frank MacDonald, Donald MacLeod, Lachlan MacQuarrie, Dee Mahan, John Malcolm, Peter Malecha, Samvel Malkhasyan, Delyan Manchev, Antonie et Marie, David Marle, Amy Marsh, Joanna Marshall, Cathy & Kevin Marston, Alberto Martin, Alina Matei, Phillip Matthews, Brent Maupin, Richard Maurice, Olivier Mauron, Eileen Mazur, Florence & Michael McBride, Richard McBride, Damian McCormack, Edmund McCosh, Jennifer & Bruce McCoy, Christine McDermott, Shirley McDermott, Tom McElderry, Ian McElmoyle, Angela McEwan, David McGowan, John McKellar, Ian McLoughlin, Kaare Meier, ER Mein, Matiss Melecis, Silvia Merli, Regine Mertens, Majda Mesic, Muhamed Mesic, Nedim Mesic, Bas Metolli, Matthias Meyer, Robin Meyerhoff, Vicky Michels, Petya Milkova, Aubree Miller, Nicolas Minec, Kenny Mitchell, Sarah Moffat, Sonja Moker, Shane Monks, Gary Moon, William A Morgan, Richard Moriarty, Ian & Veronica Moseley, Brian Moulton, Gabe Murtagh, Kathryn Murtagh, Mari Mutanen, Petra Naavalinna, Dan Nadel, Susan Nagy, Rudy Narine, Gavin Nathan, Aleksander Necakovski, Julie Nelson, Trinh Nguyen, Kate Nicholson, Marjan Nieuwland, Borut Nikolas, Jamie Norris, LE Nowosielska, Rudy Nuytten, Davor Obradovic, Erin K O'Brien, Judith O'Brien, Julie O'Brien, Jacqui O'Connell, Robin O'Donoghue, Mary Beth O'Donovan, Ronan O'Driscoll, Mick Ogrizek, Lars Olberg, Dana Olson, Carlos Ortiz, Rikke Ortved, Karl Otta, Aino Oura, Manuel Padilla, Shelia Paine, Gregory A Palermo, Rolf Palmberg, Casimir Paltinger, Athanasios Panagiotopoulos, Lars Pardo, James Parkhurst, Michael Parsons, Kate Partridge, Tanya Pashkuleva, S Patel, Max Patrick, Stuart Pattullo, Justin Peach, Jerry Peek, Jan M Pennington, Claus Penz, Miguel A Pérez-Torres, Jane Perry, Sam Perry, Julie Pervan, Piergiorgio Pescali, Michael Phillips, Stacey Piesner, Michael Pike, Michel Pinton, Paul Plaza, Mads Pockel, Magdalena Polan, Robert Pontnau, Ezra Pound, Kevin Presto, Georgina Preston, Kevin Preston, Kelsey Price, Kathy Prunty, Anna Ptaszynska, Duncan Pullen, Viara Rashkova, Stefan Ratschan, Ron Regan, Werner Reindorf, Catherine Rentz, Diane C Reynolds, Grant Reynolds, Reuben Rich, Tony Richmond, Ronald Jan Rieger, Melina Rodde, Carla Rodriguez, Francoise Rohaut, Clare Rose, Julian Ross, Vicki Roubicek, Melanie Rubenstein, Jaroslaw Rudnik, Kym Ryan, Patti Ryan, Marcin Sadurski, Mike Sampson, Rachel Samsonowitz, Stefan Samuelsson, Claudio Sandroni, Dietmar Schaeper, Frank Schaer, Carola Schellack, Wilhelm Scherz, Joe Schill, Christian Schmidt, Matthias Schmoll, Jake Schwartz, Larry Schwarz, Allan Sealy, Kerstin Seja, Amber Senneck, Brett Shackelford, Tal Shany, Joshua Sharkey, John Sherman, Michael Sherman, Alex Shore, Lori Shortreed, Dragon Simic, Lorraine & Murray Sinderberry, Helene Sinnreich, Frank Sitchler, Ella Smit, Anna Smith, Christopher Smith, Jonathon Smith, Sharon Smith, Gregor Socan, Jone Solvik, Raewyn Somerville, Tina Souvlis, Nicola & Steve Spencer, Steven Stahl, Maarten Stam, Kevin Stanes, Georgeta Stefan, Steven Stefanovic, Peter Stein, Carmen Stern-Blumenhein, Martin Stich, Marjan Stojkov, Lisa Stone, James E Storm, Samo Stritof, Paul Sullivan, Donna Sutton, Clare Szilagyi, Bea Szirti, Lamija Didic Tabak, Lamija M Tabak-Didic, Steve Talley, Ana Tanceva, Patricia Tandy, Chester Tapley, Ivo Tence, Mark Teramae, Ravindran Thanikaimoni, Anja Thijssen, Kate Thomas, Fred Thornett, Paul Jacob Tiberg, Stuart Toben, Sylvia Tomlinson-Hoehndorf, Valer Tosa, Chris Touwaide, Abi Tovarloza, Helmut Tramposch, Anna Travali, Adonis Tsilialis, Pauliina Tuominen, Ronaldo Uliana de Oliveria, Boaz Ur, Teune va der Wildt, Sergio Valdes, Natalia Valdivieso, Ted Valentin, Caroliena van den Bos, Karel van Muyden, Leo Van Steensel, Philip Vandenbroeck, Mathieu Vandermissen, Toby Vanhegan, Philline Vanhelleputte, Walter Verdonk, Maarten Vermeulen, Lea Vesine, Marco Veul, Manfred Von Carstein, Amanda Voolstra, Tijana Vukicevic, Colin Waite, Andrew Wallace, Mike Wallace, Astrid Walstra, Damian Wampler, Julian & Steve Warner, Dawn Watson, James Webb, Julie Webb, Danielle Weber, Renee Webster, Tom Wellings, Diana Wernicke, Mark Westerdale, Kate Wierciak, Janne Wikman, David Williams, Ernst Williams, Fiona Wilson, Tracy Wilson, Graham C Witt, Alex & Rhonda Wittmann, Kate Wrigley, Michael Wuerfel, John Yates, David Young, Matteo Zamboni, Hester Zegers, Alexander Zhuravlev, Maike Ziesemer, Eric Zimmerman, Paul Zoglin, Anne Zouridakis, Will Zucker

LONELY PLANET

ON THE ROAD

Travel Guides explore cities, regions and countries, and supply information on transport, restaurants and accommodation, covering all budgets. They come with reliable, easy-to-use maps, practical advice, cultural and historical facts and a rundown on attractions both on and off the beaten track. There are over 200 titles in this classic series, covering nearly every country in the world.

 Lonely Planet Upgrades extend the shelf life of existing travel guides by detailing any changes that may affect travel in a region since a book has been published. Upgrades can be downloaded for free from **www.lonelyplanet.com/upgrades**

For travellers with more time than money, **Shoestring** guides offer dependable, first-hand information with hundreds of detailed maps, plus insider tips for stretching money as far as possible. Covering entire continents in most cases, the six-volume shoestring guides are known around the world as 'backpackers bibles'.

For the discerning short-term visitor, **Condensed** guides highlight the best a destination has to offer in a full-colour, pocket-sized format designed for quick access. They include everything from top sights and walking tours to opinionated reviews of where to eat, stay, shop and have fun.

CitySync lets travellers use their Palm™ or Visor™ hand-held computers to guide them through a city with handy tips on transport, history, cultural life, major sights, and shopping and entertainment options. It can also quickly search and sort hundreds of reviews of hotels, restaurants and attractions, and pinpoint their location on scrollable street maps. CitySync can be downloaded from **www.citysync.com**

MAPS & ATLASES

Lonely Planet's **City Maps** feature downtown and metropolitan maps, as well as transit routes and walking tours. The maps come complete with an index of streets, a listing of sights and a plastic coat for extra durability.

Road Atlases are an essential navigation tool for serious travellers. Cross-referenced with the guidebooks, they also feature distance and climate charts and a complete site index.

LONELY PLANET

ESSENTIALS

Read This First books help new travellers to hit the road with confidence. These invaluable predeparture guides give step-by-step advice on preparing for a trip, budgeting, arranging a visa, planning an itinerary and staying safe while still getting off the beaten track.

Healthy Travel pocket guides offer a regional rundown on disease hot spots and practical advice on predeparture health measures, staying well on the road and what to do in emergencies. The guides come with a user-friendly design and helpful diagrams and tables.

Lonely Planet's **Phrasebooks** cover the essential words and phrases travellers need when they're strangers in a strange land. They come in a pocket-sized format with colour tabs for quick reference, extensive vocabulary lists, easy-to-follow pronunciation keys and two-way dictionaries.

Miffed by blurry photos of the Taj Mahal? Tired of the classic 'top of the head cut off' shot? **Travel Photography: A Guide to Taking Better Pictures** will help you turn ordinary holiday snaps into striking images and give you the know-how to capture every scene, from frenetic festivals to peaceful beach sunrises.

Lonely Planet's **Travel Journal** is a lightweight but sturdy travel diary for jotting down all those on-the-road observations and significant travel moments. It comes with a handy time-zone wheel, a world map and useful travel information.

Lonely Planet's eKno is an all-in-one communication service developed especially for travellers. It offers low-cost international calls and free email and voicemail so that you can keep in touch while on the road. Check it out on **www.ekno.lonelyplanet.com**

FOOD & RESTAURANT GUIDES

Lonely Planet's **Out to Eat** guides recommend the brightest and best places to eat and drink in top international cities. These gourmet companions are arranged by neighbourhood, packed with dependable maps, garnished with scene-setting photos and served with quirky features.

For people who live to eat, drink and travel, **World Food** guides explore the culinary culture of each country. Entertaining and adventurous, each guide is packed with detail on staples and specialities, regional cuisine and local markets, as well as sumptuous recipes, comprehensive culinary dictionaries and lavish photos good enough to eat.

LONELY PLANET

OUTDOOR GUIDES

For those who believe the best way to see the world is on foot, Lonely Planet's **Walking Guides** detail everything from family strolls to difficult treks, with 'when to go and how to do it' advice supplemented by reliable maps and essential travel information.

Cycling Guides map a destination's best bike tours, long and short, in day-by-day detail. They contain all the information a cyclist needs, including advice on bike maintenance, places to eat and stay, innovative maps with detailed cues to the rides, and elevation charts.

The **Watching Wildlife** series is perfect for travellers who want authoritative information but don't want to tote a heavy field guide. Packed with advice on where, when and how to view a region's wildlife, each title features photos of over 300 species and contains engaging comments on the local flora and fauna.

With underwater colour photos throughout, **Pisces Books** explore the world's best diving and snorkelling areas. Each book contains listings of diving services and dive resorts, detailed information on depth, visibility and difficulty of dives, and a roundup of the marine life you're likely to see through your mask.

OFF THE ROAD

Journeys, the travel literature series written by renowned travel authors, capture the spirit of a place or illuminate a culture with a journalist's attention to detail and a novelist's flair for words. These are tales to soak up while you're actually on the road or dip into as an at-home armchair indulgence.

The range of lavishly illustrated **Pictorial** books is just the ticket for both travellers and dreamers. Off-beat tales and vivid photographs bring the adventure of travel to your doorstep long before the journey begins and long after it is over.

Chasing Rickshaws

Lonely Planet **Videos** encourage the same independent, tough-minded approach as the guidebooks. Currently airing throughout the world, this award-winning series features innovative footage and an original soundtrack.

Yes, we know, work is tough, so do a little bit of deskside dreaming with the spiral-bound Lonely Planet **Diary** or a Lonely Planet **Wall Calendar**, filled with great photos from around the world.

TRAVELLERS NETWORK

Lonely Planet Online. Lonely Planet's award-winning Web site has insider information on hundreds of destinations, from Amsterdam to Zimbabwe, complete with interactive maps and relevant links. The site also offers the latest travel news, recent reports from travellers on the road, guidebook upgrades, a travel links site, an online book-buying option and a lively travellers bulletin board. It can be viewed at **www.lonelyplanet.com** or AOL keyword: lp.

Planet Talk is a quarterly print newsletter, full of gossip, advice, anecdotes and author articles. It provides an antidote to the being-at-home blues and lets you plan and dream for the next trip. Contact the nearest Lonely Planet office for your free copy.

Comet, the free Lonely Planet newsletter, comes via email once a month. It's loaded with travel news, advice, dispatches from authors, travel competitions and letters from readers. To subscribe, click on the Comet subscription link on the front page of the Web site.

LONELY PLANET

Guides by Region

Lonely Planet is known worldwide for publishing practical, reliable and no-nonsense travel information in our guides and on our Web site. The Lonely Planet list covers just about every accessible part of the world. Currently there are 16 series: Travel guides, Shoestring guides, Condensed guides, Phrasebooks, Read This First, Healthy Travel, Walking guides, Cycling guides, Watching Wildlife guides, Pisces Diving & Snorkeling guides, City Maps, Road Atlases, Out to Eat, World Food, Journeys travel literature and Pictorials.

AFRICA Africa on a shoestring • Botswana • Cairo • Cairo City Map • Cape Town • Cape Town City Map • East Africa • Egypt • Egyptian Arabic phrasebook • Ethiopia, Eritrea & Djibouti • Ethiopian Amharic phrasebook • The Gambia & Senegal • Healthy Travel Africa • Kenya • Malawi • Morocco • Moroccan Arabic phrasebook • Mozambique • Namibia • Read This First: Africa • South Africa, Lesotho & Swaziland • Southern Africa • Southern Africa Road Atlas • Swahili phrasebook • Tanzania, Zanzibar & Pemba • Trekking in East Africa • Tunisia • Watching Wildlife East Africa • Watching Wildlife Southern Africa • West Africa • World Food Morocco • Zambia • Zimbabwe, Botswana & Namibia
Travel Literature: Mali Blues: Traveling to an African Beat • The Rainbird: A Central African Journey • Songs to an African Sunset: A Zimbabwean Story

AUSTRALIA & THE PACIFIC Aboriginal Australia & the Torres Strait Islands •Auckland • Australia • Australian phrasebook • Australia Road Atlas • Cycling Australia • Cycling New Zealand • Fiji • Fijian phrasebook • Healthy Travel Australia, NZ & the Pacific • Islands of Australia's Great Barrier Reef • Melbourne • Melbourne City Map • Micronesia • New Caledonia • New South Wales • New Zealand • Northern Territory • Outback Australia • Out to Eat – Melbourne • Out to Eat – Sydney • Papua New Guinea • Pidgin phrasebook • Queensland • Rarotonga & the Cook Islands • Samoa • Solomon Islands • South Australia • South Pacific • South Pacific phrasebook • Sydney • Sydney City Map • Sydney Condensed • Tahiti & French Polynesia • Tasmania • Tonga • Tramping in New Zealand • Vanuatu • Victoria • Walking in Australia • Watching Wildlife Australia • Western Australia
Travel Literature: Islands in the Clouds: Travels in the Highlands of New Guinea • Kiwi Tracks: A New Zealand Journey • Sean & David's Long Drive

CENTRAL AMERICA & THE CARIBBEAN Bahamas, Turks & Caicos • Baja California • Belize, Guatemala & Yucatán • Bermuda • Central America on a shoestring • Costa Rica • Costa Rica Spanish phrasebook • Cuba • Cycling Cuba • Dominican Republic & Haiti • Eastern Caribbean • Guatemala • Havana • Healthy Travel Central & South America • Jamaica • Mexico • Mexico City • Panama • Puerto Rico • Read This First: Central & South America • Virgin Islands • World Food Caribbean • World Food Mexico • Yucatán
Travel Literature: Green Dreams: Travels in Central America

EUROPE Amsterdam • Amsterdam City Map • Amsterdam Condensed • Andalucía • Athens • Austria • Baltic States phrasebook • Barcelona • Barcelona City Map • Belgium & Luxembourg • Berlin • Berlin City Map • Britain • British phrasebook • Brussels, Bruges & Antwerp • Brussels City Map • Budapest • Budapest City Map • Canary Islands • Catalunya & the Costa Brava • Central Europe • Central Europe phrasebook • Copenhagen • Corfu & the Ionians • Corsica • Crete • Crete Condensed • Croatia • Cycling Britain • Cycling France • Cyprus • Czech & Slovak Republics • Czech phrasebook • Denmark • Dublin • Dublin City Map • Dublin Condensed • Eastern Europe • Eastern Europe phrasebook • Edinburgh • Edinburgh City Map • England • Estonia, Latvia & Lithuania • Europe on a shoestring • Europe phrasebook • Finland • Florence • Florence City Map • France • Frankfurt City Map • Frankfurt Condensed • French phrasebook • Georgia, Armenia & Azerbaijan • Germany • German phrasebook • Greece • Greek Islands • Greek phrasebook • Hungary • Iceland, Greenland & the Faroe Islands • Ireland • Italian phrasebook • Italy • Kraków • Lisbon • The Loire • London • London City Map • London Condensed • Madrid • Madrid City Map • Malta • Mediterranean Europe • Milan, Turin & Genoa • Moscow • Munich • Netherlands • Normandy • Norway • Out to Eat – London • Out to Eat – Paris • Paris • Paris City Map • Paris Condensed • Poland • Polish phrasebook • Portugal • Portuguese phrasebook • Prague • Prague City Map • Provence & the Côte d'Azur • Read This First: Europe • Rhodes & the Dodecanese • Romania & Moldova • Rome • Rome City Map • Rome Condensed • Russia, Ukraine & Belarus • Russian phrasebook • Scandinavian & Baltic Europe • Scandinavian phrasebook • Scotland • Sicily • Slovenia • South-West France • Spain • Spanish phrasebook • Stockholm • St Petersburg • St Petersburg City Map • Sweden • Switzerland • Tuscany • Ukrainian phrasebook • Venice • Vienna • Wales • Walking in Britain • Walking in France • Walking in Ireland • Walking in Italy • Walking in Scotland • Walking in Switzerland • Western Europe • World Food France • World Food Greece • World Food Ireland • World Food Italy • World Food Spain **Travel Literature:** After Yugoslavia • Love and War in the Apennines • The Olive Grove: Travels in Greece • On the Shores of the Mediterranean • Round Ireland in Low Gear • A Small Place in Italy

LONELY PLANET

Mail Order

L onely Planet products are distributed worldwide.They are also available by mail order from Lonely Planet, so if you have difficulty finding a title please write to us. North and South American residents should write to 150 Linden St, Oakland, CA 94607, USA; European and African residents should write to 10a Spring Place, London NW5 3BH, UK; and residents of other countries to Locked Bag 1, Footscray, Victoria 3011, Australia.

INDIAN SUBCONTINENT & THE INDIAN OCEAN Bangladesh • Bengali phrasebook • Bhutan • Delhi • Goa • Healthy Travel Asia & India • Hindi & Urdu phrasebook • India • India & Bangladesh City Map • Indian Himalaya • Karakoram Highway • Kathmandu City Map • Kerala • Madagascar • Maldives • Mauritius, Réunion & Seychelles • Mumbai (Bombay) • Nepal • Nepali phrasebook • North India • Pakistan • Rajasthan • Read This First: Asia & India • South India • Sri Lanka • Sri Lanka phrasebook • Tibet • Tibetan phrasebook • Trekking in the Indian Himalaya • Trekking in the Karakoram & Hindukush • Trekking in the Nepal Himalaya • World Food India **Travel Literature:** The Age of Kali: Indian Travels and Encounters • Hello Goodnight: A Life of Goa • In Rajasthan • Maverick in Madagascar • A Season in Heaven: True Tales from the Road to Kathmandu • Shopping for Buddhas • A Short Walk in the Hindu Kush • Slowly Down the Ganges

MIDDLE EAST & CENTRAL ASIA Bahrain, Kuwait & Qatar • Central Asia • Central Asia phrasebook • Dubai • Farsi (Persian) phrasebook • Hebrew phrasebook • Iran • Israel & the Palestinian Territories • Istanbul • Istanbul City Map • Istanbul to Cairo • Istanbul to Kathmandu • Jerusalem • Jerusalem City Map • Jordan • Lebanon • Middle East • Oman & the United Arab Emirates • Syria • Turkey • Turkish phrasebook • World Food Turkey • Yemen **Travel Literature:** Black on Black: Iran Revisited • Breaking Ranks: Turbulent Travels in the Promised Land • The Gates of Damascus • Kingdom of the Film Stars: Journey into Jordan

NORTH AMERICA Alaska • Boston • Boston City Map • Boston Condensed • British Columbia • California & Nevada • California Condensed • Canada • Chicago • Chicago City Map • Chicago Condensed • Florida • Georgia & the Carolinas • Great Lakes • Hawaii • Hiking in Alaska • Hiking in the USA • Honolulu & Oahu City Map • Las Vegas • Los Angeles • Los Angeles City Map • Louisiana & the Deep South • Miami • Miami City Map • Montreal • New England • New Orleans • New Orleans City Map • New York City • New York City City Map • New York City Condensed • New York, New Jersey & Pennsylvania • Oahu • Out to Eat – San Francisco • Pacific Northwest • Rocky Mountains • San Diego & Tijuana • San Francisco • San Francisco City Map • Seattle • Seattle City Map • Southwest • Texas • Toronto • USA • USA phrasebook • Vancouver • Vancouver City Map • Virginia & the Capital Region • Washington, DC • Washington, DC City Map • World Food New Orleans **Travel Literature**: Caught Inside: A Surfer's Year on the California Coast • Drive Thru America

NORTH-EAST ASIA Beijing • Beijing City Map • Cantonese phrasebook • China • Hiking in Japan • Hong Kong & Macau • Hong Kong City Map • Hong Kong Condensed • Japan • Japanese phrasebook • Korea • Korean phrasebook • Kyoto • Mandarin phrasebook • Mongolia • Mongolian phrasebook • Seoul • Shanghai • South-West China • Taiwan • Tokyo • Tokyo Condensed • World Food Hong Kong • World Food Japan **Travel Literature:** In Xanadu: A Quest • Lost Japan

SOUTH AMERICA Argentina, Uruguay & Paraguay • Bolivia • Brazil • Brazilian phrasebook • Buenos Aires • Buenos Aires City Map • Chile & Easter Island • Colombia • Ecuador & the Galapagos Islands • Healthy Travel Central & South America • Latin American Spanish phrasebook • Peru • Quechua phrasebook • Read This First: Central & South America • Rio de Janeiro • Rio de Janeiro City Map • Santiago de Chile • South America on a shoestring • Trekking in the Patagonian Andes • Venezuela **Travel Literature:** Full Circle: A South American Journey

SOUTH-EAST ASIA Bali & Lombok • Bangkok • Bangkok City Map • Burmese phrasebook • Cambodia • Cycling Vietnam, Laos & Cambodia • East Timor phrasebook • Hanoi • Healthy Travel Asia & India • Hill Tribes phrasebook • Ho Chi Minh City (Saigon) • Indonesia • Indonesian phrasebook • Indonesia's Eastern Islands • Java • Lao phrasebook • Laos • Malay phrasebook • Malaysia, Singapore & Brunei • Myanmar (Burma) • Philippines • Pilipino (Tagalog) phrasebook • Read This First: Asia & India • Singapore • Singapore City Map • South-East Asia on a shoestring • South-East Asia phrasebook • Thailand • Thailand's Islands & Beaches • Thailand, Vietnam, Laos & Cambodia Road Atlas • Thai phrasebook • Vietnam • Vietnamese phrasebook • World Food Indonesia • World Food Thailand • World Food Vietnam

ALSO AVAILABLE: Antarctica • The Arctic • The Blue Man: Tales of Travel, Love and Coffee • Brief Encounters: Stories of Love, Sex & Travel • Buddhist Stupas in Asia: The Shape of Perfection • Chasing Rickshaws • The Last Grain Race • Lonely Planet ... On the Edge: Adventurous Escapades from Around the World • Lonely Planet Unpacked • Lonely Planet Unpacked Again • Not the Only Planet: Science Fiction Travel Stories • Ports of Call: A Journey by Sea • Sacred India • Travel Photography: A Guide to Taking Better Pictures • Travel with Children • Tuvalu: Portrait of an Island Nation

LONELY PLANET

You already know that Lonely Planet produces more than this one guidebook, but you might not be aware of the other products we have on this region. Here is a selection of titles that you may want to check out as well:

Budapest map
ISBN 1 86450 077 8
US$5.95 • UK£3.99

Prague Condensed
ISBN 1 74059 349 9
US$11.99 • UK£5.99

Eastern Europe phrasebook
ISBN 1 86450 227 4
US$8.99 • UK£4.99

St Petersberg map
ISBN 1 86450 179 0
US$5.99 • UK£3.99

Europe on a shoestring
ISBN 1 74059 314 6
US$24.99 • UK£14.99

Europe phrasebook
ISBN 1 86450 224 X
US$8.99 • UK£4.99

Read This First: Europe
ISBN 1 86450 136 7
US$14.99 • UK£8.99

Moscow
ISBN 1 86450 359 9
US$17.99 • UK£10.99

Russian phrasebook
ISBN 1 86450 106 5
US$7.95 • UK£4.50

Prague
ISBN 1 74059 354 5
US$16.99 • UK£10.99

Krakow
ISBN 0 86442 698 4
US$14.95 • UK£9.99

Czech phrasebook
ISBN 1 86450 184 7
US$7.99 • UK£4.50

Available wherever books are sold

Index

Abbreviations

Text

Bold indicates maps.

Bold indicates maps.

Bold indicates maps.

Bold indicates maps.

MAP LEGEND

CITY ROUTES

Freeway	Freeway		Unsealed Road
Highway	Primary Road		One Way Street
Road	Secondary Road		Pedestrian Street
Street	Street		Stepped Street
Lane	Lane		Tunnel
	On/Off Ramp		Footbridge

REGIONAL ROUTES

	Tollway, Freeway
	Primary Road
	Secondary Road
	Minor Road

BOUNDARIES

	International
	State
	Disputed
	Fortified Wall

HYDROGRAPHY

	River, Creek		Dry Lake; Salt Lake
	Canal		Spring; Rapids
	Lake		Waterfalls

TRANSPORT ROUTES & STATIONS

	Train		Ferry
	Underground Train		Walking Trail
	Metro		Walking Tour
	Tramway		Path
	Funicular Railway		Pier or Jetty

AREA FEATURES

	Building		Market		Beach		Forest
	Park, Gardens		Sports Ground		Cemetery		Plaza

POPULATION SYMBOLS

○ CAPITAL	National Capital	● CITY	City	● Village	Village
◉ CAPITAL	State Capital	● Town	Town		Urban Area

MAP SYMBOLS

■	Place to Stay	▼	Place to Eat	●	Point of Interest

✕	Airport		Cinema		Police Station		Synagogue
❸	Bank		Embassy, Consulate		Post Office		Taxi
❹	Border Crossing		Fountain		Pub or Bar		Telephone
	Bus Station		Hospital		Ruins		Theatre
	Cable Car, Funicular		Internet Cafe		Shopping Centre		Tomb
	Castle, Chateau		Monument		Ski Field		Tourist Information
	Cathedral, Church		Museum		Swimming Pool		Zoo

Note: not all symbols displayed above appear in this book

LONELY PLANET OFFICES

Australia
Locked Bag 1, Footscray, Victoria 3011
☎ 03 8379 8000 fax 03 8379 8111
email: talk2us@lonelyplanet.com.au

USA
150 Linden St, Oakland, CA 94607
☎ 510 893 8555 TOLL FREE: 800 275 8555
fax 510 893 8572
email: info@lonelyplanet.com

UK
10a Spring Place, London NW5 3BH
☎ 020 7428 4800 fax 020 7428 4828
email: go@lonelyplanet.co.uk

France
1 rue du Dahomey, 75011 Paris
☎ 01 55 25 33 00 fax 01 55 25 33 01
email: bip@lonelyplanet.fr
www.lonelyplanet.fr

World Wide Web: www.lonelyplanet.com *or* AOL keyword: lp
Lonely Planet Images: www.lonelyplanetimages.com.au